PSYCHOLOGY
THE CORE

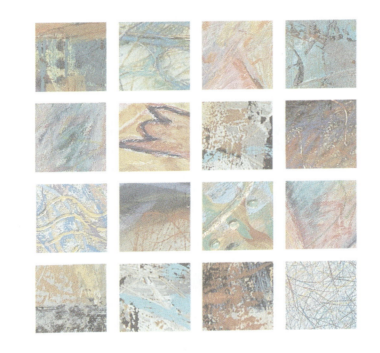

PSYCHOLOGY THE CORE

SPENCER A. RATHUS

Montclair State University

HARCOURT COLLEGE PUBLISHERS

FORT WORTH   PHILADELPHIA   SAN DIEGO   NEW YORK   ORLANDO   AUSTIN   SAN ANTONIO
TORONTO   MONTREAL   LONDON   SYDNEY   TOKYO

PUBLISHER	EARL MCPEEK
EXECUTIVE EDITOR	CAROL WADA
MARKET STRATEGIST	KATHLEEN SHARP
PROJECT EDITOR	MICHELE TOMIAK
ART DIRECTOR	CAROL KINCAID
PRODUCTION MANAGER	ANDREA ARCHER

Cover and chapter-opening art by Kevin Tolman.

ISBN: 0-15-507452-0
Library of Congress Catalog Card Number: 98-65673

Address for orders:
Harcourt College Publishers
6277 Sea Harbor Drive
Orlando, FL 32887-6777

Address for editorial correspondence:
Harcourt College Publishers
301 Commerce Street, Suite 3700
Fort Worth, TX 76102

Web site address:
http://www.harcourtcollege.com

Harcourt, Inc. will provide complimentary supplements or supplement packages to those adopters qualified under our adoption policy. Please contact your sales representative to learn how you qualify. If as an adopter or potential user you receive supplements you do not need, please return them to your sales representative or send them to: Attn: Returns Department, Troy Warehouse, 465 South Lincoln Drive, Troy, MO 63379.

Printed in the United States of America

0 1 2 3 4 5 6 7 8 048 9 8 7 6 5 4 3 2
Harcourt College Publishers

*For Carol Wada, who supplied the idea
and the energy*

Speaking of psychology textbooks, I remember when one fast-food chain served all of its hamburgers in the same way—with ketchup, mustard, pickles, lettuce, onions, on a sesame seed bun. People put up with it until the competition came out with a customizable burger and advertised "Have it your way." People appreciated the fact that they could have ketchup but not mustard, or vice versa.

Psychology: The Core has come into existence because we have learned the lesson. Introductory psychology textbooks have grown larger over the years because they have attempted to give all readers "ketchup, mustard, pickles, lettuce, onions, on a sesame seed bun." They cover topics ranging from basics like biology, learning, and memory to more applied areas like industrial/organizational psychology and environmental psychology. They are also laden with a multitude of features ranging from pedagogical devices like running glossaries and critical thinking exercises to applications like news items and suggestions for self-help. Trying to be all things to all readers creates large books with topics and features that many users consider extraneous. Thus *Psychology: The Core* provides professors with a menu of instructional materials from which they can choose.

Psychology: The Core is based on two principles: Build Your Own Book (BYOB) and Build Your Own Package (BYOP).

BUILD YOUR OWN BOOK (BYOB)

Professors may choose any combination from the following menu of chapters: Psychology as a Science, Biology and Behavior, Sensation and Perception, Consciousness, Learning, Memory, Thinking and Intelligence, Motivation and Emotion, Personality, Lifespan Development, Child and Adolescent Development, Adult Development, Psychological Disorders, Methods of Therapy, Social Psychology, Gender and Sexuality, Health Psychology, and Applied Psychology.

The Applied Psychology chapter covers industrial/organizational psychology, human factors, consumer psychology, environmental psychology, community psychology, forensic psychology, sports psychology, and educational psychology. There is also an appendix on statistics. Most chapters cover their subject matter concisely, without "boxes" and other frills.

Professors who seek a rigorous, "hard-side" but concise introduction to psychology for their students might consider adopting the following chapters:

Psychology as a Science

Biology and Behavior

Sensation and Perception

Consciousness

Learning

Memory

Thinking and Intelligence

Motivation and Emotion

Personality

Lifespan Development (or Child and Adolescent Development)

Psychological Disorders

Methods of Therapy

Social Psychology

Statistics

Professors who seek a more leisurely and applied introduction to psychology have many alternatives. For example, they can choose to use two full chapters on human growth and development: Child and Adolescent Development along with Adult Development. The Adult Development chapter provides useful information on the development of relationships and on the world of work, along with detailed information on the opportunities and problems experienced in middle age and late adulthood. Professors may elect to place the chapter or chapters on human growth and development between the "hard-side" chapters of Biology and Behavior and Sensation and Perception as a way of easing students' entry into psychology. They may also decide to include one or more of the following chapters in their textbook: Gender and Sexuality, Health Psychology, and/or Applied Psychology. In all cases, the order of the chapters is decided by the professor.

Let us note, however, that one professor's "core" topic is dispensable or superfluous to another. For example, some professors would not consider adopting a textbook without a comprehensive discussion of Gender and Sexuality because, as one professor told me, this may be the one opportunity to teach students this information from a scientific perspective. Otherwise, they will learn about gender and sex mainly from friends, TV talk shows, and popular magazines. Some professors will choose to omit the Sensation and Perception chapter or the Social Psychology chapter because they do not see it as the "core" of their mission.

You decide. You decide which chapters are at the core of your own mission in teaching introductory psychology. Select them and organize them in the order that you wish. Build Your Own Book.

Approach, Pedagogy, and Features

Once you have chosen the chapters that you consider being the core of psychology, you will find that you have a textbook that recounts psychology's rich tradition, the roots that can be traced beyond the sages of the ancient Greeks. A century ago, William James wrote, "I wished, by treating Psychology like a natural science, to help her become one." Psychology, as we enter the new millennium, is very much that science of which he spoke. Your textbook will explore psychology's tradition as an empirical science. It will cover the subject matter in psychology in a concise manner.

You will also find that each chapter contains useful and enjoyable learning aids and features. These include:

- "Truth or Fiction?" items that stimulate students to delve into the subject matter by challenging folklore and common sense (which is often common nonsense).

- Chapter outlines that serve as advance organizers of the material to be covered in each chapter.

- Running glossary items that provide quick access to the meanings of key terms so that students can maintain their concentration on the flow of material in the chapter.

- "Psychology in a World of Diversity" features that help students perceive why people of different backgrounds and genders behave and think in different ways, and how the science of psychology is enriched by addressing those differences.

- Chapter summaries that are presented in a distinct format that fosters active learning. The SQ3R and PQ4R methods of learning suggest that students preview the subject matter of each chapter, phrase questions about it, and read to answer those questions. Learning thus becomes active rather than passive. The "Truth or Fiction?" items and the chapter outlines help students preview the material. The summaries help students learn actively by posing key questions and providing the answers. However, they do not attempt to cover every concept in the chapter. Thus they point the way to active learning but intentionally leave the student some work to do.

- Key terms that are listed alphabetically, along with page numbers that indicate where the terms are defined and discussed in the text.

- References that are used in the chapter.

BUILD YOUR OWN PACKAGE (BYOP)

Psychology: The Core is more than a book. It is a book "plus." Instructors can adjust the "level" of their introductory psychology package to suit themselves. Instructors who want a more applied package may want to choose ancillaries that focus on helping students learn the material and apply it to their own lives. Instructors who want an upper-level, more rigorous package may want to choose ancillaries that contain primary sources and encourage students to think critically and to write about psychology.

Therefore, professors, "Build Your Own Package." As with the text itself, you can order precisely the ancillaries that you want for your students—exactly what you are willing to have them pay for. *Psychology: The Core* comes "kitted" with any combination of the following supplements.

Applying Psychology to Everyday Life

Many professors want their introductory psychology course to include practical advice that students can use to assess themselves and improve their lives. This 16-chapter supplement is for those professors and their students. It applies psychological principles and practices to four general areas of life today: academic life, physical health, psychological health, and the adult life your students are leading or are about to lead.

PART I is "Using Psychology to Enhance Your Academic Life." It contains chapters on "Effective Studying," "Making the Most of Classes," "Taking Tests," and "Managing Time." We recognize that it is important that your students do well in college and therefore begin with four chapters that can help them "burst out" of the starting gate.

PART II is "Using Psychology to Enhance Your Physical Health." Its chapters include "Eating Right," "Fitting in Fitness," "Getting Your Z's," and "Avoiding Problems with Drugs." College students are pressed by academic, social, and, often, financial demands, so it is not surprising that physical health often takes a back seat. Yet there are many things that students can do—often little things—to maintain and even enhance their physical health.

This part helps students marshall their resources to attend to their own health, even when the world around is filled with junk food, tensions that keep them awake at night, and substances (drugs) that promise to remove the pain but often add to it.

PART III is "Using Psychology to Enhance Your Psychological Health." The chapters in this part include "Coping with Anxiety and Tension," "Coping with Type A Behavior," "Alleviating Depression," and "Coping with Anger." Psychological health has many meanings, including resistance to stress and tension, being in charge of our emotional lives, seeing things for what they are (rather than ignoring them or blowing them out of proportion), and believing in our own ability to achieve our goals. Part III offers advice drawn from insight-oriented therapies and cognitive-behavioral therapies to help students cope with anxiety—including that most dreaded test anxiety—Type A behavior (through which we provide our own sources of stress and tension), depression, and anger and aggression.

PART IV is called "Using Psychology to Enhance Your Life as an Adult," and it covers "Building Relationships," "Making Responsible Sexual Decisions," "Managing Money," and "Making the Transition from College to the Career World." Part IV will be of use to your students whether they are fresh out of high school or returning to college after rearing a family. Social psychologists and others have studied relationships such as friendships, intimate love relationships, and professional relationships (such as student-professor relationships), and students will find a great deal of advice on how to build relationships and cope with conflict, which has a way of creeping into the best of relationships from time to time. Students are also sexual beings, and they will find valuable information on how to protect themselves and those they care about from problems such as unwanted pregnancies and sexually transmitted infections. Money is the root of all . . . purchases, and management of money is a life skill that will help students today and into their years of retirement. Finally, we will see how psychology helps students make the transition to the career world-from making career choices, to finding a job, to succeeding. Students see that psychologists have advice for succeeding and finding fulfillment in all these aspects of life.

ISBN: 0-15-507459-8

Thinking and Writing about Psychology

This supplement is designed to stimulate students to think and write about psychology. In doing so, it also helps colleges, professors, and students meet two widespread pedagogical objectives:

1. Critical thinking.
2. Writing across the curriculum.

The emphasis on critical thinking is consistent with guidelines suggested by the Association of American Colleges and by the American Psychological Association. Critical thinking has many meanings. On one level, it means taking nothing for granted. It means not believing things just because they are in print or because they were uttered by authority figures or celebrities. It means not necessarily believing that it is healthful to express all of one's feelings, even if a friend in analysis urges one to do so. On another level, critical thinking refers to a process of thoughtfully analyzing and probing the questions, statements, and arguments of others.

This book teaches students how to think critically by being skeptical, examining the definitions of terms, examining the assumptions or premises of arguments, being cautious in drawing conclusions from evidence, considering alternate interpretations of research evidence, avoiding oversimplification, avoiding overgeneralization, and applying critical thinking to all areas of life.

"Writing across the curriculum" refers to writing in every subject. Writing is essential, not only in college but also in most professional careers. Business executives need to be able to communicate their ideas through writing. Marketing plans, advertising copy, and proposals for new products must all be fleshed out in words and sentences. Very few lawyers put on courtroom shows like the fabled Perry Mason; most lawyers spend far more time writing contracts and persuasive letters. Technicians, engineers, and scientists have to be able to write precise reports.

This supplement, *Thinking and Writing about Psychology,* does more than talk about the importance of writing and list writing exercises. It also teaches students how to write. It first discusses types of papers found in psychology (reports of empirical studies, reviews of the literature, theoretical papers, and term papers). Then it provides concrete guidelines for good writing, with examples of each:

Complete the Assignment

Write for Your Audience

Write Clearly and Simply

Be Willing to Make Mistakes

Keep a Notebook or a Journal

Determine the Length of a Paper Logically

Avoid Plagiarism

Pick a Topic

Delimit the Topic

Write a Thesis Statement

Don't Wait for Inspiration—Get Going!

Make an Outline

Compose a Draft

Revise the Paper

Proofread the Paper

Produce the Final Copy

The book also contains 114 writing exercises, from which professors may make assignments or permit students to complete for extra credit. The choice is yours. This is the perfect supplement for professors who want to help their students think logically and critically and be able to set down their thoughts in writing.

ISBN: 0-15-507460-1

Primary Sources for Psychology

This supplement contains extracts from books and journals and original articles, both classic and contemporary. It is intended for instructors who want greater depth—instructors who want their students to be able to understand and criticize research articles and methods and to read primary sources in their original form. All writings are introduced by the author, and questions for discussion and critical thinking are posed at the conclusion of each selection. For example, writings by Charles Darwin include extracts from "An Unpublished Work on Species," an abstract of a letter to a professor in Boston, and an extract on sexual selection from "On the Origin of Species by Natural Selection." Writings by Sigmund Freud address his view that dreams "protect" sleep and on the Oedipus and Electra complexes, with particular focus on the supposed effects on women.

The sources include a balance of classic and contemporary writings. For example, the original articles include classics like the following:

- Fantz, R. L. (1961). The origin of form perception. *Scientific American, 204*(5), 66–72.
- Gibson, E. J., & Walk, R. D. (1960). The "visual cliff." *Scientific American, 202,* 67–71.
- Olds, J., & Milner, P. (1954). Positive reinforcement produced by electrical stimulation of the septal area and other regions of the rat brain. *Journal of Comparative and Physiological Psychology, 47,* 419–427.
- Skinner, B. F. (1948). Superstition in the pigeon. *Journal of Experimental Psychology, 38,* 168–172.
- Turnbull, C. M. (1961). Some observations regarding the experiences and behavior of the BaMouti Pygmies. *American Journal of Psychology, 74,* 304–308.
- Watson, J. B., & Rayner, R. (1920). Conditioned emotional responses. *Journal of Experimental Psychology, 3,* 1–14.

Original articles also include more recent commentaries and reports of empirical research like the following:

- Bouchard, T. J., Jr., Lykken, D. T., McGue, M., Segal, N. L., & Tellegen, A. (1990). Sources of human psychological differences: The Minnesota study of twins reared apart. *Science, 250,* 223–228.
- Bushman, B. J., Baumeister, R. F., & Stack, A. D. (1999). Catharsis, aggression, and persuasive influence: Self-fulfilling or self-defeating prophecies? *Journal of Personality and Social Psychology, 76*(3), 367–376.
- Ellis, A. (1993). Reflections on rational-emotive therapy. *Journal of Consulting and Clinical Psychology, 61,* 199–201.
- Harvey, E. (1999). Short-term and long-term effects of early parental employment on children of the National Longitudinal Survey of Youth. *Developmental Psychology, 35*(2), 445–459.
- Steinberg, L., Dornbusch, S. M., & Brown, B. B. (1992). Ethnic differences in adolescent achievement. *American Psychologist, 47,* 723–729.

Primary Sources for Psychology will give introductory psychology courses added depth by providing students with insight into the thinking, writing, and research undertakings of well-known contributors to the field.

ISBN: 0-15-507461-X

Study Guide

This supplement is designed to help students study more effectively and prepare better for tests. Each chapter of the study guide consists of learning objectives, an overview of the chapter content, a list of key terms with page references, many matching or fill-in questions, short-answer questions, a number of activities, and two multiple-choice "practice tests." Because the study guide and test bank are both written by the same author, the study guide is designed around preparing for tests. The questions, activities, and practice tests are similar in type to the test bank questions (although certainly not the same or similar questions), which ensures that students are preparing for the type of questions they will be tested on. Also included is a list of idioms or difficult words from the text that a person whose first language is not English or students who lack some facility with language may have trouble with.

ISBN: 0-15-507458-X

Other Supplements for Instructors

To help teach this course, Harcourt College Publishers provides a variety of supplements for use by instructors. These include:

INSTRUCTOR'S MANUAL WITH VIDEO INSTRUCTOR'S GUIDE Written by James E. Tremain, Midland Lutheran College, this *Instructor's Manual* provides a variety of methods to present information to the student during the class period. This includes a listing of teaching objectives for each chapter, information about people in psychology, lecture suggestions with references to other resources, classroom demonstrations created by Lawrence Weinstein, Cameron University, and reproducible in-class activities, quizzes, and figures. The Video Instructor's Guide portion lets the instructor know about the Harcourt psychology video and videodisk library. Also included is a Film Guide that lists more than 175 psychology-related films, many of them produced within the past five years. Included is distribution-contact information for each film.

ISBN: 0-15-507453-9

TEST BANK Written by Kendrick A. Thompson, Arkansas State University, the *Test Bank* includes more than 2,000 questions, primarily multiple choice and some short answer. Each question is coded in terms of correct answer, question type (factual/application/conceptual), difficulty level, and textbook page reference. Approximately a third of the test items are designated as "factual." Another third of the items are designated as "applied," measuring the student's abilities to understand and apply the learned material in real-life situations. The remaining third of the questions are "conceptual," showing how well the student understands the overall concepts presented in the chapter and their relationship to one another.

ISBN: 0-15-507454-7

EXAMASTER+™ COMPUTERIZED TEST BANK EXAMaster+™ offers easy-to-use options for computerized test creation.

- EasyTest creates a test from a single screen in just a few easy steps. Instructors choose parameters and then select questions from the database or let EasyTest randomly select them.

- FullTest offers a range of options that includes selecting, editing, adding, or linking questions or graphics; random selection of questions from a wide range of criteria; creating criteria; blocking questions; and printing up to 99 different versions of the same test and answer sheet.
- On-Line Testing allows instructors to create a test in EXAMaster+™, save it to the OLT subdirectory or diskette, and administer the test online. The results of the test can then be imported to ESAGrade.
- RequesTest is a service for instructors without access to a computer. A software specialist will compile questions according to the instructor's criteria and mail or fax the test master within 48 hours!
- The Software Support Hotline is available to answer questions 24 hours a day, 7 days a week.

(Toll-free telephone numbers for these services are provided in the preface to the printed test bank.)

ISBN: Windows version — 0-15-507457-1

ISBN: Macintosh version — 0-15-507456-3

THE HARCOURT PSYCHOLOGY AND HUMAN DEVELOPMENT MULTIMEDIA LIBRARY Consisting of a variety of videos and videodiscs for classroom presentation, this library's selections include materials exclusively created for Harcourt College Publishers as well as videos from Films for the Humanities and Sciences, Pyramid Films, PBS Video, and other sources. Please contact your sales representative for adoption requirements and other details.

THE WHOLE PSYCHOLOGY CATALOG: INSTRUCTIONAL RESOURCES TO ENHANCE STUDENT LEARNING, 1997 Written by Michael B. Reiner, Kennesaw State College, this book provides instructors with experimental exercises, questionnaires, lecture outlines, visual aids, and Internet and World Wide Web guides. These resources can be used to supplement course work and other assignments.

HARCOURT PSYCHOLOGY INSTRUCTOR'S RESOURCES ON THE WEB Come visit us at www.harcourtcollege.com.

ACKNOWLEDGMENTS

It takes many people, not just an author, to make a book. Some help the author fine-tune the wording or point out errors of commission and omission. Others design the book or do the other things that are necessary to convert the author's ideas into a bound book. Still others create a stable corporate environment that provides the setting in which the author and all the others come together. Let me begin, then, by acknowledging the debt of gratitude I owe to Ted Buchholz, President of Harcourt College Publishers, Chris Klein, Editor in Chief, and Earl McPeek, Publisher, for their general overseeing of my projects, including this one. Let me acknowledge the expert guidance I received from Carol Wada, Executive Editor for Psychology. What was good has become much better with her advice. I can truthfully say that not a word escaped her attention. (That is, she made me work very hard.) Michele Tomiak, the Senior Project Editor, carried out the myriad tasks that now make it possible for you to pick up this book and read it. I also acknowledge the Senior Production Manager, Andrea Archer. Carol Kincaid, the Art Director, created the deceptively simple, classic, and lovely design of the text. The Permissions Editors, Caroline Robbins and Sandra Lord, obtained photographs and the right to use them.

Last but far from least is Kathleen Sharp, who insisted on having her own paragraph. (Just kidding, Kathleen.) Kathleen is the Market Strategist, whose job it is to make sure that psychology professors learn about this book and why it can be of help to them and their students. Kathleen is a dynamo and an inspiration. There is no point to working on a book unless you have someone like Kathleen in your corner to promote it. Thanks, Kathleen.

I also gratefully acknowledge the feedback from reviewers. My reviewers are my professional peers, and they tell me when I have left something out or written something incorrectly. They occasionally even tell me when something is well done. The errors that remain in this text—few though they are—are mine and not theirs. (I got them off the hook.) The reviewers are:

David Baskind, Delta College, University Center, MI

Joe Bean, Shorter College, Rome, GA

Bernard Beins, Ithaca College, Ithaca, NY

Linda Brunton, Columbia State Community College, Columbia, TN

Terry Darling, Spring Arbor College, Spring Arbor, MI

Douglas Dunham, Northwest Missouri State University, Maryville, MO

Peter Ebersole, California State University–Fullerton, Fullerton, CA

Paul Fenton, University of Wisconsin–Stout, Menomonie, WI

Sandra Fiske, Onongada Community College, Syracuse, NY

Tony Fowler, Florence-Darling Technical College, Florence, SC

Bernadette Gadzella, Texas A & M–Commerce, Commerce, TX

Sam Gaft, Macomb Community College, Clinton Township, MI

Grace Galliano, Kennesaw State University, Kennesaw, GA

Dan Klaus, Beaver County Community College, Monaca, PA

Stephen Klein, Mississippi State University, Mississippi State, MS

Richard Lance, Haywood Community College, Clyde, NC

Charles Martin-Stanley, Central State University, Wilberforce, OH

Ken Murdoff, Lane Community College, Eugene, OR

David Neufeldt, Hutchinson Community College, Hutchinson, KS

William Pelz, Herkimer Community College, Herkeimer, NY

Retta Poe, Western Kentucky University, Bowling Green, KY

B. Taramanohar Rao, Ferris State University, Big Rapids, MI

Tanya Renner, Kapiolani Community College, Honolulu, HI

Carol Roberts, Springfield Technical Community College, Springfield, MA

Michael Rodman, Middlesex Community College, Bedford, MA

Robert Russell, SUNY–Delhi, Delhi, NY

Matthew Sharps, California State University–Fresno, Fresno, CA

Holly Straub, University of South Dakota, Vermillion, SD

Gordon Whitman, Sandhills Community College, Pinehurst, NC

Larry Vandervert, Spokane Falls, Community College, Spokane, WA

Kaye Young, North Iowa Area Community College, Mason City, IA

Otto Zinser, East Tennessee State University, Johnson City, TN

Finally, I thank my wife, Lois Fichner-Rathus, and my daughters Allyn, Jordan, and Taylor for creating a supportive environment that enabled me to bring this book together. I would not trade any of them for any offer I have yet received.

Spencer A. Rathus

L   LEARNING   L-1

M   MEMORY   M-1

T   THINKING AND INTELLIGENCE   T-1

ME   MOTIVATION AND EMOTION   ME-1

PD   PSYCHOLOGICAL DISORDERS   PD-1

MT   METHODS OF THERAPY   MT-1

CD   CHILD AND ADOLESCENT DEVELOPMENT   CD-1

H   STRESS AND HEALTH   H-1

A   APPLIED PSYCHOLOGY   A-1

CONTENTS

PSYCHOLOGY THE CORE

Rathus, *Psychology: The Core*
Build Your Own Book (B.Y.O.B.) & Build Your Own Package (B.Y.O.P.)

Build Your Own Book
The Core

- ❏ What Is Psychology?
- ❏ Biology & Behavior
- ❏ Lifespan Development
- ❏ Sensation & Perception
- ❏ Consciousness
- ❏ Learning
- ❏ Memory
- ❏ Thinking & Intelligence
- ❏ Motivation & Emotion
- ❏ Personality
- ❏ Psychological Disorders
- ❏ Methods of Therapy
- ❏ Social Psychology
- ❏ Applied Psychology
- ❏ Stress & Health
- ❏ Child & Adolescent Development
- ❏ Adult Development
- ❏ Gender & Sexuality

0-15-507452-X

Build Your Own Package
Study Guide

- ❏ Check here if you would like to include the corresponding Study Guide chapters for your text.

If yes, check one of the following options:

- ❏ I want all of the Study Guide chapters customized into the end of the text.

- ❏ I want the Study Guide shrink wrapped/kitted with the text.

0-15-507458-x

Build Your Own Package
Psychology Applied

- ❏ Effective Studying
- ❏ Getting the Most From Classes
- ❏ Taking Tests
- ❏ Managing Time
- ❏ Eating Right
- ❏ Fitting in Fitness
- ❏ Getting Your Z's
- ❏ Avoiding Problems w/ Drugs
- ❏ Coping with Anxiety & Tension
- ❏ Coping with Type A Behavior
- ❏ Alleviating Depression
- ❏ Coping w/ Anger
- ❏ Building Relationships
- ❏ Making Responsible Sexual Decisions
- ❏ Managing Money
- ❏ Making the Transition from College to the Workplace

0-15-507459-8

Build Your Own Package
Primary Sources

Biology & Behavior
- ❏ Olds/Milner
- ❏ Gazzaniga
- ❏ Bouchard
- ❏ Darwin
- ❏ Buss

Developmental Psychology
- ❏ Harlow
- ❏ Cernoch/Porter
- ❏ Piaget
- ❏ Steinberg/ Dornbusch/Brown
- ❏ Harvey
- ❏ Langer/Rodin

Sensation, Perception & Consciousness
- ❏ Gibson/Walk
- ❏ Fantz
- ❏ Turnbull
- ❏ Dement
- ❏ Hobson/McCarley

Learning & Cognition
- ❏ Watson/Rayner
- ❏ Skinner
- ❏ Lang/Melamed
- ❏ Miller
- ❏ Bandura/ Ross/Ross
- ❏ Tolman
- ❏ Craik/Watkins
- ❏ Loftus/Palmer
- ❏ Steele/Aronson

Motivation & Emotion
- ❏ Bexton/Heron /Scott
- ❏ Rozin/Fallon
- ❏ Festinger/ Carlsmith
- ❏ Ekman/Friesan

Personality & Psychotherapy
- ❏ Freud
- ❏ Bushman/ Baumeister/Stack
- ❏ Seligman/Maier
- ❏ Richardson/ Bernstein/Taylor
- ❏ Ellis
- ❏ Rogers
- ❏ Smith/Glass

Social & Environmental Psychology

- ❏ Freedman/Fraser
- ❏ Asch
- ❏ Milgram
- ❏ Benson
- ❏ Darley/Latane
- ❏ Calhoun
- ❏ Donnerstein/ Wilson

0-15-507461-X

Build Your Own Package
Thinking & Writing

This supplement is designed to stimulate students to think and write about psychology.

It contains 114 writing exercises that allow you to make assignments or permit students to complete for extra credit.

This supplement will help your students think logically and critically and be able to set down their thoughts in writing.

- ❏ Package with the text
- ❏ Buy separately from the text

0-15-507460-1

Psychology: The Core
By Spencer A. Rathus

Rathus's *Psychology: The Core* is a custom text that allows you to pick the exact chapters you need to make your course just the way you like it. The book you have in your hand is a sample copy that contains all the chapters from which you can choose. In addition to the main textbook, there are four other ancillaries that can also be customized to complement or extend the chapters you choose:

Psychology Applied to Everyday Life—A book of activities that help your students apply the concepts from the textbook to problems or issues in their own lives. Activities range from study skills, to coping with stress, to interpersonal relations.

Primary Sources in Psychology—A book of original source readings that provide students with the opportunity to read the actual writings of well-known psychologists and to analyze their research.

Thinking and Writing about Psychology—A book of activities that stimulate students' critical thinking and writing abilities. This ancillary is ideal for the professor who wants to emphasize analyzing and questioning the concepts presented in the class and book.

Student Study Guide—A book of studying and test-taking activities to help your students succeed in the class. Included for each chapter is a list of learning objectives, a summary of the chapter, a list of key terms with page references, matching key terms, fill-in-the-blank questions utilizing unaided recall, short answer/essay questions, activities (many of them Web-based), and practice tests.

Pick any chapter, pick any activity, pick any reading, pick any study guide chapter. . . . **It's up to you!**

And ordering is just as easy! Just pick what you want to include in your text, check the boxes on the other side of this form, tell us which order you want the chapters in, return this form to your Harcourt College Publishers representative, and a custom textbook, designed just for you, will be created. We here at Harcourt hope you enjoy the flexibility that this text offers and that your courses are a great success because of it! If you need further information or help in designing your new text, call your local Harcourt representative or our Custom Publishing division at 800/447-9479.

Harcourt Custom Publishing Order Form for
Psychology: The Core
by Spencer A. Rathus

Professor Name_____

School_____

Department_____

Course Name_____

Address_____

City/State/Zip_____

Phone #_____ FAX #_____

Email Address_____

Enrollment (please be as accurate as possible for ordering purposes)_____ ❏ per semester ❏ per year

Course Start Date_____

PSY

PSYCHOLOGY AS A SCIENCE

TRUTH OR FICTION?

_____ A book on psychology, whose contents are similar to those of the book you are now holding, was written by Aristotle more than 2,000 years ago.

_____ The ancient Greek philosopher Socrates suggested a research method that is still used in psychology.

_____ Even though she had worked to complete all the degree requirements, the first female president of the American Psychological Association turned down the doctoral degree that was offered to her.

_____ Men receive the majority of doctoral degrees in psychology.

_____ You could survey 20 million voters and still not predict the outcome of a presidential election accurately.

_____ In many experiments, neither the subjects nor the researchers know who is receiving the real treatment and who is not.

_____ Psychologists would not be able to carry out many kinds of studies without deceiving subjects as to the purposes and methods of the studies.

"**W**HAT A PIECE OF WORK IS MAN," WROTE William Shakespeare. He was writing about you: "How noble in reason! How infinite in faculty! In form and moving how express and admirable! In action how like an angel! In apprehension how like a god! The beauty of the world! The paragon of animals!"

You probably had no trouble recognizing yourself in this portrait— "noble in reason," "admirable," godlike in understanding, head and shoulders above other animals. That's you to a *tee,* isn't it? Consider some of the noble and admirable features of human behavior:

- The human abilities to think and solve problems have allowed us to build cathedrals and computers and to scan the interior of the body without surgery. Yet just what is thinking? How do we solve problems?
- The human ability to create led to the writing of great works of literature and the composition of music from opera to rap. Yet what exactly is creativity?
- Human generosity and charity have encouraged us to care for older people, people who are ill, and people who are less advantaged than we are—even to sacrifice ourselves for those we love. Why do we care for others? What motivates us to care for our children and protect our families?

Some human behavior is not as noble or admirable as these examples suggest. In fact, human behavior varies greatly. Some of it is downright puzzling. Consider some more examples:

- Although people can be generous, most adults on crowded city streets will not stop to help a person lying on the sidewalk. Why?
- Most people who overeat or smoke cigarettes know they are jeopardizing their health. Yet they continue in their bad habits. Why?
- A person claims to have raped, killed, or mutilated a victim because of insanity. The person was overcome by an irresistible impulse, or "another personality" took control. What is insanity? What is an irresistible impulse?

Human behavior has always fascinated people. Sometimes we are even surprised at ourselves. We have thoughts or impulses that seem to be out of character, or we cannot recall something that seems to be hovering on the "tip of the tongue." Psychologists, like other people, are also intrigued by the mysteries of behavior, but for them the scientific study of behavior is their life's work.

PSYCHOLOGY AS A SCIENCE

Psychology is the scientific study of behavior and mental processes. Topics of interest to psychologists include the nervous system, sensation and perception, learning and memory, intelligence, language, thought, growth and development, personality, stress and health, psychological disorders, ways of treating those disorders, sexual behavior, and the behavior of people in social settings such as groups and organizations.

Psychology, like other sciences, seeks to describe, explain, predict, and control the events it studies. Psychology thus seeks to describe, explain, predict, and control behavior and mental processes.

When possible, descriptive terms and concepts are interwoven into **theories.** Theories are formulations of apparent relationships among observed events. They allow us to derive explanations and predictions. Many psychological theories combine statements about behavior (such as eating or aggression), mental processes (such as attitudes and mental images), and biological processes. For instance, many of our responses to drugs such as alcohol and marijuana can be measured as overt behavior, and they are presumed to reflect the biochemical actions of these drugs and our (mental) expectations about their effects.

A satisfactory psychological theory allows us to predict behavior. For instance, a theory of hunger should allow us to predict when people will or will not eat. If our observations cannot be adequately explained by, or predicted from, a given theory, we should consider revising or replacing it.

What do we mean by "controlling" behavior and mental processes? Some people erroneously think that psychologists seek ways to make people do their bidding, like puppets on strings. This is not so. Psychologists are committed to a belief in the dignity of human beings, and human dignity demands that people be free to make their own decisions and choose their own behavior. Psychologists are learning more about the influences on human behavior all the time, but they implement this knowledge only on request and in order to help people clarify and meet their own goals.

The remainder of this chapter presents an overview of psychology as a science. You will see that psychologists have diverse interests and fields of specialization. We discuss the history of psychology and the major perspectives from which today's psychologists view behavior. Finally, we consider the research methods psychologists use to study behavior and mental processes.

"What a piece of work is man," wrote William Shakespeare. "How noble in reason! How infinite in faculty!" Chinese American artist Hung Liu, seen here with one of her paintings, illustrates the creativity that humans are capable of. Psychologists are interested in all aspects of human behavior and mental processes.

WHAT PSYCHOLOGISTS DO

Psychologists share a keen interest in behavior, but in other ways, they may differ markedly. Some psychologists engage primarily in basic, or **pure research.** Pure research has no immediate application to personal or social problems and therefore has been characterized as research for its own sake. Other psychologists engage in **applied research,** which is designed to find solutions to specific personal or social problems. Although pure research is sparked by curiosity and the desire to know and understand, today's pure research frequently enhances tomorrow's way of life (Leibowitz, 1996; Miller, 1995). For example, pure research on learning and motivation in lower animals done early in the century has found widespread applications in today's school systems. Pure research into the workings of the nervous system has enhanced knowledge of disorders such as epilepsy, Parkinson's disease, and Alzheimer's disease.

PSYCHOLOGY The science that studies behavior and mental processes.

THEORY A formulation of relationships underlying observed events.

PURE RESEARCH Research conducted without concern for immediate applications.

APPLIED RESEARCH Research conducted in an effort to find solutions to particular problems.

Many psychologists do not conduct research. Instead, they apply psychological knowledge to help people change their behavior so that they can meet their own goals more effectively. Many psychologists engage primarily in teaching. They share psychological knowledge in classrooms, seminars, and workshops.

Fields of Psychology

Let us now explore some of the specialties of psychologists. Although psychologists tend to wear more than one hat, most of them carry out their functions in the following fields.

Clinical psychologists help people with psychological disorders adjust to the demands of life. People's problems may range from anxiety and depression to sexual dysfunctions to loss of goals. Clinical psychologists evaluate these problems through interviews and psychological tests. They help their clients resolve their problems and change self-defeating behavior. Clinical psychologists are the largest subgroup of psychologists (see Figure PSY.1). Clinical psychologists differ from psychiatrists in that psychiatrists are *medical* doctors who specialize in the study and treatment of psychological disorders.

Counseling psychologists, like clinical psychologists, use interviews and tests to define their clients' problems. Their clients typically have adjustment problems but not serious psychological disorders. Clients may have trouble making academic or vocational decisions, or making friends in college. They may experience marital or family conflicts, have physical handicaps, or have adjustment problems such as those encountered by people who lose their jobs because of mergers or downsizing. Counseling psychologists advise clients to help them clarify their goals and overcome obstacles. Counseling psychologists are often employed in college and university counseling and testing centers. As suggested by Figure PSY.1, more than half of psychologists are clinical or counseling psychologists.

FIGURE PSY.1

RECIPIENTS OF DOCTORATES IN THE VARIOUS SUBFIELDS OF PSYCHOLOGY.

Nearly 40% of the doctorates in psychology are awarded in clinical psychology. The next most popular subfield is counseling psychology.

Source: Office of Demographic, Employment, and Educational Research (1994). Table WO4846, Summary report doctorate recipients from United States universities. Washington, D.C.: American Psychological Association.

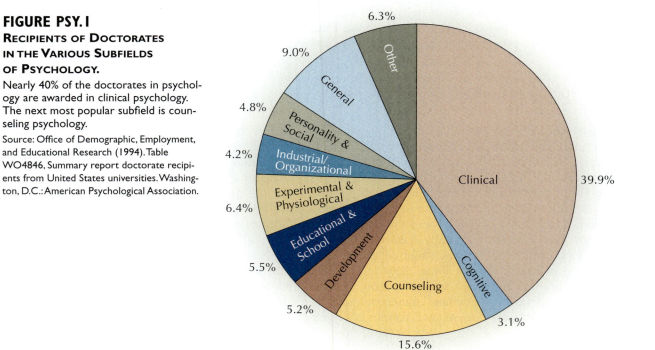

School psychologists are employed by school systems to identify and assist students who have problems that interfere with learning. Such problems range from social and family problems to emotional disturbances and learning disorders. They help make decisions about placement of students in special classes.

Educational psychologists, like school psychologists, attempt to facilitate learning. But they usually focus on course planning and instructional methods for a school system rather than on individual children. Educational psychologists research theoretical issues related to learning, measurement, and child development. For example, they study how learning is affected by psychological factors such as motivation and intelligence, sociocultural factors such as poverty and acculturation, and teacher behavior. Some educational psychologists prepare standardized tests such as the Scholastic Aptitude Tests (SATs).

Developmental psychologists study the changes—physical, emotional, cognitive, and social—that occur throughout the life span. They attempt to sort out the influences of heredity (nature) and the environment (nurture) on development. Developmental psychologists conduct research on issues such as the effects of maternal use of drugs on an embryo, the outcomes of various patterns of child rearing, children's concepts of space and time, conflicts during adolescence, and problems of adjustment among older people.

Personality psychologists attempt to define human traits; to determine influences on human thought processes, feelings, and behavior; and to explain psychological disorders. They are particularly concerned with issues such as anxiety, aggression, and gender roles.

Social psychologists are concerned primarily with the nature and causes of individuals' thoughts, feelings, and behavior in social situations. Whereas personality psychologists tend to look within the person for explanations of behavior, social psychologists tend to focus on external or social influences.

Environmental psychologists focus on the ways in which behavior influences, and is influenced by, the physical environment. They are concerned with how buildings and cities serve, or fail to serve, human needs. They investigate the effects of temperature, noise, and air pollution on behavior and mental processes.

Psychologists in all specialties may conduct experiments. However, those called *experimental psychologists* specialize in basic processes such as the nervous system, sensation and perception, learning and memory, thought, motivation, and emotion.

Industrial psychology and organizational psychology are closely related fields. *Industrial psychologists* focus on the relationships between people and work. *Organizational psychologists* study the behavior of people in organizations such as businesses. *Human factors psychologists* make technical systems such as automobile dashboards and computer keyboards more user friendly. *Consumer psychologists* study the behavior of shoppers in an effort to predict and influence their behavior. They advise store managers how to lay out the aisles of a supermarket in ways that boost impulse buying, how to arrange window displays to attract customers, and how to make newspaper ads and TV commercials more persuasive.

Health psychologists examine the ways in which behavior and mental processes such as attitudes are related to physical health. They study the effects of stress on health problems such as headaches, cardiovascular disease, and cancer. Health psychologists also guide clients toward healthier behavior patterns—such as exercising and quitting smoking—and diets.

Psychologists continue to apply their knowledge and skills in new areas.

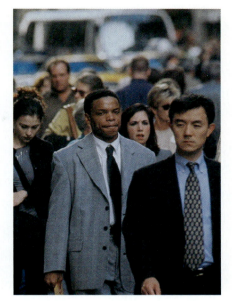

ENVIRONMENTAL PSYCHOLOGY. Environmental psychologists focus on the ways in which people affect and are affected by their physical environment. How are city dwellers affected by crowding and "stimulus overload"?

WHERE PSYCHOLOGY COMES FROM: A HISTORY

Psychology is as old as history and as modern as today. Knowledge of the history of psychology allows us to appreciate its theoretical conflicts, its place among the sciences, the evolution of its methods, and its social and political roles (McGovern et al., 1991).

Did you know that the outline for this textbook could have been written by the ancient Greek philosopher Aristotle? One of Aristotle's works is *Peri Psyches,* which translates as " About the Psyche." Like this book, *Peri Psyches* begins with a history of psychological thought and historical perspectives on the nature of the mind and behavior. Aristotle argued that human behavior, like the movements of the stars and the seas, is subject to rules and laws. Then he delved into his subject matter topic by topic: personality, sensation and perception, thought, intelligence, needs and motives, feelings and emotion, and memory. This book presents these topics in a different order, but each is here.

Aristotle also declared that people are motivated to seek pleasure and avoid pain. This view remains as current today as it was in ancient Greece.

Other ancient Greek philosophers also contributed to psychology. Around 400 B.C., Democritus suggested that we could think of behavior in terms of a body and a mind. (Contemporary psychologists still talk about the interaction of biological and mental processes.) He pointed out that our behavior is influenced by external stimulation. Democritus was one of the first to raise the question of whether there is free will or choice. Putting it another way, where do the influences of others end and our "real selves" begin?

Plato (c. 427–347 B.C.) was a disciple of the great philosopher Socrates. He recorded Socrates' advice to "Know thyself," which has remained a motto of psychology ever since. Socrates claimed that we could not attain reliable self-knowledge through our senses because the senses do not exactly mirror reality. Because the senses provide imperfect knowledge, Socrates suggested we rely on processes such as rational thought and **introspection**—careful examination of one's own thoughts and emotions— to achieve self-knowledge. He also pointed out that people are social creatures who influence one another greatly.

Had we room enough and time, we could trace psychology's roots to thinkers even further back in time than the ancient Greeks, and we could trace its development through the great thinkers of the Renaissance. As it is, we must move on to the development of psychology as a laboratory science during the second half of the 19th century. Some historians set the marker date at 1860. It was then that Gustav Theodor Fechner (1801–1887) published his landmark book *Elements of Psychophysics,* which showed how physical events (such as lights and sounds) are related to psychological sensation and perception. Fechner also showed how we can scientifically measure the effect of these events. Most historians set the debut of modern psychology as a laboratory science in the year 1879, when Wilhelm Wundt established the first psychological laboratory in Leipzig, Germany (Hergenhahn, 1997).

Structuralism

Like Aristotle, Wilhelm Wundt saw the mind as a natural event that could be studied scientifically, just like light, heat, and the flow of blood. Wundt used introspection to try to discover the basic elements of experience. When pre-

TRUTH OR FICTION REVISITED
It is true that a book on psychology, whose contents are similar to those of the book you are now holding, was written by Aristotle more than 2,000 years ago. Its title is *Peri Psyches.*

TRUTH OR FICTION REVISITED
It is true that the ancient Greek philosopher Socrates suggested a research method that is still used in psychology. That method is *introspection.*

INTROSPECTION Deliberate looking into one's own mind to examine one's own thoughts and feelings.

sented with various sights and sounds, he and his colleagues tried to look inward as objectively as possible to describe their sensations and feelings.

Wundt and his students founded the school of psychology called **structuralism.** Structuralism attempted to break conscious experience down into *objective* sensations such as sight or taste, and *subjective* feelings such as emotional responses, will, and mental images such as memories or dreams. Structuralists believed that the mind functions by combining objective and subjective elements of experience.

Functionalism

WILHELM WUNDT

> *I wished, by treating Psychology like a natural science, to help her become one.*

> WILLIAM JAMES

Toward the end of the 19th century, William James was a major figure in the development of psychology in the United States. James adopted a broad view of psychology that focused on the relation between conscious experience and behavior. He argued, for example, that the stream of consciousness is fluid and continuous. Introspection convinced him that experience cannot be broken down into objective sensations and subjective feelings as the structuralists maintained.

WILLIAM JAMES

James was a founder of the school of **functionalism,** which dealt with behavior as well as consciousness. Functionalism addressed the ways in which experience permits us to function more adaptively in our environments—for example, how the development of habits allows us to cope with commonly occurring situations. It used behavioral observation in the laboratory to supplement introspection. The structuralists tended to ask, "What are the pieces that make up thinking and experience?" The functionalists tended to ask, "What are the *purposes* (functions) of behavior and mental processes? What difference do they make?"

James was influenced by Charles Darwin's theory of evolution. Earlier in the 19th century, Darwin had argued that organisms with adaptive features—that is, the "fittest"—survive and reproduce. Functionalists adapted Darwin's theory in the study of behavior and proposed that adaptive behavior patterns are learned and maintained. Maladaptive behavior patterns tend to drop out. They are discontinued, and the "fittest" behavior patterns survive. Adaptive actions tend to be repeated and become habits. James wrote that "habit is the enormous flywheel of society." Habit keeps civilization going from day to day.

The formation of habits is seen in acts such as lifting a fork to our mouth and turning a doorknob. At first, these acts require our full attention. If you are in doubt, stand by with paper towels and watch a baby's first efforts at self-feeding. Through repetition, the acts that make up self-feeding become automatic, or habitual. The multiple acts involved in learning to drive a car also become routine through repetition. We can then perform them without much attention, freeing ourselves to focus on other matters such as our clever conversation and the CD player. The idea of learning by repetition is also basic to the behavioral tradition in psychology.

Behaviorism

Imagine you have placed a hungry rat in a maze. It meanders down a pathway that ends in a T. It can then turn left or right. If you consistently reward the rat with food for turning right at this choice point, it will learn to turn right when it arrives there, at least when it is hungry. But what does the rat

STRUCTURALISM The school of psychology that argues the mind consists of three basic elements—sensations, feelings, and images—which combine to form experience.

FUNCTIONALISM The school of psychology that emphasizes the uses or functions of the mind rather than the elements of experience.

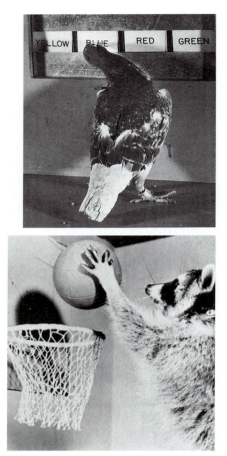

FIGURE PSY.2

EXAMPLES OF THE POWER OF REINFORCEMENT.

In the photo at the top, we see how our feathered gift to city life has earned its keep in experiments on reinforcement. Here, the pigeon pecks the blue button because pecking it has been followed (reinforced) with food. In the photo at the bottom, "Air Raccoon" shoots a basket. Behaviorists teach animals complex behaviors such as shooting baskets by first reinforcing approximations to the goal (or target behavior). As time progresses, closer approximations are demanded before reinforcement is given.

BEHAVIORISM The school of psychology that defines psychology as the study of observable behavior and studies relationships between stimuli and responses.

REINFORCEMENT A stimulus that follows a response and increases the frequency of the response.

GESTALT PSYCHOLOGY The school of psychology that emphasizes the tendency to organize perceptions into wholes and to integrate separate stimuli into meaningful patterns.

think when it is learning to turn right? "Hmm, last time I was in this situation and turned to the right, I was given some food. Think I'll try that again"?

Does it seem absurd to try to place yourself in the "mind" of a rat? So it seemed to John Broadus Watson (1878–1958), the founder of American behaviorism. But Watson was asked to consider just such a question as one of the requirements for his doctoral degree, which he received from the University of Chicago in 1903. Functionalism was the dominant view of psychology at the University of Chicago, and functionalists were concerned with the stream of consciousness as well as observable behavior. But Watson (1913) believed that if psychology was to be a natural science, like physics or chemistry, it must limit itself to observable, measurable events—that is, to behavior—hence, **behaviorism**. Observable behavior includes activities such as pressing a lever; turning left or right; eating and mating; even involuntary body functions such as heart rate, dilation of the pupils of the eyes, blood pressure, and emission of brain waves. These behaviors are *public*. They can be measured by simple observation or by laboratory instruments and different observers would readily agree about their existence and features. Behaviorists, by the way, define psychology as the scientific study of *behavior*, not of *behavior and mental processes*.

Harvard University psychologist B. F. Skinner (1904–1990) was another major contributor to behaviorism. Organisms, he believed, learn to behave in certain ways because they have been **reinforced** for doing so—that is, their behavior has had a positive outcome. He demonstrated that laboratory animals carry out behaviors, both simple and complex, because of reinforcement. They peck buttons (Figure PSY.2), turn in circles, climb ladders, and push toys across the floor. Many psychologists adopted the view that, in principle, we could explain complex human behavior in terms of thousands of instances of learning through reinforcement.

Gestalt Psychology

In the 1920s, another school of psychology—**Gestalt psychology**—was prominent in Germany. In the 1930s, the three founders of the school—Max Wertheimer (1880–1943), Kurt Koffka (1886–1941), and Wolfgang Köhler (1887–1967)—left Europe to escape the Nazi threat. They carried on their work in the United States, giving further impetus to the growing American ascendance in psychology.

Wertheimer and his colleagues focused on perception and on how perception influences thinking and problem solving. In contrast to the behaviorists, Gestalt psychologists argued that we cannot hope to understand human nature by focusing only on overt behavior. In contrast to the structuralists, they claimed that we cannot explain human perceptions, emotions, or thought processes in terms of basic units. Perceptions are *more* than the sums of their parts: Gestalt psychologists saw our perceptions as wholes that give meaning to parts.

Gestalt psychologists illustrated how we tend to perceive separate pieces of information as integrated wholes, including the contexts in which they occur. Consider Figure PSY.3. The dots in the centers of the configurations at the left are the same size, yet we may perceive them as being of different sizes because of the contexts in which they appear. The inner squares in the central figure are equally bright, but they may look different because of their contrasting backgrounds. The second symbol in each line at the right is identical, but in the top row we may perceive it as a B and in the bottom row as the number 13. The symbol has not changed, only the context in which it appears. There are many examples of this in literature and everyday life. In *The Prince and the Pauper*, Mark Twain dressed a peasant boy as a prince, and the kingdom bowed to him. Do clothes sometimes make the man or woman? Try wearing cutoffs for a job interview!

Gestalt psychologists believed that learning could be active and purposeful, not merely responsive and mechanical as in Skinner's experiments. Wolfgang Köhler and the others demonstrated that much learning, especially in learning to solve problems, is accomplished by **insight,** not by mechanical repetition. Köhler was marooned during World War I on one of the Canary Islands, where the Prussian Academy of Science kept a colony of apes, and his research while there gave him, well, insight into the process of learning by insight.

Have you ever pondered a problem for quite a while and then, suddenly, seen the solution? Did the solution seem to come out of nowhere? In a "flash"? Consider the chimpanzee in Figure PSY.4. At first, it is unsuccessful in reaching for bananas suspended from the ceiling. Then it suddenly stacks the boxes and climbs up to reach the bananas. It seems the chimp has experienced a sudden reorganization of the mental elements of the problem—that is, it has had a "flash of insight." Köhler's findings suggest that we often manipulate the elements of problems until we group them in such a way that we believe we will be able to reach a goal. The manipulations may take quite some time as mental trial and error proceeds. Once the proper grouping has been found, however, we seem to perceive it all at once.

Psychoanalysis

Psychoanalysis, the school of psychology founded by Sigmund Freud, is very different from the other schools in both background and approach. Freud's theory has invaded popular culture, and you may already be familiar with a number of its concepts. For example, on at least one TV crime show each season, an unstable person goes on a killing spree. At the end of the show, a psychiatrist explains that the killer was "unconsciously" doing away with his own mother or father. Or perhaps a friend has tried to "interpret" a slip of the tongue you made or has asked you what you thought might be the symbolic meaning of an especially vivid dream.

The notions that people are driven by hidden impulses and that verbal slips and dreams represent unconscious wishes largely reflect the influence of Freud (1856–1939), a Viennese physician who fled to England in the 1930s to escape the Nazi tyranny. While academic psychologists were conducting their research mainly in the laboratory, Freud gained his understanding of people by working with patients. He was astounded at how little insight his patients seemed to have into their motives. Some patients justified, or rationalized, the most abominable behavior with absurd explanations. Others seized the opportunity to blame themselves for nearly every misfortune that had befallen the human species.

Freud came to believe that unconscious processes, especially sexual and aggressive impulses, are more influential than conscious thought in determining human behavior. He thought that most of the mind is unconscious—a seething cauldron of conflicting impulses, urges, and wishes. People are motivated to gratify these impulses, ugly as some of them are. But at the same time, people are motivated to see themselves as decent, and hence may delude themselves about their true motives. Because Freud proposed that the motion of underlying forces of personality determines our thoughts, feelings, and behavior, his theory is referred to as **psychodynamic.**

Freud devised a method of psychotherapy called psychoanalysis. Psychoanalysis aims to help patients gain insight into many of their deep-

A. Are the circles in the center of the configurations the same size? Why not take a ruler and measure their diameters?

A B C D
12 13 14 15

B. Is the second symbol in each line the letter B or the number 13?

C. Which one of the gray squares is brighter?

FIGURE PSY.3
THE IMPORTANCE OF CONTEXT.
Gestalt psychologists have shown that our perceptions depend not only on our sensory impressions but also on the context of our impressions. You will interpret a man running toward you very differently depending on whether you are on a deserted street at night or at a track in the morning.

INSIGHT In Gestalt psychology, the sudden reorganization of perceptions, allowing the sudden solution of a problem.

PSYCHOANALYSIS The school of psychology that emphasizes the importance of unconscious motives and conflicts as determinants of human behavior.

PSYCHODYNAMIC Referring to Freud's theory, which proposes that the motion of underlying forces of personality determines our thoughts, feelings, and behavior.

FIGURE PSY.4
SOME INSIGHT INTO INSIGHT.
At first, the chimpanzee cannot reach the bananas hanging from the ceiling. After some time has passed, it has an apparent "flash of insight" and piles the boxes on top of one another to reach the fruit.

seated conflicts and find socially acceptable ways of expressing wishes and gratifying needs. It can extend for years.

Today we no longer find psychologists who describe themselves as structuralists or functionalists. Although the school of Gestalt psychology gave birth to current research approaches in perception and problem solving, few would consider themselves Gestalt psychologists. The numbers of orthodox behaviorists and psychoanalysts have also been declining. Many contemporary psychologists in the behaviorist tradition look on themselves as social-cognitive[1] theorists, and many psychoanalysts consider themselves neoanalysts rather than traditional Freudians. They have influenced or become part of contemporary perspectives in psychology.

HOW TODAY'S PSYCHOLOGISTS VIEW BEHAVIOR AND MENTAL PROCESSES

The history of psychological thought has taken many turns, and contemporary psychologists also differ in their approaches. Today there are six broad, influential perspectives in psychology: the biological, cognitive, humanistic-existential, psychodynamic, learning, and sociocultural perspec-

---

[1]Formerly termed *social-learning theorists.*

tives. Each emphasizes different topics of investigation. Each tends to approach its topics in its own ways.

The Biological Perspective

Psychologists assume that our thoughts, fantasies, and dreams are made possible by the nervous system and especially by the brain. Biologically oriented psychologists seek the links between events in the brain—such as the activity of brain cells—and mental processes. They use techniques such as CAT scans and PET scans to show what parts of the brain are involved in activities like language, mathematical problem solving, and music. We have learned how natural chemical substances in the brain are involved in the formation of memories. Among some lower animals, electrical stimulation of parts of the brain prompts the expression of innate, or built-in, sexual and aggressive behaviors.

Biological psychologists are also concerned with the influences of hormones (naturally occurring chemicals that are released into the bloodstream and regulate behavior) and heredity. In people, for instance, the hormone prolactin stimulates production of milk. In rats, however, prolactin also gives rise to maternal behavior. In lower animals, sex hormones determine whether mating behavior will follow stereotypical masculine or feminine behavior patterns. In people, hormones play a subtler role.

Psychologists are interested in the role of heredity in behavior and mental processes such as psychological disorders, criminal behavior, and thinking. Generally speaking, our heredity provides a broad range of behavioral and mental possibilities. Environmental factors interact with inherited factors to determine specific behavior and mental processes.

EVOLUTIONARY PSYCHOLOGY **Evolutionary psychologists** study the evolution of behavior and mental processes. Charles Darwin argued that in the age-old struggle for survival, only the "fittest" organisms manage to reach maturity and reproduce. For example, fish that swim faster or people who are naturally immune to certain diseases are more likely to transmit their **genes** to future generations. Their species are therefore likely to evolve in these adaptive directions. Evolutionary psychologists suggest that much human social behavior, such as tendencies toward aggression and mating patterns, also has a hereditary basis. People might also be influenced by social rules, cultural factors, and the capacity for personal choice, but evolutionary psychologists believe that inherited tendencies sort of whisper in people's ears and might tend to move them in certain directions.

The Cognitive Perspective

Cognitive psychologists venture into the realm of mental processes to understand human nature (Sperry, 1993). They investigate the ways in which we perceive and mentally represent the world, how we learn, remember the past, plan for the future, solve problems, form judgments, make decisions, and use language (Basic Behavioral Science Task Force, 1996a). Cognitive psychologists, in short, study all the things that we refer to as the *mind*.

The cognitive tradition has roots in Socrates' advice to "Know thyself" and in his suggested method of introspection. We also find cognitive psychology's roots in structuralism, functionalism, and Gestalt psychology, each of which, in its own way, addressed issues that are of interest to cognitive psychologists.

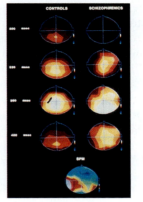

THE BIOLOGICAL PERSPECTIVE. Psychologists with a biological perspective investigate the connections among biological processes, behavior, and mental processes. They use methods such as brain electrical activity mapping (BEAM), in which electrodes measure the electrical activity of parts of the brain while people are exposed to various stimuli (photo A). The left-hand column of photo B shows the average level of electrical activity of the brains of 10 normal people at four time intervals. The right-hand column shows the average activity of 10 people diagnosed with schizophrenia, a severe psychological disorder. The more intense the activity, the brighter the color (white is most intense). The bottom diagram summarizes similarities and differences between people not diagnosed with schizophrenia and people diagnosed with schizophrenia: Areas in blue reflect smaller differences; white areas reflect larger differences.

EVOLUTIONARY PSYCHOLOGY The field of psychology that studies the evolution of behavior and mental processes. It is based on the principle of natural selection—that only the "fittest" organisms reach maturity and reproduce, thereby transmitting their genes to future generations and enabling their species to evolve in adaptive directions.

GENES The basic building blocks of heredity.

COGNITIVE Having to do with mental processes such as sensation and perception, memory, intelligence, language, thought, and problem solving.

PSYCHOLOGY IN A WORLD OF *Diversity*

THE DIVERSITY OF PSYCHOLOGISTS

Mary Whiton Calkins

Kenneth B. Clark

Women and people from various racial and ethnic backgrounds have made key contributions to the science of psychology. Consider some of the women. Christine Ladd-Franklin (1847–1930) was born during an era in American history in which women were expected to remain in the home and were excluded from careers in science (Furumoto, 1992). She nevertheless pursued a career in psychology, taught at Johns Hopkins and Columbia Universities, and formulated a theory of color vision. Margaret Floy Washburn (1871–1939) was the first woman to receive a PhD in psychology. Washburn also wrote *The Animal Mind,* a work that contained many ideas that would later become part of behaviorism.

Mary Whiton Calkins (1863–1930) became the first female president of the American Psychological Association in 1905. Calkins studied psychology with William James at Harvard University, but as a "guest student." Harvard was not yet admitting women. When she completed her degree requirements, Harvard would not award her the degree because of her gender. Instead, Harvard offered to grant her a doctorate from its sister school, Radcliffe. Calkins declined the offer because accepting it would help perpetuate discrimination against women. Even without a doctorate, Calkins pioneered research in memory at Wellesley College, where she founded a psychology laboratory in 1891. She introduced a number of methods for studying memory and other mental processes.

Numerous early psychologists came from different ethnic backgrounds. Back in 1901, Gilbert Haven Jones, an African American, received his PhD in psychology in Germany. J. Henry Alston engaged in research on perception of heat and cold and was the first African American psychologist to be published in a major psychology journal (in 1920).

In the 1940s, African American psychologist Kenneth B. Clark and his wife, psychologist Mamie Phipps Clark, conducted research showing the negative effects of school segregation on African American children. In one such study, African American children were shown white and brown dolls and asked to "Give me the pretty doll," or "Give me the doll that looks bad." Most children's choices showed that they preferred the white dolls over the brown ones. The Clarks concluded that the children had swallowed the larger society's preference for White people. The Clarks' research was cited by the Supreme Court when it overturned the "separate but equal" schools doctrine in 1954.

Hispanic American and Asian American psychologists have also made their mark. Jorge Sanchez, for example, was among the first to show how intelligence tests are culturally biased—to the disadvantage of Mexican American children. Asian American psychologist Stanley Sue has shown how discrimination may be connected with racial differences in intelligence and academic achievement.

Today more than half of the PhDs in psychology are awarded to women. African Americans and Hispanic Americans each receive 3% to 4% of the PhDs awarded in psychology (ODEER, 1994).

Put it another way: Psychology belongs to everyone. ■

TRUTH OR FICTION REVISITED

It is not true that men receive the majority of degrees in psychology. Women actually receive the majority of PhDs in psychology today.

The Humanistic-Existential Perspective

The humanistic-existential perspective is related to Gestalt psychology and is cognitive in flavor. **Humanism** stresses the human capacity for self-fulfillment and the central roles of consciousness, self-awareness, and decision making. Consciousness—our sense of being in the world—is seen as the force that unifies our personalities. **Existentialism** views people as free to choose and responsible for choosing ethical conduct.

Humanistic psychology considers personal, or subjective experience to be the most important event in psychology. Humanists believe that self-awareness, experience, and choice permit us, to a large extent, to "invent ourselves" and our ways of relating to the world as we progress through life.

The Psychodynamic Perspective

In the 1940s and 1950s, Freud's psychodynamic theory dominated the practice of psychotherapy and was influential in scientific psychology and the arts. Most psychotherapists were psychodynamically oriented. Many renowned artists and writers consulted psychodynamic therapists as a way to liberate the expression of their unconscious ideas. Freud's influence continues to be felt, although it no longer dominates methods of psychotherapy. Some psychologists even argue that Freud's ideas are of no more than historic interest.

Contemporary psychologists who follow Freud are likely to call themselves *neoanalysts*. Neoanalysts such as Karen Horney and Erik Erikson focus less on unconscious processes and more on conscious choice and self-direction.

Many Freudian ideas are retained in watered-down form by the population at large. For example, sometimes we have ideas or desires that seem atypical to us. We may say that it seems as if something is trying to get the better of us. In the Middle Ages, such thoughts and impulses were usually attributed to the devil or to demons. Dreams, likewise, were thought to enter us magically from the spirit world. Today, in part because of the influence of Sigmund Freud, many people ascribe dreams and atypical ideas or desires to unconscious processes within themselves.

Learning Perspectives

Many psychologists study the effects of experience on behavior. Learning, to them, is the essential factor in describing, explaining, predicting, and controlling behavior. The term *learning* has different meanings to psychologists of different persuasions, however. Some students of learning find roles for consciousness and insight. Others do not. This distinction is found among those who adhere to the behavioral and social-cognitive perspectives.

For John B. Watson, behaviorism was an approach to life as well as a broad guideline for psychological research. Not only did Watson despair of measuring consciousness and mental processes in the laboratory, he also applied behavioral analysis to virtually all situations in his daily life. He viewed people as doing things because of their learning histories, their situations, and rewards rather than because of conscious choice.

Behaviorists emphasize environmental influences and the learning of habits through repetition and reinforcement. **Social-cognitive theorists** (previously termed *social-learning theorists*), in contrast, suggest that people can modify or create their environments. Since the 1960s, social-cognitive theorists have gained influence in the areas of personality development,

HUMANISM The philosophy and school of psychology that asserts people are conscious, self-aware, and capable of free choice, self-fulfillment, and ethical behavior.

EXISTENTIALISM The view that people are free and responsible for their own behavior.

SOCIAL-COGNITIVE THEORY A school of psychology in the behaviorist tradition that includes cognitive factors in the explanation and prediction of behavior. Formerly termed *social-learning theory*.

HUMAN DIVERSITY.
How can psychologists understand the hopes and problems of people from a particular ethnic group without understanding that group's history and cultural heritage? The study of human diversity helps us understand and appreciate the scope of behavior and mental processes.

psychological disorders, and methods of therapy. Theorists such as Albert Bandura, Julian Rotter, and Walter Mischel see themselves as part of the behaviorist tradition because of their focus on the importance of learning. Yet they also grant cognition a key role. They note that people also engage in intentional learning by observing others. Through observational learning, we acquire a storehouse of responses to life's situations.

The Sociocultural Perspective

The profession of psychology focuses mainly on the individual and is committed to the dignity of the individual. However, psychology students cannot understand people's behavior and mental processes without reference to their diversity (Basic Behavioral Science Task Force, 1996b). Studying perspectives other than their own helps students understand the role of a culture's beliefs, values, and attitudes on behavior and mental processes. It helps students perceive why people from diverse cultures behave and think in different ways, and how the science of psychology is enriched by addressing those differences (Denmark, 1994; Reid, 1994).

People differ in many ways. The **sociocultural perspective** addresses the influences of ethnicity, gender, culture, and socioeconomic status on behavior and mental processes (Allen, 1993; Lewis-Fernández & Kleinman, 1994). For example, what is often seen as healthful, self-assertive, outspoken behavior by most U.S. women may be interpreted as brazen behavior in Hispanic American or Asian American communities (Lopez & Hernandez, 1986).

ETHNICITY One kind of diversity involves people's ethnicity. Members of an **ethnic group** are united by their cultural heritage, race, language, and common history. The experiences of various ethnic groups in the United States highlight the impact of social, political, and economic factors on human behavior and development (Basic Behavioral Science Task Force, 1996b; Phinney, 1996).

The probing of human diversity enables students to appreciate the cultural heritages and historical problems of various ethnic groups. This textbook considers many psychological issues related to ethnicity, such as the representation of ethnic minority groups in psychological research studies, substance abuse among adolescents from various ethnic minority groups, bilingualism, ethnic differences in intelligence test scores, the prevalence of suicide among members of different ethnic groups, ethnic differences in vulnerability to physical problems and disorders ranging from obesity to hypertension and cancer, multicultural issues in the practice of psychotherapy, and prejudice.

GENDER Gender is the state of being male or being female. Gender is not simply a matter of anatomic sex. It involves a complex web of cultural expectations and social roles that affect people's self-concepts and hopes and dreams as well as their behavior. How can sciences such as psychology and medicine hope to understand the particular viewpoints, qualities, and problems of women if most research is conducted with men and by men (Matthews et al., 1997)?

Just as members of ethnic minority groups have experienced prejudice, so too have women. Even much of the scientific research on gender roles and gender differences assumes that male behavior represents the norm (Ader & Johnson, 1994). Women have traditionally been channeled into domestic pursuits, regardless of their wishes as individuals. Not until rela-

SOCIOCULTURAL PERSPECTIVE The view that focuses on the roles of ethnicity, gender, culture, and socioeconomic status in behavior and mental processes.

ETHNIC GROUP A group characterized by common features such as cultural heritage, history, race, and language.

GENDER The state of being female or being male.

tively modern times were women generally considered suitable for higher education (and they are still considered unsuited to education in many parts of the world!). Women have attended college in the United States only since 1833, when Oberlin College opened its doors to women. Today, however, more than half (54.5%) of U.S. postsecondary students are women. Today women receive more than 50% of the doctoral degrees in psychology (Pion et al., 1996).

Psychology is the scientific study of behavior and mental processes. By now we have a sense of the various fields of psychology, the history of psychology, and the ways in which today's psychologists look at behavior and mental processes. Like other scientists, psychologists rely on research to seek answers to the questions of interest to them. The following section follows through on some questions of interest to psychologists to demonstrate how psychologists conduct research.

HOW PSYCHOLOGISTS STUDY BEHAVIOR AND MENTAL PROCESSES

Consider some questions of interest to psychologists: Do only humans use tools? Does alcohol cause aggression? Why do some people hardly ever think of food, whereas others are obsessed with it and snack all day long? Why do some unhappy people attempt suicide, whereas others seek other ways of coping with their problems? Does having people of different ethnic backgrounds collaborate in their work serve to decrease or increase feelings of prejudice?

Many of us have expressed opinions on questions like these at one time or another. Different psychological theories also suggest a number of possible answers. Psychology is an *empirical* science, however. In an empirical science, assumptions about the behavior of cosmic rays, chemical compounds, cells, or people must be supported by evidence. Strong arguments, reference to authority figures, even tightly knit theories are not adequate as scientific evidence. Psychologists make it their business—literally and figuratively—to be skeptical.

Psychologists use research to study behavior and mental processes empirically. To undertake our study of research methods, let us recount some famous research undertaken at Yale University more than 30 years ago.

People are capable of boundless generosity and of hideous atrocities. Throughout history, people have sacrificed themselves for the welfare of their families, friends, and nations. Throughout history, people have maimed and destroyed other people to vent their rage or please their superiors.

Let us follow up on the negative side. Soldiers have killed civilians and raped women in occupied areas to obey the orders of their superiors or to win the approval of their comrades. Millions of Native Americans, Armenians, Muslims, and Jews have been slaughtered by people who were obeying the orders of officers.

How susceptible are people—how susceptible are you and I—to the demands of authority figures such as military officers? Is there something unusual or abnormal about people who follow orders and inflict pain and

FIGURE PSY.5

THE "AGGRESSION MACHINE."

In the Milgram studies on obedience to authority, pressing levers on the "aggression machine" was the operational definition of aggression.

suffering on their fellow human beings? Are they very much unlike you and me? Or *are* they you and me?

It is easy to imagine that something must be terribly wrong with people who would hurt a stranger without provocation. There must be something abnormal about people who would slaughter innocents. But these are assumptions, and scientists are skeptical of assumptions. Psychologist Stanley Milgram also wondered whether normal people would comply with authority figures who made immoral demands. But rather than speculate on the issue, he undertook a series of classic experiments at Yale University that have become known as the Milgram studies on obedience.

In an early phase of his work, Milgram (1963) placed ads in New Haven (Connecticut) newspapers for people who would be willing to serve as **subjects** in studies on learning and memory. He enlisted 40 people ranging in age from 20 to 50—teachers, engineers, laborers, salespeople, people who had not completed elementary school, people with graduate degrees.

Let's suppose that you have answered the ad. You show up at the university in exchange for a reasonable fee ($4.50, which in the early 1960s might easily fill your gas tank) and to satisfy your own curiosity. You may be impressed. After all, Yale is a venerable institution that dominates the city. You are no less impressed by the elegant labs, where you meet a distinguished behavioral scientist dressed in a white coat and another person who has responded to the ad. The scientist explains that the purpose of the experiment is to study the *effects of punishment on learning.* The experiment requires a "teacher" and a "learner." By chance, you are appointed the teacher and the other recruit the learner.

You, the scientist, and the learner enter a laboratory room containing a threatening chair with dangling straps. The scientist straps the learner in. The learner expresses some concern, but this is, after all, for the sake of science. And this is Yale University, isn't it? What could happen to a person at Yale?

You follow the scientist to an adjacent room, from which you are to do your "teaching." This teaching promises to have an impact. You are to punish the learner's errors by pressing levers marked from 15 to 450 volts on a fearsome-looking console (see Figure PSY.5). Labels describe 28 of the 30 levers as running the gamut from "Slight Shock" to "Danger: Severe Shock." The last two levers are simply labeled "XXX." Just in case you have no idea what electric shock feels like, the scientist gives you a sample 45-volt shock. It stings. You pity the person who might receive more.

Your learner is expected to learn pairs of words, which are to be read from a list. After hearing the list once, the learner is to produce the word that pairs with the stimulus word from a list of four alternatives. This is done by pressing a switch that lights one of four panels in your room. If it is the correct panel, you proceed to the next stimulus word. If not, you are to deliver an electric shock. With each error, you are to increase the voltage of the shock (Figure PSY.6).

You probably have some misgivings. Electrodes have been strapped to the learner's wrists, and the scientist has applied electrode paste "to avoid blisters and burns." You have also been told that the shocks will cause "no permanent tissue damage," although they might be extremely painful. Still, the learner is going along. And after all, this is Yale.

The learner answers some items correctly and then makes some errors. With mild concern you press the levers up through 45 volts. You've tolerated that much yourself. Then a few more mistakes are made. You press the 60-volt lever, then 75. The learner makes another mistake. You pause and look at the scientist, who is reassuring: "Although the shocks may be painful, there is no permanent tissue damage, so please go on." The learner makes more errors, and soon you are up to a shock of 300 volts. But now the learner is pounding on the other side of the wall! Your chest tightens and you begin to perspire. 'Damn science and the $4.50!' you think. You hesitate and the scientist says, "The experiment requires that you continue." After the delivery of the next stimulus word, the learner chooses no answer at all. What are you to do? "Wait for 5 to 10 seconds," the scientist instructs, "and then treat no answer as a wrong answer." But after the next shock the pounding on the wall resumes! Now your heart is racing, and you are convinced you are causing extreme pain and discomfort. Is it possible that no lasting damage is being done? Is the experiment that important, after all? What to do? You hesitate again, and the scientist says, "It is absolutely essential that you continue." His voice is very convincing. "You have no other choice," he says, "you *must* go on." You can barely think straight, and for some unaccountable reason you feel laughter rising in your throat. Your finger shakes above the lever. *What are you to do?*

Milgram (1963, 1974) found out what most people in his sample would do. The sample was a cross section of the male population of New Haven. Of the 40 men in this phase of his research, only 5 refused to go beyond the 300-volt level, the level at which the learner first pounded the wall. Nine other "teachers" defied the scientist within the 300-volt range. But 65% of the subjects complied with the scientist throughout the series, believing they were delivering 450-volt, XXX-rated shocks.

Were these subjects unfeeling? Not at all. Milgram was impressed by their signs of stress. They trembled, they stuttered, they bit their lips. They groaned, they sweated, they dug their fingernails into their flesh. Some had fits of laughter, although laughter was inappropriate. One salesperson's laughter was so convulsive that he could not continue with the experiment.

We return to the Milgram studies later in the chapter. They are a rich mine of information about human nature. They are also useful for our discussions of research issues such as replication, the experimental method, and ethics.

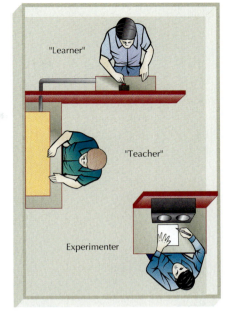

FIGURE PSY.6
THE EXPERIMENTAL SETUP IN THE MILGRAM STUDIES.
When the "learner" makes an error, the experimenter prods the "teacher" to deliver a painful electric shock.

The Scientific Method: Putting Ideas to the Test

The scientific method is an organized way of using experience and testing ideas in order to expand and refine knowledge. Psychologists do not necessarily follow the steps of the scientific method as we might follow a cookbook recipe. However, their research endeavors are guided by certain principles.

Psychologists usually begin by *formulating a research question.* Research questions can have many sources. Our daily experiences, psychological theory, even folklore all help generate questions for research. Consider some questions that may arise from daily experience. Daily experience in using day-care centers may motivate us to conduct research on whether day care influences the development of social skills or the bonds of attachment between children and mothers.

Or consider questions that might arise from psychological theory (see Figure PSY.7). Social-cognitive principles of observational learning may prompt research on the effects of TV violence. Sigmund Freud's psychoanalytic theory may prompt research on whether the verbal expression of feelings of anger helps relieve feelings of depression.

Research questions may also arise from common knowledge. Consider familiar adages such as "Misery loves company," "Opposites attract," and

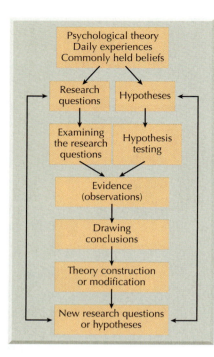

FIGURE PSY.7
THE SCIENTIFIC METHOD.
The scientific method is a systematic way of organizing and expanding scientific knowledge. Daily experiences, common beliefs, and scientific observations all contribute to the development of theories. Psychological theories explain observations and lead to hypotheses about behavior and mental processes. Observations can confirm the theory or lead to its refinement or abandonment.

HYPOTHESIS In psychology, a specific statement about behavior or mental processes that is tested through research.

SELECTION FACTOR A source of bias that may occur in research findings when subjects are allowed to choose for themselves a certain treatment in a scientific study.

REPLICATE Repeat, reproduce, copy.

"Beauty is in the eye of the beholder." Psychologists may ask, *Does* misery love company? *Do* opposites attract? *Is* beauty in the eye of the beholder?

A research question may be studied as a question or reworded as a hypothesis (see Figure PSY.7). A **hypothesis** is a specific statement about behavior or mental processes that is tested through research. One hypothesis about day care might be that preschoolers who are placed in day care will acquire greater social skills in relating to peers than preschoolers who are cared for in the home. A hypothesis about TV violence might be that elementary school children who watch more violent TV shows tend to behave more aggressively toward their peers. A hypothesis that addresses Freudian theory might be that verbally expressing feelings of anger will decrease feelings of depression.

Psychologists next examine the research question or *test the hypothesis* through controlled methods such as the experiment. For example, we could introduce children who are in day care and children who are not to a new child in a college child research center and observe how children in each group interact with the new acquaintance.

Psychologists draw conclusions about their research questions or the accuracy of their hypotheses on the basis of their observations or findings. When their observations do not bear out their hypotheses, they may modify the theories from which the hypotheses were derived (see Figure PSY.7). Research findings often suggest refinements to psychological theories and, consequently, new avenues of research.

In our research on day care, we would probably find that children in day care show greater social skills than children who are cared for in the home (Clarke-Stewart, 1991). We would probably also find that more aggressive children spend more time watching TV violence. Research on the effectiveness of psychoanalytic forms of therapy is usually based on case studies.

As psychologists draw conclusions from research evidence, they are guided by principles of critical thinking. For example, they try not to confuse correlations between findings with cause and effect. Although more aggressive children apparently spend more time watching violent TV shows, it may be erroneous to conclude from this kind of evidence that TV violence *causes* aggressive behavior. Perhaps a **selection factor** is at work—because the children studied choose (select) for themselves what they will watch. Perhaps more aggressive children are more likely than less aggressive children to tune in to violent TV shows.

To better understand the effects of the selection factor, consider a study on the relationship between exercise and health. Imagine that we were to compare a group of people who exercised regularly with a group of people who did not. We might find that the exercisers were physically healthier than the couch potatoes. But could we conclude that exercise is a causal factor in good health? Perhaps not. The selection factor—the fact that one group chose to exercise and the other did not—could also explain the results. Perhaps healthy people are more likely to *choose* to exercise.

Some psychologists include publication of research reports in professional journals as a crucial part of the scientific method. Researchers are obligated to provide enough details of their work that others will be able to repeat or **replicate** it to see if the findings hold up over time and with different subjects. Publication of research also permits the scientific community at large to evaluate the methods and conclusions of other scientists.

Samples and Populations: Representing Human Diversity

Consider a piece of history that never quite happened: The Republican candidate Alf Landon defeated the incumbent president, Franklin D.

Roosevelt, in 1936. Or at least Landon did so in a poll conducted by a popular magazine of the day, the *Literary Digest.* In the actual election, however, Roosevelt routed Landon by a landslide of 11 million votes. How, then, could the *Digest* predict a Landon victory? How was so great a discrepancy possible?

The *Digest,* you see, had surveyed voters by phone. Today telephone sampling is a widely practiced and reasonably legitimate polling technique. But the *Digest* poll was taken during the Great Depression, when people who had telephones were much wealthier than those who did not. People at higher income levels are also more likely to vote Republican. No surprise, then, that the overwhelming majority of those sampled said they would vote for Landon.

The principle involved here is that samples must accurately *represent* the population they are intended to reflect. Only representative samples allow us to **generalize**—or *extend* our findings—from research samples to populations.

In surveys such as that conducted by the *Literary Digest,* and in other research methods, the individuals who are studied are referred to as a **sample.** A sample is a segment of a **population** (the group that is targeted for study). Psychologists and other scientists need to ensure that the people they observe *represent* their target population, such as U.S. voters, and not subgroups such as southern Californians or non-Hispanic White members of the middle class.

PROBLEMS IN GENERALIZING FROM PSYCHOLOGICAL RESEARCH

All generalizations are dangerous, even this one.

ALEXANDRE DUMAS

Many factors must be considered in interpreting the accuracy of the results of scientific research. One is the nature of the research sample.

Milgram's initial research on obedience was limited to a sample of New Haven men. Could he generalize his findings to other men or to women? Would college students, who are considered to be independent thinkers, show more defiance? A replication of Milgram's study with a sample of Yale men yielded similar results. What about women, who are supposedly less aggressive than men? In subsequent research women, too, administered shocks to the learners. All this took place in a nation that values independence and free will.

Later in the chapter we consider research in which the subjects were drawn from a population of college men who were social drinkers. That is, they tended to drink at social gatherings but not when alone. Whom do college men represent, other than themselves? To whom can we extend, or generalize, the results? For one thing, the results may not extend to women, not even to college women. In the chapter on consciousness, for example, we learn that alcohol goes more quickly to women's heads than to men's.

College men also tend to be younger and more intelligent than the general adult population. We cannot be certain that the findings extend to older men of average intelligence, although it seems reasonable to assume they do. Social drinkers may also differ biologically and psychologically from alcoholics, who have difficulty controlling their drinking. Nor can we be certain that college social drinkers represent people who do not drink at all.

By and large, we must also question whether findings of research with men can be generalized to women (Ader & Johnson, 1994), and whether research with White men can be extended to members of ethnic minority groups. For example, personality tests completed by non-Hispanic White

TRUTH OR FICTION REVISITED
It is true that you could survey 20 million voters and still not predict the outcome of a presidential election accurately. Sample size alone does not guarantee that a sample will accurately represent the population from which it was drawn.

GENERALIZE To extend from the particular to the general; to apply observations based on a sample to a population.

SAMPLE Part of a population.

POPULATION A complete group of organisms or events.

Americans and by African Americans may need to be interpreted in diverse ways if accurate conclusions are to be drawn. The well-known Kinsey studies on sexual behavior (Kinsey et al., 1948, 1953) did not adequately represent African Americans, poor people, older people, and numerous other groups.

RANDOM AND STRATIFIED SAMPLING One way to achieve a representative sample is by means of **random sampling.** In a random sample, each member of a population has an equal chance of being selected to participate. Researchers can also use a **stratified sample,** which is selected so that identified subgroups in the population are represented proportionately in the sample. For instance, 12% of the American population is African American. A stratified sample would thus be 12% African American. As a practical matter, a large randomly selected sample will show reasonably accurate stratification. A random sample of 1,500 people will represent the general U.S. population reasonably well. A haphazardly drawn sample of 20 million, however, might not.

Large-scale magazine surveys of sexual behavior have asked readers to fill out and return questionnaires. Although many thousands of readers completed the questionnaires and sent them in, did they represent the general U.S. population? Probably not. These studies and similar ones may have been influenced by **volunteer bias.** People who offer or volunteer to participate in research studies differ systematically from people who do not. In the case of research on sexual behavior, volunteers may represent subgroups of the population—or of readers of the magazines in question—who are willing to disclose intimate information (Rathus et al., 2000). Volunteers may also be more interested in research than nonvolunteers, as well as have more spare time. How might such volunteers differ from the population at large? How might such differences slant or bias the research outcomes?

Methods of Observation: The Better to See You With

Many people consider themselves experts on behavior and mental processes. How many times, for example, have grandparents told us what they have seen in their lives and what it means about human nature?

We see much indeed during our lifetimes. Our personal observations tend to be fleeting and uncontrolled, however. We sift through experience for the things that interest us. We often ignore the obvious because it does not fit our assumptions about the way things ought to be. Scientists, however, have devised more controlled ways of observing others. In this section we consider the case study, survey, and naturalistic observation methods.

CASE STUDY We begin with the case study method because our own informal ideas about human nature tend to be based on **case studies,** or information we collect about individuals and small groups. But most of us gather our information haphazardly. We often see only what we want to see. Unscientific accounts of people's behavior are referred to as *anecdotes.* Psychologists attempt to gather information about individuals more carefully.

Sigmund Freud developed psychodynamic theory largely on the basis of case studies. He studied people who sought his help in great depth, seeking the factors that seemed to contribute to certain patterns of behav-

RANDDOM SAMPLE A mple drawn so that each member of a population has an equal chance of being selected to participate.

STRATIFIED SAMPLE A sample drawn so that indentified subgroups in the population are represented proportionately in the sample. How can stratified sampling be carried out to ensure that a sample represents the ethnic diversity we find in the population at large?

VOLUNTEER BIAS A source of bias or error in research reflecting the prospect that people who offer to participate in research studies differ systematically from people who do not.

CASE STUDY A carefully drawn biography that may be obtained through interviews, questionnaires, and psychological tests.

ior. He followed some people for many years, meeting with them several times a week.

Case studies are also often used to investigate rare occurrences, as in the case of "Eve." Eve was an example of a person with multiple personalities (technically termed *dissociative identity disorder*). "Eve White" was a mousy, well-intentioned woman who had two other "personalities" living inside her. One of them was "Eve Black," a promiscuous personality who now and then emerged to take control of her behavior.

Case studies can provide compelling portraits of individuals, but they also have some sources of inaccuracy. For example, there are gaps and factual inaccuracies in people's memories (Azar, 1997; Brewin et al., 1993). People may also distort their pasts to please the interviewer or because they want to remember events in certain ways. Interviewers may also have certain expectations and may subtly encourage subjects to fill in gaps in ways that are consistent with these expectations. Bandura (1986) notes, for example, that psychoanalysts have been criticized for guiding people who seek their help into viewing their own lives from the psychodynamic perspective. No wonder, then, that many people provide "evidence" that is consistent with psychodynamic theory. However, interviewers and other kinds of researchers who hold *any* theoretical viewpoint run the risk of indirectly prodding people into saying what they want to hear.

THE SURVEY In the good old days, we had to wait until the wee hours of the morning to learn the results of local and national elections. Throughout the evening and early morning hours, suspense would build as ballots from distant neighborhoods and states were tallied. Nowadays, we are barely settled with an after-dinner cup of coffee on election night when reporters announce that a computer has examined the ballots of a "scientifically selected sample" and predicted the next president of the United States. All this may occur with less than 1% of the vote tallied.

Just as computers and pollsters predict election results and report national opinion on the basis of scientifically selected samples, psychologists conduct **surveys** to learn about behavior and mental processes that cannot be observed in the natural setting or studied experimentally. Psychologists conducting surveys may employ questionnaires and interviews or examine public records. One of the great advantages to the survey is that by distributing questionnaires and analyzing answers with a computer, psychologists can study many thousands of people at a time.

We alluded earlier to the "Kinsey studies." Alfred Kinsey of Indiana University and his colleagues published two surveys of sexual behavior, based on interviews, that shocked the nation. These were *Sexual Behavior in the Human Male* (1948) and *Sexual Behavior in the Human Female* (1953). Kinsey reported that masturbation was virtually universal in his sample of men at a time when masturbation was still widely thought to impair health. He also reported that about 1 woman in 3 who was still single at age 25 had engaged in premarital intercourse.

Surveys, like case studies, have various sources of inaccuracy. People may recall their behavior inaccurately or purposefully misrepresent it. Some people try to ingratiate themselves with their interviewers by answering in what they perceive to be the socially desirable direction. The Kinsey studies all relied on male interviewers, for example. It has been speculated that female interviewees might have been more open and honest with female interviewers. Similar problems may occur when interviewers and the people surveyed are from different ethnic or socioeconomic backgrounds. Other people may falsify their attitudes and exaggerate their problems in order to draw attention to themselves or foul up the results.

SURVEY A method of scientific investigation in which a large sample of people answer questions about their attitudes or behavior.

FIGURE PSY.8

THE NATURALISTIC-OBSERVATION METHOD.

Jane Goodall has observed the behavior of chimpanzees in the field, "where it happens." She has found that chimps use sticks to grub for food and that they apparently kiss each other as a social greeting. Scientists who use this method try not to interfere with the animals or people they observe, even though this sometimes means allowing an animal to be mistreated by other animals or to die from a curable illness.

Consider some examples of survey measurement errors caused by inaccurate self-reports of behavior (Barringer, 1993). If people brushed their teeth as often as they claimed, and used the amount of toothpaste they indicated, three times as much toothpaste would be sold in the United States as is actually sold. People also appear to overreport church attendance and to underreport abortions (Barringer, 1993). Why do you think this is so?

INTELLIGENCE AND ACHIEVEMENT.
Correlations between intelligence test scores and academic achievement—as measured by school grades and achievement tests—tend to be positive and strong. Does the correlational method allow us to say that intelligence *causes* or *is responsible for* academic achievements? Why or why not?

NATURALISTIC OBSERVATION a scientific methos in which organisms are observed in their natural environments.

NATURALISTIC OBSERVATION You use **naturalistic observation**— that is, you observe people in their natural habitats—every day. So do psychologists. The next time you opt for a fast-food burger lunch, look around. Pick out slender people and overweight people and observe whether they eat their burgers and fries differently. Do the overweight people eat more rapidly? Chew less frequently? Leave less food on their plates? Psychologists have used this method to study the eating habits of normal weight and overweight people. In fact, while you're at McDonald's, if you notice people peering over sunglasses and occasionally tapping the head of a partly concealed microphone, perhaps they are recording their observations of other people's eating habits.

Naturalistic observation has the advantage of allowing psychologists and other scientists to observe behavior where it happens, or "in the field." In doing so, researchers use *unobtrusive* measures to try to avoid interfering with the behaviors they are observing. For example, Jane Goodall has observed the behavior of chimpanzees in their natural environment to learn about their social behavior, sexual behavior, use of tools, and other facts of chimp life (see Figure PSY.8). Her observations have shown us that (1) we were incorrect to think that only humans use tools; and (2) kissing, as a greeting, is apparently used by chimpanzees as well as by humans.

Correlation

Are people with higher intelligence more likely to do well in school? Are people with a stronger need for achievement likely to climb higher up the corporate ladder? What is the relationship between stress and health?

Correlation follows observation. By using the correlational method, psychologists investigate whether observed behavior or a measured trait is related to, or correlated with, another. Consider the variables of intelligence and academic performance. These variables are assigned numbers such as intelligence test scores and academic averages. Then the numbers are mathematically related and expressed as a **correlation coefficient**. A correlation coefficient is a number that varies between +1.00 and –1.00.

Studies report **positive correlations** between intelligence test scores and academic achievement, as measured, for example, by grade point averages. Generally speaking, the higher people score on intelligence tests, the better their academic performance is likely to be. The scores attained on intelligence tests tend to be positively correlated (about +0.60 to +0.70) with academic achievement (see Figure PSY.9). However, factors *other* than performance on intelligence tests also contribute to academic

CORRELATION COEFFICIENT A number from +1.00 to –1.00 that expresses the strength and direction (positive or negative) of the relationship between two variables.

POSITIVE CORRELATION A relationship between variables in which one variable increases as the other also increases.

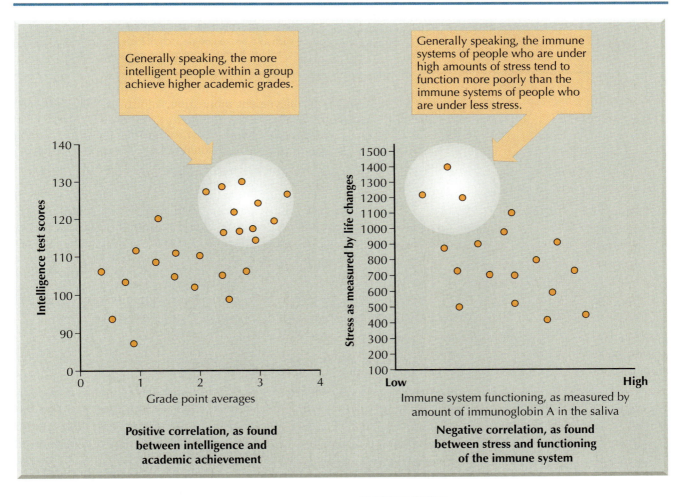

FIGURE PSY.9

POSITIVE AND NEGATIVE CORRELATIONS.

When there is a positive correlation between variables, as there is between intelligence and achievement, one increases as the other increases. By and large, the higher people score on intelligence tests, the better their academic performance is likely to be, as in the diagram to the left. (Each dot represents an individual's intelligence test score and grade point average.) But there is a negative correlation between stress and health. As the amount of stress we experience increases, the functioning of our immune systems tends to decrease. Correlational research may suggest but does not demonstrate cause and effect.

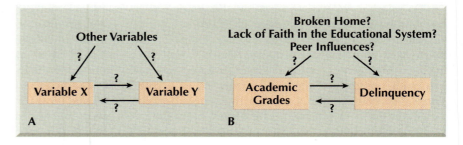

FIGURE PSY.10
CORRELATIONAL RELATIONSHIPS, CAUSE, AND EFFECT.
Correlational relationships may suggest but does not demonstrate cause and effect. In part A, there is a correlation between variables X and Y. Does this mean that either variable Y or that variable Y causes variable X? Not necessarily. Other factors could affect both variables X and Y. Consider the examples of academic grades (variable X) and juvenile delinquency (variable Y) in part B. There is a negative correlation between the two. Does this mean that poor grades contribute to delinquency? Perhaps. Does it mean that delinquency contributes to poor grades? Again, perhaps. But there could also be other variables—such as a broken home, lack of faith in the educational system, or peer influences—that contribute both to poor grades and delinquency.

success. These include achievement motivation, adjustment, and common sense (Collier, 1994; Sternberg et al., 1995).

There is a **negative correlation** between stress and health. As the amount of stress affecting us increases, the functioning of our immune systems decreases. Under high levels of stress, many people show poorer health.

Correlational research may suggest but does not prove cause and effect. For instance, it may seem logical to assume that high intelligence makes it possible for children to profit from education. Research has also shown, however, that education contributes to higher scores on intelligence tests. Preschoolers who are placed in stimulating Head Start programs later attain higher scores on intelligence tests than age-mates who did not have this experience. The relationship between intelligence and academic performance may not be as simple as you might think. What of the link between stress and health? Does stress impair health, or is it possible that people in poorer health encounter more stress? (See Figure PSY.10.)

The Experimental Method: Trying Things Out

The people who signed up for the Milgram studies participated in an elaborate experiment. The subjects received an intricate *treatment*—one that involved a well-equipped research laboratory. The experiment also involved deception. Milgram had even foreseen subjects' objections to the procedure. He had therefore conceived standardized statements that his assistants would use when subjects balked—for example: "Although the shocks may be painful, there is no permanent tissue damage, so please go on." "The experiment requires that you continue." "It is absolutely essential that you continue." "You have no other choice; you *must* go on." These statements, the bogus "aggression machine," the use of the "learner" (who was actually a confederate of the experimenter)—all these were part of the experimental treatment.

Although we can raise many questions about the Milgram studies, most psychologists agree that the preferred method for answering questions

NEGATIVE CORRELATION A relationship between two variables in which one variable increases as the other decreases.

about cause and effect is the experiment. In an **experiment,** a group of subjects obtains a **treatment,** such as a dose of alcohol, a change in room temperature, perhaps an injection of a drug. The subjects are then observed carefully to determine whether the treatment makes a difference in their behavior. Does alcohol alter the ability to take tests, for example? What about differences in room temperatures and level of background noise?

Experiments are used whenever possible because they allow psychologists to control the experiences of subjects and draw conclusions about cause and effect. A psychologist may theorize that alcohol leads to aggression because it reduces fear of consequences or because it energizes the activity levels of drinkers. She or he may then hypothesize that a treatment in which subjects receive a specified dosage of alcohol will lead to increases in aggression. Let us follow the example of the effects of alcohol on aggression to further our understanding of the experimental method.

INDEPENDENT AND DEPENDENT VARIABLES In an experiment to determine whether alcohol causes aggression, subjects would be given an amount of alcohol and its effects would be measured. In this case, alcohol is an **independent variable.** The presence of an independent variable is manipulated by the experimenters so that its effects may be determined. The independent variable of alcohol may be administered at different levels, or doses, from none or very little to enough to cause intoxication or drunkenness.

The measured results, or outcomes, in an experiment are called **dependent variables.** The presence of dependent variables presumably depends on the independent variables. In an experiment to determine whether alcohol influences aggression, aggressive behavior would be a dependent variable. Other dependent variables of interest might include sexual arousal, visual-motor coordination, and performance on intellectual tasks such as defining words or doing numerical computations.

In an experiment on the relationships between temperature and aggression, temperature would be an independent variable and aggressive behavior would be a dependent variable. We could set temperatures from below freezing to blistering hot, and study its effects. We could also use a second independent variable such as social provocation. That is, we could insult some subjects but not others. This method would allow us to study the ways in which two independent variables—temperature and social provocation—affect aggression, singly and together.

EXPERIMENTAL AND CONTROL GROUPS Ideal experiments use experimental and control groups. Subjects in **experimental groups** obtain the treatment. Members of **control groups** do not. Every effort is made to ensure that all other conditions are held constant for both groups. This method enhances the researchers' ability to draw conclusions about cause and effect. The researchers can be more confident that outcomes of the experiment are caused by the treatments and not by chance factors or chance fluctuations in behavior.

In an experiment on the effects of alcohol on aggression, members of the experimental group would ingest alcohol and members of the control group would not. In a complex experiment, different experimental groups might ingest different dosages of alcohol and be exposed to different types of social provocations.

BLINDS AND DOUBLE BLINDS One experiment on the effects of alcohol on aggression (Boyatzis, 1974) reported that men at parties where

EXPERIMENT A scientific method that seeks to confirm cause-and-effect relationships by introducing independent variables and observing their effects on dependent variables.

TREATMENT In experiments, a condition received by subjects so that its effects may be observed.

INDEPENDENT VARIABLE A condition in a scientific study that is manipulated so that its effects may be observed.

DEPENDENT VARIABLE A measure of an assumed effect of an independent variable.

EXPERIMENTAL GROUPS In experiments, groups whose members obtain the treatment.

CONTROL GROUPS In experiments, groups whose members do not obtain the treatment while other conditions are held constant.

WHAT ARE THE EFFECTS OF ALCOHOL?
Psychologists have conducted numerous studies to determine the effects of alcohol. Questions have been raised about the soundness of research in which people *know* they have drunk alcohol. Why is this research questioned?

TRUTH OR FICTION REVISITED
It is true that, in many experiments, neither the subjects nor the researchers know who is receiving the real treatment and who is receiving a placebo ("sugar pill"). Such *double-blind studies* control for the effects of subjects' and researchers' expectations.

PLACEBO A bogus treatment that has the appearance of being genuine.

BLIND In experimental terminology, unaware of whether or not one has received a treatment.

DOUBLE-BLIND STUDY A study in which neither the subjects nor the observers know who has received the treatment.

beer and liquor were served acted more aggressively than men at parties where only soft drinks were served. But subjects in the experimental group *knew* they had drunk alcohol, and those in the control group *knew* they had not. Aggression that appeared to result from alcohol might not have reflected drinking per se. Instead, it might have reflected the subjects' *expectations* about the effects of alcohol. People tend to act in stereotypical ways when they believe they have been drinking alcohol. For instance, men tend to become less anxious in social situations, more aggressive, and more sexually aroused.

A **placebo**, or "sugar pill," often results in the kind of behavior that people expect. Physicians sometimes give placebos to demanding, but healthy, people, many of whom then report that they feel better. When subjects in psychological experiments are given placebos—such as tonic water—but think they have drunk alcohol, we can conclude that changes in their behavior stem from their beliefs about alcohol, not from the alcohol itself.

Well-designed experiments control for the effects of expectations by creating conditions under which subjects are unaware of, or **blind** to, the treatment. Yet researchers may also have expectations. They may, in effect, be "rooting for" a certain treatment. For instance, tobacco company executives may wish to show that cigarette smoking is harmless. In such cases, it is useful if the people measuring the experimental outcomes are unaware of which subjects have received the treatment. Studies in which neither the subjects nor the experimenters know who has obtained the treatment are called **double-blind studies.**

The Food and Drug Administration requires double-blind studies before it allows the marketing of new drugs. The drug and the placebo look and taste alike. Experimenters assign the drug or placebo to subjects at random. Neither the subjects nor the observers know who is taking the drug and who is taking the placebo. After the final measurements have been made, a neutral panel (a group of people who have no personal stake in the outcome of the study) judges whether the effects of the drug differed from those of the placebo.

In one double-blind study on the effects of alcohol, Alan Lang and his colleagues (1975) pretested a highball of vodka and tonic water to determine that it could not be discriminated by taste from tonic water alone. They recruited college men who described themselves as social drinkers to participate in the study. Some of the men drank vodka and tonic water. Others drank tonic water only. Of the men who drank vodka, half were misled into believing they had drunk tonic water only (Figure PSY.11). Of those who drank tonic water only, half were misled into believing their drink contained vodka. Thus half the subjects were blind to their treat-

FIGURE PSY.11
THE EXPERIMENTAL CONDITIONS IN THE LANG STUDY.
The taste of vodka cannot be discerned when vodka is mixed with tonic water. For this reason, it was possible for subjects in the Lang study on the effects of alcohol to be kept "blind" as to whether or not they had actually drunk alcohol. Blind studies allow psychologists to control for the effects of subjects' expectations.

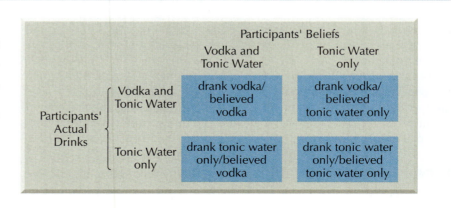

| | | Participants' Beliefs | |
		Vodka and Tonic Water	Tonic Water only
Participants' Actual Drinks	Vodka and Tonic Water	drank vodka/ believed vodka	drank vodka/ believed tonic water only
	Tonic Water only	drank tonic water only/believed vodka	drank tonic water only/believed tonic water only

ment. Experimenters who measured the men's aggressive responses were also blind concerning which subjects had drunk vodka.

The research team found that men who believed they had drunk vodka responded more aggressively to a provocation than men who believed they had drunk tonic water only. The actual content of the drink was immaterial. That is, men who had actually drunk alcohol acted no more aggressively than men who had drunk tonic water only. The results of the Lang study differ dramatically from those reported by Boyatzis, perhaps because the Boyatzis study did not control for the effects of expectations or beliefs about alcohol.

ETHICAL ISSUES IN PSYCHOLOGICAL RESEARCH AND PRACTICE

It is in the area of ethics that we raise the most serious questions about the Milgram studies. The Milgram studies on obedience made key contributions to our understanding of the limits of human nature. In fact, it is difficult for professional psychologists to imagine a history of psychology without the knowledge provided by such studies. But the subjects experienced severe psychological anguish. Were the Milgram studies **ethical?**

Psychologists adhere to a number of ethical standards that are intended to promote individual dignity, human welfare, and scientific integrity (McGovern et al., 1991). They also ensure that psychologists do not undertake research methods or treatments that are harmful to subjects or clients (American Psychological Association, 1992a). Let us look at these ethical standards as they apply to research with humans and with other animals.

Research With Humans

Lang and his colleagues (1975) gave small doses of alcohol to college students who were social drinkers. Other researchers, however, have paid alcoholics—people who have difficulty limiting their alcohol consumption—to drink in the laboratory so that they could study their reactions and those of family members (e.g., Jacob et al., 1991). Practices such as these raise ethical questions. For example, paying the alcoholics to drink in the laboratory, and providing the alcohol, could be viewed as encouraging them to engage in self-destructive behavior (Koocher, 1991).

Recall the signs of stress shown by the subjects in the Milgram studies on obedience. They trembled, stuttered, groaned, sweated, bit their lips, and dug their fingernails into their flesh. In fact, if Milgram had attempted to run his experiments in the 1990s rather than in the 1960s, he might have been denied permission to do so by a university ethics review committee. In virtually all institutional settings, including colleges, hospitals, and research foundations, **ethics review committees** help researchers consider the potential harm of their methods and review proposed studies according to ethical guidelines. When such committees find that proposed research might be unacceptably harmful to subjects, they may withhold approval until the proposal has been modified. Ethics review committees also weigh the potential benefits of research against the potential harm.

Today individuals must also provide **informed consent** before they participate in research. Having a general overview of the research and the opportunity to choose not to participate apparently gives them a sense of

ETHICAL Moral; referring to one's system of deriving standards for determining what is moral.

ETHICS REVIEW COMMITTEE A group found in an institutional setting that helps researchers consider the potential harm of their methods and reviews proposed studies according to ethical guidelines.

INFORMED CONSENT The term used by psychologists to indicate that a person has agreed to participate in research after receiving information about the purposes of the study and the nature of the treatments.

control and decreases the stress of participating (Dill et al., 1982). Is there a way in which subjects in the Milgram studies could have provided informed consent? What do you think?

Psychologists treat the records of research subjects and clients as confidential. This is because they respect people's privacy and also because people are more likely to express their true thoughts and feelings when researchers or therapists keep their disclosures confidential. Sometimes conflicts of interest arise, however, for example, when a client threatens a third party and the psychologist feels an obligation to warn that person (Nevid et al., 2000).

Ethics limit the types of research that psychologists may conduct. For example, how can we determine whether early separation from one's mother impairs social development? One way would be to observe the development of children who have been separated from their mothers at an early age. It is difficult to draw conclusions from such research, however, because of the selection factor. That is, the same factors that led to the separation—such as family tragedy or irresponsible parents—and *not* the separation, may have led to the outcome. Scientifically, it would be more sound to run experiments in which researchers separate children from their mothers at an early age and compare their development with that of other children. But psychologists would not undertake such research because of the ethical issues they pose. Yet they do run experiments with lower animals in which infants are separated from mothers.

Many psychological experiments cannot be run without deceiving the people who participate. However, the use of deception raises ethical issues. You are probably skeptical enough to wonder whether the "teachers" in the Milgram studies actually shocked the "learners" when the teachers pressed the levers on the console. They did not. The only real shock in this experiment was the 45-volt sample given to the teachers. Its purpose was to make the procedure believable.

The learners in the experiment were actually confederates of the experimenter. They had not answered the newspaper ads but were in on the truth from the start. The "teachers" were the only real subjects. They were led to believe they had been chosen at random for the teacher role, but the choosing was rigged so that newspaper recruits would always become teachers.

As you can imagine, psychologists have debated the ethics of deceiving subjects in the Milgram studies (Fisher & Fyrberg, 1994). According to the American Psychological Association's (1992a) *Ethical Principles of Psychologists and Code of Conduct,* psychologists may use deception only when they believe the benefits of the research outweigh its potential harm, they believe the individuals might have been willing to participate if they had understood the benefits of the research, and subjects are **debriefed.** Debriefing means that the purposes and methods of the research are explained afterward. Milgram provided subjects with detailed explanations of his experiment after they participated. He emphasized the fact that they had not actually harmed anyone.

Return to the Lang (Lang et al., 1975) study on alcohol and aggression. In this study, the researchers (1) misinformed subjects about the beverage they were drinking, and (2) misled them into believing they were giving other subjects electric shock when they, like the subjects in the Milgram studies, were actually only pressing switches on a dead control board. (*Aggression* was defined as pressing these switches in the study.) In the Lang study, students who believed they had drunk vodka were "more aggressive"—that is, selected higher levels of shock—than students who believed they had not. The actual content of the beverages was immaterial.

TRUTH OR FICTION REVISITED
It is true that psychologists would not be able to carry out certain kinds of research without deceiving subjects as to the purposes and methods of the studies.

DEBRIEF To elicit information about a completed procedure.

Research With Animals

Psychologists and other scientists frequently use animals to conduct research that cannot be carried out with humans. For example, experiments on the effects of early separation from the mother have been done with monkeys and other animals. Such research has helped psychologists investigate the formation of attachment bonds between parent and child.

Experiments with infant monkeys highlight some of the dilemmas faced by psychologists and other scientists who contemplate potentially harmful research. Psychologists and biologists who study the workings of the brain destroy sections of the brains of laboratory animals to learn how they influence behavior. For instance, a **lesion** in one part of a brain structure causes a rat to overeat. A lesion elsewhere causes the rat to go on a crash diet. Psychologists generalize to humans from experiments such as these in the hope of finding solutions to problems such as eating disorders. Proponents of the use of animals in research argue that major advances in medicine and psychology could not have taken place without them (Fowler, 1992).

The majority of psychologists disapprove of research in which animals are exposed to pain or killed (Plous, 1996). According to the ethical guidelines of the American Psychological Association (1992b), animals may be harmed only when there is no alternative and when researchers believe that the benefits of the research justify the harm.

ETHICS AND ANIMAL RESEARCH.
Is it ethical for researchers to harm animals in order to obtain knowledge that may benefit humans?

LESION An injury that results in impaired behavior or loss of a function.

S U M M A R Y

1. **What is psychology?** Psychology is the scientific study of behavior and mental processes.

2. **What are the goals of psychology?** Psychology seeks to describe, explain, predict, and control behavior and mental processes.

3. **What is the role of psychological theory?** Behavior and mental processes are explained through psychological theories, which are sets of statements that involve assumptions about behavior. Explanations and predictions are derived from theories. Theories are revised, as needed, to accommodate new observations.

4. **What is the difference between pure and applied research?** Basic or pure research has no immediate applications. Applied research seeks solutions to specific problems.

5. **What do different kinds of psychologists do?** Clinical psy-chologists help people with psychological disorders adjust to the demands of life. Counseling psychologists work with people with adjustment problems. School psychologists assist students with problems that interfere with learning. Developmental psychologists study the changes that occur throughout the life span. Personality psychologists study influences on our thought processes, feelings, and behavior. Social psychologists focus on the nature and causes of behavior in social situations. Experimental psychologists conduct research into basic psychological processes such as sensation and perception, learning and memory, and motivation and emotion. Industrial psychologists focus on the relationships between people and work.

6. **Where did psychology begin as a laboratory science?** Wilhelm Wundt established the first psychological laboratory in Leipzig, Germany, in 1879.

7. **What is structuralism?** Structuralism, founded by Wundt, used introspection to study the objective and subjective elements of experience.

8. **What is functionalism?** Functionalism dealt with observable behavior as well as conscious experience and focused on the importance of habit.

9. **What is behaviorism?** Behaviorism, founded by John B. Watson, argues that psychology must limit itself to observable behavior and not attempt to deal with subjective consciousness. Behaviorism focuses on learning by conditioning, and B. F. Skinner introduced the concept of reinforcement as an explanation of how learning occurs.

10. **What is Gestalt psychology?** Gestalt psychology is the school of psychology founded

by Wertheimer, Koffka, and Köhler. It is concerned with perception and argues that the wholeness of human experience is more than the sum of its parts.

11. **What is psychoanalysis?** Sigmund Freud founded the school of psychoanalysis, which asserts that people are driven by hidden impulses and that they distort reality to protect themselves from anxiety.

12. **What are the major contemporary perspectives in psychology?** They are the biological, cognitive, humanistic-existential, psychoanalytic, learning, and sociocultural perspectives. Biologically oriented psychologists study the links between behavior and biological events such as activity in the brain. Cognitive psychologists study the ways in which we mentally represent the world and process information. Humanistic-existential psychologists stress the importance of subjective experience and assert that people have the freedom to make choices. The sociocultural perspective focuses on the roles of matters of ethnicity, gender, culture, and socioeconomic status in behavior and mental processes.

13. **What is the scientific method?** The scientific method is an organized way of going about expanding and refining knowledge. Psychologists usually begin by formulating a research question, which may be reworded as a hypothesis. They reach conclusions about their research questions or the accuracy of their hypotheses on the basis of their research observations or findings.

14. **How do psychologists use samples to represent populations?** The individuals who are studied are referred to as a sample. A sample is a segment of a population. Samples must accurately represent the population they are intended to reflect. In a *random sample,* each member of a population has an equal chance of being selected to participate. Researchers can also use a *stratified sample,* which is selected so that identified subgroups in the population are represented proportionately in the sample.

15. **What methods of observation are used by psychologists?** The methods used include the case study, the survey, and naturalistic observation. Case studies gather information about the lives of individuals or small groups. The survey method uses interviews, questionnaires, or public records to gather information about behavior that cannot be observed directly. The naturalistic observation method observes behavior where it happens—"in the field."

16. **What is a correlation?** Correlations reveal relationships between variables, but do not determine cause and effect. In a positive correlation, variables increase simultaneously. In a negative correlation, one variable increases while the other decreases.

17. **What is the experimental method?** Experiments are used to discover cause and effect—that is, the effects of independent variables on dependent variables. Experimental groups receive a specific treatment, whereas control groups do not. Blinds and double blinds may be used to control for the effects of the expectations of the subjects and the researchers. Results can be generalized only to populations that have been adequately represented in the research samples.

18. **What are the ethical standards of psychologists?** Ethical standards are intended to prevent harm to humans and animals. Records of human behavior are kept confidential. Human subjects are required to give informed consent prior to participating in research. Animals may be harmed only if there is no alternative and the benefits justify the harm.

KEY TERMS

applied research (p. PSY-3)
behaviorism (p. PSY-8)
blind (p. PSY-26)
case study (p. PSY-20)
cognitive (p. PSY-11)
control groups (p. PSY-25)
correlation coefficient (p. PSY-23)
debrief (p. PSY-28)

dependent variable (p. PSY-25)
double-blind study (p. PSY-26)
ethical (p. PSY-27)
ethics review committee (p. PSY-27)
ethnic group (p. PSY-14)
evolutionary psychology (p. PSY-11)
existentialism (p. PSY-13)
experiment (p. PSY-25)

experimental groups (p. PSY-25)
functionalism (p. PSY-7)
gender (p. PSY-14)
generalize (p. PSY-19)
genes (p. PSY-11)
Gestalt psychology (p. PSY-8)
humanism (p. PSY-13)
hypothesis (p. PSY-18)

REFERENCES

Ader, D. N., & Johnson, S. B. (1994). Sample description, reporting, and analysis of sex in psychological research. *American Psychologist, 49,* 216–218.

Allen, L. (1993, August). *Integrating a sociocultural perspective into the psychology curriculum.* G. Stanley Hall lecture presented to the American Psychological Association, Toronto, Canada.

American Psychological Association. (1992a). Ethical principles of psychologists and code of conduct. *American Psychologist, 47,* 1597–1611.

American Psychological Association. (1992b). *Guidelines for ethical conduct in the care and use of animals.* Washington, DC: Author.

Azar, B. (1997). Poor recall mars research and treatment. *APA Monitor, 28*(1), 1, 29.

Bandura, A. (1986). *Social foundations of thought and action: A social-cognitive theory.* Englewood Cliffs, NJ: Prentice-Hall.

Barringer, F. (1993, April 25). Polling on sexual issues has its drawbacks. *New York Times,* p. A23.

Basic Behavioral Science Task Force of the National Advisory Mental Health Council. (1996a). Basic behavioral science research for mental health: Perception, attention, learning, and memory. *American Psychologist, 51,* 133–142.

Basic Behavioral Science Task Force of the National Advisory Mental Health Council. (1996b). Basic behavioral science research for mental health: Sociocultural and environmental practices. *American Psychologist, 51,* 722–731.

Boyatzis, R. E. (1974). The effect of alcohol consumption on the aggressive behavior of men. *Quarterly Journal for the Study of Alcohol, 35,* 959–972.

Brewin, C. R., Andrews, B., & Gotlib, I. H. (1993). Psychopathology and early experience. *Psychological Bulletin, 113,* 82–98.

Clarke-Stewart, K. A. (1991). A home is not a school: The effects of child care on children's development. *Journal of Social Issues, 47,* 105–123.

Collier, G. (1994). *Social origins of mental ability.* New York: Wiley.

Denmark, F. L. (1994). Engendering psychology. *American Psychologist, 49,* 329–334.

Dill, C. A., Gilden, E. R., Hill, P. C., & Hanselka, L. L. (1982). Federal human subjects regulations. *Personality and Social Psychology Bulletin, 8,* 417–425.

Fisher, C. B., & Fyrberg, D. (1994). Participant partners. *American Psychologist, 49,* 417–427.

Fowler, R. D. (1992). Solid support needed for animal research. *APA Monitor, 23*(6), 2.

Furumoto, L. (1992). Joining separate spheres—Christine Ladd-Franklin, woman-scientist. *American Psychologist, 47,* 175–182.

Hergenhahn, B. R. (1997). *An introduction to the history of psychology* (3rd ed.). Pacific Grove, CA: Brooks/Cole.

Jacob, T., Krahn, G. L., & Leonard, K. (1991). Parent-child interactions in families with alcoholic fathers. *Journal of Consulting and Clinical Psychology, 59,* 176–181.

Kinsey, A. C., Pomeroy, W. B., & Martin, C. E. (1948). *Sexual behavior in the human male.* Philadelphia: Saunders.

Kinsey, A. C., Pomeroy, W. B., Martin, C. E., & Gebhard, P. H. (1953). *Sexual behavior in the human female.* Philadelphia: Saunders.

Koocher, G. P. (1991). Questionable methods in alcoholism research. *Journal of Consulting and Clinical Psychology, 59,* 246–248.

Lang, A. R., Goeckner, D. J., Adesso, V. J., & Marlatt, G. A. (1975). Effects of alcohol on aggression in male social drinkers. *Journal of Abnormal Psychology, 84,* 508–518.

Leibowitz, H. W. (1996). The symbiosis between basic and applied research. *American Psychologist, 51,* 366–370.

Lewis-Fernández, R. & Kleinman, A. (1994). Culture, personality, and psychopathology. *Journal of Abnormal Psychology, 103,* 67–71.

Lopez, S., & Hernandez, P. (1986). How culture is considered in evaluations of psychopathology. *Journal of Nervous and Mental Diseases, 176,* 598–606.

Matthews, K., et al.. (1997). Women's Health Initiative. *American Psychologist, 52,* 101–116.

McGovern, T. V., Furumoto, L., Halpern, D. F., Kimble, G. A., & McKeachie, W. J. (1991). Liberal education, study in depth, and the arts and sciences major—psychology. *American Psychologist, 46,* 598–605.

Milgram, S. (1963). Behavioral study of obedience. *Journal of Abnormal and Social Psychology, 67,* 371–378.

Milgram, S. (1974). *Obedience to authority.* New York: Harper & Row.

Miller, N. E. (1995). Clinical-experimental interactions in the development of neuroscience. *American Psychologist, 50,* 901–911.

Nevid, J. S., Rathus, S. A., & Greene, B. A. (2000). *Abnormal psychology in a changing world* (4th ed.). Upper Saddle River, NJ: Prentice Hall.

ODEER (Office of Demographic, Employment, and Educational Research). (1994). Summary report on doctorate recipients from United States universities. Washington, DC: American Psychological Association.

Phinney, J. S. (1996). When we talk about American ethnic groups, what do we mean? *American Psychologist, 51,* 918–927.

Pion, G. M., Mednick, M. T., Astin, H. S., Hall, C. C. I., Kenkel, M. B., Keita, G. P., Kohout, J. L., & Kelleher, J. C. (1996). The shifting gender composition of psychology. *American Psychologist, 51,* 509–528.

Plous, S. (1996). Attitudes toward the use of animals in psychological research and education. *American Psychologist, 51,* 1167– 1180.

Rathus, S. A., Nevid, J. S., & Fichner-Rathus, L. (2000). *Human sexuality in a world of diversity* (4th ed.). Boston: Allyn & Bacon.

Reid, P. T. (1994). The real problem in the study of culture. *American Psychologist, 49,* 524–525.

Sperry, R. W. (1993). The impact and promise of the cognitive revolution. *American Psychologist, 48,* 878–885.

Sternberg, R. J., Wagner, R. K., Williams, W. M., & Horvath, J. A. (1995). Testing common sense. *American Psychologist, 50,* 912–927.

Watson, J. B. (1913). Psychology as the behaviorist views it. *Psychological Review, 20,* 158–177.

B

BIOLOGY AND BEHAVIOR

OUTLINE

ACCORDING TO THE BIG BANG THEORY, OUR UNIVERSE BEGAN WITH an enormous explosion that sent countless particles hurtling outward through space. For billions of years, these particles have been forming immense gas clouds. Galaxies and solar systems have been condensing from the clouds, sparkling for some eons, and then winking out. Human beings came into existence only recently on an unremarkable rock circling an average star in a standard spiral galaxy.

Since the beginning of time, the universe has been changing. Change has brought life and death and countless challenges. Some creatures have adapted successfully to these challenges. Others have not met the challenges and have become extinct. Some have left fossil records. Others have disappeared without a trace.

At first, human survival required a greater struggle than it does today. We fought predators such as leopards. We foraged across parched lands for food. We might have warred with creatures very much like ourselves—creatures who have since become extinct. We prevailed. The human species has survived and continues to transmit its unique traits through the generations by means of genetic material whose chemical codes are only now being cracked.

Yet exactly what is handed down through the generations? The answer is biological, or physiological, structures and processes. Our biology serves as the material base for our observable behaviors, emotions, and cognitions (our thoughts, images, and plans). Biology gives rise to specific behavioral tendencies in some organisms, such as the chick's instinctive fear of the hawk's shadow (Knight, 1994). But most psychologists believe that human behavior is flexible and is influenced by learning and choice as well as by heredity.

Biological psychologists work at the interface of psychology and biology. They study the ways in which our mental processes and behaviors are linked to biological structures and processes. In recent years, biological psychologists have been exploring these links in several areas:

1. *Neurons.* Neurons are the building blocks of the nervous system. There are billions upon billions of neurons in the body—perhaps as many as there are stars in the Milky Way galaxy. Biological psychologists are showing how neurons communicate with one another and how millions, perhaps billions, of such communications make up our mental images and thoughts.

2. *The nervous system.* Neurons combine to form the structures of the nervous system. The nervous system has branches that are responsible for muscle movement, perception, automatic functions such as breathing and the secretion of hormones, and psychological events such as thoughts and feelings.

3. *The cerebral cortex.* The cerebral cortex is the large wrinkled mass inside your head that you think of as your brain. Actually, it is only one part of the brain—the part that is the most characteristically human.

4. *The endocrine system.* Through secretion of hormones, the endocrine system controls functions ranging from growth in children to production of milk in nursing women.

5. *Heredity.* Within every cell of your body there are about 100,000 genes. These chemical substances determine just what type of creature you are, from the color of your hair to your body temperature to the fact that you have arms and legs rather than wings or fins.

NEURONS: INTO THE FABULOUS FOREST

Let us begin our journey in a fabulous forest of nerve cells, or **neurons,** that can be visualized as having branches, trunks, and roots—something like trees. As in other forests, many nerve cells lie alongside one another like a thicket of trees. Neurons can also lie end to end, however, with their "roots" intertwined with the "branches" of neurons that lie below. Trees receive sunlight, water, and nutrients from the soil. Neurons receive "messages" from a number of sources such as light, other neurons, and pressure on the skin, and they can pass these messages along.

Neurons communicate by means of chemicals called **neurotransmitters.** They release neurotransmitters, which are taken up by other neurons, muscles, and glands. Neurotransmitters cause chemical changes in the receiving neuron so that the message can travel along its "trunk," be translated back into neurotransmitters in its "branches," and then travel through the small spaces between neurons to be received by the "roots" of yet other neurons. Each neuron transmits and coordinates messages in the form of neural impulses.

We are born with more than 100 billion neurons. Most of them are found in the brain. The nervous system also contains **glial cells.** Glial cells remove dead neurons and waste products from the nervous system, nourish and insulate neurons, and direct their growth (Zheng et al., 1996). But neurons occupy center stage in the nervous system. The messages transmitted by neurons somehow account for phenomena ranging from the perception of an itch from a mosquito bite to the coordination of a skier's vision and muscles to the composition of a concerto to the solution of an algebraic equation.

The Makeup of Neurons

Neurons vary according to their functions and their location. Some neurons in the brain are only a fraction of an inch in length, whereas others in the legs are several feet long. Every neuron is a single nerve cell with a cell body, dendrites, and an axon (see Figure B.1). The cell body contains the core or *nucleus* of the cell. The nucleus uses oxygen and nutrients to generate the energy needed to carry out the work of the cell. Anywhere from a few to several hundred short fibers, or **dendrites,** extend like roots from the cell body to receive incoming messages from thousands of adjoining neurons. Each neuron has one **axon** that extends like a trunk from the cell body. Axons are very thin, but those that carry messages from the toes to the spinal cord extend for several feet.

NEURON A nerve cell.

NEUROTRANSMITTERS Chemical substances involved in the transmission of neural impulses from one neuron to another.

GLIAL CELLS Cells that nourish and insulate neurons, direct their growth, and remove waste products from the nervous system.

DENDRITES Rootlike structures, attached to the cell body of a neuron, that receive impulses from other neurons.

AXON A long, thin part of a neuron that transmits impulses to other neurons from branching structures called *terminals.*

FIGURE B.1

THE ANATOMY OF A NEURON.

Messages enter neurons through dendrites, are transmitted along the trunklike axon, and then are sent from axon terminals to muscles, glands, and other neurons. Axon terminals contain sacs of chemicals called *neurotransmitters*. Neurotransmitters are released into the synaptic cleft, where many of them are taken up by receptor sites on the dendrites of receiving neuron. Dozens of neurotransmitters have been identified.

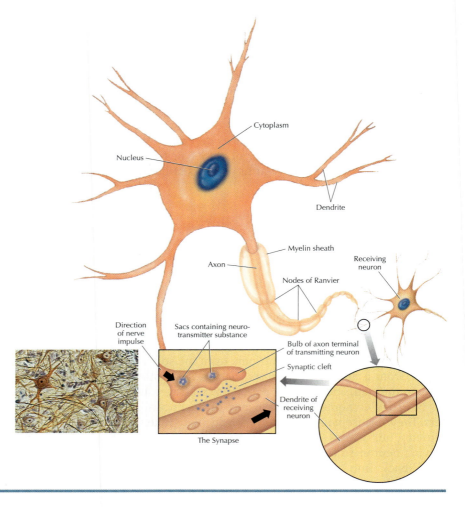

Cytoplasm

Nucleus

Dendrite

Myelin sheath

Axon

Nodes of Ranvier

Receiving neuron

Direction of nerve impulse

Sacs containing neurotransmitter substance

Bulb of axon terminal of transmitting neuron

Synaptic cleft

Dendrite of receiving neuron

The Synapse

TRUTH OR FICTION REVISITED

It is true that a single cell can stretch all the way down your back to your big toe. These cells are neurons. Question: How can cells that are this long be "microscopic"?

Like tree trunks, axons too can divide and extend in different directions. Axons end in small bulb-shaped structures, aptly named *terminals*. Neurons carry messages in one direction only: from the dendrites or cell body through the axon to the axon terminals. The messages are then transmitted from the terminals to the dendrites or cell bodies of other neurons.

As a child matures, the axons of neurons become longer and the dendrites and terminals proliferate, creating vast interconnected networks for the transmission of complex messages. The number of glial cells also increases as the nervous system develops, contributing to its dense appearance.

MYELIN The axons of many neurons are wrapped tightly with white fatty **myelin** that makes them look like strings of sausages under the microscope (bratwurst, actually). The fat insulates the axon from electrically charged atoms, or ions, found in the fluids that surround the nervous system. The myelin sheath minimizes leakage of the electric current being carried along the axon, thereby allowing messages to be conducted more efficiently.

Myelination is part of the maturation process that leads to the child's ability to crawl and walk during the first year. Infants are not physiologically "ready" to engage in visual-motor coordination and other activities until the coating process reaches certain levels. In people with the disease multiple sclerosis, myelin is replaced with a hard fibrous tissue that throws off the timing of nerve impulses and disrupts muscular control. Affliction of the neurons that control breathing can result in suffocation.

MYELIN A fatty substance that encases and insulates axons, facilitating transmission of neural impulses.

AFFERENT AND EFFERENT NEURONS If someone steps on your toes, the sensation is registered by receptors or sensory neurons near the surface of your skin. Then it is transmitted to the spinal cord and brain through **afferent neurons,** which are perhaps 2 to 3 feet long. In the brain, subsequent messages might be buffeted by associative neurons that are only a few thousandths of an inch long. You experience the pain through this process and perhaps entertain some rather nasty thoughts about the perpetrator, who is now apologizing and begging for understanding. Long before you arrive at any logical conclusions, however, motor neurons (**efferent neurons**) send messages to your foot so that you withdraw it and begin an impressive hopping routine. Other efferent neurons stimulate glands so that your heart is now beating more rapidly, you are sweating, and the hair on the back of your arms has become erect! Being a good sport, you say, "Oh, it's nothing." But considering all the neurons involved, it really is something, isn't it?

In case you think that afferent and efferent neurons will be hard to distinguish because they sound pretty much the SAME to you, remember that they *are* the "SAME"—that is, *Sensory* = *Afferent,* and *Motor* = *Efferent.* But don't tell your professor I let you in on this secret.

The Neural Impulse: Let Us "Sing the Body Electric"[1]

In the 18th century, the Italian physiologist Luigi Galvani (1737–1798) conducted a shocking experiment in a rainstorm. While his neighbors had the sense to remain indoors, Galvani and his wife were out on the porch connecting lightning rods to the heads of dissected frogs whose legs were connected by wires to a well of water. When lightning blazed above, the frogs' muscles contracted. This is not a recommended way to prepare frogs' legs. Galvani was demonstrating that the messages (**neural impulses**) that travel along neurons are electrochemical in nature.

Neural impulses travel somewhere between 2 (in nonmyelinated neurons) and 225 miles an hour (in myelinated neurons). This speed is not impressive when compared with that of an electric current in a toaster oven or a lamp, which can travel at the speed of light—over 186,000 miles per second. Distances in the body are short, however, and a message will travel from a toe to the brain in perhaps 1/50th of a second.

AN ELECTROCHEMICAL PROCESS The process by which neural impulses travel is electrochemical. Chemical changes take place within neurons that cause an electric charge to be transmitted along their lengths. Neurons and body fluids contain ions—positively or negatively charged atoms. In a resting state—that is, when a neuron is not being stimulated by its neighbors—negatively charged chloride (Cl^-) ions are plentiful within the neuron, giving it an overall negative charge in relation to the outside. The difference in electrical charge **polarizes** the neuron with a negative **resting potential** of about −70 millivolts in relation to the body fluid outside the cell membrane.

When an area on the surface of the resting neuron is adequately stimulated by other neurons, the cell membrane in the area changes its permeability to allow positively charged sodium ions to enter. Thus the area of entry becomes positively charged, or **depolarized** with respect to the outside (Figure B.2). The permeability of the cell membrane then changes again, allowing no more sodium ions to enter.

AFFERENT NEURONS Neurons that transmit messages from sensory receptors to the spinal cord and brain. Also called *sensory neurons.*

EFFERENT NEURONS Neurons that transmit messages from the brain or spinal cord to muscles and glands. Also called *motor neurons.*

NEURAL IMPULSE The electrochemical discharge of a nerve cell, or neuron.

POLARIZE To ready a neuron for firing by creating an internal negative charge in relation to the body fluid outside the cell membrane.

RESTING POTENTIAL The electrical potential across the neural membrane when it is not responding to other neurons.

DEPOLARIZE To reduce the resting potential of a cell membrane from about −70 millivolts toward zero.

---

[1] From a poem by Walt Whitman.

FIGURE B.2

NEURAL IMPULSE.

When a section of a neuron is stimulated by other neurons, the cell membrane becomes permeable to sodium ions so that an action potential of about +40 millivolts is induced. This action potential is transmitted along the axon. The neuron fires according to the all-or-none principle.

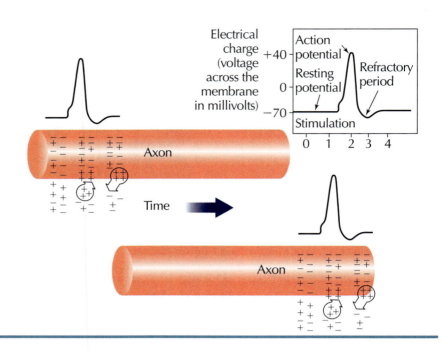

ACTION POTENTIAL The electrical impulse that provides the basis for the conduction of a neural impulse along an axon of a neuron.

ALL-OR-NONE PRINCIPLE The fact that a neuron fires an impulse of the same strength whenever its action potential is triggered.

REFRACTORY PERIOD A phase following firing during which a neuron is less sensitive to messages from other neurons and will not fire.

SYNAPSE A junction between the axon terminals of one neuron and the dendrites or cell body of another neuron.

The inside of the cell at the disturbed area has an **action potential** of 110 millivolts. This action potential, added to the −70 millivolts that characterize the resting potential, brings the membrane voltage to a positive charge of about 40 millivolts. This inner change causes the next section of the cell to become permeable to sodium ions. At the same time, other positively charged (potassium) ions are being pumped out of the area of the cell that was previously affected, which returns the area to its resting potential. In this way, the neural impulse is transmitted continuously along an axon. Because the impulse is created anew as it progresses, its strength does not change.

The conduction of the neural impulse along the length of a neuron is what is meant by "firing." Some neurons fire in less than 1/1,000th of a second. In firing, neurons attempt to transmit the message to other neurons, muscles, or glands. However, other neurons will not fire unless the incoming messages combine to reach an adequate *threshold.* A weak message may cause a temporary shift in electrical charge at some point along a neuron's cell membrane, but this charge will dissipate if the neuron is not stimulated to its threshold.

A neuron may transmit several hundred such messages in a second. Yet, in accordance with the **all-or-none principle,** each time a neuron fires, it transmits an impulse of the same strength. Neurons fire more frequently when they have been stimulated by larger numbers of other neurons. Stronger stimuli cause more frequent firing.

For a few thousandths of a second after firing, a neuron is insensitive to messages from other neurons and will not fire. It is said to be in a **refractory period.** This period is a time of recovery during which sodium is prevented from passing through the neuronal membrane. When we realize that such periods of recovery might take place hundreds of times per second, it seems a rapid recovery and a short rest indeed.

The Synapse

A neuron relays its message to another neuron across a junction called a **synapse.** A synapse consists of a "branch," or an axon terminal from the transmitting neuron; a dendrite ("root"), or the body of a receiving neuron; and a fluid-filled gap between the two that is called the *synaptic cleft* (see Figure B.1). Although the neural impulse is electrical, it does not jump across the synaptic cleft like a spark. Instead, when a nerve impulse reaches a synapse, axon terminals release chemicals into the synaptic cleft like myriad ships being cast into the sea.

Neurotransmitters

In the axon terminals are sacs, or synaptic vesicles, that contain neurotransmitters. When a neural impulse reaches the axon terminal, the vesicles release varying amounts of neurotransmitters into the synaptic cleft. From there, they influence the receiving neuron.

Dozens of neurotransmitters have been identified. Each has its own chemical structure, and each can fit into a specifically tailored harbor, or **receptor site,** on the dendrite of the receiving cell. The analogy of a key fitting into a lock is often used to describe this process. Once released, not all molecules of a neurotransmitter find their ways into receptor sites of other neurons. "Loose" neurotransmitters are usually either broken down or reabsorbed by the axon terminal (a process called reuptake).

Some neurotransmitters act to *excite* other neurons—that is, to cause other neurons to fire. Other neurotransmitters act to *inhibit* receiving neurons. That is, they prevent them from firing. The sum of the stimulation—excitatory and inhibitory—determines whether a neuron will fire and, if so, which neurotransmitters will be released.

Neurotransmitters are involved in physical processes such as muscle contraction and psychological processes such as thoughts and emotions. Excesses or deficiencies of neurotransmitters have been linked to psychological disorders such as depression and schizophrenia. Let us consider the effects of a number of key neurotransmitters: acetylcholine (ACh), dopamine, noradrenaline, serotonin, and endorphins.

ACETYLCHOLINE **Acetylcholine** (ACh) is a neurotransmitter that controls muscle contractions. It is excitatory at synapses between nerves and muscles that involve voluntary movement but inhibitory at the heart and some other locations.

The effects of curare highlight the functioning of ACh. Curare is a poison extracted from plants by South American Indians and used in hunting. If an arrow tipped with curare pierces the skin and the poison enters the body, it prevents ACh from lodging within receptor sites in neurons. Because ACh helps muscles move, curare causes paralysis. The victim is prevented from contracting the muscles used in breathing and therefore dies from suffocation. Botulism, a disease that stems from food poisoning, prevents the release of ACh and has the same effect as curare.

ACh is also normally prevalent in a part of the brain called the **hippocampus,** a structure involved in the formation of memories. When the amount of ACh available to the brain decreases, memory formation is impaired, as in Alzheimer's disease.

DOPAMINE **Dopamine** is primarily an inhibitory neurotransmitter. It is involved in voluntary movements, learning and memory, and emotional arousal. Deficiencies of dopamine are linked to Parkinson's disease, in which people progressively lose control over their muscles. They develop muscle tremors and jerky, uncoordinated movements. The drug L-dopa, a substance that stimulates the brain to produce dopamine, helps slow the progress of Parkinson's disease.

RECEPTOR SITE A location on a dendrite of a receiving neuron tailored to receive a neurotransmitter.

ACETYLCHOLINE A neurotransmitter that controls muscle contractions. Abbreviated *ACh.*

HIPPOCAMPUS A part of the limbic system of the brain involved in memory formation.

DOPAMINE A neurotransmitter involved in Parkinson's disease and that appears to play a role in schizophrenia.

RUNNER'S HIGH?
Why have thousands of people taken up
long-distance running? Running promotes
cardiovascular conditioning, muscle
strength, and weight control. But many
long-distance runners also experience
a "runner's high" that appears to be
connected with the release of endorphins.
Endorphins are naturally occurring
substances similar in function to the
narcotic morphine.

Schizophrenia has also been linked to dopamine. People with schizophrenia may have more receptor sites for dopamine in an area of the brain that is involved in emotional responding. For this reason, they may *overutilize* the dopamine available in the brain. This leads to hallucinations and disturbances of thought and emotion. The phenothiazines, a group of drugs used in the treatment of schizophrenia, block the action of dopamine by locking some dopamine out of these receptor sites (Carpenter & Buchanan, 1994). Not surprisingly, phenothiazines may have Parkinson-like side effects, which are usually treated by prescribing additional drugs, lowering the dose of phenothiazine, or switching to another drug.

NORADRENALINE **Noradrenaline** is produced largely by neurons in the brain stem. It acts both as a neurotransmitter and as a hormone. It is an excitatory neurotransmitter that speeds up the heartbeat and other body processes and is involved in general arousal, learning and memory, and eating. Excesses and deficiencies of noradrenaline have been linked to mood disorders.

The stimulants cocaine and amphetamines ("speed") facilitate the release of noradrenaline and also prevent its reabsorption by the releasing synaptic vesicles—that is, reuptake. As a result, there are excesses of noradrenaline in the nervous system, increasing the firing of neurons and leading to persistent arousal.

SEROTONIN Also primarily an inhibitory transmitter, **serotonin** is involved in emotional arousal and sleep. Deficiencies of serotonin have been linked to overeating, alcoholism, depression, aggression, and insomnia (Azar, 1997). The drug LSD decreases the action of serotonin and may also influence the utilization of dopamine. With LSD, "two no's make a yes." By inhibiting an inhibitor, it increases brain activity, in this case frequently producing hallucinations.

ENDORPHINS The word *endorphin* is the contraction of *endogenous morphine*. *Endogenous* means "developing from within." **Endorphins** occur naturally in the brain and in the bloodstream and are similar to the narcotic morphine in their functions and effects.

Endorphins are inhibitory neurotransmitters. They lock into receptor sites for chemicals that transmit pain messages to the brain. Once the endorphin "key" is in the "lock," the pain-causing chemicals are locked out. Endorphins may also increase our sense of competence and be connected with the pleasurable "runner's high" reported by many long-distance runners.

NORADRENALINE A neurotransmitter whose action is similar to that of the hormone adrenaline and that may play a role in depression.

SEROTONIN A neurotransmitter, deficiencies of which have been linked to affective disorders, anxiety, and insomnia.

ENDORPHINS Neurotransmitters composed of amino acids and that are functionally similar to morphine.

There you have it—a fabulous forest of neurons in which billions upon billions of vesicles are pouring neurotransmitters into synaptic clefts at any given time: when you are involved in strenuous activity, now as you are reading this page, even as you are passively watching television. This microscopic picture is repeated several hundred times every second. The combined activity of all these neurotransmitters determines which messages will be transmitted and which ones will not. You experience your sensations, your thoughts, and your control over your body as psychological events, but the psychological events somehow result from many billions of electrochemical events (Greenfield, 1995).

THE NERVOUS SYSTEM

As a child, I did not think it was a good thing to have a "nervous" system. After all, if your system were not so nervous, you might be less likely to jump at strange noises.

Later I learned that a nervous system is not a system that is nervous. It is a system of nerves involved in thought processes, heartbeat, visual-motor coordination, and so on. (A **nerve** is a bundle of axons and dendrites.) I also learned that the human nervous system is more complex than that of any other animal and that our brains are larger than those of any other animal. Now, this last piece of business is not quite true. A human brain weighs about 3 pounds, but the brains of elephants and whales may be four times as heavy. Still, our brains account for a greater part of our body weight than do those of elephants or whales. Our brains weigh about 1/60th of our body weight. Elephant brains weigh about 1/1,000th of their total weight, and whale brains are a paltry 1/10,000th of their weight. So humans win the brain-as-a-percentage-of-body-weight contest.

The brain is only one part of the nervous system. The nervous system consists of the brain, the spinal cord, and the nerves linking them to the sensory organs, muscles, and glands. As shown in Figure B.3, the brain and spinal cord make up the **central nervous system.** The sensory (afferent) neurons, which receive and transmit messages to the brain and spinal cord, and the motor (efferent) neurons, which transmit messages from the brain or spinal cord to the muscles and glands, make up the **peripheral nervous system.**

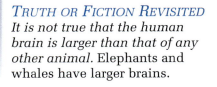

TRUTH OR FICTION REVISITED
It is not true that the human brain is larger than that of any other animal. Elephants and whales have larger brains.

The Central Nervous System

The central nervous system consists of the spinal cord and the brain. Let us take a closer look at each of these.

THE SPINAL CORD The **spinal cord** is a column of nerves about as thick as a thumb. It transmits messages from sensory receptors to the brain, and from the brain to muscles and glands throughout the body. The spinal cord

NERVE A bundle of axons and dendrites from many neurons.

CENTRAL NERVOUS SYSTEM The brain and spinal cord.

PERIPHERAL NERVOUS SYSTEM The part of the nervous system consisting of the somatic nervous system and the autonomic nervous system.

SPINAL CORD A column of nerves within the spine that transmits messages from sensory receptors to the brain and from the brain to muscles and glands throughout the body.

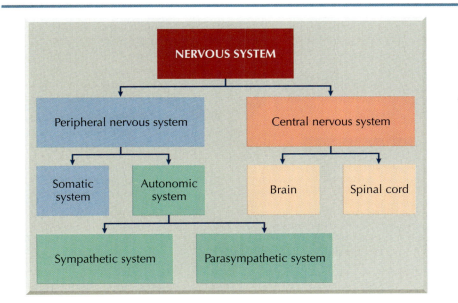

FIGURE B.3
THE DIVISIONS OF THE NERVOUS SYSTEM.
The nervous system contains two main divisions: the central nervous system and the peripheral nervous system. The central nervous system consists of the brain and spinal cord. The peripheral nervous system contains the somatic and autonomic systems. In turn, the autonomic nervous system has sympathetic and parasympathetic divisions.

is also capable of some "local government." That is, it controls some responses to external stimulation through **spinal reflexes.** A spinal reflex is an unlearned response to a stimulus that may involve only two neurons—a sensory (afferent) neuron and a motor (efferent) neuron (Figure B.4). In some reflexes, a third neuron, called an **interneuron,** transmits the neural impulse from the sensory neuron through the spinal cord to the motor neuron.

We engage in many reflexes. We blink in response to a puff of air in our faces. We swallow when food accumulates in the mouth. A physician may tap the leg below the knee to elicit the knee-jerk reflex, a sign that the nervous system is operating adequately. Urinating and defecating are reflexes that occur in response to pressure in the bladder and the rectum. Parents typically spend weeks or months toilet-training infants—in other words, teaching them to involve their brains in the process of elimination. Learning to inhibit these reflexes makes civilization possible.

Sexual response also involves many reflexes. Stimulation of the genital organs leads to erection in the male, vaginal lubrication in the female (both are reflexes that make sexual intercourse possible), and the involuntary muscle contractions of orgasm. As reflexes, these processes need not involve the brain, but most often they do. Feelings of passion, memories of an enjoyable sexual encounter, and sexual fantasies usually contribute to sexual response by transmitting messages from the brain to the genitals through the spinal cord (Rathus et al., 2000).

The spinal cord (and the brain) consists of gray matter and white matter. The **gray matter** is composed of nonmyelinated neurons. Some of these are involved in spinal reflexes. Others send their axons to the brain. The **white matter** is composed of bundles of longer, myelinated (and thus whitish) axons that carry messages to and from the brain. As you can see in Figure B.4, a cross section of the spinal cord shows that the gray matter, which includes cell bodies, is distributed in a butterfly pattern.

THE BRAIN Every show has a star, and the brain is the undisputed star of the human nervous system. The size and shape of your brain are responsible for your large, delightfully rounded head. In all the animal

SPINAL REFLEX A simple unlearned response to a stimulus that may involve only two neurons.

INTERNEURON A neuron that transmits a neural impulse from a sensory neuron to a motor neuron.

GRAY MATTER In the spinal cord, the grayish neurons and neural segments involved in spinal reflexes.

WHITE MATTER In the spinal cord, axon bundles that carry messages from and to the brain.

FIGURE B.4
THE REFLEX ARC.

A cross section of the spinal cord, showing a sensory neuron and a motor neuron, which are involved in the knee-jerk reflex. In some reflexes, interneurons link sensory and motor neurons.

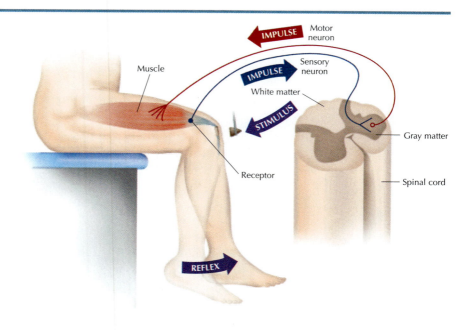

kingdom, you (and about 6 billion other people) are unique because of the capacities for learning and thought residing in the human brain. The brains of men are about 15% larger than those of women, on average (Blum, 1997), which, feminists might argue, shows that bigger is not necessarily better. In the human brain it may well be that how well connected one is (in terms of synapses) is more important than size. Moreover, women's brains "run hotter" than men's. Women metabolize more glucose and appear to use more of their brains on a given task (Blum, 1997). Let us take a closer look at the brain (see Figure B.5). We begin with the hindbrain, where the spinal cord rises to meet the brain, and we work our way upward and forward to the midbrain and the forebrain.

The lower part of the brain, or hindbrain, consists of three major structures: the medulla, the pons, and the cerebellum. Many pathways that connect the spinal cord to higher levels of the brain pass through the **medulla.** The medulla regulates vital functions such as heart rate, blood pressure, and respiration. It also plays a role in sleep, sneezing, and coughing. The **pons** is a bulge in the hindbrain that lies forward of the medulla. *Pons* is the Latin word for "bridge." The pons is so named because of the bundles of nerves that pass through it. The pons transmits information about body movement and is also involved in functions related to attention, sleep and alertness, and respiration.

Behind the pons lies the **cerebellum** ("little brain" in Latin). The two hemispheres of the cerebellum are involved in maintaining balance and in controlling motor (muscle) behavior. Injury to the cerebellum may lead to lack of motor coordination, stumbling, and loss of muscle tone.

The **reticular activating system** (RAS) begins in the hindbrain and ascends through the midbrain into the lower part of the forebrain. It is vital in the functions of attention, sleep, and arousal. Injury to the RAS may leave one in a coma. Stimulation of the RAS causes it to send messages to the cerebral cortex (the large wrinkled mass that you think of as your brain), making us more alert to sensory information. Electrical stimulation of the RAS awakens sleeping animals. Drugs known as central nervous system depressants, such as alcohol, are thought to work, in part, by lowering RAS activity.

MEDULLA An oblong area of the hindbrain involved in regulating heartbeat and respiration.

PONS A structure of the hindbrain involved in respiration, attention, and sleep and dreaming.

CEREBELLUM A part of the hindbrain involved in muscle coordination and balance.

RETICULAR ACTIVATING SYSTEM A part of the brain involved in attention, sleep, and arousal.

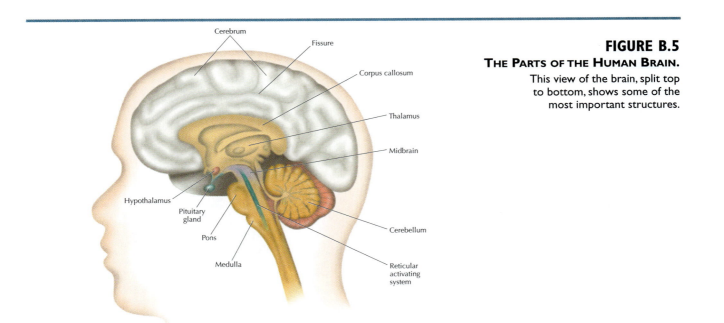

FIGURE B.5

THE PARTS OF THE HUMAN BRAIN.

This view of the brain, split top to bottom, shows some of the most important structures.

Sudden loud noises stimulate the RAS and awaken a sleeping animal or person. But the RAS may become selective through learning. That is, it comes to play a filtering role. It may allow some messages to filter through to higher brain levels and awareness while screening others out. For example, the parent who has primary responsibility for child care may be awakened by the stirring sounds of an infant while the sounds of traffic or street noise are filtered out, even though they are louder. The other parent, in contrast, may sleep through even loud crying by the infant. If the first parent must be away for several days, however, the second parent's RAS may quickly become sensitive to noises produced by the child. This sensitivity may rapidly fade again when the first parent returns.

Also located in the midbrain are areas involved in vision and hearing. These include the area that controls eye reflexes such as dilation of the pupils and eye movements.

Key areas of the forward-most part of the brain, or forebrain, are the thalamus, the hypothalamus, the limbic system, and the cerebrum (see Figures B.5 and B.6). The **thalamus** is located near the center of the brain. It consists of two joined egg- or football-shaped structures. The thalamus serves as a relay station for sensory stimulation. Nerve fibers from the sensory systems enter from below; the information carried by them is then transmitted to the cerebral cortex by way of fibers that exit from above. For instance, the thalamus relays sensory input from the eyes to the visual areas of the cerebral cortex. The thalamus is also involved in controlling sleep and attention in coordination with other brain structures, including the RAS.

The **hypothalamus** lies beneath the thalamus and above the pituitary gland. It weighs only 4 grams, yet it is vital in the regulation of body temperature, concentration of fluids, storage of nutrients, and various aspects of motivation and emotion. Experimenters learn many of the functions of the hypothalamus by implanting electrodes in parts of it and observing the effects of an electrical current. They have found that the hypothalamus is involved in hunger, thirst, sexual behavior, caring for offspring, and aggression. Among lower animals, stimulation of various areas of the hypothalamus can trigger instinctual behaviors such as fighting, mating, or even nest building.

Canadian psychologists James Olds and Peter Milner (1954) made a wonderful mistake in the 1950s. They were attempting to implant an electrode in a rat's reticular formation to see how stimulation of the area

THALAMUS An area near the center of the brain involved in the relay of sensory information to the cortex and in the functions of sleep and attention.

HYPOTHALAMUS A bundle of nuclei below the thalamus involved in body temperature, motivation, and emotion.

FIGURE B.6

THE LIMBIC SYSTEM.

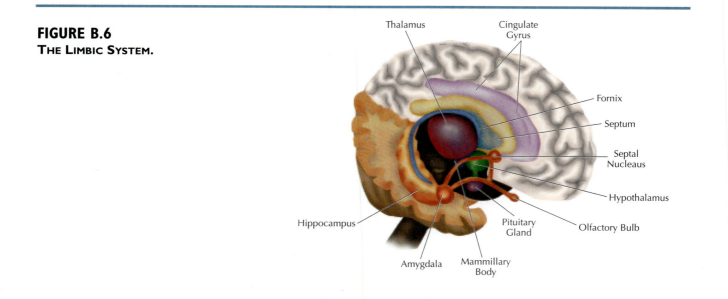

might affect learning. Olds, however, was primarily a social psychologist and not a biological psychologist. He missed his target and found a part of the animal's hypothalamus instead. Olds and Milner dubbed this area the "pleasure center" because the animal would repeat whatever it was doing when it was stimulated. The term *pleasure center* is not used too frequently because it appears to attribute human emotions to rats. Yet the "pleasure centers" must be doing something right because rats stimulate themselves in these centers by pressing a pedal several thousand times an hour, until they are exhausted (Olds, 1969).

The hypothalamus is just as important to humans as it is to lower animals. Unfortunately (or fortunately), our "pleasure centers" are not as clearly defined as those of the rat. Then, too, our responses to messages from the hypothalamus are less automatic and relatively more influenced by higher brain functions—that is, cognitive factors such as thought, choice, and value systems. It is all a part of being human.

The **limbic system** is made up of several structures, including the amygdala, hippocampus, and parts of the hypothalamus (Figure B.6). The limbic system lies along the inner edge of the cerebrum and is fully evolved only in mammals. It is involved in memory and emotion, and in the drives of hunger, sex, and aggression. People in whom operations have damaged the hippocampus can retrieve old memories but cannot permanently store new information. As a result, they may reread the same newspaper day in and day out without recalling that they read it before. Or they may have to be perpetually reintroduced to people they have met just hours earlier (Squire, 1996).

The **amygdala** looks like two little almonds. Studies using lesioning and electrical stimulation show that the amygdala is connected with aggressive behavior in monkeys, cats, and other animals. Early in the 20th century Heinrich Klüver and Paul Bucy (1939) lesioned part of the amygdala of a rhesus monkey. Rhesus monkeys are normally a scrappy lot and try to bite or grab at intruders, but destruction of this animal's amygdala made it docile. No longer did it react aggressively to people. It even allowed people to poke and pinch it. Electrical stimulation of the part of the amygdala that Klüver and Bucy had destroyed, however, triggers a so-called rage response. For example, it causes a cat to hiss and arch its back in preparation for an attack. Yet if you electrically stimulate another part of the amygdala, the cat cringes in fear when you cage it with a mouse. Not very tigerlike.

The **cerebrum** is the crowning glory of the brain. Only in human beings does the cerebrum account for such a large proportion of the brain (Figure B.5). The cerebrum is responsible for the cognitive abilities of thinking and language. The surface of the cerebrum is wrinkled, or convoluted, with ridges and valleys. This surface is termed the **cerebral cortex**. The convolutions allow a great deal of surface area to be packed into the brain—and surface area is apparently connected with human cognitive ability.

Valleys in the cortex are called *fissures*. A key fissure almost divides the cerebrum in half, creating two hemispheres. The hemispheres of the cerebral cortex are connected by the **corpus callosum** (Latin for "thick body" or "hard body"), a bundle of some 200 million nerve fibers.

Now let us consider the makeup of the peripheral nervous system. It is the peripheral nervous system that connects the brain with the world outside.

The Peripheral Nervous System

The peripheral nervous system consists of sensory and motor neurons that transmit messages to and from the central nervous system. Without the peripheral nervous system, our brains would be isolated from the world:

LIMBIC SYSTEM A group of structures involved in memory, motivation, and emotion that forms a fringe along the inner edge of the cerebrum.

AMYGDALA A part of the limbic system that apparently facilitates stereotypical aggressive responses.

CEREBRUM The large mass of the forebrain, which consists of two hemispheres.

CEREBRAL CORTEX The wrinkled surface area (gray matter) of the cerebrum.

CORPUS CALLOSUM A thick fiber bundle that connects the hemispheres of the cortex.

They would not be able to perceive it, and they would not be able to act on it. The two main divisions of the peripheral nervous system are the somatic nervous system and the autonomic nervous system.

THE SOMATIC NERVOUS SYSTEM The **somatic nervous system** contains sensory (afferent) and motor (efferent) neurons. It transmits messages about sights, sounds, smells, temperature, body positions, and so on, to the central nervous system. As a result, we can experience the beauties and the horrors of the world, its physical ecstasies and agonies. Messages transmitted from the brain and spinal cord to the somatic nervous system control purposeful body movements such as raising a hand, winking, or running, as well as movements that we hardly attend to—movements that maintain our posture and balance.

THE AUTONOMIC NERVOUS SYSTEM *Autonomic* means "automatic." The **autonomic nervous system** (ANS) regulates the glands and the muscles of internal organs. Thus the ANS controls activities such as heartbeat, respiration, digestion, and dilation of the pupils of the eyes. These activities can occur automatically, while we are asleep. But some of them can be overridden by conscious control. You can breathe at a purposeful pace, for example. Methods like biofeedback and yoga also help people gain voluntary control of functions such as heart rate and blood pressure.

The ANS has two branches, or divisions: **sympathetic** and **parasympathetic.** These branches have largely opposing effects. Many organs and glands are stimulated by both branches of the ANS (Figure B.7). When organs and glands are simultaneously stimulated by both divisions, their effects can average out to some degree. In general, the sympathetic division is most active during processes that involve the spending of body energy from stored reserves, such as in a fight-or-flight response to a predator or when you find out your rent is going to be raised. The parasympathetic

SOMATIC NERVOUS SYSTEM The division of the peripheral nervous system that connects the central nervous system with sensory receptors, skeletal muscles, and the surface of the body.

AUTONOMIC NERVOUS SYSTEM (ANS) The division of the peripheral nervous system that regulates glands and activities such as heartbeat, respiration, digestion, and dilation of the pupils.

SYMPATHETIC The branch of the ANS that is most active during emotional responses such as fear and anxiety that spend the body's reserves of energy.

PARASYMPATHETIC The branch of the ANS that is most active during processes such as digestion that restore the body's reserves of energy.

FIGURE B.7
THE BRANCHES OF THE AUTONOMIC NERVOUS SYSTEM (ANS).

The parasympathetic branch of the ANS generally acts to replenish stores of energy in the body. The sympathetic branch is most active during activities that expend energy. The two branches of the ANS frequently have antagonistic effects on the organs they service.

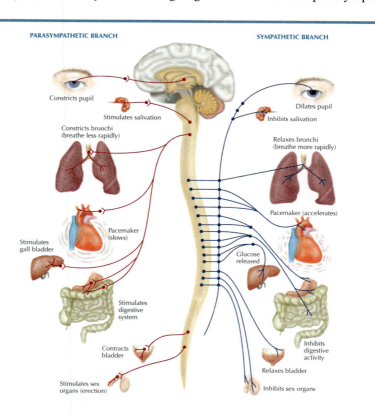

PARASYMPATHETIC BRANCH   SYMPATHETIC BRANCH

Constricts pupil
Stimulates salivation
Constricts bronchi (breathe less rapidly)
Stimulates gall bladder
Pacemaker (slows)
Stimulates digestive system
Contracts bladder
Stimulates sex organs (erection)

Dilates pupil
Inhibits salivation
Relaxes bronchi (breathe more rapidly)
Pacemaker (accelerates)
Glucose released
Inhibits digestive activity
Relaxes bladder
Inhibits sex organs

division is most active during processes that replenish reserves of energy, such as eating. When we are afraid, the sympathetic division of the ANS accelerates the heart rate. When we relax, the parasympathetic division decelerates the heart rate. The parasympathetic division stimulates digestive processes, but the sympathetic branch inhibits digestion. Because the sympathetic division predominates when we feel fear or anxiety, these feelings can cause indigestion.

The ANS is of particular interest to psychologists because its activities are linked to various emotions such as anxiety and love. Some people seem to have overly reactive sympathetic nervous systems. In the absence of external threats, their bodies still respond as though they were faced with danger. Psychologists can often help them learn to relax.

THE CEREBRAL CORTEX

The cerebral cortex is the part of the brain you think of as your brain. The cerebral cortex is involved in almost every bodily activity, including most sensations and responses. It is also the seat of the essential human activities of thinking and language. Other organisms run faster than we do, are stronger, or bite more sharply. Yet humans think faster, are intellectually "stronger," and, we might add, have a "biting" wit—all of which is made possible by the cerebral cortex.

The Geography of the Cerebral Cortex

Each of the hemispheres of the cerebral cortex is divided into four parts, or lobes, as shown in Figure B.8. The **frontal lobe** lies in front of the central fissure and the **parietal lobe** behind it. The **temporal lobe** lies below the side, or lateral, fissure—across from the frontal and parietal lobes. The **occipital lobe** lies behind the temporal lobe and behind and below the parietal lobe.

TRUTH OR FICTION REVISITED
It is true that fear can give you indigestion. Fear predominantly involves sympathetic ANS activity, whereas digestive processes involve parasympathetic activity. Because sympathetic activity can inhibit parasympathetic activity, fear can prevent digestion.

FRONTAL LOBE The lobe of the cerebral cortex that lies to the front of the central fissure.

PARIETAL LOBE The lobe that lies just behind the central fissure.

TEMPORAL LOBE The lobe that lies below the lateral fissure, near the temples of the head.

OCCIPITAL LOBE The lobe that lies behind and below the parietal lobe and behind the temporal lobe.

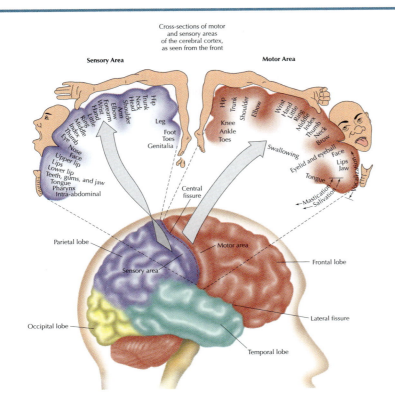

FIGURE B.8
THE GEOGRAPHY OF THE CEREBRAL CORTEX.
The cortex is divided into four lobes: frontal, parietal, temporal, and occipital. The visual area of the cortex is located in the occipital lobe. The hearing or auditory cortex lies in the temporal lobe. The sensory and motor areas face each other across the central fissure. What happens when a surgeon stimulates areas of the sensory or motor cortex during an operation?

When light strikes the eyes, neurons in the occipital lobe fire, and as a result, we "see" (that is, the image is projected in the brain). Direct artificial stimulation of the occipital lobe also produces visual sensations. If neurons in the occipital region of the cortex were stimulated with electricity, you would "see" flashes of light even if it were pitch black or your eyes were covered. The hearing or auditory area of the cortex lies in the temporal lobe along the lateral fissure. Sounds cause structures in the ear to vibrate. Messages are relayed from those structures to the auditory area of the cortex, and when you hear a noise, neurons in this area are firing.

Just behind the central fissure in the parietal lobe lies an area called the **somatosensory cortex,** which receives messages from skin senses all over the body. These sensations include warmth and cold, touch, pain, and movement. Neurons in different parts of the sensory cortex fire, depending on whether you wiggle your finger or raise your leg. If a brain surgeon were to stimulate the proper area of your somatosensory cortex with an electric probe, it might seem as if someone were touching your arm or leg.

Figure B.8 suggests how our face and head are overrepresented on this cortex compared with, say, our trunk and legs. This overrepresentation is one of the reasons our face and head are more sensitive to touch than other parts of the body.

Many years ago it was discovered that patients with injuries to one hemisphere of the brain would show sensory or motor deficits on the opposite side of the body below the head. This led to the recognition that sensory and motor nerves cross in the brain and elsewhere. The left hemisphere controls acts on, and receives inputs from, the right side of the body. The right hemisphere controls acts on, and receives inputs from, the left side of the body.

How do you make a monkey smile? One way is by inserting an electrical probe in its motor cortex and giving it a burst of electricity. Let us see what we mean by this.

The **motor cortex** lies in the frontal lobe, just across the valley of the central fissure from the somatosensory cortex. Neurons firing in the motor cortex cause parts of our body to move. More than 100 years ago, German scientists electrically stimulated the motor cortex in dogs and observed that muscles contracted in response (Fritsch & Hitzig, 1870/1960). Since then, neuroscientists have mapped the motor cortex in people and lower animals by inserting electrical probes and seeing in which parts of the body muscles contract. For example, José Delgado (1969) caused one patient to make a fist even though he tried to prevent his hand from closing. The patient said, "I guess, doctor, that your electricity is stronger than my will" (Delgado, 1969, p. 114). Delgado also made a monkey smile in this manner, many thousands of times in a row. If a surgeon were to stimulate a certain area of the right hemisphere of the motor cortex with an electric probe, you would raise your left leg. This action would be sensed in the somatosensory cortex, and you might have a devil of a time trying to figure out whether you had intended to raise that leg!

SOMATOSENSORY CORTEX The section of cortex in which sensory stimulation is projected. It lies just behind the central fissure in the parietal lobe.

MOTOR CORTEX The section of cortex that lies in the frontal lobe, just across the central fissure from the sensory cortex. Neural impulses in the motor cortex are linked to muscular responses throughout the body.

Thinking, Language, and the Cortex

Areas of the cerebral cortex that are not primarily involved in sensation or motor activity are called *association areas.* They make possible the breadth and depth of human learning, thought, memory, and language. The association areas in the frontal lobes, near the forehead, could be called the brain's executive center. It appears to be where we make plans and decisions (Goldman-Rakic, 1992).

Areas in the frontal lobes are also involved in the memory functions required for problem solving and decision making (Goldman-Rakic, 1992). These areas are connected with different sensory areas and therefore tap different kinds of sensory information. They retrieve visual, auditory, and other kinds of memories and manipulate them—similar to the way in which a computer retrieves information from files in storage and manipulates it in working memory.

Certain neurons in the visual area of the occipital lobe fire in response to the visual presentation of vertical lines. Others fire in response to presentation of horizontal lines. Although one group of cells may respond to one aspect of the visual field and another group of cells may respond to another, association areas put it all together. As a result, we see a box or an automobile or a road map and not a confusing array of verticals and horizontals.

LANGUAGE FUNCTIONS In some ways, the left and right hemispheres of the brain duplicate each other's functions. In other ways, they are very different. The left hemisphere contains language functions for nearly all right-handed people and for 2 out of 3 left-handed people (Pinker, 1994). However, the brain remains "plastic," or changeable, through about the age of 13. As a result, children who lose the left hemisphere of the brain because of surgery to control epilepsy usually transfer speech functions to the right hemisphere (Zuger, 1997).

Two key language areas lie within the hemisphere of the cortex that contains language functions (usually the left hemisphere): Broca's area and Wernicke's area (see Figure B.9). Damage to either area is likely to cause an aphasia—that is, a disruption of the ability to understand or produce language.

Wernicke's area lies in the temporal lobe near the auditory cortex. It responds mainly to auditory information. As you are reading this page, however, the visual information is registered in the visual cortex of your occipital lobe. It is then recoded as auditory information as it travels to Wernicke's area. Broca's area is located in the frontal lobe, near the section of the motor cortex that controls the muscles of the tongue, throat, and other areas of the face used when speaking (Pinker, 1994; Raichle, 1994). Broca's area processes the information and relays it to the motor cortex. The motor cortex sends the signals that cause muscles in your

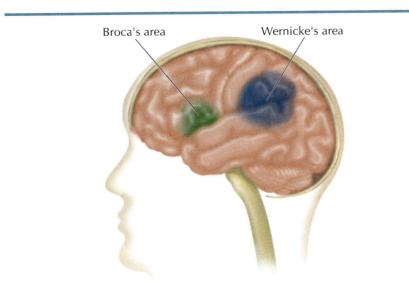

Broca's area   Wernicke's area

FIGURE B.9
BROCA'S AND WERNICKE'S AREAS OF THE CEREBRAL CORTEX.
The areas most involved in speech are Broca's area and Wernicke's area. Damage to either area can produce an *aphasia*—a disruption of the ability to understand or produce language.

throat and mouth to contract. If you are "subvocalizing"—saying what you are reading "under your breath"—that is because Wernicke's area transmits information to Broca's area via nerve fibers.

People with damage to Wernicke's area may show **Wernicke's aphasia,** which impairs their abilities to comprehend speech and to think of the proper words to express their own thoughts. Ironically, they usually speak freely and with proper syntax. Wernicke's area thus is essential to understanding the relationships between words and their meanings. When Broca's area is damaged, people usually understand language well enough but speak slowly and laboriously, in simple sentences. This pattern is termed **Broca's aphasia.**

A part of the brain called the *angular gyrus* lies between the visual cortex and Wernicke's area. The angular gyrus "translates" visual information, as is perceiving written words, into auditory information (sounds) and sends it on to Wernicke's area. It appears that problems in the angular gyrus can give rise to *dyslexia,* or serious impairment in reading, because it becomes difficult for the reader to segment words into sounds (Shaywitz, 1998).

Left Brain, Right Brain?

It has become popular to speak of people as being "left-brained" or "right-brained." The notion is that the hemispheres of the brain are involved in very different kinds of intellectual and emotional functions and responses. According to this view, left-brained people would be primarily logical and intellectual. Right-brained people would be intuitive, creative, and emotional. Those of us who are fortunate enough to have our brains "in balance" would presumably have the best of it—the capacity for logic combined with emotional richness.

Like so many other popular ideas, the left-brain—right-brain notion is at best exaggerated. Research does suggest that in right-handed individuals, the left hemisphere is relatively more involved in intellectual undertakings that require logical analysis and problem solving, language, and mathematical computation (Gazzaniga, 1995). The other hemisphere (usually the right hemisphere) is usually superior in spatial functions (it is better at putting puzzles together), recognition of faces, discrimination of colors, aesthetic and emotional responses, understanding metaphors, and creative mathematical reasoning.

Despite these differences, it would be erroneous to think that the hemispheres of the brain act independently—that some people are truly left-brained and others right-brained (Gazzaniga, 1995). The functions of the left and right hemispheres overlap to some degree, and the hemispheres tend to respond simultaneously as we focus our attention on one thing or another. The hemispheres are aided in their "cooperation" by the corpus callosum, the bundle of 200 million axons that connects them.

Now let us consider another issue involving sidedness: left-handedness. People who are left-handed are different from people who are right-handed in terms of the ways in which they write, throw a ball, and so on. But there are interesting questions as to whether people who are left-handed are psychologically different from "righties."

Handedness: Is It Gauche or Sinister to Be Left-Handed?

What do Michelangelo, Leonardo da Vinci, Pablo Picasso, and Steve Young all have in common? No, they are not all artists. Only one is a football

WERNICKE'S APHASIA A language disorder characterized by difficulty comprehending the meaning of spoken language.

BROCA'S APHASIA A language disorder characterized by slow, laborious speech.

player. But they are all left-handed. Yet being a lefty is often regarded as a deficiency. The language swarms with slurs on lefties. We speak of "left-handed compliments," of having "two left feet," of strange events as "coming out of left field." The word *sinister* means "left-hand or unlucky side" in Latin. *Gauche* is a French word that literally means "left," although in English it is used to mean awkward or ill-mannered. Compare these usages to the positive phrases "being righteous" or "being on one's right side."

Yet, 8% to 10% of us are lefties. We are usually labeled right-handed or left-handed on the basis of our handwriting preferences, yet some people write with one hand and pass a football with the other. Some people even swing a tennis racket and pitch a baseball with different hands. Left-handedness is more common in boys than girls.

Being left-handed may not be gauche or sinister, but it appears to be connected with learning disabilities (especially in reading), and health problems such as migraine headaches and allergies (Geschwind & Galaburda, 1987). But there may also be some advantages to being left-handed. According to a British study, left-handed people are twice as likely as right-handed people to be numbered among the ranks of artists, musicians, and mathematicians (Kilshaw & Annett, 1983).

The origins of handedness are likely to have a genetic component. If both of your parents are right-handed, your chances of being left-handed are about 1 in 50. If one of your parents is left-handed, your chances of being left-handed are about 1 in 6. And if both of your parents are left-handed, your chances of also being left-handed are about 1 in 2 (Springer & Deutsch, 1993). In any event, handedness comes early. A study employing ultrasound found that about 95% of fetuses suck their right thumbs rather than their left (Hepper et al., 1990).

Whether we are talking about language functions, being "left-brained" or "right-brained," or handedness, we are talking about people whose hemispheres of the cerebral cortex communicate back and forth. Now let us see what happens when the major avenue of communication between the hemispheres is shut down.

Split-Brain Experiments: When Hemispheres Stop Communicating

A number of people with severe cases of **epilepsy** have split-brain operations in which much of the corpus callosum is severed (Engel, 1996). The purpose of the operation is to try to confine epilepsy to one hemisphere of the cerebral cortex rather than allowing a neural tempest to reverberate. These operations do seem to help. People who have undergone them can be thought of as winding up with two brains, yet under most circumstances their behavior remains ordinary enough. Still, some aspects of hemispheres that have stopped talking to one another are intriguing.

As reported by pioneering brain surgeon Joseph Bogen (1969), each hemisphere may have a "mind of its own." One split-brain patient reported that her hemispheres frequently disagreed on what she should be wearing. What she meant was that one hand might undo her blouse as rapidly as the other was buttoning it. A man reported that one hemisphere (the left hemisphere, which contained language functions) liked reading but the other one did not. If he shifted a book from his right hand to his left hand, his left hand would put it down. The left hand is connected with the right hemisphere of the cerebral cortex, which in most people—including this patient—does not contain language functions.

EPILEPSY Temporary disturbances of brain functions that involve sudden neural discharges.

Michael Gazzaniga (1995) showed that people with split brains whose eyes are closed may be able to verbally describe an object such as a key when they hold it in one hand, but not when they hold it in the other hand. As shown in Figure B.10, if a person with a split brain handles a key with his left hand behind a screen, tactile impressions of the key are projected into the right hemisphere, which has little or no language ability. Thus, he will not be able to describe the key. If he holds it in his right hand, he will have no trouble describing it because sensory impressions are projected into the left hemisphere of the cortex, which contains language functions. To further confound matters, if the word *ring* is projected into the left hemisphere while the person is asked what he is handling, he will say "ring," not "key."

However, this discrepancy between what is felt and what is said occurs only in people with split brains. Most of the time the two hemispheres work together, even when we are playing the piano or solving math problems.

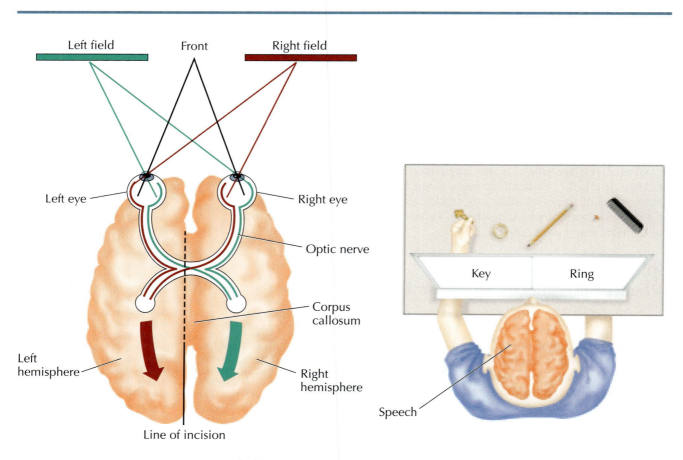

FIGURE B.10

A DIVIDED-BRAIN EXPERIMENT.

In the drawing on the left, we see that visual sensations in the left visual field are projected in the occipital cortex of the right hemisphere. Visual sensations from the right visual field are projected in the occipital cortex in the left hemisphere. In the divided-brain experiment diagrammed on the right, a person with a severed corpus callosum handles a key with his left hand and perceives the written word *key* in his left visual field. The word *key* is projected in the right hemisphere. Speech, however, is usually a function of the left hemisphere. The written word *ring,* perceived by the right visual field, is projected in the left hemisphere. So, when asked what he is handling, the divided-brain subject reports "ring," not "key."

In our discussion of the nervous system, we have described naturally occurring chemical substances—neurotransmitters—that facilitate or inhibit the transmission of neural messages. Let us now turn our attention to other naturally occurring chemical substances that influence behavior: hormones. We shall see that some hormones also function as neurotransmitters.

THE ENDOCRINE SYSTEM

The body contains two types of **glands:** glands with ducts and glands without ducts. A duct is a passageway that carries substances to specific locations. Saliva, sweat, tears, and breast milk all reach their destinations through ducts. Psychologists are interested in the substances secreted by ductless glands because of their behavioral effects. The ductless glands constitute the **endocrine system,** and they secrete **hormones** (from the Greek *horman,* meaning "to stimulate" or "to excite").

Hormones are released into the bloodstream and circulate through the body. Like neurotransmitters, hormones have specific receptor sites. That is, they act only on receptors in certain locations. Some hormones that are released by the hypothalamus influence only the **pituitary gland.** Other hormones released by the pituitary influence the adrenal cortex; still others influence the testes and ovaries, and so on.

Much hormonal action helps the body maintain steady states, as in fluid levels, blood sugar levels, and so on. Bodily mechanisms measure current levels, and when these levels deviate from optimal, they signal glands to release hormones. The maintenance of steady states requires feedback of bodily information to glands. This type of system is referred to as a *negative feedback loop.* That is, when enough of a hormone has been secreted, the gland is signaled to stop.

The hypothalamus secretes a number of releasing hormones, or factors, that influence the pituitary gland to secrete corresponding hormones. For example, growth hormone-releasing factor (hGRF) causes the pituitary to produce growth hormone. A dense network of blood vessels between the hypothalamus and the pituitary gland provides a direct route of influence for these factors.

The pituitary gland lies just below the hypothalamus (see Figure B.11). Although it is only about the size of a pea, it is so central to the body's functioning that it has been referred to as the "master gland." Despite this designation, today we know that the hypothalamus regulates much pituitary activity. The anterior (front) and posterior (back) lobes of the pituitary gland secrete many hormones. **Growth hormone** regulates the growth of muscles, bones, and glands. Children whose growth patterns are abnormally slow may catch up to their age-mates when they obtain growth hormone. **Prolactin** largely regulates maternal behavior in lower mammals such as rats and stimulates production of milk in women. As a water conservation measure, **antidiuretic hormone** (ADH) inhibits production of urine when fluid levels in the body are low. ADH is also connected with stereotypical paternal behavior in some mammals. For example, it transforms an unconcerned male prairie vole (a mouselike rodent) into an affectionate and protective mate and father. **Oxytocin** stimulates labor in pregnant women and is connected with maternal behavior (cuddling and caring for young) in some mammals. Obstetricians may induce labor by injecting pregnant women with oxytocin. During nursing, stimulation of nerve endings in and around the nipples sends messages to

GLAND An organ that secretes one or more chemical substances such as hormones, saliva, or milk.

ENDOCRINE SYSTEM The body's system of ductless glands that secrete hormones and release them directly into the bloodstream.

HORMONE A substance secreted by an endocrine gland that regulates various body functions.

PITUITARY GLAND The gland that secretes growth hormone, prolactin, antidiuretic hormone, and other hormones.

GROWTH HORMONE A pituitary hormone that regulates growth.

PROLACTIN A pituitary hormone that regulates production of milk and, in lower animals, maternal behavior.

ANTIDIURETIC HORMONE A pituitary hormone that conserves body fluids by increasing reabsorption of urine and is connected with paternal behavior in some mammals. Also called *vasopressin.*

OXYTOCIN A pituitary hormone that stimulates labor and lactation.

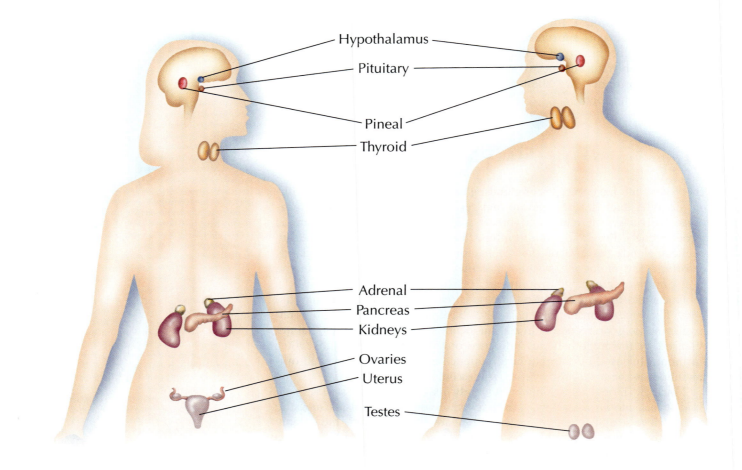

FIGURE B.11
MAJOR GLANDS OF THE ENDOCRINE SYSTEM.

the brain that cause oxytocin to be secreted. Oxytocin then causes the breasts to eject milk.

The pineal gland secretes the hormone **melatonin,** which helps regulate the sleep–wake cycle and may affect the onset of puberty. Some researchers speculate that melatonin is also connected with aging.

Thyroxin is produced by the thyroid gland. It affects the body's *metabolism*—that is, the rate at which the body uses oxygen and produces energy. Some people are overweight because of *hypothyroidism,* a condition that results from too little thyroxin. Thyroxin deficiency in children can lead to *cretinism,* a condition characterized by stunted growth and mental retardation. Adults who secrete too little thyroxin may feel tired and sluggish and may put on weight. People who produce too much thyroxin may develop *hyperthyroidism,* which is characterized by excitability, insomnia, and weight loss.

The adrenal glands, located above the kidneys, have an outer layer, or cortex, and an inner core, or medulla. The adrenal cortex is regulated by pituitary ACTH. It secretes hormones known as **corticosteroids,** or cortical steroids. These hormones increase resistance to stress; promote muscle development; and cause the liver to release stored sugar, making more

MELATONIN A hormone of the pineal gland involved in the sleep–wake cycle, the onset of puberty, and perhaps aging.

THYROXIN The thyroid hormone that increases metabolic rate.

CORTICOSTEROIDS Steroids produced by the adrenal cortex that regulate carbohydrate metabolism and increase resistance to stress by fighting inflammation and allergic reactions. Also called *cortical steroids.*

energy available in emergencies (as when you see another car veering toward your own).

Anabolic steroids (synthetic versions of the male sex hormone testosterone) have been used, sometimes in tandem with growth hormone, to enhance athletic prowess. Steroids increase the muscle mass, heighten resistance to stress, and increase the body's energy supply by signaling the liver to release sugar into the bloodstream. Steroids may also spur sex drive and raise self-esteem. Steroids are generally outlawed in amateur and professional sports. The lure of steroids is understandable. Sometimes the difference between an acceptable athletic performance and a great one is rather small. Thousands of athletes try to make it in the big leagues, and the edge offered by steroids—even if minor—can spell the difference between a fumbling attempt and success. If steroids help, why the fuss? Some of it is related to the ethics of competition—the notion that athletes should "play fair." Part of it is related to the fact that steroid use is linked to liver damage and other health problems.

Adrenaline and noradrenaline are secreted by the adrenal medulla. **Adrenaline,** also known as epinephrine, is manufactured exclusively by the adrenal glands, but noradrenaline (norepinephrine) is also produced elsewhere in the body. The sympathetic branch of the autonomic nervous system causes the adrenal medulla to release a mixture of adrenaline and noradrenaline that helps arouse the body to cope with threats and stress. Adrenaline is of interest to psychologists because it has emotional as well as physical effects. It intensifies most emotions and is crucial to the experience of fear and anxiety. Noradrenaline raises the blood pressure, and in the nervous system it acts as a neurotransmitter.

If it were not for the secretion of the male sex hormone **testosterone** about 6 weeks after conception, we would all develop into females. Testosterone is produced by the testes and, in smaller amounts, by the ovaries and adrenal glands. A few weeks after conception, testosterone causes the male sex organs to develop. (The amount produced by the ovaries and adrenal glands is normally not enough to foster development of male sex organs.)

During puberty, testosterone stokes the growth of muscle and bone and the development of primary and secondary sex characteristics. *Primary sex characteristics* such as the increased size of the penis and the sperm-producing ability of the testes are directly involved in reproduction. *Secondary sex characteristics* such as presence of a beard and a deeper voice differentiate males from females but are not directly involved in reproduction.

The ovaries produce **estrogen** and **progesterone.** Estrogen is also produced in smaller amounts by the testes. Estrogen fosters female reproductive capacity and secondary sex characteristics such as accumulation of fat in the breasts and hips. Progesterone stimulates growth of the female reproductive organs and prepares the uterus to maintain pregnancy.

Whereas testosterone levels remain fairly stable, estrogen and progesterone levels vary markedly and regulate the woman's menstrual cycle. Following menstruation—the monthly sloughing off of the inner lining of the uterus—estrogen levels increase, leading to the ripening of an ovum (egg cell) and the growth of the lining of the uterus. The ovum is released by the ovary when estrogens reach peak blood levels. Then the lining of the uterus thickens in response to the secretion of progesterone, gaining the capacity to support an embryo if fertilization should occur. If the ovum is not fertilized, estrogen and progesterone levels drop suddenly, triggering menstruation once more.

ADRENALINE A hormone produced by the adrenal medulla that stimulates sympathetic ANS activity. Also called *epinephrine.*

TESTOSTERONE A male sex hormone produced by the testes that promotes growth of male sexual characteristics and sperm.

ESTROGEN A generic term for several female sex hormones that promote growth of female sex characteristics and regulate the menstrual cycle.

PROGESTERONE A female sex hormone that promotes growth of the sex organs and helps maintain pregnancy.

CROSS-CULTURAL PERSPECTIVES ON MENSTRUATION

In Peru, they speak of a "visit from Uncle Pepé." In Samoa, menstruation is referred to as "the boogie man." One of the more common epithets given to the menstrual period throughout history is "the curse." The Fulani of Burkina Faso in Africa use a term for it that translates as "to see dirt." Some nations even blame "the curse" on their historic enemies. In earlier times, the French referred to menstruation as "the English" and to its onset as "the English are coming." Iranians used to say, "The Indians have attacked" to announce menstrual bleeding.

A common folk belief in preliterate societies is that menstrual blood is tainted (Rathus et al., 2000). Men avoid contact with menstruating women for fear of their lives. To avoid contamination, menstruating women are sent to special huts on the fringe of the village. In the traditional Navajo Indian culture, for instance, menstruating women would be consigned to huts that were set apart from other living quarters.

The Old Testament (Leviticus 15:19) warns against physical contact with a menstruating woman—including of course, sexual contact: "And if a woman have an issue, and her issue in her flesh be blood, she shall be put apart seven days; and whosoever toucheth her shall be unclean." Orthodox Jews still abstain from sex during menstruation and the week afterward. Prior to resuming sexual relations, the woman must attend a *mikvah*—a ritual cleansing.

Fears of contamination by menstruating women are nearly universal and persist today (Rathus et al., 2000). As late as the 1950s, women were not allowed in some European breweries for fear that the beer would turn sour. Some Indian castes still teach that a man who touches a woman during her period is contaminated and must be purified by a priest.

We might laugh off these misconceptions as folly were it not for their profound effects on women. Women who suffer from premenstrual syndrome may be responding to negative cultural attitudes toward menstruation as well as to menstrual symptoms themselves. The traditional view of menstruation as a time of pollution may make women highly sensitive to internal sensations at certain times of the month as well as concerned about how to dispose of the menstrual flow discreetly. ■

HEREDITY: THE NATURE OF NATURE

Consider some facts of life:

- People cannot breathe underwater (without special equipment).
- People cannot fly (again, without rather special equipment).
- Fish cannot learn to speak French or do an Irish jig even if you rear them in enriched environments and send them to finishing school.
- Chimpanzees and gorillas can use sign language but cannot speak.

People cannot breathe underwater or fly (without oxygen tanks, airplanes, or other devices) because of their **heredity.** Their heredity defines their nature—which is based in their biological structures and processes. Fish are limited in other ways by the natural traits that have been passed down from one generation to another. Chimpanzees and gorillas can understand many spoken words and express some concepts through nonverbal symbol systems such as American Sign Language. However, apes

HEREDITY The transmission of traits from one generation to another through genes.

cannot speak. They have probably failed to inherit the humanlike speech areas of the cerebral cortex. Their nature differs from ours.

Heredity is basic to the transmission of physical traits such as height, hair texture, and eye color. Animals can be selectively bred to enhance desired physical and psychological traits. We breed cattle and chickens to be bigger and fatter so that they provide more food calories for less feed. We breed animals to enhance psychological traits such as aggressiveness and intelligence. For example, poodles are relatively intelligent. Golden retrievers are gentle and patient with children. Border collies show a strong herding instinct. Even as puppies, Border collies attempt to corral people who are out for a stroll.

Heredity both makes behaviors possible and places limits on them. The subfield of biology that studies heredity is called **genetics. Behavioral genetics** bridges the sciences of psychology and biology. It is concerned with the genetic transmission of traits that give rise to patterns of behavior.

Heredity is involved in almost all human traits and behavior (Rutter, 1997). Examples include sociability, shyness, social dominance, aggressiveness, leadership, thrill seeking, effectiveness as a parent or a therapist, even interest in arts and crafts (Carey & DiLalla, 1994; Lykken et al., 1992). Genetic influences are also involved in most behavioral problems, including anxiety and depression, schizophrenia, bipolar disorder, alcoholism, even criminal behavior (DiLalla et al., 1996; Plomin et al., 1997). However, most behavior patterns also reflect life experiences and personal choice (Rose, 1995).

Heredity and Evolution

According to the British naturalist Charles Darwin (1808–1882), there is a struggle for survival as various species and individuals compete for the same territories. Organisms who are better adapted to their environments are more likely to survive (that is, to be "naturally selected"), to reproduce, and to transmit their features or traits to the next generation. Organisms evolve into more adaptive and complex creatures over time as those that are better adapted are selected and pool their genes. *Adaptation* and *natural selection* are key concepts in **evolutionary psychology.** This field of psychology studies the ways in which adaptation and natural selection—the core concepts in evolutionary theory—are connected with mental processes and behavior (Buss et al., 1998). Human evolution has given rise to such diverse activities as language, art, committed relationships, and warfare.

The "evolution" of Darwin's own thinking is fascinating. As a young man, he almost missed the boat, literally. He volunteered to serve as the scientist for an expedition by the HMS *Beagle,* but Captain Robert Fitz-Roy at first objected to Darwin because of the shape of his nose. Fitz-Roy believed you could judge a person's character by the outline of his facial features, and Darwin's nose did not fit the mode. But Fitz-Roy relented, and Darwin undertook the historic voyage that led to the development of his theory of evolution.

Darwin had always enjoyed collecting and classifying plants, minerals, and animals. He tried medical school, entered Cambridge University to become an Anglican priest, and eventually graduated with a degree in science. Independently wealthy, Darwin undertook the unpaid five-year position aboard the *Beagle.* The ship stopped at the Galápagos Islands, and Darwin noticed how species of lizards, tortoises, and plants differed somewhat on different islands. Although Darwin undertook his voyage as a believer in the Book of Genesis account of creation, his observations

GENETICS The branch of biology that studies heredity.

BEHAVIORAL GENETICS The study of the genetic transmission of structures and traits that give rise to behavior.

EVOLUTIONARY PSYCHOLOGY The field of psychology that studies the ways in which adaptation and natural selection are connected with behavior and mental processes.

Adenine   Cytosine

Thymine   Guanine

S = Sugar   P = Phosphate

FIGURE B.12
THE DOUBLE HELIX OF DNA.

GENES The basic building blocks of heredity, which consist of DNA.

CHROMOSOMES Structures consisting of genes that are found in the nuclei of the body's cells.

SEX CHROMOSOMES The 23rd pair of chromosomes, which determine whether the child will be male or female.

convinced him that the organisms he observed shared common ancestors but had *evolved* in different directions.

Darwin at first did not want his theory of evolution published until after his death. He feared it would be immensely unpopular because it contradicted religious views, and that it would bring scorn on his family. But he relented after 20 years because he learned that another naturalist, Alfred Russell Wallace, was about to publish an evolutionary theory of his own. Needless to say, Darwin's views became the standard. (Have you ever heard of Wallace's theory of evolution?)

Genes and Chromosomes

Genes are the building blocks of heredity. They are the biochemical materials that regulate the development of specific traits. Some traits, such as blood type, are controlled by a single pair of genes. (One gene is derived from each parent.) Other traits are determined by combinations of genes. The inherited component of complex psychological traits, such as intelligence, is believed to be determined by combinations of genes. We have about 100,000 genes in every cell in our bodies.

Genes are segments of **chromosomes,** each of which consists of more than 1,000 genes. Each cell in the body contains 46 chromosomes arranged in 23 pairs. Chromosomes are large complex molecules of deoxyribonucleic acid, which has several chemical components. (You can breathe a sigh of relief, for this acid is usually referred to simply as DNA.) The tightly wound structure of DNA was first demonstrated in the 1950s by James Watson and Francis Crick. It takes the form of a double helix—a twisting ladder (see Figure B.12). In all living things, the sides of the ladder consist of alternating segments of phosphate (P) and a kind of sugar (S). The "rungs" of the ladder are attached to the sugars and consist of one of two pairs of bases, either *adenine* with *thymine* (A with T) or *cytosine* with *guanine* (C with G). A single gene can contain hundreds of thousands of base pairs. The sequence of the rungs is the *genetic code* that causes the unfolding organism to grow arms or wings, skin or scales.

We normally receive 23 chromosomes from our father's sperm cell and 23 chromosomes from our mother's egg cell (ovum). When a sperm cell fertilizes an ovum, the chromosomes form 23 pairs (Figure B.13). The 23rd pair consists of **sex chromosomes,** which determine whether we are female or male. We all receive an X sex chromosome (so called because of the X shape) from our mother. If we also receive an X sex chromosome from our father, we develop into a female. If we receive a Y sex chromosome (named after the Y shape) from our father, we develop into a male.

Gender is not determined by sex chromosomes throughout the animal kingdom. Reptiles such as crocodiles, for example, do not have sex chromosomes. The crocodile's sex is determined by the temperature at which the egg develops (Crews, 1994). Some like it hot. That is, hatchlings are usually male when the eggs develop at temperatures in the mid-90s Fahrenheit or above. Some like it . . . well, not cold perhaps, but certainly cooler. When crocodile eggs develop at temperatures below the mid-80s Fahrenheit, the hatchlings are usually female.[2]

When people do not have the normal complement of 46 chromosomes, physical and behavioral abnormalities may result. The risk of these abnormalities rises with the age of the parents. Most persons with Down syndrome, for example, have an extra, or third, chromosome on the 21st pair.

---

[2] This does not mean that male crocodiles are hot-blooded. Reptiles are cold-blooded animals.

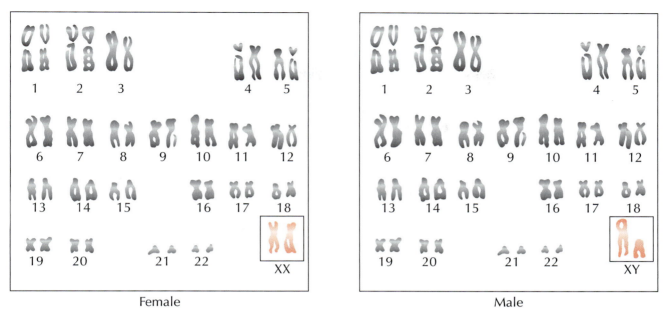

FIGURE B.13
THE 23 PAIRS OF HUMAN CHROMOSOMES.
People normally have 23 pairs of chromosomes. Whether one is female or male is determined by the 23rd pair of chromosomes. Females have two X sex chromosomes (part A), whereas males have an X and a Y sex chromosome (part B).

The extra chromosome is usually contributed by the mother, and the condition becomes increasingly likely as the mother's age at the time of pregnancy increases (Rathus et al., 2000). Persons with Down syndrome have a downward-sloping fold of skin at the inner corners of the eyes, a round face, a protruding tongue, and a broad, flat nose. They are mentally retarded and usually have physical problems that cause death by middle age.

Behavior geneticists are attempting to sort out the relative importance of **nature** (heredity) and **nurture** (environmental influences) in the origins

A PERSON WITH DOWN SYNDROME.
Down syndrome is caused by an extra chromosome on the 21st pair and becomes more likely to occur as the mother's age at the time of pregnancy increases. Persons with Down syndrome have characteristic facial features including downward-sloping fold of skin at the inner corners of the eyes, are mentally retarded, and usually have health problems that lead to death by middle age.

NATURE In behavior genetics, heredity.

NURTURE In behavior genetics, environmental influences on behavior, such as nutrition, culture, socioeconomic status, and learning.

of behavior. Psychologists are especially interested in the roles of nature and nurture in intelligence and psychological disorders. Organisms inherit physical features that set the stage for certain behaviors. But none of us is the result of heredity alone. Environmental factors such as nutrition, learning opportunities, cultural influences, exercise, and (unfortunately) accident and illness also determine whether genetically possible behaviors will be displayed. Behavior thus represents the interaction of nature and nurture. A potential Shakespeare who is reared in poverty and never taught to read or write will not create a *Hamlet.*

Kinship Studies

The more *closely* people are related, the more *genes* they have in common. Parents and children have a 50% overlap in their genetic endowments, and so do siblings (brothers and sisters). Aunts and uncles related by blood have a 25% overlap with nieces and nephews. First cousins share 12.5% of their genetic endowment. If genes are involved in a trait or behavior pattern, people who are more closely related should be more likely to show similar traits or behavior. Psychologists therefore compare the presence of traits and behavior patterns in people who are biologically related or unrelated (**kinship studies**) to help determine the role of genetic factors in their occurrence. They are especially interested in twins and adopted individuals.

TWIN STUDIES The fertilized egg cell (ovum) that carries genetic messages from both parents is called a *zygote.* Now and then, a zygote divides into two cells that separate, so instead of developing into a single person, it develops into two people with the same genetic makeup. Such people are identical, or **monozygotic (MZ), twins.** If the woman releases two ova in the same month and they are both fertilized, they develop into fraternal, or **dizygotic (DZ), twins.** DZ twins are related in the same way that other siblings are. They share 50% of their genes. MZ twins are important in the study of the relative influences of nature (heredity) and nurture (the environment) because differences between MZ twins are the result of nurture. (They cannot differ in heredity or nature because their genetic makeup is identical.)

Twin studies compare the presence of traits and behavior patterns in MZ twins, DZ twins, and other people to help determine the role of genetic factors in their occurrence. For example, twin studies show that genetic factors have a strong influence on physical features. MZ twins are more likely to look alike and to be similar in height, even to have more similar cholesterol levels than DZ twins (Heller et al., 1993). Psychologically speaking, MZ twins resemble one another more strongly than DZ twins and other siblings in the following ways:

1. Personality traits—for example, shyness, activity levels, irritability, sociability, even happiness (Adler, 1993; Goleman, 1996). Twin studies carried out by psychologist David Lykken at the University of Minnesota suggest that people inherit a tendency toward a certain level of happiness (Goleman, 1996). Despite the ups and downs of experience, people tend to drift back to their usual levels of cheerfulness or grumpiness. Factors such as availability of money, level of education, and marital status are much less influential than heredity when it comes to human happiness.

2. Developmental factors such as cognitive functioning, autism, and early signs of attachment—smiling, cuddling, and expression of fear of strangers (DeFries et al., 1987; DiLalla et al., 1996; Scarr & Kidd, 1983).

KINSHIP STUDIES Studies that compare the presence of traits and behavior patterns in people who are biologically related or unrelated in order to help determine the role of genetic factors in their occurrence.

MONOZYGOTIC (MZ) TWINS Identical twins. Twins who develop from a single zygote, thus carrying the same genetic instructions.

DIZYGOTIC (DZ) TWINS Fraternal twins. Twins who develop from separate zygotes.

3. Presence of psychological disorders such as anxiety, substance dependence, and schizophrenia (DiLalla et al., 1996).

ADOPTEE STUDIES The interpretation of kinship studies can be confused when relatives share similar environments as well as genes. This is especially true of identical twins, who may be dressed identically and encouraged to follow similar interests. Adoptee studies that compare children who have been separated from their parents at an early age (or in which identical twins are separated at an early age) and reared in different environments provide special opportunities for sorting out nature and nurture. Psychologists look for similarities between children and their adoptive and natural parents. When children reared by adoptive parents are more similar to their natural parents in a particular trait, strong evidence exists for a genetic role in the appearance of that trait.

There are thus important connections between biological factors and psychological events. Thoughts and mental images may seem like intangible pictures that float in our heads, but they have substance. They involve billions of brain cells (neurons), and the transmission of thousands of chemicals from one brain cell to another—repeated perhaps many times per second. These countless bits and pieces of microscopic activity give rise to feelings, plans, computation, art and music, and all the cognitive activities that characterize being human. We pour chemicals called hormones into our own bloodstreams, and they affect our activity levels, our anxiety levels, even our sex drives. We inherit traits that make us human, that enable us to think more deeply and act more cleverly than any other organism (after all, we write the textbooks). We also inherit unique dispositions as individuals—dispositions that affect our personalities, our patterns of development, and our psychological stability. An understanding of biology helps us grasp many psychological events that might otherwise seem elusive and without substance.

SUMMARY

1. **What are the parts of the nervous system?** The nervous system consists of neurons, which transmit information through neural impulses, and glial cells, which serve support functions. Neurons have a cell body, dendrites, and axons. Neurotransmitters transmit messages across synapses to other neurons.

2. **What is myelin?** Many neurons have a myelin coating that insulate axons, allowing for more efficient conduction of neural impulses.

3. **What are afferent and efferent neurons?** Afferent neurons transmit sensory messages to the central nervous system. Efferent neurons conduct messages from the central nervous system that stimulate glands or cause muscles to contract.

4. **How are neural impulses transmitted?** Neural transmission is electrochemical. An electric charge is conducted along an axon through a process that allows sodium ions to enter the cell and then pumps them out. The neuron has a resting potential of −70 millivolts and an action potential of about +40 millivolts.

5. **How do neurons fire?** Excitatory neurotransmitters stimulate neurons to fire. Inhibitory neurotransmitters cause them not to fire. Neurons fire according to an all-or-none principle. They may fire hundreds of times per second. Each firing is followed by a refractory period, during which neurons are insensitive to messages from other neurons.

6. **What are some important neurotransmitters?** These include acetylcholine, which is involved in muscle contractions; dopamine, imbalances of which have been linked to Parkinson's disease and schizophrenia; and noradrenaline, which accelerates the heartbeat and other body processes. Endorphins are naturally occurring painkillers.

7. **What is the central nervous system?** The brain and spinal cord make up the central nervous system. Reflexes involve the spinal cord but not the brain. The somatic and autonomic

systems make up the peripheral nervous system.

8. **What are the parts of the brain?** The hindbrain includes the medulla, pons, and cerebellum. The reticular activating system begins in the hindbrain and continues through the midbrain into the forebrain. Important structures of the forebrain include the thalamus, hypothalamus, limbic system, and cerebrum. The hypothalamus is involved in controlling body temperature and regulating motivation and emotion.

9. **What are the other parts of the nervous system?** The somatic nervous system transmits sensory information about skeletal muscles, skin, and joints to the central nervous system. It also controls skeletal muscular activity. The autonomic nervous system (ANS) regulates the glands and activities such as heartbeat, digestion, and dilation of the pupils. The sympathetic division of the ANS helps expend the body's resources, such as when fleeing from a predator, and the parasympathetic division helps build the body's reserves.

10. **What are the parts of the cerebral cortex?** The cerebral cortex is divided into the frontal, parietal, temporal, and occipital lobes. The visual cortex is in the occipital lobe, and the auditory cortex is in the temporal lobe. The somatosensory cortex lies behind the central fissure in the parietal lobe, and the motor cortex lies in the frontal lobe, across the central fissure from the somatosensory cortex.

11. **What parts of the brain are involved in thought and language?** The language areas of the cortex lie near the intersection of the frontal, temporal, and parietal lobes in one hemisphere. For right-handed people, this is usually the left hemisphere of the cortex. The notion that some people are left-brained and others are right-brained is exaggerated and largely inaccurate.

12. **How do people who have had split-brain operations behave?** For the most part, their behavior is perfectly normal. However, although they may verbally be able to describe a screened-off object such as a pencil held in the hand connected to the hemisphere that contains language functions, they cannot do so when the object is held in the other hand.

13. **What is the endocrine system?** The endocrine system consists of ductless glands that secrete hormones.

14. **What are some pituitary hormones?** The pituitary gland secretes growth hormone; prolactin, which regulates maternal behavior in lower animals and stimulates production of milk in women; and oxytocin, which stimulates labor in pregnant women.

15. **What hormones are produced by the adrenal glands?** The adrenal cortex produces steroids, which promote the development of muscle mass and increase activity level. The adrenal medulla secretes adrenaline (epinephrine), which increases the metabolic rate and is involved in general emotional arousal.

16. **What hormones are secreted by the testes and ovaries?** These are sex hormones such as testosterone, progesterone, and estrogen. Sex hormones are responsible for prenatal sexual differentiation, and female sex hormones regulate the menstrual cycle.

17. **What is genetics?** Genetics is the branch of biology concerned with the transmission of traits from generation to generation.

18. **What are genes and chromosomes?** Genes (which consist of DNA) are the basic building blocks of heredity. A thousand or more genes make up each chromosome. People normally have 46 chromosomes arranged in 23 pairs in each cell in the body. They receive 23 chromosomes from the father and 23 from the mother.

19. **What are kinship studies?** These are studies of the distribution of traits or behavior patterns among related people. When certain behaviors are shared by close relatives, such as identical twins, they may have a genetic component. This is especially so when the behaviors are shared by close blood relatives (parents and children, or identical twins) who have been separated early and reared in different environments.

KEY TERMS

acetylcholine (p. B-7)

action potential (p. B-6)

adrenaline (p. B-23)

afferent neurons (p. B-5)

all-or-none principle (p. B-6)

amygdala (p. B-13)

antidiuretic hormone (p. B-21)

autonomic nervous system (p. B-14)

axon (p. B-3)

behavioral genetics (p. B-25)

Broca's aphasia (p. B-18)

central nervous system (p. B-9)

REFERENCES

Adler, T. (1993). Shy, bold temperament? It's mostly in the genes. *APA Monitor, 24*(1), 7, 8.

Azar, B. (1997). Environment is key to serotonin levels. *APA Monitor, 28*(4), 26, 29.

Blum, D. (1997). *Sex on the brain: The biological differences between men and women.* New York: Viking.

Bogen, J. E. (1969). The other side of the brain II: An appositional mind. *Bulletin of the Los Angeles Neurological Society, 34,* 135–162.

Buss, D. M., Haselton, M. G., Shackelford, T. K., Bleske, A. L., & Wakefield, J. C. (1998). Adaptations, exaptations, and spandrels. *American Psychologist, 53,* 533–548.

Carey, G., & DiLalla, D. L. (1994). Personality and psychopathology: Genetic perspectives. *Journal of Abnormal Psychology, 103,* 32–43.

Carpenter, W. T., Jr., & Buchanan, R. W. (1994). Schizophrenia. *New England Journal of Medicine, 330,* 681–690.

Crews, D. (1994). Animal sexuality. *Scientific American, 270*(1), 108–114.

DeFries, J. C., Plomin, R., & LaBuda, M. C. (1987). Genetic stability of cognitive development from childhood to adulthood. *Developmental Psychology, 23,* 4–12.

Delgado, J. M. R. (1969). *Physical control of the mind.* New York: Harper & Row.

DiLalla, D. L., Carey, G., Gottesman, I. I., & Bouchard, T. J., Jr. (1996). Heritability of MMPI personality indicators of psychopathology in twins reared apart. *Journal of Abnormal Psychology, 105,* 491–499.

Engel, J. (1996). Surgery for seizures. *New England Journal of Medicine, 334,* 647–652.

Fritsch, G., & Hitzig, E. (1960). On the electrical excitability of the cerebrum. In G. von Bonin (Ed.), *Some papers on the cerebral cortex.* Springfield, IL: Charles C Thomas. (Original work published 1870)

Gazzaniga, M. S. (1995). Consciousness and the cerebral hemispheres. In M. S. Gazzaniga (Ed.), *The cognitive neurosciences.* Cambridge, MA: MIT Press.

Geschwind, N., & Galaburda, A. M. (1987). *Cerebral lateralization: Biological mechanisms, associations, and pathology.* Cambridge, MA: Harvard University Press.

Goldman-Rakic, P. S. (1992). Working memory and the mind. *Scientific American, 267*(3), 110–117.

Goleman, D. (1996, July 21). A set point for happiness. *New York Times,* p. E2.

Greenfield, S. A. (1995). *Journey to the center of the mind.* New York: Freeman.

Heller, D. A., de Faire, U., Pedersen, N. L., Dahlén, G., & McClearn, G. E. (1993). Genetic and environmental influences on serum lipid levels in twins. *New England Journal of Medicine, 328,* 1150–1156.

Hepper, P. G., Shahidullah, S., & White, R. (1990, October 4). Origins of fetal handedness. *Nature, 347,* 431.

Kilshaw, D., & Annett, M. (1983). Right-and left-hand skill: Effects of age, sex, and hand preferences showing superior in left-handers. *British Journal of Psychology, 74,* 253–268.

Klüver, H., & Bucy, P. C. (1939). Preliminary analysis of functions of the temporal lobe in monkeys. *Archives of Neurology and Psychiatry, 42,* 979–1000.

Knight, M. (1994). Darwinian functionalism. *The Psychological Record, 44,* 271–287.

Lykken, D. T., McGue, M., Tellegen, A., & Bouchard, T. J., Jr. (1992). Emergenesis: Genetic traits that may not run in families. *American Psychologist, 47,* 1565–1577.

Olds, J. (1969). The central nervous system and the reinforcement of behavior. *American Psychologist, 24,* 114–132.

Olds, J., & Milner, P. (1954). Positive reinforcement produced by electrical stimulation of the septal area and other regions of the rat brain. *Journal of Comparative and Physiological Psychology, 47,* 419–427.

Pinker, S. (1994). *The language instinct.* New York: Morrow.

Plomin, R., DeFries, J. C., McClearn, G., & Rutter, M. (1997). *Behavioral genetics* (3rd ed.). New York: Freeman.

Raichle, M. E. (1994). Visualizing the mind. *Scientific American, 270*(4), 58–64.

Rathus, S. A., Nevid, J. S., & Fichner-Rathus, L. (2000). *Human sexuality in a world of diversity* (4th ed.). Boston: Allyn & Bacon.

Rose, R. J. (1995). Genes and human behavior. *Annual Review of Psychology, 46,* 625–654.

Rutter, M. (1997). Nature-nurture integration. *American Psychologist, 52,* 390–398.

Scarr, S., & Kidd, K. K. (1983). Developmental behavior genetics. In M. Haith & J. J. Campos (Eds.), *Handbook of child psychology.* New York: Wiley.

Shaywitz, S. E. (1998). Dyslexia. *New England Journal of Medicine, 338,* 307–312.

Springer, S. P., & Deutsch, G. (1993). *Left brain, right brain* (4th ed.). New York: Freeman.

Squire, L. R. (1996, August). *Memory systems of the brain.* Master lecture presented to the meeting of the American Psychological Association, Toronto.

Zheng, C., Heintz, H., & Hatten, M. E. (1996). CNS gene encoding astrotacin. Which supports neural migration along glial fibers. *Science, 272,* 417–421.

Zuger, A. (1997, August 19). Removing half of brain improves young epileptics' lives. *New York Times,* p. C4.

LS

LIFESPAN DEVELOPMENT

TRUTH OR FICTION?

_____ Fertilization takes place in the uterus.

_____ Your heart started beating when you were only one fifth of an inch long and weighed a fraction of an ounce.

_____ The way to a baby's heart is through its stomach—that is, babies become emotionally attached to those who feed them.

_____ Children with strict parents are most likely to be successful.

_____ Children placed in day care are more aggressive than children cared for in the home.

_____ Child abusers frequently were abused themselves as children.

_____ A girl can become pregnant when she has her first menstrual period.

_____ Adolescents see themselves as being on stage.

_____ Menopause signals the end of a woman's sexual interest.

_____ Mothers suffer from the empty nest syndrome when their youngest child leaves home.

_____ Older people who blame health problems on aging rather than on specific factors such as a virus are more likely to die in the near future.

There is no cure for birth or death save to enjoy the interval.

GEORGE SANTAYANA

ON A SUMMERLIKE DAY IN OCTOBER, LING CHANG AND HER husband Patrick rush out to their jobs as usual. While Ling, a buyer for a New York department store, is arranging for dresses from the Chicago manufacturer to arrive in time for the spring line, a very different drama is unfolding in her body. Hormones are causing a follicle (egg container) in one of her ovaries to ovulate—that is, to rupture and release an egg cell, or ovum. Ling, like other women, possesses from birth all the egg cells she will ever have. How this particular ovum was selected to ripen and be released this month is unknown. But in any case, Ling will be capable of becoming pregnant for only a couple of days following ovulation.

When it is released, the ovum begins a slow journey down a 4-inch-long fallopian tube to the uterus. It is within this tube that one of Patrick's sperm cells will unite with the egg. The fertilized ovum, or zygote, is 1/175th of an inch across—a tiny stage for the drama that is about to unfold.

Developmental psychologists are interested in studying the development of Patrick and Ling's new child from the time of conception until death for several reasons. The discovery of early influences and developmental sequences helps psychologists understand adults. Psychologists are also interested in the effects of genetic factors, early interactions with parents and siblings (brothers and sisters), and the school and community on traits such as aggressiveness and intelligence.

Developmental psychologists also seek to learn the causes of developmental abnormalities. For instance, should pregnant women abstain from smoking and drinking? (Yes.) Is it safe for a pregnant woman to take aspirin for a headache or tetracycline to ward off a bacterial invasion? (Perhaps not. Ask your obstetrician.) What factors contribute to child abuse? Some developmental psychologists focus on adult development. For example, what conflicts and disillusionments can we expect as we journey through our 30s, 40s, and 50s? The information acquired by developmental psychologists can help us make decisions about how we rear our children and lead our own lives.

Let us begin our life story with prenatal developments—the changes that occur between conception and birth. Although they may be literally out of sight, the most dramatic biological changes occur within the short span of 9 months.

PRENATAL DEVELOPMENT: THE BEGINNING OF OUR LIFE STORY

The most dramatic gains in height and weight occur during prenatal development. Within 9 months a child develops from a nearly microscopic cell to a **neonate** (newborn) about 20 inches long. Its weight increases a billionfold.

During the months following conception, the single cell formed by the union of sperm and egg—the **zygote**—multiplies, becoming two, then four, then eight, and so on. By the time the infant is ready to be born, it contains trillions of cells.

The zygote divides repeatedly as it proceeds on its 3- to 4-day journey to the uterus. The ball-like mass of multiplying cells wanders about the uterus for another 3 to 4 days before beginning to implant in the uterine wall. Implantation takes another week or so. The period from conception to implantation is called the **germinal stage,** or the **period of the ovum.**

The **embryonic stage** lasts from implantation until about the eighth week of development. During this stage, the major body organ systems take form. As you can see from the relatively large heads of embryos (see Figure LS.1), the growth of the head precedes that of the lower parts of the body. The growth of the organs—heart, lungs, and so on—also precedes the growth of the extremities. The relatively early maturation of the brain and the organ systems allows them to participate in the nourishment and further development of the embryo. During the fourth week, a primitive heart begins to beat and pump blood—in an organism that is one fifth of an inch long. The heart continues to beat without rest every minute of every day for perhaps 80 or 90 years.

By the end of the second month, the head has become rounded and the facial features distinct—all in an embryo that is about 1 inch long and weighs 1/30th of an ounce. During the second month, the nervous system begins to transmit messages. By 5 to 6 weeks, the embryo is only a quarter to half an inch long, yet nondescript sex organs have formed. By about the seventh week, the genetic code (XY or XX) begins to assert itself, causing the sex organs to differentiate. If a Y sex chromosome is present, testes form and begin to produce **androgens** (male sex hormones), which further masculinize the sex organs. In the absence of these hormones, the embryo develops female sex organs.

As it develops, the embryo is suspended within a protective **amniotic sac** in the mother's uterus. The sac is surrounded by a clear membrane and contains amniotic fluid. The fluid serves as a sort of natural air bag, allowing the child to move or even jerk around without injury. It also helps maintain an even temperature.

From now until birth, the embryo exchanges nutrients and wastes with the mother through a pancake-shaped organ called the **placenta.** The embryo is connected to the placenta by the **umbilical cord.** The placenta is connected to the mother by the system of blood vessels in the uterine wall.

The circulatory systems of the mother and baby do not mix. A membrane in the placenta permits only certain substances to pass through. Oxygen and nutrients are passed from the mother to the embryo. Carbon dioxide and other wastes are passed from the child to the mother, where they are removed by the mother's lungs and kidneys. Unfortunately, a number of other substances can pass through the placenta. They include some microscopic disease organisms—such as those that cause syphilis and German measles—and some chemical agents, including acne drugs, aspirin, narcotics, alcohol, and tranquilizers. Because these and other agents may be harmful to the baby, pregnant women are advised to consult their physicians about the advisability of using any drugs, even those sold over the counter.

The **fetal stage** lasts from the beginning of the third month until birth. By the end of the third month, the major organ systems and the fingers and toes have been formed. In the middle of the fourth month, the mother usually detects the first fetal movements. By the end of the sixth month, the fetus moves its limbs so vigorously that the mother may complain of being kicked. The fetus opens and shuts its eyes, sucks its thumb,

---

TRUTH OR FICTION REVISITED
It is not true that fertilization takes place in the uterus. Fertilization normally occurs in a fallopian tube.

TRUTH OR FICTION REVISITED
It is true that your heart started beating when you were only one fifth of an inch long and weighed a fraction of an ounce. It started about 3 weeks after conception.

NEONATE A newly born child.

ZYGOTE A fertilized ovum (egg cell).

GERMINAL STAGE The first stage of prenatal development during which the dividing mass of cells has not become implanted in the uterine wall.

PERIOD OF THE OVUM Another term for the *germinal stage.*

EMBRYONIC STAGE The baby from the third through the eighth weeks following conception, during which time the major organ systems undergo rapid differentiation.

ANDROGENS Male sex hormones.

AMNIOTIC SAC A sac within the uterus that contains the embryo or fetus.

PLACENTA A membrane that permits the exchange of nutrients and waste products between the mother and her developing child but does not allow the maternal and fetal bloodstreams to mix.

UMBILICAL CORD A tube between the mother and her developing child through which nutrients and waste products are conducted.

FETUS The baby from the third month following conception through childbirth, during which time there is maturation of organ systems and dramatic gains in length and weight.

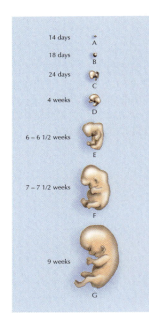

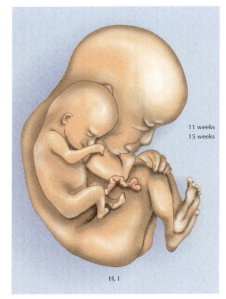

FIGURE LS.1
EMBRYOS AND FETUSES AT VARIOUS INTERVALS OF PRE-NATAL DEVELOPMENT.

REFLEX A simple unlearned response to a stimulus.

ROOTING The turning of an infant's head toward a touch, such as by the mother's nipple.

alternates between periods of wakefulness and sleep, and perceives light. It also turns somersaults, which can be clearly perceived by the mother. The umbilical cord is composed so that it will not break or become dangerously wrapped around the fetus, no matter how many acrobatic feats the fetus performs.

During the last 3 months, the organ systems of the fetus continue to mature. The heart and lungs become increasingly capable of sustaining independent life. The fetus gains about 5 1/2 pounds and doubles in length. Newborn boys average about 7 1/2 pounds and newborn girls about 7 pounds.

CHILD DEVELOPMENT

Childhood begins with birth. When my children are enjoying themselves, I kid them and say, "Stop having fun. You're a child and childhood is the worst time of life." I get a laugh because they know that childhood is supposed to be the best time of life—a time for play and learning and endless possibilities. For many children it is that, but other children suffer from problems such as malnutrition, low self-esteem, and child abuse.

Let us chronicle the events of childhood. The most obvious aspects of child development are physical. Let us therefore begin with physical development. However, we will see that cognitive developments and social and personality developments are also essential.

Physical Development

Physical development includes gains in height and weight; maturation of the nervous system; and development of bones, muscles, and organs.

During infancy—the first two years of childhood—dramatic gains in height and weight continue. Babies usually double their birth weight in about 5 months and triple it by their first birthday. Their height increases by about 10 inches in the first year. Children grow another 4 to 6 inches during the second year and gain some 4 to 7 pounds. After that, they gain about 2 to 3 inches a year until they reach the adolescent growth spurt. Weight gains also remain fairly even at about 4 to 6 pounds per year until the spurt begins.

Let us now consider other aspects of physical development in childhood: reflexes, perceptual development, and motor development.

REFLEXES Soon after you were born, a doctor or nurse probably pressed her fingers against the palms of your hands. Although you would have had no idea what to do in response, most likely you grasped the fingers firmly—so firmly that you could have been lifted from your cradle! Grasping at birth is inborn. It is one of the neonate's many **reflexes**—simple, unlearned, stereotypical responses elicited by specific stimuli. Reflexes are essential to survival and do not involve higher brain functions. They occur automatically—that is, without thinking about them.

Newborn children do not know that it is necessary to eat to survive. Fortunately, they have rooting and sucking reflexes that cause them to eat. They turn their head toward stimuli that prod or stroke the cheek, chin, or corner of the mouth. This is termed **rooting.** They suck objects that touch their lips.

Neonates have numerous other reflexes that aid in survival. They withdraw from painful stimuli. This is known as the withdrawal reflex. They draw up their legs and arch their backs in response to sudden noises, bumps, or loss of support while being held. This is the startle, or Moro, reflex. They grasp objects that press against the palms of their hands (the grasp, or palmar, reflex). They fan their toes when the soles of their feet are stimulated (the Babinski reflex). Pediatricians assess babies' neural functioning by testing these reflexes.

Babies also breathe, sneeze, cough, yawn, and blink reflexively. And it is guaranteed that you will learn about the sphincter (anal muscle) reflex if you put on your best clothes and hold an undiapered neonate on your lap for a while.

PERCEPTUAL DEVELOPMENT Newborn children spend about 16 hours a day sleeping and do not have much opportunity to learn about the world. Yet they are capable of perceiving the world reasonably well soon after birth.

Within a couple of days, infants can follow, or track, a moving light with their eyes (Kellman & von Hofsten, 1992). By the age of 3 months, they can discriminate most colors (Banks & Shannon, 1993; Teller & Lindsey, 1993). Neonates are nearsighted but by about the age of 4 months, infants seem able to focus on distant objects about as well as adults can.

The visual preferences of infants are measured by the amount of time, termed **fixation time,** they spend looking at one stimulus instead of another. In classic research by Robert Fantz (1961), 2-month-old infants preferred visual stimuli that resembled the human face to newsprint, a bull's-eye, and featureless red, white, and yellow disks. At this age the complexity of facelike patterns may be more important than their content. For example, babies have been shown facelike patterns that differ either in the number of elements they contain or the degree to which they are organized to match the human face. Five- to 10-week-old babies fixate longer on patterns with high numbers of elements. The organization of the elements—that is, the degree to which they resemble the face—is less important. By 15 to 20 weeks, the organization of the pattern also matters. At that age babies dwell longer on facelike patterns (e.g., Haaf et al., 1983).

Infants thus seem to have an inborn preference for complex visual stimuli. However, preference for faces as opposed to other equally complex stimuli may not emerge until infants have had experience with people.

Classic research has shown that infants tend to respond to cues for depth by the time they are able to crawl (at about 6 to 8 months). Most also have the good sense to avoid crawling off ledges and tabletops into open space (Campos et al., 1978). Note the setup (Figure LS.2) in the classic "visual cliff" experiment run by Walk and Gibson (1961). An 8-month-old infant crawls freely above the portion of the glass with a checkerboard pattern immediately beneath it, but hesitates to crawl over the portion of the glass beneath which the checkerboard has been dropped a few feet. Because the glass would support the infant, this is a "visual cliff," not an actual cliff.

Normal neonates hear well unless their middle ears are clogged with amniotic fluid. In such cases, hearing improves rapidly after the ears are opened up. Most neonates reflexively turn their heads toward unusual sounds, suspending other activities as they do so. This finding, along with findings about visual tracking, suggests that infants are preprogrammed to survey their environments. Speaking or singing softly in a low-pitched tone soothes infants. This is why some parents use lullabies to get infants to fall asleep.

Three-day-old babies prefer their mother's voice to those of other women, but they do not show a similar preference for their father's voice (DeCasper & Prescott, 1984; Freeman et al., 1993). By birth, of course, babies have had many months of "experience" in the uterus. For at least

AN EXERCISE CLASS FOR PREGNANT WOMEN.
Years ago pregnant women were not expected to exert themselves. Today, it is recognized that exercise is healthful for pregnant women because it promotes fitness, which is beneficial during childbirth as well as at other times.

FIGURE LS.2
THE CLASSIC VISUAL CLIFF EXPERIMENT.

This young explorer has the good sense not to crawl out onto an apparently unsupported surface, even when Mother beckons from the other side. Rats, pups, kittens, and chicks also will not try to walk across to the other side. (So don't bother asking why the chicken crossed the visual cliff.)

FIXATION TIME The amount of time spent looking at a visual stimulus.

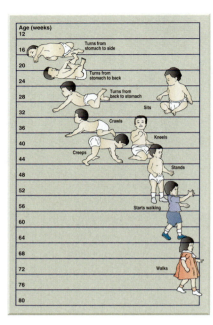

FIGURE LS.3

MOTOR DEVELOPMENT.

At birth, infants appear to be bundles of aimless nervous energy. They have reflexes but also engage in random movements that are replaced by purposeful activity as they mature. Motor development proceeds in an orderly sequence. Practice prompts sensorimotor coordination, but maturation is essential. The times in the figure are approximate: An infant who is a bit behind may develop with no problems at all, and a precocious infant will not necessarily become a rocket scientist (or gymnast).

2 or 3 months before birth, babies have been capable of hearing sounds. Because they are predominantly exposed to sounds produced by their mother, learning may contribute to neonatal preferences.

The nasal preferences of babies are similar to those of adults. Newborn infants spit, stick out their tongue, and literally wrinkle their nose at the odor of rotten eggs. They smile and make licking motions in response to chocolate, strawberry, vanilla, and honey. The sense of smell, like the sense of hearing, may provide a vehicle for mother-infant recognition. Within the first week, nursing infants prefer to turn to look at their mother's nursing pads (which can be discriminated only by smell) rather than those of strange women (Macfarlane, 1975). By 15 days, nursing infants prefer their mother's underarm odor to those of other women (Porter et al., 1992). Bottle-fed babies do not show this preference.

Shortly after birth, infants can discriminate tastes. They suck liquid solutions of sugar and milk but grimace and refuse to suck salty or bitter solutions.

Newborn babies are sensitive to touch. Many reflexes (including rooting and sucking) are activated by pressure against the skin. Newborns are relatively insensitive to pain, however. This may be adaptive, considering the squeezing that occurs during the birth process. Sensitivity to pain increases within a few days.

The sense of touch is an extremely important avenue of learning and communication for babies. Sensations of skin against skin appear to provide feelings of comfort and security that may contribute to the formation of affectionate bonds between infants and their caregivers.

MOTOR DEVELOPMENT Motor development provides some of the most fascinating changes in infants, in part because so much seems to happen so quickly—and so much of it during the first year. Children gain the capacity to move about through a sequence of activities that includes rolling over, sitting up, crawling, creeping, walking, and running. There is a great deal of variation in the ages at which infants first engage in these activities, but the sequence generally remains the same (see Figure LS.3). A number of children skip a step, however. For example, an infant may creep without ever having crawled.

Let us now consider cognitive developments during childhood. Physical development is not possible without the participation of the brain, and the brain is also the seat of cognition.

Cognitive Development

The ways in which children mentally represent and think about the world—that is, their *cognitive development*—are explored in this section. Because cognitive functioning develops over many years, young children have ideas about the world that differ considerably from those of adults. Many of these ideas are charming but illogical—at least to adults.

JEAN PIAGET'S COGNITIVE-DEVELOPMENTAL THEORY The Swiss biologist and psychologist Jean Piaget contributed significantly to our understanding of children's cognitive development. He hypothesized that children's cognitive processes develop in an orderly sequence of stages. Although some children may be more advanced than others at particular ages, the developmental sequence remains the same. Piaget (1963) identified four major stages of cognitive development: sensorimotor, preoperational, concrete operational, and formal operational (see Table LS.1).

Piaget regarded children as natural physicists who seek to learn about and control their world. In the Piagetian view, children who squish their food and laugh enthusiastically are often acting as budding scientists. In addition to enjoying the responses of their parents, they are studying the texture and consistency of their food. (Parents, of course, often wish their children would practice these experiments in the laboratory, not the dining room.)

JEAN PIAGET.

Assimilation and Accommodation   Piaget described human thought, or intelligence, in terms of two basic concepts: assimilation and accommodation. **Assimilation** means responding to a new stimulus through a reflex or existing habit. Infants, for example, usually try to place new objects in their mouth to suck, feel, or explore. Piaget would say that the child is assimilating a new toy to the sucking scheme. A **scheme** is a pattern of action or a mental structure involved in acquiring or organizing knowledge.

Accommodation is the creation of new ways of responding to objects or looking at the world. In accommodation, children transform existing schemes—action patterns or ways of organizing knowledge—to incorporate new events. Children (and adults) accommodate to objects and situations that cannot be integrated into existing schemes. (For example, children who study biology learn that whales cannot be assimilated into the "fish" scheme. They accommodate by constructing new schemes, such as "mammals without legs that live in the sea.") The ability to accommodate to novel stimuli advances as a result of maturation and experience.

Most of the time, newborn children assimilate environmental stimuli according to reflexive schemes, although adjusting the mouth to contain the nipple is a primitive kind of accommodation. Reflexive behavior, to Piaget, is not "true" intelligence. True intelligence involves adapting to the world through a smooth, fluid balancing of the processes of assimilation and accommodation. Let us now apply these concepts to the stages of cognitive development.

ASSIMILATION According to Piaget, the inclusion of a new event into an existing scheme.

SCHEME According to Piaget, a hypothetical mental structure that permits the classification and organization of new information.

ACCOMMODATION According to Piaget, the modification of schemes so that information inconsistent with existing schemes can be integrated or understood.

The Sensorimotor Stage   The newborn infant is capable of assimilating novel stimuli only to existing reflexes (or ready-made schemes) such as the rooting and sucking reflexes. But by the time an infant reaches the age of 1 month, it already shows purposeful behavior by repeating behavior patterns that are pleasurable, such as sucking its hand. During the first

TABLE LS.1

PIAGET'S STAGES OF COGNITIVE DEVELOPMENT		
STAGE	**APPROXIMATE AGE**	**DESCRIPTION**
Sensorimotor	Birth–2 years	At first, the child lacks language and does not use symbols or mental representations of objects. In time, reflexive responding ends and intentional behavior begins. The child develops the object concept and acquires the basics of language.
Preoperational	2–7 years	The child begins to represent the world mentally, but thought is egocentric. The child does not focus on two aspects of a situation at once and therefore lacks conservation. The child shows animism, artificialism, and immanent justice.
Concrete operational	7–12 years	The child develops conservation concepts, can adopt the viewpoint of others, can classify objects in series, and shows comprehension of basic relational concepts (such as one object being larger or heavier than another).
Formal operational	12 years and above	Mature, adult thought emerges. Thinking is characterized by deductive logic, consideration of various possibilities (mental trial and error), abstract thought, and the formation and testing of hypotheses.

FIGURE LS.4
OBJECT PERMANENCE.

To the infant at the top, who is in the early part of the sensorimotor stage, out of sight is truly out of mind. Once a sheet of paper is placed between the infant and the toy elephant, the infant loses all interest in it. The toy is apparently not yet mentally represented. The photos on the bottom show a child later in the sensorimotor stage. This child does mentally represent objects and pushes through a towel to reach one that has been screened from sight.

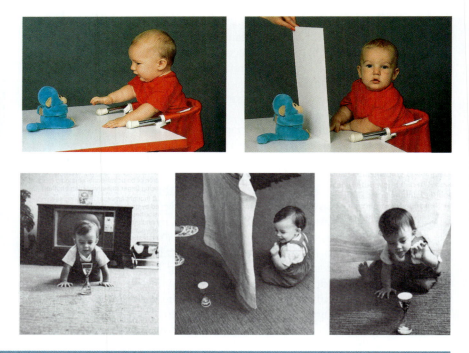

month or so, an infant apparently does not connect stimuli perceived through different senses. Reflexive turning toward sources of auditory and olfactory stimulation cannot be considered purposeful searching. But within the first few months the infant begins to coordinate vision with grasping so that it looks at what it is holding or touching.

A 3- or 4-month-old infant may be fascinated by its own hands and legs. It may become absorbed in watching itself open and close its fists. The infant becomes increasingly interested in acting on the environment to make interesting results (such as the sound of a rattle) last longer or occur again. Behavior becomes increasingly intentional and purposeful. Between 4 and 8 months of age, the infant explores cause-and-effect relationships such as the thump that can be made by tossing an object or the way kicking can cause a hanging toy to bounce.

Prior to the age of 6 months or so, out of sight is literally out of mind. Objects are not yet represented mentally. For this reason, as you can see in Figure LS.4, a child makes no effort to search for an object that has been removed or placed behind a screen. By the age of 8 to 12 months, however, infants realize that objects removed from sight still exist and attempt to find them. In this way, they show what is known as **object permanence,** thereby making it possible to play peek-a-boo.

Between 1 and 2 years of age, children begin to show interest in how things are constructed. It may be for this reason that they persistently touch and finger their parents' faces and their own. Toward the end of the second year, children begin to engage in mental trial and error before they try out overt behaviors. For instance, when they look for an object you have removed, they will no longer begin their search in the last place they saw it. Rather, they may follow you, assuming you are carrying the object even though it is not visible. It is as though they are anticipating failure in searching for the object in the place where they last saw it.

Because the first stage of development is dominated by learning to coordinate perception of the self and of the environment with motor (muscular) activity, Piaget termed it the **sensorimotor stage.** This stage comes to a close with the acquisition of the basics of language at about age 2.

OBJECT PERMANENCE Recognition that objects removed from sight still exist, as demonstrated in young children by continued pursuit.

SENSORIMOTOR STAGE The first of Piaget's stages of cognitive development, characterized by coordination of sensory information and motor activity, early exploration of the environment, and lack of language.

The Preoperational Stage The **preoperational stage** is characterized by the use of words and symbols to represent objects and relationships among them. But be warned—any resemblance between the logic of children between the ages of 2 and 7 and your own logic very often is purely coincidental. Children may use the same words that adults do, but this does not mean their views of the world are similar to adults'. A major limit on preoperational children's thinking is that it tends to be one dimensional—to focus on one aspect of a problem or situation at a time.

One consequence of one-dimensional thinking is **egocentrism.** Preoperational children cannot understand that other people do not see things the same way they do. When Allyn was 2 1/2, I asked her to tell me about a trip to the store with her mother. "You tell me," she replied. Upon questioning, it seemed she did not understand that I could not see the world through her eyes.

To egocentric preoperational children, all the world's a stage that has been erected to meet their needs and amuse them. When asked, "Why does the sun shine?" they may say, "To keep me warm." If asked, "Why is the sky blue?" they may respond, "'Cause blue's my favorite color." Preoperational children also show **animism.** They attribute life and consciousness to physical objects like the sun and the moon. They also show **artificialism.** They believe that environmental events like rain and thunder are human inventions. Asked why the sky is blue, 4-year-olds may answer, "'Cause Mommy painted it." Examples of egocentrism, animism, and artificialism are shown in Table LS.2.

To gain further insight into preoperational thinking, consider these problems:

1. Imagine that you pour water from a tall, thin glass into a low, wide glass. Now, does the low, wide glass contain more, less, or the same amount of water that was in the tall, thin glass? I won't keep you in suspense. If you said the same amount of water (with possible minor exceptions for spillage and evaporation), you were correct. Now that you're on a roll, go on to the next problem.

2. If you flatten a ball of clay into a pancake, do you wind up with more, less, or the same amount of clay? If you said the same amount of clay, you are correct once more.

PREOPERATIONAL STAGE The second of Piaget's stages, characterized by illogical use of words and symbols, spotty logic, and egocentrism.

EGOCENTRIC According to Piaget, assuming that others view the world as one does oneself.

ANIMISM The belief that inanimate objects move because of will or spirit.

ARTIFICIALISM The belief that natural objects have been created by human beings.

TABLE LS.2

EXAMPLES OF PREOPERATIONAL THOUGHT		
TYPE OF THOUGHT	**SAMPLE QUESTIONS**	**TYPICAL ANSWERS**
Egocentrism	Why does it get dark out? Why does the sun shine? Why is there snow? Why is grass green? What are TV sets for?	So I can go to sleep. To keep me warm. For me to play in. Because that's my favorite color. To watch my favorite shows and cartoons.
Animism (attributing life and consciousness to physical objects)	Why do trees have leaves? Why do stars twinkle? Why does the sun move in the sky? Where do boats go at night?	To keep them warm. Because they're happy and cheerful. To follow children and hear what they say. They sleep like we do.
Artificialism (assuming that environmental events are human inventions)	What makes it rain? Why is the sky blue? What is the wind? What causes thunder? How does a baby get in Mommy's tummy?	Someone emptying a watering can. Somebody painted it. A man blowing. A man grumbling. Just make it first. (How?) You put some eyes on it, then put on the head.

FIGURE LS.5

CONSERVATION.

The boy in these photographs agreed that the amount of water in two identical containers is equal. He then watched as water from one container was poured into a tall, thin container. In the left-hand photograph, he is examining one of the original containers and the new container. When asked whether he thinks the amounts of water in the two containers are now the same, he says no. Apparently, he is impressed by the height of the new container, and, prior to the development of conservation, he focuses on only one dimension of the situation at a time—in this case, the height of the new container.

CONSERVATION According to Piaget, recognition that basic properties of substances such as weight and mass remain the same when superficial features change.

CENTER According to Piaget, to focus one's attention.

OBJECTIVE RESPONSIBILITY According to Piaget, the assignment of blame according to the amount of damage done rather than the motives of the actor.

CONCRETE-OPERATIONAL STAGE Piaget's third stage, characterized by logical thought concerning tangible objects, conservation, and subjective morality.

DECENTRATION Simultaneous focusing on more than one dimension of a problem, so that flexible, reversible thought becomes possible.

To arrive at the correct answers to these questions, you must understand the law of **conservation.** This law holds that basic properties of substances such as mass, weight, and volume remain the same—that is, are *conserved*—when you change superficial properties such as their shape or arrangement.

Conservation requires the ability to think about, or **center** on, two aspects of a situation at once, such as height and width. Conserving the mass, weight, or volume of a substance requires the recognition that a change in one dimension can compensate for a change in another. But the preoperational boy in Figure LS.5 focuses on only one dimension at a time. First he is shown two tall, thin glasses of water and agrees that they contain the same amount of water. Then, while he watches, water is poured from a tall glass into a squat glass. Now he is asked which glass contains more water. After mulling over the problem, he points to the tall glass. Why? Because when he looks at the glasses he is "overwhelmed" by the fact that the thinner glass is taller. The preoperational child focuses on the most apparent dimension of the situation—in this case, the greater height of the thinner glass. He does not realize that the increased width of the squat glass compensates for the decreased height. By the way, if you ask him whether any water has been added or taken away in the pouring process, he readily says no. But if you then repeat the question about which glass contains *more* water, he again points to the taller glass.

If all this sounds rather illogical, that is because it is illogical—or, in Piaget's terms, preoperational.

After you have tried the experiment with the water, try the following. Make two rows of five pennies each. In the first row, place the pennies about half an inch apart. In the second row, place the pennies 2 to 3 inches apart. Ask a 4- to 5-year-old child which row has more pennies. What do you think the child will say? Why?

Piaget (1997) found that the moral judgment of preoperational children is also one dimensional. Five-year-olds are slaves to rules and authority. When you ask them why something should be done in a certain way, they may insist, "Because that's the way to do it!" or "Because my Mommy says so!" Right is right and wrong is wrong. Why? "Because!"—that's why.

According to most older children and adults, an act is a crime only when there is criminal intent. Accidents may be hurtful, but the perpetrators are usually seen as blameless. But in the court of the one-dimensional, preoperational child, there is **objective responsibility.** People are sentenced (and harshly!) on the basis of the amount of damage they have done, not their motives or intentions.

To demonstrate objective responsibility, Piaget would tell children stories and ask them which character was naughtier and why. John, for instance, accidentally breaks 15 cups when he opens a door. Henry breaks 1 cup when he sneaks into a kitchen cabinet to find forbidden jam. The preoperational child usually judges John to be naughtier. Why? Because he broke more cups.

The Concrete-Operational Stage By about age 7, the typical child is entering the stage of **concrete operations.** In this stage, which lasts until about age 12, children show the beginnings of the capacity for adult logic. However, their logical thoughts, or *operations,* generally involve tangible objects rather than abstract ideas. Concrete operational children are capable of **decentration;** they can center on two dimensions of a problem at once. This attainment has implications for moral judgments, conservation, and other intellectual undertakings.

Children now become **subjective** in their moral judgments. When assigning guilt, they center on the motives of wrongdoers as well as on the amount of damage done. Concrete-operational children judge Henry more harshly than John because John's misdeed was an accident.

Concrete-operational children understand the laws of conservation. The boy in Figure LS.5, now a few years older, would say that the squat glass still contains the same amount of water. If asked why, he might reply, "Because you can pour it back into the other one." Such an answer also suggests awareness of the concept of **reversibility**—the recognition that many processes can be reversed or undone so that things are restored to their previous condition. Centering simultaneously on the height and the width of the glasses, the boy recognizes that the loss in height compensates for the gain in width.

Concrete-operational children can conserve *number* as well as weight and mass. They recognize that the number of pennies in each of the rows described earlier is the same, even though one row may be spread out to look longer than the other.

Children in this stage are less egocentric. They are able to take on the roles of others and to view the world, and themselves, from other people's perspectives. They recognize that people see things in different ways because of different situations and different sets of values.

During the concrete-operational stage, children's own sets of values begin to emerge and acquire stability. Children come to understand that feelings of love between them and their parents can endure even when someone feels angry or disappointed at a particular moment.

We discuss the formal-operational stage and evaluate Piaget's theory in the section on adolescence.

LANGUAGE DEVELOPMENT Language is the communication of thoughts and feelings through symbols that are arranged according to rules of grammar. Language makes it possible for one person to communicate knowledge to another and for one generation to record information for another. Language allows people to learn more than they could from direct experience. It enables parents to give children advice, which now and then they heed. Language also provides many of the basic units of thinking, which is at the core of cognition.

Piaget theorized that children's cognitive development follows a specific sequence of steps. Such sequencing also applies to language development, beginning with the *prelinguistic* vocalizations of crying, cooing, and babbling. These sounds are not symbols. That is, they do not represent object or events. Therefore, they are *pre*linguistic, not linguistic.

As parents are well aware, newborn children have one inborn, highly effective form of verbal expression: crying—and more crying. During the second month, babies begin *cooing*. Babies use their tongues when they coo, so coos are more articulated than cries. Coos are often vowel-like and resemble "oohs" and "ahs." Cooing appears to be linked to feelings of pleasure. Babies do not coo when they are hungry, tired, or in pain. Parents soon learn that different cries and coos can indicate different things: hunger, gas pains, or pleasure at being held or rocked.

By the fifth or sixth month, children begin to *babble*. Babbling sort of sounds like speech. Children babble sounds that occur in many languages, including the throaty German *ch*, the clicks of certain African languages, and rolling *r*'s. In babbling, babies frequently combine consonants and vowels, as in "ba," "ga," and, sometimes, the much valued "dada." "Dada" at first is purely coincidental (sorry, dads), despite the family's delight over its appearance.

SUBJECTIVE MORAL JUDGMENT According to Piaget, moral judgments based on the motives of the perpetrator.

REVERSIBILITY According to Piaget, recognition that processes can be undone, that things can be made as they were.

Babbling, like crying and cooing, is inborn. Children from cultures whose languages sound very different all seem to babble the same sounds, including many they could not have heard (Gleason & Ratner, 1993). But children single out the sounds used in the home within a few months. By the age of 9 or 10 months they repeat them regularly and foreign sounds begin to drop out.

Babbling, like crying and cooing, is prelinguistic. Yet infants usually understand much of what others are saying well before they utter their first words. Understanding precedes the production of language, and infants show what they understand by their actions.

Development of Vocabulary Ah, that long-awaited first word! What a thrill! What a milestone! Children tend to utter their first word at about 1 year of age, but many parents miss it, often because it is not pronounced clearly or because pronunciation varies from one usage to the next. *Ball* may be pronounced "ba," "bee," or even "pah." The majority of an infant's early words are names of things (Nelson et al., 1993).

The growth of vocabulary is slow at first. It may take children 3 to 4 months to achieve a 10-word vocabulary after they have spoken their first word (Nelson, 1973). By about 18 months, children are producing nearly two dozen words. Reading to children increases their vocabulary, so parents do well to stock up on storybooks (Arnold et al., 1994; Robbins & Ehri, 1994).

Children try to talk about more objects than they have words for. As a result they often extend use of a word to refer to other things and actions for which they do not yet have words. This phenomenon is termed **overextension**. At some point, for example, many children refer to horses as *doggies*. At age 6, my daughter Allyn counted by tens as follows: sixty, seventy, eighty, ninety, *tenty*.

Development of Grammar Children's first linguistic utterances are single words, but they may express complex meanings. When they do, they are called **holophrases.** For example, *mama* may be used by the child to signify meanings as varied as "There goes Mama," "Come here, Mama," and "You are my Mama." Similarly, *poo-cat* can signify "There is a pussycat," "That stuffed animal looks just like my pussycat," or "I want you to give me my pussycat right now!" Most children readily teach their parents what they intend by augmenting their holophrases with gestures, intonations, and reinforcers. That is, they act delighted when parents do as requested and howl when they do not.

Toward the end of the second year, children begin to speak two-word sentences. These sentences are termed *telegraphic speech* because they resemble telegrams. Telegrams cut out the "unnecessary" words. "Home Tuesday" might stand for "I expect to be home on Tuesday." Similarly, only essential words are used in children's telegraphic speech—in particular, nouns, verbs, and some modifiers. When a child says, "That ball," the words *is* and *a* are implied.

Two-word utterances seem to appear at about the same time in the development of all languages (Slobin, 1983). Although two-word utterances are brief, they show understanding of grammar. The child says, "Sit chair" to tell a parent to sit in a chair, not "Chair sit." The child says, "My shoe," not "Shoe my," to show possession. "Mommy go" means Mommy is leaving. "Go Mommy" expresses the wish for Mommy to go away. (For this reason, "Go Mommy" is not heard often.)

There are different kinds of two-word utterances. Some, for example, contain nouns or pronouns and verbs ("Daddy sit"). Others contains verbs and objects ("Hit ball.") It is of interest that the sequence of

OVEREXTENSION Overgeneralizing the use of words to objects and situations to which they do not apply — a normal characteristic of the speech of young children.

HOLOPHRASE A single word used to express complex meanings.

emergence of the various kinds of two-word utterances is apparently the same in all languages—languages diverse as English, Luo (an African tongue), German, Russian, and Turkish (Slobin, 1983). The invariance of this sequence has implications for theories of language development, as we see later in the chapter.

Between the ages of 2 and 3, children's sentence structure usually expands to include the missing words in telegraphic speech. Children add articles (*a, an, the*), conjunctions (*and, but, or*), possessive and demonstrative adjectives (*your, her, that*), pronouns (*she, him, one*), and prepositions (*in, on, over, around, under,* and *through*) to their utterances. Their grasp of grammar is shown in linguistic oddities such as *your one* instead of simply *yours*, and *his one* instead of *his*.

Overregularization   One intriguing language development is **overregularization.** To understand children's use of overregularization, consider the formation of the past tense and of plurals in English. We add *d* or *ed* to make the past tense of regular verbs and *s* or *z* sounds to make regular nouns plural. Thus, *walk* becomes *walked* and *look* becomes *looked*. *Pussycat* becomes *pussycats* and *doggy* becomes *doggies*. There are also irregular verbs and nouns. For example, *see* becomes *saw, sit* becomes *sat,* and *go* becomes *went. Sheep* remains *sheep* (plural) and *child* becomes *children*.

At first children learn a small number of these irregular verbs by imitating their parents. Two-year-olds tend to form them correctly—at first! Then they become aware of the grammatical rules for forming the past tense and plurals. As a result, they tend to make charming errors (Pinker, 1994). Some 3- to 5-year-olds, for example, are more likely to say "I seed it" than "I saw it" and to say "Mommy sitted down" than "Mommy sat down." They are likely to talk about the "gooses" and "sheeps" they "seed" on the farm and about all the "childs" they ran into at the playground. This tendency to regularize the irregular is what is meant by overregularization.

Some parents recognize that at one point their children were forming the past tense of irregular verbs correctly and that they later began to make errors. The thing to remember is that overregularization reflects knowledge of grammar, not faulty language development. In another year or two, *mouses* will be boringly transformed into *mice*, and Mommy will no longer have *sitted* down. Parents might as well enjoy overregularization while they can.

Toward More Complex Language   As language develops beyond the third year, children show increasing facility in their use of pronouns (such as *it* and *she*) and prepositions (such as *in, before,* or *on*), which represent physical or temporal relationships among objects and events. Children's first questions are telegraphic and characterized by a rising pitch (which signifies a question mark) at the end. "More milky?" for example, can be translated into "May I have more milk?" or "Would you like more milk?" or "Is there more milk?"—depending on the context.

Wh questions usually appear after age 2. Consistent with the child's general cognitive development, certain *wh* questions (*what, who,* and *where*) appear earlier than others (*why, when, which,* and *how*) (Bloom et al., 1982). *Why* is usually too philosophical for the 2-year-old, and *how* is too involved. Two-year-olds are also likely to be now oriented, so *when* is of less than immediate concern. By the fourth year, however, most children are asking *why, when,* and *how* questions—and frequently their parents despair as to how to answer them.

OVERREGULARIZATION The application of regular grammatical rules for forming inflections (e.g., past tense and plurals) to irregular verbs and nouns.

EBONICS

The term *Ebonics* is derived from the words *ebony* and *phonics.* It was coined by the African American psychologist Robert Williams (Burnette, 1997). Ebonics was previously called Black English or Black Dialect (Pinker, 1994). Williams explains that a group of African American scholars convened "to name our language, which had always been named by White scholars in the past" (Burnette, 1997, p. 12).

According to linguists, Ebonics is rooted in the remnants of the West African dialects used by slaves. It reflects attempts by the slaves, who were denied formal education, to imitate the speech of the dominant White culture. Some observers believe that Ebonics uses verbs haphazardly, downgrading standard English. As a result, some school systems react to the concept of Ebonics with contempt—which is hurtful to the child who speaks Ebonics. Other observers say that Ebonics has different grammatical rules than standard English, but that the rules are consistent and allow for complex thought (Pinker, 1994). In 1996, the Oakland, California, school board recognized Ebonics as the primary language of African American students, just as Spanish had been recognized as the primary language of Hispanic American

students. "I was honored," said Williams. "And truthfully, I was shocked. It was like the truth that had been covered up in the ground for so long just exploded one day" (Burnette, 1997, p. 12).

"TO BE OR NOT TO BE": USE OF VERBS IN EBONICS

There are differences between Ebonics and standard English in the use of verbs. For example, the Ebonics usage "She-ah touch us" corresponds to the standard English "She will touch us." The Ebonics "He be gone" is the equivalent of the standard English "He has been gone for a long while." "He gone" is the same as "He is not here right now" in standard English.

Consider the rules in Ebonics that govern the use of the verb *to be.* In standard English, *be* is part of the infinitive form of the verb and is used to form the future tense, as in "I'll be angry tomorrow." Thus, "I *be* angry" is incorrect. But in Ebonics *be* refers to a continuing state of being. The Ebonics sentence "I be angry" is the same as the standard English "I have been angry for a while" and is grammatically correct.

Ebonics leaves out *to be* in cases in which standard English would use a contraction. For example, the standard

"She's the one I'm talking about" could be "*She* the one *I* talking about" in Ebonics. Ebonics also often drops *ed* from the past tense and lacks the possessive *'s.*

"NOT TO BE OR NOT TO BE NOTHING": NEGATION IN EBONICS

Consider the sentence "I don't want no trouble," which is, of course, commendable. Middle-class White children would be corrected for using double negation (do*n't* along with *no*) and would be encouraged to say "I don't want *any* trouble." Yet double negation is acceptable in Ebonics (Pinker, 1994). Nevertheless, many teachers who use standard English have demeaned African American children who speak this way.

Some African American children are bicultural and bilingual. They function competently within the dominant culture in the United States and among groups of people from their own ethnic background. They use standard English in a conference with their teacher or in a job interview, but switch to Ebonics among their friends. Other children cannot switch back and forth. The decision by the Oakland school board was intended in part to help children maintain their self-esteem and stay in school. ■

By the fourth year, children are also taking turns talking and engaging in lengthy conversations. By the age of 6, their vocabularies have expanded to 10,000 words, give or take a few thousand. By age 7 to 9, most children realize that words can have more than one meaning, and they are entertained by riddles and jokes that require some sophistication with language ("What's black and white, but read all over?").

Between the elementary school and high school years, language becomes still more complex and vocabulary continues to grow rapidly. Vocabulary, in fact, can grow for a lifetime, especially in one's fields of specialization and interest.

LAWRENCE KOHLBERG'S THEORY OF MORAL DEVELOPMENT

Another aspect of cognitive development has to do with the ways in which people arrive at judgments of right or wrong. Cognitive-developmental theorist Lawrence Kohlberg (1981) used the following tale in his research into children's moral reasoning. Before going on, why not read the tale yourself and answer the questions that follow.

> In Europe a woman was near death from a special kind of cancer. There was one drug that the doctors thought might save her. It was a form of radium that a druggist in the same town had recently discovered. The drug was expensive to make, but the druggist was charging ten times what the drug cost him to make. He paid $200 for the radium and charged $2,000 for a small dose of the drug. The sick woman's husband, Heinz, went to everyone he knew to borrow the money, but he could only get together about $1,000, which was half of what it cost. He told the druggist that his wife was dying and asked him to sell it cheaper or let him pay later. But the druggist said: "No, I discovered the drug and I'm going to make money from it." So Heinz got desperate and broke into the man's store to steal the drug for his wife. (Kohlberg, 1969)

What do you think? Should Heinz have tried to steal the drug? Was he right or wrong? The answer is more complicated than a simple yes or no. Heinz is caught up in a moral dilemma in which a legal or social rule (in this case, the law forbidding stealing) is pitted against a strong human need (his desire to save his wife). According to Kohlberg's theory, children and adults arrive at yes or no answers for different reasons. These reasons can be classified according to the level of moral development they reflect.

As a stage theorist, Kohlberg argues that the stages of moral reasoning follow a specific sequence (see Table LS.3). Children progress at different rates, and not all children (or adults) reach the highest stage. But the sequence is always the same: Children must go through stage 1 before they enter stage 2, and so on. According to Kohlberg, there are three levels of moral development and two stages within each level.

When it comes to the dilemma of Heinz, Kohlberg believed that people could justify Heinz's stealing of the drug or his decision not to steal it by the reasoning of any level or stage of moral development. In other words, Kohlberg was not as interested in the eventual "yes" or "no" as he was in *how a person reasoned* to arrive at a yes or no answer.

The Preconventional Level The **preconventional level** applies to most children through about the age of 9. Children at this level base their moral judgments on the consequences of behavior. For instance, stage 1 is oriented toward obedience and punishment. Good behavior is obedient and allows one to avoid punishment. However, a child in stage 1 can decide that Heinz should or should not steal the drug, as shown in Table LS.3.

In stage 2, good behavior allows people to satisfy their needs and those of others. (Heinz's wife needs the drug; therefore, stealing the drug—the only way of obtaining it—is not wrong.)

The Conventional Level In the **conventional level** of moral reasoning, right and wrong are judged by conformity to conventional (familial, religious, societal) standards of right and wrong. According to the stage 3,

PRECONVENTIONAL LEVEL According to Kohlberg, a period during which moral judgments are based largely on expectation of rewards or punishments.

CONVENTIONAL LEVEL According to Kohlberg, a period during which moral judgments largely reflect social conventions. A "law and order" approach to morality.

TABLE LS.3

KOHLBERG'S LEVELS AND STAGES OF MORAL DEVELOPMENT

STAGE OF DEVELOPMENT	EXAMPLES OF MORAL REASONING THAT SUPPORT HEINZ'S STEALING THE DRUG	EXAMPLES OF MORAL REASONING THAT OPPOSE HEINZ'S STEALING THE DRUG
LEVEL I: PRECONVENTIONAL		
Stage 1: Judgments guided by obedience and the prospect of punishment (the consequences of the behavior)	It isn't wrong to take the drug. Heinz did try to pay the druggist for it, and it's only worth $200, not $2,000.	Taking things without paying is wrong because it's against the law. Heinz will get caught and go to jail.
Stage 2: Naively egoistic, instrumental orientation (Things are right when they satisfy people's needs.)	Heinz ought to take the drug because his wife really needs it. He can always pay the druggist back.	Heinz shouldn't take the drug. If he gets caught and winds up in jail, it won't do his wife any good.
LEVEL II: CONVENTIONAL		
Stage 3: Good boy orientation (Moral behavior helps others and is socially approved.)	Stealing is a crime, so it's bad, but Heinz should take the drug to save his wife or else people would blame him for letting her die.	Stealing is a crime. Heinz shouldn't just take the drug because his family will be dishonored and they will blame him.
Stage 4: Law-and-order orientation (Moral behavior is doing one's duty and showing respect for authority.)	Heinz must take the drug to do his duty to save his wife. Eventually, he has to pay the druggist for it, however.	If everyone took the law into their own hands, civilization would fall apart, so Heinz shouldn't steal the drug.
LEVEL III: POSTCONVENTIONAL		
Stage 5: Contractual, legalistic orientation (One must weigh pressing human needs against society's need to maintain social order.)	This thing is complicated because society has a right to maintain law and order, but Heinz has to take the drug to save his wife.	I can see why Heinz feels he has to take the drug, but laws exist for the benefit of society as a whole and can't simply be cast aside.
Stage 6: Universal ethical principles orientation (People must follow universal ethical principles and their own conscience, even if it means breaking the law.)	In this case, the law comes into conflict with the principle of the sanctity of human life. Heinz must take the drug because his wife's life is more important than the law.	If Heinz truly believes that stealing the drug is worse than letting his wife die, he should not take it. People have to make sacrifices to do what they think is right.

"good-boy orientation," moral behavior is that which meets the needs and expectations of others. Moral behavior is what is "normal"—what the majority does. (Heinz should steal the drug because that is what a "good husband" would do. It is "natural" or "normal" to try to help one's wife. *Or,* Heinz should *not* steal the drug because "good people do not steal.")

In stage 4, moral judgments are based on rules that maintain the social order. Showing respect for authority and doing one's duty are valued highly. (Heinz *must* steal the drug; it would be his fault if he let his wife die. He would pay the druggist later, when he had the money.) Many people do not mature beyond the conventional level.

The Postconventional Level Postconventional moral reasoning is more complex and focuses on dilemmas in which individual needs are pitted against the need to maintain the social order and on personal conscience. We discuss the postconventional level of moral reasoning in the section on adolescence.

Social and Personality Development

Social relationships are crucial to us as children. When we are infants, our very survival depends on them. Later in life, they contribute to our feelings of happiness and satisfaction. In this section we discuss many aspects of social development, including Erikson's theory of psychosocial development, attachment, styles of parenting, and the effects of day care and child abuse.

ERIK ERIKSON'S STAGES OF PSYCHOSOCIAL DEVELOPMENT

According to Erik Erikson, we undergo several stages of psychosocial development (see Table LS.4). During his first stage, **trust versus mistrust,** we depend on our primary caregivers (usually our parents) and come to expect that our environments will—or will not—meet our needs. During early childhood and the preschool years, we begin to explore the environment more actively and try new things. At this time, our relationships with our parents and friends can encourage us to develop **autonomy** (self-direction) and initiative, or feelings of shame and guilt. During the elementary school years, friends and teachers take on more importance, encouraging us to become industrious or to develop feelings of inferiority.

ATTACHMENT: TIES THAT BIND At the age of 2, my daughter Allyn almost succeeded in preventing me from finishing writing a book. When I locked myself into my study, she positioned herself outside the door and called, "Daddy, oh Daddy." At other times, she would bang on the door or cry outside. When I would give in (several times a day) and open the door, she would run in and say, "I want you to pick up me" and hold out her arms or climb into my lap. Although we were separate human beings, it was as though she were very much *attached* to me.

Psychologist Mary D. Salter Ainsworth defines **attachment** as an emotional tie formed between one animal or person and another specific individual. Attachment keeps organisms together—it is vital to the survival of the infant—and it tends to endure.

The behaviors that define attachment include (1) attempts to maintain contact or nearness and (2) shows of anxiety when separated. Babies and children try to maintain contact with caregivers to whom they are attached. They engage in eye contact, pull and tug at them, ask to be picked

ALLYN.
At the age of 2 the author's daughter Allyn nearly succeeded in preventing the publication of a book by continually pulling him away from the computer when he was at work. Because of their mutual attachment, separation was painful.

TRUST VERSUS MISTRUST Erikson's first stage of psychosexual development, during which children do—or do not—come to trust that primary caregivers and the environment will meet their needs.

AUTONOMY Self-direction.

ATTACHMENT The enduring affectional tie that binds one person to another.

TABLE LS.4

ERIKSON'S STAGES OF PSYCHOSOCIAL DEVELOPMENT

TIME PERIOD	LIFE CRISIS	THE DEVELOPMENTAL TASK
Infancy (0–1)	Trust versus mistrust	Coming to trust the mother and the environment—to associate surroundings with feelings of inner goodness
Early childhood (1–3)	Autonomy versus shame and doubt	Developing the wish to make choices and the self-control to exercise choice
Preschool years (4–5)	Initiative versus guilt	Adding planning and "attacking" to choice, becoming active and on the move
Elementary school years (6–12)	Industry versus inferiority	Becoming eagerly absorbed in skills, tasks, and productivity; mastering the fundamentals of technology
Adolescence	Identity versus role diffusion	Connecting skills and social roles to formation of career objectives; developing a sense of who one is and what one stands for
Young adulthood	Intimacy versus isolation	Committing the self to another; engaging in sexual love
Middle adulthood	Generativity versus stagnation	Needing to be needed; guiding and encouraging the younger generation; being creative
Late adulthood	Integrity versus despair	Accepting the time and place of one's life cycle; achieving wisdom and dignity

Source: Erikson (1963), pp. 247–269.

ATTACHMENT.
Feelings of attachment bind most parents closely to their children. According to Mary Ainsworth, attachment is an emotional bond between an individual and another specific individual. Secure attachment paves the way for healthy social development.

up, and may even jump in front of them in such a way that they will be "run over" if they are not picked up!

The Strange Situation and Patterns of Attachment The ways in which infants behave in strange situations are connected with their bonds of attachment with their caregivers. Given this fact, Ainsworth and her colleagues (1978) innovated the *strange situation method* to measure attachment in infants. The method involves a series of separations and reunions with a caregiver (usually the mother) and a stranger. Infants are led through episodes involving the mother and a stranger in a laboratory room. For example, the mother carries the infant into the room and puts him or her down. A stranger enters and talks with the mother. The stranger then approaches the infant with a toy and the mother leaves the room. The mother and stranger take turns interacting with the infant in the room, and the infant behavior is observed in each case.

Using the strange situation, Ainsworth and her colleagues (1978) identified three major types of attachment: secure attachment and two types of insecure attachment:

1. *Secure attachment.* Securely attached infants mildly protest their mother's departure, seek interaction upon reunion, and are readily comforted by her.
2. *Avoidant attachment.* Infants who show avoidant attachment are least distressed by their mother's departure. They play by themselves without fuss and ignore their mothers when they return.
3. *Ambivalent/resistant attachment.* Infants with ambivalent/resistant attachment are the most emotional. They show severe signs of distress when their mother leaves and show ambivalence upon reunion by alternately clinging to and pushing their mother away when she returns.

Attachment is connected with the quality of care that infants receive. The parents of securely attached children are more likely to be affectionate and reliable caregivers (Cox et al., 1992; Isabella, 1993). A wealth of research literature speaks of the benefits of secure attachment. For example, securely attached children are happier, more sociable, and more cooperative than insecurely attached children (Belsky et al., 1991; Thompson, 1991a). Securely attached preschoolers have longer attention spans, are less impulsive, and are better at solving problems (Frankel & Bates, 1990; Lederberg & Mobley, 1990). At ages 5 and 6, securely attached children are liked better by their peers and teachers, are more competent, and have fewer behavior problems than insecurely attached children (Lyons-Ruth et al., 1993; Youngblade & Belsky, 1992).

Yet some research questions whether infant attachment as measured by means of the strange situation predicts adjustment later on. For example, Michael Lewis (1997) located 84 high school seniors who had been evaluated by the strange situation method at the age of 1. Extensive interviews showed that of the 49 who had been considered securely attached at the age of 1, 43% were currently maladjusted. Of the 35 who had been considered insecurely attached in infancy, only 26% were rated as currently maladjusted. Lewis (1998) suggests that childhood events such as accidents, parental divorce, and illness can be more powerful influences on adolescents' security than the quality of parenting during the first year. But most developmental psychologists continue to endorse the strange situation as a predictor of adjustment later in life (Blakeslee, 1998). For example, Alan Sroufe (1998) found that insecure attachment at the age of 1 year predicted psychological disorders at the age of 17.

Stages of Attachment Ainsworth also studied phases in the development of attachment. She and her colleagues observed infants in many societies, including infants in the African country of Uganda. She noted the efforts of infants to maintain contact with the mother, their protests when separated from her, and their use of her as a base for exploring their environment. At first, infants show **indiscriminate attachment.** That is, they prefer being held or being with someone to being alone, but they show no preferences for particular people. Specific attachment to the mother begins to develop at about 4 months of age and becomes intense by about 7 months of age. Fear of strangers, which develops in some but not all children, follows 1 or 2 months later.

From studies such as these, Ainsworth identified three stages of attachment:

1. The **initial-preattachment phase,** which lasts from birth to about 3 months and is characterized by indiscriminate attachment.

2. The **attachment-in-the-making phase,** which occurs at about 3 or 4 months and is characterized by preference for familiar figures.

3. The **clear-cut-attachment phase,** which occurs at about 6 or 7 months and is characterized by intensified dependence on the primary caregiver.

John Bowlby (1988), a colleague of Mary Ainsworth, believes that attachment is also characterized by fear of strangers ("stranger anxiety"). That is, at about 8 to 10 months of age, children may cry and cling to their parents when strangers try to befriend them. But not all children develop fear of strangers. It therefore does not seem necessary to include fear of strangers as an essential part of the process of attachment.

Theoretical Views of Attachment Early in the century, behaviorists argued that attachment behaviors are learned through experience. Caregivers feed their infants and tend to their other physiological needs. Thus, infants associate their caregivers with gratification of needs and learn to approach them to meet their needs. The feelings of gratification associated with the meeting of basic needs generalize into feelings of security when the caregiver is present.

Classic research by psychologist Harry F. Harlow suggests that skin contact may be more important than learning experiences. Harlow had noted that infant rhesus monkeys reared without mothers or companions became attached to pieces of cloth in their cages. They maintained contact with them and showed distress when separated from them. Harlow conducted a series of experiments to find out why (Harlow, 1959).

In one study, Harlow placed infant rhesus monkeys in cages with two surrogate mothers, as shown in Figure LS.6. One "mother" was made of wire mesh from which a baby bottle was extended. The other surrogate mother was made of soft, cuddly terry cloth. The infant monkeys spent most of their time clinging to the cloth mother, even though "she" did not gratify their need for food. Harlow concluded that monkeys—and perhaps humans—have an inborn need for **contact comfort** that is as basic as the need for food. Gratification of the need for contact comfort, rather than food, might be why infant monkeys (and humans) cling to their mothers.

Harlow and Zimmerman (1959) found that a surrogate mother made of terry cloth could also serve as a comforting base from which an infant monkey could explore its environment. Toys such as stuffed bears (see Figure LS.7) and oversized wooden insects were placed in cages with infant rhesus monkeys and their surrogate mothers. When the infants were alone or had wire surrogate mothers for companions, they cowered in fear as

TRUTH OR FICTION REVISITED
It is not true that the way to a baby's heart is through its stomach. Babies do not necessarily become attached to the people who feed them. Contact comfort may be a stronger wellspring of attachment. The path to a baby's heart may lie through its skin, not its stomach.

INDISCRIMINATE ATTACHMENT Showing attachment behaviors toward any person.

INITIAL-PREATTACHMENT PHASE The first phase in forming bonds of attachment, characterized by indiscriminate attachment.

ATTACHMENT-IN-THE-MAKING PHASE The second phase in forming bonds of attachment, characterized by preference for familiar figures.

CLEAR-CUT-ATTACHMENT PHASE The third phase in forming bonds of attachment, characterized by intensified dependence on the primary caregiver.

CONTACT COMFORT A hypothesized primary drive to seek physical comfort through contact with another.

FIGURE LS.6
ATTACHMENT IN INFANT MONKEYS.

Although this rhesus monkey infant is fed by the wire "mother," it spends most of its time clinging to the soft, cuddly terry-cloth "mother." It knows where to get a meal, but contact comfort is apparently more important than food in the development of attachment in infant monkeys (and infant humans?).

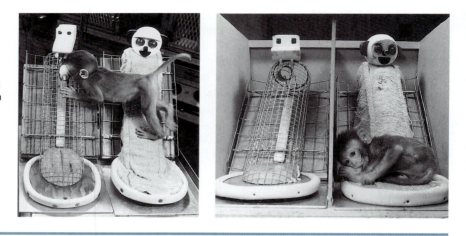

FIGURE LS.7
SECURITY.

With its terry-cloth surrogate mother nearby, this infant rhesus monkey apparently feels secure enough to explore the "bear monster" placed in its cage. But infants with wire surrogate mothers or no mothers at all cower in a corner when such "monsters" are introduced.

CRITICAL PERIOD A period of time when an instinctive response can be elicited by a particular stimulus.

IMPRINTING A process occurring during a critical period in the development of an organism, in which that organism responds to a stimulus in a manner that will afterward be difficult to modify.

long as the "bear monster" or "insect monster" was present. But when the terry-cloth mothers were present, the infants clung to them for a while and then explored the intruding "monster." With human infants, too, the bonds of mother-infant attachment appear to provide a secure base from which infants feel encouraged to express their curiosity.

Other researchers, such as ethologist Konrad Lorenz, note that for many animals, attachment is an instinct—inborn. Attachment, like other instincts, is theorized to occur in the presence of a specific stimulus and during a **critical period** of life—that is, a period during which the animal is sensitive to the stimulus.

Some animals become attached to the first moving object they encounter. The unwritten rule seems to be, "If it moves, it must be Mother." It is as if the image of the moving object becomes "imprinted" on the young animal. The formation of an attachment in this manner is therefore called **imprinting**.

Lorenz (1981) became well known when pictures of his "family" of goslings were made public (see Figure LS.8). How did Lorenz acquire his following? He was present when the goslings hatched and during their critical period, and he allowed them to follow him. The critical period for geese and some other animals is bounded, at the younger end, by the age at which they first walk and, at the older end, by the age at which they develop fear of strangers. The goslings followed Lorenz persistently, ran to him when they were frightened, honked with distress at his departure, and tried to overcome barriers between them. If you substitute crying for honking, it all sounds rather human.

Ainsworth and Bowlby (1991) consider attachment to be instinctive in humans. However, the process would not be quite the same as with ducks and geese. The upper limit for waterbirds is the age at which they develop fear of strangers, but not all children develop this fear. When children do develop fear of strangers, they do so at about 6 to 8 months of age—*prior to* independent locomotion, or crawling, which usually occurs 1 or 2 months later. Moreover, the critical period with humans would be quite extended.

Another issue in social and personality development is parenting styles. Parental behavior not only contributes to the development of attachment, but also to the development of self-esteem, self-reliance, achievement motivation, and competence.

PARENTING STYLES Many psychologists have been concerned about the relationships between parenting styles and the personality development of the child. They have asked what types of parental behavior are connected with variables such as self-esteem, achievement motivation, and independence in children. Diana Baumrind and her colleagues (1973; Lamb & Baumrind, 1978) have been particularly interested in the connections between they ways parents behavior and the development of **instrumental competence** in their children. (*Instrumental competence* refers to the ability to manipulate the environment to achieve ones goals.) Baumrind has largely focused on four aspects of parental behavior: (1) strictness; (2) demands for the child to achieve intellectual, emotional, and social maturity; (3) communication ability; and (4) warmth and involvement. The three most important parenting styles she labeled as *authoritative, authoritarian,* and *permissive* styles.

1. *Authoritative parents.* The parents of the most competent children rate high in all four areas of behavior (see Table LS.5). They are strict (restrictive) and demand mature behavior. However, they temper their strictness and demands with willingness to reason with their children, and with love and support. They expect a lot, but they explain why and offer help. Baumrind labeled these parents **authoritative parents** to suggest they know what they want but are also loving and respectful of their children.

2. *Authoritarian parents.* **Authoritarian parents** view obedience as a virtue to be pursued for its own sake. They have strict guidelines about what is right and wrong, and they demand that their children adhere to those guidelines. Both authoritative and authoritarian parents adhere to strict standards of conduct. However, authoritative parents explain their demands and are supportive, whereas authoritarian parents rely on force and communicate poorly with their children. Authoritarian parents do not respect their children's points of view, and they may be cold and rejecting. When their children ask them why they should behave in a certain way, authoritarian parents often answer, "Because I say so!"

3. *Permissive parents.* **Permissive parents** are generally easygoing with their children. As a result, the children do pretty much whatever they wish. Permissive parents are warm and supportive, but poor at communicating.

Research evidence shows that warmth is superior to coldness in rearing children. Children of warm parents are more likely to be socially and emotionally well adjusted and to internalize moral standards—that is, to develop a conscience (MacDonald, 1992; Miller et al., 1993).

FIGURE LS.8
IMPRINTING.
Quite a following? Konrad Lorenz may not look like Mommy to you, but the goslings in the photo to the left became attached to him because he was the first moving object they perceived and followed. This type of attachment process is referred to as *imprinting*.

NSTRUMENTAL COMPETENCE Ability to manipulate one's environment to achieve one's goals.

AUTHORITATIVE PARENTS Parents who are strict and warm. Authoritative parents demand mature behavior but use reason rather than force in discipline.

AUTHORITARIAN PARENTS Parents who are rigid in their rules and who demand obedience for the sake of obedience.

PERMISSIVE PARENTS Parents who impose few, if any, rules and who do not supervise their children closely.

TABLE LS.5

STYLE OF PARENTING	RESTRICTIVENESS	DEMANDS FOR MATURE BEHAVIOR	COMMUNICATION ABILITY	WARMTH AND SUPPORT
PARENTING STYLES				
		PARENTAL BEHAVIOR		
Authoritarian	High (Use of force)	Moderate	Low	Low
Authoritative	High (Use of reasoning)	High	High	High
Permissive	Low (Easygoing)	Low	Low	High

Note. According to Baumrind, the children of authoritative parents are most competent. The children of permissive parents are the least mature.

Strictness also appears to pay off, provided it is tempered with reason and warmth. Children of authoritative parents have greater self-reliance, self-esteem, social competence, and achievement motivation than other children do (Baumrind, 1991; Putallaz & Heflin, 1990). Children of authori*tarian* parents are often withdrawn or aggressive, and they usually do not do as well in school as children of authoritative parents (Olson et al., 1990; Westerman, 1990). Children of permissive parents seem to be the least mature. They are frequently impulsive, moody, and aggressive. In adolescence, lack of parental monitoring is often linked to delinquency and poor academic performance.

Let us now consider two other important areas that involve the connections between parental behavior and the social and personality development of children. The first of these, day care, considers what happens to young children's social and personality development when they spend their days in the care of people other than family members. The second of these, child abuse, considers the causes of child abuse and its effects on the development of the child.

DAY CARE As we cross over into the new millennium, only a small percentage of U.S. families fit the traditional model in which the husband is the breadwinner and the wife is a full-time homemaker. Most mothers, including more than half of mothers of children younger than 1 year of age, work outside the home (U.S. Bureau of the Census, 1998). As a consequence, millions of American preschoolers are placed in day care. Parents and psychologists are concerned about what happens to children in day care. What, for example, are the effects of day care on cognitive development and social development?

In part, the answer depends on the quality of the day-care center. A large-scale study funded by the National Institute on Child Health and Human Development found that children in high-quality day care—for example, children who have learning resources, a low children-to-caregiver ratio, and individual attention—did as well on cognitive and language tests as children who remained in the home with their mother (Azar, 1997). Children whose day-care providers spent time talking to them and asking them questions also achieved the highest scores on tests of cognitive and language ability. A Swedish study found that children in high-quality day care outperformed children who remained in the home on tests of math and language skills (Broberg et al., 1997).

Studies of the effects of day care on parent-child attachment are somewhat mixed. Children in full-time day care show less distress when their mothers leave them and are less likely to seek out their mother when they return. Some psychologists suggest that this distancing from the mother could signify insecure (avoidant) attachment (Belsky, 1990). Others suggest, however, that the children are adapting to repeated separations from, and reunions with, their mother (Field, 1991; Lamb et al., 1992; Thompson, 1991b).

Day care seems to have both positive and negative influences on children's social development. First, the positive: Children in day care are more likely to share their toys and be independent, self-confident, and outgoing (Clarke-Stewart, 1991; Field, 1991). However, some studies have found that children in day care are less compliant and more aggressive than other children (Vandell & Corasaniti, 1990). Perhaps some children in day care do not receive the individual attention or resources they need. When placed in a competitive situation, they become more aggressive in an attempt to meet their needs. Clarke-Stewart (1990), however, interprets

DAY CARE.
Because most parents in the United States are in the work force, day care is a major influence on the lives of millions of children.

the greater noncompliance and aggressiveness of children placed in day care as signs of greater independence rather than social maladjustment.

CHILD ABUSE Nearly 3 million children in the United States are neglected or abused by their parents or other caregivers each year (Fein, 1998). More than half a million of these suffer serious injuries. Nearly 1,000 die (Fein, 1998). In a national poll of 1,000 parents, 5% admitted to having physically abused their children (Lewin, 1995). One in 5 (21%) admitted to hitting their children "on the bottom" with a hard object such as a belt, stick, or hairbrush. Most parents (85%) reported that they often shouted, yelled, or screamed at their children. Nearly half (47%) reported spanking or hitting their children "on the bottom" with their hands. And 17% admitted to calling their children "dumb," "lazy," or a similar name.

These percentages may seem high, but child abuse is actually *under*reported. Why? Some family members are afraid that reporting abuse will destroy the family unit. Others are reluctant to disclose abuse because they are financially dependent on the abuser or do not trust the authorities (Seppa, 1996).

Why Do Parents Abuse Their Children? Many factors contribute to child abuse: stress, a history of child abuse in at least one of the parents' families of origin, acceptance of violence as a way of coping with stress, failure to become attached to the children, substance abuse, and rigid attitudes toward child rearing (Belsky, 1993; Kaplan, 1991). Unemployment and low socioeconomic status are common stressors that lead to abuse (Lewin, 1995; Trickett et al., 1991).

Children who are abused are quite likely to develop personal and social problems and psychological disorders. They are less likely than other children to venture out to explore the world (Aber & Allen, 1987). They are more likely to have psychological problems such as anxiety, depression, and low self-esteem (Wagner, 1997). They are less likely to be intimate with their peers and more likely to be aggressive (DeAngelis, 1997; Parker & Herrera, 1996; Rothbart & Ahadi, 1994). As adults, they are more likely to be violent toward their dates and spouses (Malinosky-Rummell, & Hansen, 1993).

Child abuse runs in families to some degree (Simons et al., 1991). That is, child abusers are more likely to have been abused than is true for the general population. Even so, *the majority of children who are abused do* not *abuse their own children as adults* (Kaufman & Zigler, 1989).

Why does abuse run in families? There are several hypotheses (Belsky, 1993). One is that parents serve as role models. According to Murray Strauss (1995), "Spanking teaches kids that when someone is doing something you don't like and they won't stop doing it, you hit them." Another is that children adopt parents' strict philosophies about discipline. Exposure to violence in their own home leads some children to view abuse as normal. A third is that being abused can create feelings of hostility that are then expressed against others, including one's own children.

The years of childhood may seem to pass rapidly, but a great deal occurs during them in terms of physical, cognitive, and social and personality development. Following childhood is the period of adolescence, which is for many a period of passage to adulthood. For many adolescents, and for their parents, the goals of adolescence and the behaviors deemed acceptable loom as huge question marks. Because of these questions, psychologists have focused a great deal of attention on adolescence, as we see next.

TRUTH OR FICTION REVISITED
It is true that child abusers have frequently been abused as children. However, the majority of victims of abuse do not abuse their own children.

ADOLESCENTS.
In our culture adolescents are "neither fish nor fowl." Although they may be old enough to reproduce and may be as large as their parents, they are often treated like children.

ADOLESCENT DEVELOPMENT

Adolescence is a time of transition from childhood to adulthood. In our society, adolescents often feel that they are "neither fish nor fowl," as the saying goes—neither children nor adults. Although adolescents may be old enough to have children and are as large as their parents, they are often treated quite differently than adults. They may not be eligible for a driver's license until they are 16 or 17. They cannot attend R-rated films unless they are accompanied by an adult. They are prevented from working long hours. They are usually required to remain in school through age 16 and may not marry until they reach the "age of consent." Let us consider the physical, cognitive, and social and personal changes of adolescence.

Physical Development

Following infancy, children gain about 2 to 3 inches a year until they reach the adolescent growth spurt. Weight gains also remain fairly even at about 4 to 6 pounds per year. The adolescent growth spurt lasts for 2 to 3 years and ends the stable patterns of growth in height and weight that characterize most of childhood. Within this short span of years, adolescents grow some 8 to 12 inches. Most boys wind up taller and heavier than most girls.

In boys, the weight of the muscle mass increases notably. The width of the shoulders and circumference of the chest also increase. Adolescents may eat enormous quantities of food to fuel their growth spurt. Adults fighting the "battle of the bulge" stare at them in wonder as they wolf down french fries and shakes at the fast-food counter and later go out for pizza.

PUBERTY **Puberty** is the period during which the body becomes sexually mature. It heralds the onset of adolescence. Puberty begins with the appearance of **secondary sex characteristics** such as body hair, deepening of the voice in males, and rounding of the breasts and hips in females. In boys, pituitary hormones stimulate the testes to increase the output of testosterone, which in turn causes enlargement of the penis and testes and the appearance of bodily hair. By the early teens, erections become common, and boys may ejaculate. Ejaculatory ability usually precedes the presence of mature sperm by at least a year. Ejaculation thus is not evidence of reproductive capacity.

In girls, a critical body weight in the neighborhood of 100 pounds is thought to trigger a cascade of hormonal secretions in the brain that cause the ovaries to secrete higher levels of the female sex hormone, estrogen (Frisch, 1997). Estrogen stimulates the growth of breast tissue and fatty and supportive tissue in the hips and buttocks. Thus the pelvis widens, rounding the hips. Small amounts of androgens produced by the adrenal glands, along with estrogen, spur the growth of pubic and underarm hair. Estrogen and androgens together stimulate the growth of female sex organs. Estrogen production becomes cyclical during puberty and regulates the menstrual cycle. The beginning of menstruation, or **menarche,** usually occurs between the ages of 11 and 14. Girls cannot become pregnant until they begin to ovulate, however, and this may occur as much as two years after menarche.

Cognitive Development

I am a college student of extremely modest means. Some crazy psychologist interested in something called "formal operational thought" has just promised to pay me $20 if I can make a

TRUTH OR FICTION REVISITED
It is not usually true that girls are capable of becoming pregnant when they have their first menstrual period. Menarche can precede ovulation by a year or more.

ADOLESCENCE The period of life bounded by puberty and the assumption of adult responsibilities.

PUBERTY The period of physical development during which sexual reproduction first becomes possible.

SECONDARY SEX CHARACTERISTICS Characteristics that distinguish the sexes, such as distribution of body hair and depth of voice, but that are not directly involved in reproduction.

MENARCHE The beginning of menstruation.

coherent logical argument for the proposition that the federal government should under no circumstances ever give or lend more to needy college students. Now what could people who believe that possibly say by way of supporting argument? Well, I suppose they could offer this line of reasoning. . . . (Adapted from Flavell et al., 1993, p. 140.)

The adolescent thinker approaches problems very differently from the elementary school child. The child sticks to the facts, to concrete reality. Speculating about abstract possibilities and what might be is very difficult. The adolescent, on the other hand, is able to deal with the abstract and the hypothetical. As shown in the above example, adolescents realize that one does not have to believe in the truth or justice of something in order to argue for it (Flavell et al., 1993). In this section we explore some of the cognitive developments of adolescence by referring to the theories of Jean Piaget and Lawrence Kohlberg.

THE FORMAL OPERATIONAL STAGE According to Piaget, children typically undergo three stages of cognitive development prior to adolescence: sensorimotor, preoperational, and concrete operational. They develop from infants who respond automatically to their environment to older children who can focus on various aspects of a situation at once and solve complex problems. The stage of **formal operations** is the final stage in Jean Piaget's theory of cognitive development, and it represents cognitive maturity. For many children in Western societies, formal operational thought begins at about the beginning of adolescence—the age of 11 or 12. However, not all individuals enter this stage at this time, and some individuals never reach it.

The major achievements of the stage of formal operations involve classification, logical thought, and the ability to hypothesize. Central features are the ability to think about ideas as well as objects and to group and classify ideas—symbols, statements, entire theories. The flexibility and reversibility of operations, when applied to statements and theories, allow adolescents to follow arguments from premises to conclusions and back again.

Several features of formal operational thought give the adolescent a generally greater capacity to manipulate and appreciate the outer environment and the world of the imagination: hypothetical thinking, the ability to use symbols to stand for symbols, and deductive reasoning.

Formal-operational adolescents (and adults) think abstractly. They become capable of solving geometric problems about circles and squares without reference to what the circles and squares may represent in the real world. Adolescents in this stage derive rules for behavior from general principles and can focus, or center, on many aspects of a situation at once in arriving at judgments and solving problems.

In a sense, it is during the stage of formal operations that adolescents tend to emerge as theoretical scientists—even though they may see themselves as having little or no interest in science. They become capable of dealing with hypothetical situations. They realize that situations can have different outcomes, and they think ahead, experimenting with different possibilities. Adolescents also conduct experiments to determine whether their hypotheses are correct. These experiments are not conducted in the laboratory. Rather, adolescents may try out different tones of voice, ways of carrying themselves, and ways of treating others to see what works best for them.

Adolescent Egocentrism: "You Just Don't Understand!" Adolescents in the formal operational stage can reason deductively, or draw conclusions about specific objects or people once they have been classified accurately.

FORMAL-OPERATIONAL STAGE Piaget's fourth stage, characterized by abstract logical thought; deduction from principles.

Adolescents can be somewhat proud of their new logical abilities, and so a new sort of egocentrism can develop in which adolescents emotionally press for acceptance of their logic without recognizing the exceptions or practical problems that are often considered by adults. Consider this example: "It is wrong to hurt people. Company A occasionally hurts people" (perhaps through pollution or economic pressures). "Therefore, Company A must be severely punished or shut down." This thinking is logical. By impatiently pressing for immediate major changes or severe penalties, however, one may not fully consider various practical problems such as the thousands of workers who would be laid off if the company were shut down. Adults frequently have undergone life experiences that lead them to see shades of gray in situations, rather than just black or white.

The thought of preschoolers is characterized by egocentrism in which they cannot take another's point of view. Adolescent thought is marked by another sort of egocentrism, in which they can understand the thoughts of others but still have trouble separating things that are of concern to others and those that are of concern only to themselves (Elkind, 1967, 1985). Adolescent egocentrism gives rise to two interesting cognition developments: *the imaginary audience* and the *personal fable*.

The concept of the **imaginary audience** refers to the belief that other people are as concerned with our thoughts and behavior as we are. As a result, adolescents see themselves as the center of attention and assume that other people are about as preoccupied with their appearance and behavior as they are (Lapsley, 1991; Milstead et al., 1993). Adolescents may feel they are on stage and all eyes are focused on them.

The concept of the imaginary audience may fuel the intense adolescent desire for privacy. It helps explain why adolescents are so self-conscious about their appearance, why they worry about every facial blemish and spend long hours grooming. Self-consciousness seems to peak at about the age of 13 and then decline. Girls tend to be more self-conscious than boys (Elkind & Bowen, 1979).

The **personal fable** is the belief that our feelings and ideas are special, even unique, and that we are invulnerable. The personal fable seems to underlie various adolescent behavior patterns, such as showing off and taking risks (Arnett, 1992; Cohn et al., 1995; Lapsley, 1990, 1991; Milstead et al., 1993). Some adolescents adopt an "It can't happen to me" attitude—assuming that they can smoke without risk of cancer or engage in sexual activity without risk of sexually transmitted infections or pregnancy. Another aspect of the personal fable is the idea that no one has ever experienced or could understand the "unique" feelings one is experiencing, such as needing independence or being in love. Perhaps the personal fable is the basis for the common teenage lament, "You just don't understand me!"

Evaluation of Piaget's Theory A number of questions have been raised concerning the accuracy of Piaget's views. Among them are these:

1. *Was Piaget's timing accurate?* Some critics argue that Piaget's methods led him to underestimate children's abilities (Bjorklund, 1995; Meltzoff & Gopnik, 1997). Other researchers using different methods have found, for example, that preschoolers are less egocentric and that children are capable of conservation at earlier ages than Piaget thought.

2. *Does cognitive development occur in stages?* Cognitive events such as egocentrism and conservation appear to develop more continuously than Piaget thought—that is, they may not occur in stages (Bjorklund, 1995; Flavell et al., 1993). Although cognitive

TRUTH OR FICTION REVISITED
It is true that adolescents tend to see themselves as being on stage. This is a manifestation of adolescent egocentrism and fuels the adolescent desires for privacy and physical perfection.

IMAGINARY AUDIENCE An aspect of adolescent egocentrism: The belief that other people are as concerned with our thoughts and behaviors as we are.

PERSONAL FABLE Another aspect of adolescent egocentrism: The belief that our feelings and ideas are special and unique and we are invulnerable.

developments appear to build on previous cognitive developments, the process may be more gradual than stagelike.

3. *Are developmental sequences always the same?* Here, Piaget's views have fared better. It seems there is no variation in the sequence in which cognitive developments occur.

In sum, Piaget's theoretical edifice has been rocked, but it has not been reduced to rubble. Psychologist Andrew Meltzoff believes that "Piaget's theories were critical for getting the field of [cognitive development] off the ground, . . . but it's time to move on" (1997, p. 9). Some of them are moving on to *information processing*. That is, they view children (and adults) as akin to computer systems. Children, like computers, obtain information (receive "input") from their environment, store it, retrieve, manipulate it (think about it), and then respond to it overtly in terms of their behavior (produce "output") (Harnishfeger & Bjorklund, 1990). One goal of the information-processing approach is to learn just how children do these things, how their "mental programs" develop. Critical issues involve children's capacity for memory and their use of cognitive strategies, such as the ways in which they focus their attention (Bjorklund, 1995; Case, 1992; Kail & Salthouse, 1994). The future of the study of cognitive development remains to be written.

THE POSTCONVENTIONAL LEVEL OF MORAL REASONING

Lawrence Kohlberg's theory of moral reasoning involves three levels: preconventional, conventional, and postconventional. Individuals can arrive at the same decision—for example, as to whether or not Heinz should save his wife by taking the drug without paying for it—but they would be doing so for a different kind of reason. (Deciding not to take the drug for fear of punishment is cognitively less complex than not taking the drug because of the belief that doing so could have negative consequences for the social order.)

None of Kohlberg's levels is tied precisely to a person's age. Although postconventional reasoning is the highest level, for example, most adolescents and adults reason conventionally. However, when postconventional reasoning does emerge, it usually does so in adolescence. Kohlberg's (1969) research showed that postconventional moral judgments were clearly absent among the 7- to 10-year-olds. But by age 16, stage 5 reasoning is shown by about 20% of adolescents, and stage 6 reasoning is shown by about 5% of adolescents.

At the **postconventional level,** moral reasoning is based on the person's own moral standards. In each instance, moral judgments are derived from personal values, not from conventional standards or authority figures. In the contractual, legalistic orientation characteristic of stage 5, it is recognized that laws stem from agreed-upon procedures and that the rule of law is in general good for society; therefore, laws should not be violated. But under exceptional circumstances laws cannot bind the individual. (Although it is illegal for Heinz to steal the drug, in this case it is the right thing to do.)

Stage 6 thinking relies on supposed universal ethical principles such as the sanctity of human life, individual dignity, justice, and the Golden Rule ("Do unto others as you would have them do unto you."). Behavior consistent with these principles is moral. If a law is unjust or contradicts the rights of the individual, it is wrong to obey it.

People at the postconventional level look to their conscience as the highest moral authority. This point has created confusion. To some it suggests that it is right to break the law when it is convenient. But this interpretation is incorrect. Kohlberg means that people at this level of moral

POSTCONVENTIONAL LEVEL According to Kohlberg, a period during which moral judgments are derived from moral principles and people look to themselves to set moral standards.

reasoning must do what they believe is right even if this action runs counter to social rules or laws or requires personal sacrifice.

Evaluation of Kohlberg's Theory Consistent with Kohlberg's theory, research suggests that moral reasoning does follow a developmental sequence (Snarey, 1985), even though most people do not reach the level of postconventional thought. Postconventional thought, when found, first occurs during adolescence. It also seems that Piaget's stage of formal operations is a prerequisite for postconventional reasoning, which requires the capacities to understand abstract moral principles and to empathize with the attitudes and emotional responses of other people (Flavell et al., 1993).

Also consistent with Kohlberg's theory, children do not appear to skip stages as they progress (Flavell et al., 1993). When children are exposed to adult models who exhibit a lower stage of moral reasoning, they can be induced to follow along (Bandura & McDonald, 1963). Children who are exposed to examples of moral reasoning above and below their own stage generally prefer the higher stage, however (Rest, 1983). The thrust of moral development would therefore appear to be from lower to higher in terms of Kohlberg's levels and stages, even if children can be influenced by the opinions of others.

Social and Personality Development

In terms of social and personality development, adolescence has been associated with turbulence. In the 19th century, psychologist G. Stanley Hall described adolescence as a time of *Sturm und Drang*—storm and stress. Certainly, many American teenagers abuse drugs, get pregnant, contract sexually transmitted diseases, become involved in violence, fail in school, and even attempt suicide (Garland & Zigler, 1993; Gentry & Eron, 1993; Kazdin, 1993). Each year nearly 1 in 10 adolescent girls becomes pregnant. Nearly 10% of teenage boys and 20% of teenage girls attempt suicide. Alcohol-related incidents are the overall leading cause of death among adolescents.

Hall attributed the conflicts and distress of adolescence to biological changes. Research evidence does suggest that hormonal changes affect the activity levels, mood swings, and aggressive tendencies of many adolescents (Buchanan et al., 1992). Overall, however, it would appear that sociocultural influences have a greater impact than hormones (Buchanan et al., 1992).

Adolescents do try to become more independent from their parents, which often leads to some bickering (Smetana et al., 1991). They usually bicker about issues such as homework, chores, money, appearance, curfews, and dating (Galambos & Almeida, 1992; Smetana et al., 1991). Arguments are common when adolescents want to make their own choices about matters such as clothes and friends (Smetana et al., 1991).

The striving for independence is also characterized by withdrawal from family life, at least relative to prior involvement. In one study, children ranging in age from 9 to 15 carried electronic pagers for a week so that they could report what they were doing and whom they were with when signaled (Larson & Richards, 1991). The amount of time spent with family members decreased dramatically with greater age. The 15-year-olds spent only half as much time with their families as the 9-year-olds. Yet this change does not mean that most adolescents spend their time on the streets. For 15-year-old boys in the study, time with the family tended to be replaced by time spent alone. For older girls, this time was divided between friends and solitude.

ARE THERE GENDER DIFFERENCES IN MORAL DEVELOPMENT?

Some studies using Heinz's dilemma have found that boys reason at higher levels of moral development than girls. However, Carol Gilligan (1982; Gilligan et al., 1989) argues that this gender difference is illusory and reflects different patterns of socialization for boys and girls.

Gilligan makes her point through two examples of responses to Heinz's dilemma. Eleven-year-old Jake views the dilemma as a math problem. He sets up an equation showing that life has greater value than property. Heinz is thus obligated to steal the drug. Eleven-year-old Amy vacil-lates. She notes that stealing the drug and letting Heinz's wife die would both be wrong. Amy searches for alternatives, such as getting a loan, stating that it would profit Heinz's wife little if he went to jail and were no longer around to help her.

According to Gilligan, Amy's reasoning is as sophisticated as Jake's, yet she would be rated as showing a lower level of moral development. Gilligan asserts that Amy, like other girls, has been socialized to focus on the needs of others and forgo simplistic judgments of right and wrong. As a consequence, Amy is more likely to exhibit stage 3 reasoning, which focuses in part on empathy for others. Jake, by contrast, has been socialized to make judgments based purely on logic. To him, clear-cut conclusions are derived from a set of premises. Amy was aware of the logical considerations that influenced Jake, but she saw them as one source of information—not as the only source. It is ironic that Amy's empathy, a trait that has "defined the 'goodness' of women," marks Amy "as deficient in moral development" (Gilligan, 1982, p. 18). Prior to his death, Kohlberg had begun to correct the sexism in his scoring system. ■

Adolescents and parents are often in conflict because adolescents experiment with many things that can be harmful to their health. Yet—apparently because of the personal fable—adolescents often do not perceive such activities to be as risky as their parents see them as being. Lawrence Cohn and his colleagues (1995) found, for example, that parents perceived drinking, smoking, failure to use seat belts, drag racing, and a number of other activities to be riskier than their teenagers saw them as being.

Some distancing from parents is beneficial for adolescents (Galambos, 1992). After all, they do have to form relationships outside the family. But greater independence does not necessarily mean that adolescents become emotionally detached from their parents or fall completely under the influence of their peers. Most adolescents continue to feel love, respect, and loyalty toward their parents (Montemayor & Flannery, 1991). Adolescents who feel close to their parents actually show greater self-reliance and independence than do those who are distant from their parents. Adolescents who retain close ties with their parents also fare better in school and have fewer adjustment problems (Davey, 1993; Papini & Roggman, 1992; Steinberg, 1996).

Despite parent-adolescent conflict over issues of control, parents and adolescents tend to share social, political, religious, and economic views (Paikoff & Collins, 1991). In sum, there are frequent differences between parents and adolescents on issues of personal control. However, there apparently is no "generation gap" on broader matters.

EGO IDENTITY VERSUS ROLE DIFFUSION According to Erik Erikson, individuals undergo eight stages of psychosocial development, each of which is characterized by a certain kind of "crisis." Four of these stages, beginning with the stage of trust versus mistrust, occur during the years of

ESTABLISHING INTIMATE RELATIONSHIPS. According to Erik Erikson, establishing intimate relationships is a central task of young adulthood.

childhood. The fifth stage, that of *ego identity versus role diffusion,* occurs during adolescence. The major challenge of adolescence is the creation of an adult identity. Identity is achieved mainly by committing oneself to a particular occupation or a role in life. But identity also extends to sexual, political, and religious beliefs and commitments.

Erikson (1963) theorized that adolescents experience a life crisis of *ego identity versus role diffusion.* **Ego identity** is a firm sense of who one is and what one stands for. It can carry one through difficult times and give meaning to one's achievements. Adolescents who do not develop ego identity may experience **role diffusion.** They spread themselves too thin, running down one blind alley after another and placing themselves at the mercy of leaders who promise to give them the sense of identity that they cannot find for themselves.

A key aspect of identity is sexual identity—how the adolescent perceives himself or herself as a sexual being. The sex organs of adolescents undergo rapid maturation, and adolescents develop the capacity for reproduction. As we see next, many of them do reproduce, before they are socially, emotionally, and financially ready to do so.

ADULT DEVELOPMENT

Development continues throughout the lifespan. Many theorists believe that adult concerns and involvements follow observable patterns, so we can speak of "stages" of adult development. Others argue that there may no longer be a standard life cycle with predictable stages or phases (Sheehy, 1995, 1998b). Age now has an "elastic quality" (Butler, 1998). People are living longer than ever before and are freer than ever to choose their own destiny. Let us consider the adult years according to three broad categories: young adulthood, middle adulthood, and late adulthood.

Young Adulthood

Young, or early, adulthood covers the period between the ages of 20 and 40. It is the period of life during which people tend to establish themselves as independent members of society. Many adults in their 20s are fueled by ambition. Journalist Gail Sheehy (1976) labeled the 20s the **Trying 20s**—a period during which people basically strive to advance their careers. They are concerned about establishing their pathway in life. They are generally responsible for their own support, make their own choices, and are largely free from parental influences. Many young adults adopt what theorist Daniel Levinson and his colleagues (1978) call the **dream**—the drive to "become" someone, to leave their mark on history—which serves as a tentative blueprint for their life.

During young adulthood, people also tend to leave their families of origin and to create families of their own. Erik Erikson (1963) characterized young adulthood as the stage of **intimacy versus isolation.** Erikson saw the establishment of intimate relationships as central to young adulthood. Young adults who have evolved a firm sense of identity during adolescence are ready to "fuse" their identities with those of other people through marriage and abiding friendships. People who do not reach out to develop intimate relationships risk retreating into isolation and loneliness.

Erikson warned that we may not be able to commit ourselves to others until we have achieved ego identity—that is, established stable life roles. Achieving ego identity is the central task of adolescence. Lack of personal stability is connected with the high divorce rate for teenage marriages.

EGO IDENTITY Erikson's term for a firm sense of who one is and what one stands for.

ROLE DIFFUSION Erikson's term for lack of clarity in one's life roles (due to failure to develop ego identity).

TRYING 20S Sheehy's term for the third decade of life, when people are frequently occupied with advancement in the career world.

DREAM In this usage, Levinson's term for the overriding drive of youth to become someone important, to leave one's mark on history.

INTIMACY VERSUS ISOLATION Erikson's life crisis of young adulthood, characterized by the task of developing abiding intimate relationships.

GENDER DIFFERENCES Most Western men consider separation and individuation to be key goals of personality development during young adulthood (Guisinger & Blatt, 1994). For women, however, the establishment and maintenance of social relationships are also of primary importance (Gilligan et al., 1990, 1991). Women, as Gilligan (1982) has pointed out, are likely to undergo a transition from being cared for by others to caring for others. In becoming adults, men are more likely to undergo a transition from being restricted by others to autonomy and perhaps control of other people.

Although there are differences in the development of women and men, between the ages of 21 and 27 college women also develop in terms of individuation and autonomy (Helson & Moane, 1987). Women, like men, assert increasing control over their own lives. College women, on average, are relatively liberated and career oriented compared with their less-well-educated peers.

Levinson labeled the ages of 28 to 33 the **age-30 transition.** For men and women, the late 20s and early 30s are commonly characterized by reassessment: "Where is my life going?" "Why am I doing this?" Sheehy (1976) labeled this period the **Catch 30s** because of this tendency toward reassessment. During our 30s, we often find that the lifestyles we adopted during our 20s do not fit as comfortably as we had expected.

One response to the disillusionments of the 30s, according to Sheehy, is the tearing up of the life we have spent most of our 20s putting together. It may mean striking out on a secondary road toward a new vision or converting a dream of "running for president" into a more realistic goal. The single person feels a push to find a partner. The woman who was previously content at home with children chafes to venture into the world. The childless couple reconsiders children. And almost everybody who is married . . . feels a discontent. (1976, p. 34)

Many psychologists find that the later 30s are characterized by settling down or planting roots. Many young adults feel a need to make a financial and emotional investment in their home. Their concerns become more focused on promotion or tenure, career advancement, and long-term mortgages.

Middle Adulthood

Middle adulthood spans the years from 40 to 60 or 65. Sheehy (1995) terms the years from 45 onward "second adulthood." Rather than viewing them as years of decline, her interviews suggest that many Americans find that these years present opportunities for new direction and fulfillment.

GENERATIVITY VERSUS STAGNATION Erikson (1963) labeled the life crisis of the middle years **generativity versus stagnation.** Generativity involves doing things that we believe are worthwhile, such as rearing children or producing on the job. Generativity enhances and maintains self-esteem. Generativity also involves helping to shape the new generation. This shaping may involve rearing our own children or making the world a better place, for example, through joining church or civic groups. Stagnation means treading water, as in keeping the same job at the same pay for 30 years, or even moving backward, as in moving into a less responsible and poorer paying job or removing oneself from rearing one's children. Stagnation has powerful destructive effects on self-esteem.

MIDLIFE TRANSITION According to Levinson and colleagues (1978), whose research involved case studies of 40 men, there is a **midlife transition** at about age 40 to 45 characterized by a shift in psychological

AGE-30 TRANSITION Levinson's term for the ages from 28 to 33, which are characterized by reassessment of the goals and values of the 20s.

CATCH 30S Sheehy's term for the fourth decade of life, when many people undergo major reassessments of their accomplishments and goals.

GENERATIVITY VERSUS STAGNATION Erikson's term for the crisis of middle adulthood, characterized by the task of being productive and contributing to younger generations.

MIDLIFE TRANSITION Levinson's term for the ages from 40 to 45, characterized by a shift in psychological perspective from viewing ourselves in terms of years lived to viewing ourselves in terms of the years we have left.

MIDLIFE CRISIS OR "MIDDLESCENCE"? According to Gail Sheehy, many middle-aged people undergo a second quest for identity (the first occurs during adolescence). They are trying to decide what they will do with their "second adulthoods"—the three to four healthy decades they may have left.

perspective. Previously, men had thought of their age in terms of the number of years that had elapsed since birth. Now they begin to think of their age in terms of the number of years they have left. Men in their 30s still think of themselves as older brothers to "kids" in their 20s. At about age 40 to 45, however, some marker event—illness, a change of job, the death of a friend or parent, or being beaten at tennis by their son—leads men to realize that they are a full generation older. Suddenly there seems to be more to look back on than forward to. It dawns on men that they will never be president or chairperson of the board. They will never play shortstop for the Dodgers. They mourn the passing of their own youth and begin to adjust to the specter of old age and the finality of death.

Research suggests that women may undergo a midlife transition a number of years earlier than men do (e.g., Reinke et al., 1985). Sheehy (1976) writes that women enter midlife about 5 years earlier than men, at about age 35 instead of 40. Why? Much of it has to do with the winding down of the "biological clock"—that is, the abilities to conceive and bear children. For example, once they turn 35, women are usually advised to have their fetuses routinely tested for Down syndrome and other chromosomal disorders. At age 35, women also enter higher risk categories for side effects from birth control pills. Yet many women today are having children in their 40s and, occasionally, even later (Clay, 1996; Matus, 1996).

THE MIDLIFE CRISIS According to Levinson, the midlife transition may trigger a crisis—the **midlife crisis.** The middle-level, middle-aged businessperson looking ahead to another 10 to 20 years of grinding out accounts in a Wall Street cubbyhole may encounter severe depression. The housewife with two teenagers, an empty house from 8 a.m. to 4 p.m., and a 40th birthday on the way may feel that she is coming apart at the seams. Both feel a sense of entrapment and loss of purpose. Some people are propelled into extramarital affairs by the desire to prove to themselves that they are still attractive.

MASTERY Sheehy (1995) is much more optimistic than Levinson. She terms the years from 45 to 65 "the Age of Mastery" because people are frequently at the height of their productive powers during this period. Sheehy believes that the key task for people aged 45 to 55 is to decide what they will do with their "second adulthoods"—the 30 to 40 healthy years that may be left for them once they reach 50. She believes that both men and women can experience great success and joy if they identify meaningful goals and pursue them wholeheartedly.

"MIDDLESCENCE" Yet people need to define themselves and their goals. Sheehy coined the term **middlescence** to describe a period of searching that is in some ways similar to adolescence. Both are times of transition. Middlescence involves a search for a new identity: "Turning backward, going around in circles, feeling lost in a buzz of confusion and unable to make decisions—all this is predictable and, for many people, a necessary precursor to making the passage into midlife" (Sheehy, 1995).

Yet women frequently experience a renewed sense of self in their 40s and 50s as they emerge from "middlescence" (Apter, 1995; Sheehy, 1995). Many women in their early 40s are already emerging from some of the fears and uncertainties that are first confronting men. For example, Helson and Moane (1987) found that women at age 43 are more likely than women in their early 30s to feel confident; to exert an influence on their community; to feel secure and committed; to feel productive, effective, and powerful; and to extend their interests beyond their family.

MIDLIFE CRISIS A crisis experienced by many people during the midlife transition when they realize that life may be more than half over and reassess their achievements in terms of their dreams.

MIDDLESCENCE Sheehy's term for a stage of life, from 45 to 55, when people seek new identity and are frequently "lost in a buzz of confusion."

MENOPAUSE **Menopause,** or cessation of menstruation, usually occurs during the late 40s or early 50s, although there are wide variations in the age at which it occurs. Menopause is the final stage of a broader female experience, the *climacteric,* which is caused by a falling off in the secretion of the hormones estrogen and progesterone, and during which many changes occur that are related to the gradual loss of reproductive ability. At this time ovulation also draws to an end. There is some loss of breast tissue and of elasticity in the skin. There can also be a loss of bone density that leads to osteoporosis (a condition in which the bones break easily) in late adulthood.

During the climacteric, many women encounter symptoms such as hot flashes (uncomfortable sensations characterized by heat and perspiration) and loss of sleep. Loss of estrogen can be accompanied be feelings of anxiety and depression, but women appear to be more likely to experience serious depression prior to menopause, when they may feel overwhelmed by the combined demands of the workplace, child rearing, and homemaking (Brody, 1993). Most women get through the mood changes that can accompany menopause without great difficulty. According to psychologist Karen Matthews, who followed a sample of hundreds of women through menopause, "The vast majority [of women] have no problem at all getting through the menopausal transition" (Matthews, 1994, p. 25).

Menopause does not signal the end of a woman's sexual interests (Brody, 1993). Many women find the separation of sex from reproduction to be sexually liberating. Some of the physical problems that may stem from the falloff in hormone production may be alleviated by hormone replacement therapy (Grodstein et al., 1997). A more important issue may be what menopause means to the individual. Women who equate menopause with loss of femininity are likely to encounter more] distress than those who do not (Rathus et al., 2000).

MANOPAUSE (*MAN*OPAUSE?) Men cannot experience menopause, of course. Yet now and then we hear the term *male menopause,* or "manopause." Middle-aged or older men may be loosely alluded to as menopausal. This epithet is doubly offensive: It reinforces the negative, harmful stereotypes of aging people, especially aging women, as crotchety and irritable. Nor is the label consistent with the biology or psychology of aging. Alternate terms are *andropause* (referring to a drop-off in androgens, or male sex hormones) and *viropause* (referring to the end of virility) (Cowley, 1996).

For women, menopause is a time of relatively acute age-related declines in sex hormones and fertility. In men, however, the decline in the production of male sex hormones and fertility is more gradual (Sheehy, 1998b). It therefore is not surprising to find a man in his 70s or older fathering a child. Moreover, some viable sperm are produced even in late adulthood. However, many men in their 50s and 60s experience intermittent problems in achieving and maintaining erections (Laumann et al., 1994), which may or may not have to do with hormone production.

Sexual performance is only one part of the story, however. Between the ages of 40 and 70, the typical American male loses 12 to 20 pounds of muscle, about 2 inches in height, and 15% of his bone mass. (Men as well as women are at risk for osteoporosis [Brody, 1996].) The amount of fat in the body nearly doubles. The eardrums thicken, as do the lenses of the eyes, resulting in some loss of hearing and vision. There is also loss of endurance as the cardiovascular system and lungs become less capable of responding effectively to exertion.

Some of these changes can be slowed or even reversed. Exercise helps maintain muscle tone and keep the growth of fatty tissue in check. A diet

TRUTH OR FICTION REVISITED
It is not true that menopause signals the end of a woman's sexual interests. Many women find the separation of sex from reproduction to be sexually liberating.

MENOPAUSE The cessation of menstruation.

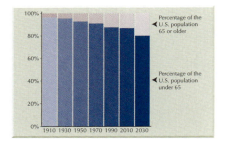

FIGURE LS.9

LIVING LONGER.

As we enter the new millennium, more people in the United States are living to be age 65 or above.

rich in calcium and vitamin D can help ward off bone loss in men as well as in women. Hormone replacement may also help, but is controversial. Although testosterone replacement appears to boost strength, energy, and the sex drive, it is connected with increased risks of prostate cancer and cardiovascular disease (Cowley, 1996). Erection is made possible by the flow of blood into the caverns within the penis (vasocongestion), which then stiffens as does a balloon when air or water is pumped in. The drug Viagra, which was first marketed in 1998, facilitates erection by relaxing the muscles that surround the caverns, enabling blood vessels in the region to dilate.

Even though sexual interest and performance decline, men can remain sexually active and father children at advanced ages (Sheehy, 1998b). For both genders, attitudes toward the biological changes of aging—along with general happiness—may affect sexual behavior as much as biological changes do.

THE EMPTY NEST SYNDROME In earlier decades, psychologists placed great emphasis on a concept referred to as the **empty nest syndrome.** This concept was applied most often to women. It was assumed that women experience a profound sense of loss when their youngest child goes off to college, gets married, or moves out of the home. Research findings paint a more optimistic picture, however. Certainly there can be problems, and these apply to both parents. Perhaps the largest of these is letting go of one's children after so many years of mutual dependence.

Many mothers report increased marital satisfaction and personal changes such as greater mellowness, self-confidence, and stability after their children have left home (Reinke et al., 1985). Middle-aged women show increased dominance and assertiveness, an orientation toward achievement, and greater influence in the worlds of politics and work. It is as if they are cut free from traditional shackles by the knowledge that their childbearing years are behind them.

Now let us consider developments in late adulthood, which begins at the age of 65.

Late Adulthood

It's never too late to be what you might have been.

GEORGE ELIOT

Did you know that an *agequake* is coming? With improved health care and knowledge of the importance of diet and exercise, more Americans than ever before are 65 or older (Abeles, 1997a). In 1900, only 1 American in 30 was over 65, as compared with 1 in 9 in 1970. By 2030, 1 American in 5 will be 65 or older ("Longer, healthier, better," 1997; see Figure LS.9).

The agequake will shake America. It has already influenced the themes of TV shows and movies. Many consumer products are designed to appeal to older consumers. Leisure communities dot the sunbelt. Older people today differ from their counterparts of a generation or two ago in that age is becoming less likely to determine their behavior and mental processes (Butler, 1998). However, the prospects are not the same for men and women, or for people from different ethnic backgrounds.

PHYSICAL DEVELOPMENT Various changes—some of them troublesome—do occur during the later years. Changes in calcium metabolism lead to increased brittleness in the bones and heightened risk of breaks due to accidents such as falls. The skin becomes less elastic and subject to wrinkles and folds.

EMPTY NEST SYNDROME A sense of depression and loss of purpose felt by some parents when the youngest child leaves home.

The senses are also affected. Older people see and hear less acutely. Because of a decline in the sense of smell, they may use more spice to flavor their food. Older people need more time (called **reaction time**) to respond to stimuli. Older drivers, for example, need more time to respond to traffic lights, other vehicles, and changing road conditions. As we grow older, our immune system also functions less effectively, leaving us more vulnerable to disease.

COGNITIVE DEVELOPMENT Although there are some declines in reaction time, intellectual functioning, and memory among older people, they are not as large as many people assume they are (Abeles, 1997b; Butler, 1998). But we understand very little about *why* they occur. Depression and losses of sensory acuity and motivation may contribute to lower cognitive test scores. B. F. Skinner (1983) argued that much of the falloff is due to an "aging environment" rather than an aging person. That is, the behavior of older people often goes unreinforced. Nursing home residents who are rewarded for remembering recent events show improved scores on tests of memory (Langer et al., 1979).

THEORIES OF AGING Although it may be hard to believe it will happen to us, every person who has walked the Earth so far has aged—which may not be a bad fate, considering the alternative. Why do we age? Various factors, some of which are theoretical, apparently contribute to aging.

The theory of **programmed senescence** sees aging as determined by a biological clock that ticks at a rate governed by instructions in the genes. Just as genes program children to grow and reach sexual maturation, they program people to deteriorate and die. There is evidence to support a role for genes in aging. Longevity runs in families. People whose parents and grandparents lived into their 80s and 90s have a better chance of reaching these ages themselves.

The **wear-and-tear theory** does not suggest that people are programmed to self-destruct. Instead, environmental factors such as pollution, disease, and ultraviolet light are assumed to contribute to wear and tear of the body over time. The body is like a machine whose parts wear out through use. Cells lose the ability to regenerate themselves, and vital organs are worn down by the ravages of time.

Behavior also influences aging. People who exercise regularly seem to live longer. Cigarette smoking, overeating, and stress can contribute to an early death. Fortunately, we can exert control over some of these factors.

PSYCHOSOCIAL VIEWS OF AGING According to Erikson, late adulthood is the stage of **ego integrity versus despair.** The basic challenge is to maintain the belief that life is meaningful and worthwhile in the face of the inevitability of death. Ego integrity derives from wisdom, as well as from the acceptance of one's lifespan as occurring at a certain point in the sweep of history and as being limited. We spend most of our lives accumulating objects and relationships. Erikson also argues that adjustment in the later years requires the ability to let go.

Other psychosocial theories of aging include disengagement theory, activity theory, and continuity theory (Berger, 1994).

1. **Disengagement theory.** Disengagement theory maintains that the individual and society withdraw from each other during the later years. Traditional roles such as those of worker and parent give way to a narrowed social circle and reduced activity.

"SUCCESSFUL AGING"?
The later years were once seen mainly as a prelude to dying. As we cross into the new millennium, however, many older people—termed "successful agers"—are seeking new challenges.

REACTION TIME The amount of time required to respond to a stimulus.

PROGRAMMED SENESCENCE The view that aging is determined by a biological clock that ticks at a rate governed by genes.

WEAR-AND-TEAR THEORY The view that factors such as pollution, disease, and ultraviolet light contribute to wear and tear on the body, so the body loses the ability to repair itself.

EGO INTEGRITY VERSUS DESPAIR Erikson's term for the crisis of late adulthood, characterized by the task of maintaining one's sense of identity despite physical deterioration.

DISENGAGEMENT THEORY The view that the individual and society withdraw from one another during the later years.

GENDER, ETHNICITY, AND AGING

Although Americans in general are living longer, there are gender and ethnic differences in life expectancy. For example, women in our society tend to live longer, but older men tend to live *better* ("Longer, healthier, better," 1997). White Americans from European backgrounds live longer on the average than do Hispanic Americans, African Americans, and Native Americans. Life expectancy for Hispanic Americans falls somewhere between the figures for African Americans and White Americans. The longevity of Asian Americans falls closer to that of White Americans than to that of African Americans. Native Americans have the lowest average longevity of the major racial/ethnic groups in our society (Nevid et al., 1998).

GENDER DIFFERENCES

Women in the United States outlive men by six to seven years. Why? For one thing, heart disease, the nation's leading killer, typically develops later in women than in men. Men are also more likely to die because of accidents, cirrhosis of the liver, strokes, suicide, homicide, AIDS, and cancer (excepting cancers of the female sex organs) (Nevid et al., 1998). Many deaths from these causes are the end result of unhealthy habits more typical of men, such as excessive drinking and reckless behavior.

Many men are also reluctant to have regular physical exams or to talk to their doctors about their health problems. "In their 20's, [men are] too strong to need a doctor; in their 30's, they're too busy, and in their 40's, too scared" ("Doctors tie male mentality," 1995). Women are much more likely to examine themselves for signs of breast cancer than men are even to recognize the early signs of prostate cancer.

Although women tend to outlive men, their prospects for a happy and healthy old age are dimmer. Men who beat the statistical odds by living beyond their 70s are far less likely than their female counterparts to live alone, suffer from chronic disabling conditions, or be poor.

Older women are more likely than men to live alone largely because they are five times more likely than men to be widowed (Nevid et al., 1998). Older women are also twice as likely to be poor than older men. Several factors account for this difference. Women now age 65 or older were less likely to hold jobs. If they had jobs, they were paid far less than men and received smaller pensions and other retirement benefits. Because more women than men live alone, they more often must shoulder the burdens of supporting a household without being able to draw on the income of a spouse or other family member.

ETHNIC DIFFERENCES

Why are there ethnic differences in life expectancy? Socioeconomic differences play a role. Members of ethnic minority groups in our society are more likely to be poor, and poor people tend to eat less nutritious diets, encounter more stress, and have less access to health care. There is a seven-year difference in life expectancy between people in the highest income brackets and those in the lowest. Yet other factors, such as cultural differences in diet and lifestyle, the stress of coping with discrimination, and genetic differences, may also partly account for ethnic group differences in life expectancy. ■

ACTIVITY THEORY The view that life satisfaction is connected with one's level of activity.

CONTINUITY THEORY The view that people tend to cope with the challenges of late adulthood in the ways they coped with earlier challenges.

2. **Activity theory.** According to this view, life satisfaction is connected with remaining active. Unfortunately, retirement and the narrowing of one's social circle often reduce activity.

3. **Continuity theory.** Continuity theory maintains that individuals tend to cope with the challenges of late adulthood the same way they coped with earlier challenges. Individual temperament and differences are more important determinants of life satisfaction than one's stage of life.

There is some merit in each of these views. As we see in the following section, "successful aging" is connected with remaining active and involved. However, biological and social realities may require older people to become more selective in their pursuits.

SUCCESSFUL AGING The later years were once seen mainly as a prelude to dying. Older people were viewed as crotchety and irritable. It was assumed that they reaped little pleasure from life. *No more.* Many stereotypes about aging are becoming less prevalent. Despite the changes that accompany aging, most people in their 70s report being generally satisfied with their lives (Margoshes, 1995). Americans are eating more wisely and exercising at later ages, so many older people are robust.

Sheehy (1995) coined the term *middlescence* to highlight her finding that people she interviewed in their 50s were thinking about what they would do with their *second adulthood*—the 30 to 40 healthy years they had left! Developmental psychologists are using another new term: *successful aging* (Margoshes, 1995). The term is not just meant to put a positive spin on the inevitable. "Successful agers" have a number of characteristics that can inspire all of us to lead more enjoyable and productive lives. There are three components of successful aging:

1. *Reshaping one's life to concentrate on what one finds to be important and meaningful.* Laura Carstensen's (1997) research on people aged 70 and above reveals that successful agers form emotional goals that bring them satisfaction. For example, rather than cast about in multiple directions, they may focus on their family and friends. Successful agers may have less time left than those of us in earlier stages of adulthood, but they tend to spend it more wisely (Garfinkel, 1995).

Researchers (Baltes, 1997; Schulz & Heckhausen, 1996) use terms such as "selective optimization and compensation" to describe the manner in which successful agers lead their lives. That is, successful agers no longer seek to compete in arenas best left to younger people—such as certain kinds of athletic or business activities. Rather, they focus on matters that allow them to maintain a sense of control over their own actions.

2. *A positive outlook.* For example, some older people attribute occasional health problems such as aches and pains to *specific* and *unstable* factors like a cold or jogging too long. Others attribute aches and pains to *global* and *stable* factors such as aging itself. Not surprisingly, those who attribute these problems to specific, unstable factors are more optimistic about surmounting them. They thus have a more positive outlook or attitude. Of particular interest here is research conducted by William Rakowski (1995). Rakowski followed 1,400 people age 70 or older with nonlethal health problems such as aches and pains. He found that those who blamed the problems on aging itself were significantly more likely to die in the near future than those who blamed the problems on specific, unstable factors.

3. *Self-challenge.* Many people look forward to late adulthood as a time when they can rest from life's challenges. But sitting back and allowing the world to pass by is a prescription for vegetating, not for living life to its fullest. Consider an experiment conducted by Curt Sandman and Francis Crinella (1995) with 175 people whose average age was 72. They randomly assigned subjects either to a foster grandparent program with neurologically impaired children or to a control group, and followed both groups for 10 years. The foster grandparents carried out various physical challenges, such as walking a few miles each day, and also engaged in new kinds of social interactions. Those in the control group did not engage in these activities. When they were assessed by the experimenters, the foster

TRUTH OR FICTION REVISITED
It is true that older people who blame health problems on aging rather than on specific factors such as a virus are more likely to die in the near future.

grandparents showed improved overall cognitive functioning, including memory functioning, and better sleep patterns. Moreover, the foster grandparents showed superior functioning in these areas compared with people assigned to the control group.

On Death and Dying

Death is the last great taboo. Psychiatrist Elisabeth Kübler-Ross commented on our denial of death in her landmark book *On Death and Dying:* "We use euphemisms, we make the dead look as if they were asleep, we ship the children off to protect them from the anxiety and turmoil around the house if the [person] is fortunate enough to die at home, [and] we don't allow children to visit their dying parents in the hospital" (1969, p. 8).

In her work with terminally ill patients, Kübler-Ross found some common responses to news of impending death. She identified five stages of dying through which many patients pass, and she suggested that older people who suspect that death is approaching may undergo similar stages:

1. *Denial.* In the denial stage, people feel "It can't be happening to me. The diagnosis must be wrong."
2. *Anger.* Denial usually gives way to anger and resentment toward the young and healthy and, sometimes, toward the medical establishment—"It's unfair. Why me?"
3. *Bargaining.* Next, people may try to bargain with God to postpone their death, promising, for example, to do good deeds if they are given another six months, another year to live.
4. *Depression.* With depression come feelings of loss and hopelessness—grief at the inevitability of leaving loved ones and life itself.
5. *Final acceptance.* Ultimately, an inner peace may come, a quiet acceptance of the inevitable. Such "peace" does not resemble contentment. It is nearly devoid of feeling.

Psychologist Edwin Shneidman, who has specialized in the concerns of suicidal and dying individuals, acknowledges the presence of feelings such as those identified by Kübler-Ross, but he does not perceive them to be linked in a sequence like the one just described. Instead, he suggests that dying people show a variety of emotional and cognitive responses that tend to be fleeting or relatively stable, to ebb and flow, and to reflect pain and bewilderment. He also points out that the kinds of responses shown by individuals reflect their personality traits and their philosophies of life.

"LYING DOWN TO PLEASANT DREAMS . . ." The American poet William Cullen Bryant is best known for his poem "Thanatopsis," which he composed at the age of 18. "Thanatopsis" expresses Erik Erikson's goal of ego integrity—optimism that we can maintain a sense of trust through life. By meeting squarely the challenges of our adult lives, perhaps we can take our leave with dignity. When our time comes to "join the innumerable caravan"—the billions who have died before us—perhaps we can depart life with integrity.

> *Live,* wrote the poet, so that
> . . . when thy summons comes to join
> The innumerable caravan that moves
> To that mysterious realm, where each shall take
> His chamber in the silent halls of death,
> Thou go not, like the quarry-slave at night,

Scourged to his dungeon, but, sustained and soothed
By an unfaltering trust, approach thy grave
Like one that wraps the drapery of his couch
About him, and lies down to pleasant dreams.

Bryant, of course, wrote "Thanatopsis" at age 18, not at 85, the age at which he died. At that advanced age, his feelings—and his verse—might have differed. But literature and poetry, unlike science, need not reflect reality. They can serve to inspire and warm us.

CONTROVERSIES IN DEVELOPMENTAL PSYCHOLOGY

Now that we have traced development through the lifespan, we are ready to consider some controversies in developmental psychology. These have to do with the relative importance of nature and nurture in development, and with whether development is continuous or occurs in stages (i.e., is discontinuous).

Does Development Reflect Nature or Nurture?

What behavior is the result of nature? That is, what aspects of behavior originate in a person's genes and are biologically programmed to unfold in the child as long as minimal needs for nutrition and social experience are met? What behavior is the result of nurture? That is, what aspects of behavior largely reflect environmental influences such as nutrition and learning?

Psychologists seek to understand the influences of nature in our genetic heritage, in the functioning of the nervous system, and in the process of **maturation** (that is, the unfolding of traits, as determined by the genetic code). Psychologists look for the influences of nurture in our nutrition, cultural and family backgrounds, and opportunities for learning, including early mental stimulation and formal education. The American psychologist Arnold Gesell (1880–1961) leaned heavily toward natural explanations of development. He argued that all areas of development are self-regulated by the unfolding of natural plans and processes. John Watson and other behaviorists, in contrast, leaned heavily toward environmental explanations. Let us consider the relative influences of nature and nurture in language development.

NATURE AND NURTURE IN LANGUAGE DEVELOPMENT

Since all normal humans talk but no house pets or house plants do, no matter how pampered, heredity must be involved in language. But since a child growing up in Japan speaks Japanese whereas the same child brought up in California would speak English, the environment is also crucial. Thus, there is no question about whether heredity or environment is involved in language, or even whether one or the other is "more important." Instead, . . . our best hope [might be] finding out how they interact.

STEVEN PINKER

Billions of children have acquired the languages spoken by their parents and passed them down, with minor changes, from generation to generation. Language development, like many other areas of development,

MATURATION The orderly unfolding of traits, as regulated by the genetic code.

apparently reflects the interactions between the influences of heredity (nature) and the environment (nurture).

Learning theorists see language as developing according to laws of learning (Gleason & Ratner, 1993). They usually refer to the concepts of imitation and reinforcement. From a social-cognitive perspective, parents serve as *models*. Children learn language, at least in part, through observation and imitation. It seems likely that many words, especially nouns and verbs (including irregular verbs), are learned by imitation.

At first children accurately repeat the irregular verb forms they observe. This repetition can probably be explained in terms of modeling, but modeling does not explain all the events involved in learning. Children later begin to overregularize irregular verb forms *because of* their knowledge of rules of grammar, not through imitation. Nor does imitative learning explain how children come to utter phrases and sentences that they have *not* observed. Parents, for example, are unlikely to model utterances such as "bye-bye sock" and "allgone Daddy," but children do say them.

Learning theory cannot account for the unchanging sequence of language development and the spurts in children's language acquisition. Even the types of two-word utterances emerge in a consistent pattern in diverse cultures. Although timing differs from one child to another, the types of questions used, passive versus active sentences, and so on, all emerge in the same order.

The nativist theory of language development holds that innate or inborn factors—which make up children's *nature*—cause children to attend to and acquire language in certain ways. From this perspective, children bring a certain neurological "prewiring" to language learning (Newport, 1998; Pinker, 1994).

According to **psycholinguistic theory,** language acquisition involves the interaction of environmental influences—such as exposure to parental speech and reinforcement—and an inborn tendency to acquire language. Noam Chomsky (1980, 1991) refers to the inborn tendency as a **language acquisition device (LAD).** Evidence for an LAD is found in the universality of human language abilities and in the specific sequence of language development.

The LAD prepares the nervous system to learn grammar. On the surface, languages differ a great deal. However, the LAD serves children all over the world because languages share what Chomsky refers to as a "universal grammar"—an underlying set of rules for turning ideas into sentences (Pinker, 1994). Consider an analogy with computers: According to psycholinguistic theory, the universal grammar that resides in the LAD is the same as a computer's basic operating system. The particular language that a child learns to use is the same as a word-processing program.

Today, most researchers would agree that both nature and nurture affect most areas of development. We can argue as to which is more prominent in a given area of development, but as in the case of language development, they are both essential.

Is Development Continuous or Discontinuous?

Do developmental changes occur gradually (continuously)? Or do they occur in major leaps (discontinuously) that dramatically alter our bodies and behavior?

Watson and other behaviorists viewed development as a continuous process in which the effects of learning mount gradually, with no major sudden changes. Maturational theorists, however, argue that people are prewired or preset to change dramatically at certain times of life. Rapid

PSYCHOLINGUISTIC THEORY The view that language learning involves an interaction between environmental factors and an inborn tendency to acquire language.

LANGUAGE ACQUISITION DEVICE (LAD) In psycholinguistic theory, neural "prewiring" that facilitates the child's learning of grammar.

qualitative changes can be ushered in in new stages of development. They point out that the environment, even when enriched, profits us little until we are ready, or mature enough, to develop in a certain direction. For example, newborn babies do not imitate their parents' speech, even when the parents speak clearly and deliberately. Nor does aided practice in "walking" during the first few months after birth significantly accelerate the date at which the child can walk on her own.

Stage theorists, such as Sigmund Freud and Jean Piaget, saw development as discontinuous. Both theorists saw biological changes as providing the potential for psychological changes. Freud focused on the ways in which sexual development might provide the basis for personality development. Piaget's research centered on the ways in which maturation of the nervous system permits cognitive advances.

Certain aspects of physical development do occur in stages. For example, from the age of 2 to the onset of puberty (the period of development during which reproduction becomes possible), children gradually grow larger. Then the adolescent growth spurt occurs. It is ushered in by hormones and characterized by rapid changes in structure and function (as in the development of the sex organs) as well as in size. Thus a new stage of life has begun. Psychologists disagree more strongly on whether aspects of development such as cognitive development, attachment, and gender typing occur in stages.

Development is a process that continues for a lifetime. If we include the formation of the genetic codes and the sperm and ova that gave rise to us and that give rise to our children, development becomes a continuous process that chronicles the existence of humans on planet earth and possibly, as we move further into the new millennium, our existence on other orbs. Development stems from the interaction of the unfolding of genetically directed processes and the effects of the environments into which we are plunged at birth. But then we grow aware of those environments and learn how to change them to better meet our needs. Learning and wisdom are as much a part of development as prenatal differentiation and the exciting changes of puberty.

SUMMARY

1. **What are the stages of prenatal development?** These are the germinal, embryonic, and fetal stages. During the germinal stage, the zygote divides as it travels through the fallopian tube and becomes implanted in the uterine wall. The major organ systems are formed during the embryonic stage, and the fetal stage is characterized by maturation and gains in size.

2. **How does physical development occur?** Physical development occurs most rapidly before birth and during the first two years after birth. There is also an adolescent growth spurt during which young people make dramatic gains in height and weight.

3. **What are reflexes?** Reflexes are inborn responses to stimuli that in many cases are essential to infant survival. Examples include breathing, sucking, and swallowing.

4. **How do babies perceive their environment?** Newborn babies can see quite well and show greater interest in complex visual stimuli than in simple ones. Infants are capable of depth perception by the time they can crawl. Newborns can normally hear and show a preference for their mother's voice. Newborns show preferences for pleasant odors and sweet foods.

5. **How did Jean Piaget view children?** Piaget saw children as budding scientists who actively strive to make sense of the perceptual world. He defined intelligence as involving the processes of assimilation

(responding to events according to existing schemes) and accommodation (changing schemes to permit effective responses to new events).

6. **What are the stages of cognitive development, according to Piaget?** Piaget's view of cognitive development includes four stages: sensorimotor (prior to the use of symbols and language); preoperational (characterized by egocentric thought, animism, artificialism, and inability to center on more than one aspect of a situation); concrete operational (characterized by conservation, less egocentrism, reversibility, and subjective moral judgments); and formal operational (characterized by abstract logic).

7. **How does language development occur?** Children make the sounds of crying, cooing, and babbling before true language develops. Single-word utterances occur at about 1 year of age; two-word utterances by the age of 2. Early language is characterized by overextension of familiar words and concepts to unfamiliar objects (calling horses *doggies*), and by overregularization of verbs ("She *sitted* down"). As time passes, vocabulary grows larger, and sentence structure grows more complex.

8. **How did Kohlberg view moral development?** Kohlberg focused on the processes of moral reasoning. He hypothesized that these processes develop through three levels, with each level consisting of two stages. Moral decisions develop from being based on pain and pleasure through necessity to maintain the social order to reliance on one's own conscience.

9. **What are the stages of attachment?** According to Ains-worth, there are three stages of attachment: the initial-preattachment phase, which is characterized by indiscriminate attachment; the attachment-in-the-making phase, which is characterized by preference for familiar figures; and the clear-cut-attachment phase, which is characterized by intensified dependence on the primary caregiver.

10. **What are the major theories of attachment?** Behaviorists have argued that children become attached to their mothers through conditioning because their mothers feed them and attend to their other needs. Harlow's studies with rhesus monkeys suggest that an innate motive, contact comfort, may be more important than conditioning in the development of attachment. Although there may be no particular time limits on the development of attachment in humans, there are critical developmental periods during which animals such as geese and ducks will become attached to (or imprinted on) an object that they follow.

11. **What are the main parenting styles?** These include the authoritative, authoritarian, and permissive styles. The children of authoritative parents are most achievement oriented and well adjusted.

12. **What is adolescence?** Adolescence is a period of life that begins at puberty and ends with assumption of adult responsibilities. Changes that lead to reproductive capacity and secondary sex characteristics are stimulated by increased levels of testosterone in the male and of estrogen and androgens in the female. During the adolescent growth spurt, young people may grow 6 or more inches in a year. Adolescents frequently yearn for greater independence from their parents.

13. **What are some of the major events of young adulthood?** Young adulthood is generally characterized by efforts to advance in the business world and the development of intimate ties. Many young adults reassess the directions of their lives during the "age-30 transition."

14. **What are some of the major events of middle adulthood?** Middle adulthood is a time of crisis (the "midlife crisis") and further reassessment for many, a time when we come to terms with the discrepancies between our achievements and the dreams of our youth. Menopause has been thought to depress many women, but research suggests that most women go through this passage without great difficulty. Some middle-aged adults become depressed when their youngest child leaves home (the so-called empty nest syndrome), but many report increased satisfaction, stability, and self-confidence. However, many people in middle adulthood experience "middlescence"—during which they redefine themselves and their goals for the 30 to 40 healthy years they expect lie ahead of them.

15. **What changes occur during late adulthood?** Older people show less sensory acuity, and their reaction time lengthens. Presumed cognitive deficits sometimes reflect declining motivation or psychological problems such as depression.

16. **What factors are involved in longevity?** Heredity plays a role in longevity. One theory (programmed senescence) suggests that aging and death are determined by our genes. An-

other theory (wear-and-tear theory) holds that factors such as pollution, disease, and ultraviolet light contribute to wear and tear on the body, so the body loses the ability to repair itself. Lifestyle factors such as exercise, good nutrition, and not smoking also contribute to longevity.

17. **What are "stages of dying"?** Kübler-Ross has identified five stages of dying among people who are terminally ill: denial, anger, bargaining, depression, and final acceptance. However, other investigators find that psychological reactions to approaching death are more varied than Kübler-Ross suggests.

18. **Does development reflect nature or nurture?** Development appears to reflect an interaction between nature (genetic factors) and nurture (environmental influences). Maturational theorists focus on the influences of nature, whereas learning theorists focus on environmental influences.

19. **How do psychologists explain language development?** The two main theories are learning theories and nativist theories. Learning theories focus on the roles of reinforcement and imitation. Nativist theories assume that innate factors cause children to attend to and perceive language in certain ways.

20. **Is development continuous or discontinuous?** Stage theorists like Freud and Piaget view development as discontinuous. According to them, people go through distinct periods of development that differ in quality and follow an orderly sequence. Learning theorists, in contrast, tend to view psychological development as a continuous process.

KEY TERMS

accommodation (p. LS-7)

activity theory (p. LS-36)

adolescence (p. LS-24)

age-30 transition (p. LS-31)

amniotic sac (p. LS-3)

androgens (p. LS-3)

animism (p. LS-9)

artificialism (p. LS-9)

assimilation (p. LS-7)

attachment (p. LS-17)

attachment-in-the-making phase (p. LS-19)

authoritarian parents (p. LS-21)

authoritative parents (p. LS-21)

autonomy (p. LS-17)

Catch 30s (p. LS-31)

center (p. LS-10)

clear-cut-attachment phase (p. LS-19)

concrete operations (p. LS-10)

conservation (p. LS-10)

contact comfort (p. LS-19)

continuity theory (p. LS-36)

conventional level (p. LS-15)

critical period (p. LS-20)

decentration (p. LS-10)

disengagement theory (p. LS-35)

dream (p. LS-30)

egocentrism (p. LS-9)

ego identity (p. LS-30)

ego integrity versus despair (p. LS-35)

embryonic stage (p. LS-3)

empty nest syndrome (p. LS-34)

fetal stage (p. LS-3)

fixation time (p. LS-5)

formal operational stage (p. LS-25)

generativity versus stagnation (p. LS-31)

germinal stage (p. LS-3)

holophrase (p. LS-12)

imaginary audience (p. LS-26)

imprinting (p. LS-20)

indiscriminate attachment (p. LS-19)

initial-preattachment phase (p. LS-19)

instrumental competence (p. LS-21)

intimacy versus isolation (p. LS-30)

language acquisition device (LAD) (p. LS-40)

maturation (p. LS-39)

menarche (p. LS-24)

menopause (p. LS-33)

middlescence (p. LS-32)

midlife crisis (p. LS-32)

midlife transition (p. LS-31)

neonate (p. LS-2)

object permanence (p. LS-8)

objective responsibility (p. LS-10)

overextension (p. LS-12)

overregularization (p. LS-13)

period of the ovum (p. LS-3)

permissive parents (p. LS-21)

personal fable (p. LS-26)

placenta (p. LS-3)

postconventional level (p. LS-27)

preconventional level (p. LS-15)

preoperational level (p. LS-9)

programmed senescence (p. LS-35)

psycholinguistic theory (p. LS-40)

puberty (p. LS-24)

reaction time (p. LS-35)

reflexes (p. LS-4)

reversibility (p. LS-11)

role diffusion (p. LS-30)

rooting (p. LS-4)

scheme (p. LS-7)

secondary sex characteristics (p. LS-24)

sensorimotor stage (p. LS-8)

subjective (p. LS-11)   Trying 20s (p. LS-30)   wear-and-tear theory (p. LS-35)

trust versus mistrust (p. LS-17)   umbilical cord (p. LS-3)   zygote (p. LS-3)

REFERENCES

Abeles, N. (1997b). Memory problems in later life. *APA Monitor, 28*(6), 2.

Aber, J. L., & Allen, J. P. (1987). Effects of maltreatment of young children on young children's socioemotional development: An attachment theory perspective. *Developmental Psychology, 23,* 406–414.

Ainsworth, M. D. S., Blehar, M. C., Waters, E., & Wall, S. (1978). *Patterns of attachment: A psychological study of the strange situation.* Hillsdale, NJ: Erlbaum.

Ainsworth, M. D. S., & Bowlby, J. (1991). An ethological approach to personality development. *American Psychologist, 46,* 333–341.

Apter, T. (1995). *Secret paths.* New York: Norton.

Arnett, J. (1992). Reckless behavior in adolescence: A developmental perspective. *Developmental Review, 12,* 339–373.

Arnold, D. H., Lonigan, C. J., Whitehurst, G. J., & Epstein, J. N. (1994). Accelerating language development through picture book reading. *Journal of Educational Psychology, 86,* 235–243.

Azar, B. (1997). It may cause anxiety, but day care can benefit kids. *APA Monitor, 28*(6), 13.

Baltes, P. B. (1997). On the incomplete architecture of human ontogeny: Selection, optimization, and compensation as foundation of developmental theory. *American Psychologist, 52,* 366–380.

Bandura, A., & McDonald, F. J. (1963). Influence of social reinforcement and the behavior of models in shaping children's moral judgments. *Journal of Abnormal and Social Psychology, 67,* 274–281.

Banks, M. S., & Shannon, E. (1993). Spatial and chromatic visual efficiency in human neonates. In C. E. Granrud (Ed.), *Visual perception and cognition in infancy.* Hillsdale, NJ: Erlbaum.

Baumrind, D. (1973). The development of instrumental competence through socialization. In A. D. Pick (Ed.), *Minnesota Symposia on Child Development* (Vol. 7). Minneapolis: University of Minnesota Press.

Baumrind, D. (1991). Parenting styles and adolescent development. In J. Brooks-Gunn, R. Lerner, & A. C. Petersen (Eds.), *Encyclopedia of Adolescence* (Vol. 2). New York: Garland.

Belsky, J. (1990). Developmental risks associated with infant day care. In I. S. Cherazi (Ed.), *Psychosocial issues in day care* (pp. 37–68). New York: American Psychiatric Press.

Belsky, J. (1993). Etiology of child maltreatment. *Psychological Bulletin, 114,* 413–434.

Belsky, J., Fish, M., & Isabella, R. (1991). Continuity and discontinuity in infant negative and positive emotionality: Family attachments and attachment consequences. *Developmental Psychology, 27,* 421–431.

Berger, K. S. (1994). *The developing person through the life span* (3rd ed.). New York: Worth.

Bjorklund, D. F. (1995). *Children's thinking* (2nd ed.). Pacific Grove, CA: Brooks/Cole.

Blakeslee, S. (1998, August 4). Re-evaluating significance of baby's bond with mother. *New York Times,* pp. F1, F2.

Bloom, L., Merkin, S., & Wootten, J. (1982). *Wh*-questions: Linguistic factors that contribute to the sequence of acquisition. *Child Development, 53,* 1084–1092.

Bowlby, J. (1988). *A secure base.* New York: Basic Books.

Broberg, A., Hwang, P., Wessels, H., & Lamb, M. (1997). Cited in Azar, B. (1997). It may cause anxiety, but day care can benefit kids. *APA Monitor, 28*(6), 13.

Brody, J. E. (1993, December 1). Liberated at last from the myths about menopause. *New York Times,* p. C15.

Brody, J. E. (1996, September 4). Osteoporosis can threaten men as well as women. *New York Times,* p. C9.

Buchanan, C. M., Eccles, J. S., & Becker, J. B. (1992). Are adolescents the victims of raging hormones? Evidence for activational effects of hormones on moods and behavior at adolescence. *Psychological Bulletin, 111,* 62–107.

Burnette, E. (1997). "Father of Ebonics" continues his crusade. *APA Monitor, 28*(4), 12.

Butler, R. (1998). Cited in CD-ROM that accompanies Nevid, J. S., Rathus, S. A., & Rubenstein, H. (1998). *Health in the new millennium.* New York: Worth.

Campos, J. J., Hiatt, S., Ramsey, D., Henderson, C., & Svejda, M. (1978). The emergence of fear on the visual cliff. In M. Lewis & L. Rosenblum (Eds.), *The origins of affect.* New York: Plenum.

Carstensen, L. (1997, August 17). *The evolution of social goals across the life span.* Paper presented to the American Psychological Association, Chicago.

Case, R. (1992). *The mind's staircase.* Hillsdale, NJ: Erlbaum.

Chomsky, N. (1980). Rules and representations. *Behavioral and Brain Sciences, 3,* 1–16.

Chomsky, N. (1991). Linguistics and cognitive science. In A. Kasher (Ed.), *The Chomskyan turn.* Cambridge, MA: Blackwell.

Clarke-Stewart, K. A. (1990). "The 'effects' of infant day care reconsidered." In N. Fox & G. G. Fein (Eds.), *Infant day care* (pp. 61–86). Norwood, NJ: Ablex.

Clarke-Stewart, K. A. (1991). A home is not a school: The effects of child care on children's development. *Journal of Social Issues, 47,* 105–123.

Clay, R. A. (1996). Beating the "biological clock" with zest. *APA Monitor, 27*(2), 37.

Cohn, L. D., Macfarlane, S., Yanez, C., & Imai, W. K. (1995). Risk-perception: Differences between adolescents and adults. *Health Psychology, 14,* 217–222.

Cowley, G. (1996, September 16). Attention: Aging men. *Newsweek,* pp. 68–77.

Cox, M. J., Owen, M. T., Henderson, V. K., & Margand, N. A. (1992). Prediction of infant-father and infant-mother attachment. *Developmental Psychology, 28,* 474–483.

Davey, L. F. (1993, March). *Developmental implications of shared and divergent perceptions in the parent-adolescent relationship.* Paper presented at the biennial meeting of the Society for Research in Child Development, New Orleans.

DeAngelis, T. (1997). Abused children have more conflicts with friends. *APA Monitor, 28*(6), 32.

DeCasper, A. J., & Prescott, P. A. (1984). Human newborns' perception of male voices. *Developmental Psychobiology, 17,* 481–491.

"Doctors tie male mentality to shorter life span." (1995, June 14). *New York Times,* p. C14.

Elkind, D. (1967). Egocentrism in adolescence. *Child Development, 38,* 1025–1034.

Elkind, D. (1985). Egocentrism redux. *Developmental Review, 5,* 218–226.

Elkind, D., & Bowen, R. (1979). Imaginary audience behavior in children and adolescents. *Developmental Psychology, 15,* 38–44.

Erikson, E. H. (1963). *Childhood and society.* New York: Norton.

Fantz, R. L. (1961). The origin of form perception. *Scientific American, 204*(5), 66–72.

Fein, E. (1998, January 5). A doctor puts herself in the world of abused children. *New York Times;* America Online.

Field, T. M. (1991). Young children's adaptations to repeated separations from their mothers. *Child Development, 62,* 539–547.

Flavell, J. H., Miller, P. H., & Miller, S. A. (1993). *Cognitive development* (3rd ed.). Englewood Cliffs, NJ: Prentice Hall.

Frankel, K. A., & Bates, J. E. (1990). Mother-toddler problem solving. *Child Development, 61,* 810–819.

Freeman, M. S., Spence, M. J., & Oliphant, C. M. (1993, June). *Newborns prefer their mothers' low-pass filtered voices over other female filtered voices.* Paper presented at the annual convention of the American Psychological Society, Chicago.

Frisch, R. (1997). Cited in Angier, N. (1997). Chemical tied to fat control could help trigger puberty. *New York Times,* pp. C1, C3.

Galambos, N. L. (1992, October). Parent-adolescent relations. *Current Directions in Psychological Science,* pp. 146–149.

Galambos, N. L., & Almeida, D. M. (1992). Does parent-adolescent conflict increase in early adolescence? *Journal of Marriage and the Family, 54,* 737–747.

Garfinkel, R. (1995). Cited in Margoshes, P. (1995). For many, old age is the prime of life. *APA Monitor, 26*(5), 36–37.

Garland, A. F., & Zigler, E. (1993). Adolescent suicide prevention. *American Psychologist, 48,* 169–182.

Gentry, J., & Eron, L. D. (1993). American Psychological Association Commission on Violence and Youth. *American Psychologist, 48,* 89.

Gilligan, C. (1982). *In a different voice.* Cambridge, MA: Harvard University Press.

Gilligan, C., Lyons, P., & Hanmer, T. J. (Eds.). (1990). *Making connections.* Cambridge, MA: Harvard University Press.

Gilligan, C., Rogers, A. G., & Tolman, D. L. (Eds.). (1991). *Women, girls, and psychotherapy.* New York: Haworth.

Gilligan, C., Ward, J. V., & Taylor, J. M. (1989). *Mapping the moral domain: A contribution of women's thinking to psychological theory and education.* Cambridge, MA: Harvard University Press.

Gleason, J. B., & Ratner, N. B. (1993). Language development in children. In J. B. Gleason & N. B. Ratner (Eds.), *Psycholinguistics.* Fort Worth: Harcourt Brace Jovanovich.

Grodstein, F., et al. (1997). Post-menopausal hormonal therapy and mortality. *New England Journal of Medicine, 336,* 1769–1775.

Guisinger, S., & Blatt, S. J. (1994). Individuality and relatedness. *American Psychologist, 49,* 104–111.

Haaf, R. A., Smith, P. H., & Smitley, S. (1983). Infant response to facelike patterns under fixed trial and infant-control procedures. *Child Development, 54,* 172–177.

Harlow, H. F. (1959). Love in infant monkeys. *Scientific American, 200,* 68–86.

Harlow, H. F., & Zimmerman, R. R. (1959). Affectional responses in the infant monkey. *Science, 130,* 421–432.

Harnishfeger, K. K., & Bjorklund, D. F. (1990). Children's strategies. In D. F. Bjorklund (Ed.), *Children's strategies* (pp. 1–184). Hillsdale, NJ: Erlbaum.

Helson, R., & Moane, G. (1987). Personality change in women from college to midlife. *Journal of Personality and Social Psychology, 53,* 176–186.

Isabella, R. A. (1993). Origins of attachment: Maternal interactive behavior across the first year. *Child Development, 64,* 605–621.

Kail, R. V., & Salthouse, T. A. (1994). Processing speed as a mental capacity. *Acta Psychologica, 86,* 199–225.

Kaplan, S. J. (1991). Physical abuse and neglect. In M. Lewis (Ed.), *Child and adolescent psychiatry: A comprehensive textbook* (pp. 1010–1019). Baltimore: Williams & Wilkins.

Kaufman, J., & Zigler, E. (1989). The intergenerational transmission of child abuse. In D. Cicchetti & V. Carlson (Eds.), *Child maltreatment: Theory and research on the causes and consequences of child abuse and neglect* (pp. 129–150). Cam-

bridge: Cambridge University Press.

Kazdin, A. E. (1993). Adolescent mental health. *American Psychologist, 48,* 127–141.

Kellman, P. J., & von Hofsten, C. (1992). The world of the moving infant. In C. Rovee-Collier & L. P. Lipsitt (Eds.), *Advances in infancy research* (Vol. 7). Norwood, NJ: Ablex.

Kohlberg, L. (1969). *Stages in the development of moral thought and action.* New York: Holt, Rinehart and Winston.

Kohlberg, L. (1981). *The philosophy of moral development.* San Francisco: Harper & Row.

Kübler-Ross E. (1969). *On death and dying.* New York: Macmillan.

Lamb, M. E., & Baumrind, D. (1978). Socialization and personality development in the preschool years. In M. E. Lamb (Ed.), *Social and personality development.* New York: Holt, Rinehart and Winston.

Lamb, M. E., Sternberg, K. J., & Prodromidis, M. (1992). Nonmaternal care and the security of infant-mother attachment. *Infant Behavior and Development, 15,* 71–83.

Langer, E. J., Rodin, J., Beck, P., Weinan, C., & Spitzer, L. (1979). Environmental determinants of memory improvement in late adulthood. *Journal of Personality and Social Psychology, 37,* 2003–2013.

Lapsley, D. K. (1990). Continuity and discontinuity in adolescent social cognitive development. In R. Montemayor, G. R. Adams, & T. P. Guillotta (Eds.), *From childhood to adolescence: A transitional period?* Newbury Park, CA: Sage.

Lapsley, D. K. (1991). Egocentrism theory and the "new look" at the imaginary audience and personal fable in adolescence. In R. M. Lerner, A. C. Petersen, & J. Brooks-Gunn (Eds.), *Ency*

clopedia of adolescence. New York: Garland.

Larson, R., & Richards, M. H. (1991). Daily companionship in late childhood and early adolescence. *Child Development, 62,* 284–300.

Laumann, E. O., Gagnon, J. H., Michael, R. T., & Michaels, S. (1994). *The social organization of sexuality.* Chicago: University of Chicago Press.

Lederberg, A. R., & Mobley, C. E. (1990). The effect of hearing impairment on the quality of attachment and mother-toddler interaction. *Child Development, 61,* 1596–1604.

Levinson, D. J., Darrow, C. N., Klein, E. B., Levinson, M. H., & McKee, B. (1978). *The seasons of a man's life.* New York: Knopf.

Lewin, T. (1995, December 7). Parents poll shows higher incidence of child abuse. *New York Times,* p. B16.

Lewis, M. (1997). *Altering fate—Why the past does not predict the future.* New York: Guilford Press.

Lewis, M. (1998). Cited in Blakeslee, S. (1998, August 4). Re-evaluating significance of baby's bond with mother. *New York Times,* pp. F1, F2.

"Longer, healthier, better." (1997, March 9). *New York Times Magazine,* pp. 44–45.

Lorenz, K. Z. (1981). *The foundations of ethology.* New York: Springer-Verlag.

Lyons-Ruth, K., Alpern, L., & Repacholi, B. (1993). Disorganized infant attachment classification and maternal psychosocial problems as predictors of hostile-aggressive behavior in the preschool classroom. *Child Development, 64,* 572–585.

MacDonald, K. (1992). Warmth as a developmental construct. *Child Development, 63,* 753–773.

Macfarlane, J. A. (1975). Olfaction in the development of social preferences in the human neonate. In M. A. Hofer (Ed.), *Parent-infant interaction.* Amsterdam: Elsevier.

Malinosky-Rummell, R., & Hansen, D. H. (1993). Long-term consequences of childhood physical abuse. *Psychological Bulletin, 114,* 68–79.

Margoshes, P. (1995). For many, old age is the prime of life. *APA Monitor, 26*(5), 36–37.

Matthews, K. (1994). Cited in Azar, B. (1994). Women are barraged by media on "the change." *APA Monitor, 25*(5), 24–25.

Matus, I. (1996). Cited in Clay, R. A. (1996). Beating the "biological clock" with zest. *APA Monitor, 27*(2), 37.

Meltzoff, A. N. (1997). Cited in Azar, B. (1997). New theory on development could usurp Piagetian beliefs. *APA Monitor, 28*(6), 9.

Meltzoff, A. N., & Gopnik, A. (1997). *Words, thoughts, and theories.* Cambridge, MA: MIT Press.

Miller, N. B., Cowan, P. A., Cowan, C. P., Hetherington, E. M., & Clingempeel, W. G. (1993). Externalizing in preschoolers and early adolescents. *Developmental Psychology, 29,* 3–18.

Milstead, M., Lapsley, D., & Hale, C. (1993, March). *A new look at imaginary audience and personal fable.* Paper presented at the meeting of the Society for Research in Child Development, New Orleans, LA.

Montemayor, R., & Flannery, D. J. (1991). Parent-adolescent relations in middle and late adolescence. In R. M. Lerner, A. C. Petersen, & J. Brooks-Gunn (Eds.), *Encyclopedia of adolescence.* New York: Garland.

Nelson, K. (1973). Structure and strategy in learning to talk. *Monographs for the Society for Research in Child Development, 38* (Whole No. 149).

Nelson, K., Hampson, J., & Shaw, L. K. (1993). Nouns in early lexicons: Evidence, explanations, and implications. *Journal of Child Language, 20,* 228.

Nevid, J. S., Rathus, S. A., & Rubenstein, H. (1998). *Health in the new millennium.* New York: Worth.

Newport, E. (1998). Cited in Azar, B. (1998). Acquiring sign language may be more innate than learned. *APA Monitor, 29*(4), 12.

Olson, S. L., Bates, J. E., & Bayles, K. (1990). Early antecedents of childhood impulsivity: The role of parent-child interaction, cognitive competence, and temperament. *Journal of Abnormal Child Psychology, 18,* 317–334.

Paikoff, R. L., & Collins, A. C. (1991). Editor's notes: Shared views in the family during adolescence. In R. L. Paikoff & A. C. Collins (Eds.), *New Directions for Child Development* (Vol. 51). San Francisco: Jossey-Bass.

Papini, D. R., & Roggman, L. A. (1992). Adolescent perceived attachment to parents in relation to competence, depression, and anxiety. *Journal of Early Adolescence, 12,* 420–440.

Parker, J. G., & Herrera, C. (1996). Interpersonal processes in friendship: A comparison of abused and nonabused children's experience. *Developmental Psychology, 32,* 1025–1038.

Piaget, J. (1963). *The origins of intelligence in children.* New York: Norton.

Piaget, J. (1997). *The moral judgment of the child.* New York: Free Press Paperbacks.

Pinker, S. (1994). *The language instinct.* New York: Morrow.

Porter, R. H., Makin, J. W., Davis, L. B., & Christensen, K. M. (1992). Breast-fed infants respond to olfactory cues from their own mother and unfamiliar lactating females. *Infant Behavior and Development, 15,* 85–93.

Putallaz, M., & Heflin, A. H. (1990). Parent-child interaction. In S. R. Asher & J. D. Coie (Eds.), *Peer rejection in childhood.* New York: Cambridge University Press.

Rakowski, W. (1995). Cited in Margoshes, P. (1995). For many, old age is the prime of life. *APA Monitor, 26*(5), 36–37.

Rathus, S. A., Nevid, J. S., & Fichner-Rathus, L. (2000). *Human sexuality in a world of diversity* (4th ed.). Boston: Allyn & Bacon.

Reinke, B. J., Holmes, D. S., & Harris, R. L. (1985). The timing of psychosocial changes in women's lives. *Journal of Personality and Social Psychology, 48,* 1353–1364.

Rest, J. R. (1983). Morality. In P. H. Mussen, J. Flavell, & E. Markman (Eds.), *Handbook of child psychology: Vol. 3. Cognitive development.* New York: Wiley.

Robbins, C., & Ehri, L. C. (1994). Reading storybooks to kindergartners helps them learn new vocabulary words. *Journal of Educational Psychology, 86,* 54–64.

Rothbart, M. K., & Ahadi, S. A. (1994). Temperament and the development of personality. *Journal of Abnormal Psychology, 103,* 55–66.

Sandman, C., & Crinella, F. (1995). Cited in Margoshes, P. (1995). For many, old age is the prime of life. *APA Monitor, 26*(5), 36–37.

Schulz, R., & Heckhausen, J. (1996). A life span model of successful aging. *American Psychologist, 51,* 702–714.

Seppa, N. (1996). APA releases study on family violence. *APA Monitor, 27*(4), 12.

Sheehy, G. (1976). *Passages.* New York: Dutton.

Sheehy, G. (1995). *New passages: Mapping your life across time.* New York: Random House.

Sheehy, G. (1998a). *Menopause—The silent passage.* New York: Random House.

Sheehy, G. (1998b). *Understanding men's passages.* New York: Random House.

Simons, R. L., Whitbeck, L. B., Conger, R. D., & Chyi-In, W. (1991). Intergenerational transmission of harsh parenting. *Developmental Psychology, 27,* 159–171.

Skinner, B. F. (1983). Intellectual self-management in old age. *American Psychologist, 38,* 239–244.

Slobin, D. I. (1983). *Crosslinguistic evidence for basic child grammar.* Paper presented to the biennial meeting of the Society for Research in Child Development, Detroit.

Smetana, J. G., Yau, J., Restrepo, A., & Braeges, J. L. (1991). Conflict and adaptation in adolescence. In M. E. Colten & S. Gore (Eds.), *Adolescent stress: Causes and consequences.* New York: deGruyter.

Snarey, J. R. (1985). Cross-cultural universality of social-moral development: A critical review of Kohlbergian research. *Psychological Bulletin, 97,* 202–232.

Sroufe, A. (1998). Cited in Blakeslee, S. (1998, August 4). Re-evaluating significance of baby's bond with mother. *New York Times,* pp. F1, F2.

Steinberg, L. (1996). *Beyond the classroom.* New York: Simon & Schuster.

Strauss, M. (1995). Cited in Collins, C. (1995, May 11). Spanking is becoming the new don't *New York Times,* p. C8.

Teller, D. Y., & Lindsey, D. T. (1993). Motion nulling techniques and infant color vision. In C. E. Granrud (Ed.), *Visual perception and cognition in infancy.* Hillsdale, NJ: Erlbaum.

Thompson, R. A. (1991a). Attachment theory and research. In M. Lewis (Ed.), *Child and adolescent psychiatry.* Baltimore: Williams & Wilkins.

Thompson, R. A. (1991b). Infant daycare. In J. V. Lerner & N. L. Galambos (Eds.), *Employed mothers and their children* (pp. 9–36). New York: Garland.

Trickett, P. K., Aber, J. L., Carlson, V., & Cicchetti, D. (1991). Relationship of socioeconomic status to the etiology and developmental sequelae of physical child abuse. *Developmental Psychology, 27,* 148–158.

U.S. Bureau of the Census. (1998). *Statistical abstract of the United States* (118th ed.). Washington, DC: U.S. Government Printing Office.

Vandell, D. L., & Corasaniti, M. A. (1990). Child care and the family. In K. McCartney (Ed.), *New directions for child development* (Vol. 49, pp. 23–37). San Francisco: Jossey-Bass.

Wagner, R. K. (1997). Intelligence, training, and employment. (1997). *American Psychologist, 52,* 1059–1069.

Walk, R. D., & Gibson, E. J. (1961). A comparative and analytical study of visual depth perception. *Psychological Monographs, 75*(15).

Westerman, M. A. (1990). Coordination of maternal directives with preschoolers' behavior in compliance-problem and healthy dyads. *Developmental Psychology, 26,* 621–630.

Youngblade, L. M., & Belsky, J. (1992). Parent-child antecedents of 5-year-olds' close friendships: A longitudinal analysis. *Developmental Psychology, 28,* 700–713.

SP

SENSATION AND PERCEPTION

TRUTH OR FICTION?

_____ People have five senses.

_____ On a clear, dark night you could probably see the light from a candle burning 30 miles away.

_____ If we could see light of slightly longer wavelengths, warm-blooded animals would seem to glow in the dark.

_____ White sunlight is composed of all the colors of the rainbow.

_____ Onions and apples have the same taste.

_____ Many amputees experience pain in limbs that have been removed.

_____ Rubbing or scratching a sore toe is often an effective way of relieving pain.

_____ We have a sense that keeps us upright.

OUTLINE

F IVE THOUSAND YEARS AGO IN CHINA, GIVE OR TAKE A DAY OR TWO, an arrow was shot into the air. Where did it land? Ancient records tell us precisely where: in the hand of a fierce warrior and master of the martial arts. As the story was told to me, the warrior had grown so fierce because of a chronic toothache. Incessant pain had ruined his disposition.

One fateful day, our hero watched as invading hordes assembled on surrounding hills. His troops were trembling in the face of the enemy's great numbers, and he raised his arms to boost their morale. A slender wooden shaft lifted into the air from a nearby rise, arced, and then descended—right into the warrior's palm. His troops cringed and muttered among themselves, but our hero said nothing. Although he saw the arrow pass through his palm, he did not scream. He did not run. He did not even complain. He was astounded. His toothache had vanished. In fact, his whole jaw was numb.

Meanwhile the invaders looked on, horrified. They, too, muttered among themselves. What sort of warrior could watch an arrow pierce his hand with such indifference? Even with a smile? If this was the caliber of the local warriors, the invaders would be better off traveling west and looking for a brawl in ancient Sumer or in Egypt. They sounded the retreat and withdrew.

Back in town, our warrior received a hero's welcome. A physician offered to remove the arrow without a fee—a tribute to bravery. But the warrior would have none of it. The arrow had worked wonders for his toothache, and he would brook no meddling. He had already discovered that if the pain threatened to return, he need only twirl the arrow and it would recede once more.

But all was not well on the home front. His wife was thrilled to find him jovial once more, but the arrow put a crimp in their romance. When he put his arm around her, she was in danger of being stabbed. Finally she gave him an ultimatum: The arrow must go, or she would.

Placed in deep conflict, our warrior consulted a psychologist, who then huddled with the physician and the village elders. After much to-do, they asked the warrior to participate in an experiment. They would remove the arrow and replace it with a pin that the warrior could twirl as needed.

To the warrior's wife's relief, the pin worked. And here, in ancient China, lay the origins of the art of *acupuncture*—the use of needles to relieve pain and treat assorted ills.

I confess that this tale is not entirely accurate. To my knowledge, there were no psychologists in ancient China (their loss). Moreover, the part about the warrior's wife is fictitious. It is claimed, however, that acupuncture as a means of dealing with pain originated in ancient China when a soldier was, in fact, wounded in the hand by an arrow and discovered that a chronic toothache had disappeared. Historians say the Chinese then set out to map the body by sticking pins into various parts of it to learn how they would influence the perception of pain.

Control of pain is just one of the many issues that interest psychologists who study the closely related concepts of sensation and perception. **Sensation** is the stimulation of sensory receptors and the transmission of sensory information to the central nervous system (the spinal cord or brain). Sensory receptors are located in sensory organs such as the eyes and ears and, as we will see, in the skin and elsewhere in the body. Stimulation of the senses is an automatic process. It results from sources of energy like light and sound or from the presence of chemicals, as in smell and taste.

Perception is not automatic. Perception is an active process in which sensations are organized and interpreted to form an inner representation of the world. Perception may begin with sensation but it also reflects our experiences and expectations as it makes sense of sensory stimuli. A human shape and a 12-inch ruler may look to be equally high; whether we interpret the shape to be a foot-long doll or a full-grown person 15 feet away is a matter of perception that depends on our experience with dolls and people.

In this chapter you will see that your personal map of reality—your ticket of admission to a world of changing sights, sounds, and other sources of sensory input—depends largely on the so-called five senses: vision, hearing, smell, taste, and touch. We will see, however, that touch is just one of several "skin senses," which also include pressure, warmth, cold, and pain. There are also senses that alert you to your own body position without your having to watch every step you take. As we explore the nature of each of these senses, we will find that similar sensations may lead to different perceptions in different people—or within the same person in different situations.

SENSATION AND PERCEPTION: YOUR TICKET OF ADMISSION TO THE WORLD OUTSIDE

Before we begin our journey through the senses, let us consider a number of concepts that apply to all of them: absolute threshold, difference threshold, signal-detection theory, and sensory adaptation. In doing so, we will learn why we might be able to dim the lights gradually to near darkness without other people becoming aware that we are doing so. We will also learn why we might grow unaware of the savory aromas of delightful dinners.

Absolute Threshold: Is It There or Isn't It?

Gustav Fechner used the term **absolute threshold** to refer to the weakest amount of a stimulus that can be distinguished from no stimulus at all. For example, the amount of physical energy required to activate the visual sensory system is the absolute threshold for light.

Psychophysicists conduct experiments to determine the absolute thresholds of the senses. These involve exposing subjects to stimuli of progressively greater intensity. In the **method of constant stimuli,** researchers present sets of stimuli with magnitudes close to the expected threshold. Subjects say yes if they detect a stimulus and no if they do not. The stimuli are presented repeatedly in random order. An individual's absolute threshold for a stimulus is the lowest magnitude of the stimulus that he or she

SENSORY THRESHOLDS.
How much stimulation is necessary before a person can detect a stimulus? How bright must the beacon from the lighthouse be to enable you to see it through the fog from several miles offshore?

TRUTH OR FICTION REVISITED
It is not true that people have five senses. People have more, as we will see.

SENSATION The stimulation of sensory receptors and the transmission of sensory information to the central nervous system.

PERCEPTION The process by which sensations are organized into an inner representation of the world.

ABSOLUTE THRESHOLD The minimal amount of energy that can produce a sensation.

PSYCHOPHYSICIST A person who studies the relationships between physical stimuli (such as light or sound) and their perception.

METHOD OF CONSTANT STIMULI A psychophysical method for determining thresholds in which the researcher presents stimuli of various magnitudes and asks the person to report detection.

reports detecting 50% of the time. Weaker stimuli are detected less than 50% of the time and stronger stimuli more than 50% of the time.

The relationship between the intensity of a stimulus (a physical event) and its perception (a psychological event) is considered to be *psychophysical*. It bridges psychological and physical events.

Absolute thresholds have been determined for the senses of vision, hearing, taste, smell, and touch. They are approximately as follows:

- For vision, the equivalent of a candle flame viewed from a distance of about 30 miles on a clear, dark night
- For hearing, the equivalent of the ticking of a watch from about 20 feet away in a quiet room
- For taste, the equivalent of about 1 teaspoon of sugar dissolved in 2 gallons of water
- For smell, the equivalent of about one drop of perfume diffused throughout a small house (1 part in 500 million)
- For touch, the equivalent of the pressure of the wing of a fly falling on a cheek from a distance of about 0.4 inch

There are individual differences in absolute thresholds. That is, some people are more sensitive to sensory stimuli than others. The same person may also differ somewhat in sensitivity from one day to the next or from one occasion to another.

If the absolute thresholds for the human senses differed significantly, our daily experiences would be unrecognizable. Our ears are particularly sensitive, especially to sounds that are low in **pitch.** If they were any more sensitive, we might hear the collisions among molecules of air. Light consists of waves of energy, and if our eyes were sensitive to light with slightly longer wavelengths, we would sense infrared light waves. Heat generates infrared light. Thus animals that are warm-blooded and give off heat—including our mates—would literally glow in the dark.

Difference Threshold: Is It the Same or Is It Different?

How much of a difference in intensity between two lights is required before you detect one as being brighter than the other? The minimum difference in magnitude of two stimuli required to tell them apart is their **difference threshold.** As with the absolute threshold, psychologists have agreed to the criterion of a difference in magnitudes that can be detected 50% of the time.

Psychophysicist Ernst Weber discovered through laboratory research that the threshold for perceiving differences in the intensity of light is about 2% (actually closer to 1/60th) of their intensity. This fraction, 1/60th, is known as **Weber's constant** for light. A closely related concept is the **just noticeable difference** (jnd), the minimal amount by which a source of energy must be increased or decreased so that a difference in intensity will be perceived. In the case of light, people can perceive a difference in intensity 50% of the time when the brightness of a light is increased or decreased by 1/60th. Weber's constant for light holds whether we are comparing two quite bright lights or two rather dull lights. However, it becomes inaccurate when we compare extremely bright or extremely dull lights.

Weber's constant for noticing differences in lifted weight is 1/53rd. (Round it off to 1/50th.) That means we would probably have to increase the weight on a 100-pound barbell by about 2 pounds before the lifter would notice the difference. Now think of the 1-pound dumbbells used by many runners. Increasing the weight of each dumbbell by 2 pounds would

PITCH The highness or lowness of a sound, as determined by the frequency of the sound waves.

DIFFERENCE THRESHOLD The minimal difference in intensity required between two sources of energy so that they will be perceived as being different.

WEBER'S CONSTANT The fraction of the intensity by which a source of physical energy must be increased or decreased so that a difference in intensity is perceived.

JUST NOTICEABLE DIFFERENCE The minimal amount by which a source of energy must be increased or decreased so that a difference in intensity is perceived.

be readily apparent to almost anyone because the increase would be threefold, not a small fraction. Yet the increase is still "only" 2 pounds. Return to our power lifter. When he is pressing 400 pounds, a 2-pound difference is less likely to be noticeable than when he is pressing 100 pounds. This is because 2 pounds is only 1/200th of 400 pounds.

People are most sensitive to changes in the pitch (frequency) of sounds. The constant for pitch is 1/333, meaning that on average, people can tell when a tone rises or falls in pitch by one third of 1%. (Singers have to be right on pitch. The smallest error makes them sound sharp or flat.) The sense of taste is much less sensitive. On average, people cannot detect differences in saltiness of less than 20%.

Signal-Detection Theory: Is Being Bright Enough?

Does our discussion so far strike you as "inhuman"? We have written about perception of sensory stimuli as if people are simply switched on by certain amounts of stimulation. This is not quite so. People are influenced by psychological factors as well as by external changes. **Signal-detection theory** considers the human aspects of sensation and perception.

The intensity of the signal is just one factor that determines whether people will perceive sensory stimuli (signals) or a difference between signals. Another is the degree to which the signal can be distinguished from background noise. It is easier to hear a friend in a quiet room than in a room in which people are talking loudly and clinking glasses. The sharpness or acuteness of a person's biological sensory system is still another factor. Is sensory capacity fully developed? Is it diminished by advanced age?

Signal-detection theory also considers psychological factors such as motivation, expectations, and learning. For example, the place in which you are reading this book may be abuzz with signals. If you are outside, perhaps a breeze is blowing against your face. Perhaps the shadows of passing clouds darken the scene now and then. If you are inside, perhaps there are the occasional clanks and hums emitted by a heating system. Perhaps the aromas of dinner are hanging in the air, or the voices from a TV set suggest a crowd in another room. Yet you are focusing your attention on this page (I hope). Thus, the other signals recede into the background of your consciousness. One psychological factor in signal detection is the focusing or narrowing of attention to signals that the person deems important.

Consider some examples. One parent may sleep through a baby's crying while the other parent is awakened. This is not necessarily because one parent is innately more sensitive to the sounds of crying (although some men may conveniently assume that mothers are). Instead, it may be because one parent has been assigned the task of caring for the baby through the night and is therefore more motivated to attend to the sounds. Because of training, an artist might notice the use of line or subtle colors that would go undetected by another person looking at the same painting.

The relationship between a physical stimulus and a sensory response is more than mechanical or mathematical. People's ability to detect stimuli such as meaningful blips on a radar screen depends not only on the intensity of the blips themselves but also on their training (learning), motivation (desire to perceive meaningful blips), and psychological states such as fatigue or alertness.

Feature Detectors

Imagine that you are standing by the curb of a busy street as a bus approaches. When neurons in your sensory organs—in this case, your eyes—are stimulated by the approach of the bus, they relay information to

Signal Detection.
The detection of signals is determined not only by the physical characteristics of the signals but also by psychological factors such as motivation and attention. The people in this photo are tuned into their newspapers for the moment, and not to each other.

SIGNAL-DETECTION THEORY The view that the perception of sensory stimuli involves the interaction of physical, biological, and psychological factors.

the sensory cortex in the brain. Nobel prizewinners David Hubel and Torsten Wiesel (1979) discovered that various neurons in the visual cortex fire in response to particular features of the visual input. Many cells, for example, fire in response to lines presented at various angles—vertical, horizontal, and in between. Other cells fire in response to specific colors. Because they respond to different aspects or features of a scene, these cells are termed **feature detectors.** In the example of the bus, visual feature detectors respond to the bus's edges, depth, contours, textures, shadows, speed, and kinds of motion (up, down, forward, and back). There are also feature detectors for other senses. Auditory feature detectors, for example, respond to the pitch, loudness, and other aspects of the sounds of the bus.

Sensory Adaptation: Where Did It Go?

Our sensory systems are admirably suited to a changing environment. We become more sensitive to stimuli of low magnitude and less sensitive to stimuli that remain the same (such as the background noises outside the window). **Sensory adaptation** refers to these processes of adjustment.

Consider how the visual sense adapts to lower intensities of light. When we first walk into a darkened movie theater, we see little but the images on the screen. As time goes by, however, we become increasingly sensitive to the faces of those around us and to the features of the theater. The process of becoming more sensitive to stimulation is referred to as **sensitization,** or positive adaptation.

But we become less sensitive to constant stimulation. Sources of light appear to grow dimmer as we adapt to them. In fact, if you could keep an image completely stable on the retinas of your eyes—which is virtually impossible to accomplish without a motionless image and stabilizing equipment—the image would fade within a few seconds and be very difficult to see. Similarly, at the beach we soon become less aware of the lapping of the waves. When we live in a city, we become desensitized to traffic sounds except for the occasional backfire or siren. And as you may have noticed from experiences with freshly painted rooms, sensitivity to disagreeable odors fades quite rapidly. The process of becoming less sensitive to stimulation is referred to as **desensitization,** or negative adaptation.

VISION: LETTING THE SUN SHINE IN

Our eyes are our "windows on the world." More than half of the cerebral cortex is devoted to visual functions (Basic Behavioral Science Task Force, 1996). Because vision is our dominant sense, we consider blindness the most debilitating type of sensory loss (Moore, 1995). To understand vision, we need to begin with the nature of light.

Light: What Is This Stuff?

In almost all cultures, light is a symbol of goodness and knowledge. We describe capable people as being "bright" or "brilliant." If we are not being complimentary, we label them as "dull." People who aren't in the know are said to be "in the dark." Just what is this stuff called light?

Visible light is the stuff that triggers visual sensations. It is just one small part of a spectrum of electromagnetic energy (see Figure SP.1). All forms of electromagnetic energy move in waves. Different kinds of

FEATURE DETECTORS Neurons in the sensory cortex that fire in response to specific features of sensory information such as lines or edges of objects.

SENSORY ADAPTATION The processes by which organisms become more sensitive to stimuli that are low in magnitude and less sensitive to stimuli that are constant or ongoing in magnitude.

SENSITIZATION The type of sensory adaptation in which we become more sensitive to stimuli that are low in magnitude. Also called *positive adaptation.*

DESENSITIZATION The type of sensory adaptation in which we become less sensitive to constant stimuli. Also called *negative adaptation.*

VISIBLE LIGHT The part of the electromagnetic spectrum that stimulates the eye and produces visual sensations.

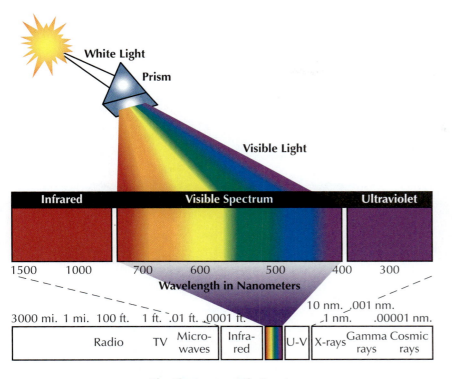

The Electromagnetic Spectrum

FIGURE SP.1
THE VISIBLE SPECTRUM.
By passing a source of white light, such as sunlight, through a prism, we break it down into the colors of the visible spectrum. The visible spectrum is just a narrow segment of the electromagnetic spectrum. The electromagnetic spectrum also includes radio waves, microwaves, X rays, cosmic rays, and many others. Different forms of electromagnetic energy have wavelengths, which vary from a few trillionths of a meter to thousands of miles. Visible light varies in wavelength from about 400 to 700 *billionths* of a meter. (A meter = 39.37 inches.)

electromagnetic energy have different wavelengths. Cosmic rays have extremely short wavelengths, only a few trillionths of an inch long. But some radio waves extend for miles. Although visible light seems to move in a steady stream, it also consists of waves of energy. Different colors have different wavelengths, with violet the shortest and red the longest. Radar, microwaves, and X rays are also forms of electromagnetic energy.

You have probably seen rainbows or light that has been broken down into several colors as it filtered through your windows. Sir Isaac Newton, the British scientist, discovered that sunlight could be broken down into different colors by means of a triangular solid of glass called a *prism* (Figure SP.1). When I took introductory psychology, I was taught to remember the colors of the spectrum, from longest to shortest wavelengths, by using the mnemonic device *Roy G. Biv* (red, orange, yellow, green, blue, indigo, violet). I must have been a backward student because I found it easier to recall them in reverse order, using the meaningless acronym *vibgyor*.

The wavelength of visible light determines its color, or **hue.** The wavelength for red is longer than the wavelength for orange, and so on through the spectrum.

The Eye: The Better to See You With

Consider that magnificent invention called the camera, which records visual experiences. In traditional cameras, light enters an opening and is focused onto a sensitive surface, or film. Chemicals on film create a lasting impression of the image that entered the camera.

The eye—our living camera—is no less remarkable. Look at its major parts, as shown in Figure SP.2. As with a film or TV camera, light enters through a narrow opening and is projected onto a sensitive surface. Light first passes through the transparent **cornea,** which covers the front of the eye's surface. (The "white" of the eye, or *sclera,* is composed of a hard

TRUTH OR FICTION REVISITED
It is true that white sunlight is actually composed of all the colors of the rainbow.

HUE The color of light, as determined by its wavelength.

CORNEA Transparent tissue forming the outer surface of the eyeball.

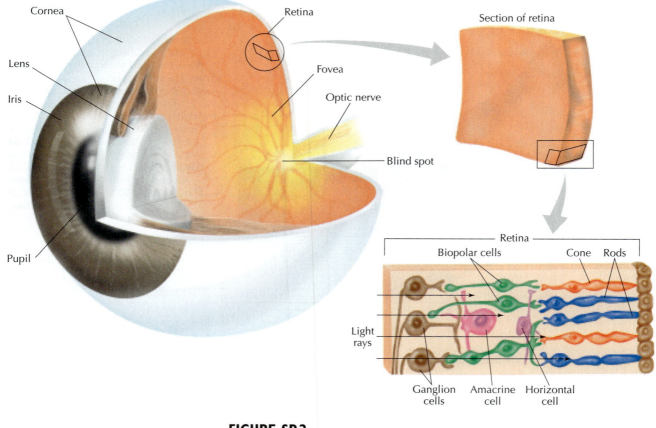

FIGURE SP.2

THE EYE.

In both the eye and a camera, light enters through a narrow opening and is projected onto a sensitive surface. In the eye, the photosensitive surface is called the retina, and information concerning the changing images on the retina is transmitted to the brain. The retina contains photoreceptors called rods and cones. Rods and cones transmit sensory input back through the bipolar neurons to the ganglion neurons. The axons of the ganglion neurons form the optic nerve, which transmits sensory stimulation through the brain to the visual cortex of the occipital lobe.

protective tissue.) The amount of light that passes through the cornea is determined by the size of the opening of the muscle called the **iris,** which is the colored part of the eye. The opening in the iris is the **pupil.** The size of the pupil adjusts automatically to the amount of light present. You do not have to try purposefully to open your eyes further to see better in low lighting conditions. The more intense the light, the smaller the opening. In a similar fashion, we adjust the amount of light allowed into a camera according to its brightness. Pupil size is also sensitive to emotional response: We can literally be "wide-eyed with fear."

Once light passes through the iris, it encounters the **lens.** The lens adjusts or accommodates to the image by changing its thickness. Changes in thickness permit a clear image of the object to be projected onto the retina. These changes focus the light according to the distance of the object from the viewer. If you hold a finger at arm's length and slowly bring it toward your nose, you will feel tension in the eye as the thickness of the lens accommodates to keep the retinal image in focus. When people squint to bring an object into focus, they are adjusting the thickness of the lens. The lens in a camera does not accommodate to the distance of

IRIS A muscular membrane whose dilation regulates the amount of light that enters the eye.

PUPIL The apparently black opening in the center of the iris, through which light enters the eye.

LENS A transparent body behind the iris that focuses an image on the retina.

objects. Instead, to focus the light that is projected onto the film, the camera lens is moved farther from the film or closer to it, as in a zoom lens.

The **retina** is like the film or image surface of the camera. However, the retina consists of cells called **photoreceptors** that are sensitive to light (photosensitive). There are two types of photoreceptors: *rods* and *cones.* The retina (see Figure SP.2) contains several layers of cells: the rods and cones, **bipolar cells,** and **ganglion cells.** All of these cells are neurons. Light travels past the ganglion cells and bipolar cells and stimulates the rods and cones. The rods and cones then send neural messages through the bipolar cells to the ganglion cells. The axons of the million or so ganglion cells in our retinae form the **optic nerve.** The optic nerve conducts sensory input to the brain, where it is relayed to the visual area of the occipital lobe. Other neurons in the retina—amacrine cells and horizontal cells—make sideways connections at a level near the receptor cells and at another level near the ganglion cells. As a result of these lateral connections, many rods and cones funnel visual information into one bipolar cell, and many bipolar cells funnel information to one ganglion cell. Receptors outnumber ganglion cells by more than 100 to 1.

The **fovea** is the most sensitive area of the retina (see Figure SP.2). Receptors there are more densely packed. The **blind spot,** in contrast, is insensitive to visual stimulation. It is the part of the retina where the axons of the ganglion cells congregate to form the optic nerve (Figure SP.3).

Visual acuity (sharpness of vision) is connected with the shape of the eye. People who have to be unusually close to an object to discriminate its details are *nearsighted.* People who see distant objects unusually clearly but have difficulty focusing on nearby objects are *farsighted.* Nearsightedness can result when the eyeball is elongated so that the images of distant objects are focused in front of the retina. When the eyeball is too short, the images of nearby objects are focused behind the retina, causing farsightedness. Eyeglasses or contact lenses can be used to help nearsighted people focus distant objects on their retinas. Farsighted people usually see well enough without eyeglasses until they reach their middle years, when they may need glasses for reading.

Beginning in the late 30s to the mid-40s, the lenses grow brittle, making it difficult to accommodate to, or focus on, objects. This condition is called **presbyopia,** from the Greek words for "old man" and "eyes," but presbyopia occurs by middle adulthood, not late adulthood. Presbyopia makes it difficult to perceive nearby visual stimuli. People who had normal visual acuity in their youth often require corrective lenses to read in middle adulthood and beyond.

RODS AND CONES Rods and **cones** are the photoreceptors in the retina. About 125 million rods and 6.5 million cones are distributed across the retina. The fovea is composed almost exclusively of cones. Cones become more sparsely distributed as you work forward from the fovea toward the lens. Rods, in contrast, are nearly absent at the fovea but are distributed more densely as you approach the lens.

Rods are sensitive only to the intensity of light. They allow us to see in black and white. Cones provide color vision. In low lighting, it is possible to photograph a clearer image with black-and-white film than with color film. Similarly, rods are more sensitive to light than cones. Therefore, as the illumination grows dim, as during the evening and nighttime hours, objects appear to lose their color well before their outlines fade from view.

LIGHT ADAPTATION Immediately after we enter it, a movie theater may seem too dark to allow us to find seats readily. But as time goes on

FIGURE SP.3
**LOCATING THE BLIND SPOTS
IN YOUR EYES.**

To try a "disappearing act," first look at Drawing 1. Close your right eye. Then move the book back and forth about a foot from your left eye while you stare at the plus sign. You will notice the circle disappear. When the circle disappears it is being projected onto the blind spot of your retina, the point at which the axons of ganglion neurons collect to form the optic nerve. Then close your left eye. Stare at the circle with your right eye and move the book back and forth. When the plus sign disappears, it is being projected onto the blind spot of your right eye. Now look at Drawing 2. You can make this figure disappear and "see" the black line continue through the spot where it was by closing your right eye and staring at the plus sign with your left. When this figure is projected onto your blind spot, your brain "fills in" the line, which is one reason you're not usually aware that you have blind spots.

RETINA The area of the inner surface of the eye that contains rods and cones.

PHOTORECEPTORS Cells that respond to light.

BIPOLAR CELLS Neurons that conduct neural impulses from rods and cones to ganglion cells.

GANGLION CELLS Neurons whose axons form the optic nerve.

OPTIC NERVE The nerve that transmits sensory information from the eye to the brain.

FOVEA An area near the center of the retina that is dense with cones and where vision is consequently most acute.

BLIND SPOT The area of the retina where axons from ganglion cells meet to form the optic nerve.

VISUAL ACUITY Sharpness of vision.

PRESBYOPIA A condition characterized by brittleness of the lens.

RODS Rod-shaped photoreceptors that are sensitive only to the intensity of light.

CONES Cone-shaped photoreceptors that transmit sensations of color.

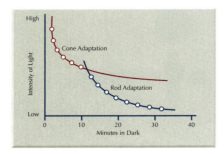

FIGURE SP.4

DARK ADAPTATION.

This illustration shows the amount of light necessary for detection as a function of the amount of time spent in the dark. Cones and rods adapt at different rates. Cones, which permit perception of color, reach maximum dark adaptation in about 10 minutes. Rods, which permit perception of dark and light only, are more sensitive than cones. Rods continue to adapt for up to about 45 minutes.

we begin to see the seats and other people clearly. The process of adjusting to lower lighting conditions is called **dark adaptation.**

Figure SP.4 shows the amount of light needed for detection as a function of the amount of time spent in the dark. The cones and rods adapt at different rates. The cones, which permit perception of color, reach their maximum adaptation to darkness in about 10 minutes. The rods, which allow perception of light and dark only, are more sensitive and continue to adapt to darkness for up to about 45 minutes.

Adaptation to brighter lighting conditions takes place much more rapidly. When you emerge from the theater into the brilliance of the afternoon, you may at first be painfully surprised by the featureless blaze around you. The visual experience is not unlike turning the brightness of the TV set to its maximum setting, at which the edges of objects seem to dissolve into light. Within a minute or so of entering the street, however, the brightness of the scene dims and objects regain their edges.

Color Vision: Creating an Inner World of Color

For most of us, the world is a place of brilliant colors—the blue-greens of the ocean, the red-oranges of the setting sun, the deepened greens of June, the glories of rhododendron and hibiscus. Color is a an emotional and aesthetic part of our everyday lives. In this section we examine theories about how we manage to convert different wavelengths of light into perceptions of color.

Adults with normal color vision can discriminate among hundreds of colors across the visible spectrum. Different colors have different wavelengths. Although we can vary the physical wavelengths of light in a continuous manner from shorter to longer, many changes in color are *dis*continuous. For example, our perception of a color shifts suddenly from blue to green, even though the change in wavelength may be smaller than that between two blues.

Our ability to perceive color depends on the eye's transmission of different messages to the brain when lights with different wavelengths stimulate the cones in the retina. Let us consider two theories of how lights with different wavelengths are perceived as different colors: the *trichromatic theory* and the *opponent-process theory*.

THE TRICHROMATIC THEORY **Trichromatic theory** is based on an experiment conducted by the British scientist Thomas Young in the early 1800s. As in Figure SP.5, Young projected three lights of different colors onto a screen so that they partly overlapped. He found he could create any color from the visible spectrum by simply varying the intensities of the lights. When all three lights fell on the same spot, they created white light, or the appearance of no color at all. The three lights manipulated by Young were red, green, and blue-violet.

The German physiologist Hermann von Helmholtz saw in Young's discovery an explanation of color vision. Von Helmholtz suggested that the eye must have three different types of photoreceptors or cones. Some must be sensitive to red light, some to green, and some to blue. We see other colors when two different types of color receptors are stimulated. The perception of yellow, for example, would result from the simultaneous stimulation of receptors for red and green. The trichromatic theory is also known as the Young-Helmholtz theory.

THE OPPONENT-PROCESS THEORY Before reading on, why don't you try a brief experiment? Look at the strangely colored American flag in

DARK ADAPTATION The process of adjusting to conditions of lower lighting by increasing the sensitivity of rods and cones.

TRICHROMATIC THEORY The theory that color vision is made possible by three types of cones, some of which respond to red light, some to green, and some to blue.

AFTERIMAGE The lingering visual impression made by a stimulus that has been removed.

OPPONENT-PROCESS THEORY The theory that color vision is made possible by three types of cones, some of which respond to red or green light, some to blue or yellow, and some only to the intensity of light.

Figure SP.6 for at least half a minute. Then look at a sheet of white or gray paper. What has happened to the flag? If your color vision is working properly, and if you looked at the miscolored flag long enough, you should see a flag composed of the familiar red, white, and blue. The flag you perceive on the white sheet of paper is an **afterimage** of the first. (If you didn't look at the green, black, and yellow flag long enough the first time, try it again. It will work any number of times.) The phenomenon of afterimages has contributed to another theory of color vision.

In 1870, Ewald Hering proposed the **opponent-process theory** of color vision: There are three types of color receptors but they are not sensitive to the simple hues of red, green, and blue. Hering suggested instead that afterimages are made possible by three types of color receptors: red-green, blue-yellow, and a type that perceives differences in brightness. A red-green cone could not transmit messages for red and green at the same time. According to Hering, staring at the green, black, and yellow flag for 30 seconds would disturb the balance of neural activity. The afterimage of red, white, and blue would represent the eye's attempt to reestablish a balance.

Research suggests that both theories of color vision are partly correct. For example, it shows that some cones are sensitive to blue, some to green, and some to red parts of the spectrum. But studies of the bipolar and ganglion neurons suggest that messages from cones are transmitted to the brain and relayed by the thalamus to the occipital lobe in an opponent-process fashion (DeValois & Jacobs, 1984). Some opponent-process cells that transmit messages to the visual centers in the brain are excited ("turned on") by green light but inhibited ("turned off") by red light. Others can be excited by red light but are inhibited by green light. A second set of opponent-process cells responds in an opposite manner to blue and yellow. A third set responds in an opposite manner to light and dark.

A neural rebound effect apparently helps explain the occurrence of afterimages. That is, a green-sensitive ganglion that had been excited by green light for half a minute or so might switch briefly to inhibitory activity when the light is shut off. The effect would be to perceive red even though no red light is present.

These theoretical updates allow for the afterimage effects with the green, black, and yellow flag and are also consistent with Young's experiments in mixing lights of different colors.

Color Blindness

If you can discriminate among the colors of the visible spectrum, you have normal color vision and are labeled a **trichromat**. This means you

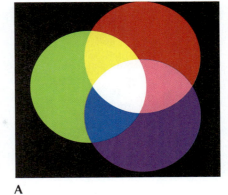

A

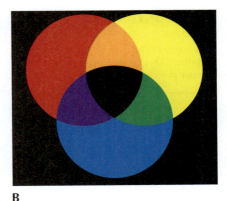

B

FIGURE SP.5

ADDITIVE AND SUBTRACTIVE COLOR MIXTURES PRODUCED BY LIGHTS AND PIGMENTS.

Thomas Young discovered that white light and all the colors of the spectrum could be produced by adding combinations of lights of red, green, and violet-blue and varying their intensities (see part A). Part B shows subtractive color mixtures, which are formed by mixing pigments, not light.

TRICHROMAT A person with normal color vision.

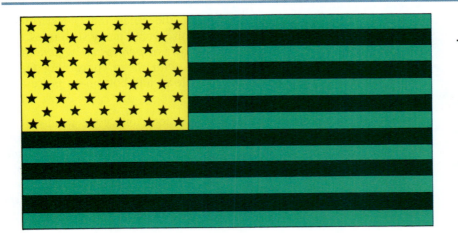

FIGURE SP.6

THREE CHEERS FOR THE . . . GREEN, BLACK, AND YELLOW?

Don't be concerned. We can readily restore Old Glory to its familiar hues. Place a sheet of white paper beneath the book, and stare at the center of the flag for 30 seconds. Then remove the book. The afterimage on the paper beneath will look familiar.

FIGURE SP.7
<small>Closure.</small>
Meaningless splotches of ink or a horse and rider? This figure illustrates the Gestalt principle of closure.

are sensitive to red-green, blue-yellow, and light-dark. People who are totally color blind, called **monochromats,** are sensitive only to lightness and darkness. Total color blindness is rare. Fully color blind individuals see the world as trichromats would on a black-and-white TV set or in a black-and-white movie.

Partial color blindness is more common than total color blindness. Partial color blindness is a sex-linked trait that affects mostly males and impairs the functioning of cones that are sensitive to red or green. People with this problem are called **dichromats,** and they find it difficult to tell red and green apart. For this reason, a dichromat might put on one red sock and one green sock, but would not mix red and blue socks. Monochromats might put on socks of any color. They would not notice a difference as long as the socks' colors did not differ in brightness.

VISUAL PERCEPTION

Perception is the process by which we organize or make sense of our sensory impressions. Although visual sensations are caused by electromagnetic energy, visual perception also relies on our knowledge, expectations, and motivations. Whereas sensation may be thought of as a mechanical process, perception is an active process through which we interpret the world around us.

For example, just what do you see in Figure SP.7? Do you see random splotches of ink or a rider on horseback? If you perceive a horse and rider, it is not just because of the visual sensations provided by the drawing. Each of the blobs is meaningless in and of itself, and the pattern they form is also less than clear. Despite the lack of clarity, however, you may still perceive a horse and rider. Why? The answer has something to do with your general knowledge and your desire to fit incoming bits and pieces of information into familiar patterns.

In the case of the horse and rider, your integration of disconnected pieces of information into a meaningful whole also reflects what Gestalt psychologists refer to as the principle of **closure,** or the tendency to perceive a complete or whole figure even when there are gaps in the sensory input. Put another way, in perception the whole can be very much more than the mere sum of the parts. A collection of parts can be meaningless. It is their configuration that matters.

Perceptual Organization

Earlier in the century, Gestalt psychologists noted certain consistencies in the way we integrate bits and pieces of sensory stimulation into meaningful wholes. They attempted to identify the rules that govern these processes. Max Wertheimer, in particular, discovered many such rules. As a group, these rules are referred to as the laws of *perceptual organization.* We examine several of them, beginning with those concerning figure-ground perception. Then we consider top-down and bottom-up processing.

FIGURE-GROUND PERCEPTION If you look out your window, you may see people, buildings, cars, and streets, or perhaps grass, trees, birds, and clouds. All these objects tend to be perceived as figures against backgrounds. Cars seen against the background of the street are easier to pick out than cars seen piled on top of each other in a junkyard. Birds seen against the sky are more likely to be perceived than birds seen "in the bush."

MONOCHROMAT A person who is sensitive to black and white only and hence color blind.

DICHROMAT A person who is insensitive to the colors of red and green and hence partially color blind.

CLOSURE The tendency to perceive a broken figure as complete or whole.

The vase in Figure SP.8 is one of psychologists' favorite illustrations of figure-ground relationships. The figure-ground relationship in part A of the figure is ambiguous. There are no cues that suggest which area must be the figure. For this reason, our perception may shift from seeing the vase as the figure to seeing two profiles as the figure. There is no such problem in part B. Because it seems that a vase has been brought forward against a colored ground, we are more likely to perceive the vase than the profiles. In part C, we are more likely to perceive the profiles than the vase because the profiles are whole and the vase is broken against the background. Of course, if we wish to, we can still perceive the vase in part C, because experience has shown us where it is. Why not have some fun with friends by covering up parts B and C and asking them what they see? (They'll catch on quickly if they can see all three drawings at once.)

OTHER GESTALT RULES FOR ORGANIZATION In addition to the law of closure, Gestalt psychologists have noted that our perceptions are guided by rules or laws of *proximity, similarity, continuity,* and *common fate*.

Without reading further, describe part A of Figure SP.9. Did you say it consists of six lines or of three groups of two parallel lines? If you said three sets of lines, you were influenced by the **proximity,** or nearness, of some of the lines. There is no other reason for perceiving them in pairs or subgroups: All of the lines are parallel and of equal length.

Now describe part B of the figure. Did you perceive the figure as a 6×6 grid, or as three columns of x's and three columns of o's? According to the law of **similarity,** we perceive similar objects as belonging together. For this reason, you may have been more likely to describe part B in terms of columns than in terms of rows or a grid.

What about part C? Is it a circle with two lines stemming from it, or is it a (broken) line that goes through a circle? If you saw it as a single (broken) line, you were probably organizing your perceptions according to the rule of **continuity.** That is, we perceive a series of points or a broken line as having unity.

According to the law of **common fate,** elements seen moving together are perceived as belonging together. A group of people running in the same direction appear unified in purpose. Birds that flock together seem to be of a feather. (Did I get that right?)

Part D of Figure SP.9 provides another example of the law of closure. The arcs tend to be perceived as a circle (or circle with gaps) rather than as just a series of arcs.

TOP-DOWN VERSUS BOTTOM-UP PROCESSING Imagine that you are trying to put together a thousand-piece puzzle—a task I usually avoid,

PROXIMITY Nearness. The perceptual tendency to group together objects that are near one another.

SIMILARITY The perceptual tendency to group together objects that are similar in appearance.

CONTINUITY The tendency to perceive a series of points or lines as having unity.

COMMON FATE The tendency to perceive elements that move together as belonging together.

A

B

C

FIGURE SP.8
THE RUBIN VASE.
A favorite drawing used by psychologists to demonstrate figure-ground perception. Part A is ambiguous, with neither the vase nor the profiles clearly the figure or the ground. In part B, the vase is the figure; in part C, the profiles are.

FIGURE SP.9
SOME GESTALT LAWS OF
PERCEPTUAL ORGANIZATION.
These drawings illustrate the Gestalt laws
of proximity, similarity, continuity, and
closure.

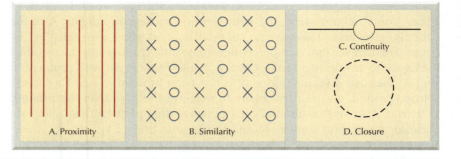

A. Proximity   B. Similarity   C. Continuity   D. Closure

despite the cajoling of my children. Now imagine that you are trying to accomplish it after someone has walked off with the box that contained the pieces—you know, the box showing the picture formed by the completed puzzle.

When you have the box—when you know what the "big picture" or pattern looks like—cognitive psychologists refer to the task of assembling the pieces as **top-down processing.** The "top" of the visual system refers to the image of the pattern in the brain, and the top-down strategy for putting the puzzle together implies that you use the pattern to guide subordinate perceptual motor tasks such as hunting for particular pieces. Without knowledge of the pattern, the assembly process is referred to as **bottom-up processing.** You begin with bits and pieces of information and become aware of the pattern formed by the assembled pieces only after you have worked at it for a while.

Perception of Movement

Moving objects—whether they are other people, animals, cars, or boulders plummeting down a hillside—are vital sources of sensory information. Moving objects capture the attention of even newborn infants.

To understand how we perceive movement, recall what it is like to be on a train that has begun to pull out of the station while the train on the adjacent track remains stationary. If your own train does not lurch as it accelerates, you might think at first that the other train is moving. Or you might not be certain whether your train is moving forward or the other train is moving backward.

The visual perception of movement is based on change of position relative to other objects. To early scientists, whose only tool for visual observation was the naked eye, it seemed logical that the sun circled the earth. You have to be able to imagine the movement of the earth around the sun as seen from a theoretical point in outer space—you cannot observe it directly.

How, then, do you determine which train is moving when your train is pulling out of the station (or the other train is pulling in)? One way is to look for objects that you know are stable, such as platform columns, houses, signs, or trees. If you are stationary in relation to them, your train is not moving. Observing people walking on the station platform may not provide the answer, however, because they are also changing their position relative to stationary objects. You might also try to sense the motion of the train in your body. You know from experience how to do these things quite well, although it may be difficult to find words to explain them.

We have been considering the perception of real movement. Psychologists have also studied several types of apparent movement, or **illusions** of movement. These include *stroboscopic motion* and the *phi phenomenon.*

TOP-DOWN PROCESSING The use of contextual information or knowledge of a pattern in order to organize parts of the pattern.

BOTTOM-UP PROCESSING The organization of the parts of a pattern to recognize, or form an image of, the pattern they compose.

ILLUSIONS Sensations that give rise to misperceptions.

FIGURE SP.10
STROBOSCOPIC MOTION.

In a motion picture, viewing a series of stationary images at the rate of about 16 to 22 frames per second provides an illusion of movement termed *stroboscopic motion.*

Stroboscopic motion makes motion pictures possible. In **stroboscopic motion,** the illusion of movement is provided by the presentation of a rapid progression of images of stationary objects. So-called motion pictures do not really consist of images that move. Rather, the audience is shown 16 to 22 pictures, or *frames,* per second. Each is slightly different from the one before (see Figure SP.10). Showing the frames in rapid succession provides the illusion of movement.

At the rate of at least 16 frames per second, the so-called motion in a film seems smooth and natural. With fewer than 16 or so frames per second, the movement looks jumpy and unnatural. That is why slow motion is achieved by filming perhaps 100 or more frames per second. When they are played back at about 22 frames per second, the movement seems slowed down, yet still smooth and natural.

Have you seen news headlines spelled out in lights that rapidly wrap around a building? Have you seen an electronic scoreboard in a baseball or football stadium? When the home team scores, some scoreboards suggest explosions of fireworks. What actually happens is that a row of lights is switched on and then off. As the first row is switched off, a second row is switched on, and so on, for dozens, perhaps hundreds of rows. When the switching occurs rapidly, the **phi phenomenon** occurs: The on-off process is perceived as movement (Figure SP.11).

Like stroboscopic motion, the phi phenomenon is an example of apparent motion. Both appear to occur because of the law of continuity. We tend to perceive a series of points as having unity, so each series of lights (points) is perceived as a moving line.

FIGURE SP.11
THE PHI PHENOMENON.

The phi phenomenon is an illusion of movement produced by lights blinking on and off in sequence, as with this New York Stock Exchange electronic "ticker."

Depth Perception

Think of the problems you might have if you could not judge depth or distance. You might bump into other people, believing them to be farther away than they really are. An outfielder might not be able to judge whether to run toward the infield or the fence to catch a fly ball. You might give your front bumper a workout in stop-and-go traffic. Fortunately, both *monocular and binocular cues* help us perceive the distance of objects.

MONOCULAR CUES Now that you have considered how difficult it would be to navigate through life without depth perception, ponder the problems of the artist who attempts to portray three-dimensional objects on a two-dimensional surface. Artists use **monocular cues**—also termed pictorial cues—to create an illusion of depth. These are cues that can be

STROBOSCOPIC MOTION A visual illusion in which the perception of motion is generated by a series of stationary images that are presented in rapid succession.

PHI PHENOMENON The perception of movement as a result of sequential presentation of visual stimuli.

MONOCULAR CUES Stimuli suggestive of depth that can be perceived with only one eye.

FRONTISPIECE TO KERBY.

FIGURE SP.12
WHAT IS WRONG WITH THESE PICTURES?

In *Waterfall,* to the left, how does Dutch artist M. C. Escher suggest that fallen water flows back upward, only to fall again? In *False Perspective,* to the right, how does English artist William Hogarth use monocular cues for depth perception to deceive the viewer?

---

perceived by one eye (*mono-* means "one"). They include perspective, relative size, clearness, interposition, shadows, and texture gradient, and cause certain objects to appear more distant from the viewer than others.

Distant objects stimulate smaller areas on the retina than nearby ones. The amount of sensory input from them is smaller, even though they may be the same size. The distances between far-off objects also appear to be smaller than equivalent distances between nearby objects. For this reason, the phenomenon known as **perspective** occurs. That is, we tend to perceive parallel lines as coming closer together, or converging, as they recede from us. However, as we will see when we discuss *size constancy,* experience teaches us that distant objects that look small are larger when they are close. In this way, their relative size also becomes a cue to their distance.

The two engravings in Figure SP.12 represent impossible scenes in which the artists use principles of perspective to fool the viewer. In the one on the left, *Waterfall,* note that the water appears to be flowing away from the viewer in a zigzag because the stream gradually becomes narrower (that is, lines we assume to be parallel are shown to be converging) and the stone sides of the aqueduct appear to be stepping down. However, given that the water arrives at the top of the fall, it must actually be flowing upward somehow. However, the spot from which it falls is no farther from the viewer than the collection point from which it appears to (but does not) begin its flow backward.

Artists normally use *relative size*—the fact that distant objects look smaller than nearby objects of the same size—to suggest depth in their

PERSPECTIVE A monocular cue for depth based on the convergence (coming together) of parallel lines as they recede into the distance.

works. The paradoxes in the engraving on the right, *False Perspective,* are made possible because more distant objects are *not* necessarily depicted as being smaller than nearby objects. Thus, what at first seems to be background suddenly becomes foreground, and vice versa.

The *clearness* of an object also suggests its distance from us. Experience teaches that we sense more details of nearby objects. For this reason, artists can suggest that objects are closer to the viewer by depicting them in greater detail. Note that the "distant" hill in the Hogarth engraving (Figure SP.12) is given less detail than the nearby plants at the bottom of the picture. Our perceptions are mocked when a man "on" the distant hill in the background is shown conversing with a woman leaning out a window in the middle ground.

We also learn that nearby objects can block our view of more-distant objects. Overlapping, or **interposition,** is the placing of one object in front of another. Experience teaches us that partly covered objects are farther away than the objects that obscure them (Figure SP.13). In the Hogarth engraving (Figure SP.12), which looks closer: the trees in the background (background?) or the moon sign hanging from the building (or is it buildings?) to the right? How does the artist use interposition to confound the viewer?

Additional information about depth is provided by **shadowing** and is based on the fact that opaque objects block light and produce shadows. Shadows and highlights give us information about an object's three-dimensional shape and its relationship to the source of light. For example, the left part of Figure SP.14 is perceived as a two-dimensional circle, but the right part tends to be perceived as a three-dimensional sphere because of the highlight on its surface and the shadow underneath. In the "sphere," the highlighted central area is perceived as being closest to us, with the surface receding to the edges.

Another monocular cue is **texture gradient.** (A gradient is a progressive change.) Closer objects are perceived as having rougher textures. In the Hogarth engraving (Figure SP.12), the building just behind the large fisherman's head has a rougher texture and therefore seems to be closer than the building with the window from which the woman is leaning. Our surprise is heightened when the moon sign is seen as hanging from both buildings.

MOTION CUES Motion cues are another kind of monocular cue. If you have ever driven in the country, you have probably noticed that distant objects such as mountains and stars appear to move along with you. Objects at an intermediate distance seem to be stationary, but nearby objects such as roadside markers, rocks, and trees seem to go by quite rapidly. The tendency of objects to seem to move backward or forward as a function of their distance is known as **motion parallax.** We learn to perceive objects that appear to move with us as being at greater distances.

Earlier we noted that nearby objects cause the lens of the eye to accommodate or bend more in order to bring them into focus. The sensations of tension in the eye muscles also provide a monocular cue to depth, especially when we are within about 4 feet of the objects.

BINOCULAR CUES **Binocular cues,** or cues that involve both eyes, also help us perceive depth. Two binocular cues are *retinal disparity* and *convergence.*

Try an experiment. Hold your index finger at arm's length. Now, gradually bring it closer until it almost touches your nose. If you keep your eyes relaxed as you do so, you will see two fingers. An image of the finger will be projected onto the retina of each eye, and each image will be slightly different because the finger will be seen from different angles.

FIGURE SP.13
THE EFFECTS OF INTERPOSITION.
The four circles are all the same size. Which circles seem closer? The complete circles or the circles with chunks bitten out of them?

FIGURE SP.14
SHADOWING AS A CUE FOR DEPTH.
Shadowing makes the circle on the right look three dimensional.

INTERPOSITION A monocular cue for depth based on the fact that a nearby object obscures a more distant object behind it.

SHADOWING A monocular cue for depth based on the fact that opaque objects block light and produce shadows.

TEXTURE GRADIENT A monocular cue for depth based on the perception that closer objects appear to have rougher (more detailed) surfaces.

MOTION PARALLAX A monocular cue for depth based on the perception that nearby objects appear to move more rapidly in relation to our own motion.

BINOCULAR CUES Stimuli suggestive of depth that involve simultaneous perception by both eyes.

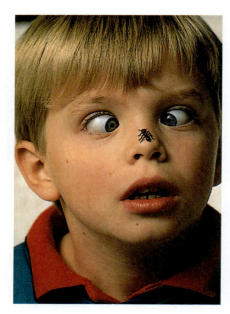

FIGURE SP.15

RETINAL DISPARITY AND CONVERGENCE AS CUES FOR DEPTH.

As an object nears your eyes, you begin to see two images of it because of retinal disparity. To maintain perception of a single image, your eyes must converge on the object.

The difference between the projected images is referred to as **retinal disparity** and serves as a binocular cue for depth perception (see Figure SP.15). Note that the closer your finger comes, the farther apart the "two fingers" appear to be. Closer objects have greater retinal disparity.

If we try to maintain a single image of the nearing finger, our eyes must turn inward, or converge on it, making us cross-eyed. **Convergence** causes feelings of tension in the eye muscles and provides another binocular cue for depth. (After convergence occurs, try looking at the finger first with one eye closed, then the other. You will readily see how different the images are in each eye.) The binocular cues of retinal disparity and convergence are strongest when objects are close.

Perceptual Constancies

The world is a constantly shifting display of visual sensations. Think how confusing it would be if we did not perceive a doorway to be the same doorway when seen from 6 feet away as when seen from 4 feet away. As we neared it, we might think it was larger than the door we were seeking, and become lost. Or consider the problems of the pet owner who recognizes his dog from the side but not from above because its shape is different when seen from above. Fortunately, these problems tend not to occur—at least with familiar objects—because perceptual constancies enable us to recognize objects even when their apparent shape or size differs.

SIZE CONSTANCY We may say that people "look like ants" when viewed from the top of a tall building, but we know they remain people even if the details of their forms are lost in the distance. We can thus say that we *perceive* people to be the same size, even when viewed from different distances.

The image of a dog seen from 20 feet away occupies about the same amount of space on your retina as an inch-long insect crawling on your hand. Yet you do not perceive the dog to be as small as the insect. Through your visual experiences you have acquired **size constancy**—that is, the tendency to perceive an object as being the same size even though the size of its image on your retina varies as a function of its distance. Experience teaches us about perspective—that the same object seen at a distance appears to be smaller than when it is nearby.

COLOR CONSTANCY We also have **color constancy**—the tendency to perceive objects as retaining their color even though lighting conditions may alter their appearance. Your bright yellow car may edge toward gray as the hours wend their way through twilight to nighttime. But when you finally locate the car in the parking lot, you may still think of it as yellow. You expect to find a yellow car and still judge it to be "more yellow" than the (faded) red and green cars on either side of it.

BRIGHTNESS CONSTANCY Similar to color constancy is **brightness constancy**. Consider Figure SP. 16. The orange squares within the blue squares are equally bright, yet the one within the dark blue square is perceived as brighter. Why? Again, consider the role of experience. If it were nighttime, we would expect orange to fade to gray. The fact that the orange within the dark square stimulates the eye with equal intensity suggests that it must be very much brighter than the orange within the lighter square.

SHAPE CONSTANCY We also perceive objects as maintaining their shape, even if we look at them from different angles so that the shape of

RETINAL DISPARITY A binocular cue for depth based on the difference in the image cast by an object on the retinas of the eyes as the object moves closer or farther away.

CONVERGENCE A binocular cue for depth based on the inward movement of the eyes as they attempt to focus on an object that is drawing nearer.

SIZE CONSTANCY The tendency to perceive an object as being the same size even as the size of its retinal image changes according to the object's distance.

COLOR CONSTANCY The tendency to perceive an object as being the same color even though lighting conditions change its appearance.

BRIGHTNESS CONSTANCY The tendency to perceive an object as being just as bright even though lighting conditions change its intensity.

their image on the retina changes dramatically. This ability is called **shape constancy.** You perceive the top of a coffee cup or a glass to be a circle even though it is a circle only when seen from above. When seen from an angle, it is an ellipse. When the cup or glass is seen on edge, its retinal image is the same as that of a straight line. So why do you still describe the rim of the cup or glass as a circle? Perhaps for two reasons: First, experience has taught you that the cup will look circular when seen from above. Second, you may have labeled the cup as circular or round. Experience and labels help make the world a stable place. Can you imagine the chaos that would prevail if we described objects as they appear as they stimulate our sensory organs with each changing moment, rather than according to stable conditions?

In another example, a door is a rectangle only when viewed straight on (Figure SP.17). When we move to the side or open it, the left or right edge comes closer and appears to be larger, changing the retinal image to a trapezoid. Yet we continue to think of doors as rectangles.

Visual Illusions

The principles of perceptual organization make it possible for our eyes to "play tricks on us." Psychologists, like magicians, enjoy pulling a rabbit out of a hat now and then. Let me demonstrate how the perceptual constancies trick the eye through *visual illusions.*

The Hering-Helmholtz and Müller-Lyer illusions (Figure SP.18, part A) are named after the people who devised them. In the Hering-Helmholtz illusion, the horizontal lines are straight and parallel. However, the radiating lines cause them to appear to be bent outward near the center. The two lines in the Müller-Lyer illusion are the same length, but the line on the left, with its reversed arrowheads, looks longer.

Let us try to explain these illusions. Because of our experience and lifelong use of perceptual cues, we tend to perceive the Hering-Helmholtz drawing as three dimensional. Because of our tendency to perceive bits of sensory information as figures against grounds, we perceive the white area in the center as a circle in front of a series of radiating lines, all of which lie in front of a white ground. Next, because of our experience with perspective, we perceive the radiating lines as parallel. We perceive the two horizontal lines as intersecting the "receding" lines, and we know that

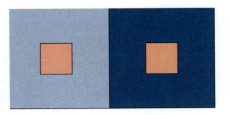

FIGURE SP.16
BRIGHTNESS CONSTANCY.
The orange squares within the blue squares are equally bright, yet the orange within the dark blue square is perceived as brighter. Why?

SHAPE CONSTANCY The tendency to perceive an object as the same shape although the retinal image varies in shape as it rotates.

FIGURE SP.17
SHAPE CONSTANCY.
When closed, this door is a rectangle. When open, the retinal image is trapezoidal. But because of shape constancy, we still perceive it as rectangular.

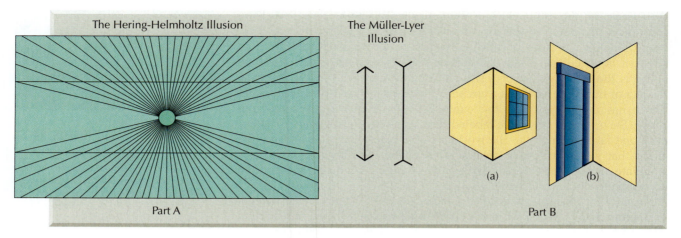

FIGURE SP.18
THE HERING-HELMHOLTZ AND MÜLLER-LYER ILLUSIONS.
In the Hering-Helmholtz illusion, are the horizontal lines straight or curved? In the Müller-Lyer illusion, are the vertical lines equal in length?

they would have to appear bent out at the center if they were to be equidistant at all points from the center of the circle.

Experience probably compels us to perceive the vertical lines in the Müller-Lyer illusion as the corners of a room as seen from inside a house, at left, and from outside a house, at right (see Figure SP.18, part B). In such an example, the reverse arrowheads to the left are lines where the walls meet the ceiling and the floor. We perceive such lines as extending toward us. They push the corner away from us. The arrowheads to the right are lines where exterior walls meet the roof and foundation. We perceive them as receding from us. They push the corner toward us. The vertical line to the left therefore is perceived as being farther away. Because both vertical lines stimulate equal expanses across the retina, the principle of size constancy encourages us to perceive the line to the left as longer.

Figure SP.19 is known as the Ponzo illusion. In this illusion, the two horizontal lines are the same length. However, do you perceive the top line as longer? The rule of size constancy may give us some insight into this illusion as well. Perhaps the converging lines again strike us as parallel lines receding into the distance, like the train tracks in the drawing in Figure SP-19. If so, we assume from experience that the horizontal line at the top is farther down the track—that is, farther away from us. And again, the rule of size constancy tells us that if two objects appear to be the same size and one is farther away, the farther object must be larger. So we perceive the top line as larger.

FIGURE SP.19
THE PONZO ILLUSION.

The horizontal lines in this drawing are equal in length, but the top line is perceived as longer. Can you use the principle of size constancy to explain why?

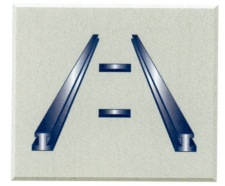

HEARING

Consider the advertising slogan for the science fiction film Alien: "In space, no one can hear you scream." It's true. Space is an almost perfect vacuum. Hearing requires a medium through which sound can travel, such as air or water.

Sound, or *auditory* stimulation, travels through the air like waves. Sound is caused by changes in air pressure that result from vibrations. These vibrations, in turn, can be created by a tuning fork, your vocal cords, guitar strings, or the slam of a book thrown down on a desk.

Figure SP.20 suggests the way in which a tuning fork creates sound waves. During a vibration back and forth, the right prong of the tuning fork moves to the right. In so doing, it pushes together, or compresses, the molecules of air immediately to the right. Then the prong moves back to the left, and the air molecules to the right expand. By vibrating back and forth, the tuning fork actually sends air waves in many directions. A cycle of compression and expansion is one wave of sound. Sound waves can occur many times in one second. The human ear is sensitive to sound waves that vary in frequency from 20 to 20,000 cycles per second.

Pitch and Loudness

Pitch and loudness are two psychological dimensions of sound. The pitch of a sound is determined by its frequency, or the number of cycles per second as expressed in the unit **Hertz** (Hz). One cycle per second is one Hz. The greater the number of cycles per second (Hz), the higher the pitch of the sound. The pitch of women's voices is usually higher than that of men's voices because women's vocal cords are usually shorter and therefore vibrate at a greater frequency. The strings of a violin are shorter than those of a viola or bass viol. They vibrate at greater frequencies, and we perceive them as higher in pitch. Pitch detectors in the brain allow us to tell the difference (Blakeslee, 1995).

The loudness of a sound is determined by the height, or amplitude, of sound waves. The higher the amplitude of the wave, the louder the sound. Frequency and amplitude are independent. Both high-and low-pitched sounds can be either high or low in loudness.

The loudness of a sound is usually expressed in **decibels** *(dB)*. Zero dB is equivalent to the threshold of hearing—the lowest sound that the typical person can hear. How loud is that? It's about as loud as the ticking of a watch 20 feet away in a very quiet room.

The decibel equivalents of many familiar sounds are shown in Figure SP.21. Twenty dB is equivalent in loudness to a whisper at 5 feet. Thirty dB is roughly the limit of loudness at which your librarian would like to keep your college library. You may suffer hearing damage if you are exposed to sounds of 85 to 90 dB for very long periods.

Now let us turn our attention to the marvelous instrument that senses all these different "vibes": the human ear.

The Ear: The Better to Hear You With

The human ear is good for lots of things—including catching dust, combing your hair around, hanging jewelry from, and nibbling. It is also admirably suited for sensing sounds. The ear is shaped and structured to capture sound waves, vibrate in sympathy with them, and transmit them to centers in the brain. In this way, you not only hear something, you can also figure out what it is. The ear has three parts: the outer ear, middle ear, and inner ear (see Figure SP.22).

THE OUTER EAR The outer ear is shaped to funnel sound waves to the **eardrum,** a thin membrane that vibrates in response to sound waves and thereby transmits them to the middle and inner ears.

THE MIDDLE EAR The middle ear contains the eardrum and three small bones—the hammer, the anvil, and the stirrup—which also transmit sound by vibrating. These bones were given their names (actually the Latin *malleus, incus,* and *stapes* [pronounced STAY-peas], which translate as

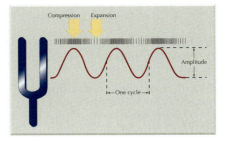

FIGURE SP.20
CREATION OF SOUND WAVES.
The vibration of the prongs of a tuning fork alternately compresses and expands air molecules, sending forth waves of sound.

HERTZ A unit expressing the frequency of sound waves. One Hertz, or *1 Hz,* equals one cycle per second.

DECIBEL A unit expressing the loudness of a sound. Abbreviated *dB.*

EARDRUM A thin membrane that vibrates in response to sound waves, transmitting the waves to the middle and inner ears.

FIGURE SP.21
DECIBEL RATINGS OF FAMILIAR SOUNDS.

Zero dB is the threshold of hearing. You may suffer hearing loss if you incur prolonged exposure to sounds of 85 to 90 dB.

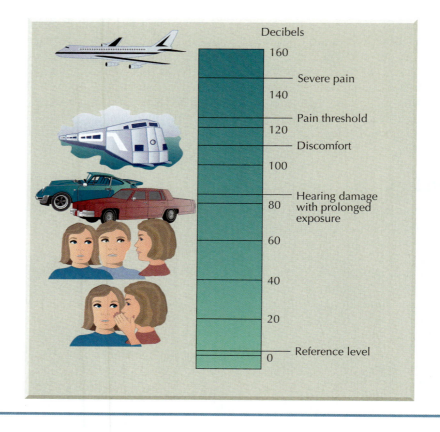

Decibels

160

140 — Severe pain

120 — Pain threshold

100 — Discomfort

80 — Hearing damage with prolonged exposure

60

40

20

0 — Reference level

hammer, anvil, and stirrup) because of their shapes. The middle ear functions as an amplifier: It increases the pressure of the air entering the ear.

The stirrup is attached to another vibrating membrane, the *oval window*. The *round* window shown in Figure SP.22 balances the pressure in the inner ear. It pushes outward when the oval window pushes in, and it is pulled inward when the oval window vibrates outward.

THE INNER EAR The oval window transmits vibrations into the inner ear, the bony tube called the **cochlea** (from the Greek for "snail"). The cochlea, which is shaped like a snail shell, contains two longitudinal membranes that divide it into three fluid-filled chambers. One of the membranes that lies coiled within the cochlea is called the **basilar membrane.** Vibrations in the fluids within the chambers of the inner ear press against the basilar membrane.

The **organ of Corti,** sometimes referred to as the "command post" of hearing, is attached to the basilar membrane. Hair cells (receptor cells that project like hair from the organ of Corti) "dance" in response to the vibrations of the basilar membrane. Their up-and-down movements generate neural impulses, which are transmitted to the brain via the 31,000 neurons that form the **auditory nerve.** Auditory input is then projected onto the hearing areas of the temporal lobes of the cerebral cortex.

Locating Sounds

How do you balance the loudness of a stereo set? You sit between the speakers and adjust the volume until the sound seems to be equally loud in each ear. If the sound to the right is louder, the musical instruments are perceived as being toward the right rather than straight ahead.

COCHLEA The inner ear; the bony tube that contains the basilar membrane and the organ of Corti.

BASILAR MEMBRANE A membrane that lies coiled within the cochlea.

ORGAN OF CORTI The receptor for hearing that lies on the basilar membrane in the cochlea.

AUDITORY NERVE The axon bundle that transmits neural impulses from the organ of Corti to the brain.

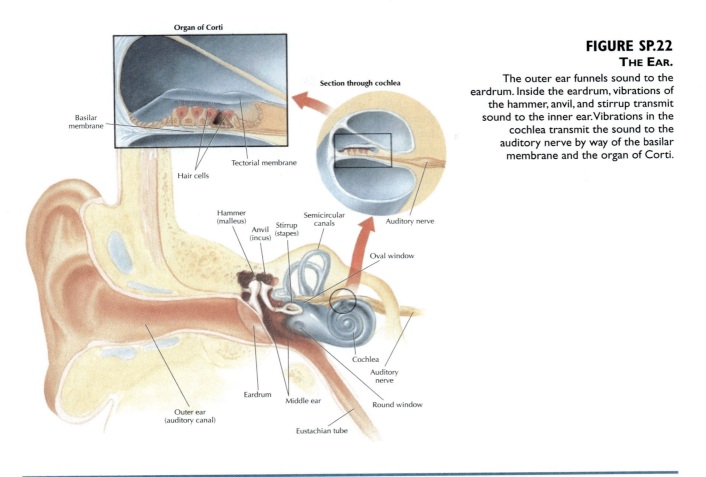

Organ of Corti

Section through cochlea

Basilar membrane

Tectorial membrane

Hair cells

Hammer (malleus)

Anvil (incus)

Stirrup (stapes)

Semicircular canals

Auditory nerve

Oval window

Cochlea

Auditory nerve

Eardrum

Middle ear

Round window

Outer ear (auditory canal)

Eustachian tube

FIGURE SP.22
THE EAR.
The outer ear funnels sound to the eardrum. Inside the eardrum, vibrations of the hammer, anvil, and stirrup transmit sound to the inner ear. Vibrations in the cochlea transmit the sound to the auditory nerve by way of the basilar membrane and the organ of Corti.

There is a resemblance between balancing a stereo set and locating sounds. A sound that is louder in the right ear is perceived as coming from the right. A sound coming from the right also reaches the right ear first. Both loudness and the sequence in which the sounds reach the ears provide directional cues.

But it may not be easy to locate a sound coming from directly in front or in back of you or overhead. Such sounds are equally distant from each ear and equally loud. So what do we do? Simple—usually we turn our head slightly to determine in which ear the sound increases. If you turn your head a few degrees to the right and the loudness increases in your left ear, the sound must be coming from in front of you. Of course, we also use vision and general knowledge in locating the source of sounds. If you hear the roar of jet engines, most of the time you can bet that the airplane is overhead.

Perception of Loudness and Pitch

Sounds are heard because they cause vibration in parts of the ear and information about these vibrations is transmitted to the brain. But what determines the loudness and pitch of our perceptions of these sounds?

The loudness and pitch of sounds appear to be related to the number of receptor neurons on the organ of Corti that fire and how often they fire. Psychologists generally agree that sounds are perceived as louder when more of these sensory neurons fire.

It takes two processes to explain perception of color: trichromatic theory and opponent-process theory. Similarly, it takes at least two processes to explain pitch perception—that is, perception of sound waves with frequencies that vary from 20 to 20,000 cycles per second: *place theory* and *frequency theory*.

Hermann von Helmholtz helped develop the place theory of pitch discrimination as well as the Young-Helmholtz (trichromatic) theory of color vision. **Place theory** holds that the pitch of a sound is sensed according to the place along the basilar membrane that vibrates in response to it. In classic research with guinea pigs and cadavers that led to the award of a Nobel prize, Georg von Békésy (1957) found evidence for place theory: He determined that receptors at different sites along the membrane fire in response to tones of differing frequencies. Receptor neurons appear to be lined up along the basilar membrane like piano keys (Azar, 1996). The higher the pitch of a sound, the closer the responsive neurons lie to the oval window. However, place theory only appears to apply to sounds higher in pitch than 4,000 Hz, and people sense pitches as low as 20 Hz.

Frequency theory accounts for pitches at the lower end of the range. **Frequency theory** notes that pitch perception depends on the stimulation of neural impulses that match the frequency of the sound waves. That is, in response to low pitches—pitches of about 20 to 1,000 cycles per second—hair cells on the basilar membrane fire at the same frequencies as the sound waves. However, neurons cannot fire more than 1,000 times per second. Therefore, frequency theory can only account for perception of pitches between 20 and 1,000 cycles per second. In actuality, frequency theory only appears to account for pitch perception between 20 and a few hundred cycles per second.

I noted that it takes at least two processes to explain how people perceive pitch. The *volley principle* is the third, and it accounts for pitch discrimination between a few hundred and 4,000 cycles per second (Matlin & Foley, 1995). In response to sound waves of these frequencies, groups of neurons take turns firing, in the way that one row of soldiers used to fire rifles while another row knelt to reload. Alternating firing—that is, volleying—appears to transmit sensory information about pitches in the intermediate range.

Unfortunately, not everyone perceives sound, and many of us do not perceive sounds of certain frequencies. Let us now turn our attention to deafness.

Deafness

An estimated 28 million Americans have impaired hearing. Two million of them are deaf (Nadol, 1993). They are thus deprived of a key source of information about the world around them. In recent years, however, society has made greater efforts to bring them into the mainstream of sensory experience. People are usually on hand to convert political and other speeches into hand signs (such as those of American Sign Language) for hearing-impaired members of the audience. Many TV shows are closed captioned so that they can be understood by people with hearing problems. Special decoders render the captions visible.

There are two major types of deafness: conductive deafness and sensorineural deafness. **Conductive deafness** is a result of damage to the structures of the middle ear—either to the eardrum or to the three bones that conduct (and amplify) sound waves from the outer ear to the inner ear (Nadol, 1993). This is the type of hearing impairment often found among

PLACE THEORY The theory that the pitch of a sound is determined by the section of the basilar membrane that vibrates in response to the sound.

FREQUENCY THEORY The theory that the pitch of a sound is reflected in the frequency of the neural impulses that are generated in response to the sound.

CONDUCTIVE DEAFNESS The forms of deafness in which there is loss of conduction of sound through the middle ear.

PSYCHOLOGY IN A WORLD OF *Diversity*

THE SIGNS OF THE TIMES ARE CHANGING

As recently as 1990, a deaf person might make the sign meaning *Japanese person* by twisting the little finger next to the eye (see Figure SP.23). Today many people who use American Sign Language have discarded this sign because it refers to the stereotypical physical feature of slanted eyes. Instead, they are adopting Japanese people's own sign for themselves: They press the thumb and index finger of both hands together and then pull them apart to sculpt the outline of Japan in the air.

"In American Sign Language, politically incorrect terms are often a visual representation of the ugly metaphors we have about people," notes psycholinguist Elissa Newport (1994). As with the sign for *Japanese,* the signs for *Chinese* and *Korean,* which are made by forming the letters *C* and *K* around the eye, are also changing. There is also a new sign for *African American.* This population group was once indicated by flattening the nose. That sign was replaced by signs for the color black—the index finger either placed by the eyebrow or wiped across the forehead.

The current sign for *African American* is still centered on the nose, however, and therefore is being replaced by a sign that outlines Africa (see Figure SP. 24).

The old sign for *gay male* was an offensive swish of the wrist. Now it is more widely acceptable to simply spell out words like *homosexual, gay male,* or *lesbian* with the hands.

Politically correct changes in American Sign Language have thus far caught on mainly among highly educated deaf people in urban settings. It is taking longer for them to catch on in the wider deaf community and to appear in dictionaries of sign language. Nevertheless, the clear trend is for the deaf—who have been victims of stereotyping themselves—to learn how to avoid stereotyping others in sign language. ■

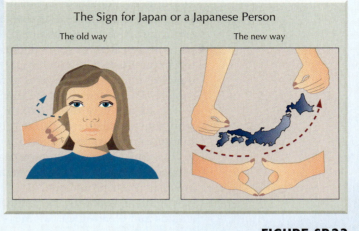

The Sign for Japan or a Japanese Person

The old way   The new way

FIGURE SP.23

OLD AND NEW SIGNS FOR JAPAN OR A JAPANESE PERSON IN AMERICAN SIGN LANGUAGE.

The old sign for Japanese is now considered offensive because it refers to the stereotypical physical feature of slanted eyes. The new sign outlines the island of Japan.

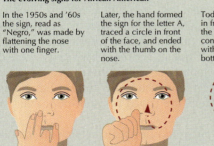

The evolving signs for African American

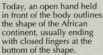

In the 1950s and '60s the sign, read as "Negro," was made by flattening the nose with one finger.

Later, the hand formed the sign for the letter A, traced a circle in front of the face, and ended with the thumb on the nose.

Today, an open hand held in front of the body outlines the shape of the African continent, usually ending with closed fingers at the bottom of the shape.

FIGURE SP.24

OLD AND NEW SIGNS FOR AFRICAN AMERICANS IN AMERICAN SIGN LANGUAGE.

The old signs for African Americans were considered offensive because they referred to the shape or location of the nose. The new sign outlines the African continent.

older people. People with conductive deafness often profit from hearing aids, which provide the amplification that the middle ear does not.

Sensorineural deafness usually stems from damage to the structures of the inner ear, most often the loss of hair cells, which will not regenerate. Sensorineural deafness can also stem from damage to the auditory nerve, for example, because of disease or because of acoustic trauma (prolonged exposure to very loud sounds). In sensorineural deafness, people tend to be more sensitive to some pitches than to others. In Hunter's notch, hearing impairment is limited to particular frequencies—in this case, the frequencies of the sound waves generated by a gun firing. Prolonged exposure to 85 dB can cause hearing loss. People who attend rock concerts, where sounds may reach 140 dB, risk damaging their ears, as do workers who run pneumatic drills or drive noisy vehicles. The ringing sensation that often follows exposure to loud sounds probably means that hair cells in the inner ear have been damaged. If you find yourself suddenly exposed to loud sounds, remember that your fingertips serve as good emergency ear protectors.

Cochlear implants, or "artificial ears," contain microphones that sense sounds and electronic equipment that transmits sounds past damaged hair cells to stimulate the auditory nerve directly. Such implants have helped many people with sensorineural deafness. However, they cannot assume the functions of damaged auditory nerves.

SMELL

Smell and taste are the chemical senses. In the cases of vision and hearing, physical energy strikes our sensory receptors. With smell and taste, we sample molecules of the substances being sensed.

You could say that we are underprivileged when it comes to the sense of smell. Dogs, for instance, devote about seven times as much of the cerebral cortex as we do to the sense of smell. Male dogs sniff in order to determine where the boundaries of other dogs' territories leave off and whether female dogs are sexually receptive. Some dogs even make a living sniffing out marijuana in closed packages and suitcases for law enforcement agencies.

Still, smell has an important role in human behavior. It makes a crucial contribution to the flavor of foods, for example (Bartoshuk & Beauchamp, 1994). If you did not have a sense of smell, an onion and an apple would taste the same to you! People's sense of smell may be deficient when we compare them to those of a dog, but we can detect the odor of 1 one millionth of a milligram of vanilla in a liter of air.

An *odor* is a sample of the substance being sensed. Odors are detected by sites on receptor neurons in the *olfactory membrane* high in each nostril. Receptor neurons fire when a few molecules of the substance in gaseous form come into contact with them. Their firing transmits information about odors to the brain via the **olfactory nerve.** That is how the substance is smelled.

It is unclear how many basic kinds of odors there are. In any event, olfactory receptors may respond to more than one kind of odor. Mixtures of smell sensations also help produce the broad range of odors that we can perceive.

The sense of smell adapts rapidly to odors, such that you lose awareness of them, even obnoxious ones. This might be fortunate if you are in a locker room or an outhouse. It might not be so fortunate if you are exposed to paint fumes or secondhand smoke because you may lose awareness of them while danger remains. One odor can mask another, which is how air fresheners work.

TRUTH OR FICTION REVISITED
It is true that onions and apples have the same taste (as sensed by taste buds). *Their flavors,* however, *which also reflect their odors and other qualities, are quite different.*

SENSORINEURAL DEAFNESS The forms of deafness that result from damage to hair cells or the auditory nerve.

OLFACTORY NERVE The nerve that transmits information concerning odors from olfactory receptors to the brain.

TASTE

Your cocker spaniel may jump at the chance to finish off your ice cream cone, but your Siamese cat may turn up her nose at the opportunity. Why? Dogs can perceive the taste quality of sweetness, as can pigs, but cats cannot.

There are four primary taste qualities: sweet, sour, salty, and bitter. The *flavor* of a food involves its taste but is more complex. Although apples and onions are similar in taste, their flavors differ greatly. After all, you wouldn't chomp into a nice cold onion on a warm day, would you? The flavor of a food depends on its odor, texture, and temperature as well as on its taste. If it were not for odor, heated tenderized shoe leather might pass for steak.

Taste is sensed through **taste cells**—receptor neurons located on **taste buds.** You have about 10,000 taste buds, most of which are located near the edges and back of your tongue. Taste buds tend to specialize a bit. Some, for example, are more responsive to sweetness, whereas others react to several tastes. Other taste receptors are found in the roof, sides, and back of the mouth, even in the throat.

We live in different taste worlds. Those of us with low sensitivity for the sweet taste may require twice the sugar to sweeten our food as others who are more sensitive to sweetness. Those of us who claim to enjoy very bitter foods may actually be taste blind to them. Sensitivities to different tastes apparently have a strong genetic component.

By eating hot foods and scraping your tongue, you regularly kill off many taste cells. But you need not be alarmed at this inadvertent oral aggression. Taste cells are the rabbits of the sense receptors. They reproduce rapidly enough to completely renew themselves about once a week.

Although older people often complain that their food has little or no "taste," they are more likely to experience a decline in the sense of smell. Because the flavor of a food represents both its tastes and its odors or aromas, older people experience loss in the *flavor* of their food. Older people often spice their food heavily to enhance its flavor.

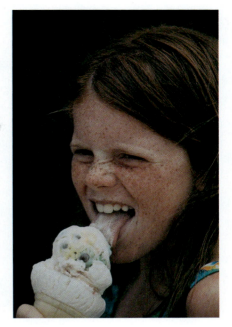

SENSATIONAL?
The flavors of foods are determined not only by their taste, but also by their odor, texture, and temperature.

THE SKIN SENSES

The skin discriminates among many kinds of sensations—touch, pressure, warmth, cold, and pain. We have distinct sensory receptors for pressure, temperature, and pain, but some nerve endings may receive more than one type of sensory input.

Touch and Pressure

Sensory receptors located around the roots of hair cells appear to fire when the surface of the skin is touched. You may have noticed that if you are trying to "get the feel of" a fabric or the texture of a friend's hair, you must move your hand over it. Otherwise the sensations quickly fade. If you pass your hand over the skin and then hold it still, again the sensations of touching will fade. This sort of "active touching" involves reception of information concerning not only touch per se but also pressure, temperature, and feedback from the muscles involved in movements of our hands.

Other structures beneath the skin are sensitive to pressure. Different parts of the body are more sensitive to touch and pressure than others. Psychophysicists use methods such as the **two-point threshold** to assess sensitivity to pressure. This method determines the smallest distance by

TASTE CELLS Receptor cells that are sensitive to taste.

TASTE BUDS The sensory organs for taste. They contain taste cells and are located on the tongue.

TWO-POINT THRESHOLD The least distance by which two rods touching the skin must be separated before the person reports there are two rods, not one, on 50% of occasions.

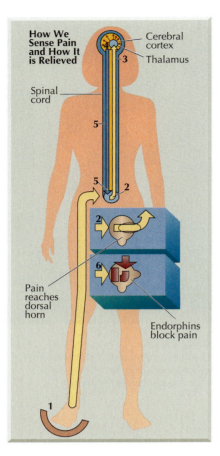

FIGURE SP.25
PERCEPTION OF PAIN.

Pain originates at the point of contact, and the pain message to the brain is initiated by the release of prostaglandins, bradykinin, and substance *P*.

How We Sense Pain and How It is Relieved
Cerebral cortex
Thalamus
Spinal cord
Pain reaches dorsal horn
Endorphins block pain

which two rods touching the skin must be separated before the (blindfolded) individual reports that there are two rods rather than one. With this method, psychophysicists have found that our fingertips, lips, noses, and cheeks are more sensitive than our shoulders, thighs, and calves. That is, the rods can be closer together but perceived as distinct when they touch the lips more than when they touch the shoulders. Why the difference in sensitivity? First, nerve endings are more densely packed in the fingertips and face than in other locations. Second, more sensory cortex is devoted to the perception of sensations in the fingertips and face.

The sense of pressure, like the sense of touch, undergoes rapid adaptation. For example, you may have undertaken several minutes of strategic movements to wind up with your hand on the arm or leg of your date, only to discover that adaptation to this delightful source of pressure reduces the sensation you experience.

Temperature

The receptors for temperature are neurons located just beneath the skin. When skin temperature increases, the receptors for warmth fire. Decreases in skin temperature cause the receptors for cold to fire.

Sensations of temperature are relative. When we are at normal body temperature, we might perceive another person's skin as warm. When we are feverish, though, the other person's skin might seem cool. We also adapt to differences in temperature. When we walk out of an air-conditioned house into the July sun, we feel intense heat at first. Then the sensations of heat tend to fade (although we may still be uncomfortable because of high humidity). Similarly, when we first enter a swimming pool, the water may seem cool or cold because it is below our body temperature. Yet after a few moments an 80° Fahrenheit pool may seem quite warm. In fact, we may chide a newcomer for not jumping right in.

Pain: The Often Unwanted Message

Headaches, backaches, toothaches—these are only a few of the types of pain that most of us encounter from time to time. Some of us also experience bouts of pain caused by arthritis, digestive disorders, cancer, or wounds.

Pain means something is wrong in the body. It is adaptive in the sense that it motivates us to do something about it. For some of us, however, chronic pain—pain that lasts once injuries or illnesses have cleared—saps our vitality and interferes with the pleasures of everyday life (Karoly & Ruehlman, 1996).

Pain originates at the point of contact, as with a stubbed toe (see Figure SP. 25). The pain message to the brain is initiated by the release of chemicals, including prostaglandins, bradykinin, and a chemical called *P* (yes, *P* stands for "pain"). Prostaglandins facilitate transmission of the pain message to the brain and heighten circulation to the injured area, causing the redness and swelling that we call inflammation. Inflammation serves the biological function of attracting infection-fighting blood cells to the affected area to protect it against invading germs. Analgesic drugs such as aspirin and ibuprofen work by inhibiting the production of prostaglandins.

The pain message is relayed from the spinal cord to the thalamus and then projected to the cerebral cortex, making us aware of the location and intensity of the damage.

TRUTH OR FICTION REVISITED

It is true that many amputees experience pain in limbs that have been removed. The pain apparently reflects activation of neural circuits that have stored memories connected with the missing limbs.

PHANTOM LIMB PAIN One of the more fascinating phenomena of psychology is the fact that many people experience pain in limbs that are no longer there (Sherman, 1997). About 2 out of 3 combat veterans with amputated limbs report feeling pain in missing, or "phantom," limbs (Kimble, 1992). In such cases, the pain occurs in the absence of (present) tissue damage, but the pain itself is real enough. It sometimes involves activation of nerves in the stump of the missing limb, but local anesthesia does not always eliminate the pain. Therefore, the pain must also reflect activation of neural circuits that have stored memories connected with the missing limb (Melzack, 1997).

GATE THEORY Simple remedies like rubbing and scratching an injured toe frequently help relieve pain. Why? One possible answer lies in the gate theory of pain originated by Melzack (1980). From this perspective, the nervous system can process only a limited amount of stimulation at a time. Rubbing or scratching the toe transmits sensations to the brain that, in a sense, compete for the attention of neurons. Many nerves are thus prevented from transmitting pain messages to the brain. The mechanism is analogous to shutting down a "gate" in the spinal cord. It is like a switch-board being flooded with calls. The flooding prevents any of the calls from getting through.

ACUPUNCTURE Thousands of years ago, the Chinese began mapping the body to learn where pins might be placed to deaden pain. Acupuncture remained largely unknown in the West, even though Western powers occupied much of China during the 1800s. But in the 1970s New York Times columnist James Reston underwent an appendectomy in China, with acupuncture his primary anesthetic. He reported no discomfort. More recently, TV journalist Bill Moyers (1993) reported on current usage of acupuncture in China. For example, one woman underwent brain surgery to remove a tumor after receiving anesthesia that consisted of a mild sedative, a small dose of narcotics, and six needles placed in her fore-head, calves, and ankles. The surgery itself and the use of a guiding CAT scan were consistent with contemporary U.S. practices.

Some of the effects of acupuncture may be due to the release of endorphins—naturally occurring chemical messengers that are similar in effect to the narcotic morphine (Richardson & Vincent, 1986). Evidence to support this suggestion is found in the fact that the drug naloxone blocks the painkilling effects of morphine. The analgesic effects of acupuncture are also blocked by naloxone (Kimble, 1992). Therefore, it may well be that the analgesic effects of acupuncture can be linked to the morphinelike endorphins.

THE PLACEBO EFFECT Some scientists have also credited endorphins with the so-called placebo effect, in which the expectation of relief some-times leads to relief from pain and other problems. They speculate that a positive attitude may lead to release of endorphins.

KINESTHESIS

Try a brief experiment. Close your eyes, and then touch your nose with your finger. If you weren't right on target, I'm sure you came close. But how? You didn't see your hand moving, and you didn't hear your arm swishing through the air.

Kinesthesis is the sense that informs you about the position and motion of parts of the body. The term is derived from the ancient Greek words for "motion" (*kinesis*) and "perception" (*aisthesis*). In kinesthesis,

TRUTH OR FICTION REVISITED
It is true that rubbing a sore toe is often an effective way of relieving pain. Rubbing or scratching may "flood" the nervous system with messages so that news of the pain does not get through to the brain.

KINESTHESIS.
This young acrobat receives information about the position and movement of the parts of her body through the sense of kinesthesis. Information is fed to her brain from sensory organs in the joints, tendons, and muscles. This allows her to follow her own movements without looking at herself.

KINESTHESIS The sense that informs us about the positions and motion of parts of our bodies.

sensory information is fed back to the brain from sensory organs in the joints, tendons, and muscles. You were able to bring your finger to your nose by employing your kinesthetic sense. When you make a muscle in your arm, the sensations of tightness and hardness are also provided by kinesthesis.

Imagine going for a walk without kinesthesis. You would have to watch the forward motion of each leg to be certain you had raised it high enough to clear the curb. And if you had tried our brief experiment without the kinesthetic sense, you would have had no sensory feedback until you felt the pressure of your finger against your nose (or cheek, or eye, or forehead), and you probably would have missed dozens of times.

Are you in the mood for another experiment? Close your eyes again. Then make a muscle in your right arm. Could you sense the muscle without looking at it or feeling it with your left hand? Of course you could. Kinesthesis also provides information about muscle contractions.

THE VESTIBULAR SENSE: ON BEING UPRIGHT

Your **vestibular sense** tells you whether you are upright (physically, not morally). Sensory organs located in the semicircular canals and elsewhere in the ears monitor your body's motion and position in relation to gravity. They tell you whether you are falling and provide cues to whether your body is changing speed such as when you are in an accelerating airplane or automobile.

TRUTH OR FICTION REVISITED
It is true that we have a sense that keeps us upright. The sense—the vestibular sense—keeps us physically upright. It apparently takes more than the vestibular sense to keep us morally upright.

VESTIBULAR SENSE The sense that informs us about our bodies' positions relative to gravity.

SUMMARY

1. **What are sensation and perception?** Sensation is a mechanical process that involves the stimulation of sensory receptors (neurons) and the transmission of sensory information to the central nervous system. Perception is not mechanical. It is the active organization of sensations into a representation of the outside world, and it reflects learning and expectations.

2. **What are absolute and difference thresholds?** The absolute threshold for a stimulus, such as light, is the lowest intensity at which it can be detected. The minimum difference in intensity that can be discriminated is the difference threshold. Difference thresholds are expressed in Weber's constants.

3. **What is signal-detection theory?** Signal-detection theory explains the ways in which stimulus characteristics and psychological factors—for example, motivation, familiarity with a stimulus, and attention—interact to influence whether a stimulus will be detected.

4. **What is light?** Light is one part of the spectrum of electromagnetic energy.

5. **How does the eye detect light and transmit it to the brain?** The eye senses and transmits visual stimulation to the occipital lobe of the cerebral cortex. After light passes through the cornea, the size of the pupil determines the amount that can pass through the lens. The lens focuses light as it projects onto the retina, which is composed of photoreceptors called *rods* and *cones*. Neurons in the visual cortex of the brain (feature detectors) fire in response to specific features of visual information, such as lines presented at particular angles and colors.

6. **What are rods and cones?** Cones are neurons in the retina that permit perception of color. Rods transmit sensations of light and dark only. Rods are more sensitive than cones to lowered lighting and continue to adapt to darkness once cones have reached their peak adaptation.

7. **What are the theories of color vision?** There are two theories of color vision. According to the trichromatic theory, there are three types of cones—some sensitive to red, others to blue, and still others to green light. The opponent-process

theory proposes three types of color receptors: red-green, blue-yellow, and light-dark.

8. **What is perceptual organization?** Perceptual organization involves recognizing patterns and processing information about relationships between parts and the whole. Gestalt rules of perceptual organization involve figure-ground relationships, proximity, similarity, continuity, common fate, and closure.

9. **How do we perceive movement?** We perceive movement when the light reflected by moving objects moves across the retina and also when objects shift in relation to one another. Distant objects appear to move more slowly than nearby objects, and objects in the middle ground may give the illusion of moving backward.

10. **How do we perceive depth?** Depth perception involves monocular and binocular cues. Monocular cues include perspective, clearness, interposition, shadows, texture gradient, motion parallax, and accommodation. Binocular cues include retinal disparity and convergence.

11. **What are the perceptual constancies?** Through experience we develop a number of perceptual constancies. For example, we learn to assume that objects retain their size, shape, brightness, and color despite their distance from us, their position, or changes in lighting conditions.

12. **What is sound?** Sound is auditory stimulation, or sound waves. It requires a medium such as air or water to be transmitted. Sound waves alternately compress and expand molecules of the medium, creating vibrations.

13. **What is the range of sounds that can be sensed by the human ear?** The human ear can hear sounds varying in frequency from 20 to 20,000 cycles per second. The greater the frequency, the higher the sound's pitch.

14. **What is meant by the loudness of a sound?** The loudness of a sound corresponds to the amplitude of sound waves as measured in decibels (dB). We can experience hearing loss if we are exposed to protracted sounds of 85 to 90 dB or more. Noise is a combination of dissonant sounds.

15. **How do we hear sound?** The eardrum, vibrating in sympathy to sound waves, transmits auditory stimuli through the bones of the middle ear to the cochlea of the inner ear. The basilar membrane of the cochlea transmits those stimuli to the organ of Corti. From there, sound travels to the brain via the auditory nerve. Sounds seem louder when more neurons of the organ of Corti fire. Two competing theories account for the perception of pitch: place theory and frequency theory.

16. **How do we detect odors?** We detect odors through the olfactory membrane in each nostril. An odor is a sample of the substance being smelled.

17. **How do we detect tastes?** There are four primary taste qualities: sweet, sour, salty, and bitter. Flavor involves the odor, texture, and temperature of food, as well as its taste. Taste is sensed through taste cells, which are located in taste buds on the tongue.

18. **What are the skin senses?** The skin senses include touch, pressure, warmth, cold, and pain.

19. **How do we detect pain?** Pain originates at the point of contact and is transmitted to the brain by various chemicals, including prostaglandins, bradykinin, and *P*.

20. **What is kinesthesis?** Kinesthesis is the sensation of body position and movement. It relies on sensory organs in the joints, tendons, and muscles. The vestibular sense is housed primarily in the semicircular canals of the ears and tells us whether we are in an upright position.

KEY TERMS

absolute threshold (p. SP-3)

afterimage (p. SP-11)

auditory nerve (p. SP-22)

basilar membrane (p. SP-22)

binocular cues (p. SP-17)

bipolar cells (p. SP-9)

blind spot (p. SP-9)

bottom-up processing (p. SP-14)

brightness constancy (p. SP-18)

closure (p. SP-12)

cochlea (p. SP-22)

color constancy (p. SP-18)

common fate (p. SP-13)

conductive deafness (p. SP-24)

cones (p. SP-9)

continuity (p. SP-13)

convergence (p. SP-18)

cornea (p. SP-7)

dark adaptation (p. SP-10)

decibel (p. SP-21)

desensitization (p. SP-6)

dichromat (p. SP-12)

difference threshold (p. SP-4)

eardrum (p. SP-21)

feature detectors (p. SP-6)

fovea (p. SP-9)

frequency theory (p. SP-24)

ganglion cells (p. SP-9)

Hertz (p. SP-21)

hue (p. SP-7)

illusions (p. SP-14)

interposition (p. SP-17)

iris (p. SP-8)

just noticeable difference (p. SP-4)

kinesthesis (p. SP-29)

lens (p. SP-8)

method of constant stimuli (p. SP-3)

monochromat (p. SP-12)

monocular cues (p. SP-15)

motion parallax (p. SP-17)

olfactory nerve (p. SP-26)

opponent-process theory (p. SP-11)

optic nerve (p. SP-9)

organ of Corti (p. SP-22)

perception (p. SP-3)

perspective (p. SP-16)

phi phenomenon (p. SP-15)

photoreceptors (p. SP-9)

pitch (p. SP-4)

place theory (p. SP-24)

presbyopia (p. SP-9)

proximity (p. SP-13)

psychophysicist (p. SP-3)

pupil (p. SP-8)

retina (p. SP-9)

retinal disparity (p. SP-18)

rods (p. SP-9)

sensation (p. SP-3)

sensitization (p. SP-6)

sensorineural deafness (p. SP-26)

sensory adaptation (p. SP-6)

shadowing (p. SP-17)

shape constancy (p. SP-19)

signal-detection theory (p. SP-5)

similarity (p. SP-13)

size constancy (p. SP-18)

stroboscopic motion (p. SP-15)

taste buds (p. SP-27)

taste cells (p. SP-27)

texture gradient (p. SP-17)

top-down processing (p. SP-14)

trichromat (p. SP-11)

trichromatic theory (p. SP-10)

two-point threshold (p. SP-27)

vestibular sense (p. SP-30)

visible light (p. SP-6)

visual acuity (p. SP-9)

Weber's constant (p. SP-4)

REFERENCES

Azar, B. (1996). Musical studies provide clues to brain functions. *APA Monitor, 27*(4), 1, 24.

Bartoshuk, L. M., & Beauchamp, G. K. (1994). Chemical senses. *Annual Review of Psychology, 45,* 419–449.

Basic Behavioral Science Task Force of the National Advisory Mental Health Council. (1996). Basic behavioral science research for mental health: Perception, attention, learning, and memory. *American Psychologist, 51,* 133–142.

Blakeslee, S. (1995, May 16). The mystery of music. *New York Times,* pp. C1, C10.

DeValois, R. L., & Jacobs, G. H. (1984). Neural mechanisms of color vision. In I. Darian-Smith (Ed.), *Handbook of physiology* (Vol. 3). Bethesda, MD: American Physiological Society.

Hubel, D. H., & Wiesel, T. N. (1979). Brain mechanisms of vision. *Scientific American, 241,* 150–162.

Karoly, P., & Ruehlman, L. S. (1996). Motivational implications of pain. *Health Psychology, 15,* 383–390.

Kimble, D. P. (1992). *Biological psychology* (2nd ed.). Fort Worth: Harcourt Brace Jovanovich.

Matlin, M. W., & Foley, H. J. (1995). *Sensation and perception* (4th ed.). Boston: Allyn & Bacon.

Melzack, R. (1980). Psychological aspects of pain. In J. J. Bonica (Ed.), *Pain.* New York: Raven Press.

Melzack, R. (1997). Phantom limbs. *Scientific American Mysteries of the Mind* [Special issue] 7(1), 84–91.

Moore, R. Y. (1995). Vision without sight. *New England Journal of Medicine, 332,* 54–55.

Moyers, B. (1993). *Healing and the mind.* New York: Doubleday.

Nadol, J. B., Jr. (1993). Hearing loss. *New England Journal of Medicine, 329,* 1092–1102.

Newport, E. L. (1994). Cited in Senior, J. (1994, January 3). Language of the deaf evolves to reflect new sensibilities. *New York Times,* pp. A1, A12.

Richardson, P. H., & Vincent, C. A. (1986). Acupuncture for the treatment of pain. *Pain, 24,* 15–40.

Sherman, R. A. (1997). *Phantom pain.* New York: Plenum.

von Békésy, G. (1957, August). The ear. *Scientific American,* pp. 66–78.

C

CONSCIOUSNESS

WHEN YOU TALK TO YOURSELF, WHO TALKS, AND WHO listens? This is the type of question posed by philosophers and scientists who study consciousness. Although it might seem that psychologists, who study the brain and mental processes, are also well equipped to look into consciousness, consciousness has not always been an acceptable topic in psychology (Crick & Koch, 1997). In 1904, for example, William James wrote an article with the intriguing title "Does Consciousness Exist?" James did not think that consciousness was a proper area of study for psychologists because no scientific method could directly observe or measure another person's consciousness.

John Watson, the "father of modern behaviorism," agreed. Watson insisted that only observable, measurable behavior is the province of psychology: "The time seems to have come when psychology must discard all references to consciousness" (1913, p. 163). In 1914, Watson was elected president of the American Psychological Association. This honor further cemented his ideas in the minds of many psychologists.

Today, however, many psychologists believe we cannot capture the richness of the human experience without referring to consciousness (Rychlak, 1997). Studies on consciousness have turned from a stream into a flood (Gorman, 1997). Psychologists, neuroscientists, philosophers, physicists, even computer scientists are searching for the elusive marvel of consciousness. Most assume that consciousness dwells within the brain. Some, like Michael Gazzaniga (1997), suggest that the biological basis for consciousness can be found in specific sites in the brain.

JUST WHAT *IS* CONSCIOUSNESS?

Consciousness is a mental concept that cannot be directly seen or touched. Yet it is real enough to most people. Mental concepts such as consciousness acquire scientific status from being tied to behavior (Kimble, 1994). The concept of consciousness has several meanings.

CONSCIOUSNESS AS SENSORY AWARENESS One meaning of consciousness is *sensory awareness* of the environment. The sense of vision enables us to see, or be *conscious* of, the sun gleaming on the snow. The sense of hearing allows us to hear, or be conscious of, a concert.

CONSCIOUSNESS AS THE SELECTIVE ASPECT OF ATTENTION Sometimes we are not aware of sensory stimulation. We may be unaware, or unconscious, of sensory stimulation when we do not pay attention to it. The world is abuzz with signals, yet you are conscious of, or focusing on, only the words on this page (I hope).

Focusing one's consciousness on a particular stimulus is referred to as **selective attention.** The concept of selective attention is important to self-control. To pay attention in class, you must screen out the pleasant aroma of the cologne or perfume wafting toward you from the person in the next seat. To keep your car on the road, you must pay more attention to driving conditions than to your hunger pangs or your feelings about an argument with a friend. If you are out in the woods at night, attending to rustling sounds in the brush nearby may be crucial to your survival.

Adaptation to our environment involves learning which stimuli must be attended to and which ones can be safely ignored. Selective attention makes our senses keener (Basic Behavioral Science Task Force, 1996). This is why we can pick out the speech of a single person across a room at a cocktail party, a phenomenon suitably termed the *cocktail party effect.*

Although we can decide where and when we will focus our attention, various kinds of stimuli also tend to capture attention. Among them are these:

- Sudden changes, as when a cool breeze enters a sweltering room or we receive a particularly high or low grade on an exam.
- Novel stimuli, as when a dog enters the classroom or a person shows up with an unusual hairdo.
- Intense stimuli, such as bright colors, loud noises, or sharp pain.
- Repetitive stimuli, as when the same TV commercial is played a dozen times throughout the course of a football game.

How do advertisers of Nike, Microsoft, or cologne use these facts to get "into" our consciousness and, they hope, into our pocketbooks?

CONSCIOUSNESS AS DIRECT INNER AWARENESS Close your eyes and imagine spilling a can of bright red paint across a black tabletop. Watch it spread across the black shiny surface and then spill onto the floor. Although this image may be vivid, you did not "see" it literally. Neither your eyes nor any other sensory organs were involved. You were *conscious* of the image through **direct inner awareness.**

We are conscious of—or have direct inner awareness of—thoughts, images, emotions, and memories. We may not be able to measure direct inner awareness scientifically. Nevertheless, many psychologists argue, "It is detectable to anyone that has it" (Miller, 1992, p. 180). These psychological processes are connected with the firings of myriads of neurons. We do not consciously experience the firing of individual neurons, but consciousness reflects the total of these millions or billions of neural events.

Sigmund Freud, the founder of psychoanalysis, differentiated between the thoughts and feelings we are conscious, or aware, of and those that are preconscious and unconscious. **Preconscious** material is not currently in awareness but is readily available. For example, if you answer the following questions, you will summon up "preconscious" information: What did you eat for dinner yesterday? About what time did you wake up this morning? What is your phone number? You can make these preconscious bits of information conscious by directing your inner awareness, or attention, to them.

According to Freud, still other mental events are **unconscious.** This means that they are unavailable to awareness under most circumstances. Freud believed that some painful memories and sexual and aggressive impulses are unacceptable to us, so we *automatically* (unconsciously) eject them from our awareness. In other words, we *repress* them. **Repression** of these memories and impulses allows us to avoid feelings of anxiety, guilt, or shame.

SELECTIVE ATTENTION The focus of one's consciousness on a particular stimulus.

DIRECT INNER AWARENESS Knowledge of one's own thoughts, feelings, and memories without use of sensory organs.

PRECONSCIOUS In psychodynamic theory, descriptive of material that is not in awareness but can be brought into awareness by focusing one's attention.

UNCONSCIOUS In psychodynamic theory, descriptive of ideas and feelings that are not available to awareness.

REPRESSION In psychodynamic theory, the automatic (unconscious) ejection of anxiety-evoking ideas, impulses, or images from awareness.

People can also *choose* to stop thinking about unacceptable ideas or distractions. When we consciously eject unwanted mental events from awareness, we are engaging in **suppression.** We may, for example, suppress thoughts of a date when we need to study for a test. We may also try to suppress thoughts of a test while we are on a date!

Some bodily processes, such as the firings of neurons, are **nonconscious.** They cannot be experienced through sensory awareness or direct inner awareness. The growing of hair and the carrying of oxygen in the blood are nonconscious. We can see that our hair has grown, but we have no sense receptors that give us sensations of growing. We can feel the need to breathe but do not directly experience the exchange of carbon dioxide and oxygen.

CONSCIOUSNESS AS PERSONAL UNITY: THE SENSE OF SELF As we develop, we differentiate ourselves from that which is not us. We develop a sense of being persons, individuals. There is a totality to our impressions, thoughts, and feelings that makes up our conscious existence—our continuing sense of self in a changing world. That self forms intentions and guides its own behavior (Rychlak, 1997). In this usage of the word, consciousness *is* self.

CONSCIOUSNESS AS THE WAKING STATE The word *conscious* also refers to the waking state as opposed, for example, to sleep. From this perspective, sleep, meditation, the hypnotic "trance," and the distorted perceptions that can accompany use of consciousness-altering drugs are considered *altered states of consciousness.*

In the remainder of this chapter, we explore various types of altered states of consciousness. They include sleep and dreams, hypnosis, meditation, biofeedback, and finally, the effects of various kinds of psychoactive drugs.

SLEEP AND DREAMS

Sleep is a fascinating topic. After all, we spend about one third of our adult lives asleep. Most adults need 8 to 9 hours of sleep, but one survey found they typically get only 7 (National Sleep Foundation, 1998). About one third get 6 hours or less of sleep a night during the workweek. One third admitted that lack of sleep impaired their ability to function during the day, and nearly 1 in 4 admitted to falling asleep at the wheel at some time within the past year.

Our alternating periods of wakefulness and sleep provide an example of an internally generated **circadian rhythm.** A circadian rhythm is a cycle that is connected with the 24-hour period of the earth's rotation. A cycle of wakefulness and sleep is normally 24 hours long. However, when people are removed from cues that signal day or night, a cycle tends to become extended to about 25 hours, and people sleep nearly 10 of them (National Sleep Foundation, 1998). Why? We do not know.

Why do we sleep? Why do we dream? Next we explore the nature of sleep, dreams, and sleep disorders.

The Stages of Sleep

A major tool of sleep researchers is the electroencephalograph, or EEG. The EEG measures the electrical activity of the brain, or brain waves. Figure C.1 shows EEG patterns that reflect the frequency and strength of brain waves that occur during the waking state, when we are relaxed, and when we are in the various stages of sleep.

SUPPRESSION The deliberate, or conscious, placing of certain ideas, impulses, or images out of awareness.

NONCONSCIOUS Descriptive of bodily processes such as the growing of hair, of which we cannot become conscious. We may "recognize" that our hair is growing but we cannot directly experience the biological process.

CIRCADIAN RHYTHM Referring to cycles connected with the 24-hour period of the earth's rotation.

Brain waves, like other waves, are cyclical. During the various stages of sleep, the brain emits waves with different *frequencies* (numbers of waves per second) and *amplitudes* (heights—an index of strength). The printouts in Figure C.1 show what happens during a period of 15 seconds or so. Brain waves that are high in frequency are associated with wakefulness. The amplitude of brain waves reflects their strength. The strength or energy of brain waves is expressed in volts (an electrical unit).

Figure C.1 shows five stages of sleep: four stages of **non-rapid-eye-movement** (NREM) sleep and one stage of **rapid-eye-movement** (REM) sleep. When we close our eyes and begin to relax before going to sleep, our brains emit many **alpha waves**. Alpha waves are low-amplitude brain waves of about 8 to 13 cycles per second.

As we enter stage 1 sleep, our brain waves slow down from the alpha rhythm and enter a pattern of **theta waves**. Theta waves, with a frequency of about 6 to 8 cycles per second, are accompanied by slow rolling eye movements. The transition from alpha waves to theta waves may be accompanied by a **hypnagogic state** during which we may experience brief dreamlike images that resemble vivid photographs. Stage 1 sleep is the lightest stage of sleep. If we are awakened from stage 1 sleep, we may feel that we have not slept at all.

NON-RAPID-EYE-MOVEMENT SLEEP Stages of sleep 1 through 4. Abbreviated *NREM* sleep.

RAPID-EYE-MOVEMENT SLEEP A stage of sleep characterized by rapid eye movements, which have been linked to dreaming. Abbreviated *REM* sleep.

ALPHA WAVES Rapid low-amplitude brain waves that have been linked to feelings of relaxation.

THETA WAVES Slow brain waves produced during the hypnagogic state.

HYPNAGOGIC STATE The drowsy interval between waking and sleeping, characterized by brief, hallucinatory, dreamlike experiences.

FIGURE C.1.
THE STAGES OF SLEEP.

This figure illustrates typical EEG patterns for the stages of sleep. During REM sleep, EEG patterns resemble those of the lightest stage of sleep, stage 1 sleep. For this reason, REM sleep is often termed *paradoxical sleep*. As sleep progresses from stage 1 to stage 4, brain waves become slower and their amplitude increases. Dreams, including normal nightmares, are most vivid during REM sleep. More disturbing sleep terrors tend to occur during deep stage 4 sleep.

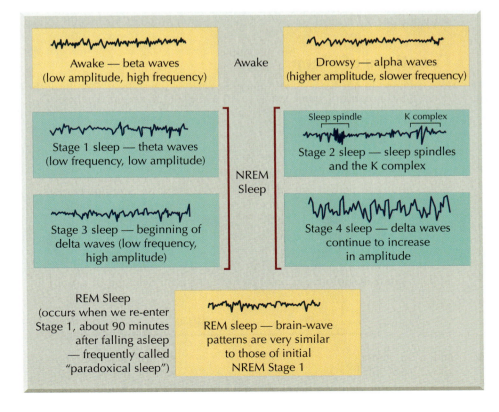

After 30 to 40 minutes of stage 1 sleep, we undergo a rather steep descent into stages 2, 3, and 4 (see Figure C.2). During stage 2, brain waves are medium in amplitude with a frequency of about 4 to 7 cycles per second, but these are punctuated by *sleep spindles*. Sleep spindles have a frequency of 12 to 16 cycles per second and represent brief bursts of rapid brain activity.

During deep sleep stages 3 and 4, our brains produce slower **delta waves**. During stage 3, the delta waves have a frequency of 1 to 3 cycles per second. Delta waves reach relatively great amplitude compared with other brain waves. Stage 4 is the deepest stage of sleep, from which it is the most difficult to be awakened. During stage 4 sleep, the delta waves slow to about 0.5 to 2 cycles per second, and their amplitude is greatest.

After perhaps half an hour of deep stage 4 sleep, we begin a relatively rapid journey back upward through the stages until we enter REM sleep (Figure C.2). REM sleep derives its name from the *rapid eye movements*, observable beneath the closed eyelids, that characterize this stage. During REM sleep we produce relatively rapid, low-amplitude brain waves that resemble those of light stage 1 sleep. REM sleep is also called *paradoxical sleep* because the EEG patterns observed suggest a level of arousal similar to that of the waking state (Figure C.1). However, it is difficult to awaken a person during REM sleep. When people are awakened during REM sleep, as is the practice in sleep research, about 80% of the time they report that they have been dreaming. (We also dream during NREM sleep, but less frequently. People report dreaming only about 20% of the time when awakened during NREM sleep.)

Each night we tend to undergo five trips through the stages of sleep (see Figure C.2). These trips include about five periods of REM sleep. Our first journey through stage 4 sleep is usually longest. Sleep tends to become lighter as the night wears on. Our periods of REM sleep tend to become longer, and toward morning our last period of REM sleep may last close to half an hour.

Now that we have some idea of what sleep is like, let us examine the question of *why* we sleep.

Functions of Sleep

DELTA WAVES Strong, slow brain waves usually emitted during stage 4 sleep.

Researchers do not have all the answers as to why we sleep. One hypothesis is that sleep helps rejuvenate a tired body. Most of us have had the

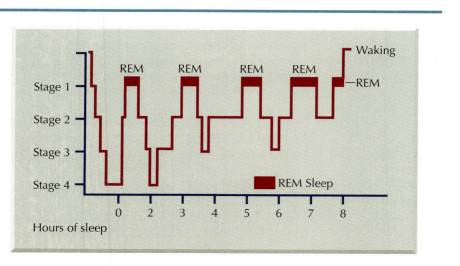

FIGURE C.2
SLEEP CYCLES.
This figure illustrates the alternation of REM and non-REM sleep for the typical sleeper. There are about five periods of REM sleep during an 8-hour night. Sleep is deeper earlier in the night, and REM sleep tends to become prolonged toward morning.

experience of going without sleep for a night and feeling "wrecked" or "out of it" the following day. Perhaps the next evening we went to bed early in order to "catch up on our sleep." What happens to you if you do not sleep for one night? For several nights?

Compare people who are highly sleep deprived with people who have been drinking heavily. Sleepless people's abilities to concentrate and perform may be seriously impaired, but they may be the last ones to recognize their limitations (Adler, 1993).

Most students can pull successful "all-nighters" (Webb, 1993). They can cram for a test through the night and then perform reasonably well the following day. When we are deprived of sleep for several nights, however, aspects of psychological functioning such as attention, learning, and memory deteriorate notably (Maas, 1998). The National Highway Traffic Safety Administration (1998) estimates that sleep deprivation is connected with 100,000 crashes and 1,500 vehicular deaths each year. Many people sleep late or nap on their days off (Webb, 1993). Perhaps they suffer from mild sleep deprivation during the week and catch up on the weekend.

The amount of sleep we need seems to be in part genetically determined (Webb, 1993). People also tend to need more sleep during periods of stress, such as a change of jobs, an increase in workload, or an episode of depression (Maas, 1998). Sleep seems to help us recover from stress.

Newborn babies may sleep 16 hours a day, and teenagers often sleep around the clock. It is widely believed that older people need less sleep than younger adults do. However, sleep in older people is often interrupted by physical discomfort or the need to go to the bathroom. Older people often sleep more during the day to make up for sleep lost at night.

DEPRIVATION OF REM SLEEP In some studies, animals or people have been deprived of REM sleep. Under these conditions they learn more slowly and forget what they have learned more rapidly (Adler, 1993). Fetuses have periods of waking and sleeping, and REM sleep may foster the development of the brain before birth (McCarley, 1992). REM sleep may also help maintain neurons in adults by "exercising" them at night. Deprivation of REM sleep is accomplished by monitoring EEG records and eye movements and waking the person during REM sleep. There is too much individual variation to conclude that people who are deprived of REM sleep learn more poorly than they otherwise would. It does seem, though, that such deprivation interferes with memory—that is, retrieval of information that has been learned previously. In any event, people and lower animals that are deprived of REM sleep tend to show *REM rebound*. They spend more time in REM sleep during subsequent sleep periods. In other words, they catch up.

It is during REM sleep that we tend to dream. Let us now turn our attention to dreams, a mystery about which philosophers, poets, and scientists have theorized for centuries.

Dreams

Just what is the "stuff"[1] of dreams? What are they "made on"? Like memories and fantasies, dreams involve imagery in the absence of external stimulation. Some dreams seem very real. In college I often had "anxiety dreams" the night before a test. I dreamed repeatedly that I had taken the test and it was all over. (Imagine the disappointment when I awakened and realized that the test still lay before me!).

---

[1] The phrase "such stuff as dreams are made on" comes from Shakespeare's *The Tempest*.

DREAM IMAGES?
In *Winter Night in Vitebsk,* Marc Chagall seems to depict images born in dreams.

Dreams are most vivid during REM sleep. Images are vaguer and more fleeting during NREM sleep. You may dream every time you are in REM sleep. Therefore, if you sleep for 8 hours and undergo five sleep cycles, you may have five dreams. Upon waking, you may think that time seemed to expand or contract during your dream, so during 10 or 15 minutes of actual time, the content of your dream ranged over days or weeks. But dreams actually tend to take place in "real time." Fifteen minutes of events fills about 15 minutes of dreaming. Your dream theater is quite flexible. You can dream in black and white or in full color.

THEORIES OF THE CONTENT OF DREAMS You may recall dreams involving fantastic adventures, but most dreams involve memories of the activities and problems of the day (Wade, 1998). If we are preoccupied with illness or death, sexual or aggressive urges, or moral dilemmas, we are likely to dream about them. The characters in our dreams are more likely to be friends and neighbors than spies, monsters, and princes.

"A dream is a wish your heart makes," is a song lyric from the Disney film *Cinderella.* Freud theorized that dreams reflect unconscious wishes and urges. He argued that through dreams we can express impulses we would censor during the day. Moreover, he said that the content of dreams is symbolic of unconscious fantasized objects such as the genitals. A key part of Freud's method of psychoanalysis involved interpretation of his clients' dreams. Freud also believed that dreams "protect sleep" by providing imagery that helps keep disturbing, repressed thoughts out of awareness.

The theory that dreams protect sleep has been challenged by the observation that disturbing events tend to be followed by disturbing dreams on the same theme—not by protective imagery (Reiser, 1992). Our behavior in dreams is also generally consistent with our waking behavior. Most dreams, then, are unlikely candidates for the expression of repressed urges (even disguised). A person who leads a moral life tends to dream moral dreams.

There are also biological views of the "meanings" of dreams. According to the **activation-synthesis model,** acetylcholine (a neurotransmitter)

TRUTH OR FICTION REVISITED
It is not true that we act out our forbidden fantasies in our dreams. Most dreams are humdrum.

ACTIVATION-SYNTHESIS MODEL The view that dreams reflect activation of cognitive activity by the reticular activating system and synthesis of this activity into a pattern by the cerebral cortex.

and the pons (a structure in the lower part of the brain) stimulate responses that lead to dreaming (Hobson & McCarley, 1977). One is *activation* of the reticular activating system (RAS), which arouses us, but not to waking. During the waking state, firing of these cells in the reticular formation is linked to movement, particularly the movements involved in walking, running, and other physical acts. During REM sleep, however, neurotransmitters generally inhibit activity, so we usually do not thrash about as we dream. In this way, we save ourselves (and our bed partners) some wear and tear. The eye muscles are stimulated and thus show the rapid eye movement associated with dreaming. The RAS also stimulates neural activity in the parts of the cortex involved in memory. The cortex then *synthesizes,* or puts together, these sources of stimulation to some degree to yield the stuff of dreams. Yet research with the PET scan shows that the frontal lobes of the brain, which make sense of experience, are pretty much shut down during sleep (Wade, 1998). Dreams are therefore more likely to be emotionally gripping than coherent in plot.

Another view of dreams is that with the brain cut off from the world outside, memories are replayed and consolidated during sleep (Wade, 1998). Another possibility is that REM activity is a way of testing whether the individual has benefitted from the restorative functions of sleep (Wade, 1998). When restoration is adequate, the brain awakens. According to this view, dreams are just the by-products of the testing.

NIGHTMARES Have you ever dreamed that something heavy was sitting on your chest and watching you as you breathed? Or that you were trying to run away from a terrible threat but couldn't gain your footing or coordinate your leg muscles?

Nightmares, like most pleasant dreams, are generally products of REM sleep. College students report an average of two nightmares a month in dream logs (Wood & Bootzin, 1990). Traumatic events can spawn nightmares, as reported in a study of survivors of the San Francisco earthquake of 1989 (Wood et al., 1992). People who suffer frequent nightmares are more likely than other people to also suffer from anxieties, depression, and other kinds of psychological discomfort (Berquier & Ashton, 1992).

THE SCREAM.
The Norwegian artist Edvard Munch's well-known painting contains the kind of imagery we might find in a nightmare.

INSOMNIA.
"You know I can't sleep at night" is a song lyric from the 1960s by the Mamas and the Papas. Why are women more likely than men to have insomnia? What can people do about insomnia?

Sleep Disorders

There are a number of sleep disorders. Some, like insomnia, are all too familiar. In this section we discuss insomnia and the deep-sleep disorders—sleep terrors, bed-wetting, and sleepwalking.

INSOMNIA According to the National Sleep Foundation (1999), more than half of American adults are affected by insomnia in any given year. Women complain of insomnia more often than men do (Kupfer & Reynolds, 1997). People who experience insomnia show greater restlessness and muscle tension than those who do not (Lacks & Morin, 1992). People with insomnia are also more likely to worry and report "racing thoughts" at bedtime (White & Nicassio, 1990). Insomnia comes and goes with many people, increasing during periods of stress (Kupfer & Reynolds, 1997).

People with insomnia tend to compound their sleep problems when they try to force themselves to fall asleep (Bootzin et al., 1991). Their concern heightens autonomic activity and muscle tension. You cannot force or will yourself to go to sleep. You can only set the stage for sleep by lying down and relaxing when you are tired. If you focus on sleep too closely, it will elude you. Yet millions of people go to bed each night dreading the possibility of insomnia.

TRUTH OR FICTION REVISITED
It is true that many people have insomnia because they try too hard to fall asleep at night. Trying to go to sleep heightens tension and anxiety, both of which counter the feelings of relaxation that help induce sleep.

DEEP-SLEEP DISORDERS: SLEEP TERRORS, BED-WETTING, AND SLEEPWALKING Sleep terrors, bed-wetting, and sleepwalking all occur during deep (stage 3 or 4) sleep, are more common among children, and may reflect immaturity of the nervous system.

Sleep terrors are similar to, but more severe than, nightmares. They usually occur during deep sleep, whereas nightmares take place during REM sleep. Sleep terrors occur during the first couple of sleep cycles; nightmares are more likely to occur later on. Experiencing a surge in the heart and respiration rates, the dreamer may suddenly sit up, talk incoherently, and move about wildly. The dreamer is never fully awake, returns to sleep, and may recall a vague image as of someone pressing on his or her chest. (Memories of nightmares tend to be more vivid.) Sleep terrors are often decreased by taking a minor tranquilizer at bedtime. The drug reduces the amount of time spent in stage 4 sleep.

Bed-wetting is often seen as a stigma that reflects parental harshness or the child's attempt to punish the parents, but this disorder, too, may stem from immaturity of the nervous system. In most cases it resolves itself before adolescence, often by age 8. Behavior therapy methods that condition children to awaken when they are about to urinate have been helpful. The drug imipramine often helps, although the reason is not fully

SLEEP TERRORS Frightening dreamlike experiences that occur during the deepest stage of NREM sleep. Nightmares, in contrast, occur during REM sleep.

known. Sometimes all that is needed is reassurance that no one is to blame for bed-wetting and that most children "outgrow" it.

Perhaps half of all children occasionally talk in their sleep. Nearly 15% walk in their sleep (Mindell, 1993). Sleepwalkers may roam about almost nightly while their parents fret about the accidents that could befall them. Sleepwalkers typically do not remember their excursions, although they may respond to questions while they are up and about. Contrary to myth, there is no evidence that sleepwalkers become violent if they are awakened, although they may be confused and upset. Mild tranquilizers and maturity typically put an end to sleepwalking.

The Greek word for "sleep" is *hypnos,* which raises the question as to whether there are connections between the state of consciousness we call sleep and another one we call hypnosis. Although many people are hypnotized by being told that they are "going to sleep," we now see many differences between sleep and hypnosis.

TRUTH OR FICTION REVISITED
It is not true that it is dangerous to awaken a sleepwalker. Sleepwalkers may be confused and startled when awakened, but they are not usually violent.

HYPNOSIS: ON BEING ENTRANCED

Perhaps you have seen films in which Count Dracula hypnotized resistant victims into a stupor. Then he could give them a bite in the neck with no further nonsense. Perhaps you have watched a fellow student try to place a friend in a "trance" after reading a book on hypnosis. Or perhaps you have seen an audience member hypnotized in a nightclub act. If so, chances are the person acted as if he or she had returned to childhood, imagined that a snake was about to have a nip, or lay rigid between two chairs for a while.

Hypnosis, a term derived from the Greek word for sleep, has only recently become a respectable subject for psychological inquiry. Modern hypnosis seems to have begun with the ideas of Franz Mesmer in the 18th century. Mesmer asserted that everything in the universe was connected by forms of magnetism—which actually may not be far from the mark. He claimed that people, too, could be drawn to one another by "animal magnetism." (No bull's-eye here.) Mesmer used bizarre props to bring people under his "spell." He did manage a respectable cure rate for minor ailments. But scientists attribute his successes to the placebo effect, not to animal magnetism.

Today hypnotism retains its popularity in nightclubs, but it is also used as an anesthetic in dentistry, childbirth, and even surgery. Some psychologists use hypnosis to teach clients how to reduce anxiety, manage pain, or overcome fears. Research shows that hypnosis is a useful supplement to other forms of therapy, especially in helping obese people lose weight (Kirsch et al., 1995). Police also use hypnosis to prompt the memories of witnesses.

The state of consciousness called the *hypnotic trance* has traditionally been induced by asking people to narrow their attention to a small light, a spot on the wall, an object held by the hypnotist, or the hypnotist's voice. The hypnotist usually suggests that the person's limbs are becoming warm, heavy, and relaxed. People may also be told that they are becoming sleepy or falling asleep. Hypnosis is *not* sleep, however. This is shown by differences between EEG recordings for the hypnotic trance and the stages of sleep. But the word *sleep* is understood by subjects to suggest a hypnotic trance.

It is also possible to induce hypnosis through instructions that direct subjects to remain active and alert (Miller et al., 1991). So the effects of hypnosis probably cannot be attributed to relaxation.

HYPNOSIS.
Hypnotized people become passive and follow the suggestions of the hypnotist. Only recently has hypnosis become a respectable subject for psychological inquiry.

HYPNOSIS A condition in which people appear to be highly suggestible and behave as though they are in a trance.

People who are readily hypnotized are said to have *hypnotic suggestibility*. Part of "suggestibility" is knowledge of what is expected during the "trance state." Generally speaking, suggestible people have positive attitudes toward hypnosis. They *want* to be hypnotized. Moreover, they attend closely to the hypnotist's instructions (Crawford et al., 1993). It is therefore extremely unlikely that someone could be hypnotized against his or her will.

Changes in Consciousness Brought About by Hypnosis

Hypnotists and people who have been hypnotized report that hypnosis can bring about the following changes in consciousness. As you read them, bear in mind that changes in "consciousness" are inferred from changes in observable behavior and self-reports.

- *Passivity.* When being hypnotized, or in a trance, people await instructions and appear to suspend planning.
- *Narrowed attention.* People focus on the hypnotist's voice or on a spot of light and avoid attending to background noise or intruding thoughts.
- *Pseudomemories and hypermnesia.* People may be instructed to report pseudomemories (false memories), or **hypermnesia.** In police investigations, for example, hypnotists attempt to heighten witnesses' memories by instructing them to focus on details of a crime and then reconstruct the scene. Studies suggest, however, that although people may report recalling more information when they are hypnotized, such information is often incorrect (Weekes et al., 1992).
- *Suggestibility.* People may respond to suggestions that an arm is becoming lighter and will rise or that the eyelids are becoming heavier and must close. They may act as though they cannot unlock hands clasped by the hypnotist or bend an arm "made rigid" by the hypnotist. Hypnotized individuals serving as witnesses may incorporate ideas presented by interviewers into their "memories" and report them as facts (Loftus, 1994).
- *Playing unusual roles.* Most people expect to play sleepy, relaxed roles, but they may also be able to play roles calling for increased strength or alertness, such as riding a bicycle with less fatigue than usual. In **age regression,** people may play themselves as infants or children. Research shows that many supposed childhood memories and characteristics are played inaccurately. Nonetheless, some people show excellent recall of such details as hairstyle or speech pattern. A person may speak a language forgotten since childhood.
- *Perceptual distortions.* Hypnotized people may act as though hypnotically induced **hallucinations** and delusions are real. In the "thirst hallucination," for example, people act as if they are parched, even if they have just had a drink. People may behave as though they cannot hear loud noises, smell odors, or feel pain (Miller & Bowers, 1993).
- *Posthypnotic amnesia.* Many people apparently cannot recall events that take place under hypnosis (Bowers & Woody, 1996) or, if so directed, that they were hypnotized at all. However, if they are hypnotized again, they can usually recall what occurred when instructed by the hypnotist to do so.
- *Posthypnotic suggestion.* People who have been hypnotized may later follow instructions to prearranged cues of which they are supposedly

HYPERMNESIA Greatly enhanced or heightened memory.

AGE REGRESSION In hypnosis, taking on the role of childhood, commonly accompanied by vivid recollections of one's past.

HALLUCINATIONS Perceptions in the absence of sensation.

unaware. For instance, during hypnosis a subject may be directed to fall into a deep trance later upon the single command "Sleep!" Smokers frequently seek the help of hypnotists to break their habit, and they may be given the suggestion that upon "waking" they will find cigarette smoke aversive.

Theories of Hypnosis

Hypnotism is no longer explained in terms of animal magnetism, but psychodynamic and learning theorists have offered explanations. According to Freud, the hypnotic trance represents **regression.** Hypnotized adults suspend "ego functioning," or conscious control of their behavior. They permit themselves to return to childish modes of responding that emphasize fantasy and impulse rather than fact and logic.

ROLE THEORY Theodore Sarbin offers a **role theory** view of hypnosis (Sarbin & Coe, 1972). He points out that the changes in behavior attributed to the hypnotic trance can be successfully imitated when people are instructed to behave *as though* they were hypnotized. For example, people can lie rigid between two chairs whether they are hypnotized or not. Also, people cannot be hypnotized unless they are familiar with the hypnotic "role"—the behavior that constitutes the trance. Sarbin is not saying that subjects *fake* the hypnotic role. Research evidence suggests that most people who are hypnotized are not faking (Kinnunen et al., 1994). Instead, Sarbin is suggesting that people *allow* themselves to enact this role under the hypnotist's directions.

Research findings that "suggestible" people are motivated to enact the hypnotic role, are good role players, and have vivid and absorbing imaginations seem to support role theory. The fact that the behaviors shown by hypnotized people can be mimicked by role players means that we need not resort to the concept of the "hypnotic trance"—an unusual and mystifying altered state of awareness—to explain hypnotic events.

DISSOCIATION Runners frequently get through the pain and tedium of long-distance races by *dissociating*—by imagining themselves elsewhere, doing other things. (My students inform me that they manage the pain and tedium of *other* instructors' classes in the same way.) Ernest Hilgard (1994) similarly explains hypnotic phenomena through **neodissociation theory.** This is the view that we can selectively focus our attention on one thing (like hypnotic suggestions) and dissociate ourselves from the things going on around us.

In one experiment related to neodissociation theory, subjects were hypnotized and instructed to submerge their arms in ice water—causing "cold pressor pain" (Miller et al., 1991). Subjects were given suggestions to the effect that they were not in pain, however. Highly hypnotizable people reported dissociative experiences that allowed them to avoid the perception of pain, such as imagining that they were at the beach or that their limbs were floating in air above the ice water.

Although hypnotized people may be focusing on the hypnotist's suggestions and perhaps imagining themselves to be somewhere else, they still tend to perceive their actual surroundings peripherally. In a sense, we do this all the time. We are not fully conscious, or aware, of everything going on about us. Rather, at any given moment we selectively focus on events such as tests, dates, or television shows that seem important or relevant. Yet while taking a test we may be peripherally aware of the color of the wall or the sound of rain.

REGRESSION Return to a form of behavior characteristic of an earlier stage of development.

ROLE THEORY A theory that explains hypnotic events in terms of the person's ability to act *as though* he or she were hypnotized. Role theory differs from faking in that subjects cooperate and focus on hypnotic suggestions instead of pretending to be hypnotized.

NEODISSOCIATION THEORY A theory of hypnotic events as the splitting of consciousness.

MEDITATION.
People use many forms of meditation to try to expand their inner awareness and experience inner harmony. The effects of meditation, like those of drugs, reflect both the bodily changes induced by meditation *and* the meditator's expectations.

Role theory and neodissociation theory do not suggest that the phenomena of hypnosis are phony. Instead, they suggest that we do not need to explain these events through an altered state of awareness called a trance. Hypnosis may not be special at all. Rather, it is *we* who are special—through our imagination, our role-playing ability, and our capacity to divide our consciousness—concentrating now on one event that we deem important, and concentrating on another event later.

Let us now consider two other states of consciousness that involve different ways of focusing our attention: meditation and biofeedback.

MEDITATION: LETTING THE WORLD FADE AWAY

The dictionary defines *meditation* as the act or process of thinking. But the concept usually suggests thinking deeply about the universe or about one's place in the world, often within a spiritual context. As the term is commonly used by psychologists, however, meditation refers to various ways of focusing one's consciousness to alter one's relationship to the world. As used by psychologists, ironically, *meditation* can also refer to a process in which people seem to suspend thinking and allow the world to fade away.

The kinds of meditation that psychologists and other kinds of helping professionals speak of are *not* the first definition you find in the dictionary. Rather they tend to refer to rituals, exercises, and even passive observation—activities that alter the normal relationship between the person and her or his environment. They are various methods of suspending problem solving, planning, worries, and awareness of the events of the day. These methods alter consciousness—that is, the normal focus of attention—and help people cope with stress by inducing feelings of relaxation.

Let us consider one common form of meditation in more detail. **Transcendental meditation (TM)** is a simplified form of Far Eastern meditation that was brought to the United States by the Maharishi Mahesh Yogi in 1959. Hundreds of thousands of Americans practice TM by repeating and concentrating on *mantras*—words or sounds that are claimed to help the person achieve an altered state of consciousness. TM has a number of spiritual goals, such as expanding consciousness so that it encompasses spiritual kinds of experiences, but there are also more worldly goals, such as reducing anxiety and normalizing blood pressure.

In early research, Herbert Benson (1975) found no scientific evidence that TM expands consciousness (how do you measure spiritual experience with earthly instruments?), despite the claims of many of its practitioners. However, TM lowered the heart and respiration rates—changes that can be measured through commonly used medical instruments—and also produced what Benson labeled a *relaxation response*. The blood pressure of people with hypertension decreased. In fact, people who meditated twice daily tended to show more normal blood pressure through the day. Meditators produced more frequent alpha waves—brain waves associated with feelings of relaxation.

Other researchers agree that TM lowers a person's level of arousal, as measured by heart rate, respiration rate, and blood pressure, but they argue that the same relaxing effects can be achieved in other ways, such as by resting quietly (Holmes, 1984). The issue is not whether meditation helps, but whether this particular approach to meditation—TM—has special measurable effects as compared with a break from a tense routine.

TRUTH OR FICTION REVISED
It is true that people have managed to bring high blood pressure under control through meditation.

TRANSCENDENTAL MEDITATION (TM) The simplified form of meditation brought to the United States by the Maharishi Mahesh Yogi and used as a method for coping with stress.

BIOFEEDBACK: GETTING IN TOUCH WITH THE UNTOUCHABLE

Let us begin our discussion of biofeedback by recounting some remarkable experiments in which psychologist Neal E. Miller (1969) trained laboratory rats to increase or decrease their heart rates. His procedure was simple but ingenious. As discovered by psychologists James Olds and Peter Milner, there is a "pleasure center" in the rat's hypothalamus. A small burst of electricity in this center is strongly reinforcing: Rats learn to do what they can, such as pressing a lever, to obtain this shock.

Miller implanted electrodes in the rats' pleasure centers. Then some rats were given an electric shock whenever their heart rate happened to increase. Other rats received a shock when their heart rate went lower. In other words, one group of rats was consistently "rewarded" (that is, shocked) when their heart rate showed an increase. The other group was consistently rewarded for a decrease in heart rate. After a single 90-minute training session, the rats learned to alter their heart rates by as much as 20% in the direction for which they had been rewarded.

Miller's research was an early example of **biofeedback training (BFT)**. Biofeedback is a system that provides, or "feeds back," information about a bodily function. Miller used electrical stimulation of the brain to feed back information to rats when they had engaged in a targeted bodily response (in this case, raised or lowered their heart rates). Somehow the rats then used this information to raise or lower their heart rates voluntarily.

Similarly, people have learned to change various bodily functions voluntarily, including heart rate, that were once considered beyond their control.

However, electrodes are not implanted in people's brains. Rather, people hear a "blip" or observe some other signal that informs them when the targeted response is being displayed.

There are many ways in which BFT helps people combat stress, tension, and anxiety. For example, people can learn to emit alpha waves (and feel somewhat more relaxed) through feedback from an EEG. A blip may increase in frequency whenever alpha waves are being emitted. The psychologist's instructions are simply to "make the blip go faster." An **electromyograph (EMG),** which monitors muscle tension, is commonly used to help people become more aware of muscle tension in the forehead and elsewhere and to learn to lower the tension. Through the use of other instruments, people have learned to lower their heart rate, their blood pressure, and the amount of sweat in the palm of the hand. All of these changes are relaxing. Biofeedback is widely used by sports psychologists to teach athletes how to relax muscle groups that are unessential to the task at hand so that they can control anxiety and tension.

People have also learned to elevate the temperature of a finger. Why bother, you ask? It happens that limbs become subjectively warmer when more blood flows into them. Increasing the temperature of a finger—that is, altering patterns of blood flow in the body—helps some people control migraine headaches, which may be caused by dysfunctional circulatory patterns.

Sleep, hypnosis, mediation, and biofeedback training all involve "natural" ways of deploying our attention or consciousness. Some altered states depend on the ingestion of psychoactive chemical substances we call "drugs." Let us now deploy our attention to the effects of alcohol and other drugs.

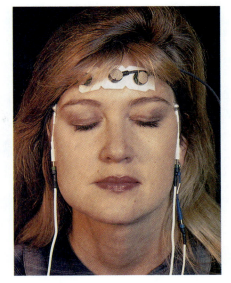

BIOFEEDBACK.
Biofeedback is a system that provides, or "feeds back," information about a bodily function to an organism. Through biofeedback training, people have learned to gain voluntary control over a number of functions that are normally automatic, such as heart rate and blood pressure.

TRUTH OR FICTION REVISITED
It is true that rats will learn to do what they can to obtain a burst of electricity in the brain—when the electricity stimulates the so-called pleasure centers of their brains.

TRUTH OR FICTION REVISITED
It is true that you can learn to change your heart rate just by thinking about it—particularly when "thinking about it" involves biofeedback training.

BIOFEEDBACK TRAINING (BFT) The systematic feeding back to an organism information about a bodily function so that the organism can gain control of that function.

ELECTROMYOGRAPH (EMG) An instrument that measures muscle tension.

ALTERING CONSCIOUSNESS THROUGH DRUGS

The world is a supermarket of **psychoactive substances,** or drugs. The United States is flooded with drugs that distort perceptions and change mood—drugs that take you up, let you down, and move you across town. Some people use drugs because their friends do or because their parents tell them not to. Some are seeking pleasure; others are seeking inner truth or escape.

For better or worse, drugs are part of American life. Young people often become involved with drugs that impair their ability to learn at school and are connected with reckless behavior (Basen-Engquist et al., 1996). Alcohol is the most popular drug on high school and college campuses (Johnston et al., 1996). More than 40% of college students have tried marijuana, and 1 in 6 or 7 smokes it regularly (see Table C.1). St. Louis Cardinal Mark McGwire slugged his way through the 1998 baseball season to a new home run record "with a little help from [his] friends" (Johnson, 1998). His "friends"? Androstenedione pills. Androstenedione is

PSYCHOACTIVE SUBSTANCES Drugs that have psychological effects such as stimulation or distortion of perceptions.

TABLE C.1

SNAPSHOT, U.S.A.: TRENDS IN DRUG USE AMONG COLLEGE STUDENTS DURING LIFETIME AND DURING LAST 30 DAYS (IN PERCENTS)

DRUG	USED . . .	1980	1982	1984	1986	1988	1990	1992	1994
Marijuana	Ever?	65.0	60.5	59.0	57.9	51.3	49.1	44.1	42.2
	Last 30 days?	34.0	26.8	23.0	22.3	16.3	14.0	14.6	15.1
Inhalants	Ever?	10.2	10.6	10.4	11.0	12.6	13.9	14.2	12.0
	Last 30 days?	1.5	0.8	0.7	1.1	1.3	1.0	1.1	0.6
Hallucinogens	Ever?	15.0	15.0	12.9	11.2	10.2	11.2	12.0	10.0
(includes LSD)	Last 30 days?	2.7	2.6	1.8	2.2	1.7	1.4	2.3	2.1
Cocaine	Ever?	22.0	22.4	21.7	23.3	15.8	11.4	7.9	5.0
(includes crack)	Last 30 days?	6.9	7.9	7.6	7.0	4.2	1.2	1.0	0.6
MDMA	Ever?	NA	NA	NA	NA	NA	3.9	2.9	2.1
	Last 30 days?	NA	NA	NA	NA	NA	0.6	0.4	0.2
Heroin	Ever?	0.9	0.5	0.5	0.4	0.3	0.3	0.5	0.1
	Last 30 days?	0.3	0.0	0.0	0.0	0.1	0.0	0.0	0.0
Stimulants	Ever?	NA	30.1	27.8	22.3	17.7	13.2	10.5	9.2
(other than cocaine)	Last 30 days?	NA	9.9	5.5	3.7	1.8	1.4	1.1	1.5
Barbiturates	Ever?	8.1	8.2	6.4	5.4	3.6	3.8	3.8	3.2
	Last 30 days?	0.9	1.0	0.7	0.6	0.5	0.2	0.7	0.4
Alcohol	Ever?	94.3	95.2	94.2	94.9	94.9	93.1	91.8	88.1
	Last 30 days?	81.8	82.8	79.1	79.7	77.0	74.5	71.4	67.5
Cigarettes	Ever?	NA	NA	NA	NA	NA	NA	NA	NA
	Last 30 days?	25.8	24.4	21.5	22.4	22.6	21.5	23.5	23.5

Source: From Johnston, L. D., O'Malley, P. M., & Bachman, J. G. (1996). *National Survey Results on Drug Use From the* Monitoring the Future Study, 1975–1994: *Vol. 2. College Students and Young Adults.* U.S. Department of Health and Human Services, Public Health Service, National Institutes of Health: National Institute on Drug Abuse. Tables 23 (p. 160) and 25 (p. 162).

converted to the male sex hormone testosterone in the body and helps pump up muscle mass. Many Americans take **depressants** to get to sleep at night and **stimulants** to get going in the morning. Karl Marx charged that "religion . . . is the opium of the people," but heroin is the real "opium of the people." Cocaine was, until recently, a toy of the well-to-do, but price breaks have brought it into the lockers of high school students.

Substance Abuse and Dependence

Where does drug use end and abuse begin? The American Psychiatric Association (1994) defines **substance abuse** as repeated use of a substance despite the fact that it is causing or compounding social, occupational, psychological, or physical problems. If you are missing school or work because you are drunk or "sleeping it off," you are abusing alcohol. The amount you drink is not as crucial as the fact that your pattern of use disrupts your life.

Dependence is more severe than abuse. Dependence has both behavioral and biological aspects (American Psychiatric Association, 1994). Behaviorally, dependence is often characterized by loss of control over one's use of the substance. Dependent people may organize their lives around getting and using a substance. Biological or physiological dependence is typified by tolerance, withdrawal symptoms, or both. **Tolerance** is the body's habituation to a substance, so that with regular usage, higher doses are required to achieve similar effects. There are characteristic withdrawal symptoms, or an **abstinence syndrome**, when the level of usage suddenly drops off. The abstinence syndrome for alcohol includes anxiety, tremors, restlessness, weakness, rapid pulse, and high blood pressure.

When doing without a drug, people who are *psychologically* dependent show signs of anxiety (such as shakiness, rapid pulse, and sweating) that may be similar to abstinence syndromes. Because of these signs, they may believe that they are physiologically dependent on a drug when they are actually psychologically dependent. But symptoms of abstinence from some drugs are unmistakably physiological. One is **delirium tremens** ("the DTs"), experienced by some chronic alcoholics when they suddenly lower their intake of alcohol. The DTs are characterized by heavy sweating, restlessness, general disorientation, and terrifying hallucinations—often of crawling animals.

Causal Factors in Substance Abuse and Dependence

Substance abuse and dependence usually begin with experimental use (Petraitis et al., 1995). Why do people experiment with drugs? Reasons include curiosity, conformity to peer pressure, parental use, rebelliousness, and escape from boredom or pressure (Chassin et al., 1996; Curran et al, 1997). Let us have a deeper look at some psychological and biological theories of substance abuse.

PSYCHOLOGICAL VIEWS Psychodynamic explanations of substance abuse propose that drugs help people control or express unconscious needs and impulses. Alcoholism, for example, is sometimes interpreted as reflecting the need to remain dependent on an overprotective mother. The idea here is that drinking alcohol is an "oral" activity. Within psychodynamic theory, dependence is considered an "oral" trait that develops from experiences during infancy.

DEPRESSANT A drug that lowers the rate of activity of the nervous system.

STIMULANT A drug that increases activity of the nervous system.

SUBSTANCE ABUSE Persistent use of a substance even though it is causing or compounding problems in meeting the demands of life.

TOLERANCE Habituation to a drug, with the result that increasingly higher doses of the drug are needed to achieve similar effects.

ABSTINENCE SYNDROME A characteristic cluster of symptoms that results from sudden decrease in an addictive drug's level of usage.

DELIRIUM TREMENS A condition characterized by sweating, restlessness, disorientation, and hallucinations. The DTs occurs in some chronic alcohol users when there is a sudden decrease in usage.

Social-cognitive theorists suggest that people commonly try tranquilizing agents such as Valium (trade name for diazepam) and alcohol on the basis of a recommendation or observation of others. Cognitive psychologists note that expectations about the effects of a substance are powerful predictors of its use (Sher et al., 1996). Use may be reinforced by the drug's positive effects on mood and its reduction of unpleasant sensations such as anxiety, fear, and tension. For people who are physiologically dependent, avoidance of withdrawal symptoms is also reinforcing. Carrying a supply of the substance is reinforcing because one need not worry about doing without it. Some people, for example, do not leave home without taking along some Valium.

Parents who use drugs may increase their children's knowledge of drugs. They also, in effect, show their children when to use them—for example, when drinking alcohol to reduce tension or to "lubricate" social interactions (Stacy et al., 1991).

BIOLOGICAL VIEWS Certain people may have a genetic predisposition toward physiological dependence on various substances, including alcohol, cocaine, and nicotine (Azar, 1999; Haney et al., 1994; Pihl et al., 1990; Pomerleau et al., 1993). For example, the biological children of alcoholics who are reared by adoptive parents seem more likely to develop alcohol-related problems than the natural children of the adoptive parents. An inherited tendency toward alcoholism may involve greater sensitivity to alcohol (that is, greater enjoyment of it) and greater tolerance of it (Pihl et al., 1990). College students with alcoholic parents exhibit better muscular control and visual-motor coordination when they drink than do college students whose parents are not alcoholics. They also feel less intoxicated when they drink (Pihl et al., 1990).

There are many kinds of psychoactive drugs. Some are depressants, others stimulants, and still others hallucinogenics. Let us consider the effects of these drugs on consciousness.

DEPRESSANTS

Depressant drugs generally act by slowing the activity of the central nervous system. There are also effects specific to each depressant drug. In this section we consider the effects of alcohol, opiates, barbiturates, and methaqualone.

Alcohol

No drug has meant so much to so many as alcohol. Alcohol is our dinnertime relaxant, our bedtime sedative, our cocktail party social facilitator. We use alcohol to celebrate holy days, applaud our accomplishments, and express joyous wishes. The young assert their maturity with alcohol. It is used at least occasionally by 8 to 9 of every 10 high school students (Johnston et al., 1996). Older people use alcohol to stimulate circulation in peripheral areas of the body. Alcohol even kills germs on surface wounds.

Alcohol is the tranquilizer you can buy without prescription. It is the relief from anxiety you can swallow in public without criticism or stigma. A man who takes a Valium tablet may look weak. A man who downs a bottle of beer may be perceived as "macho."

No drug has been so abused as alcohol. Ten million to 20 million Americans are alcoholics. In contrast, 750,000 to 1 million use heroin regularly and about 800,000 use cocaine regularly (O'Brien, 1996). Excessive

ALCOHOLISM, GENDER, AND ETHNICITY

Men are more likely than women to become alcoholics. Why? A cultural explanation is that tighter social constraints are usually placed on women. A biological explanation is that alcohol hits women harder. If, for example, you have the impression that alcohol "goes to women's heads" more quickly than to men's, you are probably correct. Women seem to be more affected by alcohol because they metabolize very little of it in the stomach. Thus alcohol reaches women's bloodstream and brain relatively intact. (Women have less of an enzyme that metabolizes alcohol in the stomach than men do [Lieber, 1990].) Women metabolize alcohol mainly in the liver. According to one health professional, for women "drinking alcohol has the same effect as injecting it intravenously" (Lieber, 1990). Strong stuff indeed.

Ethnicity is connected with alcohol abuse. Native Americans and Irish Americans have the highest rates of alcoholism in the United States (Nevid et al., 2000). Jewish Americans have relatively low rates of alcoholism, a fact for which a cultural explanation is usually offered. Jewish Americans tend to expose children to alcohol (wine) early in life, but they do so within a strong family or religious context. Wine is offered in small quantities, with consequent low blood alcohol levels. Alcohol therefore is not connected with rebellion, aggression, or failure in Jewish culture.

WHY DOES ALCOHOL AFFECT WOMEN MORE QUICKLY THAN MEN?
Alcohol "goes to women's heads" more quickly, even when we control for the factor of body weight.

There are also biological explanations for low levels of drinking among some ethnic groups (e.g., Asian Americans). Asians are more likely than White people to show a "flushing response" to alcohol, as evidenced by redness of the face, rapid heart rate, dizziness, and headaches (Ellickson et al., 1992). Such sensitivity to alcohol may inhibit immoderate drinking among Asian Americans as it may among women. ■

TRUTH OR FICTION REVISITED
It is true that alcohol goes to women's heads more quickly than to men's. Women are less likely to metabolize alcohol before it affects psychological functioning.

drinking has been linked to lower productivity, loss of employment, and downward movement in social status. Yet half of all Americans use alcohol. Despite widespread marijuana use, alcohol is the drug of choice among adolescents.

EFFECTS OF ALCOHOL The effects of alcohol vary with the dose and the duration of use. Low doses of alcohol may be stimulating. Higher doses of alcohol have a sedative effect, which is why alcohol is classified as a depressant. Alcohol relaxes people and deadens minor aches and pains. Alcohol also intoxicates: It impairs cognitive functioning, slurs the speech, and reduces motor coordination. Alcohol is involved in about half of the fatal automobile accidents in the United States.

Alcohol consumption is connected with a drop-off in sexual activity (Leigh, 1993). Yet some drinkers may do things they would not do if they were sober, such as engage in sexual activity on the first date or engage in "unprotected" sex (Cooper & Orcutt, 1997). Why? Perhaps alcohol impairs the thought processes needed to inhibit impulses (Steele & Josephs, 1990). When drunk, people may be less able to foresee the consequences of their behavior. They may also be less likely to summon up their moral beliefs. Then too, alcohol induces feelings of elation and euphoria that may wash away doubts. Alcohol is also associated with a liberated social role in our culture. Drinkers may place the blame on alcohol ("It's the alcohol, not me"), even though they choose to drink.

As a food, alcohol is fattening. Even so, chronic drinkers may be malnourished. Although it is high in calories, alcohol does not contain nutrients such as vitamins and proteins. Moreover, it can interfere with the body's absorption of vitamins, particularly thiamine, a B vitamin. Thus chronic drinking can lead to a number of disorders such as **cirrhosis of the liver**, which has been linked to protein deficiency, and **Wernicke-Korsakoff syndrome**, which has been linked to vitamin B deficiency. However, light to moderate drinking may increase levels of high-density lipoprotein (HDL, or "good" cholesterol) and decrease the risk of cardiovascular disorders (Gaziano et al., 1993). Chronic heavy drinking has been linked to cardiovascular disorders and cancer, however. In particular, heavy drinking places women at risk for breast cancer (McTiernan, 1997). Drinking by a pregnant woman may harm the embryo.

Adolescent involvement with alcohol has repeatedly been linked to poor school grades and other stressors (Wills et al., 1996). Drinking can, of course, contribute to poor grades and other problems, but people may drink to reduce academic and other stresses.

Regardless of how or why one starts drinking, regular drinking can lead to physiological dependence, which motivates people to drink to avoid withdrawal symptoms. Still, even when alcoholics have "dried out"—withdrawn from alcohol—many return to drinking (Schuckit, 1996). Perhaps they still want to use alcohol as a way of coping with stress or as an excuse for failure.

CIRRHOSIS OF THE LIVER A disease caused by protein deficiency in which connective fibers replace active liver cells, impeding circulation of the blood. Alcohol does not contain protein; therefore, persons who drink excessively may be prone to this disease.

WERNICKE-KORSAKOFF SYNDROME A cluster of symptoms associated with chronic alcohol abuse and characterized by confusion, memory impairment, and filling in gaps in memory with false information (confabulation).

TREATING ALCOHOLISM Alcoholics Anonymous (AA) is the most widely used program to treat alcoholism, yet research suggests that other approaches work as well for most people (Ouimette et al., 1997; "Tailoring treatments," 1997). The National Institute on Alcohol Abuse and Alcoholism funded an 8-year study in which more than 1,700 problem drinkers were randomly assigned to AA's 12-step program, cognitive-behavioral therapy, or "motivational-enhancement therapy." The cognitive-behavioral treatment taught problem drinkers how to cope with temptations and how to refuse offers of drinks. Motivational enhancement was designed to enhance drinkers' desires to help themselves. The treatments worked equally well for most people with some exceptions. For example, people with psychological problems fared somewhat better with cognitive-behavioral therapy.

Research is also under way on the use of medicines in treating problem drinking. Disulfiram (Antabuse), for example, cannot be mixed with alcohol. People who take disulfiram experience symptoms such as nausea and vomiting if they drink (Schuckit, 1996).

Opiates

Opiates are a group of **narcotics** derived from the opium poppy, from which they obtain their name. **Opioids** are similar in chemical structure but are synthesized in a laboratory. The ancient Sumerians gave the opium poppy its name: It means "plant of joy." Opiates include morphine, heroin, codeine, Demerol, and similar drugs whose major medical application is relief from pain.

Morphine was introduced in the United States in the 1860, at about the time of the Civil War and in Europe during the Franco-Prussian War. It was used liberally to deaden pain from wounds. Physiological dependence on morphine therefore became known as the "soldier's disease." Little stigma was attached to dependence before morphine became a legally restricted substance.

Heroin was so named because it made people feel "heroic." It was also hailed as the "hero" that would cure physiological dependence on morphine.

Heroin can provide a powerful euphoric rush. Users of heroin claim that it is so pleasurable it can eradicate any thought of food or sex. Although regular users develop tolerance for heroin, high doses can cause drowsiness, stupor, altered time perception, and impaired judgment.

Heroin is illegal. Because the penalties for possession or sale are high, it is also expensive. For this reason, many physiologically dependent people support their habit through dealing (selling heroin), prostitution, or selling stolen goods.

Methadone is a synthetic opioid. It has been used to treat physiological dependence on heroin in the same way that heroin was once used to treat physiological dependence on morphine. Methadone is slower acting than heroin and does not provide the thrilling rush. Some people must be maintained on methadone for many years before they can be gradually withdrawn from it (O'Brien, 1996). Some must be maintained on methadone indefinitely because they are unwilling to undergo any withdrawal symptoms.

Narcotics can have distressing withdrawal syndromes, especially when used in high doses. Such syndromes may begin with flulike symptoms and progress through tremors, cramps, chills alternating with sweating, rapid pulse, high blood pressure, insomnia, vomiting, and diarrhea. However, these syndromes are variable from one person to another.

Many people who obtain prescriptions for opiates for pain relief neither experience a euphoric rush nor become psychologically dependent on them (Lang & Patt, 1994). If they no longer need opiates for pain but have become physiologically dependent on them, they can usually quit with few, if any, side effects by gradually decreasing their dosage (Rosenthal, 1993). Thus difficulty or ease of withdrawal may be connected with one's motives for using psychoactive drugs. Those who are seeking habitual relief from psychological pain seem to become more dependent on them than people who are seeking time-limited relief from physical pain.

TRUTH OR FICTION REVISITED
It is true that heroin was once used as a cure for addiction to morphine. Today an opioid, methadone, is used to help addicts avert the symptoms caused by withdrawal from heroin.

OPIATES A group of narcotics derived from the opium poppy that provide a euphoric rush and depress the nervous system.

NARCOTICS Drugs used to relieve pain and induce sleep. The term is usually reserved for opiates.

OPIOIDS Chemicals that act on opiate receptors but are not derived from the opium poppy.

Barbiturates and Methaqualone

Barbiturates are depressants with a number of medical uses, including relief of anxiety and tension, deadening of pain, and treatment of epilepsy, high blood pressure, and insomnia. Barbiturates lead rapidly to physiological and psychological dependence. **Methaqualone** is a depressant whose effects are similar to those of barbiturates. Methaqualone also leads to physiological dependence and is quite dangerous.

Barbiturates and methaqualone are popular as street drugs because they are relaxing and produce mild euphoria. High doses of barbiturates result in drowsiness, motor impairment, slurred speech, irritability, and poor judgment. A physiologically dependent person who is withdrawn abruptly from barbiturates may experience severe convulsions and die. Because of additive effects, it is dangerous to mix alcohol and other depressants.

STIMULANTS

All stimulants increase the activity of the nervous system. Their other effects vary somewhat, and some contribute to feelings of euphoria and self-confidence.

Amphetamines

Amphetamines are a group of stimulants that were first used by soldiers during World War II to help them remain alert through the night. Truck drivers have used them to stay awake all night. Amphetamines have become perhaps more widely known through students, who have used them for all-night cram sessions, and through dieters, who use them because they reduce hunger.

Called speed, uppers, bennies (for Benzedrine), and dexies (for Dexedrine), these drugs are often used for the euphoric rush they can produce, especially in high doses. Some people swallow amphetamines in pill form or inject liquid methedrine, the strongest form, into their veins. They may stay awake and high for days on end. Such highs must come to an end. People who have been on prolonged highs sometimes "crash," or fall into a deep sleep or depression. Some people commit suicide when crashing.

A related stimulant, methylphenidate (Ritalin), is widely used to treat **attention-deficit hyperactivity disorder** in children. Ritalin has been shown to increase attention span, decrease aggressive and disruptive behavior, and lead to academic gains (Klorman et al., 1994). Why should Ritalin, a stimulant, calm children? Hyperactivity may be connected with immaturity of the cerebral cortex, and Ritalin may stimulate the cortex to exercise control over more primitive centers in the lower brain.

High doses of amphetamines may cause restlessness, insomnia, loss of appetite, hallucinations, paranoid delusions (e.g., false ideas that others are eavesdropping or intend to harm them), and irritability.

Cocaine

Do you recall the commercials claiming that "Coke adds life"? Given its caffeine and sugar content, "Coke"—Coca-Cola, that is—should provide quite a lift. But Coca-Cola hasn't been "the real thing" since 1906, when the company discontinued the use of cocaine in its formula. Cocaine is derived from coca leaves—the plant from which the soft drink took its name.

TRUTH OR FICTION REVISITED
It is true that a stimulant is commonly used to treat children who are hyperactive. That stimulant is methylphenidate, or Ritalin.

BARBITURATE An addictive depressant used to relieve anxiety or induce sleep.

METHAQUALONE An addictive depressant. Often called "ludes."

AMPHETAMINES Stimulants derived from *alpha-methyl-beta-phenyl-ethyl-amine*, a colorless liquid consisting of carbon, hydrogen, and nitrogen.

ATTENTION-DEFICIT/HYPERACTIVITY DISORDER A disorder that begins in childhood and is characterized by a persistent pattern of lack of attention, with or without hyperactivity and impulsive behavior.

Coca leaves contain cocaine, a stimulant that produces euphoria, reduces hunger, deadens pain, and bolsters self-confidence. Cocaine's popularity with college students seems to have peaked in the mid-1980s (Johnston et al., 1996). The majority of high school students now believe that use of cocaine is harmful (Johnston et al., 1996).

Cocaine may be brewed from coca leaves as a "tea," "snorted" in powder form, or injected in liquid form. Repeated snorting constricts blood vessels in the nose, drying the skin and sometimes exposing cartilage and perforating the nasal septum. These problems require cosmetic surgery. The potent cocaine derivatives known as "crack" and "bazooka" are inexpensive because they are unrefined.

Biologically speaking, cocaine stimulates sudden rises in blood pressure, constricts the coronary arteries (decreasing the oxygen supply to the heart), and quickens the heart rate (Kaufman et al., 1998). These events occasionally result in respiratory and cardiovascular collapse (Moliterno et al., 1994). The sudden deaths of a number of athletes have been caused in this way. Overdoses can lead to restlessness and insomnia, tremors, headaches, nausea, convulsions, hallucinations, and delusions. Use of crack has been connected with strokes.

Cocaine—also called *snow* and *coke,* like the slang term for the soft drink—has been used as a local anesthetic since the early 1800s. In 1884, it came to the attention of a young Viennese neurologist named Sigmund Freud, who used it to fight his own depression and published an article about it titled "Song of Praise." Freud's early ardor was tempered when he learned that cocaine is habit forming and can cause hallucinations and delusions. Cocaine causes physiological as well as psychological dependence (Brown & Massaro, 1996).

Cigarettes (Nicotine)

> [Smoking: a] *"custome lothesome to the Eye, hatefull to the Nose, harmefull to the Braine, dangerous to the Lungs."*
>
> KING JAMES I, 1604

Nicotine is the stimulant in cigarettes. Nicotine stimulates discharge of the hormone adrenaline and the release of many neurotransmitters, including dopamine and acetylcholine. Adrenaline creates a burst of autonomic activity that accelerates the heart rate and pours sugar into the blood. Acetylcholine is vital in memory formation, and nicotine appears to enhance memory and attention, improve performance on simple, repetitive tasks (Kinnunen et al., 1996; O'Brien, 1996), and enhance mood. Yet it also appears to relax people and reduce stress (O'Brien, 1996).

Nicotine depresses the appetite and raises the metabolic rate (Meyers et al., 1997). Thus some people smoke in order to control their weight. People also tend to eat more when they stop smoking (Klesges et al., 1997), causing some to return to the habit.

Nicotine is the agent that creates physiological dependence on cigarettes (Kessler, 1995). Regular smokers adjust their smoking to maintain fairly even levels of nicotine in their bloodstream (Shiffman et al., 1997). Symptoms of withdrawal from nicotine include nervousness, drowsiness, loss of energy, headaches, irregular bowel movements, lightheadedness, insomnia, dizziness, cramps, palpitations, tremors, and sweating. Because many of these symptoms resemble those of anxiety, it was once thought that they might reflect the anxiety of attempting to quit smoking, rather than addiction.

SNORTING COCAINE.
Cocaine is a powerful stimulant. Health professionals have become concerned about its effects, including sudden rises in blood pressure, constriction of blood vessels, and acceleration of heart rate. Several athletes have died from cocaine overdoses.

TRUTH OR FICTION REVISITED
It is true that Coca-Cola once "added life" through a powerful but now illegal stimulant. That stimulant is cocaine.

TABLE C.2

SNAPSHOT, U.S.A.: HUMAN DIVERSITY AND SMOKING

FACTOR	GROUP	PERCENT WHO SMOKE
Gender	Women	23.5
	Men	28.1
Age	18–24	22.9
	25–44	30.4
	45–64	26.9
	65–74	16.5
	75 and above	8.4
Ethnic Group	African American	29.2
	Asian American/Pacific Islander	16.0
	Hispanic American	20.2
	Native American	31.4
	Non-Hispanic White American	25.5
Level of Education	Fewer than 12 years	32.0
	12	30.0
	13–15	23.4
	16 and above	13.6
Socioeconomic Status (SES)	Below poverty level	33.3
	At poverty level or above	24.7

Source: From Office of Smoking and Health, Centers for Disease Control (1993).

TRUTH OR FICTION REVISITED
It is true that the number of people who die from smoking-related causes is greater than the total number lost to motor vehicle accidents, abuse of alcohol and all other drugs, suicide, homicide, and AIDS.

HYDROCARBONS Chemical compounds consisting of hydrogen and carbon.

THE PERILS OF SMOKING It's no secret. Cigarette packs sold in the United States carry messages like "Warning: The Surgeon General Has Determined That Cigarette Smoking Is Dangerous to Your Health." Cigarette advertising has been banned on radio and television. Nearly 420,000 Americans die from smoking-related illnesses each year (Rosenblatt, 1994). This is the equivalent of two jumbo jets colliding in midair each day with all passengers lost. It is higher than the number of people who die from motor vehicle accidents, alcohol and drug abuse, suicide, homicide, and AIDS *combined* (Rosenblatt, 1994).

The percentage of American adults who smoke overall declined from more than 40% in the mid-1960s to about 25% in recent years, but there have been increases among women, African Americans, and 8th to 12th graders (Feder, 1997). The incidence of smoking is connected with gender, age, ethnicity, level of education, and socioeconomic status (see Table C.2). Better educated people are less likely to smoke. They are also more likely to quit smoking (Rose et al., 1996).

Every cigarette smoked steals about 7 minutes of a person's life. The carbon monoxide in cigarette smoke impairs the blood's ability to carry oxygen, causing shortness of breath. It is apparently the **hydrocarbons** ("tars") in cigarette smoke that lead to lung cancer. Heavy smokers are about 10 times as likely as nonsmokers to die of lung cancer (Nevid et al., 1998). Cigarette smoking is also linked to death from heart disease, chronic lung and respiratory diseases, and other health problems. Women who smoke show reduced bone density, significantly increasing the risk of fracture of the hip and back (Hopper & Seeman, 1994). Pregnant women who smoke risk miscarriage, premature birth, and birth defects.

Passive smoking is also connected with respiratory illnesses, asthma, and other health problems and accounts for more than 50,000 deaths per year (Nevid et al., 1998). Because of the noxious effects of secondhand smoke, smoking has been banished from many public places such as airplanes, restaurants, and elevators.

Why, then, do people smoke? For many reasons—such as the desire to look sophisticated (although these days smokers may be more likely to be judged foolish than sophisticated), to have something to do with their hands, and—of course—to take in nicotine.

HALLUCINOGENICS

Hallucinogenic drugs are so named because they produce hallucinations—that is, sensations and perceptions in the absence of external stimulation. But hallucinogenic drugs may also have additional effects such as relaxation, euphoria, or, in some cases, panic.

Marijuana

Marijuana is produced from the *Cannabis sativa* plant, which grows wild in many parts of the world. Marijuana helps some people relax and can elevate their mood. It also sometimes produces mild hallucinations, which is why it is classified as a **psychedelic,** or hallucinogenic, drug. The major psychedelic substance in marijuana is delta-9-tetrahydrocannabinol, or THC. THC is found in the branches and leaves of the plant, but it is highly concentrated in the sticky resin. **Hashish,** or "hash," is derived from the resin. Hashish is more potent than marijuana.

In the 19th century marijuana was used much as aspirin is used today for headaches and minor aches and pains. It could be bought without a prescription in any drugstore. Today marijuana use and possession are illegal in most states. Marijuana also carries a number of health risks. For example, it impairs motor coordination and perceptual functions used in driving and operating machines. It impairs short-term memory and slows learning. Although it causes positive mood changes in many people, there are also disturbing instances of anxiety and confusion and occasional reports of psychotic reactions. Marijuana increases the heart rate to 140–150 beats per minute and, in some people, raises blood pressure. This higher demand on the heart and circulation poses a threat to people with hypertension and cardiovascular disorders. Moreover, marijuana smoke contains more carcinogenic hydrocarbons than tobacco smoke.

PSYCHOLOGICAL EFFECTS OF MARIJUANA
Some people report that marijuana helps them socialize at parties. Moderate to strong intoxication is linked to reports of heightened perceptions and increases in self-insight, creative thinking, and empathy for the feelings of others. Time seems to pass more slowly for people who are strongly intoxicated. A song might seem to last an hour rather than a few minutes. There is increased awareness of bodily sensations such as heartbeat. Marijuana smokers also report that strong intoxication heightens sexual sensations. Visual hallucinations are not uncommon. Strong intoxication may cause smokers to experience disorientation. If the smoker's mood is euphoric, loss of a sense of personal identity may be interpreted as being in harmony with the universe.

CIGARETTES: SMOKING GUNS?
The perils of cigarette smoking are widely known today. One surgeon general declared that cigarette smoking is the chief preventable cause of death in the United States. The numbers of Americans who die from smoking are comparable to the number of lives that would be lost if two jumbo jets crashed *every day*. If flying were that unsafe, would the government ground all flights? Would the public continue to make airline reservations?

PASSIVE SMOKING Inhaling of smoke from the tobacco products and exhalations of other people; also called *secondhand smoking.*

HALLUCINOGENIC Giving rise to hallucinations.

MARIJUANA The dried vegetable matter of the *Cannabis sativa* plant.

PSYCHEDELIC Causing hallucinations, delusions, or heightened perceptions.

HASHISH A drug derived from the resin of *Cannabis sativa.* Often called "hash."

Some marijuana smokers have negative experiences. An accelerated heart rate and heightened awareness of bodily sensations leads some smokers to fear that their heart will "run away" with them. Some smokers find disorientation threatening and are afraid that they will not regain their identity. Strong intoxication sometimes causes nausea and vomiting.

People can become psychologically dependent on marijuana, but it is not known to cause physiological dependence. Tolerance of a drug is a sign of physiological dependence. With marijuana, however, regular usage is often associated with the need for *less,* not *more,* to achieve the same effects.

Marijuana has been used to treat health problems, including glaucoma and the nausea experienced by cancer patients undergoing chemotherapy ("More research needed," 1997). However, in most cases other drugs are available for these purposes (Kolata, 1994).

LSD and Other Hallucinogenics

LSD is the abbreviation for lysergic acid diethylamide, a synthetic hallucinogenic drug. Users of "acid" claim that it "expands consciousness" and opens up new worlds to them. Sometimes people believe they have achieved great insights while using LSD, but when it wears off they often cannot apply or recall these discoveries. As a powerful hallucinogenic, LSD produces vivid and colorful hallucinations.

LSD Lysergic acid diethylamide. A hallucinogenic drug.

AN LSD TRIP?
This hallucinogenic drug can give rise to a vivid parade of colors and visual distortions. Some users claim to have achieved great insights while "tripping," but typically they have been unable to recall or apply them afterward.

Some LSD users have **flashbacks**—distorted perceptions or hallucinations that mimic the LSD "trip" but occur days, weeks, or longer after usage. Some researchers have speculated that flashbacks stem from chemical changes in the brain produced by LSD. Others suggest psychological explanations for flashbacks. Matefy (1980) found that LSD users who have flashbacks can become engrossed in role playing. Perhaps flashbacks involve enacting the role of being on a trip. This does not mean that people who claim to have flashbacks are lying. They may be more willing to surrender personal control in their quest for psychedelic experience. Users who do not have flashbacks prefer to be more in charge of their thought processes and choose to focus on the demands of daily life.

Other hallucinogenic drugs include **mescaline** (derived from the peyote cactus) and **phencyclidine** (PCP). Regular use of hallucinogenics may lead to tolerance and psychological dependence. But hallucinogenics are not known to lead to physiological dependence. High doses may induce frightening hallucinations, impaired coordination, poor judgment, mood changes, and paranoid delusions.

Consciousness is that precious thing that enables us to observe and make sense of our environment, and to act on our environment. Most conscious activity occurs in what we call the "normal" waking state, but we apparently need rest from this state through sleep. Being creative, humans have also experimented with many ways of altering consciousness, often as a way of enhancing the nature of everyday experience or gaining special insight. The widespread use of alcohol indicates that some methods of altering consciousness have become an integral part of our culture. However, as noted in this chapter, many ways of altering consciousness—including the use of alcohol—carry certain risks. Rather than focusing on ways of altering consciousness, most of us can probably do a great deal more to appreciate the normal waking state—perhaps by listening to music, exploring hobbies, getting involved in exercise, visiting museums, and thinking about our philosophies of life. It's a big universe out there, filled with endless potential, and our consciousness is our way of connecting to it.

FLASHBACKS Distorted perceptions or hallucinations that occur days or weeks after LSD usage but mimic the LSD experience.

MESCALINE A hallucinogenic drug derived from the mescal (peyote) cactus.

PHENCYCLIDINE Another hallucinogenic drug whose name is an acronym for its chemical structure. Abbreviated *PCP*.

SUMMARY

1. **What is consciousness?** The term *consciousness* has several meanings, including (1) sensory awareness, (2) direct inner awareness of cognitive processes, (3) personal unity or the sense of self, and (4) the waking state.

2. **What are the stages of sleep?** Electroencephalograph (EEG) records show different stages of sleep, as characterized by different types of brain waves. There are four stages of non-rapid-eye-movement (NREM) sleep and one stage of REM sleep. Stage 1 sleep is the lightest and stage 4 is the deepest.

3. **What are the functions of sleep?** Sleep apparently serves a restorative function, but we do not know exactly how sleep restores us or how much sleep we need.

4. **What are dreams?** Dreams are a form of cognitive activity that occurs mostly while we are sleeping. Most dreaming occurs during REM sleep. The content of most dreams is an extension of the events of the previous day. Nightmares are also dreams that occur during REM sleep.

5. **What are the sleep disorders?** A common sleep disorder is insomnia, which is most often encountered by people who are anxious and tense. Deep sleep disorders include sleep terrors, bed-wetting, and sleepwalking.

6. **What is hypnosis?** Hypnosis is an altered state of consciousness in which the individual may exhibit passivity, narrowed attention, hypermnesia (heightened memory), suggestibility, assumption of unusual roles, perceptual distortions, posthypnotic amnesia, and posthypnotic suggestion.

7. **How do psychologists explain hypnosis?** Current theories of hypnosis deny the existence of a special trance state. Rather, they emphasize people's ability to role-play the "trance" and to divide consciousness as directed by the hypnotist.

8. **What is meditation?** In meditation, one focuses "passively" on an object or a mantra in order to alter the normal relationship between oneself and the environment. In this way, consciousness (that is, the normal focuses of attention) is altered, and relaxation is often induced. TM and other forms of meditation appear to reduce high blood pressure as well as produce relaxation.

9. **What is biofeedback?** Biofeedback is a method for increasing consciousness of bodily functions. In biofeedback, the organism is continuously provided with information about a targeted biological response such as heart rate or emission of alpha waves. People and lower animals can learn to control functions such as heart rate and blood pressure through biofeedback training.

10. **What are substance abuse and dependence?** Substance abuse is use that persists even though it impairs one's functioning. Dependence has behavioral and physiological aspects. It may be characterized by organizing one's life around getting and using the substance and by the development of tolerance, withdrawal symptoms, or both.

11. **Why do people abuse drugs?** People usually try drugs out of curiosity, but usage can be reinforced by anxiety reduction, feelings of euphoria, and other positive sensations. People are also motivated to avoid withdrawal symptoms once they become physiologically dependent on a drug. Some people may have genetic predispositions to become physiologically dependent on certain substances.

12. **What are depressants?** The group of substances called depressants act by slowing the activity of the central nervous system.

13. **What are the effects of alcohol?** Alcohol is an intoxicating depressant that can lead to physiological dependence. It provides an excuse for failure or for antisocial behavior, but it has not been shown to induce such behavior directly.

14. **What are the effects of opiates?** The opiates morphine and heroin are depressants that reduce pain, but they are also bought on the street because of the euphoric rush they provide. Opiate use can lead to physiological dependence.

15. **What are the effects of barbiturates?** Barbiturates are depressants used to treat epilepsy, high blood pressure, anxiety, and insomnia. They lead rapidly to physiological dependence.

16. **What are stimulants?** Stimulants are substances that act by increasing the activity of the nervous system.

17. **What are the effects of amphetamines?** Amphetamines are stimulants that produce feelings of euphoria when taken in high doses. But high doses may also cause restlessness, insomnia, psychotic symptoms, and a crash upon withdrawal. Amphetamines

and a related stimulant, Ritalin, are commonly used to treat hyperactive children.

18. **What are the effects of cocaine?** As a psychoactive substance, cocaine provides feelings of euphoria and bolsters self-confidence. Cocaine causes sudden rises in blood pressure and constricts blood vessels. Overdoses can lead to restlessness, insomnia, psychotic reactions, and cardio-respiratory collapse.

19. **What are the effects of smoking cigarettes?** Cigarette smoke contains carbon monoxide, hydrocarbons, and the stimulant nicotine. Regular smokers adjust their smoking to maintain a consistent level of nicotine in the blood, suggestive of physiological dependence. Cigarette smoking has been linked to death from heart disease and cancer, and to other health problems.

20. **What are hallucinogenics?** Hallucinogenic substances produce hallucinations—sensations and perceptions that occur in the absence of external stimulation.

21. **What are the effects of marijuana?** Marijuana is a hallucinogenic substance whose active ingredients, including THC, often produce relaxation, heightened and distorted perceptions, feelings of empathy, and reports of new insights. Hallucinations may occur. The long-term effects of marijuana use are not fully known, although it appears that marijuana smoke itself is harmful.

22. **What are the effects of LSD?** LSD is a hallucinogenic drug that produces vivid hallucinations.

KEY TERMS

abstinence syndrome (p. C-17)

activation-synthesis model (p. C-8)

age regression (p. C-12)

alpha waves (p. C-5)

amphetamines (p. C-22)

attention-deficit/hyperactivity disorder (p. C-22)

barbiturate (p. C-22)

biofeedback training (BFT) (p. C-15)

circadian rhythm (p. C-4)

cirrhosis of the liver (p. C-20)

delirium tremens (p. C-17)

delta waves (p. C-6)

depressant (p. C-17)

direct inner awareness (p. C-3)

electromyograph (EMG) (p. C-15)

flashbacks (p. C-27)

hallucinations (p. C-12)

hallucinogenic (p. C-25)

hashish (p. C-25)

hydrocarbons (p. C-24)

hypermnesia (p. C-12)

hypnagogic state (p. C-5)

hypnosis (p. C-11)

LSD (p. C-26)

marijuana (p. C-25)

mescaline (p. C-27)

methaqualone (p. C-22)

narcotics (p. C-21)

neodissociation theory (p. C-13)

nonconscious (p. C-4)

non-rapid-eye-movement sleep (p. C-5)

opiates (p. C-21)

opioids (p. C-21)

passive smoking (p. C-25)

phencyclidine (p. C-27)

preconscious (p. C-3)

psychedelic (p. C-25)

psychoactive substances (p. C-16)

rapid-eye-movement sleep (p. C-5)

regression (p. C-13)

repression (p. C-3)

role theory (p. C-13)

selective attention (p. C-3)

sleep terrors (p. C-10)

stimulant (p. C-17)

substance abuse (p. C-17)

suppression (p. C-4)

theta waves (p. C-5)

tolerance (p. C-17)

transcendental meditation (TM) (p. C-14)

unconscious (p. C-3)

Wernicke-Korsakoff syndrome (p. C-20)

REFERENCES

Adler, T. (1993). Sleep loss impairs attention—and more. *APA Monitor, 24*(9), 22–23.

American Psychiatric Association. (1994). *Diagnostic and statistical manual of the mental disorders* (4th ed.). Washington, DC: Author.

Azar, B. (1999). New pieces filling in addiction puzzle. *APA Monitor, 30*(1), 1, 15.

Basen-Engquist, K., Edmundson, E. W., & Parcel, G. S. (1996). Structure of health risk behavior among high school students. *Journal of Consulting and Clinical Psychology, 64,* 764–775.

Basic Behavioral Science Task Force of the National Advisory Mental Health Council. (1996). Basic behavioral science research for mental health: Perception, attention, learning, and memory. *American Psychologist, 51,* 133–142.

Benson, H. (1975). *The relaxation response.* New York: Morrow.

Berquier, A., & Ashton, R. (1992). Characteristics of the frequent nightmare sufferer. *Journal of Abnormal Psychology, 101,* 246–250.

Bootzin, R. R., Epstein, D., & Wood, J. N. (1991). Stimulus control instructions. In P. Hauri (Ed.), *Case studies in insomnia.* New York: Plenum.

Bowers, K. S., & Woody, E. Z. (1996). Hypnotic amnesia and the paradox of intentional forgetting. *Journal of Abnormal Psychology, 105,* 381–390.

Brown, M., & Massaro, S. (1996). New brain studies yield insights into cocaine binging and addiction. *Journal of Addictive Diseases, 15*(4).

Chassin, L., Curran, P. J., Hussong, A. M., & Colder, C. R. (1996). The relation of parent alcoholism to adolescent substance use. *Journal of Abnormal Psychology, 105,* 70–80.

Cooper, M. L., & Orcutt, H. K. (1997). Drinking and sexual experience on first dates among adolescents. *Journal of Abnormal Psychology, 106,* 191–202.

Crawford, H. J., Brown, A. M., & Moon, C. E. (1993). Sustained attentional and disattentional abilities: Differences between low and highly hypnotizable persons. *Journal of Abnormal Psychology, 102,* 534–543.

Crick, F., & Koch, C. (1997). The problem of consciousness. *Scientific American Mysteries of the Mind* [Special issue] 7(1), 18–26.

Curran, P. J., Stice, E., & Chassin, L. (1997). The relation between adolescent alcohol use and peer alcohol use. *Journal of Consulting and Clinical Psychology, 65,* 130–140.

Ellickson, P. L., Hays, R. D., & Bell, R. M. (1992). Stepping through the drug use sequence. *Journal of Abnormal Psychology, 101,* 441–451.

Feder, B. J. (1997, April 20). Surge in the teenage smoking rate left the tobacco industry vulnerable. *New York Times,* pp. A1, A28.

Gaziano, J. M., et al. (1993). Moderate alcohol intake, increased levels of high-density lipoprotein and its subfractions, and decreased risk of myocardial infarction. *New Enland Journal of Medicine, 329,* 1829–1834.

Gazzaniga, M. S. (1997). Cited in Gorman, J. (1997, April 29). Consciousness studies: From stream to flood. *New York Times,* pp. C1, C5.

Gorman, J. (1997, April 29). Consciousness studies: From stream to flood. *New York Times,* pp. C1, C5.

Haney, M., et al. (1994). Cocaine sensitivity in Roman high and low avoidance rats is modulated by sex and gonadal hormone status. *Brain Research, 645*(1–2), 179–185.

Hilgard, E. R. (1994). Neodissociation theory. In S. J. Lynn & J. W. Rhue (Eds.), *Dissociation: Clinical, theoretical and research perspectives.* New York: Guilford Press.

Hobson, J. A., & McCarley, R. W. (1977). The brain as a dream-state generator: An activation-synthesis hypothesis of the dream process. *American Journal of Psychiatry, 134,* 1335–1348.

Holmes, D. S. (1984). Meditation and somatic arousal reduction. *American Psychologist, 39,* 1–10.

Hopper, J. L., & Seeman, E. (1994). The bone density of female twins discordant for tobacco use. *New England Journal of Medicine, 330,* 387–392.

Johnson, K. (1998, August 31). As drugs in sports proliferate, so do ethical questions. *New York Times,* pp. C1, C4.

Johnston, L. D., O'Malley, P. M., & Bachman, J. G. (1996). National survey results on drug use from the *Monitoring the Future Study, 1975–1995.* National Institute on Drug Abuse, 5600 Fishers Lane, Rockville, MD 20957; USDHHS, Public Health Service, National Institutes of Health.

Kaufman, M., et al. 1998, February 4). Cocaine-induced cerebral vasoconstriction detected in humans with magnetic resonance angiography. *Journal of the American Medical Association, 279*(5).

Kessler, D. A. (1995). Nicotine addiction in young people. *New England Journal of Medicine, 333,* 186–189.

Kimble, G. A. (1994). A frame of reference for psychology. *American Psychologist, 49,* 510–519.

Kinnunen, T., Doherty, K., Militello, F. S., & Garvey, A. J. (1996). Depression and smoking cessation. *Journal of Consulting and Clinical Psychology, 64,* 791–798.

Kinnunen, T., Zamansky, H. S., & Block, M. L. (1994). Is the hypnotized subject lying? *Journal of Abnormal Psychology, 103,* 184–191.

Kirsch, I., Montgomery, G., & Sapirstein, G. (1995). Hypnosis as an adjunct to cognitive-behavioral psychotherapy. *Journal of Consulting and Clinical Psychology, 63,* 214–220.

Klesges, R. C., et al. (1997). How much weight gain occurs following smoking cessation? *Journal of Consulting and Clinical Psychology, 65,* 286–291.

Klorman, R., Brumaghim, J. T., Fitzpatrick, P. A., Borgstedt, A. D., & Strauss, J. (1994). Clinical and cognitive effects of methylphenidate on children with attention deficit disorder as a function of aggression/oppositionality and age. *Journal of Abnormal Psychology, 103,* 206–221.

Kolata, G. (1994, February 16). Debate on using marijuana as medicine turns to question of whether it works. *New York Times,* p. C12.

Kupfer, D. J., & Reynolds, C. F. (1997). Management of insomnia. *New England Journal of Medicine, 336,* 341–346.

Lacks, P., & Morin, C. M. (1992). Recent advances in the assessment and treatment of insomnia. *Journal of Consulting and Clinical Psychology, 60,* 586–594.

Lang, S. S., & Patt, R. B. (1994). *You don't have to suffer.* New York: Oxford University Press.

Leigh, B. C. (1993). Alcohol consumption and sexual activity as reported with a diary technique. *Journal of Abnormal Psychology, 102,* 490–493.

Lieber, C. S. (1990). Cited in Barroom biology: How alcohol goes to a woman's head (January 14). *New York Times,* p. E24.

Loftus, E. F. (1994). Cited in D. Goleman (1994, May 31). Miscoding is seen as the root of false memories. *New York Times,* pp. C1, C8.

Maas, J. B. (1998). *Power sleep: Revolutionary strategies that prepare your mind and body for peak performance.* New York: Villard.

Matefy, R. (1980). Role-playing theory of psychedelic flashbacks. *Journal of Consulting and Clinical Psychology, 48,* 551–553.

McCarley, R. W. (1992). Cited in Blakeslee, S. (1992, January 7). Scientists unraveling chemistry of dreams. *New York Times,* pp. C1, C10.

McTiernan, A. (1997). Exercise and breast cancer. *New England Journal of Medicine, 336,* 1311–1312.

Meyers, A. W., et al. (1997). Are weight concerns predictive of smoking cessation? *Journal of Consulting and Clinical Psychology, 65,* 448–452.

Miller, J. L. (1992). Trouble in mind. *Scientific American, 267*(3), 180.

Miller, M. E., & Bowers, K. S. (1993). Hypnotic analgesia. *Journal of Abnormal Psychology, 102,* 29–38.

Miller, M. F., Barabasz, A. F., & Barabasz, M. (1991). Effects of active alert and relaxation hypnotic inductions on cold pressor pain. *Journal of Abnormal Psychology, 100,* 223–226.

Miller, N. E. (1969). Learning of visceral and glandular responses. *Science, 163,* 434–445.

Mindell, J. A. (1993). Sleep disorders in children. *Health Psychology, 12,* 151–162.

Moliterno, D. J., et al. (1994). Coronary-artery vasoconstriction induced by cocaine, cigarette smoking, or both. *New England Journal of Medicine, 330,* 454–459.

More research needed on medical use of marijuana. (1997). *APA Monitor, 28*(4), 9.

National Highway Traffic Safety Administration. (1998). Cited in Brody, J. E. (1998, March 31).

Facing up to the realities of sleep deprivation. *New York Times,* p. F7.

National Sleep Foundation. (1998). Cited in Brody, J. E. (1998, March 31). Facing up to the realities of sleep deprivation. *New York Times,* p. F7.

National Sleep Foundation (1999). Cited in Hellmich, N. (1999, March 23). Boomers' lifestyles lead to insomnia. *USA Today.*

Nevid, J. S., Rathus, S. A., & Greene, B. A. (2000). *Abnormal psychology in a changing world* (4th ed.). Upper Saddle River, NJ: Prentice Hall.

Nevid, J. S., Rathus, S. A., & Rubenstein, H. (1998). *Health in the new millennium.* New York: Worth.

O'Brien, C. P. (1996). Recent developments in the pharmacotherapy of substance abuse. *Journal of Consulting and Clinical Psychology, 64,* 677–686.

Ouimette, P. C., Finney, J. W., & Moos, R. H. (1997). Twelve-step and cognitive-behavioral treatment for substance abuse. *Journal of Consulting and Clinical Psychology, 65,* 230–240.

Petraitis, J., Flay, B. R., & Miller, T. Q. (1995). Reviewing theories of adolescent substance use. *Psychological Bulletin, 1995,* 67–86.

Pihl, R. O., Peterson, J. B., & Finn, P. (1990). Inherited predisposition to alcoholism. *Journal of Abnormal Psychology, 99,* 291–301.

Pomerleau, O. F., Collins, A. C., Shiffman, S., & Pomerleau, C. S. (1993). Why some people smoke and others do not. *Journal of Consulting and Clinical Psychology, 61,* 723–731.

Reiser, M. (1992). *Memory and mind and brain.* New York: Basic Books.

Rose, J. S., Chassin, L., Presson, C. C., & Sherman, S. J. (1996).

Prospective predictors of quit attempts and smoking cessation in young adults. *Health Psychology, 15,* 261–268.

Rosenblatt, R. (1994, March 20). How do tobacco executives live with themselves? *New York Times Magazine,* pp. 34–41, 55, 73–76.

Rosenthal, E. (1993, March 28). Patients in pain find relief, not addiction, in narcotics. *New York Times,* pp. A1, A24.

Rychlak, J. F. (1997). *In defense of human consciousness.* Washington, DC: American Psychological Association.

Sarbin, T. R., & Coe, W. C. (1972). *Hypnosis.* New York: Holt, Rinehart and Winston.

Schuckit, M. A. (1996). Recent developments in the pharmacotherapy of alcohol dependence. *Journal of Consulting and Clinical Psychology, 64,* 669–676.

Sher, K. J., Wood, M. D., Wood, P. K., & Raskin, G. (1996). Alcohol outcome expectancies and alcohol use. *Journal of Abnormal Psychology, 105,* 561–574.

Shiffman, S., et al. (1997). A day at a time: Predicting smoking lapse from daily urge. *Journal of Abnormal Psychology, 106,* 104–116.

Stacy, A. W., Newcomb, M. D., & Bentler, P. M. (1991). Cognitive motivation and drug use. *Journal of Abnormal Psychology, 100,* 502–515.

Steele, C. M., & Josephs, R. A. (1990). Alcohol myopia. *American Psychologist, 45,* 921–933.

Tailoring treatments for alcoholics is not the answer. (1997). *APA Monitor, 28*(2), 6–7.

Wade, N. (1998, January 6). Was Freud Wrong? Are Dreams the Brain's Start-Up Test? *New York Times.*

Watson, J. B. (1913). Psychology as the behaviorist views it. *Psychological Review, 20,* 158–177.

Webb, W. (1993). Cited in Adler, T. (1993). Sleep loss impairs attention—and more. *APA Monitor, 24*(9), 22–23.

Weekes, J. R., Lynn, S. J., Green, J. P., & Brentar, J. T. (1992). Pseudomemory in hypnotized and task-motivated subjects. *Journal of Abnormal Psychology, 101,* 356–360.

White, J. L., & Nicassio, P. M. (1990, November). *The relationship between daily stress, pre-sleep arousal and sleep disturbance in good and poor sleepers.* Paper presented at the annual meeting of the Association for the Advancement of Behavior Therapy, San Francisco.

Wills, T. A., McNamara, G., Vaccaro, D., & Hirky, A. E. (1996). Escalated substance abuse. *Journal of Abnormal Psychology, 195,* 166–180.

Wood, J. M., & Bootzin, R. R. (1990). The prevalence of nightmares and their independence from anxiety. *Journal of Abnormal Psychology, 99,* 64–68.

Wood, J. M., Bootzin, R. R., Rosenhan, D., Nolen-Hoeksema, S., & Jourden, F. (1992). Effects of the 1989 San Francisco earthquake on frequency and content of nightmares. *Journal of Abnormal Psychology, 101,* 219–224.

L

LEARNING

TRUTH OR FICTION?

——— Dogs can be trained to salivate when a bell is sounded.

——— One nauseating meal can give rise to a food aversion that persists for years.

——— Psychologists helped a young boy overcome his fear of rabbits by having him eat cookies while a rabbit was brought progressively nearer to him.

——— During World War II, a psychologist devised a plan for training pigeons to guide missiles to their targets.

——— Punishment does not work.

——— Rats can be trained to climb a ramp, cross a bridge, climb a ladder, pedal a toy car, and do several other tasks— all in sequence.

——— We must make mistakes if we are to learn.

——— Despite all the media hoopla, no scientific connection has been established between violence viewed on TV and aggressive behavior in real life.

I WAS TEACHING MY NEW DOG, PHOEBE, TO FETCH. I bought a soft yellow ball for her that squeaked when she bit into it. She enjoyed playing with it, and I assumed she would want to run after it. (Wrong!) I waved it under her nose. She sniffed at it, barked, and wagged her tail excitedly.

Then, as Phoebe watched, I tossed the ball about 20 feet away. "Fetch!" I said as the ball bounced invitingly in the grass.

"People say 'Take it!'" my teenage daughter Allyn said.

Perhaps Allyn was right. Phoebe watched the ball but didn't run after it. Instead she barked at me and snapped softly at my legs.

"Okay," I said (to both of them). I ran after the ball, picked it up, and waved it under Phoebe's nose again. She barked and wagged her tail rapidly like a reed in a brisk wind.

"Take it!" I said and tossed the ball into the air again.

Again Phoebe refused to run after it. She barked and snapped at my legs again. "This is ridiculous," I muttered, and I went to get the ball. As I brought it back to Phoebe, Allyn said, "Don't you see what's happening?"

"What?"

"Phoebe's teaching you to fetch," Allyn laughed.

"Don't you mean to 'Take it'?" I said.

Yes, Phoebe was teaching me to fetch. Somehow she got me to run after the ball. When I brought it back to her, she reinforced my behavior with a show of excitement and (apparent) glee. Phoebe used the method known as operant conditioning. In **operant conditioning,** an organism learns to engage in certain behavior because of the effects of that behavior. Phoebe taught me that fetching the ball would be followed by pleasant events, leading me to repeat the behavior.

Classical conditioning was also at work. **Classical conditioning** is a simple form of associative learning that enables organisms to anticipate events. On the next day I showed Phoebe the ball. She became excited and barked at the door of the family room, apparently because she had learned to associate the ball with the fun we had had the day before.

Classical and operant conditioning are two forms of learning, which is the subject of this chapter. In lower organisms, much behavior is instinctive, or inborn. Fish are born "knowing" how to swim. Salmon instinctively return to spawn in the stream where they were born after they have spent years roaming the seas. Robins instinctively know how to sing the song of their species and to build nests. Rats instinctively mate and rear their young. Among humans, however, the variety and complexity of behavior patterns are largely products of experience. Experience is essential to learning to walk and acquiring the language of our parents and community. We learn to read, to compute numbers, and to surf the Net.

We learn to seek out the foods that are valued in our culture when we are hungry. We get into the habit of starting our day with coffee, tea, or other beverages. We learn which behavior patterns are deemed socially acceptable and which are considered wrong. And, of course, our families and communities use verbal guidance, set examples, and apply rewards and punishments to try to teach us to stick to the straight and narrow.

Sometimes our learning experiences are direct, like Phoebe's reinforcement of my fetching the ball. But we can also learn from the experiences of others. For example, I warn my children against the perils of jumping from high places and running wild in the house. (Occasionally they heed me.) But from books and visual media, we learn about the past, about other peoples, and about how to put things together. And we learn as we invent ways of doing things that have never been done before.

Having noted these various ways of learning, let me admit that the very definition of learning stirs controversy in psychology. The term may be defined in different ways.

From the behaviorist perspective, **learning** is a relatively permanent change in behavior that arises from experience. Changes in behavior also arise from maturation and physical changes, but they do not reflect learning. For example, frogs hatch as tadpoles that swim. After they develop legs, they hop on land. The behaviorist defines learning in terms of the changes in behavior by which it is known. From the behaviorist perspective, I learned to fetch the ball (a change in behavior) because Phoebe reinforced me for doing so.

From the cognitive perspective, learning is a mental change that may or may not be displayed in behavior. Cognitive psychologists see learning in terms of experience changing the way that organisms mentally represent the environment. Changes in mental representation may affect, but do not directly cause, changes in behavior. From the cognitive perspective, learning is *demonstrated* by changes in behavior, but learning itself is a mental process. From the cognitive perspective, Phoebe's reinforcement of my fetching of the ball did not make me fetch. Rather, it gave me information. It showed me that Phoebe wanted me to repeat the act. But my continued fetching was not mechanical or automatic. (At least I don't think it was.)

Now that we have defined learning, let us consider various kinds of learning more deeply. These include classical and operant conditioning, and kinds of learning in which cognition plays a more central role.

HOW DO WE LEARN HOW TO PLAY CHESS?
Games like chess are learned, but how? Can we explain playing chess as the summation of myriad instances of conditioning, or must we explain it in terms of mental representations and cognitive maps? What developments in the nervous system make us "ready" to learn the right moves? What biological changes register the memories of games played in the past?

CLASSICAL CONDITIONING

Classical conditioning involves some of the ways in which we learn to associate events with other events. Consider: We have a distinct preference for a grade of A rather than F. We are also (usually) more likely to stop for a red light than for a green light. Why? We are not born with instinctive attitudes toward the letters *A* and *F*. Nor are we born knowing that red means stop and green means go. We learn the meanings of these symbols because they are associated with other events. A's are associated with instructor approval and the likelihood of getting into graduate school. Red lights are associated with avoiding accidents and traffic citations.

Ivan Pavlov Rings a Bell

Lower animals also learn relationships among events, as Ivan Pavlov (1927) discovered in research with dogs. Pavlov was attempting to identify neural receptors in the mouth that triggered a response from the salivary glands. But his efforts were hampered by the dogs' salivating at

OPERANT CONDITIONING A simple form of learning in which an organism learns to engage in behavior because it is reinforced.

CLASSICAL CONDITIONING A simple form of learning in which an organism comes to associate or anticipate events. A neutral stimulus comes to evoke the response usually evoked by another stimulus by being paired repeatedly with the other stimulus. (Cognitive theorists view classical conditioning as the learning of relationships among events so as to allow an organism to represent its environment.) Also referred to as *respondent conditioning* or *Pavlovian conditioning*.

LEARNING (1) According to behaviorists, a relatively permanent change in behavior that results from experience. (2) According to cognitive theorists, the process by which organisms make relatively permanent changes in the way they represent the environment because of experience. These changes influence the organism's behavior but do not fully determine it.

IVAN PAVLOV.
Pavlov, his assistants, and a professional salivator (the dog) in Russia early in the 20th century.

TRUTH OR FICTION REVISITED
It is true that dogs can be trained to salivate when a bell is sounded. The training is accomplished by means of the classical conditioning method of pairing the sound of the bell with the delivery of food.

REFLEX A simple unlearned response to a stimulus.

STIMULUS An environmental condition that elicits a response.

CONDITIONED RESPONSE (CR) In classical conditioning, a learned response to a conditioned stimulus

undesired times, such as when a laboratory assistant inadvertently clanged a food tray.

Because of its biological makeup, a dog salivates if meat powder is placed on its tongue. Salivation in response to meat powder is a **reflex.** Reflexes are simple unlearned responses to stimuli. Reflexes are evoked by stimuli. A **stimulus** is an environmental condition that evokes a response from an organism, such as meat on the tongue or tapping the leg just below the knee. Pavlov discovered that reflexes can also be learned, or *conditioned,* through association. His dogs began salivating in response to clinking food trays because in the past this noise had repeatedly been paired with the arrival of food. The dogs would also salivate when an assistant entered the laboratory. Why? In the past, the assistant had brought food.

When we are faced with novel events, we sometimes have no immediate way of knowing whether they are important. When we are striving for concrete goals, for example, we often ignore the unexpected, even when the unexpected is just as important, or more important, than the goal. So it was that Pavlov at first viewed the uncalled for canine salivation as an annoyance, a hindrance to his research. But in 1901 he decided that his "problem" was worth looking into. He set about to show that he could train, or condition, his dogs to salivate when he wished and in response to any stimulus he chose.

Pavlov termed these trained salivary responses "conditional reflexes." They were *conditional* upon the repeated pairing of a previously neutral stimulus (such as the clinking of a food tray) and a stimulus (in this case, food) that predictably elicited the target response (in this case, salivation). Today, conditional reflexes are more generally referred to as **conditioned responses (CRs).** They are responses to previously neutral stimuli that have been learned, or conditioned.

Pavlov demonstrated conditioned responses by strapping a dog into a harness like the one shown in Figure L.1. When meat powder was placed on the dog's tongue, the dog salivated. Pavlov repeated the process several times, with one difference. He preceded the meat powder by half a second or so with the sounding of a bell on each occasion. After several pairings of meat powder and bell, Pavlov sounded the bell but did *not* follow the bell with the meat powder. Still the dog salivated. It had learned to salivate in response to the bell.

Why did the dog learn to salivate in response to the bell? Behaviorists and cognitive psychologists explain the learning process in very different ways. Put on your critical thinking cap: Would behaviorists say that after a few pairings of bell and food a dog "knows" that the bell "means" food is on its way? Why or why not?

Behaviorists explain the outcome of this process, termed *classical conditioning,* in terms of the publicly observable conditions of learning. They define classical conditioning as a simple form of learning in which one stimulus comes to evoke the response usually evoked by a second stimulus by being paired repeatedly with the second stimulus. In Pavlov's demonstration, the dog learned to salivate in response to the bell *because* the sounding of the bell had been paired with meat powder. That is, in classical conditioning, the organism forms associations between stimuli because the stimuli are *contiguous*—that is, they occur at about the same time. Behaviorists do *not* say that the dog "knew" food was on the way. They argue that we cannot speak meaningfully about what a dog "knows." We can only outline the conditions under which targeted behaviors reliably occur.

Cognitive psychologists view classical conditioning as the learning of relationships among events. The relationships allow organisms to mentally

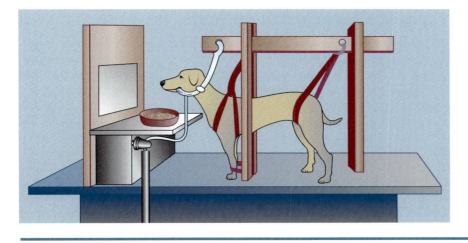

FIGURE L.1
PAVLOV'S DEMONSTRATION OF CONDITIONED REFLEXES IN LABORATORY DOGS.
From behind the two-way mirror at the left, a laboratory assistant rings a bell and then places meat on the dog's tongue. After several pairings, the dog salivates in response to the bell alone. A tube collects saliva and passes it to a vial. The quantity of saliva is taken as a measure of the strength of the animal's response.

represent their environments and make predictions (Rescorla, 1988). In Pavlov's demonstration, the dog salivated in response to the bell because the bell—from the cognitive perspective—became mentally connected with the meat powder. The cognitive focus is on *the information gained by the organism.* Organisms are viewed as seekers of information that generate and test rules about the relationships among events (Weiner, 1991).

Stimuli and Responses in Classical Conditioning

In the demonstration just described, the meat powder is an unlearned or **unconditioned stimulus (US).** Salivation in response to the meat powder is an unlearned or **unconditioned response (UR).** The bell was at first a meaningless or neutral stimulus. It might have produced an *orienting reflex* in the dog because of its distinctness. That is, the animal might have oriented itself toward the bell by turning toward it. But the bell was not yet associated with food. Then, through repeated association with the meat powder, the bell became a learned, or **conditioned stimulus (CS)** for the salivation response. Salivation in response to the bell (or CS) is a learned, or conditioned response (CR). A conditioned response is a response similar to an unconditioned response, but the response evoked by the conditioned stimulus is defined as a conditioned response, not an unconditioned response (see Figure L.2).

UNCONDITIONED STIMULUS (US) A stimulus that elicits a response from an organism prior to conditioning.

UNCONDITIONED RESPONSE (UR) An unlearned response to an unconditioned stimulus.

CONDITIONED STIMULUS (CS) A previously neutral stimulus that elicits a conditioned response because it has been paired repeatedly with a stimulus that already elicited that response.

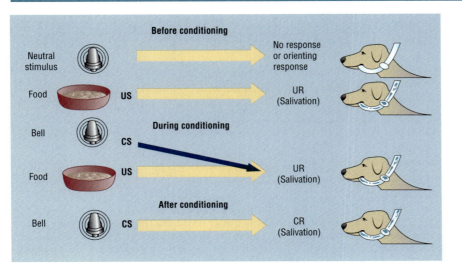

FIGURE L.2
A SCHEMATIC REPRESENTATION OF CLASSICAL CONDITIONING.
Prior to conditioning, food elicits salivation. The bell, a neutral stimulus, elicits either no response or an orienting response. During conditioning, the bell is rung just before meat is placed on the dog's tongue. After several repetitions, the bell, now a CS, elicits salivation, the CR.

Types of Classical Conditioning

Classical conditioning tends to occur most efficiently when the conditioned stimulus (CS) is presented about 0.5 second before the unconditioned stimulus (US) and is continued until the learner responds to the US. This is an example of **delayed conditioning,** in which the conditioned stimulus (for example, a light) can be presented anywhere from a fraction of a second to several seconds before the unconditioned stimulus (in this case, meat powder) and is left on until the response (salivation) is shown (see Figure L.3). Conditioning can also take place via **simultaneous conditioning.** In simultaneous conditioning, a conditioned stimulus, such as a light, is presented along with an unconditioned stimulus, such as meat powder. In **trace conditioning,** the conditioned stimulus (for example, a light) is presented and then removed (or turned off) prior to presentation of the unconditioned stimulus (meat powder). Therefore, only the memory trace of the conditioned stimulus (light) remains to be conditioned to the unconditioned stimulus.

Conditioning occurs most effectively in delayed conditioning, perhaps because it is most adaptive. That is, in delayed conditioning, the occurrence of the conditioned stimulus signals the consequent appearance of the unconditioned stimulus. As a result, organisms can learn to make predictions about their environment. Predictability is adaptive because it allows the organism to prepare for future events. Learning is inefficient

DELAYED CONDITIONING A classical conditioning procedure in which the CS is presented before the US and remains in place until the response occurs.

SIMULTANEOUS CONDITIONING A classical conditioning procedure in which the CS and US are presented at the same time.

TRACE CONDITIONING A classical conditioning procedure in which the CS is presented and then removed before the US is presented.

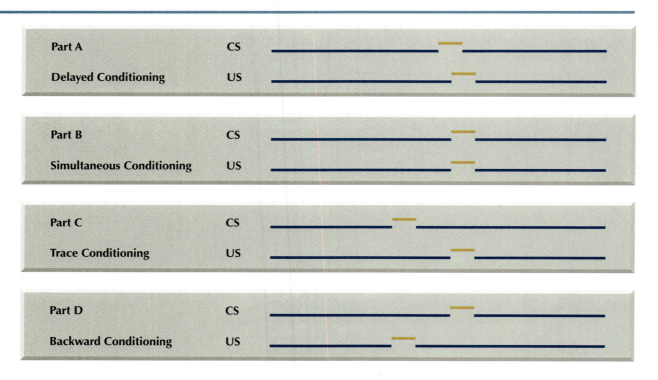

FIGURE L.3
TYPES OF CLASSICAL CONDITIONING.
In delayed conditioning (part A), the CS is presented before the US. In simultaneous conditioning (part B), the CS and US are presented together. In trace conditioning (part C), the CS is presented and removed prior to the US. Thus only the memory trace of the CS remains when the US is presented. In backward conditioning (part D), the US is presented before the CS. Delayed conditioning is most efficient, perhaps because it allows organisms to make predictions about their environments.

and may not take place at all when the unconditioned stimulus is presented before the conditioned stimulus—a sequence referred to as **backward conditioning.** Why? Perhaps because backward conditioning may not permit an organism to make predictions about its environment.

Taste Aversion

When I was a child in the Bronx, my friends and I would go to the movies on Saturday mornings. There would be a serial followed by a feature film, and the price of admission was a quarter. We would also eat candy (I loved Nonpareils and Raisinets) and popcorn. One morning my friends dared me to eat two huge containers of buttered popcorn by myself. I rose to the challenge: Down went an enormous container of buttered popcorn. More slowly—much more slowly—I stuffed down the second container. Predictably, I felt bloated and nauseated. The taste of the butter, corn, and salt lingered in my mouth and nose, and my head spun. It was obvious to me that I would have no more popcorn that day. However, I was surprised that I could not face buttered popcorn again for a year.

Years later I learned that psychologists refer to my response to buttered popcorn as a *taste aversion.* Many decades have now passed (how many is *my* business), and the odor of buttered popcorn still turns my stomach.

A taste aversion is an example of classical conditioning. Taste aversions are adaptive because they motivate organisms to avoid potentially harmful foods. Although taste aversions are acquired by association, they differ from other kinds of classical conditioning in a couple of ways. First, only one association may be required. I did not have to go back for seconds at the movies to develop my aversion for buttered popcorn! Second, whereas most kinds of classical conditioning require that the unconditioned stimulus (US) and conditioned stimulus (CS) be contiguous, in taste aversion the unconditioned stimulus (the US—in this case, nausea) can occur hours after the conditioned stimulus (the CS—in this case, the flavor of food).

Research on taste aversion also challenges the behaviorist view that organisms learn to associate any stimuli that are contiguous. In reality, not all stimuli are created equal. Instead, it seems that organisms are biologically predisposed to develop aversions that are adaptive in their environmental settings (Garcia et al., 1989). In a classic study, Garcia and Koelling (1966) conditioned two groups of rats. Each group was exposed to the same three-part conditioned stimulus (CS): a taste of sweetened water, a light, and a clicker. Afterward, one group was presented with an unconditioned stimulus (US) of nausea (induced by poison or radiation), and the other group was presented with an unconditioned stimulus (US) of electric shock.

After conditioning, the rats who had been nauseated showed an aversion for sweetened water but not to the light or clicker. Although all three stimuli had been presented at the same time, *the rats had acquired only the taste aversion.* After conditioning, the rats that had been shocked avoided both the light and the clicker, *but they did not show a taste aversion to the sweetened water.* For each group of rats, the conditioning that took place was adaptive. In the natural scheme of things, nausea is more likely to stem from poisoned food than from lights or sounds. So, for nauseated rats, acquiring the taste aversion was appropriate. Sharp pain, in contrast, is more likely to stem from natural events involving lights (fire, lightning) and sharp sounds (twigs snapping, things falling). Therefore, it was more appropriate for the shocked animals to develop an aversion to the light and the clicker than to the sweetened water.

Formation of a Taste Aversion?
Taste aversions may be acquired as a *result* of only one association of the US and the CS. Most kinds of classical conditioning require the US and CS to be contiguous, but in a taste aversion the US (nausea) can occur hours after the CS (flavor of food).

TRUTH OR FICTION REVISITED
It is true that one nauseating meal can give rise to a food aversion that persists for years.

BACKWARD CONDITIONING A classical conditioning procedure in which the unconditioned stimulus is presented prior to the conditioned stimulus.

This finding fits my experience as well. My nausea led to a taste aversion to buttered popcorn—but not to an aversion to the serials I watched (which, in retrospect, were more deserving of nausea) or the movie theater. I returned every Saturday morning to see what would happen next. Yet the serial and the theater, as much as the buttered popcorn, had been associated with my nausea. That is, the stimuli had been contiguous.

Extinction and Spontaneous Recovery

Extinction and spontaneous recovery are aspects of conditioning that help organisms adapt by updating their expectations or revising their representations of the changing environment. For example, a dog may learn to associate a new scent (a conditioned stimulus, or CS) with the appearance of a dangerous animal. It can then take evasive action when it catches a whiff of that scent. A child may learn to connect hearing a car pull into the driveway (a conditioned stimulus, or CS) with the arrival of his or her parents (an unconditioned stimulus, or US). Thus the child may begin to squeal with delight (squealing is a conditioned response, or CR) when the car is heard.

But times can change. The once dangerous animal may no longer be a threat. (What a puppy perceives to be a threat may lose its fearsomeness once the dog matures.) After moving to a new house, the child's parents may commute by means of public transportation. The sound of a car in a nearby driveway may signal a neighbor's, not a parent's, homecoming. When conditioned stimuli (such as the scent of a dog or the sound of a car) are no longer followed by unconditioned stimuli (a dangerous animal, a parent's homecoming), they lose their ability to elicit conditioned responses. In this way the organism adapts to a changing environment.

EXTINCTION In classical conditioning, **extinction** is the process by which conditioned stimuli (CSs) lose the ability to elicit conditioned responses (CRs) because the conditioned stimuli (CSs) are no longer associated with unconditioned stimuli (USs). From the cognitive perspective, extinction teaches the organism to change its representation of the environment because the learned or conditioned stimulus (CS) no longer allows it to make predictions.

In experiments on the extinction of conditioned responses (CRs), Pavlov found that repeated presentations of the conditioned stimulus (the CS—in this case, the bell) without the unconditioned stimulus (US—in this case, meat powder) led to extinction of the conditioned response (the CR—salivation in response to the bell). Figure L.4 shows that a dog that

EXTINCTION An experimental procedure in which stimuli lose their ability to evoke learned responses because the events that had followed the stimuli no longer occur. (The learned responses are said to be *extinguished*.)

FIGURE L.4

LEARNING AND EXTINCTION CURVES.

Actual data from Pavlov (1927) compose the jagged line, and the curved lines are idealized. In the acquisition phase, a dog salivates (shows a CR) in response to a bell (CS) after a few trials in which the bell is paired with meat powder (the US). Afterward, the CR is extinguished in about 10 trials during which the CS is not followed by the US. After a rest period, the CR recovers spontaneously. A second series of extinction trials leads to more rapid extinction of the CR.

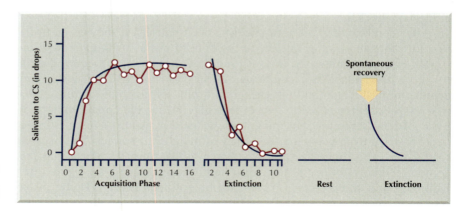

had been conditioned began to salivate (show a conditioned response, or CR) in response to a bell (the conditioned stimulus, or CS) after only a couple of pairings—referred to as *acquisition trials*—of the bell with meat powder. Continued pairings of the stimuli led to increased salivation (measured in number of drops of saliva). After seven or eight trials, salivation leveled off at 11 to 12 drops.

In the next series of experiments, salivation in response to the bell was extinguished through several trials—referred to as *extinction trials*—in which the bell was presented without the meat powder. After about 10 extinction trials, the animal no longer salivated. That is, it no longer showed the learned or conditioned response (salivation in response to the bell) when the bell was rung (the bell is the learned or conditioned stimulus).

What would happen if we were to allow a day or two to pass after we had extinguished salivation (the conditioned response, or CR) in a dog and then again rang the bell (the conditioned stimulus, or CS)? Where would you place your bet? Would the dog salivate or not?

If you bet that the dog would again show the conditioned response (the CR—in this case, salivation in response to the bell), you were correct. Organisms tend to show **spontaneous recovery** of extinguished conditioned responses (CRs) merely as a function of the passage of time. For this reason, the term *extinction* may be a bit misleading. When a species of animal becomes extinct, all the members of that species capable of reproducing have died. The species vanishes. But the experimental extinction of conditioned responses (CRs) does not lead to their permanent eradication. Rather, it seems that they *inhibit* the response. The response remains available for future performance under the "right" conditions.

Consider Figure L.4 again. When spontaneous recovery of the conditioned response (salivation in response to the bell) does occur, its strength as measured by the number of drops of saliva is weaker than it was at the end of the series of acquisition trials. A second set of extinction trials also extinguishes the conditioned response (salivation) more rapidly than the first series of trials. Although the second time around the conditioned response (salivation) is weaker at first, pairing the conditioned stimulus (the bell) with the unconditioned stimulus (meat powder) again builds response strength rapidly. That is, the animal makes the connection between the bell and the meat powder more easily the second time around.

Spontaneous recovery, like extinction, is adaptive. What would happen if the child heard no car in the driveway for several months? It could be that the next time a car entered the driveway, the child would associate the sounds with a parent's homecoming (rather than with the arrival of a neighbor). This expectation could be appropriate. After all, *something* had changed when no car entered the nearby driveway for so long. In the wild, a waterhole may contain water for only a couple of months during the year. But it is useful for animals to associate the waterhole with the thirst drive from time to time so that they will return to it at the appropriate time.

As time passes and the seasons change, things sometimes follow circular paths and arrive where they were before. Spontaneous recovery seems to provide a mechanism whereby organisms adapt to situations that recur from time to time.

Generalization and Discrimination

No two things are exactly alike. Traffic lights are hung at slightly different heights, and shades of red and green differ a little. The barking of two dogs differs, and the sound of the same animal differs slightly from one

SPONTANEOUS RECOVERY The recurrence of an extinguished response as a function of the passage of time.

bark to the next. Rustling sounds in the undergrowth differ, but rabbits and deer do well to flee when they perceive any one of many possible rustling sounds. Adaptation requires us to respond similarly (or *generalize*) to stimuli that are equivalent in function and to respond differently to (or *discriminate* between) stimuli that are not.

GENERALIZATION Pavlov noted that responding to different stimuli as though they are functionally equivalent—*generalizing*—is adaptive for animals. **Generalization** is the tendency for a conditioned response to be evoked by stimuli that are similar to the stimulus to which the response was conditioned. In a demonstration of generalization, Pavlov first conditioned a dog to salivate when a circle was presented. During each acquisition trial, the dog was shown a circle (a learned or conditioned stimulus—CS) and then given meat powder (an unlearned or unconditioned stimulus—US). After several trials the dog salivated when presented with the circle alone. Pavlov demonstrated that the dog also displayed the learned or conditioned response (the CR—in this case, salivation) in response to closed geometric figures such as ellipses, pentagons, and even squares. The more closely the figure resembled a circle, the greater the *strength* of the response (as measured by drops of saliva).

DISCRIMINATION Organisms must also learn that (1) many stimuli perceived as being similar are functionally different and (2) they must respond adaptively to each. During the first couple of months of life, babies can discriminate their mother's voice from those of other women. They often stop crying when they hear their mother but not when they hear a stranger's.

Pavlov showed that a dog conditioned to salivate in response to circles could be trained *not* to salivate in response to ellipses. The type of conditioning that trains an organism to respond to a narrow range of stimuli (in this case, circular rather than elliptical geometric figures) is termed **discrimination training**. Pavlov trained the dog by presenting it with circles and ellipses but associating the meat powder with circles only. After a while, the dog no longer salivated in response to the ellipses. Instead, it showed **discrimination**: It salivated only in response to circles.

Pavlov found that increasing the difficulty of the discrimination task apparently tormented the dog. After the dog was trained to salivate in response to circles but not ellipses, Pavlov showed it a series of progressively rounder ellipses. Eventually the dog could no longer discriminate the ellipses from circles. The animal then put on an infantile show. It urinated, defecated, barked profusely, and snapped at laboratory personnel.

How do we explain the dog's belligerent behavior? In a classic work written more than half a century ago, titled *Frustration and Aggression*, a group of behaviorally oriented psychologists suggested that frustration induces aggression (Dollard et al., 1939). Why is failure to discriminate circles from ellipses frustrating? For one thing, in such experiments, rewards—such as food—are usually contingent on correct discrimination. That is, if the dog errs, it doesn't get fed. Cognitive theorists, however, propose that organisms are motivated to construct realistic mental maps of the world. They fine-tune these maps as needed so that they fit a changing environment (Rescorla, 1988). In Pavlov's experiment, the dog lost the ability to adjust its mental map of the environment as the ellipses grew more circular. Thus it was frustrated.

Daily living requires appropriate generalization and discrimination. No two hotels are alike, but when we travel from one city to another it is adaptive to expect to stay in a hotel. It is encouraging that a green light in

GENERALIZATION In conditioning, the tendency for a conditioned response to be evoked by stimuli that are similar to the stimulus to which the response was conditioned.

DISCRIMINATION TRAINING Teaching an organism to show a learned response in the presence of only one of a series of similar stimuli, accomplished by alternating the stimuli but following only the one stimulus with the unconditioned stimulus.

DISCRIMINATION In conditioning, the tendency for an organism to distinguish between a conditioned stimulus and similar stimuli that do not forecast an unconditioned stimulus.

GENERALIZATION AT THE CROSSROADS.
Chances are that you have never seen these particular traffic lights in this particular setting. Because of generalization, however, we can safely bet you would know what to do if you were to drive up to them.

Washington has the same meaning as a green light in Paris. But returning home in the evening requires the ability to discriminate between our home and those of others. And if we could not readily discriminate our spouse from others, we might land in divorce court.

Higher-Order Conditioning

In **higher-order conditioning,** a previously neutral stimulus comes to serve as a learned or conditioned stimulus (CS) after being paired repeatedly with a stimulus that has already become a learned or conditioned stimulus (CS). Pavlov demonstrated higher-order conditioning by first conditioning a dog to salivate in response to a bell (a learned or conditioned stimulus— CS). He then repeatedly paired the shining of a light with the sounding of a bell. After several pairings, shining the light (the higher-order conditioned stimulus) came to evoke the response (salivation) that had been elicited by the bell (the first-order conditioned stimulus).

Consider children who learn that when they hear a car in the driveway their parents are about to arrive. It may be the case that a certain TV cartoon show starts a few minutes before the car enters the driveway. The TV show can come to evoke the expectation that the parents are arriving by being paired repeatedly with the car's entering the driveway. In another example, a boy may burn himself by touching a hot stove. After this experience, the sight of the stove may evoke fear (or, more technically, serve as a CS for eliciting a fear response). And because hearing the word *stove* may evoke a mental image of the stove, just hearing the word may evoke fear.

Applications of Classical Conditioning

Classical conditioning is a major means by which we learn. It is how stimuli come to serve as signals for other stimuli. It is why, for example, we come to expect that someone will be waiting outside when the doorbell is rung or why we expect a certain friend to appear when we hear a characteristic knock at the door.

THE BELL-AND-PAD TREATMENT FOR BED-WETTING By the age of 5 or 6, children normally awaken in response to the sensation of a full bladder. They inhibit the urge to urinate, which is an automatic or reflexive response to bladder tension, and instead go to the bathroom. But bed wetters tend not to respond to bladder tension while asleep. They remain asleep and frequently wet their beds.

HIGHER-ORDER CONDITIONING (1) According to behaviorists, a classical conditioning procedure in which a previously neutral stimulus comes to elicit the response brought forth by a *conditioned* stimulus by being paired repeatedly with that conditioned stimulus. (2) According to cognitive psychologists, the learning of relationships among events, none of which evokes an unleashed response.

By means of the bell-and-pad method, children are taught to wake up in response to bladder tension. They sleep on a special sheet or pad that has been placed on the bed. When the child starts to urinate, the water content of the urine causes an electrical circuit in the pad to close. The closing of the circuit triggers a bell or buzzer, and the child is awakened. (Similar buzzer circuits have been built into training pants as an aid to toilet training.) In terms of classical conditioning, the bell is a US that wakes the child (waking up is the UR). By means of repeated pairings, a stimulus that precedes the bell becomes associated with the bell and also gains the capacity to awaken the child. What is that stimulus? The sensation of a full bladder. In this way, bladder tension (the CS) gains the capacity to awaken the child *even though the child is asleep during the classical conditioning procedure.*

The bell-and-pad method is a superb example of why behaviorists prefer to explain the effects of classical conditioning in terms of the pairing of stimuli and not in terms of what the learner knows. The behaviorist may argue that we cannot assume a sleeping child "knows" that wetting the bed will cause the bell to ring. We can only note that by repeatedly pairing bladder tension with the bell, the child eventually *learns* to wake up in response to bladder tension alone. *Learning* is demonstrated by the change in the child's behavior. One can only speculate on what the child *knows* about the learning process.

THE CLASSICAL CONDITIONING OF FEAR If you happen across a gentleman nearly 80 years old who cringes at the sight of a fur coat, he may not be concerned about animal rights. Perhaps he is "Little Albert," who was conditioned to fear furry objects before he reached his first birthday.

In 1920, John B. Watson and his future wife, Rosalie Rayner, published a report of their demonstration that emotional reactions can be acquired through classical conditioning. The subject of their demonstration was a lad who has become known as "Little Albert." At the age of 11 months, Albert was not given to ready displays of emotion, but he did enjoy playing with a laboratory rat.

Using a method that many psychologists have criticized as unethical, Watson startled Little Albert by clanging steel bars behind his head whenever the infant played with the rat. After repeated pairings, Albert showed fear of the rat even when the clanging was halted. Albert's fear also generalized to objects that were similar in appearance to the rat, such as a rabbit and the fur collar on a woman's coat.

FLOODING AND SYSTEMATIC DESENSITIZATION Two behavior therapy methods for reducing specific fears are based on the classical conditioning principle of extinction (Wolpe & Plaud, 1997). In one, called **flooding,** the client is exposed to the fear-evoking stimulus until the fear response is extinguished. Little Albert, for example, might have been placed in close contact with a rat until his fear had become fully extinguished. In extinction, the learned or conditioned stimulus (the CS—in this case, the rat) is presented repeatedly in the absence of the unlearned or unconditioned stimulus (the US—in this case, the clanging of the steel bars) until the learned or conditioned response (the CR—in this case, fear) is no longer evoked.

Although flooding is usually effective, it is unpleasant. (When you are fearful of rats, being placed in a small room with one is no picnic.) For this reason, behavior therapists frequently prefer to use **systematic desensitization** (see the "Methods of Therapy" chapter), in which the client is

FLOODING A behavioral fear-reduction technique based on principles of classical conditioning. Fear-evoking stimuli (CSs) are presented continuously in the absence of actual harm so that fear responses (CRs) are extinguished.

SYSTEMATIC DESENSITIZATION A behavioral fear-reduction technique in which a hierarchy of fear-evoking stimuli are presented while the person remains relaxed.

gradually exposed to fear-evoking stimuli under circumstances in which he or she remains relaxed. For example, while feeling relaxed, Little Albert might have been given an opportunity to look at photos of rats or to see live rats from a distance before they were brought closer to him. Systematic desensitization, like flooding, is highly effective. It takes longer but it is not as unpleasant.

COUNTERCONDITIONING EARLY IN THE 20TH CENTURY John Watson's protégé Mary Cover Jones (1924) reasoned that if fears could be conditioned by painful experiences, she could *countercondition* them by substituting pleasant experiences. In counterconditioning, a pleasant stimulus is repeatedly paired with a fear-evoking object, thereby counteracting the fear response.

Two-year-old Peter had an intense fear of rabbits. Jones arranged for a rabbit to be gradually brought closer to Peter while he engaged in some of his favorite activities, such as munching on candy and cookies. They did not simply plop the rabbit in Peter's lap, as in flooding. Had she done so, the cookies on the plate, not to mention those already eaten, might have decorated the walls. Instead, she first placed the rabbit in a far corner of the room while Peter munched and crunched. Peter, to be sure, cast a wary eye, but he continued to consume the treat. Gradually the animal was brought closer until eventually, Peter ate treats and touched the rabbit at the same time. Jones theorized that the joy of eating was incompatible with fear and thus conditioned it.

Through classical conditioning, we learn to associate stimuli so a simple, usually passive, response made to one stimulus is then made in response to the other. In the case of Little Albert, clanging noises were associated with a rat, so the rat came to elicit the fear response brought forth by the noise. However, classical conditioning is only one kind of learning that occurs in these situations. After Little Albert acquired his fear of the rat, his voluntary behavior changed. He avoided the rat as a way of reducing his fear. Thus Little Albert engaged in another kind of learning—*operant conditioning*.

After I had acquired my taste aversion, I stayed away from buttered popcorn. My avoidance can also be explained in terms of operant conditioning. In *operant conditioning*, organisms learn to do things—or *not* to do things—because of the consequences of their behavior. I avoided buttered popcorn in order to prevent nausea. But we also seek fluids when we are thirsty, sex when we are aroused, and an ambient temperature of 68° to 70°F when we feel too hot or too cold. *Classical conditioning focuses on how organisms form anticipations about their environments. Operant conditioning focuses on what they* do *about them.*

OPERANT CONDITIONING

"What did you do in the war, Daddy?" is a question familiar to many who served during America's conflicts. Some stories involve heroism, others involve the unusual. When it comes to unusual war stories, few top that of Harvard University psychologist B. F. Skinner. For one of Skinner's wartime efforts was "Project Pigeon" (Bjork, 1997).

During World War II Skinner proposed that pigeons be trained to guide missiles to their targets. In their training, the pigeons would be **reinforced** with food pellets for pecking at targets projected onto a screen (see Figure L.5). Once trained, the pigeons would be placed in missiles. Their pecking at similar targets displayed on a screen would correct the missile's flight

CAN CHOCOLATE CHIP COOKIES COUNTERCONDITION FEARS?
In the 1920s, Mary Cover Jones helped a boy overcome his fear of rabbits by having him munch on cookies as the animal was brought closer.

TRUTH OR FICTION REVISITED
It is true that psychologists helped a young boy overcome fear of rabbits by having him eat cookies while a rabbit was brought progressively closer.

REINFORCE To follow a response with a stimulus that increases the frequency of the response.

FIGURE L.5
PROJECT PIGEON.

During World War II, B.F. Skinner suggested using operant conditioning to train pigeons to guide missiles to their targets. The pigeons would first be reinforced for pecking targets projected on a screen. Afterward, in combat, pecking the on-screen target would keep the missile on course.

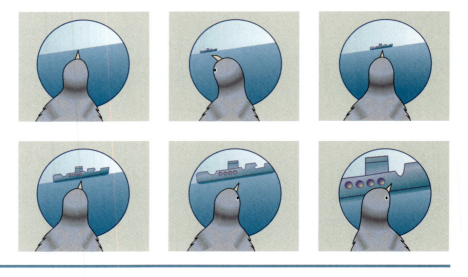

TRUTH OR FICTION REVISITED

It is true that during World War II a psychologist devised a plan for training pigeons to guide missiles to their targets. That psychologist was B. F. Skinner, and his plan employed principles of operant conditioning.

path, resulting in a "hit" and a sacrificed pigeon. However, plans for building the necessary missile—for some reason called the *Pelican* and not the *Pigeon*—were scrapped. The pigeon equipment was too bulky, and, Skinner lamented, his suggestion was not taken seriously. Apparently the Defense Department concluded that Project Pigeon was for the birds.

Project Pigeon may have been scrapped, but the principles of learning that Skinner applied to the project have found wide applications. In operant conditioning, an organism learns to *do* something because of the effects or consequences of that behavior.

This is **operant behavior,** behavior that operates on, or manipulates, the environment. In classical conditioning, involuntary responses such as salivation or eyeblinks are often conditioned. In operant conditioning, *voluntary* responses such as pecking at a target, pressing a lever, or many of the skills required for playing tennis are acquired, or conditioned.

In operant conditioning, organisms engage in operant behaviors, also known simply as *operants,* that result in presumably desirable consequences such as food, a hug, an A on a test, attention, or social approval. Some children learn to conform their behavior to social rules to earn the attention and approval of their parents and teachers. Other children, ironically, may learn to "misbehave" because misbehavior also gets attention from other people. In particular, children may learn to be "bad" when their "good" behavior is routinely ignored.

Methods of Operant Conditioning

In his most influential work, *The Behavior of Organisms,* Skinner (1938) made many theoretical and technological innovations. Among them was his focus on discrete behaviors such as lever pressing as the *unit,* or type, of behavior to be studied (Glenn et al., 1992). Other psychologists might focus on how organisms think or "feel." Skinner focused on measurable things that they do. Many psychologists have found these kinds of behavior inconsequential, especially when it comes to explaining and predicting human behavior. But Skinner's supporters point out that focusing on discrete behavior creates the potential for helpful changes. For example, in helping people combat depression, one psychologist might focus on their "feelings." A Skinnerian psychologist would focus on cataloguing (and modifying) the types of things that depressed people actually *do.* Directly modifying depressive behavior might also brighten clients' self-reports about their "feelings of depression."

OPERANT BEHAVIOR Voluntary responses that are reinforced.

FIGURE L.6
THE EFFECTS OF REINFORCEMENT.
One of the celebrities of modern psychology, an albino laboratory rat, earns its keep in a Skinner box. The animal presses a lever because of reinforcement delivered through the feeder. The habit strength of this operant is the frequency of lever pressing.

To study operant behavior efficiently, Skinner devised an animal cage (or "operant chamber") that was dubbed the *Skinner box* by another psychologist. (Skinner himself repeatedly requested that his operant chamber *not* be called a Skinner box. History has thus far failed to honor his wishes, however.[1]) Such a box is shown in Figure L.6. The cage is ideal for laboratory experimentation because experimental conditions (treatments) can be carefully introduced and removed, and the effects on laboratory animals (defined as changes in rates of lever pressing) can be carefully observed.

The rat in Figure L.6 was deprived of food and placed in a Skinner box with a lever at one end. At first it sniffed its way around the cage and engaged in random behavior. When organisms are behaving in a random manner, responses that have favorable consequences tend to occur more frequently. Responses that do not have favorable consequences tend to be performed less frequently.

The rat's first pressing of the lever was inadvertent. However, because of this action, a food pellet dropped into the cage. The arrival of the food pellet increased the probability that the rat would press the lever again. The pellet thus is said to have served as a *reinforcement* for lever pressing.

Skinner further mechanized his laboratory procedure by making use of a turning drum, or *cumulative recorder,* a tool that had previously been used by physiologists (see Figure L.7). The cumulative recorder provides a precise measure of operant behavior. The experimenter need not even be present to record the number of correct responses. In the example used, the lever in the Skinner box is connected to the recorder so that the recording pen moves upward with each correct response. The paper moves continuously to the left at a slow but regular pace. In the sample record shown in Figure L.7, lever pressings (which record correct responses) were few and far between at first. But after several reinforced responses, lever pressings became fast and furious. When the rat was no longer hungry, the lever pressing dropped off and then stopped.

THE FIRST "CORRECT" RESPONSE In operant conditioning, it matters little how the first response that is reinforced comes to be made. The organism can happen on it by chance, as in random learning. The organism can also be physically guided to make the response. You may command

---

[1] Of course, my using the term *Skinner box* does not aid Skinner's cause, either.

FIGURE L.7
THE CUMULATIVE RECORDER.

In the cumulative recorder, paper moves to the left while a pen jerks up to record each targeted response. When the pen reaches the top of the paper, it is automatically reset to the bottom.

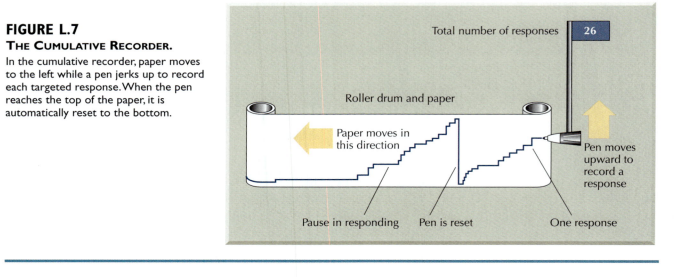

your dog to "Sit!" and then press its backside down until it is in a sitting position. Finally you reinforce sitting with food or a pat on the head and a kind word.

Animal trainers use physical guiding or coaxing to bring about the first "correct" response. Can you imagine how long it would take to train your dog if you waited for it to sit or roll over and then seized the opportunity to command it to sit or roll over? Both of you would age significantly in the process.

People, of course, can be verbally guided into desired responses when they are learning tasks such as spelling, adding numbers, or operating a machine. But they need to be informed when they have made the correct response. Knowledge of results often is all the reinforcement people need to learn new skills.

Types of Reinforcers

Any stimulus which increases the probability that responses preceding it will be repeated serves as a reinforcer. Reinforcers include food pellets when an organism has been deprived of food, water when it has been deprived of liquid, the opportunity to mate, and the sound of a bell that has previously been associated with eating.

POSITIVE AND NEGATIVE REINFORCERS Skinner distinguished between positive and negative reinforcers. **Positive reinforcers** increase the probability that an operant will occur when they are applied. Food and approval usually serve as positive reinforcers. **Negative reinforcers** increase the probability that an operant will occur when they are *removed* (see Figure L.8). People often learn to plan ahead so that they need not fear that things will go wrong. In such cases fear acts as a negative reinforcer because *removal* of fear increases the probability that the behaviors preceding it (such as planning ahead or fleeing a predator) will be repeated.

Greater reinforcers prompt more rapid learning than do lesser reinforcers. You would probably work much harder for $1,000 than for $10. (If not, get in touch with me—I have some chores that need to be taken care of.) With sufficient reinforcement, operants become *habits*. They have a high probability of recurrence in certain situations.

POSITIVE REINFORCER A reinforcer that when *presented* increases the frequency of an operant.

NEGATIVE REINFORCER A reinforcer that when *removed* increases the frequency of an operant.

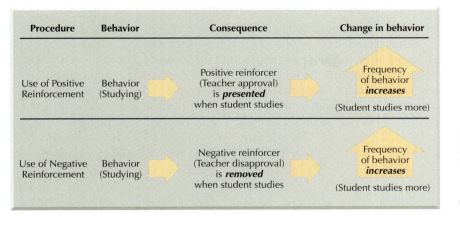

Procedure	Behavior	Consequence	Change in behavior
Use of Positive Reinforcement	Behavior (Studying)	Positive reinforcer (Teacher approval) is **presented** when student studies	Frequency of behavior **increases** (Student studies more)
Use of Negative Reinforcement	Behavior (Studying)	Negative reinforcer (Teacher disapproval) is **removed** when student studies	Frequency of behavior **increases** (Student studies more)

FIGURE L.8
POSITIVE VERSUS NEGATIVE REINFORCERS.
All reinforcers *increase* the frequency of behavior. However, negative reinforcers are aversive stimuli that increase the frequency of behavior when they are *removed*. In these examples, teacher approval functions as a positive reinforcer when students study harder because of it. Teacher *disapproval* functions as a negative reinforcer when its *removal* increases the frequency of studying. Can you think of situations in which teacher approval might function as a negative reinforcer?

IMMEDIATE VERSUS DELAYED REINFORCERS Immediate reinforcers are more effective than delayed reinforcers. Therefore, the short-term consequences of behavior often provide more of an incentive than the long-term consequences. Some students socialize when they should be studying because the pleasure of socializing is immediate. Studying may not pay off until the final exam or graduation. (This is why younger students do better with frequent tests.) It is difficult to quit smoking cigarettes because the reinforcement of nicotine is immediate and the health hazards of smoking more distant. Focusing on short-term reinforcement is also connected with careless sexual behavior.

PRIMARY AND SECONDARY REINFORCERS We can also distinguish between primary and secondary, or conditioned, reinforcers. **Primary reinforcers** are effective because of an organism's biological makeup. Food, water, adequate warmth (positive reinforcers), and pain (a negative reinforcer) all serve as primary reinforcers. **Secondary reinforcers** acquire their value through being associated with established reinforcers. For this reason they are also termed **conditioned reinforcers.** We may seek money because we have learned that it may be exchanged for primary reinforcers. Money, attention, social approval—all are conditioned reinforcers in our culture. We may be suspicious of, or not "understand," people who are not interested in money or the approval of others. Part of understanding others lies in being able to predict what they will find reinforcing.

Extinction and Spontaneous Recovery in Operant Conditioning

In operant conditioning as in classical conditioning, extinction is a process in which stimuli lose the ability to evoke learned responses because the events that followed the stimuli no longer occur. In classical conditioning, however, the "events" that normally follow and confirm the appropriateness of the learned response (that is, the conditioned response) are the unconditioned stimuli. In Pavlov's experiment, for example, the meat powder was the event that followed and confirmed the appropriateness of salivation. In operant conditioning, in contrast, the ensuing events are reinforcers. Thus in operant conditioning the extinction of learned responses (that is, operants) results from the repeated performance of operant behavior without reinforcement. After a number of trials, the

PRIMARY REINFORCER An unlearned reinforcer.

SECONDARY REINFORCER A stimulus that gains reinforcement value through association with established reinforcers.

CONDITIONED REINFORCER Another term for a secondary reinforcer.

operant behavior is no longer displayed. If you go for a month without mail, you may stop checking the mailbox.

When some time is allowed to pass after the extinction process, an organism usually performs the operant again when placed in a situation in which the operant had been reinforced previously. Such spontaneous recovery of learned responses occurs in operant conditioning as well as in classical conditioning. If the operant is reinforced at this time, it quickly regains its former strength. (Finding a few letters in the mailbox one week may again encourage you to check the mailbox daily.) Spontaneous recovery of extinguished operants suggests they are inhibited or suppressed by the extinction process and not lost permanently.

Reinforcers Versus Rewards and Punishments

Reinforcers are defined as stimuli that increase the frequency of behavior. It may be that most reinforcers—food, hugs, having the other person admit to starting the argument, and so on—are pleasant events. Yet "unpleasant" events, such as a slap on the hand or disapproval from a teacher, may be reinforcing to some—perhaps because such experiences confirm negative feelings toward teachers.

Rewards, like reinforcers, tend to increase the frequency of behavior, but rewards are defined as pleasant events. Skinner preferred the concept of reinforcement to that of reward because reinforcement does not suggest trying to "get inside the head" of an organism (whether a human or lower animal) to guess what it would find pleasant or unpleasant. A list of reinforcers is arrived at *empirically*—that is, by observing what sorts of stimuli increase the frequency of the behavior. However, note that some psychologists use the term *reward* synonymously with *positive reinforcement*.

Punishments are defined as aversive events that suppress or decrease the frequency of the behavior they follow (see Figure L.9). Punishment can rapidly suppress undesirable behavior and may be warranted in "emergencies," such as when a child tries to run into the street.

Despite the fact that punishment usually works, many learning theorists agree that punishment often fails to achieve the parent's goals (Collins, 1995). Consider the following reasons for avoiding the use of punishment:

1. Punishment does not in itself suggest an alternative acceptable form of behavior.

REWARD A pleasant stimulus that increases the frequency of the behavior it follows.

PUNISHMENT An unpleasant stimulus that suppresses the behavior it follows.

FIGURE L.9
NEGATIVE REINFORCERS VERSUS PUNISHMENTS.

Negative reinforcers and punishments both tend to be aversive stimuli. However, reinforcers *increase* the frequency of behavior. Punishments *decrease* the frequency of behavior. Negative reinforcers increase the frequency of behavior when they are *removed*. Punishments decrease or suppress the frequency of behavior when they are *applied*. Can you think of situations in which punishing students might have effects other than those desired by the teacher?

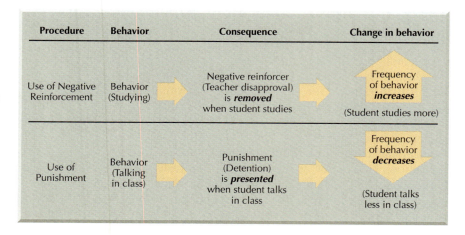

Procedure	Behavior	Consequence	Change in behavior
Use of Negative Reinforcement	Behavior (Studying)	Negative reinforcer (Teacher disapproval) is **removed** when student studies	Frequency of behavior **increases** (Student studies more)
Use of Punishment	Behavior (Talking in class)	Punishment (Detention) is **presented** when student talks in class	Frequency of behavior **decreases** (Student talks less in class)

2. Punishment tends to suppress undesirable behavior only under circumstances in which its delivery is guaranteed. It does not take children long to learn that they can "get away with murder" with one parent or teacher but not with another.

3. Punished organisms may withdraw from the situation. Severely punished children may run away, cut class, or drop out of school.

4. Punishment can create anger and hostility. Adequate punishment almost always suppresses unwanted behavior—but at what cost? The child may express accumulated feelings of hostility against other children.

5. Punishment may generalize too far. A child who is punished severely for bad table manners may stop eating altogether. Overgeneralization is more likely to occur when children do not know exactly why they are being punished and when they have not been shown alternative acceptable behaviors.

6. Punishment may be modeled as a way of solving problems or coping with stress (Straus & Smith, 1990). We will see that one way that children learn is by observing others. Even though children may not immediately perform the behavior they observe, they may perform it later on, even as adults, when their circumstances are similar to those of the model.

7. Finally, children learn responses that are punished. Whether or not children choose to perform punished responses, punishment draws their attention to these responses.

TRUTH OR FICTION REVISITED
Actually, punishment does work. Strong punishment generally suppresses the behavior it follows. The issues pertaining to punishment concern its limitations and side effects.

It is usually preferable to focus on rewarding children for desirable behavior than on punishing them for unwanted behavior. By ignoring their misbehavior, or by using **time out** from positive reinforcement, we can consistently avoid reinforcing children for misbehavior.

To reward or positively reinforce children for desired behavior takes time and care. It is not enough simply to never use punishment. First, we must pay attention to children when they are behaving well. If we take their desirable behavior for granted and respond to them only when they misbehave, we may be encouraging misbehavior. Second, we must be certain that children are aware of, and capable of performing, desired behavior. It is harmful and fruitless merely to punish children for unwanted behavior. We must also carefully guide them, either physically or verbally, into making the desired responses, and then reward them. We cannot teach children table manners by waiting for them to exhibit proper responses at random and then reinforcing them for their responses. Try holding a reward of ice cream behind your back and waiting for a child to exhibit proper manners. You will have a slippery dining room floor long before the children develop good table manners.

Discriminative Stimuli

B. F. Skinner might not have been able to get his pigeons into the drivers' seats of missiles during the war, but he had no problem training them to respond to traffic lights. Try the following experiment for yourself.

Find a pigeon. Or sit on a park bench, close your eyes, and one will find you. Place it in a Skinner box with a button on the wall. Drop a food pellet into the cage whenever the pigeon pecks the button. (Soon it will learn to peck the button whenever it has not eaten for a while.) Now place a small green light in the cage. Turn it on and off intermittently throughout the day. Reinforce button pecking with food whenever the green light is on, but not when the light is off. It will not take long for this

TIME OUT Removal of an organism from a situation in which reinforcement is available when unwanted behavior is shown.

A DISCRIMINATIVE STIMULUS.
You might not think pigeons are very discriminating, yet they readily learn that pecking will not bring food in the presence of a discriminative stimulus such as a red light.

clever city pigeon to learn that it will gain as much by grooming itself or cooing and flapping around as it will by pecking the button when the light is off.

The green light will have become a **discriminative stimulus.** Discriminative stimuli act as cues. They provide information about when an operant (in this case, pecking a button) will be reinforced (in this case, by a food pellet being dropped into the cage).

Operants that are not reinforced tend to be extinguished. For the pigeon in our experiment, the behavior of pecking the button *when the light is off* is extinguished.

A moment's reflection will suggest many ways in which discriminative stimuli influence our behavior. Isn't it more efficient to answer the telephone when it is ringing? Do you think it is wise to try to get smoochy when your date is blowing smoke in your face or downing a bottle of antacid tablets?

We noted that a pigeon learns to peck a button if food drops into its cage when it does so. What if you want the pigeon to continue to peck the button but you're running out of food? Do not despair. (Worse things have happened.) As we see in the following section, you can keep that bird pecking away indefinitely, even as you hold up on most of the food.

Schedules of Reinforcement

In operant conditioning, some responses are maintained by means of **continuous reinforcement.** You probably become warmer every time you put on heavy clothing. You probably become less thirsty every time you drink water. Yet if you have ever watched people throwing money down the maws of slot machines, you know that behavior can also be maintained by means of **partial reinforcement.**

Folklore about gambling is based on solid learning theory. You can hook a person on gambling by fixing the game so as to allow heavy winnings at first. Then you gradually space out the winnings (reinforcements) until gambling is maintained by infrequent winning—or no winning at all. Partial reinforcement schedules can maintain gambling behavior, like other behavior, for a great deal of time, even though it goes unreinforced (Pulley, 1998).

New operants or behaviors are acquired most rapidly through continuous reinforcement or, in some cases, through "one-trial learning" that meets with great reinforcement. People who cannot control their gambling often had big wins at the racetrack or casino or in the lottery in their late teens or early 20s (Greene, 1982). But once the operant has been acquired, it can be maintained by tapering off to a schedule of partial reinforcement.

There are four basic types of reinforcement schedules. They are determined by changing either the *interval* of time that must elapse between correct responses before reinforcement occurs or the *ratio* (number) of responses that must occur before reinforcement is provided. If reinforcement of responses is immediate (zero seconds), the reinforcement schedule is continuous. A larger interval of time, such as 1 or 30 seconds, is one kind of partial-reinforcement schedule. A one-to-one (1:1) ratio of correct responses to reinforcements is also a continuous-reinforcement schedule. A higher ratio such as 2:1 or 5:1 creates another kind of partial-reinforcement schedule.

More specifically, the four basic reinforcement schedules are *fixed-interval, variable-interval, fixed-ratio,* and *variable-ratio* schedules (see Figure L.10).

DISCRIMINATIVE STIMULUS In operant conditioning, a stimulus that indicates that reinforcement is available.

CONTINUOUS REINFORCEMENT A schedule of reinforcement in which every correct response is reinforced.

PARTIAL REINFORCEMENT One of several reinforcement schedules in which not every correct response is reinforced.

	Fixed	Variable
Interval	Fixed Interval	Variable Interval
Ratio	Fixed Ratio	Variable Ratio

FIGURE L.10
SCHEDULES OF REINFORCEMENT.
There are four basic reinforcement schedules, which are created by changing the amount of time that elapses between performance of a response and reinforcement, and by changing the number of responses that must be performed before reinforcement is provided. These are fixed-interval, variable-interval, fixed-ratio, and variable-ratio schedules. Which schedule is best for initially shaping a response? Which schedule(s) enable researchers to maintain responses with relatively little reinforcement?

INTERVAL SCHEDULES In a **fixed-interval schedule,** a fixed amount of time—say, a minute—must elapse between the previous and subsequent times when reinforcement for correct responses occurs. With a fixed-interval schedule, an organism's response rate falls off after each reinforcement and then picks up again as the time when reinforcement will occur approaches. For example, in a 1-minute fixed-interval schedule, a rat is reinforced with, say, a food pellet for the first operant—for example, the first pressing of a lever—that occurs after a minute has elapsed. After each reinforcement, the rat's rate of lever pressing slows down, but as the end of the 1-minute interval draws near, lever pressing increases in frequency, as suggested in Figure L.11. It is as if the rat has learned that it must wait a while before it is reinforced. The resultant record on the cumulative recorder shows a series of characteristic upward-moving waves, or scallops, which are referred to as a *fixed-interval scallop.*

Car dealers use fixed-interval reinforcement schedules when they offer incentives for buying up the remainder of the year's line every summer and fall. In a sense, they are suppressing buying at other times, except for consumers whose current cars are in their death throes or those with little self-control. Similarly, you learn to check your e-mail only at a certain time of day if your correspondent writes at that time each day.

In a **variable-interval schedule,** varying amounts of time are allowed to elapse between occurrences of reinforcement. In a so-called 3-minute variable-interval schedule, a rat would not be reinforced for pressing a lever until an average of 3 minutes had elapsed since the previous reinforcement. However, the intervals could be made to vary, say, from 1 to 5 minutes.

Reinforcement is more unpredictable in a variable-interval schedule. Therefore, the response rate is steadier but lower. If the boss calls us in for a weekly report, we probably work hard to pull things together just before the report is to be given, just as we might cram the night before a weekly quiz. But if we know that the boss might call us in for a report on the progress of a certain project at any time (variable-interval schedule), we are likely to keep things in a state of reasonable readiness at all times. However, our efforts are unlikely to have the intensity they would in a fixed-interval schedule (for example, a weekly report). Similarly, we are less likely to cram for unpredictable pop quizzes than we are to study for regularly scheduled quizzes. But we are likely to do at least some studying on a regular basis. If you receive e-mail from your correspondent at irregular intervals, you are likely to check your e-mail regularly, but with somewhat less eagerness.

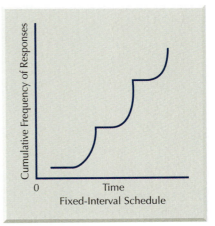

Cumulative Frequency of Responses

0 Time
Fixed-Interval Schedule

FIGURE L.11
THE "FIXED-INTERVAL SCALLOP."
Organisms who are reinforced on a fixed-interval schedule tend to slack off responding after each reinforcement. The rate of response picks up as they near the time when reinforcement will become available. The results on the cumulative recorder look like upward-moving waves, or scallops.

FIXED-INTERVAL SCHEDULE A schedule in which a fixed amount of time must elapse between the previous and subsequent times that reinforcement is available.

VARIABLE-INTERVAL SCHEDULE A schedule in which a variable amount of time must elapse between the previous and subsequent times that reinforcement is available..

RATIO SCHEDULES In a **fixed-ratio schedule,** reinforcement is provided after a fixed number of correct responses have been made. In a **variable-ratio schedule,** reinforcement is provided after a variable number of correct responses have been made. In a 10:1 variable-ratio schedule, the mean number of correct responses that would have to be made before a subsequent correct response would be reinforced is 10, but the ratio of correct responses to reinforcements might be allowed to vary from, say, 1:1 to 20:1 on a random basis.

Fixed- and variable-ratio schedules maintain a high response rate. With a fixed-ratio schedule, it is as if the organism learns that it must make several responses before being reinforced. It then "gets them out of the way" as rapidly as possible. Consider the example of piecework. If a worker must sew five shirts to receive $30, he or she is on a fixed-ratio (5:1) schedule and is likely to sew at a uniformly high rate, although there might be a brief pause after each reinforcement. With a variable-ratio schedule, reinforcement can come at any time. This unpredictability also maintains a high response rate. Slot machines tend to pay off on variable-ratio schedules, and players can be seen popping coins into them and yanking their "arms" with barely a pause. I have seen players who do not even stop to pick up their winnings. Instead, they continue to pop in the coins, whether from their original stack or from the winnings tray.

SHAPING If you are teaching the latest dance craze to people who have never danced, do not wait until they have performed it precisely before telling them they are on the right track. The foxtrot will be back in style before they have learned a thing.

We can teach complex behaviors by **shaping,** or reinforcing progressive steps toward the behavioral goal. At first, for example, it may be wise to smile and say, "Good" when a reluctant newcomer gathers the courage to get out on the dance floor, even if your feet are flattened by his initial clumsiness. If you are teaching someone to drive a car with a standard shift, at first generously reinforce the learner simply for shifting gears without stalling.

But as training proceeds, we come to expect more before we are willing to provide reinforcement. We reinforce **successive approximations** of the goal. If you want to train a rat to climb a ladder, first reinforce it with a food pellet when it turns toward the ladder. Then wait until it approaches the ladder before giving it a pellet. Then do not drop a pellet into the cage until the rat touches the ladder. In this way, the rat will reach the top of the ladder more quickly than if you had waited for the target behavior to occur at random.

Learning to drive a new standard-shift automobile to a new job also involves a complex sequence of operant behaviors. At first we actively seek out all the discriminative stimuli or landmarks that give us cues for when to turn—signs, buildings, hills, valleys. We also focus on shifting to a lower gear as we slow down so that the car won't stall. After many repetitions, these responses, or chains of behavior, become "habitual" and we need to pay very little attention to them.

Have you ever driven home from school or work and suddenly realized as you got out of your car that you couldn't recall exactly how you had returned home? Your entire trip may seem "lost." Were you in great danger? How could you allow such a thing to happen? Actually, it may be that your responses to the demands of the route and to driving your car had become so habitual that you did not have to focus on them. As you drove, you were able to think about dinner, a problem at work, or the weekend. But if something unusual had occurred on the way, such as hesitation in your engine or a severe rainstorm, you would have devoted as

TRUTH OR FICTION REVISITED
It is true that rats can be trained to climb a ramp, cross a bridge, climb a ladder, pedal a toy car, and do several other tasks—all in sequence. The procedure used to do so is called *shaping.*

FIXED-RATIO SCHEDULE A schedule in which reinforcement is provided after a fixed number of correct responses.

VARIABLE-RATIO SCHEDULE A schedule in which reinforcement is provided after a variable number of correct responses.

SHAPING A procedure for teaching complex behaviors that at first reinforces approximations of the target behavior.

SUCCESSIVE APPROXIMATIONS Behaviors that are progressively closer to a target behavior.

much attention to your driving as was needed to arrive home. Your trip was probably quite safe after all.

Applications of Operant Conditioning

Operant conditioning, like classical conditioning, is not just an exotic laboratory procedure. We use it every day in our efforts to influence other people. Parents and peers induce children to acquire so-called gender-appropriate behavior patterns through rewards and punishments. Parents also tend to praise their children for sharing their toys and to punish them for being too aggressive. Peers participate in this **socialization** process by playing with children who are generous and nonaggressive and, often, by avoiding those who are not (Etaugh & Rathus, 1995).

Operant conditioning may also play a role in attitude formation. Parents tend to reward their children for expressing attitudes that coincide with their own and to punish or ignore them for expressing attitudes that deviate. Let us now consider some specific applications of operant conditioning.

RECITING THE PLEDGE.
Operant conditioning plays a role in the socialization of children. Parents and teachers usually reward children for expressing attitudes that coincide with their own and punish or ignore them when they express "deviant" attitudes.

BIOFEEDBACK TRAINING Biofeedback training (BFT) is based on principles of operant conditioning. BFT has enabled people and lower animals to learn to control autonomic responses in order to attain reinforcement (Miller, 1969). BFT has been an important innovation in the treatment of health-related problems during the past few decades.

Through BFT, organisms can gain control of autonomic functions such as the flow of blood in a finger. They can also learn to improve their control over functions that can be manipulated voluntarily, such as muscle tension. When people receive BFT, reinforcement is given in the form of *information*. Perhaps a sound changes in pitch or frequency of occurrence to signal that they have modified the autonomic function in the desired direction. For example, we can learn to emit alpha waves—the kind of brain wave associated with feelings of relaxation—through feedback from an electroencephalograph (an instrument that measures brain waves). Through the use of other instruments, people have learned to lower their muscle tension, their heart rates, and even their blood pressure.

BFT is also used with people who have lost neuromuscular control of parts of their body as a result of an accident. A "bleep" sound informs them when they have contracted a muscle or sent an impulse down a neural pathway. By concentrating on changing the bleeps, they also gradually regain voluntary control over the damaged function.

TOKEN ECONOMIES Behavior therapists apply operant conditioning in mental hospitals to foster desired responses such as social skills and to extinguish unwanted behaviors such as social withdrawal. In a **token economy,** psychologists give hospital residents or prison inmates tokens such as poker chips as reinforcements for desired behavior. The tokens reinforce the desired behavior because they can be exchanged for time watching television, desserts, and other commodities.

Principles of operant conditioning have also enabled psychologists and educators to develop many beneficial innovations, such as behavior modification in the classroom and programmed learning.

BEHAVIOR MODIFICATION IN THE CLASSROOM Remember that reinforcers are defined as stimuli that increase the frequency of behavior—not as pleasant events. Ironically, adults frequently reinforce undesirable behavior in children by paying attention to them, or punishing them,

SOCIALIZATION Guidance of people into socially desirable behavior by means of verbal messages, the systematic use of rewards and punishments, and other methods of teaching.

TOKEN ECONOMY An environmental setting that fosters desired behavior by reinforcing it with tokens (secondary reinforcers) that can be exchanged for other reinforcers.

PRAISE.
Praise from the teacher reinforces desirable behavior in most children. Behavior modification in the classroom applies principles of operant conditioning.

TRUTH OR FICTION REVISITED
It is not true that we must make mistakes if we are to learn. The idea that we must make mistakes derives from folklore to the effect that we learn from (bad) experience. However, we also learn from good (positively reinforced) experiences and from the experiences of others.

PROGRAMMED LEARNING A method of learning in which complex tasks are broken down into simple steps, each of which is reinforced. Errors are not reinforced.

when they misbehave but ignoring them when they behave in desirable ways. Similarly, teachers who raise their voices when children misbehave may be unintentionally conferring hero status on those pupils in the eyes of their peers (Wentzel, 1994). To the teacher's surprise, some children may go out of their way to earn disapproval.

Teacher preparation and in-service programs show teachers how to use behavior modification to reverse these response patterns. Teachers are taught to pay attention to children when they are behaving appropriately and, when possible, to ignore (that is, avoid reinforcing) misbehavior (Abramowitz & O'Leary, 1991). The younger the child, the more powerful the teacher's attention and approval seem to be.

Among older children and adolescents, peer approval is often a more powerful reinforcer than teacher approval. Peer approval may maintain misbehavior, and ignoring misbehavior may only allow peers to become more disruptive. In such cases it may be necessary to separate troublesome children from less disruptive peers.

Teachers also frequently use time out from positive reinforcement to discourage misbehavior. In this method, children are placed in a drab, restrictive environment for a specified period, usually about 10 minutes, when they behave disruptively. While they are isolated, they cannot earn the attention of peers or teachers, and no reinforcers are present.

PROGRAMMED LEARNING B. F. Skinner developed an educational method called **programmed learning** that is based on operant conditioning. This method assumes that any complex task involving conceptual learning as well as motor skills can be broken down into a number of small steps. These steps can be shaped individually and then combined in sequence to form the correct behavioral chain.

Programmed learning does not punish errors. Instead, correct responses are reinforced. Every child earns "100," but at her or his own pace. Programmed learning also assumes it is the task of the teacher (or program) to structure the learning experience in such a way that errors will not be made.

COGNITIVE FACTORS IN LEARNING

Classical and operant conditioning were originally conceived of as relatively simple forms of learning. Much of conditioning's appeal is that it can be said to meet the behaviorist objective of explaining behavior in terms of observable events—in this case, laboratory conditions. Building on this theoretical base, some psychologists have suggested that the most complex human behavior involves the summation of a series of instances of conditioning. However, many psychologists believe that conditioning is too mechanical a process to explain all instances of learned behavior, even in laboratory rats (Weiner, 1991). They turn to cognitive factors to describe and explain additional findings in the psychology of learning.

In addition to concepts such as *association* and *reinforcement*, cognitive psychologists use concepts such as *mental structures, schemas, templates,* and *information processing.* Cognitive psychologists see people as searching for information, weighing evidence, and making decisions. Let us consider some classic research that points to cognitive factors in learning, as opposed to mechanical associations. These cognitive factors are not necessarily limited to humans—although, of course, people are the only species that can talk about them.

Contingency Theory: What "Really" Happens During Classical Conditioning?

Behaviorists and cognitive psychologists interpret the conditioning process in different ways. Behaviorists explain classical conditioning in terms of the pairing of stimuli. Cognitive psychologists explain classical conditioning in terms of the ways in which stimuli provide information that allows organisms to form and revise mental representations of their environment (Basic Behavioral Science Task Force, 1996).

In classical conditioning experiments with dogs, Robert Rescorla (1967) obtained some results that are difficult to explain without reference to cognitive concepts. Each phase of his work paired a tone (a learned or conditioned stimulus, or CS) with an electric shock (an unlearned or unconditioned stimulus, or US), but in different ways. With one group of animals, the shock was consistently presented after the tone. That is, the unconditioned stimulus followed on the heels of the conditioned stimulus, as in Pavlov's studies. The dogs in this group learned to show a fear response when the tone was presented.

A second group of dogs heard an equal number of tones and received an equal number of electric shocks, but the shock never immediately followed the tone. In other words, the tone and the shock were not paired. Now, from the behaviorist perspective, the dogs should not have learned to associate the tone and the shock because one did not predict the other. Actually, the dogs learned quite a lot: They learned that they had nothing to fear when the tone was sounded! They showed vigilance and fear when the laboratory was quiet—for apparently the shock could come at any time—but they were calm in the presence of the tone.

The third group of dogs also received equal numbers of tones and shocks, but the stimuli were presented at purely random intervals. Occasionally they were paired, but most often they were not. According to Rescorla, behaviorists might argue that intermittent pairing of the tones and shocks should have brought about some learning. Yet it did not. The animals showed no fear in response to the tone. Rescorla suggests that the animals in this group learned nothing because the tones did not allow them to make predictions about electric shock.

Rescorla concluded that contiguity—that is, the co-appearance of two events (the unconditioned stimulus and the conditioned stimulus)—cannot in itself explain classical conditioning. Instead, learning occurs only when the conditioned stimulus (in this case, the tone) provides information about the unconditioned stimulus (in this case, the shock). According to so-called **contingency theory,** learning occurs because a conditioned stimulus indicates that the unconditioned stimulus is likely to follow.

Behaviorists might counter, of course, that for the second group of dogs the *absence* of the tone became the signal for the shock. Shock may be a powerful enough event that the fear response becomes conditioned to the laboratory environment. For the third group of dogs, the shock was as likely to occur in the presence of the neutral stimulus as in its absence. Therefore, many behaviorists would expect no learning to occur.

Latent Learning: Forming Cognitive Maps

I'm all grown up. I know the whole mall.

THE AUTHOR'S DAUGHTER JORDAN AT AGE 7

Many behaviorists argue that organisms acquire only responses, or operants, for which they are reinforced. E. C. Tolman, however, showed that rats also learn about their environment in the absence of reinforcement.

CONTINGENCY THEORY The view that learning occurs when stimuli provide information about the likelihood of the occurrence of other stimuli.

CULTURE, ETHNICITY, AND LEARNING

Do you know where Slovenia is? In at least one respect—how well children learn in school—Slovenia is more "on the map" than the United States.

Learning is essential to competing successfully in the new millennium. The quantity of information that children and adults must absorb is leapfrogging itself every year. According to one psychologist, by the year 2110 it could take half a workday to catch up on what has happened since one left work the day before (McGuire, 1998). Much of what must be learned is technical—related to math and science. Yet children in the United States chronically fall behind children in Russia, Japan, and England in most academic subjects. According to the Third International Mathematics and Science Study, 8th graders in the United States rank 12th in science when compared with children in 41 selected countries (Murray, 1997). Math? Children in the United States rank 14th out of the 15. They lag children in Singapore, the Czech Republic, Slovenia, Hungary, and several other countries. Slovenia thus has more prominence than the United States on the math map.

Why does it matter that Asian and European children learn more about math and science than children in the United States? According to Louis Gerstner, Jr. (1994), the CEO of IBM, one reason is that U.S. businesses are forced to pick up the slack. They spend billions of dollars a year teaching workers to perform tasks and solve problems using skills that they should have learned in school. Many businesses cannot even upgrade their products or streamline their methods because they cannot teach their employees to do the necessary work. As a result, it costs them more money to produce less competitive products. This trend cannot continue if the United States is to maintain its standard of living.

BEYOND THE CLASSROOM

According to APA senior scientist Merry Bullock (1997), "Psychological research on learning can provide important input into curriculum develop-

ment." However, schools have already poured billions of dollars into reworking their curriculums and training their teachers to do a better job. A survey of 20,000 high school students from a variety of ethnic backgrounds suggests that the fault is more likely to lie with parents and teenagers themselves (Steinberg, 1996).

SERIOUSLY DISCONNECTED

In this chapter we surveyed factors in learning such as reinforcement, punishment, the formation of cognitive maps, and learning by observing others. Some of the most important "others" are parents, especially to young children. Much learning occurs in the home, long before children enter the classroom. Some of this learning is academic—learning about numbers and words and current events. But much of it is attitudinal. Parents can encourage children to learn and reward them for doing so, or they can disconnect themselves from the learning process. According to Steinberg (1996), too many parents have become seriously discon-

---

Tolman trained some rats to run through mazes for standard food goals. Other rats were permitted to explore the same mazes for several days without food goals or other rewards. After the unrewarded rats had been allowed to explore the mazes for 10 days, food rewards were placed in a box at the far end of the maze. The previously unrewarded rats reached the food box as quickly as the rewarded rats after only one or two reinforced trials (Tolman & Honzik, 1930).

Tolman concluded that rats learned about mazes in which they roamed even when they were unrewarded for doing so. He distinguished between *learning* and *performance*. Rats would acquire a cognitive map of a maze, and even though they would not be motivated to follow an efficient route

nected from their children's lives. When parents are disconnected from their children's learning, the children often drift.

Consider some of Steinberg's findings:

- Half the high school students surveyed said that it would not upset their parents if they brought home grades of C or worse;

- Forty percent of the students said that their parents never attended school functions;

- One third of the students said that their parents did not know how they were doing in school;

- One third said that they spent the day mainly "goofing off" with their friends; and

- Only one third of students said that they even had daily conversations with their parents.

Steinberg and his colleagues (1992, 1996) also looked at the situation from the parents' point of view. Many parents say that they would like to be involved in their children's school and leisure activities but are too busy to do so. By the time the children enter high school, many parents admit that they see education as the school's job, not theirs. In fact, half of the parents surveyed admitted that they do not know who their children's friends are or where their children go (and what they do) after school.

Steinberg makes some recommendations. First and foremost, parents need to be more involved with their teenagers. They should do the following:

- Communicate regularly with their teenagers about school and personal matters;

- Use consistent discipline (as opposed to being dictatorial or too permissive);

- Regularly attend school functions; and

- Consult with their children's teachers and follow through on their suggestions.

WHAT ABOUT PEERS?

Adolescents' peers also affect how well and how much they learn. Peers provide models who can encourage or discourage learning. In too many schools, it is considered socially wrong for an adolescent to be "too smart." In some schools, peers frown on adolescents doing well at all.

Overall, Steinberg and his colleagues (1996) found that some teenagers encourage others to do well in school. However, by and large, peers have a harmful effect on grades. For example, over half the students surveyed said that they did not talk about school-work with their friends. In fact, nearly 1 in 5 said he or she did not do as well as possible for fear of earning the disapproval of peers!

ETHNIC BACKGROUND

Of many possible factors, including family income and family structure, Steinberg and his colleagues (1996) conclude that ethnic background is most crucial in teenagers' attitudes toward schooling and grades. For example, consider the following:

- Many White students reported just trying to get by in school;

- African and Hispanic American students recognized the value of good grades and college education, but generally did not fear getting poor grades; and

- Asian American students spent twice as much time doing their homework as students in other ethnic groups and were most fearful of getting poor grades.

Steinberg concludes that schools are likely to continue to fight an uphill battle unless parents become more connected with their children's performance and peers become more supportive of students who do well in school.■

---

to the far end, they would learn rapid routes from one end to the other just by roaming about within the maze. Yet this learning might remain hidden, or **latent,** until they were motivated to follow the rapid routes to obtain food goals.

Observational Learning: Monkey See, Monkey May Choose to Do

How many things have you learned from watching other people in real life, in films, and on television? From films and television, you may have gathered vague ideas about how to sky dive, ride a surfboard, climb sheer

LATENT Hidden or concealed.

WHAT ARE THE EFFECTS OF MEDIA VIOLENCE?
Preschool children in the United States watch TV an average of 4 hours a day. Schoolchildren spend more hours at the TV set than in the classroom. Is it any wonder that psychologists, educators, and parents express concern about the effects of media violence?

cliffs, run a pattern to catch a touchdown pass in the Super Bowl, and dust for fingerprints, even if you have never tried these activities yourself.

In his studies of social learning, Albert Bandura and his colleagues have conducted experiments (Bandura et al., 1963) that show we can acquire operants by observing the behavior of others. We may need some practice to refine the operants, but we can learn them through observation alone. We may also allow these operants or skills to remain latent. For example, we may not imitate aggressive behavior unless we are provoked and believe that we are more likely to be rewarded than punished for it.

Observational learning may account for most human learning. It occurs when, as children, we watch our parents cook, clean, or repair a broken appliance. Observational learning takes place when we watch teachers solve problems on the blackboard or hear them speak in a foreign language. Observational learning is not mechanically acquired through reinforcement. We can learn through observation without engaging in overt responses at all. It appears sufficient to pay attention to the behavior of others.

In the terminology of observational learning, a person who engages in a response to be imitated is a **model.** When observers see a model being reinforced for displaying an operant, the observers are said to be *vicariously* reinforced. Display of the operant thus becomes more likely for the observer as well as for the model. What happens when the model is *violent*?

THE EFFECTS OF MEDIA VIOLENCE Much human learning occurs through observation. We learn by observing parents and peers, attending school, reading books, and—in one of the more controversial aspects of modern life—watching media such as TV and films. Nearly all of us have been exposed to television, videotapes, and films in the classroom. Children in day-care centers often watch *Sesame Street.* There are filmed and videotaped versions of great works of literature such as Orson Welles's *Macbeth* or Laurence Olivier's *Hamlet.* Nearly every school shows films of laboratory experiments. Sometimes we view "canned lectures" by master teachers.

But what about our viewing *outside* the classroom? Television is one of our major sources of informal observational learning. Children are routinely exposed to scenes of murder, beating, and sexual assault—just by turning on the TV set (Huesmann & Miller, 1994; Seppa, 1997). If a child watches 2 to 4 hours of TV a day, she or he will have seen 8,000 murders and another 100,000 acts of violence *by the time she or he has finished elementary school* (DeAngelis, 1993).

Moreover, violence tends to be glamorized on TV. For example, in one cartoon show, superheroes battle villains who are trying to destroy or take over the world. Violence is often shown to have only temporary or minimal effects. (How often has Wily Coyote fallen from a cliff and been pounded into the ground by a boulder, only to bounce back and pursue the Road Runner once more?) In the great majority of violent TV shows, there is no remorse, criticism, or penalty for violent behavior (Seppa, 1997). Few TV programs show harmful long-term consequences of aggressive behavior.

Why all this violence? Simple: Violence sells. But does violence do more than sell? Does media violence *cause* real violence? If so, what can parents and educators do to prevent the fictional from spilling over into the real world?

In study after study, children and adults who view violence in the media later show higher levels of aggressive behavior than people who are

OBSERVATIONAL LEARNING The acquisition of knowledge and skills through the observation of others (who are called *models*) rather than by means of direct experience.

MODEL An organism that engages in a response that is then imitated by another organism.

FIGURE L.12

CLASSIC RESEARCH ON THE IMITATION OF AGGRESSIVE MODELS.
Albert Bandura and his colleagues showed that children frequently imitate aggressive behavior they observe. In the top row, an adult model strikes a clown doll. The lower rows show a boy and a girl imitating the aggressive behavior.

not exposed to media violence (DeAngelis, 1993). Most psychologists therefore agree that media violence *contributes* to aggression (Huesmann & Miller, 1994; NIMH, 1982).

Consider a number of ways in which depictions of violence make such a contribution:

- *Observational learning.* Children learn from observation (Bandura, 1986). TV violence supplies **models** of aggressive "skills," which children may acquire. In fact, children are more likely to imitate what their parents do than to heed what they say. If adults say they disapprove of aggression but smash furniture or slap each other when frustrated, children are likely to develop the notion that aggression is the way to handle frustration. Classic experiments show that children tend to imitate the aggressive behavior they see on the media (Bandura et al., 1963) (see Figure L. 12). Media violence also provides viewers with aggressive *scripts*—that is, ideas about how to behave in situations like those they have observed (Huesmann & Miller, 1994).

- *Disinhibition.* Punishment inhibits behavior. Conversely, media violence may disinhibit aggressive behavior, especially when media characters get away with violence or are rewarded for it.

- *Increased arousal.* Media violence and aggressive video games increase viewers' level of arousal. That is, television "works them up." We are more likely to be aggressive under high levels of arousal.

- *Priming of aggressive thoughts and memories.* Media violence "primes" or arouses aggressive ideas and memories (Berkowitz, 1988).

- *Habituation.* We become "habituated to," or used to, repeated stimuli. Repeated exposure to TV violence may decrease viewers' sensitivity to real violence. If children come to perceive violence as the norm, they may become more tolerant of it and place less value on restraining aggressive urges (Huesmann & Miller, 1994).

Although media violence encourages aggression in viewers, it has its greatest impact on the children who are *already* considered the most aggressive by their teachers (Josephson, 1987). There also seems to be a circular relationship between viewing media violence and displaying aggressive behavior (DeAngelis, 1993; Eron, 1982). Yes, TV violence contributes to aggressive behavior, but aggressive children are also more likely to tune in and stay tuned to it.

TRUTH OR FICTION REVISITED
Actually, a scientific connection has been established between TV violence and aggression in real life. But does media violence *cause* aggression? What are the possible relationships between media violence and aggression (see Figure L.13)?

FIGURE L.13

WHAT ARE THE CONNECTIONS BETWEEN MEDIA VIOLENCE AND AGGRESSIVE BEHAVIOR?
Does media violence lead to aggression? Does aggressive behavior lead to a preference for viewing violence? Or does a third factor, such as a predisposition toward aggressive behavior, contribute to both? Might such a predisposition be in part genetic?

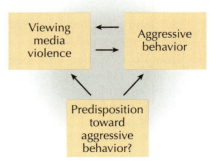

Aggressive children are frequently rejected by their nonaggressive peers—at least in middle-class culture (Eron, 1982; Patterson, 1993). Aggressive children may watch more television because their peer relationships are less fulfilling and because the high incidence of TV violence tends to confirm their view that aggressive behavior is normal (Eron, 1982). Media violence also interacts with other contributors to violence. For example, parental rejection and use of physical punishment further increase the likelihood of aggression in children (Eron, 1982).

A harsh home life may further confirm the TV viewer's vision of the world as a violent place and further encourage reliance on television for companionship.

It would be of little use to discuss how we learn if we were not capable of remembering what we learn from second to second, from day to day, or in many cases for a lifetime. In the next chapter we turn our attention to the subject of memory. And following that, we see how learning is intertwined with thinking and intelligence.

SUMMARY

1. **What is learning?** Learning is the process by which experience leads to modified representations of the environment and relatively permanent changes in behavior.

2. **What is classical conditioning?** In classical conditioning as a laboratory procedure, a previously neutral stimulus (the conditioned stimulus, or CS) comes to elicit the response evoked by a second stimulus (the unconditioned stimulus, or US) as a result of repeatedly being paired with the second stimulus.

3. **What kinds of classical conditioning procedures are there?** In the most efficient classical conditioning procedure, the CS is presented about 0.5 second before the US. Other classical conditioning procedures include trace conditioning, simultaneous conditioning, and backward conditioning, in which the US is presented first.

4. **How do extinction and spontaneous recovery occur in classical conditioning?** After a US-CS association has been learned, repeated presentation of the CS (for example, a bell) without the US (meat powder) extinguishes the CR

(salivation). But extinguished responses may show spontaneous recovery as a function of the time that has elapsed since extinction occurred.

5. **What are generalization and discrimination?** In generalization, organisms show a CR in response to a range of stimuli similar to the CS. In discrimination, organisms learn to show a CR in response to a more limited range of stimuli by pairing only the limited stimulus with the US.

6. **What is operant conditioning?** In operant conditioning, organisms learn to engage in behavior that is reinforced. Initial "correct" responses may be performed at random or as a result of physical or verbal guiding. Reinforced responses occur more frequently.

7. **What kinds of reinforcers are there?** Positive reinforcers increase the probability that operants will occur when they are applied. Negative reinforcers increase the probability that operants will occur when the reinforcers are removed. Primary reinforcers have their value because of the organism's biological makeup. Secondary reinforcers

such as money and approval acquire their value through association with established reinforcers.

8. **How do extinction and spontaneous recovery occur in operant conditioning?** In operant conditioning, learned responses are extinguished as a result of repeated performance in the absence of reinforcement. As in classical conditioning, spontaneous recovery occurs as a function of the passage of time.

9. **What are rewards and punishments?** Rewards, like reinforcers, increase the frequency of the rewarded behavior. But rewards differ from reinforcers in that they are pleasant stimuli. Punishments are aversive stimuli that suppress the frequency of the punished behavior.

10. **What is a discriminative stimulus?** A discriminative stimulus indicates when an operant will be reinforced.

11. **What kinds of schedules of reinforcement are there?** Continuous reinforcement leads to the most rapid acquisition of new responses, but operants are maintained most economically through partial

reinforcement. There are four basic schedules of reinforcement. In a fixed-interval schedule, a specific amount of time must elapse after a previous correct response before reinforcement again becomes available. In a variable-interval schedule, the amount of time is allowed to vary. In a fixed-ratio schedule, a fixed number of correct responses must be performed before one is reinforced. In a variable-ratio schedule, this number is allowed to vary.

12. **What is shaping?** In shaping, successive approximations of the target response are reinforced.

13. **What is contingency theory?** This is the view that organisms learn associations between stimuli only when stimuli provide new information about each other.

14. **What is latent learning?** In latent learning, as demonstrated by Tolman's classic research with rats, organisms can learn (that is, modify their cognitive map of the environment) in the absence of reinforcement.

15. **What is observational learning?** Bandura has shown that people can learn by observing others without emitting reinforced responses of their own. They may then choose to perform the behaviors they have observed "when the time is ripe"—that is, when they believe the learned behavior is appropriate or is likely to be rewarded.

16. **What are the effects of media violence?** Media violence often contributes to violent behavior in observers by providing violent models, disinhibiting aggressive impulses, increasing the viewer's level of arousal, priming aggressive thoughts and memories, and habituating the viewer to violence. Yet a selection factor is also at work: Aggressive children are more likely to choose to tune into violence in the media.

KEY TERMS

backward conditioning (p. L-7)

classical conditioning (p. L-2)

conditioned reinforcer (p. L-17)

conditioned response (CR) (p. L-4)

conditioned stimulus (CS) (p. L-5)

contingency theory (p. L-25)

continuous reinforcement (p. L-20)

delayed conditioning (p. L-6)

discrimination (p. L-10)

discrimination training (p. L-10)

discriminative stimulus (p. L-20)

extinction (p. L-8)

fixed-interval schedule (p. L-21)

fixed-ratio schedule (p. L-22)

flooding (p. L-12)

generalization (p. L-10)

higher-order conditioning (p. L-11)

latent (p. L-27)

learning (p. L-3)

model (p. L-29)

negative reinforcer (p. L-16)

observational learning (p. L-28)

operant behavior (p. L-14)

operant conditioning (p. L-2)

partial reinforcement (p. L-20)

positive reinforcer (p. L-16)

primary reinforcer (p. L-17)

programmed learning (p. L-24)

punishment (p. L-18)

reflex (p. L-4)

reinforce (p. L-13)

reward (p. L-18)

secondary reinforcer (p. L-17)

shaping (p. L-22)

simultaneous conditioning (p. L-6)

socialization (p. L-23)

spontaneous recovery (p. L-9)

stimulus (p. L-4)

successive approximations (p. L-22)

systematic desensitization (p. L-12)

time out (p. L-19)

token economy (p. L-23)

trace conditioning (p. L-6)

unconditioned response (UR) (p. L-5)

unconditioned stimulus (US) (p. L-5)

variable-interval schedule (p. L-21)

variable-ratio schedule (p. L-22)

REFERENCES

Abramowitz, A. J., & O'Leary S. G. (1991). Behavioral interventions for the classroom. *School Psychology Review, 20*, 220–234.

Bandura, A. (1986). *Social foundations of thought and action: A social-cognitive theory.* Englewood Cliffs, NJ: Prentice-Hall.

Bandura, A., Ross, S. A., & Ross, D. (1963). Imitation of film-mediated aggressive models. *Journal of Abnormal and Social Psychology, 66*, 3–11.

Basic Behavioral Science Task Force of the National Advisory Mental Health Council. (1996). Basic behavioral science research for mental health: Perception, attention, learning, and memory. *American Psychologist, 51*, 133–142.

Berkowitz, L. (1988). Frustrations, appraisals, and aversively stimulated aggression. *Aggressive Behavior, 14*, 3–11.

Bjork, D. W. (1997). *B. F. Skinner: A life*. Washington, DC: American Psychological Association.

Bullock, M. (1997). Cited in Murray, B. (1997). America still lags behind in mathematics test scores. *APA Monitor, 28*(1), 44.

Collins, C. (1995, May 11). Spanking is becoming the new don't. *New York Times*, p. C8.

DeAngelis, T. (1993). It's baaack: TV violence, concern for kid viewers. *APA Monitor, 24*(8), 16.

Dollard, J., Doob, L. W., Miller, N. E., Mowrer, O. H., & Sears, R. R. (1939). *Frustration and aggression*. New Haven, CT: Yale University Press.

Eron, L. D. (1982). Parent-child interaction, television violence, and aggression of children. *American Psychologist, 37*, 197–211.

Etaugh, C., & Rathus, S. A. (1995). *The world of children*. Fort Worth: Harcourt Brace.

Garcia, J., Brett, L. P., & Rusiniak, K. W. (1989). Limits of Darwinian conditioning. In S. B. Klein & R. R. Mowrer (Eds.), *Contemporary learning theories: Instrumental conditioning theory and the impact of biological constraints on learning*. Hillsdale, NJ: Erlbaum.

Garcia, J., & Koelling, R. A. (1966). Relation of cue to consequences in avoidance learning. *Psychonomic Science, 4*, 123–124.

Gerstner, L. V., Jr. (1994, May 27). Our schools are failing. Do we care? *New York Times*, p. A27.

Glenn, S. S., Ellis, J., & Greenspoon, J. (1992). On the revolutionary nature of the operant as a unit of behavioral selection. *American Psychologist, 47*, 1326–1329.

Greene, J. (1982). The gambling trap. *Psychology Today, 16*(9), 50–55.

Huesmann, L. R., & Miller, L. S. (1994). Long-term effects of repeated exposure to media violence in childhood. In L. R. Huesmann (Ed.), *Aggressive behavior*. New York: Plenum.

Jones, M. C. (1924). Elimination of children's fears. *Journal of Experimental Psychology, 7*, 381–390.

Josephson, W. D. (1987). Television violence and children's aggression: Testing the priming, social script, and disinhibition prediction. *Journal of Personality and Social Psychology, 53*, 882–890.

McGuire, P. A. (1998). Wanted: Workers with flexibility for 21st century jobs. *APA Monitor, 29*(7), 10, 12.

Miller, N. E. (1969). Learning of visceral and glandular responses. *Science, 163*, 434–445.

Murray, B. (1997). America still lags behind in mathematics test scores. *APA Monitor, 28*(1), 44.

NIMH (National Institute of Mental Health). (1982). *Television and behavior: Ten years of scientific progress and implications for the eighties*. Washington, DC: NIMH.

Patterson, G. R. (1993). Orderly change in a stable world: The antisocial trait as a chimera. *Journal of Consulting and Clinical Psychology, 61*, 911–919.

Pavlov, I. (1927). *Conditioned reflexes*. London: Oxford University Press.

Pulley, B. (1998, June 16). Those seductive snake eyes: Tales of growing up gambling. *New York Times*, A1, A28.

Rescorla, R. A. (1967). Pavlovian conditioning and its proper control procedures. *Psychological Review, 74*, 71–80.

Rescorla, R. A. (1988). Pavlovian conditioning: It's not what you think it is. *American Psychologist, 43*, 151–160.

Seppa, N. (1997). Children's TV remains steeped in violence. *APA Monitor, 28*(6), 36.

Skinner, B. F. (1938). *The behavior of organisms: An experimental analysis*. New York: Appleton.

Steinberg, L. (1996). *Beyond the classroom*. New York: Simon & Schuster.

Steinberg, L., Brown, B. B., & Dornbusch, S. M. (1996). Ethnicity and adolescent achievement. *American Educator, 20*(2), 28–35.

Steinberg, L., Lamborn, S. D., Dornbusch, S. M., & Darling, N. (1992). Impact of parenting practices on adolescent achievement: Authoritative parenting, school involvement, and encouragement to succeed. *Child Development, 63*, 1266–1281.

Straus, M. A., & Smith, C. (1990). Family patterns and child abuse. In M. A. Straus & R. J. Gelles (Eds.), *Physical violence in American families*. New Brunswick, NJ: Transaction.

Tolman, E. C., & Honzik, C. H. (1930). Introduction and removal of reward, and maze performance in rats. *University of California Publications in Psychology, 4*, 257–275.

Watson, J. B., & Rayner, R. (1920). Conditioned emotional reactions. *Journal of Experimental Psychology, 3*, 1–14.

Weiner, B. (1991). Metaphors in motivation and attribution. *American Psychologist, 46*, 921–930.

Wentzel, K. R. (1994). Relations of social goal pursuit to social acceptance, classroom behavior, and perceived social support. *Journal of Educational Psychology, 86*, 173–182.

Wolpe, J., & Plaud, J. J. (1997). Pavlov's contributions to behavior therapy: The obvious and the not so obvious. *American Psychologist, 52*, 966–972.

M

MEMORY

MY OLDEST DAUGHTER JILL WAS TALKING ABOUT HOW she had run into a friend from elementary school and they had had a splendid time recalling the goofy things they did during their school years. Her sister Allyn, age 6 at the time, was not to be outdone. "I can remember when I was born," she put in.

The family's ears perked up. Being a psychologist, I knew exactly what to say. "You can remember when you were born?" I said.

"Oh, yes," she insisted. "Mommy was there."

So far she could not be faulted. I cheered her on, and she related a remarkably detailed account of how it had been snowing in the wee hours of a bitter December morning when Mommy had to go to the hospital. You see, she said, her memory was so good that she could also summon up what it had been like *before* she was born. She wove a wonderful patchwork quilt, integrating details we had given her with her own recollections of the events surrounding the delivery of her younger sister, Jordan. All in all, she seemed quite satisfied that she had pieced together a faithful portrait of her arrival on the world stage.

Later in the chapter, we will see that children usually cannot recall events that occurred in their first two years, much less those of their first hours. But Allyn's tale dramatized the way we "remember" many of the things that have happened to us. When it comes to long-term memories, truth can take a back seat to drama and embellishment. Very often, our memories are like the bride's apparel—there's something old, something new, something borrowed, and from time to time something blue.

Memory is what this chapter is about. Without memory, there is no past. Without memory, experience is trivial and learning is lost. Shortly we will see what psychologists have learned about the ways in which we remember things. First, try to meet the following challenges to your memory.

FIVE CHALLENGES TO MEMORY

Before we go any further, let's test your memory. If you want to participate, find four sheets of blank paper and number them 1 through 4. Then follow these directions:

1. Following are 10 letters. Look at them for 15 seconds. Later in the chapter, I will ask you if you can write them on sheet number 1. (No cheating! Don't do it now.)

    THUNSTOFAM

2. Look at these nine figures for 30 seconds. Then try to draw them in the proper sequence on sheet number 2. (Yes, right after you've finished looking at them. We'll talk about your drawings later.)

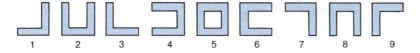

3. Okay, here's another list of letters, 17 this time. Look at the list for 60 seconds and then see whether you can reproduce it on sheet number 3. (I'm being generous this time—a full minute.)

GMC-BSI-BMA-TTC-IAF-BI

4. Which of these pennies is an accurate reproduction of the Lincoln penny you see every day? This time there's nothing to draw on another sheet; just circle or put a check mark by the penny that you think resembles the ones you throw in the back of the drawer.

5. Examine the following drawings for 1 minute. Then copy the names of the figures on sheet number 4. When you're finished, just keep reading. Soon I'll be asking you to draw those figures.

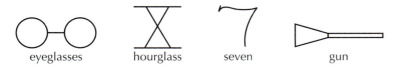

eyeglasses   hourglass   seven   gun

THREE KINDS OF MEMORY: THE "ESP" OF MEMORY

There are different kinds of memories. Endel Tulving (1985, 1991) classifies memories according to the kind of information they hold: episodic, semantic, and procedural. Return to Allyn's "recollection." Of course Allyn could not really remember her own birth. That is, she could not recall the particular event or *episode* in which she had participated. Let us first see what is meant by episodic memory.

Episodic Memory

Memories of the events that happen to a person or take place in his or her presence are referred to as **episodic memories** (Wheeler et al., 1997). Your memories of what you ate for breakfast and of what your professor said in class this afternoon are examples of episodic memory.

What Allyn did recount is more accurately characterized as generalized knowledge than as an episodic memory of her birth. From listening to her parents and from her experience with the events of her sister Jordan's birth, she had learned much about what happens during childbirth. She erroneously thought that this knowledge represented her own birth.

EPISODIC MEMORY Personal memory of specific events.

PROCEDURAL MEMORY.
Memories of how to ride a bicycle, how to type, how to turn the lights on and off, and how to drive a car are procedural memories. Procedural memories tend to persist even when we do not use them for many years. Here Jean Piaget, the cognitive-developmental theorist, demonstrates that we may never forget how to ride a bicycle.

Semantic Memory

General knowledge is referred to as **semantic memory.** *Semantics* concerns meanings. Allyn was reporting her understanding of the meaning of childbirth rather than an episode in her own life. You can "remember" that the United States has 50 states without visiting them and personally adding them up. You "remember" who authored *Hamlet*, although you were not looking over Shakespeare's shoulder as he did so. These, too, are examples of semantic memory.

Your future recollection that there are three kinds of memory is more likely to be semantic than episodic. In other words, you are more likely to "know" there are three types of memory than to recall the date on which you learned about them, where you were and how you were sitting, and whether you were also thinking about dinner at the time. We tend to use the phrase "I remember . . ." when we are referring to episodic memories, as in "I *remember* the blizzard of 1998." But we are more likely to say "I know . . ." in reference to semantic memories, as in "I *know* about—" (or, "I heard about—") "—the blizzard of 1898." Put it another way: You may *remember* that you wrote your mother, but you *know* that Shakespeare wrote *Hamlet*.

Procedural Memory

The third type of memory is **procedural memory,** also referred to as *skill memory* Procedural memory means knowing how to do things. You have learned and now "remember" how to ride a bicycle, how to swim or swing a bat, how to type, how to turn on the lights, and how to drive a car. Procedural memories tend to persist even when we have not used them for many years. (Do we ever forget how to ride a bicycle?)

Do you think it would help for a person to have ESP (which usually stands for "extrasensory perception") to remember the three types of memory? That is, E = episodic, S = semantic, and P = procedural. As we proceed, we will see that a good deal of information about memory comes in threes. We will also learn more about **mnemonic devices,** or tricks for retaining memories, such as ESP. By the way, is your use of ESP to help remember the kinds of memory an instance of episodic, semantic, or procedural memory?

Before proceeding to the next section, turn to the piece of paper on which you wrote the names of the four figures—that is, sheet number 4—and draw them from memory as exactly as you can. Do not look back at the drawings in the book. Now hold on to your drawings. We'll talk about them a bit later.

THREE PROCESSES OF MEMORY: MEMORY AS INFORMATION PROCESSING

Both psychologists and computer scientists speak of processing information. Think of using a computer to write a term paper. Once the system is up and operating, you begin to enter information. You place information in the computer's memory by typing letters and numbers on a keyboard. If you were to do some major surgery on your computer (which I am often tempted to do) and open up its memory, however, you would not find these letters inside it. This is because the computer is programmed to *change* the letters—that is, the information you have typed—into a form

SEMANTIC MEMORY General knowledge as opposed to episodic memory.

PROCEDURAL MEMORY Knowledge of ways of doing things; skill memory.

MNEMONIC DEVICES Systems for remembering in which items are related to easily recalled sets of symbols such as acronyms, phrases, or jingles.

that can be placed in its electronic memory. Similarly, when we perceive information, we must convert it into a form that can be remembered if we are to place it in our memory.

Encoding

The first stage of information processing is changing information so we can place it in memory: **encoding.** Information about the outside world reaches our senses in the form of physical and chemical stimuli. When we encode this information, we convert it into psychological formats that can be represented mentally. To do so, we commonly use visual, auditory, and semantic codes.

Let us illustrate the uses of coding by referring to the list of letters you first saw in the section on challenges to memory. Try to write the letters on sheet number 1. Go on, take a minute and then come back.

Okay, now: If you had used a **visual code** to try to remember the list, you would have mentally represented it as a picture. That is, you would have maintained—or attempted to maintain—a mental image of the letters. Some artists and art historians seem to maintain marvelous visual mental representations of works of art. This enables them to quickly recognize whether a work is authentic.

You may also have decided to read the list of letters to yourself—that is, to silently say them in sequence: "t," "h," "u," and so on. By so doing, you would have been using an **acoustic code,** or representing the stimuli as a sequence of sounds. You may also have read the list as a three-syllable word, "thun-sto-fam." This is an acoustic code, but it also involves the "meaning" of the letters, in the sense that you are interpreting the list as a word. This approach has elements of a semantic code.

Semantic codes represent stimuli in terms of their meaning. Our 10 letters were meaningless in and of themselves. However, they can also serve as an acronym—a term made up of the first letters of a phrase—for the familiar phrase "THe UNited STates OF AMerica." This observation lends them meaning.

Storage

The second memory process is **storage.** Storage means maintaining information over time. If you were given the task of storing the list of letters—that is, told to remember it—how would you attempt to place it in storage? One way would be by **maintenance rehearsal**—by mentally repeating the list, or saying it to yourself. Our awareness of the functioning of our memory, referred to by psychologists as **metamemory,** becomes more sophisticated as we develop.

You could also have condensed the amount of information you were rehearsing by reading the list as a three-syllable word; that is, you could have rehearsed three syllables (said "thun-sto-fam" over and over again) rather than 10 letters. In either case, repetition would have been the key to memory. (We talk more about such condensing, or "chunking," very soon.)

However, you could also encode the list of letters by relating it to something that you already know. This kind of coding is referred to as **elaborative rehearsal.** That is, you are elaborating or extending the semantic meaning of the letters you are trying to remember. For example, did you recognize that the list of 10 letters is an acronym for "The United States of America"? (That is, you take the first two letters of each of the words in the phrase and string them together to make up the 10 letters of THUNSTOFAM.) If you had recognized this, storage of the list of letters might have been almost instantaneous and it would probably have been permanent.

ENCODING Modifying information so that it can be placed in memory. The first stage of information processing.

VISUAL CODE Mental representation of information as a picture.

ACOUSTIC CODE Mental representation of information as a sequence of sounds.

SEMANTIC CODE Mental representation of information according to its meaning.

STORAGE Maintenance of information over time. The second stage of information processing.

MAINTENANCE REHEARSAL Mental repetition of information in order to keep it in memory.

METAMEMORY Self-awareness of the ways in which memory functions, allowing the person to encode, store, and retrieve information effectively.

ELABORATIVE REHEARSAL A method for increasing retention of new information by relating it to information that is well known.

Retrieval

The third memory process is **retrieval,** or locating stored information and returning it to consciousness. With well-known information such as our names and occupations, retrieval is effortless and, for all practical purposes, immediate. But when we are trying to remember massive quantities of information, or information that is not perfectly understood, retrieval can be tedious and not always successful. It is easiest to retrieve information stored in a computer by using the name of the file. Similarly, retrieval of information from our memories requires knowledge of the proper cues.

If you had encoded THUNSTOFAM as a three-syllable word, your retrieval strategy would involve recollection of the word and rules for decoding. In other words, you would say the "word" *thun-sto-fam* and then decode it by spelling it out. You might err in that "thun" sounds like "thumb" and "sto" could also be spelled "stow." However, using the semantic code, or recognition of the acronym for "The United States of America," could lead to flawless recollection.

I stuck out my neck by predicting that you would quickly and perhaps permanently store the list of letters if you recognized them as an acronym. Here, too, there would be recollection (of the name of our country) and rules for decoding. That is, to "remember" the 10 letters, you would have to envision the phrase ("The United States of America") and read off the first two letters of each word. Because using this semantic code is more complex than simply seeing the entire list (using a visual code), it may take a while to recall (actually, to reconstruct) the list of 10 letters. But by using the phrase, you are likely to remember the list of letters permanently.

Now, what if you were not able to remember the list of 10 letters? What would have gone wrong? In terms of the three processes of memory, it could be that you had (1) not encoded the list in a useful way, (2) not entered the encoded information into storage, or (3) stored the information but lacked the proper cues for remembering it—such as the phrase "The United States of America" or the rule for decoding the phrase.

By now you may have noticed that I have discussed three kinds of memory and three processes of memory, but I have not yet *defined* memory. No apologies—we were not ready for a definition yet. Now that we have explored some basic concepts, let us give it a try: **Memory** is the processes by which information is encoded, stored, and retrieved.

THREE STAGES OF MEMORY: MAKING *SENSE* OF THE *SHORT* AND THE *LONG* OF IT

William James (1890) was intrigued by the fact that some memories are unreliable, "going in one ear and out the other," whereas others could be recalled for a lifetime. He wrote:

> The stream of thought flows on, but most of its elements fall into the bottomless pit of oblivion. Of some, no element survives the instant of their passage. Of others, it is confined to a few moments, hours, or days. Others, again, leave vestiges which are indestructible, and by means of which they may be recalled as long as life endures.

Yes, the world is a constant display of sights and sounds and other sources of sensory stimulation, but only some of these things are remembered. James was correct in observing that we remember various "elements" of

RETRIEVAL The location of stored information and its return to consciousness. The third stage of information processing.

MEMORY The processes by which information is encoded, stored, and retrieved.

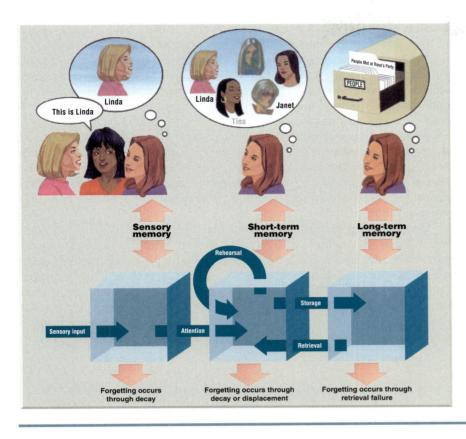

FIGURE M.1
THREE STAGES OF MEMORY.

The Atkinson-Shiffrin model proposes three distinct stages of memory. Sensory information impacts on the registers of sensory memory, where memory traces are held briefly before decaying. If we attend to the information, much of it is transferred to short-term memory (STM). Information in STM may decay or be displaced if it is not transferred to long-term memory (LTM). We can use rehearsal or elaborative strategies to transfer memories to LTM. If information in LTM is organized poorly, or if we cannot find cues to retrieve it, it may be lost.

thought for different lengths of time, and many we do not remember at all. Richard Atkinson and Richard Shiffrin (1968) proposed three stages of memory and suggested that the progress of information through these stages determines whether (and how long) it is retained (see Figure M.1). These stages are *sensory memory, short-term memory (STM),* and *long-term memory (LTM)*.

There is a saying that when you cover a topic completely, you are talking about "the long and short of it." In the case of the stages of memory, we could say we are trying to "make *sense* of the *short* and the *long* of it."

Sensory Memory

William James also wrote about the stream of thought, or consciousness:

> Consciousness . . . does not appear to itself chopped up in bits. A "river" or a "stream" are the metaphors by which it is most naturally described. In talking of it hereafter, let us call it the stream of thought, of consciousness, or of subjective life.

When we look at a visual stimulus, our impressions may seem fluid enough. Actually, however, they consist of a series of eye fixations referred to as **saccadic eye movements.** These movements jump from one point to another about four times each second. Yet the visual sensations seem continuous, or streamlike, because of **sensory memory.** Sensory memory is the type or stage of memory that is first encountered by a stimulus. Although it holds impressions briefly, it is long enough so that a series of perceptions seem to be connected.

Let us return to our example of the list of letters: THUNSTOFAM. If the list were flashed on a screen for a fraction of a second, the visual impression, or **memory trace,** of the stimulus would also last for only a

SACCADIC EYE MOVEMENT The rapid jumps made by a person's eyes as they fixate on different points.

SENSORY MEMORY The type or stage of memory first encountered by a stimulus. Sensory memory holds impressions briefly, but long enough so that series of perceptions are psychologically continuous.

MEMORY TRACE An assumed change in the nervous system that reflects the impression made by a stimulus. Memory traces are said to be "held" in sensory registers.

fraction of a second afterward. Psychologists speak of the memory trace of the list as being held in a visual **sensory register.**

If the letters had been flashed on a screen for, say, 1/10th of a second, your ability to remember them on the basis of sensory memory alone would be limited. Your memory would be based on a single eye fixation, and the trace of the image would vanish before a single second had passed. At the turn of the century, psychologist William McDougall (1904) engaged in research in which he showed people 1 to 12 letters arranged in rows—just long enough to allow a single eye fixation. Under these conditions, people could typically remember only 4 or 5 letters. Thus recollection of THUNSTOFAM, a list of 10 letters arranged in a single row, would probably depend on whether one had encoded it so that it could be processed further.

George Sperling (1960) modified McDougall's experimental method and showed that there is a difference between what people can see and what they can report. McDougall had used a *whole-report procedure,* in which people were asked to report every letter they saw in the array. Sperling used a modified *partial-report procedure,* in which people were asked to report the contents of one of three rows of letters. In a typical procedure, Sperling flashed three rows of letters like the following on a screen for 50 milliseconds (1/20th of a second):

$$A \quad G \quad R \quad E$$
$$V \quad L \quad S \quad B$$
$$N \quad K \quad B \quad T$$

Using the whole-report procedure, people could report an average of four letters from the entire display (one out of three). But if immediately after presenting the display Sperling pointed an arrow at a row he wanted viewers to report, they usually reported most of the letters in the row successfully.

If Sperling presented six letters arrayed in two rows, people could usually report either row without error. If people were flashed three rows of four letters each—a total of 12—they reported correctly an average of three of four letters in the designated row, suggesting that about nine of the 12 letters had been perceived.

Sperling found that the amount of time that elapsed before indicating the row to be reported was crucial. If he delayed pointing the arrow for a few fractions of a second after presenting the letters, people were much less successful in reporting the letters in the target row. If he allowed a full second to elapse, the arrow did not aid recall at all. From these data, Sperling concluded that the memory trace of visual stimuli *decays* within a second in the visual sensory register (see Figure M.1). With a single eye fixation, people can *see* most of a display of 12 letters clearly, as shown by their ability to immediately read off most of the letters in a designated row. Yet as the fractions of a single second are elapsing, the memory trace of the letters is fading. By the time a second has elapsed, the trace has vanished.

TRUTH OR FICTION REVISITED

It is true that some people have photographic memory. People who can see have what is actually defined as *photographic,* or *iconic,* memory. However, only a few have *eidetic imagery,* which is closer to what laypeople think of as "photographic memory."

SENSORY REGISTER A system of memory that holds information briefly, but long enough so that it can be processed further. There may be a sensory register for every sense.

ICON A mental representation of a visual stimulus that is held briefly in sensory memory.

ICONIC MEMORY The sensory register that briefly holds mental representations of visual stimuli.

ICONIC MEMORY Psychologists believe we possess a sensory register for each one of our senses. The mental representations of visual stimuli are referred to as **icons.** The sensory register that holds icons is labeled **iconic memory.** Iconic memory is one kind of sensory memory. Iconic memories are accurate, photographic memories. So those of us who mentally represent visual stimuli have "photographic memories." However, iconic memories are very brief. What most of us normally think of as a photographic memory—the ability to retain exact mental representations of visual stimuli over long periods of time—is technically referred to as *eidetic imagery.*

EIDETIC IMAGERY A few individuals retain visual stimuli, or icons, in their sensory memories for remarkably long periods of time. About 5% of children can look at a detailed picture, turn away, and several minutes later recall the particulars of the picture with exceptional clarity—as if they were still seeing it. This extraordinary visual sensory memory is referred to as **eidetic imagery** (Haber, 1980). This ability declines with age, however, all but disappearing by adolescence.

Figure M.2 provides an example of a test of eidetic imagery. Children are asked to look at the first drawing in the series for 20 to 30 seconds, after which it is removed. The children then continue to gaze at a neutral background. Several minutes later the drawing in the center is placed on the backdrop. When asked what they see, many report "a face." A face would be seen only if the children had retained a clear image of the first picture and fused it with the second so that they are, in effect, perceiving the third picture in Figure M.2 (Haber, 1980).

Eidetic imagery appears remarkably clear and detailed. It seems to be essentially a perceptual phenomenon in which encoding or rehearsal are not necessary to continue to "see" a visual stimulus. Although eidetic imagery is rare, iconic memory, as we see in the following section, universally transforms visual perceptions into smoothly unfolding impressions of the world.

ICONIC MEMORY AND SACCADIC EYE MOVEMENTS Iconic memory smooths out the bumps in the visual ride. Saccadic eye movements occur about four times every second. Iconic memory, however, holds icons for up to a second. As a consequence, the flow of visual information seems smooth and continuous. Your impression that the words you are reading flow across the page, rather than jumping across in spurts, is a product of your iconic memory. Similarly, motion pictures present 16 to 22 separate frames, or still images, each second. Iconic memory allows you to perceive the imagery in the film as being seamless (G. R. Loftus, 1983).

ECHOIC MEMORY Mental representations of sounds, or auditory stimuli, are called **echoes.** The sensory register that holds echoes is referred to as **echoic memory.**

The memory traces of auditory stimuli (that is, echoes) can last for several seconds, many times longer than the traces of visual stimuli (icons). The difference in the duration of traces is probably based on biological differences between the eye and the ear. This difference is one of the reasons that acoustic codes aid in the retention of information that has been presented visually—or why saying the letters or syllables of THUNSTOFAM makes the list easier to remember.

Yet echoes, like icons, fade with time. If they are to be retained, we must pay attention to them. By selectively attending to certain stimuli, we sort them out from the background noise. For example, in studies on the development of patterns of processing information, young children have been shown photographs of rooms full of toys and then been asked to recall as many of the toys as they can. One such study found that 2-year-old boys are more likely to attend to and remember toys such as cars, puzzles, and trains. Two-year-old girls are more likely to attend to and remember dolls, dishes, and teddy bears (Renninger & Wozniak, 1985).

FIGURE M.2
A RESEARCH STRATEGY FOR ASSESSING EIDETIC IMAGERY.
Children look at the first drawing for 20 to 30 seconds, after which it is removed. Next, the children look at a neutral background for several minutes. They are then shown the second drawing. When asked what they see, children with the capacity for eidetic imagery report a face. The face is seen only by children who retain the first image and fuse it with the second, thus perceiving the third image.

EIDETIC IMAGERY The maintenance of detailed visual memories over several minutes.

ECHO A mental representation of an auditory stimulus (sound) held briefly in sensory memory.

ECHOIC MEMORY The sensory register that briefly holds mental representations of auditory stimuli.

ECHOIC MEMORY.
The mental representations of auditory stimuli are called echoes, and the sensory register that holds echoes is referred to as echoic memory. By encoding visual information as echoes and rehearsing the echoes, we commit them to memory.

Even by this early age, the things that children attend to frequently fall into stereotypical patterns.

Short-Term Memory

If you focus on a stimulus in the sensory register, you tend to retain it in **short-term memory**—also referred to as **working memory**—for a minute or so after the trace of the stimulus decays (Baddeley, 1994). As one researcher describes it, "Working memory is the mental glue that links a thought through time from its beginning to its end" (Goldman-Rakic, 1995). When you are given a phone number by directory assistance and write it down or immediately dial the number, you are retaining the number in your short-term memory. When you are told the name of someone at a party and then use that name immediately in addressing that person, you are retaining the name in short-term memory. In short-term memory, the image tends to fade significantly after 10 to 12 seconds if it is not repeated or rehearsed. It is possible to focus on maintaining a visual image in the short-term memory, but it is more common to encode visual stimuli as sounds, or auditory stimuli. Then the sounds can be rehearsed, or repeated.

Most of us know that one way of retaining information in short-term memory—and possibly storing it permanently—is to rehearse it repeatedly. When directory assistance tells me a phone number, I usually rehearse it continuously while I am dialing it or running around frantically searching for a pencil and a scrap of paper. The more times we rehearse information, the more likely we are to remember it.

KEEPING THUNSTOFAM IN SHORT-TERM MEMORY Let us now return to the task of remembering the first list of letters in the challenges to memory at the beginning of the chapter. If you had encoded the letters as the three-syllable word THUN-STO-FAM, you would probably have recalled them by mentally rehearsing (saying to yourself) the three-syllable "word" and then spelling it out from the sounds. A few minutes later, if someone asked whether the letters had been uppercase (THUNSTOFAM) or lowercase (thunstofam), you might not have been able to answer with confidence. You used an acoustic code to help recall the list, and uppercase and lowercase letters sound alike.

Because it can be pronounced, THUNSTOFAM is not too difficult to retain in short-term memory. But what if the list of letters was TBXLFNTSDK? This list of letters cannot be pronounced as it is. You would have to find a complex acronym to code these letters, and do so within a fraction of a second—most likely an impossible task. To aid recall, you would probably choose to try to repeat the letters rapidly—to read each one as many times as possible before the memory trace fades. You might visualize each letter as you say it and try to get back to it (that is, to run through the entire list) before it decays.

Let us assume that you encoded the letters as sounds and then rehearsed the sounds. When asked to report the list, you might mistakenly say T-V-X-L-F-N-T-S-T-K. This would be an understandable error because the incorrect *V* and *T* sounds are similar, respectively, to the correct *B* and *D* sounds.

THE SERIAL-POSITION EFFECT Note that you would also be likely to recall the first and last letters in the series, *T* and *K*, more accurately than the others. Why? The tendency to recall the first and last items in a series more accurately is known as the **serial-position effect.** This effect may

SHORT-TERM MEMORY The type or stage of memory that can hold information for up to a minute or so after the trace of the stimulus decays. Also called *working memory.*

WORKING MEMORY Same as *short-term memory.*

SERIAL-POSITION EFFECT The tendency to recall more accurately the first and last items in a series.

occur because we pay more attention to the first and last stimuli in a series. They serve as the visual or auditory boundaries for the other stimuli. It may also be that the first items are likely to be rehearsed more frequently (repeated more times) than other items. The last items are likely to have been rehearsed most recently and hence are most likely to be retained in short-term memory.

According to cognitive psychologists, the tendency to recall the initial items in a list is referred to as the **primacy effect.** Social psychologists have also noted a powerful primacy effect in our formation of impressions of other people. In other words, first impressions tend to last. The tendency to recall the last items in a list is referred to as the **recency effect.** If we are asked to recall the last items in a list soon after we have been shown the list, they may still be in short-term memory. As a result, they can be "read off." Earlier items, in contrast, may have to be retrieved from long-term memory.

CHUNKING: IS SEVEN A MAGIC NUMBER OR DID THE PHONE COMPANY GET LUCKY? Rapidly rehearsing 10 meaningless letters is not an easy task. With TBXLFNTSDK there are 10 discrete elements, or **chunks,** of information that must be kept in short-term memory. When we encode THUNSTOFAM as three syllables, there are only three chunks to swallow at once—a memory task that is much easier on the digestion.

George Miller (1956) wryly noted that the average person is comfortable with digesting about seven integers at a time, the number of integers in a telephone number: "My problem is that I have been persecuted by an integer [the number *seven*]. For seven years this number has followed me around, has intruded in my most private data, and has assaulted me from the pages of our most public journals " (1956). It may sound as if Miller was being paranoid, but he was actually talking about research findings. They show that most people have little trouble recalling five chunks of information, as in a zip code. Some can remember nine, which is, for all but a few, an upper limit. So seven chunks, plus or minus one or two, is the "magic" number.

So how, you ask, do we manage to include area codes in our recollections of telephone numbers, hence making them 10 digits long? The truth of the matter is that we usually don't. We tend to recall the area code as a single chunk of information derived from our general knowledge of where a person lives. So we are more likely to remember (or "know") the 10-digit numbers of acquaintances who reside in locales with area codes that we use frequently.

Businesses pay the phone company hefty premiums so that they can attain numbers with two or three zeroes—for example, 592-2000 or 614-3300. These numbers include fewer chunks of information and hence are easier to remember. Customer recollection of business phone numbers increases sales. One financial services company uses the toll-free number CALL-IRA, which reduces the task to two chunks of information that also happen to be meaningfully related (semantically coded) to the nature of the business. Similarly, a clinic that helps people quit smoking arranged for a telephone number that can be reached by dialing the letters NO SMOKE.

Return to the third challenge to memory presented earlier. Were you able to remember the six groups of letters? Would your task have been simpler if you had grouped them differently? How about moving the dashes forward by a letter, so that they read GM-CBS-IBM-ATT-CIA-FBI? If we do this, we have the same list of letters, but we also have six chunks of information that can be coded semantically (according to what they

PRIMACY EFFECT The tendency to recall the initial items in a series of items.

RECENCY EFFECT The tendency to recall the last items in a series of items.

CHUNK A stimulus or group of stimuli perceived as a discrete piece of information.

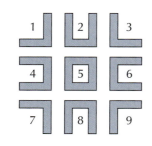

FIGURE M.3

A FAMILIAR GRID.

The nine drawings in the second challenge to memory form this familiar tic-tac-toe grid when the numbers are placed inside them and they are arranged in order. This method for recalling the shapes collapses nine chunks of information into two. One is the tic-tac-toe grid. The second is the rule for decoding the drawings from the grid.

ROTE Mechanical associative learning that is based on repetition.

mean). You may have also been able to generate the list by remembering a rule, such as "big corporations and government agencies."

If we can recall seven or perhaps nine chunks of information, how do children remember the alphabet? The alphabet contains 26 discrete pieces of information. How do children learn to encode the letters of the alphabet, which are visual symbols, as spoken sounds? There is nothing about the shape of an *A* that suggests its sound. Nor does the visual stimulus *B* sound "B-ish." One way is for children to simply learn to associate letters with their spoken names by **rote**. It is mechanical associative learning that takes time and repetition. Use of the alphabet song helps by allowing some chunking. That is, children can group letters and connect them with notes that rise and fall. In the alphabet song, children sing the group AB, then go up a note and sing CD, then go up again and sing EF, then come down a note, sing G, and pause. Later the group LMNO is sung rapidly with the same note. If you think that learning the alphabet by rote, or even with the aid of a little chunking, is a simple task, try learning the Russian alphabet.

If you had recognized THUNSTOFAM as an acronym for the first two letters of each word in the phrase "THe UNited STates OF AMerica," you would also have reduced the number of chunks of information that had to be recalled. You could have considered the phrase to be a single chunk of information. The rule that you must use the first two letters of each word of the phrase would be another chunk.

Reconsider the second challenge to memory presented earlier. You were asked to remember nine chunks of visual information. Perhaps you could have used the acoustic codes "L" and "Square" for chunks 3 and 5, but no obvious codes are available for the seven other chunks. Now look at Figure M.3. If you had recognized that the elements in the challenge could be arranged as the familiar tic-tac-toe grid, remembering the nine elements might have required two chunks of information. The first would have been the mental image of the grid and the second would have been the rule for decoding: Each element corresponds to the shape of a section of the grid if read like words on a page (from upper left to lower right). The number sequence 1 through 9 would not in itself present a problem, because you learned this series by rote many years ago and have rehearsed it in countless calculations since then.

INTERFERENCE IN SHORT-TERM MEMORY I mentioned that I often find myself running around looking for a pencil and a scrap of paper to write down a telephone number that has been given to me. If I keep on rehearsing the number while I'm looking, I'm okay. But I have also often cursed myself for failing to keep a pad and pencil by the telephone, and sometimes this has interfered with my recollection of the number. (The moral of the story? Avoid self-reproach.) It has also happened that I have actually looked up a phone number and been about to dial it when someone has asked me for the time or where I said we were going to dinner. Unless I say, "Hold on a minute!" and manage to jot down the number on something, it's back to the phone book. Attending to distracting information, even briefly, prevents me from rehearsing the number, so it falls through the cracks of my short-term memory.

In an experiment with college students, Lloyd and Margaret Peterson (1959) demonstrated how prevention of rehearsal can wreak havoc with short-term memory. They asked students to remember three-letter combinations such as HGB—normally, three easy chunks of information. They then had the students count backward from an arbitrary number, such as 181, by threes (that is, 181, 178, 175, 172, and so on). The students were told to stop counting and to report the letter sequence after the intervals of time shown in Figure M.4. The percentage of letter combinations that were recalled correctly fell precipitously within seconds. After 18 seconds of interference, counting had dislodged the letter sequences in almost all of these bright young students' memories.

Psychologists say that the appearance of new information in short-term memory **displaces** the old information. Remember: Only a few bits of information can be retained in short-term memory at the same time. Think of short-term memory as a shelf or workbench. Once it is full, some things fall off it when new items are shoved onto it. Here we have another possible explanation for the recency effect: The most recently learned bit of information is least likely to be displaced by additional information.

Displacement occurs at cocktail parties, and I'm not referring to jostling by the crowd. The point is this: When you meet Jennifer or Jonathan at the party, you should have little trouble remembering the name. But then you may meet Tamara or Timothy and, still later, Stephanie or Steven. By that time you may have a hard time dredging up Jennifer or Jonathan's name—unless, of course, you were very, very attracted to one of them. A passionate response would set a person apart and inspire a good deal of selective attention. According to signal-detection theory, if you were enamored enough, we may predict that you would "detect" the person's name (sensory signals) with a vengeance, and all the ensuing names would dissolve into background noise.

Long-Term Memory

Long-term memory is the third stage of information processing. Think of your long-term memory as a vast storehouse of information containing names, dates, places, what Johnny did to you in second grade, and what Susan said about you when you were 12.

Some psychologists (Freud was one) used to believe that nearly all of our perceptions and ideas are stored permanently. We might not be able to retrieve all of them because some memories might be "lost" because of lack of proper cues, or they might be kept unconscious by the forces of **repression.** Adherents to this view often pointed to the work of neurosurgeon Wilder Penfield (1969). When parts of their brains were electrically

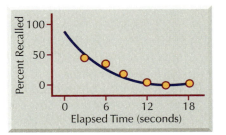

FIGURE M.4
THE EFFECT OF INTERFERENCE ON SHORT-TERM MEMORY.
In this experiment, college students were asked to remember a series of three letters while they counted backward by three's. After just 3 seconds, retention was cut by half. Ability to recall the words was almost completely lost by 15 seconds.

DISPLACE In memory theory, to cause information to be lost from short-term memory by adding new information.

LONG-TERM MEMORY The type or stage of memory capable of relatively permanent storage.

REPRESSION In Freud's psychodynamic theory, the ejection of anxiety-evoking ideas from conscious awareness.

DISPLACEMENT.
Information can be lost to short-term memory through displacement. We may have little trouble remembering the names of the first or second person we meet at a gathering. But as introductions continue, new names may displace the old ones and we may forget the names of people we met only a few minutes earlier.

stimulated, many of Penfield's patients reported the appearance of images that had something of the feel of memories.

Today most psychologists view this notion as exaggerated. Memory researcher Elizabeth Loftus, for example, notes that the "memories" stimulated by Penfield's probes lacked detail and were sometimes incorrect (Loftus & Loftus, 1980). Now let us consider some other questions about long-term memory.

HOW ACCURATE ARE LONG-TERM MEMORIES? Elizabeth Loftus notes that memories are distorted by our **schemas**—that is by the ways in which we conceptualize our worlds. Sometimes our schemas are simply our concepts or words for things. Sometimes our schemas reflect our biases and our needs.

Let me give you an example. "Retrieve" the fourth sheet of paper you prepared according to the instructions for the challenges to memory. The labels you wrote on the sheet will remind you of the figures. Take a minute or two to draw them now. Then continue reading.

Now that you have made your drawings, turn to Figure M.5. Are your drawings closer in form to those in group 1 or to those in group 2? I wouldn't be surprised if they were more like those in group 1—if, for example, your first drawing looked more like eyeglasses than a dumbbell. After all, they were labeled like the drawings in group 1. The labels serve as *schemas* for the drawings—ways of organizing your knowledge of them—and these schemas may have influenced your recollections.

Consider another example of the power of schemas in processing information. Loftus and Palmer (1973) showed people a film of a car crash and then asked them to fill out questionnaires that included a question about how fast the cars were going at the time. The language of the question varied in subtle ways, however. Some people were asked to estimate how fast the cars were going when they "hit" each other. Others were asked to estimate the cars' speed when they "smashed into" each other. On average, people who reconstructed the scene on the basis of the cue "hit" estimated a speed of 34 mph. People who watched the same film but reconstructed the scene on the basis of the cue "smashed" estimated a speed of 41 mph! In other words, the use of the word *hit* or *smashed*

SCHEMA A way of mentally representing the world, such as a belief or an expectation, that can influence perception of persons, objects, and situations.

FIGURE M.5
MEMORY AS RECONSTRUCTIVE.
In their classic experiment, Carmichael, Hogan, and Walter (1932) showed people the figures in the left-hand box and made remarks as suggested in the other boxes. For example, the experimenter might say, "This drawing looks like eyeglasses [or a dumbbell]." When people later reconstructed the drawings, they were influenced by the labels.

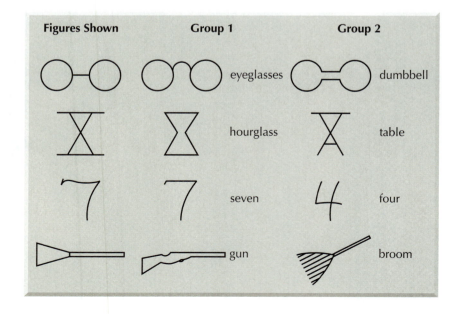

Figures Shown	Group 1	Group 2
	eyeglasses	dumbbell
	hourglass	table
	seven	four
	gun	broom

caused people to organize their knowledge about the crash in different ways. That is, the words served as diverse schemas that fostered the development of very different ways of processing information about the crash.

Subjects in the same study were questioned again a week later: "Did you see any broken glass?" Because there was no broken glass shown in the film, an answer of "yes" would be wrong. Of those who had earlier been encouraged to process information about the accident in terms of one car "hitting" the other, 14% incorrectly answered yes. But 32% of the subjects who had processed information about the crash in terms of one car "smashing into" the other reported, incorrectly, that they had seen broken glass. Findings such as these have implications for eyewitness testimony. The "Psychology in a World of Diversity" feature shows how a particular kind of schema—prejudice—can affect our memories of events.

LONG-TERM MEMORY AND EYEWITNESS TESTIMONY Jean Piaget, the investigator of children's cognitive development, distinctly remembered an attempt to kidnap him from his baby carriage as he was being wheeled along the Champs-Elysées. He recalled the excited throng, the abrasions on the face of the nurse who rescued him, the police officer's white baton, and the flight of the assailant. Although they were graphic, Piaget's memories were false. Years later, the nurse admitted that she had made up the tale.

Legal professionals are concerned about the accuracy of our memories as reflected in eyewitness testimony. Misidentifications of suspects "create a double horror: The wrong person is devastated by this personal tragedy, and the real criminal is still out on the streets" (Loftus, 1993b, p. 550). Is there reason to believe that the statements of eyewitnesses are any more factual than Piaget's?

There is cause for concern. The words chosen by an experimenter—and those chosen by a lawyer interrogating a witness—have been shown to influence the reconstruction of memories (Loftus & Palmer, 1973). For example, as in the experiment described earlier, an attorney for the plaintiff might ask the witness, "How fast was the defendant's car going when it *smashed into* the plaintiff's car?" In such a case, the car might be reported as going faster than if the question had been: "How fast was the defendant's car going when the accident occurred?" Could the attorney for the defendant claim that use of the word *smashed* biased the witness? What about jurors who heard the word *smashed?* Would they be biased toward assuming that the driver had been reckless?

Children tend to be more suggestible witnesses than adults, and preschoolers are more suggestible than older children (Ceci & Bruck, 1993). But when questioned properly, even young children may be able to provide accurate and useful testimony (Ceci & Bruck, 1993).

There are cases in which the memories of eyewitnesses have been "refreshed" by hypnosis. Sad to say, hypnosis does more than amplify memories; it can also distort them (Loftus, 1994). One problem is that witnesses may accept and embellish suggestions made by the hypnotist. Another is that hypnotized people may report fantasized occurrences as compellingly as if they were real (Loftus, 1994).

There are also problems in the identification of criminals by eyewitnesses. For one thing, witnesses may pay more attention to the suspect's clothing than to more meaningful characteristics such as facial features, height, and weight. In one experiment, viewers of a videotaped crime incorrectly identified a man as the criminal because he wore the eyeglasses and T-shirt that had been worn by the perpetrator on the tape. The man who had actually committed the crime was identified less often (Sanders, 1984).

HOW FAST WERE THESE CARS GOING WHEN THEY COLLIDED?
Our schemas influence our processing of information. When shown pictures such as these, people who were asked how fast the cars were going when they *smashed* into one another offer higher estimates than people who were told that the cars *hit* one another.

EYEWITNESS TESTIMONY?
How trustworthy is eyewitness testimony? Memories are reconstructive rather than photographic. The wording of questions also influences the content of the memory. Attorneys therefore are sometimes instructed not to phrase questions in such a way that they "lead" the witness.

Other problems with eyewitness testimony include the following:

- Identification of suspects is less accurate when suspects belong to ethnic or racial groups that differ from that of the witness (Egeth, 1993).
- Identification of suspects is confused when interrogators make misleading suggestions (Loftus, 1997).
- Witnesses are seen as more credible when they claim to be certain in their testimony, but there is little evidence that claims of certainty are accurate (Wells, 1993).

There are thus many problems with eyewitness testimony. Yet even Elizabeth Loftus (1993b), who has extensively studied the accuracy of eyewitness testimony, agrees that it is a valuable tool in the courtroom. After all, identifications made by eyewitnesses are frequently correct, and what, Loftus asks, would be the alternative to the use of eyewitnesses? If we were to prevent eyewitnesses from testifying, how many criminals would go free?

TRUTH OR FICTION REVISITED
It is true that there is no practical limit to the amount of information you can store in your memory. At least, no limit has been discovered.

HOW MUCH INFORMATION *CAN* BE STORED IN LONG-TERM MEMORY? How many gigabytes of storage are there in your most personal computer—your brain? Unlike a computer, the human ability to store information is practically unlimited (Goldman-Rakic, 1995). New information may replace older information in short-term memory, but no evidence indicates that long-term memories are lost by displacement. Long-term memories may endure for a lifetime. Now and then it may seem that we have forgotten, or "lost," a long-term memory such as the names of our elementary or high school classmates. Yet it may be that we cannot find the proper cues to help us retrieve them. If long-term memories are lost, they may be lost in the same way a misplaced object is lost. It is "lost," but we sense that it is still somewhere in the room. In other words, it is lost but not destroyed.

TRANSFERRING INFORMATION FROM SHORT-TERM TO LONG-TERM MEMORY How can you transfer information from short-term to long-term memory? By and large, the more often chunks of information are rehearsed, the more likely they are to be transferred to long-term memory. We have seen that repeating information over and over to prevent it from decaying or being displaced is termed *maintenance rehearsal*. But maintenance rehearsal does not give meaning to information by linking it to past learning. Thus it is not considered the best way to permanently store information (Craik & Watkins, 1973).

A more effective method is to make information more meaningful—to purposefully relate new information to things that are already well known (Woloshyn et al., 1994). For example, to better remember the components of levers, physics students might use seesaws, wheelbarrows, and oars as examples (Scruggs & Mastropieri, 1992). The nine chunks of information in our second challenge to memory were made easier to reconstruct once they were associated with the familiar tic-tac-toe grid in Figure M.3. We saw that relating new material to well-known material is known as *elaborative rehearsal*. For example, have you seen this word before?

FUNTHOSTAM

Say it aloud. Do you know it? If you had used an acoustic code alone to memorize THUNSTOFAM, the list of letters you first saw on page M-2, it might not have been easy to recognize FUNTHOSTAM as an incorrect spelling. Let us assume, however, that by now you have used

PSYCHOLOGY IN A WORLD OF *Diversity*

THE ROLE OF PREJUDICE IN THE RECONSTRUCTION OF MEMORIES

You might like to think that memories, especially clear memories, are fresh as the driven snow. Yet psychological research suggests that memories, even powerful memories, are often distorted by our *schemas.* And our schemas are sometimes prejudices.

To understand how schemas can distort memories, consider the problems of travelers who met up with Procrustes, the legendary hijacker of ancient Greece. Procrustes had a quirk. He was interested not only in travelers' pocketbooks but also in their height. He had a concept—a schema—of how tall people should be, and when people did not fit his schema, they were in trouble. You see, Procrustes also had a bed, the famous "Procrustean bed." He

made his victims lie down in the bed, and if they were too short for it, he stretched them to make them fit. If they were too long for the bed, he practiced surgery on their legs.

Although the myth of Procrustes may sound absurd, it reflects a quirky truth about people. People carry their cognitive Procrustean beds around with them—that is, their prejudiced schemas—and they try to make things and other people fit them. Prejudices are ways of processing social information. It is easier for people to remember instances of behavior that are consistent with their prejudices than it is to change their schemas (Devine, 1989; Fiske, 1993).

But prejudices also distort

memories. That is, people tend to reconstruct their experiences according to their prejudices, as found in an experiment reported by Elizabeth Loftus (1979). Subjects in the study were shown a picture which contained an African American man who was holding a hat and a White man who was holding a razor. Later, when they were asked what they had seen, many subjects erroneously recalled the razor as being in the hands of the African American. These subjects "chopped off the legs" of their memories; they recalled information that was consistent with their schemas. But it was wrong.

Are your own memories biased by such schemas? Are you sure? ■

---

elaborative rehearsal and encoded THUNSTOFAM semantically (according to its "meaning") as an acronym for "The United States of America." Then you would have been able to scan the spelling of the words in the phrase "The United States of America" to determine that FUNTHOSTAM is an incorrect spelling.

Rote repetition of a meaningless group of syllables, such as *thun-sto-fam,* relies on maintenance rehearsal for permanent storage. The process might be tedious (continued rehearsal) and unreliable. Elaborative rehearsal—tying THUNSTOFAM to the name of a country—might make storage almost instantaneous and retrieval foolproof.

LEVELS OF PROCESSING INFORMATION People who use elaborative rehearsal to remember things are processing information more deeply than people who use maintenance rehearsal. According to Fergus Craik and Robert Lockhart (1972), memories tend to endure when information is processed *deeply*—when it is attended to, encoded carefully, pondered, and related to things we already know. Craik and Lockhart believe that remembering relies on how deeply people process information, not on whether memories are transferred from one stage of memory to another.

Evidence for the importance of levels of processing information is found in an experiment with three groups of college students, all of whom were asked to study a picture of a living room for one minute (Bransford et al., 1977). The groups' examination of the picture entailed different

TRUTH OR FICTION REVISITED
It is not true that learning must be meaningful if we are to remember it. Nevertheless, elaborative rehearsal, which is based on the meanings of events or subject matter, is more efficient than maintenance rehearsal, which is based on rote repetition (Simpson et al., 1994).

approaches. Two groups were informed that small *x*'s were imbedded in the picture. The first of these groups was asked to find the *x*'s by scanning the picture horizontally and vertically. The second group was informed that the *x*'s could be found in the edges of the objects in the room and was asked to look for them there. The third group was asked, instead, to think about how it would use the objects pictured in the room. As a result of the divergent sets of instructions, the first two groups (the *x* hunters) processed information about the objects in the picture superficially. But the third group rehearsed the objects elaboratively—that is, members of this group thought about the objects in terms of their meanings and uses. It should not be surprising that the third group remembered many times more objects than the first two groups.

In another experiment, researchers asked subjects to indicate whether they recognized photos of faces they had been shown under one of three conditions: being asked to recall (1) the gender of the person in the photo, (2) the width of the person's nose, or (3) being asked to judge whether the person is honest (Sporer, 1991). Subjects asked to form judgments about the persons' honesty recognized more faces. It is likely that asking people to judge other people's honesty stimulates deeper processing of the features of the faces (Bloom & Mudd, 1991). That is, subjects study each face in detail, and they attempt to relate what they see to their ideas about human nature.

Language arts teachers encourage students to use new vocabulary words in sentences to process them more deeply. Each new usage is an instance of elaborative rehearsal. Usage helps build semantic codes that make it easier to retrieve the meanings of words in the future. When I was in high school, teachers of foreign languages told us that learning classical languages "exercises the mind" so that we would understand English better. Not exactly. The mind is not analogous to a muscle that responds to exercise. However, the meanings of many English words are based on foreign ones. A person who recognizes that *retrieve* stems from roots meaning "again" (*re-*) and "find" (*trouver* in French) is less likely to forget that *retrieval* means "finding again" or "bringing back."

Think, too, of all the algebra and geometry problems we were asked to solve in high school. Each problem is an application of a procedure and, perhaps, of certain formulas and theorems. By repeatedly applying the procedures, formulas, and theorems in different contexts, we rehearse them elaboratively. As a consequence, we are more likely to remember them. Knowledge of the ways in which a formula or an equation is used helps us remember the formula. Also, by building one geometry theorem on another, we relate new theorems to ones that we already understand. As a result, we process information about them more deeply and remember them better.

Before proceeding to the next section, cover the preceding paragraph with your hand. Which of the following words is spelled correctly: *retrieval* or *retreival?* The spellings sound alike, so an acoustic code for reconstructing the correct spelling would fail. Yet a semantic code, such as the spelling rule "*i* before *e* except after *c*," would allow you to reconstruct the correct spelling: retri*e*val.

FLASHBULB MEMORIES

You will always remember where you were at 8:18 Central Time on September 8, 1998.

THE ST. LOUIS SPORTSCASTER, UPON MARK MCGWIRE'S
SLAMMING HIS 62ND HOME RUN OF THE SEASON, SURPASSING
ROGER MARIS'S RECORD OF 61.

Do you remember the first time you were in love? Can you remember how the streets and the trees looked transformed? The vibrancy in your step? How generous you felt? How all of life's problems seemed suddenly solved?

We tend to remember events that occur under unusual, emotionally arousing circumstances more clearly. Many of us will never forget where we were or what we were doing when we learned that John F Kennedy, Jr.'s airplane was missing in 1999 or when Britain's Princess Diana died in an automobile accident in 1997. Many of us recall the *Challenger* disaster of 1986, or where we were when we heard that O. J. Simpson was acquitted of murder charges in 1995 (or found liable for wrongful deaths in 1997). We may also remember in detail what we were doing when we learned of a relative's death. These are examples of "flash-bulb memories," which preserve experiences in detail (Brown & Kulik, 1977; Thompson & Cowan, 1986).

Why is the memory etched when the "flashbulb" goes off? One factor is the distinctness of the memory. It is easier to discriminate stimuli that stand out. Such events are striking in themselves. The feelings caused by them are also special. It is thus relatively easy to pick them out from the storehouse of memories. Major events such as the assassination of a president or the loss of a close relative also tend to have important effects on our lives. We are likely to dwell on them and form networks of associations. That is, we are likely to rehearse them elaboratively. Our rehearsal may include great expectations, or deep fears, for the future.

ORGANIZATION IN LONG-TERM MEMORY   The storehouse of long-term memory is usually well organized. Items are not just piled on the floor or thrown into closets. We tend to gather information about rats and cats into a certain section of the storehouse, perhaps the animal or mammal section. We put information about oaks, maples, and eucalyptus into the tree section. Such categorization of stimuli is a basic cognitive function. It allows us to make predictions about specific instances and to store information efficiently (Corter & Gluck, 1992).

We tend to organize information according to a *hierarchical structure*, as shown in Figure M.6. A *hierarchy* is an arrangement of items (or chunks of information) into groups or classes according to common or distinct features. As we work our way up the hierarchy shown in Figure M.6, we find more encompassing, or *superordinate*, classes to which the items below them belong. For example, all mammals are animals, but there are many types of animals other than mammals.[1]

When items are correctly organized in long-term memory, you are more likely to recall—or know—accurate information about them (Hassel-horn, 1992; Schneider & Bjorklund, 1992). For instance, do you remember whether whales breathe underwater? If you did not know that whales are mammals (or, in Figure M.6, *subordinate* to mammals), or if you knew nothing about mammals, a correct answer might depend on some remote instance of rote learning. That is, you might be depending on chancy episodic memory rather than on reliable semantic memory. For example, you might recall some details from a public television documentary on whales. If you *did* know that whales are mammals, however, you would also know—or remember—that whales do not breathe underwater. How? You would reconstruct information about whales from knowledge about mammals, the group to which whales are subordinate. Similarly, you

FLASHBULB MEMORIES.
Where were you and what were you doing in 1997 when you learned that Britain's Princess Diana had died in an automobile accident? Major events can illuminate everything about them so that we recall everything that was happening at the time.

---

[1] A note to biological purists: Figure M.6 is not intended to represent phyla, classes, orders, and so on, accurately. Rather, it shows how an individual's classification scheme might be organized.

FIGURE M.6
THE HIERARCHICAL STRUCTURE OF LONG-TERM MEMORY.

Where are whales filed in the hierarchical cabinets of your memory? Your classification of whales may influence your answers to these questions: Do whales breathe underwater? Are they warm-blooded? Do they nurse their young?

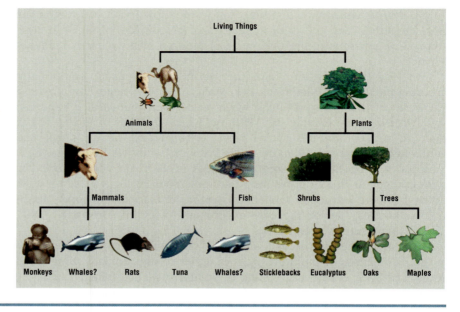

would know, or remember, that because they are mammals, whales are warm-blooded, nurse their young, and are a good deal more intelligent than, say, tunas and sharks, which are fish. Had you incorrectly classified whales as fish, you might have searched your memory and constructed the incorrect answer that they do breathe underwater.

THE TIP-OF-THE-TONGUE PHENOMENON Have you ever been so close to retrieving information that it seemed to be on "the tip of your tongue," yet you still could not quite remember it? This is a frustrating experience, similar to reeling in a fish but having it drop off the line just before it breaks the surface of the water. Psychologists term this experience the **tip-of-the-tongue (TOT) phenomenon**, or the **feeling-of-knowing experience**.

In one classic TOT experiment, Brown and McNeill (1966) defined some rather unusual words for students, such as *sampan*, a small riverboat used in China and Japan. The students were then asked to recall the words they had learned. Some of the students often had the right word "on the tip of their tongue" but reported words with similar meanings such as *junk, barge,* or *houseboat.* Still other students reported words that sounded similar, such as *Saipan, Siam, sarong,* and *sanching.* Why?

To begin with, the words were unfamiliar, so elaborative rehearsal did not take place. The students, that is, did not have an opportunity to relate the words to other things they knew. Brown and McNeill also suggested that our storage systems are indexed according to cues that include both the sounds and the meanings of words—that is, according to both acoustic and semantic codes. By scanning words similar in sound and meaning to the word on the tip of the tongue, we sometimes find a useful cue and retrieve the word for which we are searching.

The feeling-of-knowing experience also seems to reflect incomplete or imperfect learning. In such cases, our answers may be "in the ballpark" if not on the mark. In some feeling-of-knowing experiments, people are often asked trivia questions. When they do not recall an answer, they are then asked to guess how likely it is that they will recognize the right answer if it is among a group of possibilities. People turn out to be very accurate in their estimations about whether or not they will recognize the

TIP-OF-THE-TONGUE (TOT) PHENOMENON The feeling that information is stored in memory although it cannot be readily retrieved. Also called the *feeling-of-knowing experience.*

FEELING-OF-KNOWING EXPERIENCE Same as *tip-of-the-tongue phenomenon.*

answer. Similarly, Brown and McNeill found that the students in their TOT experiment proved to be very good at estimating the number of syllables in words they could not recall. The students often correctly guessed the initial sounds of the words. They sometimes recognized words that rhymed with them.

Are the three kinds of memory on the tip of your tongue now? Can you use the acronym *ESP* to recall them?

Sometimes an answer seems to be on the tip of our tongue because our knowledge of the topic is incomplete. We may not know the exact answer, but we know something. (As a matter of fact, if we have good writing skills, we may present our incomplete knowledge so forcefully that we earn a good grade on an essay question on the topic!) At such times, the problem lies not in retrieval but in the original encoding and storage.

CONTEXT-DEPENDENT MEMORY: "DÉJÀ VU ALL OVER AGAIN"?

It's déjà vu *all over again.*

YOGI BERRA

The context in which we acquire information can also play a role in retrieval. I remember walking down the halls of the apartment building where I had lived as a child. I was suddenly assaulted by images of playing under the staircase, of falling against a radiator, of the shrill voice of a former neighbor calling for her child at dinnertime. Have you ever walked the halls of an old school building and been assaulted by memories of faces and names that you would have guessed had been lost forever? Have you ever walked through your old neighborhood and recalled the faces of people or the aromas of cooking that were so real you actually salivated?

These are examples of **context-dependent memory.** Being in the proper context can dramatically enhance recall (Estes, 1972). One fascinating experiment in context-dependent memory included a number of people who were "all wet." Members of a university swimming club were asked to learn lists of words either while they were submerged or while they were literally high and dry (Godden & Baddeley, 1975). Students who learned the list underwater showed superior recall of the list when immersed. Similarly, those who had rehearsed the list ashore showed better retrieval on terra firma.

Other studies have found that students do better on tests when they study in the room where the test is to be given (Smith et al., 1978). When police are interviewing witnesses to crimes, they ask the witnesses to paint the scene verbally as vividly as possible, or they visit the scene of the crime with the witnesses. People who mentally place themselves back in the context in which they encoded and stored information frequently retrieve it more accurately.

One of the more eerie psychological experiences is **déjà vu** (French for "already seen"). Sometimes we meet someone new or find ourselves in a strange place, yet we have the feeling that we know this person or have been there before. The **déjà vu** experience seems to occur when we are in a context similar to one we have been in before—or when we meet someone who has a way of talking or moving similar to that of someone we know or once knew. Familiarity with the context leads us to think "I've been here before." Some people might even wonder if they had experienced the situation in a former life, or if their experience is something supernatural. Although your feelings and ideas are flooding in because of the similarity of the context, the sense that you have been there before, or done this thing before, can be so strong that you just stand back and wonder.

CONTEXT-DEPENDENT MEMORY Information that is better retrieved in the context in which it was encoded and stored, or learned.

DÉJÀ VU A French phrase meaning "already seen," and referring to the experience of having been in a new situation before, apparently because contextual cues trigger the retrieval of images and feelings from the past.

STATE-DEPENDENT MEMORY **State-dependent memory** is an extension of context-dependent memory. It sometimes happens that we retrieve information better when we are in a physiological or emotional state similar to the one in which we encoded and stored the information. Feeling the rush of love may trigger images of other times when we fell in love. The grip of anger may prompt memories of incidents of frustration and rage.

Gordon Bower (1981) ran experiments in which happy or sad moods were induced by hypnotic suggestion. The subjects then learned lists of words. People who learned a list while in a happy mood showed better recall when a happy state was induced again. But people who had learned the list while in a sad mood showed superior recall when they were saddened again.

Psychologists suggest that in day-to-day life a happy mood influences us to focus on positive events (Eich, 1995; Matt et al., 1992). As a result, we have better recall of these events in the future. A sad mood, unfortunately, leads us to focus on and recall the negative. Happiness may feed on happiness, but under extreme circumstances sadness can develop into a vicious cycle.

Table M.1 summarizes the "three threes of memory." It includes the three kinds of memory (episodic, semantic, and procedural), the three processes of memory (encoding, storage, and retrieval), and the three stages of memory (sensory memory, short-term memory, and long-term memory). Now that we have explored the nature of remembering, let us consider its opposite—forgetting.

STATE-DEPENDENT MEMORY Information that is better retrieved in the physiological or emotional state in which it was encoded and stored, or learned.

TABLE M.1

THREE "THREES" OF MEMORY

CONCEPT	WHAT IT MEANS	EXAMPLE
THREE KINDS OF MEMORY		
Episodic Memory	Memories of events experienced or personally witnessed by a person	Remembering what you ate for dinner last night
Semantic Memory	General knowledge (as opposed to remembering personal episodes)	Remembering the capital cities of the 50 states
Procedural Memory	Knowledge of ways of doing things; also termed skill memory	Remembering how to ride a bicycle, click a mouse, or write with a pencil
THREE PROCESSES OF MEMORY		
Encoding	Modifying information so that it can be placed in memory, sometimes from one sensory modality (e.g., vision) to another (hearing)	Mental representation of the words in this table as a sequence of sounds (an acoustic code)
Storage	Maintenance of information over time	Mental repetition (maintenance rehearsal) of the information in this chart in order to keep it in memory
Retrieval	Finding of stored information and bringing it into conscious awareness	Recall of the information in this chart; using a mnemonic device (e.g., Roy G. Biv) to recall the colors of the visible spectrum
THREE STAGES OF MEMORY		
Sensory Memory	Type or stage of memory that is first encountered by a stimulus and briefly holds impressions of it	Continuing briefly to "see" a visual stimulus after it has been removed
Short-Term Memory	Type or stage of memory that can hold information for up to a minute or so after the trace of the stimulus decays; also termed working memory	Repeating someone's name in order to remember it, or relating something new to things that are already known
Long-Term Memory teachers	Type or stage of memory that is capable of relatively permanent storage	The "file cabinets" of memory, where you store items like the names of your primary school and your memories of holidays when you were little

FORGETTING

What do DAL, RIK, BOF, and ZEX have in common? They are all **nonsense syllables.** Nonsense syllables are meaningless sets of two consonants with a vowel sandwiched in between. They were first used by Hermann Ebbinghaus to study memory and forgetting. Because nonsense syllables are intended to be meaningless, remembering them should depend on simple acoustic coding and maintenance rehearsal rather than on elaborative rehearsal, semantic coding, or other ways of making learning meaningful. Let us see how nonsense syllables are used in the measurement of forgetting.

Memory Tasks Used in Measuring Forgetting

Three basic memory tasks have been used by psychologists to measure forgetting: recognition, recall, and relearning. Nonsense syllables have been used in studying each of them. The study of these memory tasks has led to several conclusions about the nature of forgetting. Let us consider them task by task.

RECOGNITION One aspect of forgetting is failure to recognize something we have experienced. There are many ways of measuring **recognition.** In many studies, psychologists ask subjects to read a list of nonsense syllables. The subjects then read a second list of nonsense syllables and indicate whether they recognize any of the syllables as having appeared on the first list. Forgetting is defined as failure to recognize a syllable that has been read before.

In another kind of recognition study, Harry Bahrick and his colleagues (1975) studied high school graduates who had been out of school for various lengths of time. They interspersed photos of the graduates' classmates with four times as many photos of strangers. Recent graduates correctly recognized former classmates 90% of the time. Those who had been out of school for 40 years recognized former classmates 75% of the time. A chance level of recognition would have been only 20% (1 photo in 5 was of an actual classmate). Thus even older people showed rather solid long-term recognition ability.

Recognition is the easiest type of memory task. This is why multiple-choice tests are easier than fill-in-the-blank or essay tests. We can recognize correct answers more easily than we can recall them unaided.

RECALL In his own studies of **recall,** another kind of memory task, Ebbinghaus would read lists of nonsense syllables aloud to the beat of a metronome and then see how many he could produce from memory. After reading through a list once, he usually would be able to recall seven syllables—the typical limit for short-term memory.

Psychologists also often use lists of pairs of nonsense syllables, called **paired associates,** to measure recall. A list of paired associates is shown in Figure M.7. Subjects read through the lists pair by pair. Later they are shown the first member of each pair and asked to recall the second. Recall is more difficult than recognition. In a recognition task, one simply indicates whether an item has been seen before or which of a number of items is paired with a stimulus (as in a multiple-choice test). In a recall task, the person must retrieve a syllable, with another syllable serving as a cue.

Retrieval is made easier if the two syllables can be meaningfully linked—that is, encoded semantically—even if the "meaning" is stretched

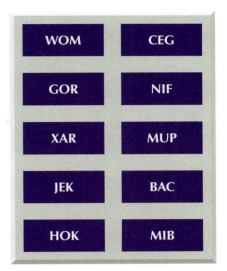

FIGURE M.7
PAIRED ASSOCIATES.

Psychologists often use paired associates to measure recall. Retrieving CEG in response to the cue WOM is made easier by an image of a WOMan smoking a "CEG-arette."

NONSENSE SYLLABLES Meaningless sets of two consonants, with a vowel sandwiched in between, that are used to study memory.

RECOGNITION In information processing, the easiest memory task, involving identification of objects or events encountered before.

RECALL Retrieval or reconstruction of learned material.

PAIRED ASSOCIATES Nonsense syllables presented in pairs in experiments that measure recall.

FIGURE M.8

EBBINGHAUS'S CLASSIC CURVE OF FORGETTING.

Recollection of lists of words drops precipitously during the first hour after learning. Losses of learning then becomes more gradual. Retention drops by half within the first hour. However, it takes a month (31 days) for retention to be cut in half again.

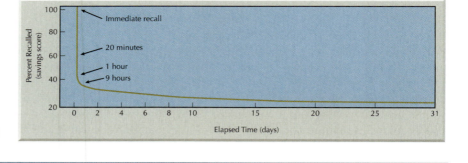
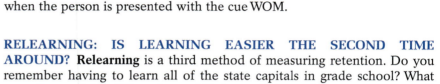

a bit. Consider the first pair of nonsense syllables in Figure M.7. The image of a WOMan smoking a CEG-arette may make CEG easier to retrieve when the person is presented with the cue WOM.

RELEARNING: IS LEARNING EASIER THE SECOND TIME AROUND? Relearning is a third method of measuring retention. Do you remember having to learn all of the state capitals in grade school? What were the capitals of Wyoming and Delaware? Even when we cannot recall or recognize material that had once been learned, such as Cheyenne for Wyoming and Dover for Delaware, we can relearn it more rapidly the second time. Similarly, as we go through our 30s and 40s we may forget a good deal of our high school French or geometry. Yet the second time around we could learn much more rapidly what previously took months or years.

To study the efficiency of relearning, Ebbinghaus (1885/1913) devised the **method of savings.** First he recorded the number of repetitions required to learn a list of nonsense syllables or words. Then he recorded the number of repetitions required to relearn the list after a certain amount of time had elapsed. Next he computed the difference in the number of repetitions to determine the **savings.** If a list had to be repeated 20 times again after a year had passed, there was no savings. Relearning, that is, was as tedious as the initial learning. However, if the list could be learned with only 10 repetitions after a year had elapsed, half the number of repetitions required for learning had been saved.

Figure M.8 shows Ebbinghaus's classic curve of forgetting. As you can see, there was no loss of memory as measured by savings immediately after a list had been learned. However, recollection dropped quite a bit, by half, during the first hour after learning a list. Losses of learning then became more gradual. It took a month (31 days) for retention to be cut in half again. In other words, forgetting occurred most rapidly right after material was learned. We continue to forget material as time elapses, but at a relatively slower rate.

Before leaving this section, I have one short question for you: What are the capitals of Wyoming and Delaware?

Interference Theory

When we do not attend to, encode, and rehearse sensory input, we may forget it through decay of the trace of the image. Material in short-term memory, like material in sensory memory, can be lost through decay. It can also be lost through displacement, as may happen when we try to remember several new names at a party.

RELEARNING A measure of retention. Material is usually relearned more quickly than it is learned initially.

METHOD OF SAVINGS A measure of retention in which the difference between the number of repetitions originally required to learn a list and the number of repetitions required to relearn the list after a certain amount of time has elapsed is calculated.

SAVINGS The difference between the number of repetitions originally required to learn a list and the number of repetitions required to relearn the list after a certain amount of time has elapsed.

According to **interference theory,** we also forget material in short-term and long-term memory because newly learned material interferes with it. The two basic types of interference are retroactive interference (also called *retroactive inhibition*) and proactive interference (also called *proactive inhibition*).

RETROACTIVE INTERFERENCE

In **retroactive interference,** new learning interferes with the retrieval of old learning. For example, a medical student may memorize the names of the bones in the leg through rote repetition. Later he or she may find that learning the names of the bones in the arm makes it more difficult to retrieve the names of the leg bones, especially if the names are similar in sound or in relative location on each limb.

PROACTIVE INTERFERENCE

In **proactive interference,** older learning interferes with the capacity to retrieve more recently learned material. High school Spanish may pop in when you are trying to retrieve college French or Italian words. All three are Romance languages, with similar roots and spellings. Previously learned Japanese words probably would not interfere with your ability to retrieve more recently learned French or Italian because the roots and sounds of Japanese differ considerably from those of the Romance languages.

Consider motor skills. You may learn to drive a standard shift on a car with three forward speeds and a clutch that must be let up slowly after shifting. Later you may learn to drive a car with five forward speeds and a clutch that must be released rapidly. For a while, you may make errors on the five-speed car because of proactive interference. (Old learning interferes with new learning.) If you return to the three-speed car after driving the five-speed car has become natural, you may stall it a few times. This is because of retroactive interference (new learning interfering with the old).

Repression

According to Sigmund Freud, we are motivated to forget painful memories and unacceptable ideas because they produce anxiety, guilt, and shame. (In terms of operant conditioning, anxiety, guilt, and shame serve as negative reinforcers. We learn to behave in ways that lead to the removal of these reinforcers—in this case, we learn *not* to think about certain events and ideas.) Psychoanalysts believe that repression is at the heart of disorders such as **dissociative amnesia.**

REPRESSION OF MEMORIES OF CHILDHOOD SEXUAL ABUSE

The popular media have recently been filled with stories of people in therapy who have recovered repressed memories of childhood sexual abuse (Pope, 1996). Symptoms such as the following have been presented as evidence of the presence of such memories: poor grades in school, difficulty concentrating, fear of new experiences, problems recollecting parts of childhood, low self-esteem, depression, sexual dysfunctions, and indecision (Hergenhahn, 1997; Loftus & Ketcham, 1994).

Loftus (1993a) does not deny that childhood sexual abuse is a serious problem, but she argues that most such recovered repressed memories are false. Consider that many people enter therapy without such memories but leave therapy with them. Because of the way in which these memories

INTERFERENCE.
In retroactive interference, new learning interferes with the retrieval of old learning. In proactive interference, older learning interferes with the capacity to retrieve material learned more recently. For example, high school French vocabulary may "pop in" when you are trying to retrieve words you have learned for a Spanish test in college.

INTERFERENCE THEORY The view that we may forget stored material because other learning interferes with it.

RETROACTIVE INTERFERENCE The interference of new learning with the ability to retrieve material learned previously.

PROACTIVE INTERFERENCE The interference by old learning with the ability to retrieve material learned recently.

DISSOCIATIVE AMNESIA Amnesia thought to stem from psychological conflict or trauma.

are "acquired," Loftus suspects that some therapists may suggest the presence of such memories to clients (Hergenhahn, 1997). Once more: Loftus is *not* arguing that memories of childhood sexual abuse are false or unimportant. She *is* suggesting that "repressed" memories of abuse that were "recovered" in therapy are suspect.

Infantile Amnesia

When he interviewed people about their early experiences, Freud discovered that they could not recall episodes that had happened prior to the age of 3 and that their recall was cloudy through the age of 5. This phenomenon is referred to as **infantile amnesia.**

Infantile amnesia has nothing to do with the fact that the episodes occurred in the distant past. Middle-aged and older people have vivid memories from the ages of 6 and 10, yet the events happened many decades ago. But 18-year-olds show steep declines in memory when they try to recall episodes that occurred earlier than the age of 6, even though they happened less than 18 years earlier (Wetzler & Sweeney, 1986).

Freud believed that young children have aggressive impulses and perverse lusts toward their parents. He attributed infantile amnesia to repression of these impulses (Bauer, 1996). However, the episodes lost to infantile amnesia are not weighted in the direction of such "primitive" impulses.

Infantile amnesia probably reflects the interaction of physiological and cognitive factors. For example, a structure of the limbic system (the **hippocampus**) that is involved in the storage of memories does not become mature until we are about 2 years old (Squire, 1993, 1996). Also, myelination of brain pathways is incomplete for the first few years, contributing to the inefficiency of information processing and memory formation. There are also cognitive reasons for infantile amnesia:

1. Infants are not particularly interested in remembering the past (Goleman, 1993).
2. Infants, in contrast to older children, tend not to weave episodes together into meaningful stories of their own lives. (Freud also recognized the second possibility [Bauer, 1996]). Information about specific episodes thus tends to be lost.
3. Infants do not make reliable use of language to symbolize or classify events. Their ability to *encode* sensory input—that is, to apply the auditory and semantic codes that facilitate memory formation—is therefore limited.

Anterograde and Retrograde Amnesia

In **anterograde amnesia,** there are memory lapses for the period following a trauma such as a blow to the head, an electric shock, or an operation. In some cases the trauma seems to interfere with all the processes of memory. The ability to pay attention, the encoding of sensory input, and rehearsal are all impaired. A number of investigators have linked certain kinds of brain damage—such as damage to the hippocampus—to amnesia (Squire, 1993).

Consider the classic case of a man with the initials H. M. Parts of the brain are sometimes lesioned to help people with epilepsy. In H. M.'s case, a section of the hippocampus was removed (Milner, 1966). Right after the operation, the man's mental functioning appeared to be normal. As time went on, however, it became quite clear that he had severe problems in processing information. For example, two years after the operation, H. M.

INFANTILE AMNESIA Inability to recall events that occur prior to the age of 2 or 3. Also termed *childhood amnesia.*

HIPPOCAMPUS A structure in the limbic system that plays an important role in the formation of new memories.

ANTEROGRADE AMNESIA Failure to remember events that occur after physical trauma because of the effects of the trauma.

believed he was 27—his age at the time of the operation. When his family moved to a new address, H. M. could not find his new home or remember the new address. He responded with appropriate grief to the death of his uncle, yet he then began to ask about his uncle and why he did not visit. Each time he was informed of his uncle's passing, he grieved as he had when he first heard of it. All in all, it seems that H. M.'s operation prevented him from transferring information from short-term to long-term memory.

In **retrograde amnesia,** the source of trauma prevents people from remembering events that took place before the accident. A football player who is knocked unconscious or a person in an auto accident may be unable to recall events that occurred for several minutes prior to the trauma. The football player may not recall taking the field. The person in the accident may not recall entering the car. It also sometimes happens that the individual cannot remember events that occurred for several years prior to the traumatic incident.

In one well-known case of retrograde amnesia, a man received a head injury in a motorcycle accident (Baddeley, 1982). When he regained consciousness, he had lost memory for all events that had occurred after the age of 11. In fact, he appeared to believe that he was still 11 years old. During the next few months he gradually recovered more knowledge of his past. He moved toward the present year by year, up until the critical motorcycle ride. But he never did recover the events just prior to the accident. The accident had apparently prevented the information that was rapidly unfolding before him from being transferred to long-term memory. In terms of stages of memory, it may be that our perceptions and ideas need to consolidate, or rest undisturbed for a while, if they are to be transferred to long-term memory.

THE BIOLOGY OF MEMORY: FROM ENGRAMS TO ADRENALINE

Psychologists assume that mental processes such as the encoding, storage, and retrieval of information—that is, memory—are accompanied by changes in the brain. Early in the century, many psychologists used the concept of the **engram** in their study of memory. Engrams were viewed as electrical circuits in the brain that corresponded to memory traces—neurological processes that paralleled experiences. Yet biological psychologists such as Karl Lashley (1950) spent many fruitless years searching for such circuits or for the structures of the brain in which they might be housed. Much contemporary research on the biology of memory focuses on the roles of neurons, neurotransmitters, and hormones.

Changes at the Neural Level

Rats who are reared in richly stimulating environments develop more dendrites and synapses in the cerebral cortex than rats reared in relatively impoverished environments (Neisser, 1997). It also has been shown that the level of visual stimulation rats receive is associated with the number of synapses they develop in the visual cortex (Turner & Greenough, 1985). In sum, there is reason to believe that the storage of experience requires the number of avenues of communication among brain cells to be increased.

Changes occur in the visual cortex as a result of visual experience. Changes occur in the auditory cortex as a result of heard experiences.

RETROGRADE AMNESIA Failure to remember events that occur prior to physical trauma because of the effects of the trauma.

ENGRAM (1) An assumed electrical circuit in the brain that corresponds to a memory trace. (2) An assumed chemical change in the brain that accompanies learning.

Information received through the other senses is likely to lead to corresponding changes in the cortical regions that represent them. Experiences perceived by several senses are also stored in numerous areas of the brain (Hilts, 1995). The recollection of experiences, as in the production of visual images, apparently involves neural activity in the appropriate regions of the brain (Kosslyn, 1994).

Research with sea snails has offered insight into the events that take place at existing synapses when learning occurs. One kind of snail, for example, has only about 20,000 neurons compared with humans' *billions*. As a result, researchers have actually been able to study how experience is reflected at the synapses of specific neurons. When sea snails are conditioned, more of the neurotransmitter serotonin is released at certain synapses. As a consequence, transmission at these synapses becomes more efficient as trials (learning) progress (Kandel & Hawkins, 1992). Transmission occurs at synapses because of naturally occurring chemical substances, such as the following:

- Serotonin. This neurotransmitter increases the efficiency of conditioning (Kandel & Hawkins, 1992).

- Acetylcholine (ACh). This neurotransmitter is vital in memory formation; low levels of ACh are connected with Alzheimer's disease.

- Adrenaline. This hormone strengthens memory when it is released into the bloodstream following learning (LeDoux, 1997).

- Vasopressin. When people sniff synthetic vasopressin (antidiuretic hormone) in the form of a nasal spray, they show significant improvement in memory. Today, excess vasopressin can have serious side effects, but future versions may target specific receptors without causing these effects.

Other research has focused on the potential of substances as diverse as estrogen and nicotine to aid in the formation of memories and to delay the progression of Alzheimer's disease. As with vasopressin, future versions may target specific receptors without causing side effects.

Changes at the Structural Level

Consider the problems that beset H. M. after his operation. Certain parts of the brain such as the hippocampus also appear to be involved in the formation of new memories—or the transfer of information from short-term to long-term memory. The hippocampus does not comprise the "storage bins" for memories themselves because H. M.'s memories prior to the operation were not destroyed. Rather, it is involved in relaying incoming sensory information to parts of the cortex. Therefore, it appears to be vital to the storage of new information even if old information can be retrieved without it (Squire, 1996).

Where are the storage bins? The brain stores parts of memories in the appropriate areas of the sensory cortex (Goleman, 1994). Sights are stored in the visual cortex, sounds in the auditory cortex, and so on (Hilts, 1995). The limbic system is largely responsible for integrating these pieces of information when we recall an event.

A specific part of the limbic system, the hippocampus, is much involved in the where and when of things. The hippocampus does not become mature until we are about 2 years old, and immaturity of the hippocampus may be connected with infantile amnesia. Adults with hippocampal damage may be able to form new procedural memories, even though they cannot form new episodic ("where and when") memories.

For example, they can acquire the skill of reading words backward even though they cannot recall individual practice sessions (Squire, 1996).

The thalamus is involved in verbal memories. Part of the thalamus of an Air Force cadet known as N. A. was damaged in a freak fencing accident. After the episode, N. A. could no longer form verbal memories, such as the names of things. However, his ability to form visual memories was not impaired (Squire, 1996).

The encoding, storage, and retrieval of information thus involve biological activity on several levels. As we learn, new synapses are developed, and changes occur at existing synapses. Various parts and structures of the brain are also involved in the formation of different kinds of memories.

SUMMARY

1. **What are the three kinds of memory?** These are episodic memory (memory for specific events that one has experienced), semantic memory (general knowledge), and procedural memory (skills).

2. **What are the three memory processes?** These are encoding, storage, and retrieval. We commonly use visual, auditory, and semantic codes in the process of encoding.

3. **What are the three stages of memory proposed by the Atkinson-Shiffrin model?** These are sensory, short-term, and long-term memory.

4. **What are sensory registers?** These hold stimuli in sensory memory. Psychologists believe that information perceived through each sense has its own register.

5. **What is the importance of Sperling's research?** Sperling demonstrated that visual stimuli are maintained in sensory memory for only a fraction of a second and that we can see more objects than we can report afterward.

6. **What are icons and echoes?** Icons are mental representations of visual stimuli; echoes are representations of auditory stimuli (sounds).

7. **What is the capacity of short-term memory?** We can hold seven chunks of information (plus or minus two) in short-term, or working, memory.

8. **How do psychologists explain the serial-position effect?** We tend to remember the initial items in a list because they are rehearsed most often (the primacy effect). We tend to remember the final items in a list because they are least likely to have been displaced by new information (the recency effect).

9. **How accurate are long-term memories?** Long-term memories are frequently biased because they are reconstructed according to our schemas—that is, our ways of mentally organizing our experiences.

10. **How is information transferred from short-term to long-term memory?** There are two paths: maintenance rehearsal (rote repetition) and elaborative rehearsal (relating information to things that are already known).

11. **How is knowledge organized in long-term memory?** Knowledge tends to be organized according to a hierarchical structure with superordinate and subordinate concepts. We know things about members

of a class when we have information about the class itself.

12. **What are context-and state-dependent memories?** Context dependence refers to the finding that we often retrieve information more efficiently when we are in the same context we were in when we acquired it. State dependence refers to the finding that we often retrieve information better when we are in the same state of consciousness or mood we were in when we learned it.

13. **What is the levels-of-processing model?** This model views memory in terms of a single dimension—not three stages. It is hypothesized that we encode, store, and retrieve information more efficiently when we have processed it more deeply.

14. **What are nonsense syllables?** These are meaningless syllables first used by Ebbinghaus as a way of measuring the functions of memory.

15. **How do psychologists measure retention?** Retention is often tested through three types of memory tasks: recognition, recall, and relearning.

16. **What is interference theory?** According to interference theory,

people forget because learning can interfere with retrieval of previously learned material. In retroactive interference, new learning interferes with old learning. In proactive interference, old learning interferes with new learning.

17. **What is repression?** This term refers to Freud's concept of motivated forgetting. Freud suggested that we are motivated to forget threatening or unacceptable material.

18. **What is infantile amnesia?** This term refers to the inability to remember events from the first couple of years of life.

19. **What are anterograde and retrograde amnesia?** In anterograde amnesia, a traumatic event such as damage to the hippocampus prevents the formation of new memories. In retrograde amnesia, shock or other trauma prevents previously known information from being retrieved.

20. **What biological processes are associated with the processes of memory?** These processes include neurotransmitters and hormones, which are connected with the development of synapses and changes at existing synapses.

KEY TERMS

acoustic code (p. M-5)

anterograde amnesia (p. M-26)

chunk (p. M-11)

context-dependent memory (p. M-21)

déjà vu (p. M-21)

displace (p. M-13)

dissociative amnesia (p. M-25)

echo (p. M-9)

echoic memory (p. M-9)

eidetic imagery (p. M-9)

elaborative rehearsal (p. M-5)

encoding (p. M-5)

engram (p. M-27)

episodic memory (p. M-3)

feeling-of-knowing experience (p. M-20)

hippocampus (p. M-26)

icon (p. M-8)

iconic memory (p. M-8)

infantile amnesia (p. M-26)

interference theory (p. M-25)

long-term memory (p. M-13)

maintenance rehearsal (p. M-5)

memory (p. M-6)

memory trace (p. M-7)

metamemory (p. M-5)

method of savings (p. M-24)

mnemonic devices (p. M-4)

nonsense syllables (p. M-23)

paired associates (p. M-23)

primacy effect (p. M-11)

proactive interference (p. M-25)

procedural memory (p. M-4)

recall (p. M-23)

recency effect (p. M-11)

recognition (p. M-23)

relearning (p. M-24)

repression (p. M-13)

retrieval (p. M-6)

retroactive interference (p. M-25)

retrograde amnesia (p. M-27)

rote (p. M-12)

saccadic eye movement (p. M-7)

savings (p. M-24)

schema (p. M-14)

semantic code (p. M-5)

semantic memory (p. M-4)

sensory memory (p. M-7)

sensory register (p. M-8)

serial-position effect (p. M-10)

short-term memory (p. M-10)

state-dependent memory (p. M-22)

storage (p. M-5)

tip-of-the-tongue (TOT) phenomenon (p. M-20)

visual code (p. M-5)

working memory (p. M-10)

REFERENCES

Atkinson, R. C., & Shiffrin, R. M. (1968). Human memory: A proposed system and its control processes. In K. Spence (Ed.), *The psychology of learning and motivation* (Vol. 2). New York: Academic Press.

Baddeley, A. (1982). *Your memory: A user's guide*. New York: Macmillan.

Baddeley, A. (1994). Working memory. In D. L. Schacter & E. Tulving (Eds.), *Memory systems 1994*. Cambridge, MA: The MIT Press, a Bradford Book.

Bahrick, H. P., Bahrick, P. O., & Wittlinger, R. P. (1975). Fifty years of memory for names and faces. *Journal of Experimental Psychology: General, 104*, 54–75.

Bauer, P. J. (1996). What do infants recall of their lives? Memory for specific events by one-to two-year-olds. *American Psychologist, 51,* 29–41.

Bloom, L., & Mudd, S. A. (1991). Depth of processing approach to face recognition: A test of two theories. *Journal of Experimental Psychology: Learning, Memory, and Cognition, 17,* 556–565.

Bower, G. H. (1981). Mood and memory. *American Psychologist, 36,* 129–148.

Bransford, J. D., Nitsch, K. E., & Franks, J. J. (1977). Schooling and the facilitation of knowing. In R. C. Anderson, R. J. Spiro, & W. E. Montague (Eds.), *Schooling and the acquisition of knowledge.* Hillsdale, NJ: Erlbaum.

Brown, R., & Kulik, J. (1977). Flashbulb memories. *Cognition, 5,* 73–99.

Brown, R., & McNeill, D. (1966). The tip-of-the-tongue phenomenon. *Journal of Verbal Learning and Verbal Behavior, 5,* 325–337.

Ceci, S. J., & Bruck, M. (1993). Suggestibility of the child witness. *Psychological Bulletin, 113,* 403–439.

Corter, J. E., & Gluck, M. A. (1992). Explaining basic categories: Feature predictability and information. *Psychological Bulletin, 111,* 291–303.

Craik, F. I. M., & Lockhart, R. S. (1972). Levels of processing. *Journal of Verbal Learning and Verbal Behavior, 11,* 671–684.

Craik, F. I. M., & Watkins, M. J. (1973). The role of rehearsal in short-term memory. *Journal of Verbal Learning and Verbal Behavior, 12,* 599–607.

Devine, P. G. (1989). Stereotypes and prejudice. *Journal of Personality and Social Psychology, 56,* 5–18.

Ebbinghaus, H. (1913). *Memory: A contribution to experimental psychology.* (H. A. Roger & C. E. Bussenius, Trans.). New York: Columbia University Press. (Original work published 1885)

Egeth, H. E. (1993). What do we *not* know about eyewitness identification? *American Psychologist, 48,* 577–580.

Eich, E. (1995). Searching for mood dependent memory. *Psychological Science, 6,* 67–75.

Estes, W. K. (1972). An associative basis for coding and organization in memory. In A. W. Melton & E. Martin (Eds.), *Coding processes in human memory.* Washington, DC: Winston.

Fiske, S. T. (1993). Controlling other people: The impact of power on stereotyping. *American Psychologist, 48,* 621–628.

Godden, D. R., & Baddeley, A. D. (1975). Context-dependent memory in two natural environments: On land and underwater. *British Journal of Psychology, 66,* 325–331.

Goldman-Rakic, P. S. (1995). Cited in Goleman, D. (1995, May 2). Biologists find site of working memory. *New York Times,* pp. C1, C9.

Goleman, D. J. (1993, April 6). Studying the secrets of childhood memory. *New York Times,* pp. C1, C11.

Goleman, D. (1994, May 31). Miscoding is seen as the root of false memories. *New York Times,* pp. C1, C8.

Haber, R. N. (1980). Eidetic images are not just imaginary. *Psychology Today, 14*(11), 72–82.

Hasselhorn, M. (1992). Task dependency and the role of typicality and metamemory in the development of an organizational strategy. *Child Development, 63,* 202–214.

Hergenhahn, B. R. (1997). *An introduction to the history of psychology* (3rd ed.). Pacific Grove, CA: Brooks/Cole.

Hilts, P. J. (1995, May 30). Brain's memory system comes into focus. *New York Times,* pp. C1, C3.

James, W. (1890). *The principles of psychology.* New York: Henry Holt.

Kandel, E. R., & Hawkins, R. D. (1992). The biological basis of learning and individuality. *Scientific American, 267*(3), 78–86.

Kosslyn, S. M. (1994). *Image and brain.* Cambridge, MA: The MIT Press, a Bradford Book.

Lashley, K. S. (1950). In search of the engram. In *Symposium of the Society for Experimental Biology* (Vol. 4). New York: Cambridge University Press.

LeDoux, J. E. (1997). Emotion, memory, and the brain. *Scientific American Mysteries of the Mind* [Special issue], 7(1), 68–75.

Loftus, E. F. (1979). *Eyewitness testimony.* Cambridge, MA: Harvard University Press.

Loftus, E. F. (1993a). The reality of repressed memories. *American Psychologist, 48,* 518–537.

Loftus, E. F. (1993b). Psychologists in the eyewitness world. *American Psychologist, 48,* 550–552.

Loftus, E. F. (1994). Conference on memory, Harvard Medical School. Cited in D. Goleman (1994, May 31). Miscoding is seen as the root of false memories. *New York Times,* pp. C1, C8.

Loftus, E. F. (1997). Cited in Loftus, Consulting in Oklahoma City bombing trial. *APA Monitor, 28*(4), 8–9.

Loftus, E. F., & Ketcham, K. (1994). *The myth of repressed memory.* New York: St. Martin's Press.

Loftus, E. F., & Loftus, G. R. (1980). On the permanence of stored information in the brain. *American Psychologist, 35*, 409–420.

Loftus, E. F., & Palmer, J. C. (1973). Reconstruction of automobile destruction. *Journal of Verbal Learning and Verbal Behavior, 13*, 585–589.

Loftus, G. R. (1983). The continuing persistence of the icon. *Behavioral and Brain Sciences, 6*, 28.

Matt, G. E., Vasquez, C., & Campbell, W. K. (1992). Mood-congruent recall of affectively toned stimuli: A meta-analytic review. *Clinical Psychology Review, 12*, 227–255.

McDougall, W. (1904). The sensations excited by a single momentary stimulation of the eye. *British Journal of Psychology, 1*, 78–113.

Miller, G. A. (1956). The magical number seven, plus or minus two: Some limits on our capacity for processing information. *Psychological Review, 63*, 81–97.

Milner, B. R. (1966). Amnesia following operation on temporal lobes. In C. W. M. Whitty & O. L. Zangwill (Eds.), *Amnesia.* London: Butterworth.

Neisser, U. (1997). Cited in Sleek, S. (1997). Can "emotional intelligence" be taught in today's schools? *APA Monitor, 28*(6), 25.

Penfield, W. (1969). Consciousness, memory, and man's conditioned reflexes. In K. H. Pribram (Ed.), *On the biology of learning.* New York: Harcourt Brace Jovanovich.

Peterson, L. R., & Peterson, M. J. (1959). Short-term retention of individual verbal items. *Journal of Experimental Psychology, 58*, 193–198.

Pope, K. S. (1996). Memory, abuse, and science: Questioning claims about the false memory syndrome epidemic. *American Psychologist, 51*, 957–974.

Renninger, K. A., & Wozniak, R. H. (1985). Effect of interest on attentional shift, recognition, and recall in young children. *Developmental Psychology, 21*, 624–632.

Sanders, G. S. (1984). Effects of context cues on eyewitness identification responses. *Journal of Applied Social Psychology, 14*, 386–397.

Schneider, W., & Bjorklund, D. (1992). Expertise, aptitude, and strategic remembering. *Child Development, 63*, 461–473.

Scruggs, T. E., & Mastropieri, M. A. (1992). Remembering the forgotten art of memory. *American Educator, 16*(4), 31–37.

Simpson, M. L., Olejnik, S., Tam, A. Y., & Supattathum, S. (1994). Elaborative verbal rehearsals and college students' cognitive performance. *Journal of Educational Psychology, 86*, 267–278.

Smith, S. M., Glenberg, A. M., & Bjork, R. A. (1978). Environmental context and human memory. *Memory and Cognition, 6*, 342–355.

Sperling, G. (1960). The information available in brief visual presentations. *Psychological Monographs, 74*, 1–29.

Sporer, S. L. (1991). Deep—deeper—deepest? Encoding strategies and the recognition of human faces. *Journal of Experimental Psychology: Learning, Memory, and Cognition, 17*, 323–333.

Squire, L. R. (1993). Memory and the hippocampus. *Psychological Review, 99*, 195–231.

Squire, L. R. (1996, August). Memory systems of the brain. Master lecture presented to the meeting of the American Psychological Association, Toronto.

Thompson, C. P., & Cowan, T. (1986). The neurobiology of learning and memory. *Science, 233*, 941–947.

Tulving, E. (1985). How many memory systems are there? *American Psychologist, 40*, 385–398.

Tulving, E. (1991). Memory research is not a zero-sum game. *American Psychologist, 46*, 41–42.

Turner, A. M., & Greenough, W. T. (1985). Differential rearing effects on rat visual cortex synapses: I. Synaptic and neuronal density and synapses per neuron. *Brain Research, 329*, 195–203.

Wells, G. L. (1993). What do we know about eyewitness identification? *American Psychologist, 48*, 553–571.

Wetzler, S. E., & Sweeney, J. A. (1986). Childhood amnesia. In D. C. Rubin (Ed.), *Autobiographical memory.* New York: Cambridge University Press.

Wheeler, M. A., Stuss, D. T., & Tulving, E. (1997). Toward a theory of episodic memory: The frontal lobes and autonoetic consciousness. *Psychological Bulletin, 121*, 331–354.

Woloshyn, V. E., Paivio, A., & Pressley, M. (1994). Use of elaborative interrogation to help students acquire information consistent with prior knowledge and information inconsistent with prior knowledge. *Journal of Educational Psychology, 86*, 79–89.

T

THINKING AND INTELLIGENCE

_____ Using a "tried and true" formula is the most efficient way to solve a problem.

_____ Only humans can solve problems by means of insight.

_____ The best way to solve a frustrating problem is to keep plugging away at it.

_____ People with great academic ability are also creative.

_____ If a couple has five sons, the sixth child is likely to be a daughter.

_____ People change their opinions when they are shown to be wrong.

_____ "Street smarts" are a kind of intelligence.

_____ The terms _intelligence_ and _IQ_ mean the same thing.

_____ Two children can answer exactly the same items on an intelligence test correctly, yet one child can be above average and the other below average in IQ.

_____ Early users of IQ tests administered them in English to immigrants who did not understand the language.

_____ Head Start programs have raised children's IQs.

A T THE AGE OF 9, MY DAUGHTER JORDAN STUMPED ME WITH A problem about a bus driver that she had heard in school. Because I firmly believe in exposing students to the kinds of torture I have undergone, see what you can do with her problem:

> You're driving a bus that's leaving from Pennsylvania. To start off with, there were 32 people on the bus. At the next bus stop, 11 people got off and 9 people got on. At the next bus stop, 2 people got off and 2 people got on. At the next bus stop, 12 people got on and 16 people got off. At the next bus stop, 5 people got on and 3 people got off. What color are the bus driver's eyes?

I was not about to be fooled when I was listening to this problem. Although it seemed clear that I should be keeping track of how many people were on the bus, I had an inkling that a trick was involved. Therefore, I first instructed myself to remember that the bus was leaving from Pennsylvania. Being clever, I also kept track of the number of stops rather than the number of people getting on and off the bus. When I was finally hit with the question about the bus driver's eyes, I was at a loss. I protested that Jordan had said nothing about the bus driver's eyes, but she insisted that she had given me enough information to answer the question.

One of the requirements of problem solving is paying attention to relevant information (de Jong & Das-Smaal, 1995). To do that, you need some familiarity with the type of problem you are dealing with. I immediately classified the bus driver problem as a trick question and paid attention to information that apparently was superfluous. But I wasn't good enough.

The Greek philosopher Aristotle pointed out that people differ from lower organisms in their capacity for rational thinking. Thinking enables us to build skyscrapers, create computers, and scan the interior of the body without surgery. Some people even manage to keep track of their children and balance their checkbooks. **Thinking** may be defined as the mental activity involved in understanding, processing, and communicating information. Thinking entails attending to information, representing it mentally, reasoning about it, and making judgments and decisions about it. The term *thinking* generally refers to conscious, planned attempts to make sense of our world.

In this chapter we explore thinking and the related topic of intelligence. We begin with concepts, which provide the building blocks of thought. But before we proceed, I have one question for you: What color were the bus driver's eyes?

CONCEPTS AND PROTOTYPES: BUILDING BLOCKS OF THOUGHT

I began the chapter with a problem posed by my daughter Jordan. Let me proceed with a riddle from my own childhood: "What's black and white and read all over?" Because this riddle was spoken, not written, and involved the colors black and white, you would probably assume that "read" was spelled "red." Thus, in seeking an answer, you might scan your memory for an object that was red although it also somehow managed to be black and white. The answer to the riddle, "newspaper, " was usually met with a groan.

The word *newspaper* is a **concept.** *Red, black,* and *white* are also concepts—color concepts. Concepts are mental categories used to group together objects, relations, events, abstractions, or qualities that have common properties. Concepts are crucial to thinking. Concepts can represent objects, events, and activities—and visions of things that never were. Much thinking has to do with categorizing new concepts and manipulating relationships among concepts.

We tend to organize concepts in *hierarchies.* The newspaper category includes objects such as your school paper and the *Los Angeles Times.* Newspapers, college textbooks, novels, and merchandise catalogs can be combined into higher-order categories such as *printed matter* or *printed devices that store information.* If you add CD-ROMs and floppy disks, you can create a still higher category, *objects that store information.* Now consider a question that requires categorical thinking: How are a newspaper and a CD-ROM alike? Answers to such questions entail supplying the category that includes both objects. In this case, we can say that both objects store information. That is, their functions are similar, even if their technology differs.

Prototypes are examples that best match the essential features of categories. In less technical terms, prototypes are good examples. When new stimuli closely match people's prototypes of concepts, they are readily recognized as examples (Sloman, 1996). Which animal seems more birdlike to you, a robin or an ostrich? Why? Which of the following better fits the prototype of a fish, a sea horse or a shark? Both self-love and maternal love may be forms of love, but more people readily agree that maternal love is a kind of love. Apparently maternal love better fits their prototype of love (Fehr & Russell, 1991).

Many simple prototypes, such as *dog* and *red,* are taught by means of **exemplars.** We point to a dog and say "dog" or "This is a dog" to a child. Dogs represent *positive instances* of the dog concept. *Negative instances*—that is, things that are not dogs—are then shown to the child while we say, "This is *not* a dog." Negative instances of one concept may be positive instances of another. So in teaching a child we may be more likely to say, "This is not a dog—it's a cat" than simply, "This is not a dog."

Children may at first include horses and other four-legged animals within the dog schema or concept until the differences between dogs and horses are pointed out. (To them, the initial category could be more appropriately labeled "fuzzy-wuzzies.") In language development, such overinclusion of instances in a category (reference to horses as dogs) is labeled *overextension.* Children's prototypes become refined after children are shown positive and negative instances and given explanations.

A GOAT OR A DOG?
Yes, yes, you know the answer, but little children may at first include goats, horses, and other four-legged animals within the dog concept until they understand the differences among the animals.

THINKING Mental activity involved in understanding, manipulating, and communicating about information. Thinking entails paying attention to information, mentally representing it, reasoning about it, and making decisions about it.

CONCEPT A mental category used to class together objects, relations, events, abstractions, or qualities that have common properties.

PROTOTYPE A concept of a category of objects or events that serves as a good example of the category.

EXEMPLAR A specific example.

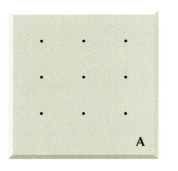

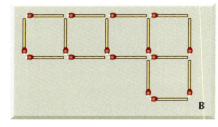

FIGURE T.I

Two Problems.

Draw straight lines through all the points in part A, using only four lines. Do not lift your pencil or retrace your steps. Move three matches in part B to make four squares equal in size. Use all the matches.

TABLE T.I

WATER JAR PROBLEMS

THREE JARS ARE PRESENT WITH THE LISTED CAPACITY (IN OUNCES)

PROBLEM	JAR A	JAR B	JAR C	GOAL
1	21	127	3	100
2	14	163	25	99
3	18	43	10	5
4	9	42	6	21
5	20	59	4	31
6	23	49	3	20
7	10	36	7	3

For each problem, how can you use some combination of the three jars given, and a tap, to obtain precisely the amount of water shown?

Source: Adapted from *Rigidity of Behavior* (p. 109), by Abraham S. Luchins and Edith H. Luchins, 1959, Eugene: University of Oregon Press.

Abstract concepts such as *bachelor* or *square root* tend to be formed through verbal explanations that involve more basic concepts.

PROBLEM SOLVING

Now I would like to share something personal with you. One of the pleasures I derived from my own introductory psychology course lay in showing friends the textbook and getting them involved in the problems in the section on problem solving. First, of course, I struggled with them myself. Now it's your turn. Get some scrap paper, take a breath, and have a go at them. The answers are discussed in the following pages, but don't peek. *Try* the problems first.

1. Provide the next two letters in the series for each of the following:
   a. ABABABAB??
   b. ABDEBCEF??
   c. OTTFFFSSE??

2. Draw straight lines through all the points in part A of Figure T.1, using only *four* lines. Do not lift your pencil from the paper or retrace your steps. (See Figure T.4 for answer.)

3. Move three matches in part B of Figure T.1 to make four squares of the same size. You must use *all* the matches. (See Figure T.4 for answer.)

4. You have three jars—A, B, and C—which hold the amounts of water, in ounces, shown in Table T.1. For each of the seven problems in Table T.1, use the jars in any way you wish in order to arrive at the indicated amount of water. Fill or empty any jar as often as you wish. How do you obtain the desired amount of water in each problem? (The solutions are discussed on p. T-6.)

Approaches to Problem Solving: Getting From Here to There

What steps did you use to try to solve parts a and b of problem 1? Did you first make sure you understood the problem by rereading the instructions? Or did you dive right in as soon as you saw them on the page? Perhaps the solutions to 1a and 1b came easily, but I'm sure you studied 1c very carefully.

After you believed you understood what was required in each problem, you probably tried to discover the structure of the cycles in each series. Series 1a has repeated cycles of two letters: *AB, AB,* and so on. Series 1b may be seen as having four cycles of two consecutive letters: *AB, DE, BC,* and so on.

Again, did you solve 1a and 1b in a flash of insight, or did you try to find rules that govern each series? In series 1a, the rule is simply to repeat the cycle. Series 1b is more complicated, and different sets of rules can be used to describe it. One correct set of rules is that odd-numbered cycles (*1 and 3,* or *AB* and *BC*) simply repeat the last letter of the previous cycle (in this case *B*) and then advance by one letter in the alphabet. The same rule applies to even-numbered cycles (*2 and 4,* or *DE* and *EF*).

If you found rules for problems 1a and 1b, you used them to produce the next letters in the series: *AB* in series 1a and *CD* in series 1b. Perhaps you then evaluated the effectiveness of your rules by checking your answers against the solutions in the preceding paragraphs.

UNDERSTANDING THE PROBLEM Let us begin our discussion of understanding problems by considering a bus driver problem very similar to the one Jordan gave me. This one, however, appeared in the psychological literature:

> Suppose you are a bus driver. On the first stop, you pick up 6 men and 2 women. At the second stop, 2 men leave and 1 woman boards the bus. At the third stop, 1 man leaves and 2 women enter the bus. At the fourth stop, 3 men get on and 3 women get off. At the fifth stop, 2 men get off, 3 men get on, 1 woman gets off and 2 women get on. What is the bus driver's name? (Halpern, 1989, p. 392)

Both versions of the bus driver problem demonstrate that a key to understanding a problem is focusing on the right information. If we assume it is crucial to keep track of the numbers of people getting on and off the bus, we focus on information that turns out to be unessential. In fact, it distracts us from the important information.

When we are faced with a novel problem, how can we know which information is relevant and which is not? Background knowledge helps. If you are given a chemistry problem, it helps if you have taken courses in chemistry. If Jordan gives you a problem, it is helpful to expect the unexpected. (In case you still haven't gotten it, the critical information you need to solve both bus driver problems is provided in the first sentence.)

Successful understanding of a problem generally requires three features:

1. *The parts or elements of our mental representation of the problem relate to one another in a meaningful way.* If we are trying to solve a problem in geometry, our mental triangles should have angles that total 180 degrees, not 360 degrees.

2. *The elements of our mental representation of the problem correspond to the elements of the problem in the outer world.* If we are neutralizing an acid in order to produce water and a salt, our mental representation of water should be H_2O, not OH. The elements of our mental representations must include the key elements for solving the problem, such as the information in the first sentence of the bus driver problem. We prepare ourselves to solve a problem by familiarizing ourselves with its elements and defining our goals.

3. *We have a storehouse of background knowledge that we can apply to the problem.* We have taken the necessary courses to solve problems in algebra and chemistry. When given a geometry problem involving a triangle, for example, we may think, "Is this problem similar to problems I've solved by using the quadratic equation?"

ALGORITHMS An **algorithm** is a specific procedure for solving a type of problem. An algorithm invariably leads to the solution—if it is used properly, that is. Mathematical formulas like the Pythagorean theorem are examples of algorithms. They yield correct answers to problems *as long as the right formula is used.* Finding the right formula to solve a problem may require scanning one's memory for all formulas that contain variables that represent one or more of the elements in the problem. The Pythagorean theorem, for example, concerns triangles with right angles. Therefore, it is appropriate to consider using this formula for problems concerning right angles, but not for others.

Consider anagram problems, in which we try to reorganize groups of letters into words. Some anagram problems require us to use every letter from the pool of letters; others allow us to use only some of the letters. How many words can you make from the pool of letters *DWARG?*

ALGORITHM A systematic procedure for solving a problem that works invariably when it is correctly applied.

If you were to use the **systematic random search** algorithm, you would list every possible letter combination, using from one to all five letters. You could use a dictionary or a spell-checking program to see whether each result is, in fact, a word. Such a method might be time consuming, but it would work.

HEURISTICS **Heuristics** are rules of thumb that help us simplify and solve problems. In contrast to algorithms, heuristics do not guarantee a correct solution to a problem. They are shortcuts. When they work, they allow for more rapid solutions. A heuristic device for solving the anagram problem would be to look for familiar letter combinations found in words and then check the remaining letters for words that include these combinations. In *DWARG*, for example, we can find the familiar combinations *dr* and *gr*. We may then quickly find *draw, drag,* and *grad*. The drawback to this method, however, is that we might miss some words.

One type of heuristic device is the **means-end analysis.** In using this heuristic device, we assess the difference between our current situation and our goals and then do what we can to reduce this discrepancy. Let's say that you are out in your car and have gotten lost. One heuristic device based on analysis of what you need to do to get to where you want to go might be to ask for directions. This approach requires no "sense of direction." An algorithm might be more complicated and require some geographical knowledge. Let us say that you know your destination is west of your current location and on the other side of the railroad tracks. You might therefore drive toward the setting sun (west) and, at the same time, watch for railroad tracks. If the road comes to an end and you must turn left or right, you can scan in both directions for tracks. If you don't see any, turn right or left, but at the next major intersection turn toward the setting sun. Eventually you may get there. If not, you can always ask for directions.

ANALOGIES An *analogy* is a partial similarity among things that are different in other ways. During the Cold War, some people in the United States believed in the so-called domino theory. Seeing the nations of Southeast Asia as analogous to dominoes, they argued that if one nation were allowed to fall to communism, its neighbor would be likely to follow. In the late 1980s, a sort of reverse domino effect actually occurred as communism collapsed in the nations of Eastern Europe. When communism collapsed in one nation, it became more likely to collapse in neighboring nations as well.

The analogy heuristic applies the solution of an earlier problem to the solution of a new one. We use the analogy heuristic whenever we try to solve a new problem by referring to a previous problem (Halpern et al., 1990). Consider the water jar problems in Table T.1. Problem 2 is analogous to problem 1. Therefore, the approach to solving problem 1 works with problem 2. (Later we consider what happens when the analogy heuristic fails.)

Let us see whether you can use the analogy heuristic to your advantage in the following number series problem: To solve problems 1a, 1b, and 1c on page T-4, you had to figure out the rules that govern the order of the letters. Scan the following series of numbers and find the rule that governs their order:

8, 5, 4, 9, 1, 7, 6, 3, 2, 0

Hint: The problem is somewhat analogous to problem 1c.[1]

---

[1] The analogous element is that there is a correspondence between these numbers and the first letter in the English word that spells them out.

Factors That Affect Problem Solving

The way you approach a problem is central to how effective you are at solving it. Other factors also influence your effectiveness at problem solving. Three of them—your level of expertise, whether you fall prey to a mental set, and whether you develop insight into the problem—reside within you. A couple of characteristics of problems also affect your ability to solve them effectively: the extent to which the elements of the problem are fixed in function, and the way the problem is defined.

EXPERTISE To appreciate the role of expertise in problem solving, unscramble the following anagrams, taken from Novick and Coté (1992). In each case use all of the letters to form an actual English word:

DNSUO
RCWDO
IASYD

How long did it take you to unscramble each anagram? Would a person whose native language is English—that is, an "expert"—unscramble each anagram more efficiently than a bilingual person who spoke another language in the home? Why or why not?

Experts solve problems more efficiently and rapidly than novices do. Generally speaking, people who are experts at solving a certain kind of problem share the following characteristics:

- They know the particular area well,
- have a good memory for the elements in the problems,
- form mental images or representations that facilitate problem solving (Clement, 1991),
- relate the problem to similar problems, and
- have efficient methods for problem solving (Hershey et al., 1990).

These factors are interrelated. Art historians, for example, acquire a database that permits them to understand the intricacies of paintings. As a result, their memory for paintings—and who painted them—expands vastly.

Novick and Coté (1992) found that among so-called experts, the solutions to the three anagram problems seemed to "pop out" in under 2 seconds. The experts apparently used more efficient methods than the novices. Experts seemed to use *parallel processing*. That is, they dealt simultaneously with two or more elements of the problems. In the case of DNSUO, for example, they may have played with the order of the vowels (*UO* or *OU*) at the same time that they tested which consonant (D, N, or S) was likely to precede them, arriving quickly at *sou* and *sound*. Novices were more likely to engage in *serial processing*—that is, to handle one element of the problem at a time.

MENTAL SETS Jordan hit me with another question: "A farmer had 17 sheep. All but 9 died. How many sheep did he have left?" Being a victim of a mental set, I assumed that this was a subtraction problem and gave the answer 8. She gleefully informed me that she hadn't said "9 died." She had said "*all but* 9 died." Therefore, the correct answer was 9. (Get it?) Put it another way: I had not *understood* the problem. My mental representation of the problem did not correspond to the actual elements of the problem.

Return to problem 1, part c (page T-4). To try to solve this problem, did you seek a pattern of letters that involved cycles and the alphabet? If so, it may be because this approach worked in solving parts a and b.

JORDAN.
The author's daughter Jordan posed this problem: "A farmer had 17 sheep. All but 9 died. How many sheep were left?" What is the answer?

FIGURE T.2

BISMARCK USES A COGNITIVE MAP TO CLAIM HIS JUST DESSERTS.

Bismarck has learned to reach dinner by climbing ladder A. But now the food goal (F) is blocked by a wire mesh barrier B. Bismarck washes his face for a while, but then, in an apparent flash of insight, he runs back down ladder A and up new ladder N to reach the goal.

TRUTH OR FICTION REVISITED

It is not true that only humans can solve problems by means of insight. Classic research evidence shows that lower animals, even rats, are also capable of insight (a sudden reorganization of the perceptual field).

TRUTH OR FICTION REVISITED

It is not true that the best way to solve a frustrating problem is to keep plugging away at it. It may be better to distance oneself from the problem for a while and allow it to "incubate." Eventually you may solve the problem in what seems to be a flash of insight.

MENTAL SET The tendency to respond to a new problem with an approach that was used successfully with similar problems.

INSIGHT In Gestalt psychology, a sudden perception of relationships among elements of the "perceptual field," permitting the solution of a problem.

INCUBATION In problem solving, a hypothetical process that sometimes occurs when we stand back from a frustrating problem for a while and the solution "suddenly" appears.

The tendency to respond to a new problem with the same approach that helped solve similar problems is termed a **mental set.** Mental sets usually make our work easier, but they can mislead us when the similarity between problems is illusory, as in part c of problem 1. Here is a clue: Part c is not an alphabet series. Each of the letters in the series *stands for* something. If you can discover what they stand for (that is, if you can discover the rule), you will be able to generate the 9th and 10th letters. (See Figure T.4 for the answer.)

INSIGHT: AHA! To gain insight into the role of **insight** in problem solving, consider the following problem posed by Janet Metcalfe (1986):

A stranger approached a museum curator and offered him an ancient bronze coin. The coin had an authentic appearance and was marked with the date 544 B.C. The curator had happily made acquisitions from suspicious sources before, but this time he promptly called the police and had the stranger arrested. Why? (p. 624)

I'm not going to give you the answer to this problem. Instead, I'll give you a guarantee. When you arrive at the solution, it will hit you all at once. You'll think "Aha!" or "Of course!" (or something less polite). It will seem as though the pieces of information in the problem have suddenly been reorganized so that the solution leaps out at you—in a flash.

Bismarck, one of University of Michigan psychologist N. R. F. Maier's rats, provided evidence of insight in laboratory rats (Maier & Schneirla, 1935). Bismarck had been trained to climb a ladder to a tabletop where food was placed. On one occasion Maier used a mesh barrier to prevent the rat from reaching his goal. But, as shown in Figure T.2, a second ladder was provided and was clearly visible to the animal. At first Bismarck sniffed and scratched and made every effort to find a path through the mesh barrier. Then he spent some time washing his face, an activity that apparently signals frustration in rats. Suddenly he jumped into the air, turned, ran down the familiar ladder and around to the new ladder, ran up the new ladder, and claimed his just desserts. It seems that Bismarck suddenly perceived the relationships between the elements of his problem so that the solution occurred by insight. He seems to have had what Gestalt psychologists have termed an "Aha! experience."

INCUBATION Let us return to the problems at the beginning of the section. How did you do with problem 1, part c, and problems 2 and 3? Students tend to fiddle around with them for a while. The solutions, when they come, appear to arrive in a flash. Students set the stage for the flash of insight by studying the elements in the problems carefully, repeating the rules to themselves, and trying to imagine what a solution might look like. If you tried out solutions that did not meet the goals, you may have become frustrated and thought, "The heck with it! I'll come back to it later." Standing back from the problem may allow for the **incubation** of insight. An incubator warms chicken eggs for a while so that they will hatch. Incubation in problem solving refers to standing back from the problem for a while as some mysterious process within us continues to work on it. Later, the answer may occur to us in a flash of insight. When standing back from the problem is helpful, it may be because it distances us from unprofitable but persistent mental sets (Azar, 1995).

Have another look at the role of incubation in helping us overcome mental sets. Consider the seventh water jar problem in Table T.1. What if we had tried several solutions involving the three water jars and none had worked? We could distance ourselves from the problem for a day or two. At some point we might recall a 10, a 7, and a 3—three elements of the problem—and suddenly realize that we can arrive at the correct answer by using only two water jars!

FUNCTIONAL FIXEDNESS **Functional fixedness** may also hinder problem solving. For example, first ask yourself what a pair of pliers is. Is it a tool for grasping, a paperweight, or a weapon? A pair of pliers could function as any of these, but your tendency to think of it as a grasping tool is fostered by your experience with it. You have probably used pliers only for grasping things. Functional fixedness is the tendency to think of an object in terms of its name or its familiar function. It can be similar to a mental set in that it makes it difficult to use familiar objects to solve problems in novel ways.

Now that you know what functional fixedness is, let's see if you can overcome it by solving the Duncker candle problem. You enter a room that has the following objects on a table: a candle, a box of matches, and some thumbtacks (see Figure T.3). Your task is to use the objects on the table to attach the candle to the wall of the room so that it will burn properly. (See Figure T.4 for the answer.)

FIGURE T.3
THE DUNCKER CANDLE PROBLEM.
Can you use the objects shown on the table to attach the candle to the wall of the room so that it will burn properly?

CREATIVITY

Creativity is the ability to do things that are novel and useful (Sternberg & Lubart, 1996). Creative people can solve problems to which there are no preexisting solutions, no tried and tested formulas. Creative people share several characteristics (Sternberg & Lubart, 1995, 1996):

- They take chances.
- They refuse to accept limitations and try to do the impossible.
- They appreciate art and music.
- They use the materials around them to make unique things.
- They challenge social norms.
- They take unpopular stands.
- They probe ideas.

A professor of mine once remarked that there is nothing new under the sun, only new combinations of existing elements. Many psychologists agree. They see creativity as the ability to make unusual, sometimes remote, associations to the elements of a problem to generate new combinations. An essential aspect of a creative response is the leap from the elements of the problem to the novel solution. A predictable solution is not creative, even if it is hard to reach.

Creativity demands divergent rather than convergent thinking. In **convergent thinking,** thought is limited to present facts; the problem solver narrows his or her thinking to find the best solution. (You use convergent thinking to arrive at the right answer to a multiple-choice question.) In **divergent thinking,** the problem solver associates freely to the elements of the problem, allowing "leads" to run a nearly limitless course. (You may use divergent thinking when you are trying to generate ideas to answer an essay question on a test.) Problem solving can involve both kinds of thinking. At first divergent thinking helps generate many possible solutions. Convergent thinking is then used to select the most likely solutions and reject the others.

FUNCTIONAL FIXEDNESS The tendency to view an object in terms of its name or familiar usage.

CREATIVITY The ability to generate novel and useful solutions to problems.

CONVERGENT THINKING A thought process that attempts to narrow in on the single best solution to a problem.

DIVERGENT THINKING A thought process that attempts to generate multiple solutions to problems.

Creativity and Academic Ability

It might seem that a creative person would also have high academic ability of the sort measured on intelligence tests. However, the relationship between intelligence test scores and creativity is only moderate (Sternberg & Williams, 1997). Intelligence test questions usually require analytical, convergent thinking to focus in on the one right answer. Tests of creativity determine how flexible a person's thinking is. Here, for example, is an item from a test used by Getzels and Jackson (1962) to measure associative ability, a factor in creativity: "Write as many meanings as you can for each of the following words: (a) duck; (b) sack; (c) pitch; (d) fair." Those who write several meanings for each word, rather than only one, are rated as potentially more creative.

Another measure of creativity might ask people to produce as many words as possible that begin with T and end with N within a minute. Still another item might give people a minute to classify a list of names in as many ways as possible. How many ways can you classify the following group of names?

MARTHA   PAUL   JEFFRY   SALLY   PABLO   JOAN

Factors That Affect Creativity

If there is only a modest connection between creativity and other aspects of intelligence, what other factors contribute to creativity? Some factors reside within the person and some involve the social setting.

PABLO PICASSO AT WORK. We know that the great artist was creative, but what about his academic ability? Academic ability and creativity often go hand in hand, but academic ability is no guarantee of imagination or of specific talents.

PERSONAL FACTORS Creative people show flexibility, fluency (in generating words and ideas), and originality. They spend time alone, thinking about who they are and exploring new ideas (McIntosh, 1996). Getzels and Jackson (1962) found that creative schoolchildren tend to express, rather than inhibit, their feelings and to be playful and independent. Creative children are often at odds with their teachers because of their independence. Faced with the chore of managing 30 or more pupils, teachers too often label quiet and submissive children as "good" and less inhibited children as "bad."

SOCIAL EVALUATION Research evidence shows that concern about evaluation by other people reduces creativity. In one experiment college students were asked to write poems under two very different sets of expectations (Amabile, 1990). Half the students were informed that the experimenter only intended to examine their handwriting—not the aesthetic value of the poetry. The remaining students were informed that judges, who were poets, would supply them with written evaluations of their poetry's content and form. The students who expected to be evaluated according to the form and content of their work turned in significantly less creative poems.

The literature is mixed as to whether people are more creative when they are rewarded for being creative. It has been argued that rewards reduce inner interest in problem solving and thereby undermine creativity. Yet the research shows that rewarding people for being creative on one task can actually enhance creativity on other tasks (Eisenberger & Cameron, 1996).

BRAINSTORMING Brainstorming is a group process intended to encourage creativity. The group leader stimulates group members to generate a great number of ideas—even wild ideas. In order to avoid inhibiting group members, judgment is suspended until a great many ideas are on the table.

BRAINSTORMING A group process that encourages creativity by stimulating a large number of ideas and suspending judgment until the process is completed.

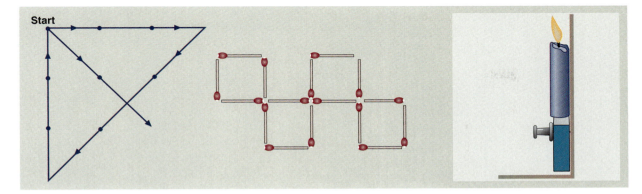

FIGURE T.4
ANSWERS TO PROBLEMS ON PAGES T-4 AND T-9.

For problem 1C, note that each of the letters is the first letter of the numbers 1 through 8. Therefore, the two missing letters are *NT,* for *nine* and *ten.* The solutions to problems 2 and 3 are shown in this illustration. To solve the Duncker candle problem, use the thumbtack to pin the matchbox to the wall. Then set the candle on top of the box. Functional fixedness prevents many people from conceptualizing the matchbox as anything more than a device to hold matches. Commonly given *wrong* answers include trying to affix the bottom of the candle to the wall with melted wax or trying to tack the candle to the wall.

Psychologists have become somewhat skeptical of the brainstorming concept, however (Matlin, 1997). For one thing, research evidence suggests that people working alone are often more creative than people working in groups. (Consider the saying, "A camel is a horse made by a committee.") Moreover, the ideas produced by brainstorming are often lower in quality than those produced by people working alone.

REASONING

We are not finished. I have more puzzles to solve, more weighty things to consider. Ponder this proposition:

If some A are B, and some B are C, then some A are C. Is it true or false? What say you?

I confess that on first seeing this proposition, I believed it was true. It seemed that we were logically progressing to higher-order categories at each step along the way (see Figure T.5, part A). For example, if apples (A) are fruit (B), and fruit (B) are food (C), then apples (A) are food (C). But I was bamboozled by the "some." My example with the apples omitted the word. Consider another example of this proposition, one that uses "some": If *some* circles (A) are shapes (B), and *some* shapes (B) are squares (C), then *some* circles (A) are squares (C). Not so! By using the qualifying term "some," we can move both up, to a higher-order category (from circles to shapes), and back down, to a lower-order category (from shapes to squares) (see Figure T.5, part B).

Types of Reasoning

We have been toying with an example of reasoning. **Reasoning** is the transformation of information in order to reach conclusions. Let us consider two kinds of reasoning: deductive and inductive.

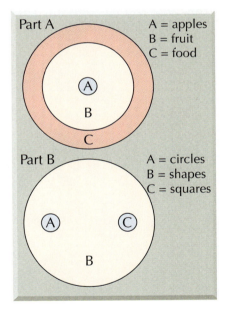

FIGURE T.5
WHEN ARE A ALSO C?

In part A of this figure, A (apples) are also C (food) because food represents a higher-order category that contains all apples. In part B, however, C (squares) is not higher order than A (circles). Therefore, C does not contain A. B (shapes), however, is higher order than both A and C and contains both.

REASONING The transforming of information to reach conclusions.

Deductive reasoning is a form of reasoning in which the conclusion must be true if the premises are true. Consider this classic three-sentence argument:

1. All persons are mortal
2. Socrates is a person.
3. Therefore, Socrates is mortal.

Sentences 1 and 2 in this argument are the *premises*. Premises provide the assumptions or basic information that allow people to draw conclusions. Sentence 3 is the conclusion. In this example, sentence 1 makes a statement about a category (persons). Sentence 2 assigns an individual (Socrates) to the category (persons). Sentence 3 concludes that what is true of the category (persons) is true for the member of the category (Socrates). The conclusion, sentence 3, is said to be *deduced* from the premises. The conclusion about Socrates is true if the premises are true.

In **inductive reasoning,** we reason from individual cases or particular facts to a general conclusion. Consider this transformation of the previous example:

1. Socrates is a person.
2. Socrates is mortal.
3. Therefore, persons are mortal.

The conclusion happens to be correct, but it is illogical. The fact that one person is mortal does not guarantee that all people are mortal.

Inductive reasoning, then, does not permit us to draw absolute conclusions (Sloman, 1996). Yet inductive reasoning is used all the time. We conclude that a certain type of food will or will not make us feel sick because of our experiences on earlier occasions. ("Buttered popcorn made me nauseous. This is buttered popcorn. Therefore, this will make me nauseous.") We assume that a cheerful smile and "Hello!" will break the ice with a new acquaintance because it has worked before. Although none of these conclusions is as logical as a deductive conclusion, inductive conclusions are correct often enough so that we can get on with our daily lives with some degree of confidence.

JUDGMENT AND DECISION MAKING

Decisions, decisions. Should you go have breakfast before classes begin or catch a few extra winks? Should you get married or remain single? Should you take a job or go on for advanced training when you complete your college program? If you opt for the job, cash will soon be jingling in your pockets. Yet later you may wonder if you have enough education to reach your full potential. By furthering your education, you may have to delay independence and gratification, but you may find a more fulfilling position later on. Ah, decisions, decisions.

Other kinds of decisions are judgments about the nature of the world. We make judgments about which route to school or work will be the least crowded. We make judgments about where it will be safe and convenient to live. We make judgments about what political candidates to vote for and which brand of ice cream to buy.

You might like to think that people are so rational that they carefully weigh all the pros and cons when they make judgments or decisions. Or you might think that they insist on finding and examining all the relevant information. Actually, people make most of their decisions on the basis of

DEDUCTIVE REASONING A form of reasoning about arguments in which conclusions are deduced from premises. The conclusions are true if the premises are true.

INDUCTIVE REASONING A form of reasoning in which we reason from individual cases or particular facts to a general conclusion.

limited information. They take shortcuts. They use heuristic devices—rules of thumb—in their judgments and decision making, just as they do in problem solving. For example, they may let a financial adviser select stocks for them rather than research the companies themselves. Or they may see a doctor recommended by a friend rather than examine the doctor's credentials. In this section we consider various factors in judgment and decision making.

Heuristics in Decision Making: If It Works, Must It Be Logical?

Let us begin by asking you to imagine that you flip a coin six times. In the following three possible outcomes, H stands for head and T for tail. Circle the most likely sequence:

H H H H H H

H H H T T T

T H H T H T

Did you select T H H T H T as the most likely sequence of events? Most people do. Why? There are two reasons. First, people recognize that the sequence of six heads in a row is unlikely. (The probability of achieving it is $1/2 \times 1/2 \times 1/2 \times 1/2 \times 1/2 \times 1/2$, or 1/64th.) Three heads and three tails are more likely than six heads (or six tails). Second, people recognize that the sequence of heads and tails ought to appear random. T H H T H T has a random look to it, whereas H H H T T T does not.

People tend to select T H H T H T because of the **representativeness heuristic**. According to this decision-making heuristic, people make judgments about events (samples) according to the populations of events that they appear to represent (Kosonen & Winne, 1995). In this case, the sample of events is six coin tosses. The "population" is an infinite number of random coin tosses. But guess what? *Each* of the sequences is equally likely (or unlikely). If the question had been whether six heads or three heads and three tails had been more likely, the correct answer would have been three and three. If the question had been whether heads and tails would be more likely to be consecutive or in random order, the correct answer would have been random order.

But each of the three sequences shown is a *specific* sequence. What is the probability of attaining the specific sequence T H H T H T? The probability that the first coin toss will result in a tail is 1/2. The probability that the second will result in a head is 1/2, and so on. Thus the probability of attaining the exact sequence T H H T H T is identical to that of achieving any other specific sequence: $1/2 \times 1/2 \times 1/2 \times 1/2 \times 1/2 \times 1/2 = 1/64$th. (Don't just sit there. Try this out on a friend.)

Or consider this question: If a couple has five children, all of whom are boys, is their sixth child more likely to be a boy or a girl? Use of the representativeness heuristic might lead us to imagine that the couple is due for a girl. That is, five boys and one girl is closer to the assumed random distribution that accounts for roughly equal numbers of boys and girls in the world. But people with some knowledge of reproductive biology might predict that another boy is actually more likely because five boys in a row may be too many to be a random biological event. If the couple's conception of a boy or girl were truly random, however, what would be the probability of conceiving another boy? Answer: 1/2.

Another heuristic device used in decision making is the **availability heuristic**. According to this heuristic, our estimates of frequency or probability are based on how easy it is to find examples of relevant events. Let

TRUTH OR FICTION REVISITED
It is not true that if a couple has five sons, the sixth child is likely to be a daughter.

REPRESENTATIVENESS HEURISTIC A decision-making heuristic in which people make judgments about samples according to the populations they appear to represent.

AVAILABILITY HEURISTIC A decision-making heuristic in which our estimates of frequency or probability of events are based on how easy it is to find examples.

me ask you whether there are more art majors or sociology majors at your college. Unless you are familiar with the enrollment statistics, you will probably answer on the basis of the numbers of art majors and sociology majors that you know personally.

The **anchoring and adjustment heuristic** suggests that there can be a good deal of inertia in our judgments. In forming opinions or making estimates, we have an initial view, or presumption. This is the anchor. As we receive additional information, we make adjustments, sometimes grudgingly. That is, if you grow up believing that one religion or one political party is the "right" one, that belief serves as a cognitive anchor. When inconsistencies show up in your religion or political party, you may adjust your views of them, but perhaps not very willingly.

Let us illustrate further by means of a math problem. Write each of the following multiplication problems on a separate piece of paper:

A. $8 \times 7 \times 6 \times 5 \times 4 \times 3 \times 2 \times 1$

B. $1 \times 2 \times 3 \times 4 \times 5 \times 6 \times 7 \times 8$

Show problem A to a few friends. Give them each 5 seconds to estimate the answer. Show problem B to some other friends and give them 5 seconds to estimate the answer.

The answers to the multiplication problems are the same because the order of the quantities being multiplied does not change the outcome. However, when Tversky and Kahneman (1982) showed these problems to high school students, the average estimate given by students who were shown version A was significantly higher than that given by students who were shown version B. Students who saw 8 in the first position offered an average estimate of 2,250. Students who saw 1 in the first position gave an average estimate of 512. That is, the estimate was larger when 8 served as the anchor. By the way, what is the correct answer to the multiplication problems? Can you use the anchoring and adjustment heuristic to explain why both groups of students were so far off?

The Framing Effect: Say That Again?

If you were on a low-fat diet, would you be more likely to choose an ice cream that is 97% fat free or one whose fat content makes up 10% of its calorie content? On one shopping excursion I was impressed with an ice cream package's claims that the product was 97% fat free. Yet when I read the label closely, I noticed that a 4-ounce serving had 160 calories, 27 of which were contributed by fat. Fat, then, accounted for 27/160ths, or about 17%, of the ice cream's calorie content. But fat accounted only for 3% of the ice cream's *weight*. The packagers of the ice cream knew all about the *framing effect*. They understood that labeling the ice cream as "97% fat free" would make it sound more healthful than "Only 17% of calories from fat."

The **framing effect** refers to the way in which wording, or the context in which information is presented, can influence decision making. Political groups are as aware as advertisers of the role of the framing effect. For example, proponents of legalized abortion refer to themselves as "prochoice," and opponents refer to themselves as "pro-life." Thus each group frames itself in a way that is positive ("pro" something) and refers to a value (freedom, life) with which it would be difficult to argue.

Parents are also aware of the framing effect. My 3-year-old, Taylor, was invited to a play date at Abigail's house. I asked Taylor, "Would you like to play with Abigail at her house?" The question met with a resounding no. I thought things over and reframed the question: "Would you like to play at

ANCHORING AND ADJUSTMENT HEURISTIC A decision-making heuristic in which a presumption or first estimate serves as a cognitive anchor. As we receive additional information, we make adjustments, but tend to remain in the proximity of the anchor.

FRAMING EFFECT The influence of wording, or the context in which information is presented, on decision making.

Abigail's house and have a real fun time? She has lots of toys and games, and I'll pick you up real soon." This time Taylor's decision was yes.

Overconfidence: Is Your Hindsight 20-20?

Whether our decisions are correct or incorrect, most of us tend to be overconfident about them (Lundeberg et al., 1994). Overconfidence applies to judgments as wide ranging as whether one will be infected by the virus that causes AIDS (Goldman & Harlow, 1993), predicting the outcome of elections (Hawkins & Hastie, 1990), asserting that one's answers to test items are correct (Lundeberg et al., 1994), and selecting stocks. Many people refuse to alter their judgments even in the face of statistical evidence that shows them to be flawed. (Have you ever known someone to maintain unrealistic confidence in a candidate who was far behind in the polls?)

We also tend to view our situations with 20-20 hindsight. When we are proven wrong, we frequently find a way to show that we "knew it all along." We also become overconfident that we would have known the actual outcome if we had had access to the information that became available after the event (Hawkins & Hastie, 1990). For example, if we had known that a key player would pull a hamstring muscle, we would have predicted a different outcome for the football game. If we had known that it would be blustery on Election Day, we would have predicted a smaller voter turnout and a different outcome.

There are several reasons for overconfidence, even when our judgments are wrong. Here are some of them:

- We tend to be unaware of how flimsy our assumptions may be.
- We tend to focus on examples that confirm our judgments and ignore those that do not.
- Because our working memories have limited space, we tend to forget information that runs counter to our judgments.
- We work to bring about the events we believe in, so they sometimes become self-fulfilling prophecies.
- Even when people are told that they tend to be overconfident in their decisions, they usually ignore this information (Gigerenzer et al., 1991).

THINKING AND LINGUISTIC RELATIVITY

What is the effect of language on thinking? Different languages have different words for the same concepts, and all concepts do not necessarily overlap. Can we be certain that English speakers can truly share or understand the thoughts of people who speak other languages? This question brings us to the linguistic-relativity hypothesis.

The **linguistic-relativity hypothesis** was proposed by Benjamin Whorf (1956). Whorf believed that language structures the way we perceive the world. That is, the categories and relationships we use to understand the world are derived from our language. Therefore, speakers of various languages conceptualize the world in different ways.

Thus most English speakers' ability to think about snow may be limited compared with that of the Inuit (Eskimos). We have only a few words for snow. The Inuit have many words. They differ according to whether the snow is hard packed, falling, melting, covered by ice, and so on. When we

TRUTH OR FICTION REVISITED
It is not necessarily true that people change their opinions when they are shown to be wrong. In some cases they may, but the statement is too general to be true.

INUIT ESKIMOS IN AN IGLOO.
The Inuit of Alaska and the Canadian Northwestern Territories have many more words for snow than most of us do. They spend most of their lives in snow, and the subtle differences among various kinds of snow are meaningful to them.

LINGUISTIC-RELATIVITY HYPOTHESIS The view that language structures the way in which we view the world.

think about snow, we have fewer words to choose from and have to search for descriptive adjectives. The Inuit, however, can readily find a single word that describes a complex weather condition. It might therefore be easier for them to think about this variety of snow in relation to other aspects of their world. Similarly, the Hanunoo people of the Philippines use 92 words for rice, depending on whether the rice is husked or unhusked and on how it is prepared. And whereas we have one word for camel, Arabs have more than 250.

In English, we have hundreds of words to describe different colors, but people who speak Shona use only three words for colors. People who speak Bassa use only two words for colors; these correspond to light and dark. The Hopi Indians had two words for flying objects, one for birds and an all-inclusive word for anything else that might be found traveling through the air.

Does this mean that the Hopi were limited in their ability to think about bumblebees and airplanes? Are English speakers limited in their ability to think about skiing conditions? Are people who speak Shona and Bassa "color-blind" for practical purposes? Probably not. People who use only a few words to distinguish among colors seem to perceive the same color variations as people with dozens of words. For example, the Dani of New Guinea, like the Bassa, have just two words for colors: one that refers to yellows and reds, and one that refers to greens and blues. Yet performance on matching and memory tasks shows that the Dani can discriminate the many colors of the spectrum when they are motivated to do so. English-speaking skiers who are concerned about different skiing conditions have developed a comprehensive vocabulary about snow, including the terms *powder, slush, ice, hard packed,* and *corn snow,* that allows them to communicate and think about snow with the facility of the Inuit. When a need to expand a language's vocabulary arises, the speakers of that language apparently have little difficulty meeting the need.

Modern cognitive scientists generally do not accept the linguistic-relativity hypothesis (Pinker, 1990). For one thing, adults use images and abstract logical propositions, as well as words, as units of thought (Larson, 1990; Miller, 1990). Infants, moreover, display considerable intelligence before they have learned to speak. Another criticism is that a language's vocabulary suggests the range of concepts that the speakers of the language have traditionally found important, not their cognitive limits. For example, people who were magically lifted from the 19th century and placed inside an airplane probably would not think they were flying inside a bird or a large insect, even if their language lacked a word for airplane.

Before leaving the section on thinking, I have a final problem for you:

> You're driving a bus that's leaving from Pennsylvania. To start off with, there were 32 people on the bus. At the next bus stop, 11 people got off and 9 people got on. At the next bus stop, 2 people got off and 2 people got on. At the next bus stop, 12 people got on and 16 people got off. At the next bus stop, 5 people got on and 3 people got off. How many people are now on the bus?

THEORIES OF INTELLIGENCE

What form of life is so adaptive that it can survive in desert temperatures of 120° F or Arctic climes of −40° F? What form of life can run, walk, climb, swim, live underwater for months on end, and fly to the moon and back?

I won't keep you in suspense any longer. We are that form of life. Yet our unclad bodies do not allow us to adapt to these extremes of temperature. Brute strength does not allow us to live underwater or travel to the moon. Rather, it is our **intelligence** that permits us to adapt to these conditions and to challenge our physical limitations. Intelligence is closely related to thinking. Whereas *thinking* involves understanding, manipulating, and communicating about information, *intelligence* is somewhat more broadly thought of as the underlying ability to understand the world and cope with its challenges.

Although these concepts overlap, psychologists tend to be concerned with *how* we think, but laypeople and psychologists are often concerned with *how much* intelligence we have. At an early age, we gain impressions of how intelligent or bright we are compared to other people. Although intelligence, like thinking, cannot be directly seen or touched, psychologists tie the concept to predictors such as school performance and occupational status (Wagner, 1997). We now discuss theories about the nature of intelligence. We see how intelligence is measured and discuss group differences in intelligence. Finally, we examine the determinants of intelligence: heredity and the environment.

Intelligence provides the cognitive basis for academic achievements. It allows us to profit from experiences such as educational experiences. Intelligence allows people to think—to understand complex ideas, reason, and solve problems—and to learn from experience and adapt effectively to the environment (Neisser et al., 1996). As we see in architecture, in the creation of mechanisms for heating and cooling, and in travel through space and under water, intelligence even permits people to create new environments. Although intelligence cannot be seen or touched, psychologists have extensively studied its nature and origins.

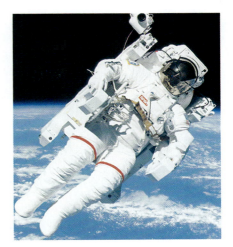

GOING FOR A "WALK."
Human intelligence permits us to live underwater for months on end or to fly to the moon and back. We are weaker than many other organisms, but intelligence enables us to adapt to the environment, to create new environments, even to go for leisurely space walks. Who can say what wonders human intelligence will devise in the new millennium?

Factor Theories

Many investigators have viewed intelligence as consisting of one or more mental abilities, or *factors*. Alfred Binet, the French psychologist who developed modern intelligence-testing methods about 100 years ago, believed that intelligence consists of several related factors. Other investigators have argued that intelligence consists of from one to hundreds of factors.

In 1904, British psychologist Charles Spearman suggested that the behaviors we consider intelligent have a common underlying factor. He labeled this factor **g,** for "general intelligence" or broad reasoning and problem-solving abilities. Spearman supported his view by noting that people rarely score very high in one area (such as knowledge of the meaning of words) and very low in another (such as the ability to compute numbers). People who excel in one area are also likely to excel in others. But he also noted that even the most capable people are relatively superior in some areas—such as music or business or poetry. For this reason, he suggested that specific, or **s,** factors account for specific abilities.

To test his views, Spearman developed **factor analysis.** Factor analysis is a statistical technique that allows researchers to determine which items on tests seem to be measuring the same things. In his research on relationships among scores on tests of verbal, mathematical, and spatial reasoning, Spearman repeatedly found evidence supporting the existence of *s* factors. The evidence for *g* was more limited.

The U.S. psychologist Louis Thurstone (1938) used factor analysis with various tests of specific abilities and also found only limited evidence for the existence of *g*. Thurstone concluded that Spearman had oversimplified the concept of intelligence. Thurstone's data suggested the presence of nine

INTELLIGENCE A complex and controversial concept. According to David Wechsler (1975), the "capacity . . . to understand the world [and] resourcefulness to cope with its challenges."

G Spearman's symbol for general intelligence, which he believed underlay more specific abilities.

S Spearman's symbol for *specific* factors, or *s factors,* which he believed accounted for individual abilities.

FACTOR ANALYSIS A statistical technique that allows researchers to determine the relationships among large number of items such as test items.

TABLE T.2

PRIMARY MENTAL ABILITIES, ACCORDING TO THURSTONE

ABILITY	DESCRIPTION
Visual and spatial abilities	Visualizing forms and spatial relationships
Perceptual speed	Grasping perceptual details rapidly, perceiving similarities and differences between stimuli
Numerical ability	Computing numbers
Verbal meaning	Knowing the meanings of words
Memory	Recalling information (words, sentences, etc.)
Word fluency	Thinking of words quickly (rhyming, doing crossword puzzles, etc.)
Deductive reasoning	Deriving examples from general rules
Inductive reasoning	Deriving general rules from examples

PRIMARY MENTAL ABILITIES According to Thurstone, the basic abilities that make up intelligence.

specific factors, which he labeled **primary mental abilities** (see Table T.2). Thurstone suggested, for example, that we might have high word fluency, enabling us to rapidly develop lists of words that rhyme but not enabling us to solve math problems efficiently.

Over the years, psychologist J. P. Guilford (1988) expanded the numbers of factors found in intellectual functioning to hundreds. The problem with this approach seems to be that the more factors we generate, the more overlap we find among them. For example, several of his "factors" deal with solving math problems and computing numbers.

FIGURE T.6

GARDNER'S THEORY OF MULTIPLE INTELLIGENCES.

According to Gardner, there are seven *intelligences,* not one, each based in a different area of the brain. Two of these involve language ability and logic, which are familiar aspects of intelligence. But Gardner also refers to bodily talents, musical ability, spatial-relations skills, and two kinds of personal intelligence—sensitivity to one's own feelings (intrapersonal sensitivity) and sensitivity to the feelings of others (interpersonal sensitivity) as *intelligences.* Gardner's critics question whether such special talents are truly "intelligences" or specific talents.

Language

Musical

Logical-mathematical

Spatial-relations skills

Intrapersonal skills

Interpersonal skills

Bodily-kinesthetic talent

Gardner's Theory of Multiple Intelligences

Howard Gardner (1983) proposes the existence of seven kinds of intelligence. He refers to each of them as "an intelligence" because they can be so different from one another (see Figure T.6). He also believes that each kind of intelligence has its neurological base in a different area of the brain. Two of these "intelligences" are familiar ones: language ability and logical-mathematical ability. However, Gardner also refers to bodily-kinesthetic talents (of the sort shown by dancers, mimes, and athletes), musical talent, spatial-relations skills, and two kinds of personal intelligence: awareness of one's own inner feelings and sensitivity to other people's feelings. According to Gardner, one can compose symphonies or advance mathematical theory yet be average in, say, language and personal skills. (Aren't some so-called academic geniuses foolish in their personal lives?)

Critics of Gardner's view grant that people do function more intelligently in some aspects of life than in others. They also concur that many people have special talents, such as bodily-kinesthetic talents, even if their overall intelligence is quite average. However, they question whether such special talents are "intelligences" per se or whether we should continue to think of them as specific talents (Neisser et al., 1996). Language skills, reasoning ability, and ability to solve math problems seem to be more closely related than musical or gymnastic talent to what most people mean by intelligence. If people have no musical ability, do we really think of them as *unintelligent*?

Sternberg's Triarchic Theory

Psychologist Robert Sternberg (1985) has constructed a three-pronged, or *triarchic*, model of intelligence (see Figure T.7). The types are *analytical*, *creative*, and *practical*.

ANALYTICAL INTELLIGENCE Analytical intelligence is what we generally think of as academic ability. It enables us to solve problems and to acquire new knowledge. Problem-solving skills include encoding information, combining and comparing pieces of information, and generating a solution. Consider Sternberg's analogy problem:

> *Washington* is to *1* as *Lincoln* is to (a) 5, (b) 10, (c) 15, (d) 50?

To solve the analogy, we must first correctly *encode* the elements—*Washington, 1,* and *Lincoln*—by identifying them and comparing them to other information. We must first encode *Washington* and *Lincoln* as the names of presidents[2] and then try to combine *Washington* and *1* in a meaningful manner. Two possibilities quickly come to mind. Washington was the first president, and his picture is on the $1 bill. We can then generate two possible solutions and try them out. First, was Lincoln the 5th, 10th, 15th, or 50th president? Second, on what bill is Lincoln's picture found? (Do you need to consult a history book or peek into your wallet at this point?)

Sternberg illustrates academic intelligence through the example of a Yale graduate student. Let's call her Ashley. Ashley scored high on standardized tests such as the Graduate Record Exam (GRE) and had a nearly perfect undergraduate record. But the GRE does not always predict success (Sternberg & Williams, 1997). Ashley did well her first year of graduate school but then dropped in academic standing because of difficulty in generating ideas for research.

---

[2] There are other possibilities. Both are the names of memorials and cities, for example.

FIGURE T.7
STERNBERG'S THEORY OF INTELLIGENCE.
According to Robert Sternberg, there are three types of intelligence: analytical (academic ability), creative, and practical ("street smarts").

Analytical Intelligence
(Academic Ability)
Abilities to solve problems, compare and contrast, judge, evaluate, and criticize

Creative Intelligence
(Creativity and Insight)
Abilities to invent, discover, suppose, or theorize

Practical Intelligence
("Street Smarts")
Abilities to adapt to the demands of one's environment, apply knowledge in practical situations

CREATIVE INTELLIGENCE Creative intelligence is defined by the abilities to cope with novel situations and to profit from experience. The ability to quickly relate novel situations to familiar situations (that is, to perceive similarities and differences) fosters adaptation. Moreover, as a result of experience, we also become able to solve problems more rapidly.

"Beth," another of Sternberg's students, had obtained excellent letters of recommendation from undergraduate instructors who found her to be highly creative. However, her undergraduate average and her standardized test scores were relatively low when compared to those of other students applying to Yale. Nevertheless, Beth's analytical skills were adequate and because of her imagination, she surpassed Ashley in performance.

TRUTH OR FICTION REVISITED
According to Sternberg, "street smarts" are a type of intelligence—practical intelligence.

PRACTICAL INTELLIGENCE Practical intelligence, or "street smarts," enables people to adapt to the demands of their environment. For example, keeping a job by adapting one's behavior to the employer's requirements is adaptive. But if the employer is making unreasonable demands, reshaping the environment (by changing the employer's attitudes) or selecting an alternate environment (by finding a more suitable job) is also adaptive (Sternberg, 1997).

A third graduate student of Sternberg's—"Cheryl"—had the greatest practical intelligence of the three. Cheryl's test scores and letters of recommendation fell between those of Ashley and Beth. Cheryl did average-quality graduate work but landed the best job of the three upon graduation—apparently because of her practical intelligence.

There are thus many views of intelligence—what intelligence is and how many types or kinds of intelligence there may be. We do not yet have the final word on the nature of intelligence, but I would like to share with you David Wechsler's definition of intelligence. Wechsler is the originator of the most widely used series of contemporary intelligence tests, and he defined intelligence as the "capacity of an individual to understand the world [and the] resourcefulness to cope with its challenges" (1975, p. 139). To Wechsler, intelligence involves accurate representation of the world and effective problem solving (adapting to one's environment, profiting from experience, selecting the appropriate formulas and strategies, and so on). His definition leaves open the kinds of resourcefulness—academic, practical, emotional—that are considered intelligent.

THE MEASUREMENT OF INTELLIGENCE

Although there are disagreements about the nature of intelligence, laypeople and psychologists are concerned with "how much" intelligence people have, because the question has important implications for their ability to profit from experiences, such as education. Thousands of intelligence tests are administered by psychologists and educators every day. In this section we examine two of the most widely used intelligence tests.

The Stanford-Binet Intelligence Scale

Many of the concepts of psychology have their origins in common sense. The commonsense notion that academic achievement depends on children's intelligence led Alfred Binet and Theodore Simon to invent measures of intelligence.

Early in this century, the French public school system was looking for a test that could identify children who were unlikely to benefit from regular classroom instruction. If these children were identified, they could be given special attention. The first version of such a test, the Binet-Simon scale, came into use in 1905. Since that time it has undergone much revision and refinement. The current version is the Stanford-Binet Intelligence Scale (SBIS).

Despite his view that many factors are involved in intellectual functioning, Binet constructed a test that would yield a single overall score so it could be easily used by the school system. He also assumed that intelligence increases with age, so older children should get more items right than younger children. Binet therefore included a series of age-graded questions, as in Table T.3, arranged in order of difficulty.

The Binet-Simon scale yielded a score called a **mental age,** or MA. The MA shows the intellectual level at which a child is functioning. For example, a child with an MA of 6 is functioning intellectually like the average 6-year-old. In taking the test, children earned "months" of credit for each correct answer. Their MA was determined by adding up the years and months of credit they attained.

Louis Terman adapted the Binet-Simon scale for use with children in the United States. The first version of the *Stanford*-Binet Intelligence Scale (SBIS) was published in 1916. (The test is so named because Terman carried out his work at Stanford University.) The SBIS included more items than the original test and was used with children aged 2 to 16. The SBIS also yielded an **intelligence quotient (IQ)** rather than an MA. As a result, American educators developed interest in learning the IQs of their pupils. The SBIS is used today with children from the age of 2 upward and with adults.

The IQ reflects the relationship between a child's mental age and his or her actual or chronological age (CA). Use of this ratio reflects the fact that the same MA score has different implications for children of different ages. That is, an MA of 8 is an above average score for a 6-year-old but below average for a 10-year-old. In 1912, the German psychologist

TRUTH OR FICTION REVISITED
The terms intelligence *and* IQ *do not mean the same thing.* Intelligence *is a hypothetical concept on whose meanings psychologists do not agree. An* IQ *is a score on an intelligence test. Can you see any danger in using the terms as if they meant the same thing?*

MENTAL AGE The accumulated months of credit that a person earns on the Stanford-Binet Intelligence Scale. Abbreviated *MA.*

INTELLIGENCE QUOTIENT (IQ) (1) Originally, a ratio obtained by dividing a child's score (or mental age) on an intelligence test by chronological age. (2) Generally, a score on an intelligence test.

	TABLE T.3

ITEMS SIMILAR TO THOSE ON THE STANFORD-BINET INTELLIGENCE SCALE

LEVEL (YEARS)	ITEM
2	1. Children show knowledge of basic vocabulary words by identifying parts of a doll, such as the mouth, ears, and hair. 2. Children show counting and spatial skills along with visual-motor coordination by building a tower of four blocks to match a model.
4	1. Children show word fluency and categorical thinking by filling in the missing words when they are asked questions such as these: "Father is a man; mother is a _____?" "Hamburgers are hot; ice cream is _____?" 2. Children show comprehension by answering correctly when they are asked questions such as these: "Why do people have automobiles?" "Why do people have medicine?"
9	1. Children can point out verbal absurdities, as in this question: "In an old cemetery, scientists unearthed a skull which they think was that of George Washington when he was only 5 years of age. What is silly about that?" 2. Children display fluency with words, as shown by answering these questions: "Can you tell me a number that rhymes with snore?" "Can you tell me a color that rhymes with glue?"
Adult	1. Adults show knowledge of the meanings of words and conceptual thinking by correctly explaining the differences between word pairs like "sickness and misery," "house and home," and "integrity and prestige." 2. Adults show spatial skills by correctly answering questions like "If a car turned to the right to head north, in what direction was it heading before it turned?"

TRUTH OR FICTION REVISITED
It is true that two children can answer exactly the same items on an intelligence test correctly, yet one can be above average and the other below average in IQ. This is because the ages of the children may differ. The more intelligent child would be the younger of the two.

Wilhelm Stern suggested the IQ as a way to deal with this problem. Stern computed IQ using this formula:

$$IQ = \frac{\text{Mental Age (MA)}}{\text{Chronological Age (CA)}} \times 100$$

According to this formula, a child with an MA of 6 and a CA of 6 would have an IQ of 100. Children who can handle intellectual problems as well as older children do have IQs above 100. For instance, an 8-year-old who does as well on the SBIS as the average 10-year-old would attain an IQ of 125. Children who do not answer as many items correctly as other children of the same age attain MAs lower than their CAs. Thus their IQ scores are below 100.

IQ scores on the SBIS today are derived by comparing their results to those of other people of the same age. People who answer more items correctly than the average for people of the same age attain IQ scores above 100. People who answer fewer items correctly than the average for their age attain scores below 100.

The Wechsler Scales

David Wechsler developed a series of scales for use with children and adults. The Wechsler scales group test questions into a number of separate subtests such as those shown in Table T.4. Each subtest measures a different type of intellectual task. For this reason, the test shows how well a person does on one type of task (such as defining words) as compared with another (such as using blocks to construct geometric designs). In this way, the Wechsler scales highlight children's relative strengths and weaknesses, as well as measure overall intellectual functioning.

As you can see in the table, Wechsler described some of his scales as measuring *verbal* tasks and others as assessing *performance* tasks. In general, verbal subtests require knowledge of verbal concepts, whereas performance subtests require familiarity with spatial-relations concepts. (Figure T.8 shows items similar to those found on the performance scales of the Wechsler tests.) But it is not that easy to distinguish between the two groupings. For example, associating to the name of the object being pieced together in subtest 11—a sign of word fluency and general knowledge as

TAKING THE WECHSLER.
The Wechsler intelligence scales consist of verbal and performance subtests such as the one shown in this photograph.

TABLE T.4	
SUBTESTS FROM THE WECHSLER ADULT INTELLIGENCE SCALE	
VERBAL SUBTESTS	**PERFORMANCE SUBTESTS**
1. *Information:* "What is the capital of the United States?" "Who was Shakespeare?"	7. *Digit Symbol:* Learning and drawing meaningless figures that are associated with numbers.
2. *Comprehension:* "Why do we have ZIP codes?" "What does 'A stitch in time saves 9' mean?"	8. *Picture Completion:* Pointing to the missing part of a picture.
3. *Arithmetic:* "If 3 candy bars cost 25 cents, how much will 18 candy bars cost?"	9. *Block Design:* Copying pictures of geometric designs using multicolored blocks.
4. *Similarities:* "How are good and bad alike?" "How are peanut butter and jelly alike?"	10. *Picture Arrangement:* Arranging cartoon pictures in sequence so that they tell a meaningful story.
5. *Digit Span:* Repeating a series of numbers forwards and backwards.	11. *Object Assembly:* Putting pieces of a puzzle together so that they form a meaningful object.
6. *Vocabulary:* "What does canal mean?"	

Note: Items for verbal subtests 1, 2, 3, 4, and 6 are similar, but not identical, to actual test items on the Wechsler Adult Intelligence Scale.

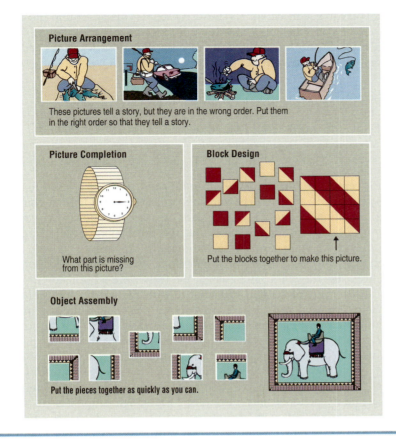

FIGURE T.8
PERFORMANCE ITEMS OF
AN INTELLIGENCE TEST.
These tasks resemble those in the
performance subtests of the
Wechsler Adult Intelligence Scale.

well as of spatial-relations ability—helps the person construct it more rapidly. In any event, Wechsler's scales permit the computation of verbal and performance IQs. It is not unusual for nontechnically oriented college students to attain higher verbal than performance IQs.

Wechsler also introduced the concept of the deviation IQ. Instead of dividing mental by chronological age to compute an IQ, he based IQ scores on how a person's answers compared with those attained by people in the same age group. The average test result at any age level is defined as an IQ score of 100. Wechsler distributed IQ scores so that the middle 50% of them were defined as the "broad average range" of 90 to 110.

TABLE T.5

VARIATIONS IN IQ SCORES

RANGE OF SCORES	PERCENT OF POPULATION	DESCRIPTION
130 and above	2	Very superior
120–129	7	Superior
110–119	16	Above average
100–109	25	High average
90–99	25	Low average
80–89	16	Slow learner
70–79	7	Borderline
Below 70	2	Intellectually deficient

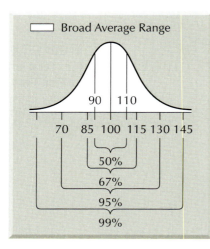

FIGURE T.9

APPROXIMATE DISTRIBUTION OF IQ SCORES.

Wechsler defined the deviation IQ so that 50% of scores fall within the broad average range of 90 to 110. This bell-shaped curve is referred to as a *normal curve* by psychologists. It describes the distribution of many traits, including height.

CULTURAL BIAS A factor that provides an advantage for test takers from certain cultural or ethnic backgrounds, such as using test items based on middle-class culture in the United States.

As you can see in Figure T.9, most IQ scores cluster around the average. Only 4% of the population have IQ scores of above 130 or below 70. Table T.5 indicates the labels that Wechsler assigned to various IQ scores and the approximate percentages of the population who attain IQ scores at those levels.

THE TESTING CONTROVERSY: JUST WHAT DO INTELLIGENCE TESTS MEASURE?

It is no secret that during the 1920s intelligence tests were used to prevent many Europeans and others from immigrating to the United States. For example, testing pioneer H. H. Goddard assessed 178 newly arrived immigrants at Ellis Island and claimed that the great majority of Hungarians, Italians, and Russians were "feeble-minded." Apparently it was of little concern to Goddard that these immigrants, by and large, did not understand English—the language in which the tests were administered!

It is now recognized that intelligence tests cannot be considered valid when they are used with people who do not understand the language. But what of cultural differences? Are the tests valid when used with ethnic minority groups or people who are poorly educated? A survey of psychologists and educational specialists by Mark Snyderman and Stanley Rothman (1987) found that most consider intelligence tests to be **culturally biased** against African Americans and members of the lower classes. Elementary and secondary schools may also place too much emphasis on them in making educational placements.

Intelligence tests measure traits that are required in developed, high-tech societies. The vocabulary and arithmetic subtests on the Wechsler scales, for example, reflect achievements in language skills and computational ability. The broad achievements measured by these tests reflect intelligence, but they also reflect familiarity with the cultural concepts required to answer test questions correctly. In particular, the tests seem to reflect middle-class White culture in the United States.

DETERMINANTS OF INTELLIGENCE: WHERE DOES INTELLIGENCE COME FROM?

Let us now discuss the roles of heredity and environmental influences on intelligence more fully. If different ethnic groups tend to score differently on intelligence tests, psychologists—like educators and other people involved in public life—want to know why. This is one debate that can make use of key empirical findings. Psychologists can point with pride to a rich mine of contemporary research on the roles of nature (genetic influences) and nurture (environmental influences) in the development of intelligence.

Genetic Influences on Intelligence

Research on genetic influences on human intelligence employs several basic strategies. These include kinship studies, twin studies, and adoptee studies (Neisser et al., 1996).

KINSHIP STUDIES We can examine the IQ scores of closely and distantly related people who have been reared together or apart. If

SOCIOECONOMIC AND ETHNIC DIFFERENCES IN INTELLIGENCE

There is a body of research suggestive of differences in intelligence between socioeconomic and ethnic groups (Suzuki & Valencia, 1997). Lower-class U.S. children obtain IQ scores some 10 to 15 points lower than those obtained by middle-and upper-class children. African American children tend to obtain IQ scores some 15 points lower than those obtained by their White age-mates (Neisser et al., 1996). Hispanic American and Native American children also tend to score below the norms for White children (Neisser et al., 1996).

Several studies of IQ have confused the factors of social class and ethnicity because disproportionate numbers of African Americans, Hispanic Americans, and Native Americans are found among the lower socioeconomic classes (Neisser et al., 1996). When we limit our observations to particular ethnic groups, however, we still find an effect for social class. That is, middle-class Whites outscore lower-class Whites. Middle-class African Americans, Hispanic Americans, and Native Americans also outscore lower-class members of their own ethnic groups.

Research has also suggested possible cognitive differences between Asians and White people. Asian Americans, for example, frequently

WHO'S SMART?
Asian children and Asian American children frequently outperform American children on tests of cognitive skills. Sue and Okazaki suggest that Asian Americans place great value on education because they have been discriminated against in careers that do not require advanced education.

outscore White Americans on the math portion of the Scholastic Aptitude Test. Students in China (Taiwan) and Japan also outscore Americans on standardized achievement tests in math and science (Stevenson et al., 1986). In the United States, moreover, people of Asian Indian, Korean, Japanese, Filipino, and Chinese descent are more likely to graduate from high school and complete four years of college than White Americans, African Americans, and Hispanic Americans are (Sue & Okazaki, 1990). Asian Americans are vastly over-

represented in competitive colleges and universities.

These ethnic differences appear to reflect cultural attitudes toward education rather than differences in intelligence per se (Neisser et al., 1996). That is, the Asian children may be more motivated to work hard in school. Research shows that Chinese and Japanese students and their mothers tend to attribute academic successes to hard work. American mothers, in contrast, are more likely to attribute their children's academic successes to "natural" ability (Basic Behavioral Science Task Force, 1996).

Sue and Okazaki (1990) agree. They note that the achievements of Asian students reflect different values in the home, the school, or the culture at large. They argue that Asian Americans have been discriminated against in careers that do not require advanced education. They therefore place relatively greater emphasis on education. Looking to other environmental factors, Steinberg and his colleagues (1992) claim that parental encouragement and supervision in combination with peer support for academic achievement partially explain the superior performances of White and Asian Americans as compared with African and Hispanic Americans. ■

heredity is involved in human intelligence, closely related people ought to have more similar IQs than distantly related or unrelated people, even when they are reared separately.

Figure T.10 is a composite of the results of more than 100 studies of IQ and heredity in human beings (Bouchard et al., 1990). The IQ scores of

FIGURE T.10

FINDINGS OF STUDIES OF THE RELATIONSHIP BETWEEN IQ SCORES AND HEREDITY

The data are a composite of studies summarized in *Science* magazine (Bouchard et al., 1990). By and large, correlations are greater between pairs of people who are more closely related. Yet people who are reared together also have more similar IQ scores than people who are reared apart. Such findings suggest that both genetic and environmental factors contribute to IQ scores.

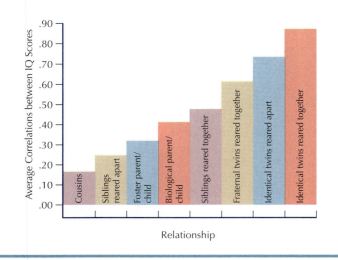

identical (monozygotic, or MZ) twins are more alike than scores for any other pairs, even when the twins have been reared apart. There are moderate correlations between the IQ scores of fraternal (dizygotic, or DZ) twins, between those of siblings, and between those of parents and their children. Correlations between the scores of children and their foster parents and between those of cousins are weak.

TWIN STUDIES The results of large-scale twin studies are consistent with the data in Figure T.10. For instance, a study of 500 pairs of MZ and DZ twins in Louisville, Kentucky (Wilson, 1983), found that the correlations in intelligence between MZ twins were about the same as that for MZ twins in Figure T.10. The correlations in intelligence between DZ twin pairs was the same as that between other siblings. Research at the University of Minnesota with sets of twins who were reared together and others who were reunited in adulthood has obtained essentially similar results (Bouchard et al., 1990). In the MacArthur Longitudinal Twin Study, Robert Emde (1993) and his colleagues examined the intellectual abilities of 200 primarily White, healthy 14-month-old pairs of twins. They found that identical (MZ) twins were more similar than fraternal (DZ) twins in spatial memory, ability to categorize things, and word comprehension. Emde and his colleagues concluded that genes tend to account for about 40% to 50% of differences in children's cognitive skills.

All in all, studies generally suggest that the **heritability** of intelligence is between 40% and 60% (Bouchard et al., 1990; Neisser et al., 1996). In other words, about half of the variations (the technical term is *variance*) in IQ scores can be accounted for by heredity. This is *not* the same as saying that you inherited about half of your intelligence. The implication of such a statement would be that you "got" the other half of your intelligence somewhere else. It means, rather, that about half of the difference between your IQ score and the IQ scores of other people can be explained in terms of genetic factors.

Note, too, that genetic pairs (such as MZ twins) who were reared together show higher correlations in their IQ scores than similar genetic pairs (such as other MZ twins) who were reared apart. This finding holds for DZ twins, siblings, parents and their children, and unrelated people. Being reared together is therefore related with similarities in IQ. *For this reason, the same group of studies used to demonstrate a role for the heritability of IQ scores also suggests that the environment plays a role in determining IQ scores.*

HERITABILITY The degree to which the variations in a trait from one person to another can be attributed to, or explained by, genetic factors.

ADOPTEE STUDIES Another strategy for exploring genetic influences on intelligence is to compare the correlations between the IQ scores of adopted children and those of their biological and adoptive parents. When children are separated from their biological parents at an early age, one can argue that strong relationships between their IQs and those of their natural parents reflect genetic influences. Strong relationships between their IQs and those of their adoptive parents might reflect environmental influences.

Several studies with 1- and 2-year-old children in Colorado (Baker et al., 1983), Texas (Horn, 1983), and Minnesota (Scarr & Weinberg, 1983) have found a stronger relationship between the IQ scores of adopted children and those of their biological parents than between the children's scores and those of their adoptive parents. The Scarr and Weinberg report concerns African American children reared by White adoptive parents. We return to its findings in the section on environmental influences on intelligence.

In sum, genetic factors may account for about half of the variation in intelligence test scores among individuals. Environmental factors also affect scores on intelligence tests.

Environmental Influences on Intelligence

Studies of environmental influences also employ a variety of research strategies. These include manipulation of the testing situation, observation of the role of the home environment, and evaluation of the effects of educational programs.

STEREOTYPE VULNERABILITY **Stereotype vulnerability** also affects test scores. Psychologist Claude Steele (1996, 1997) suggests that African American students carry an extra burden in performing scholastic tasks: They believe that they risk confirming their group's negative stereotype by doing poorly on such tasks. This concern creates performance anxiety. Performance anxiety distracts them from the tasks, and as a result they perform more poorly than White students in the same situation.

In an experiment designed to test this view, Steele and Aronson (1995) gave two groups of African American and White Stanford undergraduates the most difficult verbal skills test questions from the GRE. One group was told that the researchers were attempting to learn about the "psychological factors involved in solving verbal problems." The other group was told that the items were "a genuine test of your verbal abilities and limitations." African American students who were given the first message performed as well as White students. African American students who were given the second message—that proof of their abilities was on the line—performed significantly more poorly than the White students. Apparently the second message triggered their stereotype vulnerability, which led them to self-destruct on the test. Steele's findings are further evidence of the limits of the validity of intelligence tests as valid indicators of intelligence.

HOME ENVIRONMENT AND STYLES OF PARENTING The home environment and styles of parenting also appear to have an effect on IQ scores (Olson et al., 1992; Steinberg et al., 1992; Suzuki & Valencia, 1997). Children of mothers who are emotionally and verbally responsive, furnish appropriate play materials, are involved with their children, and provide varied daily experiences during the early years obtain higher IQ scores later on (Bradley et al., 1989; Gottfried et al., 1994). Organization and safety in the home have also been linked to higher IQs at later ages and to higher achievement test scores during the first grade (Bradley et al., 1989).

STEREOTYPE VULNERABILITY The tendency to focus on a conventional, negative belief about one's group, such that the individual risks behaving in a way that confirms that belief.

Dozens of other studies support the view that children's early environment is linked to IQ scores and academic achievement. For example, McGowan and Johnson (1984) found that good parent-child relationships and maternal encouragement of independence were both positively linked to Mexican American children's IQ scores by the age of 3. A number of studies have also found that high levels of maternal restrictiveness and punishment of children at 24 months are linked to *lower* IQ scores later on.

EDUCATION Although intelligence is viewed as permitting people to profit from education, education also apparently contributes to intelligence. For example, government-funded efforts to provide preschoolers with enriched early environments have led to measurable intellectual gains. Head Start programs, for example, enhance the IQ scores, achievement test scores, and academic skills of disadvantaged children (Barnett & Escobar, 1990; Zigler, 1995) by exposing them to materials and activities that middle-class children take for granted. These include letters and words, numbers, books, exercises in drawing, pegs and pegboards, puzzles, toy animals, and dolls.

Preschool intervention programs can have long-term positive effects on children. During the elementary and high school years, graduates of preschool programs are less likely to be left back or placed in classes for slow learners. They are more likely to graduate from high school, go on to college, and earn higher incomes.

Schooling at later ages also contributes to intelligence test scores. When children of about the same age start school a year apart because of admissions standards related to their date of birth, children who have been in school longer obtain higher IQ scores (Neisser et al., 1996). Moreover, IQ test scores tend to decrease during the summer vacation (Neisser et al., 1996).

ADOPTEE STUDIES The Minnesota adoption studies reported by Scarr and Weinberg suggest a genetic influence on intelligence. But the same studies (Scarr & Weinberg, 1976, 1977) also suggest a role for environmental influences. African American children who were adopted during their first year by White parents with above average income and education obtained IQ scores some 15 to 25 points higher than those obtained by African American children reared by their natural parents (Scarr & Weinberg, 1976). There are two cautions regarding these findings. One is that the adoptees' average IQ score, about 106, remained below those of their adoptive parents' natural children—117 (Scarr & Weinberg, 1977). The second is that follow-up studies of the adopted children at the age of 17 found that the mean IQ score of the adopted African American children had decreased by 9 points, to 97 (Weinberg et al., 1992). The meaning of the change remains to be unraveled.

Perhaps we need not be so concerned with whether we can sort out exactly how much of a person's IQ is due to heredity and how much is due to environmental influences. A majority of psychologists and educators believe that IQ reflects the complex interaction of heredity, early childhood experiences, and sociocultural factors and expectations. Psychology has traditionally supported the dignity of the individual. It might be more appropriate for us to try to identify children *of all ethnic groups* whose environments place them at risk for failure and do what we can to enrich their environments.

TRUTH OR FICTION REVISITED
It is true that Head Start programs have raised children's IQs.

HEAD START.
Preschoolers who are placed in Head Start programs have shown dramatic improvements in readiness for elementary school and in IQ scores.

SUMMARY

1. **What is thinking?** Thinking is cognitive activity involved in understanding, processing, and communicating information. It refers to conscious, planned attempts to make sense of the world.

2. **What are concepts?** Concepts are mental categories that group together objects, events, or ideas with common properties. We tend to organize concepts in hierarchies.

3. **What are prototypes?** Prototypes are good examples of particular concepts.

4. **How do people approach problem solving?** People first attempt to understand the problem. Then they use various strategies for attacking the problem, including algorithms, heuristic devices, and analogies.

5. **What are algorithms, heuristic devices, and analogies?** Algorithms are specific procedures for solving problems (such as formulas) that invariably work as long as they are applied correctly. Heuristics are rules of thumb that help us simplify and solve problems. Heuristics are less reliable than algorithms, but when they are effective, they allow us to solve problems more rapidly. One commonly used heuristic device is means-end analysis, in which we assess the difference between our current situation and our goals and do what we can to reduce the discrepancy. The analogy heuristic applies the solution of an earlier problem to the solution of a new, similar problem.

6. **What are some factors that affect problem solving?** Five key factors are level of expertise, whether one falls prey to a mental set, whether one develops insight into a problem, functional fixedness, and the definition of the problem.

7. **What is creativity?** Creativity is the ability to make unusual and sometimes remote associations to or among the elements of a problem in order to generate new combinations.

8. **What factors appear to account for creativity?** There is only a moderate relationship between creativity and academic ability. Creative people show traits such as flexibility, fluency, and independence. The pressure of social evaluation appears to reduce creativity, and the effects of brainstorming in fostering creativity are debatable.

9. **What kinds of reasoning are there?** In deductive reasoning, one reaches conclusions about premises that are true so long as the premises are true. In inductive reasoning, we reason from individual cases or particular facts to a general conclusion that is not necessarily true.

10. **How do people make decisions?** People sometimes make decisions by carefully weighing the pluses and minuses. However, people who are making decisions frequently use rules of thumb or heuristics, which are shortcuts that are correct (or correct enough) most of the time. According to the representativeness heuristic, people make judgments about events according to the populations of events that they appear to represent. According to the availability heuristic, people's estimates of frequency or proba-bility are based on how easy it is to find examples of relevant events. According to the anchoring and adjustment heuristic, we adjust our initial estimates as we receive additional information—but we often do so unwillingly.

11. **What are some factors that affect decision making?** Our decisions are influenced by the framing effect and by overconfidence.

12. **What is the relationship between thinking and language?** Thinking is possible without language, but language facilitates thinking. According to the linguistic-relativity hypothesis, language structures the ways in which we perceive the world. However, most modern cognitive scientists do not support this hypothesis.

13. **What is intelligence?** Intelligence underlies (provides the cognitive basis for) thinking and academic achievement. It has been defined by Wechsler as the "capacity . . . to understand the world . . . and . . . resourcefulness to cope with its challenges."

14. **What are Spearman and Thurstone's theories of intelligence?** Spearman and Thurstone believed that intelligence is composed of a number of factors. Spearman believed that a common factor, *g,* underlies all intelligent behavior but that people also have specific abilities, or *s* factors. Thurstone suggested several primary mental abilities, including word fluency and numerical ability.

15. **What is Gardner's theory of multiple intelligences?** Gardner believes that people have several intelligences, not one, and that each is based in a different area of the brain. Two such "intelligences" are language ability and logical-mathematical ability, but Gardner also includes bodily-kinesthetic intelligence and others.

16. **What is Sternberg's triarchic theory of intelligence?** Sternberg's triarchic theory proposes three kinds of intelligence: analytical (academic ability), creative, and practical ("street smarts").

17. **What is the IQ?** Intelligence tests yield scores called intelligence quotients, or *IQs*. The Stanford-Binet Intelligence Scale, originated by Alfred Binet, derives the IQ score by dividing a child's mental age score by chronological age and then multiplying by 100. The Wechsler scales use deviation IQs, which are derived by comparing a person's performance with that of age-mates.

18. **What kinds of items are included in intelligence tests?** The Wechsler scales contain verbal and performance subtests that measure general information, comprehension, similarities (conceptual thinking), vocabulary, mathematics, block design (copying designs), and object assembly (piecing puzzles together).

19. **How do IQ scores of people in various socioeconomic and ethnic groups differ?** Lower-class U.S. children obtain IQ scores some 10 to 15 points lower than those of middle-and upper-class children. African American children tend to obtain IQ scores some 15 to 20 points lower than those of their White age-mates. Asians and Asian Americans usually obtain higher IQ scores than White British or U.S. citizens.

20. **Where does intelligence come from?** The largest number of psychologists believe that intelligence reflects the interaction of genetic and environmental influences.

KEY TERMS

algorithm (p. T-5)

anchoring and adjustment heuristic (p. T-14)

availability heuristic (p. T-13)

brainstorming (p. T-10)

concept (p. T-3)

convergent thinking (p. T-9)

creativity (p. T-9)

cultural bias (p. T-24)

deductive reasoning (p. T-12)

divergent thinking (p. T-9)

exemplar (p. T-3)

factor analysis (p. T-17)

framing effect (p. T-14)

functional fixedness (p. T-9)

g (p. T-17)

heritability (p. T-26)

heuristics (p. T-6)

incubation (p. T-8)

inductive reasoning (p. T-12)

insight (p. T-8)

intelligence (p. T-17)

intelligence quotient (IQ) (p. T-21)

linguistic-relativity hypothesis (p. T-15)

means-end analysis (p. T-6)

mental age (p. T-21)

mental set (p. T-8)

primary mental abilities (p. T-18)

prototype (p. T-3)

reasoning (p. T-11)

representativeness heuristic (p. T-13)

s (p. T-17)

stereotype vulnerability (p. T-27)

systematic random search (p. T-6)

thinking (p. T-2)

REFERENCES

Amabile, T. M. (1990). Within you, without you: The social psychology of creativity, and beyond. In M. A. Runco & R. S. Albert (Eds.), *Theories of creativity*. Newbury Park, NY: Sage.

Azar, B. (1995). Breaking through barriers to creativity. *APA Monitor, 26*(8), 1, 20.

Baker, L. A., DeFries, J. C., & Fulker, D. W. (1983). Longitudinal stability of cognitive ability in the Colorado adoption project. *Child Development, 54*, 290–297.

Barnett, W. S., & Escobar, C. M. (1990). Economic costs and benefits of early intervention. In S. J. Meisels & J. P. Shonkoff (Eds.), *Handbook of early childhood intervention*. New York: Cambridge University Press.

Basic Behavioral Science Task Force of the National Advisory Mental Health Council. (1996). Basic behavioral science research for mental health: Sociocultural and environmental practices. *American Psychologist, 51*, 722–731.

Bouchard, T. J., Jr., Lykken, D. T., McGue, M., Segal, N. L., & Tellegen, A. (1990). Sources of human psychological differences: The Minnesota study of twins reared apart. *Science, 250*, 223–228.

Bradley, R. H., et al. (1989). Home environment and cognitive development in the first 3 years of life. *Developmental Psychology, 25,* 217–235.

Clement, J. (1991). Nonformal reasoning in experts and in science students. In J. Voss, D. Perkins, & J. Siegel (Eds.), *Informal reasoning and education.* Hillsdale, NJ: Erlbaum.

de Jong, P. F., & Das-Smaal, E. A. (1995). Attention and intelligence. *Journal of Educational Psychology, 87,* 80–92.

Eisenberger, R., & Cameron, J. (1996). Detrimental effects of reward: Reality or myth? *American Psychologist, 51,* 1153–1166.

Emde, R. (1993). Cited in Adler, T. (1993). Shy, bold temperament? It's mostly in the genes. *APA Monitor, 24*(1), 7, 8.

Fehr, B., & Russell, J. A. (1991). The concept of love viewed from a prototype perspective. *Journal of Personality and Social Psychology, 60,* 425–438.

Gardner, H. (1983). *Frames of mind.* New York: Basic Books.

Getzels, J. W., & Jackson, P. W. (1962). *Creativity and intelligence.* New York: Wiley.

Gigerenzer, G., Hoffrage, U., & Kleinbölting, H. (1991). Probabilistic mental models. *Psychological Review, 98,* 506–528.

Goldman, J. A., & Harlow, L. L. (1993). Self-perception variables that mediate AIDS-preventive behavior in college students. *Health Psychology, 12,* 489–498.

Gottfried, A. E., Fleming, J. S., & Gottfried, A. W. (1994). Role of parental motivational practices in children's academic intrinsic motivation and achievement. *Journal of Educational Psychology, 86,* 104–113.

Guilford, J. P. (1988). Some changes in the structure-of-intellect model. *Educational and Psychological Measurement, 48,* 1–4.

Halpern, D. F. (1989). *Thought and knowledge* (2nd ed.). Hillsdale, NJ: Erlbaum.

Halpern, D. F., Hansen, C., & Riefer, D. (1990). Analogies as an aid to understanding and memory. *Journal of Educational Psychology, 82,* 298–305.

Hawkins, S. A., & Hastie, R. (1990). Hindsight: Biased judgments of past events after the outcomes are known. *Psychological Bulletin, 107,* 311–327.

Hershey, D. A., Walsh, D. A., Read, S. J., & Chulef, A. S. (1990). Relationships between metamemory, memory predictions, and memory task performance in adults. *Psychology and Aging, 5,* 215–227.

Horn, J. M. (1983). The Texas adoption project. *Child Development, 54,* 268–275.

Kosonen, P., & Winne, P. H. (1995). Effects of teaching statistical laws on reasoning about everyday problems. *Journal of Educational Psychology, 87,* 33–46.

Larson, R. K. (1990). Semantics. In D. N. Osherson & H. Lasnik (Eds.), *An invitation to cognitive science: Language* (Vol. 1). Cambridge, MA: The MIT Press, a Bradford Book.

Lundeberg, M. A., Fox, P. W., & Puncochar, J. (1994). Highly confident but wrong. *Journal of Educational Psychology, 86,* 114–121.

Maier, N. R. F., & Schneirla, T. C. (1935). *Principles of animal psychology.* New York: McGraw-Hill.

Matlin, M. W. (1997). *Cognition* (4th ed.). Fort Worth: Harcourt Brace.

McGowan, R. J., & Johnson, D. L. (1984). The mother-child relationship and other antecedents of childhood intelligence. *Child Development, 55,* 810–820.

McIntosh, H. (1996). Solitude provides an emotional tune-up. *APA Monitor, 26*(3), 1, 10.

Metcalfe, J. (1986). Premonitions of insight predict impending error. *Journal of Experimental Psychology: Learning, Memory, and Cognition, 12,* 623–634.

Miller, J. L. (1990). Speech perception. In D. N. Osherson & H. Lasnik (Eds.), *An invitation to cognitive science: Language* (Vol. 1). Cambridge, MA: The MIT Press, a Bradford Book.

Neisser, U., Boodoo, G., Bouchard, T. J., Jr., Boykin, A. W., Brody, N., Ceci, S. J., Halpern, D. F., Loehlin, J. C., Perloff, R., Sternberg, R. J., & Urbina, S. (1996). Intelligence: Knowns and unknowns. *American Psychologist, 51,* 77–101.

Novick, L. R., & Coté. (1992). The nature of expertise in anagram solution. In *Proceedings of the Fourteenth Annual Conference of the Cognitive Science Society.* Hillsdale, NJ: Erlbaum.

Olson, S. L., Bates, J. E., & Kaskie, B. (1992). Caregiver-infant interaction antecedents of children's school-age cognitive ability. *Merrill-Palmer Quarterly, 38,* 309–330.

Pinker, S. (1990). Language acquisition. In D. N. Osherson & H. Lasnik (Eds.), *An invitation to cognitive science: Language* (Vol. 1). Cambridge, MA: The MIT Press, a Bradford Book.

Scarr, S., & Weinberg, R. A. (1976). IQ test performance of Black children adopted by White families. *American Psychologist, 31,* 726–739.

Scarr, S., & Weinberg, R. A. (1977). Intellectual similarities within families of both adopted and biological children. *Intelligence, 1,* 170–191.

Scarr, S., & Weinberg, R. A. (1983). The Minnesota adoption studies: Genetic differences and malleability. *Child Development, 54,* 260–267.

Sloman, S. A. (1996). The empirical case for two systems of reasoning. *Psychological Bulletin, 119,* 3–22.

Snyderman, M., & Rothman, S. (1987). Survey of expert opinion on intelligence and aptitude testing. *American Psychologist, 42,* 137–144.

Steele, C. M. (1996, August). *The role of stereotypes in shaping intellectual identity.* Master lecture presented to the meeting of the American Psychological Association, Toronto.

Steele, C. M. (1997). A threat in the air: How stereotypes shape intellectual identity and performance. *American Psychologist, 52,* 613–629.

Steele, C. M., & Aronson, J. (1995). Cited in Watters, E. (1995, September 17). Claude Steele has scores to settle. *New York Times Magazine,* pp. 44–47.

Steinberg, L., Lamborn, S. D., Dornbusch, S. M., & Darling, N. (1992). Impact of parenting practices on adolescent achievement: Authoritative parenting, school involvement, and encouragement to succeed. *Child Development, 63,* 1266–1281.

Sternberg, R. J. (1985). *Beyond IQ: A triarchic theory of human intelligence.* New York: Cambridge University Press.

Sternberg, R. J. (1997). The concept of intelligence and its role in lifelong learning and success. *American Psychologist, 52,* 1030–1037.

Sternberg, R. J., & Lubart, T. I. (1995). *Defying the crowd: Cultivating creativity in a culture of conformity.* New York: Free Press.

Sternberg, R. J., & Lubart, T. I. (1996). Investing in creativity. *American Psychologist, 51,* 677–688.

Sternberg, R. J., & Williams, W. M. (1997). Does the Graduate Record Examination predict meaningful success in the graduate training of psychologists? *American Psychologist, 52,* 630–641.

Stevenson, H. W., Lee, S. Y., & Stigler, J. W. (1986). Mathematics achievement of Chinese, Japanese, and American children. *Science, 231,* 693–699.

Sue, S., & Okazaki, S. (1990). Asian-American educational achievements. *American Psychologist, 45,* 913–920.

Suzuki, L. A., & Valencia, R. R. (1997). Race-ethnicity and measured intelligence: Educational implications. *American Psychologist, 52,* 1103–1114.

Thurstone, L. L. (1938). Primary mental abilities. *Psychometric Monographs, 1.*

Tversky, A., & Kahneman, D. (1982). Judgment under uncertainty. In D. Kahneman, P. Slovic, & A. Tversky (Eds.), *Judgment under uncertainty: Heuristics and biases.* New York: Cambridge University Press.

Wagner, R. K. (1997). Intelligence, training, and employment. *American Psychologist, 52,* 1059–1069.

Wechsler, D. (1975). Intelligence defined and undefined. *American Psychologist, 30,* 135–139.

Weinberg, R. A., Scarr, S., & Waldman, I. D. (1992). The Minnesota Transracial Adoption Study: A follow-up of IQ test performance at adolescence. *Intelligence, 16,* 117–135.

Wilson, R. S. (1983). The Louisville twin study: Developmental synchronies in behavior. *Child Development, 54,* 298–316.

Whorf, B. (1956). *Language, thought, and reality.* New York: Wiley.

Zigler, E. (1995, August 1). *Modernizing early childhood intervention to better serve children and families in poverty.* Master lecture delivered to the meeting of the American Psychological Association, New York.

ME

MOTIVATION AND EMOTION

THE SEEKERS WERE QUITE A GROUP. THEIR BRAVE LEADER, Marian Keech, dutifully recorded the messages that she believed were sent to her by the Guardians from outer space. One particular message was somewhat disturbing. It specified that the world would come to an end on December 21. A great flood would engulf Lake City, the home of Keech and many of her faithful followers.

Another message brought good news, however. Keech received word that the Seekers would be rescued from the flood. Keech reported that she received messages through "automatic writing." The messengers would communicate through her: She would write down their words, supposedly without awareness. This bit of writing was perfectly clear: The Seekers would be saved by flying saucers at the stroke of midnight on the 21st.

In their classic observational study, Leon Festinger and his colleagues (1956) described how they managed to be present in Keech's household at the fateful hour by pretending to belong to the group. Their purpose was to observe the behavior of the Seekers during and following the prophecy's failure. The cognitive theory of motivation that Festinger was working on—**cognitive-dissonance theory**—suggested that there would be a discrepancy or conflict between two key cognitions: (1) Ms. Keech is a prophet, and (2) Ms. Keech is wrong.

How might such a conflict be resolved? One way would be for the Seekers to lose faith in Keech. But the researchers argued that according to cognitive-dissonance theory, the Seekers might be motivated to resolve the conflict by going out to spread the word and find additional converts. Otherwise the group would be painfully embarrassed.

Let us return to the momentous night. Many members of the group had quit their jobs and gone on spending sprees before the anticipated end. Now they were all gathered together. As midnight approached they fidgeted, awaiting the flying saucers. Midnight came, but no saucers. Anxious glances were exchanged. Silence. Coughs. A few minutes passed, tortuously slowly. Watches were checked, more glances exchanged. At 4 a.m. a bitter and frantic Keech complained that she sensed members of the group were doubting her. At 4:45 a.m., however, she seemed suddenly relieved. Still another message was arriving, and Keech was spelling it out through automatic writing! The Seekers, it turned out, had managed to save the world through their faith. The universal powers had decided to let the world travel on along its sinful way for a while longer. Why? Because of the faith of the Seekers, there was hope!

You guessed it. The faith of most of those present was renewed. They called wire services and newspapers to spread the word. All but three psychologists from the University of Minnesota went home, weary but enlightened, and wrote a book entitled *When Prophecy Fails,* which serves as one of the key documents of cognitive-motivational theory.

What about Mr. Keech? He was a tolerant sort. He slept through it all.

The psychology of motivation is concerned with the *whys* of behavior. Why do we eat? Why do some of us strive to get ahead? Why do some of us ride motorcycles at breakneck speeds? Why do we try new things? Why were the Seekers in a state of acute discomfort?

Motives are hypothetical states within an organism that activate behavior and propel the organism toward goals. Why do we say "hypothetical states"? Because motives are not seen and measured directly. Like many other psychological concepts, they are inferred from behavior (Kimble, 1994). Highly motivated organisms act with vigor, and their activity takes specific directions, such as foraging for food or striving to advance in the corporate world.

In the following section, we explore theories of motivation. We ask, Just what is so motivating about motives?

THEORIES OF MOTIVATION: THE *WHYS* OF BEHAVIOR

Although psychologists agree that it is important to understand why humans and lower animals do things, they do not agree about the precise nature of motivation. Let us consider four theoretical perspectives on motivation.

Instinct Theory: "Doing What Comes Naturally"

Animals are "prewired"—that is, born with preprogrammed tendencies—to respond to certain situations in certain ways. Birds reared in isolation from other birds build nests during the mating season even though they have never observed another bird building a nest (or, for that matter, seen a nest). Siamese fighting fish reared in isolation from other fish assume stereotypical threatening stances and attack other males when they are introduced into their tank.

These behaviors are found in particular species (they are *species-specific*). They do not rely on learning. Such behaviors are called **instincts,** or *fixed-action patterns* (FAPs). Spiders spin webs. Bees "dance" to communicate the location of food to other bees. All of this activity is inborn. It is genetically transmitted from generation to generation.

FAPs occur in response to stimuli called *releasers.* For example, male members of many species are sexually aroused by **pheromones** secreted by females. Pheromones thus release the FAP of sexual response. Other pheromones are used to organize food gathering, maintain pecking orders, sound alarms, and mark territories (Azar, 1998).

The question arises whether humans have instincts, and if so, how many. A century ago, psychologists William James (1890) and William McDougall (1908) argued that humans have instincts that foster self-survival and social behavior. James asserted that we have social instincts such as love, sympathy, and modesty. McDougall compiled 12 "basic" instincts, including hunger, sex, and self-assertion. Other psychologists have made longer lists, and still others deny that people have any instincts. The question remains unresolved.

Sigmund Freud also used the term *instincts* to refer to physiological needs in humans. He believed that the instincts of sex and aggression give rise to *psychic energy,* which is perceived as a feeling of tension. Tension motivates us to restore ourselves to a calmer, resting state. The behavior patterns we use to reduce the tension—for example, using a weapon or a push when acting aggressively—are largely learned.

A FIXED-ACTION PATTERN.
In the presence of another male, Siamese fighting fish assume threatening stances in which they extend their fins and gills and circle each other. If neither male retreats, there will be a conflict.

COGNITIVE-DISSONANCE THEORY The view that we are motivated to make our cognitions or beliefs consistent.

MOTIVE A hypothetical state within an organism that propels the organism toward a goal.

INSTINCT An inherited disposition to activate specific behavior patterns that are designed to reach certain goals.

PHEROMONES Chemical secretions detected by other members of the same species that stimulate stereotypical behaviors.

Drive Reductionism and Homeostasis: "Steady, Steady . . ."

According to the **drive-reduction theory** of learning, as set forth by psychologist Clark Hull in the 1930s, **primary drives** such as hunger, thirst, and pain trigger arousal (tension) and activate behavior. We learn to engage in behaviors that reduce the drives. Through association, we also learn **acquired drives.** We may acquire a drive for money because money enables us to obtain food, drink, and homes, which protect us from predators and extremes of temperature. We might acquire drives for social approval and affiliation because other people, and their goodwill, help us reduce primary drives, especially when we are infants. In all cases, reduction of tension is the goal. Yet some people appear to acquire what could be considered excessive drives for money or affiliation. They gather money apparently for its own sake, long after they have obtained the things that money can buy, and some people find it difficult to be alone, even briefly.

Primary drives like hunger are triggered when we are in a state of deprivation. Sensations of hunger motivate us to act in ways that will restore the bodily balance. This tendency to maintain a steady state is called **homeostasis.** Homeostasis works much like a thermostat. When the temperature in a room drops below the set point, the heating system is triggered. The heat stays on until the set point is reached. Similarly, most animals eat until they are no longer hungry. (The fact that many people eat "recreationally"—for example, when they are presented with an appealing dessert—suggests that there is more to eating than just drive reduction.)

Humanistic Theory: "I've Got to Be Me"

Humanistic psychologists, particularly Abraham Maslow, note that the instinct and drive-reduction theories of motivation are defensive. These theories suggest that human behavior is rather mechanical and aimed toward survival and reduction of tension. As a humanist, Maslow believed that people are also motivated by the conscious desire for personal growth. Humanists note that people tolerate pain, hunger, and many other sources of tension to obtain personal fulfillment.

Maslow believed that we are separated from lower animals by our capacity for **self-actualization,** or self-initiated striving to become whatever we believe we are capable of being. Maslow considered self-actualization to be as important a need in humans as hunger. It is that need that impels people to strive to become concert pianists or chief executive officers or best-selling authors.

Maslow (1970) organized human needs into a hierarchy, from physiological needs such as hunger and thirst, through self-actualization (see Figure ME.1). He believed that we naturally strive to travel up through this hierarchy. Maslow's hierarchy consists of the following sets of needs:

1. *Physiological needs:* hunger, thirst, elimination, warmth, fatigue, pain avoidance, sexual release.
2. *Safety needs:* protection from the environment through housing and clothing; security from crime and financial hardship.
3. *Love and belongingness needs:* love and acceptance through intimate relationships, social groups, and friends. Maslow believed that in a generally well-fed society such as ours, much frustration stems from failure to meet needs at this level.
4. *Esteem needs:* achievement, competence, approval, recognition, prestige, status.

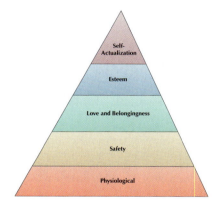

FIGURE ME.1
MASLOW'S HIERARCHY OF NEEDS.
Maslow believed we progress toward higher psychological needs once basic survival needs have been met. Where do you fit in this picture?

DRIVE-REDUCTION THEORY The view that organisms learn to engage in behaviors that have the effect of reducing drives.

PRIMARY DRIVES Unlearned, or physiological, drives.

ACQUIRED DRIVES Drives acquired through experience, or learned.

HOMEOSTASIS The tendency of the body to maintain a steady state.

SELF-ACTUALIZATION According to Maslow and other humanistic psychologists, self-initiated striving to become what one is capable of being. The motive for reaching one's full potential, for expressing one's unique capabilities.

5. *Self-actualization:* fulfillment of our unique potentials. For many individuals, self-actualization involves needs for cognitive understanding (novelty, exploration, knowledge) and aesthetic needs (music, art, poetry, beauty, order).

Cognitive Theory: "I Think, Therefore I Am Consistent"

The brain within its groove
Runs evenly and true . . .

EMILY DICKINSON

"I think, therefore I am," said the French philosopher René Descartes. If he had been a cognitive psychologist, he might have said, "I think, therefore I am *consistent.*"

Cognitive theorists note that people represent their worlds mentally. They hypothesize that people are born scientists who strive to understand the world so that they can predict and control events. In order to predict and control events, one must represent the world accurately. This means that people are also motivated to eliminate inconsistences in their worldviews.

For example, Sandra Bem (1993) argues that children try to create consistency between their own gender and their society's "gender schema"—their society's expectations of what behaviors are appropriate for males and females. As soon as they know whether they are male or female, children imitate the behavior of adults of the same gender. Leon Festinger (1957) believed that people are generally motivated to hold consistent beliefs and to justify their behavior. That is why we are more likely to appreciate what we must work to obtain.

Evaluation of Theories of Motivation

There are thus various perspectives on motivation. Let us evaluate them to see which one or ones seem to be most logical and most consistent with the research evidence.

There is no question that many animals are born with preprogrammed tendencies to respond to certain situations in certain ways. Yet instinct theory has been criticized for providing circular explanations of human behavior. In a circular explanation, we say that one thing (A) causes another (B); then, when we see B, we say it is occurring because of A. For example, we might argue a maternal instinct (A) causes mothers to care for their children (B); then we observe a mother caring for her child (B) and accept her behavior as proof of the existence of the maternal instinct (A). We have really just come full circle and explained nothing. As another example, consider William James's notion that sympathy is an instinct. Many people are cruel and cold-hearted; are we to assume that they possess less of this "instinct"? Such an explanation would also be circular.

Then, too, there is the question of how important instincts are to human beings. Some behaviors, including reflexes and the development of attachment in infants, may be considered instinctive (Ainsworth & Bowlby, 1991). However, there is so much variation in human behavior that most of it would appear to be learned, planned, or influenced by cultural values. For example, some evolutionary psychologists suggest that women but not men may be "naturally" monogamous (Bjorklund & Kipp, 1996; Buss, 1994). Their views are somewhat speculative, but let us note that U.S. cultural values in the "Swinging Sixties" motivated many women to have sexual relationships with multiple partners. Moreover, despite all the media hoopla about affairs in high places, it appears that most men in the United States adhere to marital vows of sexual faithfulness (Laumann et al., 1994).

Drive-reduction theory appears to apply in physiological drives such as hunger and thirst. However, we often eat when we are not hungry! Drive reduction also runs aground when we consider evidence showing that we often act in ways that *increase,* rather than decrease, the tensions acting on us. When we are hungry, for example, we may take the time to prepare a gourmet meal instead of a snack, even though the snack would satisfy the hunger drive sooner. We drive fast cars, ride roller coasters, and skydive for sport—all activities that heighten rather than decrease arousal.

People and many lower animals also seek novel stimulation. We may be willing to try a new dish ("just a taste") even when we feel full. We often seek novel ways of doing things—shunning the tried and the true—because of the stimulation provided by novelty. Yet the familiar tried-and-true ways would reduce tension more reliably. In view of examples like these, some psychologists have theorized the existence of stimulus motives that outweigh the motivation to reduce drives.

Critics of Maslow's theory argue that there is too much individual variation for the hierarchy of motives to apply to everyone. Some people whose physiological, safety, and love needs are met show little interest in achievement and recognition. Some artists, musicians, and writers devote themselves fully to their art, even if they have to live in an attic or basement to do so. However, people do appear to seek distant, self-actualizing goals, even while exposing themselves to great danger. This behavior is certainly more consistent with a humanistic than a drive-reductionist explanation of human behavior.

Some psychologists criticize cognitive theory for its reliance on unobservable concepts such as mental representations rather than observable behavior. However, cognitive psychologists tie their concepts to observable behavior, whenever possible. It also appears to be difficult to explain a child's active efforts to experiment with and understand other people and the world without resorting to cognitive concepts (Meltzoff & Gopnik, 1997).

It seems that each of the theories of motivation has something to offer. Each would appear to apply to certain aspects of behavior. As the chapter progresses, we will describe research that lends some support to each of these theories. Let us first describe research on the hunger drive. Hunger is based on physiological needs, and drive reduction would appear to explain some—although not all—eating behavior.

HUNGER: DO YOU GO BY "TUMMY-TIME"?

I go by tummy-time and I want my dinner.

SIR WINSTON CHURCHILL

We need food to survive, but to many of us food means more than survival. Food is a symbol of family togetherness and caring. We associate food with the nurturance of the parent-child relationship, with visits home during holidays. Friends and relatives offer us food when we enter their homes, and saying no may be viewed as a personal rejection. Bacon and eggs, coffee with cream and sugar, meat and mashed potatoes—all seem to be part of sharing U.S. values and agricultural abundance. What bodily mechanisms regulate the hunger drive? What psychological processes are at work?

HUNGER.
How do *you* feel while waiting for someone to carve the meat? Hunger is a physiological drive that motivates us to eat. Why do we feel hungry? Why do we feel satiated? Why do many people continue to eat when they have already supplied their bodies with the needed nutrients?

Bodily Mechanisms That Regulate Hunger

In considering the bodily mechanisms that regulate hunger, let us begin with the mouth. This is an appropriate choice because we are discussing eating. Chewing and swallowing provide some sensations of **satiety,** or satisfaction with the amount eaten. If they did not, we might eat for a long time after we had taken in enough food. It takes the digestive tract time to metabolize food and provide signals of satiety to the brain by way of the bloodstream.

In classic "sham feeding" experiments with dogs, researchers implanted a tube in the animals' throats so that any food swallowed fell out of the dog's body. Even though no food arrived at the stomach, the animals stopped feeding after a brief period (Janowitz & Grossman, 1949). Thus the sensations of chewing and swallowing must provide some feelings of satiety. However, the dogs in the study resumed feeding sooner than animals whose food did reach the stomach. Let us proceed to the stomach, too, as we seek further regulatory factors in hunger.

THE STOMACH An empty stomach leads to stomach contractions, which we call *hunger pangs.* Classic research suggested that stomach contractions are crucial to hunger. A man (A. L. Washburn) swallowed a balloon that was inflated in his stomach. His stomach contractions squeezed the balloon, so the contractions could be recorded by observers. Washburn also pressed a key when he felt hungry, and the researchers found a correspondence between his stomach contractions and his feelings of hunger (Cannon & Washburn, 1912).

But stomach contractions are not as influential as formerly thought. (We apparently go by more than "tummy-time.") Medical observations and classic research also find that people and animals whose stomachs have been removed still regulate food intake so as to maintain their normal weight (Tsang, 1938). (Food is absorbed through their intestines.) This finding led to the discovery of many other mechanisms that regulate hunger, including the hypothalamus, blood sugar level, and even receptors in the liver. When we are deprived of food, the level of sugar in the blood drops. The drop in blood sugar is communicated to the hypothalamus and apparently indicates that we have been burning energy and need to replenish it by eating.

THE HYPOTHALAMUS If you were just reviving from a surgical operation, fighting your way through the fog of the anesthesia, food would probably be the last thing on your mind. But when a researcher uses a probe to destroy the **ventromedial nucleus** (VMN) of a rat's hypothalamus, the rat gropes toward food as soon as its eyes open. Then it eats vast quantities of Purina Rat Chow or whatever else it likes.

The VMN seems to be able to function like a "stop-eating center" in the rat's brain. If the VMN is electrically stimulated—that is, "switched on"—the rat stops eating until the current is turned off. When the VMN is destroyed, the rat becomes **hyperphagic.** It continues to eat until it has about doubled its normal weight (see Figure ME.2). Then it levels off its eating rate and maintains the higher weight. It is as if the set point of the stop-eating center has been raised to a higher level, like turning up the thermostat in a house from 65° to 70°F (Keesey, 1986). Hyperphagic rats are also more finicky. They eat more fats or sweet-tasting food, but if their food is salty or bitter they actually eat less. Some people develop tumors near the base of the brain, damaging the ventromedial nucleus of the hypothalamus and apparently causing them to overeat and grow obese (Miller, 1995).

FIGURE ME.2
A HYPERPHAGIC RAT.
This rodent winner of the basketball look-alike contest went on a binge after it received a lesion in the ventromedial nucleus (VMN) of the hypothalamus. It is as if the lesion pushed the "set point" for body weight up several notches; the rat's weight is now about five times normal. But now it eats only enough to maintain its pleasantly plump stature, so you need not be concerned that it will eventually burst. If the lesion had been made in the lateral hypothalamus, the animal might have become the "Twiggy" of the rat world.

SATIETY The state of being satisfied; fullness.

VENTROMEDIAL NUCLEUS A central area on the underside of the hypothalamus that appears to function as a stop-eating center.

HYPERPHAGIC Characterized by excessive eating.

The **lateral hypothalamus** may function like a "start-eating center." If you electrically stimulate the lateral hypothalamus, the rat starts to eat (Miller, 1995). If you destroy the lateral hypothalamus, the rat may stop eating altogether—that is, become **aphagic.** If you force-feed an aphagic rat for a while, however, it begins to eat on its own and levels off at a relatively low body weight. It is as if you have lowered the rat's set point. It is like turning down the thermostat from, say, 70° to 40° F.

Psychological Influences

Although many areas of the body work in concert to regulate the hunger drive, this is only part of the story. In human beings, the hunger drive is more complex. Psychological as well as physiological factors play an important role. How many times have you been made hungry by the sight or aroma of food? How many times have you eaten not because you were hungry but because you were at a relative's home or in a cafeteria? The next section further explores psychological factors that affect eating.

Obesity—A Serious and Pervasive Problem

There is no sincerer love than the love of food.

GEORGE BERNARD SHAW

The two biggest sellers in any bookstore are the cookbooks and the diet books. The cookbooks tell you how to prepare the food and the diet books tell you how not to eat any of it.

ANDY ROONEY

Consider some facts about obesity:

- The prevalence of obesity in the United States has increased by 25% in the last decade (Brownell, 1997).
- One American adult in 3 is obese (Meyer, 1997).
- Nearly half of African American women are obese, possibly because they have lower metabolic rates than White women do (Brody, 1997).
- Americans eat more than a total of 800 billion calories of food each day (200 billion calories more than they need to maintain their weights). The extra calories could feed a nation of 80 million people.
- Within a few years, most dieters regain most of the weight they have lost, even when they have used diet pills "successfully" (Rosenbaum et al., 1997).
- About 300,000 Americans die each year because of excess weight (Brownell, 1997).

American culture idealizes slender heroes and heroines. For those who "more than measure up" to TV and film idols, food may have replaced sex as the central source of guilt. Obese people encounter more than their fair share of illnesses, including heart disease, diabetes, gout, respiratory problems, even certain kinds of cancer. If obesity is connected with health problems and unhappiness with the image in the mirror, why do so many people overeat? Psychological research has contributed to our understanding of obesity and what can be done about it.

BIOLOGICAL FACTORS IN OBESITY Numerous biological factors are involved in obesity, including heredity, adipose tissue (body fat), and metabolism (the rate at which the individual converts calories to energy).

TRUTH OR FICTION REVISITED
It is true that 1 adult American in 3 is obese.

TRUTH OR FICTION REVISITED
Yes, Americans do overeat by an amount great enough to feed the entire nation of Germany. The excess calories would feed another 80 million people!

LATERAL HYPOTHALAMUS An area at the side of the hypothalamus that appears to function as a start-eating center.

APHAGIC Characterized by undereating.

SOCIOCULTURAL FACTORS IN OBESITY

Rates of obesity among ethnic groups in our society. Obesity is more prevalent among people of color, especially African Americans, Hispanic Americans, and Native Americans than it is among non-Hispanic White Americans. Racial and ethnic differences are most pronounced among women (see Figure ME.3). The question is, why? Many of the answers might be found in socioeconomic factors and acculturation.

SOCIOECONOMIC FACTORS

Socioeconomic factors play a role in obesity. Obesity is more prevalent among poorer people (Ernst & Harlan, 1991; Stunkard & Sørensen, 1993). People of color are typically of lower socioeconomic status than White Americans, so it is not surprising that rates of obesity tend to be higher among Blacks and Hispanics, particularly among women (McMurtrie, 1994).

People on the lower rungs of the socioeconomic ladder appear to have a greater risk of obesity for several reasons. One is that more affluent people have greater access to information about nutrition and health. They have greater access to health-care providers. The fitness boom has been largely limited to more affluent people, so poorer people are more likely to remain sedentary. Wealthier people also have the time and income to participate in organized fitness programs. Many poor people in the inner city also turn to food as a way of coping with the stresses of poverty, discrimination, crowding, and crime.

Results from a study in San Antonio Texas provide clear evidence of the link between socioeconomic status and obesity (Hazuda et al., 1991). Obesity is less prevalent among both Mexican Americans and non-Hispanic White Americans who live in higher income neighborhoods than among those living in poorer neighborhoods. In other words, the link between socioeconomic level and obesity holds across ethnic groups.

ACCULTURATION AND OBESITY

Acculturation is the process by which immigrant or native groups adopt the cultural values, attitudes, and behaviors of the host or dominant society. Acculturation may help immigrant people to adapt more successfully to their new culture, but it can become a double-edged sword in terms of health if it involves adoption of unhealthful dietary practices of the host culture. For example, Japanese American men living in California and Hawaii eat a higher fat diet than Japanese men living in Japan do. Not surprisingly, *the prevalence of obesity is two to three times higher among the Japanese American men than among men living in Japan* (Curb & Marcus, 1991).

Acculturation may also contribute to high rates of obesity among Native Americans, who are more likely than non-Hispanic White Americans to have diseases linked to obesity, such as cardiovascular disease and diabetes (Broussard et al., 1991; Young & Sevenhuysen, 1989). A study of several hundred Cree and Ojibwa Indians in Canada found that nearly 90% of the women in the 45 to 54 age group were obese. The adoption of a high-fat Western-style diet, the destruction of physically demanding native industries, and chronic unemployment combined with low levels of physical activity are cited as factors contributing to obesity among Native Americans in the United States and Canada. ■

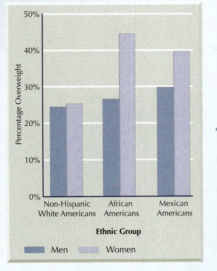

FIGURE ME.3.
PREVALENCE OF OVERWEIGHT INDIVIDUALS AMONG NON-HISPANIC WHITE AMERICANS, AFRICAN AMERICANS, AND MEXICAN AMERICANS.
What factors contribute to ethnic differences in obesity?

A Sampler of Dietary Methods. At any given time nearly half of the adult American population is on a diet. Dieting has become the "normal" pattern of eating for women. Dozens of diets vie for attention on bookstore shelves. How can we know which ones contain truth and which ones contain fiction?

Obesity runs in families. It was once assumed that obese parents encouraged their children to be overweight by serving fattening foods and setting poor examples. However, a study of Scandinavian adoptees by Stunkard and his colleagues (1990) found that children bear a closer resemblance in weight to their biological parents than to their adoptive parents. Heredity, then, plays a role in obesity (Friedman & Brownell, 1995).

The efforts of obese people to maintain a slender profile may also be sabotaged by microscopic units of life within their own bodies: fat cells. No, fat cells are not overweight cells. They are adipose tissue, or cells that store fat. Hunger might be related to the amount of fat stored in these cells. As time passes after a meal, the blood sugar level drops. Fat is then drawn from these cells to provide further nourishment. At some point, referred to as the *set point*, fat deficiency in these cells is communicated to the hypothalamus, triggering the hunger drive.

People with more adipose tissue than others feel food deprived earlier, even though they may be equal in weight. This might occur because more signals are being sent to the brain. Obese and *formerly* obese people tend to have more adipose tissue than people of normal weight. Thus many people who have lost weight complain that they are always hungry when they try to maintain normal weight levels.

Fatty tissue also metabolizes (burns) food more slowly than muscle does. For this reason, a person with a high fat-to-muscle ratio metabolizes food more slowly than a person of the same weight with a lower fat-to-muscle ratio. That is, two people who are identical in weight metabolize food at different rates, depending on the distribution of muscle and fat in their bodies. Obese people therefore are doubly handicapped in their efforts to lose weight—not only by their extra weight but by the fact that much of their body is composed of adipose tissue.

In a sense, the normal distribution of fat cells could be considered "sexist." The average man is 40% muscle and 15% fat. The average woman is 23% muscle and 25% fat. If a man and a woman with typical distributions of muscle and fat are of equal weight, therefore, the woman—who has more fat cells—has to eat less to maintain that weight.

Ironically, the very act of dieting can make it progressively more difficult to lose additional weight. This is because people on diets and those who have lost substantial amounts of weight burn fewer calories. That is, their metabolic rates slow down (Schwartz & Seeley, 1997; Wadden et al., 1997). This appears to be a built-in mechanism that helps preserve life in times of famine. However, it also makes it more difficult for dieters to continue to lose weight. The pounds seem to come off more and more reluctantly.

PSYCHOLOGICAL INFLUENCES Psychological factors, such as observational learning, stress, and emotional states, also play a role in obesity (Greeno & Wing, 1994). Our children are exposed to an average of 10,000 food commercials a year. More than 9 of 10 of these commercials are for fast foods (like McDonald's fries), sugared cereals, candy, and soft drinks (Brownell, 1997). Situations also play a role. Family celebrations, watching TV, arguments, and tension at work can all lead to overeating or going off a diet (Drapkin et al., 1995). Efforts to diet may be also impeded by negative emotions like depression and anxiety (Cools et al., 1992).

CONTROLLING YOUR WEIGHT Do you need to shed a few pounds? Perhaps, but psychologists warn that not everyone should be trying to slim down. Women in the United States today are under social pressure to conform to an unnaturally slender female ideal (Brownell & Rodin, 1994).

As a result, they tend to set unrealistic weight loss goals (Foster et al., 1997). Moreover, many attempts to lose weight are ineffective. For many obese people, however, especially those who are severely obese, shedding excess pounds lowers the risks of health problems such as diabetes and heart disease.

Research on motivation and on methods of therapy has enhanced our knowledge of healthful ways to lose weight. Sound weight control programs do not involve fad diets such as fasting, eliminating carbohydrates, or eating excessive amounts of one particular food. Instead, they involve changes in lifestyle that include improving nutritional knowledge, decreasing calorie intake, exercising, and changing eating habits (see Table ME.1).

Most people in the United States eat too much fat and not enough fruits and vegetables (Kumanyika, 1996). Eating foods low in saturated fats and cholesterol not only is good for the heart but also can contribute to weight loss. Because dietary fat is converted into bodily fat more efficiently than carbohydrates are, a low-fat diet also leads to weight loss. Nutritional knowledge leads to suggestions for taking in fewer calories, which results in lower weight. Taking in fewer calories does not just mean eating smaller portions. It means switching to some lower calorie foods—relying more on fresh, unsweetened fruits and vegetables (eating apples rather than apple pie), fish and poultry, and skim milk and cheese. It means cutting down on—or eliminating—butter, margarine, oils, and sugar.

The same foods that help control weight also tend to be high in vitamins and fiber and low in fats. Such foods therefore may also reduce the risk of developing heart disease, cancer, and a number of other illnesses.

Dieting plus exercise is more effective than dieting alone for shedding pounds and keeping them off. When we restrict our intake of calories, our metabolic rate compensates by slowing down (Wadden et al., 1997). Exercise burns calories and builds muscle tissue, which metabolizes more calories than fatty tissue does.

Cognitive and behavioral methods have also provided many strategies for losing weight. Among them are the following:

Establish calorie-intake goals and keep track of whether you are meeting them. Get a book that shows how many calories are found in foods. Keep a diary of your calorie intake.

TABLE ME.1

DIETARY RECOMMENDATIONS OF THE AMERICAN ACADEMY OF SCIENCES

Reduce your total fat intake to 30% or less of your total calorie intake.

Reduce your intake of saturated fats to less than 10% of your total calorie intake.

Reduce your cholesterol intake to less than 300 mg per day.

Eat 5 or more servings of vegetables and fruits each day.

Increase your intake of starches and other complex carbohydrates by eating 6 or more servings of breads, cereals, and legumes each day.

Keep your intake of protein to moderate levels.

Limit your total intake of sodium (salt) to 2400 mg or less per day.

Maintain adequate intake of calcium.

Source: Popkin, B. M., Siega-Riz, A. M., & Haines, P. S. (1996). A comparison of dietary trends among racial and socioeconomic groups in the United States. *New England Journal of Medicine, 335,* 716–720.

Substitute low-calorie foods for high-calorie foods. Fill your stomach with celery rather than cheesecake and enchiladas. Eat preplanned low-calorie snacks instead of binge eating a jar of peanuts or a container of ice cream.

Take a 5-minute break between helpings. Ask yourself whether you're still hungry. If not, stop eating.

Avoid temptations that have sidetracked you in the past. Shop at the mall with the Alfalfa Sprout Café, not the Cheesecake Factory. Plan your meal before entering a restaurant. (Avoid ogling that tempting full-color menu.) Attend to your own plate, not to the sumptuous dish at the next table. (Your salad probably looks greener to them, anyhow.) Shop from a list. Walk briskly through the supermarket, preferably after dinner when you're no longer hungry. Don't be sidetracked by pretty packages (fattening things may come in them). Don't linger in the kitchen. Study, watch TV, or write letters elsewhere. Don't bring fattening foods into the house. Prepare only enough food to keep within your calorie goals.

Exercise to burn more calories and increase your metabolic rate. Reach for your mate, not your plate (to coin a phrase). Take a brisk walk instead of eating an unplanned snack. Build exercise routines by adding a few minutes each week.

Reward yourself for meeting calorie goals (but not with food). Imagine how great you will look in that new swimsuit next summer. Do not go to the latest movie unless you have met your weekly calorie goal. When you meet your weekly calorie goal, put cash in the bank toward a vacation or a new camera.

Use imagery to help yourself lose weight. Tempted by a fattening dish? Imagine that it's rotten, that you would be nauseated by it and have a sick taste in your mouth for the rest of the day.

Mentally walk through solutions to problem situations. Consider what you will do when cake is handed out at the office party. Rehearse your next visit to relatives who tell you how painfully thin you look and try to stuff you with food (Drapkin et al., 1995). Imagine how you will politely (but firmly) refuse seconds and thirds, despite their objections.

Above all, if you slip from your plan for a day, don't blow things out of proportion. Dieters are often tempted to binge, especially when they rigidly see themselves either as perfect successes or as complete failures or when they experience powerful emotions—either positive or negative (Cools et al., 1992). Consider the weekly or monthly trend, not just a single day. Credit yourself for the long-term trend. If you do binge, resume dieting the next day.

Losing weight—and keeping it off—is not easy, but it can be done. Making a commitment to losing weight and establishing a workable plan for doing so are two of the keys.

STIMULUS MOTIVES

One day when my daughter Taylor was 5 months old, I was batting her feet. (Why not?) She was sitting back in her mother's lap, and I repeatedly batted her feet up toward her middle with the palms of my hands. After a while, she began to laugh. When I stopped, she pushed a foot toward me, churned her arms back and forth, and blew bubbles as forcefully as she could. So I batted her feet again. She laughed and pushed them toward me again. This went on for a while, and it dawned on me that Taylor was doing what she could to make the stimulation last.

Physical needs give rise to drives like hunger and thirst. In such cases, organisms are motivated to *reduce* the tension or stimulation that impinges on them. But in the case of **stimulus motives**, organisms seek to *increase* stimulation, as Taylor did when she sought to have me bat her feet.

STIMULUS MOTIVES Motives to increase the stimulation impinging on an organism.

Stimulus motives include sensory stimulation, activity, exploration, and manipulation of the environment.

Some stimulus motives provide a clear evolutionary advantage. Humans and lower animals that are motivated to learn about and manipulate their environment are more likely to survive. Learning about the environment increases awareness of resources and of potential dangers, and manipulation permits one to change the environment in beneficial ways. Exploring the environment helps animals locate sources of food and places to hide from predators. Learning and manipulation thus increase the animal's chances of survival until sexual maturity and of transmitting whatever genetic codes may underlie these motives to future generations.

SENSATION SEEKING?
Why do some people choose to hurl themselves into the sky? Are they raising their arousal to more stimulating levels?

Sensory Stimulation and Activity

When I was a teenager during the 1950s, I was unaware that some lucky students at McGill University in Montreal were being paid $20 a day (which, with inflation, would now be well above $100) for doing absolutely nothing. Would you like to "work" by doing nothing for $100 a day? Don't answer too quickly. According to the results of classic research on sensory deprivation, you might not like it at all.

Student volunteers were placed in quiet cubicles and blindfolded (Bexton et al., 1954). Their arms were bandaged, and they could hear nothing but the dull, continuous hum of air conditioning. With nothing to do, many of the students slept for a while. After a few hours of sensory-deprived wakefulness, most felt bored and irritable. As time went on, many of them grew more uncomfortable, and some reported hallucinations of images of dots and geometric shapes.

Many students quit the experiment during the first day despite the financial incentive. Many of those who remained for a few days found it difficult to concentrate on simple problems for a few days afterward. For many, the experimental conditions did not provide a relaxing vacation. Instead, they produced boredom and disorientation.

TRUTH OR FICTION REVISITED
It is not true that getting away from it all by going on a vacation from all sensory input for a few hours is relaxing. If it is carried out like the experiment at McGill University, such a "vacation" may be highly stressful.

Exploration and Manipulation

Have you ever brought a dog or cat into a new home? At first, it may show excitement. New kittens are also known to hide under a couch or bed for a few hours. But then they begin to explore every corner of their new environment. When placed in novel environments, many animals appear to possess an innate motive to engage in exploratory behavior.

Once they are familiar with their environment, both lower animals and humans appear to be motivated to seek novel stimulation. For example, when they have not been deprived of food for a great deal of time, rats often explore unfamiliar arms of mazes rather than head straight for the section of the maze in which they have learned to expect food. Animals who have just copulated and thereby reduced their sex drives often show renewed interest in sexual behavior when presented with a novel sex partner. Monkeys learn how to manipulate gadgets for the incentive of being able to observe novel stimulation through a window (see Figure ME.4). Children spend hour after hour manipulating the controls of video games for the pleasure of zapping video monsters.

The question has arisen of whether people and animals seek to explore and manipulate their environment *because* these activities help them reduce primary drives such as hunger and thirst or whether they engage in these activities for their own sake. Many psychologists believe that such stimulating activities are reinforcing in and of themselves. Monkeys

FIGURE ME.4
THE ALLURE OF NOVEL STIMULATION.

People and many lower animals are motivated to explore the environment and to seek novel stimulation. This monkey has learned to unlock a door for the privilege of viewing a model train.

FIGURE ME.5
MONKEYING AROUND.

Is there such a thing as a manipulation drive? These young rhesus monkeys appear to monkey around with gadgets just for the fun of it. No external incentives are needed. Children similarly enjoy manipulating gadgets that honk, squeak, rattle, and buzz, even though the resultant honks and squeaks do not satisfy physiological drives such as hunger or thirst.

do seem to get a kick out of "monkeying around" with gadgets (see Figure ME.5). They learn how to manipulate hooks and eyes and other mechanical devices without any external incentive whatsoever (Harlow et al., 1950). Young children prolong their play with "busy boxes"—boxes filled with objects that honk, squeak, rattle, and buzz when manipulated in certain ways. They seem to find discovery of the cause-and-effect relationships in these gadgets pleasurable even though they are not rewarded with food, ice cream, or even hugs from their parents.

COGNITIVE-DISSONANCE THEORY: MAKING THINGS FIT

Do I contradict myself?
Very well then I contradict myself,
(I am large, I contain multitudes.)

WALT WHITMAN, *Song of Myself*

Most of us are unlike Walt Whitman, according to cognitive-dissonance theory (Festinger, 1957; Festinger & Carlsmith, 1959). Whitman may not have minded contradicting himself, but most people do not like their attitudes (cognitions) to be inconsistent. Cognitive theorists propose that organisms are motivated to create realistic mental maps of the world. Organisms adjust their representations of the world, as needed, to make things fit. Awareness that two cognitions are dissonant, or that our attitudes are incompatible with our behavior, is unpleasant and motivates us to reduce the discrepancy.

Effort Justification: "If I Did It, It Must Be Important"?

In the first and still one of the best known studies on cognitive dissonance, one group of participants received $1 for telling someone else that a boring task was interesting (Festinger & Carlsmith, 1959). Members of a second group received $20 to describe the chore positively. Both groups were paid to engage in **attitude-discrepant behavior**—that is, behavior that ran counter to their cognitions. After "selling" the job to others, the participants were asked to rate their own liking for it. Ironically, those who were paid *less* rated the task as more interesting. Why?

According to learning theory, this result would be confusing. Learning theory would say that the more we are reinforced for doing something, the more we should like it. But that is not what happened here. In contrast, cognitive-dissonance theory would predict this "less-leads-to-more effect" for the following reason: The cognitions "I was paid very little" and "I told someone that this assignment was interesting" are dissonant. People tend to engage in **effort justification.** The discomfort of cognitive dissonance motivates them to explain their behavior to themselves in such a way that unpleasant undertakings seem worth it. Participants who were paid only $1 may have justified their lie by concluding that they may not have been lying in the first place. Similarly, we appreciate things more when they are more difficult to obtain.

Consider another situation. Many people have very strong political beliefs and fear what might happen if the "wrong" candidate was elected to public office. They tend to see their own candidates as better for their town or state or country, and some even believe that their candidate must win to save the nation from harmful forces. They are therefore strongly motivated to believe that their candidate will be elected. They pin their hopes as well as their ideology on their candidate. Cognitive dissonance

TRUTH OR FICTION REVISITED

It is true that we appreciate things more when we have to work for them. This is an example of the principle of effort justification.

ATTITUDE-DISCREPANT BEHAVIOR Behavior inconsistent with an attitude that may have the effect of modifying an attitude.

EFFORT JUSTIFICATION In cognitive-dissonance theory, the tendency to seek justification (acceptable reasons) for strenuous efforts.

would then be created if they were to believe that their candidates were likely to lose and not to win. Research shows that in presidential elections from 1952 to 1980, 4 out of 5 people reduced such dissonance by expressing the belief that their candidate would win (Granberg & Brent, 1983). Nearly half of them were wrong, of course. Yet they often clung to their prediction despite lopsided polls to the contrary. It is the triumph of dissonance reduction, and perhaps of hope, over judgment.

THE THREE A'S OF MOTIVATION: ACHIEVEMENT, AFFILIATION, AND AGGRESSION

Let us consider some of the powerful motives that bind us together or tear us asunder: achievement, affiliation, and aggression. The Harvard psychologist Henry Murray (1938) hypothesized that each of these "A's" reflects a psychological need. He also referred to them as *social motives,* which he believed differ from primary motives such as hunger in that they are acquired through social learning. However, contemporary researchers believe that hereditary predispositions may also play a role in these behavior patterns. Evolutionary psychologists believe that "genetic whisperings" influence tendencies toward achievement, affiliation, aggression, and many other aspects of personality and social behavior, even if we can also often point to environmental influences (Buss et al., 1998; Plomin et al., 1997; Rose, 1995).

Achievement: "Just Do It"

Many students persist in studying despite being surrounded by distractions. Many people strive relentlessly to get ahead, to "make it," to earn large sums of money, to invent, to accomplish the impossible. These people are said to have strong achievement motivation.

Psychologist David McClelland (1958) helped pioneer the assessment of achievement motivation through evaluation of fantasies. One method involves the Thematic Apperception Test (TAT), developed by Henry Murray. The TAT contains cards with pictures and drawings that are subject to various interpretations. Individuals are shown one or more TAT cards and asked to construct stories about the pictured theme: to indicate what led up to it, what the characters are thinking and feeling, and what is likely to happen.

One TAT card is similar to that in Figure ME.6. The meaning of the card is ambiguous—unclear. Is the girl sleeping, thinking about the book, wishing she were out with friends? Consider two stories that could be told about this card:

> Story 1: "She's upset that she's got to read the book because she's behind in her assignments and doesn't particularly like to work. She'd much rather be out with her friends, and she may very well sneak out to do just that."

> Story 2: "She's thinking, 'Someday I'll be a great scholar. I'll write books like this, and everybody will be proud of me.' She reads all the time."

The second story suggests the presence of more achievement motivation than the first. Classic studies find that people with high achievement

FIGURE ME.6

TAPPING FANTASIES IN PERSONALITY RESEARCH.

This picture is similar to a Thematic Apperception Test card used to measure the need for achievement. What is happening in this picture? What is the person thinking and feeling? What is going to happen? Your answers to these questions reflect your own needs as well as the content of the picture itself.

motivation earn higher grades than people with comparable learning ability but lower achievement motivation. They are more likely to earn high salaries and be promoted than less motivated people with similar opportunities. They perform better at math problems and at unscrambling anagrams, such as decoding RSTA into STAR, TARS, ARTS, or RATS.

McClelland (1965) used the TAT to sort college students into groups—students with high achievement motivation and students with low achievement motivation. He found that 83% of college graduates with high achievement motivation found jobs in occupations characterized by risk, decision making, and the chance for great success, such as business management, sales, or self-employment. Most (70%) of the graduates who chose nonentrepreneurial positions showed low achievement motivation. People with high achievement motivation seem to prefer challenges and are willing to take moderate risks to achieve their goals.

WHAT FLAVOR IS YOUR ACHIEVEMENT MOTIVATION? Do you want to do well in this course? If you do, why? Carol Dweck (1997) finds that achievement motivation can be driven by different forces. Are you motivated mainly by performance goals? That is, is your grade in the course of most importance? If it is, it may be in part because your motives concern tangible rewards such as getting into graduate school, landing a good job, reaping approval from parents or your instructor, or avoiding criticism. Performance goals are usually met through extrinsic rewards such as prestige and income. Parents of children who develop performance goals are likely to respond to good grades with tangible rewards such as toys or money and to respond to poor grades with anger and removal of privileges.

Or do learning goals mainly motivate you to do well? That is, is your central motive the enhancing of your knowledge and skills—your ability to understand and master the subject matter? Learning goals usually lead to intrinsic rewards, such as satisfaction with oneself. Students who develop learning goals often have parents with strong achievement motivation, parents who encourage their children to think and act independently from an early age. They help their children develop learning goals by showing warmth and praising them for their efforts to learn, exposing them to novel and stimulating experiences, and encouraging persistence, enjoyment, and independence (Dweck, 1997; Ginsburg & Bronstein, 1993; Gottfried et al., 1994). Children of such parents frequently set high standards for themselves, associate their achievements with self-worth, and attribute their achievements to their own efforts rather than to chance or to the intervention of others.

Of course, many of us strive to meet both performance and learning goals in many subjects, as well as in other areas of life. Grades are important because they are connected with (very) tangible benefits, but learning for its own sake is also of value.

Affiliation: "People Who Need People"

The motive for **affiliation** prompts us to make friends, join groups, and prefer to do things with others rather than alone. Affiliation motivation is part of the social glue that holds families and other groups together. In this sense, it is certainly a positive trait. Yet some people have such a strong need to affiliate that they find it painful to make their own decisions or to be alone. Research by Stanley Schachter suggests that a very high need to affiliate may indicate anxiety, such as when people "huddle together" in fear of some outside force.

In a classic experiment on the effects of anxiety on affiliation, Schachter (1959) manipulated participants' anxiety levels by leading them

AFFILIATION Association or connection with a group.

to believe that they would receive either painful electric shocks (the high-anxiety condition) or mild electric shocks (the low-anxiety condition). The participants were then asked to wait while the shock apparatus was supposedly being set up. They could choose to wait alone or in a room with others. The majority (63%) of those who expected a painful shock chose to wait in a room with other people. Only one third (33%) of those who expected a mild shock chose to wait with others.

Highly anxious participants were placed in two social conditions. In the first, they could choose either to wait alone or with others who would also receive painful shocks. Sixty percent of these people chose to affiliate—that is, to wait with others. In the second condition, highly anxious participants could choose to wait alone or with people they believed were not involved with the study. In this second condition, no one chose to affiliate.

Why did participants in Schachter's study wish to affiliate only with people who shared their misery? Schachter explained their choice with his **theory of social comparison.** This theory holds that in an ambiguous situation—that is, a situation in which we are not certain about what we should do or how we should feel—we affiliate with people with whom we can compare feelings and behaviors. Schachter's anxious recruits could compare their reactions with those of other "victims," but not with people who had no reason to feel anxious. Anxious participants may also have resented uninvolved people for "getting away free."

Aggression: Some Facts of Life and Death

Consider the following facts:

- After the end of the Cold War and the demise of the Soviet Union, you might have expected the world to become more peaceful. Yet civil wars and other conflicts rage on every continent.

- In the United States, violence has replaced communicable diseases as the leading cause of death among young people. Homicide has become the second leading cause of death among 15- to 24-year-olds (Lore & Schultz, 1993). (Accidents are the leading cause.)

- Aggression is not limited to foreign battlefields or dark streets and alleyways. Each year more than a million U.S. children are brought to the attention of authorities as victims of child abuse. "My sense is that something is deeply wrong with the core unit of our civilization, the family," notes former APA president Ronald Fox (1996). "It's no longer a safe haven for many Americans."

- Although the O. J. Simpson case may have brought the problem of domestic violence into the public eye, such violence is a national epidemic. At least 1 woman in 8 is subjected to violence at the hands of her partner each year, and about 2,000 of them die from it (Rathus et al., 2000). Women are more likely to be raped, injured, or killed by their current or former partners than by other types of assailants (Rathus et al., 2000).

Why do people treat each other like this? Let us consider some theories of aggression.

THE BIOLOGICAL PERSPECTIVE Numerous biological structures and chemicals appear to be involved in aggression. One is the hypothalamus. In response to certain stimuli, many lower animals show instinctive aggressive reactions. For example, the male robin responds aggressively to the red breast of another robin. The hypothalamus appears to be involved in this inborn reaction pattern: Electrical stimulation of part of the hypothalamus

TRUTH OR FICTION REVISITED
Schachter found that misery does love company—but only company of a special sort. That is, anxious people preferred to affiliate with other people who were anxious, not with people who seemed to be relaxed.

THEORY OF SOCIAL COMPARISON The view that people look to others for cues about how to behave when they are in confusing or unfamiliar situations.

triggers stereotypical aggressive behaviors in many lower animals. However, in humans, whose brains are more complex, other brain structures apparently moderate possible aggressive instincts.

Chemistry is also involved in aggression, especially in the form of the male sex hormone testosterone. Testosterone appears to affect the tendencies to dominate and control other people. Men have higher testosterone levels than women do and are also (usually) more aggressive than women, especially in contacts with male strangers (Berman et al., 1993). Testosterone levels vary somewhat with the occasion, and men's testosterone levels tend to be higher when they are "winning"—whether in athletic competitions such as football or even in chess (Christiansen & Knussman, 1987; Olweus, 1986). It could be that one reason men are more sexually aggressive than women is because of their tendency to dominate others.

The evolutionary view is that aggression is natural. Evolutionary psychologists view much social behavior, including aggressive behavior, as influenced by genetic factors such as brain structures and levels of testosterone. In his theory of evolution, Charles Darwin noted that many more individuals are produced than can find food and survive into adulthood. Therefore, there is a struggle for survival. Individuals who possess characteristics that give them an advantage in this struggle are more likely to mature and contribute their genes to the next generation. In many species, those characteristics include aggressiveness. Because aggressive individuals are more likely to survive and reproduce, whatever genes are linked to aggressive behavior are more likely to be transmitted to new generations.

In the case of humans, intelligence is also a key to survival. The capacity to outwit other species may be more important to human survival than aggressiveness. Now that humans have organized themselves into societies in which aggression is either outlawed or confined to athletic contests, it could be that intelligence and organizational skills are more important than aggressiveness in having one's genes transmitted to future generations.

THE PSYCHODYNAMIC PERSPECTIVE Sigmund Freud believed that aggressive impulses are inevitable reactions to the frustrations of daily life. Children (and adults) normally desire to vent aggressive impulses on other people, including parents, because even the most attentive parents cannot gratify all of their demands immediately. Yet children also fear punishment and loss of love, so they repress most aggressive impulses and store them in the unconscious recesses of the mind. The Freudian perspective, in a sense, sees humans as "steam engines." By holding in steam rather than venting it, we set the stage for future explosions. Pent-up aggressive impulses demand an outlet. They may be expressed toward parents in roundabout ways, such as destroying furniture; later in life they may be expressed toward strangers.

According to psychodynamic theory, the best way to prevent harmful aggression may be to encourage less harmful aggression. In the steam engine analogy, verbal aggression (through wit, sarcasm, or expression of negative feelings) may vent some of the aggressive steam in a person's unconscious mind. So might cheering on a football team or attending a prize fight. Psychoanalysts refer to the venting of aggressive impulses as **catharsis.** Catharsis thus is viewed as a safety valve. But research findings on the usefulness of catharsis are mixed. Some studies suggest that catharsis leads to pleasant reductions in tension and reduced likelihood of future aggression (e.g., Doob & Wood, 1972). Other studies, however, suggest that letting some steam escape actually encourages more aggression later on (e.g., Bushman et al., 1999). Research evidence has been hard on the psychodynamic perspective, yielding partial support for Freud's views at best.

CATHARSIS In psychodynamic theory, the purging of strong emotions or the relieving of tensions.

THE SOCIOCULTURAL PERSPECTIVE ON AGGRESSION

The sociocultural perspective focuses on ways in which ethnicity, gender, and cultural factors may be related to aggression. Note the following facts:

- African American men aged 15 to 34 are about 9 times as likely as non-Hispanic White Americans to be victims of homicide (Tomes, 1993).
- Hispanic American men are about 5 times as likely to be homicide victims (Tomes, 1993).
- Each year in the United States about 30 women per 1,000 are victims of violence at the hands of their male partners (Tomes, 1993).
- Perhaps half the women in the United States have been subjected to severe physical, sexual, or psychological abuse (Mednick, 1993).

Sociocultural theorists note that U.S. culture has a way of breeding violence. In Thailand and Jamaica, for example, aggression in children is discouraged and politeness and deference are encouraged (Tharp, 1991). Children in the United States are more likely to be argumentative, disobedient, and belligerent (Tharp, 1991).

In the United States, by contrast, competitiveness and independence are encouraged, especially among males. The lessons learned in competitive sports may particularly encourage males to violence (Levy, 1991). Coaches often urge boys to win at all costs. Boys are encouraged to dominate and vanquish their opponents, even if winning requires injuring or "taking out" the opposition. This philosophy may be carried from the playing field into social relationships. Some athletes distinguish between sports and social relationships, but others do not. ■

THE COGNITIVE PERSPECTIVE Cognitive psychologists assert that our behavior is influenced by our values, by how we interpret situations, and by choice. From the cognitive perspective, for example, people who believe that aggression is necessary and justified—as during wartime—are likely to act aggressively. People who believe that a particular war or act of aggression is unjust, or who oppose aggression regardless of the circumstances, are less likely to behave aggressively.

One cognitive theory suggests that frustration and discomfort trigger unpleasant feelings (Rule et al., 1987). These feelings, in turn, prompt aggression. Aggression is *not* automatic, however. Cognitive factors intervene (Berkowitz, 1994). People *decide*—sometimes making "split-second decisions"—whether they will strike out or not on the basis of factors such as their previous experiences with aggression and their interpretation of the other person's motives.

Researchers find that many aggressive people distort other people's motives. For example, they assume that other people wish them harm when they actually do not (Akhtar & Bradley, 1991; Dodge et al., 1990). Cognitive therapists note that we are more likely to respond aggressively to a provocation when we magnify the importance of the insult or otherwise stir up feelings of anger (e.g., Lochman & Dodge, 1994). How do you respond when someone bumps into you? If you view it as an intentional insult to your honor, you may respond with aggression. If you view it as an accident, or as a social problem in need of a solution, you are less likely to act aggressively.

LEARNING PERSPECTIVES Two types of learning perspectives are the behavioral perspective and the social-cognitive perspective. From the behavioral perspective, learning is acquired through reinforcement.

Organisms reinforced for aggressive behavior are more likely to behave aggressively in similar situations. Environmental consequences make it more likely that strong, agile organisms will be reinforced for aggressive behavior.

From the social-cognitive perspective, aggressive skills are mainly acquired by observation. Social-cognitive theorists do believe that consciousness and choice may play a role, however. In this view, we are not likely to act aggressively unless we believe that aggression is appropriate under the circumstances. The "Psychology in a World of Diversity" feature discusses the sociocultural perspective on aggression.

EMOTION: ADDING COLOR TO LIFE

Emotions color our lives. We are green with envy, red with anger, blue with sorrow. Poets paint a thoughtful mood as a "brown study." Positive emotions such as love and desire can fill our days with pleasure. Negative emotions such as fear, depression, and anger can fill us with dread and make each day a chore.

An emotion can be a response to a situation, in the way that fear is a response to a threat. An emotion can motivate behavior (e.g., anger can motivate us to act aggressively). An emotion can also be a goal in itself. We may behave in ways that lead us to experience joy or feelings of love.

Emotions are feeling states with physiological, cognitive, and behavioral components (Carlson & Hatfield, 1992). In terms of physiology, strong emotions arouse the autonomic nervous system (LeDoux, 1997). The greater the arousal, the more intense the emotion. It also appears that the type of arousal affects the emotion being experienced. Although the word *emotion* might seem to be about feeling and not about thinking, cognitions—particularly interpretations of the meanings of events—are important aspects of emotions. *Fear,* which usually occurs in response to a threat, involves cognitions that one is in danger as well as arousal of the **sympathetic nervous system** (rapid heartbeat and breathing, sweating, muscle tension). Emotions also involve behavioral tendencies. The emotion of fear is connected with behavioral tendencies to avoid or escape from the situation (see Table ME.2). As a response to a social provocation, *anger* involves cognitions that the provocateur should be paid back, arousal of both the sympathetic and **parasympathetic nervous systems,** and tendencies to attack. *Depression* usually involves cognitions of helplessness and hopelessness, parasympathetic arousal, and tendencies toward inactivity—or, sometimes—self-destruction. *Joy, grief, jealousy, disgust, embarrassment, liking*—all have cognitive, physiological, and behavioral components.

Just how many emotions are there and what are they? The ancient Chinese believed in four basic or instinctive emotions—happiness, anger,

EMOTION A state of feeling that has cognitive, physiological, and behavioral components.

SYMPATHETIC NERVOUS SYSTEM The branch of the automatic nervous system that is most active during processes that spend body energy from stored reserves, such as in a fight-or-flight response to a predator or when you are anxious about a big test. When people experience fear, the sympathetic nervous system accelerates the heart rate, raises the blood pressure, relaxes muscles, and so on.

PARASYMPATHETIC NERVOUS SYSTEM The branch of the automatic nervous system that is most actives during processes that restore reserves to the body, such a relaxing and eating. When people relax, the parasympathetic nervous system decelerates the heart rate, normalizes the blood pressure, relaxes muscles, and so on. The parasympathetic division also stimulates digestion.

TABLE ME.2

COMPONENTS OF EMOTIONS

EMOTION	PHYSIOLOGICAL	COGNITIVE	BEHAVIORAL
Fear	Sympathetic arousal	Belief that one is in danger	Avoidance tendencies
Anger	Sympathetic and parasympathetic arousal	Frustration or belief that one is being mistreated	Attack tendencies
Depression	Parasympathetic arousal	Thoughts of helplessness, hopelessness, worthlessness	Inactivity, possible self-destructive tendencies

sorrow, and fear. They arise, respectively, in the heart, liver, lungs, and kidneys (Carlson & Hatfield, 1992). (No, there is no evidence for this view.) The behaviorist psychologist John B. Watson (1924) believed that there are three basic or inborn emotions: fear, rage, and love. Others, such as Paul Ekman (1980) and Robert Plutchik (1984), have argued for larger numbers of basic emotions. The question remains unresolved (Fischer et al., 1990).

The Expression of Emotions

Joy and sadness are found in all cultures, but how can we tell when other people are happy or despondent? It turns out that the expression of many emotions may be universal (Rinn, 1991). Smiling is apparently a universal sign of friendliness and approval. Baring the teeth, as noted by Charles Darwin (1872) in the 19th century, may be a universal sign of anger. As the originator of the theory of evolution, Darwin believed that the universal recognition of facial expressions would have survival value. For example, in the absence of language, facial expressions could signal the approach of enemies (or friends).

Most investigators (e.g., Buss, 1992; Ekman, 1994; Izard, 1994) concur that certain facial expressions suggest the same emotions in all people. Moreover, people in diverse cultures recognize the emotions manifested by certain facial expressions. In a classic study, Paul Ekman (1980) took photographs of people exhibiting anger, disgust, fear, happiness, sadness, and surprise (see Figure ME.7). He then asked people around the world to indicate what emotions were being depicted. Those queried ranged from European college students to members of the Fore, a tribe that dwells in the New Guinea highlands. All groups, including the Fore, who had almost no contact with Western culture, agreed on the emotions being portrayed. The Fore also displayed familiar facial expressions when asked how they would respond if they were the characters in stories that called for basic emotional responses. Ekman and his colleagues (1987) obtained similar results in a study of 10 cultures. In that study, participants were allowed to identify more than one emotion in facial expressions. The participants generally agreed on which two emotions were being shown and which emotion was more intense.

FIGURE ME.7

PHOTOGRAPHS USED IN RESEARCH BY PAUL EKMAN.

Ekman's research suggests that the expression of several basic emotions such as happiness, anger, surprise, and fear is universally recognized.

 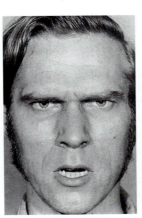 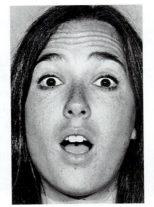 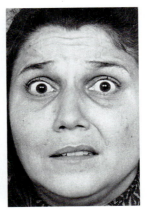

The Facial-Feedback Hypothesis

We generally recognize that facial expressions reflect emotional states. In fact, various emotional states give rise to certain patterns of electrical activity in the facial muscles and in the brain (Cacioppo et al., 1988). The **facial-feedback hypothesis** argues, however, that the causal relationship between emotions and facial expressions can also work in the opposite direction. Does this mean that smiling can give rise to feelings of goodwill? Can frowning produce anger? Perhaps.

Psychological research has yielded some interesting findings concerning the facial-feedback hypothesis (Ekman, 1993). Inducing people to smile, for example, leads them to report more positive feelings (Basic Behavioral Science Task Force, 1996) and to rate cartoons as more humorous. When induced to frown, they rate cartoons as more aggressive. When they exhibit pain through facial expressions, they rate electric shocks as more painful.

What are the possible links between facial feedback and emotion? One link is arousal. Intense contraction of facial muscles such as those used in signifying fear heightens arousal, which, in turn, boosts emotional response. Feedback from of the contraction of facial muscles may also induce feeling states. Ekman (1993) has found that engaging in the so-called Duchenne smile, characterized by "crow's feet wrinkles around the eyes and a subtle drop in the eye cover fold so that the skin above the eye moves down slightly toward the eyeball," can induce pleasant feelings.

You may have heard the British expression "Keep a stiff upper lip" as a recommendation for handling stress. It might be that a "stiff" lip suppresses emotional response—as long as the lip is relaxed rather than quivering with fear or tension. But when the lip is stiffened through strong muscle tension, facial feedback may heighten emotional response.

Theories of Emotion: "How Do You *Feel?*"

David, 32, is not sleeping well. He wakes before dawn and cannot get back to sleep. His appetite is off, his energy level is low, he has started smoking again. He has a couple of drinks at lunch and muses that it's lucky that any more alcohol makes him sick to his stomach—otherwise, he'd probably be drinking too much, too. Then he thinks, "So what difference would it make?" Sometimes he is sexually frustrated; at other times he wonders whether he has any sex drive left. Although he's awake, each day it's getting harder to drag himself out of bed in the morning. This week he missed one day of work and was late twice. His supervisor has suggested in a nonthreatening way that he "do something about it." David knows that her next warning will not be unthreatening. It's been going downhill since Sue walked out. Suicide has even crossed David's mind. He wonders if he's going crazy. (Rathus & Nevid, 1999, p. 3)

David is experiencing the emotion of depression, seriously so. Depression is to be expected following a loss, such as the end of a relationship, but David's feelings have lingered. His friends tell him that he should get out and do things, but David is so down that he hasn't the motivation to do much of anything at all. After much prompting by family and friends, David consults a psychologist who, ironically, also pushes him to get out and do things—the things he used to enjoy. The psychologist also shows David that part of his problem is that sees himself as a failure who cannot make meaningful changes.

TRUTH OR FICTION REVISITED
It is true that smiling can produce pleasant feelings. Research has shown that the Duchenne smile can indeed give rise to pleasant feelings.

FACIAL-FEEDBACK HYPOTHESIS The view that stereotypical facial expressions can contribute to stereotypical emotions.

Emotions have physiological, situational, and cognitive components, but psychologists disagree about how these components interact to produce feeling states and actions. Some psychologists argue that physiological arousal is a more basic component of emotional response than cognition and that the type of arousal we experience strongly influences our cognitive appraisal and our labeling of the emotion (e. g., Izard, 1984). For these psychologists, the body takes precedence over the mind. Do David's bodily reactions—for example, his loss of appetite and energy—take precedence over his cognitions? Other psychologists argue that cognitive appraisal and physiological arousal are so strongly intertwined that cognitive processes may determine the emotional response. Are David's ideas that he is helpless to make meaningful changes more at the heart of his feelings of depression?

The "commonsense theory" of emotions is that something happens (a situation) that is cognitively appraised (interpreted) by the person, and the feeling state (a combination of arousal and thoughts) follows. For example, you meet someone new, appraise that person as delightful, and feelings of attraction follow. Or, as in the case of David, a social relationship comes to an end, you recognize your loss, feel powerless to do anything to change it, and you feel down in the dumps.

However, both historic and contemporary theories of how the components of emotions interact are at variance with this commonsense view. Let us consider a number of theories and see if we can arrive at some useful conclusions.

THE JAMES-LANGE THEORY A century ago, William James suggested that our emotions follow, rather than cause, our behavioral responses to events. At about the same time this view was also proposed by the Danish physiologist Karl G. Lange. It is therefore termed the James-Lange theory of emotion.

According to James and Lange, certain external stimuli instinctively trigger specific patterns of arousal and action, such as fighting or fleeing (see Figure ME.8, part A). We then become angry *because* we are acting aggressively or become afraid *because* we are running away. Emotions are simply the cognitive representations (or by-products) of automatic physiological and behavioral responses.

The James-Lange theory is consistent with the facial-feedback hypothesis. That is, smiling apparently can induce pleasant feelings, even if the effect may not be strong enough to overcome feelings of sadness (Ekman, 1993). The theory also suggests that we may be able to change our feelings by changing our behavior. Changing one's behavior to change one's feelings is one aspect of behavior therapy. When David's psychologist urged him to get out and do things, she is assuming that by changing his behavior, David can have a positive effect on the way he feels.

Walter Cannon (1927) criticized the James-Lange assertion that each emotion has distinct physiological correlates. He argued that the physiological arousal associated with emotion A is not as distinct from the arousal associated with emotion B as the theory asserts. Note that the James-Lange view downplays the importance of human cognition; it denies the roles of cognitive appraisal, personal values, and personal choice in our behavioral and emotional responses to events.

THE CANNON-BARD THEORY Cannon (1927) was not content to criticize the James-Lange theory. Along with Philip Bard (1934), he suggested that an event might *simultaneously* trigger bodily responses (arousal and

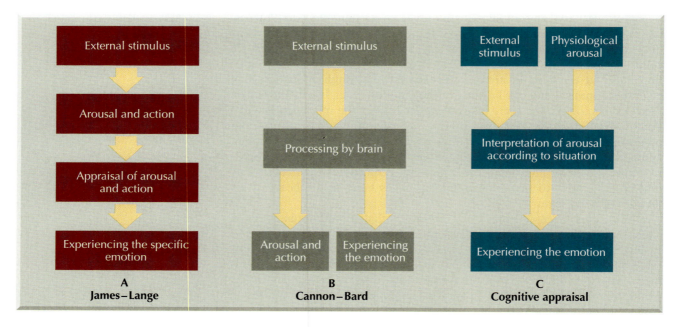

FIGURE ME.8

WHAT THEORIES OF EMOTION ARE THERE?

Several theories of emotion have been advanced, each of which proposes a different role for the components of emotional response. According to the James-Lange theory (part A), events trigger specific arousal patterns and actions. Emotions result from our appraisal of our body responses. According to the Cannon-Bard theory (part B), events are first processed by the brain. Body patterns of arousal, action, and our emotional responses are then triggered simultaneously. According to the theory of cognitive appraisal (part C), events and arousal are appraised by the individual. The emotional response stems from the person's appraisal of the situation and his or her level of arousal.

action) and the experience of an emotion. As shown in Figure ME.8 (part B), when an event is perceived (processed by the brain), the brain stimulates autonomic and muscular activity (arousal and action) *and* cognitive activity (experience of the emotion). Thus, according to the Cannon-Bard theory, emotions *accompany* bodily responses. They are not *produced by* bodily changes, as in the James-Lange theory.

The central criticism of the Cannon-Bard theory focuses on whether bodily responses (arousal and action) and emotions are actually stimulated simultaneously. For example, pain or the perception of danger may trigger arousal before we begin to feel distress or fear. Also, many of us have had the experience of having a "narrow escape" and becoming aroused and shaky afterward, when we have had time to consider the damage that might have occurred. What is needed is a theory that allows for an ongoing interaction of external events, physiological changes (such as autonomic arousal and muscular activity), and cognitive activities.

THE THEORY OF COGNITIVE APPRAISAL More recent theoretical approaches to emotion have stressed cognitive factors. Among those who argue that thinking comes first are Gordon Bower, Richard Lazarus, Stanley Schachter, and Robert Zajonc.

Stanley Schachter asserts that emotions are associated with similar patterns of bodily arousal that may be weaker or stronger, depending on the level of arousal. The label we give to an emotion depends largely on our cognitive appraisal of the situation. Cognitive appraisal is based on many factors, including our perception of external events and the ways in which other people seem to respond to those events (see Figure ME.8, part C). Given the presence of other people, we engage in social comparison to arrive at an appropriate response.

In a classic experiment, Schachter and Singer (1962) showed that arousal can be labeled quite differently, depending on the situation. The investigators told participants that they wanted to determine the effects of a vitamin on vision. Half of the participants received an injection of adrenaline, a hormone that increases the arousal of the sympathetic branch of the autonomic nervous system. A control group received an injection of an inactive solution. Those who had been given adrenaline then received one of three "cognitive manipulations," as shown in Table ME.3. Group 1 was told nothing about possible emotional effects of the "vitamin." Group 2 was deliberately misinformed; members of this group were led to expect itching, numbness, or other irrelevant symptoms. Group 3 was informed accurately about the increased arousal they would experience. Group 4 was a control group injected with an inactive substance and given no information about its effects.

After receiving injections and cognitive manipulations, the participants were asked to wait in pairs while the experimental apparatus was being set up. The participants did not know that the person with whom they were waiting was a confederate of the experimenter. The confederate's purpose was to exhibit a response that the individual would believe was caused by the injection.

Some of those who took part in the experiment waited with a confederate who acted in a happy-go-lucky manner. He flew paper airplanes about the room and tossed paper balls into a wastebasket. Other participants waited with a confederate who acted angry. He complained about the experiment, tore up a questionnaire, and left the waiting room in a huff. As the confederates worked for their Oscar awards, the real participants were observed through a one-way mirror.

The people in groups 1 and 2 were likely to imitate the behavior of the confederate. Those who were exposed to the happy-go-lucky confederate acted jovial and content. Those who were exposed to the angry confederate imitated that person's complaining, aggressive behavior. But those in groups 3 and 4 were less influenced by the confederate's behavior.

Schachter and Singer concluded that participants in groups 1 and 2 were in an ambiguous situation. Members of these groups felt arousal from the adrenaline injection but couldn't label their arousal as any specific emotion. Social comparison with a confederate led them to attribute their arousal either to happiness or to anger. Members of group 3 expected arousal from the injection, with no particular emotional consequences.

TABLE ME.3

INJECTED SUBSTANCES AND COGNITIVE MANIPULATIONS IN THE SCHACHTER-SINGER STUDY

GROUP	SUBSTANCE	COGNITIVE MANIPULATION
1	Adrenaline	No information given about effects
2	Adrenaline	Misinformation given: itching, numbness, etc.
3	Adrenaline	Accurate information given: physiological arousal
4	Inactive	None

Source: From Schachter & Singer (1962).

These participants did not imitate the confederate's display of happiness or anger because they were not in an ambiguous situation; they knew they felt arousal because of the shot of adrenaline. Members of group 4 had no physiological arousal for which they needed an attribution, except perhaps for some arousal induced by observing the confederate. They also did not imitate the behavior of the confederate.

Now, happiness and anger are quite different emotions. Happiness is a positive emotion, whereas anger, for most of us, is a negative emotion. Yet Schachter and Singer suggest that any physiological differences between these two emotions are so slight that different views of the situation can lead one person to label arousal as happiness and another person to label it as anger. The Schachter-Singer view could not be further removed from the James-Lange theory, which holds that each emotion is associated with specific and readily recognized body sensations.

The truth, it happens, may lie somewhere in between.

In science, it must be possible to replicate experiments and attain identical or similar results; otherwise a theory cannot be considered valid. The Schachter and Singer study has been replicated, but with *different* results (Ekman, 1993). For instance, a number of studies found that participants were less likely to imitate the behavior of the confederate and were likely to perceive unexplained arousal in negative terms, attributing it to nervousness, anger, even jealousy (Zimbardo et al., 1993).

EVALUATION What can we make of all this? Research by Paul Ekman and his colleagues (1993) suggests that the patterns of arousal connected with various emotions are more specific than suggested by Schachter and Singer—although less so than suggested by James and Lange. Research with the PET scan suggests that different emotions, such as happiness and sadness, involve different structures within the brain (Goleman, 1995). Moreover, lack of control over our emotions and lack of understanding of what is happening to us are disturbing experiences (Zimbardo et al., 1993). Thus our cognitive appraisals of situations apparently do affect our emotional responses, even if not quite in the way envisioned by Schachter.

The fact that emotions are accompanied by bodily arousal has led to the development of so-called lie detectors, as we see in the following section.

Arousal, Emotions, and Lie Detection

The connection between autonomic arousal and emotions has led to the development of many kinds of lie detectors. Such instruments detect something, but do they detect specific emotional responses that signify lies? Let us take a closer look at the problem of lying.

Lying—for better or worse—is a part of life (Saxe, 1991). Political leaders lie to get elected. Some students lie about why they have not completed assignments (Saxe, 1991). ('Fess up!) The great majority of people lie to their lovers—most often about other relationships (Saxe, 1991). (Is it really true that you never kissed anyone else before?) People also lie about their qualifications to obtain jobs, and of course, some people lie in denying guilt for crimes. Although we are unlikely to subject political leaders, students, and lovers to lie detector tests, such tests are frequently used in hiring and in police investigations.

Facial expressions often offer clues to deceit, but some people can lie with a straight face—or a smile. As Shakespeare pointed out in *Hamlet*, "One may smile, and smile, and be a villain." The use of devices to detect lies has a long, if not laudable, history:

The Bedouins of Arabia . . . until quite recently required conflicting witnesses to lick a hot iron; the one whose tongue was burned was thought to be lying. The Chinese, it is said, had a similar method for detecting lying: Suspects were forced to chew rice powder and spit it out; if the powder was dry, the suspect was guilty. A variation of this test was used during the Inquisition. The suspect had to swallow a "trial slice" of bread and cheese; if it stuck to the suspect's palate or throat he or she was not telling the truth. (Kleinmuntz & Szucko, 1984)

These methods may sound primitive, even bizarre, but they are broadly consistent with modern psychological knowledge. Anxiety about being caught in a lie is linked to arousal of the sympathetic division of the autonomic nervous system. One sign of sympathetic arousal is lack of saliva, or dryness in the mouth. The emotions of fear and guilt are also linked to sympathetic arousal and, hence, to dryness in the mouth.

Modern lie detectors, or polygraphs (see Figure ME.9), monitor indicators of sympathetic arousal while a witness or suspect is being examined. These indicators include heart rate, blood pressure, respiration rate, and electrodermal response (sweating). Questions have been raised about the validity of assessing truth or fiction in this way, however (Sleek, 1998).

The American Polygraph Association claims that use of the polygraph is 85% to 95% accurate. Critics find polygraph testing to be less accurate and claim that it is sensitive to more than lies (Bashore & Rapp, 1993; Saxe, 1998). Studies have found that factors such as tense muscles, drugs, and previous experience with polygraph tests can significantly reduce their accuracy rate (Steinbrook, 1992). In one experiment, people were able to reduce the accuracy of polygraph-based judgments to about 50% by biting their tongue (to produce pain) or by pressing their toes against the floor (to tense muscles) while being interviewed (Honts et al., 1985).

In a review of the literature on this subject, the government Office of Technology Assessment found little valid research on the use of the polygraph in preemployment screening, "dragnet" investigations (attempts to distinguish a guilty person from other suspects), or determining who should be given access to classified information (U.S. Congress, 1983). The government also looked into studies involving investigations of specific indictments. The studies' conclusions varied widely. In 28 studies judged to have employed adequate methodology, accurate detections of guilt ranged from 35% to 100%. Accurate judgments of innocence ranged from 12.5% to 94%.

In sum, no identifiable pattern of bodily responses pinpoints lying (Bashore & Rapp, 1993; Steinbrook, 1992). Because of validity problems, results of polygraph examinations are no longer admitted as evidence in many courts. Polygraph interviews are still often conducted in criminal investigations and job interviews, but this practice is also being questioned.

In sum, various components of an experience—cognitive, physiological, and behavioral—contribute to our emotional responses. Physiological arousal is a part of emotional response, but people appraise their situations when they feel aroused such that arousal does not appear to directly cause one emotion or another. Humans are thinking beings who gather information from all three sources in determining their behavioral responses and labeling their emotional responses. The fact that none of the theories of emotion we have discussed applies to all people in all situations is comforting. Apparently our emotions are not quite as easily understood, manipulated, or—as in the case of the polygraph—even detected as some theorists have suggested.

TRUTH OR FICTION REVISITED
It is true that you may be able to fool a lie detector by wiggling your toes. This creates patterns of autonomic arousal that may be misread in interpreting the polygraph.

FIGURE ME.9
WHAT DO "LIE DETECTORS" DETECT?
The polygraph monitors heart rate, blood pressure, respiration rate, and sweat in the palms of the hands. Is the polygraph sensitive to lying only? Is it foolproof? Because of the controversy surrounding these questions, many courts no longer admit polygraph evidence.

SUMMARY

1. **What are some psychological theories of motivation?** According to instinct theory, organisms are born with preprogrammed tendencies to behave in certain ways in certain situations. According to drive-reduction theory, we are motivated to engage in behavior that reduces drives. Humanistic psychologists argue that behavior can be growth oriented; people are motivated to strive consciously for self-fulfillment. Maslow hypothesized that people have a hierarchy of needs, including an innate need for self-actualization. According to cognitive theory, people are motivated to understand and predict events and to make their cognitions harmonious or consistent with one another.

2. **What factors give rise to hunger?** Hunger is regulated by several internal mechanisms, including stomach contractions, blood sugar level, receptors in the mouth and liver, and the responses of the hypothalamus. The ventromedial hypothalamus functions as a stop-eating center. Damage to this area leads to hyperphagia in rats, causing the animals to grow to several times their normal body weight, but their weight eventually levels off. The lateral hypothalamus has a start-eating center. External stimuli such as the aroma of food can also trigger hunger.

3. **What are stimulus motives?** Stimulus motives, like physiological motives, are innate, but they involve motives to increase rather than decrease stimulation. Sensory-deprivation studies show that lack of stimulation is aversive. People and many lower animals have needs for stimulation and activity, exploration and manipulation. Sensation seekers may seek thrills, act on impulses, and be easily bored.

4. **Do people seek cognitive consistency?** Cognitive-dissonance theory hypothesizes that people dislike situations in which their attitudes and behavior are inconsistent. Such situations apparently induce cognitive dissonance, which people can reduce by changing their attitudes. People also engage in effort justification; that is, they tend to justify attitude-discrepant behavior to themselves by concluding that their attitudes may be different than they thought they were.

5. **What is achievement motivation?** Achievement motivation is the need to accomplish things. People with high achievement motivation attain higher grades and earn more money than people of comparable ability with lower achievement motivation.

6. **What is the need for affiliation?** This is the need to be with other people. It prompts us to join groups and make friends. Anxiety tends to increase our need for affiliation, especially with people who share our predicament.

7. **Why are people aggressive?** Various theories account for aggression in different ways. Biological theory views aggression as instinctive and linked to brain structures, hormone levels, and the Darwinian concept of the "survival of the fittest." Psychodynamic theory views aggression as stemming from inevitable frustrations. Cognitive perspectives predict that people are aggressive when they see aggression as appropriate for them. Learning theories view aggression as stemming from experience and reinforcement.

8. **What is an emotion?** An emotion is a state of feeling with cognitive, physiological, and behavioral components. Emotions motivate behavior and also serve as goals.

9. **Are emotions expressed in the same way in different cultures?** According to Ekman, there are several basic emotions whose expression is recognized in cultures around the world.

10. **What is the facial-feedback hypothesis?** This is the view that intense facial expressions can heighten emotional response. Evidence for this hypothesis is mixed.

11. **What is the James-Lange theory of the activation of emotions?** According to the James-Lange theory, emotions are associated with specific patterns of arousal and action that are triggered by certain external events. The emotion follows the behavioral response.

12. **What is the Cannon-Bard theory of the activation of emotions?** The Cannon-Bard theory proposes that processing of events by the brain gives rise simultaneously to feelings and bodily responses. According to this view, feelings accompany bodily responses.

13. **What is the cognitive-appraisal theory of the activation of emotions?** According to Schachter and Singer's theory of cognitive appraisal, emotions are associated with similar patterns of arousal, but the level of arousal can differ. The emotion a person experiences in response to an external stimulus reflects that person's appraisal of the stimulus.

14. **Does research evidence support any of these theories?** Research evidence suggests that patterns of arousal are more specific than suggested by the theory of cognitive appraisal, but that cognitive appraisal also plays a role in determining our responses to events.

KEY TERMS

acquired drives (p. ME-4)

affiliation (p. ME-16)

aphagic (p. ME-8)

attitude-discrepant behavior (p. ME-14)

catharsis (p. ME-18)

cognitive-dissonance theory (p. ME-3)

drive-reduction theory (p. ME-4)

effort justification (p. ME-14)

emotion (p. ME-20)

facial-feedback hypothesis (p. ME-22)

homeostasis (p. ME-4)

hyperphagic (p. ME-7)

instinct (p. ME-3)

lateral hypothalamus (p. ME-8)

motive (p. ME-3)

parasympathetic nervous system (p. ME-20)

pheromones (p. ME-3)

primary drives (p. ME-4)

satiety (p. ME-7)

self-actualization (p. ME-4)

stimulus motives (p. ME-12)

sympathetic nervous system (p. ME-20)

theory of social comparison (p. ME-17)

ventromedial nucleus (p. ME-7)

REFERENCES

Ainsworth, M. D. S., & Bowlby, J. (1991). An ethological approach to personality development. *American Psychologist, 46*, 333–341.

Akhtar, N., & Bradley, E. J. (1991). Social information processing deficits of aggressive children. *Clinical Psychology Review, 11*, 621–644.

Azar, B. (1998). Communicating through pheromones. *APA Monitor, 29*(1), 1, 12.

Bard, P. (1934). The neurohumoral basis of emotional reactions. In C. A. Murchison (Ed.), *Handbook of general experimental psychology*. Worcester, MA: Clark University Press.

Bashore, T. R., & Rapp, P. E. (1993). Are there alternatives to traditional polygraph procedures? *Psychological Bulletin, 113*, 3–22.

Basic Behavioral Science Task Force of the National Advisory Mental Health Council. (1996). Basic behavioral science research for mental health: Sociocultural and environmental practices. *American Psychologist, 51*, 722–731.

Bem, S. L. (1993). *The lenses of gender.* New Haven: Yale University Press.

Berkowitz, L. (1994). Is something missing? Some observations prompted by the cognitive-neoassociationist view of anger and emotional aggression. In L. R. Huesmann (Ed.), *Aggressive behavior: Current perspectives.* New York: Plenum.

Berman, M., Gladue, B., & Taylor, S. (1993). The effects of hormones, Type A behavior pattern and provocation on aggression in men. *Motivation and Emotion, 17*, 182–199.

Bexton, W. H., Heron, W., & Scott, T. H. (1954). Effects of decreased variation in the sensory environment. *Canadian Journal of Psychology, 8*, 70–76.

Bjorklund, D. F., & Kipp, K. (1996). Parental investment theory and gender differences in the evolution of inhibition mechanisms. *Psychological Bulletin, 120*, 163–188.

Brody, J. E. (1997, March 26). Race and weight. *New York Times*, p. C8.

Broussard, B. A., et al. (1991). Prevalence of obesity in American Indians and Alaska Natives. *American Journal of Clinical Nutrition, 53*, 1535–1542.

Brownell, K. D. (1997). We must be more militant about food. *APA Monitor, 28*(3), 48.

Brownell, K. D., & Rodin, J. (1994). The dieting maelstrom. *American Psychologist, 49*, 781–791.

Bushman, B.J. Barmeister, R.F., & Stack, A.D. (1999). Catharsis aggression, and persuasive influence: self-fulfilling or self-defeating prophecies? *Journal of Personality and Social Psychology, 76* (3), 367–376.

Buss, D. M. (1992). Is there a universal human nature? *Contemporary Psychology, 37*, 1262–1263.

Buss, D. M. (1994). *The evolution of desire.* New York: Basic Books.

Buss, D. M., Haselton, M. G., Shackelford, T. K., Bleske, A. L., & Wakefield, J. C. (1998). Adaptations, exaptations, and spandrels. *American Psychologist, 53,* 533–548.

Cacioppo, J. T., Martzke, J. S, Petty, R. E., & Tassinary, L. G. (1988). Specific forms of facial EMG response index emotions during an interview. *Journal of Personality and Social Psychology, 54,* 552–604.

Cannon, W. B. (1927). The James-Lange theory of emotions: A critical examination and an alternative theory. *American Journal of Psychology, 39,* 106–124.

Cannon, W. B., & Washburn, A. (1912). An explanation of hunger. *American Journal of Physiology, 29,* 441–454.

Carlson, J. G., & Hatfield, E. (1992). *Psychology of emotion.* Fort Worth: Harcourt Brace Jovanovich.

Christiansen, K., & Knussman, R. (1987). Androgen levels and components of aggressive behavior in men. *Hormones and Behavior, 21,* 170–180.

Cools, J., Schotte, D. E., & McNally, R. J. (1992). Emotional arousal and overeating in restrained eaters. *Journal of Abnormal Psychology, 101,* 348–351.

Curb, J. D., & Marcus, E. B. (1991). Body fat and obesity in Japanese-Americans. *American Journal of Clinical Nutrition, 53,* 1552S–1555S.

Darwin, C. A. (1872). *The expression of the emotions in man and animals.* London: J. Murray.

Dodge, K. A., Price, J. M., Bachorowski, J., & Newman, J. P. (1990). Hostile attributional biases in severely aggressive adolescents. *Journal of Abnormal Psychology, 99,* 385–392.

Doob, A. N., & Wood, L. (1972). Catharsis and aggression. *Journal of Personality and Social Psychology, 22,* 236–245.

Drapkin, R. G., Wing, R. R., & Shiffman, S. (1995). Responses to hypothetical high risk situations. *Health Psychology, 14,* 427–434.

Dweck, C. (1997). Paper presented to the meeting of the Society for Research in Child Development. Cited in Murray, B. (1997). Verbal praise may be the best motivator of all. *APA Monitor, 28*(6), 26.

Ekman, P. (1980). *The face of man.* New York: Garland.

Ekman, P. (1993). Facial expression and emotion. *American Psychologist, 48,* 384–392.

Ekman, P. (1994). Strong evidence for universals in facial expression. *Psychological Bulletin, 115,* 268–287.

Ekman, P., et al. 1987). Universals and cultural differences in the judgments of facial expressions of emotion. *Journal of Personality and Social Psychology, 53,* 712–717.

Ernst, N. D., & Harlan, W. R. (1991). Obesity and cardiovascular disease in minority populations: Executive summary. *American Journal of Clinical Nutrition, 53,* 1507S–1511S.

Festinger, L. (1957). *A theory of cognitive dissonance.* Evanston, IL: Row, Peterson.

Festinger, L., & Carlsmith, J. M. (1959). Cognitive consequences of forced compliance. *Journal of Abnormal and Social Psychology, 58,* 203–210.

Fischer, K. W., Shaver, P. R., & Carochan, P. (1990). How emotions develop and how they organize development. *Cognition and Emotion, 4,* 81–127.

Foster, G. D., Wadden, T. A., Vogt, R. A., & Brewer, G. (1997). What is a reasonable weight loss? Patients' expectations and evaluations of obesity treatment outcomes. *Journal of Consulting and Clinical Psychology, 65,* 79–85.

Fox, R. (1996). Cited in Seppa, N. (1996). APA releases study on family violence. *APA Monitor, 26*(4), 12.

Friedman, M. A., & Brownell, K. D. (1995). Psychological correlates of obesity. *Psychological Bulletin, 117,* 3–20.

Ginsburg, G., & Bronstein, P. (1993). Family factors related to children's intrinsic/extrinsic motivational orientation and academic performance. *Child Development, 64,* 1461–1474.

Goleman, D. J. (1995, March 28). The brain manages happiness and sadness in different centers. *New York Times,* pp. C1, C9.

Gottfried, A. E., Fleming, J. S., & Gottfried, A. W. (1994). Role of parental motivational practices in children's academic intrinsic motivation and achievement. *Journal of Educational Psychology, 86,* 104–113.

Granberg, D., & Brent, E. (1983). When prophecy bends. *Journal of Personality and Social Psychology, 45,* 477–491.

Greeno, C. G., & Wing, R. R. (1994). Stress-induced eating. *Psychological Bulletin, 115,* 444–464.

Harlow, H. F., Harlow, M. K., & Meyer, D. R. (1950). Learning motivated by a manipulation drive. *Journal of Experimental Psychology, 40,* 228–234.

Hazuda, H. P., et al. (1991). Obesity in Mexican American subgroups: Findings from the San Antonio Heart Study. *American Journal of Clinical Nutrition, 53,* 1529S–1534S.

Honts, C., Hodes, R., & Raskin, D. (1985). *Journal of Applied Psychology, 70*(1).

Izard, C. E. (1984). Emotion-cognition relationships and human development. In C. E. Izard, J. Kagan, & R. B. Zajonc (Eds.), *Emotions, cognition, and behavior.* New York: Cambridge University Press.

Izard, C. E. (1994). Basic emotions, relations among emotions, and emotion-cognition relations. *Psychological Bulletin, 115,* 561–565.

James, W. (1890). *The principles of psychology.* New York: Henry Holt.

Janowitz, H. D., & Grossman, M. I. (1949). Effects of variations in nutritive density on intake of food in dogs and cats. *American Journal of Physiology, 158,* 184–193.

Keesey, R. E. (1986). A set-point theory of obesity. In K. D. Brownell & J. P. Foreyt (Eds.), *Handbook of eating disorders.* New York: Basic Books.

Kimble, G. A. (1994). A frame of reference for psychology. *American Psychologist, 49,* 510–519.

Kleinmuntz, B., & Szucko, J. J. (1984). Lie detection in ancient and modern times. *American Psychologist, 39,* 766–776.

Kumanyika, S. (1996). Improving our diet—Still a long way to go. *New England Journal of Medicine, 335,* 738–740.

Laumann, E. O., Gagnon, J. H., Michael, R. T., & Michaels, S. (1994). *The social organization of sexuality.* Chicago: University of Chicago Press.

LeDoux, J. E. (1997). Emotion, memory, and the brain. *Scientific American Mysteries of the Mind* [Special issue], 7(1), 68–75.

Levy, D. S. (1991, September 16). Why Johnny might grow up violent and sexist. *Time,* pp. 16–19.

Lochman, J. E., & Dodge, K. A. (1994). Social-cognitive processes of severely violent, moderately aggressive, and nonaggressive boys. *Journal of Consulting and Clinical Psychology, 62,* 366–374.

Lore, R. K., & Schultz, L. A. (1993). Control of human aggression. *American Psychologist, 48,* 16–25.

Maslow, A. H. (1970). *Motivation and personality* (2nd ed.). New York: Harper & Row.

McClelland, D. C. (1958). Methods of measuring human motivation. In J. W. Atkinson (Ed.), *Motives in fantasy, action, and society.* Princeton, NJ: Van Nostrand.

McClelland, D. C. (1965). Achievement and entrepreneurship. *Journal of Personality and Social Psychology, 1,* 389–392.

McDougall, W. (1908). *An introduction to social psychology.* London: Methuen.

McMurtrie, B. (1994, July 19.) Overweight fatten ranks. *New York Newsday,* p. A26.

Mednick, A. (1993). Domestic abuse is seen as worldwide "epidemic." *APA Monitor, 24*(5), 33.

Meltzoff, A. N., & Gopnik, A. (1997). *Words, thoughts, and theories.* Cambridge, MA: MIT Press.

Meyer, T. (1997). *Americans are getting fatter.* Associated Press; America Online.

Miller, N. E. (1995). Clinical-experimental interactions in the development of neuroscience. *American Psychologist, 50,* 901–911.

Murray, H. A. (1938). *Explorations in personality.* New York: Oxford University Press.

Olweus, D. (1986). Aggression and hormones: Behavioral relationship with testosterone and adrenaline. In D. Olweus, J. Block, & M. Rade-Yarrows (Eds.), *Development of antisocial and prosocial behavior* (pp. 51–72). New York: Academic Press.

Plomin, R., DeFries, J. C., McClearn, G., & Rutter, M. (1997). *Behavioral genetics* (3rd ed.). New York: Freeman.

Plutchik, R. (1984). A general psychoevolutionary theory. In K. Scherer & P. Ekman (Eds.), *Approaches to emotion.* Hillsdale, NJ: Erlbaum.

Rathus, S. A., & Nevid, J. S. (1999). *Adjustment and growth: The challenges of life* (7th ed.). Fort Worth: Harcourt Brace.

Rathus, S. A., & Nevid, J. S, & Fichner-Rathus, L. (2000). *Human sexuality in a changing world* (4th ed.). Boston: Allyn & Bacon.

Rinn, W. E. (1991). Neuropsychology of facial expression. In R. S. Feldman & B. Rime (Eds.), *Fundamentals of nonverbal behavior.* Cambridge, England: Cambridge University Press.

Rose, R. J. (1995). Genes and human behavior. *Annual Review of Psychology, 46,* 625–654.

Rosenbaum, M., Leibel, R. L., & Hirsch, J. (1997). Obesity. *New England Journal of Medicine, 337,* 396–407.

Rule, B. G., Taylor, B. R., & Dobbs, A. R. (1987). Priming effects of heat on aggressive thoughts. *Social Cognition, 5,* 131–143.

Saxe, L. (1991). Lying. *American Psychologist, 46,* 409–415.

Saxe, L. (1998). Cited in Sleek, S. (1998). Psychologists debate merits of the polygraph. *APA Monitor, 29*(6).

Schachter, S. (1959). *The psychology of affiliation.* Stanford, CA: Stanford University Press.

Schachter, S., & Singer, J. E. (1962). Cognitive, social, and physiological determinants of emotional state. *Psychological Review, 69,* 379–399.

Schwartz, M. W., & Seeley, R. J. (1997). Neuroendocrine responses to starvation and weight loss. *New England Journal of Medicine, 336,* 1802–1811.

Sleek, S. (1998). Psychologists debate merits of the polygraph. *APA Monitor, 29*(6).

Steinbrook, R. (1992). The polygraph test—A flawed diagnostic method. *New England Journal of Medicine, 327,* 122–123.

Stunkard, A. J., Harris, J. R., Pedersen, N. L., & McLearn, G. E. (1990). A separated twin study of the body mass index. *New England Journal of Medicine, 322,* 1483–1487.

Stunkard, A. J., & Sørensen, T. I. A. (1993). Obesity and socioeconomic status—A complex relation. *New England Journal of Medicine, 329,* 1036–1037.

Tharp, R. G. (1991). Cultural diversity and treatment of children. *Journal of Consulting and Clinical Psychology, 59,* 799–812.

Tomes, H. (1993). It's in the nation's interest to break abuse cycle. *APA Monitor, 24*(3), 28.

Tsang, Y. C. (1938). Hunger motivation in gastrectomized rats. *Journal of Comparative Psychology, 26,* 1–17.

U.S. Congress (1983, November). *Scientific validity of polygraph testing* (OTA-TM-H-15). Washington, DC: Office of Technology Assessment.

Wadden, T. A., et al. (1997). Exercise in the treatment of obesity. *Journal of Consulting and Clinical Psychology, 65,* 269–277.

Watson, J. B. (1924). *Behaviorism.* New York: Norton.

Young, T. K., & Sevenhuysen, G. (1989). Obesity in Northern Canadian Indians: Patterns, determinants, and consequences. *American Journal of Clinical Nutrition, 49,* 786–793.

Zimbardo, P. G., LaBerge, S., & Butler, L. D. (1993). Psychophysiological consequences of unexplained arousal. *Journal of Abnormal Psychology, 102.*

P

PERSONALITY

I WAS READING DR. SEUSS'S *ONE FISH, TWO FISH, RED FISH, BLUE FISH* to my daughter Taylor when she was 2 years old. The sneaky author had set up a trap for fathers. A part of the book reads, "Some [fish] are sad. And some are glad. And some are very, very bad. Why are they sad and glad and bad? I do not know. Go ask your dad."

Thanks, Dr. Seuss.

For many months I had just recited this section and then moved on. One day, however, Taylor's cognitive development had apparently flowered, and she would not let me get away with glossing over this. Why indeed, she wanted to know, were some fish sad, whereas others were glad and bad? I paused and then, being a typical American dad, I gave the answer I'm sure has been given by thousands of other fathers:

"Uh, some fish are sad and others are glad or bad because of, uh, the interaction of nature and nurture—I mean, you know, heredity and environmental factors."

At which Taylor laughed and replied, "Not!"

INTRODUCTION TO PERSONALITY: "WHY ARE THEY SAD AND GLAD AND BAD?"

I'm still not certain whether Taylor thought my words came out silly or that my psychological theorizing was simplistic or off base. When applied to people—that is, why are people sad or glad or bad—this is the kind of question that is of interest to psychologists who study personality.

People do not necessarily agree on what the word *personality* means. Many equate personality with liveliness, as in "She's got a lot of personality." Others characterize a person's personality as consisting of his or her most striking traits, as in a "shy personality" or a "happy-go-lucky personality." Psychologists define personality as the reasonably stable patterns of emotions, motives, and behavior that distinguish one person from another.

Psychologists also seek to explain how personality develops—that is, why some (people) are sad or glad or bad—and to predict how people with certain personality traits respond to life's demands. In this chapter we explore five perspectives on personality: the psychodynamic, trait, learning, humanistic-existential, and sociocultural perspectives. Then we discuss personality tests—the methods used to measure whether people are sad, glad, bad, and lots of other things.

THE PSYCHODYNAMIC PERSPECTIVE

There are several **psychodynamic theories** of personality, each of which owes its origin to the thinking of Sigmund Freud. These theories have a number of features in common. Each teaches that personality is characterized by conflict—by a dynamic struggle. At first the conflict is external: Drives like sex, aggression, and the need for superiority come into conflict with laws, social rules, and moral codes. But at some point laws and social rules are brought inward, or *internalized*. After that the conflict is between opposing *inner* forces. At any given moment our behavior, thoughts, and emotions represent the outcome of these inner contests.

SIGMUND FREUD

Sigmund Freud's Theory of Psychosexual Development

Sigmund Freud (1856–1939) was a mass of contradictions. He has been praised as the greatest thinker of the 20th century, the most profound of psychologists. He has been criticized as overrated, even a "false and faithless prophet." He preached liberal views on sexuality but was himself a model of sexual restraint. He invented a popular form of psychotherapy but experienced lifelong psychologically related problems such as migraine headaches, bowel problems, fainting under stress, hatred of the telephone, and an addiction to cigars. He smoked 20 cigars a day and could not or would not break the habit even after he developed cancer of the jaw.

Sigmund Freud was trained as a physician. Early in his practice he was astounded to find that some people apparently experience loss of feeling in a hand or paralysis of the legs in the absence of any medical disorder. These odd symptoms often disappear once the person has recalled and discussed stressful events and feelings of guilt or anxiety that seem to be related to the symptoms. For a long time, these events and feelings have lain hidden beneath the surface of awareness. Even so, they have the capacity to influence behavior.

From this sort of clinical evidence, Freud concluded that the human mind is like an iceberg. Only the tip of an iceberg rises above the surface of the water; the great mass of it is hidden in the depths (see Figure P.1). Freud came to believe that people, similarly, are aware of only a small portion of the ideas and impulses that dwell within their minds. He argued that a much greater portion of the mind—our deepest images, thoughts, fears, and urges—remains beneath the surface of conscious awareness, where little light shines on them.

Freud labeled the region that pokes through into the light of awareness the *conscious* part of the mind. He called the regions below the surface the *preconscious* and the *unconscious*. The **preconscious** mind contains elements of experience that are out of awareness but can be made conscious simply by focusing on them. The **unconscious** mind is shrouded in mystery. It contains biological instincts such as sex and aggression. Some unconscious urges cannot be experienced consciously because mental images and words could not portray them in all their color and fury. Other unconscious urges may be kept below the surface through repression.

Repression is the automatic ejection of anxiety-evoking ideas from awareness. Research evidence suggests that many people repress bad childhood experiences (Myers & Brewin, 1994). Perhaps "something shocking happens, and the mind pushes it into some inaccessible corner of

---

TRUTH OR FICTION REVISITED
According to Freud, it is true that the human mind is like a vast submerged iceberg. Only the top rises above the surface into conscious awareness. Most personality theorists place more emphasis on conscious thought than Freud did.

PSYCHODYNAMIC THEORY Sigmund Freud's perspective, which emphasizes the importance of unconscious motives and conflicts as forces that determine behavior. *Dynamic* refers to the concept of (psychological) forces being in motion.

PRECONSCIOUS Capable of being brought into awareness by the focusing of attention.

UNCONSCIOUS In psychodynamic theory, not available to awareness by simple focusing of attention.

REPRESSION A defense mechanism that protects the person from anxiety by ejecting anxiety-evoking ideas and impulses from awareness.

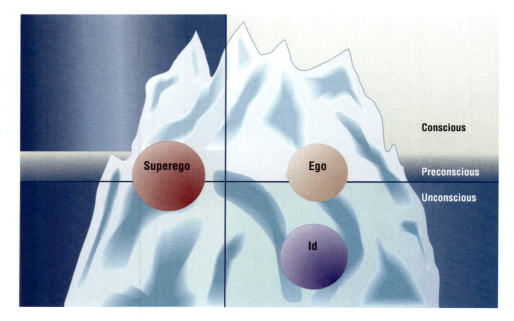

FIGURE P.1

THE HUMAN ICEBERG ACCORDING TO FREUD.

According to psychodynamic theory, only the tip of human personality rises above the surface of the mind into conscious awareness. Material in the preconscious can become conscious if we direct our attention to it. Unconscious material tends to remain shrouded in mystery.

the unconscious" (Loftus, 1993). Repression is also theorized to protect us from awareness of morally unacceptable impulses within ourselves.

In the unconscious mind, primitive drives seek expression while internalized values try to keep them in check. The resulting conflict can arouse emotional outbursts and psychological problems.

To explore the unconscious mind, Freud engaged in a form of mental detective work called **psychoanalysis.** For this reason, his theory of personality is also referred to as *psychoanalytic theory.* In psychoanalysis, people are prodded to talk about anything that pops into their mind while they remain comfortable and relaxed. They may gain self-insight by pursuing some of the thoughts that pop into awareness. But they are also motivated to evade threatening subjects. The same repression that ejects unacceptable thoughts from awareness prompts *resistance,* or the desire to avoid thinking about or discussing those thoughts. Repression and resistance can make psychoanalysis a tedious process that lasts for years, or even decades.

THE STRUCTURE OF PERSONALITY Freud spoke of mental or **psychic structures** to describe the clashing forces of personality. Psychic structures cannot be seen or measured directly, but their presence is suggested by behavior, expressed thoughts, and emotions. Freud believed that there are three psychic structures: the id, the ego, and the superego.

The **id** is present at birth. It represents physiological drives and is entirely unconscious. Freud described the id as "a chaos, a cauldron of seething excitations" (1927/1964, p. 73). The conscious mind might find it inconsistent to love and hate the same person, but Freud believed that conflicting emotions could dwell side by side in the id. In the id, one can

PSYCHOANALYSIS In this usage, Freud's method of exploring human personality.

PSYCHIC STRUCTURE In psychodynamic theory, a hypothesized mental structure that helps explain different aspects of behavior.

ID The psychic structure, present at birth, that represents physiological drives and is fully unconscious.

feel hatred for one's mother for failing to gratify immediately all of one's needs while also feeling love for her.

The id follows what Freud termed the *pleasure principle.* It demands instant gratification of instincts without consideration of law, social custom, or the needs of others.

The **ego** begins to develop during the first year of life, largely because a child's demands for gratification cannot all be met immediately. The ego stands for reason and good sense, for rational ways of coping with frustration. It curbs the appetites of the id and makes plans compatible with social convention. Thus a person can find gratification yet avoid social disapproval. The id lets you know you are hungry, but it is the ego that decides to microwave some enchiladas.

The ego is guided by the *reality principle.* It takes into account what is practical along with what is urged by the id. The ego also provides the person's conscious sense of self.

Although most of the ego is conscious, some of its business is carried out unconsciously. For instance, the ego also acts as a censor that screens the impulses of the id. When the ego senses that improper impulses are rising into awareness, it may use psychological defenses to prevent them from surfacing. Repression is one such psychological defense, or **defense mechanism.** Several defense mechanisms are described in Table P.1.

EGO The second psychic structure to develop, characterized by self-awareness, planning, and delay of gratification.

DEFENSE MECHANISM In psychodynamic theory, an unconscious function of the ego that protects it from anxiety-evoking material by preventing accurate recognition of this material.

TABLE P.1

DEFENSE MECHANISMS

DEFENSE MECHANISM	DEFINITION	EXAMPLES
Repression	Ejection of anxiety-evoking ideas from awareness.	A student forgets that a difficult term paper is due. A person in therapy forgets an appointment when anxiety-evoking material is to be discussed.
Regression	The return, under stress, to a form of behavior characteristic of an earlier stage of development.	An adolescent cries when forbidden to use the family car. An adult becomes highly dependent on his parents after the breakup of his marriage.
Rationalization	The use of self-deceiving justifications for unacceptable behavior.	A student blames her cheating on her teacher's leaving the room during a test. A man explains his cheating on his income tax by saying, "Everyone does it."
Displacement	The transfer of ideas and impulses from threatening or unsuitable objects to less threatening objects.	A worker picks a fight with her spouse after being sharply criticized by her supervisor.
Projection	The thrusting of one's own unacceptable impulses onto others so that others are assumed to have those impulses.	A hostile person perceives the world as a dangerous place. A sexually frustrated person interprets innocent gestures as sexual advances.
Reaction formation	Assumption of behavior in opposition to one's genuine impulses in order to keep those impulses repressed.	A person who is angry with a relative behaves in a "sickly sweet" manner toward that relative. A sadistic individual becomes a physician.
Denial	Refusal to accept the true nature of a threat.	Belief that one will not contract cancer or heart disease even though one smokes heavily. "It can't happen to me."
Sublimation	The channeling of primitive impulses into positive, constructive efforts.	A person paints nudes for the sake of "beauty" and "art." A hostile person becomes a tennis star.

The **superego** develops throughout early childhood, usually incorporating the moral standards and values of parents and important members of the community through **identification.** The superego functions according to the *moral principle.* The superego holds forth shining examples of an ideal self and also acts like the conscience, an internal moral guardian. Throughout life, the superego monitors the intentions of the ego and hands out judgments of right and wrong. It floods the ego with feelings of guilt and shame when the verdict is negative.

The ego does not have an easy time of it. It stands between the id and the superego, striving to satisfy the demands of the id and the moral sense of the superego. From the Freudian perspective, a healthy personality has found ways to gratify most of the id's demands without seriously offending the superego. Most of the id's remaining demands are contained or repressed. If the ego is not a good problem solver or if the superego is too stern, the ego has a hard time of it.

SUPEREGO The third psychic structure, which functions as a moral guardian and sets forth high standards for behavior.

IDENTIFICATION In psychodynamic theory, the unconscious assumption of the behavior of another person.

EROS In psychodynamic theory, the basic instinct to preserve and perpetuate life.

LIBIDO (1) In psychodynamic theory, the energy of Eros; the sexual instinct. (2) Generally, sexual interest or drive.

EROGENOUS ZONE An area of the body that is sensitive to sexual sensations.

PSYCHOSEXUAL DEVELOPMENT In psychodynamic theory, the process by which libidinal energy is expressed through different erogenous zones during different stages of development.

ORAL STAGE The first stage of psychosexual development, during which gratification is hypothesized to be attained primarily through oral activities.

STAGES OF PSYCHOSEXUAL DEVELOPMENT Freud stirred controversy by arguing that sexual impulses are a central factor in personality development, even among children. Freud believed that sexual feelings are closely linked to children's basic ways of relating to the world, such as sucking on their mother's breasts and moving their bowels.

Freud believed that a major instinct, which he termed **eros,** is aimed at preserving and perpetuating life. Eros is fueled by psychological, or psychic, energy, which Freud labeled **libido.** Libidinal energy involves sexual impulses, so Freud considered it *psychosexual.* As the child develops, libidinal energy is expressed through sexual feelings in different parts of the body, or **erogenous zones.** To Freud, human development involves the transfer of libidinal energy from one erogenous zone to another. He hypothesized five periods of **psychosexual development:** oral, anal, phallic, latency, and genital.

During the first year of life a child experiences much of its world through the mouth. If it fits, into the mouth it goes. This is the **oral stage.** Freud argued that oral activities such as sucking and biting give the child sexual gratification as well as nourishment.

THE ORAL STAGE?
According to Sigmund Freud, during the first year the child is in the oral stage of development. If it fits, into the mouth it goes. What, according to Freud, are the effects of insufficient or excessive gratification during the oral stage? Is there evidence to support his views?

Freud believed that children encounter conflict during each stage of psychosexual development. During the oral stage, conflict centers on the nature and extent of oral gratification. Early weaning (cessation of breast feeding) could lead to frustration. Excessive gratification, on the other hand, could lead an infant to expect that it will routinely be given anything it wants. Insufficient or excessive gratification in any stage could lead to **fixation** in that stage and to the development of traits characteristic of that stage. Oral traits include dependency, gullibility, and excessive optimism or pessimism (depending on the child's experiences with gratification).

Freud theorized that adults with an *oral fixation* could experience exaggerated desires for "oral activities," such as smoking, overeating, alcohol abuse, and nail biting. Like the infant whose very survival depends on the mercy of an adult, adults with oral fixations may be disposed toward clinging, dependent relationships.

During the **anal stage,** sexual gratification is attained through contraction and relaxation of the muscles that control elimination of waste products from the body. Elimination, which was controlled reflexively during most of the first year of life, comes under voluntary muscular control, even if such control is not reliable at first. The anal stage is said to begin in the second year of life.

During the anal stage children learn to delay the gratification that comes from eliminating as soon as they feel the urge. The general issue of self-control may become a source of conflict between parent and child. *Anal fixations* may stem from this conflict and lead to two sets of traits in adulthood. So-called *anal-retentive* traits involve excessive use of self-control. They include perfectionism, a strong need for order, and exaggerated neatness and cleanliness. *Anal-expulsive* traits, on the other hand, "let it all hang out." They include carelessness, messiness, even sadism.

Children enter the **phallic stage** during the third year of life. During this stage the major erogenous zone is the phallic region (the penis in boys and the **clitoris** in girls). Parent-child conflict is likely to develop over masturbation, to which parents may respond with threats or punishment. During the phallic stage children may develop strong sexual attachments to the parent of the other gender and begin to view the parent of the same gender as a rival for the other parent's affections. Thus boys may want to marry Mommy and girls may want to marry Daddy.

Children have difficulty dealing with feelings of lust and jealousy. Home life would be tense indeed if they were aware of them. These feelings, therefore, remain unconscious, but their influence is felt through fantasies about marriage with the parent of the other gender and hostility toward the parent of the same gender. In boys, this conflict is labeled the **Oedipus complex,** after the legendary Greek king who unwittingly killed his father and married his mother. Similar feelings in girls give rise to the **Electra complex.** According to Greek legend, Electra was the daughter of the king Agamemnon. She longed for him after his death and sought revenge against his slayers—her mother and her mother's lover.

The Oedipus and Electra complexes are resolved by about the ages of 5 or 6. Children then repress their hostilities toward the parent of the same gender and begin to identify with her or him. Identification leads them to play the social and gender roles of that parent and to internalize his or her values. Sexual feelings toward the parent of the other gender are repressed for a number of years. When the feelings emerge again during adolescence, they are **displaced,** or transferred, to socially appropriate members of the other gender.

TRUTH OR FICTION REVISITED
According to Freud, it is true that biting one's fingernails or smoking cigarettes as an adult is a sign of conflict during very early childhood. Freud believed that adult problems tend to have their origins in childhood conflicts that have long been lost to conscious awareness.

FIXATION In psychodynamic theory, arrested development. Attachment to objects of an earlier stage.

ANAL STAGE The second stage of psychosexual development, when gratification is attained through anal activities.

PHALLIC STAGE The third stage of psychosexual development, characterized by a shift of libido to the phallic region. (From the Greek *phallos*, referring to an image of the penis. However, Freud used the term *phallic* to refer both to boys and girls.)

CLITORIS An external female sex organ that is highly sensitive to sexual stimulation.

OEDIPUS COMPLEX A conflict of the phallic stage in which the boy wishes to possess his mother sexually and perceives his father as a rival in love.

ELECTRA COMPLEX A conflict of the phallic stage in which the girl longs for her father and resents her mother.

DISPLACED Transferred.

Freud believed that by the age of 5 or 6, children have been in conflict with their parents over sexual feelings for several years. The pressures of the Oedipus and Electra complexes cause them to repress all sexual urges. In so doing, they enter a period of **latency** during which their sexual feelings remain unconscious. During the latency phase it is not uncommon for children to prefer playmates of their own gender.

Freud believed that we enter the final stage of psychosexual development, the **genital stage,** at puberty. Adolescent males again experience sexual urges toward their mother and adolescent females experience such urges toward their father. However, the incest taboo causes them to repress these impulses and displace them onto other adults or adolescents of the other gender. Boys still might seek girls "just like the girl that married dear old Dad," as the song goes. Girls still might be attracted to men who resemble their fathers.

People in the genital stage prefer, by definition, to find sexual gratification through intercourse with a member of the other gender. In Freud's view, oral or anal stimulation, masturbation, and sexual activity with people of the same gender all represent *pregenital* fixations and immature forms of sexual conduct. They are not consistent with the life instinct, eros.

Other Psychodynamic Theorists

Several personality theorists are among Freud's intellectual heirs. Their theories, like his, include dynamic movement of psychological forces, conflict, and defensive responses to anxiety that involve repression and cognitive distortion of reality. In other respects, however, their theories differ considerably.

CARL JUNG   Carl Jung (1875–1961) was a Swiss psychiatrist who had been a member of Freud's inner circle. He fell into disfavor with Freud when he developed his own psychodynamic theory. In contrast to Freud (for whom, he said, "the brain is viewed as an appendage of the genital organs"), Jung downplayed the importance of the sexual instinct. He saw it as just one of several important instincts.

Jung, like Freud, was intrigued by unconscious processes. He believed we not only have a *personal* unconscious that contains repressed memories and impulses but also an inherited **collective unconscious.** The collective unconscious contains primitive images, or **archetypes,** that reflect the history of our species. Examples of archetypes are the all-powerful God, the young hero, the fertile and nurturing mother, the wise old man, the hostile brother—even fairy godmothers, wicked witches, and themes of rebirth or resurrection. Archetypes themselves remain unconscious, but Jung declared that they influence our thoughts and emotions and cause us to respond to cultural themes in stories and films.

ALFRED ADLER   Alfred Adler (1870–1937), another follower of Freud, also felt that Freud had placed too much emphasis on sexual impulses. Adler believed that people are basically motivated by an **inferiority complex.** In some people, feelings of inferiority may be based on physical problems and the need to compensate for them. Adler believed, however, that all of us encounter some feelings of inferiority because of our small size as children, and that these feelings give rise to a **drive for superiority.** For instance, the English poet Lord Byron, who had a crippled leg, became a champion swimmer. As a child Adler was crippled by rickets and suffered from pneumonia, and it may be that his theory developed in part from his own childhood striving to overcome repeated bouts of illness.

LATENCY A phase of psychosexual development characterized by repression of sexual impulses.

GENITAL STAGE The mature stage of psychosexual development, characterized by preferred expression of libido through intercourse with an adult of the other gender.

COLLECTIVE UNCONSCIOUS Jung's hypothesized store of vague racial memories.

ARCHETYPES Basic, primitive images or concepts hypothesized by Jung to reside in the collective unconscious.

INFERIORITY COMPLEX Feelings of inferiority hypothesized by Adler to serve as a central motivating force.

DRIVE FOR SUPERIORITY Adler's term for the desire to compensate for feelings of inferiority.

Adler believed that self-awareness plays a major role in the formation of personality. He spoke of a **creative self,** a self-aware aspect of personality that strives to overcome obstacles and develop the individual's potential.

KAREN HORNEY Karen Horney (1885–1952) agreed with Freud that childhood experiences play a major role in the development of adult personality. But she believed that sexual and aggressive impulses take a backseat in importance to social relationships. She agreed with Freud that parent-child relationships are paramount in importance. Small children are completely dependent. When parents treat them with indifference or harshness, they develop feelings of insecurity and anxiety. Children also resent neglectful parents, so anxious children are also often hostile. Like Freud, Horney thought that children repress rather than express feelings of hostility toward their parents because of fear of reprisal and, just as important, fear of driving them away. But in contrast to Freud, she also believed that genuine and consistent love could soften the effects of the most traumatic childhood (Quinn, 1987).

KAREN HORNEY

ERIK ERIKSON Erik Erikson (1902–1994) also believed that Freud had placed undue emphasis on sexual instincts. He asserted that social relationships are more crucial determinants of personality than sexual urges. To Erikson, the nature of the mother-infant relationship is more important than the details of the feeding process or the sexual feelings that might be stirred by contact with the mother. Erikson also argued that to a large extent we are the conscious architects of our own personalities. His view grants more powers to the ego than Freud did. In Erikson's theory, it is possible for us to make real choices. In Freud's theory, we may think we are making choices but may actually be merely rationalizing the compromises forced on us by internal conflicts.

ERIK ERIKSON

Erikson, like Freud, is known for devising a comprehensive theory of personality development. But whereas Freud proposed stages of psycho*sexual* development, Erikson proposed stages of psycho*social* development. Rather than label stages for various erogenous zones, Erikson labeled them for the traits that might be developed during them. Each stage is named according to its possible outcomes. For example, the first stage of **psychosocial development** is labeled the stage of *trust versus mistrust* because of its two possible outcomes: (1) A warm, loving relationship with the mother (and others) during infancy might lead to a sense of basic trust in people and the world. (2) Or a cold, ungratifying relationship might generate a pervasive sense of mistrust. Erikson believed that most people would wind up with some blend of trust and mistrust—hopefully more trust than mistrust. A basic sense of mistrust could interfere with the formation of relationships unless it was recognized and challenged.

For Erikson, the goal of adolescence is the attainment of **ego identity,** not genital sexuality. The focus is on who we see ourselves as being and what we stand for, not on sexual interests.

Evaluation of the Psychodynamic Perspective

Psychodynamic theories have tremendous appeal. They involve many concepts and explain many varieties of human behavior and traits.

Although today concepts such as "the id" and "libido" strike many psychologists as unscientific, Freud fought for the idea that human personality and behavior are subject to scientific analysis. He developed his theories at a time when many people still viewed psychological problems as

CREATIVE SELF According to Adler, the self-aware aspect of personality that strives to achieve its full potential.

PSYCHOSOCIAL DEVELOPMENT Erikson's theory of personality and development, which emphasizes social relationships and eight stages of growth.

EGO IDENTITY A firm sense of who one is and what one stands for.

signs of possession by the devil or evil spirits, as they had during the Middle Ages. Freud argued that psychological disorders stem from problems within the individual—not evil spirits. His thinking contributed to the development of compassion for people with psychological disorders and methods for helping them.

Psychodynamic theory has also focused attention on the far-reaching effects of childhood events. Freud and other psychodynamic theorists are to be credited for suggesting that personality and behavior *develop* and that it is important for parents to be aware of the emotional needs of their children.

Freud helped us recognize that sexual and aggressive urges are commonplace and that there is a difference between acknowledging these urges and acting on them. As W. Bertram Wolfe put it, "Freud found sex an outcast in the outhouse, and left it in the living room an honored guest."

Freud also noted that people have defensive ways of looking at the world. His list of defense mechanisms has become part of everyday speech. Whether or not we attribute these cognitive distortions to unconscious ego functioning, our thinking may be distorted by our efforts to avert anxiety and guilt. If these concepts no longer strike us as innovative, it is largely because of Freud's influence. Psychodynamic theorists also developed many methods of therapy.

Critics note that "psychic structures" such as the id, ego, and superego are too vague to measure scientifically (Hergenhahn, 1997). Nor can they be used to predict behavior with precision. They are little more than useful fictions—poetic ways to express inner conflict. Freud's critics thus have the right to write other "poems"—that is, to use other descriptive terms.

Nor have the stages of psychosexual development escaped criticism. Children begin to masturbate as early as the first year, not in the phallic stage. As parents know from discovering their children play "doctor," the latency stage is not as sexually latent as Freud believed. Much of Freud's thinking about the Oedipus and Electra complexes remains little more than speculation. The evidence for some of Erikson's developmental views seems somewhat sturdier. For example, people who fail to develop ego identity in adolescence seem to encounter problems developing intimate relationships later on.

Freud's method of gathering evidence from clinical sessions is also suspect (Hergenhahn, 1997). In subtle ways, therapists may influence clients to produce memories and feelings they expect to find. Therapists may also fail to separate what they are told from their own interpretations. Also, Freud and many other psychodynamic theorists restricted their evidence gathering to case studies with individuals who sought help for psychological problems. Their clients were also mostly White and from the middle and upper classes. People who seek therapy are likely to have more problems than the general population.

In the feature on diversity, we see that many theories of personality—including many psychodynamic theories—have been accused of being biased against women.

THE TRAIT PERSPECTIVE

In most of us by the age of thirty, the character has set like plaster, and will never soften again.

WILLIAM JAMES

The notion of *traits* is very familiar. If I asked you to describe yourself, you would probably do so in terms of traits such as bright, sophisticated,

Individuality Versus Relatedness

Most Western theories of personality and human development have been accused of having a "phallocentric" and individualist bias (Jordan et al., 1991). This criticism applies to the views of Freud, Erikson, Piaget, and Kohlberg, among others. Each of these uses the yardsticks of male development as the norms. Each neglects important aspects of personality development, such as the relatedness of the individual to other people (Guisinger & Blatt, 1994). In Western culture, the male view is that the self is supreme and distinct from other people. Moreover, separation and individuation are presented as the highest goal of personality development. Yet social critics (e.g., Gilligan et al., 1991; Jordan et al., 1991) consider a crucial aspect of a woman's sense of self to be her relatedness—her establishment and maintenance of social relationships.

Guisinger and Blatt (1994) suggest that the male tendency toward individualism might arise from the different developmental tasks faced by boys and girls. For example, when a boy recognizes that he and his mother are not of the same gender, he must set himself apart from her. This process of differentiation may cause boys to feel greater concern about being separate and distinct from other people. For girls, of course, such differentiation from the mother is unnecessary.

Gender stereotypes and cultural expectations also enter the picture in early childhood. True, in our society the great

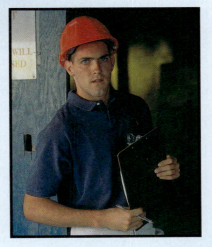

Is This "Iron John"?
The masculine gender role stereotype is characterized by separation and individuation. Do theories of personality present this stereotype as the highest goal of personality development? Women are more likely than men to emphasize interpersonal relatedness as a key goal of personality development. Although their need to be stoic may prevent men from getting in touch with their feelings, they may experience alienation and grief over lack of relatedness to other people.

majority of women are in the work force. Yet girls are still taught from an early age that they will have the primary responsibilities for homemaking and child rearing. Today women and men share child-rearing chores more than they did in the past. However, research shows that women are still more likely than men to supply the emotional glue that holds the family together (Bianchi & Spain, 1997).

Guisinger and Blatt (1994) suggest that women's and men's personality development may frustrate both genders. Women's relational development is both an undervalued strength and a source of vulnerability for women. Women are often at risk of losing themselves in their relationships and failing to develop an adequate sense of self. Although men may be more involved as fathers today than they were in the past, young daughters may still have to struggle to engage relatively distant fathers. As adults, when they attempt to engage other men in relation-

ships, they may feel that the men care less about them than they care about the men.

Men tend to underemphasize interpersonal relatedness. Although their needs to be strong individuals may prevent them from acknowledging or getting in touch with their feelings, they may suffer from feelings of alienation and grief over their loss of relatedness to others, including other men (Bly, 1990; Keen, 1991). Consider the title of Robert Bly's popular book, *Iron John.* Iron Johns are less likely than women to reveal intimate information about themselves (Dindia & Allen, 1992). They are less likely than women to have intimate friends, even though they may be part of a large sporting crowd. Iron Johns who do many things "with the guys" may still feel that they have no one to talk to. Moreover, just as women may struggle to engage distant men, men are likely to have problems in their relationships with women. ∎

and witty. (That's you, isn't it?) We also describe other people in terms of traits.

Traits are reasonably stable elements of personality that are inferred from behavior. If you describe a friend as "shy," it may be because you have observed social anxiety or withdrawal in that person's encounters with others. Traits are assumed to account for consistent behavior in diverse situations. You probably expect your "shy" friend to be retiring in most social confrontations—"all across the board," as the saying goes. The concept of traits is also found in other approaches to personality. Recall that Freud linked the development of certain traits to children's experiences in each stage of psychosexual development.

From Hippocrates to the Present

The trait approach dates back to the Greek physician Hippocrates (c. 460–377 B.C.), and could be even older (Maher & Maher, 1994). It has generally been assumed that traits are embedded in people's bodies, but *how?* Hippocrates believed that traits are embedded in bodily fluids, which give rise to certain types of personalities. In his view, an individual personality depends on the balance of four basic fluids, or "humors," in the body. Yellow bile is associated with a choleric (quick-tempered) disposition; blood with a sanguine (warm, cheerful) one; phlegm with a phlegmatic (sluggish, calm, cool) disposition; and black bile with a melancholic (gloomy, pensive) temperament. Disease was believed to reflect an imbalance among the humors. Methods such as bloodletting and vomiting were recommended to restore the balance (Maher & Maher, 1994). Although Hippocrates' theory was pure speculation, the terms *choleric, sanguine,* and so on, are still used in descriptions of personality.

More enduring trait theories assume that traits are heritable and embedded in the nervous system. They rely on the mathematical technique of factor analysis in attempting to determine basic human traits.

Sir Francis Galton was among the first scientists to suggest that many of the world's languages use single words to describe fundamental differences in personality. More than 50 years ago, Gordon Allport and a colleague (Allport & Oddbert, 1936) catalogued some 18,000 human traits from a search through word lists like dictionaries. Some were physical traits such as *short, black,* and *brunette.* Others were behavioral traits such as *shy* and *emotional.* Still others were moral traits such as *honest.* This exhaustive list has served as the basis for personality research by many other psychologists. Other researchers have used factor analysis to reduce this universe of traits to smaller lists of traits that show common features.

Hans Eysenck

British psychologist Hans J. Eysenck (Eysenck & Eysenck, 1985) has focused much of his research on the relationships between two important traits: **introversion-extraversion** and emotional stability-instability. (Emotional *in*stability is also known as **neuroticism**.) Carl Jung was first to distinguish between introverts and extraverts. Eysenck added the dimension of emotional stability-instability to introversion-extraversion. He has catalogued various personality traits according to where they are situated along these dimensions or factors (see Figure P.2). For instance, an anxious person would be high in both introversion and neuroticism—that is, preoccupied with his or her own thoughts and emotionally unstable.

TRAIT A relatively stable aspect of personality that is inferred from behavior and assumed to give rise to consistent behavior.

INTROVERSION A trait characterized by intense imagination and the tendency to inhibit impulses.

EXTRAVERSION A trait characterized by tendencies to be socially outgoing and to express feelings and impulses freely.

NEUROTICISM Eysenck's term for emotional instability.

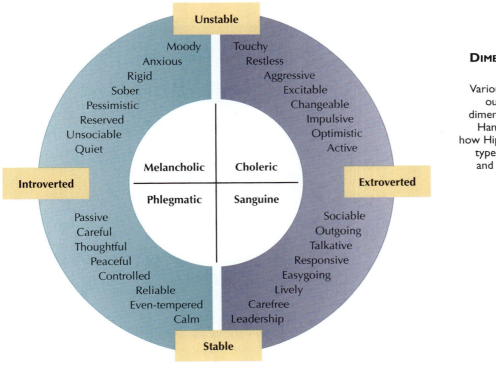

FIGURE P.2
EYSENCK'S PERSONALITY DIMENSIONS AND HIPPOCRATES'S PERSONALITY TYPES.
Various personality traits shown in the outer ring fall within the two major dimensions of personality suggested by Hans Eysenck. The inner circle shows how Hippocrates' four major personality types—choleric, sanguine, phlegmatic, and melancholic—fit within Eysenck's dimensions.

Eysenck notes that his scheme is reminiscent of that suggested by Hippocrates. According to Eysenck's dimensions, the choleric type would be extraverted and unstable; the sanguine type, extraverted and stable; the phlegmatic type, introverted and stable; and the melancholic type, introverted and unstable.

The Five-Factor Model

Recent research suggests five basic personality factors (McCrae, 1996). These include the two found by Eysenck—extraversion and neuroticism—along with conscientiousness, agreeableness, and openness to new experience (see Table P.2). Many personality theorists, especially Louis Thurstone, Donald Fiske, Robert McCrae, and Paul T. Costa, Jr., have played a role in the development of the five-factor model. The five-factor model has found applications in areas such as personnel selection and classification, and in the study of psychological disorders (Clark et al., 1994; Widiger & Costa, 1994). Moreover, cross-cultural research has found that these five factors appear to define the personality structure of American, German, Portuguese, Hebrew, Chinese, Korean, and Japanese people (McCrae & Costa, 1997). Yet many psychologists still disagree on the number of basic personality factors (Block, 1995; Zuckerman, 1992).

Evaluation of the Trait Perspective

Trait theories, like psychodynamic theories, have both strengths and weaknesses. Trait theorists have focused much attention on the development of personality tests. They have also given rise to theories about the fit between personality and certain kinds of jobs (Holland, 1996). The

TABLE P.2		
THE FIVE-FACTOR MODEL		
FACTOR	**NAME**	**TRAITS**
I	Extraversion	Contrasts talkativeness, assertiveness, and activity with silence, passivity, and reserve
II	Agreeableness	Contrasts kindness, trust, and warmth with hostility, selfishness, and distrust
III	Conscientiousness	Contrasts organization, thoroughness, and reliability with carelessness, negligence, and unreliability
IV	Neuroticism	Contrasts traits such as nervousness, moodiness, and sensitivity to negative stimuli with coping ability
V	Openness to Experience	Contrasts imagination, curiosity, and creativity with shallowness and lack of perceptiveness

qualities that suit a person for various kinds of work can be expressed in terms of abilities, personality traits, and interests. By using interviews and tests to learn about an individual's abilities and traits, testing and counseling centers can make valuable suggestions about that person's chances of success and fulfillment in various kinds of jobs.

One limitation of trait theory is that it is descriptive, not explanatory. It focuses on describing traits rather than on tracing their origins or finding out how they may be modified. Moreover, the "explanations" provided by trait theory are often criticized as being *circular*. That is, they restate what is observed and do not explain it. Saying that John failed to ask Marsha on a date *because* of shyness is an example of a circular explanation: We have merely restated John's (shy) behavior as a trait (shyness).

THE LEARNING PERSPECTIVE

The learning perspective has also contributed to our understanding of personality. In this section we focus on two learning approaches: behaviorism and social-cognitive theory.

Behaviorism

You have freedom when you're easy in your harness.

ROBERT FROST

In 1924, at Johns Hopkins University John B. Watson raised the battle cry of the behaviorist movement:

> Give me a dozen healthy infants, well-formed, and my own specified world to bring them up in and I'll guarantee to take any one at random and train him to become any type of specialist I might suggest—doctor, lawyer, merchant-chief and, yes, even beggar-man and thief, regardless of his talents, penchants, tendencies, abilities, vocations, and the race of his ancestors. (p. 82)

Watson thus proclaimed that situational variables or environmental influences—not internal, individual variables—are the key shapers of human preferences and behaviors. In contrast to the psychoanalysts and structuralists of his day, Watson argued that unseen, undetectable mental structures must be rejected in favor of that which can be seen and measured. In the 1930s, Watson's battle cry was taken up by B. F. Skinner, who agreed that psychologists should avoid trying to see into the "black box" of the organism and instead emphasized the effects of reinforcement on behavior.

The views of Watson and Skinner largely ignored the notions of personal freedom, choice, and self-direction. Most of us assume that our wants originate within us. But Skinner suggested that environmental influences such as parental approval and social custom shape us into *wanting* certain things and *not wanting* others.

In his novel *Walden Two,* Skinner (1948) described a utopian society in which people are happy and content because they are allowed to do as they please. However, from early childhood, they have been trained or conditioned to be cooperative. Because of their reinforcement histories, they *want* to behave in decent, kind, and unselfish ways. They see themselves as free because society makes no effort to force them to behave in particular ways.

Some object to behaviorist notions because they play down the importance of consciousness and choice. Others argue that humans are not blindly ruled by pleasure and pain. In some circumstances people have rebelled against the so-called necessity of survival by choosing pain and hardship over pleasure, or death over life. Many people have sacrificed their own lives to save those of others.

The behaviorist defense might be that the apparent choice of pain or death is forced on altruistic individuals just as conformity to social custom is forced on others. The altruist is also shaped by external influences, even if those influences differ from those that affect many other people.

Social-Cognitive Theory

Social-cognitive theory[1] is a contemporary view of learning developed by Albert Bandura (1986) and other psychologists (e.g., Mischel & Shoda, 1995). It focuses on the importance of learning by observation and on the cognitive processes that underlie individual differences. Social-cognitive theorists see people as influencing their environment just as their environment influences them. Bandura terms this mutual pattern of influence **reciprocal determinism.** Social-cognitive theorists agree with behaviorists and other empirical psychologists that discussions of human nature should be tied to observable experiences and behaviors. They assert, however, that variables within people—which they call **person variables**—must also be considered if we are to understand them.

One goal of psychological theories is the prediction of behavior. We cannot predict behavior from situational variables alone. Whether a person behaves in a certain way also depends on the person's **expectancies** about the outcomes of that behavior and the perceived or **subjective values** of those outcomes.

To social-cognitive theorists, people are not simply at the mercy of the environment. Instead, they are self-aware and purposefully engage in learning. They seek to learn about their environment and to alter it in order to make reinforcers available.

SOCIAL-COGNITIVE THEORY A cognitively oriented learning theory in which observational learning and person variables such as values and expectancies play major roles in individual differences. Also referred to as *social-learning theory.*

RECIPROCAL DETERMINISM Bandura's term for the social-cognitive view that people influence their environment just as their environment influences them.

PERSON VARIABLES Factors within the person, such as expectancies and competencies, that influence behavior.

EXPECTANCIES Personal predictions about the outcomes of potential behaviors.

SUBJECTIVE VALUE The desirability of an object or event.

---

[1] The name of this theory remains unsettled. It was formerly referred to as social-learning theory. Today it is also sometimes referred to as *cognitive social theory.*

OBSERVATIONAL LEARNING Observational learning (also termed **modeling** or *cognitive learning*) refers to acquiring knowledge by observing others. Observing others extends to reading about them or seeing what they do and what happens to them in books, TV, radio, and film.

Our expectations stem from our observations of what happens to ourselves and other people. For example, teachers are more likely to call on males and more accepting of "calling out" in class by males than by females (Sadker & Sadker, 1994). As a result, many males expect to be rewarded for calling out. Females, however, may learn that they will be reprimanded for behaving in what some might term an "unladylike" manner.

Social-cognitive theorists believe that behavior reflects person variables and situational variables. Person variables include competencies, encoding strategies, expectancies, emotions, and self-regulatory systems and plans (Mischel & Shoda, 1995; see Figure P.3).

COMPETENCIES: WHAT CAN YOU DO? **Competencies** include knowledge of rules that guide conduct, concepts about ourselves and other people, and skills. Our ability to use information to make plans depends on our competencies. Knowledge of the physical world and of cultural codes of conduct are important competencies. So are academic skills such as reading and writing, athletic skills such as swimming and tossing a football, social skills such as knowing how to ask someone out on a date, and many others. Individual differences in competencies reflect genetic variation, learning opportunities, and other environmental factors.

MODEL In social-cognitive theory, an organism that exhibits behaviors that others will imitate or acquire through observational learning.

COMPETENCIES Knowledge and skills.

FIGURE P.3

PERSON VARIABLES AND SITUATIONAL VARIABLES IN SOCIAL-COGNITIVE THEORY.

According to social-cognitive theory, person variables and situational variables interact to influence behavior.

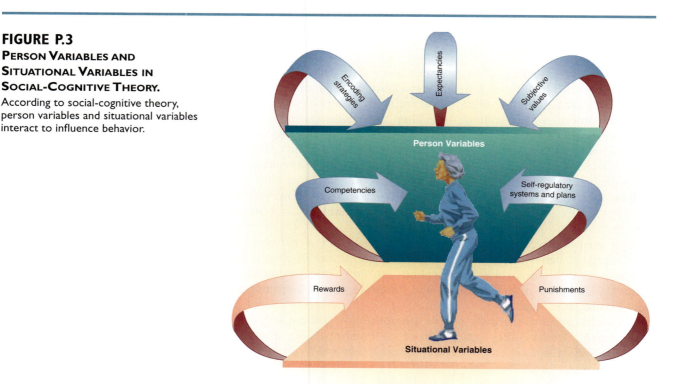

Encoding strategies · Expectancies · Subjective values

Person Variables

Competencies · Self-regulatory systems and plans

Rewards · Punishments

Situational Variables

HOW DO COMPETENCIES CONTRIBUTE TO PERFORMANCE?
What factors contribute to this girl's performance on the balance beam? Individual differences in competencies stem from variations in genetic endowment, nutrition, and learning opportunities.

ENCODING STRATEGIES: HOW DO YOU SEE IT? Different people **encode** (symbolize or represent) the same stimuli in different ways. Their encoding strategies are an important factor in their behavior. One person might encode a tennis game as a chance to bat the ball back and forth and have some fun. Another person might encode the game as a demand to perfect his or her serve. One person might encode a date that doesn't work out as a sign of personal social incompetence. Another person might encode the date as reflecting the fact that people are not always "made for each other."

Some people make themselves miserable by encoding events in self-defeating ways. A linebacker may encode an average day on the field as a failure because he did not make any sacks. Cognitive therapists foster adjustment by challenging people to view life in more optimistic ways.

EXPECTANCIES: WHAT WILL HAPPEN? There are various kinds of expectancies. Some are predictions about what will follow various stimuli or signs. For example, some people predict other people's behavior on the basis of signs such as "tight lips" or "shifty eyes." Other expectancies involve what will happen if we engage in certain behaviors. **Self-efficacy expectations** are beliefs that we can accomplish certain things, such as speaking before a group or doing a back flip into a swimming pool or solving math problems (Pajares & Miller, 1994).

Competencies influence expectancies. Expectancies, in turn, influence motivation to perform. People with positive self-efficacy expectations are more likely to try difficult tasks than people who do not believe they can

TRUTH OR FICTION REVISITED
It is true that we are more likely to persist at difficult tasks when we believe we will succeed. Positive self-efficacy expectations motivate us to persevere.

ENCODE Interpret; transform.

SELF-EFFICACY EXPECTATIONS Beliefs to the effect that one can handle a task.

master those tasks. One way that psychotherapy helps people is by changing their self-efficacy expectations from "I can't" to "I can" (Bandura, 1986). As a result, people are motivated to try new things.

EMOTIONS: HOW DOES IT FEEL? Because of our different learning histories, similar situations can arouse different feelings in us—anxiety, depression, fear, hopelessness, and anger. What frightens one person may entice another. What bores one person may excite another. From the social-cognitive perspective, in contrast to the behaviorist perspective, we are not controlled by stimuli. Instead, stimuli arouse feelings in us, and feelings influence our behavior. Hearing Chopin may make one person weep and another person switch to a rock 'n' roll station.

SELF-REGULATORY SYSTEMS AND PLANS: HOW CAN YOU ACHIEVE IT? We tend to regulate our own behavior, even in the absence of observers and external constraints. We set our own goals and standards. We make plans to achieve them. We congratulate or criticize ourselves, depending on whether or not we achieve them (Bandura, 1986).

Self-regulation helps us influence our environments. We can select the situations to which we expose ourselves and the arenas in which we will compete. Depending on our expectancies, we may choose to enter the academic or athletic worlds. We may choose marriage or the single life. And when we cannot readily select our environment, we can to some degree select our responses within an environment—even an aversive one. For example, if we are undergoing an uncomfortable medical procedure, we may try to reduce the stress by focusing on something else—an inner fantasy or an environmental feature such as the cracks in the tiles on the ceiling. This is one of the techniques used in prepared or "natural" childbirth.

Evaluation of the Learning Perspective

Learning theorists have made monumental contributions to the scientific understanding of behavior, but they have left some psychologists dissatisfied.

Psychodynamic theorists and trait theorists propose the existence of psychological structures that cannot be seen and measured directly. Learning theorists—particularly behaviorists—have dramatized the importance of referring to publicly observable variables, or behaviors, if psychology is to be accepted as a science.

Similarly, psychodynamic theorists and trait theorists focus on internal variables such as unconscious conflict and traits to explain and predict behavior. Learning theorists emphasize the importance of environmental conditions, or situational variables, as determinants of behavior. They have also elaborated on the conditions that foster learning—even automatic kinds of learning. They have shown that we can learn to do things because of reinforcements and that many behavior patterns are acquired by observing others.

On the other hand, behaviorism is limited in its ability to explain personality. Behaviorism does not describe, explain, or even suggest the richness of inner human experience. We experience thoughts and feelings and browse through our complex inner maps of the world, but behaviorism does not deal with these. To be fair, however, the so-called limitations of behaviorism are self-imposed. Personality theorists have traditionally dealt with thoughts, feelings, and behavior, whereas behaviorism deals with behavior alone.

Critics of social-cognitive theory cannot accuse its supporters of denying the importance of cognitive activity and feelings. But they often contend that social-cognitive theory has not come up with satisfying statements about the development of traits or accounted for self-awareness. Also, social-cognitive theory—like its intellectual predecessor, behaviorism—may not pay enough attention to genetic variation in explaining individual differences in behavior. Learning theories have done very little to account for the development of traits or personality types.

THE HUMANISTIC-EXISTENTIAL PERSPECTIVE

You are unique, and if that is not fulfilled, then something has been lost.

MARTHA GRAHAM

Humanists and existentialists dwell on the meaning of life. Self-awareness is the hub of the humanistic-existential search for meaning.

The term **humanism** has a long history and many meanings. It became a third force in American psychology in the 1950s and 1960s, partly in response to the predominant psychodynamic and behavioral models. Humanism also represented a reaction to the "rat race" spawned by industrialization and automation. Humanists felt that work on assembly lines produced "alienation" from inner sources of meaning. The humanistic views of Abraham Maslow and Carl Rogers emerged from these concerns.

Existentialism in part reflects the horrors of mass destruction of human life through war and genocide, frequent events in the 20th century. The European existentialist philosophers Jean-Paul Sartre and Martin Heidegger saw human life as trivial in the grand scheme of things. But psychiatrists like Viktor Frankl, Ludwig Binswanger, and Medard Boss argued that seeing human existence as meaningless could give rise to withdrawal and apathy—even suicide. Psychological salvation therefore requires giving personal meaning to things and making personal choices. Yes, there is pain in life, and yes, sooner or later life ends, but people can see the world for what it is and make genuine choices.

Freud argued that defense mechanisms prevent us from seeing the world as it is. Therefore, the concept of free choice is meaningless. Behaviorists view freedom as an illusion determined by social forces. To existentialists, we are really and painfully free to do what we choose with our lives.

Abraham Maslow and the Challenge of Self-Actualization

Humanists see Freud as preoccupied with the "basement" of the human condition. Freud wrote that people are basically motivated to gratify biological drives. The humanistic psychologist Abraham Maslow argued that people also have a need for **self-actualization**—to become all that they can be. Because people are unique, they must follow unique paths to self-actualization. Self-actualization requires taking risks. People who adhere to the tried and true may find their lives degenerating into monotony and predictability.

HUMANISM The view that people are capable of free choice, self-fulfillment, and ethical behavior.

EXISTENTIALISM The view that people are completely free and responsible for their own behavior.

SELF-ACTUALIZATION In humanistic theory, the innate tendency to strive to realize one's potential.

UNIQUE.
According to humanistic psychologists like Carl Rogers, each of us views the world from a unique frame of reference. What matters to one person may mean little to another.

Carl Rogers's Self Theory

Carl Rogers (1902–1987) wrote that people shape themselves through free choice and action. But what is your *self?*

Rogers defined the *self* as the center of experience. Your self is your ongoing sense of who and what you are, your sense of how and why you react to the environment and how you choose to act on the environment. Your choices are made on the basis of your values, and your values are also part of your self.

THE SELF-CONCEPT AND FRAMES OF REFERENCE Our self-concepts consist of our impressions of ourselves and our evaluations of our adequacy. It may be helpful to think of us as rating ourselves according to various scales or dimensions such as good-bad, intelligent-unintelligent, strong-weak, and tall-short.

Rogers believed that we all have unique ways of looking at ourselves and the world—that is, unique **frames of reference.** It may be that we each use a different set of dimensions in defining ourselves and that we judge ourselves according to different sets of values. To one person, achievement-failure may be the most important dimension. To another person, the most important dimension may be decency-indecency. A third person may not even think in terms of decency.

SELF-ESTEEM AND POSITIVE REGARD Rogers assumed that we all develop a need for self-regard, or self-esteem, as we develop and become aware of ourselves. At first, self-esteem reflects the esteem in which others hold us. Parents help children develop self-esteem when they show them **unconditional positive regard**—that is, when they accept them as having basic merit regardless of their behavior at the moment. But when parents show children **conditional positive regard**—that is, when they accept them only when they behave in a desired manner—children may develop **conditions of worth.** That is, they may come to think they have merit only if they behave as their parents wish them to behave.

FRAME OF REFERENCE One's unique patterning of perceptions and attitudes according to which one evaluates events.

UNCONDITIONAL POSITIVE REGARD A persistent expression of esteem for the value of a person, but not necessarily an unqualified acceptance of all of the person behaviors.

CONDITIONAL POSITIVE REGARD Judgment of another person's value on the basis of the acceptability of that person's behaviors.

CONDITIONS OF WORTH Standards by which the value of a person is judged.

Because each individual is thought to have a unique potential, children who develop conditions of worth must be somewhat disappointed in themselves. We cannot fully live up to the wishes of others and remain true to ourselves. This does not mean that the expression of the self inevitably leads to conflict. Rogers was optimistic about human nature. He believed that we hurt others or act in antisocial ways only when we are frustrated in our efforts to develop our potential. But when parents and others are loving and tolerant of our differentness, we, too, are loving— even if some of our preferences, abilities, and values differ from those of our parents.

However, children in some families learn that it is bad to have ideas of their own, especially about sexual, political, or religious matters. When they perceive their caretakers' disapproval, they may come to see themselves as rebels and label their feelings as selfish, wrong, or evil. If they wish to retain a consistent self-concept and self-esteem, they may have to deny many of their feelings or disown aspects of themselves. In this way the self-concept becomes distorted. According to Rogers, anxiety often stems from recognition that people have feelings and desires that are inconsistent with their distorted self-concept. Because anxiety is unpleasant, people may deny the existence of their genuine feelings and desires.

According to Rogers, the path to self-actualization requires getting in touch with our genuine feelings, accepting them, and acting on them. This is the goal of Rogers's method of psychotherapy, *client-centered therapy.*

Rogers also believed that we have mental images of what we are capable of becoming. These are termed **self-ideals.** We are motivated to reduce the discrepancy between our self-concepts and our self-ideals.

Evaluation of the Humanistic-Existential Perspective

Humanistic-existential theories have tremendous appeal for college students because of their focus on the importance of personal experience. We tend to treasure our conscious experiences (our "selves") and those of the people we care about. For lower organisms, to be alive is to move, to process food, to exchange oxygen and carbon dioxide, and to reproduce. But for human beings, an essential aspect of life is conscious experience— the sense of oneself as progressing through space and time.

Psychodynamic theories see individuals largely as victims of their childhood. Learning theories, to some degree, see people as "victims of circumstances"—or at least as victims of situational variables. But humanistic-existential theorists see humans as free to make choices. Psychodynamic theorists and learning theorists wonder whether our sense of freedom is merely an illusion. Humanistic-existential theorists, in contrast, begin by assuming personal freedom.

Ironically, the primary strength of the humanistic-existential approaches—their focus on conscious experience—is also their main weakness. Conscious experience is private and subjective. Therefore, the validity of formulating theories in terms of consciousness has been questioned. On the other hand, some psychologists (e.g., Bevan & Kessel, 1994) believe that the science of psychology can afford to loosen its methods somewhat if this will help it address the richness of human experience.

Humanistic-existential theories, like learning theories, have little to say about the development of traits and personality types. They assume that we are all unique, but they do not predict the sorts of traits, abilities, and interests we will develop.

SELF-IDEAL A mental image of what we believe we ought to be.

THE SOCIOCULTURAL PERSPECTIVE

Thirteen-year-old Hannah brought her lunch tray to the table in the cafeteria. Her mother, Julie, eyed with horror the french fries, the plate of mashed potatoes in gravy, the bag of potato chips, and the large paper cup brimming with soda. "You can't eat that!" she said. "It's garbage!"

"Oh come on, Mom! Chill, okay?" Hannah rejoined before taking her tray to sit with some friends rather than with us.

I spend Saturdays with my children at the Manhattan School of Music. Not only do they study voice and piano. They—and I—have widened our cultural perspective by relating to families and students from all parts of the world.

Julie and Hannah are Korean Americans. Flustered, Julie shook her head and said, "I've now been in the United States longer than I was in Korea, and I still can't get used to the way children act here." Alexandra, a Polish American parent, chimed in. "I never would have spoken to my parents the way Thomas speaks to me. I would have been . . . whipped or beaten."

"I try to tell Hannah she is part of the family," Julie continued. "She should think of other people. When she talks that way, it's embarrassing."

"Over here children are not part of the family," said Ken, an African American parent. "They are either part of their own crowd or they are 'individuals.'"

"Being an individual does not mean you have to talk back to your mother," Julie said. "What do you think, Spencer? You're the psychologist."

I think I made some unhelpful comments about the ketchup on the french fries having antioxidants and some slightly helpful comments about what is typical of teenagers in the United States. But I'm not sure, because I was thinking deeply about Hannah at the time. Not about her lunch, but about the formation of her personality and the influences on her behavior.

It occurred to me that in a multicultural society, personality cannot be understood without reference to the **sociocultural perspective.** Moreover, as we head toward the new millennium, trends in immigration are making the population an even richer mix. Different cultural groups within the United States have different attitudes, beliefs, norms, self-definitions, and values (Basic Behavioral Science Task Force, 1996; Triandis, 1996).

Back to Hannah. Perhaps there were some unconscious psychodynamic influences operating on her. Her traits included exceptional academic ability and musical talent, which were at least partly determined by her heredity. Clearly, she was consciously striving to become a great violinist. But one could not fully understand her personality without also considering the sociocultural influences acting on her.

Here was a youngster who was strongly influenced by her peers—she was completely at home with blue jeans and french fries. She was also a daughter in an Asian American immigrant group that views education as the key to success in our culture (Gibson & Ogbu, 1991). Belonging to this ethnic group had certainly contributed to her ambition. But being a Korean American had not prevented her from becoming an outspoken American teenager. (Would she have been outspoken if she had been reared in Korea? I wondered. Of course, this question cannot be answered with certainty.) Predictably, her outspoken behavior had struck her mother as sassy (Lopez & Hernandez, 1986). Julie was deeply offended by behavior that I consider acceptable in my own children. She reeled off the things that were "wrong" with Hannah from her Korean American perspective. I

SOCIOCULTURAL PERSPECTIVE The view that focuses on the roles of ethnicity, gender, culture, and socioeconomic status in personality formation, behavior, and mental processes.

listed some things that were very right with Hannah and encouraged Julie to worry less.

Let us consider how sociocultural factors can affect personality.

Individualism Versus Collectivism

In a sense, Julie's complaint was that Hannah saw herself as an individual and an artist to a greater extent than as a family member and a Korean girl. Cross-cultural research reveals that people in the United States and many northern European nations tend to be individualistic. **Individualists** tend to define themselves in terms of their personal identities and to give priority to their personal goals (Triandis, 1995). When asked to complete the statement "I am . . .," they are likely to respond in terms of their personality traits ("I am outgoing," "I am artistic") or their occupations ("I am a nurse," "I am a systems analyst") (Triandis, 1990). In contrast, many people from cultures in Africa, Asia, and Central and South America tend to be collectivistic (Basic Behavioral Science Task Force, 1996). **Collectivists** tend to define themselves in terms of the groups to which they belong and to give priority to the group's goals (Triandis, 1995). They feel complete in terms of their relationships with others (Markus & Kitayama, 1991; see Figure P.4). They are more likely than individualists to conform to group norms and judgments (Bond & Smith, 1996; Okazaki, 1997). When asked to complete the statement "I am . . .," they are more likely to respond in terms of their families, gender, or nation ("I am a father," "I am a Buddhist," "I am Japanese") (Triandis, 1990).

The seeds of individualism and collectivism are found in the culture in which a person grows up. The capitalist system fosters individualism to some degree. It assumes that individuals are entitled to accumulate personal fortunes and that the process of doing so creates jobs and wealth for large numbers of people. The individualist perspective is found in the self-reliant heroes and antiheroes of Western literature and mass media—from Homer's Odysseus to Clint Eastwood's gritty cowboys and Walt Disney's Pocahontas or Mulan. The traditional writings of the East have exalted people who resisted personal temptations in order to do their duty and promote the welfare of the group.

Sociocultural Factors and the Self

Sociocultural factors also affect self-concept and self-esteem. Carl Rogers noted that our self-concepts tend to reflect how other people see us. Thus members of the dominant culture in the United States are likely to have a

INDIVIDUALIST A person who defines the self in terms of personal traits and gives priority to personal goals.

COLLECTIVIST A person who defines the self in terms of relationships to other people and groups and gives priority to group goals.

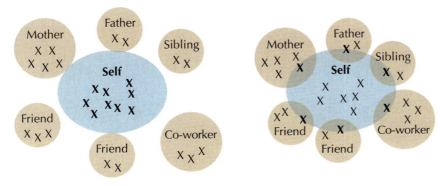

A. Independent View of Self   **B. Interdependent View of Self**

FIGURE P.4

THE SELF IN RELATION TO OTHERS FROM THE INDIVIDUALIST AND COLLECTIVIST PERSPECTIVES.

To an individualist, the self is separate from other people (part A). To a collectivist, the self is complete only in terms of relationships to other people (part B).

Based on Markus & Kitayama, 1991.

positive sense of self. They share in the expectations of personal achievement and respect that are accorded to those who rise to power. Similarly, members of ethnic groups that have been subjected to discrimination and poverty may have poorer self-concepts and lower self-esteem than members of the dominant culture (Greene, 1993, 1994; Lewis-Fernández & Kleinman, 1994).

Despite the persistence of racial prejudices, a survey by the American Association of University Women (1992) found that African American girls are likely to be happier with their appearance than White girls are. Sixty-five percent of African American elementary schoolgirls said they were happy with the way they were, compared with 55% of White girls. By high school age, 58% of African American girls remained happy with the way they were, compared with a surprisingly low 22% of White girls. Why the discrepancy? It appears that the parents of African American girls teach them that nothing is wrong with them if they do not match the ideals of the dominant culture. The world mistreats them because of prejudice, not because of who they are as individuals or what they do (Williams, 1992). The White girls are more likely to blame themselves for not attaining the unreachable ideal.

Acculturation and Self-Esteem

Should Hindu women who emigrate to the United States surrender the sari in favor of California Casuals? Should Russian immigrants try to teach their children English at home? Should African American children be acquainted with the music and art of African peoples or those of Europe? How do these activities, which are examples of **acculturation**, affect the psychological well-being of immigrants and their families?

Self-esteem is connected with patterns of acculturation among immigrants. Those patterns take various forms. Some immigrants are completely assimilated by the dominant culture. They lose the language and customs of their country of origin and become like the dominant culture in the new host country. Others maintain separation. They retain the language and customs of their country of origin and never become comfortable with those of the new country. Still others become bicultural. They remain fluent in the language of their country of origin while learning that of their new country, and they blend the customs and values of both cultures.

Research evidence suggests that people who identify with the bicultural pattern have the highest self-esteem (Phinney et al., 1992). For example, Mexican Americans who are more proficient in English are less likely to be anxious and depressed than less proficient Mexican Americans (Salgado de Snyder et al., 1990). The ability to adapt to the ways of the new society, combined with a supportive cultural tradition and a sense of ethnic identity, apparently helps people adjust.

Evaluation of the Sociocultural Perspective

The sociocultural perspective provides valuable insights into the roles of ethnicity, gender, culture, and socioeconomic status in personality formation. When we ignore sociocultural factors, we deal only with the core of the human being—the potentials that allow the person to adapt to external forces. Sociocultural factors are external forces that are internalized. They run through us deeply, touching many aspects of our cognitions, motives, emotions, and behavior. Without reference to sociocultural factors, we may be able to understand generalities about behavior and cognitive processes. However, we will not be able to understand how individuals think, behave, and feel about themselves within a given cultural setting.

ACCULTURATION The process of adaptation in which immigrants and native groups identify with a new dominant culture by learning about that culture and making behavioral and attitudinal changes.

THIS HISPANIC AMERICAN WOMAN IS HIGHLY ACCULTURATED TO LIFE IN THE UNITED STATES.
Some immigrants are completely assimilated by the dominant culture and abandon the language and customs of their country of origin. Others retain the language and customs of their country of origin and never become comfortable with those of their new country. Still others become bicultural. They become fluent in both languages and blend the customs and values of both cultures.

The sociocultural perspective enhances our sensitivity to cultural differences and expectations and allows us to appreciate the richness of human behavior and mental processes.

MEASUREMENT OF PERSONALITY

Methods of personality assessment take a sample of behavior to predict future behavior. Standardized interviews are often used. Some psychologists use computers to conduct routine interviews. **Behavior-rating scales** assess behavior in settings such as classrooms or mental hospitals. With behavior-rating scales, trained observers check off each occurrence of a behavior within a certain time frame—say, 15 minutes. However, standardized objective and projective tests are used more frequently, and we focus on them in this section.

Measures of personality are used to make important decisions, such as whether a person is suited for a certain type of work, a particular class in school, or a drug to reduce agitation. As part of their admissions process, graduate schools often ask professors to rate prospective students on scales that assess traits such as intelligence, emotional stability, and cooperation. Students may take tests to measure their aptitudes and interests to gain insight into whether they are suited for certain occupations. It is assumed that students who share the aptitudes and interests of people who function well in certain positions are also likely to function well in those positions.

Objective Tests

Objective tests present a **standardized** group of test items in the form of a questionnaire. Respondents are limited to a specific range of answers. One

BEHAVIOR-RATING SCALE A systematic means for recording the frequency with which target behaviors occur.

OBJECTIVE TESTS Tests whose items must be answered in a specified, limited manner. Tests whose items have concrete answers that are considered correct.

STANDARDIZED TEST A test given to a large number of respondents so that data concerning the typical responses can be accumulated and analyzed.

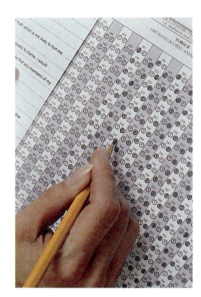

IS THIS TEST TAKER TELLING THE TRUTH?
How can psychologists determine whether or not people answer test items honestly? What are the validity scales of the MMPI?

TRUTH OR FICTION REVISITED
Psychologists cannot necessarily determine whether a person has told the truth on a personality test. However, validity scales allow them to make educated guesses.

FORCED-CHOICE FORMAT A method of presenting test questions that requires a respondent to select one of a number of possible answers.

VALIDITY SCALES Groups of test items that indicate whether a person's responses accurately reflect that individual's traits.

CLINICAL SCALES Groups of test items that measure the presence of various abnormal behavior patterns.

RESPONSE SET A tendency to answer test items according to a bias—for instance, to make oneself seem perfect or bizarre.

test might ask test takers to indicate whether items are true or false for them. Another might ask them to select the preferred activity from groups of three.

Some tests have a **forced-choice format,** in which respondents are asked to indicate which of two statements is more true for them or which of several activities they prefer. The respondents are not usually given the option of answering "none of the above." Forced-choice formats are frequently used in interest inventories, which help predict whether the person would function well in a certain occupation. The following item is similar to those found in occupational interest inventories:

I would rather

a. be a forest ranger.

b. work in a busy office.

c. play a musical instrument.

The Minnesota Multiphasic Personality Inventory (MMPI) contains hundreds of items presented in a true-false format. The MMPI is designed to be used by clinical and counseling psychologists to help diagnose psychological disorders. Accurate measurement of an individual's problems should point to appropriate treatment. The MMPI is the most widely used psychological test in clinical work (Watkins et al., 1995). It is also the most widely used instrument for personality measurement in psychological research.

Psychologists can score tests by hand, send them to computerized scoring services, or have them scored by on-site computers. Computers generate reports by interpreting the test record according to certain rules or by comparing it with records in memory.

The MMPI is usually scored for the 4 **validity scales** and 10 **clinical scales** described in Table P.3. The validity scales suggest whether answers actually represent the person's thoughts, emotions, and behaviors. However, they cannot guarantee that deception will be disclosed.

The validity scales in Table P.3 assess different **response sets,** or biases, in answering the questions. People with high L scores, for example, may be attempting to present themselves as excessively moral and well-behaved individuals. People with high F scores may be trying to seem bizarre or are answering haphazardly. Many personality measures have some kind of validity scale. The clinical scales of the MMPI assess the problems shown in Table P.3, as well as stereotypical masculine or feminine interests and introversion.

The MMPI scales were constructed *empirically*—that is, on the basis of actual clinical data rather than on the basis of psychological theory. A test-item bank of several hundred items was derived from questions that are often asked in clinical interviews. Here are some examples of the kinds of items used:

My father was a good man.	T	F
I am very seldom troubled by headaches.	T	F
My hands and feet are usually warm enough.	T	F
I have never done anything dangerous for the thrill of it.	T	F
I work under a great deal of tension.	T	F

The items were administered to people with previously identified symptoms, such as depressive or schizophrenic symptoms. Items that successfully set these people apart were included on scales named for these conditions.

TABLE P.3

MINNESOTA MULTIPHASIC PERSONALITY INVENTORY (MMPI) SCALES

SCALE	ABBREVIATION	POSSIBLE INTERPRETATIONS
VALIDITY SCALES		
Question	?	Corresponds to number of items left unanswered
Lie	L	Lies or is highly conventional
Frequency	F	Exaggerates complaints or answers items haphazardly; may have bizarre ideas
Correction	K	Denies problems
CLINICAL SCALES		
Hypochondriasis	Hs	Has bodily concerns and complaints
Depression	D	Is depressed; has feelings of guilt and helplessness
Hysteria	Hy	Reacts to stress by developing physical symptoms; lacks insight
Psychopathic deviate	Pd	Is immoral, in conflict with the law; has stormy relationships
Masculinity/Femininity	Mf	High scores suggest interests and behavior considered stereotypical of the other gender
Paranoia	Pa	Is suspicious and resentful, highly cynical about human nature
Psychasthenia	Pt	Is anxious, worried, high strung
Schizophrenia	Sc	Is confused, disorganized, disoriented; has bizarre ideas
Hypomania	Ma	Is energetic, restless, active, easily bored
Social introversion	Si	Is introverted, timid, shy; lacks self-confidence

Projective Tests

In **projective tests** there are no clear, specified answers. People are shown ambiguous stimuli such as inkblots or ambiguous drawings and asked to say what these stimuli look like to them or to tell stories about them. There is no one correct response. It is assumed that people *project* their own personalities into their responses. The meanings they attribute to these stimuli are assumed to reflect their personalities as well as the drawings or blots themselves.

THE RORSCHACH INKBLOT TEST You may have heard of a personality test that asks people what a drawing or inkblot looks like and that people commonly answer "a bat." There are a number of such tests, the best known of which is the Rorschach inkblot test, named after its originator, the Swiss psychiatrist Hermann Rorschach (1884–1922). During his last two years in the equivalent of high school, Hermann was given the nickname "Klex" by his fraternity brothers. The proper spelling of the word in German is *Klecks*, which translates as "inkblot" in English. Hermann was preoccupied with the child's game of *klecksographie*—dropping ink onto paper and arranging and folding the paper to cause the ink to take on an appealing shape (Figure P.5).

Rorschach believed that people's responses to inkblots revealed something about their personalities. He tried out dozens of inkblots with patients at a sanitarium and concluded that 15 of them helped diagnose their problems. There are only 10 Rorschach inkblots today. Why? There was not enough money to print all of the plates in Rorschach's research report.

TRUTH OR FICTION REVISITED
It is true that there is a psychological test made up of inkblots, and test takers are asked to say what the blots look like to them. It is the Rorschach Inkblot Test.

PROJECTIVE TEST A psychological test that presents ambiguous stimuli onto which the test taker projects his or her own personality in making a response.

FIGURE P.5

AN INKBLOT SIMILAR TO A RORSCHACH INKBLOT.

The Rorschach is the most widely used projective personality test. What does this look like to you? What could it be?

REALITY TESTING The capacity to perceive one's environment and oneself according to accurate sensory impressions.

People are given the inkblots, one by one, and are asked what they look like or what they could be. A response that reflects the shape of the blot is considered a sign of adequate **reality testing.** A response that richly integrates several features of the blot is considered a sign of high intellectual functioning. The Rorschach test is thought to provide insight into a person's intelligence, interests, cultural background, degree of introversion or extraversion, level of anxiety, reality testing, and many other variables.

THE THEMATIC APPERCEPTION TEST The Thematic Apperception Test (TAT) was developed in the 1930s by Henry Murray and Christiana Morgan. It consists of drawings, like the one shown in Figure P.6, that are open to a variety of interpretations. Individuals are given the cards one at a time and asked to make up stories about them.

The TAT is widely used in research on motivation and in clinical practice (Watkins et al., 1995). The notion is that we are likely to project our own needs into our responses to ambiguous situations, even if we are unaware of them or reluctant to talk about them. The TAT is also widely used to assess attitudes toward other people, especially parents, lovers, and spouses.

Although personality tests have their uses, most psychologists consider them just one source of information about people. They are best used to enrich the understanding of an individual's personality; they are not a substitute for personal contact with the individual.

FIGURE P.6

A DRAWING SIMILAR TO A TAT CARD.

Can you make up a story about this drawing? What are the characters thinking and feeling? What will happen next? What does your story reveal about yourself?

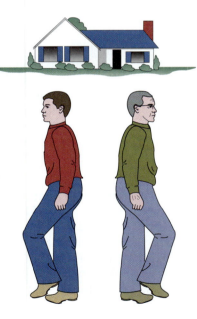

SUMMARY

1. **What is personality?** Personality is defined as the reasonably stable patterns of behavior, including thoughts and emotions, that distinguish one person from another.

2. **What is the role of conflict in Freud's psychodynamic theory?** Psychodynamic theory assumes that we are driven largely by unconscious motives. Conflict is inevitable as basic instincts of hunger, sex, and aggression come up against social pressures to follow laws, rules, and moral codes. At first this conflict is external, but as we develop, it is internalized.

3. **What are the psychic structures in psychodynamic theory?** The unconscious id is present at birth. The id represents psychological drives and seeks instant gratification. The ego is the sense of self or "I." It develops through experience and takes into account what is practical and possible in gratifying the impulses of the id. Defense mechanisms protect the ego from anxiety by repressing unacceptable ideas or distorting reality. The superego is the conscience and develops largely through identification with others.

4. **What are Freud's stages of psychosexual development?** People undergo psychosexual development as psychosexual energy, or libido, is transferred from one erogenous zone to another during childhood. There are five stages of development: oral, anal, phallic, latency, and genital.

5. **What is Carl Jung's theory?** Jung's psychodynamic theory, called analytical psychology, features a collective unconscious and numerous archetypes, both of which reflect the history of our species.

6. **What is Alfred Adler's theory?** Adler's psychodynamic theory, called individual psychology, features the inferiority complex and the compensating drive for superiority.

7. **What is Karen Horney's theory?** Horney's psychodynamic theory focuses on parent-child relationships and the possible development of feelings of anxiety and hostility.

8. **What is Erik Erikson's theory?** Erikson's psychodynamic theory of psychosocial development highlights the importance of early social relationships rather than the gratification of childhood sexual impulses. Erikson extended Freud's five developmental stages to eight, including stages that occur in adulthood.

9. **What are traits?** Traits are personality elements that are inferred from behavior and that account for behavioral consistency. Trait theory adopts a descriptive approach to personality.

10. **What are Gordon Allport's views?** Allport saw traits as embedded in the nervous system and as steering an individual's behavior.

11. **What are Hans Eysenck's views?** Eysenck theorized two broad, independent personality dimensions (introversion-extraversion and emotional stability-instability) and described personalities according to combinations of these dimensions.

12. **What is the five-factor model?** Mathematical analyses that seek common factors in multiple personality traits often arrive at a list of five factors: extraversion, agreeableness, conscientiousness, emotional stability, and openness to experience.

13. **How do behaviorists view personality?** Behaviorists emphasize the situational determinants of behavior. John B. Watson, the father of modern behaviorism, rejected notions of mind and personality altogether. Watson and B. F. Skinner opposed the idea of personal freedom and argued that environmental contingencies can shape people into wanting to do the things that society and the physical environment require of them.

14. **How do social-cognitive theorists view personality?** Social-cognitive theory, in contrast to behaviorism, has a cognitive orientation and focuses on learning by observation. To predict behavior, social-cognitive theorists consider situational variables (rewards and punishments) and person variables (competencies, encoding strategies, expectancies, emotions, and self-regulatory systems and plans).

15. **What is Carl Rogers's self theory?** Self theory begins by assuming the existence of the self. According to Rogers, the self is an organized and consistent way in which a person perceives his or her "I" in relation to others. The self attempts to actualize (develop its unique potential) when the person receives unconditional positive regard. Conditions of worth may lead to a distorted self-concept, disowning of parts of the self, and anxiety.

16. **What is the sociocultural perspective?** This view focuses on the roles of ethnicity, gender, culture, and socioeconomic status in personality formation, behavior, and mental processes. Sociocultural theorists are interested in issues such as individualism versus collectivism and the effects of sociocultural factors on the sense of self.

17. **What are objective tests?** Objective tests present test takers with a standardized set of test items to which they must respond in specific, limited ways (as in multiple-choice or true-false tests). A forced-choice format asks respondents to indicate which of two or more statements is true for them or which of several activities they prefer.

18. **What are projective tests?** Projective tests present ambiguous stimuli and allow the test taker to give a broad range of response. Examples include the Rorschach inkblot test and the Thematic Apperception Test.

KEY TERMS

acculturation (p. P-24)

anal stage (p. P-7)

archetypes (p. P-8)

behavior-rating scale (p. P-25)

clinical scales (p. P-26)

clitoris (p. P-7)

collective unconscious (p. P-8)

collectivist (p. P-23)

competencies (p. P-16)

conditional positive regard (p. P-20)

conditions of worth (p. P-20)

creative self (p. P-9)

defense mechanism (p. P-5)

displaced (p. P-7)

drive for superiority (p. P-8)

ego (p. P-5)

ego identity (p. P-9)

Electra complex (p. P-7)

encode (p. P-17)

erogenous zone (p. P-6)

eros (p. P-6)

existentialism (p. P-19)

expectancies (p. P-15)

extraversion (p. P-12)

fixation (p. P-7)

forced-choice format (p. P-26)

frame of reference (p. P-20)

genital stage (p. P-8)

humanism (p. P-19)

id (p. P-4)

identification (p. P-6)

individualist (p. P-23)

inferiority complex (p. P-8)

introversion (p. P-12)

latency (p. P-8)

libido (p. P-6)

model (p. P-16)

neuroticism (p. P-12)

objective tests (p. P-25)

Oedipus complex (p. P-7)

oral stage (p. P-6)

person variables (p. P-15)

phallic stage (p. P-7)

preconscious (p. P-3)

projective test (p. P-27)

psychic structure (p. P-4)

psychoanalysis (p. P-4)

psychodynamic theory (p. P-3)

psychosexual development (p. P-9)

psychosocial development (p. P-6)

reality testing (p. P-28)

reciprocal determinism (p. P-15)

repression (p. P-3)

response set (p. P-26)

self-actualization (p. P-19)

self-efficacy expectations (p. P-17)

self-ideal (p. P-20)

social-cognitive theory (p. P-15)

sociocultural perspective (p. P-22)

standardized test (p. P-25)

subjective value (p. P-15)

superego (p. P-6)

trait (p. P-12)

unconditional positive regard (p. P-20)

unconscious (p. P-3)

validity scales (p. P-26)

REFERENCES

Allport, G. W., & Oddbert, H. S. (1936). Trait names: A psycholexical study. *Psychological Monographs, 47,* 2–11.

American Association of University Women. (1992). *How schools shortchange women: The A.A.U.W. report.* Washington, DC: AAUW Educational Foundation.

Bandura, A. (1986). *Social foundations of thought and action: A social-cognitive theory.* Englewood Cliffs, NJ: Prentice-Hall.

Basic Behavioral Science Task Force of the National Advisory Mental Health Council. (1996). Basic behavioral science research for mental health: Sociocultural and environmental practices. *American Psychologist, 51,* 722–731.

Bevan, W., & Kessel, F. (1994). Plain truths and home cooking. *American Psychologist, 49,* 505–509.

Bianchi, S. M., & Spain, D. (1997). *Women, work and family in America.* Population Reference Bureau.

Block, J. (1995). A contrarian view of the five-factor approach to personality description. *Psychological Bulletin, 117,* 187–215.

Bond, R., & Smith, P. B. (1996). Culture and conformity. *Psychological Bulletin, 119,* 111–137.

Bly, R. (1990). *Iron John.* Reading, MA: Addison-Wesley.

Clark, L. A., Watson, D., & Mineka, S. M. (1994). Temperament, personality, and the mood and anxiety disorders. *Journal of Abnormal Psychology, 103,* 103–116.

Dindia, K., & Allen, M. (1992). Sex differences in self-disclosure. *Psychological Bulletin, 112,* 106–124.

Eysenck, H. J., & Eysenck, M. W. (1985). *Personality and individual differences.* New York: Plenum.

Freud, S. (1964). A religious experience. In J. Strachey (Ed. And Trans.), *The standard edition of the complete psychological works of Sigmund Freud* (Vol. 21). London: Hogarth Press (Original work published 1927)

Gibson, M., & Ogbu, J. (Eds.). (1991). *Minority status and schooling.* New York: Garland.

Gilligan, C., Rogers, A. G., & Tolman, D. L. (Eds.). (1991). *Women, girls, and psychotherapy.* New York: Haworth.

Greene, B. (1993). African American women. In L. Comas-Diaz & B. A. Greene (Eds.), *Women of color and mental health.* New York: Guilford.

Greene, B. (1994). Ethnic-minority lesbians and gay men. *Journal of Consulting and Clinical Psychology, 62,* 243–251.

Guisinger, S., & Blatt, S. J. (1994). Individuality and relatedness. *American Psychologist, 49,* 104–111.

Hergenhahn, B. R. (1997). *An introduction to the history of psychology* (3rd ed.). Pacific Grove, CA: Brooks/Cole.

Holland, J. L. (1996). Exploring careers with a typology. *American Psychologist, 51,* 397–406.

Jordan, J. V., Kaplan, A. G., Miller, J. B., Stiver, L. P., & Stiver, J. L. (Eds.). (1991). *Women's growth in connection.* New York: Guilford.

Keen, S. (1991). *Fire in the belly.* New York: Harper & Row.

Lewis-Fernández R., & Kleinman, A. (1994). Culture, personality, and psychopathology. *Journal of Abnormal Psychology, 103,* 67–71.

Loftus, E. F. (1993). The reality of repressed memories. *American Psychologist, 48,* 518–537.

Lopez, S., & Hernandez, P. (1986). How culture is considered in evaluations of psychopathology. *Journal of Nervous and Mental Diseases, 176,* 598–606.

Maher, B. A., & Maher, W. B. (1994). Personality and psychopathology. *Journal of Abnormal Psychology, 103,* 72–77.

Markus, H., & Kitayama, S. (1991). Culture and the self. *Psychological Review, 98*(2), 224–253.

McCrae, R. R. (1996). Social consequences of experiential openness. *Psychological Bulletin, 120,* 323–337.

McCrae, R. R., & Costa, P. T., Jr. (1997). Personality trait structure as a human universal. *American Psychologist, 52,* 509–516.

Mischel, W., & Shoda, Y. (1995). A cognitive-affective system theory of personality. *Psychological Review, 102,* 246–268.

Myers, L. B., & Brewin, C. R. (1994). Recall of early experience and the repressive coping style. *Journal of Abnormal Psychology, 103,* 288–292.

Okazaki, S. (1997). Sources of ethnic differences between Asian American and White American college students on measures of depression and social anxiety. *Journal of Abnormal Psychology, 106,* 52–60.

Pajares, F., & Miller, M. D. (1994). Role of self-efficacy and self-concept beliefs in mathematical problem solving. *Journal of Educational Psychology, 86,* 193–203.

Phinney, J. S., Chavira, V., & Williamson, L. (1992). Acculturation attitudes and self-esteem among high school and college students. *Youth and Society, 23*(3), 299–312.

Quinn, S. (1987). *A mind of her own: The life of Karen Horney.* New York: Summit Books.

Sadker, M., & Sadker, D. (1994). *How America's schools cheat girls.* New York: Scribners.

Salgado de Snyder, V. N., Cervantes, R. C., & Padilla, A. M. (1990). Gender and ethnic differences in psychosocial stress and generalized distress among Hispanics. *Sex Roles, 22,* 441–453.

Skinner, B. F. (1948). *Walden two.* New York: Macmillan.

Triandis, H. C. (1990). Cross-cultural studies of individualism and collectivism. In J. J. Berman (Ed.), *Nebraska Symposium on Motivation, 1989. Cross-cultural perspectives.* Lincoln: University of Nebraska Press.

Triandis, H. C. (1995). *Individualism and collectivism.* Boulder, CO: Westview Press.

Triandis, H. C. (1996). The psychological measurement of cultural syndromes. *American Psychologist, 51,* 407–415.

Watkins, C. E., Jr., Campbell, V. L., Nieberding, R., & Hallmark, R. (1995). Contemporary practice of psychological assessment by clinical psychologists. *Professional Psychology: Research and Practice, 26,* 54–60.

Watson, J. B. (1924). *Behaviorism.* New York: Norton.

Widiger, T. A., & Costa, P. T., Jr. (1994). Personality and personality disorders. *Journal of Abnormal Psychology, 103,* 78–91.

Williams, L. (1992, February 6). Woman's image in a mirror: Who defines what she sees? *New York Times,* pp. A1, B7.

Zuckerman, M. (1992). What is a basic factor and which factors are basic? Tumbles all the way down. *Personality and Individual Differences, 13,* 675–681.

PD

PSYCHOLOGICAL DISORDERS

URING ONE LONG FALL SEMESTER, THE OHIO STATE campus lived in terror. Four college women were abducted, forced to cash checks or obtain money from automatic teller machines, and then raped. A mysterious phone call led to the arrest of a 23-year-old drifter, William, who had been dismissed from the navy.

William was not the boy next door. Psychologists and psychiatrists who interviewed William concluded that 10 personalities—8 male and 2 female—resided within him (Scott, 1994). His personality had been fractured as a result of an abusive childhood. His personalities had distinct facial expressions, speech patterns, and memories. They even obtained different scores on psychological tests.

Arthur, the most rational personality, spoke with a British accent. Danny and Christopher were quiet adolescents. Christine was a 3-year-old girl. Tommy, a 16-year-old, had enlisted in the navy. Allen was 18 and smoked. Adelena, a 19-year-old lesbian personality, had committed the rapes. Who had made the mysterious phone call? Probably David, 9, an anxious child.

The defense claimed that William's behavior was caused by a psychological disorder termed *dissociative identity disorder* (also referred to as *multiple personality disorder*). Several distinct identities or personalities dwelled within him. Some knew of the others. Some believed they were unique. Billy, the core identity, had learned to sleep as a child in order to avoid his father's abuse. A psychiatrist asserted that Billy had also been "asleep," or in a "psychological coma," during the abductions. Billy should therefore be found not guilty by reason of insanity.

William was found not guilty. He was committed to a psychiatric institution and released six years later.

In 1982, John Hinckley was also found not guilty of the assassination attempt on President Reagan's life. Expert witnesses testified that he should be diagnosed with *schizophrenia*—a severe disorder characterized by loss of control of thought processes and inappropriate emotional responses. Hinckley, too, was committed to a psychiatric institution.

Dissociative identity disorder and schizophrenia are two **psychological disorders.** If William and Hinckley had lived in Salem, Massachusetts, in 1692, just 200 years after Columbus set foot in the New World, they might have been hanged or burned as witches. At that time, most people assumed that psychological disorders were caused by possession by the devil. A score of people were executed in Salem that year for allegedly practicing the arts of Satan.

Throughout human history people have attributed unusual behavior and psychological disorders to demons. The ancient Greeks believed that the gods punish humans by causing confusion and madness. An exception was the physician Hippocrates, who made the radical suggestion that psychological disorders are caused by an abnormality of the brain. His notion that biology could affect thoughts, feelings, and behavior was to lie dormant for about 2,000 years.

During the Middle Ages in Europe, as well as during the early period of European colonization of Massachusetts, it was generally believed that psychological disorders were signs of possession by the devil. Possession could stem from retribution, in which God caused the devil to possess a person's soul as punishment for committing certain kinds of sins. Agitation and confusion were ascribed to such retribution. Possession was also believed to result from deals with the devil, in which people traded their souls for earthly gains. Such individuals were called witches. Witches were held responsible for unfortunate events ranging from a neighbor's infertility to a poor harvest. In Europe, hundreds of thousands of accused witches were killed. The goings on at Salem were trivial by comparison.

A document authorized by Pope Innocent VIII, *The Hammer of Witches,* proposed ingenious "diagnostic" tests to identify those who were possessed. The water-float test was based on the principle that pure metals sink to the bottom during smelting. Impurities float to the surface. Suspects were thus placed in deep water. Those who sank to the bottom and drowned were judged pure. Those who managed to keep their heads above water were assumed "impure" and in league with the devil. Then they were in real trouble. This ordeal is the origin of the phrase, "Damned if you do and damned if you don't."

Few people in the United States today would argue that unusual or unacceptable behavior is caused by demons. But we continue to use phrases suggestive of demonology. How many times have you heard the expressions "Something got into me" or "The devil made me do it"?

Let us now define what is meant by psychological disorders.

WHAT ARE PSYCHOLOGICAL DISORDERS?

Psychology is the study of behavior and mental processes. Psychological disorders are behaviors or mental processes connected with various kinds of distress or disability. However, they are not predictable responses to specific events.

For example, some psychological disorders are characterized by anxiety, but many people are anxious now and then without being considered disordered. It is appropriate to be anxious before an important date or on the eve of a midterm exam. When, then, are feelings like anxiety deemed to be abnormal or signs of a psychological disorder? First, anxiety may suggest a disorder when it is not appropriate to the situation. Anxiety is inappropriate when one is entering an elevator or looking out of a fourth-story window. The magnitude of the problem may also suggest disorder. Some anxiety is common before a job interview. But feeling that your heart is pounding so intensely that it might leap out of your chest—and then avoiding the interview—are not.

Behavior or mental processes are suggestive of psychological disorders when they meet some combination of the following criteria:

1. *They are unusual.* Although people with psychological disorders are a minority, uncommon behavior or mental processes are not abnormal in themselves. Only one person holds the record for running or swimming the fastest mile. That person is different from you and me but is not abnormal. Only a few people qualify as

TRUTH OR FICTION REVISITED
It is true that a man shot the president of the United States in front of millions of television witnesses and was found not guilty by a court of law. His name is John Hinckley, and he was found not guilty by reason of insanity.

TRUTH OR FICTION REVISITED
It is true that innocent people were drowned in the Middle Ages to prove they were not possessed by the devil. This method was based on a water-float test designed to determine whether metals are pure.

TRUTH OR FICTION REVISITED
It may not be abnormal to feel anxious. It is normal to feel anxious when one is in a stressful or fearful situation.

PSYCHOLOGICAL DISORDERS Patterns of behavior or mental processes connected with emotional distress or significant impairment in functioning.

geniuses in mathematics, but mathematical genius is not a sign of a psychological disorder.

Rarity or statistical deviance may not be sufficient for behavior or mental processes to be labeled abnormal, but it helps. Most people do not see or hear things that are not there, and "seeing things" and "hearing things" are considered abnormal. We must also consider the situation. Although many of us feel "panicked" when we realize that a term paper or report is due the next day, most of us do not have panic attacks out of nowhere. Unpredictable panic attacks thus are suggestive of psychological disorder.

2. *They suggest faulty perception or interpretation of reality.* Our society considers it normal to hear people when they are talking to you, but abnormal to hear people when they are not there. "Hearing voices" and "seeing things" are considered **hallucinations.** Similarly, **ideas of persecution,** such as believing that the Mafia or the FBI are "out to get you," are considered signs of disorder. (Unless, of course, they *are* out to get you.)

3. *They suggest severe personal distress.* Anxiety, exaggerated fears, and other psychological states cause personal distress, and severe personal distress may be considered abnormal. Anxiety may also be an appropriate response to a situation, however, as in the case of a threat.

4. *They are self-defeating.* Behavior or mental processes that cause misery rather than happiness and fulfillment may suggest psychological disorder. Chronic drinking that impairs work and family life or cigarette smoking that impairs health may therefore be deemed abnormal.

5. *They are dangerous.* Behavior or mental processes hazardous to the self or others may be considered suggestive of psychological disorders. People who threaten or attempt suicide may be considered abnormal, as may people who threaten or attack others. Yet criminal behavior or aggressive behavior need not imply a psychological disorder.

6. *The individual's behavior is socially unacceptable.* The cultural context of behavior also affects whether or not it is considered normal. In

HALLUCINATION A perception in the absence of sensory stimulation that is confused with reality.

IDEAS OF PERSECUTION Erroneous beliefs that one is being victimized or persecuted.

HALLUCINATIONS.
Hallucinations are a feature of schizophrenia. They are perceptions that occur in the absence of external stimulation, as in "hearing voices" or "seeing things." Hallucinations cannot be distinguished from real perceptions. Are the cats in this Sandy Skoglund photograph real or hallucinatory?

the United States, it is deemed normal for males to be aggressive in sports and in combat. In other situations warmth and tenderness are valued. Many Americans admire women who are self-assertive, but "traditionalists" may consider outspoken women to be disrespectful.

CLASSIFYING PSYCHOLOGICAL DISORDERS

Toss some people, apes, seaweed, fish, and sponges into a room—preferably a well-ventilated one. Stir slightly. What do you have? It depends on how you classify this hodgepodge of organisms.

Classify them as plants versus animals and you lump the people, chimpanzees, fish, and, yes, sponges together. Classify them as stuff that carries on its business on land or underwater, and we throw in our lot with the chimps and none of the others. How about those that swim and those that do not? Then the chimps, the fish, and some of us are grouped together.

Classification is at the heart of science (Barlow, 1991). Without classifying psychological disorders, investigators would not be able to communicate with each other and scientific progress would come to a standstill. The most widely used classification scheme for psychological disorders is the *Diagnostic and Statistical Manual (DSM)* of the American Psychiatric Association.

The current edition of the *DSM* groups disorders on the basis of observable features or symptoms. However, early editions of the *DSM*, which was first published in 1952, grouped many disorders on the basis of assumptions about their causes. Because Freud's psychodynamic theory was widely accepted at the time, one major diagnostic category contained so-called neuroses. From the psychodynamic perspective, all neuroses—no matter how differently people with various neuroses might behave—were caused by unconscious neurotic conflict. Each neurosis was thought to reflect a way of coping with the unconscious fear that primitive impulses might break loose. As a result, sleepwalking was included as a neurosis (psychoanalysts assumed that sleepwalking reduced this unconscious fear by permitting the partial expression of impulses during the night). Now that the focus is on observable behaviors, sleepwalking is classified as a sleep disorder, not as a neurosis.

Some professionals, such as psychiatrist Thomas Szasz, believe that the categories described in the *DSM* are really "problems in living" rather than "disorders." At least, they are not disorders in the sense that high blood pressure, cancer, and the flu are disorders. Szasz argues that labeling people with problems in living as "sick" degrades them and encourages them to evade their personal and social responsibilities. Because sick people are encouraged to obey doctors' orders, Szasz (1984) also contends that labeling people as "sick" accords too much power to health professionals. Instead, he believes, troubled people need to be encouraged to take greater responsibility for solving their own problems.

Let us now consider the various kinds of psychological disorders. Some of them, like anxiety disorders, are very common; others, like dissociative identity disorder, are quite rare.

ANXIETY DISORDERS

Anxiety has subjective and physical features (Zinbarg & Barlow, 1996). Subjective features include worrying, fear of the worst things happening, fear of losing control, nervousness, and inability to relax. Physical features reflect arousal of the sympathetic branch of the autonomic nervous system. They include trembling, sweating, a pounding or racing heart, elevated blood pressure (a flushed face), and faintness. Anxiety is an appropriate response to a real threat. It can be abnormal, however, when it is excessive or when it comes out of nowhere—that is, when events do not seem to warrant it. There are different kinds of anxiety disorders, but all of them are characterized by excessive or unwarranted anxiety.

Types of Anxiety Disorders

The anxiety disorders include phobias, panic disorder, generalized anxiety, obsessive-compulsive disorder, and stress disorders.

PHOBIAS There are several types of phobias, including specific phobias, social phobia, and agoraphobia. **Specific phobias** are excessive, irrational fears of specific objects or situations such as snakes or heights. One specific phobia is fear of elevators. Some people will not enter elevators despite the hardships they incur as a result (such as walking up six flights of steps). Yes, the cable *could* break. The ventilation *could* fail. One *could* be stuck in midair waiting for repairs. These problems are uncommon, however, and it does not make sense for most people to walk up and down several flights of stairs to elude them. Similarly, some people with a specific phobia for hypodermic needles will not have injections, even to treat profound illness. Injections can be painful, but most people with a phobia for needles would gladly suffer an even more painful pinch if it would help them fight illness. Other specific phobias include **claustrophobia** (fear of tight or enclosed places), **acrophobia** (fear of heights), and fear of mice, snakes, and other creepy crawlies. Fears of animals and imaginary creatures are common among children.

Social phobias are persistent fears of scrutiny by others or of doing something that will be humiliating or embarrassing. Fear of public speaking is a common social phobia.

Agoraphobia is also widespread among adults. Agoraphobia is derived from the Greek words meaning "fear of the marketplace," or fear of being out in open, busy areas. Persons with agoraphobia fear being in places from which it might be difficult to escape or in which help might not be available if they get upset. In practice, people who receive this diagnosis often refuse to venture out of their homes, especially by themselves. They find it difficult to hold a job or to maintain an ordinary social life.

Phobias can seriously disrupt a person's life. The person may know that the phobia is irrational yet still experience acute anxiety and avoid the phobic article or circumstance.

PANIC DISORDER

My heart would start pounding so hard I was sure I was having a heart attack. I used to go to the emergency room. Sometimes I felt dizzy, like I was going to pass out. I was sure I was about to die.

KIM WEINER

Panic disorder is an abrupt attack of acute anxiety that is not triggered by a specific object or situation. People with panic disorder have strong physical symptoms such as shortness of breath, heavy sweating, tremors, and pounding of the heart. Like Kim Weiner (1992), they are particularly aware of cardiac sensations (Schmidt et al., 1997). It is not unusual for them to think they are having a heart attack (Clark et al., 1997). Many fear suffocation (McNally & Eke, 1996). People with the disorder may also

SPECIFIC PHOBIA Persistent fear of a specific object or situation.

CLAUSTROPHOBIA Fear of tight, small places.

ACROPHOBIA Fear of high places.

SOCIAL PHOBIA An irrational, excessive fear of public scrutiny.

AGORAPHOBIA Fear of open, crowded places.

PANIC DISORDER The recurrent experiencing of attacks of extreme anxiety in the absence of external stimuli that usually elicit anxiety.

experience choking sensations; nausea; numbness or tingling; flushes or chills; and fear of going crazy or losing control. Panic attacks may last minutes or hours. Afterward, the person usually feels drained.

Many people panic now and then. The diagnosis of panic disorder is reserved for those who undergo a series of attacks or live in fear of attacks.

Panic attacks seem to come from nowhere. Thus some people who have had them stay home for fear of having an attack in public. They are diagnosed as having panic disorder with agoraphobia.

GENERALIZED ANXIETY DISORDER The central feature of **generalized anxiety disorder** is persistent anxiety. As with panic disorder, the anxiety cannot be attributed to a phobic object, situation, or activity. Rather, it seems to be free floating. Features of this disorder may include motor tension (shakiness, inability to relax, furrowed brow, fidgeting); autonomic overarousal (sweating, dry mouth, racing heart, light-headedness, frequent urinating, diarrhea); feelings of dread and foreboding; and excessive vigilance, as shown by irritability, insomnia, and a tendency to be easily distracted.

OBSESSIVE-COMPULSIVE DISORDER **Obsessions** are recurrent, anxiety-provoking thoughts or images that seem irrational and beyond control. They are so compelling and recurrent that they disrupt daily life. They may include doubts about whether one has locked the doors and shut the windows, or images such as one mother's repeated fantasy that her children had been run over on the way home from school. One woman became obsessed with the idea that she had contaminated her hands with the cleaner Sani-Flush and that the chemicals were spreading to everything she touched. A 16-year-old boy found "numbers in his head" when he was about to study or take a test.

Compulsions are thoughts or behaviors that tend to reduce the anxiety connected with obsessions. They are seemingly irresistible urges to engage in specific acts, often repeatedly, such as elaborate washing after using the bathroom. The impulse is recurrent and forceful, interfering with daily life. The woman who felt contaminated by Sani-Flush spent 3 to 4 hours at the sink each day and complained, "My hands look like lobster claws."

POSTTRAUMATIC STRESS DISORDER Fires, stabbings, shootings, suicides, medical emergencies, accidents, bombs, and hazardous material explosions—these are just some of the traumatic experiences firefighters confront on a fairly regular basis. Because of such experiences, one study found that the prevalence of **posttraumatic stress disorder** (PTSD) among firefighters is 16.5%. This rate is 1% higher than the rate among Vietnam veterans and far above that for the general population, which is 1% to 3% (DeAngelis, 1995).

PTSD is characterized by a rapid heart rate and feelings of anxiety and helplessness caused by a traumatic experience. Such experiences may include a threat or assault, destruction of one's community, or witnessing a death. PTSD may occur months or years after the event. It frequently occurs among combat veterans, people whose homes and communities have been swept away by natural disasters or who have been subjected to toxic hazards, and survivors of childhood sexual abuse (Baum & Fleming, 1993; Rodriguez et al., 1997). A study of victims of Hurricane Andrew, which devastated South Florida in 1992, found that 1 man in 4 and about 1 woman in 3 (36%) had developed PTSD (Ironson, 1993). A national

A Traumatic Experience.
Traumatic experiences like the destruction of one's home can lead to posttraumatic stress disorder (PTSD). PTSD is characterized by intrusive memories of the experience, recurrent dreams about it, and the sudden feeling that it is, in fact, recurring (as in "flashbacks").

GENERALIZED ANXIETY DISORDER Feelings of dread and foreboding and sympathetic arousal of at least 6 months' duration.

OBSESSION A recurring thought or image that seems beyond control.

COMPULSION An apparently irresistible urge to repeat an act or engage in ritualistic behavior such as hand washing.

POSTTRAUMATIC STRESS DISORDER A disorder that follows a distressing event outside the range of normal human experience; characterized by features such as intense fear, avoidance of stimuli associated with the event, and reliving of the event. Abbreviated *PTSD*.

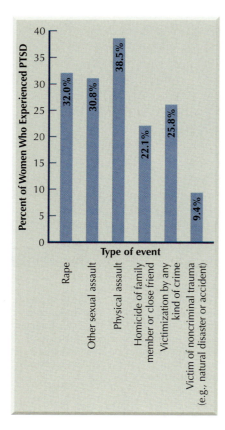

FIGURE PD.1
POSTTRAUMATIC STRESS DISORDER AMONG FEMALE VICTIMS OF CRIME AND AMONG OTHER WOMEN.
According to Resnick and her colleagues (1993), about 1 woman in 4 (25.8%) who was victimized by crime could be diagnosed with PTSD at some point following the crime. By contrast, fewer than 1 woman in 10 (9.4%) who was not victimized by crime experienced PTSD.

study of more than 4,000 women found that about 1 woman in 4 who had been victimized by crime experienced PTSD (Resnick et al., 1993; see Figure PD.1).

The traumatic event is revisited in the form of intrusive memories, recurrent dreams, and flashbacks—the sudden feeling that the event is recurring. People with PTSD typically try to avoid thoughts and activities connected to the traumatic event. They may also have sleep problems, irritable outbursts, difficulty concentrating, extreme vigilance, and an intensified "startle" response.

ACUTE STRESS DISORDER **Acute stress disorder,** like PTSD, is characterized by feelings of anxiety and helplessness caused by a traumatic event. However, PTSD can occur 6 months or more after the traumatic event and tends to persist. Acute stress disorder occurs within a month of the event and lasts from 2 days to 4 weeks. Women who have been raped, for example, experience acute distress that tends to peak in severity about 3 weeks after the assault (Davidson & Foa, 1991; Rothbaum et al., 1992).

Theoretical Views

According to the psychodynamic perspective, phobias symbolize conflicts originating in childhood. Psychodynamic theory explains generalized anxiety as persistent difficulty in repressing primitive impulses. Obsessions are explained as leakage of unconscious impulses, and compulsions are seen as acts that allow people to keep such impulses partly repressed.

Some learning theorists—particularly behaviorists—consider phobias to be conditioned fears that were acquired in early childhood. Therefore, their origins are beyond memory. Avoidance of feared stimuli is reinforced by the reduction of anxiety.

Other learning theorists—social-cognitive theorists—note that observational learning plays a role in the acquisition of fears (Basic Behavioral Science Task Force, 1996). If parents squirm, grimace, and shudder at the sight of mice, blood, or dirt on the kitchen floor, children may assume that these stimuli are awful and imitate their parents' behavior.

Cognitive theorists suggest that anxiety is maintained by thinking that one is in a terrible situation and helpless to change it. People with anxiety disorders may be cognitively biased toward paying more attention to threats than other people do (Foa et al., 1996; Mineka, 1991). Cognitive theorists note that people's appraisals of the magnitude of threats help determine whether they are traumatic and can lead to PTSD (Creamer et al., 1992). People with panic attacks tend to misinterpret bodily cues and to view them as threats (Meichenbaum, 1993). Obsessions and compulsions may serve to divert attention from more frightening issues, such as "What am I going to do with my life?" When anxieties are acquired at a young age, we may later interpret them as enduring traits and label ourselves as "people who fear _____" (you fill it in). We then live up to the labels. We also entertain thoughts that heighten and perpetuate anxiety such as "I've got to get out of here" or "My heart is going to leap out of my chest." Such ideas intensify physical signs of anxiety, disrupt planning, make stimuli seem worse than they really are, motivate avoidance, and decrease self-efficacy expectations. The belief that we will not be able to handle a threat heightens anxiety. The belief that we are in control reduces anxiety (Bandura et al., 1985).

Biological factors play a role in anxiety disorders. Genetic factors are implicated in most psychological disorders, including anxiety disorders

ACUTE STRESS DISORDER A disorder, like PTSD, characterized by feelings of anxiety and helplessness and caused by a traumatic event. Unlike PTSD, acute stress disorder occurs within a month of the event and lasts from 2 days to 4 weeks. (A category first included in *DSM-IV.*)

(Carey & DiLalla, 1994). For one thing, anxiety disorders tend to run in families (Michels & Marzuk, 1993b). Twin studies also find a higher rate of agreement for anxiety disorders among identical twins than among fraternal twins (Torgersen, 1983). Studies of adoptees who are anxious similarly show that the biological parent places the child at risk for anxiety and related traits (Pedersen et al., 1988).

Susan Mineka (1991) suggests that humans (and nonhuman primates) are genetically predisposed to respond with fear to stimuli that may have once posed a threat to their ancestors. Evolutionary forces would have favored the survival of individuals who were predisposed toward acquiring fears of large animals, spiders, snakes, heights, entrapment, sharp objects, and strangers.

Perhaps a predisposition toward anxiety—in the form of a highly reactive autonomic nervous system—can be inherited. What might make a nervous system "highly reactive"? In the case of panic disorder, faulty regulation of levels of serotonin and norepinephrine may be involved. In other anxiety disorders, receptor sites in the brain may not be sensitive enough to *gamma-aminobutyric acid* (GABA). GABA helps calm anxiety reactions. The *benzodiazepines,* a group of drugs that reduce anxiety, may work by increasing the sensitivity of receptor sites to GABA. However, it is unlikely that GABA levels fully explain anxiety disorders (Michels & Marzuk, 1993a).

In many cases anxiety disorders may reflect the interaction of biological and psychological factors. In panic disorder, biological imbalances may initially trigger attacks. However, subsequent fear of attacks—and of the bodily cues that signal their onset—may heighten discomfort and give one the idea there is nothing one can do about them (Meichenbaum, 1993). Feelings of helplessness increase fear. People with panic disorder therefore can be helped by psychological methods that provide ways of reducing physical discomfort—including regular breathing—and show them that there are, after all, things they can do to cope with attacks (Klosko et al., 1990).

DISSOCIATIVE DISORDERS

William's disorder, described at the beginning of the chapter, was a dissociative disorder. In the **dissociative disorders** there is a separation of mental processes such as thoughts, emotions, identity, memory, or consciousness—the processes that make the person feel whole. In this section we describe several types of dissociative disorders.

Types of Dissociative Disorders

The *DSM* lists several dissociative disorders. Among them are dissociative amnesia, dissociative fugue, dissociative identity disorder, and depersonalization.

DISSOCIATIVE AMNESIA In **dissociative amnesia** the person is suddenly unable to recall important personal information. The loss of memory cannot be attributed to organic problems such as a blow to the head or alcoholic intoxication. It is thus a psychological dissociative disorder and not an organic one. In the most common example, the person cannot recall events for a number of hours after a stressful incident, as in warfare or in the case of an uninjured survivor of an accident. In generalized amnesia, people forget their entire lives. Amnesia may last for hours or years.

DISSOCIATIVE DISORDERS Disorders in which there are sudden, temporary changes in consciousness or self-identity.

DISSOCIATIVE AMNESIA A dissociative disorder marked by loss of memory or self-identity; skills and general knowledge are usually retained. Previously termed *psychogenic amnesia.*

DISSOCIATIVE FUGUE In **dissociative fugue,** the person abruptly leaves his or her home or place of work and travels to another place, having lost all memory of his or her past life. While at the new location the person either does not think about the past or reports a past filled with invented memories. The new personality is often more outgoing and less inhibited than the "real" identity. Following recovery, the events that occurred during the fugue are not recalled.

DISSOCIATIVE IDENTITY DISORDER Dissociative identity disorder (formerly termed *multiple personality disorder*) is the name given to William's disorder. In dissociative identity disorder, two or more identities or personalities, each with distinct traits and memories, "occupy" the same person. Each identity may or may not be aware of the others.

The identities of people with dissociative identity disorder can be very different from one another. They might even have different eyeglass prescriptions (Braun, 1988). Braun reports cases in which assorted identities showed different allergic responses. In one person, an identity named Timmy was not sensitive to orange juice. But when other identities gained control over him and drank orange juice, he would break out with hives. Hives would also erupt if another identity emerged while the juice was being digested. If Timmy reappeared when the allergic reaction was present, the itching of the hives would cease and the blisters would start to subside. In other cases reported by Braun, different identities within a person might show various responses to the same medicine. Or one identity might exhibit color blindness while others have normal color vision.

A few celebrated cases of this disorder have been portrayed in the popular media. One of them became the subject of the film *The Three Faces of Eve.* A timid housewife named Eve White harbored two other identities. One was Eve Black, a sexually aggressive, antisocial personality. The third was Jane, an emerging identity who was able to accept the existence of her primitive impulses yet engage in socially appropriate behavior. Finally the three faces merged into one—Jane. Ironically, later on, Jane (Chris Sizemore in real life) reportedly split into 22 identities. Another well-publicized case is that of Sybil, a woman with 16 identities who was portrayed by Sally Field in the film *Sybil.*

TRUTH OR FICTION REVISITED
It is true that some people have more than one identity, and the identities may have different allergies and eyeglass prescriptions.

DISSOCIATIVE FUGUE A dissociative disorder in which one experiences amnesia and then flees to a new location. Previously termed *psychogenic fugue.*

DISSOCIATIVE IDENTITY DISORDER A disorder in which a person appears to have two or more distinct identities or personalities that may alternately emerge.

DISSOCIATIVE IDENTITY DISORDER.
In the film *The Three Faces of Eve,* Joanne Woodward played three personalities in the same woman: the shy, inhibited Eve White (lying on couch); the flirtatious, promiscuous Eve Black (in dark dress); and a third personality (Jane) who could accept her sexual and aggressive impulses and still maintain her sense of identity.

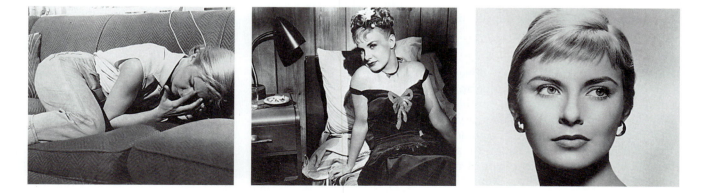

DEPERSONALIZATION DISORDER **Depersonalization disorder** is characterized by persistent or recurrent feelings that one is detached from one's own body, as if one is observing one's thought processes from the outside. For this reason, it is sometimes referred to as an "out-of-body experience." One may also feel as though he or she is functioning on automatic pilot or as if in a dream. The case of Richie illustrates a transient episode of depersonalization:

> We went to Orlando with the children after school let out. I had also been driving myself hard, and it was time to let go. We spent three days "doing" Disney World, and it got to the point where we were all wearing shirts with mice and ducks on them and singing Disney songs like "Yo ho, yo ho, a pirate's life for me." On the third day I began to feel unreal and ill at ease while we were watching these middle-American Ivory-soap teenagers singing and dancing in front of Cinderella's Castle. The day was finally cooling down, but I broke into a sweat. I became shaky and dizzy and sat down on the cement next to the 4-year-old's stroller without giving [my wife] an explanation. There were strollers and kids and [adults'] legs all around me, and for some strange reason I became fixated on the pieces of popcorn strewn on the ground. All of a sudden it was like the people around me were all silly mechanical creatures, like the dolls in the "It's a Small World" [exhibit] or the animals on the "Jungle Cruise." Things sort of seemed to slow down, the way they do when you've smoked marijuana, and there was this invisible wall of cotton between me and everyone else.
>
> Then the concert was over and my wife was like "What's the matter?" and did I want to stay for the Electrical Parade and the fireworks or was I sick? Now I was beginning to wonder if I was going crazy and I said I was sick, that my wife would have to take me by the hand and drive us back to the [motel]. Somehow we got back to the monorail and turned in the strollers. I waited in the herd [of people] at the station like a dead person, my eyes glazed over, looking out over kids with Mickey Mouse ears and Mickey Mouse balloons. The mechanical voice on the monorail almost did me in and I got really shaky.
>
> I refused to go back to the Magic Kingdom. I went with the family to Sea World, and on another day I dropped [my wife] and the kids off at the Magic Kingdom and picked them up that night. My wife thought I was goldbricking or something, and we had a helluva fight about it, but we had a life to get back to and my sanity had to come first.

Theoretical Views

According to psychodynamic theory, people with dissociative disorders use massive repression to prevent them from recognizing improper impulses or remembering ugly events (Vaillant, 1994). In dissociative amnesia and fugue, the person forgets a profoundly disturbing event or impulse. In dissociative identity disorder, the person expresses unacceptable impulses through alternate identities. In depersonalization, the person stands outside—removed from the turmoil within.

According to learning theorists, people with dissociative disorders have learned *not to think* about bad memories or disturbing impulses in order to avoid feelings of anxiety, guilt, and shame. Technically speaking, *not thinking about these matters* is reinforced by *removal* of the aversive stimulus of anxiety, guilt, or shame.

DEPERSONALIZATION DISORDER A dissociative disorder in which one experiences persistent or recurrent feelings that one is not real or is detached from one's own experiences or body.

Both psychodynamic and learning theories suggest that dissociative disorders help people keep disturbing memories or ideas out of mind. Of what could such memories be? Research suggests that many—perhaps most—cases involve memories of sexual or physical abuse during childhood, usually by a relative or caretaker (Weaver & Clum, 1995). Surveys find that the great majority of people diagnosed with dissociative identity disorder report sexual abuse in childhood (Putnam et al., 1986). Many report both physical and sexual abuse.

Perhaps all of us are capable of dividing our awareness so that we become unaware, at least temporarily, of events that we usually focus more attention on. The dissociative disorders raise fascinating questions about the nature of human self-identity and memory. Perhaps it is no surprise that attention can be divided. Perhaps the surprising thing is that human consciousness normally integrates an often chaotic set of experiences into a meaningful whole.

SOMATOFORM DISORDERS

People with **somatoform disorders** complain of physical problems such as paralysis, pain, or a persistent belief that they have a serious disease. Yet no evidence of a physical abnormality can be found. In this section we discuss two somatoform disorders: conversion disorder and hypochondriasis.

Conversion disorder is characterized by a major change in, or loss of, physical functioning, although no medical findings can explain the loss of functioning. The behaviors are not intentionally produced. That is, the person is not faking. Conversion disorder is so named because it appears to "convert" a source of stress into a physical difficulty.

If you lost the ability to see at night, or if your legs became paralyzed, you would understandably show concern. But some people with conversion disorder show indifference to their symptoms, a remarkable feature referred to as **la belle indifférence.**

During World War II, some bomber pilots developed night blindness. They could not carry out their nighttime missions, although no damage to the optic nerves was found. In rare cases, women with large families have been reported to become paralyzed in the legs, again with no medical findings. More recently, a Cambodian woman who had witnessed atrocities became blind as a result.

Another more common type of somatoform disorder is **hypochondriasis** (also called *hypochondria*). People with this disorder insist that they are suffering from a serious physical illness, even though no medical evidence of illness can be found. They become preoccupied with minor physical sensations and continue to believe that they are ill despite the reassurance of physicians that they are healthy. They may run from doctor to doctor, seeking the one who will find the causes of the sensations. Fear of illness may disrupt their work or home life.

Consistent with psychodynamic theory, early versions of the *DSM* labeled what are now referred to as somatoform disorders as "hysterical neuroses." "Hysterical" derives from the word *hystera*, the Greek word for uterus or womb. Like many other Greeks, Hippocrates believed that hysteria was a sort of female trouble caused by a wandering uterus. It was erroneously thought that the uterus could roam through the body— that it was not anchored in place! As the uterus meandered, it could cause pains and odd sensations almost anywhere. The Greeks also believed that pregnancy anchored the uterus and ended hysterical complaints. What do you think Greek physicians prescribed to end monthly aches and pains? Good guess.

SOMATOFORM DISORDERS Disorders in which people complain of physical (somatic) problems even though no physical abnormality can be found.

CONVERSION DISORDER A disorder in which anxiety or unconscious conflicts are "converted" into physical symptoms that often have the effect of helping the person cope with anxiety or conflict.

LA BELLE INDIFFÉRENCE (lah bell an-DEEF-fay-rants). A French term that describes the lack of concern sometimes shown by people with conversion disorders.

HYPOCHONDRIASIS Persistent belief that one has a medical disorder despite lack of medical findings.

Even in the earlier years of the 20th century, it was suggested that strange sensations and medically unfounded complaints were largely the province of women. Moreover, viewing the problem as a neurosis suggested that it stemmed from unconscious childhood conflicts. The psychodynamic view of conversion disorders is that the symptoms protect the individual from feelings of guilt or shame, or from another source of stress. Conversion disorders, like dissociative disorders, often seem to serve a purpose. For example, the "blindness" of the World War II pilots may have enabled them to avoid feelings of fear of being literally shot down or of guilt for killing civilians.

MOOD DISORDERS

Mood disorders are characterized by disturbance in expressed emotions. The disruption generally involves sadness or elation. Most instances of sadness are normal, or "run-of-the-mill." If you have failed an important test, if you have lost money in a business venture, or if your closest friend becomes ill, it is understandable and fitting for you to be sad about it. It would be odd, in fact, if you were *not* affected by adversity.

Types of Mood Disorders

In this section we discuss two mood disorders: major depression and bipolar disorder.

MAJOR DEPRESSION Depression is the "common cold" of psychological problems, affecting upward of 10% of adults at any given time (Alloy et al., 1990). People with run-of-the-mill depression may feel sad, blue, or "down in the dumps." They may complain of lack of energy, loss of self-esteem, difficulty concentrating, loss of interest in activities and other people, pessimism, crying, and thoughts of suicide.

These feelings are more intense in people with **major depression.** People with this disorder may also show poor appetite, serious weight loss, and agitation or great lethargy. They may be unable to concentrate and make decisions. They may say that they "don't care" anymore and in some cases attempt suicide. They may also display faulty perception of reality—so-called psychotic behaviors. These include delusions of unworthiness, guilt for imagined wrongdoings, even the notion that one is rotting from disease. There may also be delusions (e.g., of the devil administering deserved punishment) or hallucinations (e.g., of strange bodily sensations).

BIPOLAR DISORDER In **bipolar disorder,** formerly known as *manic-depressive disorder,* the person undergoes wide mood swings, from ecstatic elation to deep depression. These cycles seem to be unrelated to external events. In the elated, or manic phase, the person may show excessive excitement or silliness, carrying jokes too far. The manic person may be argumentative. He or she may show poor judgment, destroying property, making huge contributions to charity, or giving away expensive possessions. People may avoid manic individuals, finding them abrasive. Manic people often speak rapidly ("pressured speech") and jump from topic to topic, showing **rapid flight of ideas.** It is hard to get a word in edgewise. The manic individual may also be unable to sit still or sleep restfully.

MAJOR DEPRESSION A severe depressive disorder in which the person may show loss of appetite and impaired reality testing.

BIPOLAR DISORDER A disorder in which the mood alternates between two extreme poles (elation and depression). Also referred to as *manic depression.*

RAPID FLIGHT OF IDEAS Rapid speech and topic changes, characteristic of manic behavior.

WOMEN AND DEPRESSION

Women are about twice as likely as men to be diagnosed with depression (Culbertson, 1997). Hormonal changes during the menstrual cycle and childbirth may contribute to depression in women (McGrath et al., 1990). However, a panel convened by the American Psychological Association attributed most of the difference to the greater stresses placed on women (McGrath et al., 1990). Women are more likely to experience physical and sexual abuse, poverty, single parenthood, and sexism. Women are also more likely than men to help other people who are under stress. Supporting other people heaps additional caregiving burdens on themselves. One panel member, Bonnie Strickland, expressed surprise that even more women are not depressed, given that they are often treated as second-class citizens.

Social inequality creates many of the problems that lead people to seek therapy (Belle, 1990). This is particularly true among members of oppressed groups, such as women (Brown, 1992). Women—especially single mothers—have lower socioeconomic status than men, and depression and other psychological disorders are more common among poor people (Hobfoll et al., 1995). ■

Depression is the other side of the coin. People with bipolar depression often sleep more than usual and are lethargic. People with major (or unipolar) depression are more likely to have insomnia and agitation. Those with bipolar depression also exhibit social withdrawal and irritability.

Some people with bipolar disorder attempt suicide when the mood shifts from the elated phase toward depression. They will do almost anything to escape the depths of depression that lie ahead.

Theoretical Views

Depression may be a reaction to losses and unpleasant events. Problems such as marital discord, physical discomfort, incompetence, and failure or pressure at work all contribute to feelings of depression. We tend to be more depressed by things we bring on ourselves, such as academic problems, financial problems, unwanted pregnancy, conflict with the law, arguments, and fights (Simons et al., 1993). However, some people recover from depression less readily than others. People who remain depressed have lower self-esteem (Andrews & Brown, 1993), are less likely to be able to solve social problems (Marx et al., 1992), and have less social support.

PSYCHODYNAMIC VIEWS Psychoanalysts suggest various explanations for depression. In one, people are at risk for depression because they are overly concerned about hurting other people's feelings or losing their approval. As a result, they hold in feelings of anger rather than expressing them. Anger is turned inward and experienced as misery and self-hatred. From the psychodynamic perspective, bipolar disorder may be seen as alternating states in which the personality is first dominated by the superego and then by the ego. In the depressive phase of the disorder, the superego dominates, producing exaggerated ideas of wrongdoing and associated feelings of guilt and worthlessness. After a while the ego asserts supremacy, producing the elation and self-confidence often seen in the manic phase. Later, in response to the excessive display of ego, feelings of guilt return and plunge the person into depression once again.

LEARNING VIEWS Many people with depressive disorders have an external locus of control. That is, they do not believe they can control events to achieve desired outcomes (Weisz et al., 1993).

Research has also found links between depression and **learned helplessness**. In classic research, psychologist Martin Seligman taught dogs that they were helpless to escape an electric shock. The dogs were prevented from leaving a cage in which they received repeated shocks. Later, a barrier to a safe compartment was removed, offering the animals a way out. When they were shocked again, however, the dogs made no effort to escape. They had apparently learned that they were helpless. Seligman's dogs were also, in a sense, reinforced for doing nothing. That is, the shock *eventually* stopped when the dogs were showing helpless behavior—inactivity and withdrawal. "Reinforcement" might have increased the likelihood of repeating the "successful behavior"—that is, doing nothing—in a similar situation. This helpless behavior resembles that of people who are depressed.

COGNITIVE FACTORS The concept of learned helplessness bridges the learning and cognitive approaches in that it is an attitude, a broad expectation. Other cognitive factors also contribute to depression. For example, perfectionists set themselves up for depression by making irrational demands on themselves. They are likely to fall short of their (unrealistic) expectations and to feel depressed as a result (Hewitt et al., 1996).

People who ruminate about feelings of depression are more likely to prolong them (Just & Alloy, 1997). Women are more likely than men to ruminate about feelings of depression (Nolen-Hoeksema et al., 1993). Men seem more likely to try to fight off negative feelings by distracting themselves. Men are also more likely to distract themselves by turning to alcohol (Nolen-Hoeksema et al., 1993). They thus expose themselves and their families to further problems.

Seligman (1996) suggests that when things go wrong we may think of the causes of failure as either *internal* or *external, stable* or *unstable, global* or *specific*. These various **attributional styles** can be illustrated using the example of a date that does not work out. An internal attribution

LEARNED HELPLESSNESS A model for the acquisition of depressive behavior, based on findings that organisms in aversive situations learn to show inactivity when their operants go unreinforced.

ATTRIBUTIONAL STYLE One's tendency to attribute one's behavior to internal or external factors, stable or unstable factors, and so on.

WHY DID HE MISS THAT TACKLE?
This football player is compounding his feelings of depression by attributing his shortcomings on the field to factors that he cannot change. For example, he tells himself that he missed the tackle out of stupidity and lack of athletic ability. He ignores the facts that his coaching was poor and his teammates failed to support him.

involves self-blame (e.g., "I really loused it up." An external attribution places the blame elsewhere ("Some couples just don't take to each other" or "She was the wrong sign for me"). A stable attribution ("It's my personality") suggests a problem that cannot be changed. An unstable attribution ("It was because I had a head cold") suggests a temporary condition. A global attribution of failure ("I have no idea what to do when I'm with other people") suggests that the problem is quite large. A specific attribution ("I have problems making small talk at the beginning of a relationship") chops the problem down to a manageable size.

Research has shown that people who are depressed are more likely to attribute the causes of their failures to internal, stable, and global factors—factors that they are relatively powerless to change (Kinderman & Bentall, 1997; Simons et al., 1993). Such attributions can give rise to feelings of hopelessness.

BIOLOGICAL FACTORS Researchers are also searching for biological factors in mood disorders. Depression, for example, is often associated with the trait of *neuroticism*, which is heritable (Clark et al., 1994). Anxiety is also connected with neuroticism, and mood and anxiety disorders are frequently found in the same person (Clark et al., 1994).

Genetic factors appear to be involved in bipolar disorder. Mood swings tend to run in families (Wachtel, 1994). There is also a higher rate of agreement for bipolar disorder among identical twins than among fraternal twins (Goodwin & Jamison, 1990). Bipolar disorder may be associated with inappropriate levels of the neurotransmitter *glutamate*. Research with mice suggests that too little glutamate may be linked with depression, and too much, with mania (Hokin et al., 1998).

Research into depression focuses on deficiency in the level of the neurotransmitter serotonin in the brain (Cooper et al., 1991; Michels & Marzuk, 1993b). People with severe depression often respond to antidepressant drugs that heighten the action of serotonin.

Relationships between mood disorders and biological factors are complex and under intense study. Even if people are biologically predisposed toward depression, self-efficacy expectations and attitudes—particularly attitudes about whether one can change things for the better—may also play a role.

Suicide

About 30,000 people each year take their lives in the United States (Michels & Marzuk, 1993a). Most suicides are linked to feelings of depression and hopelessness (Beck et al., 1990). Other factors in suicide include anxiety, drug abuse, problems in school or at work, and social problems (Howard-Pitney et al., 1992). Exposure to other people who are committing suicide can increase the risk that an adolescent will attempt suicide (Centers for Disease Control, 1995). Copycat suicides contribute to a so-called cluster effect among adolescents.

Suicide attempts are more common after stressful events, especially events that entail loss of social support—as in the loss of a spouse, friend, or relative. People under stress who consider suicide have been found less capable of solving problems—particularly interpersonal problems—than nonsuicidal people (Sadowski & Kelley, 1993). Suicidal people thus are less likely to find other ways out of a stressful situation.

Suicide, like so many other psychological problems, tends to run in families. Nearly 1 in 4 people who attempt suicide reports that a family member has committed suicide (Sorensen & Rutter, 1991). Psychological

WHO COMMITS SUICIDE?

Suicide is not only connected with feelings of depression and stressful events, but also with educational status, gender, ethnicity, and age. Consider some facts about suicide:

- Suicide is more common among college students than among people of the same age who do not attend college. Each year about 10,000 college students attempt suicide.

- Three times as many women as men attempt suicide, but about four times as many men succeed in killing themselves (see Figure PD.2; Rich et al., 1988).

- Among people who attempt suicide, men prefer to use guns or hang themselves; women prefer to use sleeping pills. Males, that is, tend to use quicker and more lethal means (Gelman, 1994).

- Although African Americans are more likely than White Americans to live in poverty and experience the effects of discrimination, the suicide rate is about twice as high among White Americans (Figure PD.2).

- One in 4 Native American teenagers has attempted suicide—a rate four times higher than that for other U.S. teenagers (Gelman, 1994; Resnick et al., 1992). Among Zuni adolescents of New Mexico, the rate of completed suicides is more than twice the national rate (Howard-Pitney et al., 1992).

- Teenage suicides loom large in the media spotlight, but older people are actually much more likely to commit suicide (Richman, 1993; Figure PD.3). The suicide rate among older people is nearly twice the national rate. ∎

FIGURE PD.2

SUICIDE RATES ACCORDING TO GENDER AND ETHNICITY.

Men are more likely than women to commit suicide. Women, however, make more suicide attempts. How can we account for this discrepancy? White people are also more likely to commit suicide than African Americans.

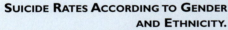
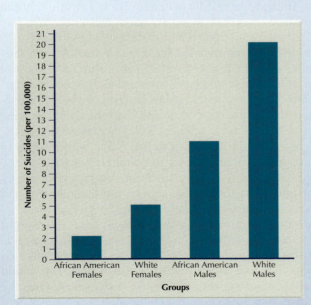

FIGURE PD.3

SUICIDE RATES ACCORDING TO AGE.

Older people (aged 65 and above) are more likely to commit suicide than the young and the middle aged, yet suicide is the second leading cause of death among college students.

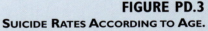
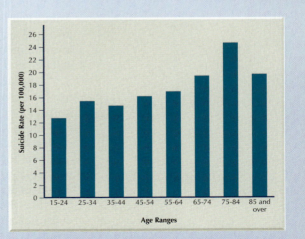

disorders among family members may also be a factor. The causal connections are unclear, however. Do people who attempt suicide inherit disorders that can lead to suicide? Does the family environment subject family members to feelings of hopelessness? Does the suicide of a family member give a person the idea of committing suicide or create the impression that he or she is somehow fated to commit suicide? What do you think?

MYTHS ABOUT SUICIDE Some people believe that individuals who threaten suicide are only seeking attention. Those who are serious just "do it." Actually, most people who commit suicide give warnings about their intentions (Brody, 1992).

Some believe that those who fail at suicide attempts are only seeking attention. But many people who commit suicide have made prior attempts (Lewinsohn et al., 1994). Contrary to widespread belief, discussing suicide with a person who is depressed does not prompt the person to attempt suicide (Centers for Disease Control, 1995). Extracting a promise not to commit suicide before calling or visiting a helping professional seems to prevent some suicides.

Some believe that only "insane" people (meaning people who are out of touch with reality) would take their own lives. However, suicidal thinking is not necessarily a sign of psychosis, neurosis, or personality disorder. Instead, contemplation of suicide can reflect a narrowing of the range of options that people believe are available to them (Schotte et al., 1990).

SCHIZOPHRENIA

Joyce was 19. Her husband Ron brought her into the emergency room because she had slit her wrists. When she was interviewed, her attention wandered. She seemed distracted by things in the air, or something she might be hearing. It was as if she had an invisible earphone.

> She explained that she had cut her wrists because the "hellsmen" had told her to. Then she seemed frightened. Later she said that the hellsmen had warned her not to reveal their existence. She had been afraid that they would punish her for talking about them.
>
> Ron and Joyce had been married for about a year. At first they had been together in a small apartment in town. But Joyce did not want to be near other people and had convinced him to rent a bungalow in the country. There she would make fantastic drawings of goblins and monsters during the days. Now and then she would become agitated and act as if invisible things were giving her instructions.
>
> "I'm bad," Joyce would mutter. "I'm bad." She would begin to jumble her words. Ron would then try to convince her to go to the hospital, but she would refuse. Then the wrist cutting would begin. Ron thought he had made the cottage safe by removing knives and blades. But Joyce would always find something.
>
> Then Joyce would be brought to the hospital, have stitches put in, be kept under observation for a while, and medicated. She would explain that she cut herself because the hellsmen had told her that she was bad and must die. After a few days she would deny hearing the hellsmen, and she would insist on leaving the hospital.
>
> Ron would take her home. The pattern continued.

When the emergency room staff examined Joyce's wrists and heard that she believed she had been following the orders of "hellsmen," they suspected that she could be diagnosed with **schizophrenia.** Schizophrenia

TRUTH OR FICTION REVISITED
It is not true that people who threaten suicide are only seeking attention.

SCHIZOPHRENIA A psychotic disorder characterized by loss of control of thought processes and inappropriate emotional responses.

touches every aspect of a person's life. It is characterized by disturbances in thought and language, perception and attention, motor activity, mood, and by withdrawal and absorption in daydreams or fantasy.

Schizophrenia has been referred to as the worst disorder affecting human beings (Carpenter & Buchanan, 1994). It afflicts nearly 1% of the population worldwide. Its onset occurs relatively early in life, and its adverse effects tend to endure.

People with schizophrenia have problems in memory, attention, and communication (Docherty et al., 1996). Their thought processes unravel. Unless we are allowing our thoughts to wander, our thinking is normally tightly knit. We start at a certain point, and thoughts that come to mind (the associations) tend to be logically connected. But people with schizophrenia often think illogically. Their speech may be jumbled. They may combine parts of words into new words or make meaningless rhymes. They may jump from topic to topic, conveying little useful information. They usually do not recognize that their thoughts and behavior are abnormal.

Many people with schizophrenia have **delusions**—for example, delusions of grandeur, persecution, or reference. In the case of delusions of grandeur, a person may believe that he is a famous historical figure such as Jesus, or a person on a special mission. He may have grand, illogical plans for saving the world. Delusions tend to be unshakable even in the face of evidence that they are not true. People with delusions of persecution may believe that they are sought by the Mafia, CIA, FBI, or some other group. A woman with delusions of reference said that news stories contained coded information about her. A man with such delusions complained that neighbors had "bugged" his walls with "radios." Other people with schizophrenia have had delusions that they have committed unpardonable sins, that they were rotting away from disease, or that they or the world did not exist.

The perceptions of people with schizophrenia often include hallucinations—imagery in the absence of external stimulation that the person cannot distinguish from reality. In Shakespeare's *Macbeth*, for example, after killing King Duncan, Macbeth apparently experiences a hallucination:

Is this a dagger which I see before me,
The handle toward my hand? Come, let me clutch thee:
I have thee not, and yet I see thee still.
Art thou not, fatal vision, sensible
To feeling as to sight? or art thou but
A dagger of the mind, a false creation,
Proceeding from the heat-oppressed brain?

Joyce apparently hallucinated the voices of "hellsmen." Other people who experience hallucinations may see colors or even obscene words spelled out in midair. Auditory hallucinations are the most common type.

In individuals with schizophrenia, motor activity may become wild or become so slow the person is said to be in a stupor. There may be strange gestures and facial expressions. The person's emotional responses may be flat or blunted, or inappropriate—as in giggling upon hearing bad news. People with schizophrenia tend to withdraw from social contacts and become wrapped up in their own thoughts and fantasies.

Types of Schizophrenia

There are three major types of schizophrenia: paranoid, disorganized, and catatonic.

PARANOID TYPE People with **paranoid schizophrenia** have systematized delusions and, frequently, related auditory hallucinations. They usually have delusions of grandeur and persecution, but they may also have

DELUSIONS False, persistent beliefs unsubstantiated by sensory or objective evidence.

PARANOID SCHIZOPHRENIA A type of schizophrenia characterized primarily by delusions — commonly of persecution — and by vivid hallucinations.

PARANOID SCHIZOPHRENIA.
People with paranoid schizophrenia have systematized delusions, often involving the idea that they are being persecuted or are on a special mission. Although they cannot be argued out of their delusions, their cognitive functioning is relatively intact compared with that of disorganized and catatonic schizophrenics.

delusions of jealousy, in which they believe that a spouse or lover has been unfaithful. They may show agitation, confusion, and fear, and may experience vivid hallucinations consistent with their delusions. People with paranoid schizophrenia often construct complex or systematized delusions involving themes of wrongdoing or persecution.

DISORGANIZED TYPE People with **disorganized schizophrenia** show incoherence, loosening of associations, disorganized behavior, disorganized delusions, fragmentary delusions or hallucinations, and flat or highly inappropriate emotional responses. Extreme social impairment is common. People with this type of schizophrenia may also exhibit silliness and giddiness of mood, giggling, and nonsensical speech. They may neglect their appearance and personal hygiene and lose control of their bladder and bowels.

CATATONIC TYPE People with **catatonic schizophrenia** show striking impairment in motor activity. It is characterized by a slowing of activity into a stupor that may suddenly change into an agitated phase. Catatonic individuals may maintain unusual, even difficult postures for hours, even as their limbs grow swollen or stiff. A striking feature of this condition is **waxy flexibility,** in which the person maintains positions into which he or she has been manipulated by others. Catatonic individuals may also show **mutism,** but afterward they usually report that they heard what others were saying at the time.

Theoretical Views

Psychologists have investigated various factors that may contribute to schizophrenia. They include psychological and biological factors.

PSYCHODYNAMIC VIEWS According to the psychodynamic perspective, schizophrenia occurs because the ego is overwhelmed by sexual or aggressive impulses from the id. The impulses threaten the ego and cause intense inner conflict. Under this threat, the person regresses to an early phase of the oral stage in which the infant has not yet learned that it and the world are separate. Fantasies become confused with reality, giving rise to hallucinations and delusions. Yet critics point out that schizophrenic behavior is not the same as infantile behavior.

LEARNING VIEWS Most learning theorists explain schizophrenia in terms of conditioning and observational learning. From this perspective, people engage in schizophrenic behavior when it is more likely to be reinforced than normal behavior. This may occur when a person is reared in a socially unrewarding or punitive situation. Inner fantasies then become more reinforcing than social realities.

Patients in a psychiatric hospital may learn what is "expected" by observing others. Hospital staff may reinforce schizophrenic behavior by paying more attention to patients who behave bizarrely. This view is consistent with folklore that the child who disrupts the class attracts more attention from the teacher than the "good" child.

Although quality of parenting is connected with the development of schizophrenia (Michels & Marzuk, 1993a; Venables, 1996), critics note that many people who are reared in socially punitive settings are apparently immune to the extinction of socially appropriate behavior. Other people develop schizophrenic behavior without having had opportunities to observe other people with schizophrenia.

DISORGANIZED SCHIZOPHRENIA A type of schizophrenia characterized by disorganized delusions and vivid hallucinations.

CATATONIC SCHIZOPHRENIA A type of schizophrenia characterized by striking impairment in motor activity.

WAXY FLEXIBILITY A feature of catatonic schizophrenia in which persons maintain postures into which they are placed.

MUTISM Refusal to talk.

SOCIOCULTURAL VIEWS Many investigators have considered whether and how social and cultural factors such as poverty, discrimination, and overcrowding contribute to schizophrenia—especially among people who are genetically vulnerable to the disorder. A classic study in New Haven, Connecticut, showed that the rate of schizophrenia was twice as high in the lowest socioeconomic class as in the next higher class on the socioeconomic ladder (Hollingshead & Redlich, 1958). Some sociocultural theorists therefore suggest that treatment of schizophrenia requires reforming society so as to alleviate poverty and other social ills, rather than trying to change people whose behavior is deviant.

Critics of this view suggest that low socioeconomic status may be a result, rather than a cause, of schizophrenia. People with schizophrenia may drift toward low social status because they lack the social skills and cognitive abilities to function at higher social-class levels. Thus they may wind up in poor neighborhoods in disproportionately high numbers.

Evidence for the hypothesis that people with schizophrenia drift downward to lower socioeconomic status is mixed (Nevid et al., 2000). Many people with schizophrenia do drift downward occupationally in comparison with their fathers' occupations. Many others, however, were reared in families in which the father came from the lowest socioeconomic class. Because the stresses of poverty may play a role in developing schizophrenia, many researchers are interested in the possible interactions between psychosocial stressors and biological factors (Carpenter & Buchanan, 1994).

BIOLOGICAL RISK FACTORS Research evidence suggests three biological risk factors for schizophrenia: heredity, complications during pregnancy and birth, and birth during winter (Carpenter & Buchanan, 1994).

Schizophrenia, like many other psychological disorders, runs in families. People with schizophrenia constitute about 1% of the population. However, children with one parent who has been diagnosed as schizophrenic have about a 10% chance of being diagnosed as schizophrenic themselves. Children with two such parents have about a 35% to 40% chance (Gottesman, 1991). Twin studies also find about a 40% to 50% rate of agreement for the diagnosis among pairs of identical (MZ) twins, whose genetic codes are the same, compared with about a 10% rate among pairs of fraternal (DZ) twins (Gottesman, 1991). Moreover, adoptee studies find that the biological parent typically places the child at greater risk for schizophrenia than the adoptive parent—even though the child has been reared by the adoptive parent (Carpenter & Buchanan, 1994; Gottesman, 1991). Sharing genes with relatives who have schizophrenia apparently places a person at risk of developing the disorder.

There seems to be strong evidence for a genetic role in schizophrenia. However, heredity cannot be the sole factor. If it were, we would expect a 100% rate of agreement between identical twins, as opposed to the 40% to 50% rate found by researchers (Carpenter & Buchanan, 1994). It also turns out that many people with schizophrenia have undergone complications during pregnancy and birth. For example, the mothers of many people with schizophrenia had influenza during the sixth or seventh month of pregnancy (Barr et al., 1990). Inadequate maternal nutrition has also been implicated (Susser & Lin, 1992). Individuals with schizophrenia are also somewhat more likely to have been born during winter than would be predicted by chance (Carpenter & Buchanan, 1994). Considered together, these three biological risk factors suggest that schizophrenia involves atypical development of the central nervous system. Problems in the nervous system may involve neurotransmitters as well as the development of brain structures, and research on these problems has led to the dopamine theory of schizophrenia.

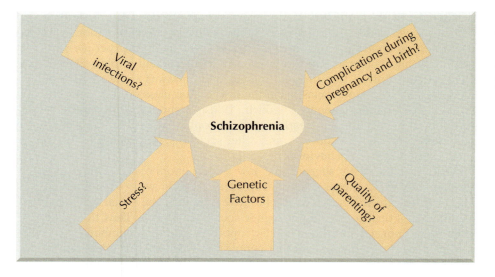

FIGURE PD.4
A MULTIFACTORIAL MODEL OF SCHIZOPHRENIA.
According to the multifactorial model of schizophrenia, people with a genetic vulnerability to the disorder experience increased risk for schizophrenia when they encounter problems such as viral infections, birth complications, stress, and poor parenting. People without the genetic vulnerability would not develop schizophrenia despite such problems.

THE DOPAMINE THEORY OF SCHIZOPHRENIA Much research has been conducted on the chemistry of schizophrenia. Numerous chemical substances have been suspected of playing a role. Much recent research has focused on the neurotransmitter dopamine (Carpenter & Buchanan, 1994). According to the dopamine theory of schizophrenia, people with schizophrenia *use* more dopamine than other people do, although they may not *produce* more of it. Why? They may have more dopamine receptors in the brain than other people, or their dopamine receptors may be hyperactive. Postmortem studies of the brains of people with schizophrenia have yielded evidence consistent with both possibilities (Davis et al., 1991). Many researchers agree that dopamine plays a role in schizophrenia but argue that other neurotransmitters are also involved. Supportive evidence is found in the fact that drugs acting on dopamine alone are not always effective in the treatment of schizophrenia (Carpenter & Buchanan, 1994).

Because so many psychological and biological factors have been implicated in schizophrenia, most investigators today favor a *multifactorial* model. According to this model, genetic factors create a predisposition toward schizophrenia (see Figure PD.4). Genetic vulnerability to the disorder interacts with other factors, such as stress, complications during pregnancy and birth, and quality of parenting, to cause the disorder to develop (Michels & Marzuk, 1993a; Venables, 1996).

PERSONALITY DISORDERS

PERSONALITY DISORDERS Enduring patterns of maladaptive behavior that are sources of distress to the individual or others.

Personality disorders, like personality traits, are characterized by enduring patterns of behavior. But personality disorders are inflexible and maladaptive. They impair personal or social functioning and are a source of distress to the individual or to other people.

Types of Personality Disorders

There are a number of personality disorders, including the paranoid, schizotypal, schizoid, antisocial, and avoidant personality types. The defining trait of the *paranoid personality disorder* is a tendency to interpret other people's behavior as threatening or demeaning. People with the disorder do not show the grossly disorganized thinking of paranoid schizophrenia. However, they are mistrustful of others, and their social relationships suffer as a result. They may be suspicious of co-workers and supervisors, but they can generally hold a job.

Schizotypal personality disorder is characterized by peculiarities of thought, perception, or behavior, such as excessive fantasy and suspiciousness, feelings of being unreal, or odd usage of words. The bizarre behaviors characterizing schizophrenia are absent, so this disorder is schizo-*typal*, not schizophrenic.

The *schizoid personality* is defined by indifference to relationships and flat emotional response. People with this disorder are loners. They do not develop warm, tender feelings for others. They have few friends and rarely get married. Some people with schizoid personality disorder do very well on the job provided that continuous social interaction is not required. They do not have hallucinations or delusions.

People with *antisocial personality disorder* persistently violate the rights of others and are often in conflict with the law (see Table PD.1). They often show a superficial charm and are at least average in intelligence. Striking features are their lack of guilt or anxiety about their misdeeds and their failure to learn from punishment or to form meaningful bonds with other people (Widiger et al., 1996). Although they are often heavily punished by their parents and rejected by peers, they continue in their impulsive, careless styles of life (Patterson, 1993). Women are more likely than men to have anxiety and depressive disorders. Men are more likely to have antisocial personality disorder (Sutker, 1994).

People with *avoidant personality disorder* are generally unwilling to enter a relationship without some assurance of acceptance because they fear rejection and criticism. As a result, they may have few close relationships outside their immediate families. Unlike people with schizoid personality disorder, however, they have some interest in, and feelings of warmth toward, other people.

TABLE PD.1

CHARACTERISTICS OF PEOPLE DIAGNOSED WITH ANTISOCIAL PERSONALITY DISORDER

KEY CHARACTERISTICS	OTHER COMMON CHARACTERISTICS
History of delinquency and truancy	Lack of loyalty or of formation of enduring relationships
Persistent violation of the rights of others	Failure to maintain good job performance over the years
Impulsiveness	Failure to develop or adhere to a life plan
Poor self-control	Sexual promiscuity
Lack of remorse for misdeeds	Substance abuse
Lack of empathy	Inability to tolerate boredom
Deceitfulness and manipulativeness	Low tolerance for frustration
Irresponsibility	Irritability
Glibness; superficial charm	
Exaggerated sense of self worth	

Sources: Harris et al., 1994; White et al., 1994; Widiger et al., 1996.

Theoretical Views

Many of the theoretical explanations of personality disorders are derived from the psychodynamic model. Traditional Freudian theory focuses on Oedipal problems as the source of many psychological disorders, including personality disorders. Faulty resolution of the Oedipus complex might lead to antisocial personality disorder because the moral conscience, or superego, is believed to depend on proper resolution of the Oedipus complex. Research evidence supports the theory that lack of guilt, a frequent characteristic of people with antisocial personality disorder, is more likely to develop among children who are rejected and punished by their parents rather than given warmth and affection (Baumeister et al., 1994; Zahn-Waxler & Kochanska, 1990). Psychodynamic theory proposed that men are more likely than women to experience feelings of guilt because men are subjected to the throes of the Oedipus complex. However, empirical research shows that *women* are actually more likely to feel guilty about moral transgressions (Baumeister et al., 1994). Men are more likely to fear being caught.

Learning theorists suggest that childhood experiences can contribute to maladaptive ways of relating to others in adulthood—that is, can lead to personality disorders. Cognitive psychologists find that antisocial adolescents encode social information in ways that bolster their misdeeds. For example, they tend to interpret other people's behavior as threatening, even when it is not (Crick & Dodge, 1994; Lochman, 1992). Cognitive therapists have encouraged some antisocial adolescents to view social provocations as problems to be solved rather than as threats to their "manhood," with some favorable initial results (Lochman, 1992).

Genetic factors are apparently involved in some personality disorders (Rutter, 1997). For example, antisocial personality disorder tends to run in families. Adoptee studies reveal higher incidences of antisocial behavior among the biological parents than among the adoptive relatives of individuals with the disorder (DiLalla & Gottesman, 1991). Yet genetic influences seem to be moderate at most (Plomin et al., 1997).

Genetic factors in antisocial personality disorder may influence the level of arousal of the nervous system. People with the disorder are unlikely to show guilt for their misdeeds or to be deterred by punishment. Low levels of guilt and anxiety may reflect lower than normal levels of arousal, which, in turn, may be partially genetically based (Lykken, 1982).

Why are people with antisocial personality disorder undeterred by punishment? Experiments show that people with antisocial personality disorder do not learn as rapidly as other people who are equal in intelligence when the payoff is ability to stop a threatened electric shock. But when their levels of arousal are increased by injections of adrenaline, they learn to avoid punishment as rapidly as others (Chesno & Kilmann, 1975; Schachter & Latané 1964).

Genetic factors such as a lower than normal level of arousal would not by itself cause the development of an antisocial personality (Rutter, 1997). Perhaps a person must also be reared under conditions that do not foster the self-concept of a law-abiding citizen. Punishment for deviant behavior would then be unlikely to induce feelings of guilt and shame. Such an individual might well be "undeterred" by punishment.

EATING DISORDERS

EATING DISORDERS Psychological disorders characterized by distortion of the body image and gross disturbances in eating patterns.

Most of us either deprive ourselves or consume vast quantities of food now and then. This is normal. The **eating disorders** listed in the *DSM* are characterized by persistent, gross disturbances in eating patterns.

Types of Eating Disorders

In this section we discuss the major types of eating disorders and some proposed explanations for them. These include anorexia nervosa and bulimia nervosa.

ANOREXIA NERVOSA   There is a saying that you can never be too rich or too thin. Excess money may be pleasant enough, but, as in the case of Karen, one can certainly be too thin.

> Karen was the 22-year-old daughter of a renowned English professor. She had begun her college career full of promise at the age of 17. But two years ago, after "social problems" occurred, she had returned to live at home and taken progressively lighter course loads at a local college. Karen had never been overweight, but about a year ago her mother noticed that she seemed to be gradually "turning into a skeleton."
>
> Karen spent hours every day shopping at the supermarket, butcher, and bakeries; and in conjuring up gourmet treats for her parents and younger siblings. Arguments over her lifestyle and eating habits had divided the family into two camps. The camp led by her father called for patience. That headed by her mother demanded confrontation. Her mother feared that Karen's father would "protect her right into her grave" and wanted Karen placed in residential treatment "for her own good." The parents finally compromised on an outpatient evaluation.
>
> At an even 5 feet, Karen looked like a prepubescent 11-year-old. Her nose and cheekbones protruded crisply, like those of an elegant young fashion model. Her lips were full, but the redness of the lipstick was unnatural, as if too much paint had been dabbed on a corpse for the funeral. Karen weighed only 78 pounds, but she had dressed in a stylish silk blouse, scarf, and baggy pants so that not one inch of her body was revealed. More striking than her mouth was the redness of her rouged cheeks. It was unclear whether she had used too much makeup or whether minimal makeup had caused the stark contrast between the parts of her face that were covered and those that were not.
>
> Karen vehemently denied that she had a problem. Her figure was "just about where I want it to be" and she engaged in aerobic exercise daily. A deal was struck in which outpatient treatment would be tried as long as Karen lost no more weight and showed steady gains back to at least 90 pounds. Treatment included a day hospital with group therapy and two meals a day. But word came back that Karen was artfully toying with her food—cutting it, licking it, and moving it about her plate—rather than eating it. After three weeks Karen had lost another pound. At that point her parents were able to persuade her to enter a residential treatment program where her eating could be carefully monitored.

Karen was diagnosed with **anorexia nervosa,** a life-threatening disorder characterized by refusal to maintain a healthful body weight, intense fear of being overweight, a distorted body image, and, in women, lack of menstruation (amenorrhea). People with anorexia usually weigh less than 85% of what would be considered a healthy weight.

By and large, eating disorders afflict women during adolescence and young adulthood (Heatherton et al., 1997). The typical person with anorexia or bulimia is a young White female of higher socioeconomic status. Women with anorexia may lose 25% or more of their body weight in a year. Severe weight loss stops ovulation. Their overall health declines.

ANOREXIA NERVOSA A life-threatening eating disorder characterized by refusal to maintain a healthful body weight, intense fear of being overweight, a distorted body image, and, in females, suspension of menstruation.

In the typical pattern, a girl notices some weight gain after menarche and decides that it must come off. However, dieting—and, often, exercise—continue at a fever pitch. They persist even after the girl reaches an average weight, and even after family members and others have told her that she is losing too much. Girls with anorexia almost always adamantly deny that they are wasting away. They may point to their fierce exercise regimens as proof. Their body image is distorted (Williamson et al., 1993). Other people perceive women with anorexia as "skin and bones." The women themselves frequently sit before the mirror and see themselves as heavy.

Many people with anorexia become obsessed with food. They engross themselves in cookbooks, take on the family shopping chores, and prepare elaborate dinners—for others.

BULIMIA NERVOSA The case of Nicole is a vivid account of a young woman who was diagnosed with bulimia nervosa:

> Nicole awakens in her cold dark room and already wishes it was time to go back to bed. She dreads the thought of going through this day, which will be like so many others in her recent past. She asks herself the question every morning, "Will I be able to make it through the day without being totally obsessed by thoughts of food, or will I blow it again and spend the day [binge eating]"? She tells herself that today she will begin a new life, today she will start to live like a normal human being. However, she is not at all convinced that the choice is hers (Boskind-White & White, 1983, p. 29).

It turns out that this day Nicole begins by eating eggs and toast. Then she binges on cookies; doughnuts; bagels smothered with butter, cream cheese, and jelly; granola; candy bars; and bowls of cereal and milk—all within 45 minutes. When she cannot take in any more food, she turns her attention to purging. She goes to the bathroom, ties back her hair, turns on the shower to mask any noise she will make, drinks a glass of water, and makes herself vomit. Afterward she vows, "Starting tomorrow, I'm going to change." But she knows that tomorrow she will probably do the same thing.

Bulimia nervosa is characterized by recurrent cycles of binge eating followed by dramatic measures to purge the food. Binge eating frequently follows food deprivation—for example, severe dieting. Purging includes self-induced vomiting, fasting or strict dieting, use of laxatives, and vigorous exercise. People with bulimia are often perfectionistic about body shape and weight (Joiner et al., 1997). Like anorexia, bulimia afflicts many more women than men.

Theoretical Views

Numerous explanations of anorexia nervosa and bulimia nervosa have been proposed. Some psychoanalysts suggest that anorexia represents an unconscious effort by the girl to cope with sexual fears, particularly the prospect of pregnancy. Because anorexia is connected with amenorrhea, some psychodynamic theorists suggest that anorexia represents an effort by the girl to revert to a prepubescent stage. Anorexia allows the girl to avoid growing up, separating from her family, and taking on adult responsibilities. Because of the loss of fatty deposits, her breasts and hips flatten. In her fantasies, perhaps, a woman with anorexia remains a child, sexually undifferentiated.

BULIMIA NERVOSA An eating disorder characterized by recurrent cycles of binge eating followed by dramatic measures to purge the food.

There is great social pressure in the United States for women to be slender. Fashion models, who represent the female ideal, are 9% taller and 16% slimmer than the average woman (Williams, 1992). As the cultural ideal grows slimmer, women with average or heavier than average figures come under more pressure to control their weight.

Although the causes of many psychological disorders remain in dispute, a variety of methods of therapy have been devised to deal with them. They are described in the "Methods of Therapy" chapter.

SUMMARY

1. **What are psychological disorders?** Psychological disorders are characterized by unusual behavior, socially unacceptable behavior, faulty perception of reality, personal distress, dangerous behavior, or self-defeating behavior.

2. **What are anxiety disorders?** Anxiety disorders are characterized by motor tension, feelings of dread, and overarousal of the sympathetic branch of the autonomic nervous system. These disorders include irrational, excessive fears, or phobias; panic disorder, characterized by sudden attacks in which people typically fear that they may be losing control or going crazy; generalized or pervasive anxiety; obsessive-compulsive disorders, in which people are troubled by intrusive thoughts or impulses to repeat some activity; and stress disorders, in which a stressful event is followed by persistent fears and intrusive thoughts about the event.

3. **How do psychologists explain anxiety disorders?** Psychoanalysts tend to view anxiety disorders as representing difficulty in repressing primitive impulses. Many learning theorists view phobias as conditioned fears. Cognitive theorists focus on ways in which people interpret threats. Some people may also be genetically predisposed to acquire certain kinds of fears. Anxiety disorders tend to run in families, and some psychologists suggest that biochemical factors that create a predisposition toward anxiety disorders may be inherited.

4. **What are dissociative disorders?** Dissociative disorders are characterized by sudden, temporary changes in consciousness or self-identity. They include dissociative amnesia; dissociative fugue, which involves forgetting plus fleeing and adopting a new identity; dissociative identity disorder (multiple personality), in which a person behaves as if more than one personality occupies his or her body; and depersonalization, characterized by feelings that one is not real or that one is standing outside oneself.

5. **How do psychologists explain dissociative disorders?** Many psychologists suggest that dissociative disorders help people keep disturbing memories or ideas out of mind. These memories may involve episodes of sexual or physical abuse during childhood.

6. **What are somatoform disorders?** People with somatoform disorders exhibit or complain of physical problems, although no medical evidence of such problems can be found. The somatoform disorders include conversion disorder and hypochondria.

7. **What are mood disorders?** Mood disorders involve disturbances in expressed emotions. Major depression is characterized by persistent feelings of sadness, loss of interest, feelings of worthlessness or guilt, inability to concentrate, and physical symptoms that may include disturbances in regulation of eating and sleeping. Feelings of unworthiness and guilt may be so excessive that they are considered delusional. Bipolar disorder is characterized by dramatic swings in mood between elation and depression.

8. **How do psychologists explain mood disorders?** Research emphasizes possible roles for learned helplessness, attributional styles, and serotonin deficiency in depression. People who are depressed are more likely than other people to make internal, stable, and global attributions for failures. Bipolar disorder may be connected with inappropriate levels of the neurotransmitter glutamate.

9. **What is schizophrenia?** Schizophrenia is characterized by disturbances in thought and language, such as loosening of

associations and delusions; in perception and attention, as found in hallucinations; in motor activity, as shown by a stupor or by excited behavior; in mood, as in flat or inappropriate emotional responses; and in social interaction, as in social withdrawal and absorption in daydreams or fantasy. The major types of schizophrenia are paranoid, disorganized, and catatonic.

10. **How do psychologists explain schizophrenia?** According to the multifactorial model, genetic vulnerability to schizophrenia may interact with other factors, such as stress, complications during pregnancy and birth, and quality of parenting, to cause the disorder to develop.

11. **What are personality disorders?** Personality disorders are inflexible, maladaptive behavior patterns that impair personal or social functioning and cause distress for the individual or others. The defining trait of paranoid personality disorder is suspiciousness. People with schizotypal personality disorders show oddities of thought, perception, and behavior. Social withdrawal is the major characteristic of schizoid personality disorder. People with antisocial personality disorders persistently violate the rights of others and are in conflict with the law. They show little or no guilt or shame over their misdeeds and are largely undeterred by punishment. People with avoidant personality disorder tend to avoid entering relationships for fear of rejection and criticism.

12. **How do psychologists explain antisocial personality disorder?** Antisocial personality disorder may develop from some combination of genetic vulnerability (which may provide lower than normal levels of arousal), inconsistent discipline, and cynical processing of social information.

13. **What are the eating disorders?** The eating disorders include anorexia nervosa and bulimia nervosa. Anorexia is characterized by refusal to eat and extreme thinness. Bulimia is characterized by cycles of binge eating and purging. Women are more likely than men to develop these disorders.

14. **How do psychologists explain eating disorders?** Although there are psychodynamic explanations of the eating disorders, most psychologists look to cultural idealization of the slender female as a major contributor.

KEY TERMS

acrophobia (p. PD-6)
acute stress disorder (p. PD-8)
agoraphobia (p. PD-6)
anorexia nervosa (p. PD-25)
attributional style (p. PD-15)
bipolar disorder (p. PD-13)
bulimia nervosa (p. PD-26)
catatonic schizophrenia (p. PD-20)
claustrophobia (p. PD-6)
compulsion (p. PD-7)
conversion disorder (p. PD-12)
delusions (p. PD-19)
depersonalization disorder (p. PD-11)
disorganized schizophrenia (p. PD-20)

dissociative amnesia (p. PD-9)
dissociative disorders (p. PD-9)
dissociative fugue (p. PD-10)
dissociative identity disorder (p. PD-10)
eating disorders (p. PD-24)
generalized anxiety disorder (p. PD-7)
hallucination (p. PD-4)
hypochondriasis (p. PD-12)
ideas of persecution (p. PD-4)
la belle indifférence (p. PD-12)
learned helplessness (p. PD-15)
major depression (p. PD-13)

mutism (p. PD-20)
obsession (p. PD-7)
panic disorder (p. PD-6)
paranoid schizophrenia (p. PD-19)
personality disorders (p. PD-22)
posttraumatic stress disorder (p. PD-7)
psychological disorders (p. PD-2)
rapid flight of ideas (p. PD-13)
schizophrenia (p. PD-18)
social phobia (p. PD-6)
somatoform disorders (p. PD-12)
specific phobia (p. PD-6)
waxy flexibility (p. PD-20)

REFERENCES

Alloy, L. B., Abramson, L. Y., & Dykman, B. M. (1990). Depressive realism and nondepressive optimistic illusions. In R. E. Ingram (Ed.), *Contemporary psychological approaches to depression*. New York: Plenum.

Andrews, B., & Brown, G. W. (1993). Self-esteem and vulnerability to depression. *Journal of Abnormal Psychology, 102,* 565–572.

Bandura, A., Taylor, C. B., Williams, S. L., Medford, I. N., & Barchas, J. D. (1985). Catecholamine secretion as a function of perceived coping self-efficacy. *Journal of Consulting and Clinical Psychology, 53,* 406–414.

Barlow, D. H. (1991). Introduction to the special issue on diagnoses, definitions, and *DSM-IV. Journal of Abnormal Psychology, 100,* 243–244.

Barr, C. E., Mednick, S. A., & Munk-Jorgensen, P. (1990). Exposure to influenza epidemics during gestation and adult schizophrenia. *Archives of General Psychiatry, 47,* 869–874.

Basic Behavioral Science Task Force of the National Advisory Mental Health Council. (1996). Basic behavioral science research for mental health: Perception, attention, learning, and memory. *American Psychologist, 51,* 133–142.

Baum, A., & Fleming, I. (1993). Implications of psychological research on stress and technological accidents. *American Psychologist, 48,* 665–672.

Baumeister, R. F., Stillwell, A. M., & Heatherton, T. F. (1994). Guilt. *Psychological Bulletin, 115,* 243–267.

Beck, A. T., Brown, G., Berchick, R. J., Stewart, B. L., & Steer, R. A.

(1990). Relationship between hopelessness and ultimate suicide. *American Journal of Psychiatry, 147,* 190–195.

Belle, D. (1990). Poverty and women's mental health. *American Psychologist, 45,* 385–389.

Boskind-White, M., & White, W. C. (1983). *Bulimarexia: The binge/purge cycle.* New York: Norton.

Braun, B. G. (1988). *Treatment of multiple personality disorder.* Washington, DC: American Psychiatric Press.

Brody, J. E. (1992, June 17). Psychotherapists warn parents not to dismiss their children's statements about suicide. *New York Times,* p. B8.

Brown, L. S. (1992). A feminist critique of the personality disorders. In L. Brown & M. Balou (Eds.), *Personality and psychopathology: Feminist reappraisals.* New York: Guilford.

Carey, G., & DiLalla, D. L. (1994). Personality and psychopathology: Genetic perspectives. *Journal of Abnormal Psychology, 103,* 32–43.

Carpenter, W. T., Jr., & Buchanan, R. W. (1994). Schizophrenia. *New England Journal of Medicine, 330,* 681–690.

Centers for Disease Control. (1995). *Suicide surveillance: 1980–1990.* Washington, DC: USDHHS.

Chesno, F. A., & Kilmann, P. R. (1975). Effects of stimulation intensity on sociopathic avoidance learning. *Journal of Abnormal Psychology, 84,* 144–151.

Clark, D. M., et al. (1997). Misinterpretation of body sensations in panic disorder. *Journal of Con-*

sulting and Clinical Psychology, 65,* 203–213.

Clark, L. A., Watson, D., & Mineka, S. M. (1994). Temperament, personality, and the mood and anxiety disorders. *Journal of Abnormal Psychology, 103,* 103–116.

Cooper, J. R., Bloom, F. E., & Roth, R. H. (1991). *The biochemical basis of neuropharmacology.* New York:Oxford University Press.

Creamer, M., Burgess, P., & Pattison, P. (1992). Reaction to trauma. *Journal of Abnormal Psychology, 101,* 452–459.

Crick, N. R., & Dodge, K. A. (1994). A review and reformulation of social information-processing mechanisms in children's social adjustment. *Psychological Bulletin, 115,* 74–101.

Culbertson, F. M. (1997). Depression and gender. *American Psychologist, 52,* 25–31.

Davidson, J. R., & Foa, E. G. (1991). Diagnostic issues in posttraumatic stress disorder. *Journal of Abnormal Psychology, 100,* 346–355.

Davis, K. L., Kahn, R. S., Ko, G., & Davidson, M. (1991). Dopamine in schizophrenia. *American Journal of Psychiatry, 148,* 1474–1486.

DeAngelis, T. (1995). Firefighters' PTSD at dangerous levels. *APA Monitor, 26*(2), 36–37.

DiLalla, D. L., & Gottesman, I. I. (1991). Biological and genetic contributors to violence—Widom's untold tale. *Psychological Bulletin, 109,* 125–129.

Docherty, N. M., et al. (1996). Working memory, attention, and communication disturbances in schizophrenia. *Journal of Abnormal Psychology, 105,* 212–219.

Foa, E. B., Franklin, M. E., Perry, K. J., & Herbert, J. D. (1996). Cognitive biases in generalized social phobia. *Journal of Abnormal Psychology, 105,* 433–439.

Gelman, D. (1994, April 18). The mystery of suicide. *Newsweek,* pp. 44–49.

Goodwin, F. K., & Jamison, K. R. (1990). *Manic-depressive illness.* New York: Oxford University Press.

Gottesman, I. I. (1991). *Schizophrenia genesis.* New York: Freeman.

Heatherton, T. F., Mahamedi, F., Striepe, M., Field, A. E., & Keel, P. (1997). A 10-year longitudinal study of body weight, dieting, and eating disorder symptoms. *Journal of Abnormal Psychology, 106,* 117–125.

Herzog, D. B., Keller, M. B., & Lavori, P. W. (1988). Outcome in anorexia and bulimia nervosa. *Journal of Nervous and Mental Disease, 176,* 131–143.

Hewitt, P. L., Flett, G. L., & Ediger, E. (1996). Perfectionism and depression. *Journal of Abnormal Psychology, 105,* 276–280.

Hobfoll, S. E., Ritter, C., Lavin, J., Hulsizer, M. R., & Cameron, R. P. (1995). Depression prevalence and incidence among inner-city pregnant and postpartum women. *Journal of Consulting and Clinical Psychology, 63,* 445–453.

Hokin, L., et al. (1998). *Proceedings of the National Academy of Sciences, 95*(14), 8363–8368.

Hollingshead, A. B., & Redlich, F. C. (1958). *Social class and mental illness.* New York: Wiley.

Howard-Pitney, B., LaFramboise, T. D., Basil, M., September, B., & Johnson, M. (1992). Psychological and social indicators of suicide ideation and suicide attempts in Zuni adolescents. *Journal of Consulting and Clinical Psychology, 60,* 473–476.

Ironson, G. (1993). Cited in Adler, T. (1993). Men and women affected by stress, but differently. *APA Monitor, 24*(7), 8–9.

Joiner, T. E., Heatherton, T. F., Rudd, M. D., & Schmidt, N. B. (1997). Perfectionism, perceived weight status, and bulimic symptoms. *Journal of Abnormal Psychology, 106,* 145–153.

Just, N., & Alloy, L. B. (1997). The response styles theory of depression. *Journal of Abnormal Psychology, 106,* 221–229.

Kinderman, P., & Bentall, R. P. (1997). Causal attributions in paranoia and depression. *Journal of Abnormal Psychology, 106,* 341–345.

Klosko, J. S., Barlow, D. H., Tassinari, R., & Cerny, J. A. (1990). A comparison of alprazolam and behavior therapy in treatment of panic disorder. *Journal of Consulting and Clinical Psychology, 58,* 77–84.

Lewinsohn, P. M., Rohde, P., & Seeley, J. R. (1994). Psychosocial risk factors for future suicide attempts. *Journal of Consulting and Clinical Psychology, 62,* 297–305.

Lochman, J. E. (1992). Cognitive-behavioral intervention with aggressive boys. *Journal of Consulting and Clinical Psychology, 60,* 426–432.

Lykken, D. T. (1982). Fearlessness. *Psychology Today, 16*(9), 20–28.

Marx, E. M., Williams, J. M. G., & Claridge, G. C. (1992). Depression and social problem solving. *Journal of Abnormal Psychology, 101,* 78–86.

McGrath, E., Keita, G. P., Strickland, B. R., & Russo, N. F. (1990). *Women and depression.* Washington, DC: American Psychological Association.

McNally, R. J., & Eke, M. (1996). Anxiety sensitivity, suffocation fear, and breath-holding duration as predictors of response to carbon dioxide challenge. *Journal of Abnormal Psychology, 105,* 146–149.

Meichenbaum, D. (1993). Changing conceptions of cognitive behavior modification. *Journal of Consulting and Clinical Psychology, 61,* 202–204.

Michels, R., & Marzuk, P. M. (1993a). Progress in psychiatry (Part 1). *New England Journal of Medicine, 329,* 552–560.

Michels, R., & Marzuk, P. M. (1993b). Progress in psychiatry (Part 2). *New England Journal of Medicine, 329,* 628–638.

Mineka, S. (1991, August). Paper presented to the annual meeting of the American Psychological Association, San Francisco. Cited in Turkington, C. (1991). Evolutionary memories may have phobia role. *APA Monitor, 22*(11), 14.

Nevid, J. S., Rathus, S. A., & Greene, B. A. (2000). *Abnormal psychology in a changing world* (4th ed.). Upper Saddle River, NJ: Prentice Hall.

Nolen-Hoeksema, S., Morrow, J., & Fredrickson, B. L. (1993). Response styles and the duration of depressed mood. *Journal of Abnormal Psychology, 102,* 20–28.

Patterson, G. R. (1993). Orderly change in a stable world: The antisocial trait as a chimera. *Journal of Consulting and Clinical Psychology, 61,* 911–919.

Pedersen, N. L., Plomin, R., McClearn, G. E., & Friberg, L. (1988). Neuroticism, extraversion, and related traits in adult twins reared apart and reared together. *Journal of Personality and Social Psychology, 55,* 950–957.

Plomin, R., DeFries, J. C., McClearn, G., & Rutter, M. (1997). *Behavioral genetics* (3rd ed.). New York: Freeman.

Putnam, F. W., Guroff, J. J., Silberman, E. K., Barban, L., & Post, R. M. (1986). The clinical phenomenology of multiple personality disorder. *Journal of Clinical Psychiatry, 47,* 285–293.

Resnick, H. S., Kilpatrick, D. G., Dansky, B. S., Saunders, B. E., & Best, C. L. (1993). Prevalence of civilian trauma and posttraumatic stress disorder in a representative national sample of women. *Journal of Consulting and Clinical Psychology, 61,* 984–991.

Resnick, M., et al. (1992, March 24). *Journal of the American Medical Association.* Cited in Young Indians prone to suicide, study finds. (1992, March 25). *New York Times,* p. D24.

Rich, C. L., Ricketts, J. E., Thaler, R. C., & Young, D. (1988). Some differences between men and women who commit suicide. *American Journal of Psychiatry, 145,* 718–722.

Richman, J. (1993). *Preventing elderly suicide.* New York: Springer.

Rodriguez, N., Ryan, S. W., Kemp, H. V., & Foy, D. W. (1997). Posttraumatic stress disorder in adult female survivors of childhood sexual abuse. *Journal of Consulting and Clinical Psychology, 65,* 53–59.

Rothbaum, B. O., Foa, E. B., Riggs, D. S., Murdock, T., & Walsh, W. (1992). A prospective examination of post-traumatic stress disorder in rape victims. *Journal of Traumatic Stress, 5,* 455–475.

Rutter, M. (1997). Nature-nurture integration. *American Psychologist, 52,* 390–398.

Sadowski, C., & Kelley, M. L. (1993). Social problem solving in suicidal adolescents. *Journal of Consulting and Clinical Psychology, 61,* 121–127.

Schachter, S., & LatanB. (1964). Crime, cognition, and the autonomic nervous system. In D. Levine (Ed.), *Nebraska Symposium on Motivation.* Lincoln: University of Nebraska Press.

Schmidt, N. B., Lerew, D. R., & Trakowski, J. H. (1997). Body vigilance in panic disorder. *Journal of Consulting and Clinical Psychology, 65,* 214–220.

Schotte, D. E., Cools, J., & Payvar, S. (1990). Problem-solving deficits in suicidal patients. *Journal of Consulting and Clinical Psychology, 58,* 562–564.

Scott, J. (1994, May 9). Multiple personality cases perplex legal system. *New York Times,* pp. A1, B10, B11.

Seligman, M. E. P. (1996, August). *Predicting and preventing depression.* Master lecture presented to the meeting of the American Psychological Association, Toronto.

Simons, A. D., Angell, K. L., Monroe, S. M., & Thase, M. E. (1993). Cognition and life stress in depression. *Journal of Abnormal Psychology, 102,* 584–591.

Sorenson, S. B., & Rutter, C. M. (1991). Transgenerational patterns of suicide attempt. *Journal of Consulting and Clinical Psychology, 59,* 861–866.

Susser, E. S., & Lin, S. P. (1992). Schizophrenia after prenatal exposure to the Dutch Hunger Winter of 1944–1945. *Archives of General Psychiatry, 49,* 983–988.

Sutker, P. B. (1994). Psychopathy: Traditional and clinical antisocial concepts. In D. C. Fowles, P. B. Sutker, & S. H. Goodman (Eds.), *Progress in experimental personality and psychopathology research* (pp. 73–120). New York: Springer.

Szasz, T. S. (1984). *The therapeutic state.* Buffalo, NY: Prometheus.

Torgersen, S. (1983). Genetic factors in anxiety disorders. *Archives of General Psychiatry, 40,* 1085–1089.

Vaillant, G. E. (1994). Ego mechanisms of defense and personality psychopathology. *Journal of Abnormal Psychology, 103,* 44–50.

Venables, P. H. (1996). Schizotypy and maternal exposure to influenza and to cold temperature. *Journal of Abnormal Psychology, 105,* 53–60.

Wachtel, P. L. (1994). Cyclical processes in personality and psychopathology. *Journal of Abnormal Psychology, 103,* 51–54.

Weaver, T. L., & Clum, G. A. (1995). Psychological distress associated with interpersonal violence. *Clinical Psychology Review, 15,* 115–140.

Weiner, K. (1992). Cited in Goleman, D. J. (1992, January 8). Heart seizure or panic attack? *New York Times,* p. C12.

Weisz, J. R., Sweeney, L., Proffitt, V., & Carr, T. (1993). Control-related beliefs and self-reported depressive symptoms in late childhood. *Journal of Abnormal Psychology, 102,* 411–418.

Widiger, T. A., et al. (1996). *DSM-IV* antisocial personality disorder field trial. *Journal of Abnormal Psychology, 105,* 3–16.

Williams, L. (1992, February 6). Woman's image in a mirror. *New York Times,* pp. A1, B7.

Williamson, D. A., Cubic, B. A., & Gleaves, D. H. (1993). Equivalence of body image disturbances in anorexia and bulimia nervosa. *Journal of Abnormal Psychology, 102,* 177–180.

Zahn-Waxler, C., & Kochanska, G. (1990). The origins of guilt. In R. A. Thompson (Ed.), *Nebraska Symposium on Motivation: Vol. 38. Socioemotional development.* Lincoln: University of Nebraska Press.

Zinbarg, R. E., & Barlow, D. H. (1996). Structure of anxiety and anxiety disorders. *Journal of Abnormal Psychology, 105,* 181–193.

MT

METHODS OF THERAPY

_____ Residents of London used to visit the local insane asylum for a night out on the town.

_____ To be effective, psychotherapy must continue for months, perhaps years.

_____ Some psychotherapists interpret clients' dreams.

_____ Other psychotherapists encourage their clients to take the lead in therapy sessions.

_____ Still other psychotherapists tell their clients precisely what to do. Lying in a reclining chair and fantasizing can be an effective way of confronting fears.

_____ Smoking cigarettes can be an effective method for helping people . . . stop smoking cigarettes.

_____ You might be able to put an end to bad habits merely by keeping a record of where and when you engage in those habits.

_____ The originator of a surgical technique designed to reduce violence learned that it was not always successful . . .

JASMINE IS A 19-YEAR-OLD COLLEGE SOPHOMORE. SHE HAS BEEN crying almost without letup for several days. She feels that her life is falling apart. Her college dreams are in a shambles. She has brought shame upon her family. Thoughts of suicide have crossed her mind. She can barely drag herself out of bed in the morning. She is avoiding her friends. She can pinpoint some sources of stress in her life: a couple of poor grades, an argument with a boyfriend, friction with roommates. Still, her misery seemed to descend on her out of nowhere.

Jasmine is depressed—so depressed that her family and friends have finally prevailed on her to seek professional help. Had she broken her leg, her treatment by a qualified professional would have followed a fairly standard course. Yet treatment of psychological problems and disorders like depression may be approached from very different perspectives. Depending on the therapist Jasmine sees, she may be doing the following:

- Lying on a couch talking about anything that pops into her awareness and exploring the hidden meanings of a recurrent dream.
- Sitting face to face with a gentle, accepting therapist who places the major responsibility for what happens in therapy on Jasmine's shoulders.
- Listening to a frank, straightforward therapist assert that Jasmine's problems stem from self-defeating attitudes and perfectionistic beliefs.
- Taking antidepressant medication.
- Participating in some combination of these approaches.

These methods, although different, all represent methods of therapy. In this chapter we explore various methods of psychotherapy and biological therapy.

WHAT IS THERAPY? THE SEARCH FOR A "SWEET OBLIVIOUS ANTIDOTE"[1]

There are many kinds of psychotherapy, but they all have certain common characteristics. **Psychotherapy** is a systematic interaction between a therapist and a client that applies psychological principles to affect the client's thoughts, feelings, or behavior in order to help the client overcome psychological disorders, adjust to problems in living, or develop as an individual.

---

[1] The phrase is from Shakespeare's *Macbeth,* as seen in the following pages.

Quite a mouthful? True. But note the essentials:

1. *Systematic interaction.* Psychotherapy is a systematic interaction between a client and a therapist. The therapist's theoretical point of view interacts with the client's to determine how the therapist and client relate to each other.
2. *Psychological principles.* Psychotherapy is based on psychological theory and research in areas such as personality, learning, motivation, and emotion.
3. *Thoughts, feelings, and behavior.* Psychotherapy influences clients' thoughts, feelings, and behavior. It can be aimed at any or all of these aspects of human psychology.
4. *Psychological disorders, adjustment problems, and personal growth.* Psychotherapy is often used with people who have psychological disorders. Other people seek help in adjusting to problems such as shyness, weight problems, or loss of a spouse. Still other clients want to learn more about themselves and to reach their full potential as individuals, parents, or creative artists.

The History of Therapies

Ancient and medieval "treatments" of psychological disorders often reflected demonological thinking. As such, they tended to involve cruel practices such as exorcism and death by hanging or burning. Some people who could not meet the demands of everyday life were tossed into prisons. Others begged in the streets, stole food, or became prostitutes. A few found their way to monasteries or other retreats that offered a kind word and some support. Generally speaking, they died early.

ASYLUMS Asylums originated in European monasteries. They were the first institutions meant primarily for people with psychological disorders. But their function was warehousing, not treatment. Their inmate populations mushroomed until the stresses created by noise, overcrowding, and disease actually aggravated the problems they were meant to ease. Inmates were frequently chained and beaten.

The word *bedlam* derives from St. Mary's of *Bethlehem*, the London asylum that opened its gates in 1547. Here unfortunate people with psychological disorders were chained, whipped, and allowed to lie in their own waste. And here the ladies and gentlemen of the British upper class might stroll on a lazy afternoon to be amused by the inmates' antics. The price of admission was one penny.

Humanitarian reform movements began in the 18th century. In Paris, the physician Philippe Pinel unchained the patients at La Bicêtre. Rather than running amok, most patients profited from kindness and freedom. Many could eventually reenter society. Later movements to reform institutions were led by the Quaker William Tuke in England and by Dorothea Dix in America.

MENTAL HOSPITALS In the United States mental hospitals gradually replaced asylums. In the mid-1950s more than a million people resided in state, county, Veterans Administration, or private facilities. The mental hospital's function is treatment, not warehousing. Still, because of high patient populations and understaffing, many patients received little attention. Even today, with somewhat improved conditions, one psychiatrist

TRUTH OR FICTION REVISITED
It is true that residents of London used to visit the insane asylum for amusement.

PSYCHOTHERAPY A systematic interaction between a therapist and a client that brings psychological principles to bear on influencing the client's thoughts, feelings, or behavior to help that client overcome abnormal behavior or adjust to problems in living.

THE UNCHAINING OF THE PATIENTS AT LA BICÊTRE.
Philippe Pinel sparked the humanitarian reform movement by unchaining the patients
at this asylum in Paris.

may be responsible for the welfare of several hundred residents on a weekend when other staff members are absent.

THE COMMUNITY MENTAL HEALTH MOVEMENT Since the 1960s, efforts have been made to maintain people with serious psychological disorders in their communities. Community mental health centers attempt to maintain new patients as outpatients and to serve patients who have been released from mental hospitals. Today most people with chronic psychological disorders live in the community, not the hospital.

Critics note that many people who had resided in hospitals for decades were suddenly discharged to "home" communities that seemed foreign and forbidding to them. Many do not receive adequate follow-up care. Many join the ranks of the homeless.

PSYCHODYNAMIC THERAPIES

Psychodynamic therapies are based on the thinking of Sigmund Freud, the founder of psychodynamic theory. They assume that psychological problems reflect early childhood experiences and internal conflicts. According to Freud, these conflicts involve the shifting of psychic, or libidinal, energy among the three psychic structures—the id, ego, and superego. These shifts of psychic energy determine our behavior. When primitive urges threaten to break through from the id or when the superego floods us with excessive guilt, defenses are established and distress is created. Freud's psychodynamic therapy method—psychoanalysis—aims to modify the flow of energy among these structures, largely to bulwark the ego against the torrents of energy loosed by the id and the superego. With impulses and feelings of guilt and shame placed under greater control, clients are freer to develop adaptive behavior.

Traditional Psychoanalysis:
"Where Id Was, There Shall Ego Be"

Canst thou not minister to a mind diseas'd,
Pluck out from the memory a rooted sorrow,
Raze out the written troubles of the brain,
And with some sweet oblivious antidote
Cleanse the stuffbosom of that perilous stuff
Which weighs upon the heart?

SHAKESPEARE, *Macbeth*

In the passage just quoted, Macbeth asks a physician to minister to Lady Macbeth after she has gone mad. In the play, her madness is caused partly by events—namely, her role in murders designed to seat her husband on the throne of Scotland. There are also hints of mysterious, deeply rooted problems, such as conflicts about infertility.

If Lady Macbeth's physician had been a traditional psychoanalyst, he might have asked her to lie on a couch in a slightly darkened room. He would have sat behind her and encouraged her to talk about anything that came to mind, no matter how trivial, no matter how personal. To avoid interfering with her self-exploration, he might have said little or nothing for session after session. That would have been par for the course. A traditional **psychoanalysis** can extend for months or even years.

Psychoanalysis is the clinical method devised by Freud for plucking "from the memory a rooted sorrow," for razing "out the written troubles of the brain." It aims to provide *insight* into the conflicts that are presumed to lie at the roots of a person's problems. Insight means many things, including knowledge of the experiences that lead to conflicts and maladaptive behavior, recognition of unconscious feelings and conflicts, and conscious evaluation of one's thoughts, feelings, and behavior.

Psychoanalysis also aims to help the client express feelings and urges that have been repressed. By so doing, Freud believed that the client spilled forth the psychic energy that had been repressed by conflicts and guilt. He called this spilling forth **catharsis.** Catharsis would provide relief by alleviating some of the forces assaulting the ego.

Freud was also fond of saying, "Where id was, there shall ego be." In part, he meant that psychoanalysis could shed light on the inner workings of the mind. He also sought to replace impulsive and defensive behavior with coping behavior. In this way, for example, a man with a phobia for knives might discover that he had been repressing the urge to harm someone who had taken advantage of him. He might also find ways to confront the person verbally.

FREE ASSOCIATION Early in his career as a therapist, Freud found that hypnosis allowed his clients to focus on repressed conflicts and talk about them. The relaxed "trance state" provided by hypnosis seemed to allow clients to "break through" to topics of which they would otherwise be unaware. Freud also found, however, that many clients denied the accuracy of this material once they were out of the trance. Other clients found them to be premature and painful. Freud therefore turned to **free association,** a more gradual method of breaking through the walls of defense that block a client's insight into unconscious processes.

In free association, the client is made comfortable—for example, lying on a couch—and asked to talk about any topic that comes to mind. No thought is to be censored—that is the basic rule. Psychoanalysts ask their clients to

PSYCHOANALYSIS Freud's method of psychotherapy.

CATHARSIS In psychoanalysis, the expression of repressed feelings and impulses to allow the release of the psychic energy associated with them.

FREE ASSOCIATION In psychoanalysis, the uncensored uttering of all thoughts that come to mind.

A VIEW OF FREUD'S CONSULTING ROOM.
Freud would sit in a chair by the head of the couch while a client free-associated. The
basic rule of free association is that no thought is censored.

wander "freely" from topic to topic, but they do not believe that the process
occurring *within* the client is fully free. Repressed impulses clamor for release.

The ego persists in trying to repress unacceptable impulses and threatening conflicts. As a result, clients might show **resistance** to recalling and
discussing threatening ideas. A client about to entertain such thoughts
might claim, "My mind is blank." The client might accuse the analyst of
being demanding or inconsiderate. He or she might "forget" the next
appointment when threatening material is about to surface.

The therapist observes the dynamic struggle between the compulsion
to utter certain thoughts and the client's resistance to uttering them.
Through discreet remarks, the analyst subtly tips the balance in favor of
utterance. A gradual process of self-discovery and self-insight ensues. Now
and then the analyst offers an **interpretation** of an utterance, showing how
it suggests resistance or deep-seated feelings and conflicts.

DREAM ANALYSIS Freud often asked clients to jot down their dreams
upon waking so that they could discuss them in therapy. Freud considered
dreams the "royal road to the unconscious." He believed that the content
of dreams is determined by unconscious processes as well as by the events
of the day. Unconscious impulses tend to be expressed in dreams as a
form of **wish fulfillment.**

But unacceptable sexual and aggressive impulses are likely to be displaced onto objects and situations that reflect the client's era and culture.
These objects become symbols of unconscious wishes. For example, long,
narrow dream objects might be **phallic symbols,** but whether the symbol
takes the form of a spear, rifle, stick shift, or spacecraft partially reflects
the dreamer's cultural background.

In psychodynamic theory, the perceived content of a dream is referred
to as its shown, or **manifest content.** Its presumed hidden or symbolic content is its **latent content.** Suppose a man dreams that he is flying. Flying is
the manifest content of the dream. Freud usually interpreted flying as
symbolic of erection, so issues concerning sexual potency might make up
the latent content of such a dream.

RESISTANCE The tendency to block the free expression of
impulses and primitive ideas — a reflection of the defense
mechanism of repression.

INTERPRETATION An explanation of a client's utterance
according to psychoanalytic theory.

WISH FULFILLMENT A primitive method used
by the id to attempt to gratify basic instincts.

PHALLIC SYMBOL A sign that represents the penis.

MANIFEST CONTENT In psychodynamic theory,
the reported content of dreams.

LATENT CONTENT In psychodynamic theory,
the symbolized or underlying content of dreams.

Modern Psychodynamic Approaches

Some psychoanalysts adhere faithfully to Freud's techniques. In recent years, however, briefer, less intense forms of psychodynamic therapy have been devised. They make treatment available to clients who do not have the time or money for long-term therapy. Many of these therapists also believe that prolonged therapy is not needed or justifiable in terms of the ratio of cost to benefits.

Some modern psychodynamic therapies continue to focus on revealing unconscious material and breaking through psychological defenses. Nevertheless, they differ from traditional psychoanalysis in several ways (Prochaska & Norcross, 1999). One is that the client and therapist usually sit face to face (the client does not lie on a couch). The therapist is usually directive. That is, modern therapists often suggest helpful behavior instead of focusing on insight alone. Finally, there is usually more focus on the ego as the "executive" of personality, and less emphasis on the id. For this reason, many modern psychodynamic therapists are considered **ego analysts.**

Many of Freud's followers, the "second generation" of psychoanalysts—from Jung and Adler to Horney and Erikson—believed that Freud had placed too much emphasis on sexual and aggressive impulses and underestimated the role of the ego. For example, Freud aimed to establish conditions under which clients could spill forth psychic energy and eventually shore up the ego. Erikson, in contrast, spoke to clients directly about their values and concerns, encouraging them to develop desired traits and behavior patterns. Even Freud's daughter, the psychoanalyst Anna Freud (1895–1982), was more concerned with the ego than with unconscious forces and conflicts.

HUMANISTIC-EXISTENTIAL THERAPIES

Psychodynamic therapies focus on internal conflicts and unconscious processes. Humanistic-existential therapies focus on the quality of the client's subjective, conscious experience. Traditional psychoanalysis focuses on early childhood experiences. Humanistic-existential therapies usually focus on what clients are experiencing here and now.

These differences, however, are mainly a matter of emphasis. The past has a way of influencing current thoughts, feelings, and behavior. Carl Rogers, the originator of client-centered therapy, believed that childhood experiences gave rise to the conditions of worth that troubled his clients here and now. He and Fritz Perls, the originator of Gestalt therapy, recognized that early incorporation of other people's values often leads clients to "disown" parts of their own personalities.

Client-Centered Therapy: Removing Roadblocks to Self-Actualization

Carl Rogers (1902–1987) spent his early years in a wealthy Chicago suburb, where he attended school with Ernest Hemingway and Frank Lloyd Wright's children. His family, with its six children, was religious and close knit. Rogers's father viewed such activities as smoking, drinking, playing cards, and going to the movies as questionable. It was all right to be tolerant of them, but relationships with those who engaged in them were discouraged. When Rogers was 12, his family moved to a farm farther from the city to protect the children from such unwholesome influences.

TRUTH OR FICTION REVISITED
It is not true that psychotherapy must continue for months, perhaps years, to be effective. There are many effective brief forms of psychotherapy.

EGO ANALYST A psychodynamically oriented therapist who focuses on the conscious, coping behavior of the ego instead of the hypothesized, unconscious functioning of the id.

CLIENT-CENTERED THERAPY. By showing the qualities of unconditional positive regard, empathic understanding, genuineness, and congruence, client-centered therapists create an atmosphere in which clients can explore their feelings.

Rogers took refuge in books and developed an interest in science. His first college major was agriculture. During a student visit to Peking, he was exposed for the first time to people from different ethnic backgrounds. He wrote his parents to proclaim his independence from their conservative views. Shortly thereafter he developed an ulcer and had to be hospitalized.

Rogers then attended New York's Union Theological Seminary with the goal of becoming a minister. At the same time he took courses in psychology and education across the street at Columbia University. After a couple of years he came to believe that psychology might be a better way of helping people, so he transferred to Columbia. Perhaps in response to his parents' efforts to "protect" him from other ways of thinking, Rogers developed a form of therapy—**client-centered therapy**—intended to help people get in touch with their genuine feelings and pursue their own interests, regardless of other people's wishes.

Rogers believed that we are free to make choices and control our destinies, despite the burdens of the past. He also believed that we have natural tendencies toward health, growth, and fulfillment. Psychological problems arise from roadblocks placed in the path of **self-actualization**—that is, what Rogers believed was an inborn tendency to strive to realize one's potential. If, when we are young, other people only approve of us when we are doing what they want us to do—as did Rogers's father—we may learn to disown the parts of ourselves to which they object. We may learn to be seen but not heard—not even by ourselves. As a result, we may experience stress and discomfort and the feeling that we—or the world—are not real.

Client-centered therapy aims to provide insight into the parts of us we have disowned so that we can feel whole. It creates a warm, therapeutic atmosphere that encourages self-exploration and self-expression. The therapist's acceptance of the client is thought to foster self-acceptance and self-esteem. Self-acceptance frees the client to make choices that develop his or her unique potential.

CLIENT-CENTERED THERAPY Carl Rogers's method of psychotherapy, which emphasizes the creation of a warm, therapeutic atmosphere that frees clients to engage in self-exploration and self-expression.

SELF-ACTUALIZATION In humanistic theory, the inborn tendency to strive to realize one's potential.

Client-centered therapy is nondirective. The client takes the lead, stating and exploring problems.

An effective client-centered therapist has several qualities:

- **Unconditional positive regard:** Respect for clients as human beings with unique values and goals.

- **Empathic understanding:** Recognition of the client's experiences and feelings. Therapists view the world through the client's **frame of reference** by setting aside their own values and listening closely.

- **Genuineness:** Openness and honesty in responding to the client. Client-centered therapists must be able to tolerate differentness because they believe that every client is different in important ways.

Client-centered therapy is practiced widely in college and university counseling centers, not just to help students experiencing, say, anxieties or depression but also to help them make decisions. Many college students have not yet made career choices or wonder whether they should become involved with particular people or in sexual activity. Client-centered therapists do not tell clients what to do. Instead, they help clients arrive at their own decisions.

Gestalt Therapy: Getting It Together

Gestalt therapy was originated by Fritz Perls (1893–1970). Like client-centered therapy, it aims to help individuals integrate conflicting parts of their personality. Perls used the term *Gestalt* to signify his interest in giving the conflicting parts of the personality an integrated form or shape. He aimed to have his clients become aware of inner conflict, accept the reality of conflict rather than deny it or keep it repressed, and make productive choices despite misgivings and fears.

Although Perls's ideas about conflicting personality elements owe much to psychodynamic theory, his form of therapy, unlike psychoanalysis, focuses on the here and now. In Gestalt therapy, clients perform exercises to heighten their awareness of their current feelings and behavior, rather than exploring the past. Perls also believed, along with Rogers, that people are free to make choices and to direct their personal growth. Unlike client-centered therapy, however, Gestalt therapy is highly directive. The therapist leads the client through planned experiences.

One Gestalt technique that increases awareness of internal conflict is the *dialogue*. The client undertakes verbal confrontations between opposing wishes and ideas. An example of these clashing personality elements is "top dog" and "underdog." One's top dog might conservatively suggest, "Don't take chances. Stick with what you have or you might lose it all." One's frustrated underdog might then rise up and assert, "You never try anything. How will you ever get out of this rut if you don't take on new challenges?" Heightened awareness of the elements of conflict can clear the path toward resolution, perhaps through a compromise of some kind.

Body language also provides insight into conflicting feelings. Clients might be instructed to attend to the ways in which they furrow their eyebrows and tense their facial muscles when they express certain ideas. In this way, they often find that their body language asserts feelings they have been denying in their spoken statements. To increase clients' understanding of opposing points of view, Gestalt therapists might encourage them to argue in favor of ideas opposed to their own.

Psychodynamic theory views dreams as the "royal road to the unconscious." Perls saw the content of dreams as representing disowned parts of the personality. Perls would often ask clients to role-play the elements of their dreams in order to get in touch with these parts of their personality.

UNCONDITIONAL POSITIVE REGARD Acceptance of the value of another person, although not necessarily acceptance of everything the person does.

EMPATHIC UNDERSTANDING Ability to perceive a client's feelings from the client's frame of reference.

FRAME OF REFERENCE One's unique perceptions and attitudes, according to which one evaluates events.

GENUINENESS Recognition and open expression of the therapist's own feelings.

GESTALT THERAPY Fritz Perls's form of psychotherapy, which attempts to integrate conflicting parts of the personality through directive methods designed to help clients perceive their whole selves.

BEHAVIOR THERAPY: ADJUSTMENT IS WHAT YOU DO

Behavior therapy—also called *behavior modification*—applies principles of learning to directly promote desired behavioral changes (Wolpe & Plaud, 1997). Behavior therapists rely heavily on principles of conditioning and observational learning. They help clients discontinue self-defeating behavior patterns such as overeating, smoking, and phobic avoidance of harmless stimuli. They also help clients acquire adaptive behavior patterns such as the social skills required to start social relationships or say no to insistent salespeople.

Behavior therapists may help clients gain "insight" into maladaptive behavior in the sense of fostering awareness of the circumstances in which it occurs. They do not foster insight in the psychoanalytic sense of unearthing the childhood origins of problems and the symbolic meanings of maladaptive behavior. Behavior therapists, like other therapists, may also build warm, therapeutic relationships with clients, but they see the efficacy of behavior therapy as deriving from specific, learning-based procedures (Wolpe, 1990). They insist that their methods be established by experimentation and that therapeutic outcomes be assessed in terms of observable, measurable behavior. In this section we consider some frequently used behavior-therapy techniques.

Fear-Reduction Methods

Behavior therapists use many methods for reducing fears. These include flooding, systematic desensitization, and modeling.

FLOODING In **flooding,** the client is exposed to a fear-evoking stimulus until fear is extinguished (Turner et al., 1994). Aaron Beck, the originator of a key approach to cognitive therapy, used flooding on himself before he became a psychiatrist. One of the reasons he went into medicine was to confront his own fear of blood. He had had a series of operations as a child, and from then on the sight of blood had made him feel faint. During his first year of medical school, he forced himself to watch operations. In his second year, he became a surgical assistant. Soon the sight of blood became normal to him. His fear of blood became extinguished because it was not connected with any real consequence, such as pain.

Flooding is an unpleasant sink-or-swim method for overcoming fears. Most behavior therapists prefer to use systematic desensitization.

SYSTEMATIC DESENSITIZATION Adam has a phobia for receiving injections. His behavior therapist treats him as he reclines in a comfortable padded chair. In a state of deep muscle relaxation, Adam observes slides projected on a screen. A slide of a nurse holding a needle has just been shown three times, 30 seconds at a time. Each time Adam has shown no anxiety. So now a slightly more discomforting slide is shown: one of the nurse aiming the needle toward someone's bare arm. After 15 seconds, our armchair adventurer notices twinges of discomfort and raises a finger as a signal (speaking might disturb his relaxation). The projector operator turns off the light, and Adam spends 2 minutes imagining his "safe scene"—lying on a beach beneath the tropical sun. Then the slide is shown again. This time Adam views it for 30 seconds before feeling anxiety.

Adam is undergoing **systematic desensitization,** a method for reducing phobic responses originated by psychiatrist Joseph Wolpe (1990). Systematic desensitization is a gradual process in which the client learns to

BEHAVIOR THERAPY Systematic application of the principles of learning to the direct modification of a client's problem behaviors.

FLOODING Exposing a person to a fear-evoking stimulus without aversive consequences until fear is extinguished.

SYSTEMATIC DESENSITIZATION Wolpe's method for reducing fears by associating a hierarchy of images of fear-evoking stimuli with muscle relaxation.

OVERCOMING A PHOBIA.
One way behavior therapists help clients overcome phobias is by having them gradually approach the feared object or situation fear while they remain relaxed.

handle increasingly disturbing stimuli while anxiety to each one is being counterconditioned. About 10 to 20 stimuli are arranged in a sequence, or hierarchy, according to their capacity to elicit anxiety. In imagination or by being shown photos, the client travels gradually up through this hierarchy, approaching the target behavior. In Adam's case, the target behavior was the ability to receive an injection without undue anxiety.

Wolpe developed systematic desensitization on the assumption that anxiety responses, like other behaviors, are learned or conditioned. He reasoned that they can be unlearned by means of counterconditioning or extinction. In counterconditioning, a response incompatible with anxiety is made to appear under conditions that usually elicit anxiety. Muscle relaxation is incompatible with anxiety. For this reason, Adam's therapist is teaching him to relax in the presence of (usually) anxiety-evoking slides of needles. (Muscle relaxation is usually achieved by means of *progressive relaxation,* a method for lowering the arousal created by anxiety reactions.)

Remaining in the presence of phobic imagery, rather than running away from it, is also likely to enhance self-efficacy expectations (Galassi, 1988). Self-efficacy expectations are negatively correlated with levels of adrenaline in the bloodstream (Bandura et al., 1985). Raising clients' self-efficacy expectations thus may help lower their adrenaline levels and reduce their feelings of nervousness.

TRUTH OR FICTION REVISITED
It is true that lying in a reclining chair and fantasizing can be an effective way of confronting fears. This is what happens in the method of systematic desensitization.

MODELING Modeling relies on observational learning. In this method clients observe, and then imitate, people who approach and cope with the objects or situations that the clients fear. Bandura and his colleagues (1969) found that modeling worked as well as systematic desensitization—and more rapidly—in reducing fear of snakes. Like systematic desensitization, modeling is likely to increase self-efficacy expectations in coping with feared stimuli.

Aversive Conditioning

Aversive conditioning is a controversial procedure. In this method painful or aversive stimuli are paired with unwanted impulses, such as desire for a cigarette or desire to engage in antisocial behavior, in order to make the impulse less appealing. For example, to help people control alcohol intake, tastes of different alcoholic beverages can be paired with drug-induced nausea and vomiting or with electric shock.

MODELING A behavior-therapy technique in which a client observes and imitates a person who approaches and copes with feared objects or situations.

AVERSIVE CONDITIONING A behavior-therapy technique in which undesired responses are inhibited by pairing repugnant or offensive stimuli with them.

AVERSIVE CONDITIONING.
In aversive conditioning, unwanted behaviors take on a noxious quality as a result of being repeatedly paired with aversive stimuli. Overexposure is making cigarette smoke aversive to this smoker.

TRUTH OR FICTION REVISITED
It is true that smoking cigarettes can be an effective treatment for helping people stop smoking cigarettes. The trick is to inhale enough smoke so it is aversive rather than enjoyable.

Aversive conditioning has been used with problems as diverse as cigarette smoking, sexual abuse (Rice et al., 1991), and retarded children's self-injurious behavior. *Rapid smoking* is an aversive-conditioning method designed to help smokers quit. In this method, the would-be quitter inhales every 6 seconds. In another method the hose of a hair dryer is hooked up to a chamber containing several lit cigarettes. Smoke is blown into the quitter's face as he or she also smokes a cigarette. A third method uses branching pipes so that the smoker draws in smoke from several cigarettes at the same time. In all of these methods overexposure causes once desirable cigarette smoke to become aversive. The quitter becomes motivated to avoid, rather than seek, cigarettes. Many reports have shown a quit rate of 60% or higher at 6-month follow-ups. Yet interest in these methods for quitting smoking has waned because of side effects such as raising blood pressure and the availability of nicotine-replacement techniques.

In one study of aversive conditioning in the treatment of alcoholism, 63% of the 685 people treated remained abstinent for 1 year afterward, and about a third remained abstinent for at least 3 years (Wiens & Menustik, 1983). It may seem ironic that punitive aversive stimulation is sometimes used to stop children from punishing themselves, but people sometimes hurt themselves in order to obtain sympathy and attention. If self-injury leads to more pain than anticipated and no sympathy, it might be discontinued.

Operant Conditioning Procedures

We usually prefer to relate to people who smile at us rather than ignore us and to take courses in which we do well rather than fail. We tend to repeat behavior that is reinforced. Behavior that is not reinforced tends to become extinguished. Behavior therapists have used these principles of operant conditioning with psychotic patients as well as with clients with milder problems.

The staff at one mental hospital was at a loss about how to encourage withdrawn schizophrenic patients to eat regularly. Ayllon and Haughton (1962) observed that staff members were making the problem worse by coaxing patients into the dining room and even feeding them. Staff attention apparently reinforced the patients' lack of cooperation. Some rules were changed. Patients who did not arrive at the dining hall within 30 minutes after serving were locked out. Staff could not interact with patients at mealtime. With uncooperative behavior no longer reinforced, patients quickly changed their eating habits. Then patients were required to pay one penny to enter the dining hall. Pennies were earned by interacting with other patients and showing other socially appropriate behaviors. These target behaviors also became more frequent.

THE TOKEN ECONOMY Many psychiatric wards and hospitals now use *token economies* in which patients must use tokens such as poker chips to purchase TV viewing time, extra visits to the canteen, or a private room. The tokens are reinforcements for productive activities such as making beds, brushing teeth, and socializing. Token economies have not eliminated all features of schizophrenia. However, they have enhanced patient activity and cooperation. Tokens have also been used to modify the behavior of children with conduct disorders. In one program, for example, children received tokens for helpful behaviors such as volunteering and lost tokens for behaviors such as arguing and failing to pay attention (Schneider & Byrne, 1987).

SUCCESSIVE APPROXIMATIONS In operant conditioning, a series of behaviors that gradually become more similar to a target behavior.

SUCCESSIVE APPROXIMATIONS The operant conditioning method of **successive approximations** is often used to help clients build good habits. Let us use a (not uncommon!) example: You want to study 3 hours each evening but can only concentrate for half an hour. Rather than attempting to increase your study time all at once, you could do so gradually by adding, say, 5 minutes each evening. After every hour or so of studying, you could reinforce yourself with 5 minutes of people-watching in a busy section of the library.

SOCIAL SKILLS TRAINING In social skills training, behavior therapists decrease social anxiety and build social skills through operant-conditioning procedures that employ self-monitoring, coaching, modeling, role playing, practice ("behavior rehearsal"), and feedback. Social skills training has been used to help formerly hospitalized mental patients maintain jobs and apartments in the community. For example, a worker can rehearse politely asking a supervisor for assistance or asking a landlord to fix the plumbing in an apartment.

Social skills training is effective in groups. Group members can role-play important people—such as parents, spouses, or potential dates—in the lives of other members.

BIOFEEDBACK TRAINING Through **biofeedback training** (BFT), therapists help clients become more aware of, and gain control over, various bodily functions. Therapists attach clients to devices that measure bodily functions such as heart rate. "Bleeps" or other electronic signals are used to indicate (and thereby reinforce) changes in the desired direction—for example, a slower heart rate. (Knowledge of results is a powerful reinforcer.) One device, the electromyograph (EMG), monitors muscle tension. It has been used to augment control over muscle tension in the forehead and elsewhere, thereby alleviating anxiety, stress, and headaches.

BFT also helps clients voluntarily regulate functions once thought to be beyond conscious control, such as heart rate and blood pressure. Hypertensive clients use a blood pressure cuff and electronic signals to gain control over their blood pressure. The electroencephalograph (EEG) monitors brain waves and can be used to teach people how to produce alpha waves, which are associated with relaxation. Some people have overcome insomnia by learning to produce the kinds of brain waves associated with sleep.

Self-Control Methods

Do mysterious forces sometimes seem to be at work in your life? Forces that delight in wreaking havoc on New Year's resolutions and other efforts to put an end to your bad habits? Just when you go on a diet, that juicy pizza stares at you from the TV set. Just when you resolve to balance your budget, that sweater goes on sale. Behavior therapists have developed a number of self-control techniques to help people cope with such temptations.

FUNCTIONAL ANALYSIS OF BEHAVIOR Behavior therapists usually begin with a **functional analysis** of the problem behavior. In this way, they help determine the stimuli that trigger the behavior and the reinforcers that maintain it. You can use a diary to jot down each instance of a problem behavior. Note the time of day, location, your activity at the time (including your thoughts and feelings), and reactions (yours and others'). Functional analysis serves a number of purposes. It makes you more aware of the environmental context of your behavior and can increase your motivation to change.

TRUTH OR FICTION REVISITED
It is true that you might be able to put an end to bad habits merely by keeping a record of where and when you engage in them. The record may help motivate you, make you more aware of the problems, and suggest strategies for behavior change.

BIOFEEDBACK TRAINING The systematic feeding back to an organism of information about a bodily function so that the organism can gain control of that function. Abbreviated *BFT*.

FUNCTIONAL ANALYSIS A systematic study of behavior in which one identifies the stimuli that trigger problem behavior and the reinforcers that maintain it.

TABLE MT.1

EXCERPTS FROM BRIAN'S DIARY OF NAIL BITING FOR APRIL 14

INCIDENT	TIME	LOCATION	ACTIVITY (THOUGHTS, FEELINGS)	REACTIONS
1	7:45 a.m.	Freeway	Driving to work, bored, not thinking	Finger bleeds; pain
2	10:30 a.m.	Office	Writing report	Self-disgust
3	2:25 p.m.	Conference	Listening to dull financial report	Embarrassment
4	6:40 p.m.	Living room	Watching evening news	Self-disgust

Note: A functional analysis of problem behavior like nail biting increases awareness of the environmental context in which it occurs, spurs motivation to change, and, in highly motivated people, might lead to significant behavioral change.

Brian used functional analysis to master his nail biting. Table MT.1 shows a few items from his notebook. He discovered that boredom and humdrum activities seemed to serve as triggers for nail biting. He began to watch out for feelings of boredom as signs to practice self-control. He also made some changes in his life so he would feel bored less often.

Numerous self-control strategies are aimed at the stimuli that trigger behavior, the behaviors themselves, and reinforcers. Table MT.2 looks briefly at some of these strategies.

COGNITIVE THERAPIES

There is nothing either good or bad, but thinking makes it so.

SHAKESPEARE, *Hamlet*

In this line from *Hamlet*, Shakespeare did not mean to suggest that injuries and misfortunes are painless or easy to manage. Rather, he meant our appraisals of unfortunate events can heighten our discomfort and impair our coping ability. In so doing, Shakespeare was providing a kind of motto for cognitive therapists.

Cognitive therapists focus on the beliefs, attitudes, and automatic types of thinking that create and compound their clients' problems. Cognitive therapists, like psychodynamic and humanistic-existential therapists, aim to foster self-insight, but they aim to heighten insight into *current cognitions* as well as those of the past. Cognitive therapists also aim to directly *change* maladaptive cognitions in order to reduce negative feelings, provide insight, and help the client solve problems.

You may have noticed that many behavior therapists incorporate cognitive procedures in their methods (Jacobson et al., 1996; Meichenbaum, 1993). For example, techniques such as systematic desensitization, covert sensitization, and covert reinforcement ask clients to focus on visual imagery. Behavioral methods for treating bulimia nervosa focus on clients' irrational attitudes toward their weight and body shape as well as foster healthful eating habits.

Let us look at the approaches and methods of some major cognitive therapists.

Cognitive Therapy: Correcting Cognitive Errors

Aaron Beck used the behavior-therapy method of flooding on himself to overcome fear of blood. However, he also experimented with himself

TRUTH OR FICTION REVISITED

It is true that some psychotherapists tell their clients precisely what to do. That is, they outline behavioral prescriptions for their clients. Behavior therapists, Gestalt therapists, and some cognitive therapists are examples.

BEHAVIORAL STRATEGIES FOR SELF-CONTROL

STRATEGY	DESCRIPTION
STRATEGIES AIMED AT STIMULI THAT TRIGGER BEHAVIOR	
Restriction of the stimulus field	Gradually exclude the problem behavior from more environments. For example, at first make smoking off limits in the car, then in the office.
Avoidance of powerful stimuli that trigger habits	Avoid obvious sources of temptation. People who go window-shopping often wind up buying more than windows. If eating at The Pizza Glutton tempts you to forget your diet, eat at home or at The Celery Stalk instead.
Stimulus control	Place yourself in an environment in which desirable behavior is likely to occur. Maybe it is difficult to lift your mood directly at times, but you can place yourself in the audience of an uplifting concert or film. It might be difficult to force yourself to study, but how about rewarding yourself for spending time in the library?
STRATEGIES AIMED AT BEHAVIOR	
Response prevention	Make unwanted behavior difficult or impossible. Impulse buying is curbed when you shred your credit cards, leave your checkbook home, and carry only a couple of dollars with you. You can't reach for the strawberry cream cheese pie in your refrigerator if you did not buy it at the supermarket.
Competing responses	Engage in behaviors that are incompatible with the bad habit. It is difficult to drink a glass of water and a fattening milk shake simultaneously. Grasping something firmly is a useful competing response for nail biting or scratching.
Chain breaking	Interfere with unwanted habitual behavior by complicating the process of engaging in it. Break the chain of reaching for a readily available cigarette and placing it in your mouth by wrapping the pack in aluminum foil and placing it on the top shelf of a closet. Rewrap the pack after taking one cigarette. Put your cigarette in the ashtray between puffs, or put your fork down between mouthfuls of dessert. Ask yourself if you really want more.
Successive approximations	Gradually approach targets through a series of relatively painless steps. Increase studying by only 5 minutes a day. Decrease smoking by pausing for a minute when the cigarette is smoked halfway, or by putting it out a minute before you would wind up eating the filter. Decrease your daily intake of food by 50 to 100 calories every couple of days, or cut out one type of fattening food every few days.
STRATEGIES AIMED AT REINFORCEMENTS	
Reinforcement of desired behavior	Why give yourself something for nothing? Make pleasant activities such as going to films, walking on the beach, or reading a new novel contingent on meeting reasonable daily behavioral goals. Each day you remain within your calorie limit, put a dollar away toward that camera or vacation trip you have been dreaming of.
Response cost	Heighten awareness of the long-term reasons for dieting or cutting down on smoking by punishing yourself for not meeting a daily goal or for engaging in a bad habit. For example, if you bite your nails or inhale that cheesecake, make out a check to a cause you oppose and mail it at once.
"Grandma's method"	How did Grandma persuade children to eat their vegetables? Simple: no veggies, no dessert. In this method, desired behaviors such as studying and brushing your teeth can be increased by insisting that those behaviors be done before you engage in a pleasant or frequently occurring activity. For example, don't watch television unless you have studied first. Don't leave the apartment until you have brushed your teeth. You can also place reminders about new attitudes you are trying to acquire on little cards and read them regularly. For example, in quitting smoking, you might write, "Every day it becomes a little easier" on one card, and "Your lungs will turn pink again" on another. Place these cards and others in your wallet, and read them each time you leave the house.
Covert sensitization	Create imaginary horror stories about problem behavior. Psychologists have successfully reduced overeating and smoking by having clients imagine that they become acutely nauseated at the thought of fattening foods or that a cigarette is made from vomit. Some horror stories are not so "imaginary." Deliberately focusing on heart strain and diseased lungs every time you overeat or smoke, rather than ignoring these long-term consequences, might also promote self-control.
Covert reinforcement	Create rewarding imagery for desired behavior. When you have achieved a behavioral goal, fantasize about how wonderful you are. Imagine friends and family members patting you on the back.

using cognitive methods. For example, he argued himself out of an irrational fear (a phobia) of tunnels. He convinced himself that the tunnels did not cause the fear because the symptoms of faintness and shallow breathing would appear before he entered them.

As a psychiatrist, Beck first practiced psychoanalysis. However, he could not find scientific evidence for psychoanalytic beliefs. Psychoanalytic theory explained depression as anger turned inward, so that it is transformed into a need to suffer. Beck's own clinical experiences led him to believe that it is more likely that depressed people experience cognitive distortions such as the *cognitive triad*. That is, they expect the worst of themselves ("I'm no good"), the world at large ("This is an awful place"), and their future ("Nothing good will ever happen").

Beck's cognitive therapy is active. Beck encourages clients to become their own personal scientists and challenge beliefs that are not supported by evidence. He questions people in a way that encourages them to see the irrationality of their ways of thinking. For example, depressed people tend to minimize their accomplishments and to assume that the worst will happen. Both distortions heighten feelings of depression. Beck (1991, 1993) notes that cognitive distortions can be fleeting and automatic, difficult to detect. His therapy methods help clients pin down such distortions and challenge them.

Beck notes the pervasive influence of cognitive errors that contribute to clients' miseries. Consider these examples:

1. Clients may *selectively perceive* the world as a harmful place and ignore evidence to the contrary.

2. Clients may *overgeneralize* on the basis of a few examples. For example, they may perceive themselves as worthless because they were laid off at work, or as unattractive because they were refused a date.

3. Clients may *magnify,* or blow out of proportion, the importance of negative events. They may catastrophize failing a test by assuming they will flunk out of college, or catastrophize losing a job by believing that they will never find another one and that serious harm will befall their family as a result.

4. Clients may engage in *absolutist thinking,* or looking at the world in black and white rather than in shades of gray. In doing so, a rejection on a date takes on the meaning of a lifetime of loneliness; an uncomfortable illness takes on life-threatening proportions.

The concept of pinpointing and modifying cognitive errors may become clearer from the following excerpt from a case in which a 53-year-old engineer obtained cognitive therapy for depression. The engineer had left his job and become inactive. As reported by Beck and his colleagues, the first goal of treatment was to foster physical activity—even chores like raking leaves and preparing dinner—because activity is incompatible with depression.

> [The engineer's] cognitive distortions were identified by comparing his assessment of each activity with that of his wife. Alternative ways of interpreting his experiences were then considered.
>
> In comparing his wife's résumé of his past experiences, he became aware that he had (1) undervalued his past by failing to mention many previous accomplishments, (2) regarded himself as far more responsible for his " failures" than she did, and (3) concluded that he was worthless since he had not succeeded in attaining certain goals in the past. When the two accounts were contrasted, he could discern many of his cognitive distortions. In subsequent sessions, his wife continued to serve as an "objectifier."
>
> In midtherapy, [he] compiled a list of new attitudes that he had acquired since initiating therapy. These included:

1. "I am starting at a lower level of functioning at my job, but it will improve if I persist."
2. "I know that once I get going in the morning, everything will run all right for the rest of the day."
3. "I can't achieve everything at once."
4. "I have my periods of ups and downs, but in the long run I feel better."
5. "My expectations from my job and life should be scaled down to a realistic level."
6. "Giving in to avoidance [e.g., staying away from work and social interactions] never helps and only leads to further avoidance."

He was instructed to reread this list daily for several weeks even though he already knew the content. (Rush et al., 1975)

The engineer gradually became less depressed and returned to work and an active social life. Along the way, he learned to combat inappropriate self-blame for problems, perfectionistic expectations, magnification of failures, and overgeneralization from failures.

Becoming aware of cognitive errors and modifying catastrophizing thoughts helps us cope with stress. Internal, stable, and global attributions of failure lead to depression and feelings of helplessness. Cognitive therapists also alert clients to cognitive errors such as these so that the clients can change their attitudes and pave the way for more effective overt behavior.

Rational Emotive Behavior Therapy: Overcoming "Musts" and "Shoulds"

Not very modestly, Albert Ellis refers to himself as "the father of REBT [**rational emotive behavior therapy**] and the grandfather of cognitive-behavioral therapy." Like Aaron Beck, Ellis first practiced psychoanalysis. However, he found Freud's methods to be slow and ineffective. He noted that people who were undergoing analysis often *felt* better, at least for a while, because of talking about their problems and getting attention from the therapist. But he did not believe they *got* better. He also was not convinced that it was useful for the therapist to be so passive, so he became more active and began to offer direct advice.

Ellis (1977, 1993) points out that our beliefs *about* events, not only the events themselves, shape our responses to them. Moreover, many of us harbor a number of irrational beliefs that can give rise to problems or magnify their impact. Two of the most important ones are the belief that we must have the love and approval of people who are important to us and the belief that we must prove ourselves as thoroughly competent, adequate, and achieving.

Ellis's methods are active and directive. He urges clients to seek out their irrational beliefs. Then he shows clients how those beliefs lead to misery and challenges them to change them. According to Ellis, we need less misery and less blaming in our lives, and more action.

Ellis also straddles behavioral and cognitive therapies. In keeping with his broad philosophy, he recently changed the name of rational emotive therapy to rational emotive *behavior* therapy.

GROUP THERAPIES

When a psychotherapist has several clients with similar problems—anxiety, depression, adjustment to divorce, lack of social skills—it often makes sense to treat them in a group rather than in individual sessions. The methods

RATIONAL EMOTIVE BEHAVIOR THERAPY Albert Ellis's form of therapy, which encourages clients to challenge and correct irrational expectations and maladaptive behaviors.

GROUP THERAPY.
Group therapy has a number of advantages over individual therapy for many clients. It is economical, provides a fund of experience for clients to draw on, elicits group support, and provides an opportunity to relate to other people. Some clients do need individual attention, however.

and characteristics of the group reflect the needs of the members and the theoretical orientation of the leader. In group psychoanalysis, clients might interpret one another's dreams. In a client-centered group, they might provide an accepting atmosphere for self-exploration. Members of behavior-therapy groups might be jointly desensitized to anxiety-evoking stimuli or might practice social skills together.

Group therapy has the following advantages:

1. It is economical (Sleek, 1995). It allows the therapist to work with several clients at once.

2. Compared with one-to-one therapy, group therapy provides more information and life experience for clients to draw on.

3. Appropriate behavior receives group support. Clients usually appreciate an outpouring of peer approval.

4. When we run into troubles, it is easy to imagine that we are different from other people or inferior to them. Affiliating with people with similar problems is reassuring.

5. Group members who show improvement provide hope for other members.

6. Many individuals seek therapy because of problems in relating to other people. People who seek therapy for other reasons also may be socially inhibited. Members of groups have the opportunity to practice social skills in a relatively nonthreatening atmosphere. In a group consisting of men and women of different ages, group members can role-play one another's employers, employees, spouses, parents, children, and friends. Members can role-play asking one another out on dates, saying no (or yes), and so on.

But group therapy is not for everyone. Some clients fare better with individual treatment. Many prefer not to disclose their problems to a group. They may be overly shy or want individual attention. It is the responsibility of the therapist to insist that group disclosures be kept confidential, to establish a supportive atmosphere, and to ensure that group members obtain the attention they need.

Many types of therapy can be conducted either individually or in groups. Encounter groups and family therapy are conducted only in groups.

Encounter Groups

Encounter groups are not appropriate for treating serious psychological problems. Rather, they are intended to promote personal growth by heightening awareness of one's own needs and feelings and those of others. This goal is sought through intense confrontations, or encounters, between strangers. Like ships in the night, group members come together out of the darkness, touch one another briefly, then sink back into the shadows of one another's lives. But something is gained from the passing. Encounter groups stress interactions between group members in the here and now. Discussion of the past may be outlawed. Interpretation is out. However, expression of genuine feelings toward others is encouraged. When group members think a person's social mask is phony, they may descend en masse to rip it off.

Encounter groups can be damaging when they urge overly rapid disclosure of intimate matters or when several members attack one member. Responsible leaders do not tolerate these abuses and try to keep the group moving in a growth-enhancing direction.

Family Therapy

In **family therapy,** one or more families constitute the group. Family therapy may be undertaken from various theoretical viewpoints. One is the "systems approach," in which family interaction is studied and modified to enhance the growth of individual family members and of the family unit as a whole (Prochaska & Norcross, 1999).

Family members with low self-esteem often cannot tolerate different attitudes and behaviors in other family members. Faulty communication within the family also creates problems. In addition, it is not uncommon for the family to present an "identified patient"—that is, the family member who has *the* problem and is *causing* all the trouble. Yet family therapists usually assume that the identified patient is a scapegoat for other problems within and among family members. It is a sort of myth: Change the bad apple—or identified patient—and the barrel—or family—will be functional once more.

The family therapist—often a specialist in this field—attempts to teach the family to communicate more effectively and encourage growth and autonomy in each family member.

DOES PSYCHOTHERAPY WORK?

Many of us know people who swear by their therapists, but the evidence is often shaky—for example, "I was a wreck before, but now . . .," or "I feel so much better now." Anecdotes like these are encouraging, but we do not know what would have happened to these people had they not sought help. Many people feel better about their problems as time goes on, with or without therapy. Sometimes, happily, problems seem to go away by themselves. Sometimes people find solutions on their own. Then, too, we hear some stories about how therapy was useless and about people who hop fruitlessly from one therapist to another.

ENCOUNTER GROUP A type of group that fosters self-awareness by focusing on how group members relate to each other in a setting that encourages open expression of feelings.

FAMILY THERAPY A form of therapy in which the family unit is treated as the client.

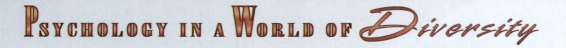
PSYCHOTHERAPY AND HUMAN DIVERSITY

The United States, they are a-changing. Most of the prescriptions for psychotherapy discussed in this chapter were originated by, and intended for use with, European Americans (Hall, 1997)—especially for male heterosexuals. People from ethnic minority groups are less likely than European Americans to seek therapy (Penn et al., 1995). Reasons for their lower participation rate include the following:

- Unawareness that therapy would help;
- Lack of information about the availability of professional services, or inability to pay for them (DeAngelis, 1995);
- Distrust of professionals, particularly White professionals and (for women) male professionals (Basic Behavioral Science Task Force, 1996);
- Language barriers (American Psychological Association, 1993);
- Reluctance to open up about personal matters to strangers—especially strangers who are not members of one's own ethnic group (LaFramboise, 1994);
- Cultural inclinations toward other approaches to problem solving, such as religious approaches and psychic healers (LaFramboise, 1994); and
- Negative experiences with professionals and authority figures.

Women and gay males and lesbians have also sometimes found therapy to be insensitive to their particular needs. Let us consider ways in which psychotherapy can be of more use to people from ethnic minority groups, women, and gay males and lesbians.

PSYCHOTHERAPY AND ETHNIC MINORITY GROUPS

Clinicians need to be sensitive to the cultural heritage, language, and values of the people they see in therapy (American Psychological Association, 1993). Let us consider some of the issues involved in conducting psychotherapy with African Americans, Asian Americans, Hispanic Americans, and Native Americans.

In addition to addressing the psychological problems of African American clients, therapists often need to help them cope with the effects of prejudice and discrimination. Beverly Greene (1993) notes that some African Americans develop low self-esteem because they internalize negative stereotypes.

African Americans often are reluctant to seek psychological help because of cultural assumptions that people should manage their own problems and because they mistrust the therapy process. They tend to assume that people are supposed to solve their own problems. Signs of emotional weakness such as tension, anxiety, and depression are stigmatized (Boyd-Franklin, 1995; Greene, 1993).

Many African Americans are also suspicious of their therapists—especially when the therapist is a non-Hispanic White American. They may withhold personal information because of the society's history of racial discrimination (Boyd-Franklin, 1995; Greene, 1993).

Asian Americans tend to stigmatize people with psychological disorders. As a result, they may deny problems and refuse to seek help for them (Sue, 1991). Asian Americans, especially recent immigrants, also may not understand or believe in Western approaches to psychotherapy. For example, Western psychotherapy typically encourages people to express their feelings openly. This mode of behavior may conflict with the Asian tradition of restraint in public. Many Asians prefer to receive concrete advice rather than Western-style encouragement to develop their own solutions (Isomura et al., 1987).

Because of a cultural tendency to turn away from painful thoughts, many Asians experience and express psychological complaints as physical symptoms (Zane & Sue, 1991). Rather than thinking of themselves as anxious, they may focus on physical features of anxiety such as a pounding heart and heavy sweating. Rather than thinking of themselves as depressed, they may focus on fatigue and low energy levels.

Therapists need to be aware of potential conflicts between the traditional Hispanic American value of interdependency in the family and the typical non-Hispanic White American belief in independence and self-reliance (De la Cancela & Guzman, 1991). Many Hispanic Americans adhere to a patriarchal (male-dominated) family structure and strong kinship ties. Measures like the following may help bridge the gaps between psychotherapists and Hispanic American clients:

1. Interacting with clients in the language requested by them or, if this is not possible, referring them to professionals who can do so.

2. Using methods consistent with the client's values and levels of *acculturation,* as suggested by fluency in English and level of education.

3. Developing therapy methods that incorporate clients' cultural values. Malgady and his colleagues (1990), for example, use *cuento therapy* with Puerto Ricans. *Cuento therapy* modifies Hispanic folktales, or *cuentos,* so the characters serve as models for adaptive behavior.

Many psychological disorders experienced by Native Americans involve the disruption of their traditional culture caused by European colonization (LaFramboise, 1994). Native Americans have also been denied full access to key institutions in Western culture (LaFramboise, 1994). Loss of cultural identity and social disorganization have set the stage for problems such as alcoholism, substance abuse, and depression. Theresa LaFramboise (1994) argues that efforts to prevent such disorders should focus on strengthening Native American cultural identity, pride, and cohesion.

Some therapists use ceremonies that reflect clients' cultural or religious traditions. Purification and cleansing rites are therapeutic for many Native Americans (Lefley, 1990). Such rites are commonly sought by Native Americans who believe that their problems are caused by failure to placate malevolent spirits or perform required rituals (Lefley, 1990).

FEMINIST PSYCHOTHERAPY

Feminist psychotherapy is not a particular method of therapy. It is an approach to therapy rooted in feminist political theory and philosophy. Feminism challenges the validity of stereotypical gender-role stereotypes and the traditional of male dominance (Greene, 1993).

Feminist therapy developed as a response to male dominance of health professions and institutions. It suggested that the mental health establishment often worked to maintain inequality between men and women by trying to help women "adjust" to traditional gender roles when they wished to challenge these roles in their own lives. Feminist therapists note that many women experience depression and other psychological problems as a result of being treated as second-class citizens, and they argue that society rather than the individual woman must change if these psychological problems are to be alleviated.

PSYCHOTHERAPY AND SEXUAL ORIENTATION

The American Psychiatric Association (1994) does not consider a gay male or a lesbian sexual orientation to be a psychological disorder. The association did list homosexuality as a mental disorder until 1973, however, and many efforts have been made to "help" gay males and lesbians change their sexual orientation. For example, William Masters and Virginia Johnson (1979) adapted methods they had devised for the treatment of sexual dysfunctions and reported that the majority of gays seen in therapy "reversed" their sexual orientations. However, most of these individuals were bisexuals and not exclusively gay. More than half were married, and they all were motivated to change their sexual behavior.

Many critics argue that it is unprofessional to try to help people change their sexual orientations (Sleek, 1997). They note that the great majority of gay males and lesbians are satisfied with their sexual orientations and only seek therapy because of conflicts that arise from social pressure and prejudice. They believe that the purpose of therapy for gay males and lesbians should be to help relieve conflicts caused by prejudice so that they will find life as gay people more gratifying.

In sum, psychotherapy is most effective when therapists attend to and respect people's sociocultural as well as individual differences. Although it is the individual who experiences psychological anguish, the fault often lies in the cultural setting and not the individual. ∎

Problems in Conducting Research on Psychotherapy

Before we report on research dealing with the effectiveness of therapy, let us review some of the problems of this kind of research. As noted by Hans Strupp, "The problem of evaluating outcomes from psychotherapy continues to bedevil the field" (1996, p. 1017).

PROBLEMS IN RUNNING EXPERIMENTS ON PSYCHOTHERAPY

The ideal method for evaluating a treatment—such as a method of therapy—is the experiment (Shadish & Ragsdale, 1996). However, experiments on therapy methods are difficult to arrange and control. The outcomes can be difficult to define and measure.

Consider psychoanalysis. In well-run experiments, people are assigned at random to experimental and control groups. A true experiment on psychoanalysis would require randomly assigning people seeking therapy to psychoanalysis and to a control group or other kinds of therapy for comparison (Luborsky et al., 1993). But a person may have to remain in traditional psychoanalysis for years to attain beneficial results. Could we create control treatments that last as long? Moreover, some people seek psychoanalysis per se, not psychotherapy in general. Would it be ethical to assign them at random to other treatments or to a no-treatment control group? Clearly not.

In an ideal experiment, participants and researchers are "blind" with regard to the treatment the participants receive. Blind research designs allow researchers to control for participants' expectations. In an ideal experiment on therapy, individuals would be blind regarding the type of therapy they are obtaining—or whether they are obtaining a placebo (Carroll et al., 1994). However, it is difficult to mask the type of therapy clients are obtaining. Even if we could conceal it from clients, could we hide it from therapists?

DOES THERAPY HELP BECAUSE OF THE METHOD OR BECAUSE OF "NONSPECIFIC FACTORS"?

Sorting out the benefits of therapy per se from other aspects of the therapy situation is a staggering task. These other aspects are termed *nonspecific factors*. They refer to features found in most therapies, such as the client's relationship with the therapist (Prochaska & Norcross, 1999). Most therapists, regardless of theoretical outlook, show warmth and empathy, encourage exploration, and instill hope (Blatt et al., 1996; Burns & Nolen-Hoeksema, 1992). The benefits of therapy thus could stem largely from these behaviors. If so, the method itself might have little more value than a placebo ("sugar pill") in combating physical ailments.

Analyses of Therapy Effectiveness

Despite these evaluation problems, research on the effectiveness of therapy has been encouraging (Barlow, 1996; Shadish et al., 1997). Some of this research has relied on a technique termed *meta-analysis*. Meta-analysis combines and averages the results of individual studies. Generally speaking, the studies included in the analysis address similar issues in a similar way. Moreover, the analysts judge them to have been conducted in a valid manner.

In their classic early use of meta-analysis, Mary Lee Smith and Gene Glass (1977) analyzed the results of dozens of outcome studies of various types of therapies. They concluded that people who obtained psychodynamic therapy showed greater well-being, on the average, than 70% to 75% of those who did not obtain treatment. Similarly, nearly 75% of the clients who obtained client-centered therapy were better off than people who did not obtain treatment. Psychodynamic and client-centered therapies appear to be most effective with well-educated, verbal, strongly motivated clients who report problems with anxiety, depression (of light to moderate proportions), and interpersonal relationships. Neither form of therapy appears to be effective with people with psychotic disorders such as major depression, bipolar disorder, and schizophrenia. Smith and Glass (1977) found that people who obtained Gestalt therapy showed greater well-being than about 60% of those who did not obtain treatment. The effectiveness of psychoanalysis and client-centered therapy thus was reasonably comparable. Gestalt therapy fell behind.

Smith and Glass (1977) did not include cognitive therapies in their meta-analysis because at the time of their study many cognitive approaches were relatively new. Because behavior therapists also incorporate many cognitive techniques, it can be difficult to sort out which aspects—cognitive or otherwise—of behavioral treatments are most effective. However, many meta-analyses of cognitive-behavioral therapy have been conducted since the early work of Smith and Glass. Their results are encouraging (Lipsey & Wilson, 1993).

A number of studies of cognitive therapy per se have also been conducted. For example, they show that modifying irrational beliefs of the type described by Albert Ellis helps people with problems such as anxiety and depression (Engels et al., 1993; Haaga & Davison, 1993). Modifying self-defeating beliefs of the sort outlined by Aaron Beck also frequently alleviates anxiety and depression (Robins & Hayes, 1993; Whisman et al., 1991). Cognitive therapy may be helpful with people with severe depression, who had been thought responsive only to biological therapies (Jacobson & Hollon, 1996; Simons et al., 1995). Cognitive therapy has also helped people with personality disorders (Beck & Freeman, 1990).

Behavioral and cognitive therapies have also provided strategies for treating anxiety disorders, social skills deficits, and problems in self-control (Chambless & Hollon, 1998; DeRubeis & Crits-Christoph, 1998). These two kinds of therapies—which are often integrated as *cognitive behavioral therapy*—have also provided empirically supported methods for helping couples and families in distress (Baucom et al., 1998), and for modifying behaviors related to health problems such as headaches (Blanchard, 1992), smoking, chronic pain, and bulimia nervosa (Compas et al., 1998). Cognitive behavioral therapists have also innovated treatments for sexual problems for which there previously were no effective treatments (Rathus et al., 2000). Cognitive therapy has helped many people with schizophrenia (who are also using drug therapy) modify their delusional beliefs (Chadwick & Lowe, 1990). Behavior therapy has helped to coordinate the care of institutionalized patients, including people with schizophrenia and mental retardation (Spreat & Behar, 1994). However, little evidence indicates that psychological therapy alone is effective in treating the quirks of thought exhibited in people with severe psychotic disorders (Wolpe, 1990).

Thus it is not enough to ask which type of therapy is most effective. We must ask which type is most effective for a particular problem and a particular patient. What are its advantages? Its limitations? Clients may successfully use systematic desensitization to overcome stage fright, as measured by ability to speak to a group of people. If clients also want to know *why* they have stage fright, however, behavior therapy alone will not provide the answer.

BIOLOGICAL THERAPIES

The kinds of therapy we have discussed so far are psychological in nature—forms of *psycho*therapy. Psychotherapies apply *psychological* principles to treatment, principles based on psychological knowledge of matters such as learning and motivation.

People with psychological disorders are also often treated with biological therapies. Biological therapies apply what is known of people's *biological* structures and processes to the amelioration of psychological disorders. For example, they may work by altering events in the nervous system, by changing the action of neurotransmitters. In this section, we discuss three biological, or medical, approaches to treating people with psychological disorders: drug therapy, electroconvulsive therapy, and psychosurgery.

Drug Therapy

In the 1950s, Fats Domino popularized the song "My Blue Heaven." Fats was singing about the sky and happiness. Today "blue heavens" is one of the street names for the 10-milligram dose of the antianxiety drug Valium. Clinicians prescribe Valium and other drugs for people with various psychological disorders.

ANTIANXIETY DRUGS Most antianxiety drugs (also called *minor tranquilizers*) belong to the chemical class known as *benzodiazepines*. Valium (diazepam) is a benzodiazepine. Other benzodiazepines include chlordiazepoxide (for example, Librium), oxazepam (Serax), and alprazolam (Xanax). Antianxiety drugs are usually prescribed for outpatients who complain of generalized anxiety or panic attacks, although many people also use them as sleeping pills. Valium and other antianxiety drugs depress the activity of the central nervous system (CNS). The CNS, in turn,

AN ARSENAL OF CHEMICAL THERAPIES. Many drugs have been developed to combat psychological disorders. They include antianxiety drugs, antipsychotic drugs, antidepressants, and lithium.

decreases sympathetic activity, reducing the heart rate, respiration rate, and feelings of nervousness and tension.

Many people come to tolerate antianxiety drugs very quickly. When tolerance occurs, dosages must be increased for the drug to remain effective.

Sedation (feelings of being tired or drowsy) is the most common side effect of antianxiety drugs. Problems associated with withdrawal from these drugs include **rebound anxiety.** That is, some people who have been using these drugs regularly report that their anxiety becomes worse than before once they discontinue them. Antianxiety drugs can induce physical dependence, as evidenced by withdrawal symptoms such as tremors, sweating, insomnia, and rapid heartbeat.

ANTIPSYCHOTIC DRUGS People with schizophrenia are often given antipsychotic drugs (also called *major tranquilizers*). In most cases these drugs reduce agitation, delusions, and hallucinations. Many antipsychotic drugs, including phenothiazines (for example, Thorazine) and clozapine (Clozaril) are thought to act by blocking dopamine receptors in the brain (Kane, 1996). Research along these lines supports the theory that schizophrenia is connected with overactivity of the neurotransmitter dopamine.

ANTIDEPRESSANTS People with major depression often take so-called **antidepressant** drugs. These drugs are also helpful for some people with eating disorders, panic disorder, obsessive-compulsive disorder, and social phobia (Abramowitz, 1997; Lydiard et al., 1996; Thase & Kupfer, 1996). Problems in the regulation of noradrenaline and serotonin may be involved in eating and panic disorders as well as in depression. Antidepressants are believed to work by increasing levels of one or both of these neurotransmitters, which can affect both depression and eating disorders. However, cognitive-behavior therapy addresses irrational attitudes concerning weight and body shape, fosters normal eating habits, and helps people resist the urges to binge and purge. Cognitive-behavior therapy therefore apparently is more effective with people with bulimia than antidepressants (Wilson & Fairburn, 1993).

LITHIUM The ancient Greeks and Romans were among the first people to use the metal lithium as a psychoactive drug. They prescribed mineral water for people with bipolar disorder. They had no inkling why this treatment sometimes helped, but it might have been because mineral water contains lithium. A salt of the metal lithium (lithium carbonate), in tablet form, flattens out cycles of manic behavior and depression in most people. It is not known precisely how lithium works, although it affects the functioning of several neurotransmitters, including—perhaps most importantly—glutamate (Hokin et al., 1998).

It might be necessary for people with bipolar disorder to use lithium indefinitely, just as a person with diabetes must continue to use insulin to control the illness. Lithium also has been shown to have side effects such as hand tremors, memory impairment, and excessive thirst and urination.

Electroconvulsive Therapy

Electroconvulsive therapy (ECT) was introduced by the Italian psychiatrist Ugo Cerletti in 1939 for use with people with psychological disorders. Cerletti had noted that some slaughterhouses used electric shock to render animals unconscious. The shocks also produced convulsions. Along

REBOUND ANXIETY Strong anxiety that can attend the suspension of usage of a tranquilizer.

ANTIDEPRESSANT Acting to relieve depression.

ELECTROCONVULSIVE THERAPY Treatment of disorders like major depression by passing an electric current (that causes a convulsion) through the head. Abbreviated *ECT*.

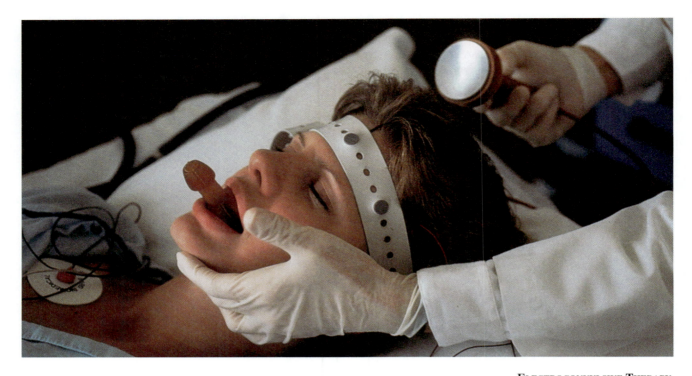

ELECTROCONVULSIVE THERAPY.
In ECT, electrodes are placed on each side of the patient's head and a current is passed between them, inducing a seizure. ECT is used mainly in cases of major depression when antidepressant drugs and psychotherapy fail.

with other European researchers of the period, Cerletti erroneously believed that convulsions were incompatible with schizophrenia and other major psychological disorders.

ECT was originally used for a variety of psychological disorders. Because of the advent of antipsychotic drugs, however, it is now used mainly for people with major depression who do not respond to antidepressants (Thase & Kupfer, 1996).

People typically obtain one ECT treatment three times a week for up to 10 sessions. Electrodes are attached to the temples and an electrical current strong enough to produce a convulsion is induced. The shock causes unconsciousness, so the patient does not recall it. Nevertheless, patients are given a **sedative** so that they are asleep during the treatment.

ECT is controversial for many reasons. First, many professionals are distressed by the idea of passing an electric shock through a patient's head and producing convulsions. Second, there are side effects, including memory problems. Third, nobody knows *why* ECT works.

Psychosurgery

Psychosurgery is more controversial than ECT. The best-known modern technique, **prefrontal lobotomy,** has been used with people with severe disorders. In this method, a picklike instrument severs the nerve pathways that link the prefrontal lobes of the brain to the thalamus. This method was pioneered by the Portuguese neurologist Antonio Egas Moniz and was brought to the United States in the 1930s. As pointed out by Valenstein (1986), the theoretical rationale for the operation was vague and

SEDATIVE A drug that relieves nervousness or agitation, or puts one to sleep.

PSYCHOSURGERY Surgery intended to promote psychological changes or to relieve disordered behavior.

PREFRONTAL LOBOTOMY The severing or destruction of a section of the frontal lobe of the brain.

misguided. Moreover, Moniz's reports of success were exaggerated. Nevertheless, by 1950 prefrontal lobotomies were performed on more than a thousand people in an effort to reduce violence and agitation. Anecdotal evidence of the method's unreliable outcomes is found in an ironic footnote to history: One of Dr. Moniz's "failures" shot the doctor, leaving a bullet lodged in his spine and paralyzing his legs.

Does Biological Therapy Work?

There is little question that drug therapy has helped many people with severe psychological disorders. For example, antipsychotic drugs largely account for the reduced need for the use of restraint and supervision (padded cells, straitjackets, hospitalization, and so on) with people diagnosed with schizophrenia. Antipsychotic drugs have allowed hundreds of thousands of former mental hospital residents to lead largely normal lives in the community, hold jobs, and maintain family lives. Most of the problems related to these drugs concern their side effects.

But many comparisons of psychotherapy (in the form of cognitive therapy) and drug therapy for depression suggest that cognitive therapy may be more effective than antidepressants (Antonuccio, 1995). Cognitive therapy provides coping skills that reduce the risk of recurrence of depression once treatment ends. Perhaps antidepressant medication is most appropriate for people who fail to respond to psychotherapy.

Many psychologists and psychiatrists are comfortable with the short-term use of antianxiety drugs to help clients manage periods of unusual anxiety or tension. However, many people use antianxiety drugs routinely to dull the arousal stemming from anxiety-producing lifestyles or interpersonal problems. Rather than make the often painful decisions required to confront their problems and change their lives, they prefer to take a pill.

Despite the controversies surrounding ECT, it helps many people who do not respond to antidepressant drugs (Thase & Kupfer, 1996). In sum, drug therapy and perhaps ECT seem to be effective for some disorders that do not respond to psychotherapy alone. Yet common sense and research evidence suggest that psychotherapy is preferable for problems such as anxiety, mild depression, and interpersonal conflict. No chemical can show a person how to change an idea or solve an interpersonal problem.

TRUTH OR FICTION REVISITED
It is true that the originator of a surgical technique intended to reduce violence learned it was not always successful . . . when one of his patients shot him. That technique is prefrontal lobotomy.

SUMMARY

1. **What is psychotherapy?** Psychotherapy is a systematic interaction between a therapist and a client that uses psychological principles to help the client overcome psychological disorders or adjust to problems in living.

2. **What are the goals of traditional psychoanalysis?** The goals are to provide self-insight, encourage the spilling forth (catharsis) of psychic energy, and replace defensive behavior with coping behavior.

3. **What are the methods of traditional psychoanalysis?** The methods include free association and dream analysis.

4. **How do modern psychodynamic approaches differ from traditional psychoanalysis?** Modern approaches are

briefer and more directive, and the therapist and client usually sit face to face.

5. **What are the goals and traits of the client-centered therapist?** The client-centered therapist uses nondirective methods to help clients overcome obstacles to self-actualization. The therapist shows unconditional positive regard, empathic understanding, and genuineness.

6. **What is behavior therapy?** Behavior therapy relies on psychological learning principles (for example, conditioning and observational learning) to help clients develop adaptive behavior patterns and discontinue maladaptive ones.

7. **What are some behavior therapy fear-reduction methods?** These include flooding, systematic desensitization, and modeling. Flooding exposes a person to fear-evoking stimuli without aversive consequences until fear is extinguished. Systematic desensitization counter conditions fears by gradually exposing clients to a hierarchy of fear-evoking stimuli while they remain deeply relaxed. Modeling encourages clients to imitate another person (the model) in approaching fear-evoking stimuli.

8. **What is aversive conditioning?** This is a behavior-therapy method for discouraging undesirable behaviors by repeatedly pairing their goals (for example, alcohol, cigarette smoke, deviant sex objects) with aversive stimuli so that the goals become aversive rather than tempting.

9. **What are operant-conditioning procedures in behavior therapy?** These are behavior-therapy methods that foster adaptive behavior through principles of reinforcement. Examples include token economies, successive approximation, social skills training, and biofeedback training.

10. **What are behavioral self-control methods?** These are behavior-therapy methods for adopting desirable behavior patterns and breaking bad habits. They focus on modifying the antecedents (stimuli that act as triggers) and consequences (reinforcers) of behavior and on modifying the behavior itself.

11. **What are the goals and methods of cognitive therapies?** Cognitive therapies aim to give clients insight into irrational beliefs and cognitive distortions and replace these cognitive errors with rational beliefs and accurate perceptions. Aaron Beck notes that clients may become depressed because they minimize accomplishments, catastrophize failures, and are generally pessimistic. Albert Ellis originated rational emotive behavior therapy, which holds that people's beliefs *about* events, not only the events themselves, shape people's responses to them. Ellis points out how irrational beliefs, such as the belief that we must have social approval, can worsen problems.

12. **What are the advantages of group therapy?** Group therapy is more economical than individual therapy. Moreover, group members benefit from the social support and experiences of other members.

13. **Does psychotherapy work?** Statistical analyses show that people who obtain most forms of psychotherapy fare better than people who do not. Psychodynamic and client-centered approaches are particularly helpful with highly verbal and motivated individuals. Cognitive and behavior therapies are probably most effective.

14. **What are the uses of drug therapy?** Antipsychotic drugs help many people with schizophrenia by blocking the action of dopamine receptors. Antidepressants often help people with severe depression, apparently by raising the levels of noradrenaline and serotonin available to the brain. Lithium often helps people with bipolar disorder, apparently by moderating levels of noradrenaline. The use of antianxiety drugs for daily tensions and anxieties is not recommended because people who use them rapidly build tolerance for the drugs. Also, these drugs do not solve personal or social problems, and people attribute their resultant calmness to the drug and not to self-efficacy.

15. **What is electroconvulsive therapy (ECT)?** In ECT an electrical current is passed through the temples, inducing a seizure and frequently relieving severe depression. ECT is controversial because of side effects such as loss of

memory and because nobody knows why it works.

16. **What is psychosurgery?** Psychosurgery is a controversial method for alleviating agitation by severing nerve pathways in the brain. The best-known psychosurgery technique, prefrontal lobot- omy, has been largely discontinued because of side effects.

KEY TERMS

antidepressant (p. MT-25)

aversive conditioning (p. MT-11)

behavior therapy (p. MT-10)

biofeedback training (p. MT-13)

cartharsis (p. MT-5)

client-centered therapy (p. MT-8)

ego analyst (p. MT-7)

electroconvulsive therapy (p. MT-25)

empathic understanding (p. MT-9)

encounter group (p. MT-19)

family therapy (p. MT-19)

flooding (p. MT-10)

frame of reference (p. MT-9)

free association (p. MT-5)

functional analysis (p. MT-13)

genuineness (p. MT-9)

Gestalt therapy (p. MT-9)

interpretation (p. MT-6)

latent content (p. MT-6)

manifest content (p. MT-6)

modeling (p. MT-19)

phallic symbol (p. MT-6)

prefrontal lobotomy (p. MT-26)

psychoanalysis (p. MT-5)

psychosurgery (p. MT-26)

psychotherapy (p. MT-2)

rational emotive behavior therapy (p. MT-17)

rebound anxiety (p. MT-25)

resistance (p. MT-6)

sedative (p. MT-26)

self-actualization (p. MT-8)

successive approximations (p. MT-12)

systematic desensitization (p. MT-10)

unconditional positive regard (p. MT-9)

wish fulfillment (p. MT-6)

REFERENCES

Abramowitz, J. S. (1997). Effectiveness of psychological and pharmacological treatments for obsessive-compulsive disorder. *Journal of Consulting and Clinical Psychology, 65,* 44–52.

American Psychiatric Association. (1994). *Diagnostic and statistical manual of the mental disorders* (4th ed.). Washington, DC: Author.

American Psychological Association. (1993). Guidelines for providers of psychological services to ethnic, linguistic, and culturally diverse populations. *American Psychologist, 48,* 45–48.

Antonuccio, D. (1995). Psychotherapy for depression: No stronger medicine. *American Psychologist, 50,* 452–454.

Ayllon, T., & Haughton, E. (1962). Control of the behavior of schizophrenic patients by food. *Journal of the Experimental Analysis of Behavior, 5,* 343–352.

Bandura, A., Blanchard, E. B., & Ritter, B. (1969). The relative efficacy of desensitization and modeling approaches for inducing behavioral, affective, and cognitive changes. *Journal of Personality and Social Psychology, 13,* 173–199.

Bandura, A., Taylor, C. B., Williams, S. L., Medford, I. N., & Barchas, J. D. (1985). Catecholamine secretion as a function of perceived coping self-efficacy. *Journal of Consulting and Clinical Psychology, 53,* 406–414.

Barlow, D. H. (1996). Health care policy, psychotherapy research, and the future of psychotherapy. *American Psychologist, 51,* 1050–1058.

Basic Behavioral Science Task Force of the National Advisory Mental Health Council. (1996). Basic behavioral science research for mental health: Sociocultural and environmental practices. *American Psychologist, 51,* 722–731.

Baucom, D. H., Shoham, V., Mueser, K. T., Daiuto, A. D., & Stickle, T. R. (1998). Empirically supported couple and family interventions for marital distress and adult mental health problems. *Journal of Consulting and Clinical Psychology, 66,* 53–88.

Beck, A. T. (1991). Cognitive therapy: A 30-year retrospective. *American Psychologist, 46,* 368–375.

Beck, A. T. (1993). Cognitive therapy: Past, present, and future. *Journal of Consulting and Clinical Psychology, 61,* 194–198.

Beck, A. T., & Freeman, A. (1990). *Cognitive therapy of personality disorders.* New York: Guilford.

Blanchard, E. B. (1992). Psychological treatment of benign headache disorders. *Journal of Consulting and Clinical Psychology, 60,* 537–551.

Blatt, S. J., Zuroff, D. C., Quinlan, D. M., & Pilkonis, P. A. (1996). Interpersonal factors in brief treatment of depression. *Journal of Consulting and Clinical Psychology, 64,* 162–171.

Boyd-Franklin, N. (1995, August). *A multisystems model for treatment interventions with inner-city African American families.* Master lecture delivered to the meeting of the American Psychological Association, New York.

Burns, D. D., & Nolen-Hoeksema, S. (1992). Therapeutic empathy and recovery from depression in cognitive-behavioral therapy. *Journal of Consulting and Clinical Psychology, 60,* 441–449.

Carroll, K. M., Rounsaville, B. J., & Nich, C. (1994). Blind man's bluff: Effectiveness and significance of psychotherapy and pharmacotherapy blinding procedures in a clinical trial. *Journal of Consulting and Clinical Psychology, 62,* 276–280.

Chadwick, P. D. J., & Lowe, C. F. (1990). Measurement and modification of delusional beliefs. *Journal of Consulting and Clinical Psychology, 58,* 225–232.

Chambless, D. L., & Hollon, S. D. (1998). Defining empirically supported therapies. *Journal of Consulting and Clinical Psychology, 66,* 7–18.

Compas, B. E., Haaga, D. A. F., Keefe, F. J., Leitenberg, H., & Williams, D. A. (1998). Sampling of empirically supported psychological treatments from health psychology: Smoking, chronic pain, cancer, and bulimia nervosa. *Journal of Consulting and Clinical Psychology, 66,* 89–112.

DeAngelis, T. (1995). Mental health care is elusive for Hispanics. *APA Monitor, 26*(7), 49.

De La Cancela, V., & Guzman, L. P. (1991). Latino mental health service needs. In H. F. Myers et al. (Eds.), *Ethnic minority perspectives on clinical training and services in psychology* (pp. 59–64). Washington, DC: American Psychological Association.

DeRubeis, R. J., & Crits-Christoph, P. (1998). Empirically supported individual and group psychological treatments for adult mental disorders. *Journal of Consulting and Clinical Psychology, 66,* 37–52.

Ellis, A. (1977). The basic clinical theory of rational-emotive therapy. In A. Ellis & R. Grieger (Eds.), *Handbook of rational-emotive therapy.* New York: Springer.

Ellis, A. (1993). Reflections on rational-emotive therapy. *Journal of Consulting and Clinical Psychology, 61,* 199–201.

Engels, G. I., Garnefski, N., & Diekstra, R. F. W. (1993). Efficacy of rational-emotive therapy. *Journal of Consulting and Clinical Psychology, 61,* 1083–1090.

Galassi, J. P. (1988). Four cognitive-behavioral approaches. *The Counseling Psychologist, 16*(1), 102–105.

Greene, B. (1993). African American women. In L. Comas-Diaz & B. A. Greene (Eds.), *Women of color and mental health.* New York: Guilford.

Haaga, D. A. F., & Davison, G. C. (1993). An appraisal of rational-emotive therapy. *Journal of Consulting and Clinical Psychology, 61,* 215–220.

Hall, G. C. I. (1997). Cultural malpractice: The growing obsolescence of psychology with the changing U.S. population. *American Psychologist, 52,* 642–651.

Hokin, L., et al. (1998). *Proceedings of the National Academy of Sciences, 95*(14), 8363–8368.

Isomura, T., Fine, S., & Lin, T. (1987). Two Japanese families. *Canadian Journal of Psychiatry, 32,* 282–286.

Jacobson, N. S., & Hollon, S. D. (1996). Cognitive-behavior therapy versus pharmacotherapy. *Journal of Consulting and Clinical Psychology, 64,* 74–80.

Jacobson, N. S., et al. (1996). A component analysis of cognitive-behavioral treatment for depression. *Journal of Consulting and Clinical Psychology, 64,* 295–304.

Kane, J. M. (1996). Schizophrenia. *New England Journal of Medicine, 334,* 34–41.

LaFramboise, T. (1994). Cited in DeAngelis, T. (1994). History, culture affect treatment for Indians. *APA Monitor, 27*(10), 36.

Lefley, H. P. (1990). Culture and chronic mental illness. *Hospital and Community Psychiatry, 41,* 277–286.

Lipsey, M. W., & Wilson, D. B. (1993). The efficacy of psychological, educational, and behavioral treatment. *American Psychologist, 48,* 1181–1209.

Luborsky, L., Barber, J. P., & Beutler, L. (1993). Introduction to special section. *Journal of Consulting and Clinical Psychology, 61,* 539–541.

Lydiard, R. B., Brawman, A., Mintzer, O., & Ballenger, J. C. (1996). Recent developments in the psychopharmacology of anxiety disorders. *Journal of Consulting and Clinical Psychology, 64,* 660–668.

Malgady, R. G., Rogler, L. H., & Costantino, G. (1990). Hero/heroine modeling for Puerto Rican adolescents. *Journal of Consulting and Clinical Psychology, 58,* 469–474.

Masters, W. H., & Johnson, V. E. (1979). *Homosexuality in perspective.* Boston: Little, Brown.

Meichenbaum, D. (1993). Changing conceptions of cognitive behavior modification. *Journal of Consulting and Clinical Psychology, 61,* 202–204.

Penn, N. E., Kar, S., Kramer, J., Skinner, J., & Zambrana, R. E. (1995). Panel VI. Ethnic minorities, health care systems, and behavior. *Health Psychology, 14,* 641–648.

Prochaska, J. O., & Norcross, J. C. (1999). *Systems of psychotherapy* (4th ed.). Pacific Grove, CA: Brooks/Cole.

Rathus, S. A., Nevid, J. S., & Fichner-Rathus, L. (2000). *Human sexuality in a world of diversity* (4th ed.). Boston: Allyn & Bacon.

Rice, M. E., Quinsey, V. L., & Harris, G. T. (1991). Sexual recidivism among child molesters released from a maximum security psychiatric institution. *Journal of Consulting and Clinical Psychology, 59,* 381–386.

Robins, C. J., & Hayes, A. M. (1993). An appraisal of cognitive therapy. *Journal of Consulting and Clinical Psychology, 61,* 205–214.

Rush, A. J., Khatami, M., & Beck, A. T. (1975). Cognitive and behavior therapy in chronic depression. *Behavior Therapy, 6,* 398–404.

Schneider, B. H., & Byrne, B. M. (1987). Individualizing social skills training for behavior-disordered children. *Journal of Consulting and Clinical Psychology, 55,* 444–445.

Shadish, W. R., & Ragsdale, K. (1996). Random versus nonrandom assignment in controlled experiments. *Journal of Consulting and Clinical Psychology, 64,* 1290–1305.

Shadish, W. R., et al. (1997). Evidence that therapy works in clinically representative conditions. *Journal of Consulting and Clinical Psychology, 65,* 355–365.

Simons, A. D., Gordon, J. S., Monroe, S. M., & Thase, M. E. (1995). Toward an integration of psychologic, social, and biologic factors in depression. *Journal of Consulting and Clinical Psychology, 63,* 369–377.

Sleek, S. (1995). Group therapy. *APA Monitor, 26*(7), 1, 38–39.

Sleek, S. (1997). Resolution raises concerns about conversion therapy. *APA Monitor, 28*(10), 15.

Smith, M. L., & Glass, G. V. (1977). Meta-analysis of psychotherapy outcome studies. *American Psychologist, 32,* 752–760.

Spreat, S., & Behar, D. (1994). Trends in the residential (inpatient) treatment of individuals with a dual diagnosis. *Journal of Consulting and Clinical Psychology, 61,* 43–48.

Strupp, H. H. (1996). The tripartite model and the *Consumer Reports* study. *American Psychologist, 51,* 1017–1024.

Sue, S. (1991). In J. D. Goodchilds (Ed.), *Psychological perspectives on human diversity in America.* Washington, DC: American Psychological Association.

Thase, M. E., & Kupfer, D. J. (1996). Recent developments in the pharmacotherapy of mood disorders. *Journal of Consulting and Clinical Psychology, 64,* 646–659.

Turner, S. M., Beidel, D. C., & Jacob, R. G. (1994). Social phobia: A comparison of behavior therapy and atenolol. *Journal of Consulting and Clinical Psychology, 62,* 350–358.

Valenstein, E. S. (1986). *Great and desperate cures.* New York: Basic Books.

Whisman, M. A., Miller, I. W., Norman, W. H., & Keitner, G. I. (1991). Cognitive therapy with depressed inpatients. *Journal of Consulting and Clinical Psychology, 59,* 282–288.

Wiens, A. N., & Menustik, C. E. (1983). Treatment outcome and patient characteristics in an aversion therapy program for alcoholism. *American Psychologist, 38,* 1089–1096.

Wilson, G. T., & Fairburn, C. G. (1993). Cognitive treatments for eating disorders. *Journal of Consulting and Clinical Psychology, 61,* 261–269.

Wolpe, J. (1990). *The practice of behavior therapy* (4th ed.). New York: Pergamon.

Wolpe, J., & Plaud, J. J. (1997). Pavlov's contributions to behavior therapy: The obvious and the not so obvious. *American Psychologist, 52,* 966–972.

Zane, N., & Sue, S. (1991). Culturally responsive mental health services for Asian Americans. In H. F. Myers et al. (Eds.), *Ethnic minority perspectives on clinical training and services in psychology* (pp. 49–58). Washington, DC: American Psychological Association.

SOCIAL PSYCHOLOGY

Candy and Stretch. A new technique for controlling weight gains? No, these are the names of a couple who have just met at a camera club. Candy and Stretch stand above the crowd—literally. Candy, an attractive woman in her early 30s, is almost 6 feet tall. Stretch is more plain looking, but wholesome, in his late 30s, and 6 feet 5 inches tall.

Stretch has been in the group for some time. Candy is a new member. Let's listen in on them as they make conversation during a coffee break.[1] Note the differences between what they say and what they are thinking:

	THEY SAY	THEY THINK
Stretch:	Well, you're certainly a welcome addition to our group.	(Can't I ever say something clever?)
Candy:	Thank you. It certainly is friendly and interesting.	(He's cute.)
Stretch:	My friends call me Stretch. It's left over from my basketball days. Silly, but I'm used to it.	(It's safer than saying my name is David Stein.)
Candy:	My name is Candy.	(At least my nickname is. He doesn't have to hear Hortense O'Brien.)
Stretch:	What kind of camera is that?	(Why couldn't a girl named Candy be Jewish? It's only a nickname, isn't it?)
Candy:	Just this old German one of my uncle's. I borrowed it from the office.	(He could be Irish. And that camera looks expensive.)
Stretch:	May I? (He takes her camera, brushing her hand and then tingling with the touch.) Fine lens. You work for your uncle?	(Now I've done it. Brought up work.)
Candy:	Ever since college. It's more than being just a secretary. I get into sales, too.	(So okay, what if I only went for a year. If he asks what I sell, I'll tell him anything except underwear.)
Stretch:	Sales? That's funny. I'm in sales, too, but mainly as an executive. I run our department. I started using cameras on trips. Last time I was in the Bahamas. I took—	(Is there a nice way to say used cars? I'd better change the subject.)
		(Great legs! And the way her hips move . . .)
Candy:	Oh! Do you go to the Bahamas, too? I love those islands.	(So I went just once, and it was for the brassiere manufacturers' convention. At least we're off the subject of jobs.)

---

[1] From G. R. Bach and R. M. Deutsch, *Pairing* (New York: Peter H. Wyden, 1970).

Stretch:		(She's probably been around. Well, at least we're off the subject of jobs.)
	I did a little underwater work there last summer. Fantastic colors. So rich in life.	(And lonelier than hell.)
Candy:		(Look at that build. He must swim like a fish. I should learn.)
	I wish I'd had time when I was there. I love the water.	(Well, I do. At the beach, anyway, where I can wade in and not go too deep.)

So begins a relationship. Candy and Stretch have a drink and talk, sharing their likes and dislikes. Amazingly, they seem to agree on everything—from cars to music to politics. The attraction is very strong, and neither is willing to risk turning the other off by disagreeing. They scrupulously avoid one topic: religion. Their religious differences become apparent when they exchange last names. But that doesn't mean they have to talk about it.

They also put off introductions to their parents. The O'Briens and the Steins are narrow-minded about religion. If the truth be known, so are Candy and Stretch.

What happens in this tangled web of deception? After some deliberation, and not without misgivings, they decide to get married. Do they live happily ever after? We can't say. "Ever after" is not here yet.

We do not have all the answers, but we have some questions. Candy and Stretch's relationship began with a powerful attraction. What is *attraction?* How do we determine who is attractive to us? Candy and Stretch pretended to share each other's attitudes. What are *attitudes?* Why didn't Candy and Stretch introduce each other to their parents? Did they fear that their parents would want them to *conform* to their own standards? Would their parents try to *persuade* them to limit dating to people of their own religions? Would they *obey?*

Attraction, attitudes, conformity, persuasion, obedience—these topics are the province of **social psychology.** Social psychologists study the nature and causes of behavior and mental processes in social situations. The social psychological topics we discuss in this chapter include attitudes, social perception, interpersonal attraction, social influence, and group behavior.

ATTITUDES

How do you feel about abortion, foreign cars, and the Republican party? The only connection I draw among these items is that people have *attitudes* toward them. They each give rise to cognitive evaluations (such as approval or disapproval), feelings (liking, disliking, or something stronger), and behavioral tendencies (such as approach or avoidance). Although I asked you how you "feel," attitudes are not just feelings or emotions. Many psychologists view thinking—or judgment—as primary. Feelings and behavior follow (Eagly & Chaiken, 1993).

Attitudes are behavioral and cognitive tendencies expressed by evaluating particular people, places, or things with favor or disfavor (Eagly & Chaiken, 1993). Attitudes are learned, and they affect behavior. They can foster love or hate. They can give rise to helping behavior or to mass destruction. They can lead to social conflict or to the resolution of conflicts. Attitudes can change, but not easily. Most people do not change their religion or political affiliation without serious reflection or coercion.

SOCIAL PSYCHOLOGY The field of psychology that studies the nature and causes of people's thoughts and behavior in social situations.

ATTITUDE An enduring mental representation of a person, place, or thing that evokes an emotional response and related behavior.

The A-B Problem: Do We Do as We Think?

Our definition of attitude implies that our behavior is consistent with our cognitions—with our beliefs and feelings. When we are free to do as we wish, it often is. But, as indicated by the term **A-B problem,** the links between attitudes (A) and behaviors (B) tend to be weak to moderate (Eagly & Chaiken, 1993). For example, research reveals that attitudes toward health-related behaviors such as use of alcohol, smoking, and drunken driving are not consistent predictors of these behaviors (Stacy et al., 1994).

A number of factors influence the likelihood that we can predict behavior from attitudes:

1. *Specificity.* We can better predict specific behavior from specific attitudes than from global attitudes. For example, we can better predict church attendance by knowing people's attitudes toward church attendance than by knowing whether they are Christian.

2. *Strength of attitudes.* Strong attitudes are more likely to determine behavior than weak attitudes (Fazio, 1990).

3. *Vested interest.* People are more likely to act on their attitudes when they have a vested interest in the outcome (Johnson & Eagly, 1989). People are more likely to vote for (or against) unionization of their workplace, for example, when they believe that their job security depends on the outcome.

4. *Accessibility.* People are more likely to express their attitudes when they are accessible—that is, when they are brought to mind (Fazio, 1990; Krosnick, 1989). Attitudes with a strong emotional impact are more accessible (Wu & Shaffer, 1987), which is one reason that politicians strive to get their supporters worked up over the issues.

Candy and Stretch avoided discussing matters on which they differed. One motive might have been to avoid heightening the *accessibility* of their clashing attitudes. By keeping them concealed, they might be less likely to act on them and go their separate ways.

Origins of Attitudes

You were not born a Republican or a Democrat. You were not born a Catholic or a Muslim—although your parents may have practiced one of these religions when you came along. Political, religious, and other attitudes are learned. In this section we describe some of the processes that result in the learning of attitudes.

Conditioning may play a role in acquiring attitudes. Experiments have shown that attitudes toward national groups can be influenced by associating them with positive words (such as *gift* or *happy*) or negative words (such as *ugly* or *failure*) (Lohr & Staats, 1973). Parents often reward children for saying and doing things that agree with their own attitudes. Patriotism is encouraged by showing approval to children when they sing the national anthem or wave the flag.

Attitudes formed through direct experience may be stronger and easier to recall, but we also acquire attitudes by observing others. The approval or disapproval of peers leads adolescents to prefer short or long hair, baggy jeans, or preppy sweaters. The media inform us that body odor, bad breath, and the frizzies are dreaded diseases—and, perhaps, that people who use harsh toilet paper are somehow un-American.

A-B PROBLEM The issue of how well we can predict behavior on the basis of attitudes.

COGNITIVE APPRAISAL Despite what we have said, the learning of attitudes is not so mechanical. Now and then we evaluate information and attitudes on the basis of evidence. We may revise **stereotypes**—fixed, conventional ideas about groups of people or objects—on the basis of new information (Weber & Crocker, 1983). For example, we may believe that a car is more reliable than we had thought if a survey by *Consumer Reports* finds that it has an excellent repair record. Still, our initial attitudes act as cognitive anchors. We often judge new ideas in terms of how much they deviate from our existing attitudes. Accepting larger deviations requires more information processing—in other words, more intellectual work (Quattrone, 1982). For this reason, perhaps, great deviations—such as changes from liberal to conservative attitudes, or vice versa—are apt to be resisted.

Changing Attitudes Through Persuasion

Rogers's social comment sounds on the mark, but he was probably wrong. It does little good to have a wonderful product if its existence remains a secret.

The **elaboration likelihood model** describes the ways in which people respond to persuasive messages (Petty et al., 1994). Consider two routes to persuading others to change attitudes. The first, or central, route inspires thoughtful consideration of arguments and evidence. The second, or peripheral, route associates objects with positive or negative cues. When politicians avow, "This bill is supported by Jesse Jackson (or Jesse Helms)," they are seeking predictable, knee-jerk reactions, not careful consideration of a bill's merits. Other cues are rewards (such as a smile or a hug), punishments (such as parental disapproval), and such factors as the trustworthiness and attractiveness of the communicator.

Advertisements, which are a form of persuasive communication, also rely on central and peripheral routes. Some ads focus on the quality of the product (central route). Others attempt to associate the product with appealing images (peripheral route). Ads for Total cereal, which highlight its nutritional benefits, provide information about the quality of the product. So, too, did the "Pepsi Challenge" taste test ads, which claimed that Pepsi tastes better than Coca-Cola. Marlboro cigarette ads that focus on the masculine, rugged image of the "Marlboro man"[2] offer no information about the product itself. Nor do ads that show football players heading for Disney World or choosing a brand of beer.

In this section we look at one central factor in persuasion—the nature of the message—and three peripheral factors: the messenger, the context of the message, and the audience. We also examine the foot-in-the-door technique.

THE PERSUASIVE MESSAGE: SAY WHAT? SAY HOW? SAY HOW OFTEN? How do we respond when TV commercials are repeated until we have memorized every dimple on the actors' faces? Research suggests that familiarity breeds content, not contempt.

You might not be crazy about *zebulons* and *afworbus* at first, but Robert Zajonc (1968) found that people began to react favorably toward these bogus foreign words on the basis of repeated exposure. In fact, repeated exposure to people and things as diverse as the following enhances their appeal (Baron & Byrne, 1997): political candidates (who are seen in repeated TV commercials), photographs of African Americans, photographs of college students, abstract art, and classical music.

TRUTH OR FICTION REVISITED
It is not true that airing a TV commercial repeatedly hurts sales. Repeated exposure frequently leads to liking and acceptance.

STEREOTYPE A fixed, conventional idea about a group.

ELABORATION LIKELIHOOD MODEL The view that persuasive messages are evaluated (elaborated) on the basis of central and peripheral cues.

---

[2] The rugged actor in the original TV commercials died of lung cancer. Apparently cigarettes were more rugged than he was.

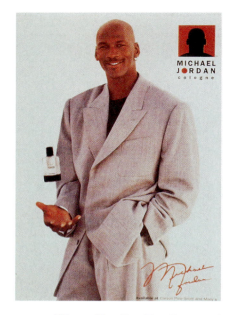

WOULD YOU BUY THIS PRODUCT?
Advertisers use a combination of central and peripheral cues to sell their products. What factors contribute to the persuasiveness of messages? To the persuasiveness of communicators? Why is Michael Jordan considered an MVE ("Most Valuable Endorser")?

FEAR APPEAL A type of persuasive communication that influences behavior on the basis of arousing fear instead of rational analysis of the issues.

SELECTIVE AVOIDANCE Diverting one's attention from information that is inconsistent with one's attitudes.

SELECTIVE EXPOSURE Deliberately seeking and attending to information that is consistent with one's attitudes.

The more complex the stimuli, the more likely that frequent exposure will have favorable effects (Smith & Dorfman, 1975). The 100th playing of a Bach fugue may be less tiresome than the 100th performance of a pop tune.

When trying to persuade someone, is it helpful or self-defeating to alert them to the arguments presented by the opposition? In two-sided arguments, the communicator recounts the arguments of the opposition in order to refute them. Theologians and politicians sometimes expose their followers to the arguments of the opposition and then refute each one. By doing so, they create a kind of psychological immunity to them in their followers. Two-sided product claims, in which advertisers admit their product's weak points in addition to highlighting its strengths, are the most believable (Bridgwater, 1982). For example, one motel chain admits that it does not offer a swimming pool or room service, but points out that the customer therefore saves money.

We would like to think that people are too sophisticated to be persuaded by a **fear appeal**. However, women who are warned of the dire risk they run if they fail to be screened for breast cancer are more likely to obtain mammograms than women who are informed of the *benefits* of mammography (Banks et al., 1995). Interestingly, although sun tanning has been shown to increase the likelihood of skin cancer, warnings against sun tanning were shown to be more effective when students were warned of risks to their *appearance* (premature aging, wrinkling, and scarring of the skin) than when the warning dealt with the risk to their health (Jones & Leary, 1994). That is, students informed of tanning's cosmetic effects were more likely to say they would protect themselves from the sun than were students informed about the risk of cancer. Fear appeals are most effective when the audience believes that the risks are serious—as in causing wrinkles!—and that the audience can change their behavior to avert the risks—as in preventing wrinkling (Eagly & Chaiken, 1993).

Audiences also tend to believe arguments that appear to run counter to the vested interests of the communicator (Eagly & Chaiken, 1993). If the president of Ford or General Motors said that Toyotas and Hondas were superior, you can bet we would pay attention.

THE PERSUASIVE COMMUNICATOR: WHO DO YOU TRUST?

Would you buy a used car from a person who had been convicted of larceny? Would you leaf through fashion magazines featuring homely models? Probably not. Research shows that persuasive communicators are characterized by expertise, trustworthiness, attractiveness, or similarity to their audiences (Mackie et al., 1990; Wilder, 1990). Because of the adoration of their fans, sports superstars such as Michael Jordan are also persuasive as endorsers of products. Fans may consider Jordan to be an MVP, or Most Valuable Player. To advertisers, however, Jordan is an MVE, or Most Valuable Endorser (Goldman, 1993).

TV news anchors enjoy high prestige. One study (Mullen et al., 1987) found that before the 1984 presidential election, Peter Jennings of ABC News had shown significantly more favorable facial expressions when reporting on Ronald Reagan than when reporting on Walter Mondale. Tom Brokaw of NBC and Dan Rather of CBS had not shown favoritism. The researchers also found that viewers of ABC News voted for Reagan in greater proportions than viewers of NBC or CBS News. It is tempting to conclude that Jennings subtly persuaded viewers to vote for Reagan—and maybe this did happen in a number of cases. But viewers do not simply absorb, spongelike, whatever the tube feeds them. Instead, they show **selective avoidance** and **selective exposure** (Sweeney & Gruber, 1984). They often switch channels when the news coverage runs counter to their own attitudes.

THE CONTEXT OF THE MESSAGE: "GET 'EM IN A GOOD MOOD"

You are too shrewd to let someone persuade you by buttering you up, but perhaps someone you know would be influenced by a sip of wine, a bite of cheese, and a sincere compliment. Aspects of the immediate environment, such as music, increase the likelihood of persuasion. When we are in a good mood, we apparently are less likely to evaluate the situation carefully (Schwarz et al., 1991).

It is also counterproductive to call your dates fools when they differ with you—even though their ideas are bound to be foolish if they do not agree with yours. Agreement and praise are more effective ways to encourage others to embrace your views. Appear sincere, or else your compliments will look manipulative. (It seems unfair to let out this information.)

THE PERSUADED AUDIENCE: ARE YOU A PERSON WHO CAN'T SAY NO?

Why do some people have sales resistance? Why do others enrich the lives of every door-to-door salesperson? It may be that people with high self-esteem and low social anxiety are more likely to resist social pressure (Santee & Maslach, 1982).

A classic study by Schwartz and Gottman (1976) reveals the cognitive nature of the social anxiety that can make it difficult for some people to refuse requests. The researchers found that people who comply with unreasonable requests are more apt to report thoughts like the following: "I was worried about what the other person would think of me if I refused." "It is better to help others than to be self-centered." "The other person might be hurt or insulted if I refused." People who refuse unreasonable requests reported thoughts like these: "It doesn't matter what the other person thinks of me." "I am perfectly free to say no." "This request is unreasonable."

THE FOOT-IN-THE-DOOR TECHNIQUE

You might suppose that contributing money to door-to-door solicitors for charity will get you off the hook. Perhaps they will take the cash and leave you alone for a while. Actually, the opposite is true. The next time they mount a campaign, they may call on you to go door to door on their behalf! Organizations compile lists of people they can rely on. Because they have gotten their "foot in the door," this is known as the **foot-in-the-door technique.**

Consider a classic experiment by Freedman and Fraser (1966). Groups of women received phone calls from a consumer group requesting that they let a six-person crew come to their home to catalog their household products. The job could take hours. Only 22% of one group acceded to this irksome request. But 53% of another group of women assented to a visit from this wrecking crew. Why was the second group more compliant? They had been phoned a few days earlier and had agreed to answer a few questions about the soap products they used. Thus they had been primed for the second request: The caller had gotten a foot in the door.

Research suggests that people who accede to small requests become more amenable to larger ones because they come to see themselves as the kind of people who help in this way (Eisenberg et al., 1987). Regardless of how the foot-in-the-door technique works, if you want to say no, it may be easier to do so (and stick to your guns) the first time a request is made. Later may be too late.

Prejudice

Prejudice is an attitude toward a group that leads people to evaluate members of that group negatively—even though they have never met these individuals. On a cognitive level, it is linked to expectations that members

FOOT-IN-THE-DOOR TECHNIQUE A method for inducing compliance in which a small request is followed by a larger request.

PREJUDICE The unfounded belief that a person or group—on the basis of assumed racial, ethnic, sexual, or other features—will possess negative characteristics or perform inadequately.

TRUTH OR FICTION REVISITED
It is true that people have condemned billions of other people without meeting them or learning their names. Such are the effects of prejudice.

of the target group will behave poorly, say, in the workplace, or engage in criminal behavior. On an emotional level, prejudice is associated with negative feelings such as dislike or hatred. In behavioral terms, it is connected with avoidance, aggression, and discrimination. Prejudice is the most troubling kind of attitude. It is connected with the genocide of millions upon millions of people.

DISCRIMINATION   One form of negative behavior that results from prejudice is **discrimination.** Many groups in the United States have experienced discrimination—women, gay males and lesbians, older people, and ethnic groups such as African Americans, Asian Americans, Hispanic Americans, Irish Americans, Jewish Americans, and Native Americans. Discrimination takes many forms, including denial of access to jobs, housing, and the voting booth.

STEREOTYPES   Are Jewish Americans shrewd and ambitious? Are African Americans superstitious and musical? Are gay men and lesbians unfit for military service? Such ideas are *stereotypes*—prejudices about certain groups that lead people to view members of those groups in a biased fashion.

SOURCES OF PREJUDICE   The sources of prejudice are many and varied. Here are some of them:

STEREOTYPING.
How well is this child doing? Research shows that our expectations concerning a child's performance on a test are linked to our awareness of that child's socio-economic background.

1. *Dissimilarity.* We are apt to like people who share our attitudes. In forming impressions of others, we are influenced by attitudinal similarity and dissimilarity (Duckitt, 1992). People of different religions and races often have different backgrounds, however, giving rise to dissimilar attitudes. Even when people of different races share values, they may assume that they do not.

2. *Social conflict.* There is a lengthy history of social and economic conflict between people of different races and religions. For example, for many decades southern White people and African Americans have competed for jobs, giving rise to negative attitudes, even lynchings (Green et al., 1998).

3. *Social learning.* Children acquire some attitudes from other people, especially their parents. Children tend to imitate their parents, and parents reinforce their children for doing so (Duckitt, 1992). In this way prejudices can be transmitted from generation to generation.

4. *Information processing.* One cognitive view is that prejudices act as cognitive filters through which we perceive the social world. Prejudice is a way of processing social information. It is easier to attend to, and remember, instances of behavior that are consistent with our prejudices than it is to change our beliefs (Devine, 1989; Fiske, 1993). If you believe Jewish Americans are stingy, it is easier to recall a Jewish American's negotiation of a price than a Jewish American's charitable donation. If you believe Californians are airheads, it may be easier to recall TV images of surfing than of scientific conferences at Caltech and Berkeley.

5. *Social categorization.* A second cognitive perspective focuses on the tendency to divide our social world into "us" and "them." People usually view those who belong to their own groups—the "in-group"—more favorably than those who do not—the "out-group" (Duckitt, 1992; Linville et al., 1989). Moreover, we tend to assume that members of the out-group are more similar in their attitudes and behavior than members of our own groups (Judd & Park,

DISCRIMINATION The denial of privileges to a person or a group on the basis of prejudice.

1988). Our isolation from the out-group makes it easier to maintain our stereotypes.

6. *Victimization by prejudice.* Ironically, people who have been victims of prejudice sometimes attempt to gain a sense of pride by asserting superiority over other socioeconomic or ethnic groups (Van Brunt, 1994).

SOCIAL PERCEPTION

An important area of social psychology concerns the ways in which we perceive other people—for example, the importance of the first impressions they make on us. Next we explore some factors that contribute to **social perception:** the primacy and recency effects, attribution theory, and body language.

Primacy and Recency Effects: The Importance of First Impressions

Why do you wear a suit to a job interview? Why do defense attorneys make sure that their clients dress neatly and get their hair cut before they are seen by the jury? Because as social psychologist Solomon Asch discovered, first impressions are important and reasonably accurate (Gleitman et al., 1997).

When I was a teenager, a young man was accepted or rejected by his date's parents the first time they were introduced. If he was considerate and made small talk, her parents would allow the couple to stay out past curfew—perhaps even to watch submarine races at the beach during the early morning hours. If he was boorish or uncommunicative, he was seen as a cad forever after. Her parents would object to him, no matter how hard he worked to gain their favor.

First impressions often make or break us. This phenomenon is known as the **primacy effect.** We infer traits from behavior. If we act considerately at first, we are labeled considerate. The trait of consideration is used to explain and predict our future behavior. If, after being labeled considerate, one keeps a date out past curfew, this lapse is likely to be seen as an exception to a rule—excused by circumstances or external causes. If one is first seen as inconsiderate, however, several months of considerate behavior may be perceived as a cynical effort to "make up for it."

Subjects in a classic experiment on the primacy effect read different stories about "Jim" (Luchins, 1957). The stories consisted of one or two paragraphs. The one-paragraph stories portrayed Jim as either friendly or unfriendly. These paragraphs were also used in the two-paragraph stories, but in this case the paragraphs were read in the reverse order. Of those reading only the "friendly" paragraph, 95% rated Jim as friendly. Of those who read just the "unfriendly" paragraph, 3% rated him as friendly. Seventy-eight percent of those who read two-paragraph stories in the "friendly-unfriendly" order labeled Jim as friendly. When they read the paragraphs in the reverse order, only 18% rated Jim as friendly.

How can we encourage people to pay more attention to impressions occurring after the first encounter? Abraham Luchins accomplished this by allowing time to elapse between the presentations of the two paragraphs. In this way, fading memories allowed more recent information to take precedence. This is known as the **recency effect.** Luchins found a second way to counter first impressions: He simply asked subjects to avoid making snap judgments and to weigh all the evidence.

TRUTH OR FICTION REVISITED
It is true that victimization by prejudice can lead people to become prejudiced themselves.

TRUTH OR FICTION REVISITED
It is true that you may never get a second chance if you don't make a good first impression. People interpret future events in the light of first impressions.

FIRST IMPRESSIONS.
Why is it important to make a good first impression? What are some ways of doing so?

SOCIAL PERCEPTION A subfield of social psychology that studies the ways in which we form and modify impressions of others.

PRIMACY EFFECT The tendency to evaluate others in terms of first impressions.

RECENCY EFFECT The tendency to evaluate others in terms of the most recent impression.

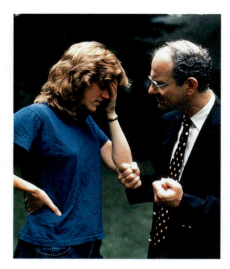

THE ACTOR-OBSERVER EFFECT.
Who is at fault here? When parents and teenagers argue about the teenagers' choices of friends or dates, the parents tend to perceive the teenagers as stubborn and independent. But the children may perceive their parents as bossy and controlling. Parents and children alike make dispositional attributions for each other's behavior. But the parents and teenagers both tend to see their own behavior as motivated by situational factors. Teenagers often see themselves as caught between peer pressures and parental restrictiveness. Parents, in contrast, tend to see themselves as forced to act out of love of their impetuous children and fear for what might happen to them.

ATTRIBUTION A belief concerning why people behave in a certain way.

ATTRIBUTION PROCESS The process by which people draw inferences about the motives and traits of others.

DISPOSITIONAL ATTRIBUTION An assumption that a person's behavior is determined by internal causes such as personal attitudes or goals.

SITUATIONAL ATTRIBUTION An assumption that a person's behavior is determined by external circumstances such as the social pressure found in a situation.

FUNDAMENTAL ATTRIBUTION ERROR The tendency to assume that others act predominantly on the basis of their dispositions, even when there is evidence suggesting the importance of their situations.

ACTOR-OBSERVER EFFECT The tendency to attribute our own behavior to situational factors but to attribute the behavior of others to dispositional factors.

Attribution Theory: You're Free, but I'm Caught in the Middle?

At the age of 3, one of my daughters believed a friend's son was a boy because he *wanted* to be a boy. Because she was 3 at the time, this error in my daughter's **attribution** of the boy's gender is understandable. Adults tend to make somewhat similar attribution errors, however. Although they do not believe that people's preferences have much to do with their gender, they do tend to exaggerate the role of choice in their behavior.

An assumption about why people do things is an attribution (Jones, 1990). When you assume that one child is mistreating another child because she is "mean," you are making an attribution. The process by which we make inferences about the motives and traits of others through observation of their behavior is the **attribution process.** In this section we focus on attribution theory, or the processes by which people draw conclusions about the factors that influence one another's behavior. Attribution theory is important because attributions lead us to perceive others either as purposeful actors or as victims of circumstances.

DISPOSITIONAL AND SITUATIONAL ATTRIBUTIONS Social psychologists describe two types of attributions. **Dispositional attributions** ascribe a person's behavior to internal factors such as personality traits and free will. The assumption that one child is mistreating another child because she is mean is a dispositional attribution. **Situational attributions** attribute a person's actions to external factors such as social influence or socialization. If you assume that one child is mistreating the other because her parents have given her certain attitudes toward the other child, you are making a situational attribution.

THE FUNDAMENTAL ATTRIBUTION ERROR In cultures that view the self as independent, such as ours, people tend to attribute other people's behavior primarily to internal factors such as personality, attitudes, and free will (Basic Behavioral Science Task Force, 1996). This bias in the attribution process is known as the **fundamental attribution error.** In such individualistic societies, people tend to focus on the behavior of others rather than on the circumstances surrounding their behavior. For example, if a teenager gets into trouble with the law, individualistic societies are more likely to blame the teenager than the social environment in which the teenager lives.

THE ACTOR-OBSERVER EFFECT When we see people (including ourselves) doing things we do not like, we tend to see the others as willful actors but to see ourselves as victims of circumstances (Baron & Byrne, 1997). The tendency to attribute other people's behavior to dispositional factors and our own behavior to situational influences is called the **actor-observer effect.**

Consider an example. Parents and children often argue about the children's choice of friends or dates. When they do, the parents tend to infer traits from behavior and to see the children as stubborn and resistant. The children also infer traits from behavior. Thus they may see their parents as bossy and controlling. Parents and children alike attribute the others' behavior to internal causes. That is, both make dispositional attributions about other people's behavior.

How do the parents and children perceive themselves? The parents probably see themselves as being forced into combat by their children's foolishness. If they become insistent, it is in response to the children's stubbornness. The children probably see themselves as responding to peer pressures and, perhaps, to sexual urges that may have come from within but seem like a source of outside pressure. The parents and the children both tend to see their own behavior as motivated by external forces. That is, they make situational attributions for their own behavior.

The actor-observer effect extends to our perceptions of both the in-group (an extension of ourselves) and the out-group. Consider conflicts between nations, for example. Both sides may engage in brutal acts of violence. Each side usually considers the other to be calculating, inflexible, and—not infrequently—sinister. Each side also typically views its own people as victims of circumstances and its own violent actions as justified or dictated by the situation. After all, we may look at the other side as being in the wrong, but can we expect them to agree with us?[3]

THE SELF-SERVING BIAS There is also a **self-serving bias** in the attribution process. We are likely to ascribe our successes to internal, dispositional factors but our failures to external, situational influences (Baumgardner et al., 1986). When we have done well on a test or impressed a date, we are likely to credit our intelligence and charm. But when we fail, we are likely to blame bad luck, an unfair test, or our date's bad mood.

It seems that we extend the self-serving bias to others in our perceptions of why we win or lose when we gamble. If we win a bet on a football game, we tend to attribute our success to the greater ability of the winning team—a dispositional factor (Gilovich, 1983). But when we lose the bet, we tend to ascribe the outcome to a fluke such as an error by a referee.

There are exceptions to the self-serving bias. For example, depressed people are more likely than other people to ascribe their failures to internal factors, even when external forces are mostly to blame.

Another interesting attribution bias is a gender difference in attributions for friendly behavior. Men are more likely than women to interpret a woman's friendliness toward a man as flirting (Abbey, 1987). Perhaps traditional differences in gender roles still lead men to expect that a "decent" woman will be passive.

FACTORS CONTRIBUTING TO THE ATTRIBUTION PROCESS Our attribution of behavior to internal or external causes can apparently be influenced by three factors: *consensus, consistency,* and *distinctiveness* (Kelley & Michela, 1980). When few people act in a certain way—that is, when the **consensus** is low—we are likely to attribute behavior to internal factors. Consistency refers to the degree to which the same person acts in the same way on other occasions. Highly consistent behavior can often be attributed to internal factors. Distinctiveness is the extent to which the person responds differently in different situations. If the person acts similarly in different situations, distinctiveness is low. We therefore are likely to attribute his or her behavior to internal factors.

Let us apply the criteria of consensus, consistency, and distinctiveness to the behavior of a customer in a restaurant. She takes one bite of her blueberry cheesecake and calls the waiter. She tells him that her food is inedible; she demands that it be replaced. The question is whether she complained as a result of internal causes (for example, because she is hard to please) or external causes (that is, because the food really is bad). Under the following circumstances, we are likely to attribute her behavior to internal causes: (1) No one else at the table is complaining, so consensus

TRUTH OR FICTION REVISITED
It is true that we take others to task for their misdeeds but tend to see ourselves as victims of circumstances when our conduct falls short of our ideals. This bias in the attribution process is referred to as the actor-observer effect.

---

[3] I am not suggesting that all nations are equally blameless (or blameworthy) for their brutality toward other nations. I am pointing out that there is a tendency for the people of a nation to perceive themselves as driven to undesirable behavior. Yet they are also likely to perceive other nations' negative behavior as willful.

SELF-SERVING BIAS The tendency to view one's successes as stemming from internal factors and one's failures as stemming from external factors.

CONSENSUS General agreement.

TABLE S.1		
FACTORS LEADING TO INTERNAL OR EXTERNAL ATTRIBUTIONS OF BEHAVIOR		
	INTERNAL ATTRIBUTION	**EXTERNAL ATTRIBUTION**
Consensus	Low: Few people behave this way.	High: Most people behave this way.
Consistency	High: The person behaves this way frequently.	Low: The person does not behave this way frequently.
Distinctiveness	Low: The person behaves this way in many situations.	High: The person behaves this way in few situations.

is low. (2) She has returned her food on other occasions, so consistency is high. (3) She complains in other restaurants also, so distinctiveness is low (see Table S.1). Given these circumstances, we are likely to believe that the customer is just a complainer.

Under the following circumstances, however, we are likely to attribute the customer's behavior to external causes: (1) Everyone else at the table is also complaining, so consensus is high. (2) She does not usually return food, so consistency is low. (3) She usually does not complain at restaurants, so distinctiveness is high. Given these conditions, we are likely to believe that the blueberry cheesecake really is awful and that the customer is justified in her response.

Body Language

Body language is important in social perception. At an early age we learn that the way people carry themselves provides cues about how they feel and are likely to behave (Saarni, 1990). You may have noticed that when people are "uptight" they may also be rigid and straight-backed. People who are relaxed are more likely to "hang loose." Factors such as eye contact, posture, and the distance between two people provide cues to the individuals' moods and their feelings toward their companions. When people face us and lean toward us, we may assume that they like us or are interested in what we are saying. If we overhear a conversation between a couple and observe that the woman is leaning toward the man but the man is sitting back and toying with his hair, we are likely to infer that he is not interested in what she is saying.

TOUCHING: PUT THE ARM ON PEOPLE (LITERALLY) Touching also communicates. Women are more likely than men to touch other people when they are interacting with them (Stier & Hall, 1984). In one "touching" experiment, Kleinke (1977) showed that appeals for help can be more effective when the distressed person makes physical contact with people who are asked for aid. A woman obtained more coins for phone calls when she touched the arm of the person she was asking for money. In another experiment, waitresses obtained higher tips when they touched patrons on the hand or the shoulder while making change (Crusco & Wetzel, 1984).

In these experiments, the touching was noncontroversial. It was usually gentle, brief, and done in familiar settings. However, when touching suggests greater intimacy than desired, it can be seen as negative. A study in a nursing home found that responses to being touched depended on factors such as the status of the staff member, the type of touch, and the part of the body that was touched (Hollinger & Buschmann, 1993). Touching was considered positive when it was appropriate to the situation and did not appear to be condescending. It was seen as negative when it was controlling, unnecessary, or overly intimate.

Body language can also be used to establish and maintain territorial control, as any student who has had to step aside because a football player was walking down the hall knows. Werner and her colleagues (1981) found that players in a game arcade used touching as a way of signaling others to keep their distance. Solo players engaged in more touching than did groups, perhaps because they were surrounded by strangers.

GAZING AND STARING: THE EYES HAVE IT We usually feel that we can learn much from eye contact. When other people "look us squarely in the eye," we may assume they are being assertive or open with us. Avoidance of eye contact may suggest deception or depression. Gazing is interpreted as a sign of liking or friendliness (Kleinke, 1986). In one penetrating study, men and women were asked to gaze into each other's eyes for 2 minutes (Kellerman et al., 1989). After doing so, they reported having passionate feelings toward one another. (Watch out!)

Of course, a gaze is not the same as a persistent hard stare. A hard stare is interpreted as a provocation or a sign of anger. Adolescent males sometimes engage in staring contests as an assertion of dominance. The male who looks away first loses the contest. In a classic series of field experiments, Phoebe Ellsworth and her colleagues (1972) subjected drivers stopped at red lights to hard stares by riders of motor scooters (see Figure S.1). When the light changed, people who were stared at crossed the intersection more rapidly than people who were not. People who are stared at show higher levels of anxiety as measured by heart rate, blood pressure, and so on, than people who are not (Strom & Buck, 1979).

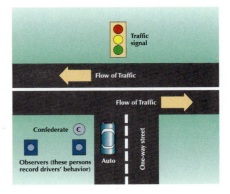

FIGURE S.1

DIAGRAM OF AN EXPERIMENT IN HARD STARING AND AVOIDANCE.

In the study by Phoebe Ellsworth and her colleagues, the confederate of the experimenter stared at some drivers and not at others. Recipients of the stares drove across the intersection more rapidly once the light turned green. Why?

INTERPERSONAL ATTRACTION: ON LIKING AND LOVING

One of the more fascinating topics within social psychology is that of interpersonal attraction. Whether we are discussing the science of physics, a pair of magnetic toy dogs, or Candy and Stretch, attraction is a force that draws bodies together. In psychology and sociology, attraction is defined as an attitude of liking ("positive attraction") or disliking ("negative attraction"). Magnetic "kissing" dogs are usually made so that the heads attract one another, but (unlike their real counterparts) a head and tail repel one another. We shall see that when there is a matching of the heads—that is, a meeting of the minds—people are also more likely to be attracted to one another. And, as with the toy dogs, when we believe that another person's attitudes and opinions are, well, asinine, we are likely to be repelled. Among the factors contributing to attraction are physical appearance, matching, and reciprocity.

Physical Appearance: How Important Is Looking Good?

Physical appearance is a key factor in attraction and in considering partners for dates and marriage. What determines physical allure? Are our standards subjective—that is, "in the eye of the beholder"? Or is there general agreement on what is appealing?

Some aspects of beauty appear to be cross cultural. For example, a study of people in England and Japan found that both British and Japanese men consider women with large eyes, high cheekbones, and narrow jaws to be most attractive (Perret, 1994). In his research, Perret created computer composites of the faces of 60 women and, as shown in part A of

"LOOKING GOOD."
Naomi Campbell, Claudia Schiffer, and Christie Turlington are among those who set the standards for beauty in contemporary American culture. How important is physical attractiveness?

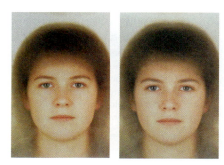

FIGURE S.2

WHAT FEATURES CONTRIBUTE TO FACIAL ATTRACTIVENESS?

In both England and Japan, features such as large eyes, high cheekbones, and narrow jaws contribute to perceptions of the attractiveness of women. Part A shows a composite of the faces of 15 women rated as the most attractive of a group of 60. Part B is a composite in which the features of these 15 women are exaggerated—that is, developed further in the direction that separates them from the average of the entire 60.

MATCHING HYPOTHESIS The view that people tend to choose persons similar to themselves in attractiveness and attitudes in the formation of interpersonal relationships.

Figure S.2, of the 15 women who were rated the most attractive. He then used computer enhancement to exaggerate the differences between the composite of the 60 and the composite of the 15 most attractive women. He arrived at the image shown in part B of Figure S.2. Part B, which shows higher cheekbones and a narrower jaw than part A, was rated as the most attractive image. Similar results were found for the image of a Japanese woman. Works of art suggest that the ancient Greeks and Egyptians favored similar facial features.

In our society, tallness is an asset for men, but tall women are viewed less positively (Sheppard & Strathman, 1989). College women prefer their dates to be about 6 inches taller than they are. College men tend to favor women who are about 4½ inches shorter than they are (Gillis & Avis, 1980).

Although preferences for facial features may transcend time and culture, preferences for body weight and shape may be more culturally determined. For example, plumpness has been valued in many cultures. Grandmothers who worry that their granddaughters are starving themselves often come from cultures in which stoutness is acceptable or desirable. In contemporary Western society, both genders find slenderness appealing (Franzoi & Herzog, 1987). Women generally favor men with a V taper—broad shoulders and a narrow waist.

Although generally men and women both perceive overweight people as unappealing, there are fascinating gender differences in perceptions of desirable body shapes. College men tend to consider their current physique similar to the ideal male build and to the one that women find most appealing (Fallon & Rozin, 1985). College women, in contrast, generally see themselves as markedly heavier than the figure that is most appealing to men and heavier still than the ideal (see Figure S.3). Both mothers and fathers of college students see themselves as heavier than their ideal weight (Rozin & Fallon, 1988). Both genders err in their estimates of the other gender's preferences, however. Men of both generations actually prefer women to be heavier than the women presume. Both college women and their mothers prefer men who are slimmer than the men presume.

"PRETTY IS AS PRETTY DOES"? Both men and women are perceived as more attractive when they are smiling (Reis et al., 1990). There is thus ample reason to, as the song goes, "put on a happy face" when you are meeting people or looking for a date.

Other aspects of behavior also affect interpersonal attraction. Women who are shown videotapes of prospective dates prefer men who act outgoing and self-assertive (Riggio & Woll, 1984). College men who exhibit dominance (defined as control over a social interaction with a professor) in a videotape are rated as more attractive by women (Sadalla et al., 1987). However, college men respond negatively to women who show self-assertion and social dominance (Riggio & Woll, 1984; Sadalla et al., 1987). Despite the liberating trends of recent years, the cultural stereotype of the ideal woman still includes modesty. I am *not* suggesting that self-assertive women should take a back seat in order to make themselves more appealing to traditional men. Assertive women might find nothing but conflict in their interactions with such men in any case.

The Matching Hypothesis: Do "Opposites Attract" or Do "Birds of a Feather Flock Together"?

Although we may rate highly attractive people as most desirable, most of us are not left to blend in with the wallpaper. According to the **matching hypothesis,** we tend to date people who are similar to ourselves in physi-

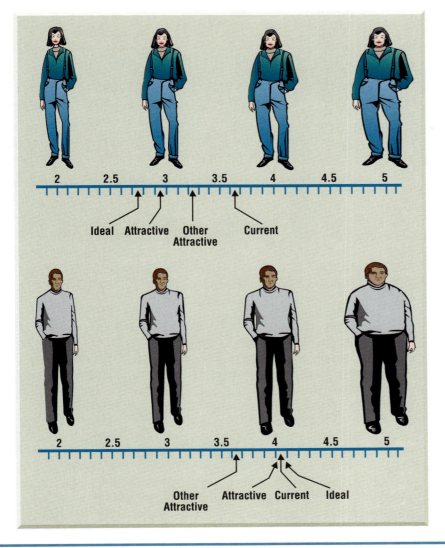

cal attractiveness rather than the local Will Smith or Sandra Bullock look-alike. One motive for asking out "matches" seems to be fear of rejection by more attractive people (Bernstein et al., 1983).

The quest for similarity extends beyond physical attractiveness. Our marital and sex partners tend to be similar to us in race/ethnicity, age, level of education, and religion. Consider some findings of the National Health and Social Life Survey (Michael et al., 1994, pp. 45–47):

- Nearly 94% of single White men have White women as their sex partners; 2% are partnered with Hispanic American women, 2% with Asian American women, and less than 1% with African American women.

- About 82% of African American men have African American women as their sex partners; nearly 8% are partnered with White women and almost 5% with Hispanic American women.

- About 83% of the women and men in the study chose partners within five years of their own age and of the same or a similar religion.

- Of nearly 2,000 women in the study, not one with a graduate college degree had a partner who had not finished high school.

Why do most people have partners from the same background as their own? One reason is that marriages are made in the neighborhood and not

"YOUR DADDY'S RICH AND YOUR MA IS GOOD LOOKIN'": GENDER DIFFERENCES IN THE IMPORTANCE OF PHYSICAL ATTRACTIVENESS

Your Daddy's rich
And your Ma is good
      lookin',
So hush, little baby,
Don't you cry.

FROM "SUMMERTIME" (FROM THE OPERA *PORGY & BESS*)

How important to you is your partner's physical appearance? Studies on mate selection find that women tend to place greater emphasis than men on traits such as professional status, consideration, dependability, kindness, and fondness for children. Men place relatively greater emphasis on physical allure, cooking ability (can't they turn on the microwave oven themselves?), even thrift (Buss, 1994; Feingold, 1992a). Evolutionary psychologists believe that evolutionary forces favor the survival of women who desire status in their mates and men who emphasize

physical allure because these preferences provide reproductive advantages. Some physical features such as cleanliness, good complexion, clear eyes, strong teeth and healthy hair, firm muscle tone, and a steady gait are found universally appealing to both genders (Rathus et al., 2000). Perhaps such traits have value as markers of better reproductive potential in prospective mates. According to the "parental investment model," a woman's appeal is more strongly connected with her age and health, both of which are markers of reproductive capacity. The value of men as reproducers, however, is more intertwined with factors that contribute to a stable environment for child rearing—such as social standing and reliability (Feingold, 1992a). For such reasons, evolutionary psychologists speculate that these qualities may

have grown relatively more alluring to women over the millennia (e.g., Buss, 1994).

This theory is largely speculative, however, and not fully consistent with all the evidence. Women, like men, are attracted to physically appealing partners, and women tend to marry men similar to them in physical attractiveness and socioeconomic standing. Aging men are more likely than younger men to die from natural causes. The wealth they accrue may not always be transmitted to their spouses and children, either. Many women may be more able to find reproductive success by mating with a fit, younger male than with an older, higher-status male. Even evolutionary psychologists allow that despite any innate predispositions, many men desire older women. Human behavior is certainly flexible. ■

in heaven (Michael et al., 1994). We tend to live among people who are similar to us in background, and we therefore come into contact with them more often than with people from other backgrounds. Another reason is that we are drawn to people whose attitudes are similar to ours. People from a similar background are more likely to have similar attitudes. Similarity in attitudes and tastes is a key contributor to friendships and romantic relationships (Griffin & Sparks, 1990; Laumann et al., 1994).

Reciprocity: If You Like Me, You Must Have Excellent Judgment

Has anyone told you how good looking, brilliant, and mature you are? That your taste is refined? That all in all, you are really something special? If so, have you been impressed by his or her fine judgment?

Reciprocity is a powerful determinant of attraction. We tend to return feelings of admiration. We tend to be more open, warm, and help-

RECIPROCITY The tendency to return feelings and attitudes that are expressed about us.

ful when we are interacting with strangers who seem to like us (Curtis & Miller, 1986).

Feelings of attraction are influenced by factors such as physical appearance and similarity. Let us explore what we mean when we say that feelings of attraction have blossomed into love.

STEREOTYPES OF ATTRACTIVE PEOPLE: DO GOOD THINGS COME IN PRETTY PACKAGES? By and large, we rate what is beautiful as good (Aronson et al., 1998). That is, stereotypes of attractive people are connected with *positive* prejudice. We expect physically attractive people to be poised, sociable, popular, mentally healthy, and fulfilled (Eagly et al., 1991; Feingold, 1992b). We expect them to be persuasive and hold prestigious jobs. We even expect them to be good parents and have stable marriages.

These stereotypes seem to have some basis in reality. For one thing, it seems that more attractive individuals are less likely to develop psychological disorders and that the disorders of unattractive individuals are more severe (Archer & Cash, 1985; Burns & Farina, 1987). For another, attractiveness correlates positively with popularity and social skills (Feingold, 1992b). The correlations between physical attractiveness and most measures of mental ability and personality are trivial, however (Feingold, 1992b).

One way to interpret the data on the correlates of physical attractiveness is to assume that these links are all innate—in other words, we can believe that beauty and competence genetically go hand in hand. We can believe that biology is destiny and throw up our hands in despair. But a more useful way to interpret this data is to assume that we can do things to make ourselves more attractive and also more successful and fulfilled. Recall that having a decent physique or figure (which is something we can work on), good grooming, and attending to the ways in which we dress are linked to attractiveness. So don't give up the ship.

Attractive people are also more likely to be found innocent of burglary and cheating in mock jury experiments (Mazzella & Feingold, 1994). When found guilty, they are handed down less severe sentences. Perhaps we assume that more attractive people are less likely to need to resort to deviant behavior to achieve their goals. Even when they have erred, perhaps we assume that they will have more opportunity for personal growth and will be more likely to change their evil ways.

TRUTH OR FICTION REVISITED
It is true that juries are less likely to find attractive individuals guilty of burglary or of cheating on an exam. "Good things" are apparently expected to "come in pretty packages."

Love: Doing What Comes . . . Culturally?

Love—the ideal for which we make great sacrifice. Love—the sentiment that launched a thousand ships in Homer's epic poem *The Iliad*. Through the millennia, poets have sought to capture love in words. Dante, the Italian poet who shed some light on the Dark Ages, wrote of "the love that moves the sun and the other stars." The Scottish poet Robert Burns wrote that his love was like "a red, red rose." Love is beautiful and elusive. Passion and romantic love are also lusty, surging with sexual desire. Let us now consider a theoretical view of romantic love.

THE LOVE TRIANGLE No, this love triangle does not refer to two men wooing the same woman. It refers to Robert Sternberg's **triangular model of love.** Sternberg (1988) believes that love can include combinations of three components: intimacy, passion, and commitment (see Figure S.4).

Intimacy refers to a couple's closeness, to their mutual concern and sharing of feelings and resources. **Passion** means romance and sexual

TRIANGULAR MODEL OF LOVE Sternberg's view that love involves combinations of three components: intimacy, passion, and commitment.

INTIMACY Close acquaintance and familiarity; a characteristic of a relationship in which partners share their inmost feelings.

PASSION Strong romantic and sexual feelings.

FIGURE S.4
THE TRIANGULAR MODEL OF LOVE.

According to this model, love has three components: intimacy, passion, and commitment. The ideal of consummate love consists of romantic love plus commitment.

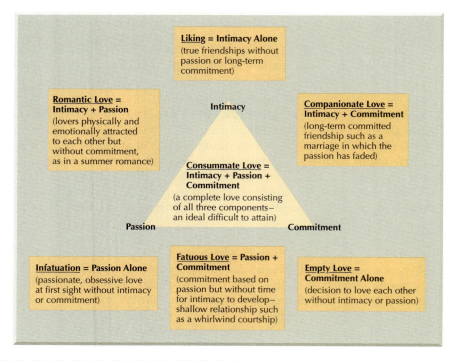

Liking = Intimacy Alone
(true friendships without passion or long-term commitment)

Romantic Love = Intimacy + Passion
(lovers physically and emotionally attracted to each other but without commitment, as in a summer romance)

Intimacy

Companionate Love = Intimacy + Commitment
(long-term committed friendship such as a marriage in which the passion has faded)

Consummate Love = Intimacy + Passion + Commitment
(a complete love consisting of all three components—an ideal difficult to attain)

Passion

Commitment

Infatuation = Passion Alone
(passionate, obsessive love at first sight without intimacy or commitment)

Fatuous Love = Passion + Commitment
(commitment based on passion but without time for intimacy to develop—shallow relationship such as a whirlwind courtship)

Empty Love = Commitment Alone
(decision to love each other without intimacy or passion)

feelings. Commitment means deciding to enhance and maintain the relationship. Passion is most crucial in short-term relationships. Intimacy and commitment are relatively more important in enduring relationships. The ideal form of love, which combines all three, is **consummate love.** Consummate love, in this model, is romantic love plus commitment.

Romantic love is characterized by passion and intimacy. Passion involves fascination (preoccupation with the loved one); sexual craving; and the desire for exclusiveness (a special relationship with the loved one). Intimacy involves caring—championing the interests of the loved one, even if it entails sacrificing one's own. People who are dating, or who expect to be dating each other, are cognitively biased toward evaluating each other positively (Fiske, 1993). They tend to pay attention to information that confirms their romantic interests. In less technical terms, romantic lovers often idealize each another. They magnify each other's positive features and overlook their flaws.

To experience romantic love, in contrast to attachment or sexual arousal, one must be exposed to a culture that idealizes the concept. In Western culture, romantic love blossoms in fairy tales about Sleeping Beauty, Cinderella, Snow White, and all their princes charming. It matures with romantic novels, television tales and films, and the personal accounts of friends and relatives about dates and romances.

Men seem to be somewhat more reluctant than women to make commitments in their romantic relationships (Rathus et al., 2000). Evolutionary psychologists suggest that men may be naturally more promiscuous because they are the genetic heirs of ancestors whose reproductive success was connected with the number of women they could impregnate (Bjorklund & Kipp, 1996; Buss, 1994). But women can produce relatively few children in their lifetimes. Thus, the theory suggests, women need to be more selective with respect to their mating partners. Is it possible that the man's "roving eye" and the woman's selectivity are embedded in their genes (Townsend, 1995)? (This possibility is *not* intended to provide male readers with the excuse, "But how can I make a commitment? Running around is in my genes.")

CONSUMMATE LOVE The ideal form of love within Sternberg's model, which combines passion, intimacy, and commitment.

ROMANTIC LOVE An intense, positive emotion that involves sexual attraction, feelings of caring, and the belief that one is in love.

SOCIAL INFLUENCE

Most people would be reluctant to wear blue jeans to a funeral, walk naked on city streets, or, for that matter, wear clothes at a nudist colony. This is because other people and groups can exert enormous pressure on us to behave according to their norms. **Social influence** is the area of social psychology that studies the ways in which people alter the thoughts, feelings, and behavior of others. We already learned how attitudes can be changed through persuasion. In this section we describe a couple of classic experiments that demonstrate how people influence others to engage in destructive obedience or conform to social norms.

Obedience to Authority: Does Might Make Right?

Throughout history soldiers have followed orders—even when it comes to slaughtering innocent civilians. The Turkish slaughter of Armenians, the Nazi slaughter of Jews, the Serbian slaughter of Albanians and Bosnian Muslims, the mutual slaughter of Hutus and Tutsis in Rwanda—these are all examples of the tragedies that can arise from simply following orders. We may say we are horrified by such crimes and we cannot imagine why people engage in them. But how many of us would refuse to follow orders issued by authority figures?

THE MILGRAM STUDIES Stanley Milgram also wondered how many people would resist immoral requests made by authority figures. To find out, he ran the series of experiments described in the "Psychology as a Science" chapter (Milgram, 1974). People responded to newspapers ads seeking subjects for an experiment on "the effects of punishment on learning." The experiment required a "teacher" and a "learner." The newspaper recruit was assigned the role of teacher—supposedly by chance.

Figures PSY.5 and PSY.6 show the bogus shock apparatus employed in the experiment and the layout of the laboratory. "Teachers" were given the task of administering shock to learners when they made errors. The level of shock was to increase with each consecutive error. Despite the professed purpose of the research, Milgram's sole aim was to determine how many people would deliver high levels of apparently painful electric shock to "learners."

In various phases of Milgram's research, nearly half or the majority of the subjects complied throughout the series, believing they were delivering 450-volt, XXX-rated shocks. These findings held for men from the New Haven community, for male students at Yale, and for women.

Many people obey the commands of others even when they are required to perform immoral tasks. But *why?* Why did Germans "just follow orders" during the Holocaust? Why did "teachers" obey the experimenter in Milgram's study? We do not have all the answers, but we can offer a number of hypotheses:

1. *Socialization.* Despite the expressed American ideal of independence, we are socialized from early childhood to obey authority figures such as parents and teachers. Obedience to immoral demands may be the ugly sibling of socially desirable respect for authority figures.

2. *Lack of social comparison.* In Milgram's experimental settings, experimenters displayed command of the situation. Teachers (subjects), however, were on the experimenter's ground and very much on their own so they did not have the opportunity to compare their ideas and

SOCIAL INFLUENCE The area of social psychology that studies the ways in which people influence the thoughts, feelings, and behavior of others.

feelings with those of other people in the same situation. They therefore were less likely to have a clear impression of what to do.

3. *Perception of legitimate authority.* One phase of Milgram's research took place within the hallowed halls of Yale University. Subjects might have been overpowered by the reputation and authority of the setting. An experimenter at Yale might have appeared to be a highly legitimate authority figure—as might a government official or a high-ranking officer in the military. Yet further research showed that the university setting contributed to compliance but was not fully responsible for it. The percentage of individuals who complied with the experimenter's demands dropped from 65% to 48% when Milgram (1974) replicated the study in a dingy storefront in a nearby town. At first glance, this finding might seem encouraging. But the main point of the Milgram studies is that most people are willing to engage in morally reprehensible acts at the behest of a legitimate-looking authority figure. Hitler and his henchmen were authority figures in Nazi Germany. "Science" and Yale University legitimized the authority of the experimenters in the Milgram studies.

4. *The foot-in-the-door technique.* The foot-in-the-door technique might also have contributed to the obedience of the teachers. Once they had begun to deliver shocks to learners, they might have found it progressively more difficult to extricate themselves from the situation. Soldiers, similarly, are first taught to obey orders unquestioningly in unimportant matters such as dress and drill. By the time they are ordered to risk their lives, they have been saluting smartly and following commands without question for a long time.

5. *Inaccessibility of values.* People are more likely to act in accordance with their attitudes when their attitudes are readily available, or accessible. Most people believe that it is wrong to harm innocent people. But strong emotions interfere with clear thinking. As the teachers in the Milgram experiments became more upset, their attitudes might have become less "accessible." As a result, it might have become progressively more difficult for them to behave according to these attitudes.

6. *Buffers.* Several buffers decreased the effect of the learners' pain on the teachers. For example, the "learners" (who were actually confederates of the experimenter) were in another room. When they were in the same room with the teachers—that is, when the teachers had full view of their victims—the compliance rate dropped from 65% to 40%. Moreover, when the teacher held the learner's hand on the shock plate, the compliance rate dropped to 30%. In modern warfare, opposing military forces may be separated by great distances. They may be little more than a blip on a radar screen. It is one thing to press a button to launch a missile or aim a piece of artillery at a distant troop carrier or a faraway mountain ridge. It is quite another to hold a weapon to a victim's throat.

Thus there are many possible explanations for obedience. Milgram's research has alerted us to a real danger—the tendency of many, if not most, people to obey the orders of an authority figure even when they run counter to moral values. It has happened before. It is happening now. What will you do to stop it?

Conformity: Do Many Make Right?

CONFORM To change one's attitudes or overt behavior to adhere to social norms.

SOCIAL NORMS Explicit and implicit rules that reflect social expectations and influence the ways people behave in social situations.

We are said to **conform** when we change our behavior in order to adhere to social norms. **Social norms** are widely accepted expectations concerning social behavior. Explicit social norms are often made into rules and laws such as those that require us to whisper in libraries and to slow down when driving past a school. There are also unspoken or implicit social norms, such as those that cause us to face front in an elevator or to be "fashionably late" for social gatherings.

The tendency to conform to social norms is often good. Many norms have evolved because they promote comfort and survival. Group pressure can also promote maladaptive behavior, as when people engage in risky behavior because "everyone is doing it."

Let us look at a classic experiment on conformity conducted by Solomon Asch in the early 1950s. We then examine factors that promote conformity.

SEVEN LINE JUDGES CAN'T BE WRONG: THE ASCH STUDY Can you believe what you see with your own eyes? Seeing is believing, isn't it? Not if you were a subject in Asch's (1952) study.

You entered a laboratory room with seven other subjects, supposedly taking part in an experiment on visual discrimination. At the front of the room stood a man holding cards with lines drawn on them.

The eight of you were seated in a series. You were given the seventh seat, a minor fact at the time. The man explained the task. There was a single line on the card on the left. Three lines were drawn on the card at the right (Figure S.5). One line was the same length as the line on the other card. You and the other subjects were to call out, one at a time, which of the three lines—1, 2, or 3—was the same length as the one on the card on the left. Simple.

The subjects to your right spoke out in order: "3," "3," "3," "3," "3," "3." Now it was your turn. Line 3 was clearly the same length as the line on the first card, so you said "3." The fellow after you then chimed in: "3." That's all there was to it. Then two other cards were set up at the front of the room. This time line 2 was clearly the same length as the line on the first card. The answers were "2," "2," "2," "2," "2," "2." Again it was your turn. You said "2," and perhaps your mind began to wander. Your stomach was gurgling a bit. The fellow after you said "2."

Another pair of cards was held up. Line 3 was clearly the correct answer. The six people on your right spoke in turn: "1," "1 . . ." Wait a second! ". . . 1," "1." You forgot about dinner and studied the lines briefly. No, line 1 was too short by a good half inch. But the next two subjects said "1," and suddenly it was your turn. Your hands had become sweaty and there was a lump in your throat. You wanted to say "3," but was it right? There was really no time, and you had already paused noticeably. You said "1," and so did the last fellow.

Now your attention was riveted on the task. Much of the time you agreed with the other seven judges, but sometimes you did not. And for some reason beyond your understanding, they were in perfect agreement

CONFORMITY.
In the military, individuals are taught to conform until the group functions in machinelike fashion. What pressures to conform do you experience? Do you surrender to them? Why or why not?

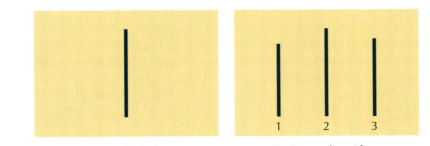

A. Standard Line   **B. Comparison Lines**

1 2 3

FIGURE S.5
CARDS USED IN THE ASCH STUDY ON CONFORMITY.
Which line on card B—1, 2, or 3—is the same length as the line on card A? Line 2, right? But would you say "2" if you were a member of a group and six people answering ahead of you all said "3"? Are you sure?

even when they were wrong—assuming you could trust your eyes. The experiment was becoming an uncomfortable experience, and you began to doubt your judgment.

The discomfort in the Asch study was caused by the pressure to conform. Actually, the other seven recruits were confederates of the experimenter. They prearranged a number of incorrect responses. The sole purpose of the study was to see whether you would conform to the erroneous group judgments.

How many people in Asch's study caved in? How many went along with the crowd rather than give what they thought to be the right answer? Seventy-five percent. *Three out of four agreed with the majority's wrong answer at least once.*

FACTORS THAT INFLUENCE CONFORMITY Several factors increase the tendency to conform. They include the following:

- belonging to a collectivist rather than an individualistic society (Bond & Smith, 1996),
- the desire to be liked by other members of the group (but valuing being right over being liked *decreases* the tendency to conform),
- low self-esteem,
- social shyness (Santee & Maslach, 1982), and
- lack of familiarity with the task.

Other factors in conformity include group size and social support. The likelihood of conformity, even to incorrect group judgments, increases rapidly as group size grows to five members, then rises more slowly to about eight members. At about that point the maximum chance of conformity is reached. Yet finding just one other person who supports your minority opinion apparently is enough to encourage you to stick to your opinion (Morris et al., 1977).

TRUTH OR FICTION REVISITED
Research evidence reveals that seeing is not necessarily believing—at least when most people seem to see things differently than we do.

GROUP BEHAVIOR

To be human is to belong to groups. Groups have much to offer us. They help us satisfy our needs for affection, attention, and belonging. They empower us to do things we could not manage by ourselves. But groups can also pressure us into doing things we might not do if we were acting alone, such as taking great risks or attacking other people.

This section considers ways in which people behave differently as group members than they would as individuals. We begin with social facilitation.

Social Facilitation: Monkey See, Monkey Do Faster?

One effect of groups on individual behavior is **social facilitation,** or the effects on performance that result from the presence of others. Bicycle riders and runners tend to move faster when they are members of a group. This effect is not limited to people. Dogs and cats eat more rapidly around others. Even roaches—yes, roaches—run more rapidly when other roaches are present (Zajonc, 1980).

According to Robert Zajonc (1980), the presence of other people increases our levels of arousal, or motivation. At high levels of arousal, our performance of simple tasks is facilitated. Our performance of complex responses may be impaired, however. For this reason, a well-rehearsed

SOCIAL FACILITATION The process by which a person's performance is increased when other members of a group engage in similar behavior.

speech may be delivered more masterfully before a larger audience. An offhand speech or a question-and-answer session may be hampered by a large audience.

Social facilitation may be influenced by **evaluation apprehension** as well as arousal (Sanna & Shotland, 1990). Our performance before a group is affected not only by the presence of others but also by concern that they are evaluating us. When giving a speech, we may "lose our thread" if we are distracted by the audience and focus too much on its apparent reaction. If we believe we have begun to flounder, evaluation apprehension may sky-rocket. As a result, our performance may falter even more.

The presence of others can also impair performance—not when we are acting *before* a group but when we are anonymous members *of* a group (Shepperd, 1993). Workers, for example, may "goof off" or engage in *social loafing* on humdrum jobs when they believe they will not be found out and held accountable. Under these conditions there is no evaluation apprehension. There may also be **diffusion of responsibility** in groups. Each person may feel less obligation to help because others are present. Group members may also reduce their efforts if an apparently capable member makes no contribution but "rides free" on the efforts of others.

How would you perform in a tug of war? Would the presence of other people pulling motivate you to pull harder? (If so, we would attribute the result to "social facilitation.") Or would the fact that no one can tell how hard you are pulling encourage you to "loaf"? (If so, we would attribute the result to "diffusion of responsibility.")

SOCIAL FACILITATION.
Runners tend to move faster when they are members of a group. Does the presence of other people raise our levels of arousal or produce "evaluation apprehension"?

Group Decision Making

Organizations use groups such as committees or juries to make decisions in the belief that group decisions are more accurate than individual decisions (Gigone & Hastie, 1997). How are group decisions made? Social psychologists have discovered a number of "rules," or *social decision schemes,* that govern much of group decision making. Here are some examples:

1. *The majority-wins scheme.* In this commonly used scheme, the group arrives at the decision that was initially supported by the majority. This scheme appears to guide decision making most often when there is no single objectively correct decision. An example would be a decision about what kind of election campaign ads to run when their popularity has not been tested in the court of public opinion.

2. *The truth-wins scheme.* In this scheme, as more information is provided and opinions are discussed, the group comes to recognize that one approach is objectively correct. For example, a group deciding whether to use SAT scores in admitting students to college would profit from information about whether the scores do predict college success.

3. *The two-thirds majority scheme.* Juries tend to convict defendants when two thirds of the jury initially favors conviction.

4. *The first-shift scheme.* In this scheme, the group tends to adopt the decision that reflects the first shift in opinion expressed by any group member. If a car manufacturing group is divided on whether to produce a convertible, it may opt to do so after one member of the group who initially was opposed to the idea changes her mind. Similarly, if a jury is deadlocked, the members may eventually follow the lead of the first juror to switch his position.

EVALUATION APPREHENSION Concern that others are evaluating our behavior.

DIFFUSION OF RESPONSIBILITY The spreading or sharing of responsibility for a decision or behavior within a group.

Polarization and the "Risky Shift"

We might think that a group decision would be more conservative than an individual decision. After all, shouldn't there be an effort to compromise, to "split the difference"? We might also expect that a few mature individuals would be able to balance the opinions of daredevils. Groups do not generally seem to work in these ways, however.

Consider the *polarization* effect. As an individual, you might recommend that your company risk an investment of $500,000 to develop a new product. Other company executives, polled individually, might risk similar amounts. If you were gathered together to make a group decision, however, you would probably recommend either an amount well above this figure or nothing at all (Burnstein, 1983). This group effect is called **polarization,** or the taking of an extreme position. If you had to gamble on which way the decision would go, however, you would do better to place your money on movement toward the higher sum—that is, to bet on a **risky shift.** Why?

One possibility is that one member of the group may reveal information the others were not aware of. This information may clearly point in one direction or the other. With doubts removed, the group becomes polarized. It moves decisively in the appropriate direction. It is also possible that social facilitation occurs in the group setting and that the resulting greater motivation prompts more extreme decisions.

Why, however, do groups tend to take *greater* risks than those their members would take as individuals? One answer is diffusion of responsibility (Burnstein, 1983). If the venture flops, the blame will not be placed on you alone. Remember the self-serving bias: You can always say (and think) that the failure was the result of a group decision. You thus protect your self-esteem (Larrick, 1993). If the venture pays off, however, you can attribute the outcome to your cool analysis and boast of your influence on the group.

Groupthink

Groupthink is a problem that sometimes arises in group decision making. In **groupthink,** group members tend to be more influenced by group cohesiveness and a dynamic leader than by the realities of the situation (Janis, 1982). Group problem solving may degenerate into groupthink when a group senses an external threat. The external threat heightens the cohesiveness of the group and is a source of stress. Group members under stress tend not to consider all their options carefully (Keinan, 1987). Flawed decisions are frequently made as a result.

Groupthink has been connected with fiascos such as the Bay of Pigs invasion of Cuba (when President Kennedy supported a misguided invasion of the island of Cuba by Cuban exiles), the Watergate scandal (in which President Nixon helped cover up a robbery of Democratic headquarters), the Iran-contra affair (in which people high up in President Reagan's administration made a deal with Iran that would enable them to illegally send guns to anticommunist rebels in Latin America), and NASA's decision to launch the *Challenger* space shuttle despite engineers' warnings about the dangers created by cold weather (Aldag & Fuller, 1993). Irving Janis notes five characteristics of groupthink that contribute to such flawed group decisions:

1. *Feelings of invulnerability*. Each decision-making group might have believed it was beyond the reach of critics or the law—in some cases, because the groups consisted of powerful people who were close to the president of the United States.

TRUTH OR FICTION REVISITED

It is not true that group decisions tend to represent conservative compromises among the opinions of the group's members. Group decisions tend to be riskier than the average decision that would be made by each member of the group acting as an individual— probably because of diffusion of responsibility.

POLARIZATION In social psychology, taking an extreme position or attitude on an issue.

RISKY SHIFT The tendency to make riskier decisions as a member of a group than as an individual acting independently.

GROUPTHINK A process in which group members are influenced by cohesiveness and a dynamic leader to ignore external realities as they make decisions.

2. *The group's belief in its rightness.* These groups apparently believed in the rightness of what they were doing. In some cases, they were carrying out the president's wishes. In the case of the *Challenger* launch, NASA had a track record of successful launches.

3. *Discrediting of information contrary to the group's decision.* The government group involved in the Iran-contra affair knowingly broke the law. Its members apparently discredited the law by (1) deciding that it was inconsistent with the best interests of the United States, and (2) enlisting private citizens to do the dirty work so that the government was not directly involved.

4. *Pressures on group members to conform.* Group cohesiveness and a dynamic leader pressure group members to conform.

5. *Stereotyping of members of the out-group.* Members of the group that broke the law in the Iran-contra affair reportedly stereotyped people who would oppose them as "communist sympathizers" and "knee-jerk liberals."

Groupthink can be averted if group leaders encourage members to remain skeptical about options and to feel free to ask probing questions and disagree with one another.

Mob Behavior and Deindividuation

The Frenchman Gustave Le Bon (1895/1960) branded mobs and crowds as irrational, resembling a "beast with many heads." Mob actions such as race riots and lynchings sometimes seem to operate on a psychology of their own. Do mobs bring out the beast in us? How is it that mild-mannered people commit mayhem when they are part of a mob? In seeking an answer, let us examine a lynching.

THE LYNCHING OF ARTHUR STEVENS In their classic volume *Social Learning and Imitation,* Neal Miller and John Dollard (1941) vividly describe a lynching that occurred in the South in the 1930s. Arthur Stevens, an African American, was accused of murdering his lover, a White woman, when she wanted to break up with him. Stevens was arrested, and he confessed to the crime. Fearing violence, the sheriff moved Stevens to a town 200 miles away during the night. But his location was discovered. The next day a mob of 100 people stormed the jail and returned Stevens to the scene of the crime.

Outrage spread from one member of the mob to another like a plague bacillus. Laborers, professionals, women, adolescents, and law enforcement officers alike were infected. Stevens was tortured and murdered. His corpse was dragged through the streets. The mob then went on a rampage, chasing and assaulting other African Americans. The riot ended only when troops were sent in to restore law and order.

Why did the mob engage in behavior that its members might have rejected as individuals acting alone? One possible answer is *deindividuation.*

DEINDIVIDUATION When people act as individuals, fear of consequences and self-evaluation tend to prevent them from engaging in antisocial behavior. But in a mob, they may experience **deindividuation,** a state of reduced self-awareness and lowered concern for social evaluation. Many factors lead to deindividuation. These include anonymity, diffusion of responsibility, arousal due to noise and crowding, and a focus on emerging group norms rather than on one's own values (Baron & Byrne, 1997). Under these circumstances crowd members behave more aggressively than they would as individuals.

AN ANGRY MOB IS CONTAINED BY POLICE.
Gustave Le Bon branded mobs as irrational, like a "beast with many heads."

DEINDIVIDUATION The process by which group members may discontinue self-evaluation and adopt group norms and attitudes.

Police know that mob actions are best averted early by dispersing small groups that could gather into a crowd. On an individual level, perhaps we can resist deindividuation by instructing ourselves to stop and think whenever we begin to feel highly emotional in a group. If we dissociate ourselves from such groups when they are forming, we are more likely to remain critical and avoid behavior that we might later regret.

Altruism and the Bystander Effect: Some Watch While Others Die

TRUTH OR FICTION REVISITED
It is true that nearly 40 people stood by and did nothing while a woman was stabbed to death. Their failure to come to her aid has been termed the *bystander effect*.

People throughout the nation were shocked by the murder of 28-year-old Kitty Genovese in New York City. Murder was not unheard of in the Big Apple, but Kitty had screamed for help as her killer stalked her for more than half an hour and stabbed her in three separate attacks (Rosenthal, 1994). Thirty-eight neighbors heard the commotion. Twice the assault was interrupted by their voices and bedroom lights. Each time the attacker returned. Yet nobody came to the victim's aid. No one even called the police. Why? Some witnesses said matter-of-factly that they did not want to get involved. One said that he was tired. Still others said, "I don't know." As a nation, are we a callous bunch who would rather watch than help when others are in trouble?

THE HELPER: WHO HELPS?   Many factors affect helping behavior:

1. Empathic observers who are in good moods are more likely to help. Most psychologists focus on the roles of a helper's mood and personality traits. By and large, we are more likely to help others when we are in a good mood (Baron & Byrne, 1997). Perhaps good moods impart a sense of personal power. People who are empathic are also more likely to help people in need (Darley, 1993). Empathic people feel the distress of others, feel concern for them, and can imagine what it must be like to be in need. Women are more likely than men to be empathic, and thus more likely to help people in need (Trobst et al., 1994).

2. Bystanders may not help unless they believe an emergency exists (Baron & Byrne, 1997). Perhaps some people who heard Kitty Genovese's calls for help were not certain what was happening. (But remember that others admitted they did not want to get involved.)

3. Observers must assume the responsibility to act (Baron & Byrne, 1997). It may seem logical that a group of people would be more likely to have come to the aid of Kitty Genovese than a lone person. After all, a group could more effectively have overpowered her attacker. Yet research by Darley and Latané (1968) suggests that a lone person may have been more likely to try to help her.

   In their classic experiment, male subjects were performing meaningless tasks in cubicles when they heard a (convincing) recording of a person apparently having an epileptic seizure. When the men thought that four other persons were immediately available, only 31% tried to help the victim. When they thought no one else was available, however, 85% of them tried to help. As in other areas of group behavior, it seems that *diffusion of responsibility* inhibits helping behavior in groups or crowds. When we are in a group, we are often willing to let George (or Georgette) do it. When George is not around, we are more willing to help others ourselves. (Perhaps some who heard Kitty Genovese thought, "Why should I get involved? Other people can hear her too.")

4. Observers must know what to do (Baron & Byrne, 1997). We hear of cases in which people impulsively jump into the water to save a drowning child and then drown themselves. Most of the time, however, people do not try to help unless they know what to do. For example, nurses are more likely than people without medical training to try to help accident victims (Cramer et al., 1988). Observers who are not sure they can take charge of the situation may stay on the sidelines for fear of making a social blunder and being ridiculed. Or they may fear getting hurt themselves. (Perhaps some who heard Kitty Genovese thought, "If I try to intervene, I may get killed or make an idiot of myself.")

5. Observers are more likely to help people they know (Rutkowski et al., 1983). Aren't we also more likely to give to charity when asked directly by a co-worker or supervisor in the socially exposed situation of the office as compared with a letter received in the privacy of our own homes?

Evolutionary psychologists suggest that **altruism** is a natural aspect of human nature (Guisinger & Blatt, 1994). Self-sacrifice sometimes helps close relatives or others who are similar to us to survive. That is, by battling courageously against the enemy— whether a natural predator or a another human—we may assure that members of our family survive even if we lose our individual lives. Ironically, self-sacrifice is selfish from an evolutionary point of view. It helps us perpetuate a genetic code similar to our own. This view suggests that we are more likely to be altruistic with our relatives rather than strangers, however. The Kitty Genoveses of the world may remain out of luck unless they are surrounded by kinfolk or friends.

6. Observers are more likely to help people who are similar to themselves. Similarity also seems to promote helping behavior. Poorly dressed people are more likely to succeed in requests for a dime with poorly dressed strangers. Well-dressed people are more likely to get money from well-dressed strangers (Hensley, 1981).

THE VICTIM: WHO IS HELPED? Although women are more likely than men to help people in need, it is traditional for men to help women, particularly in the South. Women were more likely than men to receive help, especially from men, when they dropped coins in Atlanta (a southern city) than in Seattle or Columbus (northern cities) (Latané & Dabbs, 1975). Why? The researchers suggest that traditional gender roles persist more strongly in the South.

Women are also more likely than men to be helped when their cars have broken down on the highway or they are hitchhiking. Is this gallantry or are there sexual overtones to some of this "altruism"? There may be, because attractive and unaccompanied women are most likely to be helped by men (Benson et al., 1976).

And so we conclude our discussion of the nature and causes of behavior and mental processes in social situations. People do many things in social situations that they would not do as individuals, and sometimes they do nothing—not even come to the aid of a person in danger—when other people are present. People are social beings. We cannot live without other people, and many times people lose their lives because of other people. So it has been; so it would appear to be. How do you behave when you are a member of a group—a family, a class, a crowd of friends, a crowd on a city sidewalk, a religious group, the armed services? Is your behavior the same as it would be if you were acting alone? Why or why not?

ALTRUISM Unselfish concern for the welfare of others.

SUMMARY

1. **What do social psychologists do?** Social psychologists study the factors that influence our thoughts, feelings, and behaviors in social situations.

2. **What are attitudes?** Attitudes are enduring mental representations of people, places, and things that elicit emotional reactions and influence behavior.

3. **What is the elaboration likelihood model for understanding persuasive messages?** According to this model, persuasion occurs through both central and peripheral routes. Change occurs through the central route by means of consideration of arguments and evidence. Peripheral routes involve associating the objects of attitudes with positive or negative cues, such as attractive or unattractive communicators.

4. **What factors affect the persuasiveness of messages?** Repeated messages generally sell better than messages delivered only once. People tend to show greater response to fear appeals than to purely factual presentations. This is especially so when the appeals offer concrete advice for avoiding negative outcomes. Persuasive communicators tend to show expertise, trustworthiness, attractiveness, or similarity to the audience.

5. **What is the foot-in-the-door technique?** In this technique, people are asked to accede to larger requests after they have acceded to smaller ones.

6. **What is the importance of first impressions?** First impressions can last (the primacy effect) because we tend to label or describe people in terms of the behavior we see initially.

7. **What is the attribution process?** Inference of the motives and traits of others through observation of their behavior is referred to as the attribution process. In dispositional attributions, we attribute people's behavior to internal factors such as their personality traits and decisions. In situational attributions, we attribute people's behavior to their circumstances or external forces.

8. **What are some biases in the attribution process?** According to the actor-observer effect, we tend to attribute the behavior of others to internal, dispositional factors. However, we tend to attribute our own behavior to external, situational factors. The so-called fundamental attribution error is the tendency to attribute too much of other people's behavior to dispositional factors.

9. **What can we infer from body language?** People who feel positively toward one another position themselves closer together and are more likely to touch. Gazing into another's eyes can be a sign of love, but a hard stare is an aversive challenge.

10. **What is interpersonal attraction?** In social psychology, attraction is an attitude of liking (positive attraction) or disliking (negative attraction).

11. **What factors contribute to attraction?** In our culture, slenderness is considered attractive in both men and women, and tallness is valued in men. We are more attracted to good-looking people. Similarity in attitudes and reciprocity in feelings of admiration also enhance attraction.

12. **What is the matching hypothesis?** According to the matching hypothesis, we tend to seek dates and mates at our own level of attractiveness, largely because of fear of rejection.

13. **What is love?** Sternberg's theory suggests that love has three components: intimacy, passion, and commitment. Different kinds of love combine these components in different ways. Romantic love is characterized by the combination of passion and intimacy.

14. **Will people obey authority figures who order them to engage in improper behavior?** Many people in the Milgram studies on obedience complied with the demands of authority figures even when the demands seemed immoral. Factors contributing to obedience include socialization, lack of social comparison, perception of legitimate authority figures, the foot-in-the-door technique, inaccessibility of values, and buffers between perpetrator and victim.

15. **What factors contribute to conformity?** Personal factors such as low self-esteem, high self-consciousness, and shyness contribute to conformity. Group size is also a factor.

16. **What is social facilitation?** Social facilitation refers to the effects on performance that result from the presence of other people. The presence of others may facilitate performance for reasons such as increased arousal and evaluation apprehension. However, when we are anonymous group members, task performance may fall off. This phenomenon is termed *social loafing*.

17. **How do group decisions differ from individual decisions?** Group decisions tend to be more polarized and riskier than individual decisions, largely because groups diffuse responsibility. Group decisions may be highly productive when group members are knowledgeable, there is an explicit procedure for arriving at decisions, and there is a process of give and take.

18. **How do groups make decisions?** Social psychologists have identified several decision-making schemes, including the majority-wins scheme, the truth-wins scheme, the two-thirds majority scheme, and the first-shift rule.

19. **What is groupthink?** Groupthink is an unrealistic kind of decision making fueled by the perception of external threats to the group or to those whom the group wishes to protect. It is facilitated by feelings of invulnerability, the group's belief in its rightness, discrediting of information that contradicts the group's decision, conformity, and stereotyping of members of the out-group.

20. **How do social psychologists explain mob behavior?** Highly emotional crowds may induce attitude-discrepant behavior through the process of deindividuation, which is a state of reduced self-awareness and lowered concern for social evaluation.

21. **What is the bystander effect?** According to the bystander effect, we are unlikely to aid people in distress when we are members of crowds. Crowds tend to diffuse responsibility.

KEY TERMS

A-B problem (p. S-4)
actor-observer effect (p. S-10)
altruism (p. S-27)
attitude (p. S-3)
attribution (p. S-10)
attribution process (p. S-10)
conform (p. S-20)
consensus (p. S-11)
consummate love (p. S-18)
deindividuation (p. S-25)
diffusion of responsibility (p. S-23)
discrimination (p. S-8)
dispositional attribution (p. S-10)
elaboration likelihood model (p. S-5)

evaluation apprehension (p. S-23)
fear appeal (p. S-6)
foot-in-the-door technique (p. S-7)
fundamental attribution error (p. S-10)
groupthink (p. S-24)
intimacy (p. S-17)
matching hypothesis (p. S-14)
passion (p. S-17)
polarization (p. S-24)
prejudice (p. S-7)
primacy effect (p. S-9)
recency effect (p. S-9)
reciprocity (p. S-16)

risky shift (p. S-24)
romantic love (p. S-18)
selective avoidance (p. S-6)
selective exposure (p. S-6)
self-serving bias (p. S-11)
situational attribution (p. S-10)
social facilitation (p. S-22)
social influence (p. S-19)
social norms (p. S-20)
social perception (p. S-9)
social psychology (p. S-3)
stereotype (p. S-5)
triangular model of love (p. S-17)

REFERENCES

Abbey, A. (1987). Misperceptions of friendly behavior as sexual interest. *Psychology of Women Quarterly, 11,* 173–194.

Aldag, R. J., & Fuller, S. R. (1993). Beyond fiasco: A reappraisal of the groupthink phenomenon and a new model of group decision processes. *Psychological Bulletin, 113,* 533–552.

Archer, R. P., & Cash, T. F. (1985). Physical attractiveness and maladjustment among psychiatric patients. *Journal of Social and Clinical Psychology, 3,* 170–180.

Aronson, E., Wilson, T. D., & Akert, R. M. (1998). *Social psychology* (3rd ed.). New York: Addison Wesley Longman.

Asch, S. E. (1952). *Social psychology.* Englewood Cliffs, NJ: Prentice-Hall.

Banks, S. M., et al. (1995). The effects of message framing on mammography utilization. *Health Psychology, 14,* 178–184.

Baron, R. A., & Byrne, D. (1997). *Social psychology* (8th ed.). Boston: Allyn & Bacon.

Basic Behavioral Science Task Force of the National Advisory Mental Health Council. (1996). Basic behavioral science research for mental health:

Sociocultural and environmental practices. *American Psychologist, 51,* 722–731.

Baumgardner, A. H., Heppner, P. P., & Arkin, R. M. (1986). Role of causal attribution in personal problem solving. *Journal of Personality and Social Psychology, 50,* 636–643.

Benson, P. L., Karabenick, S. A., & Lerner, R. M. (1976). Pretty pleases: The effects of physical attractiveness, race, and sex on receiving help. *Journal of Experimental Social Psychology, 12,* 409–415.

Bernstein, W. M., Stephenson, B. O., Snyder, M. L., & Wicklund, R. A. (1983). Causal ambiguity and heterosexual affiliation. *Journal of Experimental Social Psychology, 19,* 78–92.

Bjorklund, D. F., & Kipp, K. (1996). Parental investment theory and gender differences in the evolution of inhibition mechanisms. *Psychological Bulletin, 120,* 163–188.

Bond, R., & Smith, P. B. (1996). Culture and conformity. *Psychological Bulletin, 119,* 111–137.

Bridgwater, C. A. (1982). What candor can do. *Psychology Today, 16*(5), 16.

Burns, G. L., & Farina, A. (1987). Physical attractiveness and self-perception of mental disorder. *Journal of Abnormal Psychology, 96,* 161–163.

Burnstein, E. (1983). Persuasion as argument processing. In M. Brandstatter, J. H. Davis, & G. Stocker-Kreichgauer (Eds.), *Group decision processes.* London: Academic Press.

Buss, D. M. (1994). *The evolution of desire.* New York: Basic Books.

Cramer, R. E., McMaster, M. R., Bartell, P. A., & Dragna, M. (1988). Subject competence and minimization of the bystander effect. *Journal of Applied Social Psychology, 18,* 1133–1148.

Crusco, A. H., & Wetzel, C. G. (1984). The Midas touch: The effects of interpersonal touch on restaurant tipping. *Personality and Social Psychology Bulletin, 10,* 512–517.

Curtis, R. C., & Miller, K. (1986). Believing another likes or dislikes you: Behavior making the beliefs come true. *Journal of Personality and Social Psychology, 51,* 284–290.

Darley, J. M. (1993). Research on morality. *Psychological Science, 4,* 353–357.

Darley, J. M., & Latané, B. (1968). Bystander intervention in emergencies: Diffusion of responsibility. *Journal of Personality and Social Psychology, 8,* 377–383.

Devine, P. G. (1989). Stereotypes and prejudice. *Journal of Personality and Social Psychology, 56,* 5–18.

Duckitt, J. (1992). Psychology and prejudice. *American Psychologist, 47,* 1182–1193.

Eagly, A. H., Ashmore, R. D., Makhijani, M. G., & Longo, L. C. (1991). What is beautiful is good, but . . . *Psychological Bulletin, 110,* 109–128.

Eagly, A. H., & Chaiken, S. (1993). *The psychology of attitudes.* Fort Worth: Harcourt Brace Jovanovich.

Eisenberg, N., Cialdini, R. B., McCreath, H., & Shell, R. (1987). Consistency-based compliance: When and why do children become vulnerable? *Journal of Personality and Social Psychology, 52,* 1174–1181.

Ellsworth, P. C., Carlsmith, J. M., & Henson, A. (1972). The stare as a stimulus to flight in human subjects. *Journal of Personality and Social Psychology, 21,* 302–311.

Fallon, A. E., & Rozin, P. (1985). Sex differences in perceptions of desirable body shape. *Journal of Abnormal Psychology, 94,* 102–105.

Fazio, R. H. (1990). Multiple processes by which attitudes guide behavior. In M. P. Zanna (Ed.), *Advances in experimental social psychology.* San Diego, CA: Academic Press.

Feingold, A. (1992a). Gender differences in mate selection preferences. *Psychological Bulletin, 112,* 125–139.

Feingold, A. (1992b). Good-looking people are not what we think. *Psychological Bulletin, 111,* 304–341.

Fiske, S. T. (1993). Controlling other people: The impact of power on stereotyping. *American Psychologist, 48,* 621–628.

Franzoi, S. L., & Herzog, M. E. (1987). Judging physical attractiveness. *Personality and Social Psychology Bulletin, 13,* 19–33.

Freedman, J. L., & Fraser, S. C. (1966). Compliance without pressure: The foot-in-the-door technique. *Journal of Personality and Social Psychology, 4,* 195–202.

Gigone, D., & Hastie, R. (1997). Proper analysis of the accuracy of group judgments. *Psychological Bulletin, 121,* 149–167.

Gillis, J. S., & Avis, W. E. (1980). The male-taller norm in mate selection. *Personality and Social Psychology Bulletin, 6,* 396–401.

Gilovich, T. (1983). Biased evaluation and persistence in gambling. *Journal of Personality and Social Psychology, 44,* 1110–1126.

Gleitman, H., Rozin, P., & Sabini, J. (1997). Solomon E. Asch (1907–1996). *American Psychologist, 52,* 984–985.

Goldman, K. (1993, June 1). Jordan & Co. play ball on Madison Avenue. *The Wall Street Journal,* p. B9.

Green, D. P., Glaser, J., & Rich, A. (1998). From lynching to gay bashing: The elusive connection between economic condition and hate crime. *Journal of Personality and Social Psychology, 75*, 82–92.

Griffin, E., & Sparks, G. G. (1990). Friends forever. *Journal of Social and Personal Relationships, 7*, 29–46.

Guisinger, S., & Blatt, S. J. (1994). Individuality and relatedness. *American Psychologist, 49*, 104–111.

Hensley, W. E. (1981). The effects of attire, location, and sex on aiding behavior. *Journal of Nonverbal Behavior, 6*, 3–11.

Hollinger, L. M., & Buschmann, M. B. (1993). Factors influencing the perception of touch by elderly nursing home residents and their health caregivers. *International Journal of Nursing Studies, 30*, 445–461.

Janis, I. L. (1982). *Groupthink* (2nd ed.). Boston: Houghton Mifflin.

Johnson, B. T., & Eagly, A. H. (1989). Effects of involvement on persuasion. *Psychological Bulletin, 106*, 290–314.

Jones, E. E. (1990). *Interpersonal perception.* New York: Freeman.

Jones, J. L., & Leary, M. R. (1994). Effects of appearance-based admonitions against sun exposure on tanning intentions in young adults. *Health Psychology, 13*, 86–90.

Judd, C. M., & Park, B. (1988). Outgroup homogeneity. *Journal of Personality and Social Psychology, 54*, 778–788.

Keinan, G. (1987). Decision making under stress. *Journal of Personality and Social Psychology, 52*, 639–644.

Kellerman, J., Lewis, J., & Laird, J. D. (1989). Looking and loving: The effects of mutual gaze on feelings of romantic love. *Journal of Research in Personality, 23*, 145–161.

Kelley, H. H., & Michela, J. L. (1980). Attribution theory and research. *Annual Review of Psychology, 31*, 457–501.

Kleinke, C. L. (1977). Compliance to requests made by gazing and touching experimenters in field settings. *Journal of Experimental Social Psychology, 13*, 218–223.

Kleinke, C. L. (1986). Gaze and eye contact. *Psychological Review, 100*, 78–100.

Krosnick, J. A. (1989). Attitude importance and attitude accessibility. *Personality and Social Psychology Bulletin, 15*, 297–308.

Larrick, R. P. (1993). Motivational factors in decision theories. *Psychological Bulletin, 113*, 440–450.

Latané B., & Dabbs, J. M. (1975). Sex, group size, and helping in three cities. *Sociometry, 38*, 180–194.

Laumann, E. O., Gagnon, J. H., Michael, R. T., & Michaels, S. (1994). *The social organization of sexuality.* Chicago: University of Chicago Press.

Le Bon, G. (1960). *The crowd.* New York: Viking. (Original work published 1895)

Linville, P. W., Fischer, G. W., & Salovey, P. (1989). Perceived distribution of the characteristics of in-group and out-group members. *Journal of Personality and Social Psychology, 57*, 165–188.

Lohr, J. M., & Staats, A. (1973). Attitude conditioning in Sino-Tibetan languages. *Journal of Personality and Social Psychology, 26*, 196–200.

Luchins, A. S. (1957). Primacy-recency in impression formation. In C. I. Hovland (Ed.), *The order of presentation in persuasion.* New Haven, CT: Yale University Press.

Mackie, D. M., Worth, L. T., & Asuncion, A. G. (1990). Processing of persuasive in-group messages. *Journal of Personality and Social Psychology, 58*, 812–822.

Mazzella, R., & Feingold, A. (1994). The effects of physical attractiveness, race, socioeconomic status, and gender of defendants and victims on judgments of mock jurors. *Journal of Applied Social Psychology, 24*(15), 1315–1344.

Michael, R. T., Gagnon, J. H., Laumann, E. O., & Kolata, G. (1994). *Sex in America: A definitive survey.* Boston: Little, Brown.

Milgram, S. (1974). *Obedience to authority.* New York: Harper & Row.

Miller, N. E., & Dollard, J. (1941). *Social learning and imitation.* New Haven, CT: Yale University Press.

Morris, W. N., Miller, R. S., & Spangenberg, S. (1977). The effects of dissenter position and task difficulty on conformity and response conflict. *Journal of Personality, 45*, 251–256.

Mullen, B., et al. (1987). Newscasters'facial expressions and voting behavior of viewers. *Journal of Personality and Social Psychology, 53*.

Perrett, D. I. (1994). *Nature.* Cited in Brody, J. E. (1994, March 21). Notions of beauty transcend culture, new study suggests. *New York Times*, p. A14.

Petty, R. E., Cacioppo, J. T., Strathman, A. J., & Priester, J. R. (1994). To think or not to think: Exploring two routes to persuasion. In S. Shavitt & T. C. Brock (Eds.), *Persuasion* (pp. 113–147). Boston: Allyn & Bacon.

Quattrone, G. A. (1982). Overattribution and unit formation. *Journal of Personality and Social Psychology, 42*, 593–607.

Rathus, S. A., Nevid, J. S., & Fichner-Rathus, L. (2000). *Human sexuality in a world of diversity* (4th ed.). Boston: Allyn & Bacon.

Reis, H. T., et al. (1990). What is smiling is beautiful and good. *European Journal of Social Psychology, 20,* 259–267.

Riggio, R. E., & Woll, S. B. (1984). The role of nonverbal cues and physical attractiveness in the selection of dating partners. *Journal of Social and Personal Relationships, 1,* 347–357.

Rosenthal, A. M. (1994, March 15). The way she died. *New York Times,* p. A23.

Rozin, P., & Fallon, A. (1988). Body image, attitudes to weight, and misperceptions of figure preferences of the opposite sex. *Journal of Abnormal Psychology, 97,* 342–345.

Rutkowski, G. K., Gruder, C. L., & Romer, D. (1983). Group cohesiveness, social norms, and bystander intervention. *Journal of Personality and Social Psychology, 44,* 545–552.

Saarni, C. (1990). Emotional competence. In R. Thompson (Ed.), *Nebraska Symposium on Motivation: Vol. 36. Socioemotional development.* Lincoln: University of Nebraska Press.

Sadalla, E. K., Kenrick, D. T., & Vershure, B. (1987). Dominance and heterosexual attraction. *Journal of Personality and Social Psychology, 52,* 730–738.

Sanna, L. J., & Shotland, R. L. (1990). Valence of anticipated evaluation and social facilitation. *Journal of Experimental Social Psychology, 26,* 82–92.

Santee, R. T., & Maslach, C. (1982). To agree or not to agree: Personal dissent amid social pressure to conform. *Journal of Personality and Social Psychology, 42,* 690–700.

Schwartz, R. M., & Gottman, J. M. (1976). Toward a task analysis of assertive behavior. *Journal of Consulting and Clinical Psychology, 44,* 910–920.

Schwarz, N., Bless, H., & Bohner, G. (1991). Mood and persuasion. In M. Zanna (Ed.), *Advances in experimental social psychology* (Vol. 24). New York: Academic Press.

Sheppard, J. A., & Strathman, A. J. (1989). Attractiveness and height. *Personality and Social Psychology Bulletin, 15,* 617–627.

Shepperd, J. A. (1993). Productivity loss in performance groups. *Psychological Bulletin, 113,* 67–81.

Smith, G. F., & Dorfman, D. (1975). The effect of stimulus uncertainty on the relationship between frequency of exposure and liking. *Journal of Personality and Social Psychology, 31,* 150–155.

Stacy, A. W., Bentler, P. M., & Flay, B. R. (1994). Attitudes and health behavior in diverse populations. *Health Psychology, 13,* 73–85.

Sternberg, R. J. (1988). *The triangle of love: Intimacy, passion, commitment.* New York: Basic Books.

Stier, D. S., & Hall, J. A. (1984). Gender differences in touch. *Journal of Personality and Social Psychology, 47,* 440–459.

Strom, J. C., & Buck, R. W. (1979). Staring and participants' sex. *Personality and Social Psychology Bulletin, 5,* 114–117.

Sweeney, P. D., & Gruber, K. L. (1984). Selective exposure. *Journal of Personality and Social Psychology, 46,* 1208–1221.

Townsend, J. M. (1995). Sex without emotional involvement: An evolutionary interpretation of sex differences. *Archives of Sexual Behavior, 24,* 173–206.

Trobst, K. K., Collins, R. L., & Embree, J. M. (1994). The role of emotion in social support provision. *Journal of Social and Personal Relationships, 11,* 45–62.

Van Brunt, L. (1994, March 27). About men: Whites without money. *New York Times Magazine,* p. 38.

Weber, R., & Crocker, J. (1983). Cognitive processes in the revision of stereotypic beliefs. *Journal of Personality and Social Psychology, 45,* 961–977.

Werner, C. M., Brown, B. B., & Damron, G. (1981). Territorial marking in a game arcade. *Journal of Personality and Social Psychology, 41,* 1094–1104.

Wilder, D. A. (1990). Some determinants of the persuasive power of in-groups and out-groups. *Journal of Personality and Social Psychology, 59,* 1202–1213.

Wu, C., & Shaffer, C. R. (1987). Susceptibility to persuasive appeals as a function of source credibility and prior experience with the attitude object. *Journal of Personality and Social Psychology, 52,* 677–688.

Zajonc, R. B. (1968). Attitudinal effects of mere exposure. *Journal of Personality and Social Psychology, Monograph Supplement* 2(9), 1–27.

Zajonc, R. B. (1980). Compresence. In P. Paulus (Ed.), *The psychology of group influence.* Hillsdale, NJ: Erlbaum.

CHILD AND ADOLESCENT DEVELOPMENT

TRUTH OR FICTION?

_____ Fertilization takes place in the uterus.

_____ Your heart started beating when you were only one fifth of an inch long and weighed a fraction of an ounce.

_____ The saying "Out of sight, out of mind" applies to babies who are a few months old. When an object is removed from sight, it no longer exists so far as they are concerned.

_____ Four-year-old children may believe that the sun shines in order to keep them warm.

_____ The majority of people around the world speak at least two languages.

_____ The way to a baby's heart is through its stomach—that is, babies become emotionally attached to those who feed them.

_____ Children with strict parents are most likely to be successful.

_____ Children placed in day care are more aggressive than children cared for in the home.

_____ Child abusers frequently were abused themselves as children.

_____ A girl can become pregnant when she has her first menstrual period.

_____ Adolescents see themselves as being on stage.

IN A SUMMERLIKE DAY IN OCTOBER, LING CHANG AND her husband Patrick rush out to their jobs as usual. While Ling, a buyer for a New York department store, is arranging for dresses from the Chicago manufacturer to arrive in time for the spring line, a very different drama is unfolding in her body. Hormones are causing a follicle (egg container) in one of her ovaries to ovulate—that is, to rupture and release an egg cell, or ovum. Ling, like other women, possesses from birth all the egg cells she will ever have. How this particular ovum was selected to ripen and be released this month is unknown. But in any case, Ling will be capable of becoming pregnant for only a couple of days following ovulation.

When it is released, the ovum begins a slow journey down a 4-inch-long fallopian tube to the uterus. It is within this tube that one of Patrick's sperm cells will unite with the egg. The fertilized ovum, or zygote, is 1/175th of an inch across—a tiny stage for the drama that is about to unfold.

Developmental psychologists are interested in studying the development of Patrick and Ling's new child from the time of conception until death. There are several reasons for this. One is that the discovery of early influences and developmental sequences helps psychologists understand adults. Psychologists are also interested in the effects of genetic factors, early interactions with parents and siblings (brothers and sisters), and school and community on traits such as aggressiveness and intelligence.

Developmental psychologists also seek to learn the causes of developmental abnormalities. For instance, should pregnant women abstain from smoking and drinking? (Yes.) Is it safe for a pregnant woman to take aspirin for a headache or tetracycline to ward off a bacterial invasion? (Perhaps not. Ask your obstetrician.) What factors contribute to child abuse? Are all adolescents rebellious? The information acquired by developmental psychologists can help us make decisions about how we rear our children and lead our own lives.

Let us begin our story with prenatal developments—the changes that occur between conception and birth. Although they may be literally "out of sight," the most dramatic biological changes occur within the short span of 9 months.

PRENATAL DEVELOPMENT: THE BEGINNING OF OUR LIFE STORY

The most dramatic gains in height and weight occur during prenatal development. Within 9 months a child develops from a nearly microscopic cell to a **neonate** (newborn) about 20 inches long. Its weight increases a billionfold.

During the months following conception, the single cell formed by the union of sperm and egg—the **zygote**—multiplies, becoming two, then four, then eight, and so on. By the time the infant is ready to be born, it contains trillions of cells.

The zygote divides repeatedly as it proceeds on its 3-to 4-day journey to the uterus. The ball-like mass of multiplying cells wanders about the uterus for another 3 to 4 days before beginning to implant in the uterine wall. Implantation takes another week or so. The period from conception to implantation is called the **germinal stage,** or the *period of the ovum.*

The **embryonic stage** lasts from implantation until about the eighth week of development. During this stage, the major body organ systems take form. As you can see from the relatively large heads of embryos (see Figure CD.1), the growth of the head precedes that of the lower parts of the body. The growth of the organs—heart, lungs, and so on—also precedes the growth of the extremities. The relatively early maturation of the brain and the organ systems allows them to participate in the nourishment and further development of the embryo. During the fourth week, a primitive heart begins to beat and pump blood—in an organism that is one fifth of an inch long. The heart will continue to beat without rest every minute of every day for perhaps 80 or 90 years.

By the end of the second month, the head has become rounded and the facial features distinct—all in an embryo that is about 1 inch long and weighs 1/30th of an ounce. During the second month, the nervous system begins to transmit messages. By 5 to 6 weeks, the embryo is only a quarter to half an inch long, yet nondescript sex organs have formed. By about the seventh week, the genetic code begins to assert itself, causing the sex organs to differentiate. If a Y sex chromosome is present, testes form and begin to produce **androgens** (male sex hormones), which further masculinize the sex organs. In the absence of these hormones, the embryo develops female sex organs.

As it develops, the embryo is suspended within a protective **amniotic sac** in the mother's uterus. The sac is surrounded by a clear membrane and contains amniotic fluid. The fluid serves as a sort of natural air bag, allowing the child to move or even jerk around without injury. It also helps maintain an even temperature.

From now until birth, the embryo exchanges nutrients and wastes with the mother through a pancake-shaped organ called the **placenta.** The

NEONATE A newly born child.

ZYGOTE A fertilized ovum (egg cell).

GERMINAL STAGE The first stage of prenatal development during which the dividing mass of cells has not become implanted in the uterine wall.

EMBRYONIC STAGE The stage of development from the third through the eighth weeks following conception, during which time the major organ systems undergo rapid differentiation.

ANDROGENS Male sex hormones.

AMNIOTIC SAC A sac within the uterus that contains the embryo or fetus.

PLACENTA A membrane that permits the exchange of nutrients and waste products between the mother and her developing child but does not allow the maternal and fetal bloodstreams to mix.

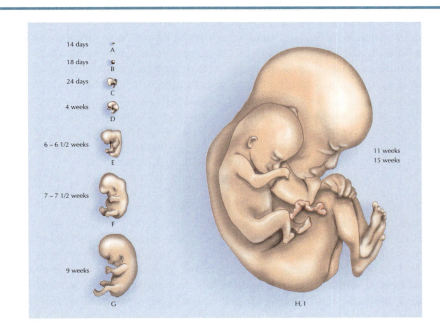

14 days — A
18 days — B
24 days — C
4 weeks — D
6 – 6 1/2 weeks — E
7 – 7 1/2 weeks — F
9 weeks — G
11 weeks / 15 weeks — H, I

FIGURE CD.1
EMBRYOS AND FETUSES AT VARIOUS INTERVALS OF PRENATAL DEVELOPMENT.

AN EXERCISE CLASS FOR PREGNANT WOMEN.
Years ago pregnant women were not expected to exert themselves. Today, it is recognized that exercise is healthful for pregnant women because it promotes fitness, which is beneficial during childbirth as well as at other times.

embryo is connected to the placenta by the **umbilical cord.** The placenta is connected to the mother by the system of blood vessels in the uterine wall.

The circulatory systems of the mother and baby do not mix. A membrane in the placenta permits only certain substances to pass through. Oxygen and nutrients are passed from the mother to the embryo. Carbon dioxide and other wastes are passed from the child to the mother, where they are removed by the mother's lungs and kidneys. Unfortunately, a number of other substances can pass through the placenta. They include some microscopic disease organisms—such as those that cause syphilis and German measles—and some chemical agents, including acne drugs, aspirin, narcotics, alcohol, and tranquilizers. Because these and other agents may be harmful to the baby, pregnant women are advised to consult their physicians about the advisability of using any drugs, even those sold over the counter.

The **fetal stage** lasts from the beginning of the third month until birth. By the end of the third month, the major organ systems and the fingers and toes have been formed. In the middle of the fourth month, the mother usually detects the first fetal movements. By the end of the sixth month, the fetus moves its limbs so vigorously that the mother may complain of being kicked. The fetus opens and shuts its eyes, sucks its thumb, alternates between periods of wakefulness and sleep, and perceives light. It also turns somersaults, which can be clearly perceived by the mother. The umbilical cord is composed so that it will not break or become dangerously wrapped around the fetus, no matter how many acrobatic feats the fetus performs.

Genetic and Chromosomal Abnormalities

The genes that direct our development sometimes move it in unhealthful directions or threaten our very lives. Moreover, some of us do not have the normal complement of chromosomes. A number of genetic and chromosomal abnormalities are described in Table CD.1.

Genetic counselors obtain information about a couple's medical background to assess the risk that they might pass along genetic defects to their children. Some couples who face a high risk of doing so choose to adopt instead of conceiving their own children. Other couples choose to have an abortion if the fetus is found to have certain abnormalities.

Various procedures are used to learn whether the fetus has these disorders. *Amniocentesis* is usually performed about four months into pregnancy. In this procedure, fluid containing fetal cells is drawn from the amniotic sac (or "bag of waters") with a syringe. The cells are then grown in a culture and examined for the presence of abnormalities. *Chorionic villus sampling (CVS)* is performed several weeks earlier. A narrow tube is used to snip off material from the chorion, a membrane that contains the amniotic sac and fetus, and the material is analyzed. CVS is somewhat riskier than amniocentesis, so most obstetricians prefer to use the latter. These tests are used to detect the presence of Down syndrome, sickle-cell anemia, Tay-Sachs disease, spina bifida, muscular dystrophy, Rh incompatibility, and other disorders. They also reveal the gender of the fetus.

Ultrasound bounces high-pitched sound waves off the fetus, revealing a picture of the fetus on a monitor and allowing the obstetrician to detect certain abnormalities. Obstetricians also use ultrasound during amniocentesis to locate the fetus in order to avoid hitting it with the syringe.

Parental blood tests can suggest the presence of problems such as sickle-cell anemia, Tay-Sachs disease, and neural tube defects. Still other tests examine fetal DNA and can indicate the presence of Huntington's chorea, cystic fibrosis, and other disorders.

UMBILICAL CORD A tube between the mother and her developing child through which nutrients and waste products are conducted.

FETAL STAGE The stage of development from the third month following conception through childbirth, during which time there is maturation of organ systems and dramatic gains in length and weight.

TABLE CD.1

SOME GENETIC AND CHROMOSOMAL ABNORMALITIES

HEALTH PROBLEM	CHARACTERISTICS
Cystic fibrosis	Genetic disease in which the pancreas and lungs become clogged with mucus, which impairs the processes of respiration and digestion.
Down syndrome	Condition caused by a 3rd chromosome on the 21st pair. The child with Down syndrome has a characteristic fold of skin over the eye and mental retardation. The risk of having a child with the syndrome increases as parents increase in age.
Hemophilia	Disorder in which the blood fails to clot properly.
Huntington's chorea	Fatal neurological disorder whose onset occurs in middle adulthood.
Neural tube defects	Disorders of the brain or spine, such as anencephaly, in which part of the brain is missing, and spina bifida, in which part of the spine is exposed or missing. Anencephaly is fatal shortly after birth, but some spina bifida victims survive for a number of years, albeit with severe handicaps.
Phenylketonuria	Disorder in which children cannot metabolize phenylalanine, which builds up in the form of phenylpyruvic acid and causes mental retardation. The disorder can be diagnosed at birth and controlled by diet.
Retina blastoma	Genetic form of blindness.
Sickle-cell anemia	Blood disorder that mostly afflicts African Americans, in which deformed blood cells obstruct small blood vessels, decreasing their capacity to carry oxygen and heightening the risk of occasionally fatal infections.
Tay-Sachs disease	Fatal neurological disorder that primarily afflicts Jews of European origin.

Source: Etaugh & Rathus (1995).

During the last 3 months, the organ systems of the fetus continue to mature. The heart and lungs become increasingly capable of sustaining independent life. The fetus gains about 5½ pounds and doubles in length. Newborn boys average about 7½ pounds and newborn girls about 7 pounds.

CHILD DEVELOPMENT

Childhood begins with birth. When my children are enjoying themselves, I kid them and say, "Stop having fun. You're a child and childhood is the worst time of life." I get a laugh because they know that childhood is supposed to be the best time of life—a time for play and learning and endless possibilities. For many children it is that, but other children suffer from problems such as malnutrition, low self-esteem, and child abuse.

Let us chronicle the events of childhood. The most obvious aspects of child development are physical. Let us therefore begin with physical development. However, we will see that cognitive developments and social and personality developments are also essential.

PHYSICAL DEVELOPMENT

Physical development includes gains in height and weight, maturation of the nervous system, and development of bones, muscles, and organs.

During infancy—the first 2 years of childhood—dramatic gains in height and weight continue. Babies usually double their birth weight in about 5 months and triple it by their first birthday. Their height increases by about 10 inches in the first year. Children grow another 4 to 6 inches during the second year and gain some 4 to 7 pounds. After that, they gain about 2 to 3 inches a year until they reach the adolescent growth spurt. Weight gains also remain fairly even at about 4 to 6 pounds per year until the spurt begins.

Let us now consider other aspects of physical development in childhood: reflexes, perceptual development, and motor development.

Reflexes

Soon after you were born, a doctor or nurse probably pressed her fingers against the palms of your hands. Although you would have had no idea what to do in response, most likely you grasped the fingers firmly—so firmly that you could have been lifted from your cradle! Grasping at birth is inborn. It is one of the neonate's many **reflexes**—simple, unlearned, stereotypical responses elicited by specific stimuli. Reflexes are essential to survival and do not involve higher brain functions. They occur automatically—that is, without thinking about them.

Newborn children do not know that it is necessary to eat to survive. Fortunately, they have rooting and sucking reflexes that cause them to eat. They turn their head toward stimuli that prod or stroke the cheek, chin, or corner of the mouth. This is termed **rooting.** They suck objects that touch their lips.

Neonates have numerous other reflexes that aid in survival. They withdraw from painful stimuli. This is known as the withdrawal reflex. They draw up their legs and arch their backs in response to sudden noises, bumps, or loss of support while being held. This is the startle, or Moro, reflex. They grasp objects that press against the palms of their hands (the grasp, or palmar, reflex). They fan their toes when the soles of their feet are stimulated (the Babinski reflex). Pediatricians assess babies' neural functioning by testing these reflexes.

Babies also breathe, sneeze, cough, yawn, and blink reflexively. And it is guaranteed that you will learn about the sphincter (anal muscle) reflex if you put on your best clothes and hold an undiapered neonate on your lap for a while.

Perceptual Development

Newborn children spend about 16 hours a day sleeping and do not have much opportunity to learn about the world. Yet they are capable of perceiving the world reasonably well soon after birth.

Within a couple of days, infants can follow, or track, a moving light with their eyes (Kellman & von Hofsten, 1992). By the age of 3 months, they can discriminate most colors (Banks & Shannon, 1993; Teller & Lindsey, 1993). Neonates are nearsighted but by about the age of 4 months, infants seem able to focus on distant objects about as well as adults can.

The visual preferences of infants are measured by the amount of time, termed **fixation time,** they spend looking at one stimulus instead of another. In classic research by Robert Fantz (1961), 2-month-old infants preferred visual stimuli that resembled the human face to newsprint, a bull's-eye, and featureless red, white, and yellow disks. At this age the complexity of facelike patterns may be more important than their content. For example, babies have been shown facelike patterns that differ either in the number of elements they contain or the degree to which they are organized to match the human face. Five- to 10-week-old babies fixate longer on patterns with high numbers of elements. The organization of the elements—that is, the degree to which they resemble the face—is less important. By 15 to 20 weeks, the organization of the pattern also matters. At that age babies dwell longer on facelike patterns (e.g., Haaf et al., 1983).

REFLEX A simple unlearned response to a stimulus.

ROOTING The turning of an infant's head toward a touch, such as by the mother's nipple.

FIXATION TIME The amount of time spent looking at a visual stimulus.

Infants thus seem to have an inborn preference for complex visual stimuli. However, preference for faces as opposed to other equally complex stimuli may not emerge until infants have had experience with people.

Classic research has shown that infants tend to respond to cues for depth by the time they are able to crawl (at about 6 to 8 months). Most also have the good sense to avoid crawling off ledges and tabletops into open space (Campos et al., 1978). Note the setup (Figure CD.2) in the classic "visual cliff" experiment run by Walk and Gibson (1961). An 8-month-old infant crawls freely above the portion of the glass with a checkerboard pattern immediately beneath it, but hesitates to crawl over the portion of the glass beneath which the checkerboard has been dropped a few feet. Because the glass alone would support the infant, this is a "visual cliff," not an actual cliff.

Normal neonates hear well unless their middle ears are clogged with amniotic fluid. In such cases, hearing improves rapidly after the ears are opened up. Most neonates reflexively turn their heads toward unusual sounds, suspending other activities as they do so. This finding, along with findings about visual tracking, suggests that infants are preprogrammed to survey their environments. Speaking or singing softly in a low-pitched tone soothes infants (Papousek et al., 1991). This is why some parents use lullabies to get infants to fall asleep.

Three-day-old babies prefer their mother's voice to those of other women, but they do not show a similar preference for their father's voice (DeCasper & Prescott, 1984; Freeman et al., 1993). By birth, of course, babies have had many months of "experience" in the uterus. For at least 2 or 3 months before birth, babies have been capable of hearing sounds. Because they are predominantly exposed to sounds produced by their mother, learning may contribute to neonatal preferences.

The nasal preferences of babies are similar to those of adults. Newborn infants spit, stick out their tongue, and literally wrinkle their nose at the odor of rotten eggs. They smile and make licking motions in response to chocolate, strawberry, vanilla, and honey. The sense of smell, like the sense of hearing, may provide a vehicle for mother-infant recognition. Within the first week, nursing infants prefer to turn to look at their mother's nursing pads (which can be discriminated only by smell) rather than those of strange women (Macfarlane, 1975). By 15 days, nursing infants prefer

FIGURE CD.2
THE CLASSIC VISUAL CLIFF EXPERIMENT.
This young explorer has the good sense not to crawl out onto an apparently unsupported surface, even when Mother beckons from the other side. Rats, pups, kittens, and chicks also will not try to walk across to the other side. (So don't bother asking why the chicken crossed the visual cliff.)

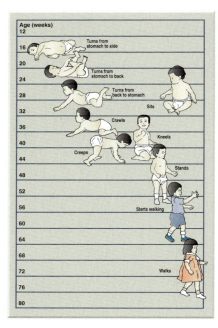

Age (weeks)
12
16 Turns from stomach to side
20
24 Turns from stomach to back
28 Turns from back to stomach
32 Sits
36 Crawls
40 Kneels
44 Creeps
48 Stands
52
56 Starts walking
60
64
68
72 Walks
76
80

FIGURE CD.3
MOTOR DEVELOPMENT.

At birth, infants appear to be bundles of aimless nervous energy. They have reflexes but also engage in random movements that are replaced by purposeful activity as they mature. Motor development proceeds in an orderly sequence. Practice prompts sensorimotor coordination, but maturation is essential. The times in the figure are approximate: An infant who is a bit behind may develop with no problems at all, and a precocious infant will not necessarily become a rocket scientist (or gymnast).

their mother's underarm odor to those of other women (Porter et al., 1992). Bottle-fed babies do not show this preference.

Shortly after birth, infants can discriminate tastes. They suck liquid solutions of sugar and milk but grimace and refuse to suck salty or bitter solutions.

Newborn babies are sensitive to touch. Many reflexes (including rooting and sucking) are activated by pressure against the skin. Newborns are relatively insensitive to pain, however. This may be adaptive, considering the squeezing that occurs during the birth process. Sensitivity to pain increases within a few days.

The sense of touch is an extremely important avenue of learning and communication for babies. Sensations of skin against skin appear to provide feelings of comfort and security that may contribute to the formation of affectionate bonds between infants and their caregivers.

Motor Development

"When did your baby first sit up?" "When did he walk?" "Allyn couldn't walk yet at 10 months, but she zoomed after me in her walker, giggling her head off." "Anthony was walking forward and backward by the age of 13 months."

These are some of the types of comments parents make about their children's motor development. Motor development provides some of the most fascinating changes in infants, in part because so much seems to happen so quickly—and so much of it during the first year. Children gain the capacity to move about through a sequence of activities that includes rolling over, sitting up, crawling, creeping, walking, and running. There is a great deal of variation in the ages at which infants first engage in these activities, but the sequence generally remains the same (see Figure CD.3). A number of children skip a step, however. For example, an infant may creep without ever having crawled.

Let us now consider cognitive developments during childhood. Physical development is not possible without the participation of the brain, and the brain is also the seat of cognition.

COGNITIVE DEVELOPMENT

The ways in which children mentally represent and think about the world—that is, their *cognitive development*—are explored in this section. Because cognitive functioning develops over many years, young children have ideas about the world that differ considerably from those of adults. Many of these ideas are charming but illogical—at least to adults.

Jean Piaget's Cognitive-Developmental Theory

The Swiss biologist and psychologist Jean Piaget (1896–1980) was once offered the curatorship of a museum in Geneva, but he had to turn it down. Why? He was only 11 at the time. Piaget's first intellectual love was biology, and he published his first scientific article at the age of 10. He then became a laboratory assistant to the director of a museum of natural history and engaged in research on mollusks (oysters, clams, snails, and such). The director soon died, and Piaget published the research findings himself. On the basis of these papers, he was offered the curatorship.

During adolescence Piaget studied philosophy, logic, and mathematics, but he earned his PhD in biology. In 1920, he obtained a job at the Binet Institute in Paris, where work on intelligence tests was being conducted. His first task was to adapt English verbal reasoning items for use with

JEAN PIAGET

French children. To do so, he had to try out the items on children in various age groups and see whether they could arrive at correct answers. The task was boring until Piaget became intrigued by the children's *wrong* answers. Another investigator might have shrugged them off and forgotten them, but young Piaget realized that there were methods in the children's madness. The wrong answers seemed to reflect consistent, if illogical, cognitive processes. Piaget investigated these "wrong" answers by probing the children's responses to discover the underlying patterns of thought that led to them. These early probings eventually resulted in Piaget's influential theory of cognitive development.

Jean Piaget hypothesized that children's cognitive processes develop in an orderly sequence of stages. Although some children may be more advanced than others at particular ages, the developmental sequence remains the same. Piaget (1963) identified four major stages of cognitive development: sensorimotor, preoperational, concrete operational, and formal operational (see Table CD.2).

Piaget regarded children as natural physicists who seek to learn about and control their world. In the Piagetian view, children who squish their food and laugh enthusiastically are often acting as budding scientists. In addition to enjoying the responses of their parents, they are studying the texture and consistency of their food. (Parents, of course, often wish that their children would practice these experiments in the laboratory, not the dining room.)

ASSIMILATION AND ACCOMMODATION Piaget described human thought, or intelligence, in terms of two basic concepts: assimilation and accommodation. **Assimilation** means responding to a new stimulus through a reflex or existing habit. Infants, for example, usually try to place new objects in their mouth to suck, feel, or explore. Piaget would say that the child is assimilating a new toy to the sucking scheme. A **scheme** is a pattern of action or a mental structure involved in acquiring or organizing knowledge.

Accommodation is the creation of new ways of responding to objects or looking at the world. In accommodation, children transform existing schemes—action patterns or ways of organizing knowledge—to incorporate new events. Children (and adults) accommodate to objects and situations that cannot be integrated into existing schemes. (For example, children who study biology learn that whales cannot be assimilated into the "fish" scheme. They accommodate by constructing new schemes, such as

ASSIMILATION According to Piaget, the inclusion of a new event into an existing scheme.

SCHEME According to Piaget, a hypothetical mental structure that permits the classification and organization of new information.

ACCOMMODATION According to Piaget, the modification of schemes so that information inconsistent with existing schemes can be integrated or understood.

TABLE CD.2

PIAGET'S STAGES OF COGNITIVE DEVELOPMENT		
Sensorimotor	Birth–2 years	At first, the child lacks language and does not use symbols or mental representations of objects. In time, reflexive responding ends and intentional behavior begins. The child develops the object concept and acquires the basics of language.
Preoperational	2–7 years	The child begins to represent the world mentally, but thought is egocentric. The child does not focus on two aspects of a situation at once and therefore lacks conservation. The child shows animism, artificialism, and immanent justice.
Concrete operational	7–12 years	The child develops conservation concepts, can adopt the viewpoint of others, can classify objects in series, and shows comprehension of basic relational concepts (such as one object being larger or heavier than another).
Formal operational	12 years and above	Mature, adult thought emerges. Thinking seems to be characterized by deductive logic, consideration of various possibilities (mental trial and error), abstract thought, and the formation and testing of hypotheses.

"mammals without legs that live in the seas.") The ability to accommodate to novel stimuli advances as a result of maturation and experience.

Most of the time, newborn children assimilate environmental stimuli according to reflexive schemes, although adjusting the mouth to contain the nipple is a primitive kind of accommodation. Reflexive behavior, to Piaget, is not "true" intelligence. True intelligence involves adapting to the world through a smooth, fluid balancing of the processes of assimilation and accommodation. Let us now apply these concepts to the stages of cognitive development. We will see that infants in the sensorimotor stage mostly assimilate novel stimuli, but that children in more advanced stages of cognitive development balance assimilation and accommodation.

THE SENSORIMOTOR STAGE The newborn infant is capable of assimilating novel stimuli only to existing reflexes (or ready-made schemes) such as the rooting and sucking reflexes. But by the time an infant reaches the age of 1 month, it already shows purposeful behavior by repeating behavior patterns that are pleasurable, such as sucking its hand. During the first month or so, an infant apparently does not connect stimuli perceived through different senses. Reflexive turning toward sources of auditory and olfactory stimulation cannot be considered purposeful searching. But within the first few months the infant begins to coordinate vision with grasping so that it looks at what it is holding or touching.

A 3- or 4-month-old infant may be fascinated by its own hands and legs. It may become absorbed in watching itself open and close its fists. The infant becomes increasingly interested in acting on the environment to make interesting results (such as the sound of a rattle) last longer or occur again. Behavior becomes increasingly intentional and purposeful. Between 4 and 8 months of age, the infant explores cause-and-effect relationships such as the thump that can be made by tossing an object or the way kicking can cause a hanging toy to bounce.

Prior to the age of 6 months or so, out of sight is literally out of mind. Objects are not yet represented mentally. For this reason, as you can see in Figure CD.4, a child makes no effort to search for an object that has been removed or placed behind a screen. By the age of 8 to 12 months, however, infants realize that objects removed from sight still exist, and

FIGURE CD.4

OBJECT PERMANENCE.

To the infant at the top, who is in the early part of the sensorimotor stage, out of sight is truly out of mind. Once a sheet of paper is placed between the infant and the toy elephant, the infant loses all interest in it. The toy is apparently not yet mentally represented. The photos on the bottom shows a child later in the sensorimotor stage. This child does mentally represent objects and pushes through a towel to reach one that has been screened from sight.

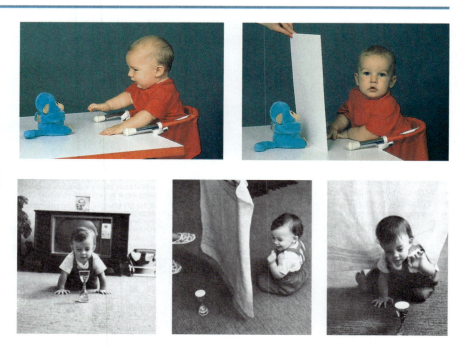

attempt to find them. In this way, they show what is known as **object permanence,** thereby making it possible to play peek-a-boo.

Between 1 and 2 years of age, children begin to show interest in how things are constructed. It may be why they persistently touch and finger their parents' faces and their own. Toward the end of the second year, children begin to engage in mental trial and error before they try out overt behaviors. For instance, when they look for an object you have removed, they no longer begin their search in the last place they saw it. Rather, they may follow you, assuming that you are carrying the object even though it is not visible. It is as though they are anticipating failure in searching for the object in the place where they last saw it.

Because the first stage of development is dominated by learning to coordinate perception of the self and of the environment with motor (muscular) activity, Piaget termed it the **sensorimotor stage.** This stage comes to a close with the acquisition of the basics of language at about age 2.

THE PREOPERATIONAL STAGE The **preoperational stage** is characterized by the use of words and symbols to represent objects and relationships among them. But be warned—any resemblance between the logic of children between the ages of 2 and 7 and your own logic very often is purely coincidental. Children may use the same words that adults do, but this does not mean that their views of the world are similar to adults'. A major limit on preoperational children's thinking is that it tends to be one dimensional—to focus on one aspect of a problem or situation at a time.

One consequence of one-dimensional thinking is **egocentrism.** Preoperational children cannot understand that other people do not see things the same way they do. When Allyn was 2½, I asked her to tell me about a trip to the store with her mother. "You tell me," she replied. Upon questioning, it seemed she did not understand that I could not see the world through her eyes.

To egocentric preoperational children, all the world's a stage that has been erected to meet their needs and amuse them. When asked, "Why does the sun shine?" they may say, "To keep me warm." If asked, "Why is the sky blue?" they may respond, "'Cause blue's my favorite color." Preoperational children also show **animism.** They attribute life and consciousness to physical objects like the sun and the moon. They also show **artificialism.** They believe that environmental events like rain and thunder are human inventions. Asked why the sky is blue, 4-year-olds may answer, "'Cause Mommy painted it." Examples of egocentrism, animism, and artificialism are shown in Table CD.3.

To gain further insight into preoperational thinking, consider these problems:

1. Imagine that you pour water from a tall, thin glass into a low, wide glass. Now, does the low, wide glass contain more, less, or the same amount of water that was in the tall, thin glass? I won't keep you in suspense. If you said the same amount of water (with possible minor exceptions for spillage and evaporation), you were correct. Now that you're on a roll, go on to the next problem.

2. If you flatten a ball of clay into a pancake, do you wind up with more, less, or the same amount of clay? If you said the same amount of clay, you are correct once more.

To arrive at the correct answers to these questions, you must understand the law of **conservation.** This law holds that basic properties of substances such as mass, weight, and volume remain the same—that is, are *conserved*—when you change superficial properties such as their shape or arrangement.

TRUTH OR FICTION REVISITED
It is true that 4-year-old children may believe the sun shines in order to keep them warm. Such egocentric thinking is an example of preoperational thinking.

OBJECT PERMANENCE Recognition that objects removed from sight still exist, as demonstrated in young children by continued pursuit.

SENSORIMOTOR STAGE The first of Piaget's stages of cognitive development, characterized by coordination of sensory information and motor activity, early exploration of the environment, and lack of language.

PREOPERATIONAL STAGE The second of Piaget's stages, characterized by illogical use of words and symbols, spotty logic, and egocentrism.

EGOCENTRIC According to Piaget, assuming that others view the world as one does oneself.

ANIMISM The belief that inanimate objects move because of will or spirit.

ARTIFICIALISM The belief that natural objects have been created by human beings.

CONSERVATION According to Piaget, recognition that basic properties of substances such as weight and mass remain the same when superficial features change.

TABLE CD.3

EXAMPLES OF PREOPERATIONAL THOUGHT

TYPE OF THOUGHT	SAMPLE QUESTIONS	TYPICAL ANSWERS
Egocentrism	Why does it get dark out? Why does the sun shine? Why is there snow? Why is grass green? What are TV sets for?	So I can go to sleep. To keep me warm. For me to play in. Because that's my favorite color. To watch my favorite shows and cartoons.
Animism (attributing life and consciousness to physical objects)	Why do trees have leaves? Why do stars twinkle? Why does the sun move in the sky? Where do boats go at night?	To keep them warm. Because they're happy and cheerful. To follow children and hear what they say. They sleep like we do.
Artificialism (assuming that environmental events are human inventions)	What makes it rain? Why is the sky blue? What is the wind? What causes thunder? How does a baby get in Mommy's tummy?	Someone emptying a watering can. Somebody painted it. A man blowing. A man grumbling. Just make it first. (How?) You put some eyes on it, then put on the head.

Conservation requires the ability to think about, or **center** on, two aspects of a situation at once, such as height and width. Conserving the mass, weight, or volume of a substance requires the recognition that a change in one dimension can compensate for a change in another. But the preoperational boy in Figure CD.5 focuses on only one dimension at a time. First he is shown two tall, thin glasses of water and agrees that they contain the same amount of water. Then, while he watches, water is poured from a tall glass into a squat glass. Now he is asked which glass contains more water. After mulling over the problem, he points to the tall glass. Why? Because when he looks at the glasses he is "overwhelmed" by the fact that the thinner glass is taller. The preoperational child focuses on the most apparent dimension of the situation—in this case, the greater height of the thinner glass. He does not realize that the increased width of the squat glass compensates for the decreased height. By the way, if you ask him whether any water has been added or taken away in the pouring process, he readily says no. But if you then repeat the question about which glass contains *more* water, he again points to the taller glass.

If all this sounds rather illogical, that is because it is illogical—or, in Piaget's terms, preoperational.

After you have tried the experiment with the water, try the following. Make two rows of five pennies each. In the first row, place the pennies about half an inch apart. In the second row, place the pennies 2 to 3 inches apart. Ask a 4- to 5-year-old child which row has more pennies. What do you think the child will say? Why?

Piaget (1997) found that the moral judgment of preoperational children is also one dimensional. Five-year-olds are slaves to rules and authority. When you ask them why something should be done in a certain way, they may insist, "Because that's the way to do it!" or "Because my Mommy says so!" Right is right and wrong is wrong. Why? "Because!"— that's why.

According to most older children and adults, an act is a crime only when there is criminal intent. Accidents may be hurtful, but the perpetrators are usually seen as blameless. But in the court of the one-dimensional, preoperational child, there is **objective responsibility.** People are sentenced (and harshly!) on the basis of the amount of damage they have done, not their motives or intentions.

CENTER According to Piaget, to focus one's attention.

OBJECTIVE RESPONSIBILITY According to Piaget, the assignment of blame according to the amount of damage done rather than the motives of the actor.

To demonstrate objective responsibility, Piaget would tell children stories and ask them which character was naughtier and why. John, for instance, accidentally breaks 15 cups when he opens a door. Henry breaks 1 cup when he sneaks into a kitchen cabinet to find forbidden jam. The preoperational child usually judges John to be naughtier. Why? Because he broke more cups.

THE CONCRETE-OPERATIONAL STAGE By about age 7, the typical child is entering the stage of **concrete operations.** In this stage, which lasts until about age 12, children show the beginnings of the capacity for adult logic. However, their logical thoughts, or *operations,* generally involve tangible objects rather than abstract ideas. Concrete operational children are capable of **decentration;** they can center on two dimensions of a problem at once. This attainment has implications for moral judgments, conservation, and other intellectual undertakings.

Children now become **subjective** in their moral judgments. When assigning guilt, they center on the motives of wrongdoers as well as on the amount of damage done. Concrete-operational children judge Henry more harshly than John because John's misdeed was an accident.

Concrete-operational children understand the laws of conservation. The boy in Figure CD.5, now a few years older, would say that the squat glass still contains the same amount of water. If asked why, he might reply, "Because you can pour it back into the other one." Such an answer also suggests awareness of the concept of **reversibility**—the recognition that many processes can be reversed or undone so that things are restored to their previous condition. Centering simultaneously on the height and the width of the glasses, the boy recognizes that the loss in height compensates for the gain in width.

Concrete-operational children can conserve *number* as well as weight and mass. They recognize that the number of pennies in each of the rows described earlier is the same, even though one row may be spread out to look longer than the other.

Children in this stage are less egocentric. They are able to take on the roles of others and to view the world, and themselves, from other people's perspectives. They recognize that people see things in different ways because of different situations and different sets of values.

During the concrete-operational stage, children's own sets of values begin to emerge and acquire stability. Children come to understand that feelings of love between them and their parents can endure even when someone feels angry or disappointed at a particular moment.

We discuss the formal-operational stage and evaluate Piaget's theory in the section on adolescence.

Language Development

Language is the communication of thoughts and feelings through symbols that are arranged according to rules of grammar. Language makes it possible for one person to communicate knowledge to another and for one generation to record information for another. Language allows people to learn more than they could from direct experience. It enables parents to give children advice, which now and then they heed. Language also provides many of the basic units of thinking, which is at the core of cognition.

Piaget theorized that children's cognitive development follows a specific sequence of steps. Such sequencing also applies to language development, beginning with the *prelinguistic* vocalizations of crying, cooing, and babbling. These sounds are not symbols. That is, they do not represent object or events. Therefore, they are *pre*linguistic, not linguistic.

FIGURE CD.5
CONSERVATION.
The boy in these photographs agreed that the amount of water in two identical containers is equal. He then watched as water from one container was poured into a tall, thin container. In the top photograph, he is examining one of the original containers and the new container. When asked whether he thinks the amounts of water in the two containers are now the same, he says no. Apparently, he is impressed by the height of the new container, and, prior to the development of conservation, he focuses on only one dimension of the situation at a time—in this case, the height of the new container.

CONCRETE-OPERATIONAL STAGE Piaget's third stage, characterized by logical thought concerning tangible objects, conservation, and subjective morality.

DECENTRATION Simultaneous focusing on more than one dimension of a problem, so that flexible, reversible thought becomes possible.

SUBJECTIVE MORAL JUDGMENT According to Piaget, moral judgments based on the motives of the perpetrator.

REVERSIBILITY According to Piaget, recognition that processes can be undone, that things can be made as they were.

As parents are well aware, newborn children have one inborn, highly effective form of verbal expression: crying—and more crying. During the second month, babies begin *cooing*. Babies use their tongues when they coo, so coos are more articulated than cries. Coos are often vowel-like and resemble "oohs" and "ahs." Cooing appears to be linked to feelings of pleasure. Babies do not coo when they are hungry, tired, or in pain. Parents soon learn that different cries and coos can indicate different things: hunger, gas pains, or pleasure at being held or rocked.

By the fifth or sixth month, children begin to *babble*. Babbling sort of sounds like speech. Children babble sounds that occur in many languages, including the throaty German *ch*, the clicks of certain African languages, and rolling *r*'s. In babbling, babies frequently combine consonants and vowels, as in "ba," "ga," and, sometimes, the much valued "dada." "Dada" at first is purely coincidental (sorry, Dads), despite the family's delight over its appearance.

Babbling, like crying and cooing, is inborn. Children from cultures whose languages sound very different all seem to babble the same sounds, including many they could not have heard (Gleason & Ratner, 1993). But children single out the sounds used in the home within a few months. By the age of 9 or 10 months they repeat them regularly and foreign sounds begin to drop out.

Babbling, like crying and cooing, is prelinguistic. Yet infants usually understand much of what others are saying well before they utter their first words. Understanding precedes the production of language, and infants show what they understand by their actions.

PATTERNS OF DEVELOPMENT Ah, that long-awaited first word! What a thrill! What a milestone! Children tend to utter their first word at about 1 year of age, but many parents miss it, often because it is not pronounced clearly or because pronunciation varies from one usage to the next. *Ball* may be pronounced "ba," "bee," or even "pah." The majority of an infant's early words are names of things (Nelson et al., 1993).

The growth of vocabulary is slow at first. It may take children 3 to 4 months to achieve a 10-word vocabulary after they have spoken their first word (Nelson, 1973). By about 18 months, children are producing nearly two dozen words. Reading to children increases their vocabulary, so parents do well to stock up on storybooks (Arnold et al., 1994; Robbins & Ehri, 1994).

Children try to talk about more objects than they have words for. As a result they often extend use of a word to refer to other things and actions for which they do not yet have words. This phenomenon is termed **overextension.** At some point, for example, many children refer to horses as *doggies*. At age 6, my daughter Allyn counted by tens as follows: sixty, seventy, eighty, ninety, *tenty*.

DEVELOPMENT OF GRAMMAR Children's first linguistic utterances are single words, but they may express complex meanings. When they do, they are called **holophrases.** For example, *mama* may be used by the child to signify meanings as varied as "There goes Mama," "Come here, Mama," and "You are my Mama." Similarly, *poo-cat* can signify "There is a pussycat," "That stuffed animal looks just like my pussycat," or "I want you to give me my pussycat right now!" Most children readily teach their parents what they intend by augmenting their holophrases with gestures, intonations, and reinforcers. That is, they act delighted when parents do as requested and howl when they do not.

Toward the end of the second year, children begin to speak two-word sentences. These sentences are termed *telegraphic speech* because they resemble telegrams. Telegrams cut out the "unnecessary" words. "Home

OVEREXTENSION Overgeneralizing the use of words to objects and situations to which they do not apply—a normal characteristic of the speech of young children.

HOLOPHRASE A single word used to express complex meanings.

Tuesday" might stand for "I expect to be home on Tuesday." Similarly, only essential words are used in children's telegraphic speech—in particular, nouns, verbs, and some modifiers. When a child says "That ball," the words *is* and *a* are implied.

Two-word utterances seem to appear at about the same time in the development of all languages (Slobin, 1983). Although two-word utterances are brief, they show understanding of grammar. The child says, "Sit chair" to tell a parent to sit in a chair, not "Chair sit." The child says, " My shoe," not "Shoe my," to show possession. "Mommy go" means Mommy is leaving. "Go Mommy" expresses the wish for Mommy to go away. (For this reason, "Go Mommy" is not heard often.)

There are different kinds of two-word utterances. Some, for example, contain nouns or pronouns and verbs ("Daddy sit"). Others contain verbs and objects ("Hit ball"). It is of interest that the sequence of emergence of the various kinds of two-word utterances is apparently the same in all languages—languages diverse as English, Luo (an African tongue), German, Russian, and Turkish (Slobin, 1983). The invariance of this sequence has implications for theories of language development, as we see later in the chapter.

Between the ages of 2 and 3, children's sentence structure usually expands to include the missing words in telegraphic speech. Children add articles (*a, an, the*), conjunctions (*and, but, or*), possessive and demonstrative adjectives (*your, her, that*), pronouns (*she, him, one*), and prepositions (*in, on, over, around, under, through*) to their utterances. Their grasp of grammar is shown in linguistic oddities such as *your one* instead of simply *yours,* and *his one* instead of *his.*

One intriguing language development is **overregularization.** To understand children's use of overregularization, consider the formation of the past tense and of plurals in English. We add *d* or *ed* to make the past tense of regular verbs and *s* or *z* sounds to make regular nouns plural. Thus *walk* becomes *walked* and *look* becomes *looked. Pussycat* becomes *pussycats* and *doggy* becomes *doggies.* There are also irregular verbs and nouns. For example, *see* becomes *saw, sit* becomes *sat,* and *go* becomes *went. Sheep* remains *sheep* (plural) and *child* becomes *children.*

At first, children learn a small number of these irregular verbs by imitating their parents. Two-year-olds tend to form them correctly—at first! Then they become aware of the grammatical rules for forming the past tense and plurals. As a result, they tend to make charming errors (Pinker, 1994). Some 3- to 5-year-olds, for example, are more likely to say "I seed it" than "I saw it" and to say "Mommy sitted down" than " Mommy sat down." They are likely to talk about the "gooses" and "sheeps" they "seed" on the farm and about all the "childs" they ran into at the playground. This tendency to regularize the irregular is what is meant by overregularization.

Some parents recognize that at one point their children were forming the past tense of irregular verbs correctly and that they later began to make errors. The thing to remember is that overregularization reflects knowledge of grammar, not faulty language development. In another year or two, *mouses* will be boringly transformed into *mice,* and Mommy will no longer have *sitted* down. Parents might as well enjoy overregularization while they can.

As language ability develops beyond the third year, children show increasing facility in their use of pronouns (such as *it* and *she*) and prepositions (such as *in, before,* or *on*), which represent physical or time relationships among objects and events. Children's first questions are characterized by a rising pitch (which signifies a question mark) at the end. One or two words are also used to represent complete sentences. "More milky?" for example, can be translated into "May I have more milk?" or "Would you like more milk?" or "Is there more milk?"—depending on the context.

OVERREGULARIZATION The application of regular grammatical rules for forming inflections (e.g., past tense and plurals) to irregular verbs and nouns.

Why questions usually appear after age 2. Consistent with the child's general cognitive development, certain *wh* questions (*what, who,* and *where*) appear earlier than others (*why, when, which,* and *how*) (Bloom et al., 1982). *Why* is usually too philosophical for the 2-year-old, and *how* is too involved. Two-year-olds are also likely to be now oriented, so *when* is of less than immediate concern. By the fourth year, however, most children are asking *why, when,* and *how* questions—and frequently their parents despair as to how to answer them.

By the fourth year, children are also taking turns talking and engaging in lengthy conversations. By the age of 6, their vocabularies have expanded to 10, 000 words, give or take a few thousand. By age 7 to 9, most children realize that words can have more than one meaning, and they are entertained by riddles and jokes that require some sophistication with language ("What's black and white, but read all over?").

Between the elementary school and high school years, language becomes more complex and vocabulary continues to grow rapidly. Vocabulary, in fact, can grow for a lifetime, especially in one's fields of specialization and interest.

TRUTH OR FICTION REVISITED
It is true that the majority of people around the world speak at least two languages. Bilingualism thus is the normal state of affairs, not merely an issue of concern to immigrants.

BILINGUALISM AND COGNITIVE DEVELOPMENT Most people throughout the world speak two or more languages. Most countries have minority populations whose languages differ from the national tongue. Nearly all Europeans are taught English and the languages of neighboring nations. Consider the Netherlands. Dutch is the native tongue, but all children are also taught French, German, and English and are expected to become fluent in all of them.

For more than 30 million people in the United States, English is a second language (Barringer, 1993). Spanish, French, Chinese, Russian, or Arabic is spoken in the home and, perhaps, the neighborhood.

Early in the century it was widely believed that children reared in bilingual homes were retarded in their cognitive development. The theory was that cognitive capacity is limited, so people who store two linguistic systems are crowding their mental abilities (Lambert, 1990). However, the U.S. Bureau of the Census reports that more than 75% of Americans who first spoke another language in the home also speak English "well" or "very well" (Barringer, 1993). Moreover, a careful analysis of older studies in bilingualism shows that the bilingual children observed often lived in families with low socioeconomic status and little education. Yet these bilingual children were compared to middle-class monolingual children. In addition, achievement and intelligence tests were conducted in the language of the dominant culture, which was the second language of the bilingual child (Reynolds, 1991). Lack of education and inadequate testing methods, rather than bilingualism per se, accounted for the apparent differences in cognitive development.

Today most linguists consider it advantageous for children to be bilingual. For one thing, knowledge of more than one language expands children's cognitive understanding of different cultures and broadens their perspectives (Cavaliere, 1996). For example, bilingual children are more likely to understand that the symbols used in language are arbitrary. Monolingual children are more likely to think erroneously that the word *dog* is somehow intertwined with the nature of the beast. Bilingual children therefore have somewhat more cognitive flexibility. Second, learning a second language does not crowd children's available "cognitive space." Instead, learning a second language has been shown to increase children's expertise in their first (native) language. For example, research evidence reveals that learning French enhances knowledge of the structure of English among Canadian children whose native language is English (Lambert et al., 1991). It now seems clear that bilingualism enhances rather than detracts from children's cognitive development.

EBONICS

The term *Ebonics* is derived from the words *ebony* and *phonics.* It was coined by the African American psychologist Robert Williams (Burnette, 1997). Ebonics was previously called Black English or Black Dialect (Pinker, 1994). Williams explains that a group of African American scholars convened "to name our language, which had always been named by White scholars in the past" (Burnette, 1997, p. 12).

According to linguists, Ebonics is rooted in the remnants of the West African dialects used by slaves. It reflects attempts by the slaves, who were denied formal education, to imitate the speech of the dominant White culture. Some observers believe that Ebonics uses verbs haphazardly, downgrading standard English. As a result, some school systems react to the concept of Ebonics with contempt—which is hurtful to the child who speaks Ebonics. Other observers say that Ebonics has different grammatical rules than standard English, but that the rules are consistent and allow for complex thought (Pinker, 1994). In 1996, the Oakland, California, school board recognized Ebonics as the primary language of African American students, just as Spanish had been recognized as the primary language of Hispanic American students. "I was honored," said Williams. "And truthfully, I was shocked. It was like the truth that had been covered up in the ground for so long just exploded one day" (Burnette, 1997, p. 12).

ROBERT WILLIAMS

"TO BE OR NOT TO BE": USE OF VERBS IN EBONICS

There are differences between Ebonics and standard English in the use of verbs. For example, the Ebonics usage "She-ah touch us" corresponds to the standard English "She will touch us." The Ebonics "He be gone" is the equivalent of the standard English "He has been gone for a long while." "He gone" is the same as "He is not here right now" in standard English.

Consider the rules in Ebonics that govern the use of the verb *to be.* In standard English, *be* is part of the infinitive form of the verb and used to form the future tense, as in "I'll be angry tomorrow." Thus "I *be* angry" is incorrect. But in Ebonics *be* refers to a continuing state of being. The Ebonics sentence "I be angry" is the same as the standard English "I have been angry for a while" and is grammatically correct.

Ebonics leaves out *to be* in cases in which standard English would use a contraction. For example, the standard "She's the one I'm talking about" could be "*She* the one *I* talking about" in Ebonics. Ebonics also often drops *ed* from the past tense and lacks the possessive *'s.*

"NOT TO BE OR NOT TO BE NOTHING": NEGATION IN EBONICS

Consider the sentence "I don't want no trouble," which is, of course, commendable. Middle-class White children would be corrected for using double negation (do*n't* along with *no*) and would be encouraged to say "I don't want *any* trouble." Yet double negation is acceptable in Ebonics (Pinker, 1994). Nevertheless, many teachers who use standard English have demeaned African American children who speak this way.

Some African American children are bicultural and bilingual. They function competently within the dominant culture in the United States and among groups of people from their own ethnic background. They use standard English in a conference with their teacher or in a job interview, but switch to Ebonics among their friends. Other children cannot switch back and forth. The decision by the Oakland school board was intended in part to help children maintain their self-esteem and stay in school. ■

LAWRENCE KOHLBERG

Lawrence Kohlberg's Theory of Moral Development

Another aspect of cognitive development has to do with the ways in which people arrive at judgments of right or wrong. Cognitive-developmental theorist Lawrence Kohlberg (1981) used the following tale in his research into children's moral reasoning. Before going on, why not read the tale yourself and answer the questions that follow.

> In Europe a woman was near death from a special kind of cancer. There was one drug that the doctors thought might save her. It was a form of radium that a druggist in the same town had recently discovered. The drug was expensive to make, but the druggist was charging ten times what the drug cost him to make. He paid $200 for the radium and charged $2,000 for a small dose of the drug. The sick woman's husband, Heinz, went to everyone he knew to borrow the money, but he could only get together about $1,000, which was half of what it cost. He told the druggist that his wife was dying and asked him to sell it cheaper or let him pay later. But the druggist said: "No, I discovered the drug and I'm going to make money from it." So Heinz got desperate and broke into the man's store to steal the drug for his wife. (Kohlberg, 1969)

What do you think? Should Heinz have tried to steal the drug? Was he right or wrong? The answer is more complicated than a simple yes or no. Heinz is caught up in a moral dilemma in which a legal or social rule (in this case, the law forbidding stealing) is pitted against a strong human need (his desire to save his wife). According to Kohlberg's theory, children and adults arrive at yes or no answers for different reasons. These reasons can be classified according to the level of moral development they reflect.

THE STORY OF LAWRENCE KOHLBERG Kohlberg's own life story sheds light on his views on moral development. In 1987, his car was found parked beside Boston Harbor. Three months later his body washed up onto the shore. He had discussed the moral dilemma posed by suicide with a friend, and perhaps Lawrence Kohlberg had taken his own life. He was suffering from a painful parasitic intestinal disease that he had acquired 40 years earlier while smuggling Jewish refugees from Europe past the British blockade into Palestine (now Israel). There had also been recent disappointments in his work. Nevertheless, Carol Gilligan wrote that he had "almost singlehanded established moral development as a central concern of developmental psychology" (Hunt, 1993, p. 381).

Kohlberg was born in 1927 into a wealthy family in suburban New York. He graduated from Phillips Academy as World War II came to an end. Rather than go on immediately to college, he became a merchant mariner and helped save people who had been displaced by the war. He was captured and imprisoned on the Mediterranean island of Cyprus. He did escape, but not before acquiring the disease that would bring him a lifetime of pain. Between high school and college, Kohlberg had already decided that one must attend more to one's own conscience than to law and authority figures in determining what was right and wrong.

As a stage theorist, Kohlberg believed that making moral judgments according to one's own conscience reflected a certain stage of moral development. He believed the stages of moral reasoning follow a specific sequence (see Table CD.4). Children progress at different rates, and not all children (or adults) reach the highest stage. But the sequence is always the same: Children must go through stage 1 before they enter stage 2, and so on. According to Kohlberg, there are three levels of moral development and two stages within each level.

When it comes to the dilemma of Heinz, Kohlberg believed that people could justify Heinz's stealing of the drug or his decision not to steal it by the reasoning of any level or stage of moral development. In other words, Kohlberg was not as interested in the eventual "yes" or "no" as he was in *how a person reasoned* to arrive at a yes or no answer.

THE PRECONVENTIONAL LEVEL   The **preconventional level** applies to most children through about the age of 9. Children at this level base their moral judgments on the consequences of behavior. For instance, stage 1 is oriented toward obedience and punishment. Good behavior is obedient and allows one to avoid punishment. However, a child in stage 1 can decide that Heinz should or should not steal the drug, as shown in Table CD.4.

In stage 2, good behavior allows people to satisfy their needs and those of others. (Heinz's wife needs the drug; therefore, stealing the drug—the only way of obtaining it—is not wrong.)

PRECONVENTIONAL LEVEL According to Kohlberg, a period during which moral judgments are based largely on expectation of rewards or punishments.

TABLE CD.4

KOHLBERG'S LEVELS AND STAGES OF MORAL DEVELOPMENT

STAGE OF DEVELOPMENT	EXAMPLES OF MORAL REASONING THAT SUPPORT HEINZ'S STEALING THE DRUG	EXAMPLES OF MORAL REASONING THAT OPPOSE HEINZ'S STEALING THE DRUG
LEVEL I: PRECONVENTIONAL		
Stage 1: Judgments guided by obedience and the prospect of punishment (the consequences of the behavior)	It isn't wrong to take the drug. Heinz did try to pay the druggist for it, and it's only worth $200, not $2,000.	Taking things without paying is wrong because it's against the law. Heinz will get caught and go to jail.
Stage 2: Naively egoistic, instrumental orientation (Things are right when they satisfy people's needs.)	Heinz ought to take the drug because his wife really needs it. He can always pay the druggist back.	Heinz ought to take the drug because his wife really needs it. He can always pay the druggist back.
LEVEL II: CONVENTIONAL		
Stage 3: Good boy orientation (Moral behavior helps others and is socially approved.)	Stealing is a crime, so it's bad, but Heinz should take the drug to save his wife or else people would blame him for letting her die.	Stealing is a crime. Heinz shouldn't just take the drug because his family will be dishonored and they will blame him.
Stage 4: Law-and-order orientation (Moral behavior is doing one's duty and showing respect for authority.)	Heinz must take the drug to do his duty to save his wife. Eventually, he has to pay the druggist for it, however.	If everyone took the law into their own hands, civilization would fall apart, so Heinz shouldn't steal the drug.
LEVEL III: POSTCONVENTIONAL		
Stage 5: Contractual, legalistic orientation (One must weigh pressing human needs against society's need to maintain social order.)	This thing is complicated because society has a right to maintain law and order, but Heinz has to take the drug to save his wife.	I can see why Heinz feels he has to take the drug, but laws exist for the benefit of society as a whole and can't simply be cast aside.
Stage 6: Universal ethical principles orientation (People must follow universal ethical principles and their own conscience, even if it means breaking the law.)	In this case, the law comes into conflict with the principle of the sanctity of human life. Heinz must take the drug because his wife's life is more important than the law.	If Heinz truly believes that stealing the drug is worse than letting his wife die, he should not take it. People have to make sacrifices to do what they think is right.

THE CONVENTIONAL LEVEL In the **conventional level** of moral reasoning, right and wrong are judged by conformity to conventional (familial, religious, societal) standards of right and wrong. According to the stage 3, "good-boy orientation," moral behavior is that which meets the needs and expectations of others. Moral behavior is what is "normal"—what the majority does. (Heinz should steal the drug because that is what a "good husband" would do. It is "natural" or "normal" to try to help one's wife. *Or,* Heinz should *not* steal the drug because "good people do not steal.")

In stage 4, moral judgments are based on rules that maintain the social order. Showing respect for authority and doing one's duty are valued highly. (Heinz *must* steal the drug; it would be his fault if he let his wife die. He would pay the druggist later, when he had the money.) Many people do not mature beyond the conventional level.

THE POSTCONVENTIONAL LEVEL Postconventional moral reasoning is more complex and focuses on dilemmas in which individual needs are pitted against the need to maintain the social order and on personal conscience. We discuss the postconventional level of moral reasoning in the section on adolescence.

SOCIAL AND PERSONALITY DEVELOPMENT

Social relationships are crucial to us as children. When we are infants, our very survival depends on them. Later in life, they contribute to our feelings of happiness and satisfaction. In this section we discuss many aspects of social development, including Erikson's theory of psychosocial development, attachment, styles of parenting, day care, and child abuse.

Erik Erikson's Stages of Psychosocial Development

According to Erik Erikson, we undergo several stages of psychosocial development (see Table CD.5). During his first stage, **trust versus mistrust,** we depend on our primary caregivers (usually our parents) and come to expect that our environments will—or will not—meet our needs. During early childhood and the preschool years, we begin to explore the environment more actively and try new things. At this time, our relationships with our parents and friends can encourage us to develop **autonomy** (self-direction) and initiative, or feelings of shame and guilt. During the elementary school years, friends and teachers take on more importance, encouraging us to become industrious or to develop feelings of inferiority.

Attachment: Ties That Bind

At the age of 2, my daughter Allyn almost succeeded in preventing me from finishing writing a book. When I locked myself into my study, she positioned herself outside the door and called, "Daddy, oh Daddy." At other times, she would bang on the door or cry outside. When I would give in (several times a day) and open the door, she would run in and say, "I want you to pick up me" and hold out her arms or climb into my lap. Although we were separate human beings, it was as though she were very much *attached* to me.

Psychologist Mary D. Salter Ainsworth defines **attachment** as an emotional tie formed between one animal or person and another specific individual. Attachment keeps organisms together—it is vital to the survival of the infant—and it tends to endure.

CONVENTIONAL LEVEL According to Kohlberg, a period during which moral judgments largely reflect social conventions. A "law and order" approach to morality.

TRUST VERSUS MISTRUST Erikson's first stage of psychosexual development, during which children do—or do not—come to trust that primary caregivers and the environment will meet their needs.

AUTONOMY Self-direction.

ATTACHMENT The enduring affectional tie that binds one person to another.

TABLE CD.5

ERIKSON'S STAGES OF PSYCHOSOCIAL DEVELOPMENT

TIME PERIOD	LIFE CRISIS	THE DEVELOPMENTAL TASK
Infancy (0–1)	Trust versus mistrust	Coming to trust the mother and the environment—to associate surroundings with feelings of inner goodness
Early childhood (1–3)	Autonomy versus shame and doubt	Developing the wish to make choices and the self-control to exercise choice
Preschool years (4–5)	Initiative versus guilt	Adding planning and "attacking" to choice, becoming active and on the move
Elementary school years (6–12)	Industry versus inferiority	Becoming eagerly absorbed in skills, tasks, and productivity; mastering the fundamentals of technology
Adolescence	Identity versus role diffusion	Connecting skills and social roles to formation of career objectives; developing a sense of who one is and what one stands for
Young adulthood	Intimacy versus isolation	Committing the self to another; engaging in sexual love
Middle adulthood	Generativity versus stagnation	Needing to be needed; guiding and encouraging the younger generation; being creative
Late adulthood	Integrity versus despair	Accepting the time and place of one's life cycle; achieving wisdom and dignity

Source: Erikson 1963, pp. 247–269.

The behaviors that define attachment include (1) attempts to maintain contact or nearness, and (2) shows of anxiety when separated. Babies and children try to maintain contact with caregivers to whom they are attached. They engage in eye contact, pull and tug at them, ask to be picked up, and may even jump in front of them in such a way that they will be "run over" if they are not picked up!

THE STRANGE SITUATION AND PATTERNS OF ATTACHMENT

The ways in which infants behave in strange situations are connected with their bonds of attachment with their caregivers. Given this fact, Ainsworth and her colleagues (1978) innovated the *strange situation method* to measure attachment in infants. The method involves a series of separations and reunions with a caregiver (usually the mother) and a stranger. Infants are led through episodes involving the mother and a stranger in a laboratory room. For example, the mother carries the infant into the room and puts him or her down. A stranger enters and talks with the mother. The stranger then approaches the infant with a toy and the mother leaves the room. The mother and stranger take turns interacting with the infant in the room, and the infant's behavior is observed in each case.

Using the strange situation, Ainsworth and her colleagues (1978) identified three major types of attachment: secure attachment and two types of insecure attachment:

1. *Secure attachment.* Securely attached infants mildly protest their mother's departure, seek interaction upon reunion, and are readily comforted by her.

2. *Avoidant attachment.* Infants who show avoidant attachment are least distressed by their mother's departure. They play by themselves without fuss and ignore their mothers when they return.

3. *Ambivalent/resistant attachment.* Infants with ambivalent/resistant attachment are the most emotional. They show severe signs of distress when their mother leaves and show ambivalence upon

ALLYN.
At the age of 2 the author's daughter Allyn nearly succeeded in preventing the publication of a book by continually pulling him away from the computer when he was at work. Because of their mutual attachment, separation was painful.

ATTACHMENT.
Feelings of attachment bind most parents closely to their children. According to Mary Ainsworth, attachment is an emotional bond between an individual and another specific individual. Secure attachment paves the way for healthy social development.

reunion by alternately clinging to and pushing their mother away when she returns.

Attachment is connected with the quality of care that infants receive. The parents of securely attached children are more likely to be affectionate and reliable caregivers (Cox et al., 1992; Isabella, 1993). There is also a wealth of research literature that speaks of the benefits of secure attachment. For example, securely attached children are happier, more sociable, and more cooperative than insecurely attached children (Belsky et al., 1991; Thompson, 1991a). Securely attached preschoolers have longer attention spans, are less impulsive, and are better at solving problems (Frankel & Bates, 1990; Lederberg & Mobley, 1990). At ages 5 and 6, securely attached children are liked better by their peers and teachers, are more competent, and have fewer behavior problems than insecurely attached children (Lyons-Ruth et al., 1993; Youngblade & Belsky, 1992).

Yet some research questions whether infant attachment as measured by means of the strange situation predicts adjustment later on. For example, Michael Lewis (1997) located 84 high school seniors who had been evaluated by the strange situation method at the age of 1. Extensive interviews showed that of the 49 who had been considered securely attached at the age of 1, 43% were currently maladjusted. Of the 35 who had been considered insecurely attached in infancy, only 26% were rated as currently maladjusted. Lewis (1998) suggests that childhood events such as accidents, parental divorce, and illness can be more powerful influences on adolescents' security than the quality of parenting during the first year. But most developmental psychologists continue to endorse the strange situation as a predictor of adjustment later in life (Blakeslee, 1998). For example, Alan Sroufe (1998) found that insecure attachment at the age of 1 year predicted psychological disorders at the age of 17.

STAGES OF ATTACHMENT Ainsworth also studied phases in the development of attachment. She and her colleagues observed infants in many societies, including infants in the African country of Uganda. She noted the efforts of infants to maintain contact with the mother, their protests when separated from her, and their use of her as a base for exploring their environment. At first, infants show **indiscriminate attachment.** That is, they prefer being held or being with someone to being alone, but they show no preferences for particular people. Specific attachment to the mother begins to develop at about 4 months of age and becomes intense by about 7 months of age. Fear of strangers, which develops in some but not all children, follows 1 or 2 months later.

From studies such as these, Ainsworth identified three stages of attachment:

1. The **initial-preattachment phase,** which lasts from birth to about 3 months and is characterized by indiscriminate attachment.

2. The **attachment-in-the-making phase,** which occurs at about 3 or 4 months and is characterized by preference for familiar figures.

3. The **clear-cut-attachment phase,** which occurs at about 6 or 7 months and is characterized by intensified dependence on the primary caregiver.

INDISCRIMINATE ATTACHMENT Showing attachment behaviors toward any person.

INITIAL-PREATTACHMENT PHASE The first phase in forming bonds of attachment, characterized by indiscriminate attachment.

ATTACHMENT-IN-THE-MAKING PHASE The second phase in forming bonds of attachment, characterized by preference for familiar figures.

CLEAR-CUT-ATTACHMENT PHASE The third phase in forming bonds of attachment, characterized by intensified dependence on the primary caregiver.

John Bowlby (1988), a colleague of Mary Ainsworth, believes that attachment is also characterized by fear of strangers ("stranger anxiety"). That is, at about 8 to 10 months of age, children may cry and cling to their parents when strangers try to befriend them. But not all children develop fear of strangers. It therefore does not seem necessary to include fear of strangers as an essential part of the process of attachment.

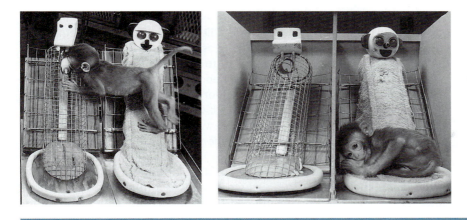

FIGURE CD.6
ATTACHMENT IN INFANT MONKEYS.
Although this rhesus monkey infant is fed by the wire mother, it spends most of its time clinging to the soft, cuddly terry-cloth mother. It knows where to get a meal, but contact comfort is apparently more important than food in the development of attachment in infant monkeys (and infant humans?).

THEORETICAL VIEWS OF ATTACHMENT Early in the century, behaviorists argued that attachment behaviors are learned through experience. Caregivers feed their infants and tend to their other physiological needs. Thus infants associate their caregivers with gratification of needs and learn to approach them to meet their needs. The feelings of gratification associated with the meeting of basic needs generalize into feelings of security when the caregiver is present.

Classic research by psychologist Harry F. Harlow suggests that skin contact may be more important than learning experiences. Harlow had noted that infant rhesus monkeys reared without mothers or companions became attached to pieces of cloth in their cages. They maintained contact with them and showed distress when separated from them. Harlow conducted a series of experiments to find out why (Harlow, 1959).

In one study, Harlow placed infant rhesus monkeys in cages with two surrogate mothers, as shown in Figure CD.6. One mother was made of wire mesh from which a baby bottle was extended. The other surrogate mother was made of soft, cuddly terry cloth. The infant monkeys spent most of their time clinging to the cloth mother, even though "she" did not gratify their need for food. Harlow concluded that monkeys—and perhaps humans—have an inborn need for **contact comfort** that is as basic as the need for food. Gratification of the need for contact comfort, rather than food, might be why infant monkeys (and humans) cling to their mothers.

Harlow and Zimmerman (1959) found that a surrogate mother made of terry cloth could also serve as a comforting base from which an infant monkey could explore its environment. Toys such as stuffed bears (see Figure CD.7) and oversized wooden insects were placed in cages with infant rhesus monkeys and their surrogate mothers. When the infants were alone or had wire surrogate mothers for companions, they cowered in fear as long as the "bear monster" or "insect monster" was present. But when the terry-cloth mothers were present, the infants clung to them for a while and then explored the intruding "monster." With human infants, too, the bonds of mother-infant attachment appear to provide a secure base from which infants feel encouraged to express their curiosity.

Other researchers, such as ethologist Konrad Lorenz, note that for many animals, attachment is an instinct—an inborn **fixed-action pattern.** Attachment, like other instincts, is theorized to occur in the presence of a specific stimulus and during a **critical period** of life—that is, a period during which the animal is sensitive to the stimulus.

Some animals become attached to the first moving object they encounter. The unwritten rule seems to be, "If it moves, it must be Mother." It is as if the image of the moving object becomes "imprinted" on the young animal. The formation of an attachment in this manner is therefore called **imprinting.**

FIGURE CD.7
SECURITY.
With its terry-cloth surrogate mother nearby, this infant rhesus monkey apparently feels secure enough to explore the "bear monster" placed in its cage. But infants with wire surrogate mothers or no mothers at all cower in a corner when such monsters are introduced.

CONTACT COMFORT A hypothesized primary drive to seek physical comfort through contact with another.

FIXED-ACTION PATTERN An instinct; a stereotyped response to a stimulus shown by members of a given species.

CRITICAL PERIOD A period of time when a fixed action pattern can be elicited by a releasing stimulus.

IMPRINTING A process occurring during a critical period in the development of an organism, in which that organism responds to a stimulus in a manner that will afterward be difficult to modify.

FIGURE CD.8

IMPRINTING.

Quite a following? Konrad Lorenz may not look like Mommy to you, but the goslings in the photo became attached to him because he was the first moving object they perceived and followed. This type of attachment process is referred to as *imprinting.*

INSTRUMENTAL COMPETENCE Ability to manipulate one's environment to achieve one's goals.

AUTHORITATIVE PARENTS Parents who are strict and warm. Authoritative parents demand mature behavior but use reason rather than force in discipline.

AUTHORITARIAN PARENTS Parents who are rigid in their rules and who demand obedience for the sake of obedience.

Lorenz (1981) became well known when pictures of his "family" of goslings were made public (see Figure CD.8). How did Lorenz acquire his following? He was present when the goslings hatched and during their critical period, and he allowed them to follow him. The critical period for geese and some other animals is bounded, at the younger end, by the age at which they first walk and, at the older end, by the age at which they develop fear of strangers. The goslings followed Lorenz persistently, ran to him when they were frightened, honked with distress at his departure, and tried to overcome barriers between them. If you substitute crying for honking, it all sounds rather human.

Ainsworth and Bowlby (1991) consider attachment to be instinctive in humans. However, the process would not be quite the same as with ducks and geese. The upper limit for waterbirds is the age at which they develop fear of strangers, but not all children develop this fear. When children do develop fear of strangers, they do so at about 6 to 8 months of age—*prior to* independent locomotion, or crawling, which usually occurs 1 or 2 months later. Moreover, the critical period with humans would be quite extended.

Another issue in social and personality development is parenting styles. Parental behavior not only contributes to the development of attachment, but also to the development of self-esteem, self-reliance, achievement motivation, and competence.

Parenting Styles

Many psychologists have been concerned about the relationships between parenting styles and the personality development of the child. They have asked what types of parental behavior are connected with variables such as self-esteem, achievement motivation, and independence in children. Diana Baumrind and her colleagues (1973; Lamb & Baumrind, 1978) have been particularly interested in the connections between the ways parents behave and the development of **instrumental competence** in their children. (*Instrumental competence* refers to the ability to manipulate the environment to achieve one's goals.) Baumrind has largely focused on four aspects of parental behavior: (1) strictness; (2) demands for the child to achieve intellectual, emotional, and social maturity; (3) communication ability; and (4) warmth and involvement. The three most important parenting styles she labeled as *authoritative, authoritarian,* and *permissive* styles.

1. *Authoritative parents.* The parents of the most competent children rate high in all four areas of behavior (see Table CD.6). They are strict (restrictive) and demand mature behavior. However, they temper their strictness and demands with willingness to reason with their children, and with love and support. They expect a lot, but they explain why and offer help. Baumrind labeled these parents **authoritative parents** to suggest that they know what they want but are also loving and respectful toward their children.

2. *Authoritarian parents.* **Authoritarian parents** view obedience as a virtue to be pursued for its own sake. They have strict guidelines about what is right and wrong, and they demand that their children adhere to those guidelines. Both authoritative and authoritarian parents adhere to strict standards of conduct. However, authoritative parents explain their demands and are supportive, whereas authoritarian parents rely on force and communicate poorly with their children. Authoritarian parents do not respect their children's points of view, and they may be cold and rejecting. When their children ask them why they should behave in a certain way, authoritarian parents often answer, "Because I say so!"

TABLE CD.6

PARENTING STYLES

STYLE OF PARENTING	RESTRICTIVENESS	DEMANDS FOR MATURE BEHAVIOR	COMMUNICATION ABILITY	WARMTH AND SUPPORT
		PARENTAL BEHAVIOR		
Authoritarian	High (Use of force)	Moderate	Low	Low
Authoritative	High (Use of reasoning)	High	High	High
Permissive	Low (Easygoing)	Low	Low	High

Note: According to Baumrind, the children of authoritative parents are most competent. The children of permissive parents are the least mature.

3. *Permissive parents.* **Permissive parents** are generally easygoing with their children. As a result, the children do pretty much whatever they wish. Permissive parents are warm and supportive, but poor at communicating.

Research evidence shows that warmth is superior to coldness in rearing children. Children of warm parents are more likely to be socially and emotionally well adjusted and to internalize moral standards—that is, to develop a conscience (MacDonald, 1992; Miller et al., 1993).

Strictness also appears to pay off, provided it is tempered with reason and warmth. Children of authoritative parents have greater self-reliance, self-esteem, social competence, and achievement motivation than other children do (Baumrind, 1991; Putallaz & Hefflin, 1990). Children of authori*tarian* parents are often withdrawn or aggressive, and they usually do not do as well in school as children of authoritative parents (Olson et al., 1990; Westerman, 1990). Children of permissive parents seem to be the least mature. They are frequently impulsive, moody, and aggressive. In adolescence, lack of parental monitoring is often linked to delinquency and poor academic performance.

Let us now consider two other important areas that involve the connections between parental behavior and the social and personality development of children. The first of these, day care, considers what happens to young children's social and personality development when they spend their days in the care of people *other than* family members. The second of these, child abuse, considers the causes of child abuse and its effects on the development of the child.

Day Care

As we cross over into the new millennium, only a small percentage of U.S. families fit the traditional model in which the husband is the breadwinner and the wife is a full-time homemaker. Most mothers, including more than half of mothers of children younger than 1 year of age, work outside the home (U.S. Bureau of the Census, 1998). As a consequence, millions of American preschoolers are placed in day care. Parents and psychologists are concerned about what happens to children in day care. What, for example, are the effects of day care on cognitive development and social development?

In part, the answer depends on the quality of the day-care center. A large-scale study funded by the National Institute on Child Health and Human Development found that children in high-quality day care—for example, children who have learning resources, a low children-to-care-

TRUTH OR FICTION REVISITED
It is true that children with strict parents are most likely to be successful. This is especially so when the parents also reason with their children and are loving and supportive.

PERMISSIVE PARENTS Parents who impose few, if any, rules and who do not supervise their children closely.

DAY CARE.
Because most parents in the United States are in the work force, day care is a major influence on the lives of millions of children.

TRUTH OR FICTION REVISITED
It is true that children placed in day care are more aggressive than children cared for in the home. Perhaps they are so because they have become more independent.

giver ratio, and individual attention—did as well on cognitive and language tests as children who remained in the home with their mother (Azar, 1997). Children whose day-care providers spent time talking to them and asking them questions also achieved the highest scores on tests of cognitive and language ability. A Swedish study found that children in high-quality day care outperformed children who remained in the home on tests of math and language skills (Broberg et al., 1997).

Studies of the effects of day care on parent-child attachment are somewhat mixed. Children in full-time day care show less distress when their mothers leave them and are less likely to seek out their mother when they return. Some psychologists suggest that this distancing from the mother could signify insecure (avoidant) attachment (Belsky, 1990). Others suggest, however, that the children are adapting to repeated separations from, and reunions with, their mother (Field, 1991; Lamb et al., 1992; Thompson, 1991b).

Day care seems to have both positive and negative influences on children's social development. First, the positive: Children in day care are more likely to share their toys and to be independent, self-confident, and outgoing (Clarke-Stewart, 1991; Field, 1991). However, some studies have found that children in day care are less compliant and more aggressive than other children (Vandell & Corasaniti, 1990). Perhaps some children in day care do not receive the individual attention or resources they need. When placed in a competitive situation, they become more aggressive in an attempt to meet their needs. But Clarke-Stewart (1990) interprets the greater noncompliance and aggressiveness of children placed in day care as signs of greater independence rather than social maladjustment.

SELECTING A DAY-CARE CENTER Because it is economically, vocationally, and socially unrealistic for most parents to spend the day at home, most parents strive to secure day care that will foster the social and emotional development of their children. Yet selecting a day-care center can be an overwhelming task. Standards for day-care centers vary from locale to locale, so licensing is no guarantee of adequate care. To help make a successful choice, parents can weigh factors such as the following:

1. Is the center licensed? By what agency? What standards must be met to acquire a license?

2. What is the ratio of children to caregivers? Everything else being equal, caregivers can do a better job when there are fewer children in their charge.

3. What are the qualifications of the center's caregivers? How well aware are they of children's needs and patterns of development? Have they been screened for criminal backgrounds? Children fare better when their caregivers have specific training in child development. Years of day-care experience and formal degrees are less important. If the administrators of a day-care center are reluctant to discuss the training and experience of their caregivers, consider another center.

4. How safe is the environment? Do toys and swings seem to be in good condition? Are dangerous objects out of reach? Would strangers have a difficult time breaking in? Ask something like, "Have children been injured in this center?" Administrators should report previous injuries without hesitation.

5. What is served at mealtime? Is it nutritious and appetizing? Will *your child* eat it? Some babies are placed in day care at age 6 months or younger, and parents need to know what formulas are used.

6. Which caregivers will be responsible for your child? What are their backgrounds? How do they seem to relate to children? To *your* child?

7. What toys, games, books, and other educational materials are provided?

8. What facilities are provided to promote the motor development of your child? How well supervised are children when they use equipment like swings and tricycles?

9. Are the hours offered by the center convenient for your schedule?

10. Is the location of the center convenient?

11. Do you like the overall environment and "feel" of the center?

As you can see, the considerations can be overwhelming. Perhaps no day-care center within reach will score perfectly on every factor. Some factors are more important than others, however, and this list may help you focus on what is most important to you.

One of the primary concerns of parents selecting a day-care center is that their children not be abused. Yet as we see in the following section, much child abuse occurs in the home.

Child Abuse

Nearly 3 million children in the United States are neglected or abused by their parents or other caregivers each year (Fein, 1998). More than half a million of these suffer serious injuries. Nearly 1,000 die (Fein, 1998). In a national poll of 1,000 parents, 5% admitted to having physically abused their children (Lewin, 1995). One in 5 (21%) admitted to hitting their children "on the bottom" with a hard object such as a belt, stick, or hairbrush. Most parents (85%) reported that they often shouted, yelled, or screamed at their children. Nearly half (47%) reported spanking or hitting their children on the bottom with their bare hands. And 17% admitted to calling their children "dumb," "lazy," or a similar name.

These percentages may seem high, but child abuse is actually *under* reported. Why? Some family members are afraid that reporting abuse will destroy the family unit. Others are reluctant to disclose abuse because they are financially dependent on the abuser or do not trust the authorities (Seppa, 1996).

Why do parents abuse their children? Many factors contribute to child abuse: stress, a history of child abuse in at least one of the parents' families of origin, acceptance of violence as a way of coping with stress, failure to become attached to the children, substance abuse, and rigid attitudes toward child rearing (Belsky, 1993; Kaplan, 1991). Unemployment and low socioeconomic status are common stressors that lead to abuse (Lewin, 1995; Trickett et al., 1991).

Children who are abused are quite likely to develop personal and social problems and psychological disorders. They are less likely than other children to venture out to explore the world (Aber & Allen, 1987). They are more likely to have psychological problems such as anxiety, depression, and low self-esteem (Wagner, 1997). They are less likely to be intimate with their peers and more likely to be aggressive (DeAngelis, 1997; Parker & Herrera, 1996; Rothbart & Ahadi, 1994). As adults, they are more likely to be violent toward their dates and spouses (Malinosky-Rummell & Hansen, 1993).

Child abuse runs in families to some degree (Simons et al., 1991). That is, child abusers are more likely to have been abused than is the general population. Even so, *the majority of children who are abused do* not *abuse their own children as adults* (Kaufman & Zigler, 1989).

TRUTH OR FICTION REVISITED
It is true that child abusers have frequently been abused as children. However, the majority of victims of abuse do not abuse their own children.

Why does abuse run in families? There are several hypotheses (Belsky, 1993). One is that parents serve as role models. According to Murray Strauss (1995), "Spanking teaches kids that when someone is doing something you don't like and they won't stop doing it, you hit them." Another is that children adopt parents' strict philosophies about discipline. Exposure to violence in their own home leads some children to view abuse as normal. A third is that being abused can create feelings of hostility that are then expressed against others, including one's own children.

WHAT TO DO Dealing with child abuse is frustrating in itself. Social agencies and courts can find it difficult to distinguish between "normal" hitting or spanking and abuse. Because of the widespread belief that parents have the right to rear their children as they wish, police and courts usually try to avoid involvement in "domestic quarrels" and "family disputes."

However, the alarming incidence of child abuse has spawned new efforts at detection and prevention. Many states require helping professionals such as psychologists and physicians to report any suspicion of child abuse. Many states legally require *anyone* who suspects child abuse to report it to authorities.

Many locales also have child abuse "hot lines." Their phone numbers are available from the telephone information service. Private citizens who suspect child abuse may call for advice. Parents who are having difficulty controlling aggressive impulses toward their children are encouraged to use the hot lines. Some hot lines are serviced by groups such as Parents Anonymous, which involve parents who have had similar difficulties and may help callers diffuse feelings of anger in less harmful ways. When in doubt, call a psychologist, your doctor, or the police to ask whom you can speak to in confidence about known or suspected child abuse.

The years of childhood may seem to pass rapidly, but a great deal occurs during them in terms of physical, cognitive, and social and personality development. Following childhood is the period of adolescence, which is for many a period of passage to adulthood. For many adolescents, and for their parents, the goals of adolescence and the behaviors that are deemed acceptable loom as huge question marks. Because of these questions, psychologists have focused a great deal of attention on adolescence, as we see next.

ADOLESCENT DEVELOPMENT

Adolescence is a time of transition from childhood to adulthood. In our society, adolescents often feel they are "neither fish nor fowl," as the saying goes—neither children nor adults. Although adolescents may be old enough to have children and physically are as large as their parents, they are often treated quite differently than adults. They may not be eligible for a driver's license until they are 16 or 17. They cannot attend R-rated films unless they are accompanied by an adult. They are prevented from working long hours. They are usually required to remain in school through age 16 and may not marry until they reach the "age of consent." Let us consider the physical, cognitive, and social and personal changes of adolescence.

PHYSICAL DEVELOPMENT

ADOLESCENCE The period of life bounded by puberty and the assumption of adult responsibilities.

Following infancy, children gain about 2 to 3 inches a year until they reach the adolescent growth spurt. Weight gains also remain fairly even at about

4 to 6 pounds per year. The adolescent growth spurt lasts for 2 to 3 years and ends the stable patterns of growth in height and weight that characterize most of childhood. Within this short span of years, adolescents grow some 8 to 12 inches. Most boys wind up taller and heavier than most girls.

In boys, the weight of the muscle mass increases notably. The width of the shoulders and circumference of the chest also increase. Adolescents may eat enormous quantities of food to fuel their growth spurt. Adults fighting the "battle of the bulge" stare in wonder as teens wolf down french fries and shakes at the fast-food counter and later go out for pizza.

Puberty

Puberty is the period during which the body becomes sexually mature. It heralds the onset of adolescence. Puberty begins with the appearance of **secondary sex characteristics** such as body hair, deepening of the voice in males, and rounding of the breasts and hips in females (see Table CD.7). In boys, pituitary hormones stimulate the testes to increase the output of testosterone, which in turn causes enlargement of the penis and testes and the appearance of bodily hair. By the early teens, erections become common, and boys may ejaculate. Ejaculatory ability usually precedes the presence of mature sperm by at least a year. Ejaculation thus is not evidence of reproductive capacity.

In girls, a critical body weight in the neighborhood of 100 pounds is thought to trigger a cascade of hormonal secretions in the brain that cause the ovaries to secrete higher levels of the female sex hormone, estrogen (Frisch, 1997). Estrogen stimulates the growth of breast tissue and fatty and supportive tissue in the hips and buttocks. Thus the pelvis widens, rounding the hips. Small amounts of androgens produced by the adrenal glands, along with estrogen, spur the growth of pubic and underarm hair. Estrogen and androgens together stimulate the growth of female sex organs. Estrogen production becomes cyclical during puberty and regulates the menstrual cycle. The beginning of menstruation, or **menarche,** usually occurs between the ages of 11 and 14. Girls cannot become pregnant until they begin to ovulate, however, and this may occur as much as 2 years after menarche.

COGNITIVE DEVELOPMENT

> I am a college student of extremely modest means. Some crazy psychologist interested in something called "format operational thought" has just promised to pay me $20 if I can make a coherent logical argument for the proposition that the federal government should under no circumstances ever give or lend more to needy college students. Now what could people who believe *that* possibly say by way of supporting argument? Well, I suppose they *could* offer this line of reasoning. . . . (Adapted from Flavell et al., 1993, p. 140)

The adolescent thinker approaches problems very differently from the elementary school child. The child sticks to the facts, to concrete reality. Speculating about abstract possibilities and what might be is very difficult. The adolescent, on the other hand, is able to deal with the abstract and the hypothetical. As shown in the above example, adolescents realize that one does not have to believe in the truth or justice of something in order to argue for it (Flavell et al., 1993). In this

ADOLESCENTS.
In our culture adolescents are "neither fish nor fowl." Although they may be old enough to reproduce and may be as large as their parents, they are often treated like children.

TRUTH OR FICTION REVISITED
It is not usually true that girls are capable of becoming pregnant when they have their first menstrual period.
Menarche can precede ovulation by a year or more.

PUBERTY The period of physical development during which sexual reproduction first becomes possible.

SECONDARY SEX CHARACTERISTICS Characteristics that distinguish the males from females, such as distribution of body hair and depth of voice, but that are not directly involved in reproduction.

MENARCHE The beginning of menstruation.

TABLE CD.7

PUBERTAL DEVELOPMENT

IN FEMALES	
Beginning between the ages of 8 and 11	Pituitary hormones stimulate ovaries to increase the production of estrogen. The internal reproductive organs begin to grow.
Beginning between the ages of 9 and 15	First the areola (darker area around the nipple) and then the breasts increase in size and become more rounded. Pubic hair becomes darker and coarser. Growth in height continues. Body fat continues to round body contours. A (normal) vaginal discharge becomes noticeable. Sweat and oil glands increase in activity, and acne may appear. Internal and external reproductive organs and genitals grow, which makes the vagina longer and the vaginal lips more pronounced.
Beginning between the ages of 10 and 16	Pubic hair begins to grow in a triangular shape. Underarm hair appears. Menarche occurs. The internal reproductive organs continue to develop. The ovaries may begin to release mature eggs (eggs capable of being fertilized). Growth in height slows.
Beginning between the ages of 12 and 19	The breasts near adult size and shape. Pubic hair spreads to the top of the thighs. The voice may deepen slightly (but not as deeply as in males). Menstrual cycles gradually become more regular.
IN MALES	
Beginning between the ages of 9 and 15	The testicles begin to grow. The skin of the scrotum (the sac that contains the testicles) becomes redder and coarser. A few straight pubic hairs appear at the base of the penis. The muscle mass develops, and the boy begins to grow taller. The areola (the darker area around the nipple) grows larger and darker.
Beginning between the ages of 11 and 17	The penis begins to lengthen. The testicles and scrotum continue to grow. Pubic hair becomes coarser and curlier and spreads to cover the area between the legs. Growth in height continues. The shoulders broaden. The hips narrow. The larynx enlarges, resulting in a deepening of the voice. Sparse facial and underarm hair appears.
Beginning between the ages of 14 and 17	The penis begins to widen as well as to continue to lengthen (although more slowly). The testicles continue to increase in size. The texture of the pubic hair becomes more like an adult's. Growth of facial and underarm hair increases, so the boy begins to shave. First ejaculation occurs. In nearly half of all boys, gynecomastia (breast enlargement) occurs, which then decreases in a year or two. Increased skin oils may produce acne.
Beginning between the ages of 14 and 18	The body nears final adult height, and the genitals achieve adult shape and size, with pubic hair spreading to the thighs and slightly upward toward the belly. Chest hair appears. Facial hair reaches full growth so shaving becomes more frequent. Further increases in height, body hair, and muscle growth and strength can continue into the early 20s.

This table is a general guideline. Changes may occur earlier or later and not always in this sequence.
Source: Adapted from Reinisch, J. M. (1990). *The Kinsey Institute new report on sex: What you must know to be sexually literate.* New York: St. Martin's Press.

section we explore some of the cognitive developments of adolescence by referring to the theories of Jean Piaget and Lawrence Kohlberg.

The Formal-Operational Stage

According to Piaget, children typically undergo three stages of cognitive development prior to adolescence: sensorimotor, preoperational, and concrete operational. They develop from infants who respond automatically to their environment to older children who can focus on various aspects of a situation at once and solve complex problems. The stage of **formal operations** is the final stage in Jean Piaget's theory of cognitive development, and it represents cognitive maturity. For many children in Western societies, formal operational thought begins at about the onset of adolescence—the age of 11 or 12. However, not all individuals enter this stage at this time, and some individuals never reach it.

The major achievements of the stage of formal operations involve classification, logical thought, and the ability to hypothesize. Central features are the ability to think about ideas as well as objects and to group and classify ideas—symbols, statements, entire theories. The flexibility and reversibility of operations, when applied to statements and theories, allow adolescents to follow arguments from premises to conclusions and back again.

Several features of formal operational thought give the adolescent a generally greater capacity to manipulate and appreciate the outer environment and the world of the imagination: hypothetical thinking, the ability to use symbols to stand for symbols, and deductive reasoning.

Formal-operational adolescents (and adults) think abstractly. They become capable of solving geometric problems about circles and squares without reference to what the circles and squares may represent in the real world. Adolescents in this stage derive rules for behavior from general principles and can focus, or center, on many aspects of a situation at once in arriving at judgments and solving problems.

In a sense, it is during the stage of formal operations that adolescents tend to emerge as theoretical scientists—even though they may see themselves as having little or no interest in science. They become capable of dealing with hypothetical situations. They realize that situations can have different outcomes, and they think ahead, experimenting with different possibilities. Adolescents also conduct experiments to determine whether their hypotheses are correct. These experiments are not conducted in the laboratory. Rather, adolescents may try out different tones of voice, ways of carrying themselves, and ways of treating others to see what works best for them.

ADOLESCENT EGOCENTRISM: "YOU JUST DON'T UNDERSTAND!" Adolescents in the formal operational stage can reason deductively, or draw conclusions about specific objects or people once they have been classified accurately. Adolescents can be somewhat proud of their new logical abilities, and so a new sort of egocentrism can develop in which adolescents emotionally press for acceptance of their logic without recognizing the exceptions or practical problems that are often considered by adults. Consider this example: "It is wrong to hurt people. Company A occasionally hurts people" (perhaps through pollution or economic pressures). "Therefore, Company A must be severely punished or shut down." This thinking is logical. By impatiently pressing for immediate major changes or severe penalties, however, one may not fully consider various practical problems such as the thousands of workers who would be laid off if the company were shut down. Adults frequently have undergone life experiences that lead them to see things in shades of gray, rather than just black or white.

FORMAL-OPERATIONAL STAGE Piaget's fourth stage, characterized by abstract logical thought and deduction from principles.

The thought of preschoolers is characterized by egocentrism in which they cannot take another's point of view. Adolescent thought is marked by another sort of egocentrism, in which they can understand the thoughts of others but still have trouble separating things of concern to others and those of concern only to themselves (Elkind, 1967, 1985). Adolescent egocentrism gives rise to two interesting cognition developments: *the imaginary audience* and the *personal fable*.

The concept of the **imaginary audience** refers to the belief that other people are as concerned with our thoughts and behavior as we are. As a result, adolescents see themselves as the center of attention and assume that other people are about as preoccupied with their appearance and behavior as they are (Lapsley, 1991; Milstead et al., 1993). Adolescents feel they are on stage and all eyes are focused on them.

The concept of the imaginary audience may fuel the intense adolescent desire for privacy. It helps explain why adolescents are so self-conscious about their appearance, why they worry about every facial blemish and spend long hours grooming. Self-consciousness seems to peak at about the age of 13 and then decline. Girls tend to be more self-conscious than boys (Elkind & Bowen, 1979).

The **personal fable** is the belief that our feelings and ideas are special, even unique, and that we are invulnerable. The personal fable seems to underlie various adolescent behavior patterns, such as showing off and taking risks (Arnett, 1992; Cohn et al., 1995; Lapsley, 1991; Milstead et al., 1993). Some adolescents adopt an "It can't happen to me" attitude; they assume that they can smoke without risk of cancer or engage in sexual activity without risk of sexually transmitted infections or pregnancy. Another aspect of the personal fable is the idea that no one has ever experienced or could understand the "unique" feelings one is experiencing, such as needing independence or being in love. Perhaps the personal fable is the basis for the common teenage lament, "You just don't understand me!"

EVALUATION OF PIAGET'S THEORY A number of questions have been raised concerning the accuracy of Piaget's views. Among them are these:

1. *Was Piaget's timing accurate?* Some critics argue that Piaget's methods led him to underestimate children's abilities (Bjorklund, 1995; Meltzoff & Gopnik, 1997). Other researchers using different methods have found, for example, that preschoolers are less egocentric and that children are capable of conservation at earlier ages than Piaget thought.

2. *Does cognitive development occur in stages?* Cognitive events such as egocentrism and conservation appear to develop more continuously than Piaget thought—that is, they may not occur in stages (Bjorklund, 1995; Flavell et al., 1993). Although cognitive developments appear to build on previous cognitive developments, the process may be more gradual than stagelike.

3. *Are developmental sequences always the same?* Here, Piaget's views have fared better. It seems there is no variation in the sequence in which cognitive developments occur.

In sum, Piaget's theoretical edifice has been rocked, but it has not been reduced to rubble. Psychologist Andrew Meltzoff believes that " Piaget's theories were critical for getting the field of [cognitive development] off the ground, . . . but it's time to move on" (1997, p. 9). Some researchers are moving on to *information processing*. That is, they view children (and adults) as akin to computer systems. Children, like computers, obtain

---

TRUTH OR FICTION REVISITED
It is true that adolescents tend to see themselves as being on stage. This is a manifestation of adolescent egocentrism and fuels the adolescent desires for privacy and physical perfection.

IMAGINARY AUDIENCE An aspect of adolescent egocentrism: The belief that other people are as concerned with our thoughts and behaviors as we are.

PERSONAL FABLE Another aspect of adolescent egocentrism: The belief that our feelings and ideas are special and unique and we are invulnerable.

information (receive "input") from their environment, store it, retrieve, manipulate it (think about it), and then respond to it overtly in terms of their behavior (produce "output") (Harnishfeger & Bjorklund, 1990). One goal of the information-processing approach is to learn just how children do these things, how their "mental programs" develop. Critical issues involve children's capacity for memory and their use of cognitive strategies, such as the ways in which they focus their attention (Bjorklund, 1995; Case, 1992; Kail & Salthouse, 1994). The future of the study of cognitive development remains to be written.

The Postconventional Level of Moral Reasoning

Lawrence Kohlberg's theory of moral reasoning involves three levels: preconventional, conventional, and postconventional. Individuals can arrive at the same decision—for example, as to whether or not Heinz should save his wife by taking the drug without paying for it—but they would be doing so for a different kind of reason. (Deciding not to take the drug for fear of punishment is cognitively less complex than not taking the drug because of the belief that doing so could have negative consequences for the social order.)

None of Kohlberg's levels is tied precisely to a person's age. Although postconventional reasoning is the highest level, for example, most adolescents and adults reason conventionally. However, when postconventional reasoning does emerge, it usually does so in adolescence. Kohlberg's (1969) research showed that postconventional moral judgments were clearly absent among the 7- to 10-year-olds. But by age 16, stage 5 reasoning is shown by about 20% of adolescents, and stage 6 reasoning is shown by about 5% of adolescents.

At the **postconventional level,** moral reasoning is based on the person's own moral standards. In each instance, moral judgments are derived from personal values, not from conventional standards or authority figures. In the contractual, legalistic orientation characteristic of stage 5, it is recognized that laws stem from agreed on procedures and that the rule of law is in general good for society; therefore, laws should not be violated. But under exceptional circumstances laws cannot bind the individual. (Although it is illegal for Heinz to steal the drug, in this case it is the right thing to do.)

Stage 6 thinking relies on supposed universal ethical principles such as the sanctity of human life, individual dignity, justice, and the Golden Rule ("Do unto others as you would have them do unto you."). Behavior consistent with these principles is moral. If a law is unjust or contradicts the rights of the individual, it is wrong to obey it.

People at the postconventional level look to their conscience as the highest moral authority. This point has created confusion. To some it suggests that it is right to break the law when it is convenient. But this interpretation is incorrect. Kohlberg means that people at this level of moral reasoning must do what they believe is right even if this action runs counter to social rules or laws or requires personal sacrifice.

EVALUATION OF KOHLBERG'S THEORY Research suggests that moral reasoning does follow a developmental sequence (Snarey, 1985), even though most people do not reach the level of postconventional thought. Postconventional thought, when found, first occurs during adolescence. It also seems that Piaget's stage of formal operations is a prerequisite for postconventional reasoning, which requires the capacities to understand abstract moral principles and to empathize with the attitudes and emotional responses of other people (Flavell et al., 1993).

Consistent with Kohlberg's theory, children do not appear to skip stages as they progress (Flavell et al., 1993). When children are exposed to

POSTCONVENTIONAL LEVEL According to Kohlberg, a period during which moral judgments are derived from moral principles and people look to themselves to set moral standards.

ARE THERE GENDER DIFFERENCES IN MORAL DEVELOPMENT?

Some studies using Heinz's dilemma have found that boys reason at higher levels of moral devel-opment than girls. However, Carol Gilligan (1982; Gilligan et al., 1989) argues that this gender difference is illusory and reflects different patterns of socialization for boys and girls.

Gilligan makes her point through two examples of responses to Heinz's dilemma. Eleven-year-old Jake views the dilemma as a math problem. He sets up an equation showing that life has greater value than property. Heinz is thus obligated to steal the drug. Eleven-year-old Amy vacillates. She notes that stealing the drug and letting Heinz's wife die would both be wrong. Amy searches for alternatives, such as getting a loan, stating it would profit Heinz's wife little if he went to jail and was no longer around to help her.

According to Gilligan, Amy's reasoning is as sophisticated as Jake's, yet she would be rated as showing a lower level of moral development. Gilligan asserts that Amy, like other girls, has been socialized to focus on the needs of others and forgo simplistic judgments of right and wrong. As a consequence, Amy is more likely to exhibit stage 3 reasoning, which focuses in part on empathy for others. Jake, by contrast, has been socialized to make judgments based purely on logic. To him, clear-cut conclusions are to be derived from a set of premises. Amy was aware of the logical considerations that influenced Jake, but she saw them as one source of information—not as the only source. It is ironic that Amy's empathy, a trait that has "defined the 'goodness' of women," marks Amy "as deficient in moral development" (Gilligan, 1982, p. 18). Prior to his death, Kohlberg had begun to correct the sexism in his scoring system. ■

adult models who exhibit a lower stage of moral reasoning, they can be induced to follow along (Bandura & McDonald, 1963). Children exposed to examples of moral reasoning above and below their own stage generally prefer the higher stage, however (Rest, 1983). The thrust of moral development would therefore appear to be from lower to higher in terms of Kohlberg's levels and stages, even if children can be influenced by the opinions of others.

SOCIAL AND PERSONALITY DEVELOPMENT

In terms of social and personality development, adolescence has been associated with turbulence. In the 19th century, psychologist G. Stanley Hall described adolescence as a time of *Sturm und Drang*—storm and stress. Certainly, many American teenagers abuse drugs, get pregnant, contract sexually transmitted diseases, become involved in violence, fail in school, and even attempt suicide (Garland & Zigler, 1993; Gentry & Eron, 1993; Kazdin, 1993). Each year nearly 1 in 10 adolescent girls becomes pregnant. Nearly 10% of teenage boys and 20% of teenage girls attempt suicide. Alcohol-related incidents are the overall leading cause of death among adolescents.

Hall attributed the conflicts and distress of adolescence to biological changes. Research evidence does suggest that hormonal changes affect the activity levels, mood swings, and aggressive tendencies of many adolescents (Buchanan et al., 1992). Overall, however, it would appear that sociocultural influences have a greater impact than hormones (Buchanan et al., 1992).

Striving for Independence

Adolescents try to become more independent from their parents, which often leads to some bickering (Smetana et al., 1991). They usually argue about issues such as homework, chores, money, appearance, curfews, and dating (Galambos & Almeida, 1992; Smetana et al., 1991). Arguments are common when adolescents want to make their own choices about matters such as clothes and friends (Smetana et al., 1991).

The striving for independence is also characterized by withdrawal from family life, at least relative to prior involvement. In one study, children ranging in age from 9 to 15 carried electronic pagers for a week so that they could report what they were doing and whom they were with when signaled (Larson & Richards, 1991). The amount of time spent with family members decreased dramatically with greater age. The 15-year-olds spent only half as much time with their families as the 9-year-olds. Yet this change does not mean that most adolescents spend their time on the streets. For 15-year-old boys in the study, time with the family tended to be replaced by time spent alone. For older girls, this time was divided between friends and solitude.

Adolescents and parents are often in conflict because adolescents experiment with many things that can be harmful to their health. Yet—apparently because of the personal fable—adolescents often do not perceive such activities to be as risky as their parents see them as being. Lawrence Cohn and his colleagues (1995) found, for example, that parents perceived drinking, smoking, failure to use seat belts, drag racing, and a number of other activities to be riskier than their teenagers saw them as being (Table CD.8).

Some distancing from parents is beneficial for adolescents (Galambos, 1992). After all, they do have to form relationships outside the family. But greater independence does not necessarily mean that adolescents become emotionally detached from their parents or fall completely under the influence of their peers. Most adolescents continue to feel love, respect, and loyalty toward their parents (Montemayor & Flannery, 1991). Adolescents who feel close to their parents actually show greater self-reliance

TABLE CD.8

MEAN RATINGS OF PERCEIVED HARMFULNESS OF VARIOUS ACTIVITIES

ACTIVITY	EXPERIMENTAL INVOLVEMENT (DOING ACTIVITY ONCE OR TWICE TO SEE WHAT IT IS LIKE)		FREQUENT INVOLVEMENT	
	TEENAGER	TEENAGER'S PARENTS	TEENAGER	TEENAGER'S PARENTS
Drinking alcohol	2.6	3.5	4.4	4.8
Smoking cigarettes	3.0	3.6	4.4	4.8
Using diet pills	2.8	3.8	4.1	4.7
Not using seat belts	3.0	4.3	4.0	4.8
Getting drunk	3.2	4.2	4.4	4.8
Sniffing glue	3.6	4.6	4.6	4.9
Driving home after drinking a few beers	3.8	4.5	4.6	4.8
Drag racing	3.8	4.6	4.5	4.8
Using steroids	3.8	4.4	4.7	4.9

Source: Adapted from Cohn et al. (1995), p. 219.

and independence than do those who are distant from their parents. Adolescents who retain close ties with their parents also fare better in school and have fewer adjustment problems (Davey, 1993; Papini & Roggman, 1992; Steinberg, 1996).

Despite parent-adolescent conflict over issues of control, parents and adolescents tend to share social, political, religious, and economic views (Paikoff & Collins, 1991). In sum, there are frequent differences between parents and adolescents on issues of personal control. However, there apparently is little or no "generation gap" on broader matters.

Ego Identity Versus Role Diffusion

According to Erik Erikson, individuals undergo eight stages of psychosocial development, each characterized by a certain kind of "crisis." Four of these stages, beginning with the stage of trust versus mistrust, occur during the years of childhood. The fifth stage, *ego identity versus role diffusion*, occurs during adolescence. The major challenge of adolescence is the creation of an adult identity. Identity is achieved mainly by committing oneself to a particular occupation or a role in life. But identity also extends to sexual, political, and religious beliefs and commitments.

Erikson (1963) theorized that adolescents experience a life crisis of *ego identity versus role diffusion*. **Ego identity** is a firm sense of who one is and what one stands for. It can carry one through difficult times and give meaning to one's achievements. Adolescents who do not develop ego identity may experience **role diffusion**. They spread themselves too thin, running down one blind alley after another and placing themselves at the mercy of leaders who promise to give them the sense of identity that they cannot find for themselves.

A key aspect of identity is sexual identity—how the adolescent perceives himself or herself as a sexual being. The sex organs of adolescents undergo rapid maturation, and adolescents develop the capacity for reproduction. As we see next, many of them do reproduce, before they are socially, emotionally, and financially ready to do so.

Adolescent Sexuality

My first sexual experience occurred in a car after the high school junior prom. We were both virgins, very uncertain but very much in love. We had been going together since eighth grade. The experience was somewhat painful. I remember wondering if I would look different to my mother the next day. I guess I didn't because nothing was said. (Adapted from Morrison et al., 1980, p. 108)

Although adolescents may not form enduring romantic relationships or be able to support themselves, the changes of puberty ready their bodies for sexual activity. High hormone levels also prompt great interest in sex. Adolescents therefore wrestle with issues of how and when to express their awakening sexuality. To complicate matters, adults in Western society often send mixed messages concerning sexual behavior. Teenagers may be advised to wait to engage in sexual activity until they have married or at least entered into meaningful relationships, but they are also bombarded by sexual messages in films, TV and radio commercials, print advertising, and virtually every other medium (Rathus et al., 2000).

As we enter the new millennium, a federal survey found that about half of the high school students in the United States are sexually active (Kolbe, 1998). No statistics were available for high school dropouts, who make up about 5% of the teenage population.

Adolescent girls by and large obtain little advice at home or in school about how to resist sexual pressures. Nor do most of them have ready

EGO IDENTITY Erikson's term for a firm sense of who we are and what we stand for.

ROLE DIFFUSION Erikson's term for lack of clarity in our life roles (because of failure to develop ego identity).

access to effective contraception. According to the Alan Guttmacher Institute (1998), fewer than half of the adolescents who are sexually active report using contraceptives consistently. As a result, about 10% of American adolescent girls—about 1 million teenage girls—get pregnant each year (Meckler, 1998). This rate is higher than that for teens in other Western nations. For example, the U.S. rate is twice as high as the comparable rate in England and Canada. It is nine times as high as the rate in Japan (Brody, 1998). More than 200,000 of them have abortions (Shalala, 1998). Nearly 3 million teenagers in the United States also contract a sexually transmitted infection each year.

Why is teenage pregnancy so common? Some teenage girls become pregnant as a way of eliciting a commitment from their partner or rebelling against their parents. But most become pregnant because they misunderstand reproduction and contraception or miscalculate the odds of conception. Even those who are well informed about contraception often do not use it consistently (Rathus et al., 2000). Peers also play an important role in determining the sexual behavior of adolescents. When 1,000 teenagers were asked why they had not waited to have sexual intercourse until they were older, the top reason given was peer pressure, cited by 34% of girls and 26% of boys (Kelley & Byrne, 1992).

The medical, social, and economic costs of unplanned teenage pregnancies are enormous to teenage mothers and their children. Teenage mothers are more likely to have medical complications during pregnancy and to have prolonged labor. Their babies are more likely to be born prematurely and to have low birth weight. It appears that these medical problems are largely due not to the young age of the mother, but to the inadequate prenatal care and poor nutrition often experienced by teenage mothers living in conditions of poverty (Etaugh & Rathus, 1995).

Teenage mothers are also less likely to graduate from high school or attend college. Their lack of educational achievement makes it more difficult for them to obtain adequate employment. They have a lower standard of living and are more likely to require public assistance (Center for the Study of Social Policy, 1993). Few receive consistent financial or emotional help from the fathers, who generally are unable to support themselves, let alone a family (Klein, 1993).

Still, there is some encouraging news. The 1990s saw a decline in the teenage pregnancy rate because of increased use of contraception as well as the leveling off of sexual activity among teenagers (Kolbe, 1998; Meckler, 1998). Perhaps sex education programs and the increased availability of contraceptive and family planning services are beginning to make inroads.

Many controversies surround adolescent behavior and society's response to it. For example, should adolescents have sex education? Should school districts make contraceptive devices available to adolescents? Most parents favor sex education, but they disagree on what should be taught. Consider a comment from Anke Ehrhardt (1998), a professor of psychiatry at Columbia University: "In other countries, sex education is put in a positive context of loving relationships, but here we spread fear. And it hasn't worked. We have a much higher rate of teen pregnancy."

There are also broad controversies in the field of developmental psychology, as we see next. These controversies refer to all aspects of development: physical, cognitive, and social and personality development.

CONTROVERSIES IN DEVELOPMENTAL PSYCHOLOGY

Now that we have traced development from childhood through adolescence, we are ready to consider some controversies in developmental psychology. These have to do with the relative importance of nature and nurture in development, and with whether development is continuous or occurs in stages (i.e., is discontinuous).

Does Development Reflect Nature or Nurture?

What behavior is the result of nature? That is, what aspects of behavior originate in a person's genes and are biologically programmed to unfold in the child as long as minimal needs for nutrition and social experience are met? What behavior is the result of nurture? That is, what aspects of behavior largely reflect environmental influences such as nutrition and learning?

Psychologists seek to understand the influences of nature in our genetic heritage, in the functioning of the nervous system, and in the process of **maturation** (that is, the unfolding of traits, as determined by the genetic code). Psychologists look for the influences of nurture in our nutrition, cultural and family backgrounds, and opportunities for learning, including early mental stimulation and formal education. The American psychologist Arnold Gesell (1880–1961) leaned heavily toward natural explanations of development. He argued that all areas of development are self-regulated by the unfolding of natural plans and processes. John Watson and other behaviorists, in contrast, leaned heavily toward environmental explanations. To better understand this controversy, let us consider the relative influences of nature and nurture in motor development and in language development.

NATURE AND NURTURE IN MOTOR DEVELOPMENT Both maturation (nature) and experience (nurture) play indispensable roles in motor development (Jouen & Lepecq, 1990). Certain motor activities do not seem possible until the cortex of the brain has matured. Infants also need some opportunity for motor experimentation before they can engage in milestones such as sitting up and walking. But although it may take them several months to sit up and still more months to take their first steps, most of this time can apparently be attributed to maturation. In a classic study, Wayne and Marsena Dennis (1940) reported on the motor development of Native American Hopi children who spent their first year strapped to a cradleboard. Although denied a full year of experience in locomotion, the Hopi infants gained the capacity to walk early in their second year, at about the same time as children reared in other cultures. Another cross-cultural study (Hindley et al., 1966) reported that infants in five European cities began to walk at about the same time (generally, between 12 and 15 months), despite cultural differences in encouragement to walk.

But evidence is mixed whether specific training can accelerate the appearance of motor skills. For example, in a classic study with identical twins, Arnold Gesell (1929) gave one twin extensive training in hand coordination, block building, and stair climbing from early infancy. The other was allowed to develop on his own. But as time passed, the untrained twin became as skilled in these activities as the other.

Although the development of motor skills can be accelerated by training (Zelazo et al., 1993), this effect is slight at best. Guided practice in the absence of neural maturation can have only limited results. No evidence indicates that this sort of training leads to eventual superior motor skills or other advantages.

Nature appears to provide limits for behavior. Nurture determines whether the child develops skills in accord with the upper boundaries of these limits. Even fundamental locomotion skills are apparently deter-

MATURATION Orderly unfolding of traits, as regulated by the genetic code.

mined by a complex interplay of maturational and environmental factors (Thelen, 1990; Thelen & Adolph, 1992). There may be little purpose in trying to train children to enhance their motor skills before they are ready. Once they are ready, however, teaching and practice make a difference. One does not become an Olympic athlete without "good genes." But one also does not become an Olympic athlete without high-quality training.

NATURE AND NURTURE IN LANGUAGE DEVELOPMENT

> Since all normal humans talk but no house pets or house plants do, no matter how pampered, heredity must be involved in language. But since a child growing up in Japan speaks Japanese whereas the same child brought up in California would speak English, the environment is also crucial. Thus, there is no question about whether heredity or environment is involved in language, or even whether one or the other is "more important." Instead, . . . our best hope [might be] finding out *how* they interact. (Pinker, 1994)

Billions of children have acquired the languages spoken by their parents and passed them down, with minor changes, from generation to generation. Language development, like many other areas of development, apparently reflects the interactions between the influences of nature and nurture.

Learning theorists focus on nurture. They see language as developing according to laws of learning (Gleason & Ratner, 1993). They usually refer to the concepts of imitation and reinforcement. From a social-cognitive perspective, parents serve as *models*. Children learn language, at least in part, through observation and imitation. It seems likely that many words, especially nouns and verbs (including irregular verbs), are learned by imitation.

At first children accurately repeat the irregular verb forms they observe. This repetition can probably be explained in terms of modeling, but modeling does not explain all the events involved in learning. Children later begin to overregularize irregular verb forms *because of* their knowledge of rules of grammar, not through imitation. Nor does imitative learning explain how children come to utter phrases and sentences they have *not* observed. Parents, for example, are unlikely to model utterances such as "bye-bye sock" and "allgone Daddy," but children do say them.

Theorists who focus on the importance of heredity or nature argue that learning theory cannot account for the unchanging sequence of language development and the spurts in children's language acquisition. Even the types of two-word utterances emerge in a consistent pattern in diverse cultures. Although timing differs from one child to another, the types of questions used, passive versus active sentences, and so on, all emerge in the same order.

The nativist theory of language development holds that innate or inborn factors—which make up children's *nature*—cause children to attend to and acquire language in certain ways. From this perspective, children bring a certain neurological "prewiring" to language learning (Newport, 1998; Pinker, 1994).

According to **psycholinguistic theory**, language acquisition involves the interaction of environmental influences—such as exposure to parental speech and reinforcement—and an inborn tendency to acquire language. Noam Chomsky (1980, 1991) refers to the inborn tendency as a **language acquisition device** (LAD). The LAD involves the structure of the human brain, and its development is directed by genes. Evidence for an LAD is found in the universality of human language abilities and in the specific sequence of language development.

PSYCHOLINGUISTIC THEORY The view that language learning involves an interaction between environmental factors and an inborn tendency to acquire language.

LANGUAGE ACQUISITION DEVICE In psycholinguistic theory, neural "prewiring" that facilitates the child's learning of grammar. Abbreviated *LAD*.

The LAD prepares the nervous system to learn grammar. On the surface, languages differ a great deal. However, the LAD serves children all over the world because languages share what Chomsky refers to as a "universal grammar"—an underlying set of rules for turning ideas into sentences (Pinker, 1990, 1994). Consider an analogy with computers: According to psycholinguistic theory, the universal grammar that resides in the LAD is the same as a computer's basic operating system (e.g., Windows, Macintosh, Unix, Linux). The particular language that a child learns to use is the same as a word-processing program.

So which is the key to language development: nature or nurture? Today, most researchers would agree that both nature and nurture affect most areas of development (Azar, 1997). We can argue about which is more prominent in a given area of development, but as in the case of language development, they are both essential.

Is Development Continuous or Discontinuous?

Do developmental changes occur gradually (continuously)? Or do they occur in major leaps (discontinuously) that dramatically alter our bodies and behavior?

Watson and other behaviorists viewed development as a continuous process in which the effects of learning mount gradually, with no major sudden changes. Maturational theorists, however, argue that people are prewired or preset to change dramatically at certain times of life. They point out that the environment, even when enriched, profits us little until we are ready, or mature enough, to develop in a certain direction. For example, newborn babies do not imitate their parents' speech, even when the parents speak clearly and deliberately. Nor does aided practice in "walking" during the first few months after birth significantly accelerate the date at which the child can walk independently.

Stage theorists, such as Sigmund Freud and Jean Piaget, saw development as discontinuous. Both theorists saw biological changes as providing the potential for psychological changes. Freud focused on the ways in which sexual development might provide the basis for personality development. Piaget's research centered on the ways in which maturation of the nervous system permits cognitive advances.

Certain aspects of physical development do occur in stages. For example, from the age of 2 to the onset of puberty (the period of development during which reproduction becomes possible), children gradually grow larger. Then the adolescent growth spurt occurs. It is ushered in by hormones and characterized by rapid changes in structure and function (as in the development of the sex organs) as well as in size. Thus a new stage of life has begun. Psychologists disagree more strongly on whether aspects of development such as cognitive development, attachment, and gender typing occur in stages.

The developments of childhood and adolescence set the stage for adult life. They are also fascinating in their own right. Development stems from the interaction of the unfolding of genetically directed processes and the effects of the environments into which we are plunged at birth. But then we grow aware of those environments and learn how to change them to better meet our needs. Development is a process that continues for a lifetime.

SUMMARY

1. **What are the stages of prenatal development?** These are the germinal, embryonic, and fetal stages. During the germinal stage, the zygote divides as it travels through the fallopian tube and becomes implanted in the uterine wall. The major organ systems are formed during the embryonic stage, and the fetal stage is characterized by maturation and gains in size.

2. **How does physical development occur?** Physical development occurs most rapidly before birth and during the first two years after birth. There is also an adolescent growth spurt during which young people make dramatic gains in height and weight.

3. **What are reflexes?** Reflexes are inborn responses to stimuli that in many cases are essential to infant survival. Examples include breathing, sucking, and swallowing.

4. **How do babies perceive their environment?** Newborn babies can see quite well and show greater interest in complex visual stimuli than in simple ones. Infants are capable of depth perception by the time they can crawl. Newborns can normally hear and show a preference for their mother's voice. Newborns show preferences for pleasant odors and sweet foods.

5. **How did Jean Piaget view children?** Piaget saw children as budding scientists who actively strive to make sense of the perceptual world. He defined intelligence as involving the processes of assimilation (responding to events according to existing schemes) and accommodation (changing schemes to permit effective responses to new events).

6. **What are the stages of cognitive development, according to Piaget?** Piaget's view of cognitive development includes four stages: sensorimotor (prior to the use of symbols and language); preoperational (characterized by egocentric thought, animism, artificialism, and inability to center on more than one aspect of a situation); concrete operational (characterized by conservation, less egocentrism, reversibility, and subjective moral judgments); and formal operational (characterized by abstract logic).

7. **How does language development occur?** Children make the sounds of crying, cooing, and babbling before true language develops. Single-word utterances occur at about 1 year of age, and 2-word utterances by the age of 2. Early language is characterized by overextension of familiar words and concepts to unfamiliar objects (calling horses *doggies*) and by overregularization of verbs ("She *sitted* down"). As time passes, vocabulary grows larger, and sentence structure grows more complex.

8. **How did Kohlberg view moral development?** Kohlberg focus-ed on the processes of moral reasoning. He hypothesized that these processes develop through three "levels," with each level consisting of two stages. Moral decisions develop from being based on pain and pleasure through necessity to maintain the social order to reliance on one's own conscience.

9. **What are the stages of attachment?** According to Ainsworth, there are three stages of attachment: the initial-preattachment phase, characterized by indiscriminate attachment; the attachment-in-the-makin phase, characterized by preference for familiar figures; and the clear-cut-attachment phase, characterized by intensified dependence on the primary caregiver.

10. **What are the major theories of attachment?** Behaviorists have argued that children become attached to their mothers through conditioning because their mothers feed them and attend to their other needs. Harlow's studies with rhesus monkeys suggest that an innate motive, contact comfort, may be more important than conditioning in the development of attachment. Although there may be no particular time limits on the development of attachment in humans, there are critical developmental periods during which animals such as geese and ducks become attached to (or imprinted on) an object that they follow.

11. **What are the main parenting styles?** These include the authoritative, authoritarian, and permissive styles. The children of authoritative parents are most achievement oriented and well adjusted.

12. **What physical changes take place during adolescence?** Adolescence begins at puberty and ends with assumption of adult responsibilities. Changes that lead to reproductive capacity and secondary sex characteristics are stimulated by increased levels of testosterone in the male and of estrogen and

androgens in the female. During the adolescent growth spurt, young people may grow 6 or more inches in a year.

13. **What cognitive developments occur during adolescence?** It is during adolescence that formal operational thought and postconventional moral reasoning develop, although not everyone reaches these stages of cognitive development. Formal operational thought involved the ability to think hypothetically, to think about ideas as well as objects, and to group and classify ideas—symbols, statements, even entire theories. Adolescent thought is also characterized by the imaginary audience, connected with the adolescent's desire for privacy, and the personal fable, connected with the adolescent's sense of invulnerability.

The first stage of postconventional moral reasoning enables people to weigh important human needs against society's need to maintain the social order (the contractual, legalistic orientation). The ultimate stage requires people to follow their own conscience, even if it means breaking the law (the universal ethical principles orientation).

14. **What personality and social developments occur during adolescence?** Adolescents frequently yearn for greater independence from their parents. According to Erikson, the psychosocial stage of ego identity versus role diffusion occurs during adolescence. Ego identity is our sense of who we are and what we believe in. At least half of high school students are sexually active. About 1 Ameri-

can adolescent girl in 10 gets pregnant each year.

15. **Does development reflect nature or nurture?** Development appears to reflect an interaction between nature (genetic factors) and nurture (environmental influences). Maturational theorists focus on the influences of nature, whereas learning theorists focus on environmental influences.

16. **Is development continuous or discontinuous?** Stage theorists like Freud and Piaget view development as discontinuous. According to them, people go through distinct periods of development that differ in quality and follow an orderly sequence. Learning theorists, in contrast, tend to view psychological development as a continuous process.

KEY TERMS

accommodation (p. CD-9)

adolescence (p. CD-28)

amniotic sac (p. CD-3)

androgens (p. CD-3)

animism (p. CD-11)

artificialism (p. CD-11)

assimilation (p. CD-9)

attachment (p. CD-20)

attachment-in-the-making phase (p. CD-22)

authoritarian parents (p. CD-24)

authoritative parents (p. CD-24)

autonomy (p. CD-20)

center (p. CD-12)

clear-cut-attachment phase (p. CD-22)

concrete-operational stage (p. CD-13)

conservation (p. CD-11)

contact comfort (p. CD-23)

conventional level (p. CD-20)

critical period (p. CD-23)

decentration (p. CD-13)

ego identity (p. CD-36)

egocentric (p. CD-11)

embryonic stage (p. CD-3)

fetal stage (p. CD-4)

fixation time (p. CD-6)

fixed-action pattern (p. CD-23)

formal-operational stage (p. CD-31)

germinal stage (p. CD-3)

holophrase (p. CD-14)

imaginary audience (p. CD-32)

imprinting (p. CD-23)

indiscriminate attachment (p. CD-22)

initial-preattachment phase (p. CD-22)

instrumental competence (p. CD-24)

language acquisition device (p. CD-39)

maturation (p. CD-38)

menarche (p. CD-29)

neonate (p. CD-2)

object permanence (p. CD-11)

objective responsibility (p. CD-12)

overextension (p. CD-14)

overregularization (p. CD-14)

permissive parents (p. CD-25)

personal fable (p. CD-32)

placenta (p. CD-3)

postconventional level (p. CD-33)

preconventional level (p. CD-19)

REFERENCES

Aber, J. L., & Allen, J. P. (1987). Effects of maltreatment of young children on young children's socioemotional development: An attachment theory perspective. *Developmental Psychology, 23,* 406–414.

Ainsworth, M. D. S., Blehar, M. C., Waters, E., & Wall, S. (1978). *Patterns of attachment: A psychological study of the strange situation.* Hillsdale, NJ: Erlbaum.

Ainsworth, M. D. S., & Bowlby, J. (1991). An ethological approach to personality development. *American Psychologist, 46,* 333–341.

Alan Guttmacher Institute. (1998). Cited in Brody, J. E. (1998, September 15). Teenagers and sex: Younger and more at risk. *New York Times;* America Online.

Arnett, J. (1992). Reckless behavior in adolescence: A developmental perspective. *Developmental Review, 12,* 339–373.

Arnold, D. H., Lonigan, C. J., Whitehurst, G. J., & Epstein, J. N. (1994). Accelerating language development through picture book reading. *Journal of Educational Psychology, 86,* 235–243.

Azar, B. (1997). It may cause anxiety, but day care can benefit kids. *APA Monitor, 28*(6), 13.

Bandura, A., & McDonald, F. J. (1963). Influence of social reinforcement and the behavior of models in shaping children's moral judgments. *Journal of Abnormal and Social Psychology, 67,* 274–281.

Banks, M. S., & Shannon, E. (1993). Spatial and chromatic visual efficiency in human neonates. In C. E. Granrud (Ed.), *Visual perception and cognition in infancy.* Hillsdale, NJ: Erlbaum.

Barringer, F. (1993, April 28). For 32 million Americans, English is a second language. *New York Times,* p. A18.

Baumrind, D. (1973). The development of instrumental competence through socialization. In A. D. Pick (Ed.), *Minnesota symposia on child development* (Vol. 7). Minneapolis: University of Minnesota Press.

Baumrind, D. (1991). Parenting styles and adolescent development. In J. Brooks-Gunn, R. Lerner, & A. C. Petersen (Eds.), *Encyclopedia of adolescence* (Vol. 2). New York: Garland.

Belsky, J. (1990). Developmental risks associated with infant day care. In I. S. Cherazi (Ed.), *Psychosocial issues in day care* (pp. 37–68). New York: American Psychiatric Press.

Belsky, J. (1993). Etiology of child maltreatment. *Psychological Bulletin, 114,* 413–434.

Belsky, J., Fish, M., & Isabella, R. (1991). Continuity and discontinuity in infant negative and positive emotionality: Family attachments and attachment consequences. *Developmental Psychology, 27,* 421–431.

Bjorklund, D. F. (1995). *Children's thinking* (2nd ed.). Pacific Grove, CA: Brooks/Cole.

Blakeslee, S. (1998, August 4). Reevaluating significance of baby's bond with mother. *New York Times,* pp. F1, F2.

Bloom, L., Merkin, S., & Wootten, J. (1982). *Wh*-questions: Linguistic factors that contribute to the sequence of acquisition. *Child Development, 53,* 1084–1092.

Bowlby, J. (1988). *A secure base.* New York: Basic Books.

Broberg, A., Hwang, P., Wessels, H., & Lamb, M. (1997). Cited in Azar, B. (1997). It may cause anxiety, but day care can benefit kids. *APA Monitor, 28*(6), 13.

Brody, J. E. (1998, September 15). Teen-agers and sex: Younger and more at risk. *New York Times;* America Online.

Buchanan, C. M., Eccles, J. S., & Becker, J. B. (1992). Are adolescents the victims of raging hormones? Evidence for activational effects of hormones on moods and behavior at adolescence. *Psychological Bulletin, 111,* 62–107.

Burnette, E. (1997). "Father of Ebonics" continues his crusade. *APA Monitor, 28*(4), 12.

Campos, J. J., Hiatt, S., Ramsey, D., Henderson, C., & Svejda, M. (1978). The emergence of fear on the visual cliff. In M. Lewis & L. Rosenblum (Eds.), *The origins of affect.* New York: Plenum.

Case, R. (1992). *The mind's staircase.* Hillsdale, NJ: Erlbaum.

Cavaliere, F. (1996). Bilingual schools face big political challenges. *APA Monitor, 27*(2), 36.

Center for the Study of Social Policy. (1993). *Kids count data book.* Washington, DC: Author.

Chomsky, N. (1980). Rules and representations. *Behavioral and Brain Sciences, 3,* 1–16.

Chomsky, N. (1991). Linguistics and cognitive science. In A. Kasher (Ed.), *The Chomskyan turn.* Cambridge, MA: Blackwell.

Clarke-Stewart, K. A. (1990). "The 'effects' of infant day care reconsidered." In N. Fox & G. G. Fein (Eds.), *Infant day care* (pp. 61–86). Norwood, NJ: Ablex.

Clarke-Stewart, K. A. (1991). A home is not a school: The effects of child care on children's development. *Journal of Social Issues, 47,* 105–123.

Cohn, L. D., Macfarlane, S., Yanez, C., & Imai, W. K. (1995). Risk-perception: Differences between adolescents and adults. *Health Psychology, 14,* 217–222.

Cox, M. J., Owen, M. T., Henderson, V. K., & Margand, N. A. (1992). Prediction of infant-father and infant-mother attachment. *Developmental Psychology, 28,* 474–483.

Davey, L. F. (1993, March). *Developmental implications of shared and divergent perceptions in the parent-adolescent relationship.* Paper presented at the biennial meeting of the Society for Research in Child Development, New Orleans.

DeAngelis, T. (1997). Abused children have more conflicts with friends. *APA Monitor, 28*(6), 32.

DeCasper, A. J., & Prescott, P. A. (1984). Human newborns' perception of male voices. *Developmental Psychobiology, 17,* 481–491.

Dennis, W., & Dennis, M. G. (1940). The effect of cradling practices upon the onset of walking in Hopi children. *Journal of Genetic Psychology, 56,* 77–86.

Ehrhardt, A. A. (1998). Cited in Bronner, E. (1998, February 1). Just say maybe. "No sexology, please. We're Americans." *New York Times,* p. WK6.

Elkind, D. (1967). Egocentrism in adolescence. *Child Development, 38,* 1025–1034.

Elkind, D. (1985). Egocentrism redux. *Developmental Review, 5,* 218–226.

Elkind, D., & Bowen, R. (1979). Imaginary audience behavior in children and adolescents. *Developmental Psychology, 15,* 38–44.

Erikson, E. H. (1963). *Childhood and society.* New York: Norton.

Etaugh, C., & Rathus, S. A. (1995). *The world of children.* Fort Worth: Harcourt Brace.

Fantz, R. L. (1961). The origin of form perception. *Scientific American, 204*(5), 66–72.

Fein, E. (1998, January 5). A doctor puts herself in the world of abused children. *New York Times;* America Online.

Field, T. M. (1991). Young children's adaptations to repeated separations from their mothers. *Child Development, 62,* 539–547.

Flavell, J. H., Miller, P. H., & Miller, S. A. (1993). *Cognitive development* (3rd ed.). Englewood Cliffs, NJ: Prentice Hall.

Frankel, K. A., & Bates, J. E. (1990). Mother-toddler problem solving. *Child Development, 61,* 810–819.

Freeman, M. S., Spence, M. J., & Oliphant, C. M. (1993, June). *Newborns prefer their mothers' low-pass filtered voices over other female filtered voices.* Paper presented at the annual convention of the American Psychological Society, Chicago.

Frisch, R. (1997). Cited in Angier, N. (1997). Chemical tied to fat control could help trigger puberty. *New York Times,* pp. C1, C3.

Galambos, N. L. (1992, October). Parent-adolescent relations. *Current Directions in Psychological Science,* pp. 146–149.

Galambos, N. L., & Almeida, D. M. (1992). Does parent-adolescent conflict increase in early adolescence? *Journal of Marriage and the Family, 54,* 737–747.

Garland, A. F., & Zigler, E. (1993). Adolescent suicide prevention.

American Psychologist, 48, 169–182.

Gentry, J., & Eron, L. D. (1993). American Psychological Association Commission on Violence and Youth. *American Psychologist, 48,* 89.

Gesell, A. (1929). Maturation and infant behavior patterns. *Psychological Review, 36,* 307–319.

Gilligan, C. (1982). *In a different voice.* Cambridge, MA: Harvard University Press.

Gilligan, C., Ward, J. V., & Taylor, J. M. (1989). *Mapping the moral domain: A contribution of women's thinking to psychological theory and education.* Cambridge, MA: Harvard University Press.

Gleason, J. B., & Ratner, N. B. (1993). Language development in children. In J. B. Gleason & N. B. Ratner (Eds.), *Psycholinguistics.* Fort Worth: Harcourt Brace Jovanovich.

Haaf, R. A., Smith, P. H., & Smitley, S. (1983). Infant response to facelike patterns under fixed trial and infant-control procedures. *Child Development, 54,* 172–177.

Harlow, H. F. (1959). Love in infant monkeys. *Scientific American, 200,* 68–86.

Harlow, H. F., & Zimmermann, R. R. (1959). Affectional responses in the infant monkey. *Science, 130,* 421–432.

Harnishfeger, K. K., & Bjorklund, D. F. (1990). Children's strategies. In D. F. Bjorklund (Ed.), *Children's strategies* (pp. 1–184). Hillsdale, NJ: Erlbaum.

Hindley, C. B., Filliozat, A. M., Klackenberg, G., Nicolet-Neister, D., & Sand, E. A. (1966).

Differences in age of walking for five European longitudinal samples. *Human Biology, 38,* 364–379.

Hunt, M. (1993). *The story of psychology.* New York: Anchor Books.

Isabella, R. A. (1993). Origins of attachment: Maternal interactive behavior across the first year. *Child Development, 64,* 605–621.

Jouen, F., & Lepecq, J. (1990). Early perceptuo-motor development: Posture and locomotion. In C. A. Hauert (Ed.), *Developmental psychology: Cognitive, perceptuo-motor and neuropsychological perspectives.* Amsterdam: North-Holland.

Kail, R. V., & Salthouse, T. A. (1994). Processing speed as a mental capacity. *Acta Psychologica, 86,* 199–225.

Kaplan, S. J. (1991). Physical abuse and neglect. In M. Lewis (Ed.), *Child and adolescent psychiatry: A comprehensive textbook* (pp. 1010–1019). Baltimore: Williams & Wilkins.

Kaufman, J., & Zigler, E. (1989). The intergenerational transmission of child abuse. In D. Cicchetti & V. Carlson (Eds.), *Child maltreatment: Theory and research on the causes and consequences of child abuse and neglect* (pp. 129–150). Cambridge: Cambridge University Press.

Kazdin, A. E. (1993). Adolescent mental health. *American Psychologist, 48,* 127–141.

Kelley, K., & Byrne, D. (1992). *Human sexuality.* Englewood Cliffs, NJ: Prentice Hall.

Kellman, P. J., & von Hofsetn, C. (1992). The world of the mov-

ing infant. In C. Rovee-Collier & L. P. Lipsitt (Eds.), *Advances in infancy research* (Vol. 7). Norwood, NJ: Ablex.

Klein, J. (1993, June 21). Make the daddies pay. *Newsweek,* p. 33.

Kohlberg, L. (1969). *Stages in the development of moral thought and action.* New York: Holt, Rinehart and Winston.

Kohlberg, L. (1981). *The philosophy of moral development.* San Francisco: Harper & Row.

Kolbe, L. (1998). Cited in Poll shows decline in sex by high school students. (1998, September 18). *New York Times,* p. A26.

Lamb, M. E., & Baumrind, D. (1978). Socialization and personality development in the preschool years. In M. E. Lamb (Ed.), *Social and personality development.* New York: Holt, Rinehart and Winston.

Lamb, M. E., Sternberg, K. J., & Prodromidis, M. (1992). Nonmaternal care and the security of infant-mother attachment. *Infant Behavior and Development, 15,* 71–83.

Lambert, W. E. (1990). Persistent issues in bilingualism. In B. Harley et al. (Eds.), *The development of second language proficiency.* Cambridge, England: Cambridge University Press.

Lambert, W. E., Genesee, F., Holobow, N., & Chartrand, L. (1991). *Bilingual education for majority English-speaking children.* Montreal: McGill University.

Lapsley, D. K. (1991). Egocentrism theory and the "new look" at the imaginary audience and personal fable in adolescence. In R. M. Lerner, A. C. Petersen,

& J. Brooks-Gunn (Eds.), *Encyclopedia of adolescence*. New York: Garland.

Larson, R., & Richards, M. H. (1991). Daily companionship in late childhood and early adolescence. *Child Development, 62*, 284–300.

Lederberg, A. R., & Mobley, C. E. (1990). The effect of hearing impairment on the quality of attachment and mother-toddler interaction. *Child Development, 61*, 1596–1604.

Lewin, T. (1995, December 7). Parents poll shows higher incidence of child abuse. *New York Times*, p. B16.

Lewis, M. (1997). *Altering fate—Why the past does not predict the future*. New York: Guilford Press.

Lewis, M. (1998). Cited in Blakeslee, S. (1998, August 4). Re-evaluating significance of baby's bond with mother. *New York Times*, pp. F1, F2.

Lorenz, K. Z. (1981). *The foundations of ethology*. New York: Springer-Verlag.

Lyons-Ruth, K., Alpern, L., & Repacholi, B. (1993). Disorganized infant attachment classification and maternal psychosocial problems as predictors of hostile-aggressive behavior in the preschool classroom. *Child Development, 64*, 572–585.

MacDonald, K. (1992). Warmth as a developmental construct. *Child Development, 63*, 753–773.

Macfarlane, J. A. (1975). Olfaction in the development of social preferences in the human neonate. In M. A. Hofer (Ed.), *Parent-infant interaction*. Amsterdam: Elsevier.

Malinosky-Rummell, R., & Hansen, D. H. (1993). Long-term consequences of childhood physical abuse. *Psychological Bulletin, 114*, 68–79.

Meckler, L. (1998, June 26). *Teen abortion, pregnancy rates fall*. Associated Press; America Online.

Meltzoff, A. N. (1997). Cited in Azar, B. (1997). New theory on development could usurp Piagetian beliefs. *APA Monitor, 28*(6), 9.

Meltzoff, A. N., & Gopnik, A. (1997). *Words, thoughts, and theories*. Cambridge, MA: MIT Press.

Miller, N. B., Cowan, P. A., Cowan, C. P., Hetherington, E. M., & Clingempeel, W. G. (1993). Externalizing in preschoolers and early adolescents. *Developmental Psychology, 29*, 3–18.

Milstead, M., Lapsley, D., & Hale, C. (1993, March). *A new look at imaginary audience and personal fable*. Paper presented at the meeting of the Society for Research in Child Development, New Orleans.

Montemayor, R., & Flannery, D. J. (1991). Parent-adolescent relations in middle and late adolescence. In R. M. Lerner, A. C. Petersen, & J. Brooks-Gunn (Eds.), *Encyclopedia of adolescence*. New York: Garland.

Morrison, E. S., et al. (1980). *Growing up sexual*. New York: Van Nostrand Reinhold.

Nelson, K. (1973). Structure and strategy in learning to talk. *Monographs for the Society for Research in Child Development, 38* (Whole No. 149).

Nelson, K., Hampson, J., & Shaw, L. K. (1993). Nouns in early lexicons: Evidence, explanations, and implications. *Journal of Child Language, 20*, 228.

Newport, E. (1998). Cited in Azar, B. (1998). Acquiring sign language may be more innate than learned. *APA Monitor, 29*(4), 12.

Olson, S. L., Bates, J. E., & Bayles, K. (1990). Early antecedents of childhood impulsivity: The role of parent-child interaction, cognitive competence, and temperament. *Journal of Abnormal Child Psychology, 18*, 317–334.

Paikoff, R. L., & Collins, A. C. (1991). Editor's notes: Shared views in the family during adolescence. In R. L. Paikoff & A. C. Collins (Eds.), *New directions for child development* (Vol. 51). San Francisco: Jossey-Bass.

Papini, D. R., & Roggman, L. A. (1992). Adolescent perceived attachment to parents in relation to competence, depression, and anxiety. *Journal of Early Adolescence, 12*, 420–440.

Papousek, M., Papousek, H., & Symmes, D. (1991). The meanings of melodies in motherese in tone and stress languages. *Infant Behavior and Development, 14*, 415–440.

Parker, J. G., & Herrera, C. (1996). Interpersonal processes in friendship: A comparison of abused and nonabused children's experience. *Developmental Psychology, 32*, 1025–1038.

Piaget, J. (1963). *The origins of intelligence in children*. New York: Norton.

Piaget. J. (1997). *The moral judgment of the child*. New York: Free Press Paperbacks.

Pinker, S. (1990). Language acquisition. In D. N. Osherson & H. Lasnik (Eds.), *An invitation to cognitive science: Language* (Vol. 1). Cambridge, MA: The MIT Press, a Bradford Book.

Pinker, S. (1994). *The language instinct.* New York: Morrow.

Porter, R. H., Makin, J. W., Davis, L. B., & Christensen, K. M. (1992). Breast-fed infants respond to olfactory cues from their own mother and unfamiliar lactating females. *Infant Behavior and Development, 15,* 85–93.

Putallaz, M., & Heflin, A. H. (1990). Parent-child interaction. In S. R. Asher & J. D. Coie (Eds.), *Peer rejection in childhood.* New York: Cambridge University Press.

Rathus, S. A., Nevid, J. S., & Fichner-Rathus, L. (2000). *Human sexuality in a world of diversity* (4th ed.). Boston: Allyn & Bacon.

Rest, J. R. (1983). Morality. In P. H. Mussen, J. Flavell, & E. Markman (Eds.), *Handbook of child psychology: Vol. 3. Cognitive development.* New York: Wiley.

Reynolds, A. G. (1991). The cognitive consequences of bilingualism. In A. G. Reynolds (Ed.), *Bilingualism, multiculturalism, and second language learning.* Hillsdale, NJ: Erlbaum.

Robbins, C., & Ehri, L. C. (1994). Reading storybooks to kindergartners helps them learn new vocabulary words. *Journal of Educational Psychology, 86,* 54–64.

Rothbart, M. K., & Ahadi, S. A. (1994). Temperament and the development of personality. *Journal of Abnormal Psychology, 103,* 55–66.

Seppa, N. (1996). APA releases study on family violence. *APA Monitor, 27* (4), 12.

Shalala, D. (1998). Cited in Meckler, L. (1998, June 26). *Teen abortion, pregnancy rates fall.* Associated Press; America Online.

Simons, R. L., Whitbeck, L. B., Conger, R. D., & Chyi-In, W. (1991). Intergenerational transmission of harsh parenting. *Developmental Psychology, 27,* 159–171.

Slobin, D. I. (1983). *Crosslinguistic evidence for basic child grammar.* Paper presented to the biennial meeting of the Society for Research in Child Development, Detroit.

Smetana, J. G., Yau, J., Restrepo, A., & Braeges, J. L. (1991). Conflict and adaptation in adolescence. In M. E. Colten & S. Gore (Eds.), *Adolescent stress: Causes and consequences.* New York: Aldine deGruyter.

Snarey, J. R. (1985). Cross-cultural universality of social-moral development: A critical review of Kohlbergian research. *Psychological Bulletin, 97,* 202–232.

Sroufe, A. (1998). Cited in Blakeslee, S. (1998, August 4). Re-evaluating significance of baby's bond with mother. *New York Times,* pp. F1, F2.

Steinberg, L. (1996). *Beyond the classroom.* New York: Simon & Schuster.

Strauss, M. (1995). Cited in Collins, C. (1995, May 11). Spanking is becoming the new don't. *New York Times,* p. C8.

Teller, D. Y., & Lindsey, D. T. (1993). Motion nulling techniques and infant color vision. In C. E. Granrud (Ed.), *Visual perception and cognition in infancy.* Hillsdale, NJ: Erlbaum.

Thelen, E. (1990). Dynamical systems and the generation of individual differences. In J. Colombo & J. W. Fagen (Eds.), *Individual differences in infancy: Reliability, stability and prediction.* Hillsdale, NJ: Erlbaum.

Thelen, E., & Adolph, K. E. (1992). Arnold L. Gesell: The paradox of nature and nurture. *Developmental Psychology, 28,* 368–380.

Thompson, R. A. (1991a). Attachment theory and research. In M. Lewis (Ed.), *Child and adolescent psychiatry.* Baltimore: Williams & Wilkins.

Thompson, R. A. (1991b). Infant daycare. In J. V. Lerner & N. L. Galambos (Eds.), *Employed mothers and their children* (pp. 9–36). New York: Garland.

Trickett, P. K., Aber, J. L., Carlson, V., & Cicchetti, D. (1991). Relationship of socioeco-nomic status to the etiology and developmental sequelae of physical child abuse. *Developmental Psychology, 27,* 148–158.

U.S. Bureau of the Census. (1998). *Statistical abstract of the United States* (118th ed.). Washington, DC: U.S. Government Printing Office.

Vandell, D. L., & Corasaniti, M. A. (1990). Child care and the family. In K. McCartney (Ed.), *New directions for child development* (Vol. 49, pp. 23–37). San Francisco: Jossey-Bass.

Wagner, R. K. (1997). Intelligence, training, and employment. *American Psychologist, 52,* 1059–1069.

Walk, R. D., & Gibson, E. J. (1961). A comparative and analytical study of visual depth perception. *Psychological Monographs, 75*(15).

Westerman, M. A. (1990). Coordination of maternal directives with preschoolers' behavior in compliance-problem and healthy dyads. *Developmental Psychology, 26,* 621–630.

Youngblade, L. M., & Belsky, J. (1992). Parent-child antecedents of 5-year-olds' close friendships: A longitudinal analysis. *Developmental Psychology, 28,* 700–713.

Zelazo, N. A., Zelazo, P. R., Cohen, K. M., & Zelazo, P. D. (1993). Specificity of practice effects on elementary neuromotor patterns. *Developmental Psychology, 29,* 686–691.

AD

ADULT
DEVELOPMENT

TRUTH OR FICTION?

_____ Single people are "swingers."

_____ Cohabitation is most common among college students.

_____ Most Americans would continue to work even if they did not need the money.

_____ Menopause signals the end of a woman's sexual interest.

_____ Mothers suffer from the empty nest syndrome when their youngest child leaves home.

_____ The percentage of the U.S. population aged 65 and above more than tripled during the 20th century.

_____ Frank Lloyd Wright created the innovative design for the Guggenheim Museum at the age of 65.

_____ Alzheimer's disease is a normal part of growing old.

_____ Older people who blame health problems on aging rather than on specific factors such as a virus are more likely to die in the near future.

WHAT NOW? YOU'VE BEEN THROUGH THE EARLY CHILD-hood years of utter dependency on adults. You've come through elementary school and high school. You're developing plans about a career, and you may be thinking about marriage and a family. Maybe you already have your early career laid out. Some of you are already involved in an enduring relationship or a marriage. Some of you have children. Because there are many returning students today, some of you may even have grandchildren.

What will happen as you journey through the remaining years of your adult life? Is everything going to come up roses, right on course? What are some of the typical life experiences of 40-, 50-, and 60-year-olds? Do you ever think about middle and late adulthood? Are you so young that it is almost impossible to imagine these periods of life will arrive? Given the alternative, let us hope they do. If you hold negative stereotypes of what it will be like to be a 45-year-old or a 55-year-old, let us also hope this chapter will replace some of your prejudices with accurate information and positive expectations.

I admit that I cannot foresee what your world, or your life, will be in 20 years or in 40 years. Gail Sheehy (1995, 1998b) suggests there may no longer be a "standard" life cycle with predictable stages or phases. Aging now has an "elastic quality" (Butler, 1998). People are living longer than ever before and are freer than ever to choose their own destiny. Lifestyle changes are accelerating. Perhaps our homes and our work will bear little resemblance to what they are today. Still, researchers have made enormous strides in cataloguing and accounting for many of the changes we undergo as we travel through young, middle, and late adulthood. Although we are unique as individuals, we also have a number of common experiences. These experiences are beneficial because they allow us to have some predictive power concerning our own futures. And, so to speak, "forewarned is forearmed." Predictability helps us exert control over our destinies. We can brace ourselves for inevitable negative life changes. We can prepare ourselves to take advantage of our opportunities.

The weight of theory and research concerning adult development is uplifting. There is much future to look forward to. Yes, there are alligators in the streams, and some of the strands of our rope bridges get frayed. Yes, accidents, illnesses, and failures can foreclose opportunities at any time. But for most of us the outlook is reasonably bright—in terms of our physical, cognitive, and social and personality development. Let us consider the adult years according to three broad categories: young adulthood, middle adulthood, and late adulthood.

YOUNG ADULTHOOD

Young, or early, adulthood covers the period between the ages of 20 and 40. Let us consider the changes that occur in physical, cognitive, and social and personality development.

Physical Development

Physical development peaks in young adulthood. Most people are at the apex of their sensory sharpness, strength, reaction time, and cardiovascular fitness. Women gymnasts find themselves going downhill in their early 20s because they accumulate body fat and lose suppleness and flexibility. Other kinds of athletes are more likely to experience a decline in their 30s. Most athletes retire before they reach 40.

Sexually speaking, most people in early adulthood become readily aroused. They tend to attain and maintain erections as desired, and to lubricate readily. A man in his 20s is more likely to be concerned about ejaculating too quickly than about whether or not he will be able to obtain an erection (Rathus et al., 2000).

Cognitive Development

People are also at the height of their cognitive powers during early adulthood. Many professionals show the broadest knowledge of their fields at about the time they are graduating from college or graduate school. At this time their course work is freshest. They may have just recently studied for comprehensive examinations. Once they enter their fields, they often specialize. As a result, knowledge deepens in certain areas, but understanding of related areas may grow relatively superficial.

Social and Personality Development

According to Erikson (1963), young adulthood is the stage of **intimacy versus isolation.** Erikson saw the establishment of intimate relationships as central to young adulthood. Young adults who have evolved a firm sense of identity during adolescence are ready to fuse their identities with those of other people through marriage and lasting friendships. People who do not reach out to develop intimate relationships risk retreating into isolation and loneliness.

Erikson warned that we may not be able to commit ourselves to others until we have achieved ego identity—that is, established stable life roles. Achieving ego identity is the central task of adolescence. Lack of personal stability is connected with the high divorce rate for teenage marriages.

Adults in their 20s tend to be fueled by ambition. Journalist Gail Sheehy (1976) labeled this period the **Trying 20s**—a period during which people basically strive to advance their careers. They are concerned about establishing their pathway in life. They are generally responsible for their own support, make their own choices, and are largely free from parental influences.

GENDER DIFFERENCES Most Western men consider separation and individuation to be key goals of personality development during young adulthood (Guisinger & Blatt, 1994). For women, however, the establishment and maintenance of social relationships are also of primary importance (Gilligan et al., 1991). Women, as Gilligan (1982) has pointed out, are likely to undergo a transition from being cared for by others to caring for others. In becoming adults, men are more likely to undergo a transition from being restricted by others to autonomy and perhaps control of other people.

According to an in-depth study of 40 men by Daniel Levinson and his colleagues (1978), men enter the adult world in their early 20s. Upon entry, they are faced with the tasks of exploring adult roles (in terms of careers, intimate relationships, and so on) and establishing stability in the

ESTABLISHING INTIMATE RELATIONSHIPS. According to Erik Erikson, establishing intimate relationships is a central task of young adulthood.

INTIMACY VERSUS ISOLATION Erikson's life crisis of young adulthood, characterized by the task of developing abiding intimate relationships.

TRYING 20S Sheehy's term for the third decade of life, when people are frequently occupied with advancement in the career world.

chosen roles. At this time, men also often adopt a **dream**—the drive to "become" someone, to leave their mark on history—which serves as a tentative blueprint for their life.

Although there are differences in the development of women and men, between the ages of 21 and 27 college women also develop in terms of individuation and autonomy (Helson & Moane, 1987). Women, like men, assert increasing control over their own lives. College women, on average, are relatively liberated and career oriented compared with their less-well-educated peers.

Levinson labeled the ages of 28 to 33 the **age-30 transition.** For men and women, the late 20s and early 30s are commonly characterized by reassessment: "Where is my life going?" "Why am I doing this?" Sheehy (1976) labeled this period the **Catch 30s** because of this tendency toward reassessment. During our 30s, we often find that the lifestyles we adopted during our 20s do not fit as comfortably as we had expected.

One response to the disillusionments of the 30s, according to Sheehy,

> is the tearing up of the life we have spent most of our 20s putting together. It may mean striking out on a secondary road toward a new vision or converting a dream of "running for president" into a more realistic goal. The single person feels a push to find a partner. The woman who was previously content at home with children chafes to venture into the world. The childless couple reconsiders children. And almost everybody who is married . . . feels a discontent. (1976, p. 34)

Many psychologists find that the later 30s are characterized by settling down or planting roots. Many young adults feel a need to make a financial and emotional investment in their home. Their concerns become more focused on promotion or tenure, career advancement, and long-term mortgages.

Lifestyles of the Rich and Famous— And of the Rest of Us

Part of social and personality development involves cultivating intimate relationships with other people. Erikson, for example, believed that a key issue of young adulthood is intimacy versus isolation—that is, whether we join our life with that of another person through an abiding relationship or remain alone. Developmental psychologist Robert Havighurst (1972) believed that each stage of development involves certain tasks. His developmental tasks for young adulthood include the following:

1. Getting started in an occupation
2. Selecting and courting a mate
3. Learning to live contentedly with one's partner
4. Starting a family and becoming a parent
5. Assuming the responsibilities of managing a home
6. Assuming civic responsibilities
7. Finding a congenial social group.

Erikson and Havighurst were theorizing 30 or 40 years ago, when it was widely assumed that young adults would want to get married and start families. Many young adults in the United States, perhaps most, still have these goals. But there are many different lifestyles today. Some people, for example, choose to remain single. Others choose to live together without getting married.

DREAM In this usage, Levinson's term for the overriding drive of youth to become someone important, to leave one's mark on history.

AGE-30 TRANSITION Levinson's term for the ages from 28 to 33, characterized by reassessment of the goals and values of the 20s.

CATCH 30S Sheehy's term for the fourth decade of life, when many people undergo major reassessments of their accomplishments and goals.

THE SINGLES SCENE: SWINGING, LONELY, OR ALL OF THE ABOVE? The final years of the 20th century saw a dramatic increase in the numbers of young adults who remained single. Being single became the nation's most common lifestyle for people in their early 20s. Young adults were delaying marriage for a variety of reasons. More people were going for advanced education, and many women were placing career objectives ahead of marriage.

But many young adults do not view being single as a stage of life that precedes marriage. Because career women are no longer financially dependent on men, a number of them choose to remain single (Lamott, 1993). Many young adults are single by choice and see being single as an alternative, open-ended lifestyle. Although most single mothers in the United States are young and poorly educated, larger numbers of single, older, well-educated professional women chose to become mothers in recent years (Lamott, 1993).

There is no single "singles scene." Being single is varied in intent and style of life. For some, it means singles bars and a string of one-night affairs. Some "swinging singles" do not want to be "trapped" with a single partner. They opt for many partners for the sake of novel sexual stimulation, the personal growth that can be attained through meeting many people, and the maintenance of independence. Yet many singles have become disillusioned with frequent casual sexual involvements. The singles bar provokes anxieties about physical and sexual abuse, fear of sexually transmitted diseases, and feelings of alienation as well as opportunities for sexual experience.

Other single people limit sex to affectionate relationships only. Many singles are delaying marriage until they find Mr. or Ms. Right. Along the way many practice *serial monogamy.* That is, they become involved in one exclusive relationship after another, rather than having multiple sexual relationships at the same time.

Many single people find that being single is not always as free as it seems. Some complain that employers and co-workers view them with skepticism and are reluctant to assign them responsibility. Their families may see them as selfish, as failures, or as sexually loose. Many single women complain that once they have entered their middle 20s, men are less willing to accept a "No" at the end of a date.

The goals and values that seem rock solid in the 20s may be shaken in the 30s. In their late 20s and 30s, many people who had chosen to remain single decide they would prefer to get married and have children. For women, of course, the "biological clock" may seem to be running out during the 30s. Yet some people choose to remain single for a lifetime.

COHABITATION: "THERE'S NOTHING THAT I WOULDN'T DO IF YOU WOULD BE MY POSSLQ" *There's Nothing That I Wouldn't Do If You Would Be My POSSLQ* is the name of a book by television commentator Charles Osgood. *POSSLQ?* That's the unromantic abbreviation for "Person of Opposite Sex Sharing Living Quarters"—the official term used for cohabitors by the U.S. Bureau of the Census.

Some social scientists believe that **cohabitation** has become accepted within the social mainstream (Steinhauer, 1995). Whether or not this is so, society in general has become more tolerant of it. We seldom hear cohabitation referred to as "living in sin" or "shacking up" as we once did. People today are more likely to refer to cohabitation with value-free expressions such as "living together."

Perhaps the current tolerance reflects societal adjustment to the increase in the numbers of cohabiting couples. Or perhaps the numbers of

TRUTH OR FICTION REVISITED
It is not true that single people are swingers. The statement is too general to be accurate. Single people follow a number of different kinds of styles of life.

COHABITATION An intimate relationship in which—pardon me—POSSLQs (pronounced POSS-L-CUE) live as though they are married, but without legal sanction.

TRUTH OR FICTION REVISITED
It is not true that cohabitation is most common among college students. Cohabitation is actually more prevalent among the less well educated and less affluent.

cohabiting couples have increased as a consequence of tolerance. The numbers of households consisting of unmarried adults of the other gender living together in the United States doubled between 1980 and the early 1990s (Steinhauer, 1995). They grew from 1.6 million couples in 1980 to more than 3 million couples in the 1990s (Saluter, 1995).

Much of the attention on cohabitation has focused on college students living together, but cohabitation is more prevalent among the less well educated and less affluent classes (Willis & Michael, 1994). The cohabitation rate is about twice as high among African American couples as White couples. Children live with about 1 cohabiting couple in 3 (Saluter, 1995).

About 1 cohabitor in 3 is divorced. Divorced people are more likely than people who have never been married to cohabit. The experience of divorce may make some people more willing to share their lives than their bank accounts—the second or third time around (Steinhauer, 1995).

Willingness to cohabit is related to more liberal attitudes toward sexual behavior, less traditional views of marriage, and less traditional views of gender roles (Huffman et al., 1994). Cohabitors are less likely than married people to attend church regularly (Laumann et al., 1994).

Why do people cohabit? Cohabitation is an alternative to the loneliness that can accompany living alone. Cohabitation, like marriage, creates a home life. Romantic partners may have deep feelings for each other but not be ready to get married. Some couples prefer cohabitation because it provides a consistent relationship without the legal entanglements of marriage (Steinhauer, 1995).

Economic factors also come into play. Some couples decide to cohabit because of the economic advantages of sharing household expenses. Cohabiting individuals who receive public assistance (social security or welfare checks) risk losing support if they get married (Steinhauer, 1995). Some older people live together rather than marry because of resistance from adult children. Some children fear that a parent will be victimized by a needy senior citizen. Others may not want their inheritances jeopardized or may not want to have to decide where to bury the remaining parent.

Many cohabitors feel less commitment toward their relationships than married people do (Nock, 1995). Ruth, an 84-year-old woman, has been living with her partner, age 85, for 4 years. "I'm a free spirit," she says. "I need my space. Sometimes we think of marriage, but then I think that I don't want to be tied down" (cited in Steinhauer, 1995, p. C7).

Ruth's comments are of interest because they counter stereotypes of women and older people. However, it is more often the man who is unwilling to make a marital commitment. Consider the case of Mark, a 44-year-old computer consultant who lives with Nancy and their 7-year-old daughter, Janet. Mark says, "We feel we are not primarily a couple but rather primarily individuals who happen to be in a couple. It allows me to be a little more at arm's length. Men don't like committing, so maybe this is just some sort of excuse" (cited in Steinhauer, 1995, p. C7).

MARRIAGE

Marriage is a great institution, but I'm not ready for an institution, yet.

MAE WEST

Marriage is our most popular lifestyle. In the United States 75% to 80% of people get married at least once (Saluter, 1995). Throughout Western history, marriage has helped people meet their personal and social needs. Marriage regulates and legitimizes sexual relations. Marriage creates a home life and provides an institution for the financial support and socialization of children. Marriage also permits the orderly transmission of wealth from one generation to another, and from one family to another.

Notions such as romantic love, equality, and the radical concept that men, like women, should be faithful are recent additions to the structure of marriage. Today many people believe that sex is acceptable within the bounds of an affectionate relationship, so the desire for a sexual relationship is less likely to motivate marriage. But marriage still offers a sense of emotional and psychological security—a partner with whom to share feelings, experiences, and goals. Among the highly educated, intimacy and companionship are central motives.

We tend to marry people to whom we are attracted. They are usually similar to us in physical attractiveness and hold similar attitudes on major issues. The concept of like marrying like is termed **homogamy**. In the United States, we only rarely marry people of different races or socioeconomic classes. According to the U.S. Bureau of the Census (USBC, 1998), only 2% of U.S. marriages are interracial. More than 90% of married couples are of the same religion.

We also follow *age homogamy*. Husbands tend to be 2 to 3 years older than their wives. Age homogamy reflects the tendencies to get married soon after achieving adulthood and to select partners, such as classmates, with whom we have been in close contact. People who are getting remarried, or marrying at later ages, are less likely to marry partners so close in age.

By and large, however, we seem to be attracted to and to get married to the boy or girl (almost) next door in a quite predictable manner. Marriages seem to be made in the neighborhood—not in heaven.

DIVORCE

> It is so far from being natural for a man and woman to live in a state of marriage that we find all the motives which they have for remaining in that connection, and the restraints which civilized society imposes to prevent separation, are hardly sufficient to keep them together.
>
> SAMUEL JOHNSON

> Whenever I date a guy, I think, is this the man I want my children to spend their weekends with?
>
> RITA RUDNER

> My wife and I were considering a divorce, but after pricing lawyers we decided to buy a new car instead.
>
> HENNY YOUNGMAN

In 1920, about 1 marriage in 7 ended in divorce. By 1960, this figure had risen to 1 in 4. Today nearly half of the marriages in the United States end in divorce (Laumann et al., 1994). More than one quarter (27%) of children under the age of 18 live in single-parent households (Saluter, 1995). Divorced women outnumber divorced men, in part because men are more likely to remarry (Saluter, 1995).

Why do so many people get divorced? One reason is the relaxation of legal restrictions on divorce, especially the introduction of the so-called no-fault divorce. Until the 1960s, adultery was the only legal grounds for divorce in New York State. Other states were equally strict. But no-fault divorce laws have since been enacted in nearly every state, allowing a divorce to be granted without a finding of marital misconduct. Another reason is the increased economic independence of women. Today a higher percentage of women in the United States have the financial means to break away from a troubled marriage. Today, more people regard marriage as an alterable condition than in prior generations.

HOMOGAMY The principle of like marrying like.

It is ironic that another reason for the high divorce rate is that people today hold higher expectations of marriage than their parents or grandparents did. They expect marriage to be personally fulfilling as well as meet the traditional expectation of marriage as an institution for rearing children. Many demand the right to be happy in marriage. The most common reasons given for a divorce today are problems in communication and a lack of understanding. Years ago it was more likely to be lack of financial support.

Divorce usually has financial and emotional repercussions. When a couple split, their resources may not be sufficient to maintain the former standard of living for both of them. A divorced woman's income drops by one quarter on the average, whereas a divorced man's income drops by less than 10% (Bianchi & Spain, 1997). The divorced woman who has not pursued a career may find herself competing for work with younger, more experienced people. Because women usually have custody of the children, they are also likely to bear—or to continue to bear—the main or sole responsibility for rearing the children as well as attempting to increase their income. The divorced man may not be able to manage alimony and child support and also establish a new home of his own.

People who are separated and divorced have the highest rates of mental and physical illness in the population (Rathus et al., 2000). Divorced people are subject to greater stress and feel that they exert less control over their lives. Feelings of failure as a spouse and parent, loneliness, and uncertainty prompt feelings of depression. But divorce can enable an individual to become a whole, autonomous person once more—or for the first time. Some people find that despite the pain and aggravation, the experience of divorce provides opportunities for self-renewal.

Divorce also has repercussions for the children. Research shows that divorce has a relatively greater effect on boys as measured in terms of dependence, anxiety, and conduct problems in school—perhaps because boys tend to be less mature than girls of the same age (Grych & Fincham, 1993; Holden & Ritchie, 1991). Problems can develop many years after a divorce, even among children who seem to have gotten through relatively unfazed. As adults, some may fear or assume that their own partners will not be capable of making permanent commitments to them (Wallerstein & Blakeslee, 1989). The emergence of such problems does not mean that it is best for parents to stay together for the sake of the children, however. Marital conflicts make relationships between parents and children more difficult and are also connected with eventual marital conflict in the children (Erel & Burman, 1995; Harold et al., 1997). That is, parental conflict and arguments seem to be as harmful or more harmful than divorce, and may even account for much of the harmful effects of divorce.

It also seems that it is not so much the divorce per se that has an impact on the children, but the breakdown in the quality of parenting that often follows the divorce (Erel & Burman, 1995; Harold et al., 1997). In order to protect the children, psychologists usually advise parents who are getting divorced to try to agree on how they will treat the children (e.g., children often ask a parent for something after the other parent has said no), help each other maintain a good parent-child relationship, and not criticize each other to or in front of the children.

The World of Work

Work is the refuge of people who have nothing better to do.

OSCAR WILDE

A century ago, the British playwright George Bernard Shaw pronounced, "Drink is the greatest evil of the working class." Upon sober reflection, he added, "Work is the greatest evil of the drinking class."

Humor aside, work in Shaw's day for most people involved backbreaking labor or mind-numbing factory work, sunrise to sunset, 6 days a week. Although most of today's workers put in fewer hours and are as likely to exercise their brains as their arms and backs, work is still at the core of the lives of many adults.

EXTRINSIC VERSUS INTRINSIC MOTIVES FOR WORKING Why do people work? One of the major reasons for working, if not *the* major reason, is economic. Work provides us with the means to pay our bills. The paycheck, fringe benefits, security in old age—all these are external or extrinsic motives for working. But work also satisfies many internal or intrinsic motives, including the opportunity to engage in stimulating and satisfying activities (Katzell & Thompson, 1990). Three Americans in four say they would work even if they did not have to, and half would stay in their present jobs (Hugick & Leonard, 1991).

Intrinsic reasons for working include the work ethic, self-identity, self-fulfillment, self-worth, and the social values of work. Occupational identity becomes intertwined with self-identity so we are likely to think, "I *am* a nurse" or "I *am* a lawyer" rather than "I work as a nurse" or "as an attorney." We often express our personal needs, interests, and values through our work. The self-fulfilling values of the work of the astronaut, scientist, and athlete may seem obvious. But factory workers, plumbers, police officers, and firefighters can also find self-enrichment as well as cash rewards for their work. Recognition and respect for a job well done contribute to self-esteem. The workplace also extends our social contacts. It introduces us to friends, lovers, challenging adversaries. At work, we may meet others who share our interests. We may form social networks that in our highly mobile society sometimes substitute for family.

VOCATIONAL DEVELOPMENT

> [I]f one advances confidently in the direction of his dreams, and endeavors to live the life which he has imagined, he will meet with a success unexpected in common hours.
>
> HENRY DAVID THOREAU, *WALDEN*

"Any child can grow up to be president." "My child—the doctor." "You can do anything, if you set your mind to it." America—land of opportunity. America—land of decision anxiety.

In societies with caste systems, such as Old England or India, children grew up to do what their parents did. They assumed that they would follow in their parents' footsteps. The caste system saved people the need to decide what they would "do" with themselves. Unfortunately, it also squandered special talents and made a mockery of personal freedom.

In the United States, choosing and becoming established in a career are among the developmental tasks of young adulthood. Yet there is a bewildering array of career possibilities. *The Dictionary of Occupational Titles,* published by the U.S. Department of Labor, lists more than 20,000 occupations. Nevertheless, most of us make our choices from a relatively narrow group of occupations, based on our experiences and our personalities. Some of us postpone career decisions so that when we have graduated from college we are no closer to settling on a career than when we began college. Many of us fall into careers not because of particular skills and interests, but because of what is available at the time, family pressures, or the lure of high income or a certain lifestyle.

Because of the overwhelming abundance of occupations, psychologists have devised methods of helping people make choices that are likely to work out for them. For example, psychologist John Holland (1997) predicts how well people will enjoy a certain kind of work by matching the

TRUTH OR FICTION REVISITED
It is true that most Americans would continue to work even if they did not need the money. We work not only for extrinsic rewards such as the paycheck and financial security, but also for intrinsic rewards, such as the opportunity to engage in challenging activities and broaden social contacts.

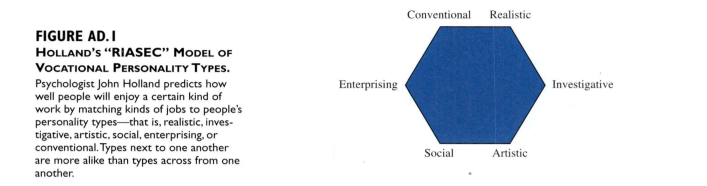

FIGURE AD.1

HOLLAND'S "RIASEC" MODEL OF VOCATIONAL PERSONALITY TYPES.
Psychologist John Holland predicts how well people will enjoy a certain kind of work by matching kinds of jobs to people's personality types—that is, realistic, investigative, artistic, social, enterprising, or conventional. Types next to one another are more alike than types across from one another.

kinds of jobs available to people's vocational personality types—that is, realistic, investigative, artistic, social, enterprising, or conventional (see Figure AD.1). In Holland's scheme, types next to one another are more alike than types across from one another. For example, people who are "conventional" are more likely to also be realistic or enterprising than they are to be artistic. Research shows that these six types are found among African, Asian, Mexican, Native, and White Americans (Day & Rounds, 1998), and they can be assessed by Holland's Vocational Preference Inventory and other tests. Consider each of them:

1. *Realistic.* Realistic people tend to be concrete in their thinking, mechanically oriented, and interested in jobs that involve motor activity.

   Examples include farming; unskilled labor, such as attending gas stations; and skilled trades, such as construction and electrical work.

2. *Investigative.* Investigative people tend to be creative, introverted, and abstract in their thinking. They are frequently well adjusted in research and college and university teaching.

3. *Artistic.* Artistic individuals tend to be creative, emotional, interested in subjective feelings, and intuitive. They tend to gravitate toward the visual and performing arts.

4. *Social.* Socially oriented people tend to be extraverted and socially concerned. They frequently show high verbal ability and strong needs for affiliating with others. They are often well suited to jobs such as social work, counseling, and teaching children.

5. *Enterprising.* Enterprising individuals tend to be adventurous and impulsive, domineering, and extraverted. They gravitate toward leadership and planning roles in industry, government, and social organizations. The successful small business owner or business manager is usually enterprising.

6. *Conventional.* Conventional people tend to enjoy routines. They show high self-control, a need for order, and a desire for social approval. They are not particularly imaginative. Jobs that suit them include banking, accounting, and clerical work.

Many occupations call for combinations of these traits. A copywriter in an advertising agency might be both artistic and enterprising. Clinical and counseling psychologists tend to be investigative, artistic, and socially oriented. Military personnel and beauticians tend to be realistic and conventional. (But military leaders who plan major operations and form governments are also enterprising; and individuals who create new hairstyles and fashions are also artistic.)

WOMEN IN THE WORKPLACE Working women usually work two shifts, one in the workplace and one at home. Nearly 90% of working women—including married and single mothers—continue to bear the major responsibility for child care (Lewin, 1995). (Nevertheless, a sizable minority of fathers—about 13%—are the primary care providers for their children [Casper, 1997].) Women miss work twice as often as men do when the kids are sick (Wasserman, 1993). Women, moreover, still carry out the great majority of the household chores—including cleaning, cooking, and shopping (see Figure AD.2). Between work, commuting, child care, and housework, American working women are putting in nearly 15 hours a day!

So *why* do women work? So the family can afford a second car? So the family can go on vacation? To send the kids off to camp in the summer? Not according to a poll by Louis Harris and Associates (cited in Lewin, 1995). These stereotypes are long outdated. Women no longer work to provide the family with a supplemental income. Women, like men, work to support the family.

Perhaps we are more familiar with high-powered mothers like Jane Pauley, Demi Moore, even Hillary Rodham Clinton. These women either outearn their husbands or provide the major support for their children. But out of the spotlight, the earning power of the ordinary woman has been growing significantly. According to the Harris poll, wives share about equally with their husbands in supporting their families. Nearly half of them—48%—reported that they provide at least half of their family's income. We are not talking vacation money here. We mean half of the mortgage, half of the clothing, half of the medical bills, even half of the new pairs of Nikes and the mountain bikes (Lewin, 1995).

So why do most of us still think of women as primarily mothers? Why haven't we paid more attention to their roles as providers? Perhaps it is because working mothers continue to do what mothers were doing before they became so vital a part of the work force. That is, 9 of 10 working mothers still bear the primary responsibility for the children, the cooking, and the cleaning (Lewin, 1995).

So Mom is still "traditional." That is, she is still looking after the house and kids. But now she also pays half the bills.

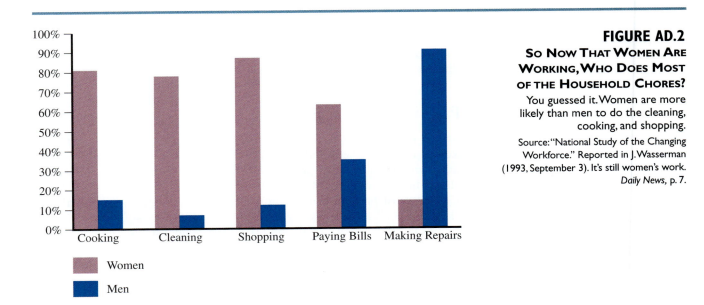

FIGURE AD.2
So Now That Women Are Working, Who Does Most of the Household Chores?
You guessed it. Women are more likely than men to do the cleaning, cooking, and shopping.
Source: "National Study of the Changing Workforce." Reported in J. Wasserman (1993, September 3). It's still women's work. *Daily News*, p. 7.

THE WORKPLACE FOR WOMEN

Despite some recent breaking down of traditional gender segregation, many occupations largely remain "men's work" or "women's work." According to the U.S. Department of Labor (1998), women still account for more than 90% of secretaries and kindergarten teachers, but for less than 5% of truck drivers and carpenters. But the percentage of women in medical and law schools has risen to nearly equal the numbers of men entering these professions. In other professional fields, however, the gap has not narrowed as much, particularly in fields such as math, science, and engineering.

THE EARNINGS GAP

Note these sad but fascinating examples of the earnings gap (Bianchi & Spain, 1997; Valian, 1998):

- Women overall earn about 72% of the income of men.

- Male physicians earn about $7 more an hour than female physicians.

- Male college professors advance more quickly than female college professors and earn about 30% more.

- The median salary of female scientists with bachelor's degrees and up to 2 years of experience was 73% that of their male colleagues in 1990. Those with doctorates made 88% of the median male salary.

- The average female high school graduate earns less than the average male grade-school *dropout*.

- Men with only an eighth-grade education earn more than the average female *college graduate*.

Why this gap in earnings? Some of it can be explained by the fact that most women still work in traditionally low-paying occupations such as waitress, housekeeper, clerk, salesperson, and light factory worker (Valian,

1998). Even in the same job area, such as sales, men are usually given higher-paying, more responsible positions. Men in sales are more likely to vend high-ticket items such as automobiles, microcomputers, and appliances.

Even though nearly as many women as men now graduate from medical schools, men tend to gravitate toward higher paying specialties, such as surgery. Female physicians are more likely to enter lower paying medical specialties, such as pediatrics and psychiatry. Men are also more likely than women to be in positions of power on medical school faculties.

Male college professors earn more than women for several reasons (Valian, 1998). Because women are relative newcomers to academia, they are more likely to be found in lower-paying entry positions, such as assistant professorships. When men and women reach full professor-

MIDDLE ADULTHOOD

Middle adulthood spans the years from 40 to 60 or 65. Let us consider the changes in physical, cognitive, and social and personality development that occur during this period.

Physical Development

At age 40 we do not possess quite the strength, coordination, and stamina we had during our 20s and 30s. This decline is most obvious in the professional ranks where peak performance is at a premium. Gordie Howe still played hockey at 50 and George Blanda was still kicking field goals at that age, but most professionals at those ages can no longer keep up with the "kids."

But the years between 40 and 60 are reasonably stable. There is gradual physical decline, but it is minor and only likely to be of concern if we insist on competing with young adults—or with idealized memories of ourselves. And many of us first make time to develop our physical potentials during middle adulthood. The 20-year-old couch potato occasionally becomes the

ships, the gap in pay narrows to under 10%. Another reason is that women are more likely than men to choose lower-paying academic fields, such as education and English. Men are more likely to be found on faculties in business, engineering, and the hard sciences, where the pay is higher. But women in the same academic field are promoted less rapidly than men are, in part because they publish fewer articles. Why the publication gap? Hunter College psychologist Virginia Valian (1998) notes that women's articles are written more painstakingly, as if they are less willing to make errors. Male academics seem more willing to take chances, perhaps because they feel less pressure to show they can do the job.

REDUCING THE EARNINGS GAP

Measures such as the following can improve the quality of work life and reduce the earnings gap for women:

1. *More realistic career planning.* The average woman today spends three decades in the work force, but may plan for a much shorter tenure. Young women should assume that they will be working for several decades and avail themselves of opportunities for education and training.

2. *Providing employers with accurate information about women in the work force.* If more employers recognized that women spend so many years in the work force, and that commitment to a job reflects the type of work rather than the gender of the worker, they might be more motivated to open the doors to women.

3. *Heightening awareness of the importance of the woman's career in dual-career marriages.* Husbands may also hold stereotypes that damage their wives' chances for career advancement and fulfillment. A couple should not blindly assume that the man's career always comes first. The man can

share child rearing and house-keeping chores so that each may reap the benefits of employment.

4. *Maintaining employment continuity and stability.* Promotions and entry into training programs are usually earned by showing a stable commitment to a career and, often, one's employer. Many couples permit both partners to achieve these benefits by postponing childbearing or sharing child rearing.

5. *Increasing job flexibility and providing child-care facilities.* Employers can also assist women workers through flex-time, providing on-site child-care facilities, and granting extended maternity and *paternity* leaves.

6. *Recruiting qualified women into training programs and jobs.* Educational institutions, unions, and employers can actively recruit qualified women for positions that have been traditionally held by men. ■

50-year-old marathoner. By any reasonable standard, we can maintain excellent cardiorespiratory condition throughout middle adulthood.

Because the physical decline in middle adulthood is gradual, people who begin to eat more nutritious diets (e.g., decrease intake of fats and increase intake of fruits and vegetables) and to exercise during this stage of life may find themselves looking and feeling better than they did in young adulthood. Sedentary people in young adulthood may gasp for air if they rush half a block to catch a bus, whereas fit people in middle adulthood—even in late adulthood—may run for miles before they feel fatigued.

MENOPAUSE **Menopause,** or cessation of menstruation, usually occurs during the late 40s or early 50s, although there are wide variations in the age at which it occurs. Menopause is the final stage of a broader female experience, the *climacteric,* which is caused by a falling off in the secretion of the hormones estrogen and progesterone, and during which many changes occur that are related to the gradual loss of reproductive ability. At this time ovulation also draws to an end. There is some loss of breast tissue and of elasticity in the skin. There can also be a loss of bone density that leads to osteoporosis (a condition in which the bones break easily) in late adulthood.

MENOPAUSE The cessation of menstruation.

During the climacteric, many women encounter symptoms such as hot flashes (uncomfortable sensations characterized by heat and perspiration) and loss of sleep. Loss of estrogen can be accompanied by feelings of anxiety and depression, but women appear to be more likely to experience serious depression prior to menopause, when they may feel overwhelmed by the combined demands of the workplace, child rearing, and homemaking (Brody, 1993). Most women get through the mood changes that can accompany menopause without great difficulty. According to psychologist Karen Matthews, who followed a sample of hundreds of women through menopause, "The vast majority [of women] have no problem at all getting through the menopausal transition" (Matthews, 1994, p. 25).

MYTHS ABOUT MENOPAUSE We are better able to adjust to life's changes when we have accurate information about them. Menopause is a major life change for most women, and many of us harbor misleading and maladaptive ideas about it. Consider the following myths and realities about menopause:

Myth 1.   *Menopause is abnormal.* No, menopause is a normal development in women's lives.

Myth 2.   *The medical establishment defines menopause as a disease.* No longer. Today menopause is conceptualized as a "deficiency syndrome," in recognition of the drop-off in secretion of estrogen and progesterone. Sad to say, the term *deficiency* also has negative connotations.

Myth 3.   *After menopause, women need complete replacement of estrogen.* Not necessarily. Some estrogen is still produced by the adrenal glands, fatty tissue, and the brain. The pros and cons of estrogen replacement therapy are still being debated.

Myth 4.   *Menopause is accompanied by depression and anxiety.* Not necessarily. Much of the emotional response to menopause reflects its meaning to the individual rather than physiological changes.

Myth 5.   *At menopause, women suffer debilitating hot flashes.* Many women do not have them at all. Those who do usually find them mild.

Myth 6.   *Menopause signals an end to women's sexual interests.* Not so (Brody, 1993). Many women find the separation of sex from reproduction to be sexually liberating. Some of the physical problems that may stem from the falloff in hormone production may be alleviated by hormone replacement therapy (Grodstein et al., 1997). A more important issue may be what menopause means to the individual (Sheehy, 1998a). Women who equate menopause with loss of femininity are likely to encounter more distress than those who do not (Rathus et al., 2000).

Myth 7.   *Menopause brings an end to a woman's childbearing years.* Not necessarily! After menopause, women no longer produce ova. However, ova from donors have been fertilized in laboratory dishes, and the developing embryos have been successfully implanted in the uteruses of postmenopausal women.

Myth 8.   *A woman's general level of activity is lower after menopause.* Research shows that many postmenopausal women become peppier and more assertive.

TRUTH OR FICTION REVISITED
It is not true that menopause signals the end of a woman's sexual interests. Some women, in fact, feel sexually liberated because of the separation of sexual expression and reproduction.

MANOPAUSE (MANOPAUSE?) Men cannot experience menopause, of course. Yet now and then we hear the term *male menopause,* or "manopause." Middle-aged or older men may be loosely alluded to as menopausal. This epithet is doubly offensive: It reinforces the negative, harmful stereotypes of aging people, especially aging women, as crotchety and irritable. Nor is the label consistent with the biology or psychology of aging. Alternate terms are *andropause* (referring to a drop-off in androgens, or male sex hormones) and *viropause* (referring to the end of virility) (Cowley, 1996).

For women, menopause is a time of relatively acute age-related declines in sex hormones and fertility. In men, however, the decline in the production of male sex hormones and fertility is more gradual (Sheehy, 1998b). Moreover, some viable sperm are produced even in late adulthood. It therefore is not surprising to find a man in his 70s or older fathering a child. But many men in their 50s and 60s have problems in achieving and maintaining erections (Laumann et al., 1994), which may or may not have to do with hormone production.

Sexual performance is only one part of the story, however. Between the ages of 40 and 70, the typical American male loses 12 to 20 pounds of muscle, about 2 inches in height, and 15% of his bone mass. (Men as well as women are at risk for osteoporosis [Brody, 1996].) The amount of fat in the body nearly doubles. The eardrums thicken, as do the lenses of the eyes, resulting in some loss of hearing and vision. There is also loss of endurance as the cardiovascular system and lungs become less capable of responding effectively to exertion.

Some of these changes can be slowed or even reversed. Exercise helps maintain muscle tone and keep the growth of fatty tissue in check. A diet rich in calcium and vitamin D can help ward off bone loss in men as well as in women. Hormone replacement may also help, but is controversial. Although testosterone replacement appears to boost strength, energy, and the sex drive, it is connected with increased risks of prostate cancer and cardiovascular disease (Cowley, 1996). Erection is made possible by the flow of blood into the caverns within the penis (vasocongestion), which then stiffens as a balloon does when air or water is pumped in. The drug Viagra facilitates erection by relaxing the muscles that surround the caverns, enabling blood vessels in the region to dilate.

Even though sexual interest and performance decline, men can remain sexually active and father children at advanced ages (Sheehy, 1998b). For both genders, attitudes toward the biological changes of aging—along with general happiness—may affect sexual behavior as much as biological changes do.

Social and Personality Development

Sheehy (1995) terms the years from 45 onward "second adulthood." Rather than viewing them as years of decline, her interviews suggest that many Americans find that these years present opportunities for new direction and fulfillment.

Researchers find that many people today make career changes in middle adulthood and beyond. Some do so because they find their jobs boring or unchallenging. Some are looking for better pay, more prestige, or the feeling of being more valued by an employer. Many workers are successful in terms of money and occupational prestige, but decide to pursue careers that may bring them more personal pleasure and satisfaction (Michelozzi, 1992; Steers & Porter, 1991). Some workers, of course, are laid off because of changes in technology or the popularity of the goods or services they had provided. Yet many people during the middle years are

MIDLIFE CRISIS OR "MIDDLESCENCE"? According to Gail Sheehy, many middle-aged people undergo a second quest for identity (the first occurs during adolescence). They are trying to decide what they will do with their "second adulthoods"— the three to four healthy decades they may have left.

secure enough but looking for something better, something that will better enable them to express their talents and interests.

GENERATIVITY VERSUS STAGNATION Erikson (1963) labeled the life crisis of the middle years **generativity versus stagnation.** Generativity involves doing things we believe are worthwhile, such as rearing children or producing on the job. Generativity enhances and maintains self-esteem. Generativity also involves helping shape the new generation. This shaping may involve rearing our own children or making the world a better place, for example, through joining church or civic groups. People who are unproductive during the middle years risk becoming stagnant, which means they may lose their sense of forward motion and encounter feelings of depression.

MIDLIFE TRANSITION According to Levinson, there is a **midlife transition** at about age 40 to 45 that is characterized by a shift in psychological perspective. Previously, we thought of our age in terms of the number of years that have elapsed since birth. Now we begin to think of our age in terms of the number of years we have left to live. Men in their 30s still think of themselves as part of the Pepsi generation, older brothers to "kids" in their 20s. At about age 40 to 45, however, some marker event— illness, a change of job, the death of a friend or parent, or being beaten at tennis by their son—leads men to realize that they are a full generation older. Suddenly there seems to be more to look back on than forward to. It dawns on men that they will never be president or chairman of the board. They will never play shortstop for the Dodgers. They mourn the passing of their own youth and begin to adjust to the specter of old age and the finality of death.

THE MIDLIFE CRISIS Again, according to Levinson, the midlife transition may trigger a crisis—a so-called **midlife crisis.** The middle-level, middle-aged businessperson looking ahead to another 10 to 20 years of grinding out accounts in a Wall Street cubbyhole might encounter this crisis as a severe depression. The housewife with two teenagers, an empty house from 8 a.m. to 4 p.m., and a 40th birthday on the way could feel she is coming apart at the seams. Both could feel a sense of entrapment, that options are closing down forever, and a loss of purpose. Some people are propelled into extramarital affairs by the desire to prove to themselves that they are still attractive.

It seems to make some sense that the midlife transition would or could trigger such a crisis, but does it? Levinson's conclusions are based on interviews with 40 men, yet survey research calls the very existence of such a crisis into question. The midlife crisis is defined as involving feelings of mortality, loss of meaning, emotional instability, and dissatisfaction with one's life at home and on the job. But a survey of over 10,000 adults aged 30 to 60 found no evidence of any particular crisis at age 40 (McCrae & Costa, 1990). Nor was there any particular "bump" in the measures of instability and dissatisfaction at any time during the 40s.

In retrospect, Levinson's view seems to have been too pessimistic. Even if his sample experienced such a crisis, perhaps it was because medicine was less advanced during the 1970s, resulting in poorer health at midlife. Gail Sheehy's (1995) research yields a very different picture.

MASTERY AND "SECOND ADULTHOOD" Sheehy (1995) is more optimistic than Levinson. She terms the years from 45 to 65 the "Age of

GENERATIVITY VERSUS STAGNATION Erikson's term for the crisis of middle adulthood, characterized by the task of being productive and contributing to younger generations.

MIDLIFE TRANSITION Levinson's term for the ages from 40 to 45, characterized by a shift in psychological perspective from viewing ourselves in terms of years lived to viewing ourselves in terms of the years we have left.

MIDLIFE CRISIS A crisis experienced by many people during the midlife transition when they realize that life may be more than halfway over and reassess their achievements in terms of their dreams.

Mastery" because people are frequently at the height of their productive powers during this period. Sheehy believes that the key task for people aged 45 to 55 is to decide what they will do with their "second adulthoods"—the 30 to 40 healthy years that may be left for them once they reach 50. She believes that both men and women can experience great success and personal fulfillment if they identify meaningful goals and pursue them wholeheartedly.

"MIDDLESCENCE" Yet people do need to define themselves and their goals. Sheehy coined the term **middlescence** to describe a period of searching that is in some ways similar to adolescence. Both are times of transition. Middlescence involves a search for a new identity: "Turning backward, going around in circles, feeling lost in a buzz of confusion and unable to make decisions—all this is predictable and, for many people, a necessary precursor to making the passage into midlife" (Sheehy, 1995).

It may be that women undergo a sort of midlife transition a number of years earlier than men do (e.g., Reinke et al., 1985). Sheehy (1976) writes that women enter midlife about 5 years earlier than men, at about age 35 instead of 40. Once they turn 35, women are usually advised to have their fetuses routinely tested for Down syndrome and other chromosomal disorders. At age 35, women also enter higher risk categories for side effects from birth control pills.

Yet women frequently experience a renewed sense of self in their 40s and 50s as they emerge from "middlescence" (Apter, 1995; Sheehy, 1995). Many women in their early 40s are already emerging from some of the fears and uncertainties that are first confronting men. For example, Helson and Moane (1987) found that women at age 43 are more likely than women in their early 30s to feel confident; to exert an influence on their community; to feel secure and committed; to feel productive, effective, and powerful; and to extend their interests beyond their family.

THE EMPTY NEST SYNDROME In earlier decades, psychologists placed great emphasis on a concept referred to as the **empty nest syndrome.** This concept was applied most often to women. It was assumed that women experience a profound sense of loss when their youngest child goes off to college, gets married, or moves out of the home. Research findings paint a more optimistic picture, however. Certainly there can be problems, and these apply to both parents. Perhaps the largest of these is letting go of one's children after so many years of mutual dependence.

Many mothers report increased marital satisfaction and personal changes such as greater mellowness, self-confidence, and stability after their children have left home (Reinke et al., 1985). Middle-aged women show increased dominance and assertiveness, an orientation toward achievement, and greater influence in the worlds of politics and work. It is as if they are cut free from traditional shackles by the knowledge that their childbearing years are behind them.

Family role reversals are not uncommon once the children have left home (Wink & Helson, 1993). Given traditional sociocultural expectations of men and women, men are frequently more competent than their wives in the world outside the family during the early stages of marriage, and their wives are more emotionally dependent. But in the postparental period these differences may decrease or reverse direction, both because of women's enhanced status in the workplace and because of the decreased influence of the mother role.

Now let us consider developments in late adulthood, which begins at the age of 65.

TRUTH OR FICTION REVISITED
It is not true that mothers in general suffer from the empty nest syndrome when their youngest child leaves home. Most mothers (and fathers) do *not* suffer when their youngest child leaves home.

MIDDLESCENCE Sheehy's term for a stage of life, from 45 to 55, when people seek new identity and are frequently "lost in a buzz of confusion."

EMPTY NEST SYNDROME A sense of depression and loss of purpose felt by some parents when the youngest child leaves home.

LATE ADULTHOOD

It's never too late to be what you might have been.

GEORGE ELIOT

Did you know that an *agequake* is coming? With improved health care and knowledge of the importance of diet and exercise, more Americans than ever before are 65 or older (Abeles, 1997a). The percentage of people aged 65 and above more than tripled during the 20th century (APA Task Force, 1998). In 1900, only 1 American in 30 was over 65, as compared with 1 in 9 in 1970. By 2030, 1 American in 5 will be 65 or older ("Longer," 1997; see Figure AD.3).

The agequake will shake America. It has already influenced the themes of TV shows and movies. Many consumer products are designed to appeal to older consumers. Leisure communities dot the sunbelt. Older people today differ from their counterparts of a generation or two ago in that age is becoming less likely to determine their behavior and mental processes (Butler, 1998). However, the prospects are not the same for men and women, or for people from different ethnic backgrounds.

Physical Development

More people in the United States are living into late adulthood. Some are benefitting from innovations in health care. Many are prolonging life by eating a healthful diet and by exercising. Nevertheless, the functioning of the immune system declines, leaving older people more vulnerable to disease. These changes eventually result in death.

Some changes of aging seem to be largely unavoidable (see Figure AD.4). These include changes in the skin, hair, and nails, in the senses, in reaction time, and in lung capacity. Other changes may be moderated to some degree by means such as exercise and diet. These include changes in metabolism (the rate at which the body converts food to energy), muscle mass, strength, bone density, lung capacity, tolerance of sugar in the blood (blood-sugar level), and the ability to regulate one's body temperature (Evans & Rosenberg, 1991). Let us consider some of these changes in depth.

COSMETIC CHANGES People develop wrinkles and gray hair if they live long enough. The hair grows gray as the production of *melanin,* the pigment responsible for hair color, declines. Hair loss also accelerates as people age, especially in men.

The aging body produces less *collagen* and *elastin,* proteins that make the skin elastic, soft, and supple. The body also produces fewer of the kinds of cells found in the outer layer of skin, so the skin becomes drier, more brittle, and prone to wrinkles. The tendency to wrinkling reflects one's heredity as well as hormonal balances and environmental influences such as diet and exposure to the sun. Exposure to ultraviolet (UV) rays accelerates the aging of the skin. People—including older people—who lie on the beach, especially at midday, are not only aging their skin; they are also heightening their risk of skin cancer.

SENSORY CHANGES Age-related changes in vision usually begin in the mid-30s. The lenses of the eyes become more brittle so they are less capable of focusing on fine print (which is why people tend to need reading glasses as they age) or nearby objects. Other changes of aging can lead to eye problems such as *cataracts* and *glaucoma.* Cataracts cloud the lens, impairing the focusing of light on the retina, resulting in blurred vision

FIGURE AD.3

LIVING LONGER.

As we enter the new millennium, more people in the United States are living to age 65 or above.

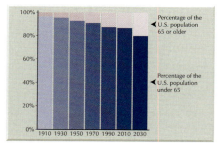

HAIR AND NAILS
Hair often turns gray and
thins out. Men may go bald.
Fingernails can thicken.

BRAIN
The brain shrinks, but
it is not known if that affects
mental functions.

THE SENSES
The sensitivity of hearing,
sight, taste, and smell can
all decline with age.

SKIN
Wrinkles occur as the skin thins
and the underlying fat shrinks,
and age spots often crop up.

GLANDS AND HORMONES
Levels of many hormones
drop, or the body becomes
less responsive to them.

IMMUNE SYSTEM
The body becomes less able
to resist some pathogens.

LUNGS
It doesn't just seem
harder to climb those stairs;
lung capacity drops.

HEART AND BLOOD VESSELS
Cardiovascular problems
become more common.

MUSCLES
Strength usually peaks
in the 20s, then declines.

KIDNEY AND URINARY TRACT
The kidneys become less efficient.
The bladder can't hold as much,
so urination is more frequent.

DIGESTIVE SYSTEM
Digestion slows down
as the secretion of digestive
enzymes decreases.

REPRODUCTIVE SYSTEM
Women go through
menopause, and testosterone
levels drop for men.

BONES AND JOINTS
Wear and tear can lead to
arthritic joints, and osteoporosis is
common, especially in women.

FIGURE AD.4
THE RELENTLESS MARCH OF TIME.
A number of physical changes occur during the later years.

GENDER, ETHNICITY, AND AGING

Although Americans in general are living longer, there are gender and ethnic differences in life expectancy. For example, women in our society tend to live longer, but older men tend to live *better* ("Longer," 1997). White Americans from European backgrounds live longer on the average than do Hispanic Americans, African Americans, and Native Americans. The longevity of Asian Americans is similar to that of White Americans. Native Americans have the lowest average longevity of the major racial/ethnic groups in our society (Rathus et al., 2000).

GENDER DIFFERENCES

Women in the United States outlive men by 6 to 7 years. Why? For one thing, heart disease, the nation's leading killer, typically develops later in women than in men. Men are also more likely to die because of accidents, cirrhosis of the liver, strokes, suicide, homicide, AIDS, and cancer (excepting cancers of the female sex organs) (Nevid et al., 1998). Many deaths from these causes are the end result of unhealthy habits that are more typical of men, such as excessive drinking and reckless behavior.

Many men are also reluctant to have regular physical exams or to talk to their doctors about their health problems (Brody, 1998). "In their 20's, [men are] too strong to need a doctor; in their 30's, they're too busy, and in their 40's, too scared" ("Doctors," 1995). Women are much more likely to examine themselves for signs of breast cancer than men are even to recognize the early signs of prostate cancer.

Although women tend to outlive men, their prospects for a happy and healthy old age are dimmer. Men who beat the statistical odds by living beyond their 70s are far less likely than their female counterparts to live alone, suffer from chronic disabling conditions, or be poor.

Older women are more likely than men to live alone largely because they are five times more likely than men to be widowed (Nevid et al., 1998). Older women are also twice as likely to be poor than older men. Several factors account for this difference. Women now age 65 or older were less likely to hold jobs. If they had jobs, they were paid far less than men and received smaller pensions and other retirement benefits. Because more women than men live alone, they more often must shoulder the burdens of supporting a household without being able to draw on the income of a spouse or other family member.

ETHNIC DIFFERENCES

Why are there ethnic differences in life expectancy? Socioeconomic differences play a role. Members of ethnic minority groups in our society are more likely to be poor, and poor people tend to eat less nutritious diets, encounter more stress, and have less access to health care. There is a 7-year difference in life expectancy between people in the highest income brackets and those in the lowest. Yet other factors, such as cultural differences in diet and lifestyle, the stress of coping with discrimination, and genetic differences, may also partly account for ethnic group differences in life expectancy. ∎

and possible blindness. Glaucoma is caused by increased pressure within the eyeball, causing the eyeball to harden, tunnel vision (loss of peripheral vision), and possible blindness. These conditions are treated with medication or surgery.

The sense of hearing also declines with age, more quickly in men than women. Many older people secrete more ear wax, which can impair hearing. But hearing loss in late adulthood frequently results from loss of flexibility in the bones and membranes of the middle and inner ears, and decreased circulation in the inner ear. Hearing aids amplify sounds and often compensate for hearing loss.

Smell and taste lose their sharpness as people age, so food loses much of its flavor. The sense of smell declines more sharply. Older people often spice their food heavily to obtain flavor.

REACTION TIME   Age-related changes in the nervous system increase reaction time—the amount of time it takes to respond to a stimulus. Older people cannot catch rapidly moving baseballs or footballs or dodge other cars as easily when driving.

CHANGES IN LUNG CAPACITY, MUSCLE MASS, AND METABOLISM   The walls of the lungs stiffen as people age, no longer expanding as readily as when people were younger. Between the ages of 20 and 70, lung capacity may decline by 40% or so. Regular exercise can prevent much of this decline, however (Kotre & Hall, 1990).

The very composition of the body changes. Muscle cells are lost with age, especially after the age of 45 (Evans & Rosenberg, 1991). Fat replaces muscle. There is a consequent reshaping of the body and loss of muscle strength. However, exercise can compensate for much of the loss by increasing the size of the muscle cells that remain.

The metabolic rate declines as we age, largely because of the loss of muscle tissue and the corresponding increase in body fat. Muscle burns more calories—has a faster metabolic rate—than fat. People also require fewer calories to maintain their weight as they age, and extra calories are deposited as fat. Older people are thus likely to gain weight if they eat as much as they did when they were younger. Regular exercise helps older people maintain a healthful weight just as it does with younger people. Not only does exercising burn calories; it also builds the muscle mass, and muscle burns calories more efficiently than fat.

The cardiovascular system becomes less efficient with age. The heart pumps less blood and the blood vessels carry less blood, which has implications for sexual functioning, as we see later.

CHANGES IN BONE DENSITY   Bones consist mainly of calcium, and they begin to lose density in early middle age, frequently leading to osteoporosis. *Osteoporosis* literally translates as "porous bone," meaning that the bone becomes porous rather than maintaining its density. As a result, the risk of fractures increases. Osteoporosis poses a greater threat to women because men usually begin with a larger bone mass, providing some protection against the disease. Bone loss in women is connected with low levels of estrogen at menopause (Delmas et al., 1997). Following menopause, women may have only half the bone density they had in young adulthood ("Size Up," 1996). Women are three times as likely as men to suffer fractures of the hip ("Size Up," 1996). Seven of 8 hip fractures occur in people aged 65 or older (Brody, 1992). Hip fractures can be deadly among older people. Nearly one quarter of those who have them die within a year ("Size Up," 1996). Loss of bone density can also shorten people by inches and lead to deformities such as curvature of the spine ("dowager's hump").

Loss of estrogen can also have psychological effects. It can impair cognitive functioning—making it more difficult to solve problems. It can also give rise to feelings of anxiety and depression, which further impair the ability to cope with stress (Sourander, 1994).

Some women use synthetic estrogen and progesterone (hormone replacement therapy) to prevent the kinds of physical and psychological problems that can attend menopause. Estrogen has the added benefits of helping protect people from heart disease, which is why women are less likely than men to suffer heart attacks until after menopause. Estrogen replacement also lowers the risks of colon cancer and Alzheimer's disease (Grodstein et al., 1996, 1997). But estrogen replacement can heighten the risk of breast cancer and some other health problems, so it is not used universally. Researchers are now developing forms of estrogen replacement that do not increase the risk of breast cancer and other disorders.

CHANGES IN SEXUAL FUNCTIONING Age-related changes affect sexual functioning as well as other areas of functioning (see Table AD.1). Yet people are capable of enjoying sexual experience for a lifetime if they make some adjustments, including adjustments to their expectations. Older men and women may both experience less interest in sex, which is apparently related to lowered levels of testosterone (yes, women naturally produce some testosterone) in both genders.

Many physical changes in older women reflect the lower estrogen levels of menopause. The vaginal opening becomes constricted and the vaginal walls become less elastic. The vagina shrinks in size. Less vaginal lubrication is produced. All these changes can make sexual activity irritating. Some of these changes may be arrested or reversed through estrogen replacement therapy. Natural lubrication may be increased through elaborate foreplay. An artificial lubricant can also be of help.

The muscle tone of the pelvic region decreases so that orgasms become less intense. Still, women can retain the ability to reach orgasm into advanced old age. The experience of orgasm can remain very satisfying, regardless of the intensity of muscle contractions.

Age-related changes are more gradual in men and not connected to any single biological event like menopause. Male adolescents can attain erection in seconds through sexual fantasy alone. Older men take more time to attain erections, and the erections are less firm, possibly because of lowered testosterone production. Fantasy may no longer do it; extensive direct stimulation (stroking) may be needed. Many, perhaps half, of men have at least intermittent difficulty attaining erections in middle and late adulthood. They also usually require more time to reach orgasm. Couples can adjust to these changes by extending the length and variety of foreplay. Viagra and similar drugs help men attain erections (and also help women become aroused, as shown, for example, by lubrication of the vaginal barrel) by increasing the flow of blood to the genitals when sexual activity alone does not do it.

The testes may decrease slightly in size and produce less testosterone with age. Testosterone production usually declines gradually through

TABLE AD.1

CHANGES IN SEXUAL RESPONSE CONNECTED WITH AGING

CHANGES THAT OCCUR IN WOMEN	CHANGES THAT OCCUR IN MEN
Less interest in sex	Less interest in sex
Less blood flow to the genitals	Less blood flow to the genitals
Less vaginal lubrication	More time needed to attain erection and reach orgasm
Less elasticity in vaginal walls	More need for direct stimulation (touch) to attain erection
Smaller increases in breast size	Less firm erections
Less intense orgasms	Less ejaculate
	Less intense orgasms
	More time needed to become aroused (erect) again

middle adulthood and begins to level off in late adulthood. An adolescent may require but a few minutes to regain erection and ejaculate again after a first orgasm, whereas older men may require hours. Older men produce less ejaculate, and it may seep out rather than gush out. Orgasms become weaker as measured by the physical aspects of orgasm—that is, the strength and number of muscle contractions at the base of the penis. But physical measures do not translate exactly into pleasure. An older man may enjoy orgasms as much as he did when younger. Again, attitudes and expectations are crucial to the continued enjoyment of sexual activity.

In sum, late adulthood need not bring a man's or a woman's sex life to a halt. Their expectations and the willingness of their partners to help them adjust are crucial factors in sexual fulfillment.

Theories of Aging

Although it may be hard to believe it will happen to us, every person who has walked the Earth so far has aged—which may not be a bad fate, considering the alternative. Why do we age? Various factors, some of which are theoretical, apparently contribute to aging.

The theory of **programmed senescence** sees aging as determined by a biological clock that ticks at a rate governed by instructions in the genes. Just as genes program children to grow and reach sexual maturation, they program people to deteriorate and die. There is evidence to support a role for genes in aging. Longevity runs in families. People whose parents and grandparents lived into their 80s and 90s have a better chance of reaching these ages themselves.

The **wear-and-tear theory** does not suggest that people are programmed to self-destruct. Instead, environmental factors such as pollution, disease, and ultraviolet light are assumed to contribute to wear and tear of the body over time. The body is like a machine whose parts wear out through use. Cells lose the ability to regenerate themselves, and vital organs are worn down by the ravages of time.

Behavior also influences aging. People who exercise regularly seem to live longer. Cigarette smoking, overeating, and stress can contribute to an early death. Fortunately, we can exert control over some of these factors.

Americans are living longer than ever, and part of the reason is that many of them are taking charge of their own lives, influencing not only how long they live, but how well they live. Regular medical evaluations, proper diet (for example, consuming less fat), and exercise all help people live longer.

Exercise helps older people maintain flexibility and cardiovascular condition. The exercise need not be of the type that pounds the body and produces rivers of sweat. Because older people tend to have more brittle bones and more rigid joints, fast or prolonged walking are excellent aerobic choices for them.

Amy Hakim of the University of Virginia School of Medicine and her colleagues (1998) provided dramatic evidence of the value of exercise—in this case, walking—for older people. They reviewed 12 years of data on 707 retired men from the Honolulu Heart Program and found that 43.1% of the men who walked less than a mile per day died during that period, as compared with 27.7% of those who walked from 1 to 2 miles a day and 21.5% of those who walked at least 2 miles daily. Additional findings: 6.6% of the men who walked less than a mile a day died from coronary heart disease or strokes, as compared with only 2.1% of those who walked upward of 2 miles (see Figure AD.5). Moreover, 13.4% of the men who walked less than a mile died from cancer, as compared with 5.3% who walked more than 2 miles a day. Because the study was not experimental,

PROGRAMMED SENESCENCE The view that aging is determined by a biological clock that ticks at a rate governed by genes.

WEAR-AND-TEAR THEORY The view that factors such as pollution, disease, and ultraviolet light contribute to wear and tear on the body, so the body loses the ability to repair itself.

FIGURE AD.5

CAUSES OF DEATH AND DISTANCE WALKED IN MILES PER DAY AMONG PARTICIPANTS IN THE HONOLULU HEART PROGRAM.

Men who walked more than 2 miles a day had a lower mortality rate than men who walked between 1 and 2 miles a day and men who walked less than a mile a day. Men who took long walks were less likely to die from cancer and heart disease (Hakim et al., 1998).

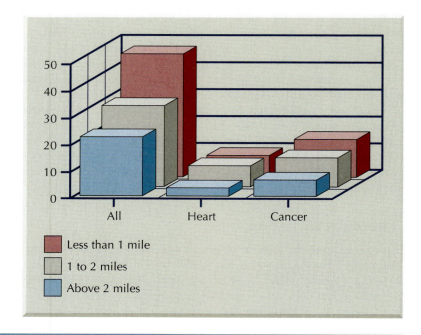

one can ask whether those who walked less died sooner because they were hobbled by health problems that made them less able or willing to walk. Hakim and her colleagues recognized this problem and got around it partly by using data only on nonsmokers who were physically able to walk a few miles. Older people can also continue to fight heart disease and cancer by eating diets low in cholesterol and saturated fats (Wolk et al., 1998).

Cognitive Development

Cognitive development in adulthood has many aspects—creativity, memory functioning, and intelligence. People can be creative for a lifetime. Picasso was painting in his 90s. Grandma Moses did not even begin painting until she was 78 years old. The architect Frank Lloyd Wright designed New York's spiral-shaped Guggenheim Museum when he was 89 years old.

People are probably at their height in terms of learning and memory in young adulthood. Memory functioning declines with age. It is common enough for older people to have trouble recalling the names of common objects or people they know. Memory lapses can be embarrassing, and older people sometimes lose confidence in their memories, which then lowers their motivation to remember things (Cavanaugh & Green, 1990). But declines in memory are not usually as large as people assume (Abeles, 1997b). Memory tests usually measure ability to recall meaningless information. Older people show better memory functioning in areas in which they can apply their experience, especially in their areas of specialization, to new challenges (Graf, 1990). For example, who would do a better job of learning and remembering how to solve problems in chemistry—a college history major or a retired professor of chemistry?

People also obtain the highest intelligence test scores in young adulthood (Baltes, 1997). Yet people tend to retain their verbal skills, as demonstrated by their vocabularies and general knowledge, into advanced old age. It is their performance on tasks that require speed and visual-spatial skills, such as putting puzzles together, that tends to fall off (Lindenberger et al., 1993; Schaie, 1994; Schaie & Willis, 1991).

TRUTH OR FICTION REVISITED
It is not true that Frank Lloyd Wright created the innovative design for the Guggenheim Museum at the age of 65. But the reason is that he created the New York City museum at the age of 89!

CRYSTALLIZED VERSUS FLUID INTELLIGENCE Consider the difference between *crystallized intelligence* and *fluid intelligence.* **Crystallized intelligence** represents one's lifetime of intellectual attainments, as shown by vocabulary and accumulated facts about world affairs. Therefore, crystallized intelligence generally increases over the decades. **Fluid intelligence** is defined as mental flexibility, demonstrated by the ability to process information rapidly, as in learning and solving problems in new areas of endeavor.

In terms of people's worth to their employers, familiarity in solving the kinds of problems found on the job (their crystallized intelligence) may be more important than their fluid intelligence. Experience on the job enhances people's specialized vocabularies and their knowledge of the area. People draw on fluid intelligence when the usual solutions no longer work, but experience is often more valuable than fluid intelligence.

The role of experience brings us to what some developmental theorists refer to as **postformal thought** (Labouvie-Vief, 1992), which is shown by some adults, including some in late adulthood. *Formal* operational thought is the highest stage of intellectual development within Jean Piaget's theory. It is characterized by deductive logic, consideration of various ways of solving problems (mental trial and error), abstract thought, and the formation and testing of hypotheses. *Post*formal thought is characterized by creative thinking, the ability to solve complex problems, and the posing of new questions. People usually show postformal thinking in their areas of expertise or specialization, providing one more suggestion that experience often compensates for age-related losses in intellectual functioning.

THE SEATTLE LONGITUDINAL STUDY Psychologist Walter Schaie and his colleagues (Schaie, 1994) have been studying the cognitive development of adults for four decades and discovered factors that contribute to intellectual functioning across the lifespan:

1. *General health.* People in good health tend to retain higher levels of intellectual functioning into late adulthood. Therefore, paying attention to one's diet, exercising, and having regular medical checkups contribute to intellectual functioning as well as physical health.

2. *Socioeconomic status (SES).* People with high SES tend to maintain intellectual functioning more adequately than people with low SES. High SES is also connected with above-average income and levels of education, a history of stimulating occupational pursuits, maintenance of intact families, and better health.

3. *Stimulating activities.* Cultural events, travel, participation in professional organizations, and extensive reading contribute to intellectual functioning.

4. *Marriage to a spouse with a high level of intellectual functioning.* The spouse whose level of intellectual functioning is lower at the beginning of a marriage tends to increase in intellectual functioning as time goes by. Perhaps that partner is continually challenged by the other.

5. *Openness to new experience.* Being open to new challenges of life apparently helps keep us young—at any age.

ALZHEIMER'S DISEASE **Alzheimer's disease** is a progressive form of mental deterioration that affects about 10% of people over the age of 65. The risk increases dramatically with advanced age. Although Alzheimer's is connected with aging, it is a disease and not part of the normal aging process.

CRYSTALLIZED INTELLIGENCE A person's lifetime of intellectual attainments, as shown by vocabulary, accumulated facts about world affairs, and ability to solve problems within one's areas of expertise.

FLUID INTELLIGENCE Mental flexibility, as shown by the ability to process information rapidly, as in learning and solving problems in new areas of endeavor.

POSTFORMAL THOUGHT A hypothesized stage of cognitive development that follows formal operational thought and is characterized by creative thinking, the ability to solve complex problems, and the posing of new questions.

ALZHEIMER'S DISEASE A disease that causes progressive mental deterioration and that affects about 10% of people over the age of 65.

We consider Alzheimer's disease within the section on cognitive development because it is characterized by general, gradual deterioration in mental processes such as memory, language, and problem solving. As the disease progresses, people may fail to recognize familiar faces or forget their names. At the most severe stage, people with Alzheimer's disease become helpless. They become unable to communicate or walk and require help in toileting and feeding. More isolated memory losses (for example, forgetting where one put one's glasses) may be a normal feature of aging (Abeles, 1997b). Alzheimer, in contrast, seriously impairs vocational and social functioning.

In Alzheimer's disease, there is a loss of synapses in the hippocampus and the frontal cortex (Tanzi, 1995). Acetylcholine (ACh) is normally prevalent in the hippocampus, but people with Alzheimer's have reduced levels of ACh in their brains. Thus drug therapy has aimed at heightening ACh levels. Drugs achieve modest benefits with many people by inhibiting the breakdown of ACh.

Alzheimer's is a disease and does not reflect the normal aging process. However, there are normal, more gradual declines in intellectual functioning and memory among older people, although they are not as large as many people assume they are (Abeles, 1997b; Butler, 1998). But we understand very little about *why* these declines occur. Depression and losses of sensory acuity and motivation may contribute to lower cognitive test scores. B. F. Skinner (1983) argued that much of the falloff is due to an "aging environment" rather than an aging person. That is, the behavior of older people often goes unreinforced. This idea is substantiated by a study of nursing home residents who were rewarded for remembering recent events and showed improved scores on tests of memory (Langer et al., 1979).

Social and Personality Development

According to Erikson, late adulthood is the stage of **ego integrity versus despair.** The basic challenge is to maintain the belief that life is meaningful and worthwhile in the face of the inevitability of death. Ego integrity derives from wisdom, as well as from the acceptance of one's lifespan as occurring at a certain point in the sweep of history and as being limited. We spend most of our lives accumulating objects and relationships. Erikson also argues that adjustment in the later years requires the ability to let go.

Other psychosocial theories of aging include disengagement theory, activity theory, and continuity theory (Berger, 1994).

1. **Disengagement theory.** Disengagement theory maintains that the individual and society withdraw from each other during the later years. Traditional roles such as those of worker and parent give way to a narrowed social circle and reduced activity.

2. **Activity theory.** According to this view, life satisfaction is connected with remaining active. Unfortunately, retirement and the narrowing of one's social circle often reduce activity.

3. **Continuity theory.** Continuity theory maintains that individuals tend to cope with the challenges of late adulthood the same way they coped with earlier challenges. Individual temperament and differences are more important determinants of life satisfaction than one's stage of life.

There is some merit in each of these views. As we see in the following section, so-called successful aging is connected with remaining active and involved. But biological and social realities may require older people to become more selective in their pursuits.

EGO INTEGRITY VERSUS DESPAIR Erikson's term for the crisis of late adulthood, characterized by the task of maintaining one's sense of identity despite physical deterioration.

DISENGAGEMENT THEORY The view that the individual and society withdraw from one another during the later years.

ACTIVITY THEORY The view that life satisfaction is connected with one's level of activity.

CONTINUITY THEORY The view that people tend to cope with the challenges of late adulthood in the ways that they coped with earlier challenges.

SUCCESSFUL AGING The later years were once seen mainly as a prelude to dying. Older people were viewed as crotchety and irritable. It was assumed that they reaped little pleasure from life. *No more.* Many stereotypes about aging are becoming less prevalent. Despite the changes that accompany aging, most people in their 70s report being generally satisfied with their lives (Margoshes, 1995). Americans are eating more wisely and exercising at later ages, so many older people are robust.

Sheehy (1995) coined the term *middlescence* to highlight her finding that people she interviewed in their 50s were thinking about what they would do with their *second adulthood*—the 30 to 40 healthy years they had left! Developmental psychologists are using another new term: *successful aging* (Margoshes, 1995). The term is not just meant to put a positive spin on the inevitable. Successful agers have a number of characteristics that can inspire all of us to lead more enjoyable and productive lives. There are three components of successful aging:

1. *Reshaping one's life to concentrate on what one finds to be important and meaningful.* Laura Carstensen's (1997) research on people aged 70 and above reveals that successful agers form emotional goals that bring them satisfaction. For example, rather than cast about in multiple directions, they may focus on their family and friends. Successful agers may have less time left than those of us in earlier stages of adulthood, but they tend to spend it more wisely (Margoshes, 1995).

Researchers (Baltes, 1997; Schulz & Heckhausen, 1996) use terms such as "selective optimization and compensation" to describe the manner in which successful agers lead their lives. That is, successful agers no longer seek to compete in arenas best left to younger people—such as certain kinds of athletic or business activities. Rather, they focus on matters that allow them to maintain a sense of control over their own actions. Moreover, they use available resources to make up for losses. If their memory is not quite what it once was, they make notes or other reminders. For example, if their senses are no longer as acute, they use devices such as hearing aids or allow themselves more time to take in information. There are also some ingenious individual strategies. The great pianist Arthur Rubinstein performed into his 80s, even after he had lost much of his pianistic speed. In his later years, he would slow down before playing faster passages in order to enhance the impression of speed during those passages.

2. *Maintaining a positive outlook.* For example, some older people attribute occasional health problems such as aches and pains to *specific* and *unstable* factors like a cold or jogging too long. Others attribute aches and pains to *global* and *stable* factors such as aging itself. Not surprisingly, those who attribute these problems to specific, unstable factors are more optimistic about surmounting them. They thus have a more positive outlook or attitude. Of particular interest here is research conducted by William Rakowski (Margoshes, 1995). Rakowski followed 1,400 people age 70 or older with nonlethal health problems such as aches and pains. He found that those who blamed the problems on aging itself were significantly more likely to die in the near future than those who blamed the problems on specific, unstable factors.

3. *Challenging oneself.* Many people look forward to late adulthood as a time when they can rest from life's challenges. But sitting back and allowing the world to pass by is a prescription for vegetating, not for living life to its fullest. Consider an experiment conducted by Curt Sandman and Francis Crinella with 175 people whose average age was 72 (Margoshes, 1995). They randomly assigned subjects either to a foster grandparent program with neurologically impaired children or to a control group, and they followed both groups for 10 years. The foster grandparents were

"SUCCESSFUL AGING"?
The later years were once seen mainly as a prelude to dying. As we approach the new millennium, however, many older people—termed "successful agers"—are seeking new challenges.

TRUTH OR FICTION REVISITED
It is true that older people who blame health problems on aging rather than on specific factors such as a virus are more likely to die in the near future.

encouraged to carry out various physical challenges, such as walking a few miles each day, and also engaged in new kinds of social interactions. Those in the control group were not encouraged to engage in any particular activities. Ten years later, the foster grandparents showed superior overall cognitive functioning, including memory functioning, and better sleep patterns as compared with people assigned to the control group.

ON DEATH AND DYING

Death is the last great taboo. Psychiatrist Elisabeth Kübler-Ross commented on our denial of death in her book *On Death and Dying:*

> We use euphemisms, we make the dead look as if they were asleep, we ship the children off to protect them from the anxiety and turmoil around the house if the [person] is fortunate enough to die at home, [and] we don't allow children to visit their dying parents in the hospital. (1969, p. 8)

Stages of Dying

In her work with terminally ill patients, Kübler-Ross found some common responses to news of impending death. She identified five stages of dying through which many patients pass, and she suggested that older people who suspect death is approaching may undergo similar stages:

1. Denial. In the denial stage, people feel that "It can't be happening to me. The diagnosis must be wrong."
2. *Anger.* Denial usually gives way to anger and resentment toward the young and healthy and, sometimes, toward the medical establishment—"It unfair. Why me?"
3. *Bargaining.* Next, people may try to bargain with God to postpone their death, promising, for example, to do good deeds if they are given another six months, another year to live.
4. *Depression.* With depression come feelings of loss and hopelessness—grief at the inevitability of leaving loved ones and life itself.
5. *Final acceptance.* Ultimately, an inner peace may come, a quiet acceptance of the inevitable. Such "peace" does not resemble contentment. Instead, it is nearly devoid of feeling.

Psychologist Edwin Shneidman, who has specialized in the concerns of suicidal and dying individuals, acknowledges the presence of feelings such as those identified by Kübler-Ross. However, he does not perceive them to be linked in a particular sequence. Instead, he suggests that dying people show a variety of emotional and cognitive responses that may ebb and flow, and reflect pain and bewilderment. He also points out that people's responses reflect their individual personality traits and philosophies of life.

"Lying Down to Pleasant Dreams . . ."

The American poet William Cullen Bryant is best known for his poem "Thanatopsis," which he composed at the age of 18. "Thanatopsis" expresses Erik Erikson's goal of ego integrity, Erikson's optimism that we can maintain a sense of trust through life. By meeting squarely the challenges of our adult lives, perhaps we can take our leave with dignity. When our time comes to "join the innumerable caravan"—the billions who have died before us—perhaps we can depart life with integrity.

Live, wrote the poet, so that
. . . when thy summons comes to join
The innumerable caravan that moves
To the pale realms of shade, where each shall take
His chamber in the silent halls of death,
Thou go not, like the quarry-slave at night,
Scourged to his dungeon, but, sustained and soothed
By an unfaltering trust, approach thy grave
Like one who wraps the drapery of his couch
About him, and lies down to pleasant dreams.

Bryant, of course, wrote "Thanatopsis" at 18, not 85, the age at which he died. At that advanced age his feelings, his pen, might have differed. But literature and poetry, unlike science, need not reflect reality. They can serve to inspire and warm us.

SUMMARY

1. **What are some of the major events of young adulthood?** Physical and cognitive development usually peak in early adulthood. Young adulthood is generally characterized by efforts to advance in the business world and by the development of intimate relationships.

2. **What are the common lifestyles of young adulthood?** Many people remain single because they have not found the right marital partner. Others prefer sexual variety and wish to avoid making a commitment. Cohabitation is living together without being married. Much of the attention on cohabitation has been focused on college students living together, but cohabitation is more common among the less well educated and less affluent people. Marriage is the most popular lifestyle in the United States today. Today's marriages are usually based on attraction and love and the desires for emotional and psychological intimacy and security.

3. **Why do people work?** Workers are motivated both by extrinsic rewards (money, status, security) and intrinsic rewards (the work ethic, self-identity, self-fulfillment, self-worth, and the social values of work).

4. **What is Holland's method for helping people make vocational choices?** Holland predicts how well people will enjoy a certain kind of work by matching the kinds of jobs that are available to people's vocational personality types— that is, realistic, investigative, artistic, social, enterprising, or conventional.

5. **What can be done to improve the workplace for women?** Women profit from more realistic career planning, maintaining employment continuity, child-care facilities, and training programs.

6. **What are some physical and cognitive developments of middle adulthood?** Physical strength declines gradually during middle adulthood. Decline in production of sex hormones leads to menopause, or cessation of menstruation, in women. Women's adjustment to menopause is connected with what menopause means to them. There is little change in intellectual function during the middle years.

7. **What are some of the major personal and social developments of middle adulthood?** Sheehy refers to the middle years as "second adulthood." She is more optimistic than theorists who have seen middle adulthood as a time of crisis and reassessment during which people must come to terms with the discrepancies between their achievements and the dreams of youth. Some middle-aged adults become depressed when their youngest child leaves home (the so-called empty nest syndrome), but many report increased satisfaction, stability, and self-confidence. According to Sheehy, many people in middle adulthood experience "middlescence"—during which they redefine themselves and their goals for the 30 to 40 healthy years they expect lie ahead of them.

8. **What are some physical changes of late adulthood?** As people age, the skin wrinkles and heart and lung capacity decline. Older people show less sensory acuity, and their reaction time lengthens. Bone density decreases. Sexual functioning declines.

9. **What factors are involved in longevity?** Heredity plays a role in longevity. One theory (programmed senescence) suggests that aging and death are determined by our genes. Another theory (wear-and-tear theory) hold that factors such as pollution, disease, and ultraviolet light contribute to wear and tear on the body, so the body loses the ability to repair itself. Lifestyle factors such as exercise, good nutrition, and not smoking also contribute to longevity.

10. **What are some cognitive changes of late adulthood?** People can be creative for a lifetime. There is normally a decline in learning ability and memory functioning as people age. People show decline in fluid intelligence, but crystallized intelligence may peak in late adulthood. General health, socioeconomic status, and stimulating activities all contribute to intellectual functioning in late adulthood. Alzheimer's disease occurs most often during late adulthood, but it is a disease and not a normal part of the aging process.

11. **What are some personal and social changes of late adulthood?** According to Erikson, late adulthood is the stage of ego integrity versus despair. Other psychosocial theories of aging include disengagement theory, activity theory, and continuity theory. So-called successful agers reshape their lives to focus on what they consider important and meaningful, have a positive outlook, and challenge themselves.

12. **Are there "stages of dying"?** Kübler-Ross has identified five stages of dying among people who are terminally ill: denial, anger, bargaining, depression, and final acceptance. Other investigators find that psychological reactions to approaching death are more varied than Kübler-Ross suggests, however.

KEY TERMS

activity theory (p. AD-26)

age-30 transition (p. AD-4)

Alzheimer's disease (p. AD-25)

Catch 30s (p. AD-4)

cohabitation (p. AD-5)

continuity theory (p. AD-26)

crystallized intelligence (p. AD-25)

disengagement theory (p. AD-26)

dream (p. AD-4)

ego integrity versus despair (p. AD-26)

empty nest syndrome (p. AD-17)

fluid intelligence (p. AD-25)

generativity versus stagnation (p. AD-16)

homogamy (p. AD-7)

intimacy versus isolation (p. AD-3)

menopause (p. AD-13)

middlescence (p. AD-17)

midlife crisis (p. AD-16)

midlife transition (p. AD-16)

postformal thought (p. AD-25)

programmed senescence (p. AD-23)

Trying 20s (p. AD-3)

wear-and-tear theory (p. AD-23)

REFERENCES

Abeles, N. (1997a). Psychology and the aging revolution. *APA Monitor, 28*(4), 2.

Abeles, N. (1997b). Memory problems in later life. *APA Monitor, 28*(6), 2.

APA Task Force on Diversity Issues at the Precollege and Undergraduate Levels of Education in Psychology. (1998). *APA Monitor, 29*(8), 46.

Apter, T. (1995). *Secret paths.* New York: Norton.

Baltes, P. B. (1997). On the incomplete architecture of human ontogeny: Selection, optimization, and compensation as foundation of developmental theory. *American Psychologist, 52,* 366–380.

Berger, K. S. (1994). *The developing person through the life span* (3rd ed.). New York: Worth.

Bianchi, S. M., & Spain, D. (1997). *Women, work and family in America.* Population Reference Bureau.

Boksay, I. (1998, February 11). *Mourning spouse's death: Two years.* Associated Press; America Online.

Brody, J. E. (1992, December 9). Hip fracture: A potential killer that can be avoided. *New York Times,* p. C16.

Brody, J. E. (1993, December 1). Liberated at last from the myths about menopause. *New York Times,* p. C15.

Brody, J. E. (1996, September 4). Osteoporosis can threaten men as well as women. *New York Times,* p. C9.

Brody, J. E. (1998, August 4). Personal health: Giving men directions to the road to better health. *New York Times;* America Online.

Butler, R. (1998). Cited in CD-ROM that accompanies Nevid, J. S., Rathus, S. A., & Rubenstein, H. (1998). *Health in the new millennium.* New York: Worth.

Carstensen, L. (1997, August 17). *The evolution of social goals across the life span.* Paper presented to the American Psychological Association, Chicago.

Casper, L. (1997). My daddy takes care of me! Fathers as care providers. U.S. Bureau of the Census: *Current Population Reports* (P70-59).

Cavanaugh, J. C., & Green, E. E. (1990). I believe, therefore I can: Self-efficacy beliefs in memory aging. In E. A. Lovelace (Ed.), *Aging and cognition: Mental processes, self-awareness, and interventions.* North-Holland, Elsevier.

Cowley, G. (1996, September 16). Attention: Aging men. *Newsweek,* pp. 68–77.

Cunningham, R. (1996). *Hospice: A special kind of caring.* Hospice Federation of Massachusetts.

Day, S. X., & Rounds, J. (1998). Universality of vocational interest structure among racial and ethnic minorities. *American Psychologist, 53,* 728–736.

Delmas, P. D., et al. (1997). Effects of raloxifene on bone mineral density, serum cholesterol concentrations, and uterine endometrium in postmenopausal women. *New England Journal of Medicine, 337,* 1641–1648.

"Doctors tie male mentality to shorter life span." (1995, June 14). *New York Times,* p. C14.

Erel, O., & Burman, B. (1995). Interrelatedness of marital relations and parent-child relations: A meta-analytic review. *Psychological Bulletin, 118,* 108–132.

Erikson, E. H. (1963). *Childhood and society.* New York: Norton.

Evans, W., & Rosenberg, I. H. (1991). *Biomarkers: The 10 determinants of aging you can control.* New York: Simon & Schuster.

Gilligan, C. (1982). *In a different voice.* Cambridge, MA: Harvard University Press.

Gilligan, C., Lyons, P., & Hanmer, T. J. (Eds.). (1990). *Making connections.* Cambridge, MA: Harvard University Press.

Gilligan, C., Rogers, A. G., & Tolman, D. L. (Eds.). (1991). *Women, girls, and psychotherapy.* New York: Haworth.

Graf, P. (1990). Life-span changes in implicit and explicit memory. *Bulletin of the Psychonomic Society, 28,* 353–358.

Grodstein, F., et al. (1996). Postmenopausal estrogen and progestin use and the risk of cardiovascular disease. *New England Journal of Medicine, 335,* 453–461.

Grodstein, F., et al. (1997). Postmenopausal hormonal therapy and mortality. *New England Journal of Medicine, 336,* 1769–1775.

Grych, J. H., & Fincham, F. D. (1993). Children's appraisals of marital conflict. *Child Development, 64,* 215–230.

Guisinger, S., & Blatt, S. J. (1994). Individuality and relatedness. *American Psychologist, 49,* 104–111.

Hakim, A. A., et al. (1998). Effects of walking on mortality among nonsmoking retired men. *New England Journal of Medicine, 338,* 94–99.

Harold, G. T., Fincham, F. D., Osborne, L. N., & Conger, R. D. (1997). Mom and Dad are at it again: Adolescent perceptions of marital conflict and adolescent psychological distress. *Developmental Psychology, 33,* 333–350.

Havighurst, R. J. (1972). *Developmental tasks and education* (3rd ed.). New York: McKay.

Helson, R., & Moane, G. (1987). Personality change in women from college to midlife. *Journal of Personality and Social Psychology, 53,* 176–186.

Holden, G. W., & Ritchie, K. L. (1991). Linking extreme marital discord, child rearing, and child behavior problems. *Child Development, 62,* 311–327.

Holland, J. L. (1997). *Making vocational choices: A theory of vocational personalities and work environments* (3rd ed.). Odessa, FL: Psychological Assessment Resources.

Huffman, T., Chang, K., Rausch, P., & Schaffer, N. (1994). Gender differences and factors related to the disposition toward cohabitation. *Family Therapy, 21*(3), 171–184.

Hugick, L., & Leonard, J. (1991). Job dissatisfaction grows: "Moonlighting" on the rise. *Gallup Poll Monthly, No. 312,* 2–15.

Katzell, R. A., & Thompson, D. E. (1990). Work motivation: Theory and practice. *American Psychologist, 45,* 144–153.

Kotre, J., & Hall, E. (1990). *Seasons of life: Our dramatic journey from birth to death.* Boston: Little, Brown.

Kübler-Ross, E. (1969). *On death and dying.* New York: Macmillan.

Labouvie-Vief, G. (1992). A neo-Piagetan perspective on adult cognitive development. In R. J. Sternberg & C. A. Berg (Eds.), *Intellectual development* (pp. 197–228). Cambridge, England: Cambridge University Press.

Lamott, A. (1993, August 5). When going it alone turns out to be not so alone at all. *New York Times,* pp. C1, C9.

Langer, E. J., Rodin, J., Beck, P., Weinan, C., & Spitzer, L. (1979). Environmental determinants of memory improvement in late adulthood. *Journal of Personality and Social Psychology, 37,* 2003–2013.

Laumann, E. O., Gagnon, J. H., Michael, R. T., & Michaels, S. (1994). *The social organization of sexuality.* Chicago: University of Chicago Press.

Levinson, D. J., Darrow, C. N., Klein, E. B., Levinson, M. H., & McKee, B. (1978). *The seasons of a man's life.* New York: Knopf.

Lewin, T. (1995). Women are becoming equal providers. *New York Times,* p. A27.

Lindenberger, U., Mayr, U., & Kliegl, R. (1993). Speed and intelligence in old age. *Psychology and Aging, 8,* 207–220.

"Longer, healthier, better." (1997, March 9). *New York Times Magazine,* pp. 44–45.

Margoshes, P. (1995). For many, old age is the prime of life. *APA Monitor, 26*(5), 36–37.

Matthews, K. (1994). Cited in Azar, B. (1994). Women are barraged by media on "the change." *APA Monitor, 25*(5), 24–25.

McCrae, R. R., & Costa, P. T., Jr. (1990). *Personality in adulthood.* New York: Guilford.

Michelozzi, B. N. (1992). *Coming alive from nine to five* (4th ed.). Palo Alto, CA: Mayfield.

Nevid, J. S., Rathus, S. A., & Greene, B. A. (2000). *Abnormal psychology in a changing world* (4th ed.). Upper Saddle River, NJ: Prentice Hall.

Nevid, J. S., Rathus, S. A., & Rubenstein, H. (1998). *Health in the new millennium.* New York: Worth.

Nock, S. L. (1995). A comparison of marriages and cohabiting relationships. *Journal of Family Issues, 16*(1), 53–76.

Quill, T. E. (1993). *Death and dignity: Making choices and taking charge.* New York: Norton.

Rathus, S. A., Nevid, J. S., & Fichner-Rathus, L. (2000). *Human sexuality in a world of diversity* (4th ed.). Boston: Allyn & Bacon.

Reinke, B. J., Holmes, D. S., & Harris, R. L. (1985). The timing of psychosocial changes in women's lives. *Journal of Personality and Social Psychology, 48,* 1353–1364.

Saluter, A. F. (1995). Marital status and living arrangements: March 1995. *Current Population Reports,* Series P20–491.

Schaie, K. W. (1994). The course of adult intellectual development. *American Psychologist, 49,* 304–313.

Schaie, K. W., & Willis, S. L. (1991). Adult personality and psychomotor performance. *Journal of Gerontology: Psychological Sciences, 46,* 275–284.

Schulz, R., & Heckhausen, J. (1996). A life span model of successful aging. *American Psychologist, 51,* 702–714.

Sheehy, G. (1976). *Passages.* New York: Dutton.

Sheehy, G. (1995). *New passages: Mapping your life across time.* New York: Random House.

Sheehy, G. (1998a). *Menopause—The silent passage.* New York: Random House.

Sheehy, G. (1998b). *Understanding men's passages.* New York: Random House.

Size up your bones . . . now! (1996, February). *Prevention,* p. 76.

Skinner, B. F. (1983). Intellectual self-management in old age. *American Psychologist, 38,* 239–244.

Sourander, L. B. (1994). Geriatric aspects on estrogen effects and sexuality. *Gerontology, 40* (Suppl. 3), 14–17.

Steers, R. M., & Porter, L. W. (1991). *Motivation and work behavior* (5th ed.). New York: Macmillan.

Steinhauer, J. (1995, July 6). No marriage, no apologies. *New York Times,* pp. C1, C7.

Tanzi, R. E. (1995). A promising animal model of Alzheimer's disease. *New England Journal of Medicine, 332,* 1512–1513.

U.S. Bureau of the Census. (1998). *Statistical abstract of the United States* (118th ed.). Washington, DC: U.S. Government Printing Office.

U.S. Department of Labor. (1998). Washington, DC.

Valian, V. (1998). *Why so slow? The advancement of women.* Cambridge, MA: MIT Press.

Wallerstein, J. S., & Blakeslee, S. (1989). *Second chances: Women and children a decade after divorce.* New York: Ticknor & Fields.

Wasserman, J. (1993, September 3). It's still women's work. *Daily News,* p. 7.

Willis, R. J., & Michael, R. T. (1994). Innovation in family formation: Evidence on cohabitation in the United States. In J. Eruisch & K. Ogawa (Eds.), *The family, the market and the state in aging societies.* London: Oxford University Press.

Wink, P., & Helson, R. (1993). Personality change in women and their partners. *Journal of Personality and Social Psychology, 65,* 597–606.

Wolk, A., et al. (1998, January 12). *Archives of Internal Medicine.* Cited in *Study: Some fats reduce cancer risk.* (1998, January 11). Associated Press; America Online.

GS

GENDER AND SEXUALITY

OFF THE MISTY COAST OF IRELAND LIES THE SMALL ISLAND OF INIS Beag. From the air it is a green jewel, warm and inviting. At ground level, life is somewhat different.

For example, the residents of Inis Beag do not believe that women experience orgasm. The woman who chances to find pleasure in sex is considered deviant. Premarital sex is all but unknown. Women engage in sexual relations to conceive children and to appease their husbands' carnal cravings. They need not worry about being called on for frequent performances, however, because the men of Inis Beag believe, erroneously, that sex saps their strength. Sex on Inis Beag is carried out in the dark—both literally and figuratively—and with nightclothes on. The man lies on top in the so-called missionary position. In accordance with local concepts of masculinity, he ejaculates as fast as he can. Then he rolls over and falls asleep.

If Inis Beag does not sound like your cup of tea, you may find the atmosphere of Mangaia more congenial. Mangaia is a Polynesian pearl of an island, lifting lazily from the blue waters of the Pacific. It is on the other side of the world from Inis Beag—in more ways than one.

From an early age, Mangaian children are encouraged to get in touch with their sexuality through masturbation. Mangaian adolescents are expected to engage in sexual intercourse. They may be found on secluded beaches or beneath the swaying fronds of palms, diligently practicing techniques learned from village elders.

Mangaian women are expected to reach orgasm several times before their partners do. Young men want their partners to reach orgasm, and they compete to see who is more effective at bringing young women to multiple orgasms.

On the island of Inis Beag, a woman who has an orgasm is considered deviant. On Mangaia, multiple orgasms are the norm (Rathus et al., 2000). If we take a quick tour of the world of sexual diversity, we also find the following:

• Nearly every society has an incest taboo, but some societies believe that a brother and sister who eat at the same table are engaging in a mildly sexual act. The practice is therefore forbidden.

• What is considered sexually arousing varies enormously among different cultures. Women's breasts and armpits stimulate a sexual response in some cultures, but not in others.

• Kissing is a nearly universal form of petting in the United States but is unpopular in Japan and unknown among some cultures in Africa and South America. Upon seeing European visitors kissing, a member of an African tribe remarked, "Look at them—they eat each other's saliva and dirt."

- Sexual exclusiveness in marriage is valued highly in most parts of the United States, but among the people of Alaska's Aleutian Islands it is considered good manners for a man to offer his wife to a houseguest.

- The United States has its romantic Valentine's Day, but Japan has eroticized another day—Christmas Eve. (You read that right: Christmas Eve.) Christmas Eve may be a time of religious devotion in many Western nations, but it has become a time of sexual devotion in Japan. On Christmas Eve every single person must have a date that includes an overnight visit (Reid, 1990). During the weeks prior to Christmas, the media brim with reports on hotels for overnight stays, proper attire, and breakfast ideas for the morning after. Where do Tokyo singles like to go before their overnighter? Tokyo Disneyland.

The residents of Inis Beag and Mangaia have similar anatomical features but vastly different attitudes toward sex. Their sociocultural settings influence their patterns of sexual behavior and the pleasure they gain—or do not gain—from sex. Sex may be a natural function, but few natural functions have been influenced so strongly by religious and moral beliefs, cultural tradition, folklore, and superstition.

This chapter is about gender and sexuality. We begin by exploring gender polarization—the behaviors that make up the stereotypes of "masculinity" and "femininity." We then examine *actual* psychological differences between males and females and consider the development of these differences. Next we turn our attention to sexual orientation; we ask why some people are attracted to people of their own gender, whereas most are attracted to people of the other gender. We describe sexual anatomy and sexual response, and we see that women and men are probably more alike in their sexual response than you may have thought. Then we consider sexual dysfunctions and their treatment. Finally, we turn to the dark side of gender and sexuality: issues in sexual coercion, including rape and sexual harassment.

TRUTH OR FICTION REVISITED
It is true that Christmas Eve has become a time of sexual devotion in Japan, although it is a time of religious devotion in most Western nations. There is a good deal of social pressure on single people to have a date that includes an overnight stay.

GENDER POLARIZATION: GENDER STEREOTYPES AND THEIR COSTS

"Why Can't a Woman Be More Like a Man?" You may recognize this song title from the musical *My Fair Lady*. In the song, Henry Higgins laments that women are emotional and fickle, whereas men are logical and dependable.

The excitable woman is a **stereotype.** Stereotypes are fixed, conventional ideas about a group of people that can give rise to prejudice and discrimination. The logical man is a **gender** stereotype. Higgins's stereotypes reflect cultural beliefs. Cultural beliefs about men and women involve clusters of stereotypes called **gender roles.** Gender roles define the ways in which men and women are expected to behave.

Sandra Lipsitz Bem (1993) writes that three beliefs about women and men have prevailed throughout the history of Western culture:

1. Women and men have basically different psychological and sexual natures.

2. Men are the superior, dominant gender.

3. Gender differences and male superiority are "natural."

STEREOTYPE A fixed, conventional idea about a group.

GENDER The state of being male or female.

GENDER ROLE A cluster of behaviors that characterizes traditional female or male behaviors within a cultural setting.

These beliefs have tended to polarize our views of women and men. It is thought that gender differences in power and psychological traits are natural, but what does "natural" mean? Throughout most of history, people viewed naturalness in terms of religion, or God's scheme of things (Bem, 1993). For the past century or so, naturalness has been seen in biological, evolutionary terms—at least by most scientists. But these views ignore cultural influences.

What are perceived as the so-called natural gender roles? In our society, people tend to see the feminine gender role as warm, emotional, dependent, gentle, helpful, mild, patient, submissive, and interested in the arts (Bem, 1993). The typical masculine gender role is perceived as independent, competitive, tough, protective, logical, and competent at busi-

TABLE GS.1

GENDER-ROLE STEREOTYPES AROUND THE WORLD

STEREOTYPES OF MALES		STEREOTYPES OF FEMALES	
Active	Opinionated	Affectionate	Nervous
Adventurous	Pleasure-seeking	Appreciative	Patient
Aggressive	Precise	Cautious	Pleasant
Arrogant	Quick	Changeable	Prudish
Autocratic	Rational	Charming	Self-pitying
Capable	Realistic	Complaining	Sensitive
Coarse	Reckless	Complicated	Sentimental
Conceited	Resourceful	Confused	Sexy
Confident	Rigid	Dependent	Shy
Courageous	Robust	Dreamy	Softhearted
Cruel	Sharp-witted	Emotional	Sophisticated
Determined	Show-off	Excitable	Submissive
Disorderly	Steady	Fault-finding	Suggestible
Enterprising	Stern	Fearful	Superstitious
Hardheaded	Stingy	Fickle	Talkative
Individualistic	Stolid	Foolish	Timid
Inventive	Tough	Forgiving	Touchy
Loud	Unscrupulous	Frivolous	Unambitious
Obnoxious		Fussy	Understanding
		Gentle	Unstable
		Imaginative	Warm
		Kind	Weak
		Mild	Worrying
		Modest	

Source of data: Williams & Best, 1994, p. 193, Table 1.

Psychologists John Williams and Deborah Best (1994) found that people in 30 nations around the world tended to agree on the nature of masculine and feminine gender-role stereotypes. Men are largely seen as more adventurous and hardheaded than women. Women are generally seen as more emotional and dependent.

PSYCHOLOGY IN A WORLD OF Diversity

MACHISMO/MARIANISMO STEREOTYPES AND HISPANIC CULTURE[1]

Machismo is a Hispanic American cultural stereotype that defines masculinity in terms of an idealized view of manliness. To be macho is to be strong, virile, and dominant. Each Hispanic culture puts its own particular cultural stamp on the meaning of machismo, however. In the Spanish-speaking cultures of the Caribbean and Central America, the macho code encourages men to restrain their feelings and maintain an emotional distance. In my travels in Argentina and some other Latin American countries, however, I have observed that men who are sensitive and emotionally expressive are not perceived as compromising their macho code.

In counterpoint to the macho ideal among Hispanic peoples is the cultural idealization of femininity embodied in the concept of **marianismo.** The marianismo stereotype, which derives its name from the Virgin Mary, refers to the ideal of the virtuous woman as one who "suffers in silence," submerging her needs and desires to those of her husband and children. With the marianismo stereotype, the image of a woman's role as a martyr is raised to the level of a cultural ideal. According to this cultural stereotype, a woman is expected to demonstrate her love for her husband by waiting patiently at home and having dinner prepared for him at any time of day or night he happens to come home, to have his slippers ready for him, and so on. The feminine ideal involves self-sacrifice and providing joy, even in the face of pain. Strongly influenced by the patriarchal Spanish tradition, the marianismo stereotype has historically been used to maintain women in a subordinate position in relation to men.

Acculturation has challenged this traditional machismo/marianismo division of marital roles among Hispanic couples in the United States. I have seen in my own work treating Hispanic American couples in therapy that marriages are under increasing strain from the conflict between traditional and modern expectations about marital roles. Hispanic American women have been entering the work force in increasing numbers, usually in domestic or childcare positions. Yet they are still expected to assume responsibility for tending their own children, keeping the house, and serving their husbands' needs when they return home. In many cases, a reversal of traditional roles occurs in which the wife works and supports the family while the husband remains at home because he is unable to find or maintain employment.

It is often the Hispanic American husband who has the greater difficulty accepting a more flexible distribution of roles within the marriage and giving up a rigid set of expectations tied to traditional machismo/marianismo gender expectations. Although some couples manage to reshape their expectations and marital roles in the face of changing conditions, many relationships buckle under the strain and end in divorce. ∎

[1] This feature on diversity was written by Rafael Art Javier, a clinical professor of psychology and director of the Center for Psychological services and Clincal Studies at St. John's University in Jamaica, New York.

ness, math, and science. Women are typically expected to care for the kids and cook the meals. Cross-cultural studies confirm that these gender-role stereotypes are widespread (see Table GS.1). For example, in their survey of 30 countries, John Williams and Deborah Best (1994) found that men are more likely judged as active, adventurous, aggressive, arrogant, and autocratic (and we have only gotten through the *a*'s.) Women are more likely seen as fearful, fickle, foolish, frivolous, and fussy (and these are only a handful of *f*'s.)

MACHISMO The Hispanic cultural stereotype of the male as strong, virile, and dominant.

MARIANISMO The Hispanic cultural stereotype of the virtuous woman as one who "suffers in silence," submerging her needs and desires to those of her husband and children.

Gender polarization in the United States is linked to the traditional view of men as breadwinners and women as homemakers (Eagly & Steffen, 1984). Stereotypes also affect the opportunities open to men and women in Hispanic communities, as you can see in the feature discussion on *machismo* and *marianismo*.

Costs of Gender Polarization

Gender polarization can be costly in terms of education, activities, careers, psychological well-being, and interpersonal relationships. Let us take a closer look at each of these areas.

EDUCATION Polarization has historically worked to the disadvantage of women. In past centuries, girls were considered unable to learn. Even the great Swiss-French philosopher Jean-Jacques Rousseau, who was in the forefront of a movement toward a more open approach to education, believed that girls are basically irrational and naturally disposed to child rearing and homemaking—certainly not to commerce, science, and industry, pursuits for which education is required.

Intelligence tests show that boys and girls are about equal in overall learning ability. Nevertheless, girls are expected to excel in language arts, and boys in math and science. Such expectations dissuade girls from taking advanced courses in the so-called male domain. Boys take more math courses in high school than girls do (American Association of University Women, 1992). Math courses open doors for them in fields such as natural science, engineering, and economics. There are several reasons why boys are more likely than girls to feel at home with math:

1. Fathers are more likely than mothers to help children with math homework.
2. Advanced math courses are more likely to be taught by men.
3. Teachers often show higher expectations for boys in math courses.
4. Math teachers spend more time working with boys than with girls.

Given these experiences, we should not be surprised that by junior high, boys view themselves as more competent in math than girls do, even when they receive the same grades. Boys are more likely to have positive feelings about math. Girls are more likely to have math anxiety. Even girls who excel in math and science are less likely than boys to choose courses or careers in these fields (American Association of University Women, 1992).

If women are to find their places in professions related to math, science, and engineering, we may need to provide more female role models in these professions. Such models will help shatter the stereotype that these are men's fields. We also need to encourage girls to take more courses in math and science.

CAREERS

I have yet to hear a man ask for advice on how to combine marriage and a career.

GLORIA STEINEM

Women are less likely than men to enter higher paying careers in math, science, and engineering. They account for perhaps 1 in 6 of the nation's scientists and engineers. Although women are awarded more than half of the bachelor's degrees in the United States, they receive fewer than one

A FEMALE ARCHITECTURAL ENGINEER. Women remain underrepresented in many kinds of careers. Although women have made marked gains in medicine and law, their numbers remain relatively low in math and engineering. Why?

third of the degrees in science and engineering. Why? It is partly because math, science, and engineering are perceived as inconsistent with the feminine gender role. Many little girls are dissuaded from thinking about professions such as engineering and architecture because they are given dolls, rather than trucks and blocks, as toys. Many boys are likewise deterred from entering child-care and nursing professions because others scorn them when they play with dolls.

There are also inequalities in the workplace that are based on gender polarization. For example, women's wages average only about 72% of men's (Bianchi & Spain, 1997). Women physicians and college professors earn less than men in the same positions (Honan, 1996; "Study Finds," 1996). Women are less likely than men to be promoted into high-level managerial positions (Valian, 1998). Once in managerial positions, women often feel pressured to be "tougher" than men in order to seem just as tough. They feel pressured to be careful about their appearance because co-workers pay more attention to what they wear, how they style their hair, and so forth. If they do not look crisp and tailored every day, others may think they are not in command. But if they dress up too much, they may be denounced as fashion plates rather than serious workers! Female managers who are deliberate and take time making decisions may be seen as weak. What happens when female managers change their minds? They run the risk of being labeled fickle and indecisive rather than flexible.

Women in the workplace are also often expected to make the coffee or clean up after the conference lunch, along with the jobs they were hired to do. Women who work also usually have the responsibility of being the major caretaker for children in the home (Bianchi & Spain, 1997). Yet in the 1990s women's wages averaged 72% of men's compared to 59% in 1970 (Bianchi & Spain, 1997). Wives share about equally with their husbands in supporting their families (Lewin, 1995).

PSYCHOLOGICAL WELL-BEING AND RELATIONSHIPS Gender polarization also interferes with psychological well-being and relationships. Women who adhere to the traditional feminine gender role are likely to believe that women, like children, should be seen and not heard. They therefore are unlikely to assert themselves to make their needs and wants known. They are likely to feel frustrated as a result.

Men who accept the traditional masculine gender role are less likely to feel comfortable performing the activities involved in caring for children, such as bathing them, dressing them, and feeding them (Bem, 1993). Such men are less likely to ask for help—including medical help—when they need it ("Doctors Tie," 1995). They are also less likely to be sympathetic and tender or express feelings of love in their marital relationships (Coleman & Ganong, 1985).

PSYCHOLOGICAL GENDER DIFFERENCES: VIVE LA DIFFÉRENCE OR VIVE LA SIMILARITÉ?

The French have an expression "Vive la différence," which means "Long live the difference" (between men and women). Yet modern life has challenged our concepts of what it means to be a woman or a man. The obvious anatomical differences between women and men are connected with the biological aspects of reproduction. Biologists therefore have a relatively easy time describing and interpreting the gender differences they study. The task of psychology is more complex and wrapped up with sociocultural and political issues (Eagly, 1995; Marecek, 1995). Psychological gender differences are not as obvious as biological gender differences. In fact, in many ways women and men are more similar than different.

To put it another way: To reproduce, women and men have to be biologically different. Throughout history, it has also been assumed that women and men must be psychologically different in order to fulfill different roles in the family and society (Bem, 1993). But what are the psychological differences between women and men? Key studies on this question span three decades.

Cognitive Abilities

It was once believed that males were more intelligent than females because of their greater knowledge of world affairs and their skill in science and industry. We now know that greater male knowledge and skill did not reflect differences in intelligence. Rather, it reflected the systematic exclusion of females from world affairs, science, and industry. Assessments of intelligence do not show overall gender differences in cognitive abilities. However, reviews of the research suggest that girls are somewhat superior to boys in verbal abilities, such as verbal fluency, ability to generate words that are similar in meaning to other words, spelling, knowledge of foreign languages, and pronunciation (Halpern, 1997). Males, however, seem to be somewhat superior in visual-spatial abilities. Differences in mathematical ability are more complex (Neisser et al., 1996).

Girls seem to acquire language somewhat faster than boys do (Hyde & Linn, 1988). Also, in the United States far more boys than girls have reading problems, ranging from reading below grade level to severe disabilities (Halpern, 1997; Neisser et al., 1996). But at least the males headed for college seem to catch up in verbal skills.

Males apparently excel in visual-spatial abilities of the sort used in math, science, and even reading a map (Voyer et al., 1995). Tests of spatial ability assess skills such as mentally rotating figures in space (see Figure GS.1) and finding figures embedded within larger designs (see Figure GS.2).

FIGURE GS.1
ROTATING FIGURES IN SPACE.

Males as a group outperform females on spatial relations tasks, such as rotating figures in space and picturing the results. However, females do as well as males when they receive training in the task.

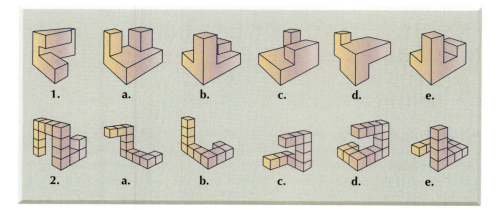

In math, differences at all ages are small and seem to be narrowing (Hyde et al., 1990). Females excel in computational ability in elementary school, however. Males excel in mathematical problem solving in high school and college (Hyde et al., 1990). Boys outperform girls on the math part of the Scholastic Aptitude Test (Byrnes & Takahira, 1993). According to Byrnes and Takahira (1993), boys' superiority in math does not reflect gender per se. Instead, boys do as well as they do because of greater experience in solving math problems.

In any event, psychologists note three factors that should caution us not to attach too much importance to apparent gender differences in cognition:

1. In most cases, the differences are small (Hyde & Plant, 1995). In addition, differences in verbal, mathematical, and spatial abilities are getting smaller (Hyde et al., 1990; Voyer et al., 1995).

2. These gender differences are *group* differences. There is greater variation in these skills between individuals *within* the groups than between males and females (Maccoby, 1990). That is, there may be a greater difference in, say, verbal skills between two women than between a woman and a man. Millions of females outdistance the "average" male in math and spatial abilities. Men have produced their Shakespeares. Women have produced their Madame Curies.

3. Some differences may largely reflect sociocultural influences. In our culture, spatial and math abilities are stereotyped as masculine. Women who are given just a few hours of training in spatial skills— for example, rotating geometric figures or studying floor plans—perform at least as well as men on tests of these skills (Azar, 1997).

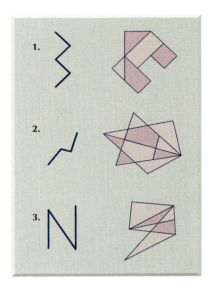

FIGURE GS.2
ITEMS FROM AN EMBEDDED-FIGURES TEST.

Social Behavior

There are many other psychological differences between males and females. For example, women exceed men in extraversion, anxiety, trust, and nurturance (Feingold, 1994). Men exceed women in assertiveness and tough-mindedness. In the arena of social behavior, women seem more likely than men to cooperate with other people and hold groups, such as families, together (Bjorklund & Kipp, 1996).

Despite the stereotype of women as gossips and chatterboxes, research in communication styles suggests that in many situations men spend more time talking than women do. Men are more likely to introduce new topics and to interrupt (Hall, 1984). Women, in contrast, seem more willing to reveal their feelings and personal experiences (Dindia & Allen, 1992).

Women interact at closer distances than men do. They also seek to keep more space between themselves and strangers of the other gender than men do (Rüstemli, 1986). Men are made more uncomfortable by strangers who sit across from them, whereas women are more likely to feel "invaded" by strangers who sit next to them. In libraries, men tend to pile books protectively in front of them. Women place books and coats in adjacent seats to discourage others from taking them.

There are also gender differences in three major areas of social behavior (Archer, 1996): sex and relationships, mate selection, and aggression.

SEX AND RELATIONSHIPS Men are more interested than women in casual sex and in having more than one sex partner (Leitenberg & Henning, 1995). In our society there are constraints on unbridled sexual behavior, so most men are not promiscuous (Archer, 1996). Women are more likely to want to combine sex with a romantic relationship.

GENDER DIFFERENCES IN MATE SELECTION Susan Sprecher and her colleagues (1994) surveyed more than 13,000 people in the United States. They asked how willing they would be to marry someone who was older, younger, of a different religion, unlikely to hold a steady job, not good looking, and so on. Each item was answered by checking off a 7-point scale in which 1 meant "not at all" and 7 meant "very willing." Women were more willing than men to marry someone who was not good looking (see Figure GS.3). But they were less willing to marry someone who was unlikely to hold a steady job.

TRUTH OR FICTION REVISITED
It is true that men behave more aggressively than women do—at least in most cultures. The issue is whether this gender difference is inborn or reflects sociocultural factors.

AGGRESSION In most cultures, it is the males who march off to war and battle for glory (and sneaker ads in TV commercials). Psychological studies of aggression find that male children and adults behave more aggressively than females do (Archer, 1996).

In a classic review of 72 studies concerning gender differences in aggression, Ann Frodi and her colleagues (1977) found that females are more likely to act aggressively under some circumstances than others:

1. Females are more likely to feel anxious or guilty about aggression. Such feelings inhibit aggressive behavior.
2. Females behave as aggressively as males when they have the means to do so and believe that aggression is justified.
3. Females are more likely to empathize with the victim—to imagine themselves in the victim's place. Empathy encourages helping behavior, not aggression.
4. Gender differences in aggression decrease when the victim is anonymous. Anonymity may prevent females from empathizing with their victims.

FIGURE GS.3
GENDER DIFFERENCES IN MATE PREFERENCES.
Susan Sprecher and her colleagues found that men are more willing than women to marry someone who is several years younger and less well educated. Women are more willing than men to marry someone who is not good looking and who earns more money than they do.

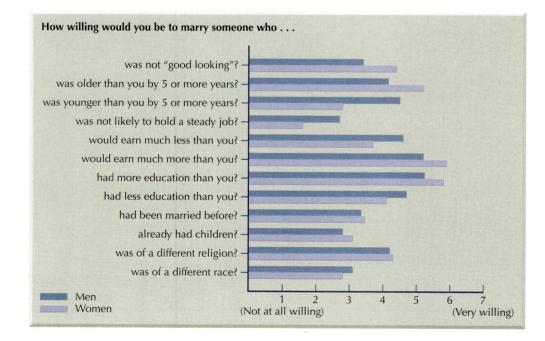

GENDER TYPING: ON BECOMING A WOMAN OR A MAN

There are thus a number of psychological gender differences. They include minor differences in cognitive functioning and differences in personality and social behavior. The process by which these differences develop is termed **gender typing.** In this section we explore several possible sources of gender typing, both biological and psychological.

Biological Influences

According to evolutionary psychologists like David Buss (1999), gender differences were fashioned by natural selection in response to problems in adaptation that were repeatedly encountered by humans over thousands of generations. On a biological level, the psychological differences that have evolved between men and women may largely reflect differences in brain organization and sex hormones.

BRAIN ORGANIZATION A number of studies suggest that we can speak of "left brain" versus "right brain" functions (Springer & Deutsch, 1993). Some psychological activities, such as language, seem to be controlled largely by the left side of the brain. Other psychological activities, such as spatial relations and aesthetic and emotional responses, seem to be controlled largely by the right side. Brain-imaging research suggests that the brain hemispheres are more specialized in males than in females (Shaywitz et al., 1995). For example, men with damage to the left hemisphere are more likely to experience difficulties in verbal functioning than women with similar damage. Men with damage to the right hemisphere are more likely to have problems with spatial relations than women with similar injuries.

Gender differences in brain organization might, in part, explain why women exceed men in verbal skills that require some spatial organization, such as reading, spelling, and crisp articulation of speech. Men, however, might be superior at more specialized spatial-relations tasks such as interpreting road maps and visualizing objects in space.

SEX HORMONES Sex hormones are responsible for the prenatal differentiation of sex organs. Prenatal sex hormones may also "masculinize" or "feminize" the brain by creating predispositions consistent with some gender-role stereotypes (Collaer & Hines, 1995; Crews, 1994). Yet John Money (1987) argues that social learning plays a stronger role in the development of **gender identity,** personality traits, and preferences. Money (1987) claims that social learning is powerful enough to counteract many prenatal predispositions.

Some evidence for the possible role of hormonal influences has been obtained from animal studies (Collaer & Hines, 1995; Crews, 1994). For example, male rats are generally superior to females in maze-learning ability, a task that requires spatial skills. Female rats exposed to male sex hormones in the uterus (e.g., because they have several male siblings in the uterus with them) or soon after birth learn maze routes as rapidly as males, however. They also roam over larger distances and mark larger territories than most females do (Vandenbergh, 1993).

Men are more aggressive than women, and aggression in lower animals has been connected with the male sex hormone testosterone (Collaer & Hines, 1995). However, cognitive psychologists argue that boys (and girls)

GENDER TYPING The process by which people acquire a sense of being female or male and acquire the traits considered typical of females or males within a cultural setting.

GENDER IDENTITY One's psychological sense of being female or male.

can choose whether or not to act aggressively, regardless of the levels of hormones in their bloodstreams.

Psychological Influences

The two most prominent psychological perspectives on gender typing today are cognitive-social theory and gender-schema theory.

SOCIAL-COGNITIVE THEORY Social-cognitive theorists explain gender typing in terms of observational learning, identification, and socialization. Children learn much of what is considered masculine or feminine by observational learning, as suggested by a classic experiment conducted by David Perry and Kay Bussey (1979). In this study, children learned how behaviors are gender typed by observing the *relative frequencies* with which men and women performed them. The adult role models expressed arbitrary preferences for one item from each of 16 pairs of items—pairs such as oranges versus apples and toy cows versus toy horses—while 8- and 9-year-old boys and girls watched them. The children were then asked to show their own preferences. Boys selected an average of 14 of 16 items that agreed with the "preferences" of the men. Girls selected an average of only 3 of 16 items that agreed with the choices of the men. In other words, boys and girls learned gender-typed preferences even though those preferences were completely arbitrary.

Social-cognitive theorists view **identification** as a continuous learning process in which children are influenced by rewards and punishments to imitate adults of the same gender—particularly the parent of the same gender. In identification, as opposed to imitation, children do not simply imitate a certain behavior pattern. They also try to become similar to the model.

Socialization also plays a role. Parents and other adults—even other children—inform children about how they are expected to behave. They reward children for behavior they consider appropriate for their gender. They punish (or fail to reinforce) children for behavior they consider inappropriate. Girls, for example, are given dolls while they are still sleeping in their cribs. They are encouraged to use the dolls to rehearse caretaking behaviors in preparation for traditional feminine adult roles.

IDENTIFICATION The process of becoming broadly like another person.

SOCIALIZATION The guiding of behavior through instruction and rewards and punishments.

ACQUIRING GENDER ROLES.
How do people develop gender roles? What contributions are made by biological and psychological factors? Social-cognitive theory focuses on imitation of the behavior of adults of the same gender and reinforcement by parents and peers.

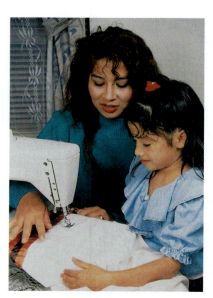

Concerning gender and aggression, Maccoby and Jacklin (1974) note that aggression is more actively discouraged in girls through punishment, withdrawal of affection, or being told that "girls don't act that way." If girls retaliate when they are insulted or attacked, they usually experience social disapproval. They therefore learn to feel anxious about the possibility of acting aggressively. Boys, in contrast, are usually encouraged to strike back (Frodi et al., 1977).

Classic experiments point up the importance of social learning in female aggressiveness. In one study, for example, college women competed with men to see who could respond to a stimulus more quickly (Richardson et al., 1979). There were four blocks of trials, with six trials in each block. The subjects could not see their opponents. The loser of each trial received an electric shock whose intensity was set by the opponent. Women competed under one of three experimental conditions: public, private, or with a supportive other. In the public condition, another woman observed the subject silently. In the private condition, there was no observer. In the supportive-other condition, another woman urged the subject to retaliate strongly when her opponent selected high shock levels. As shown in Figure GS.4, women in the private and supportive-other conditions selected increasingly higher levels of shock in retaliation. Presumably, the women assumed that an observer, although silent, would frown on aggressive behavior. This assumption is likely to reflect the women's own early socialization experiences. Women who were not observed or who were urged on by another person apparently felt free to violate the gender norm of nonaggressiveness when their situations called for aggressive responses.

Social-cognitive theory outlines ways in which rewards, punishments, and modeling foster "gender-appropriate" behavior. Gender-schema theory suggests that we tend to assume gender-appropriate behavior patterns by blending our self-concept with cultural expectations.

GENDER-SCHEMA THEORY You have probably heard the expression, "looking at the world through rose-colored glasses." According to Sandra Bem (1993), the originator of **gender-schema theory,** people look at the social world through "the lenses of gender." Bem argues that our culture polarizes females and males by organizing social life around mutually exclusive gender roles. Children come to accept the polarizing scripts without realizing it. Unless parents or unusual events encourage them to challenge the validity of gender polarization, children attempt to construct identities that are consistent with the "proper" script. Most children reject behavior—in others and in themselves—that deviates from it. Children's self-esteem soon becomes wrapped up in the ways in which they measure up to the gender schema. For example, boys soon learn to hold a high opinion of themselves if they excel in sports.

Once children understand the labels *boy* and *girl,* they have a basis for blending their self-concepts with the gender schema of their culture. No external pressure is required. Children who have developed a sense of being male or being female, which usually occurs by the age of 3, actively seek information about their gender schema. As in social-cognitive theory, children seek to learn through observation what is considered appropriate for them.

Powerful evidence indicates that the polarized female-male scripts influence cognitive activity (Bowes & Goodnow, 1996). Researchers in one study showed 5- and 6-year-old boys and girls pictures of actors engaged in "gender-consistent" or "gender-inconsistent" activities. The gender-consistent pictures showed boys playing with trains or sawing wood. Girls

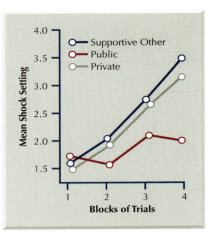

FIGURE GS.4

MEAN SHOCK SETTINGS SELECTED BY WOMEN IN RETALIATION AGAINST MALE OPPONENTS.

Women in the Richardson study chose higher shock levels for their opponents when they were alone or when another person (a "supportive other") urged them on.

GENDER-SCHEMA THEORY The view that gender identity plus knowledge of the distribution of behavior patterns into feminine and masculine roles motivate and guide the gender typing of the child.

were shown cooking and cleaning. Gender-inconsistent pictures showed actors of the other gender engaged in these gender-typed activities. Each child was shown a randomized set of pictures that included only one picture of each activity. One week later, the children were asked who had engaged in the activity, a male or a female. Both boys and girls gave wrong answers more often when the picture they had seen showed gender-*inconsistent* activity. In other words, they distorted what they had seen to conform to the gender schema.

In sum, brain organization and sex hormones may contribute to gender-typed behavior and play a role in verbal ability, math skills, and aggression. Yet the effects of social learning may counteract biological influences. Social-cognitive theory outlines the environmental factors that influence children to engage in so-called gender-appropriate behavior. Gender-schema theory focuses on how children blend their self-identities with the gender schema of their culture.

SEXUAL ORIENTATION

Sexual orientation refers to the organization or direction of one's erotic interests. **Heterosexual** people are sexually attracted to people of the other gender and interested in forming romantic relationships with them. **Homosexual** people are sexually attracted to people of their own gender and interested in forming romantic relationships with them. Homosexual males are also referred to as **gay males** and homosexual females as **lesbians. Bisexual** people are sexually attracted to and interested in forming romantic relationships with both women and men.

Do not confuse the concept of *sexual orientation* with *sexual activity*. For example, engaging in sexual activity with people of one's own gender does not necessarily mean that one has a homosexual orientation. Sexual activity between males sometimes reflects limited sexual opportunities. Adolescent males may manually stimulate one another while fantasizing about girls. Men in prisons may similarly turn to each other as sexual outlets. Young Sambian men in New Guinea engage in sexual practices exclusively with older males because it is believed that they must drink "men's milk" to achieve the fierce manhood of the headhunter (Money, 1987). Once they reach marrying age, however, their sexual activities are limited to female partners.

Surveys find that about 3% of men in the United States identify themselves as gay (e.g., Laumann et al., 1994). About 2% of the U.S. women surveyed say that they have a lesbian sexual orientation (Laumann et al., 1994). The nearby "Psychology in a World of Diversity" feature describes the experiences of gay people from various ethnic groups.

Origins of Sexual Orientation

There are psychological and biological theories of sexual orientation, as well as theories that bridge the two.

PSYCHOLOGICAL APPROACHES Psychodynamic theory ties sexual orientation to identification with male or female figures. Identification, in turn, is related to resolution of the Oedipus and Electra complexes. In men, faulty resolution of the **Oedipus complex** would stem from a "classic pattern" of child rearing in which there is a "close binding" mother and a "detached hostile" father. Boys reared in such a home environment would identify with their mother and not with their father. Psychodynamic theory has been criticized, however, because many gay males have had

SEXUAL ORIENTATION The directionality of one's erotic interests — that is, whether one is sexually attracted to and interested in forming romantic relationships with people of the other or the same gender.

HETEROSEXUAL Referring to people who are sexually aroused by and interested in forming romantic relationships with people of the other gender.

HOMOSEXUAL Referring to people who are sexually aroused by and interested in forming romantic relationships with people of the same gender.

GAY MALE A male homosexual.

LESBIAN A female homosexual.

BISEXUAL A person who is sexually aroused by and interested in forming romantic relationships with people of either gender.

OEDIPUS COMPLEX Within psychodynamic theory, a conflict of the phallic stage characterized by romantic feelings toward the parent of the other gender and feelings of rivalry toward the parent of the same gender.

excellent relationships with both parents (Isay, 1990). Also, the childhoods of many heterosexuals fit the "classic pattern."

From a learning theory point of view, early reinforcement of sexual behavior (e.g., by orgasm achieved through interaction with people of one's own gender) can influence one's sexual orientation. But most people are aware of their sexual orientation before they have sexual contacts (Bell et al., 1981).

BIOLOGICAL APPROACHES Biopsychologists note evidence of familial patterns in sexual orientation (Pillard, 1990; Pillard & Weinrich, 1986). In one study, 22% of the brothers of 51 primarily gay men were either gay or bisexual themselves. This is about four times the percentage found in the general population (Pillard & Weinrich, 1986). Genes connected with sexual orientation might be found on the X sex chromosome and be transmitted from mother to child (Hamer et al., 1993). Moreover, identical (MZ) twins have a higher agreement rate for a gay male sexual orientation

PSYCHOLOGY IN A WORLD OF *Diversity*

ETHNICITY AND SEXUAL ORIENTATION: A MATTER OF BELONGING

Societal prejudices make it difficult for many young people to come to terms with an emerging homosexual orientation (American Psychological Association, 1998b). You might assume that members of ethnic minority groups in the United States, who themselves have been subjected to prejudice and discrimination, would be more tolerant of a homosexual orientation. However, according to psychologist Beverly Greene (1994) of St. John's University, you might be wrong.

Greene (1994) notes that it is difficult to generalize about ethnic groups in the United States. For example, African Americans may find their cultural origins in the tribes of West Africa, but they have also been influenced by Christianity and the local subcultures of North American towns and cities. Native Americans represent hundreds of tribal groups, languages, and cultures. By and large, homosexuality is rejected by ethnic minority groups in the United States. Lesbians and gay males are pressured to keep their sexual orientation a secret or to move to communities where they can express it without condemnation.

In traditional Hispanic American culture, the family is the primary social unit. Men are expected to support and defend the family, and women are expected to be submissive, respectful, and deferential (Morales, 1992). Also, Hispanic American culture frequently denies the sexuality of women. Thus lesbians are doubly condemned—because of their sexual orientation and because their independence from men threatens the tradition of male dominance (Trujillo, 1991).

Asian American cultures emphasize respect for one's elders, obedience to one's parents, and distinct masculine and feminine gender roles (Chan, 1992). The topic of sex is generally taboo within the family. Asian Americans, like Hispanic Americans, tend to assume that sex is unimportant to women. Women are also considered less important than men. Open admission of a homosexual orientation is seen as a rejection of one's traditional cultural roles and a threat to the continuity of the family line (Chan, 1992).

Because many African American men have had difficulty finding jobs, gender roles among African Americans have been more flexible than those found among most other ethnic minority groups and among White Americans (Greene, 1994). Nevertheless, the African American community appears to reject gay men and lesbians strongly, pressuring them to remain secretive about their sexual orientation (Gomez & Smith, 1990; Poussaint, 1990). One factor that influences African Americans to be hostile toward lesbians and gay men is allegiance to Christian beliefs and biblical Scripture (Greene, 1994).

Prior to the European conquest of the Americas, sex was seen as a natural part of life. Native American individuals who incorporated both traditional feminine and masculine styles were generally accepted, even admired. The influence of colonists' religions led to greater rejection of lesbians and gay men and pressure on them to move from reservations to large cities (Greene, 1994). Native American lesbians and gay men thus often feel doubly removed from their families.

If any generalization is possible, it may be that lesbians and gay men find a greater sense of belonging in the gay community than in their ethnic communities. ■

than do fraternal (DZ) twins: 52% for MZ twins versus 22% for DZ twins (Bailey & Pillard, 1991). Although genetic factors may partly determine sexual orientation, psychologist John Money, who has specialized in research on sexual behavior, concludes that sexual orientation is "not under the direct governance of chromosomes and genes" (1987, p. 384).

Sex hormones may play a role in sexual orientation. These hormones promote biological sexual differentiation and regulate the menstrual cycle. They also have organizing and activating effects on sexual behavior. They predispose lower animals toward masculine or feminine mating patterns—

a directional or **organizing effect** (Crews, 1994). They also affect the sex drive and promote sexual response; these are **activating effects.**

Sexual behavior among many lower animals is almost completely governed by hormones (Crews, 1994). In many species, if the sex organs and brains of fetuses are exposed to large doses of **testosterone** in the uterus (which occurs naturally when they share the uterus with many brothers, or artificially as a result of hormone injections), they become masculine in structure (Crews, 1994). Prenatal testosterone organizes the brains of females in the masculine direction, predisposing them toward masculine behaviors in adulthood. Testosterone in adulthood then apparently activates the masculine behavior patterns.

Because sex hormones predispose lower animals toward masculine or feminine mating patterns, some have asked whether gay males and lesbians might differ from heterosexuals in levels of sex hormones. However, a gay male or lesbian sexual orientation has not been reliably linked to current (adult) levels of male or female sex hormones (Friedman & Downey, 1994). What about the effects of sex hormones on the developing fetus? As just noted, we know that prenatal sex hormones can masculinize or feminize the brains of laboratory animals.

Lee Ellis (1990; Ellis & Ames, 1987) theorizes that sexual orientation is hormonally determined prior to birth and affected by genetic factors, synthetic hormones (such as male sex hormones), and maternal stress. Why maternal stress? Stress causes the release of hormones such as **adrenaline** and **cortisol,** which can masculinize the embryonic brain. Perhaps the brains of some gay males have been feminized and the brains of some lesbians masculinized prior to birth (Collaer & Hines, 1995; Friedman & Downey, 1994).

In sum, the determinants of sexual orientation are mysterious and complex (American Psychological Association, 1998b). Research suggests that they may involve prenatal hormone levels—which can be affected by factors such as heredity, drugs, and maternal stress—and postnatal socialization. But the precise interaction among these influences is not yet understood.

Sexual orientation probably involves the interaction of psychological and biological factors. Let us now consider the biological aspects of human sexuality more deeply.

SEXUAL ANATOMY AND SEXUAL RESPONSE

Although we may consider ourselves sophisticated about sex, it is surprising how little we know about sexual biology. How many male readers know that women have different orifices for urination and sexual intercourse? How many readers, male and female, know that the penis—sometimes referred to by the slang term "boner" when erect—contains no bones?

In this section we survey some of the details of female and male sexual anatomy. Then we consider how female and male sexual anatomy respond to sexual stimulation—that is, the so-called sexual response cycle.

Female Sexual Anatomy

The external female genital organs are called the **vulva,** from the Latin for "covering." The vulva is also known as the **pudendum,** from "something

ORGANIZING EFFECT The directional effect of sex hormones—for example, along stereotypically masculine or feminine lines.

ACTIVATING EFFECT The arousal-producing effects of sex hormones that increase the likelihood of sexual behavior.

TESTOSTERONE A male sex hormone that promotes development of male sexual characteristics and that has activating effects on sexual arousal.

ADRENALINE A hormone produced by the adrenal glands that generally arouses people and heightens their emotional responsiveness.

CORTISOL A hormone produced by the adrenal glands that increases resistance to stress.

VULVA The female external genital organs.

PUDENDUM Another term for the *vulva.*

TRUTH OR FICTION REVISITED
It is true that a word for the female genital organs (pudendum) *is derived from the Latin for "something to be ashamed of."* Ingrained cultural attitudes cause many women to feel embarrassed about their genital organs.

FIGURE GS.5
FEMALE SEXUAL ANATOMY.

The top drawing is a cross section of the internal reproductive organs of the female. The bottom drawing is an external view of the vulva.

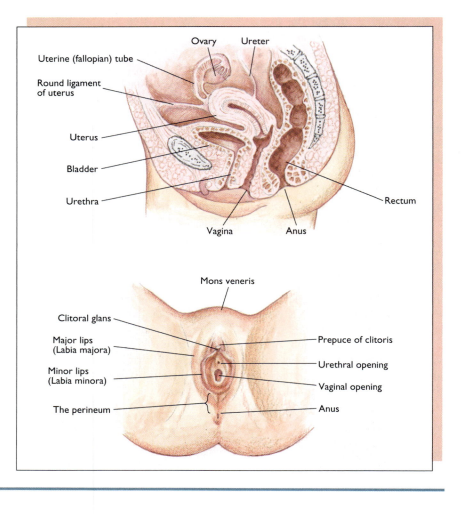

URETHRA A tube that conducts urine from the body and, in males, the ejaculate.

MONS VENERIS The mound of fatty tissue that covers the joint of the pubic bones and cushions the female during intercourse.

CLITORIS The female sex organ whose only known function is the reception and transmission of sensations of sexual pleasure.

GLANS Tip or head.

MAJOR LIPS Large folds of skin that run along the sides of the vulva. (In Latin, *labia majora*.)

MINOR LIPS Folds of skin that lie within the major lips and enclose the urethral and vaginal openings. (In Latin, *labia minora*.)

to be ashamed of"—a clear reflection of some ancient Mediterranean sexism. The vulva has several parts (see the bottom part of Figure GS.5): the mons veneris, clitoris, major and minor lips, and vaginal opening. Females urinate through the **urethral** opening.

The **mons veneris** (Latin for "hill of love") is a fatty cushion that lies above the pubic bone and is covered with short, curly pubic hair. The mons and pubic hair cushion the woman during intercourse. The woman's most sensitive sex organ, the **clitoris** (from the Greek for "hill"), lies below the mons and above the urethral opening. The only known function of the clitoris is to receive and transmit pleasurable sensations.

During sexual arousal, the clitoris becomes engorged with blood and expands. The clitoris has a shaft and a tip, or **glans.** The glans is the more sensitive of the two and may become irritated if approached too early during foreplay, or by prolonged stimulation.

Two layers of fatty tissue, the outer, or **major lips,** and the inner, or **minor lips,** line the entrance to the vagina. The outer lips are covered with hair and are less sensitive to touch than the smooth, pinkish inner lips.

The woman's internal sexual and reproductive organs consist of the vagina, cervix, fallopian tubes, and ovaries (see the top part of Figure GS.5). The vagina contains the penis during intercourse. At rest the vagina is a flattened tube 3 to 5 inches in length. When aroused, it can lengthen by several inches and dilate (open) to a diameter of about 2 inches. A large penis is not required to "fill" the vagina in order for a woman to experience sexual pleasure. The vagina expands as needed. The pelvic muscles that surround the vagina may also be contracted during intercourse to heighten sensation. The outer third of the vagina is highly sensitive to touch.

When a woman is sexually aroused, the vaginal walls produce moisture that serves as lubrication. Sexual relations can be painful for unaroused, unlubricated women. Adequate arousal usually stems from sexual attraction, positive feelings like liking and loving, fantasies, and foreplay. Anxieties concerning sex or a partner may inhibit sexual arousal—for either gender.

High in the vagina is a small opening called the **cervix** (Latin for "neck") that connects the vagina to the uterus. Strawlike fallopian tubes lead from the uterus to the abdominal cavity. Ovaries, which produce ova and the hormones estrogen and progesterone, lie near the uterus and the fallopian tubes. When an ovum is released from an ovary, it normally finds its way into the nearby fallopian tube (although we do not know *how* it does so) and makes its way to the uterus. Conception normally takes place in the tube, but the embryo becomes implanted and grows in the uterus. During labor the cervix dilates, and the baby passes through the cervix and distended vagina.

Male Sexual Anatomy

The major male sex organs consist of the penis, testes (or testicles), scrotum, and the series of ducts, canals, and glands that store and transport sperm and produce **semen.** Whereas the female vulva has been viewed historically as "something to be ashamed of," the male sex organs were prized in ancient Greece and Rome. Citizens wore phallic-shaped trinkets, and the Greeks held their testes when offering testimony, in the same way that we swear on a Bible. *Testimony* and *testicle* both derive from the Greek *testis,* meaning "witness." Given this tradition of masculine pride, it is not surprising that Sigmund Freud believed that girls were riddled with penis envy.

The **testes** produce sperm and the male sex hormone testosterone. The **scrotum** allows the testes to hang away from the body. (Sperm require a lower-than-body temperature.) Sperm travel through ducts up over the bladder and back down to the ejaculatory duct (see Figure GS.6), which

CERVIX The lower part of the uterus that opens into the vagina.

SEMEN The whitish fluid that carries sperm. Also called the *ejaculate.*

TESTES Male reproductive organs that produce sperm cells and male sex hormones. Also called *testicles.*

SCROTUM A pouch of loose skin that houses the testes.

FIGURE GS.6
MALE SEXUAL ANATOMY.
A cross section of the internal and external reproductive organs of the male.

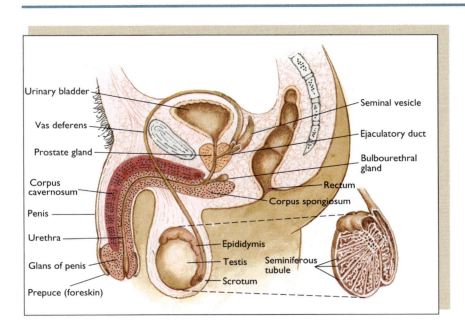

Urinary bladder
Vas deferens
Prostate gland
Corpus cavernosum
Penis
Urethra
Glans of penis
Prepuce (foreskin)
Seminal vesicle
Ejaculatory duct
Bulbourethral gland
Rectum
Corpus spongiosum
Epididymis
Testis
Seminiferous tubule
Scrotum

empties into the urethra. In females, the urethral opening and the orifice for transporting the ejaculate are different; in males they are one and the same. Although the male urethra transports urine as well as sperm, a valve shuts off the bladder during ejaculation. Thus sperm and urine do not mix. Several glands, including the prostate, produce semen. Semen transports, activates, and nourishes sperm, enhancing their ability to swim and fertilize the ovum.

The penis consists mainly of loose erectile tissue. Like the clitoris, the penis has a shaft and tip, or glans, that is highly sensitive to sexual stimulation, especially on the underside. Within seconds following sexual stimulation, blood rushes reflexively into caverns within the penis, just as blood engorges the clitoris. Engorgement with blood—not bone—produces erection.

The Sexual Response Cycle

Although we may be culturally attuned to focus on gender differences rather than similarities, William Masters and Virginia Johnson (1966) found that the biological responses of males and females to sexual stimulation are quite similar. They use the term *sexual response cycle* to describe the changes that occur in the body as men and women become sexually aroused. Masters and Johnson divide the **sexual response cycle** into four phases: *excitement, plateau, orgasm,* and *resolution.* Figure GS.7 suggests the levels of sexual arousal associated with each phase.

SEXUAL RESPONSE CYCLE Masters and Johnson's model of sexual response, which consists of four stages or phases.

FIGURE GS.7

LEVELS OF SEXUAL AROUSAL DURING THE PHASES OF THE SEXUAL RESPONSE CYCLE.

Masters and Johnson divide the sexual response cycle into four phases: excitement, plateau, orgasm, and resolution. During the resolution phase, the level of sexual arousal returns to the prearoused state. For men there is a refractory period following orgasm. As shown by the broken line, however, men can become rearoused to orgasm once the refractory period is past and their levels of sexual arousal have returned to preplateau levels. Pattern A for women shows a typical response cycle, with the broken line suggesting multiple orgasms. Pattern B shows the cycle of a woman who reaches the plateau phase but for whom arousal is "resolved" without reaching the orgasmic phase. Pattern C shows the possibility of orgasm in a highly aroused woman who passes quickly through the plateau phase.

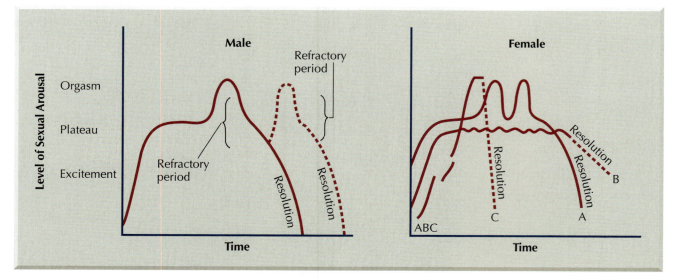

The sexual response cycle is characterized by vasocongestion and myotonia. **Vasocongestion** is the swelling of the genital tissues with blood. It causes erection of the penis and swelling of the area surrounding the vaginal opening. The testes, the nipples, and even the earlobes swell as blood vessels dilate in these areas.

Myotonia is muscle tension. It causes facial grimaces, spasms in the hands and feet, and then the spasms of orgasm. In this section we explore these and other bodily changes that make up the sexual response cycle.

TRUTH OR FICTION REVISITED
It is true that the earlobes swell when people become sexually aroused.

EXCITEMENT PHASE Vasocongestion during the **excitement phase** can cause erection in young men as soon as 3 to 8 seconds after sexual stimulation begins. The scrotal skin also thickens, becoming less baggy. The testes increase in size and become elevated.

In the female, excitement is characterized by vaginal lubrication, which may start 10 to 30 seconds after sexual stimulation begins. Vasocongestion swells the clitoris and flattens and spreads the vaginal lips. The inner part of the vagina expands. The breasts enlarge, and blood vessels near the surface become more prominent. The nipples may become erect in both men and women. Heart rate and blood pressure also increase.

PLATEAU PHASE The level of sexual arousal remains somewhat stable during the **plateau phase** of the cycle. Because of vasocongestion, men show some increase in the circumference of the head of the penis, which also takes on a purplish hue. The testes are elevated into position for **ejaculation** and may reach one and a half times their unaroused size.

In women, vasocongestion swells the outer part of the vagina, contracting the vaginal opening in preparation for grasping the penis. The inner part of the vagina expands further. The clitoris withdraws beneath the clitoral hood and shortens.

Breathing becomes rapid, like panting. Heart rate may increase to 100 to 160 beats per minute. Blood pressure continues to rise.

ORGASMIC PHASE The orgasmic phase in the male consists of two stages of muscular contractions. In the first stage, **seminal fluid** collects at the base of the penis. The internal sphincter of the urinary bladder prevents urine from mixing with semen. In the second stage, muscle contractions propel the ejaculate out of the body. Sensations of pleasure tend to be related to the strength of the contractions and the amount of seminal fluid present. The first 3 to 4 contractions are generally most intense and occur at 0.8-second intervals (5 contractions every 4 seconds). Another 2 to 4 contractions occur at a somewhat slower pace. Rates and patterns can vary from one man to another.

Orgasm in the female is manifested by 3 to 15 contractions of the pelvic muscles that surround the vaginal barrel. The contractions first occur at 0. 8-second intervals. As in the male, they produce release of sexual tension. Weaker and slower contractions follow.

Blood pressure and heart rate reach a peak, with the heart beating up to 180 times per minute. Respiration may increase to 40 breaths per minute.

RESOLUTION PHASE After orgasm the body returns to its unaroused state. This is called the **resolution phase.** After ejaculation, blood is released from engorged areas, so the erection disappears. The testes return to their normal size.

VASOCONGESTION Engorgement of blood vessels with blood, which swells the genitals and breasts during sexual arousal.

MYOTONIA Muscle tension.

EXCITEMENT PHASE The first phase of the sexual response cycle, characterized by muscle tension, increases in the heart rate, and erection in the male and vaginal lubrication in the female.

PLATEAU PHASE The second phase of the sexual response cycle, characterized by increases in vasocongestion, muscle tension, heart rate, and blood pressure in preparation for orgasm.

EJACULATION The ejection of semen from the penis.

SEMINAL FLUID The fluid produced by the prostate and other glands that carries and nourishes sperm. Also called *semen.*

ORGASM The height or climax of sexual excitement, involving involuntary muscle contractions, release of sexual tensions, and, usually, subjective feelings of pleasure.

RESOLUTION PHASE The fourth phase of the sexual response cycle, during which the body gradually returns to its prearoused state.

In women, orgasm also triggers the release of blood from engorged areas. The nipples return to their normal size. The clitoris and vaginal barrel gradually shrink to their unaroused sizes. Blood pressure, heart rate, and breathing also return to their levels before arousal. Both partners may feel relaxed and satisfied.

Unlike women, men enter a **refractory period** during which they cannot experience another orgasm or ejaculate. The refractory period of adolescent males may last only minutes, whereas that of men age 50 and above may last from several minutes to a day. Women do not undergo a refractory period and therefore can become quickly rearoused to the point of repeated (multiple) orgasm if they desire and receive continued sexual stimulation.

Sexual Dysfunctions and Sex Therapy

Sexual dysfunctions are persistent problems in becoming sexually aroused or reaching orgasm. Many people are troubled by a sexual dysfunction at one time or another. Let us take a look at the main types of sexual dysfunctions and their causes.

TYPES OF SEXUAL DYSFUNCTIONS The sexual dysfunctions include hypoactive sexual desire disorder, female sexual arousal disorder, male erectile disorder, orgasmic disorder, premature ejaculation, dyspareunia, and vaginismus.

In **hypoactive sexual desire disorder,** a person lacks interest in sexual activity and frequently reports a lack of sexual fantasies. This diagnosis exists because it is assumed that sexual fantasies and interests are normal responses that may be blocked by anxiety or other factors.

In women, sexual arousal is characterized by lubrication of the vaginal walls, which facilitates entry by the penis. Sexual arousal in men is characterized by erection. Almost all women sometimes have difficulty becoming or remaining lubricated. Almost all men have occasional difficulty attaining or maintaining an erection through intercourse. When these events are persistent or recurrent, they are considered dysfunctions (**female sexual arousal disorder** and **male erectile disorder**).

In **orgasmic disorder,** the man or woman, although sexually excited, takes a long time to reach orgasm or does not reach it at all. Orgasmic disorder is more common among women than among men. In **premature ejaculation,** the male ejaculates after minimal sexual stimulation, too soon to permit his partner or himself to enjoy sexual relations fully. Other dysfunctions include **dyspareunia** (painful sexual activity) and **vaginismus** (involuntary contraction of the muscles surrounding the vaginal opening, which makes entry painful and/or difficult).

CAUSES OF SEXUAL DYSFUNCTIONS Some sexual dysfunctions reflect biological problems. Lack of desire, for example, can be due to diabetes or to diseases of the heart and lungs. Fatigue can reduce sexual desire and inhibit orgasm. Depressants such as alcohol, narcotics, and tranquilizers can also impair sexual response. Physical factors sometimes interact with psychological factors. For instance, dyspareunia can heighten anxiety, and extremes of anxiety can damp sexual arousal. The changes of aging can lead to erectile problems in men and orgasmic problems in women.

Physically or psychologically painful sexual experiences, such as rape, can block future sexual response (Koss, 1993). Moreover, a sexual relationship is usually no better than other aspects of a relationship or mar-

---

REFRACTORY PERIOD In the sexual response cycle, a period of time following orgasm during which an individual is not responsive to sexual stimulation.

SEXUAL DYSFUNCTION A persistent or recurrent problem in becoming sexually aroused or reaching orgasm.

HYPOACTIVE SEXUAL DESIRE DISORDER A sexual dysfunction in which people lack sexual desire.

FEMALE SEXUAL AROUSAL DISORDER A sexual dysfunction in which females fail to become adequately sexually aroused to engage in sexual intercourse.

MALE ERECTILE DISORDER A sexual dysfunction in which males fail to obtain or maintain erections that are adequate for sexual intercourse.

ORGASMIC DISORDER A sexual dysfunction in which people have persistent or recurrent problems in reaching orgasm.

PREMATURE EJACULATION Ejaculation that occurs before the couple are satisfied with the duration of sexual relations.

DYSPAREUNIA A sexual dysfunction characterized by persistent or recurrent pain during sexual intercourse. (From roots meaning "badly paired.")

VAGINISMUS A sexual dysfunction characterized by involuntary contraction of the muscles surrounding the vagina, preventing entry by the penis or making entry painful.

riage. Couples who have difficulty communicating are at a disadvantage in expressing their sexual desires.

Cognitive psychologists point out that irrational beliefs and attitudes can contribute to sexual dysfunctions. If we believe that we need a lover's approval at all times, we may view a disappointing sexual episode as a catastrophe. If we demand that every sexual encounter be perfect, we set ourselves up for failure.

In most cases of sexual dysfunction, the physical and psychological factors we have outlined lead to yet another psychological factor—**performance anxiety,** or fear of not being able to perform sexually. People with performance anxiety may focus on past failures and expectations of another disaster rather than enjoying present erotic sensations and fantasies. Performance anxiety can make it difficult for a man to attain erection, yet also spur him to ejaculate prematurely. It can prevent a woman from becoming adequately lubricated and can contribute to vaginismus.

SEX THERAPY **Sex therapy** is a collection of techniques that help people overcome sexual dysfunctions. It is largely indebted to the pioneering work of Masters and Johnson (1970), although other therapists have also developed important techniques. It generally focuses on reducing performance anxiety, changing self-defeating attitudes and expectations, teaching sexual skills, enhancing sexual knowledge, and improving sexual communication. Moreover, a number of biological treatments are available for various problems, such as male erectile disorder. Readers interested in learning more about sex therapy are advised to consult a human sexuality textbook, contact their state's psychological association, or ask their professors or college counseling centers for referral.

Sexual dysfunctions are one category of problems in sexual interaction. Let us now consider a darker side of human interaction: sexual coercion. In sexual dysfunctions, individuals and couples generally wish to remove obstacles to having a fulfilling sexual relationship. In the case of sexual coercion, individuals—usually women—need effective barriers to prevent other people from damaging their physical and psychological well-being.

SEXUAL COERCION

Sexual coercion includes rape and other forms of sexual pressure. It also includes *any* sexual activity between an adult and a child. Even when children cooperate, sexual relations with children are coercive because the child is below the legal age of consent. In this section we focus on rape and sexual harassment.

Rape

As many as 1 woman in 4 in the United States has been raped (Koss, 1993). Parents regularly encourage their daughters to be wary of strangers and strange places—places where they could fall prey to rapists. Certainly the threat of rape from strangers is real enough. Yet 4 out of 5 rapes are committed by acquaintances (Laumann et al., 1994).

Date rape is a pressing concern on college campuses, where thousands of women have been victimized and there is much controversy over what exactly constitutes rape. Nine percent of one sample of 6,159 college women reported that they had given in to sexual intercourse as a result of threats or physical force (Koss et al., 1987).

PERFORMANCE ANXIETY Anxiety concerning one's ability to perform, especially when performance may be evaluated by other people.

SEX THERAPY A collective term for short-term cognitive-behavioral models for treatment of sexual dysfunctions.

KRISTINE, AMY, AND KAREN. These college women are among the thousands who have been raped by their dates. The great majority of rapes are committed by dates or acquaintances, not by strangers.

If we add to these statistics instances in which women are subjected to forced kissing and petting, the numbers grow even more alarming. At a major university, 40% of 201 male students surveyed admitted to using force to unfasten a woman's clothing, and 13% reported that they had forced a woman to engage in sexual intercourse (Rapoport & Burkhart, 1984). Forty-four percent of the college women in the Koss study (Koss et al., 1987) reported that they had "given in to sex play" because of a "man's continual arguments and pressure."

WHY DO MEN RAPE WOMEN? Why do men force women into sexual activity? Sex is not the only reason. Many social scientists argue that rape is often a man's way of expressing social dominance over, or anger toward, women (Hall & Barongan, 1997). With some rapists, violence appears to enhance sexual arousal. They therefore seek to combine sex and aggression (Barbaree & Marshall, 1991).

Many social critics contend that American culture socializes men— including the nice young man next door—into becoming rapists (Powell, 1996). This occurs because males are often reinforced for aggressive and competitive behavior (Hall & Barongan, 1997). The date rapist could be said to be asserting culturally expected dominance over women.

College men frequently perceive a date's protests as part of an adversarial sex game. One male undergraduate said, "Hell, no" when asked whether a date had consented to sex. He added, "[B]ut she didn't say no, so she must have wanted it, too. . . . It's the way it works" (Celis, 1991).

TRUTH OR FICTION REVISITED
It is true that most Americans believe that some women like to be talked into sex. A majority of Americans— including a majority of American *women*—share this belief. Does this belief encourage men to pressure their dates into sex?

MYTHS ABOUT RAPE In the United States there are numerous myths about rape—myths that tend to blame the victim, not the aggressor. For example, a majority of Americans aged 50 and older believe that the woman is partly responsible for being raped if she dresses provocatively (Gibbs, 1991). As a result, they are unlikely to be sympathetic if such a woman complains of being raped. A majority of Americans believe that some women like to be talked into sex.

Other myths include the notions that "women say no when they mean yes," "all women like a man who is pushy and forceful," and "rapists are crazed by sexual desire" (Powell, 1996, p. 139). Still another myth is that deep down inside, women *want* to be raped. All these myths deny the impact of the assault and transfer blame onto the victim. They contribute to a social climate that is too often lenient toward rapists and unsympathetic toward victims.

TRUTH OR FICTION REVISITED
It is not *true that women say no when they mean yes.* Myths such as this foster a social climate that encourages rape.

PREVENTING RAPE (SHOUT "FIRE!" NOT "RAPE!") Let us begin this section with a disclaimer. We are going to talk about measures that women can take to reduce their vulnerability to rapists. However, we are *not* implying that the prevention of rape is the responsibility of the victim. Society at large harbors many attitudes that have the effect of supporting rape. For example, large numbers of people believe that a woman loses the right to say no if she has "led on" a man or even goes with him to his apartment. Also, men are reinforced for aggressive behavior in our society. Many people even expect men to exert social dominance over women. These social attitudes and expectations have catastrophic consequences for women and even for men who are uncomfortable with the stereotypes. It is thus the responsibility of any people who can communicate, such as your author, to lay the blame at the proper door and to insist on social change. We are doing precisely that—*now.*

Social change is a tedious process, however, and it may never come to pass. Women, unfortunately, can thus profit from being armed with strategies for preventing rape in this less-than-ideal society.

The Boston Women's Health Book Collective (1992) lists a number of such strategies that women can use to lower the likelihood of rape at the hands of strangers:

- Establish signals and arrangements with other women in an apartment building or neighborhood.
- List only first initials in the telephone directory or on the mailbox.
- Use dead-bolt locks.
- Keep windows locked and obtain iron grids for first-floor windows.
- Keep entrances and doorways brightly lit.
- Have keys ready for the front door or the car.
- Do not walk alone in the dark.
- Avoid deserted areas.
- Never allow a strange man into your apartment or home without checking his credentials.
- Drive with the car windows up and the door locked.
- Check the rear seat of the car before entering.
- Avoid living in an unsafe building (if you can).
- Do not pick up hitchhikers (including women).
- Do not talk to strange men in the street.
- Shout "Fire!" not "Rape!" People crowd around fires but avoid scenes of violence.

The following tactics may help prevent *date rape* (Rathus et al., 2000):

- Avoid getting into secluded situations until you know your date very well. But be aware that victims of date rapes have sometimes gotten to know their assailants.

- Be wary when a date attempts to control you in any way, such as frightening you by driving rapidly or taking you some place you would rather not go.

- Be very assertive and clear concerning your sexual intentions. Some rapists, particularly date rapists, tend to misinterpret women's wishes. If their dates begin to implore them to stop during kissing or petting, they construe pleading as "female game playing." So if kissing or petting is leading where you don't want it to go, speak up.

- When dating a person for the first time, try to date in a group.

- Encourage your college or university to offer educational programs about date rape. The University of Washington, for example, offers students lectures and seminars on date rape and provides women with escorts to get home. Brown University requires all first-year students to attend orientation sessions on rape. Men need to learn that "No" means "No," despite the widespread belief that some women like to be "talked into" sex.

- Talk to your date about his attitudes toward women. If you get the feeling that he believes that men are in a war with women, or that women "play games" with men, you may be better off dating someone else.

Sexual Harassment

SEXUAL HARASSMENT Deliberate or repeated verbal comments, gestures, or physical contact of a sexual nature that is unwanted by the recipient.

Sexual harassment is frequent on college campuses, in the business world, and in the military (Seppa, 1997). It is sometimes difficult to draw the line between sexual persuasion and attempted rape. It can be even *more* difficult to distinguish between a legitimate (if unwelcome) sexual invita-

TABLE GS.2

SEXUAL HARASSMENT: MYTHS AND REALITIES

MYTHS	REALITIES
Sexual harassment is rare.	Sexual harassment is extremely widespread. It touches the lives of 40% to 60% of working women, and similar proportions of female students in colleges and universities.
The seriousness of sexual harassment has been exaggerated; most so-called harassment is really trivial and harmless flirtation.	Sexual harassment can be devastating. Studies indicate that most harassment has nothing to do with "flirtation" or sincere sexual or social interest. Rather, it is offensive, often frightening, and insulting to women. Research shows that women are often forced to leave school or jobs to avoid harassment. They may experience serious psychological and health problems.
Many women make up and report stories of sexual harassment to get back at their employers or others who have angered them.	Research shows that less than 1% of complaints are false. Women rarely file complaints even when they are justified in doing so.
Women who are sexually harassed generally provoke harassment by the way they look, dress, and behave.	Harassment does not occur because women dress provocatively or initiate sexual activity in the hope of getting promoted and advancing their careers. Studies have found that victims of sexual harassment vary in physical appearance, type of dress, age, and behavior. The only thing they have in common is that over 99% of them are female.
If you ignore harassment, it will go away.	It will not. Research has shown that simply ignoring the behavior is ineffective; harassers generally do not stop on their own. Ignoring such behavior may even be seen as agreement or encouragement.

Source: American Psychological Association (1998, March 16). Sexual harassment: Myths and realities. APA Public Information Home Page; www.apa.org.

tion and sexual harassment. People accused of sexual harassment often claim that the charges are exaggerated. They say that the victim "overreacted" to normal male-female interaction, or "She took me too seriously." Sexual harassment *is* a serious problem, however, and most harassers know very well what they are doing (see Table GS.2).

Where does "normal male-female interaction" end and sexual harassment begin? Sexual harassment involves deliberate or repeated unwanted comments, gestures, or physical contact of a sexual nature (Powell, 1996). Consider some examples:

- Verbal abuse
- Unwelcome sexual overtures or advances
- Pressure to engage in sexual activity
- Remarks about a person's body, clothing, or sexual activities
- Leering at, or ogling, someone
- Telling unwanted dirty jokes in mixed company
- Unnecessarily touching, patting, or pinching
- Whistles and catcalls
- Brushing up against someone
- Demands for sex that are accompanied by threats, such as being fired from a job or not getting a promotion.

Your college may publish guidelines about sexual harassment. Check with the dean of students or the president's office.

College students are sexually harassed by other students and sometimes by professors. Professors are sometimes harassed by students. Most often the victims of sexual harassment are women. Some cases are so serious that women switch majors or schools to avoid it. Ironically, as with rape, society often blames the victim of sexual harassment for being provocative or for not saying no firmly enough (Powell, 1996).

Gender and sexuality may be "the facts of life," but many of the "facts" we have taken for granted may be little more than myth. Some of the more questionable facts have to do with the nature and extent of supposed gender differences, and the burdens that these supposed differences have placed historically on women. Both in terms of personality and sexual response, males and females are apparently more alike than most people have assumed. Nevertheless, we all differ greatly as individuals, and one of the great lessons of research in gender and sexuality is that we need to respect our differences as individuals.

SEXUAL HARASSMENT.
Is this behavior acceptable in the workplace? Many women have switched jobs or colleges because of sexual harassment.

SUMMARY

1. **What are gender stereotypes?** Cultures have broad expectations of men and women that are termed *gender-role stereotypes*. In our culture women are expected to be gentle, dependent, kind, helpful, patient, and submissive. Men are expected to be tough, competitive, gentlemanly, and protective.

2. **What are some psychological gender differences?** Boys have historically been seen as excelling in math and spatial relations skills, whereas girls have been viewed as excelling in language skills. Males are also more aggressive than females.

3. **What are some biological views of gender typing?** Biological views of gender typing focus on the roles of evolution, genetics, and prenatal influences in predisposing men and women to gender-linked behavior patterns. Testosterone in the brains of male fetuses spurs greater growth of the right hemisphere of the brain, which may be connected with the ability to manage spatial relations tasks.

4. **What are some psychological views of gender typing?** Social-cognitive theorists explain the development of gender-typed behavior in terms of processes such as observa-tional learning, identification, and socialization. Gender-schema theory proposes that children develop a gender schema as a means of organizing their perceptions of the world. Once children acquire a gender schema, they begin to judge themselves according to traits that are considered relevant to their gender.

5. **How do psychologists explain gay male and lesbian sexual orientations?** Psychoanalytic theory connects sexual orientation with unconscious castration anxiety and improper resolution of the Oedipus complex. Learning theorists focus on the role of reinforcement of early patterns of sexual behavior. Evidence of a genetic contribution to sexual orientation is accumulating. Research has failed to connect sexual orientation with differences in current (adult) levels of sex hormones. But prenatal sex hormones may play a role in determining sexual orientation in humans.

6. **What biological features are connected with sexual arousal and sexual behavior?** The male and female sex organs respond to sexual stimulation and make reproduction possible. Although the male sex organs are more visible than the female organs, females' organs are complex and, like men's, are oriented toward sexual pleasure.

7. **What are the phases of the sexual response cycle?** The sexual response cycle includes the excitement, plateau, orgasm, and resolution phases.

8. **What are sexual dysfunctions?** Sexual dysfunctions are persistent or recurrent problems in becoming sexually aroused or reaching orgasm. They include hypoactive sexual desire disorder, female sexual arousal disorder, male erectile disorder, orgasmic disorder, premature ejaculation, dyspareunia, and vaginismus.

9. **What are the causes of sexual dysfunctions?** Sexual dysfunctions may be caused by physical problems, negative attitudes toward sex, lack of sexual knowledge and skills, problems in the relationship, and performance anxiety.

10. **Why do men rape women?** Social attitudes such as gender-role stereotyping, seeing sex as adversarial, and acceptance of violence in interpersonal relationships help create a climate that encourages rape.

11. **What is sexual harassment?** Sexual harassment consists of gestures, verbal comments, or physical contact of a sexual nature that is unwelcome to the recipient.

KEY TERMS

activating effect (p. GS-17)

adrenaline (p. GS-17)

bisexual (p. GS-14)

cervix (p. GS-19)

clitoris (p. GS-18)

cortisol (p. GS-17)

dyspareunia (p. GS-22)

ejaculation (p. GS-21)

excitement phase (p. GS-21)

female sexual arousal disorder (p. GS-22)

gay male (p. GS-14)

gender (p. GS-3)

gender identity (p. GS-11)

gender role (p. GS-3)

gender-schema theory (p. GS-13)

gender typing (p. GS-11)

glans (p. GS-18)

heterosexual (p. GS-14)

homosexual (p. GS-14)

hypoactive sexual desire disorder (p. GS-22)

identification (p. GS-12)

lesbian (p. GS-14)

machismo (p. GS-5)

major lips (p. GS-18)

male erectile disorder (p. GS-22)

marianismo (p. GS-5)

minor lips (p. GS-18)

mons veneris (p. GS-18)

myotonia (p. GS-21)

Oedipus complex (p. GS-14)

organizing effect (p. GS-17)

orgasm (p. GS-21)

orgasmic disorder (p. GS-22)

performance anxiety (p. GS-23)

plateau phase (p. GS-21)

premature ejaculation (p. GS-22)

pudendum (p. GS-17)

refractory period (p. GS-22)

resolution phase (p. GS-21)

scrotum (p. GS-19)

semen (p. GS-19)

seminal fluid (p. GS-21)

sex therapy (p. GS-23)

sexual dysfunction (p. GS-22)

sexual harassment (p. GS-26)

sexual orientation (p. GS-14)

sexual response cycle (p. GS-20)

socialization (p. GS-12)

stereotype (p. GS-3)

testes (p. GS-19)

testosterone (p. GS-17)

urethra (p. GS-18)

vaginismus (p. GS-22)

vasocongestion (p. GS-21)

vulva (p. GS-17)

REFERENCES

American Association of University Women. (1992). *How schools shortchange women: The A.A.U.W. report.* Washington, DC: AAUW Educational Foundation.

American Psychological Association (1998a, March 16). Sexual harassment: Myths and realities. APA Public Information Home Page; www.apa.org.

American Psychological Association (1998b, October 4). Answers to your questions about sexual orientation and homosexuality. APA Public Information Home Page; www.apa.org.

Archer, J. (1996). Sex differences in social behavior. *American Psychologist, 51,* 909–917.

Azar, B. (1997). Environment can mitigate differences in spatial ability. *APA Monitor, 28*(6), 28.

Bailey, J. M., & Pillard, R. C. (1991). A genetic study of male sexual orientation. *Archives of General Psychiatry, 48,* 1089–1096.

Barbaree, H. E., & Marshall, W. L. (1991). The role of male sexual arousal in rape. *Journal of Consulting and Clinical Psychology, 59,* 621–631.

Bell, A. P., Weinberg, M. S., & Hammersmith, S. K. (1981). *Sexual preference: Its development in men and women.* Bloomington: University of Indiana Press.

Bem, S. L. (1993). *The lenses of gender.* New Haven: Yale University Press.

Bianchi, S. M., & Spain, D. (1997). *Women, work and family in America.* Population Reference Bureau.

Bjorklund, D. F., & Kipp, K. (1996). Parental investment theory and gender differences in the evolution of inhibition mechanisms. *Psychological Bulletin, 120,* 163–188.

Boston Women's Health Book Collective. (1992). *The new our bodies, ourselves.* New York: Simon & Schuster.

Bowes, J. M., & Goodnow, J. J. (1996). Work for home, school, or labor force. *Psychological Bulletin, 119,* 300–321.

Buss, D. M. (1999, June 1). Evolutionary science ponders: Where is fancy bred? *New York Times Online.*

Byrnes, J., & Takahira, S. (1993). Explaining gender differences on SAT-math items. *Developmental Psychology, 29,* 805–810.

Celis, W. (1991, January 2). Students trying to draw line between sex and an assault. *New York Times,* pp. 1, B8.

Chan, C. (1992). Cultural considerations in counseling Asian American lesbians and gay men. In S. Dworkin & F. Gutierrez (Eds.), *Counseling gay men and lesbians.* Alexandria, VA: American Association for Counseling and Development.

Coleman, M., & Ganong, L. H. (1985). Love and sex role stereotypes. *Journal of Personality and Social Psychology, 49,* 170–176.

Collaer, M. L., & Hines, M. (1995). Human behavioral sex differences: A role for gonadal hormones during early development? *Psychological Bulletin, 118,* 55–107.

Crews, D. (1994). Animal sexuality. *Scientific American, 270*(1), 108–114.

Dindia, K., & Allen, M. (1992). Sex differences in self-disclosure. *Psychological Bulletin, 112,* 106–124.

Doctors tie male mentality to shorter life span. (1995, June 14). *New York Times,* p. C14.

Eagly, A. H. (1995). The science and politics of comparing women and men. *American Psychologist, 50,* 145–158.

Eagly, A. H., & Steffen, V. J. (1984). Gender stereotypes stem from the distribution of men and women into social roles. *Journal of Personality and Social Psychology, 46,* 735–754.

Ellis, L. (1990). Prenatal stress may effect sex-typical behaviors of a child. *Brown University Child Behavior and Development Letter, 6*(1), 1–3.

Ellis, L., & Ames, M. A. (1987). Neurohormonal functioning and sexual orientation. *Psychological Bulletin, 101,* 233–258.

Feingold, A. (1994). Gender differences in personality: A meta-analysis. *Psychological Bulletin, 116,* 429–456.

Friedman, R. C., & Downey, J. I. (1994). Homosexuality. *New England Journal of Medicine, 331,* 923–930.

Frodi, A. M., Macauley, J., & Thome, P. R. (1977). Are women always less aggressive than men? A review of the experimental literature. *Psychological Bulletin, 84,* 634–660.

Gibbs, N. (1991, June 3). When is it rape? *Time,* pp. 48–54.

Gomez, J., & Smith, B. (1990). Taking the home out of homophobia: Black lesbian health. In E. C. White (Ed.), *The Black women's health book.* Seattle: Seal Press.

Greene, B. (1994). Ethnic-minority lesbians and gay men. *Journal of Consulting and Clinical Psychology, 62,* 243–251.

Hall, C. S. (1984). "A ubiquitous sex difference in dreams" revisited. *Journal of Personality and Social Psychology, 46,* 1109–1117.

Hall, G. C. I., & Barongan, C. (1997). Prevention of sexual aggression. *American Psychologist, 52,* 5–14.

Halpern, D. F. (1997). Sex differences in intelligence: Implications for education. *American Psychologist, 52,* 1091–1102.

Hamer, D. H., et al. (1993, July 16). A linkage between DNA markers on the X chromosome and male sexual orientation. *Science, 261,* 321–327.

Honan, W. H. (1996, April 11). Male professors keep 30% lead in pay over women, study says. *New York Times,* p. B9.

Hyde, J. S., Fennema, E., & Lamon, S. J. (1990). Gender differences in mathematics performance. *Psychological Bulletin, 107,* 139–155.

Hyde, J. S., & Linn, M. C. (1988). Gender differences in verbal ability. *Psychological Bulletin, 104,* 53–69.

Hyde, J. S., & Plant, E. A. (1995). Magnitude of psychological gender differences. *American Psychologist, 50,* 159–161.

Isay, R. A. (1990). Psychoanalytic theory and the therapy of gay men. In D. P. McWhirter, S. A. Sanders, & J. M. Reinisch (Eds.), *Homosexuality/heterosexuality* (pp. 283–303). New York: Oxford University Press.

Koss, M. P. (1993). Rape. *American Psychologist, 48,* 1062–1069.

Koss, M. P., Gidycz, C. A., & Wisniewski, N. (1987). The scope of rape. *Journal of Consulting and Clinical Psychology, 55,* 162–170.

Laumann, E. O., Gagnon, J. H., Michael, R. T., & Michaels, S. (1994). *The social organization of sexuality.* Chicago: University of Chicago Press.

Leitenberg, H., & Henning, K. (1995). Sexual fantasy. *Psychological Bulletin, 117,* 469–496.

Lewin, T. (1995). Women are becoming equal providers. *New York Times,* p. A27.

Maccoby, E. E. (1990). Gender and relationships. *American Psychologist, 45,* 513–520.

Maccoby, E. E., & Jacklin, C. N. (1974). *The psychology of sex differences.* Stanford, CA: Stanford University Press.

Marecek, J. (1995). Gender, politics, and psychology's ways of knowing. *American Psychologist, 50,* 162–163.

Masters, W. H., & Johnson, V. E. (1966). *Human sexual response.* Boston: Little, Brown.

Masters, W. H., & Johnson, V. E. (1970). *Human sexual inadequacy.* Boston: Little, Brown.

Money, J. (1987). Sin, sickness, or status? Homosexual gender identity and psychoneuroendocrinology. *American Psychologist, 42,* 384–399.

Morales, E. (1992). Latino gays and Latina lesbians. In S. Dworkin & F. Gutierrez (Eds.), *Counseling gay men and lesbians.* Alexandria, VA: American Association for Counseling and Development.

Neisser, U., Boodoo, G., Bouchard, T. J., Jr., Boykin, A. W., Brody, N., Ceci, S. J., Halpern, D. F., Loehlin, J. C., Perloff, R., Sternberg, R. J., & Urbina, S. (1996). Intelligence: Knowns and unknowns. *American Psychologist, 51,* 77–101.

Perry, D. G., & Bussey, K. (1979). The social learning theory of sex differences. *Journal of Personality and Social Psychology, 37,* 1699–1712.

Pillard, R. C. (1990). The Kinsey Scale: Is it familial? In D. P. McWhirter, S. A. Sanders, & J. M. Reinisch (Eds.), *Homosexuality/heterosexuality: Concepts of sexual orientation* (pp. 88–100). New York: Oxford University Press.

Pillard, R. C., & Weinrich, J. D. (1986). Evidence of familial nature of male homosexuality. *Archives of Sexual Behavior, 43,* 808–812.

Poussaint, A. (1990, September). An honest look at Black gays and lesbians. *Ebony,* pp. 124, 126, 130–131.

Powell, E. (1996). *Sex on your terms.* Boston: Allyn & Bacon.

Rapoport, K., & Burkhart, B. R. (1984). Personality and attitudinal characteristics of sexually coercive college males. *Journal of Abnormal Psychology, 93,* 216–221.

Rathus, S. A., Nevid, J. S., & Fichner-Rathus, L. (2000). *Human sexuality in a world of diversity* (4th ed.). Boston: Allyn & Bacon.

Reid, T. R. (1990, December 24). Snug in their beds for Christmas Eve: In Japan, December 24th has become the hottest night of the year. *Washington Post.*

Richardson, D. C., Bernstein, S., & Taylor, S. P. (1979). The effect of situational contingencies on female retaliative behavior. *Journal of Personality and Social Psychology, 37,* 2044–2048.

Rüstemli, A. (1986). Male and female personal space needs and escape reactions under intrusion: A Turkish sample. *International Journal of Psychology.*

Seppa, N. (1997). Sexual harassment in the military lingers on. *APA Monitor, 28*(5), 40–41.

Shaywitz, B. A., et al. (1995). Sex differences in the functional organization of the brain for language. *Nature, 373,* 607–609.

Sprecher, S., Sullivan, Q., & Hatfield, E. (1994). Mate selection preferences. *Journal of Personality and Social Psychology, 66*(6), 1074–1080.

Springer, S. P., & Deutsch, G. (1993). *Left brain, right brain* (4th ed.). New York: Freeman.

Study finds smaller pay gap for male and female doctors. (1996, April 11). *New York Times,* p. B9.

Trujillo, C. (Ed.). (1991). *Chicana lesbians: The girls our mothers warned us about.* Berkeley, CA: Third Woman Press.

Valian, V. (1998). *Why so slow? The advancement of women.* Cambridge, MA: MIT Press.

Vandenbergh, J. G. (1993). Cited in Angier, N. (1993, August 24).

Female gerbil born with males is found to be begetter of sons. *New York Times,* p. C4.

Voyer, D., Voyer, S., & Bryden, M. P. (1995). Magnitude of sex differences in spatial abilities. *Psychological Bulletin, 117,* 250–270.

Williams, J. E., & Best, D. L. (1994). Cross-cultural views of women and men. In W. J. Lonner & R. Malpass (Eds.), *Psychology and culture.* Boston: Allyn & Bacon.

STRESS AND HEALTH

TRUTH OR FICTION?

_____ Going on vacation is stressful.

_____ Because variety is the spice of life, the more change the better.

_____ People with a strong need for social approval are setting themselves up for feelings of anxiety and depression.

_____ A sense of humor can moderate the impact of stress.

_____ At any given moment, countless microscopic warriors within our bodies are carrying out search-and-destroy missions against foreign agents.

_____ Poor people in the United States eat less than more affluent people do.

S IRENS. AMBULANCES. STRETCHERS. THE EMERGENCY room at Dallas's public Parkland Memorial Hospital is a busy place. Sirens wail endlessly as ambulances pull up to the doors and discharge people who need prompt attention. Because of the volume of patients, beds line the halls, and people who do not require immediate care cram the waiting room. Many hours may pass before they are seen by a doctor. It is not unusual for people who are not considered in danger to wait 10 to 12 hours.

All this may sound rather foreboding, but good things are happening at Parkland as well. One of them is the attention physicians are devoting to patients' psychological needs as well as to their physical needs. For example, influenced both by his own clinical experience and by Native American wisdom about the healing process, Dr. Ron Anderson teaches his medical students that caring about patients is not an outdated ideal. Rather, it is a powerful weapon against disease.

TV journalist Bill Moyers describes Anderson on his medical rounds with students:

> I listen as he stops at the bedside of an elderly woman suffering from chronic asthma. He asks the usual questions: "How did you sleep last night?" "Is the breathing getting any easier?" His next questions surprise the medical students: "Is your son still looking for work?" "Is he still drinking?" "Tell us what happened right before the asthma attack." He explains to his puzzled students. "We know that anxiety aggravates many illnesses, especially chronic conditions like asthma. So we have to find out what may be causing her episodes of stress and help her find some way of coping with it. Otherwise she will land in here again, and next time we might not be able to save her. We cannot just prescribe medication and walk away. That is medical neglect. We have to take the time to get to know her, how she lives, her values, what her social supports are. If we don't know that her son is her sole support and that he's out of work, we will be much less effective in dealing with her asthma." (Moyers, 1993, p. 2)

HEALTH PSYCHOLOGY

Note some key concepts from the slice of hospital life reported by Moyers: "Anxiety aggravates many illnesses." "We have to find out what may be causing . . . stress and . . . find some way of coping with it." "We cannot just prescribe medication and walk away." "We have to take the time to get to know [patients], how [they] live, [their] values, what [their] social supports are."

Anderson and Moyers have given us a fine introduction to the field of **health psychology,** which studies the relationships between psychological factors and the prevention and treatment of physical illness (Taylor, 1990). The case of the woman with asthma is a useful springboard for discussion because health psychologists study the ways in which

- psychological factors such as stress, behavior patterns, and attitudes can lead to or aggravate illness
- people can cope with stress
- stress and **pathogens** (disease-causing organisms such as bacteria and viruses) interact to influence the immune system
- people decide whether or not to seek health care
- psychological forms of intervention such as health education (e.g., concerning nutrition, smoking, and exercise) and behavior modification can contribute to physical health.

In this chapter we consider a number of issues in health psychology: sources of stress, factors that moderate the impact of stress, and the body's response to stress.

STRESS: PRESSES, PUSHES, AND PULLS

Americans will put up with anything provided it doesn't block traffic.

DAN RATHER

In physics, stress is defined as a pressure or force exerted on a body. Tons of rock pressing on the earth, one car smashing into another, a rubber band stretching—all are types of physical stress. Psychological forces, or stresses, also press, push, or pull. We may feel "crushed" by the weight of a big decision, "smashed" by adversity, or "stretched" to the point of snapping.

In psychology, **stress** is the demand made on an organism to adapt, cope, or adjust. Some stress is healthful and necessary to keep us alert and occupied. Stress researcher Hans Selye (1980) referred to such healthful stress as **eustress** (pronounced YOU-STRESS). But intense or prolonged stress can overtax our adjustive capacity, affect our moods, impair our ability to experience pleasure, and harm the body (Berenbaum & Connelly, 1993; Cohen et al., 1993).

A DAILY HASSLE.
Daily hassles are notable daily conditions and experiences that are threatening or harmful to a person's well-being. The hassles shown in this photograph center on commuting. What are some of the daily hassles in your life?

Sources of Stress: Don't Hassle Me?

DAILY HASSLES Which straw will break the camel's back? The last straw, according to the saying. Similarly, stresses can pile up until we can no longer cope with them. Some of these stresses are **daily hassles**—regularly occurring conditions and experiences that can threaten or harm our well-being. Others are life changes. Lazarus and his colleagues (1985) analyzed a scale that measures daily hassles and their opposites—termed **uplifts**—and found that hassles could be grouped as follows:

1. *Household hassles:* preparing meals, shopping, and home maintenance
2. *Health hassles:* physical illness, concern about medical treatment, and side effects of medication

HEALTH PSYCHOLOGY The field of psychology that studies the relationships between psychological factors (e.g., attitudes, beliefs, situational influences, and behavior patterns) and the prevention and treatment of physical illness.

PATHOGEN A microscopic organism (e.g., bacterium or virus) that can cause disease.

STRESS The demand made on an organism to adapt.

EUSTRESS Stress that is healthful.

DAILY HASSLES Notable daily conditions and experiences that are threatening or harmful to a person's well-being.

UPLIFTS Notable pleasant daily conditions and experiences.

3. *Time-pressure hassles:* having too many things to do, too many responsibilities, and not enough time

4. *Inner concern hassles:* being lonely and fearful of confrontation

5. *Environmental hassles:* crime, neighborhood deterioration, and traffic noise

6. *Financial responsibility hassles:* concern about owing money such as mortgage payments and loan installments

7. *Work hassles:* job dissatisfaction, not liking one's duties at work, and problems with co-workers

8. *Future security hassles:* concerns about job security, taxes, property investments, stock market swings, and retirement.

These hassles are linked to psychological variables such as nervousness, worrying, inability to get started, feelings of sadness, and feelings of loneliness. For example, 83% of people in the United States will be victimized by a violent crime at some time, and victimization is connected with problems such as anxiety, physical complaints, hostility, and depression (Norris & Kaniasty, 1994).

LIFE CHANGES.
Life changes differ from daily hassles in that they tend to be more episodic. Also, life changes can be positive as well as negative. What is the relationship between life changes and illness? Is the relationship causal?

LIFE CHANGES You might think that marrying Mr. or Ms. Right, finding a good job, and moving to a better neighborhood all in the same year would propel you into a state of bliss. It might. But too much of a good thing may also make you ill. All of these events, coming one after another, may also lead to headaches, high blood pressure, and other symptoms. As pleasant as they may be, they entail life changes. Life changes require adjustment and thus are a source of stress.

Life changes differ from daily hassles in two key ways:

1. Many life changes are positive and desirable. Hassles, by definition, are negative.

2. Hassles occur regularly. Life changes occur at irregular intervals.

Peggy Blake and her colleagues (1984) constructed a scale to measure the impact of life changes among college students. Surveys in students' weighted life changes revealed that death of a spouse or parent were considered the most stressful life changes (94 and 88 life-change units, respectively; see Table H.1). Academic failure (77 units) and graduation from college (68 units) were also considered highly stressful, even though graduation from college is a positive event—considering the alternative. Positive life changes such as an outstanding personal achievement (49 units) and going on vacation (30 units) also made the list.

TRUTH OR FICTION REVISITED
It is true that going on vacation is stressful. A vacation is a life change, and change requires adjustment.

TRUTH OR FICTION REVISITED
Although variety may be the spice of life, psychologists have not found that more change is better. Changes, even changes for the better, are sources of stress that require adjustment.

HASSLES, LIFE CHANGES, AND HEALTH PROBLEMS Hassles and life changes—especially negative life changes—affect us psychologically. They can cause us to worry and can affect our moods. But stressors such as hassles and life changes also predict health problems such as heart disease and cancer, even athletic injuries (Smith et al., 1990). Holmes and Rahe (1967) found that people who "earned" a high number of life-change units within a year, according to their own scale, were at greater risk for health problems. Eight of 10 developed health problems, compared with only 1 of 3 people whose totals of life-change units for the year were at a low level.

Moreover, people who remain married to the same person live longer than people who experience marital breakups and remarry (Tucker et al., 1996). Apparently the life changes of divorce and remarriage—or the instability associated with them—can be harmful to health.

TABLE H.1

LIFE-CHANGE UNITS CONNECTED WITH VARIOUS EVENTS

	EVENT	LIFE-CHANGE UNITS
1.	Death of a spouse, lover, or child	94
2.	Death of a parent or sibling	88
3.	Beginning formal higher education	84
4.	Jail sentence	82
5.	Divorce or marital separation	82
6.	Unwanted pregnancy of self, spouse, or lover	80
7.	Abortion of unwanted pregnancy of self, spouse, or lover	80
8.	Academic failure	77
9.	Marrying or living with lover against parents' wishes	75
10.	Change in love relationship or important friendship	74
11.	Change in marital status of parents	73
12.	Hospitalization of a parent or sibling	70
13.	Graduation from college	68
14.	Major personal injury or illness	68
15.	Wanted pregnancy of self, spouse, or lover	67
16.	Preparing for an important exam or writing a major paper	65
17.	Major financial difficulties	65
18.	Change in academic status	64
19.	Change in relationship with members of your immediate family	62
20.	Hospitalization of yourself or a close relative	61
21.	Change in course of study, major field, vocational goals, or work status	60
22.	Change in own financial status	59
23.	Beginning or ceasing service in the armed forces	57
24.	Change in living arrangements, conditions, or environment	55
25.	Change in frequency or nature of sexual experiences	55
26.	Change in degree of interest in college or attitudes toward education	55
27.	Academic success	54
28.	Change to a new college or university	54
29.	Change in number or type of arguments with roommate	52
30.	Change in responsibility at work	50
31.	Change in amount or nature of social activities	50
32.	Change in routine at college or work	49
33.	Change in amount of leisure time	49
34.	Outstanding personal achievement	49
35.	Improvement of own health	47
36.	Change in study habits	46
37.	Change in religious affiliation	44
38.	Change in address or residence	43
39.	Change in weight or eating habits	39
40.	Vacation or travel	30

Source: Adapted from *Self-Assessment and Behavior Change Manual* (pp. 43–47), by Peggy Blake, Robert Fry, & Michael Pesjack, 1984, New York: Random House. Reprinted by permission of Random House, Inc.

EVALUATION Although the links among daily hassles, life changes, and illness seem to have been supported by a good deal of research, a careful evaluation reveals a number of limitations:

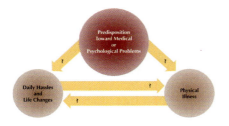

Figure H.1
WHAT ARE THE RELATIONSHIPS AMONG DAILY HASSLES, LIFE CHANGES, AND PHYSICAL ILLNESS?

There are positive correlations between daily hassles and life events, on the one hand, and illness on the other. It may seem logical that hassles and life changes cause illness, but research into the issue is correlational and not experimental. The results are therefore subject to rival interpretations. One is that people who are predisposed toward medical or psychological problems encounter or generate more hassles and amass more life-change units.

1. *Correlational evidence.* The links that have been uncovered among hassles, life changes, and illness are correlational rather than experimental. It may seem logical that the hassles and life changes caused the disorders, but these variables were not manipulated experimentally. Other explanations of the data are possible (Figure H.1). One possible explanation is that people who are predisposed toward medical or psychological problems encounter more hassles and amass more life-change units. For example, undiagnosed medical disorders may contribute to sexual problems, arguments with spouses or in-laws, changes in living conditions and personal habits, and changes in sleeping habits. People may also make certain changes in their lives that lead to physical and psychological disorders (Simons et al., 1993).

2. *Positive versus negative life changes.* Other aspects of the research on the relationship between life changes and illness have also been challenged. For instance, positive life changes may be less disturbing than hassles and negative life changes, even though the number of life-change units assigned to them is high (Lefcourt et al., 1981).

3. *Personality differences.* People with different kinds of personalities respond to life stresses in different ways (Vaillant, 1994). For example, people who are easygoing or psychologically hardy are less likely to become ill under the impact of stress.

4. *Cognitive appraisal.* The stress of an event reflects the meaning of the event to the individual (Whitehead, 1994). Pregnancy, for example, can be a positive or negative life change, depending on whether one wants and is prepared to have a child. We appraise the hassles, traumatic experiences, and life changes that we encounter (Creamer et al., 1992; Kiecolt-Glaser, 1993). In responding to them, we take into account their perceived danger, our values and goals, our beliefs in our coping ability, our social support, and so on. The same event is less taxing to someone with greater coping ability and support than to someone who lacks these advantages.

Despite these research problems, hassles and life changes require adjustment. It seems wise to be aware of hassles and life changes and how they may affect us.

CONFLICT Have you ever felt "damned if you do and damned if you don't"? Regretted that you couldn't do two things, or be in two places, at the same time? In psychology this is termed **conflict**. It is the feeling of being pulled in two or more directions by opposing motives. Conflict is frustrating and stressful. Psychologists often classify conflicts into four types: approach-approach, avoidance-avoidance, approach-avoidance, and multiple approach-avoidance.

Approach-approach conflict (Figure H.2, part A) is the least stressful type. Here, each of two goals is desirable, and both are within reach. You may not be able to decide between pizza or tacos, Tom or Dick, or a trip to Nassau or Hawaii. Such conflicts are usually resolved by making a decision. People who experience this type of conflict may vacillate until they make a decision.

Avoidance-avoidance conflict (Figure H.2, part B) is more stressful because you are motivated to avoid each of two negative goals. However, avoiding one of them requires approaching the other. You may be fearful of visiting the dentist but also afraid that your teeth will decay if you do not make an appointment and go. You may not want to contribute to the Association for the Advancement of Lost Causes, but you fear that your friends will consider you cheap or uncommitted if you do not. Each goal

CONFLICT Being torn in different directions by opposing motives. Feelings produced by being in conflict.

APPROACH-APPROACH CONFLICT A type of conflict in which the goals that produce opposing motives are positive and within reach.

AVOIDANCE-AVOIDANCE CONFLICT A type of conflict in which the goals are negative, but avoidance of one requires approaching the other.

in an avoidance-avoidance conflict is negative. When an avoidance-avoidance conflict is highly stressful and no resolution is in sight, some people withdraw from the conflict by focusing on other matters or doing nothing. Highly conflicted people have been known to refuse to get up in the morning and start the day.

When the same goal produces both approach and avoidance motives, we have an **approach-avoidance conflict** (Figure H.2, part C). People and things have their pluses and minuses, their good points and their bad points. Cream cheese pie may be delicious, but oh, the calories! Goals that produce mixed motives may seem more attractive from a distance but undesirable from up close. Many couples repeatedly break up and then reunite. When they are apart and lonely, they may recall each other fondly and swear that they could make the relationship work if they got together again. But after they spend time together again, they may find themselves thinking, "How could I ever have believed that this so-and-so would change?"

The most complex form of conflict is the **multiple approach-avoidance conflict,** in which each of several alternative courses of action has both promising and distressing aspects. An example with two goals is shown in Figure H.2, part D. This sort of conflict might arise on the eve of an examination, when you are faced with the choice of studying or, say, going to a film. Each alternative has both positive and negative aspects: "Studying's a bore, but I won't have to worry about flunking. I'd love to see the movie, but I'd just be worrying about how I'll do tomorrow."

All forms of conflict entail motives that aim in opposite directions. When one motive is much stronger than the other—such as when you feel "starved" and are only slightly concerned about your weight—it will probably not be too stressful to act in accordance with the powerful motive—in this case, to eat. When each conflicting motive is powerful, however, you may experience high levels of stress and confusion about the proper course of action. At such times you are faced with the need to make a decision. Yet decision making can also be stressful, especially when there is no clear correct choice.

APPROACH-AVOIDANCE CONFLICT A type of conflict in which the same goal produces approach and avoidance motives.

MULTIPLE APPROACH-AVOIDANCE CONFLICT A type of conflict in which each of a number of goals produces approach and avoidance motives.

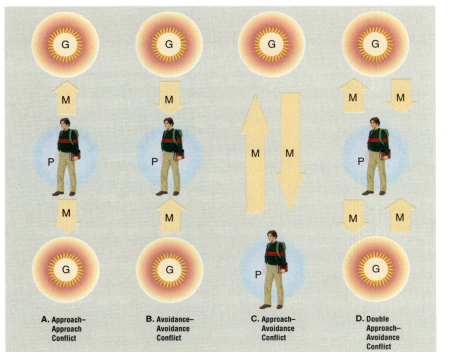

A. Approach–Approach Conflict **B. Avoidance–Avoidance Conflict** **C. Approach–Avoidance Conflict** **D. Double Approach–Avoidance Conflict**

Figure H.2
MODELS FOR CONFLICT.
Part A shows an approach-approach conflict, in which a person (P) has motives (M) to reach two goals (G) that are desirable, but approach of one requires exclusion of the other. Part B shows an avoidance-avoidance conflict in which both goals are negative, but avoiding one requires approaching the other. Part C shows an approach-avoidance conflict, in which the same goal has desirable and undesirable properties. Part D shows a double approach-avoidance conflict, which is the simplest kind of *multiple* approach-avoidance conflict. In a multiple approach-avoidance conflict, two or more goals have mixed properties.

IRRATIONAL BELIEFS: TEN DOORWAYS TO DISTRESS Psychologist Albert Ellis (1977, 1993) notes that our beliefs about events, as well as the events themselves, can be stressors. Consider a case in which a person is fired from a job and is anxious and depressed about it. It may seem logical that losing the job is responsible for the misery, but Ellis points out how the individual's beliefs about the loss compound his or her misery.

Let us examine this situation according to Ellis's A→B→C approach: Losing the job is an *activating event* (A). The eventual outcome, or *consequence* (C), is misery. Between the activating event (A) and the consequence (C), however, lie *beliefs* (B), such as these: "This job was the most important thing in my life," "What a no-good failure I am," "My family will starve," "I'll never find a job as good," "There's nothing I can do about it." Beliefs such as these compound misery, foster helplessness, and divert us from planning and deciding what to do next. The belief that "There's nothing I can do about it" fosters helplessness. The belief that "I am a no-good failure" internalizes the blame and may be an exaggeration. The belief that "My family will starve" may also be an exaggeration.

We can diagram the situation like this:

Activating events → Beliefs → Consequences or A → B → C

Anxieties about the future and depression over a loss are normal and to be expected. However, the beliefs of the person who lost the job tend to **catastrophize** the extent of the loss and contribute to anxiety and depression. By heightening the individual's emotional reaction to the loss and fostering feelings of helplessness, these beliefs also impair coping ability. They lower the person's self-efficacy expectations.

Ellis proposes that many of us carry with us the irrational beliefs shown in Table H.2. They are our personal doorways to distress. In fact, they can give rise to problems in themselves. When problems assault us from other sources, these beliefs can magnify their effect. How many of these beliefs do you harbor? Are you sure?

Ellis finds it understandable that we would want the approval of others but irrational to believe we cannot survive without it. It would be nice to be competent in everything we do, but it is unreasonable to *expect* it. Sure, it would be great to be able to serve and volley like a tennis pro, but

CATASTROPHIZE To interpret negative events as being disastrous; to "blow out of proportion."

TABLE H.2	
IRRATIONAL BELIEFS	
Irrational Belief 1:	You must have sincere love and approval almost all the time from the people who are important to you.
Irrational Belief 2:	You must prove yourself to be thoroughly competent, adequate, and achieving at something important.
Irrational Belief 3:	Things must go the way you want them to go. Life is awful when you don't get your first choice in everything.
Irrational Belief 4:	Other people must treat everyone fairly and justly. When people act unfairly or unethically, they are rotten.
Irrational Belief 5:	When there is danger or fear in your world, you must be preoccupied with and upset by it.
Irrational Belief 6:	People and things should turn out better than they do. It's awful and horrible when you don't find quick solutions to life's hassles.
Irrational Belief 7:	Your emotional misery stems from external pressures that you have little or no ability to control. Unless these external pressures change, you must remain miserable.
Irrational Belief 8:	It is easier to evade life's responsibilities and problems than to face them and undertake more rewarding forms of self-discipline.
Irrational Belief 9:	Your past influenced you immensely and must therefore continue to determine your feelings and behavior today.
Irrational Belief 10:	You can achieve happiness by inertia and inaction, or by just enjoying yourself from day to day.

most of us do not have the time or natural ability to perfect the game. Demanding perfection prevents us from going out on the court on weekends and batting the ball back and forth just for fun. Belief number 5 is a prescription for perpetual emotional upheaval. Beliefs numbers 7 and 9 lead to feelings of helplessness and demoralization. Sure, Ellis might say, childhood experiences can explain the origins of irrational beliefs, but it is our own cognitive appraisal—here and now—that makes us miserable.

Research findings support the connections between irrational beliefs (e.g., excessive dependence on social approval and perfectionism) and feelings of anxiety and depression (Blatt, 1995). Perfectionists are also more likely than other people to commit suicide when they are depressed (Pilkonis, 1996).

TYPE A BEHAVIOR Some people create stress for themselves through the **Type A behavior** pattern. Type A people are highly driven, competitive, impatient, and aggressive (Thoresen & Powell, 1992). They feel rushed and under pressure all the time and keep one eye constantly on the clock. They are not only prompt for appointments but often early. They eat, walk, and talk rapidly and become restless when others work slowly. They attempt to dominate group discussions. Type A people find it difficult to give up control or share power. They are often reluctant to delegate authority in the workplace, and because of this they increase their own workloads. Type A people criticize themselves mercilessly when they fail at a task (Moser & Dyck, 1989). They even seek out negative information about themselves in order to improve themselves (Cooney & Zeichner, 1985).

Type A people find it difficult just to go out on the tennis court and bat the ball back and forth. They watch their form, perfect their strokes, and demand continual self-improvement. They hold to the irrational belief that they must be perfectly competent and achieving in everything they undertake.

Type B people, in contrast, relax more readily and focus more on the quality of life. They are less ambitious and less impatient, and they pace themselves. Type A people earn higher grades and more money than Type B's of equal intelligence. Type A people also seek greater challenges than Type B's (Ortega & Pipal, 1984).

Psychological Moderators of Stress

There is no one-to-one relationship between the amount of stress we undergo and the physical illnesses or psychological distress we experience. Physical factors account for some of the variability in our responses: Some people inherit predispositions toward specific disorders. Psychological factors also play a role, however (Holahan & Moos, 1990). They can influence, or *moderate*, the effects of stress. In this section we discuss several psychological moderators of stress: self-efficacy expectations, psychological hardiness, a sense of humor, predictability, and social support.

SELF-EFFICACY EXPECTATIONS: "THE LITTLE ENGINE THAT COULD" Our **self-efficacy expectations** affect our ability to withstand stress (Basic Behavioral Science Task Force, 1996). For example, when we are faced with fear-inducing objects, high self-efficacy expectations are accompanied by relatively *lower* levels of adrenaline and noradrenaline in the bloodstream (Bandura et al., 1985). Adrenaline is secreted when we are under stress. It arouses the body in several ways, such as accelerating the heart rate and releasing glucose from the liver. As a result, we may

TYPE A BEHAVIOR.
The Type A behavior pattern is characterized by a sense of time urgency, competitiveness, and hostility.

TYPE A BEHAVIOR Behavior characterized by a sense of time urgency, competitiveness, and hostility.

SELF-EFFICACY EXPECTATIONS Our beliefs that we can bring about desired changes through our own efforts.

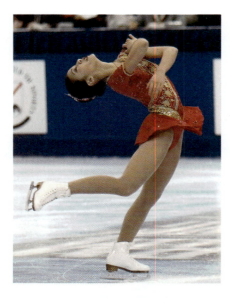

SELF-EFFICACY EXPECTATIONS AND PERFORMANCE.
Outstanding athletes like figure skater Michelle Kwan tend to have high self-efficacy expectations. That is, they believe in themselves. These expectations moderate the amount of stress that affects us.

have "butterflies in the stomach" and feel nervous. Excessive arousal can impair our ability to manage stress by boosting our motivation beyond optimal levels and by distracting us from the tasks at hand. People with higher self-efficacy expectations thus have biological as well as psychological reasons for remaining calmer.

People who are self-confident are less prone to be disturbed by adverse events (Benight et al., 1997; Holahan & Moos, 1991). People with higher self-efficacy expectations are more likely to lose weight or quit smoking and less likely to relapse afterward (DiClemente et al., 1991). They are better able to function in spite of pain (Lackner et al., 1996).

People are more likely to comply with medical advice when they believe it will work. Women, for example, are more likely to engage in breast self-examination when they believe they will really be able to detect abnormal growths (Miller et al., 1996). People with diabetes are more likely to use insulin when they believe that it will help control their blood-sugar level (Brownlee-Duffeck et al., 1987). People are more likely to try to quit smoking when they believe they can do so successfully (Mischel & Shoda, 1995).

PSYCHOLOGICAL HARDINESS Psychological hardiness also helps people resist stress. Our understanding of this phenomenon is derived largely from the pioneering work of Suzanne Kobasa and her colleagues (1994). They studied business executives who seemed able to resist illness despite stress. In one phase of the research, executives completed a battery of psychological tests. Kobasa (1990) found that the psychologically hardy executives had three important characteristics:

1. They were high in *commitment*. They tended to involve themselves in, rather than feel alienated from, whatever they were doing or encountering.

2. They were high in *challenge*. They believed that change, rather than stability, is normal in life. They appraised change as an interesting incentive to personal growth, not as a threat to security.

3. They were high in perceived *control* over their lives. They felt and behaved as though they were influential, rather than helpless, in facing the various rewards and punishments of life. Psychologically hardy people tend to have what Julian B. Rotter (1990) terms an internal **locus of control.**

Hardy people are more resistant to stress because they *choose* to face it (Kobasa, 1990). They also interpret stress as making life more interesting. For example, they see a conference with a supervisor as an opportunity to persuade the supervisor rather than as a risk to their positions.

SENSE OF HUMOR: "A MERRY HEART DOETH GOOD LIKE A MEDICINE" The idea that humor lightens the burdens of life and helps people cope with stress has been with us for millennia (Lefcourt & Martin, 1986). Consider the biblical maxim "A merry heart doeth good like a medicine" (Proverbs 17:22).

In *Anatomy of an Illness*, writer Norman Cousins (1979) reported on his bout with a painful collagen illness that is similar to arthritis. He found that 10 minutes of belly laughter of the sort he experienced while watching Marx Brothers movies relieved much of his pain. Laughter allowed him to sleep. It may also have reduced the inflammation he suffered. This is consistent with some findings that emotional responses such as happiness and anger may have beneficial effects on the immune system (Kemeny, 1993).

PSYCHOLOGICAL HARDINESS A cluster of traits that buffer stress and are characterized by commitment, challenge, and control.

LOCUS OF CONTROL The place (locus) to which an individual attributes control over the receiving of reinforcers — either inside or outside the self.

Research has also shown that humor can moderate the effects of stress. In one study, students completed a checklist of negative life events and a measure of mood disturbance (Martin & Lefcourt, 1983). The measure of mood disturbance also yielded a stress score. The students also rated their sense of humor. Behavioral assessments were made of their ability to produce humor under stress. Overall, there was a significant relationship between negative life events and stress scores: High accumulations of negative life events predicted higher levels of stress. However, students who had a greater sense of humor and produced humor in difficult situations were less affected by negative life events than other students. In other studies, Lefcourt (1997) found that watching humorous videotapes raised the level of immunoglobin A (a measure of the functioning of the immune system) in students' saliva.

PREDICTABILITY The ability to predict a stressor apparently moderates its impact. Predictability allows us to brace ourselves for the inevitable and, in many cases, plan ways of coping with it. There is also a relationship between the desire to assume control over one's situation and the usefulness of information about impending stressors (Lazarus & Folkman, 1984). Predictability is of greater benefit to **"internals"**—that is, to people who wish to exercise control over their situations—than to **"externals."** People who want information about medical procedures and what they will experience cope better with pain when they undergo those procedures (Ludwick-Rosenthal & Neufeld, 1993).

SOCIAL SUPPORT Social support also seems to act as a buffer against the effects of stress (Burman & Margolin, 1992; Uchino et al., 1996).

Sources of social support include the following:

1. *Emotional concern*—listening to people's problems and expressing feelings of sympathy, caring, understanding, and reassurance.
2. *Instrumental aid*—the material supports and services that facilitate adaptive behavior. For example, after a disaster the government may arrange for low-interest loans so that survivors can rebuild. Relief organizations may provide foodstuffs, medicines, and temporary living quarters.
3. *Information*—guidance and advice that enhances people's ability to cope.
4. *Appraisal*—feedback from others about how one is doing. This kind of support involves helping people interpret, or "make sense of," what has happened to them.
5. *Socializing*—simple conversation, recreation, even going shopping with another person. Socializing has beneficial effects, even when it is not oriented specifically toward solving problems.

Research supports the value of social support. Introverts, people who lack social skills, and people who live by themselves seem more prone to developing infectious diseases such as colds when they are under stress (Cohen & Williamson, 1991; Gilbert, 1997). Social support helps people cope with the stresses of cancer and other health problems (Azar, 1996a; Wilcox et al., 1994). People find caring for persons with Alzheimer's disease less stressful when they have social support (Haley et al., 1996). People who have buddies who help them start exercising or quit drinking or smoking are more likely to succeed (Gruder et al., 1993; Nides et al., 1995). Social support helped children cope with the stresses of Hurricane Andrew (Vernberg et al., 1996). It appears to protect people from feelings

TRUTH OR FICTION REVISITED
It is true that a sense of humor can moderate the impact of stress. In an experiment run by Martin and Lefcourt, humor was shown to serve as a buffer against stress.

"INTERNALS" People who perceive the ability to attain reinforcements as being largely within themselves.

"EXTERNALS" People who perceive the ability to attain reinforcements as being largely outside themselves.

ARE THEIR ALARM SYSTEMS GOING OFF AS THEY TAKE OUT A LOAN?
The alarm reaction of the general adaptation syndrome can be triggered by daily hassles and life changes—such as taking out a large loan—as well as by physical threats. When the stressor persists, diseases of adaptation may develop.

GENERAL ADAPTATION SYNDROME Selye's term for a hypothesized three-stage response to stress. Abbreviated *GAS*.

ALARM REACTION The first stage of the GAS, which is triggered by the impact of a stressor and characterized by sympathetic activity.

FIGHT-OR-FLIGHT REACTION An innate adaptive response to the perception of danger.

of depression and to aid in recovery from depression (Holahan et al., 1995; Lewinsohn et al., 1994b). Stress is also less likely to lead to high blood pressure or alcohol abuse in people who have social support (Linden et al., 1993).

The General Adaptation Syndrome

How can stress make us ill? Hans Selye suggested that under stress the body is like a clock with an alarm system that does not shut off until its energy has been depleted.

Selye (1976) observed that the body's response to different stressors shows certain similarities whether the stressor is a bacterial invasion, perceived danger, or a major life change. For this reason, he labeled this response the **general adaptation syndrome** (GAS). The GAS consists of three stages: an alarm reaction, a resistance stage, and an exhaustion stage.

THE ALARM REACTION The **alarm reaction** is triggered by perception of a stressor. This reaction mobilizes or arouses the body in preparation for defense. Early in the century, physiologist Walter Cannon termed this alarm system the **fight-or-flight reaction**. The alarm reaction involves a number of body changes that are initiated by the brain and further regulated by the endocrine system and the sympathetic division of the autonomic nervous system (ANS). Let us consider the roles of these systems.

Stress has a domino effect on the endocrine system (Figure H.3). The hypothalamus secretes corticotrophin-releasing hormone (CRH). CRH causes the pituitary gland to secrete adrenocorticotrophic hormone (ACTH). ACTH then causes the adrenal cortex to secrete cortisol and other corticosteroids (steroidal hormones produced by the adrenal cortex). Corticosteroids help protect the body by combating allergic reactions (such as difficulty breathing) and producing inflammation. Inflammation increases circulation to parts of the body that are injured. It ferries in hordes of white blood cells to fend off invading pathogens.

Two other hormones that play a major role in the alarm reaction are secreted by the adrenal medulla. The sympathetic division of the ANS activates the adrenal medulla, causing it to release a mixture of adrenaline and noradrenaline. This mixture arouses the body by accelerating the

Figure H.3
STRESS AND THE ENDOCRINE SYSTEM.
Stress has a domino effect on the endocrine system, leading to the release of corticosteroids and a mixture of adrenaline and noradrenaline. Corticosteroids combat allergic reactions (such as difficulty in breathing) and cause inflammation. Adrenaline and noradrenaline arouse the body to cope by accelerating the heart rate and providing energy for the fight-or-flight reaction.

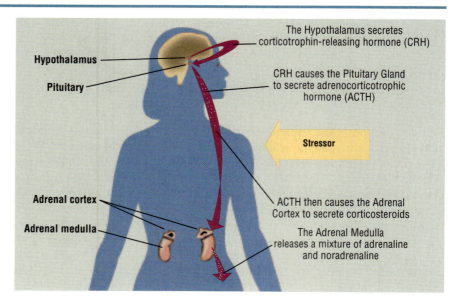

Hypothalamus
Pituitary
Adrenal cortex
Adrenal medulla

The Hypothalamus secretes corticotrophin-releasing hormone (CRH)

CRH causes the Pituitary Gland to secrete adrenocorticotrophic hormone (ACTH)

Stressor

ACTH then causes the Adrenal Cortex to secrete corticosteroids

The Adrenal Medulla releases a mixture of adrenaline and noradrenaline

heart rate and causing the liver to release glucose (sugar). This provides the energy that fuels the fight-or-flight reaction, which activates the body so that it is prepared to fight or flee from a predator.

The fight-or-flight reaction stems from a period in human prehistory when many stressors were life threatening. It was triggered by the sight of a predator at the edge of a thicket or by a sudden rustling in the undergrowth. Today it may be aroused when you are caught in stop-and-go traffic or learn that your mortgage payments are going to increase. Once the threat is removed, the body returns to a lower state of arousal. Many of the bodily changes that occur in the alarm reaction are outlined in Table H.3.

THE RESISTANCE STAGE If the alarm reaction mobilizes the body and the stressor is not removed, we enter the adaptation, or **resistance stage** of the GAS. Levels of endocrine and sympathetic activity are lower than in the alarm reaction but still higher than normal. In this stage the body attempts to restore lost energy and repair bodily damage.

THE EXHAUSTION STAGE If the stressor is still not dealt with adequately, we may enter the **exhaustion stage** of the GAS. Individual capacities for resisting stress vary, but anyone will eventually become exhausted when stress continues indefinitely. The muscles become fatigued. The body is depleted of the resources required for combating stress. With exhaustion, the parasympathetic division of the ANS may predominate. As a result, our heartbeat and respiration rate slow down and many aspects of sympathetic activity are reversed. It might sound as if we would profit from the respite, but remember that we are still under stress—possibly an external threat. Continued stress in the exhaustion stage may lead to what Selye terms "diseases of adaptation." These are connected with constriction of blood vessels and alternation of the heart rhythm, and can range from allergies and hives to ulcers and coronary heart disease—and, ultimately, death.

Let us now consider the effects of stress on the body's immune system. Our discussion will pave the way for understanding the links between various psychological factors and physical illnesses.

Effects of Stress on the Immune System

Research shows that stress suppresses the **immune system** (Delahanty et al., 1996; O'Leary 1990). Psychological factors such as feelings of control and social support moderate these effects (Gilbert, 1997).

HOW THE IMMUNE SYSTEM WORKS Given the complexity of the human body and the fast pace of scientific change, we often feel we must depend on trained professionals to cope with illness. Yet we actually do most of this coping by ourselves, by means of the immune system.

The immune system has several functions that combat disease. One of these is the production of white blood cells, which engulf and kill pathogens such as bacteria, fungi, and viruses as well as worn-out body cells and even cancerous cells. The technical term for white blood cells is **leukocytes** (Figure H.4). Leukocytes carry on microscopic warfare. They engage in search-and-destroy missions in which they "recognize" and eradicate foreign agents and unhealthy cells.

Leukocytes recognize foreign substances by their shapes. These substances are also termed **antigens** because the body reacts to them by generating specialized proteins, or **antibodies.** Antibodies attach themselves to the foreign substances, deactivating them and marking them for

---

TABLE H.3

COMPONENTS OF THE ALARM REACTION

Corticosteroids are secreted

Adrenaline is secreted

Noradrenaline is secreted

Respiration rate increases

Heart rate increases

Blood pressure increases

Muscles tense

Blood shifts from internal organs to the skeletal musculature

Digestion is inhibited

Sugar is released from the liver

Blood coagulability increases

The alarm reaction is triggered by various types of stressors. It is defined by the release of corticosteroids and adrenaline and by activity of the sympathetic branch of the autonomic nervous system. It prepares the body to fight or flee from a source of danger.

TRUTH OR FICTION REVISITED
It is true that countless microscopic warriors within our bodies are carrying out search-and-destroy missions against foreign agents at any given moment. The warriors are the white blood cells of the immune system.

RESISTANCE STAGE The second stage of the GAS, characterized by prolonged sympathetic activity in an effort to restore lost energy and repair damage. Also called the *adaptation stage.*

EXHAUSTION STAGE The third stage of the GAS, characterized by weakened resistance and possible deterioration.

IMMUNE SYSTEM The system of the body that recognizes and destroys foreign agents (antigens) that invade the body.

LEUKOCYTES White blood cells.

ANTIGEN A substance that stimulates the body to mount an immune system response to it. (The contraction for *anti*body *gen*erator.)

ANTIBODIES Substances formed by white blood cells that recognize and destroy antigens.

Figure H.4
MICROSCOPIC WARFARE.
The immune system helps us to combat disease. It produces white blood cells (leukocytes), shown here, which routinely engulf and kill pathogens like bacteria and viruses.

destruction. The immune system "remembers" how to battle antigens by maintaining their antibodies in the bloodstream, often for years.

Inflammation is another function of the immune system. When injury occurs, blood vessels in the area first contract (to stem bleeding) and then dilate. Dilation increases the flow of blood to the damaged area, causing the redness and warmth that characterize inflammation. The increased blood supply also floods the region with white blood cells to combat invading microscopic life-forms such as bacteria, which otherwise might use the local damage as a port of entry into the body.

STRESS AND THE IMMUNE SYSTEM Psychologists, biologists, and medical researchers have combined their efforts in a field of study that addresses the relationships among psychological factors, the nervous system, the endocrine system, the immune system, and disease. This field is called **psychoneuroimmunology** (Maier et al., 1994). One of its major concerns is the effect of stress on the immune system.

One of the reasons that stress eventually exhausts us is that it stimulates the production of steroids. Steroids suppress the functioning of the immune system. Suppression has negligible effects when steroids are secreted intermittently. However, persistent secretion of steroids decreases inflammation and interferes with the formation of antibodies. As a consequence, we become more vulnerable to various illnesses, including the common cold (Cohen et al., 1993).

In one study, dental students showed lower immune system functioning, as measured by lower levels of antibodies in their saliva, during stressful periods of the school year than immediately following vacations (Jemmott et al., 1983). In contrast, social support buffers the effects of stress and enhances the functioning of the immune system (Gilbert, 1997; Uchino et al., 1996). In the Jemmott study, students who had many friends showed less suppression of immune system functioning than students with few friends.

Other studies have shown that the stress of exams depresses the immune system's response to the Epstein-Barr virus, which causes fatigue and other problems (Glaser et al., 1991, 1993). Here too, students who were lonely showed greater suppression of the immune system than students who had more social support. A study of older people found that a combination of relaxation training, which decreases sympathetic nervous system activity, and training in coping skills *improves* the functioning of the immune system (Glaser et al., 1991). Moreover, psychological methods that reduce stress and anxiety in cancer patients may prolong their survival by boosting the functioning of their immune system (Azar, 1996b).

Coping With Stress

What do these strategies have in common: (1) telling yourself you can live with another person's disappointment, (2) taking a deep breath and telling yourself to relax, (3) taking the scenic route to work, and (4) jogging for half an hour? These are all methods suggested by psychologists to help people cope with the stresses of modern life.

Stress takes many forms and can harm our psychological well-being and physical health. Here we highlight ways of coping with stress: controlling irrational thoughts, lowering arousal, modifying the Type A behavior pattern, and exercising.

CONTROLLING IRRATIONAL THOUGHTS People often feel pressure from their own thoughts. Consider the following experiences:

INFLAMMATION Increased blood flow to an injured area of the body, resulting in redness, warmth, and an increased supply of white blood cells.

PSYCHONEUROIMMUNOLOGY The field that studies the relationships between psychological factors (e.g., attitudes and overt behavior patterns) and the functioning of the immune system.

1. You have difficulty with the first item on a test and become convinced that you will flunk.

2. You want to express your genuine feelings but think that if you do so you might make another person angry or upset.

3. You haven't been able to get to sleep for 15 minutes and assume that you will lie awake all night and feel "wrecked" in the morning.

4. You're not sure what decision to make, so you try to put the problem out of your mind by going out, playing cards, or watching TV.

5. You decide not to play tennis because your form isn't perfect and you're in less than perfect condition.

If you have had these or similar experiences, it may be because you harbor some of the irrational beliefs identified by Albert Ellis (see Table H.4). These beliefs may make you overly concerned about the approval of others (item 2 in the preceding list) or perfectionistic (item 5). They may lead you to think that you can solve problems by pretending they do not exist (item 4) or that a minor setback will invariably lead to greater problems (items 1 and 3).

How, then, do we change irrational thoughts? The answer is deceptively simple: We just change them. However, this may require work. Moreover, before we can change our thoughts we must become aware of them.

THREE STEPS FOR CONTROLLING IRRATIONAL THOUGHTS

Meichenbaum and Jaremko (1983) suggest a three-step procedure for controlling the irrational or catastrophizing thoughts that often accompany feelings of anxiety, conflict, or tension:

1. Develop awareness of these thoughts through careful self-examination. Study the examples at the beginning of this section or in Tables H.2 or H.4 to see if they apply to you. When you encounter anxiety or frustration, pay close attention to your thoughts. Are they guiding you toward a solution, or are they compounding your problems?

TABLE H.4

CONTROLLING IRRATIONAL BELIEFS AND THOUGHTS	
IRRATIONAL THOUGHTS	**INCOMPATIBLE (COPING) THOUGHTS**
"Oh my God, I'm going to completely lose control!"	"This is painful and upsetting, but I don't have to go to pieces over it."
"This will never end."	"This will end even if it's hard to see the end right now."
"It'll be awful if Mom gives me that look again."	"It's more pleasant when Mom's happy with me, but I can live with it if she isn't."
"How can I go out there? I'll look like a fool."	"So you're not perfect. That doesn't mean that you're going to look stupid. And so what if someone thinks you look stupid? You can live with that, too. Just stop worrying and have some fun."
"My heart's going to leap out of my chest! How much can I stand?"	"Easy—hearts don't leap out of chests. Stop and think! Distract yourself. Breathe slowly, in and out."
"What can I do? There's nothing I can do!"	"Easy—stop and think. Just because you can't think of a solution right now doesn't mean there's nothing you can do. Take it a minute at a time. Breathe easy."

Do irrational beliefs or catastrophizing thoughts compound the stress you experience? Cognitive psychologists suggest that you can cope with stress by becoming aware of your self-defeating beliefs and thoughts and replacing them with rational, calming beliefs and thoughts.

2. Prepare thoughts that are incompatible with the irrational or catastrophizing thoughts, and practice saying them firmly to yourself. (If nobody is nearby, why not say them firmly aloud?)

3. Reward yourself with a mental pat on the back for making effective changes in your beliefs and thought patterns.

LOWERING AROUSAL Stress tends to trigger intense activity in the sympathetic branch of the autonomic nervous system—in other words, arousal. Arousal is a sign that something may be wrong. It is a message telling us to survey the situation and take appropriate action. But once we are aware that a stressor is acting on us and have developed a plan to cope with it, it is no longer helpful to have blood pounding fiercely through our arteries. Psychologists and other scientists have developed many methods for teaching people to reduce arousal. These include meditation, biofeedback (both discussed in the "Learning" chapter), and progressive relaxation.

PROGRESSIVE RELAXATION In progressive relaxation, people purposefully tense a particular muscle group before relaxing it. This sequence allows them to develop awareness of their muscle tensions and also to differentiate between feelings of tension and relaxation.

Progressive relaxation lowers the arousal produced by the alarm reaction. It has been found useful for stress-related illnesses ranging from headaches (Blanchard et al., 1990a) to hypertension (Agras et al., 1983). You can experience muscle relaxation in the arms by doing the exercise described next.

Settle down in a reclining chair, dim the lights, and loosen any tight clothing. Use the instructions given here. They can be memorized (slight variations from the text are all right), recorded and played back, or read aloud by a friend. For instructions about relaxation of the entire body, consult a psychologist or other helping professional who is familiar with the technique.

Settle back as comfortably as you can. Let yourself relax to the best of your ability. . . . Now, as you relax like that, clench your right fist, just clench your fist tighter and tighter, and study the tension as you do so. Keep it clenched and feel the tension in your right fist, hand, forearm . . . and now relax. Let the fingers of your right hand become loose, and observe the contrast in your feelings. . . . Now, let yourself go and try to become more relaxed all over. . . . Once more, clench your right fist really tight . . . hold it, and notice the tension again. . . . Now let go, relax; your fingers straighten out, and you notice the difference once more. . . . Now repeat that with your left fist. Clench your left fist while the rest of your body relaxes; clench that fist tighter and feel the tension . . . and now relax. Again enjoy the contrast. . . . Repeat that once more, clench the left fist, tight and tense. . . . Now do the opposite of tension—relax and feel the difference. Continue relaxing like that for a while. . . . Clench both fists tighter and together, both fists tense, forearms tense, study the sensations . . . and relax; straighten out your fingers and feel that relaxation. Continue relaxing your hands and forearms more and more. . . . Now bend your elbows and tense your biceps, tense them harder and study the tension feelings . . . all right, straighten out your arms, let them relax and feel that difference again. Let the relaxation develop. . . . Once more, tense your biceps; hold the tension and observe it carefully. . . . Straighten the arms and relax; relax to the best of your ability. . . . Each time, pay close attention to your feelings when you tense up and when you relax. Now straighten your arms, straighten them so that you feel most tension in the triceps muscles along the back of your arms; stretch your arms and feel that tension. . . . And now relax. Get your arms back into a comfortable position. Let the relaxation proceed on its own. The arms should feel comfortably heavy as you allow them to relax. . . . Straighten the arms once more so that you feel the tension in the triceps muscles; straighten them. Feel that tension . . . and relax. Now let's concentrate on pure relaxation in the arms without any tension. Get your arms comfortable and let them relax further and further. Continue relaxing your arms even further. Even when your arms seem fully relaxed, try to go that extra bit further; try to achieve deeper and deeper levels of relaxation. (Wolpe & Lazarus, 1966, p. 177)

Together, controlling irrational thoughts and reducing arousal lessen the impact of the stressor. These methods give you a chance to develop a plan for effective action. When effective action is not possible, controlling your thoughts and your level of arousal can enhance your capacity to tolerate discomfort.

EXERCISING: RUN FOR YOUR LIFE?

I like long walks, especially when they are taken by people who annoy me.

FRED ALLEN

Exercise, particularly aerobic exercise, not only fosters physical health but can also enhance our psychological well-being and help in coping with stress (Hays, 1995). *Aerobic exercise* refers to exercise that requires a sustained increase in consumption of oxygen. Aerobic exercise promotes cardiovascular fitness. Aerobic exercises include, but are not limited to, running and jogging, running in place, walking (at more than a leisurely pace), aerobic dancing, jumping rope, swimming, bicycle riding, basketball, racquetball, and cross-country skiing.

Anaerobic exercises, in contrast, involve short bursts of muscle activity. Examples of anaerobic exercises are weight training, calisthenics (which usually allow rest periods between exercises), and sports such as baseball, in which there are infrequent bursts of strenuous activity. Anaerobic exercises can strengthen muscles and improve flexibility.

The major physiological effect of exercise is greater fitness. Fitness includes muscle strength; muscle endurance; suppleness or flexibility; cardiorespiratory, or aerobic, fitness; and a higher ratio of muscle to fat (usually due to both building muscle and reducing fat). Cardiovascular fitness, or "condition," means that the body can use more oxygen during vigorous activity and pump more blood with each heartbeat. Because conditioned athletes' hearts pump more blood with each beat, they usually have a slower pulse rate—that is, fewer heartbeats per minute. However, during aerobic exercise they may double or triple their resting heart rate for minutes at a time.

Sustained physical activity does more than promote fitness. It also increases longevity by reducing the risk of heart attacks and other health problems (Curfman, 1993a). Amy Hakim of the University of Virginia School of Medicine and her colleagues (1998) reviewed 12 years of data on 707 retired men from the Honolulu Heart Program and found that 43.1% of the men who walked less than a mile per day died during that

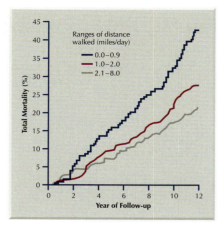

Figure H.5
**CUMULATIVE MORTALITY ACCORD-
ING TO YEAR OF FOLLOW-UP AND
DISTANCE WALKED PER DAY AMONG
PARTICIPANTS IN THE HONOLULU
HEART PROGRAM.**
After 12 years of follow-ups, retired men
who walked more than 2 miles a day had
lower mortality rates than men who
walked shorter distances
Source: Hakim et al., 1998.

period, as compared with 27.7% of those who walked from 1 to 2 miles a day and 21.5% of those who walked at least 2 miles daily (see Figure H.5). Additional findings: 6.6% of the men who walked less than a mile a day died from coronary heart disease or strokes, as compared with only 2.1% of those who walked upward of 2 miles. Moreover, 13.4% of men who walked less than a mile died from cancer, as compared with 5.3% of men who walked more than 2 miles a day.

There is an important limitation to such studies: They are correlational and not experimental. It is possible that people who are in better health *choose* to engage in higher levels of physical activity. If such is the case, then their lower mortality rates due to heart attacks and cancer would be attributable to their initial superior health, not to their physical activity. Hakim and her colleagues recognized this problem and got around it partly by using data only on nonsmokers who were physically able to walk a few miles.

Aerobic exercise raises blood levels of high-density lipoproteins (HDL, or "good cholesterol") (Curfman, 1993b). HDL lowers the amount of low-density lipoproteins (LDL, or "bad cholesterol") in the blood. This is another way in which exercise may reduce the risk of heart attacks. Psychologists are also interested in the effects of exercise on psychological variables. Articles have appeared on exercise as "therapy"—for example, "running therapy."

Consider depression. Depression is characterized by inactivity and feelings of helplessness. Exercise is, in a sense, the opposite of inactivity. Exercise might also help alleviate feelings of helplessness. In one experiment, McCann and Holmes (1984) randomly assigned mildly depressed college women to aerobic exercise, progressive relaxation, and a no-treatment control group. The relaxation group showed some improvement, but aerobic exercise dramatically reduced students' depression. Other experiments also find that exercise alleviates feelings of depression, at least among mildly and moderately depressed individuals (Buffone, 1984; Greist, 1984; Norvell & Belles, 1993). Exercise has also been shown to decrease anxiety and hostility and to boost self-esteem (Norvell & Belles, 1993).

How about you? Are you thinking of climbing onto the exercise bandwagon? If so, consider these suggestions:

1. Unless you have engaged in sustained and vigorous exercise recently, seek the advice of a medical expert. If you smoke, have a family history of heart disease, are overweight, or over 40, get a stress test.

2. Consider joining a beginner's aerobics class. Group leaders are not usually experts in physiology, but at least they "know the steps." You will also be among other beginners and derive the benefits of social support.

3. Get the proper equipment to facilitate performance and avert injury.

4. Read up on the activity you are considering. Books, magazines, and newspaper articles can give you ideas on how to get started and how fast to progress.

5. Try to select activities that you can sustain for a lifetime. Don't worry about building yourself up rapidly. Enjoy yourself. Your strength and endurance will progress on their own. If you do not enjoy what you're doing, you're not likely to stick to it.

6. If you feel severe pain, don't try to exercise "through" it. Soreness is to be expected for beginners (and for old-timers now and then). In

that sense, soreness, at least when it is intermittent, is normal. But sharp pain is abnormal and a sign that something is wrong.

7. Have fun!

A MULTIFACTORIAL APPROACH TO HEALTH AND ILLNESS

Why do people become ill? Why do some people develop cancer? Why do others have heart attacks? Why do still others seem to be immune to these illnesses? Why do some of us seem to come down with everything that is going around, whereas others ride out the roughest winters without a sniffle? There is no single, simple answer to these questions. The likelihood of contracting an illness—be it a case of the flu or a kind of cancer—can reflect the interaction of many factors (Coie et al., 1993; Stokols, 1992).

"An Opportunity to Keep Those Nasty Genes From Expressing Themselves"

Biological factors such as pathogens, inoculations, injuries, age, gender, and a family history of disease may strike us as the most obvious causes of illness. Genetics, in particular, tempts some people to assume there is little they can do about their health. But genes only create *predispositions* toward illness. As *The New York Times* health columnist Jane Brody (1995) notes, predispositions "need a conducive environment in which to express themselves. A bad family medical history should not be considered a portent of doom. Rather, it should be welcomed as an opportunity to keep those nasty genes from expressing themselves."

As shown in Figure H.6, psychological and other factors also play key roles in health and illness (Ader, 1993; Mischel & Shoda, 1995). As shown in Table H.5, nearly 1 million deaths each year in the United States are preventable (National Center for Health Statistics, 1996). Stopping smoking, eating right, exercising, and controlling alcohol use would prevent nearly 80% of these. Psychological states such as anxiety and depression can impair the functioning of the immune system, rendering us more vulnerable to physical disorders (Esterling et al., 1993; Herbert & Cohen, 1993; Kemeny et al., 1994).

The nearby "Psychology in a World of Diversity" feature focuses on some of the sociocultural factors connected with health and illness, as reflected in human diversity. Let us now consider the health problems of headaches, heart disease, and cancer. In each case we consider the interplay of biological, psychological, social, technological, and environmental factors. Although these are medical problems, they have very real psychological consequences. Moreover, psychologists have made important contributions to their treatment.

Headaches

Headaches are among the most common stress-related physical ailments. Nearly 20% of people in the United States suffer from severe headaches. Let us consider the common muscle tension headache and the more severe migraine headache.

MUSCLE TENSION HEADACHE The single most frequent kind of headache is the muscle tension headache. During the first two stages of

---

TABLE H.5

ANNUAL PREVENTABLE DEATHS IN THE UNITED STATES

Elimination of tobacco use could prevent 400,000 deaths each year from cancer, heart and lung diseases, and stroke.

Improved diet and exercise could prevent 300,000 deaths from conditions like heart disease, stroke, diabetes, and cancer.

Control of underage and excess drinking of alcohol could prevent 100,000 deaths from motor vehicle accidents, falls, drownings, and other alcohol-related injuries.

Immunizations for infectious diseases could prevent up to 100,000 deaths.

Safer sex or sexual abstinence could prevent 30,000 deaths from sexually transmitted infections (STIs).

Other measures for preventing needless deaths include improved worker training and safety to prevent accidents in the workplace, wider screening for breast and cervical cancer, and control of high blood pressure and elevated blood cholesterol levels.

Biological Factors

Family history of illness
Exposure to infectious organisms
    (e.g., bacteria and viruses)
Functioning of the immune system
Inoculations
Medication history
Congenital disabilities, birth complications
Physiological conditions (e.g., hypertension,
    serum cholesterol level)
Reactivity of the cardiovascular system to stress
    (e.g., "hot reactor")
Pain and discomfort
Age
Gender
Ethnicity (e.g., genetic vulnerability to
    Tay-Sachs disease or sickle-cell anemia)

Sociocultural Factors

Socioeconomic status
Family circumstances (social class, family size, family conflict, family disorganization)
Access to health care (e.g., adequacy of available health care, availability of health
    insurance, availability of transportation to health care facilities)
Prejudice and discrimination
Health-related cultural and religious beliefs and practices
Health promotion in the workplace or community
Health-related legislation

Personality

Seeking (or avoiding) information about
    health risks and stressors
Self-efficacy expectations
Psychological hardiness
Psychological conflict (approach-approach,
    avoidance-avoidance, approach-avoidance)
Optimism or pessimism
Attributional style (how one explains one's
    failures and health problems to oneself)
Health locus of control (belief that one is or
    is not in charge of one's own health)
Introversion/extroversion
Coronary-prone (Type A) personality
Tendencies to express or hold in feelings of
    anger and frustration
Depression/anxiety
Hostility/suspiciousness

Environmental Factors

Vehicular safety
Architectural features (e.g., crowding,
    injury-resistant design, nontoxic
    construction materials, aesthetic
    design, air quality, noise insulation)
Aesthetics of residential, workplace,
    and communal architecture and
    landscape architecture
Water quality
Solid waste treatment and sanitation
Pollution
Radiation
Global warming
Ozone depletion
Natural disasters (earthquakes, blizzards,
    floods, hurricanes, drought, extremes
    of temperature, tornadoes)

Behavior

Diet (intake of calories, fats, fiber, vitamins, etc.)
Consumption of alcohol
Cigarette smoking
Level of physical activity
Sleep patterns
Safety practices (e.g., using seat belts; careful driving; practice
    of sexual abstinence, monogamy, or "safer sex"; adequate
    prenatal care)
Having (or not having) regular medical and dental checkups
Compliance with medical and dental advice
Interpersonal/social skills

Stressors

Daily hassles (e.g., preparing meals, illness, time pressure,
    loneliness, crime, financial insecurity, problems with co-workers,
    day care)
Major life changes such as divorce, death of a spouse,
    taking out a mortgage, losing a job
Frustration
Pain and discomfort
Availability and use of social support vs. peer rejection or isolation
Climate in the workplace (e.g., job overload, sexual harassment)

Figure H.6
FACTORS IN HEALTH AND ILLNESS.

Various factors figure in to a person's state of health or illness. Which of the factors in this figure are you capable of controlling? Which are beyond your control?

the GAS we are likely to contract muscles in the shoulders, neck, fore-head, and scalp. Persistent stress can lead to persistent contraction of these muscles, giving rise to muscle tension headaches. Psychological factors, such as the tendency to catastrophize negative events—that is, blow them out of proportion—can bring on a tension headache (Ukestad & Wittrock, 1996). Tension headaches usually come on gradually. They are most often characterized by dull, steady pain on both sides of the head and feelings of tightness or pressure.

MIGRAINE HEADACHE Most other headaches, including severe **migraine headaches,** are vascular in nature. That is, they stem from changes in the blood supply to the head (Welch, 1993). These involve the dilation and consequent expansion of blood vessels in the head, which then place pressure against nerve endings. There is often a warning aura that may include vision problems and perception of unusual odors. The attacks themselves are often accompanied by sensitivity to light, loss of appetite, nausea, vomiting, sensory and motor disturbances such as loss of balance, and changes in mood. The so-called common migraine headache is identified by sudden onset and throbbing on one side of the head. The so-called classic migraine is characterized by sensory and motor distur-bances that precede the pain.

The origins of migraine headaches are not clearly understood. It is believed, however, that they can be induced by barometric pressure; pollen; certain drugs; monosodium glutamate (MSG), a chemical often used to enhance flavor; chocolate; aged cheese; beer, champagne, and red wine; and the hormonal changes connected with menstruation. Type A behavior may also contribute to migraine headaches. In one study, 53% of people who had migraine headaches showed the Type A behavior pattern, compared with 23% of people who had muscle tension headaches (Rappaport et al., 1988).

Regardless of the source of the headache, we can unwittingly propel ourselves into a vicious cycle. Headache pain is a stressor that can lead us to increase, rather than relax, muscle tension in the neck, shoulders, scalp, and face.

TREATMENT Aspirin and ibuprofen are frequently used to decrease pain, including headache pain. They inhibit the production of the prostaglandins that help initiate transmission of pain messages to the brain. Drugs that affect the blood flow in the brain help many people with migraine (Welch, 1993). Many of these medications include the drug caf-feine, which occurs naturally in foods such as coffee, tea, colas, and choco-late, and which functions as a *vasoconstrictor.* This means that caffeine acts to constrict blood vessels in the head, counteracting their dilation. (Yes, a cup of coffee can help some people with a migraine headache, but caffeine is a stimulant and might intensify muscle tension headaches.)

Behavioral methods also help in the treatment of headaches. Progres-sive relaxation focuses on decreasing muscle tension and has been shown to be highly effective in relieving muscle tension headaches (Blanchard et al., 1990a). Biofeedback training that alters the flow of blood to the head has helped many people with migraine headaches (Blanchard et al., 1990b). People who are sensitive to MSG or red wine can request meals without MSG and switch to white wine.

When we encounter stress, why do some of us develop coronary heart disease or other health problems while other people suffer no physical prob-lems? In the following sections we see a possible interaction between stress and certain biological and psychological differences between individuals.

MIGRAINE HEADACHES Throbbing headaches connected with changes in the supply of blood to the head.

HUMAN DIVERSITY AND HEALTH: NATIONS WITHIN THE NATION

Today we know more about the connections between behavior and health than ever before. The United States also has the resources to provide the most advanced health care in the world. But not all Americans take advantage of contemporary knowledge. Nor do all pro fit equally from the health-care system. Health psychologists note, therefore, that from the perspective of health and health care we are many nations and not just one. Many factors influence whether people engage in good health practices or let themselves go. Many factors affect whether they act to prevent illness or succumb to it. These include ethnicity, gender, level of education, and socioeconomic status.

ETHNICITY AND HEALTH

The life expectancy of African Americans is 7 years shorter than that of White Americans (Flack et al., 1995). It is unclear whether this difference is connected with ethnicity per se or with factors such as income and level of education (Angell, 1993; Guralnik et al., 1993).

Because of lower socioeconomic status, African Americans have less access to health care than White Americans do (Flack et al., 1995; Penn et al., 1995). They are also more likely to live in unhealthful neighborhoods, eat high-fat diets, and smoke (Pappas et al., 1993).

African Americans also experience different treatment by medical practitioners. Even when they have the same medical conditions as White people, African Americans are less likely to receive treatments such as coronary artery bypass surgery, hip and knee replacements, kidney transplants, mammography, and flu shots (Geiger, 1996). Why? Various explanations have been offered, including cultural differences, patient preferences, and lack of information about health care. Another possible explanation, of course, is racism (Geiger, 1996)

Disproportionate numbers of deaths from AIDS occur within ethnic minority groups in the United States, predominantly among African Americans and Hispanic Americans (Rathus et al., 2000). Only 12% of the U.S. population is African American, but African American men account for 31% of people with AIDS. African American women account for 55% of women with AIDS. Only 9% of the population is Hispanic American, but Hispanic American men account for 17% of the men with AIDS. Hispanic American women account for 20% of women with AIDS.

African Americans are five to seven times more likely than European Americans to have hypertension (Leary, 1991). However, African Americans are also more likely to suffer from hypertension than Black Africans are. Many health professionals thus infer that environmental factors found among many African Americans—such as stress, diet, and smoking—contribute to high blood pressure in people who are genetically vulnerable to it (Betancourt & López, 1993; Leary, 1991).

African Americans are more likely than White Americans to have heart attacks and to die from them (Becker et al., 1993). Early diagnosis and treatment might help decrease the racial gap (Ayanian, 1993). African Americans with heart disease are less likely than White Americans to obtain procedures such as bypass surgery, even when it appears that they would benefit equally from the procedure (Peterson et al., 1997).

African Americans are also more likely than White Americans to contract most forms of cancer. Possibly because of genetic factors, the incidences of colon cancer and lung cancer are significantly higher among African Americans than White Americans (Blakeslee, 1994). Once they contract cancer, African Americans are more likely than White Americans to die from it (Bal, 1992). The results for African Americans are connected with their lower socioeconomic status (Baquet et al., 1991).

Also consider some cultural differences in health. Death rates from cancer are higher in nations like the Netherlands, Denmark, England, Canada, and—yes—the United States, where average rates of daily fat intake are high (Cohen, 1987). Death rates from cancer are much lower in such nations like Thailand, the Philippines, and Japan, where average daily fat intake is much lower. Do not assume that the difference is racial just because Thailand, the Philippines, and Japan are Asian nations! The diets of Japanese Americans are similar in fat content to those of other Americans—and so are their rates of death from cancer.

There are health-care "overusers" and "underusers" among cultural groups. For example, Hispanic Americans visit physicians less often than African Americans and non-Hispanic White Americans do because of lack of health insurance, difficulty speaking English, misgivings about medical technology, and—for illegal immigrants—fear of deportation (Ziv & Lo, 1995).

GENDER AND HEALTH

Also consider a few gender differences. Men are more likely than women to have coronary heart disease. Women are apparently "protected" by high levels of estrogen until menopause. After menopause, women are dramatically more likely to incur heart disease, although this tendency can be counteracted by estrogen replacement therapy (Brody, 1997).

The gender of the physician can also make a difference. According to a study of more than 90,000 women, those whose internists or family practitioners are women are more likely to have screening for cancer (mammograms and Pap smears) than those whose internists or family practitioners are men (Lurie et al., 1993). It is unclear from this study, however, whether female physicians are more likely than their male counterparts to encourage women to seek preventive care, or whether women who choose female physicians are also more likely to seek preventive care. Other research shows that female physicians are more likely than male physicians to conduct breast examinations properly (Hall et al., 1990).

Men's life expectancy is 7 years shorter, on the average, than women's. Surveys of physicians ("Doctors Tie Male Mentality," 1995) and of the general population (Brody, 1998) suggest that this difference is due, at least in part, to women's greater willingness to seek health care. Men often let symptoms go until a problem that could have been prevented or readily treated becomes serious or life threatening.

HEALTH AND SOCIOECONOMIC STATUS: THE RICH GET RICHER AND THE POOR GET . . . SICKER?

Socioeconomic status (SES) and health are intimately connected. Generally speaking, people with higher SES enjoy better health and lead longer lives (Goode, 1999). The question is *why*.

Consider three possibilities (Adler et al., 1994). One is that there is no causal connection between health and SES. Perhaps both SES and health reflect genetic factors. For example, "good genes" might lead both to good health and to high social standing. Second, poor health might lead to socioeconomic "drift" (that is, loss of social standing). Third, SES might affect biological functions that, in turn, influence health.

How might SES influence health? SES is defined in part in terms of education. That is, people who attain low levels of education are also likely to have low SES. Less well educated people are more likely to smoke (Winkleby et al., 1991), and smoking has been linked to many physical illnesses. People with lower SES are also less likely to exercise and more likely to be obese—both of which, again, are linked to poor health outcomes (Ford et al., 1991).

Anorexia and bulimia nervosa are uncommon among poor people, but obesity is most prevalent among the poor. The incidence of obesity is also greater in cultures that associate obesity with happiness and health—as is true of some Haitian and Puerto Rican groups. People living in poor urban neighborhoods are more likely to be obese because junk food is heavily promoted in those neighborhoods and many residents tend to eat as a way of coping with stress (Johnson et al., 1995).

Let us also not forget that poorer people also have less access to health care (Goode, 1999). The problem is compounded by the fact that people with low SES are less likely to be educated about the benefits of regular health checkups and early medical intervention when symptoms arise. ■

TRUTH OR FICTION REVISITED
It is not true that poor people in the United States eat less than more affluent people. Obesity is actually most prevalent among the lowest socioeconomic groups. (This is not to deny the fact that some poor people in the United States cannot afford food.)

COPING WITH THE TYPE A SENSE OF TIME URGENCY.
The San Francisco Recurrent Coronary Prevention Project has helped Type A heart attack victims modify their behavior in order to avert future attacks. Type A individuals are taught to alleviate their sense of time urgency and their hostility.

Coronary Heart Disease

Coronary heart disease (CHD) is the leading cause of death in the United States, most often from heart attacks (National Center for Health Statistics, 1996). Consider the risk factors for CHD:

1. *Family history.* People with a family history of CHD are more likely to develop the disease themselves (Marenberg et al., 1994).

2. *Physiological conditions.* Obesity, high **serum cholesterol** levels (Stampfer et al., 1991), and **hypertension** are risk factors for CHD.

   About 1 American in 5 has hypertension, or abnormally high blood pressure (Leary, 1991). When high blood pressure has no identifiable cause, it is referred to as *essential hypertension.* This condition appears to have a genetic component (Caulfield et al., 1994). However, blood pressure also rises when we inhibit the expression of strong feelings or are angry or on guard against threats (Jorgensen et al., 1996; Suls et al., 1995). When we are under stress, we may believe we can feel our blood pressure "pounding through the roof," but this notion is usually false. Most people cannot recognize hypertension. Therefore it is important to have blood pressure checked regularly.

3. *Patterns of consumption.* Patterns include heavy drinking, smoking, overeating, and eating food high in cholesterol, like saturated fats (Jeffery, 1991).

4. *Type A behavior.* Most studies suggest at least a modest relationship between Type A behavior and CHD (Thoresen & Powell, 1992). It also seems that alleviating Type A behavior may reduce the risk of *recurrent* heart attacks (Friedman & Ulmer, 1984).

5. *Hostility and holding in feelings of anger* (Miller et al., 1996; Powch & Houston, 1996).

6. *Job strain.* Overtime work, assembly-line labor, and exposure to conflicting demands can all contribute to CHD. High-strain work, which makes heavy demands on workers but gives them little personal control, puts workers at the highest risk (Karasek et al., 1982; Krantz et al., 1988). As shown in Figure H.7, the work of many waiters and waitresses fits this description.

7. *Chronic fatigue and chronic emotional strain.*

8. *Sudden stressors.* For example, after the 1994 Los Angeles earthquake, there was an increased incidence of death from heart attacks in people with heart disease (Leor et al., 1996).

9. *A physically inactive lifestyle* (Dubbert, 1992; Lakka et al., 1994).

REDUCING THE RISK OF CHD THROUGH BEHAVIOR MODIFICATION Once CHD has been diagnosed, a number of medical treatments, including surgery and medication, are available. However, people who have not had CHD (as well as those who have) can profit from behavior modification techniques designed to reduce the risk factors. These methods include the following:

1. *Stopping smoking.*

2. *Weight control.*

3. *Reducing hypertension.* There is medication for reducing hypertension, but behavioral changes such as the following often do the trick: relaxation training (Agras et al., 1983), meditation (Benson et al., 1973), aerobic exercise (Danforth et al., 1990), and eating more fruits and vegetables and less fat (Appel et al., 1997).

SERUM CHOLESTEROL Cholesterol found in the blood.

HYPERTENSION High blood pressure.

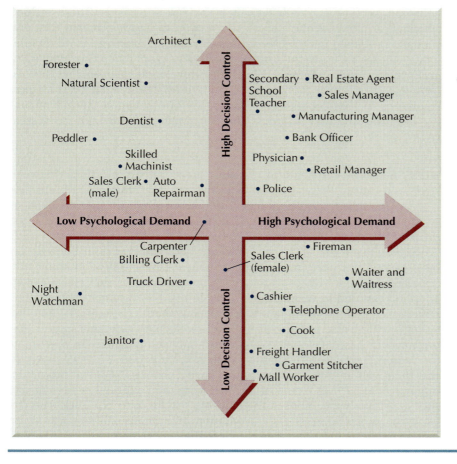

Figure H.7
THE JOB-STRAIN MODEL.
This model highlights the psychological demands made by various occupations and the amount of personal (decision) control they allow. Occupations characterized by high demand and low decision control place workers at greatest risk for heart disease.

4. *Lowering low-density lipoprotein (harmful serum cholesterol).* Major methods involve exercise, medication, and cutting down on foods that are high in cholesterol and saturated fats (Shepherd et al., 1995).

5. *Changing Type A behavior* (Friedman & Ulmer, 1984).

6. *Exercise.* Sustained physical activity protects people from CHD (Curfman, 1993b).

Cancer

Cancer is the number one killer of women in the United States, and the number two killer of men (Andersen, 1996). Cancer is characterized by the development of abnormal, or mutant, cells that may take root anywhere in the body: in the blood, bones, digestive tract, lungs, and genital organs. If their spread is not controlled early, the cancerous cells may *metastasize*—that is, establish colonies elsewhere in the body. It appears that our bodies develop cancerous cells frequently. However, these are normally destroyed by the immune system. People whose immune system is damaged by physical or psychological factors are more likely to develop tumors (Azar, 1996b).

RISK FACTORS As with many other disorders, people can inherit a disposition toward cancer (Lerman et al., 1997). Carcinogenic genes may remove the brakes from cell division, allowing cells to multiply wildly. Or they may allow mutations to accumulate unchecked. However, many

HOW HAVE HEALTH PSYCHOLOGISTS HELPED THIS YOUNGSTER COPE WITH CANCER?
Cancer is a medical condition, but psychologists have contributed to the treatment of people with cancer. For example, psychologists help people with cancer remain in charge of their lives, combat feelings of hopelessness, manage stress, and cope with the side effects of chemotherapy.

behavior patterns markedly heighten the risk for cancer. These include smoking, drinking alcohol (especially in women), eating animal fats, and sunbathing (which may cause skin cancer due to exposure to ultraviolet light). Agents in cigarette smoke, such as benzopyrene, may damage a gene that would otherwise block the development of many tumors, including lung cancer ("Damaged Gene," 1996). Prolonged psychological conditions such as depression or stress may also heighten the risk of cancer because they, too, suppress the functioning of the immune system (Azar, 1996b).

STRESS AND CANCER Researchers have uncovered links between stress and cancer (Azar, 1996b). One study revealed that a significant percentage of children with cancer had encountered severe life changes within a year of the diagnosis (Jacobs & Charles, 1980). These often involved the death of a loved one or the loss of a close relationship.

Experimental research that could not be conducted with humans has been carried out using rats and other animals. In one type of study, animals are injected with cancerous cells or with viruses that cause cancer and then exposed to various conditions. In this way researchers can determine which conditions influence the likelihood that the animals' immune systems will be able to fend off the disease. Such experiments suggest that once cancer has developed, stress can influence its course. In one study, for example, rats were implanted with small numbers of cancer cells so that their own immune systems would have a chance to combat them (Visintainer et al., 1982). Some of the rats were then exposed to inescapable shocks. Others were exposed to escapable shocks or to no shock. The rats exposed to the most stressful condition—the inescapable shock—were half as likely as the other rats to reject the cancer and twice as likely to die from it.

In sum, cancer is frightening, and in many cases, little can be done about its eventual outcome. However, we are not helpless in the face of cancer. Cure rates have been improving, and we can take preventive measures like the following:

1. Limit exposure to behavioral risk factors for cancer.
2. Modify diet by reducing intake of fats and increasing intake of fruits and vegetables (Mevkens, 1990). Tomatoes, broccoli, cauliflower, cabbage, grapes, and raspberries appear to be especially helpful. (Yes, Grandma was right about veggies.)
3. Have regular medical checkups so that cancer will be detected early. Cancer is most treatable in the early stages.
4. Regulate exposure to stress.
5. If we are struck by cancer, we can fight it energetically rather than become passive victims.

We conclude this chapter with good news for readers of this book: *Better educated* people—that means *you*—are more likely to modify health-impairing behavior and reap the benefits of change (Angell, 1993; Guralnik et al., 1993; Pappas et al., 1993).

SUMMARY

1. **What is health psychology?** Health psychology studies the relationships between psychological factors and the prevention and treatment of physical illness.

2. **What is stress?** Stress is the demand made on an organism to adjust. Whereas some stress is desirable to keep us alert and occupied, too much stress can tax our adjustive capacities and contribute to physical illness.

3. **What are some sources of stress?** Sources of stress include daily hassles, life changes, conflict, irrational beliefs, and Type A behavior. Type A behavior is characterized by aggressiveness, time urgency, and competitiveness.

4. **What psychological factors moderate the impact of stress?** These include positive self-efficacy expectations, psychological hardiness, a sense of humor, predictability of stressors, and social support. Self-efficacy expectations encourage us to persist in difficult tasks and to endure discomfort. Psychological hardiness is characterized by com-mitment, challenge, and control.

5. **What is the general adaptation syndrome (GAS)?** The GAS is a body response triggered by the perception of a stressor. It consists of three stages: alarm, resistance, and exhaustion.

6. **What is the role of the endocrine system in the body's response to stress?** The hypothalamus and pituitary glands secrete hormones that stimulate the adrenal cortex to release corticosteroids. Corticosteroids help resist stress by fighting inflammation and allergic reactions. Adrenaline and noradrenaline are secreted by the adrenal medulla. Adrenaline arouses the body by activating the sympathetic nervous system.

7. **What is the role of the autonomic nervous system (ANS) in the body's response to stress?** The sympathetic division of the ANS is highly active during the alarm and resistance stages of the GAS. This activity is characterized by rapid heartbeat and respiration rate, release of stores of sugar, muscle tension, and other responses that deplete the body's supply of energy. The parasympathetic division of the ANS predominates during the exhaustion stage of the GAS. Its activity is characterized by responses such as digestive processes that help restore the body's reserves of energy.

8. **What are the functions of the immune system?** One function of the immune system is to engulf and kill pathogens, worn-out body cells, and cancerous cells. Another is to "remember" pathogens and combat them in the future. A third function is to facilitate inflammation, which increases the number of white blood cells brought to a damaged area.

9. **What are the effects of stress on the immune system?** By stimulating the release of corticosteroids, stress depresses the functioning of the immune system. (For example, steroids counter inflammation.)

10. **What kinds of headaches are there, and how are they related to stress?** The most common kinds are muscle tension headaches and migraine headaches. Stress causes headache pain by stimulating muscle tension.

11. **What are the risk factors for coronary heart disease?** They include family history; physiological conditions such as hypertension and high levels of serum cholesterol; behavior patterns such as heavy drinking, smoking, eating fatty foods, and Type A behavior; work overload; chronic tension and fatigue; and physical inactivity.

12. **What are the risk factors for cancer?** Risk factors for cancer include family history, smoking, drinking alcohol, eating animal fats, sunbathing, and stress.

13. **What behavioral measures contribute to the prevention and treatment of cancer?** The following measures can be helpful: controlling exposure to behavioral risk factors for cancer, having regular medical checkups, regulating exposure to stress, and vigorously fighting cancer if it develops.

KEY TERMS

alarm reaction (p. H-12)

antibodies (p. H-13)

antigen (p. H-13)

approach-approach conflict (p. H-6)

approach-avoidance conflict (p. H-7)

avoidance-avoidance conflict (p. H-6)

catastrophize (p. H-8)

conflict (p. H-6)

daily hassles (p. H-3)

eustress (p. H-3)

exhaustion stage (p. H-13)

"externals" (p. H-11)

fight-or-flight reaction (p. H-12)

general adaptation syndrome (p. H-12)

health psychology (p. H-3)

hypertension (p. H-24)

immune system (p. H-13)

inflammation (p. H-14)

"internals" (p. H-11)

leukocytes (p. H-13)

locus of control (p. H-10)

migraine headaches (p. H-21)

multiple approach-avoidance conflict (p. H-7)

pathogen (p. H-3)

psychological hardiness (p. H-10)

psychoneuroimmunology (p. H-14)

resistance stage (p. H-13)

self-efficacy expectations (p. H-9)

serum cholesterol (p. H-24)

stress (p. H-3)

Type A behavior (p. H-9)

uplifts (p. H-3)

REFERENCES

Ader, R. (1993). Conditioned responses. In B. Moyers (Ed.), *Healing and the mind.* New York: Doubleday.

Adler, N. E., et al. (1994). Socioeconomic status and health. *American Psychologist, 49,* 15–24.

Agras, W. S., Southam, M. A., & Taylor, C. B. (1983). Long-term persistence of relaxation-induced blood pressure lowering during the working day. *Journal of Consulting and Clinical Psychology, 51,* 792–794.

Andersen, B. L. (1996). Psychological and behavioral studies in cancer prevention and control. *Health Psychology, 15,* 411–412.

Angell, M. (1993). Privilege and health—What is the connection? *New England Journal of Medicine, 329,* 126–127.

Appel, L. J., et al. (1997). A clinical trial of the effects of dietary patterns on blood pressure. *New England Journal of Medicine, 336,* 1117–1124.

Ayanian, J. Z. (1993). Heart disease in Black and White. *New England Journal of Medicine, 329,* 656–658.

Azar, B. (1996a). Scientists examine cancer patients' fears. *APA Monitor, 27*(8), 32.

Azar, B. (1996b). Studies investigate the link between stress and immunity. *APA Monitor, 27*(8), 32.

Bal, D. G. (1992). Cancer in African Americans. *Ca—A Cancer Journal for Clinicians, 42,* 5–6.

Bandura, A., Taylor, C. B., Williams, S. L., Medford, I. N., & Barchas, J. D. (1985). Catecholamine secretion as a function of perceived coping self-efficacy. *Journal of Consulting and Clinical Psychology, 53,* 406–414.

Baquet, C. R., Horm, J. W., Gibbs, T., & Greenwald, P. (1991). Socioeconomic factors and cancer incidence among Blacks and Whites. *Journal of the National Cancer Institute, 83,* 551–557.

Basic Behavioral Science Task Force of the National Advisory Mental Health Council. (1996). Basic behavioral science research for mental health: Vulnerability and resilience. *American Psychologist, 51,* 22–28.

Becker, L. B., et al. (1993). Racial differences in the incidence of cardiac arrest and subsequent survival. *New England Journal of Medicine, 329,* 600–606.

Benight, C. C., et al. (1997). Coping self-efficacy buffers psychological and physiological disturbances in HIV-infected men following a natural disaster. *Health Psychology, 16,* 248–255.

Benson, H., Manzetta, B. R., & Rosner, B. (1973). Decreased systolic blood pressure in hypertensive subjects who practiced meditation. *Journal of Clinical Investigation, 52,* 8.

Berenbaum, H., & Connelly, J. (1993). The effect of stress on hedonic capacity. *Journal of Abnormal Psychology, 102,* 474–481.

Betancourt, H., & López, S. R. (1993). The study of culture, ethnicity, and race in American psychology. *American Psychologist, 48,* 629–637.

Blanchard, E. B., et al. (1990a). Placebo-controlled evaluation of abbreviated progressive muscle relaxation and of relaxation combined with cognitive therapy in the treatment of tension headache. *Journal of Consulting and Clinical Psychology, 58,* 210–215.

Blanchard, E. B., et al. (1990b). A controlled evaluation of thermal biofeedback and thermal feedback combined with cognitive therapy in the treatment of vascular headache. *Journal of Consulting and Clinical Psychology, 58,* 216–224.

Blake, P., Fry, R., & Pesjack, M. (1984). *Self-assessment and behavior change manual* (pp. 43–47). New York: Random House.

Blakeslee, S. (1994, April 13). Black smokers' higher risk of cancer may be genetic. *New York Times,* p. C14.

Blatt, S. J.(1995). The destructiveness of perfectionism: Implications for the treatment of depression. *American Psychologist, 50,* 1003–1020.

Brody, J. E. (1995). Cited in DeAngelis, T. (1995), Eat well, keep fit, and let go of stress. *APA Monitor, 26*(10), 20.

Brody, J. E. (1997, August 20). Estrogen after menopause? A tough dilemma. *New York Times,* p. C8.

Brody, J. E. (1998, August 4). Personal health: Giving men directions to the road to better health. *New York Times;* America Online.

Brownlee-Duffeck, M., et al. (1987). The role of health beliefs in the regimen adherence and metabolic control of adolescents and adults with diabetes mellitus. *Journal of Consulting and Clinical Psychology, 55,* 139–144.

Buffone, G. W. (1984). Running and depression. In M. L. Sachs & G. W. Buffone (Eds.), *Running as therapy: An integrated approach.* Lincoln: University of Nebraska Press.

Burman, B., & Margolin, G. (1992). Analysis of the association between marital relationships and health problems. *Psychological Bulletin, 112,* 39–63.

Caulfield, M., et al. (1994). Linkage of the angiotensinogen gene to essential hypertension. *New England Journal of Medicine, 330,* 1629–1633.

Cohen, L. A. (1987, November). Diet and cancer. *Scientific American,* pp. 42–48, 53–54.

Cohen, S., Tyrrell, D. A. J., & Smith, A. P. (1993). Negative life events, perceived stress, negative affect, and susceptibility to the common cold. *Journal of Personality and Social Psychology, 64,* 131–140.

Cohen, S., & Williamson, G. M. (1991). Stress and infectious disease in humans. *Psychological Bulletin, 109,* 5–24.

Coie, J. D., et al. (1993). The science of prevention. *American Psychologist, 48,* 1013–1022.

Cooney, J. L., & Zeichner, A. (1985). Selective attention to negative feedback in Type A and Type B individuals. *Journal of Abnormal Psychology, 94,* 110–112.

Cousins, N. (1979). *Anatomy of an illness as perceived by the patient.* New York: Norton.

Creamer, M., Burgess, P., & Pattison, P. (1992). Reaction to trauma. *Journal of Abnormal Psychology, 101,* 452–459.

Curfman, G. D. (1993a). The health benefits of exercise. *New England Journal of Medicine, 328,* 574–576.

Curfman, G. D. (1993b). Is exercise beneficial—or hazardous—to your heart? *New England Journal of Medicine, 329,* 1730–1731.

Damaged gene is linked to lung cancer. (1996, April 6). *New York Times,* p. A24.

Danforth, J. S., et al. (1990). Exercise as a treatment for hypertension in low-socioeconomic-status Black children. *Journal of Consulting and Clinical Psychology, 58,* 237–239.

Delahanty, D. L., et al. (1996). Time course of natural killer cell activity and lymphocyte proliferation in response to two acute stressors in healthy men. *Health Psychology, 15,* 48–55.

DiClemente, C. C., et al. (1991). The process of smoking cessation. *Journal of Consulting and Clinical Psychology, 59,* 295–304.

Doctors tie male mentality to shorter life span. (1995, June 14). *New York Times,* p. C14.

Dubbert, P. M. (1992). Exercise in behavioral medicine. *Journal of Consulting and Clinical Psychology, 60,* 613–618.

Ellis, A. (1977). The basic clinical theory of rational-emotive therapy. In A. Ellis & R. Grieger (Eds.), *Handbook of rational-emotive therapy.* New York: Springer.

Ellis, A. (1993). Reflections on rational-emotive therapy. *Journal of Consulting and Clinical Psychology, 61,* 199–201.

Esterling, B. A., Antoni, M. H., Kumar, M., & Schneiderman, N. (1993). Defensiveness, trait anxiety, and Epstein-Barr viral capsid antigen antibody titers in healthy college students. *Health Psychology, 12,* 132–139.

Flack, J. M., et al. (1995). Panel I: Epidemiology of minority health. *Health Psychology, 14,* 592–600.

Ford, E. S., et al. (1991). Physical activity behaviors in lower and higher socioeconomic status populations. *American Journal of Epidemiology, 133,* 1246–1256.

Friedman, M., & Ulmer, D. (1984). *Treating Type A behavior and your heart*. New York: Fawcett Crest.

Geiger, H. J. (1996). Race and health care. *New England Journal of Medicine, 335*, 815–816.

Gilbert, S. (1997, June 25). Social ties reduce risk of a cold. *New York Times*, p. C11.

Glaser, R., et al. (1991). Stress-related activation of Epstein-Barr virus. *Brain, Behavior, and Immunity, 5*, 219–232.

Glaser, R., et al. (1993). Stress and the memory T-cell response to the Epstein-Barr virus. *Health Psychology, 12*, 435–442.

Goode, E. (1999, June 1). For good health, it helps to be rich and important. *New York Times Online*.

Greist, J. H. (1984). Exercise in the treatment of depression. *Coping with mental stress: The potential and limits of exercise intervention*. Washington, DC: National Institute of Mental Health.

Gruder, C. L., et al. (1993). Effects of social support and relapse prevention training as adjuncts to a televised smoking-cessation intervention. *Journal of Consulting and Clinical Psychology, 61*, 113–120.

Guralnik, J. M., Land, K. C., Blazer, D., Fillenbaum, G. G., & Branch, L. G. (1993). Educational status and active life expectancy among older Blacks and Whites. *New England Journal of Medicine, 329*, 110–116.

Hakim, A. A., et al. (1998). Effects of walking on mortality among nonsmoking retired men. *New England Journal of Medicine, 338*, 94–99.

Haley, W. E., et al. (1996). Appraisal, coping, and social support as mediators of well-being in Black and White caregivers of patients with Alzheimer's disease. *Journal of Consulting and Clinical Psychology, 64*, 121–129.

Hall, J. A., et al. (1990). Performance quality, gender, and professional role. *Medical Care, 28*, 489–501.

Hays, K. F. (1995). Putting sport psychology into (your) practice. *Professional Psychology: Research and Practice, 26*, 33–40.

Herbert, T. B., & Cohen, S. (1993). Depression and immunity. *Psychological Bulletin, 113*, 472–486.

Holahan, C. J., & Moos, R. H. (1990). Life stressors, resistance factors, and psychological health. *Journal of Personality and Social Psychology, 58*, 909–917.

Holahan, C. J., & Moos, R. H. (1991). Life stressors, personal and social resources, and depression. *Journal of Abnormal Psychology, 100*, 31–38.

Holahan, C. J., Moos, R. H., Holahan, C. K., & Brennan, P. L. (1995). Social support, coping, and depressive symptoms in a late-middle-aged sample of patients reporting cardiac illness. *Health Psychology, 14*, 152–163.

Holmes, T. H., & Rahe, R. H. (1967). The social readjustment rating scale. *Journal of Psychosomatic Research, 11*, 213–218.

Jacobs, T. J., & Charles, E. (1980). Life events and the occurrence of cancer in children. *Psychosomatic Medicine, 42*, 11–24.

Jeffery, R. W. (1991). Population perspectives on the prevention and treatment of obesity in minority populations. *American Journal of Clinical Nutrition, 53*, 1621S–1624S.

Jemmott, J. B., et al. (1983). Academic stress, power motivation, and decrease in secretion rate of salivary secretory immunoglobin A. *Lancet, 1*, 1400–1402.

Johnson, K. W., et al. (1995). Panel II: Macrosocial and environmental influences on minority health. *Health Psychology, 14*, 601–612.

Jorgensen, R. S., Johnson, B. T., Kolodziej, M. E., & Schreer, G. E. (1996). Elevated blood pressure and personality. *Psychological Bulletin, 120*, 293–320.

Karasek, R. A., et al. (1982). Job, psychological factors and coronary heart disease. *Advances in Cardiology, 29*, 62–67.

Kemeny, M. E. (1993). Emotions and the immune system. In B. Moyers (Ed.), *Healing and the mind*. New York: Doubleday.

Kemeny, M. E., Weiner, H., Taylor, S. E., Schneider, S., Visscher, B., & Fahey, J. L. (1994). Repeated bereavement, depressed mood, and immune parameters in HIV seropositive and seronegative gay men. *Health Psychology, 13*, 14–24.

Kiecolt-Glaser, J. K. (1993). Cited in Adler, T. (1993). Men and women affected by stress, but differently. *APA Monitor, 24*(7), 8–9.

Kobasa, S. C. O. (1990). Stress-resistant personality. In R. E. Ornstein & C. Swencionis (Eds.), *The healing brain* (pp. 219–230). New York: Guilford Press.

Kobasa, S. C. O., Maddi, S. R., Puccetti, M. C., & Zola, M. A. (1994). Effectiveness of hardiness, exercise, and social support as resources against illness. In A. Steptoe & J. Wardle (Eds.), *Psychosocial processes and health* (pp. 247–260). Cambridge, England: Cambridge University Press.

Krantz, D. S., Contrada, R. J., Hill, D. R., & Friedler, E. (1988). Environmental stress and biobehavioral antecedents of coronary heart disease. *Journal of Consulting and Clinical Psychology, 56*, 333–341.

Lackner, J. M., Carosella, A. M., & Feuerstein, M. (1996). Pain expectancies, pain, and functional self-efficacy expectancies as determinants of disability in patients with chronic low back disorders. *Journal of Consulting and Clinical Psychology, 64,* 212–220.

Lakka, T. A., et al. (1994). Relation of leisure-time physical activity and cardiorespiratory fitness to the risk of acute myocardial infarction in men. *New England Journal of Medicine, 330,* 1549–1554.

Lazarus, R. S., DeLongis, A., Folkman, S., & Gruen, R. (1985). Stress and adaptational outcomes. *American Psychologist, 40,* 770–779.

Lazarus, R. S., & Folkman, S. (1984). *Stress, appraisal, and coping.* New York: Springer.

Leary, W. E. (1991, October 22). Black hypertension may reflect other ills. *New York Times,* p. C3.

Lefcourt, H. M. (1997). Cited in Clay, R. A. (1997). Researchers harness the power of humor. *APA Monitor, 28*(9), 1, 18.

Lefcourt, H. M., & Martin, R. A. (1986). *Humor and life stress.* New York: Springer-Verlag.

Lefcourt, H. M., Miller, R. S., Ware, E. E., & Sherk, D. (1981). Locus of control as a modifier of the relationship between stressors and moods. *Journal of Personality and Social Psychology, 41,* 357–369.

Leor, J., Poole, K., & Kloner, R. A. (1996). Sudden cardiac death triggered by an earthquake. *New England Journal of Medicine, 334,* 413–419.

Lerman, C., et al. (1997). Incorporating biomarkers of exposure and genetic susceptibility into smoking cessation treatment. *Health Psychology, 16,* 87–99.

Lewinsohn, P. M., et al. (1994b). Adolescent psychopathology: II. Psychosocial risk factors for depression. *Journal of Abnormal Psychology, 103,* 302–315.

Linden, W., Chambers, L., Maurice, J., & Lenz, J. W. (1993). Sex differences in social support, self-deception, hostility, and ambulatory cardiovascular activity. *Health Psychology, 12,* 376–380.

Ludwick-Rosenthal, R., & Neufeld, R. W. J. (1993). Preparation for undergoing an invasive medical procedure. *Journal of Consulting and Clinical Psychology, 61,* 156–164.

Lurie, N., et al. (1993). Preventive care for women? *New England Journal of Medicine, 329,* 478–482.

Maier, S. F., Watkins, L. R., & Fleshner, M. (1994). Psychoneuroimmunology: The interface between behavior, brain, and immunity. *American Psychologist, 49,* 1004–1017.

Marenberg, M. E., et al. (1994). Genetic susceptibility to death from coronary heart disease in a study of twins. *New England Journal of Medicine, 330,* 1041–1046.

Martin, R. A., & Lefcourt, H. M. (1983). Sense of humor as a moderator of the relation between stressors and moods. *Journal of Personality and Social Psychology, 45,* 1313–1324.

McCann, I. L., & Holmes, D. S. (1984). Influence of aerobic exercise on depression. *Journal of Personality and Social Psychology, 46,* 1142–1147.

Meichenbaum, D., & Jaremko, M. E. (Eds.). (1983). *Stress reduction and prevention.* New York: Plenum.

Mevkens, F. L. (1990). Coming of age—The chemoprevention of cancer. *New England Journal of Medicine, 323,* 825–827.

Miller, S. M., Shoda, Y., & Hurley, K. (1996). Applying cognitive-social theory to health-protective behavior: Breast self-examination in cancer screening. *Psychological Bulletin, 199,* 70–94.

Miller, T. Q., Smith, T. W., Turner, C. W., Guijarro, M. L., & Hallet, A. J. (1996). A meta-analytic review of research on hostility and physical health. *Psychological Bulletin, 119,* 322–348.

Mischel, W., & Shoda, Y. (1995). A cognitive-affective system theory of personality. *Psychological Review, 102,* 246–268.

Moser, C. G., & Dyck, D. G. (1989). Type A behavior, uncontrollability, and the activation of hostile self-schema responding. *Journal of Research in Personality, 23,* 248–267.

Moyers, B. (1993). *Healing and the mind.* New York: Doubleday.

National Center for Health Statistics. (1996, March). News Releases and Fact Sheets. *Monitoring Health Care in America: Quarterly Fact Sheet.*

Nides, M. A., et al. (1995). Predictors of initial smoking cessation and relapse through the first 2 years of the lung health study. *Journal of Consulting and Clinical Psychology, 63,* 60–69.

Norris, F. H., & Kaniasty, K. (1994). Psychological distress following criminal victimization in the general population: Cross-sectional, longitudinal, and prospective analyses. *Journal of Consulting and Clinical Psychology, 62,* 111–123.

Norvell, N., & Belles, D. (1993). Psychological and physical benefits of circuit weight training in law enforcement personnel. *Journal of Consulting and Clinical Psychology, 61,* 520–527.

O'Leary, A. (1990). Stress, emotion, and human immune function. *Psychological Bulletin, 108,* 363–382.

Ortega, D. F., & Pipal, J. E. (1984). Challenge seeking and the Type A coronary-prone behavior pattern. *Journal of Personality and Social Psychology, 46,* 1328–1334.

Pappas, G., Queen, S., Hadden, W., & Fisher, G. (1993). The increasing disparity of mortality between socioeconomic groups in the United States, 1960 and 1986. *New England Journal of Medicine, 329,* 103–109.

Penn, N. E., Kar, S., Kramer, J., Skinner, J., & Zambrana, R. E. (1995). Panel VI. Ethnic minorities, health care systems, and behavior. *Health Psychology, 14,* 641–648.

Peterson, E. D., et al. (1997). Racial variation in the use of coronary-revascularization procedures. *New England Journal of Medicine, 336,* 480–486.

Pilkonis, P. (1996). Cited in Goleman, D. J. (1996, May 1). Higher suicide risk for perfectionists. *New York Times,* p. C12.

Powch, I. G., & Houston, B. K. (1996). Hostility, anger-in, and cardiovascular reactivity in White women. *Health Psychology, 15,* 200–208.

Rappaport, N. B., McAnulty, D. P., & Brantley, P. J. (1988). Exploration of the Type A behavior pattern in chronic headache sufferers. *Journal of Consulting and Clinical Psychology, 56,* 621–623.

Rathus, S. A., Nevid, J. S., & Fichner-Rathus, L. (2000). *Human sexuality in a world of diversity* (4th ed.). Boston: Allyn & Bacon.

Rotter, J. B. (1990). Internal versus external control of reinforcement. *American Psychologist, 45,* 489–493.

Selye, H. (1976). *The stress of life* (rev. ed.). New York: McGraw-Hill.

Selye, H. (1980). The stress concept today. In I. L. Kutash et al. (Eds.), *Handbook on stress and*

anxiety. San Francisco: Jossey-Bass.

Shepherd, J., et al. (1995). Prevention of coronary heart disease with pravastatin in men with hypercholesterolemia. *New England Journal of Medicine, 333,* 1301–1307.

Simons, A. D., Angell, K. L., Monroe, S. M., & Thase, M. E. (1993). Cognition and life stress in depression. *Journal of Abnormal Psychology, 102,* 584–591.

Smith, R. E., Smoll, F. L., & Ptacek, J. T. (1990). Conjunctive moderator variables in vulnerability and resiliency research. *Journal of Personality and Social Psychology, 58,* 360–370.

Stampfer, M. J., et al. (1991). A prospective study of cholesterol, apolipoproteins, and the risk of myocardial infarction. *New England Journal of Medicine, 325,* 373–381.

Stokols, D. (1992). Establishing and maintaining healthy environments. *American Psychologist, 47,* 6–22.

Suls, J., Wan, C. K., & Costa, P. T., Jr. (1995). Relationship of trait anger to resting blood pressure. *Health Psychology, 14,* 444–456.

Taylor, S. E. (1990). Health psychology: The science and the field. *American Psychologist, 45,* 40–50.

Thoresen, C., & Powell, L. H. (1992). Type A behavior pattern. *Journal of Consulting and Clinical Psychology, 60,* 595–604.

Tucker, J. S., Friedman, H. S., Wingard, D. L., & Schwartz, J. E. (1996). Marital history at midlife as a predictor of longevity. *Health Psychology, 15,* 94–101.

Uchino, B. N., Cacioppo, J. T., & Kiecolt-Glaser, J. K. (1996). The

relationship between social support and physiological processes. *Psychological Bulletin, 119,* 488–531.

Ukestad, L. K., & Wittrock, D. A. (1996). Pain perception and coping in female tension headache sufferers and headache-free controls. *Health Psychology, 15,* 65–68.

Vaillant, G. E. (1994). Ego mechanisms of defense and personality psychopathology. *Journal of Abnormal Psychology, 103,* 44–50.

Vernberg, E. M., La Greca, A. M., Silverman, W. K., & Prinstein, M. J. (1996). Prediction of posttraumatic stress symptoms in children after Hurricane Andrew. *Journal of Abnormal Psychology, 105,* 237–248.

Visintainer, M. A., Volpicelli, J. R., & Seligman, M. E. P. (1982). Tumor rejection in rats after inescapable or escapable shock. *Science, 216*(23), 437–439.

Welch, K. M. A. (1993). Drug therapy of migraine. *New England Journal of Medicine, 329,* 1476–1483.

Whitehead, W. E. (1994). Assessing the effects of stress on physical symptoms. *Health Psychology, 13,* 99–102.

Wilcox, V. L., Kasl, S. V., & Berkman, L. F. (1994). Social support and physical disability in older people after hospitalization. *Health Psychology, 13,* 170–179.

Winkleby, M., Fortmann, S., & Barrett, D. (1991). Social class disparities in risk factors for disease. *Preventive Medicine, 19,* 1–12.

Wolpe, J., & Lazarus, A. A. (1966). *Behavior therapy techniques.* New York: Pergamon Press.

Ziv, T. A., & Lo, B. (1995). Denial of care to illegal immigrants. *New England Journal of Medicine, 332,* 1095–1098.

A

APPLIED PSYCHOLOGY

TRUTH OR FICTION?

_____ Efficient, skillful employees are evaluated more highly than hardworking employees who must struggle to get the job done.

_____ Allowing employees to piece together their own work schedules is demoralizing to workers and interferes with productivity.

_____ Psychologists help design computer keyboards and aircraft controls.

_____ TV commercials must be likable if they are to influence us to buy the advertised products.

_____ Heat makes some people hot under the collar. That is, high temperatures are connected with aggression.

_____ In community psychology, "An ounce of prevention is worth a pound of cure."

_____ The insanity plea is presented as a defense in about one third of felony cases.

_____ You can improve your athletic performance by imagining yourself making the right moves.

_____ Teachers who know more about a subject do a better job of teaching it.

COLUMNIST RUSSELL BAKER ONCE WROTE, "THE GOAL of all inanimate objects is to resist man and ultimately to defeat him." He must know my stove personally. Each morning it tries to do me in. It has four burners, two in back and two in front, but the burner controls are lined up in a neat row. Unless I strain my eyes looking for the tiny "F" or "B" that shows which one governs which burner, I wind up minutes later with a pot of cold water and a red-eyed burner glaring angrily at me. Then I hop into my shower—the one with the single knob that is turned clockwise for hot (or is it cold?) and counterclockwise for cold (or is it hot?). Each morning I risk burning or freezing as I relearn which is which.

Next, I encounter my car, whose "smart sticks" are much smarter than I. I usually turn on the lights when it begins to rain and the windshield wipers to welcome the twilight. I know that if I turn one of them clockwise (or is it counterclockwise?), I get intermittent wiping, and if I turn it counterclockwise (or is it clockwise?), I get rapid wiping, but I'm not sure which. To gas up, I have to release the gas tank cover. Unfortunately, the control is out of sight on the floor to the side of the driver's seat, next to two others that feel just like it. So I'm as likely to pop open the hood or the trunk as the door to the gas tank. (The attendant always smiles.)

If I were not a psychologist, I would think that I'm just inept. But as a professional, I recognize all these problems as shortcomings in human factors engineering. The field called **human factors**, or human factors in engineering, ensures that equipment and facilities are compatible with human behavior patterns and mental processes. That is, they are reasonably easy to work, or work in, and safe. But the machines surrounding me were either designed by fiends or left to chance.

Human factors in engineering is one example of **applied psychology.** There are many kinds of applied psychologists, but they all use psychological knowledge and methods to solve problems in the world outside the laboratory. They apply knowledge from psychology's basic areas—for example, biology and behavior, sensation and perception, learning, memory, motivation, and personality—to meet people's needs. Clinical psychologists are the largest subgroup of applied psychologists. Clinical psychologists apply psychological knowledge from areas such as biology, learning, motivation, and personality to the evaluation and treatment of psychological disorders. Counseling psychologists apply psychological knowledge to help people with academic, vocational, and adjustment problems. Health psychologists apply psychological knowledge to the prevention and treatment of illness. In this chapter, we explore a number of other areas of applied psychology including industrial/organizational psychology and the related fields of human factors and consumer psychology, environmental psychology, community psychology, forensic psychology, sports psychology, and educational psychology.

INDUSTRIAL/ORGANIZATIONAL PSYCHOLOGY

The world of work is in transition as we cross over into the new millennium. Workers are now affected by such far-ranging factors as global competition, information technology, downsizing of businesses, and the shift from making products to providing services.

Psychologists are employed by businesses and organizations to help them cope with flux and the realities of daily business life. **Industrial/ organizational (I/O) psychologists** engage in activities such as the following:

- Devising psychological tests for recruitment of people for positions in industry and organizations
- Interviewing individuals who are being recruited for such positions
- Measuring performance on the job
- Motivating workers to increase productivity
- Enhancing job satisfaction
- Helping organizations function more efficiently
- Identifying and modifying stressors in the workplace
- Making person-machine systems user friendly and efficient
- Studying and modifying the behavior of consumers.

Currents in Industrial/Organizational Psychology

We have gone from an era in which we have tried to get the most out of people, to the soft, touchy-feely age. Now we have to go back and balance the two.

LILY KELLY-RADFORD (1998)

Various schools and fields of psychology have given birth to I/O psychology and influenced the directions it has taken. First is the testing movement, which focuses on the measurement of individual differences in personality and aptitudes (Landy, 1992). It assumes relationships among a person's intelligence, personality traits (e.g., sociable or shy, domineering or self-abasing), and aptitudes (e. g., mechanical or musical) on the one hand and the requirements of jobs on the other. People whose personal attributes fit the requirements of their jobs are better adjusted and more productive in their work.

Second is the human relations (or human potential) movement, as set forth by Carl Rogers and Abraham Maslow. Rogers argued that we possess unique talents and abilities. Ideally, the environment ought to encourage each of us to develop them. Abraham Maslow pointed out that people not only have needs for food, clothing, housing, and freedom from financial hardship. They also have needs for social interaction, achievement, approval and recognition, prestige and status, and the opportunity to explore and fulfill their unique potentials. From the human relations perspective, our work ought to help us meet these higher needs as well as supply a paycheck.

Third is the industrial-engineering movement. This movement has sparked interest in efficient, user-friendly person-machine systems and has prompted psychologists to become involved in human factors.

Many I/O psychologists also apply the behavioral and cognitive perspectives (Landy, 1992). Behavioral principles have been used in industry,

HUMAN FACTORS The field of psychology that focuses on making equipment and facilities compatible with human behavior patterns and mental processes.

APPLIED PSYCHOLOGY The application of fundamental psychological methods and knowledge to the investigation and solution of human problems.

INDUSTRIAL PSYCHOLOGY The field of psychology that studies the relationships between people and work.

ORGANIZATIONAL PSYCHOLOGY The field of psychology that studies the structure and functions of organizations.

for example, to train workers in step-by-step fashion, to modify problem work behaviors, and to make sure that workers are rewarded for targeted behaviors. When required work behaviors are made explicit and the reinforcers (e.g., raises, bonuses, promotions, and time off) for completing tasks are spelled out, morale rises and complaints about favoritism decrease. Companies as diverse as Chase Manhattan, Procter & Gamble, Ford, Standard Oil of Ohio, Emery Air Freight, General Electric, B. F. Goodrich, and Connecticut General Life Insurance have used behavior modification in some form.

The influences of cognitive psychology are being felt in issues ranging from biases in the appraisal of worker performance to the ways in which workers' information-processing capacities affect the design of work environments. Concerning appraisal of workers, for example, supervisors tend to rate employees according to how much they like them (Landy, 1992). They also evaluate hard workers more positively than other workers, even if they accomplish less (Tsui & O'Reilly, 1989). Concerning workers' ability to process information, psychologists help design work stations, such as computer work stations, which help workers understand how to use their electronic equipment. For example, they try to select user-friendly software that people can use in a more or less intuitive manner.

We consider some of the functions and findings of I/O psychologists in the areas of job recruitment, training, and evaluation.

Recruitment and Placement

People sometimes get hired for reasons that are irrelevant to their potential to perform in the job. Now and then, people are hired because they are physically attractive (Mack & Rainey, 1990). On other occasions, nepotism reigns, meaning that relatives or friends of friends get hired. By and large, however, businesses seek employees who can do the job and are likely to be reasonably satisfied with it. Employees who are satisfied with their jobs have lower absenteeism and turnover (quit) rates (Fowler, 1998). I/O psychologists facilitate recruitment by analyzing jobs, specifying the skills and personal attributes needed in a position, and constructing tests and interview procedures to determine whether job candidates have these skills and attributes. Hiring the right person for the job enhances job satisfaction and productivity (Katzell & Thompson, 1990; McGuire, 1998).

PERSONNEL TESTS Different kinds of jobs require different job skills, and many of these skills—or the ability to develop them—can be measured on personnel tests. The kinds of personnel tests commonly used in industry and by organizations include tests of (1) intellectual abilities, (2) spatial and mechanical abilities, (3) perceptual accuracy, (4) motor abilities, and (5) personality and interests. Assuming an individual is adequate in general intellectual functioning, an industry seeking to hire trainees for airplane mechanics is more likely to be interested in candidates' mechanical abilities, perceptual accuracy, and motor abilities—especially the fine motor skills involved in using tools. Test performances are correlated with success on the job to make sure that the tests predict what they are supposed to predict. As a matter of fact, people whose general intellectual ability is too high for humdrum assembly-line types of work may be considered "overqualified" and therefore poor risks for such positions.

Tests of mechanical comprehension are appropriate for many factory workers, construction workers, and of course, mechanics. They include items such as indicating which of two pairs of shears would cut metal better. Spatial-relations ability is needed in any job that requires the ability to visualize objects in three dimensions. Examples include drafting, clothing design, and architecture. Tests of perceptual accuracy are useful for clerical positions, such as bank tellers and secretaries. Some items on these tests require respondents to compare columns of letters, words, or numbers and indicate which do or do not match. Tests of motor abilities are useful for jobs that require strength, coordination, rapid reaction time, or dexterity. Moving furniture, driving certain kinds of equipment, and sewing all require some motor skills.

The relationships between personality and performance in a job are somewhat less clear. It seems logical that one might wish to hire a candidate for a sales position who has a strong need to persuade others. Many businesses have used personality tests to measure candidates' general "stability," however. Such use has sometimes been criticized as an invasion of privacy.

Interest inventories—tests that assess what people are and are not interested in—also help predict whether a person will function well in a certain occupation. For example, a person who is not interested in outdoor activities would probably not adjust well to life as a forest ranger or landscaper. A person who is interested in biological functions and in helping other people might perform well in one of the health professions. The level at which one functions also reflects specific aptitudes or general academic ability. For example, medical technicians (X-ray technicians, dental hygienists, blood analysts, and so on) may not require as high a level of intellectual functioning as that required of nurses, physical therapists, physicians, psychologists, and many other health professionals. Assessment of interests and aptitudes can help one zero in on a potentially fulfilling career.

Training and Instruction

One expert predicts that by 2110 it will take 50 percent of a work day to come up to speed with what's transpired since you left the day before.

PATRICK MCGUIRE (1998)

How can we prepare our organizations or our people to function in [the new millennium]? The way you will thrive in the marketplace is by living on chaos. There is the challenge of balancing work and home life when operating globally, 24 hours a day. With digital phones you can be reached any time. E-mail is filling up every hour. New items are coming in 24 hours a day. How do you balance that?

SEYMOUR ADLER (1998)

Worker training and instruction is the most commonly reported way of enhancing productivity (Katzell & Thompson, 1990). Training provides workers with appropriate skills. Equipping them to solve job problems also reduces the stress they encounter and enhances their feelings of self-worth. More than 90% of American corporations train their workers (Goldstein & Buxton, 1982). As we enter the new millennium, training is more important than ever because technology "continuously spawns new products and new markets that expect new and fast ways of doing things" (McGuire, 1998). I/O psychologists help organizations establish training goals and methods on the basis of (1) organizational analysis, (2) task analysis, and (3) person or worker analysis.

Organizational analysis is appraisal of the goals and resources—including its personnel and physical facilities—of the corporation or other institution. Consider IBM. The goals of IBM include such varied items as helping other organizations understand the ways in which electronic information processing can benefit them and how they can efficiently install it, manufacturing and selling microchips (the "brains" of computers) and computers, writing and selling software, identifying future markets, and pure scientific development (advancement of the sciences for their own sake, although commercial opportunities are certainly acted on). The resources of IBM include factory workers, managers, sales personnel, doctoral-level scientists, assorted assistants, and numerous physical facilities around the world. Organizational analysis helps organizations such as IBM determine what they need to accomplish. Then they can translate these needs into the refinement or creation of jobs and begin to focus on how to recruit and train people to do them.

Once jobs have been identified and defined, **task analysis** involves appraisal of the duties (breaking them down into subparts) required of a person placed in a given job. For example, a police officer is expected to carry out a wide range of duties, including but certainly not limited to patrolling neighborhoods to prevent crime, coming to the assistance of victims of crime, apprehending people suspected of committing crimes, counseling juveniles, giving street directions, controlling crowds, using weapons, even chasing animals and operating vehicles under varied weather conditions. I/O psychologists help organizations arrive at accurate lists of the duties required in a job title so that organizations can begin to consider how to train and instruct the people in these positions.

Person analysis deals with the question of who should be trained. Trainees can include the people who are already in a job and new recruits. A number of years ago, IBM had a policy of lifetime employment. When they eliminated a type of job, they always offered to retrain the workers for positions they needed to fill rather than sever them from the corporation. A former security guard at IBM told me that the company was going to be in trouble because they were retraining him to write software rather than hiring a more qualified outsider to replace him. Within a couple of years, it turned out that IBM went into a tailspin as its profits shrank. They then ended the lifetime employment policy and the company has since rebounded and moved ahead in new directions. I/O psychologists would probably have advised IBM that people who become security guards often (not always, of course) differ in personality and mental abilities from people who write software, and that training in itself may not be sufficient to enable an individual who has worked well in one of these areas to perform well and adjust to a job in the other area.

Once organization, task, and person analyses have been accomplished, I/O psychologists apply psychological knowledge of the principles of learning to help create training programs. They begin by listing learning objectives for employees that are consistent with the needs analysis. The learning objectives are designed to give employees the specific skills, the cognitive knowledge, and, sometimes, the attitudes they need to perform well on the job. Why attitudes? A factory worker might resist wearing protective devices, even when taught how to do so, if he has the attitude that safety devices are for sissies. I have observed barehanded gardeners injuring themselves on thorns and barehanded construction cleanup workers injuring themselves on glass shards, nails, and so on, all because of the self-defeating attitude that "real men" do not use protective gloves. A learning objective may be to train factory workers (and gardeners) to appreciate the value of wearing protective devices.

Once learning objectives are established, psychologists help devise ways to gain and maintain the workers' attention, to present materials in

ORGANIZATIONAL ANALYSIS Evaluation of the goals and resources of an organization.

TASK ANALYSIS The breaking down of a job or behavior pattern into its component parts.

PERSON ANALYSIS Determination of *who* should be trained to perform a given task.

TABLE A.1

CRITICISM—THE GOOD, THE BAD, AND THE UGLY	
CONSTRUCTIVE CRITICISM (GOOD)	**DESTRUCTIVE CRITICISM (BAD AND UGLY)**
Specific: The supervisor is specific about what the employee is doing wrong. For example, she or he says "This is what you did that caused the problem, and this is why it caused the problem."	**Vague:** The supervisor makes a blanket condemnation, such as, "That was an awful thing to do," or "That was a lousy job." No specifics are given.
Supportive: The supervisor gives the employee the feeling that the criticism is meant to help him or her perform better on the job.	**Condemnatory of the employee:** The supervisor attributes the problem to an unchangeable cause such as the employee's personality.
Helpful in problem solving: The supervisor helps employees improve things or solve their problems on the job.	**Threatening:** The supervisor attacks the employee, saying for example, "If you do this again, you'll be docked," or "Next time, you're fired."
Timely: The supervisor offers the criticism as soon as possible after the problem occurs.	**Pessimistic:** The supervisor seems doubtful that the employee will be able to improve.

step-by-step fashion, to promote retention, and to evaluate the effectiveness of the training program.

Appraisal of Workers' Performance

Workers fare better and productivity is enhanced when workers receive individualized guidance and reinforcers are based on accurate appraisal of their performance (Fowler, 1998). Criticism of workers' performance is necessary if workers are to improve, and it is important that criticisms be delivered constructively (Weisinger, 1990; see Table A.1). Destructive criticism saps workers' motivation and belief in their own ability to perform adequately. Constructive criticism helps workers feel that they are being shown how to perform better (Baron, 1990).

BIASES IN THE APPRAISAL PROCESS In an ideal world, appraisal of workers' performances would be based solely on how well they do their jobs (Fowler, 1998). Managers do give the largest salary increments to workers whose objective performances are rated most positively (Alexander & Barrett, 1982), but research into appraisal of performance shows that biases are also at work. One bias is a tendency for supervisors to focus on the *worker* rather than the worker's performance. Raters may form general impressions of workers and then evaluate them on the basis of these impressions rather than on how well they carry out their tasks (Isen & Baron, 1990). It also turns out that a supervisor is more likely to positively appraise the performance of a subordinate who is also a friend (Fiske, 1993; Hogan et al., 1994).

The tendency to rate workers according to general impressions (e.g., of liking or disliking) is an example of the **halo effect.** The halo effect can be overcome by instructing raters to focus on how well workers perform specific tasks rather than on their feelings about them.

Behavioral I/O psychologists suggest that the criteria for appraisal be objective. They should be publicly observable behaviors that are outlined to workers and supervisors beforehand (Katzell & Thompson, 1990). Workers are ideally rated according to whether they complete their tasks. Workers are not penalized for things that are difficult to define, such as "poor attitude." Task analysis allows managers to create objective standards.

Another bias in appraisal is the tendency to evaluate workers according to how much effort they put into their work (Dugan, 1989; Knowlton

HALO EFFECT The tendency for one's general impression of a person to influence one's perception of aspects of, or performances by, that person.

& Mitchell, 1980). Supervisors often focus on employees' efforts, sometime more so than on their performance. Hard work is not necessarily good work, however. (Should students who work harder than you do be given higher grades on tests, even when you get the answers right and they make errors?)

Social psychologists have observed that we tend to overestimate the role of dispositional (internal) factors in our attributions for other people's behavior. That is, we assume they do what they do because of their own choice and will (dispositional or internal factors), and not because of the situations in which they find themselves (situational or external factors). This tendency to overestimate the role of dispositional factors extends into the workplace (Mohrman et al., 1989). For example, in the 1980s U.S. workers were criticized for flagging productivity. As productivity in Japan and some other nations began to equal or surpass our own, there was a tendency to assume that U.S. workers were lazy (a dispositional factor). More perceptive critics of the workplace noted that situational factors such as the greater use of robots in foreign countries have contributed to the (apparent) lagging of U.S. workers. However, at the turn of the millennium, U.S. productivity is up, and it has become clearer that external factors such as interest rates, technological innovations, and corporate efficiency may be more important keys to productivity than internal factors are. This recognition brings us to a consideration of the nature of organizations—how they work, and why.

Organizational Theory

The real challenge for organizations that I think psychology is going to be uniquely capable of helping is creating coordination and commitment.

SEYMOUR ADLER (1998)

Organizations are moving toward flatter, more flexible structures with fewer levels of supervision and more wide-ranging job descriptions. So there is less likelihood of a very stable structured job where you can write down what you will do for the next 20 years.

KEVIN MURPHY (1998)

You're going to need leaders who can manage diversity beyond the traditional sense of race and gender. I mean diversity in individuals with different psychological needs, like outsourced contractors or in-house team players.

MITCHELL MARKS (1998)

CORPORATE IDENTITY.
Corporations, like people, can be thought of as having personalities or identities. The Transamerica "pyramid" in San Francisco was designed to help lend the corporation a jaunty, upward-looking appearance. The pyramid also dominates the San Francisco skyline, which may be suggestive of permanence and strength.

Organizations are composed of individuals, but they can have natures of their own. Organizations have formal characteristics such as chains of command, channels of communication, and policies concerning hiring, compensation, and retirement. They also have informal characteristics such as "personalities," which may be impersonal and cold, warm and familylike, authoritarian, or permissive (Schein, 1990). Netscape recently merged with America Online. Netscape employees had traditionally worn blue jeans, brought their dogs to work, and tossed Frisbees around the lawn during breaks. America Online was more straitlaced or "buttoned down." When the merger took place, executives on both sides were concerned about a clashing of corporate cultures.

The traits of individuals involve relatively stable ways of responding to the demands of life. The characteristics of organizations also form traits.

These traits are consistent ways in which organizations respond to economic, political, and other challenges to organizational life. As with individuals, we speak of corporations as adapting or failing to adapt to environments, such as a recession, inflation, a booming market, and laws and regulations. We speak of them as growing and thriving or as being sick and dying or disintegrating.

Organizational adaptations may be required if businesses are to remain competitive. Many corporations heighten their competitiveness by restructuring the organization of the company to cut costs, for example. We speak of them as becoming "leaner and meaner." Many corporations once considered too large and bound by tradition to adapt to a rapidly changing business world, such as IBM and AT&T, have changed their personalities and acquired "lean and hungry" looks.

As with other areas of psychology, there are different theoretical approaches to structuring organizations. Three broad approaches are in use today: *classic organization theories, contingency theories,* and *human relations theories*. **Classic organization theories** propose that there is one best way to structure an organization—from the skeleton outward. Organization is based on the required levels of authority and supervision. Classic organization theories frequently rely on a **bureaucracy**, which ideally frees workers from the injustices of favoritism and nepotism and enables them to make long-range plans. From these required levels of authority and supervision come division of labor and the delegation of authority.

Contingency theories hold that there are many valid ways to structure organizations and that organizational approaches are *contingent on* factors such as organizational goals, workers' characteristics, and the political or economic environment. A classic bureaucracy might make sense when timeliness and accuracy in production are central corporate objectives. When scientific innovation is the major goal, however, a less centralized and authoritarian organization—such as the one that characterized Netscape—might encourage individual experimentation and creativity.

Human relations theories begin structuring with the individual, the worker. They argue that the behavior of the organization cannot be predicted or controlled without considering the characteristics and needs of the worker. From this perspective, efficient organizational structure reflects the cognitive processes of individuals as these processes are applied to problem solving, decision making, and the quests for self-expression and self-fulfillment. Let us consider three human relations approaches: McGregor's Theory Y, Argyris's developmental theory, and Ouichi's Theory Z.

HUMAN RELATIONS APPROACHES Douglas McGregor's (1960) **Theory Y** is based on the idea that workers are motivated to assume responsibility and that worker indifference and misbehavior stem from shortcomings of the organization. Theory Y holds that management's central task is to structure the organization so that organizational goals fit with workers'-goals. Workers cannot be expected to be productive if their personal goals are at odds with those of the organization.

Chris Argyris (1972) notes a number of developmental principles and suggests that organizations are structured efficiently when they allow their workers to develop. Argyris notes that individuals develop (1) from passive to active organisms, (2) from dependent to independent organisms, (3) from organisms capable of dealing with concrete issues to organisms capable of dealing with abstract issues, and (4) from organisms with few abilities to organisms with many abilities.

CLASSIC ORGANIZATION THEORIES Theories that hold that organizations should be structured from the skeleton (governing body) outward.

BUREAUCRACY An administrative system characterized by departments and subdivisions whose members frequently are given long tenure and inflexible work tasks.

CONTINGENCY THEORIES Theories that hold that organizational structure should depend on factors such as goals, workers' characteristics, and the overall economic or political environment.

HUMAN-RELATIONS THEORIES Theories that hold that efficient organizations are structured according to the characteristics and needs of the individual worker.

THEORY Y McGregor's view that organizational goals should be congruent with workers' goals.

Organizations should therefore encourage workers to assume more responsibility and develop their skills as time goes on. Otherwise, workers may experience frustration, which hurts job satisfaction and productivity.

Ouchi's (1981) **Theory Z** combined some of the positive features of the Japanese workplace with some of the realities of the U.S. workplace to foster company loyalty and heighten productivity. Perhaps the most prominent feature of many Japanese workplaces has been their paternalism. That is, they offered security through lifetime employment, involvement of workers' families in company activities, and the subsidizing of housing and education for workers' families. Many U.S. firms, in contrast, lay off workers with every economic downturn. Ouchi's theory compromised by suggesting that U. S. firms offer long-term employment when possible. Restructuring to avoid layoffs would also enhance workers' loyalty.

There is traditionally a high division of labor and specialization in the U.S. workplace, leading to feelings of being pigeonholed and lack of a sense of control over the whole product. Japanese career paths have tended to be relatively nonspecialized, allowing for sideways movement and variety. Again, Theory Z suggests the compromise of a moderately specialized career path. In the traditional U.S. workplace, decision making and responsibility are in the hands of relatively few supervisors. In Japan, decision making tends to be consensual—and responsibility collective. In Japan, moreover, managers often eat with laborers and share their bathrooms. Theory Z also suggests that managers in the United States can enhance employee job satisfaction, loyalty, and productivity by taking measures that increase employees' sense of participation in the decision-making process. Although the Japanese are highly competitive in the world marketplace, managers within given firms tend to reach decisions by means of consensus, in contrast to the typical U.S. winner-take-all approach. Therefore, another Theory-Z Japanese import is a consensus management system in which managers tend to feel that "nobody has lost."

Theory Z was developed at a time when the Japanese economy was on the upswing and many organizations and workers in the United States were concerned about the ability of the United States to sustain economic growth, compete in the world marketplace, and create new jobs. But as the world was preparing to enter the new millennium, Japan's organizations were becoming less paternalistic and the economy of the United States was once again booming. Therefore, many business people concluded that Theory Z held few answers for them.

Psychologists are highly concerned with the dignity of the individual. They thus tend to gravitate toward human relations approaches—organizational structures that allow for workers' self-development and self-satisfaction. In many cases, this leaning also heightens productivity.

WORK SCHEDULES   When there is no company reason for maintaining a strict 9 to 5 schedule, workers frequently profit from **flextime,** being able to modify their own schedules to meet their personal needs. In one approach to flextime, workers put in four 10-hour workdays, rather than five 8-hour days. In another, workers select 4-hour work blocs (Kahn & Rohe, 1998). Such policies are family friendly in that they better enable workers to meet both the demands of their employers and their children (Clay, 1998). Flextime increases worker effectiveness and job satisfaction, and lowers the absentee and quit rates (Clay, 1998).

At Honeywell, a "mothers' shift" allows women to coordinate their work schedules with school hours. Mothers may also have college students fill in for them during their children's summer vacations. Are we ready for a "fathers' shift"?

TRUTH OR FICTION REVISITED
It is not true that allowing employees to piece together their own work schedules (flextime) is demoralizing to workers and interferes with productivity. Flextime can help workers cope with parenthood, for example, and as a result boost their morale on the job.

THEORY Z Ouchi's view that adapts positive features of the Japanese workplace to the U.S. workplace.

FLEXTIME Adaptation of work schedules to help meet workers' personal needs.

PSYCHOLOGY IN A WORLD OF *Diversity*

TRIBAL PRACTICES RAISE WORKER MORALE[1]

Integrating Native American tribal practices into the management of a work team may improve morale and increase workers' sense of purpose, according to an evaluation of a workplace intervention.

Psychologist Ira S. Katz was looking for a way to improve morale, effectiveness, and communication among the members of a research team at Silver Dollar City, a family entertainment company in Branson, Missouri. The team surveys the general public to help the company better understand its customers. The workers, most of them part-time employees, were bored, generally unhappy, and not working well as a team.

Katz proposed to the team's manager, Mark Acosta, that they try to integrate some Native American themes into the team's management. In particular, Katz and Acosta wanted to give workers more of a sense of meaning and purpose through certain tribal practices, including the idea that everyone on the team has an equal voice.

For example, the group calls its meetings "tribal councils." And everyone has equal status at the meetings. When someone wishes to talk—and everyone is encouraged to do so—he or she holds the "talking stick." Everyone must be silent and listen. "Using the talking stick is a lesson in living in the moment," says Katz. "These techniques give people undiluted air time, and suddenly we begin to see walls [people have put up] become less of a barrier to communication."

Although the team has a hierarchical structure, Acosta tries to emphasize that all levels of the team are integral. "Just like a totem pole, you can't have the highest level without the lowest," says Katz. "We teach them to be reverential of others' abilities and expertise.

Through a series of employee surveys and interviews comparing the research team with another team at Silver Dollar City that does not use the tribal practices, Katz finds that the intervention is improving morale and the effectiveness of the team. "People are raising issues and being more open with their ideas and concerns," says Katz. "I've seen a wonderful transition from a highly dependent culture to a more independent culture. And team members are noticeably happier in their jobs." ∎

[1]Adapted from Azar, B. (1998). Tribal practices raise worker morale. *APA Monitor* 29(7), 8.

HUMAN FACTORS

I was griping earlier about the ways in which displays are coded. The controls of my stove, shower, and car hassle me because they are arbitrary, inconvenient, and, to some degree, dangerous. In other words, they are "user unfriendly." Psychologists in human factors apply knowledge of biology, sensation and perception, learning, memory, and motivation in enhancing the efficiency and safety of person-machine systems and work environments.

Criteria for Evaluating Person-Machine Systems and Work Environments

Psychologists have been involved in human factors for more than 100 years. In 1898, APA president Hugo Munsterberg studied industrial safety.

In evaluating the efficiency and safety of stoves and other kinds of equipment, human-factors psychologists use performance criteria, physiological criteria, subjective criteria, and accident-and-injury criteria.

Performance criteria involve the quality of the performance made possible by the design. For example, how rapidly can the task (such as finding the proper water temperature in the shower!) be carried out? Can it be performed without making errors? (Am I likely to turn on the correct burner of the stove?)

Physiological criteria involve the physical changes caused by operating the equipment. For example, are switches difficult to throw? Does working in a certain factory raise the blood pressure or damage the lungs? Does the screen of the computer monitor cause eye strain? Does the keyboard contribute to carpal tunnel syndrome?

Subjective criteria include psychological factors such as boredom and job satisfaction. For many people, assembly-line work is boring and non-satisfying. There can be high absenteeism and turnover in such humdrum positions. Keyboards are more enjoyable to work when they make responsive clacks. Quiet keyboards are frustrating. Computer programmers also attempt to choose pleasing color combinations for the screen.

Accident and injury criteria involve the ways in which industrial designs foster or prevent accidents and injuries. Are we at risk of burning our hands (or our houses down!) when we cannot readily find the control that governs the burner? Fortunately, I have not yet been injured in the shower, but making the water hotter when I think I am cooling it down could have dangerous consequences. How many times do we injure ourselves by using dangerous tools? Part of the problem may lie in failure to follow rules of safety. Tools are often not as safe in design as they could be, however.

Criteria for Evaluating the Coding in Displays

I don't want you to think that I'm obsessed with my stove, so I'll talk about word processing for a minute. My computer keyboard has nicely marked keys that say "Insert" and "Delete." With an old keyboard, however, I had to press a function key simultaneously with keys for regular letters. It wasn't too difficult, however, because the "D" key was used for deleting and the "S" key, which is next to it, was used for inserting. Think of the designer's quandary: Should the "S" or "I" key be used to insert material? The "I" key begins with the proper letter, but the "S" key sits next to the "D" key and in the section of the keyboard that houses all the codes. It worked out fine.

The MEN and WOMEN rest room signs are adequate for people who read English, and CABALLEROS and DAMAS are helpful for speakers of Spanish. But the universal nonverbal code is a stick figure of a man or woman. Here the code (the figure) is inherently related to the function of the design. That is, one door is meant for men to walk through, the other for women. Consider, however, an arbitrary but popular code: Decaffeinated coffee is often served from pots that are color coded orange. If you think about it logically, perhaps decaffeinated coffee should be color coded green or blue. Orange is a warm color, and oranges and reds are more likely than greens and blues to be used to signal danger or increases in intensity. Because caffeine is the "dangerous" substance, shouldn't caffeinated coffee be coded orange or red? Nevertheless, practice seems to defeat logic.

Good codes have the following characteristics:

- *Detectability.* Good codes are readily detected or sensed. I have difficulty detecting the gas tank cover release lever because it is out of

AN INTIMIDATING DISPLAY.
Display panels of modern instruments can be overwhelming unless their coding is helpful. I/O psychologists attribute the following characteristics to good coding: detectability, discriminability, compatibility, meaningfulness, standardizations, and multidimensionality.

sight (down along the side of my seat). We place "shortcuts" to programs on our computer "desktops" to make them more readily detectable than the program-execute files, which are hidden somewhere within the "file folders" of the computer.

- *Discriminability.* Good codes can be discriminated from other symbols of the same kind. My gas tank cover release switch is next to the hood and trunk releases, and the three are similar in design—not easy to tell apart.

- *Compatibility.* Good codes are consistent with our expectations. The stick figure of a man is compatible with our expectation that the room being coded is the "men's room." For reasons noted, the color orange is incompatible with *de*caffeinated coffee.

- *Meaningfulness.* When possible, good codes symbolize the information in question. The stick figure of the man symbolizes men. The "do not enter" symbol is a meaningful barrier. The meaning of orange as the symbol for decaffeinated coffee runs contrary to the color's "meaning," however. One icon on the toolbar of my word-processing program is an opening file; you click it to access a file (Figure A.1). Another icon is a drawing of a diskette; you click it to save the file you are working on. You click a boldfaced **b** to boldface, and you click an italicized *i* to italicize. All these are meaningful icons.

- *Standardization.* When possible, the same code should be used universally. Consistency in usage could be the saving grace of using the color orange to signify decaffeinated coffee. Using green to mean "go" and red to mean "stop" is universal in traffic lights. Nearly all programs for Windows have the word "File" in a bar across the top of the monitor, and when you click the bar you can expect a "drop-down" menu to appear that allows you to "Close" the file or "Exit" the program, among other things. (It drives me to . . . read the "Methods of Therapy" chapter . . . when I am playing with my 8-year-old in one of her programs and there is no apparent way to exit the thing!)

- *Multidimensionality.* Codes are made easier to recognize when they employ two or more dimensions. Traffic stop signs, for example, employ a hexagonal shape and are red in color. A green stop sign would confuse drivers and create hazardous crossings. Red traffic lights are always on top or on the left. They are also always arranged red, amber, green. You might not ever think about this array, but if you drove up to an intersection with a different grouping, it would not feel right, and there might be accidents. Two senses alert me to the presence of e-mail when I go online: A red flag pops up and I hear "You've Got Mail."

Psychologists who engage in human-factors design, like other psychologists, use research methods to develop and test their ideas. In addition to deriving design concepts from psychological theory, they try them out

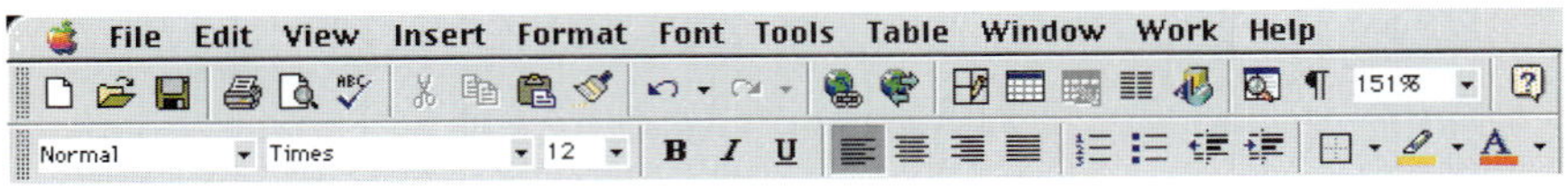

FIGURE A.1
THE TOOLBAR OF A WORD-PROCESSING PROGRAM.
The icons such as the opening file, the diskette, the boldfaced **b,** and the italicized *i* are intended to be meaningful so the user can easily determine what to click to achieve a certain result.

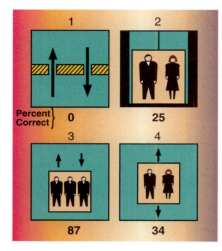

FIGURE A.2
ELEVATOR SYMBOLS.

Psychologists in human factors evaluate symbols' effectiveness at communicating ideas. Which of these symbols best signifies an elevator to you?

CONSUMER PSYCHOLOGY The field of psychology that studies the nature, causes, and modification of consumer behavior and mental processes.

before implementing them. Consider, for example, the four designs in Figure A.2. Which telegraphs itself as the best symbol for an elevator? As you can see from the numbers beneath the designs, the third was identified as the symbol for an elevator by 87% of the participants in one study (Mackett-Stout & Dewar, 1981). *None* correctly identified the symbol on the left. From this type of research, the more effective designs would be selected. If no code were correctly identified by the great majority of those queried, perhaps designers would return to the drawing board.

Figure A.3 provides some other examples of good symbols. Part A of Figure A.4 shows my problem with the electric stove: The burners are grouped in a square, but the controls form a line. In his book *The Psychology of Everyday Things,* psychologist Donald Norman (1988) agrees with me that if the controls were in a square pattern that corresponded to the arrangement of the burners (see part B of Figure A.4), I wouldn't be heating the air and pouring ice-cold water over my poor wife's tea bags. (I wouldn't refer to Norman if he disagreed with me.) Finally, note how the shape-coded cockpit control knobs in Figure A.5 discourage a pilot from accidentally activating the wrong mechanism.

Human-factors engineers participate in the development of products for consumers. In the following section, we see how psychologists study and help influence the behavior of consumers.

CONSUMER PSYCHOLOGY

Consumer psychology applies psychological research methods to the investigation and modification of consumer behavior and mental processes. We encounter topics of concern to consumer psychologists every day. Here is just a brief list:

- Why are consumers loyal to a brand? For example, why do consumers buy Miller beer or Budweiser?

- What characteristics do consumers attribute to various brands? For example, what are consumers' impressions of American cars compared with Japanese cars and German cars?

- How can consumer attitudes toward products be modified? How can brand images be enhanced? For example, how can consumers be persuaded that the reliability of American cars and electronic devices is improving? Why did American Express Company hire Jerry Seinfeld to promote the use of its credit cards?

FIGURE A.3
VISUAL-CODE SYMBOLS.

Psychologists in human factors apply knowledge of sensation and perception in the design of effective visual-code symbols.

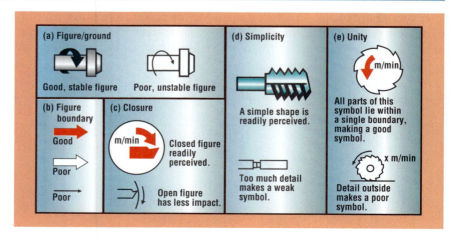

• What is the best way to market a new product? Should there be a national advertising blitz, or should the product first be tested in a local market?

Task Analysis of Consumer Behavior

Consumer psychologists have undertaken task analyses of consumer behavior and found that it often involves a number of steps: deciding to make a purchase, selecting the brand, shopping, buying the product, and evaluating how well it meets one's needs (Robertson et al., 1984). Consumer psychologists study ways of intervening at each stage to enhance the probability that consumers will decide to make a purchase and choose a certain brand. Advertising is used not only to help consumers tell brands apart but also to encourage them to buy. Packaging similarly helps consumers distinguish between brands. If the packages are "pretty" enough, consumers may assume that "good things" come in them. First impressions count in the supermarket as well as in interpersonal relationships.

An experiment by Julie Baker and her colleagues provides an example of research into consumer behavior. The researchers recruited 147 undergraduates and exposed them to a combination of environmental factors (music and lighting) and social factors (such as the friendliness of employees) in a store. The environmental and social factors stimulated the students and made them feel good. As a result, they were more likely to make purchases. There is an expression in business—"The customer comes first." Psychological research suggests that when store managers put the customer first by creating a pleasant physical environment and training employees to "put on a happy face," sales go up.

Marketing Research

Consumer psychologists have shown marketing managers how to test hypotheses concerning the effectiveness of advertising and marketing through marketing research. In this method, a consumer population is targeted—for example, women, baby boomers, or teenagers. Representative samples are then drawn from the target population. Their responses to product names, ads, packages, and the products themselves are measured. Taste tests of soft drinks apply methods used by psychologists who study sensation and perception. Consumer psychologists find ways of having drinkers indicate their preferences for the flavors of various beverages. Participants may simply report that they prefer brand A over the notorious brand X. Or they may rate each drink on, for example, scales from 1 to 10 according to variables such as sweetness, general liking, and so on.

In applying principles of social psychology, consumer psychologists also study the factors that enhance advertisements' persuasiveness. For example, does sex sell? Are cars made more appealing to viewers when an attractive woman drives them or yearns for the male driver? And what about all those sexy jeans ads? Consumer psychologists have found that although some ads catch the eye, you may remember the models but forget the product when the ad is too sexy (Rathus et al., 2000).

Social psychologists have found that if we like people, we are more likely to approach them and talk to them. Do you think that if we like an advertisement, we are more likely to buy the product, however? Not necessarily. Consumer psychologists have found that it does not matter whether a commercial is likable or irritating. What is important is that the viewer can remember the product and when to use it (Baron & Byrne, 1997).

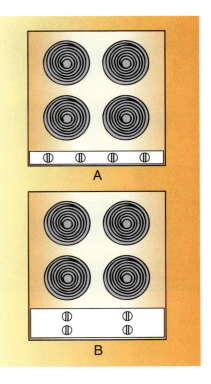

FIGURE A.4

TWO STOVE-TOP CONFIGURATIONS.

Well-designed regulation systems are readily interpreted by users (are user friendly). Which control regulates which burner? Is it easier to determine which regulates which in stove-top A or stove-top B?

TRUTH OR FICTION REVISITED
It is not true that TV commercials must be likable if they are to influence us to buy the advertised products. It is sufficient that commercials prompt the viewer to remember the product and when to use it.

FIGURE A.5

SHAPE-CODED CONTROL KNOBS.

How does the shape of each airplane control knob help signal its function?

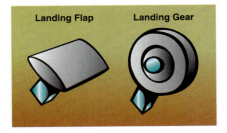

WHAT IS OUR IMPACT ON PLANET EARTH?
People's impact on planet Earth has been less than benevolent. Environmental psychologists study the ways in which people and the physical environment influence each other. One concern of environmental psychologists is finding ways to persuade people to change their environmental behavior.

We noted that customers are more likely to make purchases when store managers create pleasant physical environments for them. Let us now consider what psychologists have learned about the ways in which people behave within the larger physical environment—the world at large.

ENVIRONMENTAL PSYCHOLOGY

What do you picture when you hear the phrase "the environment"? Is it vast acres of wilderness? Is it deep, rolling oceans? Or do you picture seagulls and ducks coated in gunk as a result of an oil spill? Do you think of billowing summer storm clouds and refreshing rain, or do you conjure up visions of crowded sidewalks and acid rain? All this—the beauty and the horror—is the territory of environmental psychology.

Environmental psychologists study the ways in which people and the physical environment influence each other. As people, we have needs that must be met if we are to remain physically and psychologically healthy. Environmental conditions such as temperature and population density affect our capacities to meet these needs. People also affect the environment. We have pushed back forests and driven many species to extinction. In recent years, our impact has mushroomed. So have the controversies over the greenhouse effect, the diminution of the ozone layer, and acid rain. Many of us have an aesthetic interest in the environment and appreciate the remaining pockets of wilderness. Protecting the environment also ultimately means protecting ourselves—for it is in the environment that we flourish or fade away.

In this section, we touch on environmental activism. We then consider some findings of environmental psychologists concerning the effects of atmospheric conditions, noise, heat, and crowding.

Environmental Activism

Because people cause much environmental damage, environmental psychologists try to find ways to persuade people to change their environmental behavior (Stokols, 1992). Most people consider themselves pro-environment. Many think of themselves as "environmentalists." People may not put their behaviors where their mouths are, however, as shown by the fact that many people believe that they are conserving natural resources more so than they actually are (Hamilton, 1985). Many people are unaware of the individual impact they have on the environment—for example, how much electricity, natural gas, and water they consume (Kushler, 1989). Research has shown that when people obtain accurate information on the resources they use—and squander—they are more likely to modify their behavior. When home owners begin to read their meters and check for drafts, they become more likely to weatherize their homes (Aronson, 1990).

According to **cognitive-dissonance theory,** people find it unpleasant when they hold conflicting views on an issue or when they behave in a way that is inconsistent with their attitudes. People are therefore motivated to behave in ways that are consistent with their beliefs. Research into cognitive-dissonance theory has shown that we may change our attitudes when we are compelled to change our behavior. In that way, we reduce the discrepancy between our attitudes and our behavior. People who must conform to antidiscrimination laws may become less prejudiced. People may similarly grumble when "bottle bills" are passed—laws that require them to pay high deposits on bottled beverages and return the used bottles to regain their money. As time passes, however, their

ENVIRONMENTAL PSYCHOLOGY The field of psychology that studies the ways in which people and the environment influence each other.

COGNITIVE-DISSONANCE THEORY The view that we are motivated to make our cognitions or beliefs consistent.

behavior tends to conform and their attitudes tend to grow positive (Kahle & Beatty, 1987). Similar patterns are found when communities legislate the recycling of aluminum cans, newspapers, and bottles.

Noise: Of Muzak, Rock 'n' Roll, and Low-Flying Aircraft

Environmental psychologists apply knowledge of sensation and perception to design environments that produce positive emotional responses and contribute to human performance. They may thus suggest soundproofing certain environments or using pleasant background sounds such as music or recordings of water in natural environments (rain, the beach, brooks, and so on). Noise can be aversive, however—especially loud noise (Staples, 1996). How do you react when chalk is scraped on the blackboard or when an airplane screeches low overhead?

The decibel (dB) is used to express the loudness of noise. The hearing threshold is defined as zero dB. Your school library is probably about 30 to 40 dB. A freeway is about 70 dB. One hundred forty dB is painfully loud, and 150 dB can rupture your eardrums. After 8 hours of exposure to 110 to 120 dB, your hearing may be damaged (rock groups play at this level). High noise levels are stressful and can lead to illnesses such as hypertension, neurological and intestinal disorders, and ulcers (Cohen et al., 1986; Staples, 1996).

High noise levels also impair daily functioning. They foster forgetfulness, perceptual errors, even dropping things (Cohen et al., 1986). Children exposed to greater traffic noise on the lower floors of apartment complexes or to loud noise from low-flying airplanes at their schools may experience stress, hearing loss, and impairments in learning and memory. Time to adjust and subsequent noise abatement do not seem to reverse their cognitive and perceptual deficits (Cohen et al., 1986).

Couples may enjoy high noise levels at the disco, but grating noises of 80 dB seem to decrease feelings of attraction. They cause couples to stand farther apart. Loud noise also dampens helping behavior. People are less likely to help pick up a dropped package when the background noise of a construction crew is at 92 dB than when it is at 72 dB (Staples, 1996). They are even less willing to make change for a quarter.

If you and your date have had a fight and are then exposed to a sudden tire blowout, look out. Angered people are more likely to behave aggressively when exposed to a sudden noise of 95 dB than one of 55 dB (Donnerstein & Wilson, 1976).

Temperature: Getting Hot Under the Collar

Environmental psychologists also study the ways in which temperature can facilitate or impair behavior and mental processes. Extremes of heat can make excessive demands on our bodies' circulatory systems, leading to dehydration, heat exhaustion, and heat stroke. When it is too cold, the body responds by attempting to generate and retain heat. For example, the metabolism increases and blood vessels in the skin constrict, decreasing flow of blood to the periphery of the body.

Despite their obvious differences, both hot and cold temperatures are aversive events with some similar consequences, the first of which is increased arousal. A number of studies suggest that moderate shifts in temperature are mildly arousing. They may thus facilitate learning and performance, increase feelings of attraction, and have other positive effects. Extreme temperatures cause performance and activity levels to decline, however.

AT THE DISCO. Couples may enjoy high noise levels (up to 140 dB) at the discotheque. Less desirable noises of only 80 dB, however, can decrease feelings of attraction, put a damper on helping behavior, and contribute to aggressive behavior.

Environmental psychologists point out that small changes in arousal tend to get our attention, motivate us to perform, and facilitate the performance of tasks—whether we are talking about writing a term paper, working on an assembly line, or public speaking. Great increases in arousal, like those that can result from very high or very low temperatures, are uncomfortable and interfere with performing complex tasks. We try to cope with uncomfortable temperatures through clothing, air conditioning, or traveling to areas with milder climes. Extreme temperatures can sap our ability to cope.

Heat apparently makes some people hot under the collar. That is, high temperatures are connected with aggression. The frequency of car honking at traffic lights in Phoenix increases with the temperature (Kenrick & Mac-Farlane, 1986). In Houston, murders and rapes are most likely to occur when the temperature is in the 90s F (Anderson & DeNeve, 1992). In Raleigh, North Carolina, the incidence of rape and aggravated assault escalates with the average monthly temperature (Cohn, 1990; Simpson & Perry, 1990).

Some psychologists (e.g., Anderson & DeNeve, 1992) suggest that the probability of aggressive behavior continues to increase as the temperature soars. Other psychologists (e.g., Bell, 1992) argue that once temperatures become extreme, people tend to avoid aggressive behavior so that they will not be doubly struck by hot temper and hot temperature. The evidence does not absolutely support either view. Thus the issue remains, well, heated.

Truth or Fiction Revisited
It is true that heat makes some people hot under the collar—that is, it increases the likelihood of aggression.

Of Aromas and Air Pollution: Facilitating, Fussing, and Fuming

Environmental psychologists also investigate the effects of odors ranging from perfumes to auto fumes, industrial smog, cigarette smoke, fireplaces, even burning leaves. For example, the lead in auto fumes may impair children's intellectual functioning in the same way that eating lead paint does.

Carbon monoxide, a colorless, odorless gas found in cigarette smoke, auto fumes, and smog, decreases the capacity of the blood to carry oxygen. Carbon monoxide impairs learning ability and perception of the passage of time. It may also contribute to highway accidents. Residents of Los Angeles, New York, and various other major cities are accustomed to warnings to remain indoors or to be inactive in order to reduce air consumption when atmospheric conditions allow smog to accumulate. In December 1952, high amounts of smog collected in London, causing nearly 4,000 deaths (Schenker, 1993). High levels of air pollution have also been connected with higher mortality rates in U.S. cities (Dockery et al., 1993).

People tend to become psychologically accustomed to air pollution. For example, newcomers to polluted regions such as Southern California are more concerned about the air quality than long-term residents (Evans et al., 1982). Acceptance of pollution backfires when long-term illnesses result.

Unpleasant smelling pollutants, like other forms of aversive stimulation, decrease feelings of attraction and heighten aggression (Baron & Byrne, 1997).

Crowding and Personal Space: "Don't Burst My Bubble, Please"

Psychologists distinguish between "density" and "crowding." *Density* refers to the number of people in an area. *Crowding* suggests an aversive high-density social situation. (In other words, *crowding* is used to mean that we are "too close for comfort.")

When are we too close for comfort? It happens that all instances of density are not equal. Whether we feel crowded depends on who is thrown in with us and our interpretation of the situation (Baron & Byrne, 1997). (One student of mine reported that she had not at all minded being crowded in by the Dallas Cowboys football players who surrounded her on an airplane ride.) Environmental psychologists apply principles of information processing and social psychology in explaining why.

A fascinating experiment illustrates the importance of cognitive factors—in this case, our interpretations of our arousal—in transforming high density into crowding. Worchel and Brown (1984) showed small groups of people films when the people were spaced comfortably apart or uncomfortably close. There were four different films. Three were arousing (either humorous, sexual, or violent), and one was just plain boring.

As shown in Figure A.6, viewers who sat more closely together generally felt more crowded than those seated farther apart. Note that those who were seated far enough apart uniformly rated the seating arrangements as uncrowded. Among those who were seated too close for comfort, viewers of the boring (unarousing) film felt most crowded. Viewers of the arousing films felt less crowded. Why? The researchers suggest that viewers who were packed in could explain their arousal in terms of their response to the content of the films. Viewers of the unarousing film could not. They were therefore likely to attribute their arousal to the seating arrangements.

PSYCHOLOGICAL MODERATORS OF THE IMPACT OF HIGH DEN-SITY A sense of control enhances psychological hardiness. Examples from everyday life suggest that a sense of control—of choice—over the situation also helps us cope with the stress of being packed in. When we are at a concert, a disco, or a sports event, we may encounter higher density than we do in those frustrating ticket lines. But we may be having a wonderful time.

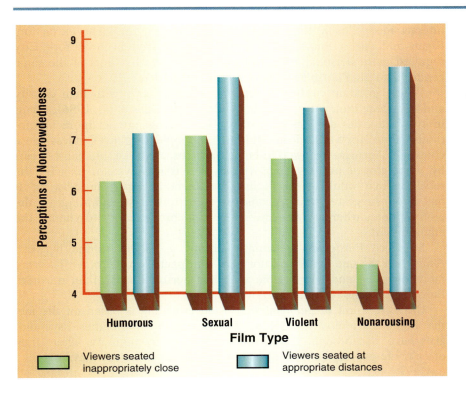

FIGURE A.6

TYPE OF FILM AND APPRAISAL OF HIGH-DENSITY SEATING.

In a study by Worchel and Brown (1984), viewers seated inappropriately close or at appropriate distances watched four kinds of films. Of the individuals seated too closely, those who could attribute their arousal to the film were less likely to experience crowding than those who could not.

Why? We have *chosen* to be at the concert and are focusing on our good time (unless a tall or noisy person sits in front of us). We feel in control.

We tend to moderate the effects of high density in subway cars and other mass transportation vehicles by ignoring fellow passengers and daydreaming, by reading newspapers and books, and by finding humor in the situation. Some people catch a snooze and wake up just before their stop.

SOME EFFECTS OF CITY LIFE Big city dwellers are more likely to experience stimulus overload and fear crime than suburbanites and rural folk. Overwhelming crowd stimulation, bright lights, shop windows, and so on, cause them to narrow their perceptions to a particular face, destination, or job. The pace of life literally picks up—pedestrians walk faster in bigger cities (Sadalla et al., 1990).

City dwellers are less willing to shake hands with, make eye contact with, or help, strangers (Milgram, 1977; Newman & McCauley, 1977). People who move to the city from more rural areas adjust by becoming more deliberate in their daily activities. They plan ahead to take safety precautions, and they increase their alertness to potential dangers.

Farming, anyone?

PERSONAL SPACE One adverse effect of crowding is the invasion of **personal space,** which is an invisible boundary, sort of a bubble, that surrounds you. You are likely to become anxious and, perhaps, angry when others invade your space. This may happen when someone sits down across from or next to you in an otherwise empty cafeteria or stands too close in an elevator. Personal space appears to serve protective and communicative functions.

People sit and stand closer to people of the same race, similar age, or similar socioeconomic status. Dating couples come closer together as the attraction between them increases.

North Americans and northern Europeans apparently distance themselves from others more so than southern Europeans, Asians, and Middle Easterners do (Baron & Byrne, 1997). A study by Pagan and Aiello (1982) suggests the contribution of cultural experiences. Puerto Ricans tend to interact more closely than Americans of northern European extraction. Pagan and Aiello found that Puerto Ricans reared in New York City required more personal space when interacting with others of the same gender than did Puerto Ricans reared in Puerto Rico.

People in some cultures apparently learn to cope with high density and also share their ways of coping with others (Gillis et al., 1986). Asians in crowded cities such as Tokyo and Hong Kong interact more harmoniously than North Americans and English people, who dwell in less dense cities. The Japanese are used to being packed sardinelike into subway cars by white-gloved pushers employed by the transit system. Imagine the rebellion that would occur at such treatment in American subways! It has been suggested that Asians are accustomed to adapting to the environment, whereas Westerners are more prone to try to change the environment.

Southern Europeans apparently occupy a middle ground between Asians, on the one hand, and northern Europeans, on the other. They are more outgoing and comfortable with less personal space than northern Europeans but not as tolerant of it as Asians are.

Our discussion of personal space and crowding is based on the fact that humans are mostly social beings who live in communities. Psychologists have also brought their expertise into the community, where they often try to prevent behavioral and mental problems before they begin.

PERSONAL SPACE An invisible boundary that surrounds a person and serves protective functions.

COMMUNITY PSYCHOLOGY

Clinical psychologists treat psychological disorders. **Community psychologists** use their knowledge of biology, learning, motivation, and personality to *prevent* them. Community mental health centers (CMHCs) deal with psychological problems in the community rather than in the hospital. Hospitalization has not been shown to be of help with many people who have psychological disorders (Kiesler, 1982). Moreover, removal of the individual from the community can sever ties to social realities and obligations and to social support. As a result, disorders are sometimes intensified rather than alleviated. Some functions of the CMHC are to help people with disorders live in the community. Partial hospitalization allows them to sleep in a community hospital and work outside during the day. Through community consultation and education, problems may be averted or identified during their formative stages.

Levels of Prevention

Prevention of psychological disorders takes place at three levels: primary, secondary, and tertiary. **Primary prevention** aims to stop potential problems before they start. Psychology has a lengthy tradition of working in the community. More than 100 years ago, the American founder of clinical psychology, Lightner Witmer, tried to help children by changing harmful social conditions. Community psychologists cannot alter genetic predispositions toward psychological disorders, but genetic predispositions interact with psychological and sociocultural factors to produce disorders. Such factors include unemployment, lack of education, drug abuse, teenage pregnancy, marital conflict, and substandard housing. By consulting with community leaders, agencies and institutions, and lawmakers, community psychologists alleviate stressful conditions that contribute to psychological disorders (Edgerton, 1994). Community psychologists apply their knowledge of developmental psychology, psychological disorders, and social psychology when they consult with groups such as Big Brothers and Boys' Clubs to help high-risk youth avoid delinquency. Yoshikawa (1994) has shown, for example, that a combination of family support and early childhood education can reduce the prevalence of juvenile delinquency. Many community psychologists follow a systems or ecological approach, which means that they study the ways in which the criminal justice, educational, welfare, and health-care systems can work together to foster psychological well-being among groups at risk (Boyd-Franklin, 1995).

The aim of **secondary prevention** is to catch psychological problems early and halt their advancement. Groups such as Parents Anonymous and suicide prevention centers provide ways for distressed people to express their concerns before child abuse gets out of hand or they kill themselves. Community psychologists also work with teachers and others to help them identify early signs of psychological disorders or abuse.

Tertiary prevention deals with psychological disorders that have been diagnosed and are being treated. There is much overlap between psychological treatment (e.g., psychotherapy and behavior therapy) and tertiary prevention. In tertiary prevention, however, there is a community emphasis. The focus is on rallying community forces to strengthen troubled people's ties to their families and jobs.

The community problems connected with the development of psychological disorders are also often associated with criminal behavior. We now consider the field of psychology that applies psychological expertise to the criminal justice system.

TRUTH OR FICTION REVISITED
It seems to be true that "an ounce of prevention is worth a pound of cure" in community psychology—at least if you don't hold us to exact measurements. That is, investment in organizations such as Big Brothers, in family support, and in early childhood education can reduce the prevalence of juvenile delinquency.

COMMUNITY PSYCHOLOGY A field of psychology, related to clinical psychology, that focuses on preventing psychological problems and maintaining distressed persons in the community.

PRIMARY PREVENTION In community psychology, the deterrence of psychological problems.

SECONDARY PREVENTION In community psychology, the early detection and treatment of psychological problems.

TERTIARY PREVENTION In community psychology, the treatment of ripened psychological problems.

FORENSIC PSYCHOLOGY

Forensic psychologists apply psychological knowledge to the functioning of the criminal justice system. Some forensic psychologists apply their knowledge of social psychology and information processing to study the behavior and mental processes of people involved in the criminal justice system. For example, they study the accuracy of eyewitness testimony because it has an impact on juries. They also investigate ways in which the behavior of judges, attorneys, and defendants influences jury decisions. For example, they have learned that jurors are influenced by how defendants dress. Therefore, their attorneys have them dress neatly. They have also learned many things about the functioning of juries. For example, if a jury is split on a decision, it usually follows the lead of the first juror who changes his or her mind (Baron & Byrne, 1997).

Many forensic psychologists are employed by law enforcement agencies. They apply their knowledge of personality, personality assessment, and the psychology of learning to facilitate the recruitment and training of police officers. There is a high burnout rate among police officers, and some psychologists apply therapy methods to help police find ways of coping with stress. They apply knowledge of psychological disorders and social psychology to help train police to handle special problems—for example, assessing the dangerousness of persons they suspect of crimes or handling suicide threats, hostage crises, and family disputes.

One of the obvious overlaps between crime and psychology involves the insanity plea. Defendants who use the insanity plea claim to have committed a crime because of a psychological disorder and not by choice. Let us consider the origins of the insanity plea and its use today.

The Insanity Plea

Some forensic psychologists apply psychological knowledge in the evaluation of persons who commit crimes. They testify about defendants' competence to stand trial or participate in their own defense, as well as about whether defendants should be found not guilty by reason of insanity. For example, John Hinckley was found not guilty of an assassination attempt on President Reagan by reason of insanity. Hinckley was diagnosed with schizophrenia and committed to a psychiatric institution rather than given a prison sentence. He remains there to this day.

In pleading insanity, lawyers use the M'Naghten rule, named after Daniel M'Naghten, who tried to assassinate the British prime minister, Sir Robert Peel, in 1843. M'Naghten had delusions that Peel was persecuting him, and he killed Peel's secretary in the attempt. The court found M'Naghten not guilty by reason of insanity, referring to what has become the M'Naghten rule. It states that the accused did not understand what she or he was doing at the time of the act, did not realize it was wrong, or was succumbing to an irresistible impulse.

Many people, including some government officials, would like to ban the insanity plea (DeAngelis, 1994b). Such banning "is an attempt to deal with a perception that the world is getting more violent," notes psychologist/lawyer Donald Bersoff (1994, p. 28). "That's combined with the perception that people are literally getting away with murder because of the insanity defense." Practically speaking, there may not be all that much cause for concern, however. Although the public estimates that the insanity defense is used in about 37% of felony cases, it is actually raised in only 1% (Silver et al., 1994).

TRUTH OR FICTION REVISITED
It is not true that the insanity plea is presented as a defense in about one third of felony cases. It is only used in about 1% of such cases.

FORENSIC PSYCHOLOGY The field that applies psychological knowledge within the criminal justice system.

SPORTS PSYCHOLOGY

Among the noise of a spirited tennis crowd, I overheard a conversation between two women:

> "Do you think there's anything I could do to play like Steffi Graf?"
> "The first thing you've got to do is get Steffi Graf's genes."
> A pause. Then: "But she's wearing a skirt."

Clothes may make the man, or woman, but probably not the athlete. Why does Steffi Graf outplay nearly every other woman on the tennis circuit? There is a combination of reasons, including motivation, dedication, long hours of training, superb coaching—as well as her ability to cope with stardom and the crowds. And, yes, "genes"—not jeans. Heredity plays a role in terms of her physical strength, her coordination, her reaction time, and her eyesight.

Task Analysis of Athletic Performances

Sports psychologists apply psychological methods and knowledge to the study and modification of the behavior and mental processes of people involved in sports (Hays, 1995). Sports psychologists do task analyses of athletic performances just as I/O psychologists do task analyses of work performances. They break athletic performances down into their components to discover ways of enhancing the performance of each. In doing so, they apply knowledge about biology (the facts concerning human limits and health hazards), motivation, learning (e.g., the roles of cognitive understanding, repetition, and reinforcement), self-efficacy expectations ("I can do it"), and coping with stress. They apply this knowledge and knowledge about group processes to help coaches. Many amateur and professional teams have psychologists as well as coaches.

Note some of the issues sports psychologists deal with:

- How can athletes focus their attention on their own performance and not on the crowd or on competing athletes?
- How can athletes use cognitive strategies such as mental practice and positive visualization to enhance performance?
- What is the role of emotions in performance? For example, did tennis pro John McEnroe's on-court cursing and arguing spark his achievement motivation and concentration, or did they distract him and cost him matches?
- What are the relationships between sports and psychological well-being?
- How can knowledge of group behavior be applied to enhance team cohesiveness?
- How can psychologists help athletes handle "choking"?

Let us consider this last issue further—the problem of "choking."

How Sports Psychologists Help Athletes Handle "Choking"

Buffalo Bills kicker Scott Norwood had worked for many years preparing for the 1991 Super Bowl. For several hours a day, he perfected his form on the field. He kicked field goals from various distances and in all extremes of weather. Then, when his opportunity to win the game with a short field goal arose, he "choked." He shanked the ball in the final

SPORTS PSYCHOLOGY The field of psychology that studies the nature, causes, and modification of the behavior and mental processes of people involved in sports.

SCOTT NORWOOD AT THE SUPER BOWL. Buffalo Bills placekicker Scott Norwood trained for years, under extremes of weather. Then, in the waning seconds of the January 1991 Super Bowl—when a relatively short kick would have given the Bills a victory over the Giants—he choked. Instead of splitting the uprights, the ball spun off to the side. One of the functions of sports psychologists is to help athletes handle choking through techniques like relaxation and positive visualization.

TRUTH OR FICTION REVISITED
It is true that you can improve your athletic performance by imagining yourself making the right moves. This is an example of the technique of positive visualization. Positive visualization helps you rehearse the desired behavior and enhances self-efficacy expectations.

seconds of the game, handing the victory to Buffalo's downstate rivals—the New York Giants.

A critical outing also had a devastating effect one fall on Penn State placekicker Herb Menhardt. Penn State was facing its second loss in three games. With a fourth down on the Iowa 37-yard line and 50 seconds to play, the coach took a chance on the untested Menhardt, a first-year student. As 75,000 anxious Penn State fans looked on at Beaver Stadium, Menhardt hooked the 54-yard kick wide to the left, leaving Iowa with a 7-6 victory. As a result, Matt Bahr got the starting placekicking job, which eventually landed him in the pros.

Menhardt quit the team and did not return until his junior year. "I had to live with that kick for years," Menhardt noted. "Matt won the starting job, and I had to accept being a failure. I had nightmares about it, and all my so-called friends mocked me. I decided to give up on football. I knew I could kick, but I had to live with that one kick."

Choking during an athletic contest, like when taking a test, is especially cruel. The athlete, like the student, may have sweated long hours preparing for a crucial performance. Then it is over in a matter of seconds or minutes. Yet it may devastate one's self-esteem and taint one's life.

Fortunately, Menhardt had an opportunity to work with sports psychologists Charles Stebbins and Kevin Hickey. They taught him a variety of coping skills. Some were largely perceptual and physical—such as helping him develop his peripheral vision, sense of balance, and response time. They taught him relaxation skills. Menhardt learned to breathe deeply and regularly under stress. He was shown how to relax muscle groups as he told himself to relax.

Positive Visualization

Like many other performers, Menhardt was also shown how to use the technique of positive visualization. He envisioned himself going through the motions in a critical game situation. He pictured blocking the crowd out of his mind and focusing on the ball. He moved fluidly toward the ball as if in a trance—as if he and the performance were one—and booted the ball flawlessly through the posts.

After his new combination of athletic, behavioral, and cognitive training, Menhardt returned to the team and made a last-second 54-yard goal against North Carolina State. He gave Penn State the winning margin: 9-6. That season, he went on to convert 14 field goals in 20 attempts and all of his 28 kicks after touchdowns.

Peak Performance

Menhardt was now engaging in what sports psychologists refer to as "peak performances," which are characterized by the following:

- intense concentration
- ability to screen out the crowd and, when appropriate, the competitors (successful field-goal kickers and quarterbacks do not usually "hear footsteps" or focus on the opposition's defenders rushing in)
- a sense of power and control over the situation
- lack of pain and fatigue
- the sense that time has slowed down, as if the performance is being carried out in slow motion (Browne & Mahoney, 1984). Great hitters in baseball have fine eyesight and timing. They report that they can "see" the ball exceptionally clearly. When they are at their peak, even fast balls seem to linger in the air as they come across the plate.

It also seems that peak performances can elude athletes who pursue them intentionally, or who "try too hard." A useful prescription includes these elements:

1. Training adequately—that is, enhancing endurance and fine-tuning skills
2. Learning how to regulate one's breathing to obtain enough oxygen but not so rapidly as to become lightheaded
3. Learning how to relax muscle groups that are unessential to performance as a way of remaining relaxed and conserving energy
4. Spending some practice time picturing oneself performing flawlessly under adverse conditions (that is, engaging in positive visualization).

We could say that sports psychology is about educating athletes to enhance their performance. Let us now turn our attention to educational psychology, which is concerned with the enhancement of learning in general.

EDUCATIONAL PSYCHOLOGY

Discussion of educational psychology brings our book full circle. After all, educating students in psychology is what it is all about.

Educational psychologists apply knowledge from many areas of psychology to the processes of teaching and learning (Woolfolk, 1998). They apply knowledge of developmental psychology to determine when children are ready to undertake certain kinds of learning and whether teaching practices can be modified to meet the needs of older people. They apply knowledge of learning and memory to present instructional materials in ways that will foster comprehension and retention. They apply knowledge of motivation to find ways to encourage students to pay attention to the subject matter. They apply knowledge of test construction and statistics to develop tests that assess aptitudes and achievement. They apply knowledge of social psychology to enhance teacher-student and student-student relationships.

Let us survey some of the concerns of educational psychologists. We begin with the area of teaching practices because teaching lies at the core of education.

Teaching Practices

Consider the way in which one psychology professor teaches his students about neurons. Joseph Palladino (1994) involves his students in neuropsychology by having them pretend they are neurons. He motivates students to pay attention to the similarities and differences between psychological disorders by having them act them out in class. These are examples of learning by doing.

Educational psychologists help instructors find ways to teach effectively. A first step involves analyzing the outcomes of learning—that is, whether students are expected to show changes in their attitudes, motor skills, verbal information, intellectual skills (e.g., knowing how to add and subtract), or cognitive strategies for processing information (e.g., paying attention and rehearsing information).

Analyzing the outcomes of learning enables the setting of **instructional objectives.** Communication of objectives helps students focus on the essential aspects of the material. Objectives can be general (the student should be able to reason in solving simple math problems) and specific (the student should be able to add single digits when written in the form,

EDUCATIONAL PSYCHOLOGY The field of psychology that studies the nature, causes, and enhancement of teaching and learning.

INSTRUCTIONAL OBJECTIVE A clear statement of what is to be learned.

A CLASS ACT.
Educational psychologists help instructors find ways of teaching effectively. For example, they connect various teaching methods to the outcomes of learning (e.g., whether students are expected to show changes in their attitudes, motor skills, verbal information, intellectual skills, or cognitive strategies for processing information).

TAXONOMY Classification system.

RECITATION A teaching format in which teachers pose questions that are answered by students.

EXPOSITORY TEACHING Ausubel's method of presenting material in an organized form, moving from broad to specific concepts.

DISCOVERY LEARNING Bruner's view that children should work on their own to discover basic principles.

TRUTH OR FICTION REVISITED

It is not true teachers who know more about a subject do a better job of teaching it—at least in the lower grades. The statement is too general to be true and discounts other key teaching factors, such as communication skills and organization. With young children, such factors seem to be just as important, if not more important, than knowledge of content areas. The situation may differ in college, where students are better able to organize subject matter for themselves.

$3 + 5 = x$). A classification system, or **taxonomy**, of instructional objectives divides them into three domains: cognitive, affective (emotional), and psychomotor (concerning the development of physical abilities and skills). Examples of objectives in the cognitive domain include acquisition of knowledge, comprehension of subject matter, and ability to apply concepts to solve problems.

Educational psychologists conduct research into which teaching formats best enable teachers to meet instructional objectives. For example, in the **recitation** approach, teachers pose questions that students answer. Research has shown that teachers who are too busy or unwilling to answer student questions discourage learning and inhibit students from participating in class discussions (Newman, 1990). Teachers who encourage students to ask questions and provide clear answers motivate students to take an active role in learning (Karabenick & Sharma, 1994).

Other basic teaching formats include the lecture approach (**expository teaching**), group discussion, seatwork and homework, and individualized instruction. A number of psychologists, such as Jerome Bruner, argue in favor of **discovery learning** for children in lower grades. That is, they claim that children should be placed in resource-rich environments and be allowed to work on their own to discover basic principles. The practice of discovery learning relies on the assumption that children are naturally curious and strive to make sense of stimulating events.

Individualized instruction teaches students on a one-to-one basis. They are then given time to read about or apply the subject matter on their own. It is interesting to note that individualized instruction, which is usually prized because of the presumably ideal teacher-to-student ratio, has *not* been shown to be superior for elementary and secondary students. Perhaps it leaves immature students too much time on their own. However, individualized instruction seems to benefit college students, who are presumably better able to manage their time.

There are some interesting findings concerning teacher characteristics and student learning. For example, it has *not* been shown that teachers who know more about a subject do a better job of teaching it, particularly at the elementary level. Students learn more when their teachers manage the classroom well and present material in a clear, organized fashion (Cantrell et al., 1977; Hines et al., 1985).

Teaching, of course, is the core of the job of the teacher. However, teachers do much more than teach. For example, they manage classrooms.

Let us consider some of the contributions of educational psychologists to methods of classroom management.

Classroom Management

One of the areas educational psychologists study is ways of managing students in the classroom setting. Students, especially young children, are interested in many things beyond the subject matter. They may be interested in playing with one another or looking out the window rather than paying attention to the teacher. In some cases, they get into arguments or fights. Educational psychologists have found that teachers can help manage classrooms by creating conditions that meet students' needs for stimulation, affiliation, and safety (DeAngelis, 1994a; Woolfolk, 1998). Teachers can do so in these ways:

1. By making the classroom and the lesson interesting and inviting
2. By ensuring that students can fulfill their needs for affiliation and belonging
3. By making the classroom a safe and pleasant place
4. By recognizing that students' backgrounds can give rise to diverse patterns of needs
5. By helping students take appropriate responsibility for their successes and failures
6. By encouraging students to perceive the links between their own efforts and their achievements
7. By helping students set attainable short-term goals.

Classrooms are special environments crowded with people, learning resources, tasks, and time pressures (Doyle, 1986). Everything seems to happen at once. Some events—such as the burning out of a light bulb or a child's becoming ill—can make them unpredictable places. Despite the unpredictables, classrooms become more manageable when concrete procedures and rules are spelled out to students. For example, elementary school students need rules concerning being polite and helpful, taking care of the school, avoiding aggressive behavior, keeping the bathroom neat, and behaving in the cafeteria. Young students need concrete examples. Saying "Be good" is not enough. Children need examples of "good" behavior spelled out. Class procedures involve ways in which students are expected to enter and leave the room, whether they must raise their hands to participate in class discussion, and how they will find out about and hand in assignments. Teachers who state rules clearly and insist that they be followed during the early weeks of school usually encounter fewer behavior problems as the year progresses. Educational psychologists also devise ways for dealing with defiant and violent students. Many teachers are instructed in the methods of behavior modification to help students with behavior problems.

Teachers usually assess what students have learned through tests and provide students with feedback about their accomplishments through grades. Let us now see how educational psychologists have contributed to test construction and the use of grades.

Tests and Grades

Educational psychologists also develop methods for assessing students and assigning grades. Assessment includes standardized tests that measure intelligence (e.g., the Wechsler and Stanford-Binet scales), aptitudes (e.g., the SATs and GREs), achievement in specific subjects (e.g., the California Achievement Tests and the advanced tests of the GREs), and problems that affect learning (e.g., perceptual and motor problems, as measured by the Bender Gestalt Test). Schools use such tests to assess learning ability and to see how well children are reading or computing math problems as compared with age-mates. Colleges and graduate programs use tests to make admissions decisions.

Such tests can be *norm referenced* or *criterion referenced*. Students' performances on **norm-referenced** tests are compared with the average performance of others. That is, the test results are "curved." Our performance on the Wechsler scales or on the GREs depends on how well we perform relative to other people who take the tests. On the Wechsler scales for children, test takers' performances are compared with a nationwide sample that represents their age-mates. Norms for the GRE are based on numbers of items answered correctly by young adults interested in pursuing graduate education—a select group.

In **criterion-referenced** testing, test takers' scores are compared with a fixed performance standard. In other words, criterion-referenced testing might be used to determine whether we can use long division, type 60 words a minute, or speak Spanish fluently. A good score on the norm-referenced GRE advanced test in Spanish means that you answered more questions correctly than the average test taker, not that you can understand or speak Spanish. A road test for a driver's license is a criterion-referenced test; either you can drive successfully according to the set standard or you cannot.

Educational psychologists are also interested in classroom evaluation and testing. They study the reliability and validity of various kinds of tests such as multiple-choice tests versus essay tests. They have found, for example, that long tests are more reliable than brief tests. They have learned that the grading of multiple-choice tests is more objective, or fair, than the grading of essay tests. The grading of essays (and course grades themselves), like the appraisal of workers, can also be influenced by the halo effect—that is, the teacher's general impression of the student. However, the consistency of essay test grades can be enhanced by writing a model answer and then assigning points to its various parts (Gronlund, 1985). Covering students' names while grading also increases fairness. (But penmanship can also affect grades!)

Educational psychologists also investigate the effects of grading. Grades provide students with more than just feedback about how much they have achieved. They also affect students' self-esteem and motivation. For that reason, some teachers try to encourage students they perceive as underachievers by grading them on their (presumed) abilities and not on their actual achievements. In elementary schools, teachers are frequently allowed to give children two grades for the same subject matter area: One reflects achievement and the other is based on judgment calls and intangibles such as effort.

NORM-REFERENCED TESTING A testing approach in which scores are derived by comparing the number of items answered correctly with the average performance of others.

CRITERION-REFERENCED TESTING A testing approach in which scores are based on whether or not one can perform up to a set standard.

Psychology's applications continue to grow. Applications in the areas of psychological disorders are obvious, but there are also applications for personal health, for the workplace, for people's interactions with the environment, for the criminal justice system, for athletics, and for education. It is no accident that psychology is the second most popular undergraduate major—right behind business administration and management (Murray, 1996). Moreover, the numbers of psychology majors are growing at a rapid pace. People are applying psychology to every area of life.

SUMMARY

1. **What is applied psychology?** Applied psychology refers to a number of fields of psychology such as industrial/organizational or environmental psychology that apply fundamental psychological methods and knowledge to the investigation and solution of human problems.

2. **What is industrial/organizational (I/O) psychology?** I/O psychologists apply psychological expertise to assist in worker recruitment, training, and appraisal; enhance job satisfaction; and structure organizations to function efficiently.

3. **How do I/O psychologists facilitate recruitment?** I/O psychologists facilitate recruitment procedures by analyzing jobs in order to specify the skills and personal attributes that are required. They also construct personnel tests and interview procedures to assess the presence of these skills and attributes.

4. **How do I/O psychologists facilitate training?** Training programs usually follow when managers identify a need for improved performance in a given job. Steps in devising training programs include assessing needs, establishing learning objectives, devising methods for gaining and maintaining attention, presenting material, and evaluating program effectiveness.

5. **What have I/O psychologists learned about employee appraisal?** Appraisal of a worker's performance is a cognitive process that is subject to distortions. For example, workers may be judged on the basis of general impressions instead of work performance.

6. **What are the various approaches to organizational theory?** There are three basic approaches to organizational theory: the classic approach, which tends to rely on a bureaucracy, division of labor, and delegation of authority; contingency approaches, which tie organizational structures to organizational objectives and environmental demands; and human relations approaches, which place the worker first.

7. **What are the major human relations approaches?** Three important human relations theories are McGregor's Theory Y, based on the assumption that workers are motivated to take responsibility for their work behavior; Argyris's view that organizations are structured efficiently when they allow their workers to develop; and Ouchi's Theory Z, which combines some of the positive features of the Japanese workplace with some of the realities of the American workplace.

8. **What is human-factors psychology?** This is the field that ensures that equipment and facilities are compatible with human behavior patterns and mental processes—that is, they are reasonably easy to work, or work in, and safe.

9. **What criteria do human-factors psychologists use in evaluating person-machine systems and work environments?** They use performance criteria, physiological criteria, subjective criteria, and accident-and-injury criteria.

10. **What criteria do human-factors psychologists use for evaluating the coding in displays?** They consider the displays' detectability, discriminability, compatibility, meaningfulness, standardization, and multidimensionality.

11. **What is consumer psychology?** Consumer psychology applies psychological methods to the investigation and modification of consumer behavior and mental processes.

12. **What kinds of questions are considered by consumer psychologists?** They consider issues such as why consumers are loyal to one brand over another, the qualities or characteristics that consumers associate with various brands, and how consumer attitudes toward products can be modified.

13. **What is environmental psychology?** Environmental psychologists study the ways in which people and the physical environment influence each other. They investigate the ways in which factors such as noise, temperature, pollution, and population density affect human behavior and mental processes.

14. **What is community psychology?** Community psychology is related to clinical psychology but focuses on the prevention of psychological problems and the maintenance of distressed individuals in the community.

15. **What kinds of prevention are there?** Primary prevention is the modification of the community environment to preclude the emergence of problems. Secondary prevention is the early detection and treatment of problems. Tertiary prevention is the treatment of developed problems.

16. **What is forensic psychology?** Forensic psychology is the

application of psychological knowledge to the functioning of the criminal justice system.

17. **What kinds of issues are dealt with by forensic psychologists?** Forensic psychologists study ways in which witnesses, judges, defendants, and attorneys affect the legal process. Forensic psychologists participate in the recruitment, training, and counseling of police personnel. They also testify as to the competence of defendants to participate in their own defense.

18. **What is sports psychology?** Sports psychology is the application of psychological methods and knowledge to the study and modification of the behavior and mental processes of people involved in sports.

19. **What kinds of issues do sports psychologists deal with?** In addition to task analysis of athletic performances, sports psychologists are concerned with issues such as how athletes can use cognitive strategies like mental practice and positive visualization to enhance performance, how sports contribute to mental health, how team cohesiveness can be enhanced, how coaching methods can be improved, how athletes can handle choking, and how athletes can attain peak performance.

20. **What is educational psychology?** Educational psychologists apply knowledge from many areas of psychology to the processes of teaching and learning.

21. **How do educational psychologists contribute to teaching practices?** Educational psychologists explain how to use instructional objectives according to a taxonomy. They conduct research into which teaching formats best enable teachers to meet their objectives.

22. **How do educational psychologists contribute to classroom management?** They study ways of motivating and managing students in the classroom setting. They relate instructional methods to students' needs and point out the value of concrete school rules and procedures.

KEY TERMS

applied psychology (p. A-3)

bureaucracy (p. A-9)

classic organization theories (p. A-9)

cognitive-dissonance theory (p. A-16)

community psychology (p. A-21)

consumer psychology (p. A-14)

contingency theories (p. A-9)

criterion-referenced testing (p. A-28)

discovery learning (p. A-26)

educational psychology (p. A-25)

environmental psychology (p. A-16)

expository teaching (p. A-26)

flextime (p. A-10)

forensic psychology (p. A-22)

halo effect (p. A-7)

human factors (p. A-3)

human relations theories (p. A-9)

industrial psychology (p. A-3)

instructional objective (p. A-25)

norm-referenced testing (p. A-28)

organizational analysis (p. A-6)

organizational psychology (p. A-3)

person analysis (p. A-6)

personal space (p. A-20)

primary prevention (p. A-21)

recitation (p. A-26)

secondary prevention (p. A-21)

sports psychology (p. A-23)

task analysis (p. A-6)

taxonomy (p. A-26)

tertiary prevention (p. A-21)

Theory Y (p. A-9)

Theory Z (p. A-10)

REFERENCES

Adler, S. (1998). Cited in McGuire, P. A. (1998). Wanted: Workers with flexibility for 21st century jobs. *APA Monitor, 29*(7), 10, 12.

Alexander, R. A., & Barrett, G. U. (1982). Equitable salary increase judgments based upon merit and nonmerit considerations: A cross-national comparison. *International Review of Applied Psychology, 31,* 443–454.

Anderson, C. A., & DeNeve, K. M. (1992). Temperature, aggression, and the negative affect escape model. *Psychological Bulletin, 111,* 347–351.

Argyris, C. (1972). *The applicability of organizational psychology.* Cambridge, England: Cambridge University Press.

Aronson, E. (1990). Applying social psychology to desegregation and energy conservation. *Personality and Social Psychology Bulletin, 16,* 118–132.

Azar, B. (1998). Tribal practices raise worker morale. *APA Monitor, 29*(7), 8.

Baron, R. A. (1990). Countering the effects of destructive criticism. *Journal of Applied Psychology, 75,* 235–245.

Baron, R. A., & Byrne, D. (1997). *Social psychology* (8th ed.). Boston: Allyn & Bacon.

Bell, P. A. (1992). In defense of the negative affect escape model of heat and aggression. *Psychological Bulletin, 111,* 342–346.

Bersoff, D. (1994). Cited in DeAngelis, T. (1994). Experts see little impact from insanity plea ruling. *APA Monitor, 25*(6), 28.

Boyd-Franklin, N. (1995, August). *A multisystems model for treatment interventions with inner-city African American families.* Master lecture delivered to the meeting of the American Psychological Association, New York.

Browne, M. A., & Mahoney, M. J. (1984). Sport psychology. *Annual Review of Psychology, 35,* 605–625.

Cantrell, R. P., Stenner, A. J., & Katzenmeyer, W. G. (1977). Teacher knowledge, attributes, and classroom teaching correlates of student achievement. *Journal of Educational Psychology, 69,* 180–190.

Clay, R. A. (1998). Many managers frown on use of flexible work options. *APA Monitor, 29*(7), 11.

Cohen, S., Evans, G. W., Stokols, D., & Krantz, D. S. (1986). *Behavior, health, and environmental stress.* New York: Plenum.

Cohn, E. G. (1990). Weather and violent crime. *Environment and Behavior, 22,* 280–294.

DeAngelis, T. (1994a). Educators reveal keys to success in classroom. *APA Monitor, 25*(1), 39–40.

DeAngelis, T. (1994b). Experts see little impact from insanity plea ruling. *APA Monitor, 25*(6), 28.

Dockery, D. W., et al. (1993). An association between air pollution and mortality in six U.S. cities. *New England Journal of Medicine, 329,* 1753–1759.

Donnerstein, E. I., & Wilson, D. W. (1976). Effects of noise and perceived control on ongoing and subsequent aggressive behavior. *Journal of Personality and Social Psychology, 34,* 774–781.

Doyle, W. (1986). Classroom organization and management. In M. Wittrock (Ed.), *Handbook of research on teaching* (3rd ed.). New York: Macmillan.

Dugan, K. W. (1989). Ability and effort attributions. *Academy of Management Journal, 32,* 87–114.

Edgerton, J. W. (1994). Working with key players for psychological and mental health services. *American Psychologist, 49,* 314–321.

Evans, G. W., Jacobs, S. V., & Frager, N. B. (1982). Behavioral responses to air pollution. In A. Baum & J. E. Singer (Eds.), *Advances in environmental psychology* (Vol. 4). Hillsdale, NJ: Erlbaum.

Fiske, S. T. (1993). Controlling other people: The impact of power on stereotyping. *American Psychologist, 48,* 621–628.

Fowler, R. D. (1998). Fairness in the workplace. *APA Monitor, 29*(7), 3.

Gillis, A. R., Richard, M. A., & Hagan, J. (1986). Ethnic susceptibility to crowding. *Environment and Behavior, 18,* 683–706.

Goldstein, I. L., & Buxton, V. M. (1982). Training and human performance. In M. D. Dunnette & E. A. Fleishman (Eds.), *Human Performance and Productivity 1,* 135–177.

Gronlund, N. E. (1985). *Measurement and evaluation in teaching* (5th ed.). New York: Macmillan.

Hamilton, L. C. (1985). Self-reported and actual savings in a water conservation campaign. *Environment and Behavior, 17,* 315–326.

Hays, K. F. (1995). Putting sport psychology into (your) practice. *Professional Psychology: Research and Practice, 26,* 33–40.

Hines, C. V., Cruickshank, D. R., & Kennedy, J. (1985). Teacher clarity and its relation to student achievement and satisfaction. *American Educational Research Journal, 22,* 87–99.

Hogan, R., Curphy, G. J., & Hogan, J. (1994). What we know about leadership. *American Psychologist, 49,* 493–504.

Isen, A. M., & Baron, R. A. (1990). Positive affect and organizational behavior. In B. M. Staw & L. L. Cummings (Eds.), *Advances in experimental social psychology* (Vol. 12). Greenwich, CT: JAI Press.

Kahle, L. R., & Beatty, S. E. (1987). Cognitive consequences of post-purchase behavior. *Journal of Applied Social Psychology, 17,* 828–843.

Kahn, R. L., & Rowe, J. (1998). *Successful aging.* New York: Pantheon.

Karabenick, S. A., & Sharma, R. (1994). Perceived teacher support of student questioning in the college classroom: Its relationship to student characteristics and role in the classroom questioning process. *Journal of*

Educational Psychology, 86, 90–103.

Katzell, R. A., & Thompson, D. E. (1990). Work motivation. *American Psychologist, 45,* 144–153.

Kelly-Radford, L. (1998). Cited in McGuire, P. A. (1998). Wanted: Workers with flexibility for 21st century jobs. *APA Monitor, 29*(7), 10, 12.

Kenrick, D. T., & MacFarlane, S. W. (1986). Ambient temperature and horn honking. *Environment and Behavior, 18,* 179–191.

Kiesler, C. A. (1982). Mental hospitalization and alternative care. *American Psychologist, 37,* 349–360.

Knowlton, W. A., Jr., & Mitchell, T. R. (1980). Effects of causal attributions on a supervisor's evaluation of subordinate performance. *Journal of Applied Psychology, 65,* 459–466.

Kushler, M. G. (1989). Use of evaluation to improve energy conservation programs. *Journal of Social Issues, 45,* 153–168.

Landy, F. J. (1992, August). *The roots of organizational and industrial psychology.* Master lecture presented to the annual meeting of the American Psychological Association, Washington, DC.

Mack, D., & Rainey, D. (1990). Female applicants' grooming and personnel selection. *Journal of Social Behavior and Personality, 5,* 399–407.

Mackett-Stout, J., & Dewar, R. (1981). Evaluation of public information signs. *Human Factors, 23*(2), 139–151.

Marks, M. (1998). Cited in McGuire, P. A. (1998). Wanted: Workers with flexibility for 21st century jobs. *APA Monitor, 29*(7), 10, 12.

McGregor, D. (1960). *The human side of enterprise.* New York: McGraw-Hill.

McGuire, P. A. (1998). Wanted: Workers with flexibility for 21st century jobs. *APA Monitor, 29*(7), 10, 12.

Milgram, S. (1977). *The individual in a social world.* Reading, MA: Addison-Wesley.

Mohrman, A. M., Jr., Resnick-West, S. M., & Lawler, E. E., III. (1989). *Designing performance appraisal systems: Aligning appraisals and organizational realities.* San Francisco: Jossey-Bass.

Murphy, K. (1998). Cited in McGuire, P. A. (1998). Wanted: Workers with flexibility for 21st century jobs. *APA Monitor, 29*(7), 10, 12.

Murray, B. (1996). Psychology remains top college major. *APA Monitor, 27*(2), 1, 42.

Newman, J., & McCauley, C. (1977). Eye contact with strangers in city, suburb, and small town. *Environment and Behavior, 9,* 547–558.

Newman, R. S. (1990). Children help seeking in the classroom: The role of motivational factors and attitudes. *Journal of Educational Psychology, 82,* 71–80.

Norman, D. A. (1988). *The psychology of everyday things.* New York: Basic Books.

Ouchi, W. (1981). *Theory Z: How American business can meet the Japanese challenge.* Reading, MA: Addison-Wesley.

Pagan, G., & Aiello, J. R. (1982). Development of personal space among Puerto Ricans. *Journal of Nonverbal Behavior, 7,* 59–68.

Palladino, J. (1994). Cited in DeAngelis, T. (1994). Educators reveal keys to success in classroom. *APA Monitor, 25*(1), 39–40.

Rathus, S. A., Nevid, J. S., & Fichner-Rathus, L. (2000). *Human sexuality in a world of diversity* (4th ed.). Boston: Allyn & Bacon.

Robertson, T. S., Zielinski, J., & Ward, S. (1984). *Consumer behavior.* Glenview, IL: Scott Foresman.

Sadalla, E. K., Sheets, V., & McCreath, H. (1990). The cognition of urban tempo. *Environment and Behavior, 22,* 230–254.

Schein, E. H. (1990). Organizational culture. *American Psychologist, 45,* 109–119.

Schenker, M. (1993). Air pollution and mortality. *New England Journal of Medicine, 329,* 1807–1808.

Silver, E., Cirincione, C., & Steadman, H. J. (1994, February). *Law and human behavior.* Cited in DeAngelis, T. (1994b). Experts see little impact from insanity plea ruling. *APA Monitor, 25*(6), 28.

Simpson, M., & Perry, J. D. (1990). Crime and climate. *Environment and Behavior, 22,* 295–300.

Staples, S. I. (1996). Human responses to environmental noise. *American Psychologist, 51,* 143–150.

Stokols, D. (1992). Establishing and maintaining healthy environments. *American Psychologist, 47,* 6–22.

Tsui, A. S., & O'Reilly, C. A., III. (1989). Beyond simple demographic effects. *Academy of Management Journal, 32,* 402–423.

Weisinger, H. (1990). *The critical edge: How to criticize up and down your organization and make it pay off.* New York: Harper & Row.

Woolfolk, A. E. (1998). *Educational psychology* (8th ed.). Boston: Allyn & Bacon.

Worchel, S., & Brown, E. H. (1984). The role of plausibility in influencing environmental attributions. *Journal of Experimental Social Psychology, 20,* 86–96.

Yoshikawa, H. (1994). Prevention as cumulative protection: Effects of early family support and education on chronic delinquency and its risks. *Psychological Bulletin, 115,* 28–54.

STA

STATISTICS

TRUTH OR FICTION?

Basketball players are abnormal.

Being a "10" is not necessarily a good thing.

Researchers can group their data either to highlight or to hide their findings.

Adding people's incomes and then dividing them by the number of people can be an awful way of showing the average income.

Psychologists may express your IQ score in terms of how deviant you are.

An IQ score of 130 may be more impressive than an SAT score of 500.

Correlational research shows that smoking cigarettes causes cancer.

We cannot conclude that men are taller than women unless we know the average heights of men and women and how much the heights within each group vary.

I MAGINE THAT SOME VISITORS FROM OUTER SPACE ARRIVE OUTSIDE Madison Square Garden in New York City. Their goal this dark and numbing winter evening is to learn all they can about the inhabitants of planet Earth. They are drawn inside the Garden by lights, shouts, and warmth. The spotlighting inside rivets their attention to a wood-floored arena where the New York Stales are hosting the California Quakes in a briskly contested basketball game.

Our visitors use their sophisticated instruments to take some measurements of the players. Some surprising statistics are sent back to the planet of their origin: It staears that (1) 100% of Earthlings are male, and (2) the height of Earthlings ranges from 6 feet 1 inch to 7 feet 2 inches.

Statistics is the name given the science concerned with obtaining and organizing numerical measurements or information. Our imagined visitors have sent home some statistics about the sex and size of human beings that are at once accurate and misleading. Although they accurately measured the basketball players, their small **sample** of Earth's **population** was quite distorted. Fortunately for us Earthlings, about half of us are female. And the **range** of heights observed by the aliens, of 6 feet 1 to 7 feet 2, is both restricted and too high. People vary in height by more than 1 foot and 1 inch. And our **average** height is not between 6 feet 1 inch and 7 feet 2 inches but a number of inches below.

Psychologists, like our imagined visitors, are vitally concerned with measuring human as well as animal characteristics and traits—not just physical characteristics like sex and height but also psychological traits like intelligence, aggressiveness, anxiety, or self-assertiveness. By observing the central tendencies (averages) and variations in measurements from person to person, psychologists can state that some person is average or above average in intelligence or that another person is less assertive than, say, 60% of the population.

But psychologists, unlike our aliens, are careful in their attempts to select a sample that accurately represents the entire population. Professional basketball players do not represent the human species. They are taller, stronger, and more agile than the rest of us, and they make more shaving cream commercials.

In this staendix, we survey some of the statistical methods used by psychologists to draw conclusions about the measurements they take in research activities. First, we discuss *descriptive statistics* and learn what types of statements we can make about the heights of basketball players and some other human traits. Then, we discuss the *normal curve* and learn why basketball players are abnormal—at least in terms of height. We explore *correlation coefficients* and provide you with some less-than-shocking news: More intelligent people attain higher grades than less intelligent people. Finally, we have a brief look at *inferential statistics* and see why we can be bold enough to say that the difference in height between basketball players and other people is not just a chance accident, or fluke. Basketball players are in fact statistically significantly taller than the general population.

DESCRIPTIVE STATISTICS

Being told that someone is a "10" is not very descriptive unless you know something about how possible scores are distributed and how frequently one finds a 10. Fortunately—for 10s, if not for the rest of us—one is usually informed that someone is a 10 on a scale of 1 to 10 and that 10 is the positive end of the scale. If this is not sufficient, one will also be told that 10s are few and far between—rather unusual statistical events.

This business of a scale from 1 to 10 is not very scientific, to be sure, but it does suggest something about **descriptive statistics**. We can use descriptive statistics to clarify our understanding of a distribution of scores such as heights, test grades, IQs, or increases or decreases in measures of sexual arousal following the drinking of alcohol. For example, descriptive statistics can help us to determine measures of central tendency, or averages, and to determine how much variability there is in the scores. Being a 10 loses some of its charm if the average score is an 11. Being a 10 is more remarkable in a distribution whose scores range from 1 to 10 than in one that ranges from 9 to 10.

Let us now examine some of the concerns of descriptive statistics: the frequency distribution, measures of central tendency (types of averages), and measures of variability.

The Frequency Distribution

A **frequency distribution** takes scores or items of raw data, puts them into order as from lowest to highest, and groups them according to class intervals. Table STA.1 shows the rosters for a recent California Quakes—New

TRUTH OR FICTION REVISITED
It is true that basketball players are abnormal—statistically speaking. They are much taller than average and also possess better-than-average athletic skills.

TRUTH OR FICTION REVISITED
It is true that being a "10" is not necessarily a good thing. Being a 10 may be good if the scale varies from 1 to 10, but not if the scale varies from 1 to, say, 100.

STATISTICS Numerical facts assembled in such a manner that they provide significant information about measures or scores. (From the Latin word *status*, meaning "standing" or "position.")

SAMPLE Part of a population.

POPULATION A complete group from which a sample is selected.

RANGE A measure of variability; the distance between extreme measures or scores.

AVERAGE Central tendency of a group of measures, expressed as mean, median, and mode.

DESCRIPTIVE STATISTICS The branch of statistics that is concerned with providing information about a distribution of scores.

FREQUENCY DISTRIBUTION An ordered set of data that indicates how frequently scores staear.

Table STA.1

ROSTERS OF QUAKES VERSUS APPLES AT NEW YORK			
CALIFORNIA		**NEW YORK**	
2 Callahan	6'7"	3 Roosevelt	6'1"
5 Daly	6'11"	12 Chaffee	6'5"
6 Chico	6'2"	13 Baldwin	6'9"
12 Capistrano	6'3"	25 Delmar	6'6"
21 Brentwood	6'5"	27 Merrick	6'8"
25 Van Nuys	6'3"	28 Hewlett	6'6"
31 Clemente	6'9"	33 Hollis	6'9"
32 Whittier	6'8"	42 Bedford	6'5"
41 Fernando	7'2"	43 Coram	6'2"
43 Watts	6'9"	45 Hampton	6'10"
53 Huntington	6'6"	53 Ardsley	6'10"

A glance at the rosters for a recent California Quakes—New York Apples basketball game shows you that the heights of the team members, combined, ranged from 6 feet 1 inch to 7 feet 2 inches. Are the heights of the team members representative of those of the general male population?

TABLE STA.2

FREQUENCY DISTRIBUTION OF HEIGHTS OF BASKETBALL PLAYERS. WITH A ONE-INCH CLASS INTERVAL

CLASS INTERVAL	NUMBER OF PLAYERS IN CLASS
6'1"–6'1.9"	1
6'2"–6'2.9"	2
6'3"–6'3.9"	2
6'4"–6'4.9"	0
6'5"–6'5.9"	3
6'6"–6'6.9"	3
6'7"–6'7.9"	1
6'8"–6'8.9"	2
6'9"–6'9.9"	4
6'10"–6'10.9"	2
6'11"–6'11.9"	1
7'0"–7'0.9"	0
7'1"–7'1.9"	0
7'2"–7'2.9"	1

TRUTH OR FICTION REVISITED

It is true that researchers can often group their data to highlight or to hide their findings. In the example shown in the text, they can highlight the fact that no basketball player they measured was 6' 4" tall, which could give the impression that basketball players are not that tall.

York Apples basketball game. The members of each team are listed according to the numbers on their uniforms. Table STA.2 shows a frequency distribution of the heights of the players of both teams combined, with a class interval of 1 inch.

It would also be possible to use 3-inch class intervals, as in Table STA.3. In determining how large a class interval should be, a researcher attempts to collapse that data into a small enough number of classes to ensure that they will staear meaningful at a glance. But the researcher also attempts to maintain a large enough number of categories to ensure that important differences are not obscured.

Table STA.3 obscures the fact that no players are 6 feet 4 inches tall. If the researcher believes that this information is extremely important, a class interval of 1 inch may be maintained.

Figure STA.1 shows two methods for representing the information in Table STA.3 with graphs. Both in frequency **histograms** and frequency **polygons,** the class intervals are typically drawn along the horizontal line,

TABLE STA.3

FREQUENCY DISTRIBUTION OF HEIGHTS OF BASKETBALL PLAYERS. WITH A THREE-INCH CLASS INTERVAL

CLASS INTERVAL	NUMBER OF PLAYERS IN CLASS
6'1"–6'3.9"	5
6'4"–6'6.9"	6
6'7"–6'9.9"	7
6'10"–7'0.9"	3
7'1"–7'3.9"	1

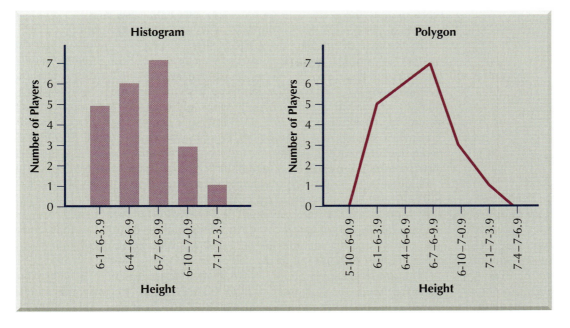

FIGURE STA.1
TWO GRAPHICAL REPRESENTATIONS OF THE DATA IN TABLE STA.3.

or X-axis, and the number of scores (persons, cases, or events) in each class is drawn along the vertical line, or Y-axis. In a histogram, the number of scores in each class interval is represented by a rectangular solid so that the graph resembles a series of steps. In a polygon, the number of scores in each class interval is plotted as a point, and the points are then connected to form a many-sided geometric figure. Note that class intervals were added at both ends of the horizontal axis of the frequency polygon so that the lines could be brought down to the axis to close the geometric figure.

Measures of Central Tendency

Never try to walk across a river just because it has an average depth of four feet.

MARTIN FRIEDMAN

There are three types of measures of central tendency, or averages: *mean, median,* and *mode.* Each tells us something about the way in which the scores in a distribution may be summarized by a typical or representative number.

The **mean** is what most people think of as "the average." The mean is obtained by adding up all the scores in a distribution and then dividing this sum by the number of scores. In the case of our basketball players, it would be advisable first to convert all heights into one unit, such as inches (6'1" becomes 73", and so on). If we add all the heights in inches, then divide by the number of players, or 22, we obtain a mean height of 78.73", or 6'6.73".

The **median** is the score of the middle case in a frequency distribution. It is the score beneath which 50% of the cases fall. In a distribution with an even number of cases, such as the distribution of the heights of the 22 basketball players in Table STA.2, the median is determined by finding the mean of the two middle cases. Listing these 22 cases in ascending order,

HISTOGRAM A graphic representation of a frequency distribution that uses rectangular solids. (From the Greek *historia,* meaning "narrative," and *gramma,* meaning "writing" or "drawing.")

POLYGON A closed figure. (From the Greek *polys,* meaning "many," and *gonia,* meaning "angle.")

MEAN A type of average calculated by dividing the sum of scores by the number of scores. (From the Latin *medius,* meaning "middle.")

MEDIAN The score beneath which 50% of the class falls. (From the Latin *medius,* meaning "middle.")

we find that the 11th case is 6′6″ and the 12th case is 6′7″. Thus the median is (6′6″ + 6′7″)/2, or 6′6 1/2″.

In the case of the heights of the basketball players, the mean and the median are similar, and either serves as a useful indicator of the central tendency of the data. But suppose we are attempting to determine the average savings of 30 families living on a suburban block. Let us assume that 29 of the 30 families have savings between $8,000 and $12,000, adding up to $294,000. But the 30th family has savings of $1,400,000! The mean savings for a family on this block would thus be $56,467. A mean can be greatly distorted by one or two extreme scores, and for such distributions the median is a better indicator of the central tendency. The median savings on our hypothetical block would lie between $8,000 and $12,000 and so would be more representative of the central tendency of savings. Studies of the incomes of American families usually report median rather than mean incomes just to avoid the distortions that would result from treating incomes of the small numbers of multimillionaires in the same way as other incomes.

The **mode** is simply the most frequently occurring score in a distribution. The mode of the data in Table STA.1 is 6′9″ because this height occurs most often. The median class interval for the data in Table STA.3 is 6′6 1/2″ to 6′9 1/2″. In these cases, the mode is somewhat higher than the mean or median height.

In some cases, the mode is a more staropriate description of a distribution than the mean or median. Figure STA.2 shows a **bimodal** distribution, or a distribution with two modes. In this hypothetical distribution of the test scores, the mode at the left indicates the most common class interval for students who did not study, and the mode at the right indicates the most frequent class interval for students who did. The mean and median test scores would probably lie within the 55–59 class interval, yet use of that interval as a measure of central tendency would not provide very meaningful information about the distribution of scores. It might suggest that the test was too hard, not that a number of students chose not to study. One would be better able to visualize the distribution of scores if it were reported as a bimodal distribution. Even in similar cases in which the modes are not exactly equal, it might be more staropriate to describe a distribution as bimodal or even multimodal.

Measures of Variability

Measures of variability of a distribution inform us about the spread of scores, or about the typical distances of scores from the average score. Measures of variability include the *range* of scores and the *standard deviation*.

The **range** of scores in a distribution is defined as the difference between the highest score and the lowest score, and it is obtained by

MODE The most frequently occurring number or score in a distribution. (From the Latin *modus,* meaning "measure.")

BIMODAL Having two modes.

RANGE The difference between the highest and the lowest scores in a distribution.

FIGURE STA.2

A BIMODAL DISTRIBUTION.

This hypothetical distribution represents students' scores on a test. The mode at the left represents the central tendency of students who did not study, and the mode at the right represents the mode of students who did study.

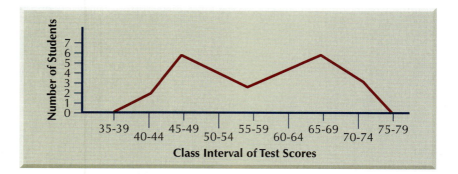

subtracting the lowest score from the highest score. The range of heights in Table STA.2 is 7′2″ minus 6′1″, or 1′1″. It is important to know the range of temperatures if we move to a new climate so we may anticipate the weather and dress staropriately. A teacher must have some understanding of the range of abilities or skills in a class to teach effectively.

The range is an imperfect measure of variability because of the manner in which it is influenced by extreme scores. In our earlier discussion of the savings of 30 families on a suburban block, the range of savings is $1,400,000 to $8,000, or $1,392,000. This tells us little about the typical variability of savings accounts, which lie within a restricted range of $8,000 to $12,000. The **standard deviation** is a statistic that indicates how scores are distributed about a mean of a distribution.

The standard deviation considers every score in a distribution, not just the extreme scores. Thus the standard deviation for the distribution on the right in Figure STA.3 would be smaller than that of the distribution on the left. Note that each distribution has the same number of scores, the same mean, and the same range of scores. But the standard deviation for the distribution on the right is smaller than that of the distribution on the left, because the scores tend to cluster more closely about the mean.

The standard deviation (S.D.) is calculated by the formula

$$\text{S.D.} = \sqrt{\frac{\text{Sum of } d^2}{N}}$$

where d equals the deviation of each score from the mean of the distribution, and N equals the number of scores in the distribution.

Let us find the mean and standard deviation of the IQ scores listed in column 1 of Table STA.4. To obtain the mean, we add all the scores, attain 1,500, and then divide by the number of scores (15) to obtain a mean of 100. We obtain the deviation score (d) for each IQ score by subtracting the score from 100. The d for an IQ of 85 equals 100 minus 85, or 15, and so on. Then we square each d and add these squares. The S.D. equals the square root of the sum of squares (1,426) divided by the number of scores (15), or 9.75.

TRUTH OR FICTION REVISITED
It is true that psychologists may express your IQ score in terms of how deviant you are. The more extreme high (and low) IQ scores deviate more from the mean score.

STANDARD DEVIATION A measure of the variability of a distribution, attained by the formula

$$\sqrt{\frac{\text{Sum of } d^2}{N}}$$

FIGURE STA.3
HYPOTHETICAL DISTRIBUTIONS OF STUDENT TEST SCORES.
Each distribution has the same number of scores, the same mean, and even the same range, but the standard deviation is greater for the distribution on the left because the scores tend to be farther from the mean.

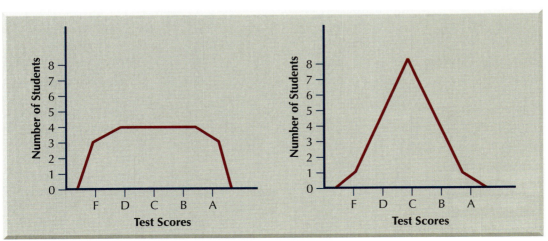

TABLE STA.4

HYPOTHETICAL SCORES ATTAINED FROM AN IQ TESTING

IQ SCORE	d (DEVIATION SCORE)	d² (DEVIATION SCORE SQUARED)
85	15	225
87	13	169
89	11	121
90	10	100
93	7	49
97	3	9
97	3	9
100	0	0
101	−1	1
104	−4	16
105	−5	25
110	−10	100
112	−12	144
113	−13	169
117	−17	289

Sum of IQ scores = 1,500   Sum of d^2 scores = 1,426

$$\text{Mean} = \frac{\text{Sum of scores}}{\text{Number of scores}} = \frac{1,500}{15} = 100$$

$$\text{Standard Deviation (S.D.)} = \sqrt{\frac{\text{Sum of } d^2}{\text{Number of scores}}} = \sqrt{\frac{1,426}{15}} = \sqrt{95.07} = 9.75$$

As an additional exercise, we can show that the S.D. of the test scores on the left (in Figure STA.3) is greater than that for the scores on the right by assigning the grades points according to a 4.0 system. Let A = 4, B = 3, C = 2, D = 1, and F = 0. The S.D. for each distribution of test scores is computed in Table STA.5. The greater S.D. for the distribution on the left indicates that the scores in that distribution are more variable, or tend to be farther from the mean.

THE NORMAL CURVE

Many human traits and characteristics such as height and intelligence seem to be distributed in a pattern known as a normal distribution. In a **normal distribution,** the mean, median, and mode all fall at the same data point or score. Scores cluster most heavily about the mean, fall off rapidly in either direction at first (as shown in Figure STA.4), and then taper off more gradually.

The curve in Figure STA.4 is bell shaped. This type of distribution is also called a **normal curve.** It is hypothesized to reflect the distribution of variables in which different scores are determined by chance variation. Height is thought to be largely determined by chance combinations of genetic material. A distribution of the heights of a random sample of the

NORMAL DISTRIBUTION A symmetrical distribution in which staroximately 68% of cases lie within a standard deviation of the mean.

NORMAL CURVE Graphic presentation of a normal distribution, showing a bell shape.

TABLE STA.5

COMPUTATION OF STANDARD DEVIATIONS FOR TEST-SCORE DISTRIBUTIONS IN FIGURE STA.3

DISTRIBUTION AT LEFT			DISTRIBUTION AT RIGHT		
GRADE	d	d^2	GRADE	d	d^2
A (4)	2	4	A (4)	2	4
A (4)	2	4	B (3)	1	1
A (4)	2	4	B (3)	1	1
B (3)	1	1	B (3)	1	1
B (3)	1	1	B (3)	1	1
B (3)	1	1	C (2)	0	0
B (3)	1	1	C (2)	0	0
C (2)	0	0	C (2)	0	0
C (2)	0	0	C (2)	0	0
C (2)	0	0	C (2)	0	0
C (2)	0	0	C (2)	0	0
D (1)	−1	1	C (2)	0	0
D (1)	−1	1	C (2)	0	0
D (1)	−1	1	D (1)	−1	1
D (1)	−1	1	D (1)	−1	1
F (0)	−2	4	D (1)	−1	1
F (0)	−2	4	D (1)	−1	1
F (0)	−2	4	F (0)	−2	4

Sum of grades = 36
Mean grade = 36/18 = 2
Sum of d^2 = 32

S.D. = $\sqrt{32/18}$ = 1.33

Sum of grades = 36
Mean grade = 36/18 = 2
Sum of d^2 = 16

S.D. = $\sqrt{16/18}$ = 0.94

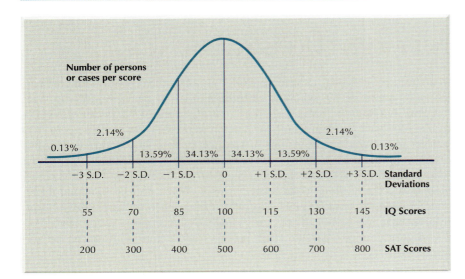

FIGURE STA.4
A BELL-SHAPED OR NORMAL CURVE.

In a normal curve, staroximately 68% of the cases lie within a standard deviation (S.D.) from the mean, and the mean, median, and mode all lie at the same score. IQ tests and Scholastic Assessment Tests have been constructed so that distri- butions of scores staroximate the normal curve.

population staroximates normal distributions for men and women, with the mean of the distribution for men a few inches higher than the mean for women.

Test developers traditionally assumed that intelligence was also randomly or normally distributed among the population. For that reason, they constructed intelligence tests so scores would be distributed as close to "normal" as possible. In actuality, IQ scores are also influenced by environmental factors and chromosomal abnormalities, so the resultant curves are not perfectly normal. Most IQ tests have means defined as scores of 100 points, and the Wechsler scales are constructed to have standard deviations of 15 points, as shown in Figure STA.4. This means that 50% of the Wechsler scores fall between 90 and 100 (the "broad average" range), about 68% (or two of three) fall between 85 and 115, and more than 95% fall between 70 and 130—that is, within two S.D.s of the mean.

The Scholastic Assessment Tests (SATs) were constructed so the mean scores would be 500 points, and an S.D. would be 100 points. Thus a score of 600 would equal or excel that of some 84% to 85% of the test takers. Because of the complex interaction of variables determining SAT scores, the distribution of SAT scores is not exactly normal either. The normal curve is an idealized curve.

TRUTH OR FICTION REVISITED
It is true that an IQ score of 130 may be more impressive than an SAT score of 500. The IQ score of 130 is two standard deviations above the mean and exceeds that of more than 97% of the population. An SAT score of 500 is the mean SAT score.

THE CORRELATION COEFFICIENT

What is the relationship between intelligence and educational achievement? Between cigarette smoking and lung cancer in human beings? Between introversion and frequency of dating among college students? We cannot run experiments to determine whether the relationships between these variables are causal, because we cannot manipulate the independent variable. For example, we cannot randomly assign a group of people to cigarette smoking and another group to nonsmoking. People must be permitted to make their own choices, and so it is possible that the same factors that lead people to choose to smoke may also lead to lung cancer. However, the **correlation coefficient** may be used to show there is a relationship between smoking and cancer.

The correlation coefficient is a statistic that describes the relationship between two variables. It varies from +1.00 to –1.00; therefore, a correlation coefficient of +1.00 is called a perfect positive correlation, a coefficient of –1.00 is a perfect negative correlation, and a coefficient of 0.00 shows no correlation between variables.

TRUTH OR FICTION REVISITED
It is not true that correlational research shows that smoking cigarettes causes cancer. Correlational research shows that smoking and cancer are related but does not reveal cause and effect. (Other kinds of research do strongly suggest that smoking causes cancer, however.)

INFERENTIAL STATISTICS

In a study on learning, children enrolled in a Head Start program earned a mean IQ score of 99, whereas children similar in background who were not enrolled in Head Start earned a mean IQ score of 93. Is this difference of six points in IQ significant, or does it represent chance fluctuation of scores? In a study on the effects of alcohol, people who believed they had drunk alcohol chose higher levels of electric shock to be stalied to persons who had provoked them than people who believed they had not drunk alcohol. Did the difference in level of shock chosen reflect an actual difference between the two groups, or could it have been a chance fluctuation? Inferential statistics help us make decisions about whether differences found between such groups reflect real differences or just fluctuations.

CORRELATION COEFFICIENT A number between –1.00 and +1.00 that indicates the degree of relationship between two variables.

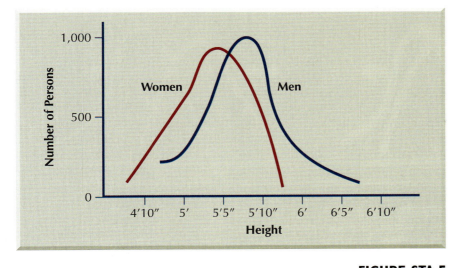

FIGURE STA.5

DISTRIBUTION OF HEIGHTS FOR RANDOM SAMPLES OF MEN AND WOMEN.
Inferential statistics permit us to staly our findings to the populations sampled.

Figure STA.5 shows the distribution of heights of 1,000 men and 1,000 women selected at random. The mean height for men is greater than the mean height for women. Can we draw the conclusion, or **infer**, that this difference in heights represents the general population of men and women? Or must we avoid such an inference and summarize our results by stating only that the sample of 1,000 men in the study had a higher mean height than that of the sample of 1,000 women in the study?

If we could not draw inferences about populations from studies of samples, our research findings would be very limited indeed—limited only to the specific individuals studied. However, the branch of statistics known as **inferential statistics** uses mathematical techniques in such a way that we can draw conclusions about populations from which samples have been drawn.

Statistically Significant Differences

In determining whether differences in measures taken of research samples may be stalied to the populations from which they were drawn, psychologists use mathematical techniques that indicate whether differences are statistically significant. Was the difference in IQ scores for children attending and those not attending Head Start significant? Did it represent only the children participating in the study, or can it be stalied to all children represented by the sample? Is the difference between the height of men and the height of women in Figure STA.5 statistically significant? Can we staly our findings to all men and women?

Psychologists use formulas involving the means and standard deviations of sample groups to determine whether group differences are statistically significant. As you can see in Figure STA.6, the farther apart the group means are, the more likely it is that the difference between them is statistically significant. This makes a good deal of common sense. After all, if you were told that your neighbor's car had gotten one tenth of a mile more per gallon of gasoline than your car had last year, you might assume that this was a chance difference. But if the difference was farther apart,

INFER To draw a conclusion, to conclude. (From the Latin *in,* meaning "in," and *ferre,* meaning "to bear.")

INFERENTIAL STATISTICS The branch of statistics concerned with the confidence with which conclusions drawn about samples may be extended to the populations from which they were drawn.

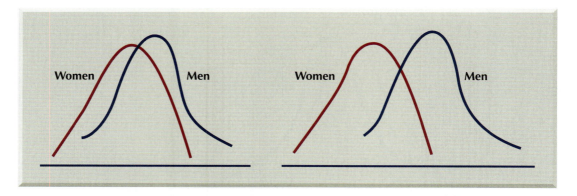

FIGURE STA.6
Psychologists use group means and standard deviations to determine whether the difference between group means is statistically significant. The difference between the means of the groups on the right is greater and thus more likely to be statistically significant.

say 14 miles per gallon, you might readily believe this difference reflected an actual difference in driving habits or efficiency of the automobiles.

As you can see in Figure STA.7, the smaller the standard deviations (a measure of variability) of the two groups, the more likely it is that the difference of the means is statistically significant. As an extreme example, if all women sampled were exactly 5′5″ tall, and all men sampled were exactly 5′10″, we would be highly likely to assume that the difference of 5 inches in group means is statistically significant. But if the heights of women varied from 2′ to 14′, and the heights of men varied from 2′1″ to 14′3″, we might be more likely to assume that the 5-inch difference in group means could be attributed to chance fluctuation.

Samples and Populations

Inferential statistics are mathematical tools that psychologists staly to samples of scores to determine whether they can generalize their findings to populations of scores. Thus they must be quite certain that the samples involved actually represent the populations from which they were drawn.

FIGURE STA.7
The variability of the groups on the left is smaller than the variability of the groups on the right. Thus it is more likely that the difference between the means of the groups on the left is statistically significant.

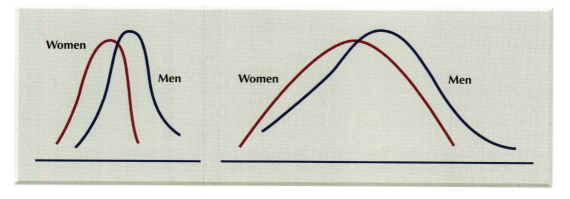

Psychologists often use the techniques of random sampling and stratified sampling of populations to draw representative samples. If the samples studied do not accurately represent their intended populations, it matters very little how sophisticated the statistical techniques of the psychologist may be. We could use a variety of statistical techniques on the heights of the New York Stales and California Quakes, but none would tell us much about the height of the general population.

SUMMARY

1. **What is statistics?** Statistics is the science that assembles data in such a way that they provide useful information about measures or scores. Such measures or scores include people's height, weight, and scores on psychological tests such as IQ tests.

2. **What are samples and populations?** A sample is part of a population. A population is a complete group from which a sample is drawn. The example with basketball players shows that a sample must represent its population if it is to provide accurate information about the population.

3. **What is descriptive statistics?** Descriptive statistics is the branch of statistics that provides information about distributions of scores.

4. **What is a frequency distribution?** A frequency distribution organizes a set of data, usually from low scores to high scores, and indicates how frequently a score appears. Class intervals may be used on large sets of data to provide a quick impression of how the data tend to cluster. The histogram and frequency polygon are two ways of graphing data to help people visualize the way in which the data are distributed.

5. **What are measures of central tendency?** Measures of central tendency are "averages" that show the center or balancing points of a frequency distribution. The mean—which is what most people consider the average—is obtained by adding the scores in a distribution and dividing by the number of scores. The median is the score of the middle or central case in a distribution. The mode is the most common score in a distribution. Distributions can be bimodal (having two modes) or multimodal.

6. **What are measures of variability?** Measures of variability provide information about the spread of scores in a distribution. The range is defined as the difference between the highest and lowest scores. The standard deviation is a statistic that shows how scores cluster around the mean. Distributions with higher standard deviations are more spread out.

7. **What is the normal curve?** The normal or bell-shaped curve is hypothesized to occur when the scores in a distribution occur by chance. The normal curve has one mode, and approximately two of three scores (68%) are found within one standard deviation from the mean. Fewer than 5% of cases are found beyond two standard deviations from the mean.

8. **What is the correlation coefficient?** The correlation coefficient is a statistic that describes how variables such as IQ and grade point averages are related. It varies from +1.00 to −1.00. When correlations between two variables are positive, it means that one (such as school grades) tends to rise as the other (such as IQ) rises.

9. **What are inferential statistics?** Inferential statistics is the branch of statistics that indicates whether researchers can extend their findings with samples to the populations from which they were drawn.

10. **What are statistically significant differences?** Statistically significant differences are believed to represent real differences between groups, and not chance fluctuation.

KEY TERMS

average (p. STA-2)
bimodal (p. STA-6)
correlation coefficient
     (p. STA-10)
descriptive statistics
     (p. STA-3)
frequency distribution (p. STA-3)

histogram (p. STA-4)
infer (p. STA-11)
inferential statistics (p. STA-11)
mean (p. STA-5)
median (p. STA-5)
mode (p. STA-6)
normal curve (p. STA-8)

normal distribution (p. STA-8)
polygon (p. STA-4)
population (p. STA-2)
range (p. STA-2)
sample (p. STA-2)
standard deviation (p. STA-7)
statistics (p. STA-2)

LEARNING
Page L-3, © H. Dratch/The Image Works; page L-4, The Bettmann Archive; page L-7, © Susan McElhinney; page L-11, © Frank Cezus/Tony Stone Images; page L-13, © Sandra Lord/Photoright; page L-15, © Walter Dawn/Photo Researchers; page L-20, © Hank Morgan/Rainbow; page L-23, © Will & Deni McIntyre/Photo Researchers; page L-24, © Robin Sachs/PhotoEdit; page L-28, © David E. Dempster/Offshoot; page L-29, Albert Bandura.

MEMORY
Page M-4, © Yves De Braine/Black Star; page M-10, © Mary Kate Denny/PhotoEdit; page M-13, © Myrleen Ferguson/PhotoEdit; page M-15, © B. Daemmrich/The Image Works; page M-19, Reuters/Paul Hackett/Archive Photos; page M-25, © Robert Finken/The Picture Cube.

THINKING AND INTELLIGENCE
Page T-3, © Frozen Images, Inc.; page T-7, The Image Maker, Berkeley Heights-Mendham, NJ; page T-10, © 1950 Gjon Mili—Life Magazine—Time Warner Inc.; page T-15, © Wayne R. Bilenduke/Tony Stone Images; page T-17, NASA/Johnson Space Center; page T-22, © 1988 David E. Dempster/Offshoot; page T-25, © Mary Kate Denny/Tony Stone Images; page T-28, © Paul Conklin/PhotoEdit.

MOTIVATION AND EMOTION
Page ME-3, © 1987 Comstock; page ME-6, © Tom McCarthy/PhotoEdit; page ME-7, Dr. Neal Miller/Yale University; page ME-10, © Carolyn Smith; page ME-13 (top), Lockheed; page ME-13 (bottom), Harlow Primate Lab University of Wisconsin; page ME-14, Harlow Primate Lab University of Wisconsin; page ME-21, © 1976 Paul Ekman/Human Interaction Lab, UCSF; page ME-27, © John Boykin/The Picture Cube.

PERSONALITY
Page P-3, The Bettmann Archive; page P-6, © Lawrence Migdale/Photo Researchers; page P-9, UPI/Corbis-Bettmann; page P-11, © 1996 Richard Lord; page P-17, © Diane Johnson/Tony Stone Images; page P-20, © Jeff Isaac Greenberg/Photo Researchers; page P-25, © 1995 Richard Lord; page P-26, © Bob Daemmrich/The Image Works.

PSYCHOLOGICAL DISORDERS
Page PD-4, © Sandy Skoglund/Janet Borden, Inc.; page PD-7, © Mark Richards/PhotoEdit; page PD-10, Museum of Modern Art/Film Stills Archive; page PD-15, © SuperStock; page PD-20, © Frieman Photography/Photo Researchers.

METHODS OF THERAPY
Page MT-4, Culver Pictures; page MT-6, Freud Museum, London; page MT-8, © Zigy Kaluzny/Tony Stone Images; page MT-11, © Rick Friedman/Black Star; page MT-12, © 1985 Lester Sloan /Woodfin Camp & Associates, Inc.; page MT-18, © Bob Daemmrich/Stock, Boston; page MT-24, © Phil Degginger/Tony Stone Images; page MT-26, © Will McIntyre/Photo Researchers, Inc.

SOCIAL PSYCHOLOGY
Page S-6, © Spencer Grant/PhotoEdit; page S-8, © Jeff Greenberg/The Picture Cube; page S-9, © Michael Newman/PhotoEdit; page S-10, © H.

Gans/The Image Works; page S-13, Reuters/Ian Waldie/Archive Photos; page S-14, D. Perrett, K. May, S. Yoshikawa—University of St. Andrews/Science Photo Library/Photo Researchers; page S-21, © Dennis MacDonald/PhotoEdit; page S-23, © B. Daemmrich/The Image Works; page S-25, © Fritz Hoffmann/The Image Works.

CHILD AND ADOLESCENT DEVELOPMENT

Page CD-4, © Julie Marcotte/Stock, Boston; page CD-8, The Granger Collection, New York; page CD-10 (top), © Doug Goodman/Monkmeyer; page CD-10 (bottom), © George Zimbel/Monkmeyer; page CD-13, © Tony Freeman/PhotoEdit; page CD-17, Photo by Washington University Photo Services; page CD-18, Harvard University Archives; page CD-21, Courtesy of author; page CD-22, © DPA/The Image Works; page CD-23 (all), Harlow Primate Lab/University of Wisconsin; page CD-24, © Nina Leen/Life Magazine—Time Inc.; pages CD-26 and CD-29, © Elizabeth Crews.

ADULT DEVELOPMENT

Page AD-3, © Arlene Collins/The Image Works; page AD-16, © Michael Dwyer/Stock, Boston; page AD-27, © Bob Daemmrich/Stock, Boston.

GENDER AND SEXUALITY

Page GS-6, © Dan McCoy/Rainbow; page GS-12 (left), © Myrleen Cate/Tony Stone Images; page GS-12 (right), © Michael Greenlar/The Image Works; page GS-15, http://www.planetout.com; page GS-24, © Per Breiehagen/Time Magazine; page GS-27, © W. Hill, Jr./The Image Works.

STRESS AND HEALTH

Page H-3, © David Harding/Tony Stone Images; page H-4 (top), © Vanessa Vick/Photo Researchers, Inc.; page H-4 (bottom), © Lawrence Migdale/Tony Stone Images; page H-9, © Peter Correz/Tony Stone Images; page H-10, AP/Wide World; page H-12, © David Young-Wolff/PhotoEdit; page H-14, © Biology Media/Photo Researchers; page H-24, © Joseph Nettis/Tony Stone Images; page H-26, © Zigy Kaluzny/Tony Stone Images.

APPLIED PSYCHOLOGY

Page A-8, © Frank Pedrick/The Image Works; page A-12, © Michael Newman/PhotoEdit; page A-16 (top), AP/Wide World Photos; page A-16 (bottom), © Gamma Liaison; page A-17, © A. Gottfried/The Image Works; page A-24, © Focus on Sports; page A-26, © Elizabeth Crews.